D0624363

Q
591   cop.1
The New Larousse
encyclopedia of animal
life. $60.00

The New Larousse Encyclopedia of ANIMAL LIFE

SISKIYOU COUNTY PUBLIC LIBRARY
719 FOURTH STREET
YREKA, CALIFORNIA 96097

Based on *La Vie des Animaux* by Léon Bertin with
contributions by Maurice and Robert Burton, J.A.L. Cooke,
F.E.G. Cox, R. Phillips Dales, R.G. Davies,
Benjamin Dawes, J.F.D. Frazer, James Green,
Shirley Hawkins, J.W. Jones, Peter Walker,
Alwynne Wheeler and Sir Maurice Yonge.

Foreword to revised edition by Maurice Burton;
to first edition by Robert Cushman Murphy,
Lamont Curator Emeritus of Birds,
American Museum of Natural History.

All photographs supplied by
Bruce Coleman Ltd.

Bonanza Books
New York

The
New Larousse
Encyclopedia of

ANIMAL LIFE

R
591
cop. 1 ✓

CONTENTS

The *New Larousse Encyclopedia of Animal Life*, with original
contributions to the English edition, is based on Léon Bertin's
La Vie des Animaux, first published in France by Augé, Gillon,
Hollier-Larousse, Moreau et Cie (Librairie Larousse), Paris.

Copyright © Paul Hamlyn Limited 1967

Copyright © revised material The Hamlyn Publishing Group Limited 1980

All rights reserved. No part of this publication may be reproduced, stored in
a retrieval system, or transmitted, in any form or by any means, electronic,
mechanical, photocopying, recording or otherwise, without the permission of
The Hamlyn Publishing Group Limited.

Phototypeset by Tradespools Limited, Frome, Somerset.
Printed and bound in Spain by Graficromo, S. A. – Córdoba

This edition published by Bonanza Books, 1981,
distributed by Crown Publishers, Inc.,
by arrangement with The Hamlyn Publishing Group Limited

h g f e d c b a

Library of Congress Cataloging in Publication Data

The New Larousse encyclopedia of animal life.

Rev. ed. of: Larousse encyclopedia of animal life. 1967.
Bibliography: p.
Includes index.
I. Zoology. I. Burton, Maurice, 1898-
II. Bertin, Léon, 1896-1956. Vie des animaux.
QL50.N48 1981   591   81-17030
ISBN 0-517-36055-1   AACR2

FOREWORD TO FIRST EDITION

Robert Cushman Murphy
Lamont Curator Emeritus of Birds
American Museum of Natural History

Proof of man's interest in his fellow creatures on earth is his aptitude for recording information about them even before he had invented the art of writing. We know this from the vivid and highly sophisticated portraits of animals left us by the cavemen at Lascaux in France, at Altamira in Spain, and on the walls of hundreds of other grottoes and caverns between Siberia and South Africa.

In the fourth century B.C., many thousands of years after the time of the prehistoric cave painters, Aristotle wrote the first encyclopedic *History of Animals*. Within its limitations, this work is so astonishingly accurate that for centuries afterward it was judged almost heretical to question any of the Greek philosopher's statements. Even where he had obviously erred, as in reporting that the housefly has eight legs, medieval scholars seemed inclined to trust the master's testimony rather than their own eyes.

Throughout a very long succeeding period, the greater part of published natural history, in Europe and the East alike, was far less realistic than that given the world by Aristotle. As late as the eighteenth century, for instance, Oliver Goldsmith—during his lifetime one of the most popular authors of any age—composed with grace, vivacity, and utter irresponsibility his *Animated Nature*, for which a London publisher paid him the then handsome sum of 800 guineas. Despite the allure of this book, it is a medley of the false and the absurd.

On the other hand, Count de Buffon, a French contemporary of Goldsmith, was steeped in the natural history of his day. Throughout the entire latter half of the eighteenth century this savant was engaged in the preparation of the forty-four exquisite volumes of his brilliant compendium *Histoire Naturelle*, a work that has had enormous influence all over the reading world and retains its usefulness even today. In this magnum opus Buffon took full advantage of the wonderful and all but incredible findings made by naturalists in the course of the worldwide voyages of exploration undertaken during the Golden Age of Discovery from the time of Columbus to Captain James Cook.

Though Buffon foresaw at least vague aspects of the evolutionary concept, he carried out his labours before the enlightenment—the true renaissance of biological understanding—that came in 1859 with the publication of Darwin's *Origin of Species*. Only after this date could consideration of the ancestry, relationships, distribution and behaviour of animals and plants begin to be 'modern'. All that had gone before, however truthful or however entertaining, had lacked the key to broadest significance as well as the key to a rational comprehension of man's place among the several million other species of living organisms that inhabit the earth and the sea.

Since Darwin, books of vast coverage in various natural history fields have been published in nearly every modern language. A few of them have aimed at global scope and, as nearly as possible, at zoological universality. In other words, they have embraced the whole animal kingdom. Brehm's *Tierleben*, which has gone through several revisions in Germany, is one example, and the Larousse *La Vie des Animaux*, another.

This second, an eminent French work, first appeared in 1949 in two quarto volumes as attractive as they are impressive, under the able authorship of the late Professor Léon Bertin, of the Musée National d'Histoire Naturelle, of Paris. This book was heir not only to the sound older knowledge of Buffon, the great Baron Cuvier, and their international colleagues, but equally to the subsequent wisdom of Fabre and Pasteur, and to still later researchers in physiology, biochemistry, genetics, animal psychology and other experimental disciplines who, during recent years, have cast new and bright illumination on the meaning of life. It is this valuable work of Bertin, newly clothed, completely reillustrated, and thoroughly revised to the threshold of today, that is offered now in English. This is a fresh structure on a tried and substantial base. The comprehensive and detailed text on invertebrates has been newly commissioned from distinguished authorities for the English-language edition. The rest, covering the whole of the vertebrate world, has been extensively revised by equally knowledgeable British and American specialists. The result is a text of approximately 400,000 words, extended by some 40,000 more in pithy captions to illustrations.

Descriptive as well as basic science has altered markedly during the last twenty-five years. For this new encyclopedia the systematic sequence of animal forms has been brought into harmony wih the latest conclusions of specialists; major and up-to-date revisions in international classification systems are embodied in the basic organisation of the book, particularly those resulting from the work of American ornithologists. Editorial policy has been zealous to extend accounts of species especially characteristic of each of the continents. Readers in the United States, for example, will therefore discover that the species of North America, and indeed all the New World, receive no less adequate treatment than the longer-known fauna of Europe.

In short, here is a widely encompassing yet compact, scrupulously indexed book that surveys the animal world from the single-celled protozoans to the most advanced primates (excluding only man himself). Introductions to each phylum or major grouping of organisms deal with general principles of form and function, with rearing of young, ecological relationships, heritage, and way of life. Both common names and specific names are used throughout. In short, this is a volume that will save the enquiring reader in search of information from the need to consult printed bibliographies, drawers of title cards, and shelves of books. Its pictures and text are filled with clarity and enthusiasm, added to authority. It is at once pleasant reading and a practical source of reference for the individual and for schools and libraries.

FOREWORD TO REVISED EDITION

Maurice Burton
Former Deputy Keeper of the Department of Zoology
British Museum (Natural History)

It is now thirty years since *La Vie des Animaux* was first published and a decade since it was translated from the original French into the English edition. It is now reissued in a new form, the most obvious and marked feature being the complete replacement of the black-and-white illustrations by colour pictures. The opportunity has also been taken to bring up to date the information contained in the text. In a few groups this has meant an almost total revision. In many sections, especially in the invertebrates, there has been little or no alteration. This does not mean that information on any particular group has stood still. The reverse is, indeed, correct. Day by day, week by week, year by year, there has been steady accretion of knowledge of the living world, but for many invertebrates this has been in minor details only.

An encyclopedia should contain all that is to be known on a subject, from beginning to end. However, with the present state of our knowledge of the animal kingdom, this would be impossible within the confines of single volume. So our aim has been to give priority to the basic information. This information must of necessity still be mainly the classification, because this is the framework on which everything else is hung. In some areas such as the mammals and birds, reptiles and amphibians, the classification has reached a point where it is more or less stable and unlikely to be radically altered. However, in areas such as the fishes there is still considerable debate as to the most satisfactory classification. Perhaps, at last, with the present classification we are nearing the finality already evident in mammals and birds.

In the world of invertebrates, the classification of some groups has altered little over the past century. In other groups the classification has been in a state of flux from the beginning and there is little sign yet of finality. Therefore, there would have been little point in upsetting the text as it originally appeared merely to introduce another classification which might be outdated almost as soon as these pages began to roll off the press.

The biggest change in the text between this edition and the last will be found in the pages devoted to the vertebrates, especially in those sections dealing with fishes, birds and mammals. In these is reflected how much more is known about the behaviour of animals as compared with thirty or even ten years ago. Another striking difference is, of course, in the extensive use of colour photographs. This reflects the advances in photography and visual presentation, both of which play a highly important part in the study of natural history. Without question one learns far more from a colour photograph than from a black-and-white one and to this extent this new edition of the *Larousse Encyclopedia of Animal Life* represents an enormous and a new contribution to our literature from its illustrations alone.

INTRODUCTION

Over a million species of animals have been described and there must certainly be many more as yet unknown. Yet, diverse as this assemblage is, it can be divided into groups of clearly related forms. In one way or another man has sought since earliest times to classify the animals which surround him. The need for classification is twofold. First, to identify, and secondly, to group related kinds into larger associations which reflect their evolutionary relationship. For example, the American wolf is *Canis lupus*. It belongs, as its scientific name indicates, to the genus *Canis*, which includes dogs, and is related to other dog-like animals. These all belong to the family Canidae which is itself a member of the order Carnivora. The Carnivora include not only dogs but, weasels and so on, all of which are carnivorous in habit and have certain features in common: tooth pattern, claws and form of the skull and bones. The Carnivora resemble elephants (order Proboscidea) much less closely than they do one another, but both orders are mammalian, characterised by hair and suckling their young, so they may be placed in class Mammalia. The mammals, while very different from, say, birds or reptiles, share with them the feature of a backbone of vertebrae and all may therefore be placed in the subphylum Vertebrata. The vertebrates share with apparently unlikely relatives, the sea-squirts and lancelets, a characteristic axial stiffening rod, the notochord, so that all may be placed in the phylum Chordata.

The Latin name, *Canis lupus*, identifies the animal. Vernacular names like 'wolf' and 'tiger' may be confusing for such names are often applied in different places to different creatures. There are also many animals that have no common name. These short-comings were appreciated especially by the botanist Linnaeus, who was the first real exponent of the 'binary' system we use now in naming living things: the first name is the generic one showing where the species—indicated by the second name—belongs. In some groups there may be a third name (subgenus or subspecies) indicating another category of relationship.

Thus, while the name identifies the animal, the higher categories to which it belongs tell us something about it. To take our example, *Canis lupus* may be 'classified' as a member of the family Canidae, order Carnivora and class Mammalia, each category telling us something of its structure and mode of life. It is important, therefore, that the classification adopted should be as 'natural' as possible, in other words it should reflect the way in which the group has evolved. If identification were the sole object a variety of classificatory systems could be adopted which would be practicable, but some quite useless in conveying any further information about the animal. The classification adopted in this book represents the result of study by many experts, constantly improved as our understanding of evolution has increased.

The species is the basic unit, and as applied to most animals may perhaps best be defined as interbreeding populations of individuals, or at least populations which can interbreed and produce viable offspring when mixed. Species are grouped into genera. Different species of a genus can sometimes be crossed to produce offspring, but these are usually sterile. Crosses between tiger and lion, or horse and ass, come into this category. Neither of these would occur in nature.

While the species is the basic unit, species can be grouped into genera, genera into families, families into orders and so on. These categories are roughly comparable from one group to the next. But, because each has evolved along rather different lines, some groups may have further subdivisions—subfamilies, superorders, subclasses or even subphyla. These divisions express relationship and help to indicate where the animal fits in the general scheme.

The family is a fairly coherent group of recognisably related genera. The order represents a group of families which are clearly, though obviously more distantly, related. The class is a major group with very distinct differences in both structure and way of life from other classes; the phyla differ even more widely in their appearance and organisation. If there are fewer 'links' between phyla than between families, this should cause no surprise for the divergences which have produced phyla have had a longer history and so more opportunities for the elimination of intermediate forms. The differences between species are, from an evolutionary viewpoint, more recent than those between families; family distinctions have come about more recently than those between orders, and so on.

Of the million and more known species of animals over three-quarters are insects. And new species are being discovered and described every day. It is less often that a previously unknown bird is discovered and described for the first time than, for example, some insect. According to Prof. C.B. Williams there are almost certainly as many insects unrecognised as already described. Differences in different groups between the proportions of species described to those awaiting discovery are not only an indication of their size or the fact that some species or groups attract attention while others do not, but also of the fact that the human population is itself unevenly distributed over the globe. The insect faunas of Western Europe and of North America are best known simply because there are more biologists in these areas. Undoubtedly as human affluence and civilisation spreads many more species will be revealed in other regions.

Distribution and abundance of particular groups show similar differences. There may not be many elephants to the square kilometre in the regions where they occur, but smaller species of animals may be represented by much larger numbers of individuals. It has been calculated, for example, that a hectare of north temperate forest land may support 1,700 million mites in the soil. And a swarm of locusts in the Middle East may be made up of over 10,000 million individuals. On the other hand there may be fewer than 500 St Kilda wrens on the island of St Kilda in the Outer Hebrides. Larger animals are generally represented by fewer numbers than small animals. The female elephant produces only one young at a time and is about thirty years old before it does so; a female fruit fly, on the other hand, can lay 300 eggs and complete its whole life-cycle in ten days. Even so, populations are largely stable and death rate roughly balances birth rate, though in any one season other factors may cause an imbalance; thus there may be 'plagues' of certain animals in certain seasons, or a species may be rare in some years and abundant in others. The number of offspring produced is an indication of the dangers in life. The individuals which survive are those best adapted to the conditions at the time, and while populations of species tend to remain stable as long as the factors influencing them remain the same, when these factors change so can the numbers and distribution of species. In this context it is important to realise that the world is always changing, and all species are in dynamic equilibrium with the environment, always coming into existence and dying out. If these changes are not readily perceived it is because man's own life-span is relatively so short.

New species can be formed by a population becoming divided. It is clear that possibilities for divergence and evolution may be greater and occur more rapidly in animals which produce large numbers of offspring or have a short life-span than in those which produce few young and have a long life-span. Some groups therefore reveal more species than others. For example, there are, perhaps, 25,000 species of fishes, but, as already noted, almost a million species of insects. This does not mean that animals less fecund and of greater longevity are incapable of evolution but rather that evolution must take longer and environmental changes must be slower for such animals to adapt themselves. The more specialised animals, such as many of the mammals, may have reached dominant positions in various habitats in our own times, but if faced with radical changes it is unlikely that they will survive. Some insect species, of course, succumb to radical change, but it is more likely that of those represented by large numbers of individuals, all of which are slightly different, some individuals at least will be better adapted to the changing conditions than others, so that the species as a whole survives while changing imperceptibly. There was no sudden creation of all species as earlier generations thought, but a gradual evolution of the species we know today. Many species have been lost on the way, and many more will disappear in the future, but others will take their place. Our own species is increasing all too rapidly in number. The result must be, directly or indirectly, the extinction of many others.

All evolution has come about by small changes which occur continually. These multitudinous changes have added up over hundreds of millions of years to the major divergences which we call phyla. No phylum has been produced by a single, major evolutionary 'step'. Nor have orders appeared as results of sudden evolutionary changes of greater magnitude than those that have produced differences shown between two families. All have come about by the cumulative effect of equally small steps in different directions.

Let us now look very briefly, but in more detail, at this succession of life. All animals fall into one or other of the two groups 'Invertebrata' or 'Chordata'. The division came about by the elaboration of an internal axial strengthening rod, later developed into a series of bony vertebrae. We may, perhaps, more readily appreciate the elaborations within the vertebrates because we are vertebrates ourselves. The invertebrates are more of a mixed bag: a heterogeneous collection of animals without backbones, some distinctly related, others apparently without near relatives, each individual phylum representing an exploitation of a distinct structural type.

The invertebrates include a succession of grades in structural complexity from minute acellular organisms to complex creatures like snails and starfishes. They include many phyla, most exploiting structures as different one from another as the chordates from any invertebrate. We tend to make a sharp mental distinction between 'vertebrates' and 'invertebrates', but this is somewhat egocentric, since we are ourselves vertebrates, and we should remember that all the vertebrates from fish to man are members of a single phylum (Chordata), in the evolutionary scheme no more than the equivalent in one of the many invertebrate phyla. The phylum Mollusca and the phylum Arthropoda, for example, both show a range of animal forms as wide as that from fish to man. The differences between a fish and man are really no greater than those between an arthropod like a brine shrimp and a fruit fly, or a pond snail and an octopus.

Can an evolutionary series be traced through these many invertebrate phyla? The answer is not straight-forward. A series can be traced in so far as each step represents one of increasing complexity of structure in one direction or another. But each phylum as we now know it has been evolving for many hundreds of millions of years and each is much more specialised than the ancestral group which first gave rise to the next step. Thus, the Protozoa, while they are all acellular, are in fact highly specialised. The cnidarians have only tissues, no organs and no body cavity other than that which serves as a gut, but the representatives of the phylum found in rock pools on the seashore or elsewhere are animals which have exploited these limitations to the full. The platyhelminth flatworms have a third layer, but no body cavity; the annelids have a true (coelomic) body cavity, their organisation being converted in the arthropods by the external cuticle which covers the skin forming an exoskeleton, and by each segment coming to bear a pair of jointed appendages. These changes can all be related to changing needs and ways of life. They do indeed represent steps in increasing complexity. But to regard the Protozoa as 'more primitive' than the cnidarians, or the annelids as 'more primitive' than the arthropods, is to overlook the fact that the representatives of each have survived to the present day by their adaptation to niches which have survived with them. The real ancestors, the links between each step, have long since disappeared.

Among the true vertebrates there is a clear series of classes representing successive evolutionary steps: the fishes, the amphibians, the reptiles, the birds and the mammals. At different times in the past there were first only fishes, then fishes and amphibious creatures probably not very different in external appearance from our modern salamanders; later there were amphibians and reptiles, and finally all the classes known today. The expansion is one which has taken steps in time with the changing global climates and flora. The step from fish to amphibian was essentially one from water to land for the adult stage of the life-cycle; that from amphibian to reptile was one of increasingly proficient adaptation to land life at all stages of the life-cycle. From the reptiles both birds on the one hand and mammals on the other evolved; the first in adaption to an arboreal and finally flying life, the second as a further advance in adoption of homoeothermy—the maintenance of an even (and high) body temperature—by combining an insulating external layer (feathers or hair) with a variety of physiological thermostats. The reptiles and amphibians which survive today are, compared with their ancestors, specialised forms which owe their survival to successful adaptation to the particular environmental niches in which

they are found. Even so, there are some remarkable links between classes, but known only as fossils: one or two birds which retain many reptile characters, many animals truly intermediate between reptiles and mammals, and one or two fossils linking the fishes with the first land vertebrates. The fishes which gave rise to the first land tetrapods were related most closely to the strange tassel-finned fishes like *Latimeria* and the lungfishes (Dipnoi). There is no doubt that the series is a natural one, but one must always remember that the fishes we know now are more specialised than those from which the first land vertebrates were derived.

We need not here expand on the details of these varied groups of vertebrate and invertebrate animals, except to note two further facets which may help the reader to a broader view of the whole animal kingdom. The first is that many of the different types of animal are different solutions to similar problems. Life began in the sea; to live in water that is fresh, let alone on dry land or in the air, posed many problems. The impetus to conquer these initially inhospitable realms came from competition, and those animals which overcame the problems initiated waves of adaptive radiation into new kinds of animals. The passage from sea to freshwater has been achieved by many invertebrates as well as by vertebrates; the insects, birds and bats all fly, the insects by wings moved by independent muscles distorting the exoskeletal box of which the wings are a thin expansion, the birds by flapping their fore limbs enlarged by feathers evolved primarily as body lagging, and the bats by skin stretched between the fingers and the body. To bear such facts in mind helps to reduce what at first may seem an enormous assemblage of very different forms to a semblance of order.

The second facet is that of geographical distribution: some species are fairly closely restricted in distribution, others are found all over the world. The marsupials are found almost entirely in Australasia and South America; the tiger is found only in the Indian-Malayan region, while the lion is restricted mainly to Africa. This pattern reflects the way in which these groups have evolved in relation to the evolution of the physical world. Marsupials are found in their present location because they have been protected from the superior placentals by isolation; the tiger and lion, two species of the same genus, have diverged from earlier cats in adaptation to different conditions, and are now separated by inhospitable country. The world presents widely varied physical and climatic conditions, and those animals distributed over large parts of it are usually the most adaptable.

This book is purposely systematic in its presentation to develop an understanding of the relationships of animals, and every effort has been made to provide illustrations of species which are representative of the groups to which they belong. But, if the knowledge and entertainment derived from this encyclopedia leads the reader to observe animals more closely and with greater understanding then its real object will have been achieved. For there is no true substitute for a knowledge of animals in their natural habitat.

Measurements given in this book are metric, but the imperial units can be found by noting the metric measurement and using the following conversion table

LENGTH		MASS	
1 millimetre (mm) 0.039 inches		1 gram (g) 0.035 ounces	
1 centimetre (cm) 0.39 inches		1 kilogram (kg) 2.2 pounds	
1 metre (m) 3.2 feet			
1 kilometre (km) 0.6 miles			

For conversion of temperatures from Centigrade to Fahrenheit multiply by $\frac{9}{5}$ and add 32.

PROTOZOANS
(Phylum Protozoa)

The term Protozoa embraces the vast assemblage of living organisms, some free-living, some parasitic, that appear to organise their whole lives as single cells. Estimates of the total number of species are difficult to make because the definition of the term species is particularly unclear in the Protozoa. It is safe to say that over 80,000 species have been described and that there are more than three times this number as yet undescribed. Although a few are visible to the unaided eye, being up to five millimetres long, the vast majority require a good microscope to reveal them and their structure. Whether they are animal or plant, whether this or that group is truly protozoan, whether they form a subkingdom, superphylum or phylum are all matters that have produced diverse opinions. But the one generally accepted criterion for the inclusion of a particular organism in the phylum is that all functions are confined to a unicellular structure. It is therefore valuable to consider cell construction and function before reviewing the more varied and complex aspects of micro-organisms. Without a knowledge of basic structure it is impossible to begin to make sense of the enormous variety of this versatile and cosmopolitan group.

Historically protozoology is relatively recent. Protozoans were first seen in 1674 by Van Leeuwenhoek using a simple microscope. Their small size has meant that knowledge about them has been linked with the slow development of the microscope. Improved techniques and instruments have brought with them wider understanding of the form, physiology and behaviour of these tiny creatures.

Structure on a small scale

Certain functions are essential to life in its highest and lowest forms. In man, for example, the essentials are: movement in search of food and away from harmful agents; awareness of environment through the senses and integration of responses; capture and processing of food; respiration through the lungs; controlling the water content and soluble substances of the body by means of the urinary system; and reproduction by means of specialised organs. In man these six functions demand specialised structures or organ systems in which each organ consists of many minute, and usually specialised cells. In other words the cell is the lowest structural denominator of life. In higher forms some cells are so specialised that they cannot exist or multiply outside the organism of which they are part. But in other organisms a single cell makes up the whole individual; these are the unicellular animals, the protozoans ('first animals'). Some of these micro-organisms are among the simplest forms of animal life, yet within a structure reduced to minimal size, all the functions essential to life are performed.

Basic cell plan

In its basic form the plan of most cells, including most protozoans, is that shown in the diagram of a hypothetical cell below. It will be seen at once that the traditional definition of a cell as a single nucleus surrounded by cytoplasm is now no more than a convenient simplification. Even *Amoeba*, one of the simplest known forms of animal life, cannot be reduced to quite such fundamentals. With the recent advent of the electron microscope the cell membrane, the mitochondria, the golgi apparatus and other structures have been elevated from the

Opposite
Until relatively recently, it was possible to say with confidence that an animal was any living organism that was not plant. Today, that confidence has been sapped. This is because there is a greater realization that the living world cannot be neatly divided between the subkingdoms of plants and animals. *Volvox*, pictured here, illustrates how nature abhors the strict line of demarcation, for it is a protozoan which by definition means a single-celled animal, that lives in colonies and manufactures its own food, as a plant would, by the use of chlorophyll.

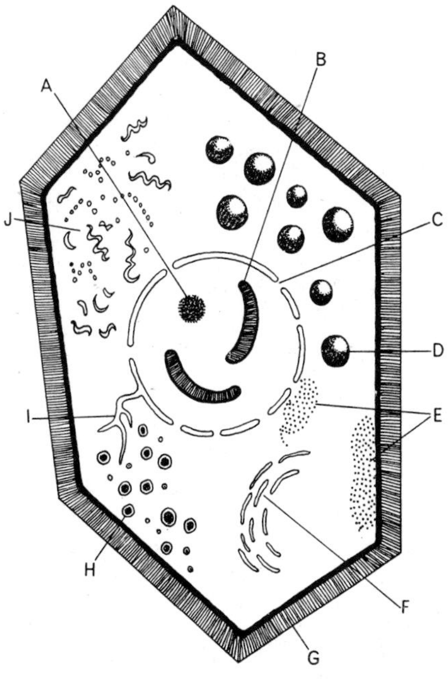

A diagram of a 'typical' cell showing the nucleus—which consists of (A) the nucleolus, (B) chromosomes and (C) the nuclear membrane and pores, (D) chloroplasts, (E) ribosomes, (F) Golgi complex, (G) the cell membrane with inner and outer layers, (H) the secretory product, (I) endoplasmic reticulum and (J) mitochondria.

The Slipper Animalcule, or *Paramoecium* as it is customarily known, lives in freshwater, feeding on bacteria, and is propelled through the water by the cilia on its surface beating in metachronal rhythm. These same cilia create feeding currents that waft food particles into the so-called gullet, or oral groove. The star-shaped organelle is the contractile vacuole complex in which the radial arms of the star collect water from the cell. This drains into the central vacuole and is periodically discharged to the surface.

Astasia sp., a euglenoid phytomast in its typical freshwater habitat, lying between filaments of an alga. The vibratile flagellum, the organ of locomotion, shows up clearly. Although so like the more familiar *Euglena* in structure it lacks chloroplasts and therefore the ability to manufacture its own food with the aid of sunlight.

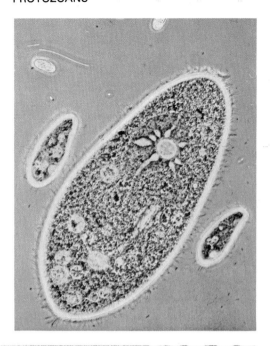

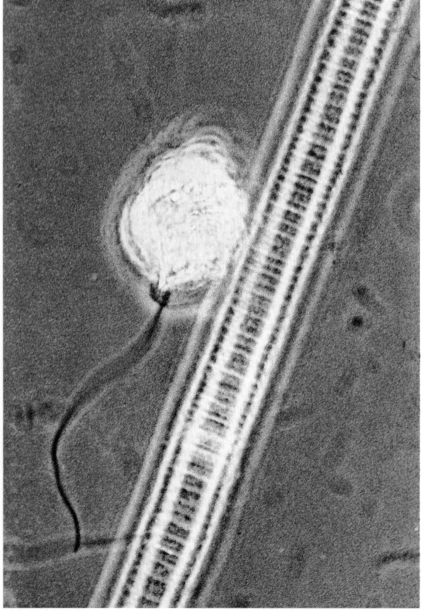

area of hypothesis to that of common and certain knowledge. The existence of other structures (ribosomes, nuclear pores and the endoplasmic reticulum) was not even suspected by earlier cytologists using light microscopes.

The cell membrane is composed of two asymmetrical layers, each one formed by a complex of fatty and protein substances known as lipoprotein. The molecules are composed of fat at one end and protein at the other. In a membrane they are arranged in such a way that the fatty ends are together and the two protein ends face outwards. This typical structure is known as a unit membrane and forms not only the covering of all animal cells, but also their projecting organelles and some internal structures.

Mitochondria of cells other than those of protozoans are ovoid structures with an internal anatomy consisting of cristae or layers of double unit membranes crossing transversely. It is these cristae which characterise mitochondria, and are particularly important, as protozoan mitochondria are seldom ovoid, but generally elongated to various extents. In trypanosomes mitochondria change in size and function during the life-history. In one phase, the bloodstream form, mitochondria are very reduced and poor in cristae, by which characteristic such forms are distinguished. The function of mitochondria is to release energy in usable form to the cell in the process called cellular respiration.

Chloroplasts are structures somewhat resembling mitochondria but which contain colour pigments. They give most plants their characteristic green colour. In some flagellated protozoans chloroplasts are green, but more typically they are yellowish brown. These organelles serve to absorb energy from sunlight and convert light energy into chemical energy of sugar or starch. This is a process requiring dissolved carbon dioxide and water, and is generally known as photosynthesis.

Golgi apparatus and lysosomes are structures about which there is still some controversy. Typically the golgi body has been shown to consist of flattened sacules arranged like a pile of paper bags. Electron micrographs strongly indicate that small bodies called lysosomes develop at the tips of the sacules and are freed into the cytoplasm. They are characterised by their typical content of enzymes, which perform a catalytic function in breaking down many biological substances in acid conditions. Lysosomes seem to function as the start of some digestive processes and also in protecting cells against noxious substances.

Cilia and flagella are organelles of locomotion and have essentially the same basic structure. The unit is the flagellum and is composed of eleven hollow fibres inside a cylinder of 200–300mμ in diameter. Two fibres lie together in the centre with nine outer fibres arranged in a ring around them. At the base of a flagellum, where it is inserted into the cell body, the centre fibres disappear, leaving only the ring of nine which may become fused. The fused region is known variously as the basal body or basal granule. Flagella vary in length from 6μ to 250μ and are found singly or only a few attached to each cell. Cilia, on the other hand, occur typically in rows, when many hundreds may more or less cover the cell, and are seldom longer

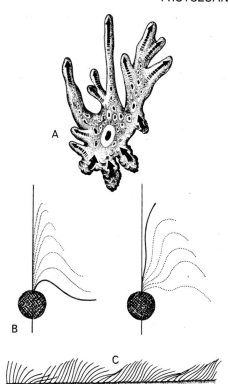

than 30μ. In a few ciliates, however, the cilia are much reduced in number or fused together to form paddle-like membranelles or tufted cirri. Thus it is difficult to generalise and it may well be that the distinction between cilia and flagella is artificial. When cilia occur in large numbers they beat in a co-ordinated way, controlled by additional structures running along, and some between, the rows of cilia immediately below the cell membrane.

Protozoan nuclei are so similar that it is best to describe first the structures of a mammalian nucleus and then draw contrasts with the protozoans. These structures are chromosomes, centrioles and spindle (when the nucleus is dividing), nucleolus, and nuclear membrane with its associated pores.

The chromosomes usually are seen clearly only during cell division, when they appear as sausage-shaped elements. The number in each cell is usually constant within a species but can be as low as four or as high as several hundred. It has been demonstrated that the chromosomes contain deoxyribonucleic acid (DNA), the substance which in all animal cells constitutes the encoded genetic information. Between divisions chromosomes are diffuse in the nucleus and not usually visible.

The centrioles and spindle, like the chromosomes, become visible only at division. The centrioles are short cylinders and are frequently regarded as the same type of structure as the basal granule of a flagellum. From them arise numerous hollow fibres to which the chromosomes are attached. In a dividing nucleus there are two diametrically opposed centrioles (see diagram p. 17). The fibres from each centriole approach each other from the poles.

The nucleolus is a body within the nucleus. Characteristically it appears between divisions. It contains ribonucleic acid. Between divisions the nucleus can be seen to be made of a mesh of fibres or diffuse granules and one or more distinct bodies called karyosomes or endosomes.

The nuclear membrane is a typical unit membrane surrounding the nucleus and separating it from the surrounding cytoplasm. It was once thought that the nuclear membrane acted as a barrier against the flow of materials across it in either direction. Recent electromicrographs have shown that the nuclear membrane is pierced by numerous pores 8–20mμ in diameter. This fact makes its supposed role as a barrier rather less than certain.

The foregoing is a brief account of generalised nuclear structure. The variations found in different protozoans inevitably strain this generalisation as they strain most others. Some protozoans appear not to have chromosomes; others appear to divide without either centrioles or spindle; some appear to have no nucleolus; some (typically of the class Ciliata) have two nuclei; and others (the Trypanosomatidae) have a fragment of DNA associated with the flagellum, and so on. The diversity has two main explanations.

First, the protozoans are an ancient group of organisms and have undergone extensive evolutionary diversification; second, some of the diversity may be only apparent either because the descriptions of the many species have been made by different authors using different techniques at different times, or because many of the structures are very close to the limit of resolution of the light microscope and are therefore difficult or impossible to see clearly. The electron microscope has aided greatly the study of the smaller protozoan components both nuclear and extra-nuclear. In some cases a unity of structure has been demonstrated (unit membrane, fibrillar structure of cilia and flagella). In other cases a considerable diversity has been shown (e.g. variety of cytoplasmic inclusions).

Symmetry

Applied to other animals the term means the spatial arrangement of parts according to some geometrical design. Thus most animals including man have bilateral symmetry, otherwise called

There are three types of protozoan locomotion. (A) Amoeboid locomotion, illustrated here by *Amoebus proteus*, in which a pseudopodium is pushed out and the nucleus moves into it. Other pseudopodia are produced at the same time and the nucleus subsequently moves into one of these. (B) Flagellate locomotion, presented here in schematised form, is by means of one or more flagella, used oar-fashion, except that the flagellum is flexible on the recovery stroke. This is the method used by the majority of flagellates, but others twist the flagellum so that a vortex is created in the water and the animal is sucked into it. (C) Ciliate locomotion is produced by rows of short filaments or cilia that cover the surface of the animal and are interconnected by a network of subpellicular fibrils. The cilia behave rather like flagella, except that the strokes are co-ordinated by the subpellicular fibrils to beat in waves, and this is known as metachronal rhythm.

Amoeba was the 'primeval blob of jelly' of the early protagonists of the theory of organic evolution. So familiar did the name of this single-celled animal become that many people who had only a faint knowledge of zoology and had never heard the word 'Protozoa' spoke the name as if on familiar terms. Far from being a blob of jelly, the body of amoeba, as the advanced microscopes have revealed, is a complex structure with a diversity of organelles.

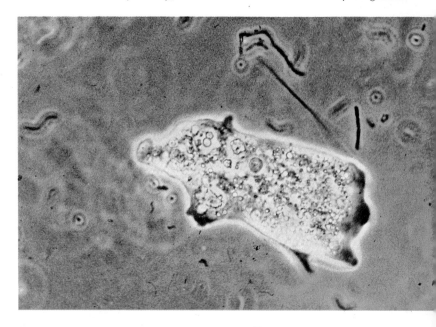

mirror-image or two-fold symmetry. Here, the animal body has mirror-image right and left halves. Adult echinoderms such as starfishes with a five-fold radial symmetry (the symmetry of cylinders and wheels), break the more usual pattern.

Among protozoans, the protean nature of the body form of some (amoebas) dictates that they be considered asymmetrical. Others, with a more constant body form, may be imperfectly bilateral (and this group includes the majority, especially hypotrichous ciliates), radial (choanoflagellates), or even spherical (heliozoans and radiolarians).

Energy production

Energy is needed for all life processes. Animals obtain it by enzymatically breaking down complex molecules containing much energy into smaller molecules with less total energy. The difference between the two energy levels is available to the organism if it is capable of using it. The most frequent method of breakdown is cellular respiration, summarised in the overall equation:

$$\text{sugar} + \text{oxygen} \rightarrow \text{carbon dioxide} + \text{water} + \text{energy}$$
$$C_6H_{12}O_6 + 6O_2 \rightarrow 6CO_2 + 6H_2O + \text{energy}$$

The oxygen required for this aerobic respiration is obtained directly or indirectly from the air by respiration. In those protozoans which require oxygen, it is acquired by aerobic respiration, dissolved in the environmental medium (freshwater, seawater, host's blood) and enters the cell by simple diffusion through the cell membrane. No special respiratory organs are known in the protozoan orders.

Anaerobic protozoans (e.g. entodiniomorphs) do not require oxygen to produce energy. These are typically the parasitic species which live in a nutrient-rich but oxygen-poor environment of the host, whose metabolism deals with the waste product, lactic acid. The conversion of sugars to these substances extracts only about one fifth of the total energy that would be available if the complete process took place. Therefore, to obtain a given amount of energy, anaerobic organisms utilise much more sugar than aerobic species.

Aerobic respiration may be considered as a three-stage process: glycolosis or splitting of simple sugar molecules into two 3-carbon molecules; the tricarboxylic acid cycle, in which the 3-carbon molecules are progressively broken down in the mitochondria to liberate carbon dioxide and some energy; and oxygen transport, the major energy source, in which oxygen is combined ultimately with hydrogen.

The energy so produced is used to make a common cell fuel, adenosine triphosphate or ATP. This molecule gives up energy to whatever synthetic system needs it by the liberation of one phosphate group and becomes adenosine diphosphate or ADP.

Homeostasis and osmoregulation

A cell, whether protozoan or metazoan, has numerous substances within it which are essential for its proper function. Some of these constantly are being broken down and utilised and must therefore be replaced. Also, metabolic activity produces waste products which have to be eliminated if the cell is not to be self-poisoned. The functioning of cells is such that the internal constituents, both of cytoplasm and nucleus, tend to remain constant, except for necessary changes in growth and cell division. The general condition keeping each cell in a state of constant composition is called homeostasis.

One feature of biological membranes is that they are selectively permeable; water and some small ions and molecules can flow more easily through them than larger molecules, although size is not the only regulating factor. This is the basis for the phenomenon of osmosis. In freshwater habitats it is mostly water molecules that bombard the outside of the cell, while the inside is bombarded by water containing dissolved salts, sugars and proteins. There is therefore a net gain of water into the cell without any corresponding loss of the larger molecules. If this osmosis of water continued unchecked the cell would distend and finally burst. Normally this does not happen because energy is spent in the cell membrane keeping the water out, though it is not clear by what mechanism this occurs. However, in many freshwater species some water gets past this barrier and is removed from the cell through the expenditure of energy by membranes which form the pulsating vesicle called the tractile vacuole. This process permits the simultaneous excretion of waste products.

Cell membranes, by using energy, are able to regulate the rate of flow of many kinds of ions and molecules into and from cells. The mechanisms involved are mostly not understood but are called active transport.

The general principle demonstrated is that cells can conserve and in some cases concentrate necessary materials within themselves. The emphasis lies on the properties of the cell membrane and on the healthy cell being able to keep this organelle in good repair to function properly.

Locomotion

In the Protozoa this is as varied as the main body forms, amoeboid, flagellate or ciliate. The general principles of each method are shown on page 13. Descriptions of mechanical processes which often happen at considerable speed cannot replace direct observation or, especially, 'slow motion' cinematographs.

A radiolarian from the Mediterranean in which the protoplasm of the body is supported by long needle-like spicules that radiate from a central point in a definite geometrical pattern. Attached to each spicule are contractile strands, like miniature muscle fibres, stretching from the outer layers of the protoplasm. By the expansion and contraction of these strands the volume of the radiolarian's body is altered and with it the hydrostatic balance, enabling the animal to rise or sink in the water.

Amoeboid movement, a very slow form of progress, has been closely investigated recently and several theories have been proposed. Seen from above, amoebas move by a smooth and continuous process of pushing out a pseudopodium ('false foot'). The nucleus (one of the few reference points) moves slowly into it. In the meantime newer pseudopodia have been formed and movement is then in the direction of one of them. A newly formed pseudopodium has a clear margin, known as the ectoplasm, and an inner granular endoplasm. The granular bodies have been shown by the electron microscope to be numerous vacuoles, mitochondria and lysosomes.

The earlier sol-gel hypothesis supposed that the ectoplasm at the tip of a growing pseudopodium was thinner and weaker than that surrounding the rest of the organism, especially at the rear. And so the jelly-like ectoplasm (gel) tended to contract, forcing the more fluid endoplasm (sol) forwards and thereby extending the weakest part, the new pseudopodium.

A more recent theory has been put forward proposing that the ectoplasm is made up of parallel protein molecules which strengthen it. In the ectoplasm of a forming pseudopodium a folding and regimentation of these molecules occurs near the tip. The result is that endoplasm flows into the tip to occupy the newly formed space.

Still more recently amoebas have been viewed from the side instead of from above. Seen from this angle, they seem to move on small strut-like projections which hold the main pseudopodia clear of the substratum. This important matter is still under active study.

Another type of locomotion related to amoeboid movement is found in the Actinopoda, which have fine stiff filaments projecting from the main cell body. Cytoplasm streams along these filaments, carrying with it bits of matter stuck to the surface. The organic bits serve as food when they reach the main cell body. Those pseudopodia in contact with the substratum slowly ease the animal along.

A third type, flagellate movement, is invariably by means of one or more flagella. The exact method of obtaining the relatively high speeds achieved by such small creatures (often 250μ per second or about a metre an hour) depends on the species. The movement of the flagellum is by locally-formed waves which can pass in either direction along the length of the organelle. The waves act on the surrounding water to push or pull

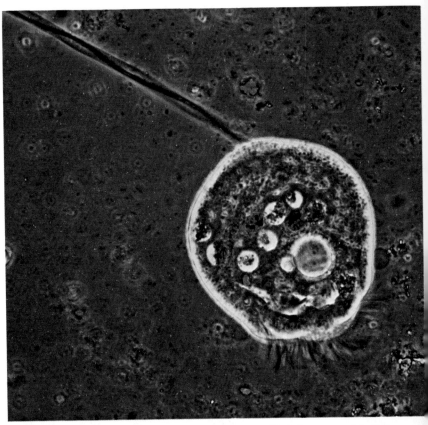

the animal forward. Most flagellates use the pulling method of propulsion and the flagellum moves first. Some species move by twisting the forward-projecting flagellum back on itself and then by whirling the tip to create a vortex into which the rest of the animal is sucked. The variations on the method are many.

Slow-motion ciné studies have shown that the flagella of trypanosomes are subject to waves of contraction passing from the tip to the base. Since flagella can be observed to stop and start, the control for starting a wave presumably originates in the cell and some signal must travel along the flagellum from base to tip to trigger a contraction.

Euglenoid movement is an alternation of shape of the body of *Euglena* and other similar flagellates apparently determined by the subpellicular fibrils. It is well developed in *Euglena* and is used to move the whole body. In others it appears to be less involved in locomotion although its exact function is not known.

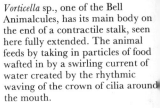

Vorticella sp., one of the Bell Animalcules, has its main body on the end of a contractile stalk, seen here fully extended. The animal feeds by taking in particles of food wafted in by a swirling current of water created by the rhythmic waving of the crown of cilia around the mouth.

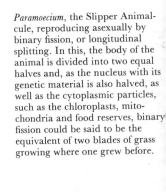

Paramoecium, the Slipper Animalcule, reproducing asexually by binary fission, or longitudinal splitting. In this, the body of the animal is divided into two equal halves and, as the nucleus with its genetic material is also halved, as well as the cytoplasmic particles, such as the chloroplasts, mitochondria and food reserves, binary fission could be said to be the equivalent of two blades of grass growing where one grew before.

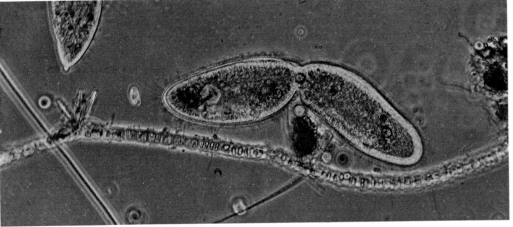

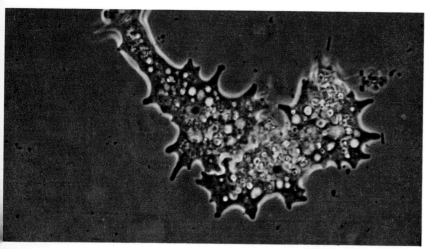

The familiar form of the well-known amoeba is of a shapeless body pushing out blunt, rounded pseudopodia, or false-feet, as it gropes its way through its micro-environment. There are, however, many kinds of amoeba and in some species smaller rhizopodia extend from the broader, blunt pseudopodia.

Yet another method of locomotion is found in the ciliates, which sweep themselves along by using the cilia with which most are more or less covered. Each cilium beats in a characteristic way. In the power stroke the filament is stiff and extended while in the recovery stroke it is bent and offers least resistance to the water. The cilia lie in rows interconnected by a complex network of subpellicular fibrils. The result is that the whole ciliated surface of the animal can beat in a co-ordinated way. The term metachronal rhythm is used to describe the beating, as the cilia do not all exhibit the power stroke simultaneously but in an orderly sequence. This sends waves of power and recovery strokes alternately down the body.

The varied and advanced methods of locomotion found especially in the *Spirotricha* are produced partly by the loss of some rows of cilia and partly by fusion of others into cirri and membranellae. Many organisms in this group are able to 'run' over the surface of water plants with astonishing speed. The cirri serve as stronger leg-like units than single cilia, and although more widely separated from each other still beat in a co-ordinated way.

Nutrition

In the Protozoa this is so varied that it serves to emphasise their claim as founders of the animal kingdom. Some, like *Euglena*, are green and are very close to plants; some like *Didinium* ingest large

particles or the whole bodies of other protozoans; some 'drink' in nutrients by forming small pockets in the cell membrane; some filter off particles in the surrounding water by setting up wide-ranging currents; and there are some in which the feeding mechanisms are still obscure.

The commonest methods of obtaining food are undoubtedly filter feeding, phagocytosis—both phagotrophic feeding methods—and saprozoic feeding. Phagotrophy is the general term applied to feeding on particulate matter. If the particles are in suspension then the method usually employed is filter feeding. As practised by *Vorticella*, a sessile ciliate, a current of water is produced by the beating of the cilia around the crown of the body, causing a vortex that draws food into the mouth.

Particles may also be taken when they are on the surface of water plants or in among other materials such as soil or intestinal contents. The process is a modification of amoeboid movement and consists of forming a hollow conical pseudopod with the particle in the depression. The pseudopod rejoins with itself on the other side of the particle, which is now enclosed within the protozoan. This process is known as phagocytosis.

Saprozoic feeding was earlier thought to be diffusion of soluble food through the cell membrane. Two things have changed this concept considerably. First, the distinction between a solution and a suspension is no longer clear cut. For example, protein molecules which appear to form a stable solution under normal conditions can be thrown down to the bottom of the vessel by ultra-centrifugation. The distinction, then, is one of convenience: small particles (e.g. proteins) cannot be seen when in solution; larger particles can be seen and the mixture is then called a suspension. The second point is that more careful observation of cells revealed pinocytosis (cell drinking), a process in which the cell membrane, instead of absorbing material in solution, forms very deep cones, smaller and more tube-like than in phagocytosis, into which the solution is drawn. The tube closes behind it and so cuts off a pinocytosis vacuole. Pinocytosis may be considered, rather crudely, as a modification of phagocytosis or *vice versa*. The mechanisms are similar but are far removed from the original diffusion theory of saprozoic feeding.

Mitosis is the usual process during which a cell divides into two. At first the nucleus is resting (A), then the chromosomes appear as threads (B) which shorten and coil into spirals. At this point the centrioles or poles begin to move apart, and a spindle forms between them. The chromosomes lie across the spindle (C), attached to it by their spindle attachments. By now the nuclear membrane has dissolved (D), and the duplicates of each chromosome separate and move towards the poles (E) and the spindle itself elongates, pushing the groups of chromosomes further apart. The chromosomes uncoil (F), elongate and disappear, and a new nuclear membrane forms to give two distinct new cells.

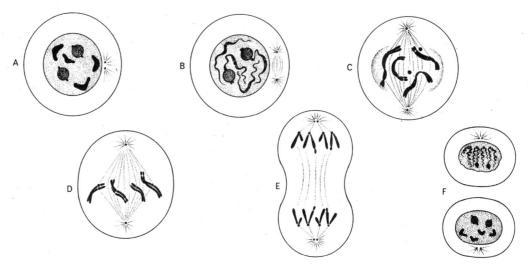

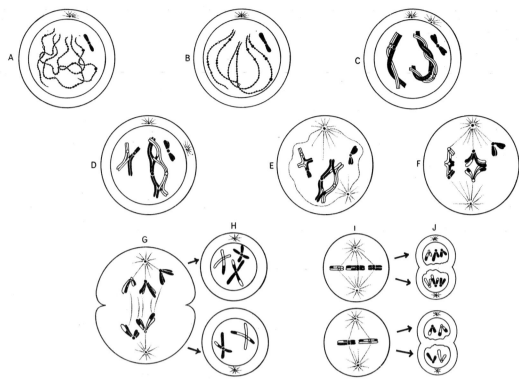

Meiosis consists of two successive cell divisions that both resemble mitosis, but the number of chromosomes is only duplicated once in the whole process so that the number present in each of the four resulting cells is half that of the original cell. When the chromosomes first appear in meiosis (A) they are single pairs—in mitosis they are already double. The two homologous members of each pair of chromosomes begin to associate side by side (B). The centrioles begin to move apart and in a process called pairing or synapsis the associated pairs form bivalents (C). Each chromosome duplicates so that each bivalent becomes four separate chromatids. The two chromatids derived from one chromosome remain paired, but separate from the other two chromatids derived from the homologous chromosome. In certain places they are held together by chiasms or interchanges, and it appears that one chromatid from each of the original chromosomes breaks at corresponding places and fuses with the broken ends of the other, so that a crossing over of genes takes place (D). The chromatids, still in pairs, now begin to go to the poles, two from each original chromosome to opposite ends (E, F) and the nuclear membrane dissolves (G), but the chromatids are still in pairs. At this point there may be a short resting stage, or the second division may follow at once (H). The chromatids go to opposite poles as before (I) and now four cells are produced (J).

Recent studies of trypanosomes have shown the passing of ferritin (a marker substance for the electron microscope) across the membrane surrounding the base of the flagellum. Few of the other saprozoic protozoa have been investigated, but it is to be expected that in the absence of clearly differentiated feeding organelles similar movement of soluble compounds will be found.

Reproduction

In the Protozoa this is a general term that includes both the process of increasing the number of identical cells and also the process of 'shuffling' the genetic material. No single method of achieving both ends is common throughout the group. Differences occur among genera and even among species within a genus. For the proper understanding of reproduction, however, the following distinctions may be made:

For increasing numbers, mitosis, in the Metazoa or many-celled animals, is the process in which the chromosomes form replicates (copies) of themselves and then are so distributed to the two daughter cells that each daughter cell receives a representative of each of the parent cell's chromosomes. The genetic information-containing DNA molecule of each chromosome is perfectly replicated by a process in which a lengthwise 'unzippering' of the molecule occurs, each half then directing the synthesis of its missing portion. Thus each daughter cell contains genetic information identical to that of the parent cell.

The movement of the chromosomes to their respective daughter cells is directed and assisted by the centrioles and spindle fibres. The nucleus as a formed body breaks down at the beginning of the process and a new one forms around the chromosomes in each daughter cell.

Various modifications and simplifications of this process are found in protozoans, though most do not qualify for the strict definition of mitosis.

In sexually reproducing organisms, the union of sperm and ovum in fertilisation would produce a doubling of chromosome number at each generation unless, somewhere, a corresponding reduction occurred. This reduction takes place in the process called meiosis by which the sperm and ovum are produced. Meiosis is a sequence of two cell divisions with, however, only one set of chromosome replications. The result is a halving of the chromosome number in each sex cell.

In the body cells (somatic cells) of animals more complex than protozoans there are almost always two chromosomes of each particular size and shape. This is spoken of as the diploid condition. At the beginning of the first meiotic division (reduction division) the pair members become closely associated (synapsis) and each chromosome replicates. The genetic material is reorganised between the members of each chromosome pair by the process of crossing over, and then the pair members separate to different daughter cells thus halving the number of chromosomes in each daughter cell. Each cell now has only one member of each pair. During the second division the replicates of each chromosome separate, the number in each gamete remaining half the usual number.

Since the nuclei of many protozoans appear more or less homogeneous it is impossible to see and count chromosomes, but the state of the nucleus can frequently be inferred from the phase of the life-cycle. It should be noted that as most protozoans exist as single cells there is nothing remarkable if at some stage in the life-cycle they exist as single haploid cells and at others as single diploid cells.

Without the necessary experimental or observational evidence it is unwise to assign the terms diploid or haploid to stages of the life-cycle before first observing it as a whole and making estimates of the DNA content of the nuclei. In many species a resistant stage develops with a dark and thick protective wall. In other species the complete life-cycle is not known. It is obvious that in such species the situation cannot be determined.

Gametes are the vehicles of genetic material from one sexual generation to another and exist in considerable variety. They are the bodies which are most important in sexual processes. The (female) macrogamete is not motile and the micro-gamete actively swims to it and fuses with it. This is typical of the behaviour of female and male gametes of the metazoans and these types of germ cells are called heterogametes. Isogametes are germ cells which fuse together but are of the same size. In this process mixing of genetic material is achieved but usually little food reserve capable of supporting future divisions is carried as the macrogamete is absent. The cell formed by the fusion of gametes is called a zygote, and the new organism develops from this by mitotic divisions.

A reproductive pattern found quite commonly in protozoa is multiple fission. This can be observed very clearly in the malarial parasite. When the feeding stage is complete, one parasite divides repeatedly to produce eight, sixteen or more schizonts, each theoretically capable of infecting a further red cell. The vast potential increase in number is not fully realised in practice. For example, about three-quarters of *Plasmodium berghei* schizonts have been shown to be capable of increasing the infection. Even so, the efficiency of this method of increasing the number of parasites is considerably higher than that of mitosis or some simplified form of division or binary fission.

Other specialisations of reproductive processes in protozoans will be described in the section dealing with species. The general picture in this phylum is of diversity and lack of uniformity. In many functions and especially in reproduction the protozoans can be regarded as a group in which the experiments of nature are still going on. The selective forces driving the evolution of single cells are so different from those acting on multicellular organisms that many different systems of performing the same function are suited to the diverse ways of life of their possessors.

Protozoans and their environments

Protozoa have free-living and parasitic representatives. In both forms the environment is strikingly different from that of the larger metazoans such as insects or mammals. They occur in very varied conditions: freshwater, salt water and all types of soil.

They are exposed to changing temperatures, salinities, acidities and other chemical factors to a degree unknown to larger animals because the small size, with its consequent slow movement, and water dependence of the free-living protozoans allow the surroundings to change faster than the organisms can escape. This has inevitably developed in most free-living species a general tolerance (but only in the sense of survival and not for reproduction) of a wide variety of conditions. Even in temperate countries the surface soil temperature may well exceed a range from $-10°C$. to $+45°C$. In addition to temperature variations the soil undergoes other changes: it dries out and is wetted again, is frozen and thawed, is flooded and

rendered without oxygen, perhaps inundated by the sea or locally altered by the faeces or urine of a large mammal such as a horse. None of these conditions causes total sterilisation of the soil, though changed conditions do determine which species are most numerous. Some adaptations are known, such as the remarkable transformation of the amoebo-flagellate *Naegleria gruberi* (*see* page 23). The success of the phylum obviously suggests that most protozoans are capable of considerable tolerance of change.

The parasitic forms are exposed to quite the opposite situation so long as they stay within one metazoan host. A characteristic requirement of life for all organisms is to be able to regulate the internal environment of the body (*see* homeostasis in vertebrates, p. 206). The constancy of mammalian blood is a remarkable feature surpassed only by the supreme constancy of mammalian cerebro-spinal fluid. Thus parasites may live out many generations within the highly regulated environment of the body of their host. This solves many problems but creates a major difficulty.

The life of a parasite is easier because it is supplied with food, water and, in the case of homothermic hosts, uniform temperature. Most other factors are well stabilised within greater or lesser limits. If the parasites' metabolic products do not exceed a small proportion of the host's products—and here one is thinking of the total waste products from all the parasites in a host compared with all the waste products from the host itself—the host will take care of the disposal of such products. This simplifies the need for excretory mechanisms in parasites. Most protozoan parasites (and also many helminth parasites and tumours) have done away with a large part of the energy production metabolism. Since food is plentiful, waste products disposable, and oxygen possibly scarce (for gut parasites) only the first steps in carbohydrate breakdown are found. Thus glycolysis predominates although it is an inefficient form of energy production; pyruvate so produced is metabolised by the host.

The difficulty introduced by simplification of structural and biochemical features is that of finding a new host. If the old host dies all the parasites die with it unless they find a new one. Most parasitic protozoans have evolved complex life-histories to overcome this danger. For example, anopheline mosquitoes regularly bite man and so transmit the protozoans which cause malaria. Reproduction continues in the insect host. In short, getting from host to host is a chancy business for a highly specialised parasite. To increase the odds for success extreme emphasis is placed on prolific reproduction.

The variety of protozoans

It has been explained in the Introduction (*see* pp. 7–9) that animals are classified in a way which signifies their mutual relationships. This aim is less satisfactorily pursued in classifying Protozoa than other phyla. The classification used here, although not the latest, is that most generally adopted. It conveniently divides the phylum into four major classes. Mastigophora, Rhizopoda, Sporozoa and Ciliata, and a minor one, Cnidospora.

The flagellates (Class Mastigophora)

This class contains organisms which are actively motile by means of flagella. They may have a single flagellum or they may have hundreds, so that they bear a strong superficial resemblance to ciliates. The nuclei are usually restricted to one per cell but if there is more than one they are all similar and do not display sexual reproduction of the kinds found in the ciliates. They are usually without pseudopodia, and are small (under 100μ). There are both parasitic and free-living members in this class.

Reproduction varies: in some species hetero- or iso-gametes are found, in others no sexual processes are yet known.

There are two subclasses, Phytomastigophora and Zoomastigophora.

Phytomasts (Subclass Phytomastigophora)

The theoretical distinction between the two subclasses, Phytomastigophora and Zoomastigophora, is that the former, being plant-like, have chloroplasts and produce their own food with the agency of chlorophyll or related pigments, whereas the latter, true animals, rely on ingesting other micro-organisms. Difficulty arises when a particular organism looks in every way like a phytomast but does not have chloroplasts. Common sense classifies such organisms with those to which they have most resemblance and we presume the colourless forms have lost their chloroplasts. The flagellates are most readily thought of as a class made up of some fourteen orders of which eight are of general importance (and dealt with here). Apart from the major classification based on chloroplasts, each order has a characteristic shape and is therefore generally recognisable.

Phytomonads (Order Phytomonadida)

This is the protozoan group clearly the nearest to plants. The chloroplasts contain a bright green chlorophyll and the cell walls, firm and resistant to distortion, are made of cellulose or a close chemical relative. The typical organism is *Chlamydomonas*, which has two flagella, a pigment spot (stigma), is small (about 20μ) and is found in freshwater. Both iso- and hetero-gametes are known in the different species of this genus. Reproduction by sexual methods is readily induced in the laboratory.

In early spring colonial phytomonads are commonly found in freshwater. These are organisms formed by 4, 8, 16, 32 or more cells, each cell more or less like *Chlamydomonas*. The arrangement of cells is usually regular, flattened in *Gonium*, and spherical in *Eudorina* and *Pleodorina*. A larger colonial form consisting of several thousand flagellated cells is *Volvox*. Reproduction may be by asexual or sexual method. If by the first, daughter colonies are formed inside the sphere and freed when the mother colony opens; if by a sexual process, male and female gametes occur and the two unite to produce a zygote, or fertilised egg. The zygote is a resistant stage with a thick cell wall, and *Volvox* usually overwinters in this form.

The niche occupied by most phytomonads is that of small motile plants. Some are most numerous in early spring, when they make use of bright sunshine and the high carbon dioxide concentration of water only a few degrees above the freezing-point. Colonies may be seen actively swimming near the surface of slow streams. One may assume that motility enables them to enjoy an optimum light intensity by day and avoid being frozen at night by descending to lower levels.

In contrast to the plant-like behaviour of the green phytomonads the genus *Polytoma* is clearly saprozoic in its nutrition. It has no chloroplasts but is otherwise similar to *Chlamydomonas*. Since it has no cytostome (cell mouth) the only possible means for food intake would appear to be by diffusion.

Euglenoids (Order Euglenoidida)

The members of this common freshwater order are typically bright green and have only one flagellum, used in locomotion. (In some forms a short second flagellum is seen in stained preparations.) The flagellum arises from within a pit in the anterior end of the cell. Also in this pit, sometimes called a gullet, is a reddish coloured body called a stigma.

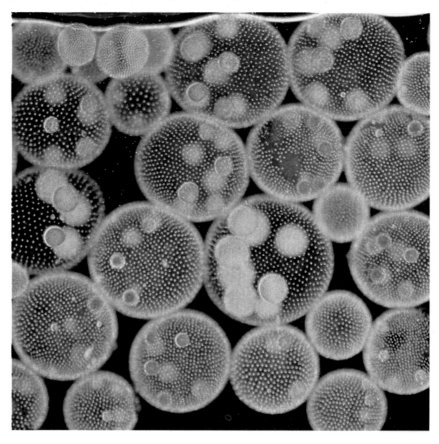

Volvox crowding to the surface in strong sunlight. The colonial phytomasts rise and sink in the water of ponds as the strength of daylight waxes and wanes. They may be scattered or they may be aggregated, as here, when the colour of these living spheres imparts a greenish tinge to the water.

PROTOZOANS

Euglena viridis is one of the best-known members of a group of phytomasts living in freshwater and noted for their characteristic motility. From this has arisen the term euglenoid movement. Typically, in this form of movement, the flagellum is lashed sideways and backwards, the body rotates on its long axis and at the same time worm-like, semi-amoeboid changes of shape in the body are evident.

A characteristic feature of euglenoids is their food reserve, paramylum, which, although a carbohydrate like starch, does not stain with iodine as do other starches. The cells are otherwise very variable; some secrete flask-shaped loricas (inanimate protective coverings) in which they live, others are naked; some have stiff cell walls, others are very flexible and are shaped by complex changes in subpellicular fibrils; some live on the end of fixed stalks, but most of them are free-swimming.

The genus *Euglena* has members which range from 30μ to 400μ in length. While most are green, have upwards of fifteen chloroplasts, and are found in freshwater, *E. halophila* is a marine species and is most tolerant of very high concentrations of salt. *E. rubra* is reddish and commonly occurs in late summer as the scum on stagnant waters rich in organic matter, such as farmyard ponds.

Phacus is common in freshwater. The body is rigid and flattened in the shape of a conventional lover's heart. In some species the body is twisted spirally at the posterior end and produced to a point. Numerous spiral ridges cover the body.

Nutritionally *Astasia* is among the most interesting of the order. Structurally it resembles *Euglena* but is without chloroplasts. The cells form paramylum when cultured in media devoid of complex substances like sugars or proteins. This property is typical of plants and has been retained despite the loss of chloroplasts.

Peranema, like *Astasia*, is colourless. It is found in situations rich in organic matter. The flagellum is noteworthy in this genus for it is held out stiff in front of the body. Only the very tip moves and causes locomotion. Related genera have two flagella, one held as described, the other, the shorter one, trails alongside the body.

Cryptomonads (Order Cryptomonadida)

This is a small order whose members usually have two flagella which arise in a pit, are small (15–40μ long) and have one or two yellow or brown chloroplasts. The cells are usually flattened in section. *Chilomonas* deserves mention because it has an abundance of infusions of plant material although devoid of chloroplasts. It grows so readily that it is frequently used as food for particle feeders, e.g. ciliates.

Chrysomonads (Order Chrysomonadida)

This order is probably large in terms of number of species and is certainly very large when numbers of individuals are considered. These are the yellowish-brown, very small flagellates ubiquitous in fresh, brackish and seawater. In size they seldom exceed 20μ in length. They have one or two flagella, and one to a few chloroplasts. Owing to their small size, frequently marine habit and the difficulty experienced in making permanent preparations, the study of this order has been largely neglected. Their habits are varied. Colonial forms similar to *Gonium* exist but others form tips of much-branched stalks. Some are solitary. Silica-containing cysts is a feature of the order.

Chromulina is an example of a solitary species. The flagellate stage with one flagellum and one chloroplast is dominant but it also has an amoeboid stage. In the latter the flagellum is entirely absent and locomotion is by means of a single pseudopodium (a blunt-ended lobopodium). *Mallomonas* is more elongate than *Chromulina* and has siliceous spines covering its body. Members of this genus are larger (40–80μ) than is general for the order.

Ochromonas has in the past few years become of considerable importance as a gauge in the estimation of the amounts of vitamin B_{12} present in certain foods. This organism cannot synthesise the vitamin and cannot grow without it. Thus the extent of growth of a culture on food media affords a measure of the vitamin B_{12} content in the food. The organisms have the appearance of a small, round cell with two stubby flagella, one slightly longer than the other.

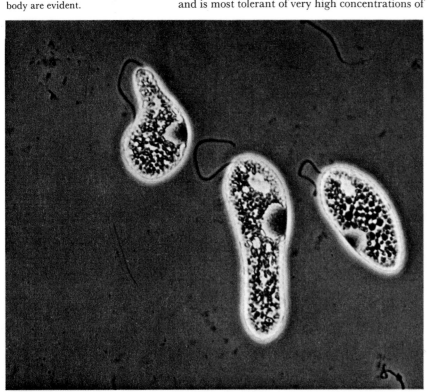

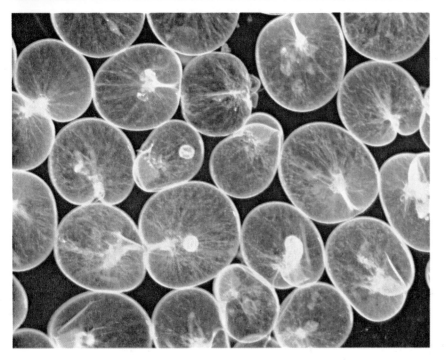

Dinoflagellates (Order Dinoflagellata)

This comprises a fairly homogeneous assemblage of mostly marine organisms characterised by their sculptured cellulose cell walls. They have two flagella. One lies in a groove on the equatorial plane while the other projects to the posterior of the organism from a groove, the sulcus, confluent with the equatorial groove or girdle. By this arrangement both flagella arise close together though their tips are far apart. The longitudinal flagellum is used for propulsion. The equatorial flagellum rotates the animal and may serve in orientation. Except for *Ceratium* and *Noctiluca* the size range is 20–80μ.

Although some species have a variety of chlorophylls and the food reserves are starch and lipids, there appears to be a tendency to holozoic nutrition, that is, taking in food through permanent openings. Particulate food is ingested in many species and in *Ceratium* there is evidence that food is also captured by means of a fine pseudopodial network. Of more doubtful function are the two pusules or vacuoles containing a pink fluid. These are connected to the outside by fine pores and may be used to intake suspended matter.

Gymnodinium is an example of a 'naked' dinoflagellate. No thickened, sculptured plates are carried. Structurally it is probably the simplest of the order. Members of the genus are found in lakes, freshwater ponds and also in the sea. Some are green and holophytic; that is, they make complex organic substances by photosynthesis and from simple substances absorbed through the body surface. Others are holozoic. Occasionally the balance of nature controlling the number of organisms is disturbed and vast numbers are found in some subtropical waters. For example it occurs on the Florida coast at times in such numbers that fish are poisoned. The species concerned is reddish and the plague is known as the 'red tide'.

Another red dinoflagellate is *Gonyaulax*. The genus has armoured plates surrounding the body. The plates are of a characteristic shape and have regularly pitted surfaces. As in the last genus sporadic increases in number occur, giving the sea a reddish tinge and killing fishes and crustaceans. The organism contains a toxic alkaloid.

Ceratium has elaborate armouring. The epicone or covering on the top half of the body has one long process and the hypocone covering the lower half has three. Diameter is 100–700μ. Numerous coloured granules, possibly chloroplasts, are arranged in five groups. Food is captured by a pseudopodial web and a large single pseudopodium which can appear through the sulcus. Food vacuoles are clearly visible in the cytoplasm, and contain the remnants of other dinoflagellates, diatoms and phytomasts.

Noctiluca is well known as an organism causing phosphorescence of the sea at night. It is a large and aberrant dinoflagellate up to two millimetres in diameter and with a permanent tentacle formed for the hypocone. Phosphorescent granules in rows form a close mesh in the cytoplasm. The discharge of light occurs mainly when the water is disturbed.

Parasitic dinoflagellates are known, and these are harmful to fishes and some marine invertebrates. They are all small and usually without flagella and the characteristic structures while in the parasitic phase. It is only during the free-swimming phase that they can be identified as belonging to the order.

Zoomasts (Subclass Zoomastigophora)

These are flagella-bearing protozoans which have truly animal methods of nutrition. Many are parasitic and have been extensively studied as they affect the life of man. The number of free-living species is not certain. They are morphologically diverse and are best considered in their orders.

Protomonads (Order Protomonadida)

All members have only one or two flagella, but are otherwise probably unrelated.

In the family Codosigidae are the remarkable collar flagellates. The collar is a contractile cylindrical process from the cytoplasm which covers about one fifth of the flagellum. Food is apparently directed by the flagellum to a pocket between the cell and its test or shell, travelling down the outside of the collar. The particle is ingested by movement of the cell against its test.

The genus *Bodo* (Bodonidae) is common in freshwater. It has two flagella; one leads and the other is bent back round the body so as to trail. It is small, about 14μ in diameter, and rather difficult to observe. Stained preparations show that it has a DNA-containing body called a kinetoplast at the base of the flagella.

The kinetoplast is also found in the trypanosomatids, of which one species causes sleeping sickness in man and related diseases in vertebrate animals. *Trypanosoma* is a genus of variable morphology but members usually have one flagellum. Sufficient work has elucidated the relations between apparently dissimilar organisms. Change in shape bears a clear relation to the environment of the parasite and to the evolutionary stage attained by a particular species. For example, a simple insect parasite, which seems to do no harm to its host, like *Crithidia gerridis* of water bugs (*Gerris* sp.) is found in crithidial, leptomonad and leishmanial stages. *Trypanosoma brucei* which has a life-history in the Tsetse Fly and in cattle, is known in all stages except leishmania in the vertebrate. *T. cruzi* even has a leishmanial stage. Although in the leishmanial form the flagellum is absent, rudimentary organelles remain and from these the new flagellum grows.

Slender body and vigorous movement are typical of trypanosomes, which are found in a wide range of vertebrates and invertebrates. As the blood is the easiest organ in which to see moving objects it is not surprising that trypanosomes are considered to be blood parasites. But much of the damage they do is not produced in the blood but is destruction or poisoning of the brain (by *T. rhodesiense*) or of the heart muscle (by *Schizotry-*

Opposite
Noctiluca scintillans is a large dinoflagellate protozoan. It is spherical, the size of a pin's head, and found in large numbers in the sea. The body is filled with a gelatinous substance through which strands of protoplasm radiate from a central point. It has lost all power of active movement so that it drifts with the currents. It is one of the marine animals responsible for bioluminescence.

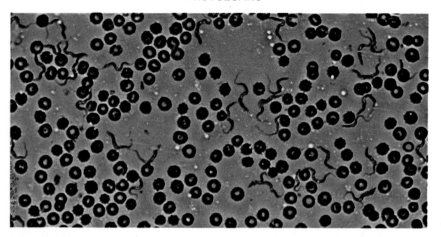

Trypanosomes lying among blood corpuscles. A parasitic zoomast, it is responsible for diseases in vertebrates and for sleeping sickness and Chagas's disease in man. Sleeping sickness is caused by subspecies of *Trypanosoma brucei* in tropical Africa and Chagas's disease is indigenous to America, from Chile and Argentina to Texas.

panum cruzi). The 'undulating membrane' of the textbooks which was supposed to attach the flagellum to the body is not a real membrane but a loose pellicle pulled out by the movement of the flagellum. The names given to the organelles at the base of the flagellum have caused much confusion. Basal granule is the centriole-like structure at the root of the flagellum, while the kinetoplast is the larger, darkly staining body which contains DNA and has been shown to be associated with mitochondria. The size of trypanosomatids varies from 2μ in leishmania to several hundred μ for the trypanosome form of certain marine fish parasites.

In the disease called leishmaniasis the trypanosome form is never seen. The form found in mammals is the leishmania, and the vector, *Phlebotomus* sp., develops a leptomonad and so indicates that the causative organism (*Leishmania* sp.) is related to other trypanosomes.

Order Polymastigida
These flagellates have more than two flagella. Their other features are variable, as are the number of nuclei.

The genus *Trichomonas* ($3–20\mu$ in length) consists of parasites of man and other animals. Typically there are four flagella, three fairly short and projecting forward from their bases, the fourth, although arising with the others, is much longer and is united with the body to form an undulating membrane extending beyond the posterior of the body. In addition there is an axostyle as a stiffening rod running the length of the body. These organisms are found in the gut of many vertebrates and invertebrates where for the most part they do little harm. *Trichomonas vaginalis*, however, is found in the genital tract of women,

commonly in some geographic regions, and to a lesser extent in men. Under certain conditions the numbers become excessive and inflammation results.

Giardia is another genus commonly found in the gut of vertebrates. It is sometimes included in the order Distomatina. The body has a characteristic kite shape and bilateral symmetry is strictly observed in all organelles including the nuclei, of which there are two. There are six flagella. Normally no inconvenience is experienced by the host of these parasites, but occasionally the numbers rise and cause a severe diarrhoea.

Order Trichomonadida
Trichonympha and its allies are found in the gut of termites and orthopterans such as cockroaches and woodroaches. They are mutualistic symbionts in that they are essential to the economy of many of their wood-feeding hosts, breaking down cellulose particles that the host's own enzymes cannot digest. Length ranges between 50μ and 300μ. But some species are as small as 5μ. The number of flagella is very large. This genus is not classified among the ciliates because it has only a single nucleus and an amoeboid posterior, which is used to ingest particles of wood. Food vacuoles and their contents are clearly visible in the living organism. It has been shown recently that sexual phenomena occur when the host moults. The onset of meiosis is controlled by the host moulting hormone.

Order Opalinida
This order even more closely resembles the ciliates than does the Trichomonadida. Cilia arise all over the body and are of uniform size with interconnected bases. *Opalina* used to be classified as protociliates but now the genus is included somewhat tentatively in the zoomasts because the many nuclei are of identical size, and any resemblance to the ciliates is superficial.

When sexual phenomena occur the cells fuse permanently like gametes, and not temporarily, for the exchange of nuclei (the latter process known as conjugation). The various species are found in the rectum of frogs and toads. They are generally rather large, ranging from $100–800\mu$ long. Infection is transmitted from one frog by encysted forms produced during the frogs' breeding season. Experiments have shown that sex hormones injected into the host can induce cyst formation though it is not clear whether this has a direct or indirect effect on the parasites.

Class Sarcodina, Subclass Rhizopoda

This class includes the various species of amoebas. Typically amoebas crawl on the surface of mud, submerged plants, in the spaces between soil particles, or inside animals as parasites. Locomotion is by means of pseudopodia, which may be long and thin but usually unbranched (filopodia), long, thin and branched, uniting with one another to form a network (rhizopodia) or shorter, broader and usually blunt (lobopodia). A generalised cell contains all the usual complement of organelles

and, if found in freshwater, a contractile vacuole as well. The shape is highly plastic. There are few or no reference points on the surface or within the cell. This makes classification difficult. Confusion is made worse by some amoebas having flagella or being readily able to assume a flagellate phase in the right conditions. The fundamental level of the structural-functional components of these organisms can be gauged from considering their counterparts in man's body where many white blood cells function like amoebas, his trachea is lined with cells which bear cilia and his spermatozoa move by means of a flagellum. In all these, typical protozoan features are retained for integrated use by advanced metazoans. It is a question whether the whole stock of animals arose from an organism which had both flagella and pseudopodia, or whether these features have been lost and redeveloped over and over again. There is no fossil record to help us.

The classification of the rhizopods is therefore based on other features: whether it lives in a 'house' or shell, or whether it is naked. If in a 'house', what shape is it and of what is it made? And, if naked, is a flagellate stage known? At this stage in our knowledge it is inevitable that the classification should be based to some extent on negative factors, e.g. flagellate stage *not* known. These remarks serve as a caution to those who may like to compare the classification used here with that of any other author. Almost certainly they will be different. Such are the problems of incomplete knowledge.

Order Rhizomastigida

These are naked amoebas with a flagellate stage in their life-history. Perhaps the most studied species is *Naegleria gruberi* which lives in organically rich soils. It is a small limax-type amoeba (*see below*) in dry conditions or in high osmotic pressure liquids. When placed in distilled water a rapid transformation occurs: first the posterior (uroid) develops long filaments of cytoplasm which move about; the thickest of these become flagella and as soon as they are fully formed the earlier processes are withdrawn; finally, the two to four flagella migrate to the anterior end and the flagella beat more vigorously until the body breaks its attachment with the substrate. The flagellate swims with rotatory movement. The reverse process has been shown to be very sudden: the flagellate sticks to a surface, the flagellum stops and after a few minutes is quickly withdrawn and the amoeba crawls away. *Dientamoeba* is a small (5–18μ) limax-type amoeba sometimes found in the intestine of man. It has been shown to have a flagellate phase. Apart from having two nuclei it is very similar to other entamoebas.

Histomonas is an amoeba with one to four flagella. The comb and wattles of poultry infected by this parasite, known as 'blackhead', turn black. The parasite is flagellated in the lumen of the intestine but becomes amoeboid upon invading the liver.

Mastigamoeba is large (150–200μ long) and has both pseudopodia and a flagellum at the same time. The pseudopodia are radial or terminal (posterior). Some species are free-living, others are parasitic, especially in the gut of amphibians.

Typical amoebas (Order Amoebina)

These are amoebas in which a flagellate stage is not known. The size range is great, from very small soil species of 3–15μ to large, sometimes multinucleate, freshwater species up to three millimetres in length. Reproduction is believed to be asexual and may be by promitosis (binary fission) or true mitosis. The habits are both free-living and parasitic.

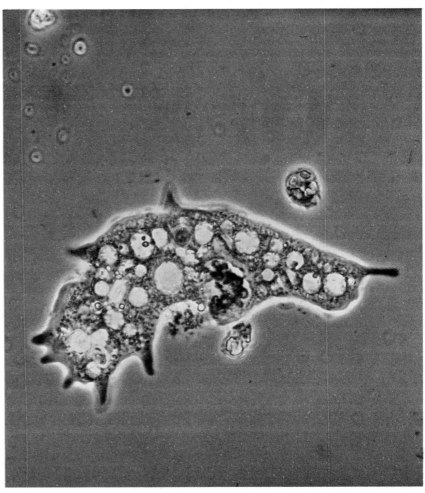

Amoeba proteus is probably the most commonly studied organism in schools. It has also been known as *Chaos diffluens*. But it is doubtful whether the various organisms from all over the world which roughly fit the pictures in textbooks are the species *proteus*.

This type of amoeba has several large pseudopodia which contain ectoplasm and endoplasm. It is usually seen to move in one direction at once and the spent pseudopodia collect as small bumps in the uroid. Also in or near the uroid is the contractile vacuole, while the nucleus may be close but somewhat anterior. In the endoplasm of many species of free-living amoeba are bipyramidal crystals of uncertain function. Few pseudopodia reveal much of taxonomic value because the shape is ever changing. The genera are distinguished principally by nuclear and cyst structure. Therefore identification is possible only by the specialist.

The limax-amoebas are the small amoebas which abound in soil. They are distinguished from the other free-living forms by their single pseudopodium which contains relatively more ectoplasm. The smallest are only 3μ across and the majority are under 20μ, though up to 40μ has been reported. They are extremely simple in structure. They feed on bacteria and round up into resistant cysts when food is in short supply or conditions are otherwise unfavourable. The Hartmanellidae are amoebas in this group which show true mitosis.

The parasitic amoebas are typically found in the gut of vertebrates and invertebrates. Frequently

Amoeba moves and captures its food by sending out temporary protoplasmic processes in different directions, the so-called pseudopodia or false-feet. Its movement is, however, less random than was formerly supposed, since the protoplasm of the body as a whole streams more persistently in one direction, the pseudopodia that have been pushed out in other directions, then withdrawing.

23

Foraminiferan shells: most foraminiferans secrete a calcareous shell, starting with a small chamber, the proloculum, and adding larger and larger chambers as they grow. These are often arranged in a spiral. The shells are typically perforated by a large number of small holes through which issue slender strands of protoplasm, the pseudopodia.

there is little morphological distinction between the species found in different hosts. They are mostly $20-40\mu$ in diameter. Amoebic dysentery is caused by *Entamoeba hystolytica*, which invades the walls of the large intestine and causes loss of blood and excessive secretion of mucus. An almost identical species, *Entamoeba coli*, is found in the same part of the gut but is non-pathogenic. The precise conditions in which one species gains a numerical advantage over the other are difficult to determine as many apparently healthy humans are 'cyst-passers' and clearly infected carriers. The cysts are most resistant to chemical treatment and even to gentle drying. Amoebic dysentery is therefore easily spread by contamination of food. A related parasite, *Entamoeba invadens*, causes great damage in snakes and other reptiles. It does not infect man.

Testaceans (Order Testacida)
This order contains amoebas which build a shell or test in which they live. They are distinguished from the foraminifers by having only one test. The type of test determines classification within the order. In some the test is simple, made of secreted substances and not complicated by plates. The genus *Arcella* belongs here. Its test is pale brown and shaped like the cap of a young mushroom. The organism lives outside the test and extends blunt pseudopodia through a hole where, in the mushroom, the stalk would join the cap. These organisms are $25-100\mu$ and are found on surfaces of decaying plants in freshwater.

The arenaceous testaceans are so-called because they cement grains of sand to their tests and so add

to the protective advantage of their armour. *Difflugia* has a symmetrical round test with a pointed apex and a rim round the opening. The pseudopodia are blunt and in other respects the organisms are similar to those above.

Foraminifers (Order Foraminifera)
Foraminifers taken collectively are important because they concentrate calcium or silica with which they form their tests. They are abundant and typically marine. The accumulations of their tests are found to make up a substantial part of certain geological formations, in particular the chalk deposits of the Cretaceous. A young foraminiferan in the process of developing from amoebulae (formed by asexual reproduction) secretes a proloculum around itself. It feeds on particles captured by fine pseudopodia. These shorten and drag the food to the organism for ingestion. Growth ensues and instead of enlarging the existing proloculum by adding to it on a conical principle like a snail it secretes a new loculum which remains attached to the proloculum. Cytoplasm continues in the old proloculum and a thin covering of it invests old, new and later locula. New locula are added when needed. This pattern affords the system of classification. Growth may be spiral, linear, concentric or in a complicated fashion of overlapping tubes. The tests are composed of calcareous or porcelaneous material depending on the genus. In all cases they are perforated by holes through which pseudopodia emerge.

This is a large, well-known order, partly because accurate identification of the tests has a practical application: because many oil deposits occur below foraminiferous strata the presence of certain species may be indicative of the mineral's proximity.

The life-history of all species is not fully known, but in those studied it involves an alternation of generations. When the (gamont) stage described above becomes mature it forms gametes. These fuse and the zygote forms a small microspheric proloculum (smaller than the proloculum of the early gamont, which is megalospheric). As the zygote grows it forms new locula of the agamont generation and when mature divides to become amoebulae, at the start of the gamont generation.

Elphidium is a spirally arranged foraminifer common on seaweeds in littoral areas. It creeps slowly and can climb the glass sides of a tank. *Globigerina*, known from Jurassic times to the present day and forming globigerina ooze on the floor of deep oceans in warm regions, has spherical locula arranged in spirals.

Heliozoans (Order Heliozoida)
The 'sun animalcules', beloved of Victorian microscopists, are freshwater organisms found in peat and other acid pools. The various species are generally more than 40μ in diameter and as much as one millimetre. The cytoplasm of *Actinosphaerium* is clearly divided into two concentric spheres. The outer is vacuolated and considered to be ectoplasm. The inner sphere is dense and contains the food vacuoles and most other organelles. The roots of the axial filaments arise in the dense cytoplasm. This and the related genus

Radiolarians live in the plankton of the sea, usually in warm waters, When they die the protoplasm disintegrates and the finely sculptured shells, like those seen here, sink slowly to the ocean bed where they form vast areas of radiolarian ooze, especially underneath the warmer seas.

Actinosphaerium sp., a freshwater Heliozoan or Sun Animalcule, showing the cytoplasm clearly differentiated into two concentric spheres. In life, fine pseudopodia radiate from the surface, giving the effect of the sun and its peripheral light rays.

Actinophrys are both naked, that is, without a stiffening skeleton. *Raphidiophrys* and *Clathrulina* have siliceous skeletons.

In the genera studied in detail cysts form in well-fed individuals. Within the cyst gametes are formed and these fuse with each other. Hatching of the zygote seems to require winter conditions. Reproduction is also by repeated binary fission.

Radiolarians (Order Radiolarida)

These are all marine and mostly pelagic. Structurally they are separated from the heliozoans by having a distinct membrane between the ectoplasm and endoplasm. The ectoplasm in some species appears to be capable of secreting freshwater into vacuoles. The presence of such vacuoles clearly lightens a skeleton-bearing animal and enables it to rise to the surface of the sea. Not all radiolarians have massive skeletons. The suborder *Actipylina* have radial spicules and some members of the suborder *Peripylaria* have four-pronged spicules or none at all. Silica is the principal skeletal constituent. The best-known radiolarians are those with full and persistent skeletons, which sink to the bottom of the ocean to form thick 'radiolarian ooze'. The variety and detail make these remains beautiful objects for microscopy.

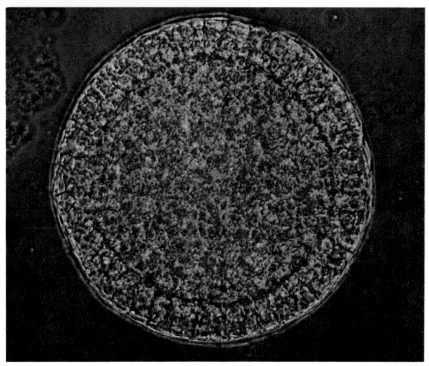

The spore-formers (Class Sporozoa)

This class was formerly thought to be an artificial grouping but the electron microscope has revealed fundamental characteristics in all its members that justify the grouping. First, all are well-adapted parasites. To this end reproductive efficiency is exaggerated and structural complexity reduced. The same stages, though not the names, are found in trypanosomatids, some foraminifers, trematodes and some cestodes, and are typical of alternation of generations in the lower plants.

In the Sporozoa, as in the other cases in which it occurs, alternation of generation serves to increase the number of organisms by asexual reproduction. Exchange and recombination of genetic material is achieved through occasional sexual reproduction. The life-history of a sporozoan species may be in a single host (monogenetic) or in two hosts (digenetic). The names given to the various reproductive stages do not indicate where there is a change of host. The life-cycle is as follows: sporozoites which are usually long and motile infect a host and change into the feeding form (trophozoite) which grows until it is able to undertake multiple fission (schizont stage); when fission is complete the daughter cells are liberated. Merozoites are often similar to sporozoites and can either become trophozoites or they can become sporonts which give rise to gametocytes; the latter may be large (macrogametocyte) or small (microgametocyte) and in turn change into macrogametes and microgametes respectively. After fusion of the gametes the zygote enlarges and develops a protective wall, the oocyst; inside the oocyst repeated division takes place to produce sporozoites. When the sporozoites are ripe the oocyst wall breaks down liberating sporozoites and starting a new cycle.

Gregarina lumbriculus, one of the common parasites within the gut of certain invertebrates, especially earthworms.

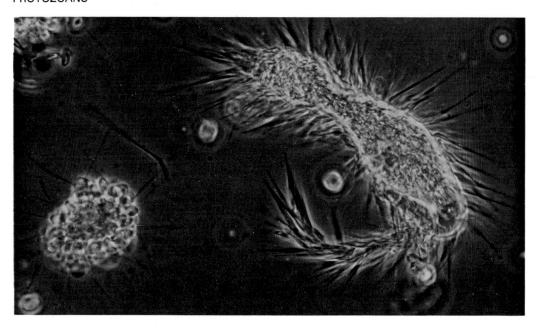

Subclass Gregarinomorpha

In this group are placed various parasites with reproductive similarities. The trophozoite is large and feeds in the lumen of the host's gut or between cells. Genetic exchange is achieved by a union of two sporonts (mature trophozoites) prior to gametogenesis. This union and the formation of gametocysts ensures that gametes can find each other. When gametes develop they do so in a gametocyst and fuse in pairs.

Order Archigregarinida

These are considered to be primitive gregarines because some species display schizogony, which is lost in the eugragarines. The trophozoites of *Selenidium* are found in the gut wall of various marine annelid worms and are about $80\mu \times 25\mu$. The elongate body has numerous longitudinal myonemes and the nucleus is situated anteriorly. The extreme anterior carries a knob-like process which serves to attach the parasite to its host's cells. Very little is known about these parasites.

Order Eugregarinida

The parasites of the two suborders making up this order are morphologically very different but neither displays asexual reproduction by means of schizogony. Numerical increase occurs by sporogony, that is, the development of eight sporozoites from each zygote, and also by the production of several to numerous gametes from each gametocyte.

Cephalines (Suborder Cephalina)

Many insects have these highly developed parasites as gut parasites. Species of *Dermestes* and *Tenebrio* are often heavily infected. There are many species of the genus *Gregarina*. The body of the trophozoite (cephalont) which may be up to 400μ long, has a marked knob (epimerite) on the anterior tip and the remaining part is two-jointed. The epimerite is lost when the trophozoite is

mature and is no longer anchored by it to intestinal cells. This stage (sporont) moves slowly in the gut contents and unites with another sporont. Whether these are symbionts or parasites and harm their hosts is not clear. In some species of *Dermestes* the proportion of beetles infected can be variable. No difference in health or reproductive capacity of the hosts is noted. Sometimes a host benefits from a symbiont (as in *Trichonympha*) and sometimes it may be weakened, as with poorly-adjusted parasites. That neither advantage nor disadvantage is known in this instance indicates a condition of apparent neutrality. Transmission between hosts is by contamination of food with gametocysts containing mature sporocysts.

Acephalines (Suborder Acephalina)

As the name suggests these gregarines are without either epimerite or two-jointed body. The mature trophozoite (sporont) is large by comparison with other stages but seldom exceeds 200μ long. A typical genus is *Monocystis* which has its life-history in the seminal vesicles of earthworms. The sporont is elongate and has a small distention of the anterior which is used as an anchoring device. The life-history is similar to that of the cephalines and need not be repeated here. A characteristic feature is the invasion of a sperm mother cell of the host by a sporozoite at a time when the nuclei have just divided. The young trophozoite is intracellular and takes up a central position surrounded by the host's sperm nuclei. The latter continue to develop and at a later stage the trophozoite is seen in sections or smears to be covered with sperm tails. Having grown as large as possible in this cell the parasite escapes and continues to feed between the cells of the seminal vesicles. Sporogony is started when two sporonts come together and form a single gametocyst around themselves. Infection is believed to be by ingestion of soil infected with sporocysts.

Subclass Coccidiomorpha

This group is distinguished from the previous one by spending the whole of its trophozoite life intracellularly, and by effecting massive reproduction with schizogony. There is only one major order which contains three suborders. These are markedly different from one another.

Order Eucocciida

These are parasites of epithelial cells of invertebrates and vertebrates, though variations do occur.

Suborder Adeleidea

In this group the young gametocytes associate and during their development produce only a few gametes. This is, as already noted, an efficient fertilisation method. The life-history is monogenetic in some genera but digenetic in others. Among the digenetic ones a variety of blood-sucking arthropods including tsetse flies, lice, mites and ticks act as the insect vector. In *Haemogregarina* sexual reproduction occurs in leeches and asexual reproduction in turtles. All classes of vertebrates can serve as hosts for the different species. The parasites seem to be well adjusted to their hosts as these appear to remain healthy.

Suborder Eimeriidea

The parasites causing 'coccidiosis' in chickens illustrate the severity of maladjusted parasitism. They are distinguished from the previous suborder by having gametocytes which develop independently. Many wild birds and mammals pass cysts of coccidia and live normal lives. But poultry suffer heavy losses from outbreaks of this disease.

Eimeria tenella or *E. necatrix* infections are usually fatal to chickens. Young birds become infected when they ingest cysts passed in the faeces of infected animals. The cysts hatch and liberate sporozoites which invade the wall of the caecum (one of a pair of blind sacs from the hind gut). Intracellular development proceeds and schizogony occurs in less than three days after infection. As many as nine hundred merozoites ($3\mu \times 1\mu$) may be produced from one sporozoite. Usually these first-generation merozoites invade other cells and cause haemorrhage in the caeca. Second-generation merozoites appear at about six days and the bird is very sick. On the seventh and eighth days the second-generation merozoites have developed independently into macro- and micro-gametocysts and fusion of gametes occurs. The microgametes are liberated from the microgametocyte and swarm towards the macrogametes. Only one macrogamete forms each macrogametocyte, which after fusion with a microgamete becomes an oocyst with a resistant wall. Development of four sporoblasts continues within the oocyst, each sporoblast forming its own protective wall. Two sporozoites form in each sporoblast. The birds die at 8–10 days unless kept under ideal conditions. If they survive the first attack some immunity may develop but death can occur at any age. It is normal practice in many countries to keep young chickens on wire grids to cut down the ingestion rate of faecal material and also to add traces of drugs to the feed and thus suppress multiplication of the initial stages.

Haemosporidians
(Suborder Haemosporidia)

True digenetic intracellular blood parasites which cause malaria in man and related diseases in other mammals make up this uniform group. The devastation to human populations by malaria is even today very large. In the recent past, before drugs were used and the method of transmission known, this disease covered much of the world between 50° north and south of the equator, and was one of the major causes of a stable population number despite man's high reproductive potential. Only two hundred years ago ague (malaria) was prevalent in the marshy lands of Norfolk, England. At that time the climate was more continental, giving very hot summers and cold winters. The disease was thus able to develop in the vector, anopheline mosquitoes, in the summer and so spread from host to host, while it overwintered in man. The present climate with cooler summers is not favourable for mosquito development.

On a world-wide basis, over the years 1945 to 1960, there were 100 million cases per year, a reduction to one third of the annual number of cases reported before World War II. New techniques of control developed during and just after that war have been refined and applied on a worldwide scale by many nations with the aid of the World Health Organisation. Even so, as late as 1962, malaria was reported to disable more people than any other disease.

In the United States, malaria was formerly extensive geographically, reaching even into New England. The great bulk of cases, however, lay in the South. A survey made in 1916 and 1917, of over 31,000 people in Mississippi, determined that almost half of the population had detectable malaria parasites in the blood, a history of attacks of malaria fever during the twelve months prior to the survey or both. Even as late as 1938 in the United States, it was estimated that there were three to four million cases annually. Today, malaria is almost non-existent in the United States.

Mosquitoes do not become infective until seven to twenty days after taking an infected blood meal. The time lapse depends on temperature: lower temperature prolongs development to twenty days. An infection in man is initiated by sporozoites which are inoculated together with anticoagulant by the mosquito prior to sucking up blood. The sporozoites migrate into the main circulation and enter or are ingested by endothelial cells of the liver. Here each one divides repeatedly to form a large multinucleate pre-erythrocytic form. When mature, at about six days, this liberates a thousand or more merozoites which can infect red blood cells. Thereafter the schizogony cycle is mostly in the red cells and occurs repeatedly. The bouts of fever, which occur every two or three days depending on the species, coincide with the liberation of merozoites from blood cells. Some of these merozoites enter a long tissue phase similar to the pre–erythrocytic forms in the liver cells (this is the exo–erythrocytic cycle) while others form gametocytes and continue to circulate in the blood. Gametocytes are taken up in a blood meal and pass into the stomach of the mosquito. Liberation of microgametes and fusion takes place. The motile zygote invades the gut wall and develops an oocyst. This divides repeatedly and forms thousands of sporozoites which are freed when the oocyst ruptures. The sporozoites then migrate to the salivary glands for injection just prior to the next blood meal. Relapses after self- or drug-cure of malaria are due to the exo-erythrocytic forms again entering active schizogony and infecting the red cells.

Other haemosporidians include *Haemoproteus* (found in birds and reptiles) and *Babesia*, a species of which causes Texas cattle fever. *Haemoproteus* is carried by blood-sucking flies, *Babesia* by ticks.

Class Cnidosporidea

This class is characterised by non-motile spores, each containing two or more polar filaments, small sacs with curled spring-like structures within. They are all parasitic and small, with a host range that includes both invertebrates and vertebrates. The infections caused are mostly mild or occur in non-domestic animals. An exception is *Nosema* (order Microsporidia) of silkworms and honey bees, where a debilitating and often fatal disease results from infection.

The ciliates (Class Ciliata)

These protozoans have many cilia and nuclei of two sizes. Because the mastigophoran *Opalina* also have many flagella (or cilia), it is the nuclei that act as the criterion and establish the true ciliates as a distinct group. Other features include a kinety system of fibrils and granules for co-ordinating the cilia, characteristic cross-wise fission and a characteristic form of sexual reproduction called conjugation. The range of form exhibited in this class is so great that it suggests a very long independent evolutionary history. While it is relatively easy to place a protozoan as a ciliate it is often quite difficult to determine its order unless the genus is already known, because elaborations and fusion of some cilia, often accompanied by loss of others, has occurred in each order. This type of parallel evolution produces genera that are superficially similar. The only sure method of identification is the application of one of the silver line staining techniques, in which it is possible to show portions of the kinety system and so obtain the necessary characterisation upon which their taxonomy is based. But this method is not easily performed.

The habitats are various: parasitic, commensal and free-living species are found in many orders. The degree of morphological specialisation in some of the spirotrichs is noteworthy as an example of elaboration in a single cell: adaptation to unusual habitats such as the interstitial spaces in sand has lead to great elongation of up to five millimetres in some species, while some free-living freshwater species are only 15μ long.

Holotrichs (Subclass Holotricha)

This group is regarded as more primitive than the other subclass for there is lack of development in the peristomial membranelles. A feature which cuts across all other complications and simplifications of structure is the way the cilia are fused to form accessory organelles in the funnel-shaped cytopharynx, or cell mouth. It is characteristic of this subclass that no fused structures are present and the mouth is plainly open. Typically the body (somatic) cilia are of about the same length and present all over the cell.

Gymnostomes (Order Gymnostomatida)
As the name suggests the mouth is without ciliary organelles. This is a most diverse group of structurally simple ciliates. But diversity has led to considerable changes in the classification in recent years. Most species in the order contain one meganucleus and one or more micronuclei. The mouth may be anterior and terminal or lateral. If the mouth is lateral then the body is produced into a thin extension to form the new anterior end. This is the basis for the classification of the suborder Rhabdophorina, in which the cytopharynx (the space immediately within the cell opening, the cytostome) is extensible. The other suborder is the Cyrtophorina which has a rigid inextensible cytopharynx.

Suborder Rhabdophorina
In this group are found some remarkably voracious feeders, carnivorous in every sense of the word despite their smallish size. A simple form like *Holophrya* is oval and about 160μ long. It is found on the surface of freshwater where it feeds on dinoflagellates. The remains of past meals are clearly visible in several food vacuoles in the cytoplasm. A contractile vacuole partly maintains the water balance in the cell. *Didinium* is similar in shape but has much reduced ciliary fields. Only two bands are left, one round the mouth and one near the equator. This organism can ingest a

whole *Paramecium* although the prey is several times larger than itself. The vigour with which the prey is attacked, apparently paralysed and then drawn into a mouth, which seems far too small, is fascinating to watch. Other genera include *Dileptus* and *Lionotus* which have extended trichocyst and cilia-bearing anterior processes giving a comb-like appearance to the region in front of the mouth. This shape is an adaptation to living between sand grains and where free swimming is impossible.

Suborder Cyrtophorina

The ventrally placed mouth is believed to be of evolutionary significance in view of the fact that the majority of ciliates are like this but have additional elaborations. This is a small group. A typical genus is *Chilodonella*. The ventral mouth is visible from the dorsal side through the cell. The anterior process is considerably thinner than the main posterior part. A line of cilia, the dorsal brush; runs from the edge of the cell to a region over the mouth, and should not be confused with the feeding organelles in other ciliates which sweep food into the mouth.

Suctorians (Order Suctorida)

The suctorians are a compact group. The adult form is sessile and without cilia. Food is captured by long knob-ended tentacles which are capable of paralysing prey. After capture the prey is not drawn to the body, for there is no mouth, but is sucked dry by the tentacles. Film studies show the steady flow of cytoplasm from an organism such as *Tetrahymena* into a suctorian. Reproduction is by several methods. The commonest is internal budding. After division of the nucleus the anterior pellicle sinks into the cytoplasm in a circle and a young ciliated suctorian develops around the new nucleus. When mature the daughter cell leaves the parent and swims freely. Later it settles down on some object, secretes a non-contractile stalk and loses its cilia to become a small adult. Stained preparations of suctorians show that at all stages of development the kinety system is present even when cilia are not. Typical genera are *Tokophyra*, *Podophyra* and *Acineta*.

Trichostomes (Order Trichostomatida)

This group has many features in common with the gymnostomes but is distinguished from them by the presence of a vestibulum. This organ is a depression of the pellicle complete with the cilia which forms a tube leading to the mouth. The cilia of the vestibulum urge food into the mouth. The cytoplasm adjoining the mouth appears to be highly vacuolated, and algae or bacteria upon which a free-living genus, *Coelosomides*, feeds, are digested here.

The structure of the gut parasite of amphibians and mammals, *Balantidium coli*, superficially resembles some hymenostomes or heterotrichs. The mouth, however, is fed by vestibular cilia which are derived from and develop in a way similar to the normal somatic cilia covering the cell. A common freshwater genus is *Colpoda*, characteristically kidney-shaped and about 75μ long. The mouth is on the indented side, and the vestibular cilia, clearly visible in stained preparations, are a little shorter than the somatic cilia.

Hymenostomes (Order Hymenostomatida)

This order marks the starting point for the elaborations found in the remaining ciliates. The feeding apparatus is described in some detail here and the names of structures are applicable later. The first of these structures is the buccal cavity between the cytostome and the buccal overture, which is a line of demarcation between the somatic cilia and the buccal cilia. The buccal cavity has two types of ciliary organelles: the adoral zone of membranellae (AZM) on the left of the cytostome and the undulating membrane (UM) on the right. (Left and right are used for the organism whose mouth is considered to be ventral when the observer is looking from the dorsal surface to the ventral, as left and right are on our own bodies. In order to get clear pictures and because of the standard way microscopical preparations are made the organisms are always viewed from the ventral surface. So, in drawings and photographs, left and right are transposed, as when two people look at each other face to face.) The UM is a row of cilia which are fused together and beat in co-ordination. The AZM is variable and may be a row of fused cilia as in the spirotrichs or may be divided into several sheets of fused cilia as in *Tetrahymena*. The buccal cavity has no cilia except for those contained in the UM and the AZM.

The hymenostomes are mostly free living and found in freshwater. A simple member of the group is *Tetrahymena*. This genus has become well known because of its usefulness in laboratory studies on cell division. The pellicle, measuring $50\mu \times 30\mu$ is somewhat flexible and ovoid. The oral apparatus is near the anterior end and is ventral. The UM is single but the AZM is represented as three fused bands of cilia. A macronucleus is always found but many strains are without micronuclei. The latter cannot reproduce sexually. There is one contractile vacuole and also a cytoproct (cellanus) for the elimination of solid waste.

Paramecium is a genus which abounds in nature and is large enough for ready observation. The size of the different species ranges from $80\mu - 200\mu$. The oral ciliature is developed into two fields of cilia in the buccal cavity which opens into a vestibulum lying in a shallow oral groove. *Paramecium* feeds largely on bacteria which are gathered by a feeding current created by cilia in the oral groove. The particles are swept down this groove into the shallow vestibulum and, if accepted into the buccal cavity, to the cytostome. Particles can be rejected, in which case they are swept across the buccal cavity at right angles to the normal ciliary beat.

Movement in *Paramecium* is, as in most ciliates, by means of the somatic cilia covering the body. The cilia beat in a co-ordinated pattern to give waves of propulsion running down the surface. The cilia lie in rows called meridians, running in the anteroposterior direction. Each row or kinety has cilia connected by fibrils running under the pellicle. The kineties are cross-connected by transverse fibrils at a level deeper than the longitudinal fibrils. The whole of these interconnections beneath the pellicle is known as the infra-ciliature. *Paramecium* is well known for its avoidance reaction. The normal course of swimming is forwards

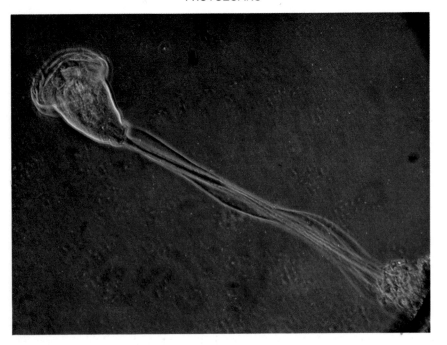

Vorticella campanula, one of the so-called Wheel Animalcules that lives in freshwater with the lower end of its stalk anchored to the surface of a water plant. Periodically the stalk is contracted into a spiral and then extended again to resume feeding after a brief pause.

thus receives two mitotically derived micronuclei and one whole macronucleus.

The second form of sexual reproduction is autogamy. Here a single organism goes through the motions of conjugation without another conjugant. Two homozygous gametic nuclei are formed and these fuse to form a zygote. Thereafter divisions and a new macronucleus are formed as in conjugation. Genetically autogamy brings about recombination of genetic material in a wasteful manner as the genes contained in the daughter micronuclei are lost for ever. The process is similar to the endomeiosis in aphids.

Recent genetical studies have shown that *Paramecium* species have classical Mendelian inheritance for many characters. Although cytological studies have suggested the above description of sexual reproduction for some eighty years it was only from genetical analysis that certain divisions could be more surely determined as meiotic. Further, some characters were found to be inconstant, in particular the properties of the surface protein of cilia. These proteins developed in response to the temperature of the environment.

Peritrichs (Order Peritrichida)

These include the sessile ciliates (Sessilina), which live on contractile stalks and are common near the surface of overgrown aquaria, and motile forms (Mobilina) which are believed to be derived from the sessile forms. The characteristics of the order are three specialised rows of cilia around the mouth and the general absence of somatic cilia. Viewed from the anterior the oral cilia are seen to wind counter-clockwise into the mouth.

Vorticella is a typical and common genus. The body is bell shaped and mounted with the pointed end on a contractile stalk. During feeding the stalk is elongated and the crown of peristomial cilia expanded. The slightest disturbance causes both structures to contract. Vorticellids live in clusters and as they are, in the expanded condition, about 500μ long, contraction of a whole cluster is conspicuous. Food is drawn in particulate form from the surrounding water in the swirling currents set up by the peristomial cilia. Reproduction is by binary fission and conjugation. In binary fission one of the daughter cells leaves the stalk to swim away and settle elsewhere. In conjugation one organism remains on its stalk while another assumes male function and swims to the sessile one. Fusion takes place and genetic recombination results.

Order Astomatida

Holotrichs characterised by the absence of any kind of mouth. This is probably to be correlated with their parasitic habit, for all are parasites of invertebrates.

and rotating about its own long axis. But when an unpleasant stimulus is reached the organism stops, reverses at a slight angle for two to four lengths and then moves forward again at a slight angle to the reverse direction. The net result is that the organism turns from its original course and heads away from the unpleasant stimulus. It appears not to feed when moving quickly.

Reproduction can be by fission or by a sexual process. Binary fission may occur two or three times a day and the micronucleus divides mitotically while the macronucleus divides by splitting without the characteristic mitotic apparatus. The methods of sexual reproduction in the ciliates are conjugation and autogamy.

In conjugation two individuals come together and join at their oral surfaces. Both macronuclei partially degenerate by enlarging and becoming diffuse and then drawing out into strands which later break down to give numerous weakly staining remnants of the original nuclei. The micronuclei, of which *Paramecium aurelia* has two, divide meiotically, giving eight daughter nuclei. Seven of the eight degenerate and the remaining one divides again to produce two homozygous gametic nuclei. One gametic nucleus from each partner migrates into the other partner and fuses with the stationary gametic nucleus. The zygotic nucleus divides twice and while these divisions are occurring the conjugants separate. Of the four resultant micronuclei two become macronuclei and two micronuclei. The latter divide again and the exconjugant divides, one macronucleus going to one daughter while the other goes to the second. Each daughter

Spirotrichs (Subclass Spirotricha)

Members of this subclass are mostly free living and have a more highly developed AZM than the primitive hymenostomes. The AZM winds clockwise to the cytostome. Many of the more advanced spirotrichs have no somatic cilia but this loss is secondary. There is wide variety of structure which prevents generalisations on morphology; most of the orders are relatively compact.

Heterotrichs (Order Heterotrichida)

The somatic cilia are more or less well represented and of uniform size. The oral cilia are several times larger than the somatic cilia and may be fused into cirri. Various habitats are used: *Clevelandella* and *Nyctotherus* are both invertebrate gut symbionts, *Spirostomum* is found in freshwater and is highly motile, and *Stentor* is found in freshwater but is sessile. *Spirostomum* and *Stentor* are both large and may be three millimetres long. Both are highly contractile and can shorten to less than one quarter of the original length. *Spirostomum* has its cytostome situated about two-thirds of the way down the body and is fed by particles passing down the oral groove. The latter is wound spirally round the animal for between half and one turn. A contractile vacuole is in the posterior and from it a single tubule for drainage of the cytoplasm extends nearly the whole length of the organism. *Spirostomum* feeds on bacteria and other protozoans. Food vacuoles take a regular course, first passing forward to the anterior tip and then journeying to the posteriorly situated permanent cytoproct.

Stentor is sessile when feeding, being attached by a 'foot' at the thin end of the conical body. The base of the cone carries the oral cilia (AZM) as a single row on the rim. Only at the buccal region is there an indentation and the food particles are led to the cytostome. The macronucleus is in the form of a string of beads with up to twenty segments. There are many micronuclei.

Hypotrichs (Order Hypotrichida)

Examples of this order are among the most active and commonly found ciliates. They are generally of medium size ($70–150\mu$ long) and occur in mud and rotting vegetation. There are no generally distributed somatic cilia. These are replaced by bristle-like cirri composed of fused cilia on the dorsal surface. The distribution of cirri is a factor used in the separation of the several families and genera. The AZM is the main feature of the oral ciliature. *Euplotes* and *Stylonichia* are good examples of the order. In *Euplotes* the macronucleus is horseshoe-shaped. Adjacent to the centre of the macronucleus and on its outer surface is a single micronucleus. The dorsal cirri are reduced to only eighteen bristles. Some of the posterior cirri are connected by a system of subpellicular fibrils to a centre, the motorium, at the anterior of the cell. The other cirri have several fibrils running from their bases at different angles. Experiments in which some fibrils are cut suggest that they serve to co-ordinate the posterior cirri.

Entodiniomorphs (Order Entodiniomorphida)

Structurally these are the most complex of the ciliates and therefore of the whole phylum. Somatic cilia are absent, and tufts of cirri are confined to a maximum of three regions. The posterior is sometimes produced into spines. They are found in the rumen and reticulum portions of the stomach of ruminants, where they always occur in great numbers. Being extremely specialised to this bizarre environment with its continuous comings and goings of food materials, low pH and near absence of oxygen, the order is, not surprisingly, most difficult to culture. In consequence little is

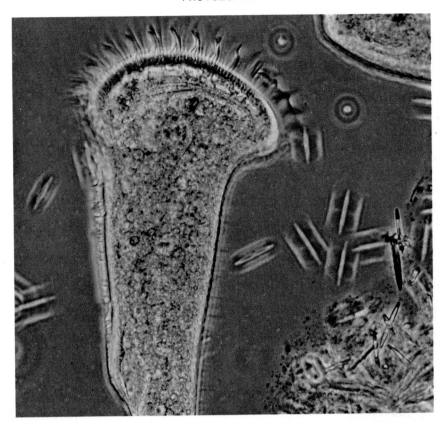

known about them except their morphology. The question of importance is how does the presence of perhaps 10^{10} 100μ long ciliates affect the nutrition of a cow. It was once thought that the ciliates converted cellulose into digestible carbohydrate, which would be of considerable benefit to the host. Later work has shown that cattle thrive every bit as well when their rumens have been sterilised of ciliates. It has been claimed that the frequently fatal disease, bloat, is caused by cattle feeding on too rich pasture, which in turn provides food for and produces many bacteria which are ingested too readily by the ciliates. The overfed ciliates burst in the rumen, liberating their cell proteins which stabilise the foam of normally produced gases. The foam cannot escape and the rumen swells.

The morphology of our example, *Epidinium*, is complex in derivation but simple in the reduced number of features. There is a macronucleus, a micronucleus, a permanent cytoproct and two contractile vacuoles. A motorium has a co-ordinating function. The AZM is the only feeding ciliature. Another group of cilia, the dorsal zone of membranelles, is close to the AZM.

Comparison of the organisms described in this chapter with those in the rest of the book leaves no doubt that the Protozoa are strikingly different in both structure and function. This is not all, for their small size brings with it difficulties in observation. It is not at all surprising when one considers that a trypanosome is about the same size as a large human chromosome, and inevitably the chromosomes of trypanosomes are scaled down to be below the resolution of the light microscope. In no other phylum does this type of difficulty occur and in its wake an area of uncertainty follows.

Stentor sp., a trumpet-shaped heterotrich living in freshwater fastened by the base of its upright stalk to the surface of a water plant. Some stentors are green, others blue, and many are colourless. The larger of them may be as much as two millimetres long, large enough to be seen with the naked eye.

MESOZOANS
(Phylum Mesozoa)

The mesozoans are tiny parasitic animalcules found in certain marine invertebrates. There are two orders, the Dicyemida and the Orthonectida, whose simple multicellular structure has provoked much speculation over the years about their place in any systematic classification of the animal kingdom.

The fifty species of mesozoans parasitise worms, crustaceans, starfishes and molluscs, living free or attached within their body cavities. No mesozoan possesses distinct body systems, whether nervous, digestive or circulatory, so that all functions must be carried out by individual cells. The complex life-cycle involves both asexual and sexual reproduction. Mating normally takes place within the host but many species produce free-swimming larvae. In a few species only the adults leave the host to mate in the sea.

In a way still unknown, the worm-like dicyemids infect the kidneys of young squids and octopuses. Typically, each is up to seven millimetres long and consists usually of fewer than 25 elongated cells, the so-called axial cells. Within these, other cells are produced, each of which develops into a new individual before breaking out. This development from unfertilised 'agametes', formed without meiosis, never occurs in the Metazoa. The new individuals remain in the kidney of the host and give rise to a further generation in the same way. When the host reaches sexual maturity, this type of reproduction ceases and the dicyemid differs slightly in appearance and reproduces in a different manner: clusters of cells are produced inside the axial cell, the outer cells in the cluster separating off and dividing to form free-swimming ciliated larvae. These leave the kidney of the host species, but whether they also infect an intermediate host is not known.

At one stage of their cycle the orthonectids exist as multinucleate amoeboid plasmodia in the tissues of their hosts, which may be flatworms, nemertine worms, annelids, brittle stars or bivalve molluscs. The plasmodia reproduce by fragmentation for a time, but eventually, like the dicyemids, they produce agametes, which give rise to distinct sexual forms (male, female or hermaphrodite) with an outer ciliated cell layer, as in dicyemids, but marked off in rings. An inner mass of cells replaces the single axial cell. Generally the males are about 0·1 millimetres long and the females two or three times this length. As adults they leave the host and enter the sea, where they copulate. The resulting fertilised eggs develop into ciliated larvae, which then escape from the parent and infect new hosts. At this point the larvae lose their outer layer of cells, and the inner cells scatter, each giving rise to a new plasmodium to complete the cycle.

In lacking a well-defined ectoderm and endoderm, the mesozoans are clearly outside the main body of multicellular organisms, the Metazoa. They could represent a stage in the evolution of that group from unicellular organisms, in which case the first mesozoans can hardly have inhabited the bodies of invertebrates, as they do now. It has also been suggested that they owe their simple structure and complex life-cycles to their parasitic way of life, since these are two common features of parasites. This would make them degenerate forms, and one hypothesis is that they could have evolved from flatworms, although there is little to support this. It is, however, more probable that, like the sponges, they represent an independent line of evolution.

SPONGES
(Phylum Porifera)

All sponges are aquatic and most of them are marine. Freshwater sponges are found in fair numbers—but belonging to relatively few species—in ponds and lakes, streams and rivers, even in lakes formed in the craters of extinct volcanoes 3,000 metres above sea-level. Marine sponges exist in large numbers from mid-tide level on the shore down to the greatest depths of the oceans. The smallest are about one millimetre high when fully grown; the largest are the size of a medium-sized barrel as in *Spheciospongia vesparia*, the so-called Loggerhead Sponge of the West Indies. On the shore they tend to encrust rocks where, by the coalescence of adjacent growths, certain species may be found in continuous sheets of varying thickness covering areas of several square metres. In the shallow and deep seas the form is more varied, ranging from a crust on stones, shells and dead coral to spherical, finger-shaped, bush or tree-like, tubular, cup-shaped and funnel-shaped sponges. In general the greater the depth at which they grow the more their form tends to be regular and symmetrical. Those living in shallow seas are the more colourful, and colour becomes more noticeable as the mean annual temperature of the water increases, as in the tropics, but usually sponges are monochrome with reds, browns, yellows and purples predominating, green less common and usually due to symbiotic algae, and blue very rare and usually the result of symbiotic blue-green algae or bacteria. The texture varies from soft and readily compressible (as in sponges lacking a skeleton, such as *Oscarella*) to as hard as stone (as in the polyphyletic—i.e. not descended from a common ancestor—group known as the Lithistida).

The characteristic feature of a sponge is that it bears one or more usually conspicuous rounded openings. These used to be called oscula (little mouths) but are better described as vents. Under the microscope the rest of the surface is seen to be punctured by minute openings or pores, for which reason sponges are collectively known as the Porifera or pore-bearers.

Aristotle was the first to recognise, 2,000 years ago, the animal nature of sponges, and yet it is only within the last 200 years that this verdict has been generally accepted. In the sixteenth century sponges were believed to be solidified sea foam, and in the seventeenth century it was suggested that they were the homes of marine worms, made by the worms themselves. Otherwise the general impression was that sponges belonged to the plant kingdom. Not until 1766, when John Ellis discovered that they eject currents of water and thus established that they were animals, was Aristotle's view accepted, and then not by everyone. Even as late as 1841 John Hogg was still arguing before the British Royal Society that sponges were plants.

Hogg based his ideas on freshwater sponges. Some of these have long, slender branches springing from a basal crust, and all are green, but turn yellow when growing in places shielded from daylight, just as green plants do. Moreover in summer they are filled with small brown seed-like

Sponges with a fibrous skeleton, related to the bath sponge, from the shallow seas of the Caribbean. The tubular shape is commonly seen in sponges, the opening at the top representing a vent for the discharge of water after it has circulated through the body of the sponge.

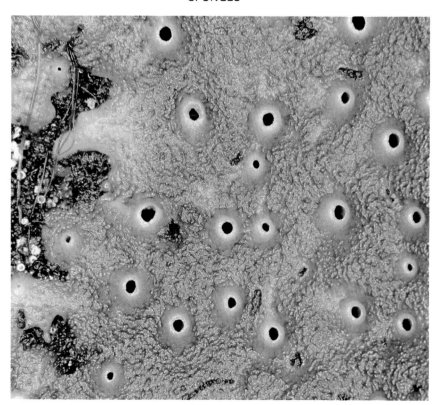

The Crumb-o'-Bread Sponge (*Halichondria panicea*) may form flat encrustations or irregular masses on rocks and seaweeds throughout a large part of the world. When dried it looks like mouldy bread and readily crumbles when handled. Its skeleton is composed of needle-like spicules of silica, loosely aggregated in a felt-like mass.

bodies. But we now know that the green colour of freshwater sponges is due to symbiotic algae and that the 'seeds' are gemmules, asexual reproductive bodies enclosed in brown, spherical capsules.

Many marine sponges are also plant-like, and some could very easily pass for seaweeds, but no sponge contains cellulose, the typical constituent of plant tissues. Moreover some sponges possess true muscle fibres in the outer layers, and recent research has suggested that others may possess a rudimentary nervous system, largely in the form of scattered nerve-cells. In addition the sponge larva is decidedly more animal than plant-like in its structure and behaviour. Yet some zoologists contend that sponges are not animals in the strict sense, and opinion today is increasingly tending to regard them as an aberrant offshoot from the main line of animal evolution, best placed in a separate subkingdom, the Parazoa.

Whatever view one takes it is difficult not to see them as being on the border-line between single-celled animals (Protozoa) and multicellular animals (Metazoa). Their relationship to the Protozoa is somewhat distant, but certain scientists have regarded sponges as little more than colonies of Protozoa. This view was based on the behaviour of the cells in the sponge body, particularly in the process known as dissociation and regeneration, which will be described later.

The relationship of sponges to the rest of the multicellular animals is equally obscure. Most Metazoa are triploblastic. That is, early in the development of the embryo three primary layers are laid down. Leaving aside the problematic Mesozoa, we can say that the most primitive Metazoa are diploblastic, and have two layers in the embryo. But no such clear-cut distinctions can be seen at any stage in the development of a sponge. The embryo consists typically of a single layer of cells, although in some species there is an

incipient migration of a few cells from the single layer to the interior of the embryo, which some authorities have equated with a rudimentary diploblastic condition, but such analogies are not generally accepted.

It is also difficult to relate the tissues of the adult sponge to those seen in other multicellular animals, although many attempts have been made to do so. The body of a sponge has none of the definite organisation or orientation seen in the bodies of higher animals. It has no upper, lower, anterior, or posterior parts, except in so far as these are determined by its position in the water. Experimentally, a sponge can be turned on its side or even upside-down and it will continue to function effectively, or, if full functioning is impeded, it will re-organise its tissues so that what was originally the underside will become the upper surface.

Body structure

Probably the best way to describe the body of a sponge is to define its various parts:

The skin or ectosome is the outer layer or layers of cells; usually this is a single or double layer, but in a few species it takes the form of a thick cortex made up largely of muscle fibres.

The pores are very minute openings in the skin through which water is drawn into the sponge, and in this way they form the inhalant current.

The vents are rather larger openings in the skin through which the exhalant current of water is passed out of the sponge. As previously explained, these are usually called oscula, a word which tends to mislead as to their function.

The canals are tubes or channels running through the body along which water flows continuously, except when the sponge is quiescent. The water is drawn in through the pores and driven out forcibly through the vents.

The flagellated chambers are typically spherical or thimble-shaped chambers into which the canals open, and from which run similar canals. Those leading into a chamber are called inhalant, and those leading out are called exhalant. The exhalant canals in most sponges soon join up with neighbouring exhalant canals to form larger canals and so on progressively until a single large exhalant canal (cloaca) carries water to the vent. The flagellated chambers are so called because they are lined with cells, each of which bears a flagellum surrounded by a protoplasmic collar. (Although this definition holds for the majority of sponges, in the glass sponges (Hexactinellida) the flagellated chambers are large and thimble-shaped, and are not equipped with inhalant or exhalant canals. By contrast, in the so-called ascon sponges (*Leucosolenia*) the whole central cavity, the spongocoel, is lined with collared cells. It receives the inhalant current directly through pores, and communicates direct with the exterior through a vent.)

The collared cells or choanocytes line the flagellated chambers. Each collared cell has a spherical or columnar body bearing at its free end a protoplasmic funnel-like collar, from the bottom centre of which springs a protoplasmic whip or flagellum. As the flagellum lashes a vortex is created around the collar, and the result of the concerted action of thousands of collared cells is to suck water in through the pores, drive it through the canals and forcibly eject it through the vents. The inhalant current brings in food and oxygen and the exhalant current carries away the waste products of digestion and respiration. Collared cells are very small and their structure in life was for a long time impossible to determine satisfactorily, even using the higher powers of ordinary microscopes. Consequently, their collars were thought to be made up of thin sheets of protoplasm of uniform consistency. With improved microscopes they have been shown to have a fine structure which includes numerous longitudinal fibrillae.

Since the choanocytes form the most conspicuous feature of the sponge body, this is sometimes regarded as consisting of an ectosome, or skin, and a choanosome comprising everything internal to it.

Food obtained by the collared cells is passed on to wandering cells or amoebocytes which transport it to other parts of the body.

Star-shaped or stellate cells form a loose network filling the spaces between the labyrinth formed by the inhalant and exhalant canals. (Alternatively we can regard the body of a sponge as filled with a network of star-shaped cells through which the canals run.)

The amoebocytes are cells which wander about in the spaces between the star-shaped cells. They are called amoebocytes because when active they are continually changing shape, like the protozoan animal *Amoeba*. There are various kinds of amoebocytes, some carry oil-globules and other nutrients, while others build the skeleton or have functions that are not, as yet, fully understood.

The skeleton and the various reproductive cells will be discussed in detail below.

Sponges have no special organs of locomotion and are mainly sedentary, although a small amount of creeping movement can take place, especially in the post-larval stages, and in some species even in the adult. They have no special sense-organs, although a few species show some sensitivity to light and touch, but how far this is dependent upon the possible presence of rudimentary nerve-cells or is a property of all the cells in the body has yet to be determined. The food of sponges is believed to be either finely divided organic particles or bacteria, or both, and there is evidence that freshwater sponges feed to some extent on their symbiotic algae. The normal food must clearly be of minute proportions, otherwise it would not enter the microscopic pores in the ectosome. Furthermore, sponges grow to unusually large size in water contaminated with decaying matter and rich in organic particles and bacteria.

Some sponges, especially those with large vents and deep tubular cloacae, contain numerous commensals. These may number thousands for a single sponge and include a variety of small crustaceans and polychaete annelid worms. In contrast, sponges have few predators. A few are eaten by nudibranch or small gastropod molluscs, but almost as fast as these eat the wounds heal.

Reproduction

This is by both sexual and a variety of non-sexual methods. All sponges appear to bear both ova and spermatozoa, although there has recently been a suggestion that this is not invariable, and fertilisation may be internal or external. With internal fertilisation the embryos develop inside the sponge, which is then said to be viviparous; with external fertilisation the sponge is regarded as oviparous or 'egg-laying'. When fertilisation is internal the spermatozoa are presumably carried into the body by the inhalant currents. In the breeding season viviparous sponges bear large numbers of embryos scattered through the body.

Non-sexual reproduction includes purely vegetative methods, in which the body may fragment, each piece being capable of forming a new sponge, or buds may be formed, either on the surface of the body or internally; the seed-like gemmules of freshwater sponges belong to this second category. In addition, asexual larvae identical in appearance with sexually formed larvae may be produced.

In oviparous sponges the ova can be seen lying in the choanosome, but sperms and larvae have never been identified. Presumably the ova are fertilised in the sea after leaving through the exhalant canals and vents.

We know more about the sexual process in the viviparous species. Arthur Dendy was the first to investigate fully the origin and growth of the ovum. According to him the first step is the migration of a collared cell from the flagellated chamber into the tissues surrounding it. As it migrates it withdraws its collar and flagellum, and becomes amoeboid. Other amoebocytes heavily laden with nutrients move towards it, and these Dendy named 'nurse-cells', assuming that they pass their nutrients into the developing ovum, which becomes extremely large and is filled with yolk granules. There is some doubt whether the ova may not, in some species at least, be derived from amoebocytes already within the choanosome.

The segmentation of the embryos is sometimes regular and sometimes irregular, but in all instances a larva leaves the parent body by one of the vents. There are no special reproductive organs or special sex-cells, and in the few instances investigated sperm mother-cells and ova appear to be derived from modified collared cells or amoebocytes.

The ovum segments form a spherical embryo, which later becomes oval, while a layer of cells forms a capsule enclosing it. Just before the embryo leaves the parent body its cells put out flagella which, by their lashing, cause the embryo to rotate, rupturing the wall of the capsule. The embryo, now transformed into a swimming larva, bursts through the wall of the nearest exhalant canal, and is carried out through the vent.

The larva is typically a hollow oval body with all or most of the cells bearing flagella which drive it through the water. After being ejected the larva swims with a spiral movement for some 24 hours before settling on the bottom to undergo metamorphosis into a post-larva, or small platelet of semi-transparent tissue with an irregular outline and no sign of pores or vents.

In the calcareous sponges, cells which develop with flagella initially pointing inward are turned through 180° in a curious process called inversion so that the flagella are on the outside. The larva breaks free from the parent at this time and the flagella function as locomotor structures. When settling of the larva occurs an infolding of the body wall brings the flagella again to the interior.

The further developments of species living between tidemarks can be watched at low tide. The platelets appear static to the casual observer but they are constantly moving very slowly in an amoeboid manner, advancing towards or away from each other, with movements of a few millimetres only in the course of twenty-four hours. Two may meet and coalesce at the point of contact, though later tearing away with one partner taking a portion of the other. In this way there must be exchange of tissue between post-larvae.

The appearance of a vent in about the centre of the upper surface marks the time when a post-larva is settling into its final position. In those species that form encrustations or irregular masses, later growth takes place laterally so that eventually the separate sponges from hundreds of larvae may join to form a continuous sheet covering several square metres of rock surface.

Typically an individual animal is the product of one fertilised ovum, but a single sponge may be the product of many fertilised ova. This is one reason why the problem of individuality in a sponge has never been satisfactorily settled. Even the larvae may coalesce, either while swimming, or after settling and before metamorphosis into post-larvae. Adult sponges can also grow towards each other and coalesce completely. Theoretically, therefore, it should be possible—were it practicable—to collect all the individuals of a species and cause them to coalesce into a single mass, in which event the species would be the individual.

In contrast to this wholesale coalescence, in some species the larva may settle and grow into a creeping stolon which branches repeatedly, with adults arising from various points on the stolon, so that when later the stolon disappears a dozen or more sponges are left, all derived from a single fertilised ovum. To complicate matters, often one or more of the sponges so produced may give rise to further sponges by budding from the base, and these may either remain together throughout life or separate.

Thus it is not possible to speak with precision about an 'individual', nor is it justifiable to speak of a colony. Some authorities have sought to get over the difficulty by referring to the 'sponge person'—which is only another way of calling it an individual, or of the 'sponge body', meaning a sponge that looks like a single individual, although it may be composed of several that have coalesced, or may be one of many that originated from a single ovum.

This plasticity is reflected in other ways, one of which can be demonstrated by the classic experiment of squeezing a piece of living sponge through fine silk. The tissues become dissociated and pass through the meshes of the silk as a milky fluid, consisting of hundreds of cells separated from their fellows and amoeboid in shape and behaviour. Usually the collared cells withdraw their collars and flagella and cannot be recognised as such. All the cells wander at random, moving by means of pseudopodia, but after a lapse of several hours they begin to gather together in clusters.

In some species the individual cell walls seem to disappear as the clusters grow, so that syncytia—continuous masses of cytoplasm with many nuclei—are formed. These behave like giant multinucleate amoebas and in their turn wander, meet and coalesce. Eventually rounded masses are formed in which the cell walls have reappeared, so that they do not differ from normal post-larvae. Such regenerative cell-masses have been kept in aquaria for several months until they were sexually mature and producing their own larvae.

Under natural conditions multiplication by regenerative cell-masses takes place in several ways. One is the formation of internal buds or gemmules. These are most typical of freshwater sponges but have also been found in a few marine sponges. The formation of a gemmule is preceded by the streaming together of numerous small amoebocytes, heavily charged with granules, presumably nutrients. These eventually form a spherical mass around which other amoebocytes lay down a horny capsule. A third set of cells secretes special spicules in the parent choanosome, and transports these to the developing gemmule where they are laid down in the walls of the capsule and so strengthen it.

In freshwater sponges the parent body dies and disintegrates in due course, leaving the gemmules to tide over the winter and provide the crop of sponges for the ensuing year. In the spring the contents of each gemmule flow out from the shelter of the capsule and proceed to behave like normal sexually produced post-larvae.

There is evidence that when spicules are extruded some of the amoebocytes transporting them are carried to the exterior on the spicules. They fall with them to the sea bed, move about, meet and form regenerative cell-masses, which it seems may develop into adult sponges.

Another variation of reproduction by means of a regenerative cell-mass is seen in external budding. The Sea-orange (*Tethya aurantium*), which is oviparous, regularly reproduces by means of buds. The skeleton in this species is composed of bundles of long, needle-shaped spicules radiating from the centre of the body to the surface. Amoebocytes migrate along these bundles and collect beneath the ectosome, which is consequently pushed up into low warts. Eventually these grow out into stalked buds, the amoebocytes inside meanwhile becoming organised into tissues complete with collared cells. As the buds ripen their stalks become enormously long and attenuated, and when they break the miniature sponges float away to settle on a rock surface and grow into adults.

Perhaps the most remarkable method of reproduction involving regenerative cell-masses is the formation, non-sexually, of larvae that simulate sexually produced larvae. Instead of an embryo produced by segmentation of an ovum there is formed a precisely similar structure through an aggregation of amoebocytes, resulting in a larva that is indistinguishable from one derived from the fertilised ovum.

This ability of separate or separated sponge cells to come together to form multicellular bodies supports the views of those who regard sponges as little more than colonial protozoans.

However, recent research has shown that certain mammalian cells grown in culture media behave in a similar way, coming together to form rounded masses surrounded by a single-layered capsule. The implications of this are not easy to see.

Non-sexual reproduction is not peculiar to sponges, but they are remarkable for the variety of ways in which they multiply without the intervention of the sexual process. Although non-sexual reproduction is more characteristic of the plant kingdom than the animal kingdom, this multiplicity of non-sexual methods in sponges was unknown in the days when they were mistakenly regarded as plants.

The remaining non-sexual methods of reproduction involve fragmentation. That seen in the sponge *Halichondria coalita*, for instance, is a simple natural example. This sponge often forms reticulations of slender branches, and is most abundant just offshore. During violent storms it may be broken up into many pieces, and occasionally tens of thousands of these may be cast up on the beaches, their damaged surfaces already beginning to heal. Doubtless many become attached to pebbles and rocks and grow into new sponges.

Similarly commercial sponges can be artificially propagated by cutting a mature sponge into a number of small 'seed sponges', fastening each to a concrete disc, and returning them to the sea. There are several species that can be said to adopt this process naturally. The first in which this was fully demonstrated was the Purse Sponge (*Grantia compressa*), which grows between tide-marks, and is usually twenty-five to fifty millimetres high. It has also been seen in *Scypha ciliata*, another common littoral species of calcareous sponge, and the indications are that it may be more widespread. In these two species fragmentation takes place by the formation of lines of weakness across the sponge body, associated with folding and splitting, the end result being that the sponge breaks up in a variety of stereotyped patterns, sometimes accompanied by budding, the two processes proceeding simultaneously. It has been possible to show that such fragments reform to produce a shape like that of the parent, with the formation of a vent and a stalk for attachment. And although it has not been satisfactorily demonstrated that all such fragments become attached and thereafter grow in the normal manner, enough is known to postulate reasonably that a high percentage of such fragments may survive.

Skeleton

With few exceptions the body of a sponge is supported by a skeleton made up either of spongin fibres, usually forming a network, as in the bath sponges (*Spongia*), or of spicules (little spikes) of silica or carbonate of lime. Although we speak of the spicules as constituting a skeleton there are some remarkable differences between the skeleton of the majority of sponges and a skeleton as normally understood.

In the bath sponges and the others which have a fibrous skeleton, this is laid down *in situ* and is permanent. However, where the skeleton consists of spicules, as in the majority of the 2,500 known species of sponge, each spicule is laid down in the interior of the sponge and is then transported to its position by several amoebocytes.

In most sponges the skeleton is made up of separate spicules, loosely aggregated. These are constantly extruded and replaced by fresh spicules. They fall to the sea bed, after extrusion, where they mingle with the other detritus, like the foraminiferan that figures so prominently in this picture.

The calcareous spicules are fashioned on a three-rayed or triradiate plan, whereas siliceous or flinty spicules are of two kinds: those that are basically four-rayed and those that are six-rayed. These forms provide the primary divisions in the classification of sponges: the Calcarea; the Tetraxonida (four-rayed), and the Hexactinellida (six-rayed) with siliceous spicules; and the Keratosa with fibrous skeletons.

The greatest range of modification of the primary form of the spicules is seen in the Tetraxonida, but it is hardly less in the Hexactinellida. In the Tetraxonida the siliceous spicules are modified to form forks, anchors, needles, stars, plates, keyholes, and a great variety of other forms. The important feature in these modifications is that it is possible to see in them an almost complete series indicating an evolution from the basic tetraxon (or hexaster, in Hexactinellida) to forms which, on their own, give no hint of the basic pattern.

Distribution

Calcareous sponges are largely confined to the littoral and the shallow seas, although a few have been dredged at depths down to 180 metres or beyond, to a maximum depth of 820 metres. Hexactinellida are typically deep-sea, the majority of species living at depths greater than 180 metres, but around the Indo-Pacific islands they seem to be fairly common in shallower waters, up to thirty-six metres. The Tetraxonida range from mid-tide level to the greatest depths so far dredged, and probably occur in the deepest trenches in the oceans.

The density of populations of littoral sponges varies according to the range of the tide as well as the substratum and other environmental factors. Where the tidal rise and fall is small there are few sponges, or where there is a racing current giving a scouring action. They are almost non-existent also on sandy beaches, although *Hymeniacidon perlevis* can grow half-buried in sand, or on mud-flats, where *Halichondria coalita* will also grow half-buried. Pebbly beaches also are barren. Much the same relation between substratum and sponge is

seen for shallow and deep seas, the sponges usually requiring a solid substratum on which to grow, but there are many species adapted to life on fine mud or ooze. These have either a long stalk embedded in the mud, which holds the body well up from the substratum, as in *Stylocordyla borealis*, or there is a tuft or raft of long spicules serving the same purpose, as in *Pheronema carpenteri* or *Euplectella aspergillum*. One of the most remarkable adaptations is seen in the Single-rod Sponge (*Monoraphis chuni*), a deep-sea hexactinellid in the Indian Ocean, which has one spicule a metre long with the sponge itself situated near the upper end, the lower end being embedded in the sea-floor mud.

In the shallow seas or at middle depths in the deep seas there is a profusion of sponges in tropical and subtropical waters, and again in polar waters, with less profusion in temperate waters.

At depths of around 180 metres and in the deeper seas sponges tend to be spaced out, and it is probably in these situations, where individuals are widely separated, that asexual reproduction offers the greater advantages.

The commercial sponges (i.e. the bath sponge and related species) reach their maximum development in special areas. The group Keratosa, to which they belong, is almost entirely confined to tropical and subtropical seas, with very few species ranging into temperate or polar waters. Commercial sponges are most numerous in the Mediterranean, especially in the eastern half, and in the Gulf of Mexico, especially around the Bahamas and Mexico.

Outside these broad generalisations it is not easy to plot the geographical distribution. The sponge-fauna of the Arctic spreads south around the continental shelf of north-west Europe, north-east and north-west America and north-east Asia. Further south it merges into subtropical faunas, typified by those found in the Mediterranean and the Gulf of Mexico, and the subtropical faunas in turn merge into tropical faunas. There is a similar succession starting from the Antarctic and passing northwards to the Equator. The genera tend to be cosmopolitan and the species differ, although in outward form there is little to differentiate them, the identification being largely based on differences in their skeletons. Moreover there are many

The Purse Sponge (*Grantia compressa*), one of the calcareous sponges with a skeleton of three-rayed spicules of calcite. It is common, often found in large numbers, between tide-marks and in the shallow seas, over a large part of the world.

The Venus' Flower Basket (*Euplectella aspergillum*), a hexactinellid sponge from 200 metres off the Philippines, one of the most beautiful of all sponges, showing the symmetry characteristic of deep-sea sponges. It was commonly displayed as a curiosity in Victorian parlours in England alongside the wax fruits and stuffed birds.

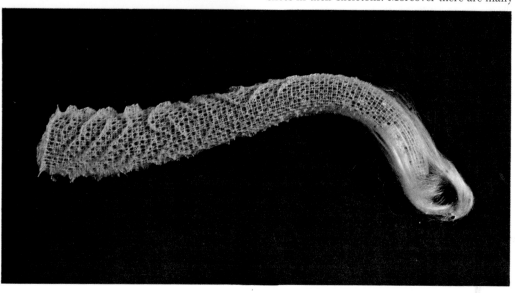

species, such as the Crumb-o'-bread Sponge (*Halichondria panicea*), *Hymeniacidon perlevis*, *Scypha ciliata* and *Haliclona oculata*, which are common around the coasts of Europe and are found elsewhere in the world, as far away as Australia and the Pacific coast of Canada. *Scypha ciliata* and others may, in fact, be truly cosmopolitan.

Classification

Many different systems of classification have been suggested for sponges. Two of the leading workers in this field were Emile Topsent and Arthur Dendy and both, after studying the subject for forty years, evolved their own systems of classification. Critical examination of these shows that they differ more in detail than in principle. Almost forty years of study in the same field, and a deep and comprehensive comparison of all the systems of classification proposed, would seem to suggest that Dendy's scheme, modified to some degree towards that of Topsent, seems the most satisfactory. This gives the following scheme:

Calcareous sponges (Class Calcarea)

These are sponges with spicules of calcite that have a triradiate form or some modification of the three-rayed pattern. All are exclusively marine, have a simple construction and vary in shape from vase-shaped to cylindrical. Sometimes the sponge may form a honeycomb-shape. Calcarea often exist as single individuals or as a colony of individuals joined at the base. Their colour varies from white or cream to a variety of pastel shades. Examples are *Sycon* and *Leucosolenia*.

Glass sponges (Class Hexactinellida)

These sponges are characterised by having siliceous spicules based on a hexaradiate or six-rayed plan. They are exclusively marine and more common in the deep seas than in shallow waters. In addition to having spicules lying free in the tissues, many species have a framework of spicules fused more or less and forming a solid lattice-work, as in the beautiful Venus' flower basket (*Euplectella*). All are white or yellow, frequently with a large rooting tuft of spicules which may at times form an extensive raft, an adaptation to living on a soft seabed, such as mud or ooze.

Class Demospongiae

This class includes the great bulk of all living species, as found in freshwaters and in the seas from mid-tide level down to the greatest depths. A few are without spicules, but where spicules are present they have a four-rayed form, known as a tetract or tetraxon, but in many the siliceous spicules are either partially replaced by a fibrous material known as spongin or entirely replaced by it as in the bath sponges. Demospongiae show a wide variety of colours and of shapes.

Coralline sponges (Class Sclerospongiae)

This class is best known from fossils and only a very few living species have been found, and those in recent years, living on coral reefs in the Pacific and the Caribbean. They are exclusively marine and are characterised by having a skeleton composed of calcium carbonate and silica, plus spongin. The sponge forms a thin layer covering a mass of underlying skeleton of aragonite.

HYDROIDS, JELLYFISHES AND CORALS
(Phylum Cnidaria, formerly Coelenterata)

A medusa of the sea-fir *Obelia*. This tiny jellyfish represents the sexual phase in the alternation of generations characteristic of the hydroids. The gonads (reproductive organs) can be seen as four dark spherical bodies. The manubrium, bearing at its apex the mouth, is the dark club-shaped organ at the centre. The other, asexual, generation is represented by the small tree-like colony of polyps found attached to rocks and seaweeds, looking like a kind of moss.

The phylum Cnidaria is predominantly marine and contains many common shore animals such as sea anemones and sea firs (hydroids), as well as deeper water forms such as the Portuguese Man-o'-War. Freshwater forms are less common, but one group, the hydras, is probably the best-known member of the phylum. There are three classes: Hydrozoa (hydroids or sea firs), Scyphozoa (large jellyfishes) and Anthozoa (sea anemones and corals). All are animals with a low grade of organisation, simpler structures being found only in sponges, mesozoans and protozoans. The body wall is composed of two layers of cells, ectoderm and endoderm, separated by a layer of non-cellular material, the mesogloea. There is a single internal cavity, the coelenteron (gastrovascular cavity or, simply, enteron) which has both digestive and circulatory functions. The coelenteron has only one opening to the exterior, the mouth, which is generally surrounded by tentacles. Both tentacles and general ectoderm bear nematocysts (cnidae or thread capsules) specialised for stinging or otherwise capturing prey. Cnidarians may be solitary or colonial, many of the latter producing a calcareous exoskeleton, as in corals.

The most obvious external feature is radial symmetry; a plane taken through any lengthwise direction gives identical halves. The main axis of symmetry is from mouth to base (oral/aboral) with the parts arranged concentrically around this axis. There is no definite head and the nervous system is not centralised. There are no defined respiratory, circulatory or excretory organs.

A feature of the Cnidaria is polymorphism, there being two main types of individual, the polyp and the medusa. The polyp or hydroid is the sessile form resembling a cylinder, closed at one end and with mouth and tentacles at the open end. It may occur in a variety of forms even within the same species. The medusa or jellyfish is a free-swimming form in which the cylindrical part of the polyp is shortened, the mesogloea thickened and the diameter increased, giving a bell- or saucer-shaped animal with a central mouth and tentacles round the bell margin.

When both polyp and medusa are present in the same species, as in many hydroids, they occur in alternate generations. A sedentary polyp generation asexually produces a medusa capable of sexual reproduction, the fertilised ovum producing a larva which transforms into a polyp. In scyphozoan jellyfishes the medusa is the dominant stage, the polyp generation often being omitted, whereas hydras, sea anemones and corals are exclusively polypoid.

The polyp can be divided into three regions: basal, oral and column. In solitary forms the basal region or pedal disc adheres to the substratum and in colonial cnidarians it is connected by a root-like stolon to the base of the next polyp. The oral region bears solid or hollow tentacles commonly arranged round the mouth, which is usually circular. The third region, the column, lies between the basal and oral regions. The body wall encloses the sole cavity, the coelenteron, which in hydrozoans is simple and tubular, but in scyphozoan and anthozoan polyps is divided by ridges or septa extending from the body wall.

This generalised form of the polyp may be modified. In some colonies polyps occur whose only function is to bud off medusae (*Obelia*), or

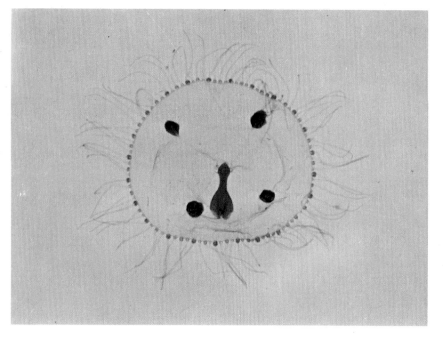

they may have a solely defensive role (*Hydractinia*), in which case there is no mouth but only tentacles bearing considerable numbers of nematocysts.

The free-swimming medusa, which can be likened to a deep or shallow bowl of gelatin, swims with the convex, aboral surface (the exumbrella) uppermost and the concave, oral or subumbrella surface beneath. A short projection or manubrium from the middle of the subumbrella surface contains the mouth. Leading internally from the mouth there is a small central 'stomach' region from which radial canals extend towards the bell margin where they connect into a ring or circular canal. The mesogloea is much more developed than in the polypoid form so that ectoderm and endoderm are separated by some distance, the ectoderm forming a thin layer on the exumbrella and subumbrella surfaces and the endoderm lining the manubrium and canal system. The bell margin bears a varying number of tentacles and sense-organs, the latter being generally concerned with maintaining balance.

The medusa swims by a form of jet propulsion, alternately contracting a ring of muscle fibres round the bell margin and passively expanding via the elasticity of the mesogloea.

Medusae are usually produced by budding from the polypoid colony. The parent may be a modified polyp, a feeding polyp, or some other part of the colony, e.g. the stolon. The medusa is generally the sexually mature form producing gametes, but in certain cases may be modified by loss of structures such as tentacles, mouth and reproductive organs to become a float or swimming organelle, or it may lose mouth and tentacles to function as a reproductive body only, often on the parent colony.

Structure

Musculo-epithelial cells

The major cell types of the Cnidaria are the musculo-epithelial cells, nerve cells and nematoblasts which produce nematocysts. The 'body' is composed mainly of musculo-epithelial cells. These cells, found only in the cnidarians, are a means of producing an epithelium combined with a contractile system. Each cell consists of two parts, epithelial and muscular, linked by cytoplasm. The epithelial portion lies externally and forms the outer covering of the animal in the ectoderm as well as the lining of the enteron in the endoderm. The muscular portion contains muscle fibres that lie next to the mesogloea along the base of the cell. The muscle fibres are arranged longitudinally in the ectoderm and transversely in the endoderm, so that they work antagonistically.

The musculo-epithelial cells of the endoderm may be modified into glandular and digestive cells bearing flagella. Glandular cells produce enzymes which are secreted into the enteron and break food material into small particles. Digestive cells engulf these particles which then undergo further digestion in the food vacuoles within the cells.

Nerve cells

Nerve cells have been positively identified only in medusae and anthozoans. The nervous system in cnidarians takes the form of a nerve-net composed

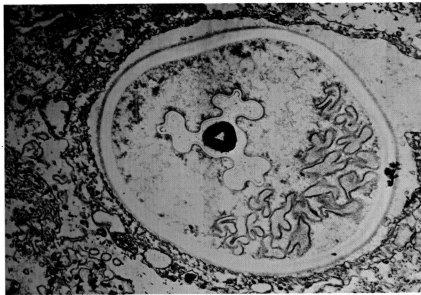

of a large number of multipolar nerve cells, that is, nerve cells with many dendrites or connecting links. Because any stimulus must cross the numerous synapses or gaps between cells, transmission of the impulse is very slow. In some species transmission is accelerated by the development of through-conduction paths, which are regions where the nerve-net is composed of bipolar cells orientated to form a pathway where synaptic resistance is reduced.

Mesogloea

The mesogloea is a secretion lying between the two cell layers of the body wall. In medusae the mesogloea constitutes the bulk of the animal. Thought to be produced mainly by the cells of the ectoderm, this secretion is composed of a protein similar to collagen. Its function is important because it forms a base upon which the muscle system can operate and therefore acts in a skeletal capacity, preventing excessive deformation of the body.

Feeding habits

Cnidarians are carnivorous, feeding on living animals such as small fishes and their eggs, small crustaceans, molluscs, worms and other cnidarians. They capture their prey and convey it to the mouth by means of their tentacles which possess nematocysts. Nematocysts are characteristic of the phylum, but some molluscs and some flatworms which prey on cnidarians are able to collect them in their own tissues and use them. They are double-walled capsules containing a coiled and sometimes barbed thread which is ejected when the cnidocil or trigger comes in contact with a foreign body. As the coiled thread is ejected from the capsule it turns inside out, and its fine point pierces the prey, injecting a paralysing toxin. A toxin from the nematocysts of a large jellyfish or Portuguese Man o' War can produce a kind of 'allergic' response in the form of rashes and weals in human beings, and the poison of some siphonophores is lethal. Other types of nematocyst have adhesive powers and some coil around the victim. Nematocysts are not controlled by the nervous system, but are discharged by chemical

A transverse section through a nematocyst or stinging cell of *Hydra*, the freshwater polyp. A nematocyst is not strictly a cell but a cell organoid, contained within an epithelial cell. It consists of a subspherical capsule, filled with fluid, in which lies coiled an inverted thread-like tube which can be shot out to penetrate the skin of a prey or an enemy. Poison then flows down the tube.

and mechanical stimulation. Large numbers are released and are continually replaced, as once released they are expended.

The tentacles then deliver the prey to the mouth and enteron where it is broken down into small particles for ingestion by the cells lining the enteron. Soluble food is distributed, possibly by diffusion, to cells of the body wall of the polyp, and via the canal system in medusae.

Reproduction and development

Cnidarians are usually dioecious, that is, the sexes are separate, but may be hermaphrodite. Gametes are usually shed into the sea water, where fertilisation occurs. In general, medusae produce gametes, but in instances where only the polyp occurs (e.g. in anthozoans) gonads are borne on the projecting internal septa or (e.g in hydras) as protruberances on the outside of the body wall. Often the medusa

is reduced in size and never leaves the parent colony; in these cases the eggs are fertilised *in situ* by free-swimming spermatozoa.

After fertilisation the zygote divides, giving rise to cells of equal size; cleavage is said to be radial and indeterminate, for it is possible to remove any cell without damage to the embyro. (This should be contrasted with the Ctenophora.) The cell ball develops into a ciliated larva or planula which is found swimming in the plankton. The mass of cells then forms two layers with a central cavity and the minute planula settles on the substratum where it develops into a polyp. When there is a medusa stage only in the life-history, the planula often develops into an actinula, a tentacled larva, which then develops into a medusa. In some cases eggs are retained by the parent in special brood-pouches from which the progeny emerge as young adults.

Sea firs (hydroids), hydras and siphonophores (Class Hydrozoa)

Below
Hydra oligactis, one of the species of green or brown freshwater polyps, showing the cylindrical body with the mouth at the top and the thread-like tentacles surrounding the mouth. When in repose the tentacles are retracted and appear as small knobs around the mouth. For feeding purposes, the tentacles are extended to a great length and gently waved in the water. The nematocysts in the 'beads' are ready to come into action immediately a small animal brushes against the tentacles, stimulating them to shoot out their poison-conducting threads.

Below right
Hydra oligactis has stung, paralysed and swallowed (ingested) a chironomid (gnat) larva larger than itself. This picture illustrates strikingly the elasticity of the hydra's body wall, as the animal hangs from a water plant withdrawing its tentacles prior to digesting the prey so recently captured.

The class Hydrozoa comprises over 2,700 species and is subdivided into seven orders: Athecata, Thecata, Limnomedusae, Trachymedusae, Narcomedusae, Siphonophora and Hydrocorallinae. Both polyp and medusa are generally present, but the latter may be reduced and then does not always leave the parent colony. Many members of the class live between tidemarks or in shallow coastal waters, while others are deep-water forms rarely seen. Most members are small, both polyps and medusae measuring only a few millimetres. The class contains both colonial and solitary forms, is marine with the exception of the few species of freshwater hydras and jellyfishes, and shows the most extreme polymorphism. Many are able to lay down a skeleton, either a chitinous secretion (termed the 'perisarc') of the ectodermal cells round the stolons and polyps of the colony, or a calcareous material as in the hydrocorallines.

The hydrozoan polyp is the simplest in the

phylum; the two body layers enclose a coelenteron which lacks septa, and the nervous system is a nerve-net whose properties are, as yet, scarcely investigated.

The medusa generally has four radial canals, a variable number of solid or hollow tentacles, as well as sense-organs and light-sensitive ocelli which appear as red, brown or black spots at the bases of the tentacles. In addition a velum is generally present; this is a circular shelf which projects inwards from the bell margin. According to the order to which they belong, some medusae are referred to as anthomedusae, others as leptomedusae. Anthomedusae (order Athecata) are thimble-shaped and bear gonads on the manubrium while the leptomedusae (order Thecata) are saucer-shaped and the gonads develop on the radial canals. In addition, leptomedusae possess statocysts, special cells at the base of the velum and considered to be organs of equilibrium. Each

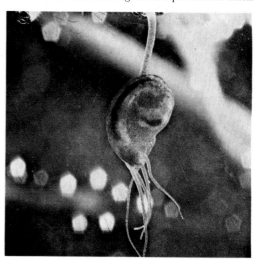

contains a calcareous concretion or statolith which, pulled in various directions by gravity according to the tilt of the medusa, touches against sensory 'hairs' and so indicates orientation with respect to gravity.

In the medusa there is evidence of two distinct nerve-nets. One, situated at the bell margin and overlying the ring of muscle fibres, is a through-conducting system of bipolar nerve cells which causes the contraction of the whole bell. It probably evolved with the use of the bell as a swimming organ. The second nerve-net consists of multipolar cells spread over the exumbrella and subumbrella and is responsible for local contractions of the bell.

Order Athecata
Most of the hydrozoans belong to this order or to the Thecata. The Athecata include the sea firs or hydroids of the intertidal zones as well as the freshwater hydras and By-the-wind-sailor (*Velella*). Generally there are both polyp and medusa forms, although the medusa is often reduced and is not always free-living. In colonial forms the chitinous perisarc surrounds the stolons and continues to just below the head of the polyp. In solitary forms the perisarc is often lacking.

Medusae begin their growth as gonophores produced as asexual buds. The gonophores are oval, stalked bodies lacking a perisarc and are produced from various parts of the polyp colony according to the species. In only about a third of the Athecata do the gonophores produce free-living anthomedusae. In the remaining two-thirds the gonophores remain attached and the eggs are fertilised *in situ*. In these instances the planula often develops into an actinula before its release into the sea.

Classification into families is usually based on such details as the type of tentacles borne on the feeding polyp.

Tubularia (family Tubulariidae) is a colonial hydroid with a set of long, thin tentacles round the mouth and another set at the base of the polyp. Between the two sets are gonophores resembling bunches of grapes. There are no free-living medusae; the eggs are fertilised *in situ* and develop into actinulae. Each polyp, often rose-pink in colour, rises from a long stem originating in a mass of rooting stolons. Species of *Tubularia* are common in the British Isles and America, especially in strong currents, and are found at low tide levels on rocks and seaweeds like the kelps or oarweeds, *Laminaria*.

Other genera are often found between tidemarks. *Clava* (family Clavidae) forms pinkish colonies on seaweeds, particularly the wracks. *Coryne* (family Corynidae) has rose-coloured polyps bearing knobbed tentacles and is found on larger seaweeds or rocks. Gonophores produced on the polyp head in *Coryne* release anthomedusae with four long tentacles on the bell margin, four radial canals and a long manubrium. *Hydractinia* (family Bougainvilliidae) forms a thick mat of stolons on shells occupied by hermit crabs. It is polymorphic, the main forms being feeding polyps, protective spines, reproductive polyps and defensive polyps with tentacles only.

The freshwater hydras (family Hydridae) are probably the most familiar of the hydrozoans, numerous species occurring in ponds, lakes and streams throughout the world. The best-known species in Britain and the United States are the Green Hydra (*Chlorohydra viridissima*) and the Brown Hydra (*Pelmatohydra oligactis*). Hydras are atypical of the phylum in that they inhabit freshwater, and must be capable of controlling the amount of water entering the body due to differences in the ionic concentration of cells and freshwater. As a phylum cnidarians seem unable to make this adjustment and are confined to the sea. Hydras are also atypical hydrozoans in that they lack any evidence of a medusa stage; in existing as solitary individuals rather than colonies; in some species being hermaphrodite and in all lacking a perisarc.

The polyp is elongate with a mouth surrounded by five to six tentacles, a columnar region varying from a few millimetres in some species to fifteen millimetres in others, and a basal disc. There is no medusoid phase in the life-history. Instead, eggs produced as bulges on the column are fertilised *in situ*, usually in the autumn, and the developing embryo secretes a chitinous material on its surface. The resistant embryo then drops off the parent and lies dormant for a period, before hatching in the spring as a small hydra. This phase in the life-history is thought to be a secondary adaptation to life in freshwater ponds liable to dry up. When ample food is available hydras reproduce asexually by budding. A small bulge appears on the column and develops tentacles at the end furthest from the parent. The continuous coelenterons of parent and bud become separated by constriction at the base of the young polyp, which then drops off.

Hydras, like other members of the Athecata, are able to regenerate lost parts. The colours of the hydras are given by the presence of symbiotic algae in the endodermal cells.

Two unusual genera of the order Athecata are By-the-wind-sailor (*Velella*) and *Porpita*. They resemble an enlarged, inverted and solitary version of a polyp such as *Tubularia*, floating on the surface. They have a round or oval float, which in *Velella* has an extension or sail, and under this is a central mouth surrounded by gonophores and with tentacles round the margin. The float contains air chambers and it is claimed that air is pumped through, constituting a respiratory

Hydra was one of the first cnidarians to be named, for its ability to regrow a new 'head' when this had been cut off or injured, after the Hydra of mythology. Thereafter, small polyps related to *Hydra* became known as hydroids (= like hydra). Most hydroids are marine and consist of a colony of tiny polyps on a branching stalk. *Tubularia* sp., shown here, is unusual in that each polyp is borne on its own stalk.

43

The freshwater hydra is remarkable for its budding, a form of asexual reproduction. A tiny pimple appears on the surface of the body. This grows in height, a hole (the mouth) appears at the apex while tentacles grow out around it. Finally, the new individual so formed becomes constricted at the base, and the young hydra eventually breaks away from the parent body to start life on its own.

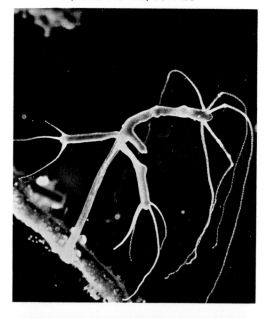

A hydroid or Sea-fir (*Plumularia setacea*) growing on the green alga (*Codium tomentosum*). Tiny sea-slugs (*Eubranchus cingulatus*) can be seen spawning. This picture presents a typical scene from the miniature sea gardens coating the rocks on the sea-shores everywhere. This one is from the intertidal zone of the coasts of Europe. The polyps of *Plumularia* are arranged in a zig-zag fashion, so forming erect colonies.

This tiny jellyfish is one of the Trachymedusae. The transparent umbrella-shaped body is traversed by four radial canals on which lie the gonads (reproductive organs). The stinging tentacles hang from the rim of the umbrella. Trachymedusae have no hydroid phase, new individuals being developed from a planula, a free-swimming larva formed by the union of a sperm and an ovum from the gonads.

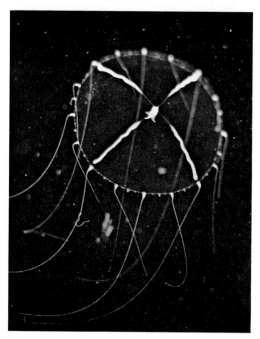

system. The small medusae released by *Velella* are known as *Chrysomitra*, since they were originally thought to be a separate genus. They have no mouth and die after releasing gametes. *Porpita* has a yellow float and *Velella* a purple sail. Both are widely distributed. *Velella* is often washed up on the south-west coasts of the British Isles.

Thecate hydroids (Order Thecata)

This order comprises the sea firs in which the chitinous perisarc surrounds the stolons and forms a protective cup, the theca, round the head of the polyp. Medusae are produced asexually by budding from a modified feeding polyp, the blastostyle, around which the perisarc forms a protective case or gonotheca. Blastostyles may be produced from the stolons or polyp stems. The free-swimming medusae of the order, when released, are termed leptomedusae. Only a fifth of the thecate hydroids produce these. In the rest the medusae may become very much modified and are difficult to identify. Thecates are widely distributed geographically. They and hydroids in general flourish especially in temperate and cold waters. Thecates are found on algae and stones (many prefer red algae) or between tidemarks, while others prefer deep water.

The order includes *Obelia* (family Campanulariidae), common on oarweeds, with polyps in open goblet-shaped thecae and releasing free medusae; *Clytia* (family Campanulariidae), a delicate branching colony on red weeds, releasing free medusae; *Lafoea* (family Lafoeidae) with colonies formed of parallel stolons giving mechanical support and polyps growing at right angles to the stolons in elongated thecae without lids. *Sertularia* (family Sertulariidae) is common on wracks, with polyps growing in pairs opposite each other in thecae with lids. Known commercially as 'white weed', many species of *Sertularia* growing offshore are dried, stained and sold for decorative purposes.

Order Limnomedusae

This order comprises a collection of saucer-shaped medusae with four to six radial canals and numerous tentacles in sets round the bell margin. In *Olindias*, found in shallow tropical waters, some of the tentacles bear suckers, enabling it to walk on seaweeds. *Gonionemus* also has suckers and is recorded from the British Isles and America. An uncommon freshwater species, *Craspedacusta sowerbii*, is a large hydrozoan medusa up to twenty millimetres in diameter. It was first found in London in 1880 in a pond containing an Amazonian water lily brought from Brazil and has since been found in certain ponds and lakes in America. It has a minute polyp, called *Microhydra* before its relation to the medusa was discovered, which buds off small medusae.

Order Trachymedusae

In this small group of medusae the mouth is borne at the end of a long pseudomanubrium which is an extension of the subumbrella surface. There are four to six radial canals and few tentacles. There is no polyp phase, the planula developing into an actinula, which then expands radially to become a medusa. Some authorities consider this type of life-history to be ancestral. Examples of the order which live in warmer waters are *Geryonia* and *Liriope*.

Order Narcomedusae

This is another small group of medusae which have no polyp phase. They have broad flat bells and lack a manubrium. The mouth opens directly into the stomach region. Tentacles around the bell margin actually arise above the margin and ecto-dermal extensions (peronia) of the tentacles run along the outer surface of the bell to indentations in its margin, giving the bell a scalloped edge. In *Cunina* the planula becomes parasitic, attaching itself to the trachymedusa *Geryonia* and developing as an elongated stolon which then buds off medusae.

Siphonophores (Order Siphonophora)

Siphonophores form swimming or floating colonies composed of both polypoid and medusoid forms. They display the highest degree of polymorphism found in the cnidarians. They are found in all seas, but prefer warmer waters. Relatively small and transparent, they are often unnoticed. Two examples are *Halistemma* and *Agalma*. Forms derived from polyps include feeding polyps with a single long tentacle bearing nematocysts, palpons or 'feeling' polyps which have a tentacle but no mouth, and gonozooids which bear gonophores. Medusoid forms include swimming bells, floats and bracts, in addition to gonophores.

The float is usually the only part of the colony visible above water-level and often contains a gland which secretes gas into the float, enabling the colony to rise and fall beneath the waves. Below the float are numerous swimming bells, medusae which are unable to feed or reproduce and act only as swimming organelles. And below them are clusters of feeding and reproductive individuals on a long central axis.

Some colonies have no float and the summit of the colony consists of swimming bells. *Muggiaea*, a genus with a single bell, often occurs off the south-west coasts of the British Isles.

The Portuguese Man o' War (*Physalia physalis*) is a familiar siphonophore. Its long axis is shor-tened so that the feeding and reproductive forms lie underneath a large, oval contractile float. The float is generally blue in colour and may be very large, from ten to thirty centimetres long, with the tentacles of the feeding polyps extending for many metres. The nematocysts of this species contain powerful toxins and their sting is dangerous to man. A small fish *Nomeus*, however, habitually swims about among the tentacles without coming to harm and never lives independently. Normally an inhabitant of the open Atlantic, *Physalia* may appear around the south and west coasts of the British Isles after prolonged southwesterly winds and along the Atlantic coast of the United States.

The Portuguese Man-o'-War (*Physalia physalis*), so named for the shape of its bladder-like float which has a passing resemblance to the Portuguese fighting ships of former times. Each Portuguese Man-o'-War comprises a colony of polyps, the float being one which carries on its undersurface a cluster of others, some being feeding polyps, others reproductive, with a third group forming the long stinging tentacles.

Order Hydrocorallinae

This order consists of a few genera which lay down a calcareous skeleton. There are two suborders.

The Milleporina consists of one genus, *Mille-pora*, found in tropical shallow seas, where it often forms extensive reefs or contributes to true coral reefs. It forms upright, white or whitish-yellow leaf-like or branching growths. The surface of the calcareous skeleton is pitted with a ring of small pores surrounding each of the larger pores. When alive, the feeding polyp occupies the centre pore and is connected by stolons to other feeding polyps and to defensive dactylozooids which occupy the smaller pores. The dactylozooids are feeding polyps reduced to tentacled forms with powerful nematocysts which produce a burning sensation on contact with the skin. The small reduced medusae of this suborder live only for a few hours and shed their gametes.

The Stylasterina resemble the Milleporina, but the distribution of feeding and defensive polyps is different and there are no free medusae. They form upright, branching, calcareous growths, often pink or purple, and inhabit tropical and subtropical seas.

Jellyfishes (Class Scyphozoa)

In the large jellyfishes or Scyphozoa the medusoid phase is dominant, the polyp, known as the hydratuba or scyphistoma, being a small tubular organism resembling *Hydra*. The class comprises five orders: Semaeostomeae, Rhizostomeae, Coronatae, Cubomedusae and Stauromedusae.

Chrysaora hyoscella, one of the semaeostome jellyfishes, common towards the end of summer in the European Atlantic waters. It has 24 tentacles around the margin of the umbrella and four feeding arms, hanging from the manubrium (mouth), which can be greatly extended to catch prey. The arms are then retracted and the prey licked from them by the lips of the manubrium.

A portion of the jellyfish (*Cyanea lamarcki*). This is the Violet Jellyfish, its colour ranging from deep blue to purple. It is also the largest jellyfish known. Although its diameter is most usually up to forty centimetres or so, individuals two metres across have been met in the Arctic. As *Cyanea* drifts through the water its long stinging tentacles spread out in the water like a giant spider's web.

The most noticeable external feature of the class is its four-rayed symmetry. The bell of the scyphomedusae, the medusoid phase, varies in shape according to the order and is generally gelatinous due to the extensive formation of mesogloea.

There is a varying number of tentacles round the bell margin and a four-cornered mouth at the end of a manubrium. The mouth may be drawn out at the corners into lobes or oral arms, which in some jellyfishes may be extensive. Both the arms and ectoderm of the bell bear many nematocysts. The mouth leads into a central cavity, off which are four gastric pouches from which run radial canals leading to a circular canal at the bell margin, and from which other canals lead back to pores at the bases of the oral arms. The canals are ciliated and by their action food materials, subjected to preliminary digestion, are circulated through the bell. The gonads are found in the gastric pouches. Round the perimeter of the bell is a well-developed muscle-band which, like that of hydrozoan medusae, contracts to close the bell and eject water, propelling the animal forwards. To co-ordinate swimming movements there is an elaborate nervous system similar to that of the other medusae. On the bell margin are sense-organs responsible for maintaining equilibrium.

The polyp stage, the scyphistoma or hydratuba, when present, develops from the ciliated planula. The zygote often remains in brood-pouches formed from the oral arms until it reaches the planula stage. The larva settles and becomes a cylindrical scyphistoma with a basal disc and a tentacled oral disc. Although superficially like *Hydra*, internally it differs: the enteron is incompletely divided into four by septa which project from the wall into the centre. The septa bear longitudinal muscles and have a curious feature, a peristomial pit, which runs from the oral disc to near the base of the polyp.

During the summer months the scyphistoma feeds and buds off other scyphistomae, but during the winter a process known as strobilation occurs: the polyp becomes multiply constricted in the transverse plane so that it resembles a pile of plates. From each disc eight lobes or lappets grow out. One by one the discs are constricted off from the parent by contraction of the longitudinal muscles in the septa. These discs are tiny medusae known as ephyra larvae. Each newly liberated ephyra is about one millimetre in diameter and swims in the plankton, feeding and growing until it reaches adult size. The parent scyphistoma produces more oral tentacles and feeds again, living for several years and under favourable conditions producing ephyrae every winter.

Order Semaeostomeae

The jellyfishes in this order are among the most familiar members of the class, being those usually seen in temperate waters, and they are also the most typical. There are numerous tentacles round the bell margin and the oral arms are long and frilly. The musculature is usually obvious and there are numerous simple or branched canals. The order is found in coastal waters of all seas, warm and temperate, while some species of *Cyanea* are found in polar regions. *Pelagia* occurs in deeper waters and lacks the fixed scyphistoma, the planulae developing directly into small medusae. Jellyfishes vary in size from five to forty centimetres in diameter; species of *Cyanea* with a diameter of over two metres have been recorded. They are often coloured in patches and streaks. In many instances the gonads are highly coloured and many jellyfishes fluoresce in the dark.

The Common Jellyfish (genus *Aurelia*) is seven to twenty centimetres in diameter and sometimes larger, with numerous short tentacles round the bell margin giving it a frilly appearance. In *Aurelia aurita*, which is often found washed ashore on beaches, the four crescent-shaped gonads are purple and very noticeable. *Chrysaora isoceles*, found occasionally off the coasts of Britain and with related American species, is a whitish jellyfish with long tentacles hanging down from a lobed edge, each lobe having a dark brown spot. There are long, frilly, brown oral arms, a brown spot in the centre of the exumbrella and twenty-four brown triangular patches radiating from it.

Species of *Cyanea* are found off the coasts of Britain and America and can be identified by the lobed bell margin with eight bundles of tentacles arranged round it. Small specimens are often thirty centimetres in diameter and even bigger individuals have been recorded from the North Atlantic. They are variously coloured, ranging from yellows to purples and blue. Species of *Pelagia*, especially *P. noctiluca*, are luminescent. They have a scalloped bell margin and long, thin tentacles. In addition the oral arms are very long and the bell is spotted with purples and red-browns.

Order Rhizostomeae

Members of this order closely resemble the semaeostome jellyfishes, the differences being the lack of tentacles round the bell margin and the great increase in size and fusion of the oral arms. These are much branched and the original grooves of the arms close over to form a canal. The main mouth generally becomes part of the fused system, and the numerous branches lead to the so-called suctorial mouths. In some genera additional mouth-bearing outgrowths, the shoulder ruffles, occur on the outer edges of the arms. The arms also bear elongated appendages with many nematocysts, assisting in the capture of food. The fused mouth leads into a central stomach region, and numerous branched radial canals extend to the bell margin. They are generally good swimmers with well-developed muscles round the bell margin and usually live in warm shallow waters, although species of *Rhizostoma* may extend into temperate waters. Little is known about their development, but it is thought there is a scyphistoma which produces ephyrae.

Rhizostoma is a widely distributed genus with eight long terminal appendages and is occasionally found on the south and west coasts of the British Isles. *R. octopus* is grey-green in colour, up to sixty centimetres in diameter, and its bell has a purple edge. Often associated with it in the subumbrella is an amphipod crustacean, or Sandhoppper (*Hypera galba*).

Cassiopeia, common round Florida and the West Indies, contains more sluggish forms which have

eight branching mouth arms with suctorial mouths. A flattened bell with a marginal ridge gives the appearance of a saucer. These jellyfishes lie upside-down in shallow lagoons with the exumbrella facing downwards and adhering by the bell ridge. Pulsations of the bell cause water currents to flow over the outstretched arms, bringing food and oxygen.

Order Coronatae

Typically inhabitants of deeper waters, the jellyfishes in this order generally have conical or flattened bells and are characterised by the presence of a coronal groove midway between the centre of the bell and the margin. Below this groove is a deeply scalloped bell margin with lappets and tentacle-bearing organs. The mouth is on a short manubrium opening into a central stomach.

Little is known about their development, many members being known only from collections taken on deep-sea dredging expeditions. For instance, *Atolla* with a shallow, dark red bell is not usually found above 200 metres. *Periphylla* with a dome-shaped, purple bell is common in deeper waters but is sometimes seen on the surface. *Nausithoe* and the small thimble-shaped *Linuche* inhabit shallow waters in the Bahamas and Florida region of the western Atlantic.

Pelagia noctiluca, the luminescent jellyfish. Its scientific name can be approximately translated as the drifting nightlight. The jellyfish has the appearance at night of a ball of molten metal at white heat. There have been occasions when the sea has been so filled with these jellyfish that the fishing vessels have had to suspend operations.

Cassiopeia sp., from the New Hebrides, a jellyfish that has brought easy living to a fine art. The animal has a flat disc in place of the usual umbrella of jellyfish. It lies on its back on the sandy bed of a tropical sea and stretches out its shrubby arms to suck in the plankton drifting by, each arm being spongy and covered with numerous small openings.

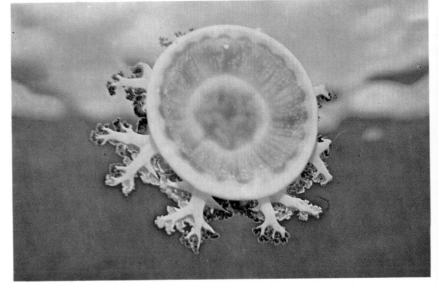

Sea wasps (Order Cubomedusae)

These jellyfishes are unlike the other orders because the bells are cuboid with four flattened sides. They have a simple bell margin with groups of tentacles hanging from the four corners. Each tentacle consists of a wide portion near the bell and a narrower portion armed with nematocysts. The mouth at the centre of a short manubrium is deeply set in the subumbrella cavity and four septa divide the internal stomach region. They are found in open seas but are characteristic of tropical shallow waters, where they are powerful swimmers and feed on fishes. They are generally colourless and the best known is *Charabdea* with four single tentacles at the bell margin. All are noted for their powerful and often lethal sting and are feared by swimmers in coastal waters of south Japan, the Philippines and Australia, where they occur. Little is known about their life-history. *Chiropsalmus quadrigatus* is an example from northern Australian waters.

Stalked jellyfishes (Order Stauromedusae)

Unlike the other members of the Scyphozoa, these jellyfishes are sessile and live fastened to seaweeds or stone by the exumbrella surface, feeding on small crustaceans. The bell is trumpet-shaped with a flattened subumbrella surface bearing tentacles and with a central mouth. The short, stalk-like body is anchored by an adhesive disc which in some cases is detachable, allowing the animal to move. They never swim but live in bays, sounds and coastal waters, generally in colder areas. Typically the margin of the bell is drawn out into eight lobes or four bifurcated lobes, each with a bundle of short tentacles at the tips. In between these lobes there may be dark patches representing adhesive organs.

Internally, stauromedusae resemble scyphistomae, having an enteron divided by four septa. Typical planulae are produced which settle down and may bud off more larvae before growing into stalked, trumpet-shaped adults. Generally greenish or rose-pink in colour, they may measure several centimetres in diameter. The commonest genera are *Haliclystus* with eight dark patches and *Lucernaria* which has none. Whether this is a jellyfish which has become sessile, a scyphistoma which has become sexually mature, or an early member of the Cnidaria has not been resolved.

Sea anemones and corals (Class Anthozoa)

This class, the 'flower animals', comprises 6,100 marine species, many of which are well known: sea anemones, corals, sea feathers, sea pens and sea fans. There are three subclasses: Octocorallia or Alcyonaria, Zoantharia and Ceriantipatharia. The most important feature is that the class is exclusively polypoid. Members may be solitary or colonial, with or without the skeleton. The latter when present may be massive as in corals, or may be internal spicules as in the sea pens. General features of the polyp are its relatively short main axis as compared with that of hydrozoan polyps, and its flattened oral region giving a wide disc. Unlike hydrozoan polyps it has a coelenteron that is subdivided by septa (sometimes known as mesenteries) which are partitions composed of a central axis of mesogloea surrounded by endoderm and bearing at the free ends digestive filaments— groups of cells producing enzymes, and nematocysts. Gonads develop in the septa towards the base of the polyp. The number and arrangement of the septa is characteristic of the various orders.

With this increase in body size, circulation of sea water carrying respiratory gases becomes a problem and an effective circulation in the coelenteron is maintained by ciliated grooves and septa with flagella. The mouth opens into a throat which then opens into the coelenteron. The throat bears one or two ciliated grooves or siphonoglyphs. The cilia beat inwards, drawing water and oxygen into the polyp. Water is directed out of the polyp by the action of flagella on two or more special septa known as directives. The siphonoglyphs and directives confer a bilateral symmetry to the class.

The muscular and nervous systems are much more developed, polyps being able to contract rapidly, either forming a smaller, more firm mass or withdrawing into a protective skeleton. Longitudinal muscles are located in the septa and in the same area the nerve-net is concentrated into a through-conduction path, where transmission is rapid. In addition there is a diffuse nerve-net composed of multipolar nerve cells controlling local responses.

Soft corals, sea pens and sea feathers (Subclass Octocorallia)

This subclass is distinguished from all the other polyps by its obvious eight-rayed symmetry and eight subdivided tentacles. Internally there are eight septa which all join to the throat at the oral end. There is one siphonoglyph and in an approxi-mately opposite position, two flagellated directives in the free region below the throat. All the members of this subclass are colonial, the polyps being connected to each other by tubular extensions of the body wall from which other polyps may be budded. Generally ectodermal cells lay down spicules of calcium carbonate, which can be massed together and compacted to form an apparently internal axis. The muscular system is comparatively less developed and it is known that nervous communication exists between polyps in a colony, an adverse stimulus causing contraction of several polyps.

There are three orders in this subclass: Alcyonacea, Gorgonacea and Pennatulacea.

Order Alcyonacea

This order is mainly composed of species of soft corals, but there are a few other forms originally placed in separate orders. The soft corals, typified by Dead Men's Fingers (*Alcyonium digitatum*) found off the shores of the British Isles, are usually masses of gelatinous material in which are embedded the polyps with their long, extended bodies reaching through the colony. The mesogloea is well developed and embedded in it are many spicules, often of characteristic shape. Generally members of the group live in littoral, warm waters, but a number are deep-water forms. Those found in the polar regions tend to be very massive with many spicules. On the whole they are dull brown in colour, but some may be whitish.

Polyps of the Organ Pipe Coral (*Tubipora*) grow in long, upright, parallel tubes of compacted spicules, united at levels by transverse stolons. The skeleton, the form generally seen, resembles a set of organ pipes connected by platforms at intervals. Its dull red colour is thought to be caused by iron salts. *Tubipora* is generally found on coral reefs.

The Blue Coral (*Helipora*) forms a massive skeleton of an amorphous type, not spicules. The polyps and living tissue overlie the lobed skeletal mass and are brownish in colour. The skeleton itself is a blue colour, due to the incorporation of iron salts.

Horny corals (Order Gorgonacea)

This is a group of tropical and subtropical forms known variously as sea whips, sea fans and sea feathers. In all there is a central axis of fused spicules or horn-like material known as gorgonin, with the living polyps and their interconnecting tubes on the outside. In the majority of species growth resembles that of a plant, with a short main trunk fastened to the ground and lateral branching stems which may be in the same plane, as in sea fans. Preferring warmer seas, these forms live from low tide to deep waters and may form colonies up to about three metres in diameter. They are common on coral reefs, the spicules which lie loosely in the mesogloea in some species giving colour to the colonies, with yellows, reds, oranges and purples being the common colours. One cold water form is *Eunicella*, whitish in colour, which is often dredged around the south-west coasts of Britain. The best known member from the Mediterranean and Japan is the precious coral *Corallium rubrum* whose red, solid axis of fused spicules is used to make coral jewellery.

Sea pens (Order Pennatulacea)

The sea pens are fleshy colonies with a degree of motility. Originating from one polyp, which develops from a planula and later degenerates, lateral secondary polyps arise occupying the summit of the colony, while an area devoid of polyps, the stalk, is used to anchor the colony in soft, muddy bottoms. The arrangement of the secondary polyps varies, but all have two types of polyp, a feature that also occurs in some other orders. Polyps of one type are solely feeding forms with septa but lacking siphonoglyphs and directives, while the others have siphonoglyphs and directives, but lack tentacles and digestive septa. In the most highly evolved families the polyps are arranged in rows which become fused to form fleshy projections or 'leaves'. The stalk contains four large canals which can be filled with water to give a digging organ, and in this way the sea pen can burrow in soft mud. They are generally most abundant in warmer seas although some species have been found in colder seas such as the North Atlantic. Species of *Pennatula* are reddish or yellow

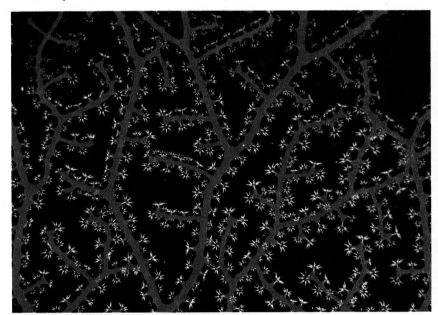

A gorgonian coral or sea fan from the Red Sea. Gorgonians are most common in the warm seas and live to depths of 1000 metres. Each consists of a plant-like growth, with a short stalk fixed to a pebble or rock bearing branches arranged mainly in one plane. The stalk and branches have a central axis of calcareous spicules or of a horny substance known as gorgonin.

Sarcophyllum sp., one of the sea pens, found mainly in warm seas. This one was living at 13 metres off Curragong, New South Wales, Australia. Sea pens were so called because of their feather-like shape, the first specimens examined by scientists reminding them of the quill pens then in use.

The Beadlet Anemone (*Actinia equina*) is almost worldwide in distribution. Although known at times under different names according to the area in which it is found, anemones of this species have been identified from as far apart as Europe, South Africa and Australia, as well as Bermuda. The species is also famous because one of these anemones was known to have lived for 66 years in captivity.

Calliactis parasitica, a sea-anemone well-known for its symbiotic association with a hermit crab. Most commonly it is seated on the large whelk shell inhabited by a hermit crab, but this association is not invariable. The anemone may be attached to a rock or a large pebble, even to the claw of a large crab.

in colour with the polyps arranged in 'leaves'. *Umbellula*, found in deep waters, is less evolved, with a long primary axis bearing secondary polyps at intervals, and has been found in the Antarctic as

well as the Atlantic, Pacific and Indian oceans. Many sea pens are luminescent when stimulated and a flash of light will pass outwards over the colony.

Sea anemones and stony corals (Subclass Zoantharia)

This subclass includes the sea anemones and corals together with a few less-known forms. These polyps possess hollow tentacles, either in a single marginal circle round the oral disc or in radiating rows. Internally, many septa (always paired) are present; some reach the throat, others never grow as far.

Members may be solitary or colonial. They are generally found in all seas but many prefer warmer

regions. There are four orders: Actiniaria, Corallimorpharia, Scleractinea and Zoanthiniaria.

Sea anemones (Order Actiniaria)
The most familiar animals of rocky shores, the sea anemones, so-called because of the flower-like appearance of the expanded oral disc, are worldwide in distribution, more abundant in warmer seas but with a considerable number of species in colder regions. In Great Britain alone there are at least thirty-nine species. They are generally attached to rocks or weeds, but some species are able to burrow into mud using a burrowing organ developed from the basal disc, while one tropical family, the Minyadidae, are able to float, the basal region having become a chitinous float.

They never form a skeleton and are all solitary. They have two siphonoglyphs, two pairs of directive septa and paired digestive septa.

Fertilisation of eggs may be external or internal. If internal, young anemones develop in the parent enteron to be released later. Young ciliated anemones progressively develop septa and are found in the plankton. Later they settle down, producing tentacles as well as septa. In addition, asexual reproduction occurs, longitudinal fission being most common, but laceration of small quantities of material from the pedal regions also produces small anemones. Wide variation in colour, shape, numbers of septa, etc. makes identification of anemones difficult.

The Plumose Anemone (*Metridium*), with species in Great Britain and North America, has numerous white tentacles giving it a feathery appearance. *Calliactis*, an offshore variety, lives on the shell of a whelk inhabited by a Hermit Crab. The crab breaks up large prey and the anemone takes some of the smaller pieces. It is pale brown-cream with brown stripes. Another commensal form, *Adamsia*, is cream with purple spots and is always found in association with a Hermit Crab. Here the basal region of the anemone is modified into two large wings which clasp the whelk shell and fuse.

Order Corallimorpharia
Probably more closely related to corals than anemones, *Corynactis* is a small anemone which although solitary, grows in groups so that it appears colonial. It is a delicate green animal about a half to one-and-a-half centimetres in height, but may be orange, grey or scarlet, with numerous knobbed tentacles.

True or stony corals (Order Scleractinia)
The stony corals are builders of coral reefs and are generally colonial. The polyp can be visualised as

The biggest and most famous coral reef in the world is the Great Barrier Reef of Australia. Its substance is made up of a diversity of dead and living corals, with which a great variety of other sessile animals are associated, notably all manner of sponges. The picture shows a mass of coral rock from the Great Barrier Reef with profusely branched stony corals growing on it.

an anemone which forms a skeleton, the base of the polyp being situated in a calcareous cup or theca secreted by the animal. The oral disc bears cycles of short tentacles with terminal knobs of nematocysts. There is no siphonoglyph, and internally there are pairs of complete and incomplete septa. The polyps are connected to one another by extensions of the body wall above the level of the skeleton, so that the coral colony sits above its massive skeleton.

On examining the calcareous material it is easy to see the thecae in which the living polyps sat. The theca is not a simple cup, but has calcareous septa radiating from the outer margin inwards and, in addition, septa radiating from an inner central knob or columella. The living polyp lies over these septa. The way in which the skeleton is laid down is not fully understood, but it is secreted by ectodermal cells and the rate of growth is dependent on the type of skeleton, solid and massive or lighter and perforated. The polyps may be widely separated, giving a branching structure, or very close to each other so that they may have walls of thecae in common. Several polyps may also share a common trough-like theca, as in the Brain Coral (*Meandrina*). Symbiotic algae in the endoderm are believed to facilitate the laying down of the skeleton.

Reef-building corals require certain minimal conditions; warm, shallow waters, the temperature of which must not fall below 18°C, although flourishing coral growth only occurs above 22°C. They must not be exposed to sun or rain for long periods, and require a low silt content. Thus reefs are absent from many areas and confined to the Caribbean and related waters, Indo-pacific and the Pacific east of Australia. At great depths reefs are not formed, and generally only solitary cup corals are found.

Reefs are usually considered to be of three types, fringing and barrier reefs and atolls. Fringing reefs extend from shores a metre or so to half a kilometre out and consist initially of a reef front, where the most active coral growth occurs. There is a reef flat behind, composed of coral, sand, mud, dead corals and debris, together with living corals and other animals. The reef front is subjected to continuous surf, which breaks off pieces of reef and

deposits them in front, thus the reef grows, usually sharply, over debris, front shelving to the ocean bed.

A barrier reef is similar but larger, and is separated from the land by a lagoon eighteen to ninety metres deep and one to sixteen kilometres wide. The most famous example is the Great Barrier Reef of Australia. An atoll is more or less circular or horse-shoe shaped and encircles a lagoon.

Chief among reef-building corals are astraeid corals with massive forms, e.g. *Orbicella, Favia*; some perforate corals, *Acropora, Porites*, and brain corals, *Meandrina*. Although corals are the principal animal builders of reefs, other animals are important, e.g. *Millepora*, and there are also sponges, sea anemones, sea urchins, etc.

The solitary coral *Fungia* has an interesting life-history. When the young planula settles down and becomes attached the oral end expands into a disc and lays down a calcareous skeleton. This disc breaks off and the adult remains unattached.

The massive form of stony corals is the consequence of asexual reproduction, which occurs so commonly in the lower invertebrates. The coral animal, or polyp, starts life as a single individual which then buds, the new individual so formed remaining in organic continuity with the parent. By repeated budding, with each individual laying down its own calcareous skeleton, the massive stony structure is built. The living parts of the coral, the polyps, look like the related but larger sea-anemones, as in the Tubastrea coral shown here.

One of the largest of the stony corals is the hemispherical Brain Coral, which may be a metre or more in height and diameter. When the polyps die and their flesh has disintegrated the stony skeleton is exposed revealing a pattern resembling that of the brain with its convolutions.

These corals can tolerate quantities of silt which is removed from the disc by ciliary action.

The Astrangidae form small encrusting colonies and are found along the coasts of the Americas, one species, *Astrangia danae*, occurring from North Carolina to Massachusetts.

The Caryophyllidae are a family of solitary corals with goblet or horn-shaped thecae which are found in colder waters. The Devonshire Cup Coral (*Caryophyllia smithii*) can be found occasionally in south-west Britain. This is a whitish animal with brownish tentacles when expanded. When contracted, the radiating ribs of the theca can be seen.

Balanophyllia regia (family Eupsammidae) is another rare solitary form, known as the Scarlet-and-gold Star Coral. It resembles *Caryophyllia* but is scarlet or orange with transparent tentacles. This species is also found in California.

Order Zoanthiniaria

These are a small group of colonial forms which lack a skeleton. They resemble small anemones, but there is a different arrangement of septa. Generally found in warm, shallow waters, there are some littoral and deeper-water forms. They often grow as encrusting organisms on sponges, corals and shells. Localities for species of *Epizoanthus* include south-west Britain and Bermuda.

Thorny corals (Subclass Ceriantipatharia)

This is a smaller subclass containing two orders: Antipatharia (black corals) and Cerianthidea.

Black or thorny corals (Order Antipatharia)

Members of this order resemble the Gorgonacea and consist of a skeletal axis covered by a thin layer of living material. The axis, consisting of horny material, is brown or black and covered with thorns. The polyps have generally six simple, non-retractile tentacles and in some genera are drawn out along the branches of the axis so that they appear as three polyps each with two tentacles. Internally there are relatively few septa, up to twelve in number. These animals live in deep abyssal waters and little is known about their biology. An example of the order is *Antipathes* with polyps spread along the axis.

Order Cerianthidea

These anthozoans resemble anemones but have much more elongated bodies and two sets of tentacles, one encircling the mouth, the other on the edge of the disc. There is one complete cycle of septa internally and new pairs are added. Most interesting is the development of muscles in the ectodermal layer giving the appearance of a three-layered animal. They live on sandy bottoms in vertical cavities into which they contract when disturbed. The cavities are lined by secretions, shed nematocysts and sand grains, which give the animal an iridescent appearance. *Cerianthus membranaceus* is a Mediterranean species and most species are tropical or subtropical, but a few inhabit colder waters. *Cerianthus lloydi* is a small species found in Devon.

Phylogeny

The evolution of the phylum is a widely discussed subject, the major problem being whether the original form is the polyp or the medusa. Some authorities consider the ancestral form to have been a primitive medusa developing from a planula larva through an actinula stage and they therefore regard the Hydrozoa as the earliest Cnidaria, the Scyphozoa and Anthozoa being developed independently from the early medusa. Other authorities suggest that the polyp is the ancestral form, developing from the planula which settles on the substratum. They therefore consider the Anthozoa, which have only polyp forms, to be the most primitive class from which the Scyphozoa and later the Hydrozoa evolved.

COMB JELLIES
OR SEA WALNUTS
(Phylum Ctenophora)

Although some zoologists still classify the Cnidaria and Ctenophora as subphyla in the phylum Coelenterata, they are now generally recognised as distinct phyla.

The ctenophores or comb jellies are small marine animals with a cosmopolitan distribution. The gelatinous body is composed of two cell layers, ectoderm and endoderm, separated by the non-cellular mesogloea. Like cnidarians they have only one internal space, the digestive cavity, but in ctenophores it is much more complex. Most species have a pair of tentacles but, with the exception of *Euchlora rubra*, do not have nematocysts, prey being caught by means of adhesive cells known as lasso cells or colloblasts. Members of the phylum are carnivorous and are generally found in the plankton, with a few species which have become modified for a creeping existence. They are biradially symmetrical and show no trace of polymorphism.

Ctenophores swim by means of transverse rows of fused cilia. There are eight rows of these comb-like plates arranged meridionally and they beat in an orderly fashion. Ctenophores are noted for their bioluminescence: after being placed in the dark for some while, light can be seen in the region of the comb plates, originating from the canal system lying below them.

General structure and physiology

The general plan of the phylum can be seen best in members of the order Cydippida, the commonest genus being the sea gooseberries (*Pleurobrachia*) which are about two centimetres long. They are shaped rather like a hen's egg, somewhat flattened in one plane so that they appear oval in cross-section. There is a central mouth at the pointed end and a statocyst at the aboral end. On the exterior surface are the eight rows of comb plates positioned meridionally. At opposite points on the surface and between two comb rows are two deep pouches containing long retractile tentacles. These bear the colloblasts.

As the two tentacle sheaths are arranged on opposite sides of the body, the symmetry of the animal is biradial, there being two vertical planes of symmetry, tentacular and sagittal. For the purposes of this description the plane which bisects the tentacle sheaths symmetrically is termed the tentacular plane. Identical halves can be obtained by cutting along the tentacular plane, but the halves obtained by cutting in the sagittal plane are related as mirror-images. The comb rows do not lie on the principal planes but in an adradial position, with two rows in each quadrant formed by cutting the animal along both planes.

Digestive system

The digestive system branches in a complex manner through the thick mesogloea. The mouth leads into a long pharynx with folded walls which extends about two-thirds of the distance between oral and aboral poles and then opens into a

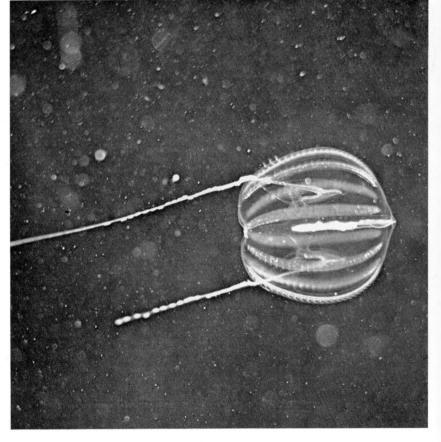

Pleurobrachia sp., one of the comb jellies or sea gooseberries, subspherical, with the mouth at one pole and eight meridian rows of comb-plates. A pair of tentacles trail behind the animal as it swims by pulsations of the jelly-like body. Comb jellies often occur in large swarms, kept together by the action of currents, as, for example, when they are swept into a bay.

stomach from which canals leave and pass into the mesogloea. From the roof of the stomach one aboral canal leads to just below the statocyst where it divides into four excretory canals, two of which open to the exterior by small pores and eject indigestible material. From the oral surface of the stomach two canals run towards the mouth, parallel with the pharynx, and end blindly near the mouth. From each side of the stomach in the tentacular plane, a large canal proceeds horizontally, giving off on each side an interradial canal and ending blindly in the tentacle sheath. Each interradial canal divides into two so that there are four in each tentacular half of the body. These canals, termed meridional canals, extend under the rows of comb plates. Circulation along this canal system is maintained by cilia.

The food of ctenophores consists of fishes, crustaceans, medusae and other ctenophores which are caught on the sticky tentacles. After capturing an animal, the tentacle shortens and the food is drawn against the mouth and swallowed. In the pharynx extracellular digestion takes place, i.e. digestive enzymes are produced by the cells of the pharynx and pass into its lumen where digestion occurs, and partially digested material enters the canal system where it is circulated. This particulate food material is taken up by phagocytosis and digestion continues in the cells of the canal walls.

Swimming

The comb rows beat synchronously in each quadrant. The beat is a strong flap of the plate from oral to aboral so that the animal swims mouth forwards. The actual wave of movement of comb plates starts at the aboral end and proceeds along the rows. Stimulation of the oral end by an object causes reversal of the wave of movement, i.e. from oral to aboral, and the effective stroke also reverses so that the animal swims backwards.

In the centre of the aboral pole is a sense-organ, the statocyst, lying in a concavity. Removal of the statocyst causes lack of co-ordination and inability to maintain the vertical resting position.

The nervous system, as in the cnidarians, consists of multipolar cells forming a nerve-net, and this system is concentrated under the comb rows giving an impression of a nerve. The cells are long and bipolar with fewer synaptic junctions, thus transmission along the length of the comb row is faster.

Development

All ctenophores are hermaphrodite, gonads being found on the walls of the meridional canals. The gametes are usually shed into the sea where fertilisation occurs. A few species retain the young in brood-pouches. After fertilisation, cleavage occurs. At the third cleavage the eight cells formed are of uneven size, four small micromeres and four large macromeres. Division of the larger cells continues unevenly, producing small and large cells, while the smaller cells divide evenly. The embryo consists of cells of two sizes, the micromeres which give rise to the outer ectoderm and which spread over the larger macromeres. These latter cells give rise to the endoderm. This type of cleavage is known as spiral and determinate, and, in contrast to the indeterminate development of the cnidarians, removal of cells at an early stage in development results in the absence of some component in the adult.

Development continues to give a free-swimming larva, the cydippid, which resembles the adults of the order Cydippida, but which can undergo changes to give the adults of other orders.

There are at least eighty species of Ctenophora comprising two classes: Tentaculata (forms with tentacles) and Nuda (forms lacking tentacles).

Class Tentaculata

Order Cydippida

Members of this order are the least modified and are generally globular with two long tentacles bearing colloblasts. Of the genera which include *Pleurobrachia*, *Hormiphora* and *Callianira*, the only ones commonly seen along the coasts of the British Isles and North America are species of *Pleurobrachia*. These tend to be seen in shoals and are sometimes very common. Occasionally they can be found stranded in rock pools, but are more generally seen in deeper water.

Order Lobata

Members of this order are compressed in the tentacular plane, i.e. laterally, and the oral end is expanded in the opposite plane on each side into a contractile lobe. The tentacles lack a sheath, lie on either side of the mouth and are reduced. Four comb rows are reduced while the other four rows are extended down the oral lobes. From the lower, oral ends of the four reduced rows are processes, of varying length, known as auricles, which have a ciliated edge. These project above the mouth, two on each side, and are important in capturing food. The digestive system is altered in detail due to the shift in tentacle position and development of the oral lobes. The cydippid larva has typical tentacles with sheaths, but the latter disappear and the tentacles shift their position during development.

Of the genera, species of *Bolinopsis* (*Bolina*) are found off the coasts of the British Isles and the Atlantic coasts of America from Maine north to the Arctic, during the summer months. Species of *Mnemiopsis* are found in coastal waters of America from Cape Cod southwards to Carolina. Other genera occur in the tropical Atlantic.

Order Cestida

The peculiarities of the Lobata are exaggerated in the Cestida, of which there are but two genera, *Cestum*, containing Venus's Girdle (*Cestum veneris*) and *Velamen*. These forms are restricted to tropical and subtropical waters and the Mediterranean. Some species of each may be seen around Florida.

In the Cestida the process of compression has occurred to such an extent that the body is

elongated in the sagittal plane to a flattened gelatinous ribbon, which may be more than one metre long. Four comb rows are very reduced and four are very elongated. The tentacles are reduced and move orally. These animals do not swim by their comb plates but by undulation of the body.

Order Platyctenea

The Platyctenea are ctenophores that have taken to creeping along surfaces and as a consequence are very much modified. They are flattened orally/ aborally and the additional oral surface is really the flattened pharynx. Because they are so unlike other ctenophores, the identity of some genera was in doubt until larvae of the typical cydippid type were found in adult brood-pouches.

Coeloplana, found originally in the Red Sea and later off Japan, is a flattened oval animal which, although possessing tentacles, lacks comb plates and is ectocommensal on species of soft coral (order Alcyonacea). Developing eggs are attached to the mother and a cydippid larva is produced which takes to creeping, loses its comb plates and everts the pharynx.

Tjalfiella is even less recognisable as a ctenophore and occurs on the pennatulid *Umbellula*, found off Greenland. Flattened orally/aborally and lacking comb plates, this animal has a strange appearance because the tentacles arise through upturned 'chimneys' at either end of the body. The young animal is a typical cydippid larva.

Beroë cucumis is the largest and oddest of the ctenophorans. Up to twenty centimetres long it is thimble-shaped, somewhat flattened laterally and is little more than a bag with jelly-like walls and a mouth at one end. It has been described as looking like a marrow or like the famous Zeppelin airship as it swims lazily around. Then suddenly its mouth opens wide to engulf its prey, which is often another smaller ctenophoran, a jellyfish, a copepod or a fish.

Class Nuda

Order Beroida

The beroids are thimble-shaped ctenophores which are compressed in the tentacular plane. They have a very large mouth opening and pharynx. The stomach lies very close under the statocyst and because of the increase in the size of the pharynx, the canals of the digestive system run close to the surface of the animal. The canals give off many branches and the comb plates are very obvious, extending the whole length of the body in some species. The main genus is *Beroë*, which is ubiquitous and can be up to twenty centimetres in length. It tends to be pinkish in colour when found in colder waters.

Phylogeny

The discovery of creeping ctenophores immediately led to the suggestion that these were the missing link between Cnidaria and Platyhelminthes, from a two-layered to a three-layered organisation. It is now clear that the Platyctenea are aberrant forms highly modified for their habit.

There are two main lines of thought regarding the origin of ctenophores: either that they are derived from the Platyhelminthes as a degenerate group, and this seems very unlikely, or that they are a group which diverged early from the original bilayered stock before the evolution of the Cnidaria.

FLATWORMS, FLUKES AND TAPEWORMS
(Phylum Platyhelminthes)

This large group comprises some hundreds of families, several thousand genera and about 7,000 species of worm-like forms which differ so much that to formulate the general characteristics is hardly possible. Representatives of the group are planarian worms, flukes and tapeworms. With some exceptions all show bilateral symmetry, have no body cavity (coelom) and are triploblastic, that is, they are composed of cells derived from the three primary germinal layers, the ectoderm, endoderm and mesoderm. The body may be covered by an epithelium of ciliated cells or by a protective cuticle secreted and maintained by underlying cells. Beneath this surface, muscles responsible for the co-ordinated movements of the worm are arranged in circular and longitudinal layers, and there is sometimes an intervening oblique layer.

The internal organs comprise a nervous system with sensory and motor components acting through a centralised 'brain', male and female (hermaphrodite) genital organs, and an excretory system of branching canals terminating in distinctive flame cells or multicellular flame bulbs, the long internal cilia of which undulate to produce a flow of liquid. The internal organs are surrounded by the parenchyma, loosely packed branching cells and intercellular spaces, which fills all available space beneath the muscle layers. Many flatworms have an alimentary system comprising a mouth, muscular pharynx and simple or branched intestine but rarely anal openings. (This system is conspicuously absent in tapeworms.) Notably, there are no structural modifications forming skeletal, vascular and respiratory systems, so that problems of structural support and the circulation

A flatworm living on the coast of South Africa. Its body is extremely motile, its margins crenated. Marine flatworms are often beautifully coloured and this, with the grace of their movement as they move flowingly through the water, has a strong aesthetic appeal not usually evoked by animals classified as 'worms'.

of nutrients and gases involved in metabolism are overcome by more makeshift arrangements than those in coelomate animals. Bodily movements maintain an ebb and flow circulation within the parenchyma and so constitute a rudimentary lymphatic system in some.

The three classes of flatworms are the turbellarians (Turbellaria), flukes (Trematoda) and tapeworms (Cestoda), which are not difficult to distinguish. Turbellarians are usually free-living forms found in freshwater, the sea and moist situations on land; they glide over weeds or stones by means of their external ciliation but can swim by co-ordinated muscular movements when necessary. In the early larval stage trematodes are ciliated but as adults have sacrificed the ciliated epidermis and acquired a cuticle. Like turbellarians, they have a well-developed alimentary system and their larvae have brief periods of free life, but as adults they invariably live as ectoparasites on the bodies of vertebrates which provide their sustenance, or as endoparasites inside the host. Cestodes have an external cuticle but no alimentary system; they are usually very long, ribbon-like forms which imbibe nutriment through the cuticle, and when adult are obligatory endoparasites in vertebrate intestines.

A few other worm-like animals are sometimes included in the platyhelminths. The remarkable forms known as Temnocephalida have been included in the Turbellaria in some taxonomic schemes but referred to a separate class in others. The first alternative will be accepted here. The thorny-headed worms, or Acanthocephala, have been included in the platyhelminths somewhat more often than in the roundworms (Nematoda). They are probably more closely related to tapeworms than to roundworms but are now generally regarded as constituting a separate phylum and are considered separately (*see* p. 75).

Turbellarians (Class Turbellaria)

Many turbellarians are about two centimetres in length but very elongate terrestrial forms may be more than thirty centimetres long. Shape undergoes constant change with movement but the body is often oval and flattened, colourless and transparent or coloured in drab shades of brown or grey. Some brilliantly coloured forms are known, however, and land planarians often have stripes of white, yellow or orange pigment on a dark ground. The worms often seem to creep over weeds, using their cilia, but sometimes swim freely by muscular undulations of the margins of the body. Cells of the epidermis secrete a mucus-like substance invariably associated with ciliary activity, and special cells produce rod-like bodies of various kinds, including rhabdites, which macerate in water and contribute to the slimy investment of the body. This contains toxic substances which repel wouldbe adversaries and is thus protective. The subepidermal musculature contains outer circular and inner longitudinal fibres which operate in coordinated, complementary ways to extend and contract the body and there may be an intervening layer of fibres arranged diagonally. Vertically arranged muscles exist also to control the thickness of the body. Beneath the integumentary muscles there is well-developed parenchyma within which amoebocytes or wandering cells may play some part in the transport of nutrients, thus supplementing the ebb and flow circulation of nutrients brought about by muscular movements of the body. In some turbellarians (*Syndesmis*, *Derostoma*) the lymph-like liquid within the parenchymatous spaces is coloured red by haemoglobin, indicating possible oxygen-carrying or oxygenstoring properties.

Many turbellarians feed avidly on diatoms, protozoans, small crustaceans, rotifers, annelids and other small organisms, which are seized at the mouth, swallowed by the muscular pharynx and forced into a simple or branched intestine to be broken down as food. Larger turbellarians, which attack prey too large to be swallowed, extrude and unfold a pharynx and wrap it about the prey, gradually killing and partially digesting it externally so that tissue remnants or homogenised liquid remains may be sucked in. The kind of food taken is related to the structure and function of the pharynx and the course of digestion rather than to increase in size and complexity. A turbellarian with a simple pharynx engulfs small organisms whole but one with a large plicate pharynx can utilise larger prey and extend the variety of its diet.

Sense-organs acting through a central nervous system give turbellarians an awareness of changing conditions in their aqueous environment. The commonest type of sensory cell seems to be the tango-receptor, the tactile cell, terminating in hairs or bristles which project beyond the limits of the external ciliation. Such receptors may be concentrated on tentacles to form definite sensory regions. Chemoreceptors, cells which respond to chemical stimulation, may also be restricted mainly to the anterior region and located in pits or grooves. Extirpation of such pits results in a loss of ability to detect nutrient substances in solution and, as a result, a loss of power to orient in relation to food. Cilia that produce water currents impinging on such receptors are an integral part of the chemo-receptive process. Rheoreceptors enable turbellarians to detect external water currents which may contain food, and the statocyst serves as an aid to equilibration. The photoreceptors, cells sensitive to light, are most important, and various turbellarians have one pair of eyes, sometimes two or three pairs, and even numerous eyes arranged in clusters or along the margins of the body. Each eye consists of a bowl of pigmented cells and an inner group of rod-like photosensitive retinal elements which, like other receptors, are linked by fibres with the central nervous system. This comprises a 'brain' containing various kinds of nerve cells, and bundles of emergent nerve fibres form ventral or dorsal and ventral nerve trunks which vary in number according to species. In these nervous arrangements nerve endings are

A flatworm (*Dalyellia* sp.) found throughout the Arctic, in both fresh and salt water. It feeds on diatoms.

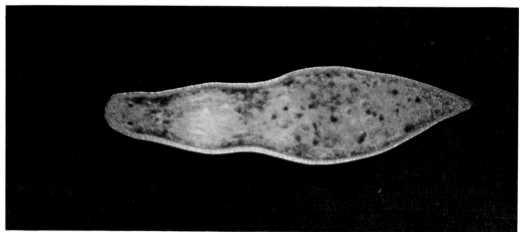

supplied to appropriate effector organs, mainly to the muscles of the integument and also to internal organs, which produce appropriate responses to various kinds of stimulation affecting the sense-organs and other receptors.

Most turbellarians are hermaphrodite and the gonads (organs producing gametes or germ cells) arise from free cells in the parenchyma which migrate to certain locations where gametogenesis (the process of gamete formation) occurs. There may be a single testis and one ovary, a pair of each of these gonads, or sometimes several or numerous gonads ultimately giving a follicular arrangement. The terminal parts of male and female systems are ducts which open into a depression or depressions of the body wall, an antrum, and may have separate pores or a common gonopore. Sperms are of usual type, generally long and filamentous with two flagella near the tip, but they may be spindle-like and are sometimes gathered into sper-matophores. They are discharged during copula-tion along with nourishing secretions formed by special glands *en route*, and the male organ—cirrus or penis according to introversibility or fixed form—has an associated storage place (the semi-nal vesicle) for the sperms and prostate glands. The copulatory organ may bear spines which serve to hold it in position, and a common feature of some turbellarians is a multiplicity of male ducts and copulatory organs in complex and varied arrangements.

The terminal part of the female system is even more variable and complex and is sometimes modified to aid copulation. The ducts are often lined with glandular or ciliated epithelium and muscles provide for peristaltic movements of their contents. One part of the female system is con-cerned with the reception and maintenance of sperms from another individual during and after copulation, and there is often a pouch, or a copulatory bursa, which receives the male organ. The ova may have yolk, although nutrients are generally confined to special (vitelline) cells grouped to form vitellaria. The egg may have a hard shell formed from secretions of the vitelline cells, and special glands secrete gelatinous mate-rials which bind the eggs together in strings or plates. Otherwise, the egg may have a soft and delicate capsule but often forms a rigid cocoon, and vitelline cells and sperms are enclosed with an ovum in one capsule, which usually darkens and hardens after laying. Such eggs may be attached to

external objects by cement-like secretions. During the breeding season copulation occurs frequently and eggs are laid every few days, taking some weeks to develop into free-living larvae or minia-ture worms, according to species. In some inst-ances eggs develop within the parenchyma, or the intestinal lumen.

Copulation is an indication that cross-fertilis-ation occurs, and self-fertilisation, though possible, is unusual. One unusual method of insemination is a form of hypodermic impregnation by means of a modified penis through the integument, after which sperms wander through the parenchyma to their meeting with the ova. The more usual forms of copulation are sometimes accompanied by a sexual interlude that can be termed 'courtship', which may last a few minutes or over an hour.

The active and versatile turbellarians form associations with other animals such as starfishes, sea urchins, holothurians and crustaceans and it is noteworthy that all the main orders of the class contain some forms which have acquired parasitic habits, living either as ectoparasites or endopara-sites and thus indicating how the obligatory forms of parasitism seen in the trematodes have arisen from free-living animals of related stock.

Classification

The most recent classification scheme (by Beau-champ) places the turbellarians in seven orders.

Polyclads (Order Polycladida)

This is a group of large marine forms with a plicate pharynx and an intestine with many branches. Forms having a small pseudosucker (e.g. *Anony-mus*) are placed in a suborder Cotylea, families and forms without it (e.g. *Leptoplana*) in a suborder Acotylea.

Triclads (Order Tricladida)

These are forms in which the intestine has three main branches, one directed forward and the others backward. Marine forms (e.g. *Procerodes*) are placed in a suborder Maricola, freshwater forms (e.g. *Dendrocoelum*) in the Paludicola and terrestrial forms (e.g. *Geoplana*) in the Terricola, which hunt their prey in the humus of forests in warm countries.

Protriclads (Order Protricladida)

These are mainly marine forms with a triclad type of pharynx and a simple undivided intestine (e.g.

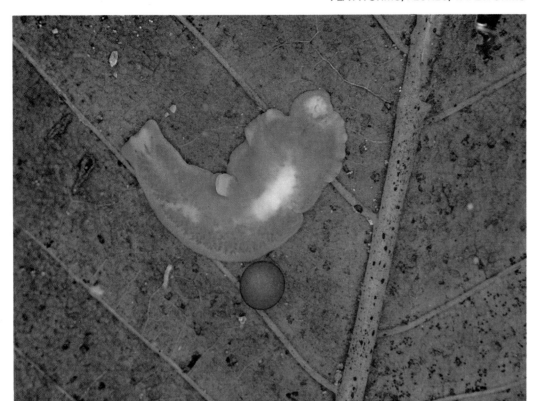

A freshwater flatworm of Britain (*Dendrocoelum lacteum*), one of the triclads, creeping over the leaf of a water plant, with its newly-laid cocoon.

Monocelis, *Otoplana*, *Otomesostoma* of the suborder Crossocoela and the *Bothrioplana semperi*, the single species of the suborder Cyclocoela.

Order Eulecithophora

This group contains most forms with a simple intestine once placed in the Rhabdocoela, along with some Alloeocoela. It is a complex group with four suborders, twenty-two families and more than 200 genera (e.g. *Plagiostomum*, *Dalyellia*).

Order Perilecithophora

This small group has one family and two principal genera (*Polycystis* and *Koinocystis*) with an anterior protrusible proboscis.

Order Archoophora

This is a diverse group of seven suborders, one of which is the Acoela, forms without an intestine (e.g. *Convoluta*). The remaining suborders contain about twenty-four genera (e.g. *Macrostomum*, *Hofstenia*).

Order Temnocephala

A group of leech-like forms (e.g. *Temnocephala*, *Craspedella*) with anterior tentacles.

Flukes (Class Monogenea)

Most Monogenea are ectoparasites on the gills, fins or skin of fishes but some occur in the cloaca of rays, the eyes of fishes and the bladder of amphibians. They creep about and attach themselves by haptors, the special organs of adhesion. There is an anterior prohaptor comprising paired glands which produce sticky secretions, lappets (sucker-like organs on the body margin) or a muscular oral sucker around the mouth, and a posterior opisthaptor of more variable structure. In some forms the opisthaptor is a simple sucker, in others it is a paired series of suckers. Large curved hooks and hooklets which characterise larval forms may be carried over into adult life to function alone or to augment suctorial action and these may be associated with paired clamp-like structures which, pincer fashion, can grasp gill filaments singly or in groups. Suckers and hooks serve for attachment to plane surfaces and their actions allow for greater freedom of translatory movement.

The body is covered by a protective cuticle which may be a secretionary product of underlying cells but is sometimes a modified epithelium. The openings on the surface of the body include mouth, genital pore or pores, vaginal pores and excretory pores, most of which are anterior. The mouth is round, oval or slit-like, sometimes terminal and sometimes not, and it may lead into an eversible tube with a pair of buccal suckers in its wall. Male and female genital systems may open by separate pores—which may be close together, widely separated or even on opposite sides of the body—or by a common gonopore at the outer end of a genital atrium. The hermaphrodite organs follow the pattern seen in some turbellarians but vaginae are usually associated with the vitelline ducts and open by one pore or a pair of pores. The main criteria of distinction amongst Monogenea are external characters. Internal structure is not as well known as in Digenea (*see* page 60) but the reproductive system is more varied.

The male system may comprise one testis or several, with sperms sometimes being temporarily stored in a seminal vesicle. The male organ may be simple or complicated by accessories of ill-defined function. It may be a protrusible and eversible cirrus or a fleshy penis with sclerotised lining, and there may be spines to aid copulation.

The ovary of the female system is rarely globular as in Digenea but more usually elongate and folded. Ova develop in all parts of the body but mature only in the terminal region before passing into an oviduct, one part of which (the ootype) is specialised to ensure fertilisation and encapsulation of the eggs. Unicellular glands around the ootype extrude secretions which play some part in shell formation but the shell-forming materials are derived from the secretions of vitelline cells. The shell appears almost instantaneously when an ovum, some vitelline cells and a rivulet of spermatozoa have been assembled in the ootype, a mould that shapes the eggs. These have one or two polar filaments and may be laid in chains. As the eggs are formed they are passed with assembly-line precision into the uterus, which opens by a pore or the common gonopore.

Other organs follow a turbellarian pattern. There is a 'brain' and systems of nerves to or from all parts of the body, and paired ventral nerves are prominent. Little is known about sense-organs but some Monogenea have eyes, and nerve endings and tactile organs occur in the integument. The protonephridial excretory system comprises branched canals ending in flame cells. Little is known about food and feeding in Monogenea but the alimentary canal comprises a muscular pharynx, a short oesophagus and an intestine which may be simple, bifurcate or ring-like and is sometimes branched.

The larvae
The minute, newly hatched larvae of Monogenea swim about for only a day or so to locate a host and then begin their creeping but somewhat sedentary life. They swim by means of incomplete ciliated bands on the body and creep by using their muscles. They have a rudimentary 'brain' and associated nerves, one or two pairs of eyes with pigmented cups and lenses, flame cells and a pair of excretory pores, an alimentary canal with pharynx and simple or bifurcate intestine, and a genital rudiment. Once established on their hosts, they grow, perfect the haptors already present, and mature. Some species mature in about one week; others take some months. *Polystoma* requires three years for full development of normal kind. During post-larval development the larval opisthaptor may increase in size and develop hooks or other accessories, or it may persist without enlargement, to be superseded by a definitive adult haptor. These changes may illustrate the mode of evolution of turbellarian-like ancestral forms of present-day Monogenea.

Life-cycles
The monogenetic life-cycle is so called because it occurs within a single host. It is usually envisaged as a simple sequence of events—the hatching of the larva from the egg, maturation phenomena and the final production of eggs by the adult. But it is not a uniform process throughout the group. The fertilised egg may develop into an embryo within the body of the parent (as in *Gryodactylus*), it

may hatch as a miniature adult after protracted embryonic development (as in *Sphyranura*), or after hatching as a larva it may take a peculiar form (diporpa) which unites with another individual of the same kind to produce pairs united in permanent copula (as in *Diplozoon*). Apart from such specialisations, the life-cycle is usually oversimplified by considering a single generation, and should perhaps include a series of generations and events of a seasonal kind leading to the appearance of an individual which is as nearly equivalent to the original parental fluke as may be in every respect. Changes in the host during its own life-cycle and the cycle of annual changes in external environment shared by host and parasite mean that there are changes in the parasitism.

The gill parasite *Dactylogyrus vastator* may infect carp less than one month old. However, the flukes begin to reproduce during early spring and the parasite populations greatly increase during the summer but are reduced at the onset of winter until only isolated individuals survive. Infections during the following spring are due partly to these survivors but also to overwintering eggs. At first the older fishes are infected, then young fishes as these appear.

The life-cycle of *Polystoma integerrimum*, which occurs in the bladder of frogs, is notable for synchronisation between the young stages of parasite and host. The ciliated larval trematodes are free-swimming for a maximum of twenty-four hours before they pass into the gill chambers of tadpoles, attach to the gills, develop slowly and wander through the alimentary canal to the excretory bladder when the tadpoles metamorphose. They take three years to attain maturity in this way. But when larvae attach externally to young tadpoles they develop rapidly and neotenic forms arise, small and much modified in structure, sexually mature in a very short time and laying fertile eggs within a few weeks. The eggs produce normal larvae which infect well-developed tadpoles and proceed with their development in the usual manner. As a result of the neotenic cycle these larvae avoid a period of high tadpole mortality and, provided they find hosts, stand a better chance of survival in tadpoles just about to metamorphose.

Trematodes (Class Digenea)
The digenetic trematodes are often described as flat, oval or elongate and leaf-like, but they are really lively worms with no fixed shape. They move briskly by the combined action of various systems of muscles and are constantly altering the topographical relationships between their organs and parts. The entire body is covered by cuticle, beneath which are layers of muscles and deeper organ systems lodged in parenchyma, as in Monogenea. Their haptors are simpler than those of monogenetic trematodes, taking the form of two muscular suckers of nearly spherical shape, and they have no hooks or other sclerotised accessories. An oral sucker surrounds the mouth, and the ventral or posterior sucker may occupy any ventral position because of differential growth of the hind part of the body. The internal organs of Digenea have much in common with those of Monogenea but more varied arrangements occur in the more

numerous forms which exist.

Some types of Digenea can be identified by simple characters; they serve to illustrate diversity of structure but are not taxonomic units. Distomes have an oral sucker around the mouth and a ventral sucker somewhere on the ventral surface of the body. Echinostomes have a spinous head-collar with collar-spines around the anterior extremity. Amphistomes have a large posterior sucker and sometimes a huge genital atrium. Monostomes lack the oral or the ventral sucker, sometimes both. Holostomes are constricted to form a fore body carrying the suckers and an accessory adhesive organ (tribocytic organ), and a hind body containing the genital organs. Schistosomes are elongate and somewhat spindle-like unisexual forms which live in the blood vascular system of their hosts.

The variable structure of the Digenea is reflected in all the organ systems. The alimentary canal may have a tubular prepharynx, pharynx, long or short oesophagus, and simple or branched intestinal crura. The caeca usually end blindly but a few forms have anal pores. In the excretory system the mode of branching of canals and the ultimate numbers of blind terminations and flame cells are matters of taxonomic importance usually expressed by a formula. Added complexity of structure is often brought about by the branching of internal organs. In the Liver Fluke of sheep (*Fasciola hepatica*) both the intestine and the gonads are profusely branched, whereas in the Human Liver Fluke (*Clonorchis sinensis* also known as *Opisthorcis sinensis*) there is a similar arrangement.

The hermaphrodite genital system of Digenea has many complications. Male and female ducts usually open together in a genital atrium with a terminal common gonopore, but this region may be much modified. The essential male organs are a pair of testes, vasa efferentia, vas deferens, seminal vesicle and cirrus pouch enclosing the cirrus, ejaculatory duct and prostate glands. However,

some forms have one testis, others several testes or else a follicular arrangement of many testes. The components of the female system are an ovary, oviduct, ootype, receptaculum seminis, uterus and Laurer's canal, which has a dorsal pore and may be used in copulation, although this usually takes place through the gonopore. As in Monogenea, the egg is formed in the ootype and then passed into the uterus, where some development may occur so that larvae (miracidia) hatch as soon as eggs are laid, although in *Fasciola* they are undeveloped at this time. The egg shell is formed largely from secretions of vitelline cells which wander down to the ootype, and the sperms from another individual are stored in the receptaculum seminis and passed as required into this part of the oviduct, to mingle with the ova.

The larvae

The digenetic trematodes pass through a series of larval stages and undergo a process of asexual reproduction and multiplication before reaching the juvenile stage. From each egg some hundreds and even thousands of juvenile flukes arise. The successive larval stages are known as the miracidium, sporocyst, redia and cercaria, and usually an encysted form called a metacercaria. The miracidium is a ciliated form liberated at hatching. It has no structure even remotely resembling the opisthaptor of larval Monogenea and there are other reasons for doubting that the two kinds of larvae are comparable. There are points of resemblance—a pair of eyes, a rudimentary 'brain', and a protonephridial excretory system— but only a vestigial alimentary system with associated unicellular glands.

The distinctive feature of the miracidium is the presence of clusters of germinal cells (germinal balls) which are destined to give rise to succeeding larval generations as they multiply and develop. These never appear in Monogenea, which have never been known to infect molluscs, whereas the

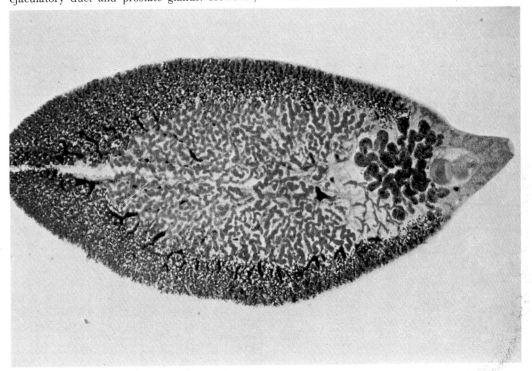

The Sheep Liver Fluke (*Fasciola hepatica*) infests the bile duct of sheep. It is soft-bodied and leaf-shaped, with a head lobe in front. It feeds on the blood and the dark biliary matter of the sheep. Another name for the flounder is fluke and it was the outline and the flattened shape, so like those of the flatfish, that gained this alternative name for the parasitic worms.

Opposite
Sponges are low in the animal
scale, of little economic value apart
from the bath sponge and so
difficult to study that they have
been called the pariahs of science.
With the advent of skin-diving and
underwater photography it is now
being realized how large a part
they constitute of the animal
growths on the seabed.

miracidium can develop only when its component vital parts enter a snail. Entry is effected by suctorial adhesion to the snail's body, followed by the extrusion of secretions which break down the snail's integument locally. During the penetration process the miracidium loses its ciliated epithelium so that a rounded mother sporocyst is formed. The entered mother sporocyst thus has a delicate surface admirably adapted to absorb nutrients derived from the snail's tissues, and it grows rapidly while the contained larvae of the next generation undergo development. In some digenetic life-cycles the mother sporocyst gives rise to other sporocyst generations but the more usual pattern is for the next larval stage, the rediae, to take the place of sporocysts.

Rediae are tissue-feeding forms with a pharynx and simple intestine, and they make extensive burrows within the digestive gland or gonad of the snail as they feed. During growth, germinal cells passed on during sporocyst development multiply and develop to form the final larval stage, cercariae, which are tailed forms with the rudiments of the adult body. Cercariae are free-swimming forms which leave the snail but must find a suitable host in which to mature.

The life-cycle

The swimming ability of cercariae varies enormously. Some swim vigorously and float or are suspended in water, others are poor swimmers and remain near the bottom of their freshwater or marine environment. In some instances, notably in the transmission of schistosomes, the cercariae can penetrate the skin of the host and pass as juveniles to the final location. Other cercariae may penetrate the skin of a fish and become walled off

in underlying muscles, to be transmitted to a final host subsequently. The transmission of cercariae often depends on the feeding habits of the hosts. The cercariae of *Fasciola* encyst on herbage, secreting about the body a protective covering, and only when cysts and herbage have been ingested by cattle or sheep does development continue. The Human Intestinal Fluke (*Fasciolopsis buski*) is acquired by eating the tubers of plants on which snails feed and cercariae encyst. Birds may become infected with echinostomes and monostomes by devouring snails on or in which cercariae encyst, or with other trematodes by eating infected bivalve molluscs containing cysts. The Human Lung Fluke (*Paragonimus westermani*) encysts as a metacercaria in many freshwater crayfishes favoured as food in the Far East, and the Human Liver Fluke (*Clonorchis sinensis*) encysts in many species of freshwater fishes, some of which are used for food and similarly serve as vectors of parasitic disease. Larvae of the Lancet Fluke (*Dicrocoelium dendriticum*) must pass through land snails before achieving adulthood in their mammalian hosts which include sheep, cattle, deer and many others.

It will be noted that while *Schistosoma* and *Fasciola* require two hosts, a snail and a vertebrate, other digenetic trematodes require three hosts: snails, crayfishes or fishes and vertebrates. More complex life-cycles are known, species of *Alaria* requiring four hosts: snails, amphibians, rats or mice, and mammals such as cats, dogs, mink or weasels. Some digenetic trematodes come to full maturity within the tissues of snails, however, and such instances of progenesis tempt us to believe that this may have been the primitive mode before vertebrates appeared in the seas or on the earth.

Tapeworms and allies (Class Cestoda)

Adult cestodes do not possess an alimentary system. They live in the intestines of vertebrates amidst much predigested food and they absorb nutriment through the external cuticle. Most of them are ribbon-like and the body has three parts: the minute scolex or head, which usually has suckers, hooks or both; the neck composed of embryonic cells; and the long chain, or strobila, of segments produced by a budding process of the neck region. The segments do not correspond to those of coelomate worms, for each mature seg-

ment contains a complete set of hermaphrodite genital organs, and is on this account usually termed a proglottis. The scolex clings to the intestinal mucosa of the host, gaining anchorage for small tapeworms. Large tapeworms avoid being swept out of the host's body by creating muscular movements which act against the peristalsis of the intestines. If the strobila breaks away from the scolex, perhaps as a result of antihelminthic drug treatment, a new strobila can be formed by a regenerative process in the neck region.

Monozoic cestodes (Subclass Cestodaria) (= Cestoda Monozoa)

These small forms do not strobilate and the entire body may be regarded as a single proglottis. They form two orders, Gyrocotylidea and Amphilinidea, two contrasting types which may be represented by the genera *Gyrocotyle* and *Amphilina* species of which occur in sturgeons and rabbitfishes respectively. These are difficult to compare because, in the absence of an alimentary canal, it is not easy to distinguish one end from the other. *Gyrocotyle* has a deep, funnel-like organ with a frilled margin at one

end of the body and a sucker at the other; *Amphilina* has only one distinctive organ, a terminal rectractile proboscis.

One important character which distinguishes monozoic cestodes from tapeworms, however, is their characteristic larva or lycophore with five pairs of hooks. In contrast, tapeworms have a hexacanth larva or onchosphere with three pairs of hooks. This indication of close affinity may represent an early dichotomy of ancestral cestodes.

Merozoic cestodes (Subclass Eucestoda) (= Cestoda Merozoa)

Opposite
A newly-hatched Ram's-horn
Snail (*Planorbis* sp.). This is one of
the commoner species of freshwater molluscs in Europe. The
shell is in a flattened coil.

Tapeworms vary greatly in size. Whereas *Echinococcus granulosus* is about eight millimetres long and has no more than four to five proglottides, the broad tapeworm of man (*Diphyllobothrium latum*) may become twenty metres long and comprise 3,000 to 4,000 proglottides.

The scolex

The minute scolex shows great variety of structure and many kinds of haptors, often suckers and hooks but sometimes more elaborate and complex muscular organs (phyllidea) with sucking grooves (bothridia), and in some forms protrusible and eversible proboscides beset with numerous hooklets of various kinds. In Pseudophyllidea a simple type of scolex comprises grooves with raised muscular margins forming a pair. The scolex of *Diphyllobothrium* is of this type and often described as almond-shaped, although in life it is a very extensile and contractile organ used for exploring the substrate as well as securing anchorage to it. The scolex of Tetraphyllidea has four bothridia. In Diphyllidea they are fused two by two and there is an armed peduncle or head-stalk and distinctive apical hooks. In Tetrarhynchidea there is a more complex arrangement: four bothridia and four eversible and protrusible armed proboscides are used to secure anchorage. The most elaborate type of all is seen in Phyllobothriidae, where the phyllidea may be sessile or stalked, with simple or much-folded margins and multiloculate bothridia, and sometimes accessory sucker-like organs. Perhaps the best known and simplest type of scolex is that of Cyclophyllidea, which has four more or less globular muscular suckers distinct and separate from the musculature of the scolex wall, and a fleshy terminal rostellum bearing a circlet of hooks of characteristic shapes. This kind of scolex occurs in *Taenia*, although in the Beef Tapeworm (*T. saginata*) there are no hooks present. Less ornate scoleces are known, some without haptorial organs. In these the entire scolex is able to penetrate into the host's mucosa, there to fuse with the tissues in more or less permanent attachment, as in *Disculiceps*.

Strobila and proglottides

The proglottides or segments are short and broad when formed but they become long and narrow in the terminal parts of the strobila or chain. They are covered with cuticle, beneath which are typical muscle layers and deeper internal organs embedded in parenchyma. The 'brain' is located in the scolex; the nerves occur in the strobila, usually in the lateral region. Some nerves are ganglionated and connected by ring commisures. The main canals of the excretory system are also lateral, the genital organs taking up the median region of the proglottides. The reproductive system is protandrous, that is, the male organs usually develop before the female organs. Both male and female organs may be duplicated in each proglottis, their pores opening separately, or after union with one another, on both sides of the strobila instead of only one side. This duplication of genital systems is common in some families of Cyclophyllidea, rarer in Tetrarhynchidea and Pseudophyllidea, and unknown in Tetraphyllidea and Diphyllidea. In a few genera only the male organs are duplicated. It will be obvious that the tremendous fecundity of tapeworms is due to the multiplicity of genital systems present in adult forms. The tapeworm of man may produce a million eggs a day.

The male system is simpler than the female, but variable. Some forms have one, others two, three or four testes, and yet others hundreds. The sperms are thread-like and pass by way of vasa efferentia into a vas deferens, dilated at one part to form a seminal vesicle, and they are nourished by secretions of prostate glands. The cirrus is large, muscular and sometimes spinous to facilitate copulation, which occurs between different proglottides of the strobila or between proglottides of different individuals.

The female system comprises an ovary, vitellaria, oviduct, ootype, vagina and uterus. The vagina leads from the genital atrium to the oviduct and along it sperms pass from the cirrus of another segment (or individual) to the ootype, and to a receptaculum seminis for temporary storage. The uterus is the more variable organ; it is often sac-like, with or without lateral branches, and provided with a pore or not. When there is no pore eggs are liberated when cast off proglottides decompose in the external world. Otherwise the eggs are shed into the host's intestines. In some forms the uterus breaks down to form numerous small egg capsules, or is modified to form an accessory fibrous capsule, or paruterine organ, which may be duplicated in the same proglottis. The eggs are of various kinds. The operculate eggs of Pseudophyllidea resemble those of digenetic trematodes, and probably have the same origin. The formed egg of Cyclophyllidea is quite different, comprising several membranes which arise during development, including a thick embryophore formed of wedge-like blocks united by a cement-like matrix to form a striated shell.

The larvae

All cestode eggs come to contain a hexacanth larva or onchosphere, distributed in various ways. The embryophore of the pseudophyllidean egg is a delicate cellular envelope around the hexacanth, and the entire larva is called a coracidium, which is often ciliated. This larva has a short, free life subsequent to hatching. With the exception of a few Cyclophyllidea, the hexacanth must enter the body of an intermediate host in order to continue its development. In Pseudophyllidea the first host is a copepod, which eats the coracidium, but in most other cestodes the hexacanth is ingested by the intermediate host whilst it is still in the egg capsule. In both instances the hexacanth develops into a small elongate larva called the procercoid. But whereas in most cestodes this develops further into a juvenile tapeworm within the first host, the procercoid of Pseudophyllidea can develop only in

63

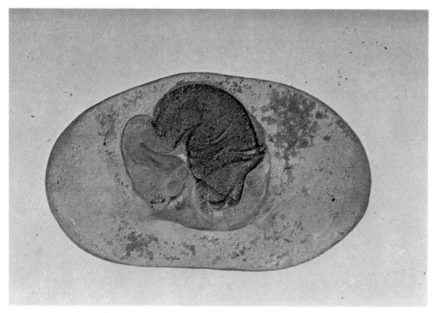

The cysticercus or bladderworm, the larval stage of *Taenia solium*, the tapeworm that can afflict human beings. If a portion of pig muscle, containing cysticerci which have not been killed by cooking, is taken into a human stomach, the bladder is thrown off and the larva attaches itself by the hooks on its scolex (head-end) to the walls of the intestine and grows into a tapeworm.

Tapeworms maintain the continuity of their species mainly by two means. First, they have adapted to a parasitic life by producing offspring in very high numbers, each of the many proglottides being in the end little more than a bag of eggs passed to the outer world in the faeces of the host. Secondly, they maintain a tenacious grip on their host by means of a scolex (head) armed with a battery of suckers and numerous minute hooks, as seen here.

a second intermediate host, usually a fish, within which it develops into a larger juvenile worm, or plerocercoid.

In addition to the hooks, the hexacanth of the tapeworm possesses unicellular glands which secrete enzymatic juices that liquify by cytolysis host tissues with which they come into contact, thus enabling larvae to wander through the host's tissues. The procercoid is a modified hexacanth of elongate form and has developed a cuticle, muscle layers and parenchyma and sometimes an anterior pit and related 'frontal glands'. The plerocercoid of Pseudophyllidea is an enlarged and modified procercoid which has elaborated bothridia, nervous system and excretory system but only the merest rudiments of genital organs, which develop in a third and final host, usually a fish-eating vertebrate. The term *Sparganum* is given to certain plerocercoids which undergo an unusual process of budding and become branched.

The term metacestode is sometimes applied to the successive stages passed through by developing Eucestoda. The procercoid and plerocercoid are two such stages. Two others are the cysticercoid and cysticercus types, which result from the development of the hexacanth in the Cyclophyllidea. Each type has various modified forms. The common tapeworm of the dog (*Dipylidium caninum*) and other carnivores, has a typical cysticercoid— a minute solid juvenile form comprising little more than a scolex and neck, together with a surrounding coat of protective tissue. It occurs in either dog fleas or cat fleas which ingest the hexacanths during their larval life. Certain cysticercoids arise by a process of budding and occur in clusters resembling a bunch of grapes; the cluster is known as a staphylocystis, and if individuals become detached each is called a urocystis. The cysticercoid of *Hymenolepis* with adults in birds and mammals has a tail-like outgrowth bearing larval hooks and is sometimes termed a cercocystis type, whereas the corresponding form of *Dipylidium* may not show the outgrowth and is referred to as a cryptocystis type.

The cysticercus is a common juvenile form usually known as a bladder worm because the inverted developing scolex lies within a vesicle filled with liquid. Some forms of cysticerci were discovered and named before the corresponding adults were known, so that *Cysticercus pisiformis*, for example, is the bladder worm corresponding to *Taenia pisiformis*. The most unusual cysticercus, *C. longicollis*, undergoes an unusual process of budding before developing into the adult form *Taenia crassiceps*. Cysticerci commonly occur in herbivorous animals such as rodents, their corresponding adults in carnivores which acquire their parasites from the herbivores which they devour. The main characteristic of the cysticercus is its single scolex. Some species of *Taenia*, however, develop as large vesicular forms with multiple scoleces, the outstanding example of multiplicative asexual reproduction in the cestodes. In the coenurus-type bladder, numerous scoleces arise from the wall of a large vesicle, the hydatid, but in echinococcus-type bladders secondary vesicles arise from the wall of the hydatid, their formation being either internal (endogenous) or external (exogenous), and from both hydatid wall and contained vesicles numerous scoleces arise. The corresponding adults are numerous but minute. *Echinococcus granulosus*, for example, has only about four proglottides. Helminthic hydatidosis (Echinococcosis) is a disease of global importance in carnivorous or omnivorous mammals, including man, which are infected by ingesting 'hydatid sand', the grains of which are minute juveniles, the ultimate products of *Echinococcus* development within the body of some herbivore.

The life-cycle

Some features of the life-cycle have already become apparent. The origin of the cestode life-cycle is just as obscure as that of Digenea, and for the same reason—the progenitors probably existed long before vertebrates appeared on the earth but ancestral forms died without leaving recognisable remains. The proto-cestodes were perhaps parasites of crustaceans and then of mites and insects, and the universal occurrence of the onchosphere and procercoid cannot be without significance in evolution. Both forms are well adapted to penetrate animal tissues and were probably preadapted to continue existence as parasites of vertebrates, when these appeared. Before strobilisation was possible an intestinal location was necessary, this advance calling for a spacious environment with minimal restriction from adjacent tissues. At some point in evolution new methods of dispersal made possible a conquest of mammals and birds as hosts and these were related to the novel method of providing the fertilised ovum with a hard embryophore or shell capable of resisting desiccation in a terrestrial environment.

There are two main types of life-cycle in the strobilate cestodes. The first type is evinced by Pseudophyllidea (and Tetraphyllidea) which occur in fishes, notably by *Haplobothrium globuliforme*, a parasite of the Bowfin (*Amia calva*). The hexacanth, enveloped in a ciliated embryophore, the coracidium, hatches from the egg and is eaten by the first host, usually an entomostracan and often a copepod (*Cyclops*). The procercoid is later transferred by means of a predator to a second intermediate host and transformed into a plerocercoid, and when this host is eaten by the final host, maturity is obtained. This type of cycle is characteristic of the broad tapeworm of man (*Diphyllobothrium latum*) and respective hosts are the copepod, a fish and man or some other fish-eating vertebrate.

The second type of life-cycle is characteristic of Cyclophyllidea. Although it displays various modes with a variety of stages, it is essentially a two-host cycle involving one intermediate host and a final host. In some species of *Hymenolepis* even the intermediate host is optional. Where there is a two-host cycle the post larval forms are cysticercoids or their derivatives, or cysticerci in various forms, including the coenurus and echinococcus. In some instances the first host is an arthropod (commonly an insect or acarine) but sometimes a herbivorous mammal. *Dipylidium* utilises fleas, *Moniezia* of sheep and other ruminants is transmitted by mites (Oribatoidea), and *Taenia* by a pig, ox or other mammal. Cestodes having this two-host cycle belong to various families of Cyclophyllidea.

Classification

The classification of tapeworms has proved as troublesome as that of other flatworms. In 1959 Yamaguti's scheme recognised 51 families, 435 genera and more than 3,000 species, and revealed the unequal distribution of cestodes in the classes of vertebrate hosts. Fishes support 37 families, amphibians 4, reptiles 6, birds 16 and mammals 10 families. But only 42 families occur solely in one class of host: 33 in fishes, 1 in amphibians, 6 in birds and 2 in mammals, no family being represented in reptiles alone. Other families share two or more classes of hosts. In contrast with the distribution of digenetic trematodes, not one family of tapeworms is represented in all the classes of vertebrates, or even in four of the five.

Another scheme based largely on extremely variable and complex characters of the scolex was put forward by Joyeux and Baer in 1961. This broke the class into nine orders: Haplobothrioidea, Pseudophyllidea, Tetrarhynchidea, Diphyllidea, Tetraphyllidea, Nippotaeniidea, Ichthyotaeniidea, Tetrabothridea and Cyclophyllidea. The common cestodes of man and domesticated animals belong to the Pseudophyllidea and Cyclophyllidea, mainly to the latter order. *Diphyllobothrium latum* is a notorious pseudophyllidean tapeworm and well-known cyclophyllideans are species of *Taenia*, *Multiceps* and *Echinococcus* (Taeniidae) in man and animals, *Hymenolepis* (Hymenolepididae), *Dipylidium* (Dilepididae), *Anoplocephala* and *Moniezia* (Anoplocephalidae). Well-known species in poultry belong to genera of *Davainea*, *Raillietina* and *Amoebotaenia*.

Parasitology

As free-living forms turbellarians have traditional interest for the ecologist, but the importance of the platyhelminths lies in the development of the parasitic habit by numerous species. Trematodes and cestodes are numerous and widely distributed parasites and some have veterinary or medical importance. The science and parasitology has its roots in morphology and taxonomy. It is necessary first to name and classify a parasite in order to study it and then to determine its structure as a prerequisite of further investigation. In recent times parasitologists have become more and more concerned with the delicately poised and balanced association known as the host-parasite relationship, which often has to be sustained. The unit of study is no longer the parasite alone but the parasite and its host. The composite nature of the life-cycle with its sequences of larval forms in flatworms adds difficulty and interest to the problems. Within the modern field of biological science, therefore, physiological and biochemical efforts are being made to study the chemistry and physiology not only of the parasite in all its larval phases but also the host. Trematodes and cestodes, together with their hosts, are being subjected to the methods of histochemistry, electron microscopy, chromatography, immunology and other disciplines. Flatworms are no longer objects of individual interest only, but are recognised as the agents of biological phenomena which cannot be investigated in free-living forms apart from parasitism because they transcend the phenomena of free life.

Opposite
The growth of a tapeworm is by the budding of fresh segments (proglottides) just behind the scolex. Here may be seen three sets of proglottides in various stages of development. These are short and broad when first formed and become long and narrow as they mature. Each then becomes little more than a bag of gonads.

RIBBON WORMS (Phylum Nemertina or Rhynchocoela)

Ribbon worms or nemertines are long, flat, worm-like creatures in which it is difficult to distinguish the head and the tail. They may reach a length of thirty metres although two metres is usually the maximum size attained by common forms such as *Lineus*. When nemertines are found along the shore they look like shiny, wet coils of seaweed ranging from a yellowish white to brown, green, orange or red and may be distinctively patterned. They break easily and entire specimens are difficult to collect.

Most ribbon worms live in shallow water, sheltering under stones in sand and mud on the marine bottom, but some species inhabit freshwater and a few are terrestrial. They are distributed throughout the world, including the Arctic and Antarctic regions, but are most common in the temperate zones, particularly along the north European and Mediterranean coasts. All are carnivorous and feed by extruding a proboscis which lies in a sheath dorsal to the intestine and distinguishes this phylum from all other animals. The proboscis is wrapped round the prey and drawn back towards the mouth. Even the commensal forms are active carnivores, feeding on other small animals which may enter the mantle chambers of the molluscs on which they live. Nemertines feed on a variety of invertebrates and their young, including protozoans, turbellarians and other worms, as well as some species of molluscs and crustaceans. Some nemertines only suck in the body juices of the prey, but in other species the mouth is highly distensible, enabling them to swallow prey as large as their own diameter.

The phylum is usually divided into two classes: the Anopla, in which the mouth is posterior to the brain and the proboscis is typically unarmed, and the Enopla, in which the mouth is anterior to the brain and the proboscis may be armed. There are two orders in the class Anopla: Palaeonemertini and Heteronemertini. The Palaeonemertini, which includes the common littoral forms such as *Cephalothrix*, are the most primitive nemertines. Their body wall has two or three layers of muscles. In the forms with two muscle layers the inner layer is longitudinal but in the three-layered forms one longitudinal layer is sandwiched between outer and inner layers of circular muscles. In the Heteronemertini there are also three muscle layers

but the inner and outer ones are longitudinal while the middle one is circular and the muscles are themselves surrounded by a thick fibrous dermis. Many familiar nemertines belong to this order, including *Cerebratulus* and *Lineus*. One species, *Lineus ruber*, is common throughout the world.

In the class Enopla, which includes the orders Hoplonemertini and Bdellonemertini, the proboscis, is either armed or derived from the armed condition. The Hoplonemertini is an important and varied order in which the proboscis is armed with one or more stylets. It includes some unusual nemertines such as *Dichonemertes*, which is hermaphrodite, *Prostoma*, a common freshwater form in northern latitudes, and the terrestrial nemertine, *Geonemertes*, which is found in tropical regions in the southern hemisphere. The Bdellonemertini is a small order in which the proboscis is unarmed.

Reproduction and development

The sexes are separate, but a few species are hermaphrodite, and fertilisation is external except in the viviparous forms, in which the embryo develops within the parent. Cleavage is of the spiral determinate type. Some forms, such as *Malacobdella*, have no larval stage and develop directly into adults. In *Cerebratulus*, and in many other forms, there is a free-swimming larva known as the pilidium and this is generally regarded as being typical of the nemertines. A third type of development involves a larva which resembles the pilidium but remains within the egg. This form is known as Desor's larva and is found in *Lineus*.

Relationships

The phylum Nemertina may be regarded as the culmination of the acoelomate grade of organisation. The space between the body wall and the intestine is filled with mesenchyme and this character links the nemertines with the acoelomates and separates them from the pseudocoelomates and coelomates. The nemertines, however, show several advances over the flatworms, especially in the possession of a through gut with an anus and a circulatory system. These advanced characters suggest that the nemertines have evolved from flatworm ancestors but, as it is not possible to derive any other group from them, they are regarded as members of a distinct phylum.

ROUNDWORMS, ROTIFERS AND ALLIES
(Phylum Aschelminthes)

The phylum Aschelminthes contains six classes, some of which have had a varied history of association with other groups and, although the phylum was originally proposed in 1910, the name has only been in general use since 1951. The members of the phylum are pseudocoelomates, the blastocoel or blastula cavity persisting in the adult as a space unlined by epithelium, which lies between the gut and the body wall. They possess a through digestive tract with a highly developed pharynx and an anus. All are worm-like in appearance and the bodies are not segmented although there may be superficial indications that they are.

A characteristic of the group is that during embryonic development cleavage is spiral and determinate as in the annelids and molluscs. Another is that of cell constancy, for after the young animal has hatched or been born the number of cells in the body never increases although size usually increases. The six classes are: Nematoda, 10,000 species; Rotifera, containing about 1,500 species; Gastrotricha, 140 species; Kinorhyncha, 100 species; Priapulida, three

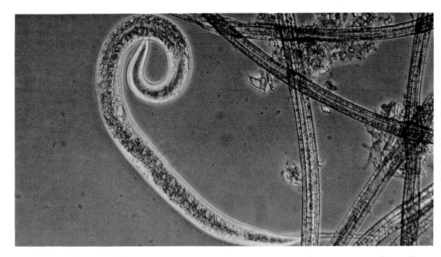

species; and Nematomorpha, 250 species. The nematodes are the most important class, both in terms of number of species and also their effects as parasites of man, his domestic animals and his crops.

Threadworms are usually small and all are very slender. Many are found in water and have given rise in the past to a legend, that they have developed from horse-hairs that have found their way into water and will later develop into snakes. Such threadworms are usually the adult stages of animals parasitizing plants in their immature stages.

Roundworms (Class Nematoda)

The class Nematoda is the largest and most important class in the phylum Aschelminthes and includes many parasites of medical, veterinary and agricultural importance. Roundworms or nematodes occur throughout the world wherever life is possible and occupy a range of habitats more varied even than those of the arthropods. They occur in the soil and in freshwater, in the sea and as parasites in animals and plants. Undue emphasis is often placed on their role in the destruction of domestic animals and plants but probably their most important function is in the breakdown of organic material in the soil or at the bottom of ponds, lakes and seas. Any rotting material is almost invariably infested with nematodes and a decaying apple has been found to contain ninety thousand individuals. Large numbers occur in the soil, three thousand million having been estimated from an acre of topsoil, and they are of major importance in the circulation of

substances in food chains. The parasitic nematodes and in particular those of man, have been known and feared throughout recorded history. A dramatic example is the metre-long Guinea-worm (*Dracunculus medinensis*), the fiery serpent of the Old Testament, which is removed from the human host by winding it round a stick.

Structure

Nematodes are uniformly cylindrical animals which taper at both ends, a feature that distinguishes them from the other aschelminths in which the body can be divided into separate regions at some stage of the life-cycle. The body is covered with a thick cuticle which is often smooth but may be ornamented, and the mouth is at the anterior tip. The cylindrical shape may be modified in various ways, the commonest form being the expansion of the cuticle into alae or 'wings' which are usually at the posterior end of the males of particular groups and in such a position are known as caudal alae. In some species the cylindrical shape may become almost spherical and in others, particularly some larvae such as those which inhabit the blood of vertebrates, the tapering at the two ends may disappear altogether.

The free-living nematodes are seldom seen, in spite of their abundance, because they are so small. For the majority are less than three millimetres in length although marine species tend to be bigger. Among parasitic forms are the largest nematodes known and a common species, *Ascaris lumbricoides*, found in vertebrates including man, reaches a length of about thirty-five centimetres with a diameter of over five millimetres. The giant kidney worm in dogs (*Dioctophyme renale*) is even larger and may measure 100 centimetres in length and one centimetre in diameter. The uniform shape of roundworms is interesting in that one would normally expect considerable variation in such a large group of animals. The reason for uniformity is probably a mechanical one and due to the combination of a firm but slightly flexible cuticle and a high internal pressure, features which limit the type of movement available to nematodes. Evolution has produced adaptations of other kinds, the complex life-cycles for example. This group provides one of the best examples in the animal kingdom of the variations which are possible on a single theme.

Classification

The most acceptable scheme of classification is that which divides roundworms into two subclasses on the basis of the presence or absence of a pair of minute pore-like sensory structures called phasmids, which occur on either side of the posterior end of certain nematodes. The subclass possessing these structures is known as the Phasmida and the other is the Aphasmida. The use of the phasmids as a basis for dividing the class into subclasses can be criticised on the grounds that these minute pores are not sufficiently important criteria for such a major distinction. On the other hand this character, when coupled with others, provides a useful and probably realistic basis for the classification of the nematodes and will be accepted here.

The subclass Aphasmida consists of two orders: Chromadorida and Enoplida. The Chromadorida are never parasitic and are found free-living in freshwater or marine habitats and in the soil. The order Enoplida also contains freshwater, marine and terrestrial members and, in addition, certain parasitic forms, such as *Mermis* in arthropods, the giant kidney worm of dogs (*Dioctophyme renale*) and two parasites of man, *Trichinella spiralis* and *Trichuris trichiura*. The diagnostic feature separating the Chromadorida from the Enoplida is the form of the amphids, sensory structures which may be pores or tubes, found towards the anterior end of the nematode, and spiral in the Chromadorida but pore-like in the Enoplida. In the second subclass, the Phasmida, there are five orders and it is within this group that most of the discussion concerning the limits of the orders occurs. The orders are separated from one another on a number of characteristics and it is only possible to summarise these. In the first four

orders, Rhabditida, Strongylida, Ascaridida and Tylenchida, the oesophagus may be divided into three parts including a bulb. In members of the fifth order, Spirurida, this bulb is absent. Members of the Tylenchida possess an anterior piercing tube called a stylet and this is absent in the remaining orders. The males of the Strongylida possess caudal alae which are reinforced with a number of rays, usually thirteen, and the whole structure, which is quite characteristic, is known as a bursa. The Rhabditida can be distinguished from the Ascaridida by the presence of a muscular vagina in the females of the latter whereas in the former it is hardly muscular at all. Most Rhabditida live on decaying organic material in the soil but a number are parasitic in annelids, molluscs, arthropods and vertebrates while others invade the tissues of plants. *Rhabditis maupasi* is a common parasite of earthworms and is found as a juvenile in the nephridia or 'kidneys', where it encysts, and as an adult feeding on the body of the earthworm when it dies. One species within this group, *Strongyloides stercoralis*, is a parasite of man.

Several important parasites occur within the Strongylida, the best known of which are the hookworms of man, *Ancylostoma duodenale* and *Necator americanus*, and the trichostrongyles and lungworms of domestic animals. In all of these the adults are parasitic and the larvae are free-living. Other representatives of this order are parasitic in annelids and molluscs while some lead a freeliving saprophagous existence in the soil.

The ascarids are parasitic in the guts of terrestrial molluscs, arthropods and vertebrates and there are no free-living stages in the life-cycle. An example of this order is *Ascaris lumbricoides* which is a parasite of both man and the pig.

The most important nematode parasites of plants occur in the order Tylenchida and these include the eelworms (*Anguina*), the stem and bulb eelworms (*Ditylenchus*) and the cyst eelworms (*Heterodera*). The stylet, a characteristic feature of these nematodes, is used for sucking the cell contents of the living plant. Not all the members of this order are plant parasites, as the group contains carnivores and parasites of invertebrates.

The parasites with the most complex life-cycles among the nematodes are found in the Spirurida and all of these have two hosts: a vertebrate in which the adult nematode lives, and an invertebrate intermediate host (usually an arthropod) for the larva. The filarial worms of man and other animals are members of this order and include *Wuchereria bancrofti* and *Brugia malayi* which are transmitted by mosquitoes and cause elephantiasis. *Onchocerca volvulus* and *Loa loa*, which cause blindness, are also filarial worms and these are transmitted by black flies (genus *Simulinum*) and deer flies (family Tabanidae) respectively in Western Africa. The larval forms, known as microfilariae, circulate in the blood of the host until they are taken up by a blood-sucking insect. The Guineaworm (*Dracunculus medinensis*) belongs to this order.

Life-cycles

There are numerous types of life-cycle among the nematodes but when these are examined in detail they are seen to be variations on a common theme. The life-cycle begins with the egg and, in the simplest situation, a young juvenile hatches from this. The juvenile nematode typically resembles the adult except in size and the maturity of its sex organs. As in other aschelminths there is no increase in the number of cells after hatching, and growth comes with an increase in the size of the cells and not an increase in their number. The juvenile which hatches from the egg moults four times during growth, each time shedding the whole of the cuticle including the lining of the mouth and rectum. After the fourth moult the nematode is a mature adult but may grow slightly after this. The main variation on this pattern is that the juvenile may moult within the egg and emerge as a second-stage larva. The third-stage larva is the most important in the life-cycle of parasitic forms and is usually the stage when the parasite transfers from one type of environment to another.

In the 'typical' vertebrate parasites the juvenile hatches from the egg and begins a free-living existence, moulting twice before it becomes an infective third-stage larva. This infective stage then gains access to the vertebrate host, moults twice more and grows into an adult. Examples of this type of life-cycle are found in the hookworms (*Ancylostoma* and *Necator*) in man. The third-stage larvae are picked up on the bare feet of the host and bore through the skin until they reach a blood vessel and are carried to the lungs. From the lungs they make their way to the oesophagus, moulting once on the way, and are swallowed and enter the intestine where they moult again before growing into adults.

The life-cycles of the trichostrongyles, some of the most serious parasites of domestic animals, are similar to those of the human hookworms. *Haemonchus* and *Ostertagia* in ruminants are examples. In other groups of parasites the pre-infective stage develops in the egg and, in *Ascaris*, the second-stage larvae emerge after the egg has been swallowed, penetrate the wall of the mucosa, enter blood vessels and are eventually carried to the lungs. As in the hookworms, the larvae migrate up the respiratory passage and down the oesophagus. By this time they are fourth-stage larvae and these moult into adults.

Why this complicated life-cycle should have evolved is not certain but it is thought that in the primitive life-cycle the third-stage larvae encysted before being eaten by a final host. This theory adds weight to the suggestion that the third-stage larva is always the infective stage. Parasitic nematodes tend to be very host specific and if humans swallow the eggs of ascarids of other animals, for example *Toxocara canis* from dogs or *Toxocara cati* from cats, the larvae migrate around the body but cannot establish themselves. They may produce serious symptoms, even blindness, if they happen to enter the eye.

The third-stage larvae are the effective infective stages of the filarial worms in which two hosts are involved in the life-cycle. The adults live in the lymphatic vessels of man and shed their larvae into the blood from which they are taken up by a suitable insect when it feeds. The third-stage larvae develop in the insect and are injected into a new host. In a life-cycle such as this the parasites are never exposed to the outside environment.

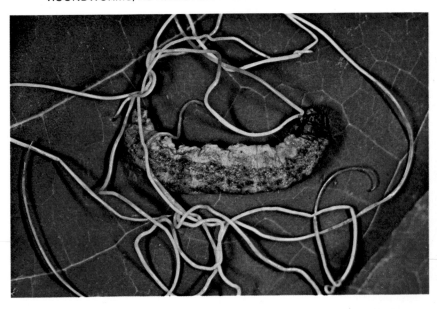

Threadworms or roundworms (Nematoda) of the type that infest the bodies of insects.

An equally complicated life-cycle, but with a short free-living phase, occurs in the Guinea-worm (*Dracunculus medinensis*). The larvae hatch within the female nematode which makes her way to the subcutaneous tissue of the human host and forms a small ulcer to which the nematode applies her genital opening. When the ulcer comes in contact with water large numbers of juveniles are set free and swim around until they are eaten by copepod crustaceans of the genus *Cyclops*. Within the crustacean the parasites develop to their infective stage and when humans accidentally swallow water containing the crustaceans they become infected. There is a third type of life-cycle in which the juveniles are parasitic and the adults free-living. In this case the third-stage larva leaves the host whereas this is usually the stage which enters it.

The third-stage larva is less important in the parasites of plants and the second and fourth stages are frequently the infective ones. In *Heterodera*, a root parasite on a great variety of plants including potatoes, beets and parsnips, the second-stage larva penetrates the host cell and, using the stylet, sucks out the cell contents. The plant responds by forming a gall and the nematode becomes a lemon-shaped adult after a series of moults. The eggs which are produced are liberated from the gall within the body of the dead female which acts as a protective cyst until the second-stage larvae are formed and ready to escape into the soil to repeat the cycle.

Relationships

The relationships of the nematodes are with the pseudocoelomates. There is no doubt that the class belongs to the phylum Aschelminthes and is related to the kinorhynchs and priapulids. Within the Nematoda all the parasitic phasmidian nematodes, of plants as well as animals, can be traced back to the Rhabditida and cannot be derived from any marine ancestors. The widespread incidence of parasitism in this class is very interesting and may be due to the fact that the nematodes of mud were adapted to a habitat with abundant organic matter and a low oxygen tension and that the guts of invertebrates, and later vertebrates, provided similar conditions.

69

Rotifers (Class Rotifera)

Rotifers are amongst the smallest and most common metazoa encountered in any sample of freshwater. Few exceed 0·5 millimetres in length and the great majority are no longer than the ciliated protozoans among which they occur and with which they are frequently confused. All have an elongate or rounded body covered by a thin cuticle which in some species forms a hard transparent shell known as a lorica. The body is divided into an anterior portion, which may be broad, narrow or lobed, a trunk which is also variable in shape, and a foot. The anterior end bears a ciliated corona by means of which the animals swim and cause currents which bring food to their mouths. In the most common rotifers such as *Philodina*, the corona is elaborated into two circlets of cilia which give the appearance of revolving wheels as they move. It is these structures which give the rotifers their common name of wheel animalcules. Basically, a ciliary zone surrounds the ventral mouth of creeping forms but in the course of evolution this has become very much elaborated in some genera and reduced in others. This means that, although the most commonly encountered rotifers have two wheel-like anterior organs, there is much variation. The pharynx is modified into a grinding structure known as a mastax and this, like the corona, is a distinctive feature and varies greatly in form according to the diet of the species.

Classification

There are three orders in the class Rotifera. The smallest of these, the Seisonidea, contains one genus, *Seison*, which is known only from European seas. *Seison* has a small head with a corona reduced to a few tufts, a long thin neck, and a stout trunk. It lives on the crustacean *Nebalia*, attaching itself by an adhesive disc at the posterior end. The other two orders, Bdelloidea and Monogononta, are large and embrace a wide variety of different forms.

The Bdelloidea are familiar freshwater rotifers and although a few are capable of living in brackish water none is truly marine. Bdelloid rotifers such as *Philodina* and *Rotaria* are typically bottom-dwellers in lakes, streams, ponds or any patch of freshwater and are also found among mosses, lichens and liverworts. In fact, they are found wherever water is retained for any period. The bdelloid rotifers are usually resistant to freezing and desiccation and this accounts for their wide geographical distribution which includes Antarctic lakes and hot water springs. They have quite a distinctive appearance for they have sixteen joints, those in the centre of the body being larger in diameter than those at either end so that the whole animal is able to contract, withdrawing the head and foot into the trunk. The paired ciliary wheels, which are typical of the family Philodinidae, are in many other groups reduced to ciliated ventral areas and cannot be used to differentiate bdelloid rotifers from the others. The main internal structures, which are useful in grouping rotifers, are the female reproductive organs which take the form of paired ovaries and vitellaria or yolk glands in the bdelloid rotifers,

paired ovaries only in the Seisonidea and only one ovary and vitellarium in the Monogononta.

The members of the Monogononta are the most varied of the class. There are three suborders: Ploima, Flosculariacea and Collothecacea. Unlike the bdelloids, the Monogononta inhabit both freshwater and marine habitats but only a few are truly marine, most of the forms found in the sea being freshwater species which are able to tolerate a high salinity. The majority of these marine rotifers belong to the suborder Ploima and most of the members of this group have a normal body shape and a well-defined corona. All possible types of habit are encountered in the suborder Ploima, ranging from a free-living pelagic or littoral existence to one of obligate parasitism. The better-known parasitic rotifers, such as *Proales*, occur in this group, parasitising both plants and animals.

Intermediate between the free-living and parasitic forms are a number of epizoic animals but the evolution of parasitism within the rotifers has not been studied. Whereas the majority of the bdelloid rotifers are bottom-dwellers and many of the Ploima are free-swimming organisms, the sessile rotifers are found in the suborders Flosculariacea and Collothecacea. The Flosculariacea tend to be encased in gelatinous sheaths which are sometimes fused to form a colony, as in two British species, *Conochilus hippocrepis* and *C. unicornis*. In the Collothecacea the anterior end of the sessile forms, e.g. species of *Collotheca*, is expanded into a funnel which is used for the capture and ingestion of large

Opposite
Acropora sp., one of the stony corals that form reefs in tropical seas. In this picture we are looking down on a single colony with its jagged branches pointing to the surface of the sea.

Two rotifers, *Asplanchia* sp. These have a bladder-like body, an eversible stomach equipped with jaws and feed on other rotifers. One of their prey is the rotifer *Brachionus calyciflorus*. This rotifer produces young with spines when the predator *Asplanchna* is present in the water and not in its absence. Presumably the spines make it difficult for the predator to swallow the young.

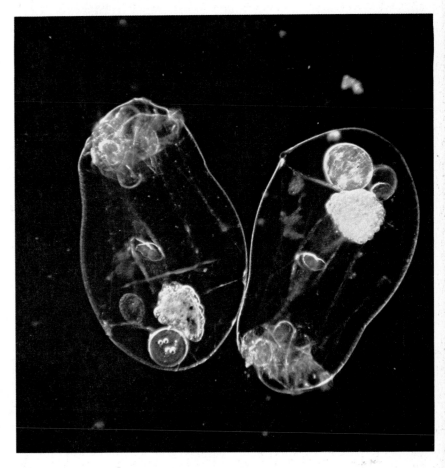

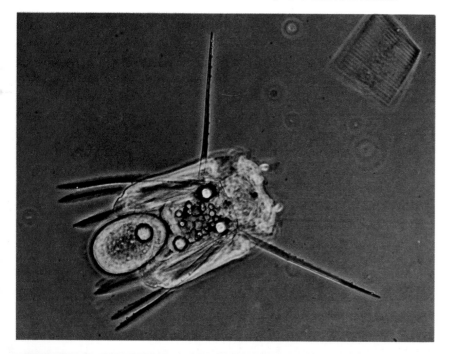

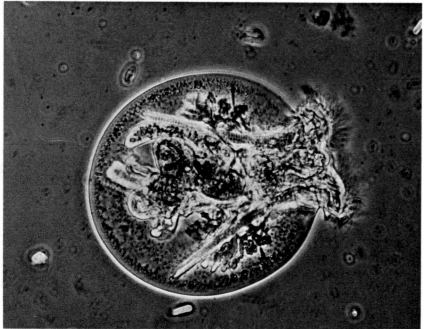

Some rotifers look and behave like crustacean larvae. This *Polyarthra* is one of them. It swims by means of fringed bristles actuated by muscles at their bases.

Testudinella patina, a rotifer in which the body is protected by a transparent coat or lorica. This is one of the rotifers found attached to the crustacean known as the fish-louse. It benefits from fragments of the crustacean's food as well as deriving the enhanced oxygen supply from the crustacean's movements through water.

prey. In these carnivorous forms the anterior end of the body bears a number of bristles on lobes and these close around the prey in a kind of trap. Free-swimming carnivores in other groups swim actively after their prey and seize them with their protruded mouth parts and either chew them or suck their body fluids. The bottom-dwelling Ploima use the corona for both swimming and feeding and waft small organisms and pieces of food into their mouths by setting up feeding currents. This type of feeding reaches its most specialised condition in the sessile flosculariaceans and bottom-dwelling bdelloids which use the corona almost solely for setting up feeding currents.

Reproduction and development

Two sexes are characteristically present in the rotifers but males are very seldom seen and for some groups they are unknown. In those species where males do occur their presence is limited to a short period of time and often they are much reduced in size. In the Seisonidea the males are very little different from the females except that they are smaller, in the Bdelloidea males are unknown, and an intermediate situation exists in the Monogononta where males are uncommon and much modified.

The type of egg produced by rotifers reflects the position of the males in the various groups. In the Seisonidea one type of egg is produced and develops into a male or female. The bdelloids produce only one type of egg which develops partheno-genetically into a female. In the sub-order Ploima, within the Monogononta, three kinds of egg are formed. Amictic eggs are thin-shelled ones which cannot be fertilised and develop into amictic females. Mictic eggs develop into males if unfertilised or into females if fertil-ised. The fertilised mictic eggs do not develop directly into young female rotifers but undergo a period of dormancy during which a thick egg wall is produced. The different types of egg, which are found in several groups of rotifers, are important because they allow the species to cope with diverse and changing environmental conditions and, in particular, the thick-walled eggs ensure survival in times of drought. Cleavage is basically the same in all types of rotifers and is of a modified spiral type. The young forms which hatch from the eggs differ according to whether they are to be males, females, free-living or sessile. Females usually emerge from the eggs with all the adult features except reproductive organs and grow into adults, while the males usually emerge as sexually mature individuals. The young of sedentary forms are free-swimming and these are responsible for the distribution of the species.

Histology

Practically all rotifer organs are syncytial, the cells fusing together in such a way that their limits cannot be identified with the aid of ordinary microscopical techniques. This type of organis-ation occurs in some turbellarians or flatworms and in certain organs in other aschelminths but nowhere is it so marked as in the rotifers.

The number of cells or at least of nuclei in a rotifer can easily be counted and is usually less than a thousand and once the number has been fixed it does not alter. This cell or nuclear constancy is a feature common to all aschelminths. In rotifers various organs are formed from a constant number of cells and in some cases the same number is found throughout the whole class. Each vitellarium, for instance, is formed from eight cells and each gastric gland from six. One of the disadvantages of constancy in cell numbers is that cell replacement is impossible and so regener-ation cannot take place. It is therefore possible to calculate the rate of ageing and length of life of these animals and the life-span is known for many species. In the genus *Philodina*, for example, it is less than three weeks. This short life-span and an established rate of ageing, and the ease with which rotifers can be maintained makes them very useful in studies on the nature of senescence.

Relationships

The rotifers have been classified with nearly every group of animals from the ciliates to the arthropods but now there is no doubt that they belong to the phylum Aschelminthes. Although it is difficult to establish the exact relationship with the other classes in this phylum, it is the group which is probably most clearly related to the turbellarians and thus links platyhelminths and aschelminths.

Gastrotrichs (Class Gastrotricha)

Gastrotrichs are common aquatic animals but, because of their small size, usually less than 0·5 millimetres they are seldom noticed. They are ventrally flattened creatures with a bristly or spiny appearance and may be seen gliding about on ventral cilia in much the same way as free-living flatworms. The body is covered with scales which are usually elaborated into spines but may sometimes be fused to form plates.

There are two orders: Chaetonotoidea and Macrodasyoidea. The Chaetonotoidea are mainly freshwater inhabitants and the body is differentiated into a head, neck and trunk, while the Macrodasyoidea are marine and the body is undivided. The freshwater forms are commonly found at the bottoms of ponds or lakes, and even in aquarium tanks or protozoan cultures, where they feed on detritus, bacteria, diatoms or protozoans by means of a long sucking pharynx. *Chaetonotus* is a common freshwater form and is found throughout the world.

The marine forms are less well known than the freshwater forms, probably because they have been almost ignored by the majority of zoologists until fairly recently. Practically all the marine species live in the spaces between grains of sand at a depth of about a metre below the surface, mainly in the sublittoral zone. These creatures seldom move from the sand grains, to which they attach themselves by means of secretions produced by special adhesive organs, and, like their freshwater relatives, feed on detritus, bacteria, diatoms and protozoans.

At one time it was thought that the order Macrodasyoidea was exclusively European but species have now been recorded from Africa, Japan and the Atlantic and Pacific coasts of America and there is every reason to suppose that they are distributed as widely as the freshwater forms.

Reproduction and development

Unlike all the other members of the aschelminths the gastrotrichs are hermaphrodite but in the Chaetonotoidea the male reproductive system degenerates so that all the adults are functionally females. Both reproductive systems remain in the Macrodasyoidea. The freshwater forms, which may be regarded as parthenogenetic, lay two types of eggs; one kind hatches in one to three days and the other is a dormant type similar to that found among the rotifers. The cleavage of the developing egg is of a modified spiral type.

Relationships

In many ways the gastrotrichs resemble the rotifers but they also share similarities with the nematodes. Current opinion is that they are related to the nematodes and also, but less closely, to the rotifers.

Kinorhynchs (Class Kinorhyncha)

Kinorhynchs are small marine creatures less than one millimetre long. They are bristly in appearance but differ from the gastrotrichs in having a segmented body. The first segment is the head which is spiny and can be retracted into the second segment, known as the neck. Behind the neck there are usually eleven, but sometimes twelve, other segments which constitute the trunk. Each segment is covered with a cuticle consisting of one dorsal and two ventral plates. The dorsal plate usually bears one median and two lateral spines, as in *Echinoderella*. In cross-section a typical kinorhynch is roughly triangular with a slightly concave ventral surface. Kinorhynchs burrow in the mud of coastal waters, feeding as they move. Some species feed on diatoms but the majority feed on various organic materials in the mud. The collection of kinorhynchs from the mud is a tedious occupation but large numbers can be obtained by bubbling air through sea water containing suitable samples and collecting the tiny creatures from the surface film. Most kinorhynchs are European but, like the gastrotrichs, more and more are being recognised in other areas and they probably occur at the edges of all seas. One of the most widespread genera, *Echinoderella*, is known from America, Europe and Asia.

Sexes are separate in the kinorhynchs but it is practically impossible to distinguish them externally, and little is known of their early embryology. The young larvae are not segmented and have no head but adult characters become apparent after the cuticle has been moulted a number of times.

Relationships

The relationships of the kinorhynchs are probably with the gastrotrichs and nematodes but it is very difficult to be sure about this because their embryology is not well charted. It is probably best to regard them as off-shoots of the general stock which gave rise to these two groups.

Priapulids (Class Priapuloidea)

This is a small class, containing three species of marine mud-dwelling animals which reach eight centimetres in length. There are three species, *Priapulus caudatus*, *Priapulus bicaudatus* and *Halicryptus spinulosus*, all of which are cylindrical, worm-like creatures with a warty, segmented trunk and a proboscis which can be partially retracted into the remainder of the body. The segmentation is only superficial but may trap the unwary into thinking he is dealing with an annelid. At the end of the proboscis there is a mouth, with a number of spines, and this may be retracted into the proboscis. At the posterior end of the trunk there are structures known as caudal appendages in *Priapulus* but, although these are very distinctive, nothing is known of their function. Priapulids are found in soft mud and sand in the littoral and sublittoral regions of the colder seas. Most records are known from northern waters but *Priapulus caudatus* also occurs in the Antarctic and this unusual bipolar distribution is of interest.

In general, priapulids are rare animals but are sometimes locally abundant even in England where both species of *Priapulus* occur along the south and west coasts but not in the north or east. *Priapulus* and *Halicryptus* are active predators and feed on any soft-bodied slow-moving animals, especially polychaetes, and they frequently attack one another using their spiny mouths. The sexes are separate but little is known of their reproduction or embryology. The young larva resembles the adult except that it is encased in a lorica, but the juvenile sheds this and emerges as a smaller version of the adult.

Relationships

The absence of information concerning the embryology of the priapulids makes it difficult to establish their relationships and some zoologists suggest that the body cavity is a true coelom and that the class should be removed from the aschelminths. But many zoologists maintain that the priapulids are pseudocoelomates and, although the larvae possess a number of rotifer characters, they are probably related to the kinorhynchs and less closely related to the nematodes.

Nematomorphs (Class Nematomorpha)

The nematomorphs are pseudocoelomates which are parasitic as juveniles and free-living as adults. In the adult form they are long, cylindrical worms which measure up to one metre long and are very thin in relation to their length, being only about one millimetre in diameter. Their long, thin appearance, coupled with the fact that they are usually brown or black, gives this group its familiar name of horse-hair worms. The nematomorphs are distributed throughout the world in temperate and tropical regions and the adults are always found in water or in damp soil.

Classification and life-cycles

There are two orders in the class, the Gordioidea, which live in freshwater habitats, and the Nectonematoidea, represented by four species in the genus *Nectonema*, which are all marine. The adults of both orders are similar and, apart from their general shape, lack any outstanding diagnostic features. The larvae are not nearly as long in relation to their width as the adults. They have an armed retractile proboscis and the trunk is superficially segmented in some species. Resemblance to the kinorhynchs and priapulids is very striking. The larvae are parasitic in various arthropods. The life-cycle of the freshwater forms begins when the fertilised eggs are deposited by the adult female and hatch in the water. The young larva emerges immediately and may be ingested by a small aquatic animal or it may encyst. If it is eaten by an appropriate host it makes its way through the gut wall and develops into a juvenile within the haemocoel or primary body cavity. There is a certain degree of host specificity, the usual hosts being the larvae of caddis flies and dragonflies. If the host is not an appropriate one the larva enters the haemocoel and encysts and the life-cycle may or may not terminate at this stage, depending on whether or not this host is eaten by a more suitable host. Unsuitable hosts include the larvae of mayflies and stoneflies but these hatch into adults which may be eaten by various carnivores including centipedes and millipedes, in which development of the parasite can continue. If the larvae are not eaten by a small aquatic animal they are able to encyst and such forms may then be eaten by terrestrial arthropods, including beetles and cockroaches, and eventually come to lie within the haemocoel of these hosts. Within the appropriate terrestrial host, regardless of whether the cycle has been direct or indirect, the larvae develop into juveniles which resemble the adults except that they are still covered with the larval cuticle. These moult and leave their hosts in or near water and the adults take to a free-living but non-feeding existence. The life-cycle of the nematomorphs is remarkable in that the adults are aquatic and the larvae are parasitic in aquatic or terrestrial arthropods and also that many other hosts, including frogs and even humans, may harbour the encysted larvae. The life-cycles of the marine species are similar to those of the freshwater species except that the hosts are crustaceans such as hermit crabs and true crabs of various kinds.

Relationships

The nematomorphs have often been associated with the nematodes but, although they are related in as far as they belong to the same phylum, the resemblances are superficial. The larva is the most important form in the establishment of relationships and this indicates that it is probable that the nematomorphs are related to the priapulids.

THORNY-HEADED WORMS
(Phylum Acanthocephala)

Acanthocephalans or thorny-headed worms comprise about 500 species of parasitic animals having a retractile proboscis which bears a number of thorn-shaped spines. The body is cylindrical and varies greatly in length, some species measuring only two millimetres while others exceed fifty centimetres. The larger parasites generally occur in the larger hosts, and the males are usually smaller than the females of the same species. There are several negative features associated with the parasitic mode of life: the absence of a digestive tract, circulatory system or sense-organs. The adults are found in various vertebrates, particularly fishes, birds and mammals, and their distribution is world-wide in terrestrial, freshwater and marine habitats.

Life-cycles
The sexes are separate and fertilisation occurs within the gut of the host. The larva develops in the egg before it is liberated by the female. The embryonated eggs are shed in the faeces of the host and lie dormant in the water or in the soil until eaten by an appropriate intermediate host which is usually an arthropod. The actual intermediate host depends on the species of the parasite but the larvae of insects and some crustaceans (isopods and amphipods) are frequently infected. When the egg is eaten by the intermediate host the young larva is liberated and makes its way through the gut wall until it reaches the haemocoel or primary body cavity, where it develops into a juvenile with all the features of a small adult. The life-cycle then stops until the intermediate host is eaten by the final host in which the juvenile parasite is set free and attaches to the wall of the gut by means of its spiny proboscis. Within the gut of the host the acanthocephalan becomes sexually mature and the life-cycle is repeated. In some cases the cycle is complicated by the fact that the juvenile form in an arthropod has to be ingested by a vertebrate other than the final host and this vertebrate must, in its turn, be eaten before the adult can mature. This seems to be an elaboration required only when the final host is unlikely to eat the arthropod.

Representative species
No species of acanthocephalan is a specific parasite of man but two are sometimes found in the human intestine. These cosmopolitan species are *Macracanthorhynchus hirudinaceus* found in pigs and dung beetle larvae and *Moniliformis dubius*, normally parasitic in rats and cockroaches. Some species cause serious diseases in domestic animals, one of the best known being *Polymorphus minutus*, which is a parasite of ducks and other birds. Its intermediate host is usually a freshwater shrimp. The bright orange juvenile parasite shows through the body of the shrimp and it is thought that this may attract the attention of the duck, thus ensuring the completion of the life-cycle. *Filicollis anatis* is another important parasite of ducks and freshwater isopods. The two most important acanthocephalan genera in fishes are *Echinorhynchus* and *Acanthocephalus* and these are frequently found throughout the world. *Acanthocephalus* also occurs in amphibia.

Relationships
The relationships of the acanthocephalans are obscure for the structure of the adult suggests affinities with the aschelminths while the modified spiral cleavage during embryonic development is of the type found in tapeworms (platyhelminths). The formation of the coelom or body cavity separates the group from aschelminths and it is probably best to regard the acanthocephalans as pseudocoelomates and to place them near the aschelminths as a separate phylum.

PHYLUM ENTOPROCTA

Portion of a sea mat (*Membranipora* sp.) of the kind commonly found coating rocks, seashells and the fronds of seaweeds. Each compartment is a box (or zooecium) containing one individual, known as a polypide because of its superficial resemblance to the true polyps of the phylum Cnidaria.

The Entoprocta, also known as Kamptozoa, are small aquatic animals less than one millimetre in length. They bear a superficial resemblance to hydroids (p. 40) but are closely related to the polyzoans (opposite) with which they were originally classified. Each consists of a jointed calcareous stalk which supports a rounded or bell-shaped body known as the polyp. The rim of the polyp forms a platform, the lophophore, which bears an oval circlet of ciliated tentacles. The tentacles do not retract but fold inwards and can be covered with a flap formed by the body wall. The body contains a simple gut, with a mouth and an anus, which opens within the circlet of tentacles. There is no coelom or body cavity, the space between the gut and the body wall being filled with a parenchymatous tissue. There is a pair of primitive excretory organs, the protonephridia, ending in flame bulbs, a nerve ganglion and gonads with their own ducts.

The sexes may be separate as in *Loxosoma* which also reproduces asexually by budding, or hermaphrodite as in *Pedicellina*, a colonial form in which the individuals are arranged on a common stolon.

There are three families, Loxosomatidae, Pedicellinidae and Urnatellidae, comprising about sixty species. Except for the genus *Urnatella*, found in India and the eastern United States, they are all marine, living on the sea shore or in adjacent shallow waters.

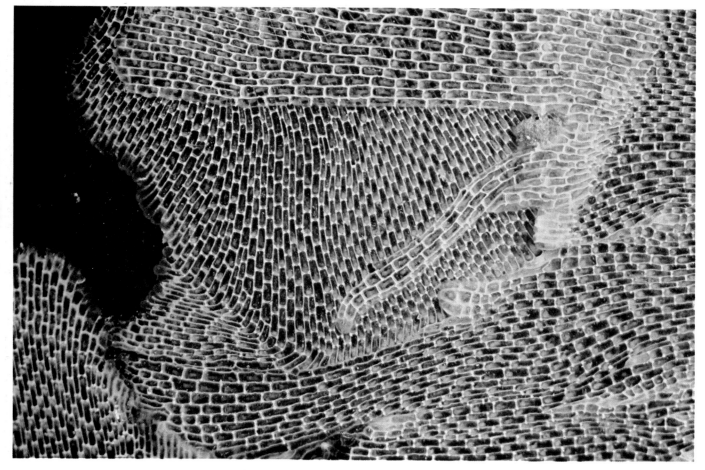

MOSS ANIMALS
(Phylum Bryozoa)

The Bryozoa, formerly known as Polyzoa, Ecto-procta, or moss animals, are small colonial animals found mainly in the sea, but some species inhabit freshwater. There are about 4,000 described existing species and 15,000 extinct ones. Although individuals, known as zooids, are usually only one millimetre in length, colonies may extend for a few metres, attached to rocks, seaweed or shells. In some species the colonies are erect, with broad lobes or cylindrical branches, while others form flat, moss-like encrustations. Three genera are commonly found washed up on ocean shores: *Flustra* whose flattened, seaweed-like colonies are drab brown and friable. *Alcyonidium* which forms erect finger-like colonies with the zooids embedded in a firm gelatinous matrix, and *Bugula* which forms elongate spirally branched colonies. There are two classes: Phylactolaemata, comprising such freshwater forms as *Cristatella* and *Plumatella*, and Gymnolaemata which are chiefly marine.

Structure

Each zooid consists of two parts: the zooecium or body wall and the polypide, which can be retracted into the zooecium. The wall is membranous and often strengthened by calcium carbonate deposited by the polypide which is not unlike one of the polyps in a hydroid colony.

The structure of the polypide is remarkably simple. The mouth is surrounded by a hollow circular or crescentric ridge extended into a variable number of hollow, ciliated tentacles, the whole structure being termed a lophophore. The mouth leads into a U-shaped digestive tube which ends in an anus situated outside the tentacles. There are no special organs for respiration and excretion and no blood vessels. The nervous system consists of a single ganglion situated between the mouth and the anus. The reproductive cells are produced in the lining of the coelom or body cavity and when ripe they are discharged through a special tube, the intertentacular organ, leading to an opening at the base of the tentacles.

Contraction of a set of muscles on the body wall produces internal pressure, causing the polypide to emerge. At any disturbance the polypides are rapidly withdrawn by a retractor muscle running from the lophophore to the opposite end of the zooecium. In some species the opening of the zooecium is covered by a calcareous lid, the operculum, after the polypide has withdrawn.

Bryozoa feed on minute particles of organic matter in the water. These particles are picked up by cilia on the tentacles, and passed into the mouth.

Many species of Cheilostomata (class Gym-

Plumatella repens, one of the moss animals in which the polypides form branching colonies that extend over the substratum. Shown here is the end portion of one of the branches with five polypides that have their crown of tentacles arranged in a characteristic horseshoe.

nolaemata) are polymorphic, the body form of some polypides being modified so that they function as specialised organs. Two kinds of modified zooids are vibracula and avicularia. A vibraculum takes the form of a long bristle which sweeps backwards and forwards over the surface of a colony. The avicularium, which resembles a bird's head, is a modified zooid attached to the colony by a long stalk. It has a movable lower jaw derived from the operculum which is provided with powerful muscles and can seize and in some types of avicularia swallow small animals. These modified zooids keep the colony clean by removing larvae and preventing overgrowth by other sedentary animals.

Reproduction and formation of colonies

Bryozoa are hermaphrodite and both sexual and asexual reproduction occur. Species such as *Crisia* (order Cyclostomata) reproduce by embryonic fission, the fertilised egg developing into an embryo in a modified zooecium, known as an ovicell, giving rise to numerous secondary embryos, each of which becomes a free-swimming larva.

Each colony begins as a free-swimming larva which, after settling on the substratum, undergoes metamorphosis into a zooid. It then produces buds, each of which becomes a zooid and produces other buds, the young zooids being on the periphery or on the tips of branches in branched species. The life-span of each polypide is very short and the zooecia are occupied by a succession of polypides. In winter the polypides degenerate and form a minute brown mass in each zooecium. Simultaneously a new polypide bud develops to take its place, the brown body being enveloped by the stomach of the young polypide and evacuated. It is arguable whether death results from the accumulation of nitrogenous waste, there being no excretory system, or because the polypide ruptures when discharging its larvae.

Class Phylactolaemata

Members of this class inhabit freshwater and are characterised by the horseshoe shape of the lophophore and arrangement of the tentacles, and the presence of a lip or epistome protecting the mouth. The coelom is continuous from one zooid to another. They reproduce sexually and by means of statoblasts, a form of internal budding. The statoblasts are lens-shaped masses of cells enclosed in a chitonous envelope capable of withstanding desiccation in periods of drought and freezing. When the parent colony dies in the autumn, in temperate regions, the statoblasts germinate in the following spring. Statoblasts are a means of dispersal; they may be carried on the feet of water-birds.

Some freshwater Bryozoa form bushy clumps or tufts on stones and the stems of water plants; others are invested in a mass of gelatinous material, in *Pectinatella* up to a metre or more in diameter, coating stones and other submerged objects. Most Bryozoa are sedentary but *Cristatella* and *Lophopus* can creep slowly over the surfaces of water plants, aided by a gelatinous secretion which serves the same purpose as the slime track of slugs. Movement is probably effected by the concerted action of the muscles in the body wall of each zooid. Colonies of *Cristatella* may divide into two by a constriction in the middle, the two parts then continuing to grow to full size. Alternatively, separate colonies may fuse together, forming a network, as, for example, on the leaf of a water lily.

Class Gymnolaemata

The Gymnolaemata are chiefly marine and occur on driftwood and other floating objects including ships. Many species have a world-wide distribution. The three orders, Cyclostomata, Cheilostomata and Ctenostomata, are characterised by the circular arrangement of the tentacles and absence of an epistome. Various types of free-swimming larvae occur.

In Cheilostomata, which is the largest order and includes such species as *Bugula* and *Flustra*, the orifice is closed by a chitinous operculum and the zooecium, which is box-shaped, is often very calcareous. Protrusion of the tentacles is effected with a compensation sac which fills with water.

The zooecia are tubular in the Cyclostomata and lack an operculum. Embryonic fission is common.

The Ctenostomata have a comb-like circlet of rods which close the opening of the zooecium when the tentacles are withdrawn. One of its species, *Victorella pavida*, was first discovered in brackish water in the London docks, and also occurs in the freshwaters of Lake Tanganyika. Several members of this order burrow into the shells of marine molluscs, dissolving the lime of the shell.

Some gymnolaemate colonies form low-growing mats on rocks, molluscs and crustacean shells and seaweeds. These may be fan-like (*Schizoporella*), circular (older colonies of *Membranipora*), or irregular in adjustment to the shape of the substrata.

Marine bryozoans are among the organisms causing fouling of ship bottoms with resultant increased drag and loss of speed.

The freshwater bryozoans grow rapidly under suitable conditions and gelatinous forms have caused clogging of conduits in public water supply systems and hydro-electric plants.

As filter-feeders upon bacteria, protozoans and other minute organisms, bryozoans play an important part in the total economy of nature, controlling, together with many other kinds of filter-feeder, the population size of their prey. Bryozoans are fed upon by flatworms, naidid annelids, snails, orbatid mites, insect larvae and fishes.

PHORONIDS
(Phylum Phoronida)

Phoronids are sessile, marine animals which live in membranous tubes. They are usually gregarious, the tubes being irregularly woven around each other like a tangle of string, but some species are solitary. Fifteen species are known from areas as far apart as the Mediterranean, North Atlantic, California and Australia. Most of them are less than twenty centimetres long and some measure little more than 0·5 millimetres. One of the largest species, *Phoronopsis californica*, which is found in estuaries, is worm-like, forty-five centimetres long and about six millimetres in diameter. Others are found in shallow coastal water on pier-piles, sand or mud flats.

At the upper end of the soft, unsegmented body is a horseshoe-shaped platform, the lophophore. This bears a crown of ciliated tentacles which can be protruded from the top of the tube and spread out fanwise. Particles of organic matter in the water are caught on the film of mucus covering the tentacles and passed by ciliary action to the mouth at the base of the lophophore.

The gut is U-shaped with both mouth and anus situated at the base of the lophophore. An epistome, a small lobe lying between the mouth and the anus, prevents waste matter from re-entering the body. The gut consists of a gullet, stomach and intestine. There is a system of blood vessels with contractile walls and red blood containing haemoglobin. The nerve-cells are distributed generally over the body but are especially concentrated in a ring just below the mouth, which is thickened at one point to form a ganglion. There are no special sense-organs. Two excretory organs, the nephridia, at their inner ends open into the coelom or body cavity.

Phoronids are hermaphrodite, and genital cells on the inner wall of the coelom produce both eggs and sperms which pass to the exterior through the nephridial tubes. On being shed, the eggs adhere to the tentacles, where they are fertilised by sperms from one or more other phoronids. After undergoing the early stages of development within the egg membrane attached to the tentacles, each egg hatches into a free-swimming larva known as an actinotrocha, in which tentacles and gut are already present. Then it settles on the bottom and starts to secrete a tube.

The position of the Phoronida in the classification of the invertebrates has always been uncertain. There is a superficial resemblance to the bryozoans and the internal anatomy has affinities with the annelids. There are also similarities in some details with forms like the pogonophores, which are regarded as being near the base of chordate evolution (*see* p. 198).

LAMP-SHELLS
(Phylum Brachiopoda)

Brachiopods or lamp-shells, which are exclusively marine, are represented in some of the earliest fossil-bearing rocks in the Cambrian period and reached their greatest development in the Ordovician period about 500 million years ago. They are represented in the seas today by some 250 species, whereas 30,000 fossil species are known. The body is enclosed in a shell composed of two bilaterally symmetrical but dissimilar valves, placed on the upper and lower surfaces as in some bivalve molluscs such as oysters and jingle shells (species of *Anomia*). But whereas the valves of oysters and jingle shells are placed one on each side of the body and the animal grows lying on its side, in brachiopods the two halves are dorsoventrally arranged and the animal occurs right side up. The larger ventral valve ends in a projecting beak pierced by an opening for the stalk or peduncle which anchors the animal to the substratum, usually a rock or a coral. The whole shell resembles a Roman lamp.

The largest living lamp-shells are about eight centimetres in diameter, but most are only five centimetres or less in diameter. The largest fossil species has a diameter of thirty centimetres, and extinct forms were often heavily ornamented with spines. Typically a lamp-shell has a muscular stalk by which it is attached to the substratum, but in species of the genus *Crania*, found in waters off western Ireland and in the West Indies, the ventral shell is cemented to the rock surface.

There are two classes: the Inarticulata which have muscles connecting the valves, and the Articulata with hinged valves. The Articulata have shells containing calcium carbonate and are typically dredged from deep waters, whereas most of the Inarticulata have shells containing calcium phosphate and a higher proportion of horn-like material.

The biology of the two classes is essentially the same except that the horny-shelled brachiopods have a much longer peduncle, the shell is more flattened and they live up to thirty centimetres deep in burrows in mud. The horny-shelled brachiopods are represented by the genus *Lingula*, with species in shallow waters off the shores of Japan, the Indo-Pacific islands and Queensland, Australia. Found in the rocks of the Cambrian period, *Lingula* has survived almost unchanged for over 500 million years. In contrast with the limy-shelled brachiopods, its fossils are not numerous at any period.

Internally the most conspicuous part of the soft body is a pair of complex loops or arms, one on each side of the mouth, bearing numerous ciliated tentacles. They recall the lophophore of Bryozoa and Phoronida and have the same function, the ciliated loops creating currents of water as the shell gapes. Micro-organisms and food particles brought in by an inhalant current are trapped by the mucus-covered loops and passed by the cilia down to the mouth. The loops also have a respiratory function, taking up oxygen from the incoming water. In *Terebratulina septentrionalis*, the loops form a stirrup-shaped ring with only a small hole at its centre.

The mouth, situated in a groove at the base of the lophophore, leads into a stomach into which opens a branched digestive gland. Most of the digestion takes place in the cavity of this gland. In the Articulata the short intestine running from the stomach ends blindly, but in the Inarticulata there is an anus. The coelom or body cavity is spacious and divided into two parts. It is continued into the lophophore and into the tentacles.

The excretory system consists of segmental organs or metanephridia which are short tubes ending in large nephrostomes. There is a simple system of blood vessels, which includes a dorsal vessel, part of which functions as a heart. The nervous system consists of a ganglion behind the mouth and one in front of it, connected by a nerve-ring, and with a nerve running into each tentacle. There are no special sense-organs.

The sexes are usually separate. Ova or sperms are found in patches on the coelomic epithelium. They are shed into the coelom and reach the cavity of the shell through the tubes of the segmental organs.

Embryonic development in a few species takes place in the parent shell, sometimes in a special brood-pouch. Usually, however, the gametes are shed into the sea where fertilisation occurs and a free-swimming larva, known as a trochosphere or trophophore develops. It is propelled through the water by the rows of cilia on its three-lobed body, but after a few days the larva sinks to the bottom and undergoes metamorphosis. The posterior lobe becomes elongated into a stalk, the middle lobe secretes a shell and a lophophore is formed.

MOLLUSCS (Phylum Mollusca)

The molluscs, or soft-bodied animals, are a large (128,000 species) and most important invertebrate phylum, members of which occupy many habitats in the sea, in freshwater and on land. They include slugs, snails, oysters, mussels, cuttlefishes and squids. Although all conforming in fundamental structure to the same ground plan, molluscs are exceptionally diverse in outward appearance and in habits. With the possible exception of the recently discovered monoplacophoran *Neopilina* (*see below*), they are not segmented and, in the active and often large cephalopods (squids, cuttlefishes and octopods), display the highest non-segmented organisation.

Body form

All molluscs are divisible into four regions: a usually well-developed head with tentacles and eyes (this has been lost in the bivalves); a ventral and muscular foot, originally probably possessing a flat 'sole' on which the mollusc crawled, as many still do, on hard surfaces (the foot can be greatly modified but is seldom lost); a dorsal visceral mass—coiled in the gastropods—in which the internal organs are concentrated in a rounded mass; and a mantle or pallium consisting of a sheet of tissue which grows over the visceral mass and secretes a calcareous shell laid down as crystals within an organic matrix. The shell takes many forms; it is usually in one piece (even in the bivalves where the two lateral valves and the dorsal connecting ligament together form the shell), although in the polyplacophorans or chitons it consists of eight plates. The shell may become enclosed in the mantle and so reduced as in the slugs, some chitons, and the squids.

Consideration of the basic form in molluscs reveals that, unlike that of any other phylum, it has two growth axes: the antero-posterior axis of the head-foot such as occurs in all bilaterally symmetrical animals, and—what must have appeared when the earliest mollusc evolved—a second dorsoventral axis. This is associated with the visceral mass and mantle or visceropallium. Growth in this instance takes place radially by marginal increment around the edge of the mantle where new shell is added. Many complications of molluscan form can only be understood by reference to the interacting symmetries of the bilateral head-foot and the radial (or biradial) visceropallium. They may achieve a balance or one may dominate the other.

Mantle cavity and respiration

Space between the edge of the mantle and the underlying tissues constitutes the mantle cavity. Originally this probably consisted of a groove between the mantle skirt and the foot into which the anus opened posteriorly and the paired kidneys and reproductive system opened laterally; the groove also contained paired series of gills. This is the pattern in the monoplacophoran *Neopilina* illustrated on page 82. However, it is clear that with further evolution the groove enlarged to form a combined respiratory and cloacal cavity at the posterior end into which the foot could be withdrawn. This is certainly the basic pattern of the respiratory cavity in the majority of molluscs. In it the highly characteristic molluscan gills or ctenidia lie protected.

Each ctenidium consists of an axis containing blood vessels, muscle and nerve and bears on each side alternately disposed rows of elongated filaments. Between these, upward-beating rows of cilia create a current of water in the direction opposed to the blood flow within the thin-walled filaments. Efficient respiratory exchange is thus ensured. Associated with the paired ctenidia are osphradia, sense-organs situated near the opening of the cavity and, at least primitively, probably concerned with estimating the amount of sediment

A beautifully marked sea-snail, known as the Partridge Tun, of the Great Barrier Reef, gliding along on its fleshy foot.

carried in with the respiratory current created by the cilia. Hypobranchial glands on the roof of the cavity produce mucus which entangles sediment.

Circulatory system

The heart lies within the pericardium which represents part of the much reduced coelom or body cavity. It consists of a single muscular ventricle into which open usually one pair, but in a few cases two pairs, of auricles. Contractions of the ventricle force blood into anterior and posterior aortae; it then circulates round the body in sinuses (only the highly organised cephalopods have capillaries), passing through the kidneys and finally returning to the auricles by way of the ctenidia. The blood is either colourless or contains the blue respiratory pigment haemocyanin. Blood is extensively used in molluscs for hydrostatic purposes as well as for respiration: it forces the body out of the shell, extends the foot, and so on.

Alimentary system

The mouth, which may bear 'jaws', lies at the anterior end of the head. Just within the cavity and capable of being protruded is the radula or lingual ribbon. This typically molluscan structure, lacking only in the bivalves, is a horny ribbon which bears rows of teeth and is capable of wide modification for scraping, piercing, seizing or even poisoning prey. It also acts as a conveyor belt carrying food into the gut. It is continually being worn away but at the same time being added to in the radular sac

whence it originates. It is carried over a muscular pad known as the odontophore and lubricated by mucus from salivary glands which in some cases may be modified to produce digestive enzymes or even poison. Digestive glands may occur in the oesophagus leading to the stomach into which open a mass of blind-ended tubules or digestive diverticula. Universally present in molluscs, these tubules are concerned, in varying degrees in different groups, with intracellular (i.e. phagocytic) digestion, absorption, secretion of digestive enzymes, excretion and, in some gastropods, with storage of the calcium needed for the formation of the shell.

The stomach itself is a largely ciliated organ broadly concerned with sorting material into finer particles which pass into the tubules of the digestive diverticula and larger ones which pass into the mid gut or intestine for consolidation into faecal pellets. Varying extents of the stomach wall are covered with a translucent, firm gastric shield. This is frequently in functional association with the crystalline style, a rod-like structure formed from globulin (a protein). This is secreted in a style-sac which forms the posterior extension of the stomach. Cilia lining the sac cause the style to rotate. The head of the revolving style assists in drawing food into the stomach and in its mixing while, as the style slowly dissolves, it liberates digestive enzymes which break down sugars, and even in some cases cellulose, and also fats. Universally present in the bivalves, this remarkable structure (possibly the only revolving structure in animals) also occurs in the monoplacophoran *Neopilina* and in many gastropods.

The anus opens into the mantle cavity. In association with this the mid and hind gut (or rectum) are primarily concerned with consolidation of faeces which would foul the respiratory chamber. The anus opens above the ctenidia and the faeces are carried away in the exhalant stream.

Nervous system and sense-organs

The most primitive nervous system occurs in the monoplacophorans and amphineurans (e.g. chitons), where it consists of a central nerve ring round the anterior oesophagus with pleurovisceral and pedal cords running back, the former encircling the margin of the mantle, the latter running down the foot, with cross connections between the two. Nerve cells lie largely within the cords and are not concentrated into ganglia as they are in the other molluscan classes, which typically possess paired cerebral, pleural, pedal and visceral ganglia, that is ganglia associated with the four regions of the body.

Sense-organs are primitively located in the head where tentacles carry eyes and are also probably concerned with chemoreception. Statocysts (organs of balance) occur in the foot near the pedal ganglia.

Locomotion

While the ventrally placed muscular foot with its primitively broad 'sole' is responsible for temporary attachment to a hard substrate, it is also the prime means of locomotion. It is attached to the dorsal shell by a series of shell muscles, paired in all but the gastropods where, following torsion (*see*

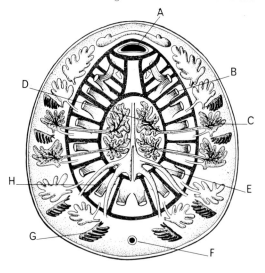

Diagrammatic view of the structure of the monoplacophoran *Neopilina*, viewed from above. (A) is the mouth, (B) the shell muscles, (C) the kidneys, (D) the gonads, (E) the ventricles, (F) the anus, (G) the gills and (H) the auricles.

The Great Scallop (*Pecten maximus*), of Europe, lying free, as is normal, on the rocks. It is a bivalve mollusc and when the valves part they reveal jewel-like eyes as well as numerous small tentacles fringing the mantle that lines the interior of the shell.

p. 86), they are reduced to a single, enlarged columellar muscle. Extension of the foot is achieved by hydrostatic pressure and withdrawal by muscular contraction. Contractions of intrinsic muscles within the foot produce the rhythmic propulsive wave which carries the animal slowly on. The foot can be extensively modified to permit movement through sand or other soft substrates, as in typical bivalves, or as 'wings' or 'fins' for swimming in surface-dwelling gastropods. In a few cases where the animal becomes permanently attached the foot is lost. Rapid movement in the cephalopods and in the bivalve scallops is produced by jet propulsion when water is expelled from the mantle cavity by sudden muscular contractions. In the cephalopods the direction of the jet is controlled by the foot, converted into a tubular funnel.

Excretory system

Primarily this consists of kidneys which open internally into the pericardium and externally into the mantle cavity, where the dissolved nitrogenous and other wastes are carried away in the exhalant stream. Most usually a single pair, they may be more numerous when there is more than one pair of auricles, as in the monoplacophorans and in the primitive cephalopod *Nautilus*. Throughout the gastropods there is only a single functional kidney which, as well as controlling blood concentration, removes waste products of metabolism from circulating blood. Other organs may assist in excretion, for example pericardial glands in bivalves and regions of the digestive diverticula, notably in the cephalopods.

Reproductive system

Reproductive tissue lines forward extensions of the body cavity which are initially in free communication which are initially in free communication with the pericardium into which the sexual products are discharged before being conveyed to the exterior through the kidneys. The general effect of evolution within the molluscs is to separate the reproductive from the excretory system with provision of separate ducts. Although most often of separate sexes, there is a strong tendency for hermaphroditism to occur in a variety of forms, especially in the bivalves and the gastropods; protandry (a male condition preceding a female one) is particularly common. Most primitively, egg and sperm are liberated for fertilisation to occur in the sea but the higher gastropods and the cephalopods have evolved complicated methods of internal fertilisation. In the former these have made land colonisation possible.

Development

Following fertilisation, usually in the sea, a trochophore larva (also found in annelid worms) is produced, followed by the typically molluscan shelled veliger larva which has a ciliated velum which can be protruded from or withdrawn into the cavity of the increasingly large shell. This is the organ of propulsion and of feeding. After a variable free-swimming period the larva settles on a suitable substrate to undergo metamorphosis to the adult form. Following internal fertilisation elaborate capsules may be formed containing yolky eggs which develop to a late larval stage in many gastropods or to an adult stage in the higher pulmonate snails and cephalopods. Direct development is more abundant in cold water than warm.

Affinities

While the occurence in both molluscs and annelids of spiral cleavage in development and of trochophore larvae has long indicated some affinity between the two phyla, it has long been assumed that separation occurred before the appearance of the segmentation so characteristic of the annelids. However, *Neopilina*, a living monoplacophoran genus, makes some reconsideration necessary. As seen in the diagram opposite, these animals possess serially-repeated gills, kidneys, gonads and shell muscles and are regarded by some as truly segmental. There is no doubt that they are very primitive and it is possible, although not absolutely certain, that they are segmented. But the remainder of the molluscs show no trace of true segmentation, and if *Neopilina* does indicate primitive structure then it is necessary to postulate much secondary simplification involving loss of all indications of segmentation before the appearance of the basically much simpler pattern which permitted the radiating evolution of the remaining five molluscan classes. Initial simplicity of underlying pattern is probably the major factor in the great success of this phylum.

Roman Snails (*Helix pomatia*) in the process of mating. The animals, hermaphrodite like all land snails, are fully extended with their under surfaces applied. The two pairs of tentacles with eyes at the summit of the hind pair are characteristic of the Stylommatophora (Pulmonata).

Class Monoplacophora

Although the class was established some years previously by palaeontologists to accommodate a group of Palaeozoic limpets characterised by the presence of a series of paired muscle scars which indicated that they were *not* gastropods, the first living monoplacophoran (*Neopilina galatheae*

Lemche) was dredged in 1952 in 3,590 metres off the Pacific coast of Mexico. Three other species were taken, all off the Pacific coast of America within fifteen degrees of the Equator, from depths between 1,500 and 3,500 metres. In appearance a somewhat flattened limpet about 35 millimetres long with the apex, which bears a spirally coiled embryonic shell near the anterior end, *N. galatheae* possesses many archaic features. Unlike gastropod limpets it is bilaterally symmetrical with the mouth in front and the anus in the midline posteriorly. Eight pairs of shell muscle run between the disc-shaped foot and the shell. There is no enlarged posterior mantle cavity but in the pallial grooves lie five pairs of gills, certainly not identical with ctenidia although showing some common features and possibly representing a derivative from some common prectenidial structure. The head is unusual. It has a pair of small tentacles, a pair of lateral flaps and, behind the mouth, a pair of much-branched tentacular tufts. The animal lives on a relatively firm bottom of abyssal ooze and these organs (not yet observed in life) presumably convey detritus into the mouth. However, unlike the bivalves, it has a long radular sac. The remainder of the gut, with a style-sac opening into a simple stomach and a long, coiled intestine, is typical of fine particle or deposit feeding molluscs.

The body cavity is relatively large; posteriorly it consists of paired pericardial cavities containing a longitudinally divided ventricle with two pairs of auricles. A more anterior pair of cavities dubiously connect with these but ventral to them are paired spaces containing the two pairs of gonads. These communicate with the pallial groove by way of the third and fourth of the six pairs of kidneys. The nervous system conforms closely to the primitive pattern as already described, consisting of small cerebral ganglia, an anterior oesophageal ring and a pair of cords with many rung-like connections.

There can be no doubt that *Neopilina* represents the earliest type of mollusc yet found alive. It occupies, however, what is far from being a primitive habitat and probably retreated into abyssal depths before the competition of more recently evolved—and more simply constructed—molluscs. The serial repetition of shell muscles (8), kidneys (6), gills (5), auricles (2) and gonads (2) may indicate that the molluscs were primitively segmented, although it is noteworthy that neither the body surface nor the nervous system are involved as they so notably are in the annelids. Moreover, it may represent an extreme example of the tendency found in some other molluscs, notably the polyplacophorans (*see below*) for repetition of certain organs. In any case it is difficult to regard the monoplacophorans as in any way ancestral to modern molluscs, all five classes of which have a fundamentally simpler structure. *Neopilina* may be presumed to have survived because it has been able to live in a habitat where there is little competition.

Class Amphineura

This group consists of a thousand species of marine molluscs which possess a variety of primitive characters, notably in the nervous system, but which are also in many respects very specialised. Some of their apparent simplicity is due to loss of organs. All are elongated. The polyplacophorans have a shell consisting of eight plates; the aplacophorans, as their name infers, have no shell.

Chitons and allies (Subclass Polyplacophorea = Loricata)

These chitons possess an elongate, flattened body, and a foot covered with a linear series of eight articulating plates, each with separate shell muscles. The visceropallium may be said to dominate the head-foot, which it completely covers. Neither foot nor head is ever visible from above. Here association with a hard substrate has been taken to the furthest extreme consistent with mobility. They are essentially elongated limpets. The mantle extends beyond the shell plates to form the girdle, which is in contact with the substrate below and bears spicules on the upper surface. The articulating plates enable the foot and girdle to conform to irregular surfaces and, should the animal be torn off the rocks in very heavy seas, permit it to curl up with the undersurface, including the all-important pallial grooves, well protected. Chitons may be rolled about without damage. While usually covering the greater part of the dorsal surface, the plates may be reduced and may finally be completely enclosed within the leathery mantle, as in the largest of all chitons, *Cryptochiton stelleri*, a species that is found in the waters of the northern Pacific.

The narrow pallial grooves between the girdle and the massive foot contain series of ctenidia varying in number from four to eighty pairs and so valueless as evidence for segmentation. This multiplication is clearly associated with the restricted space available. The ctenidia are attached to the roof of the groove and, whatever their number, they act as a unit linked by interlocking zones of cilia on the edges of the filaments. The cilia create a current of water which is drawn in anteriorly at any point where the girdle may be raised. Water passes between the filaments to form exhalant currents which run back to unite behind the foot. The separate renal and reproductive ducts open into the inner space and the anus opens into it in the mid-line posteriorly. Blood flows from the gills into the two pairs of auricles which open into a median ventricle in a dorsal and posterior pericardium. Circulation is of the normal molluscan type.

The mouth is invariably applied to the rocky substrate from which the broad radula scrapes largely plant matter and conveys it into the gut. The primitive oesophagael glands are represented by two pouches, the posterior and larger one forming the 'sugar glands' which secrete amylase for digestion of starch. The stomach is relatively simple with the digestive diverticula secreting protease and absorbing (but with no intracellular digestion). The intestine is divisible into four regions, the first two concerned with digestion, the last two with consolidation of the faecal pellets.

The nervous system is very primitive and without conspicuous ganglia. Sense-organs are confined to a subradular organ below the head and clearly used to test the substrate for food; strips of sensory epithelium in the pallial groove or on the axes of the ctenidia may have the same function as osphradia. There are no eyes on the head but megalaesthetes furnished with elementary retina, lens and cornea and smaller micraesthetes penetrate the shell plates. These are probably sensitive to stimuli of light, pressure and tactile contact. They enable the animals to react to light and

contact. Pedal movement is extremely slow.

The kidneys extend far forward from the pericardium but then loop back with their external openings on a line with the pericardium. The gonads have lost connection with the pericardium and are usually fused although they retain the paired ducts which open just anterior to the renal pores. Sexes are usually separate with external fertilisation but one species is viviparous. Lunar periodicity in spawning occurs, as in *Acanthozostera*.

The polyplacophorans are a homogeneous group highly specialised for life on hard uneven surfaces and occur on all rocky shores not scoured by ice. They are particularly common along the Pacific coast of North America where many are large and brightly and variously coloured. They probably evolved in shallow and intertidal waters where the great majority live. Members of one order (Lepidopleurida) inhabit deep and even abyssal seas where, like *Neopilina*, they must live on consolidated deposits. Although with a less efficient respiratory system and less complex plates than those living in shallow water, they are able to consolidate sediment in the inhalant chamber (before it reaches the ctenidia). This is probably an adaptation for life on a muddy bottom in still water.

Subclass Aplacophorea

This very small group of worm-like molluscs, sometimes considered as a separate class, is more specialised, although less successfully, than the polyplacophorans. The mantle, which almost or entirely surrounds the body, forms a thick cuticle in which spicules are embedded. The foot, where it is present, is confined to a narrow ventral groove. The mantle cavity (or cloaca) is represented by a posterior depression into which the anus and renal ducts open. A pair of what are probably ctenidia occur in some, while in others respiration takes place through a series of folds. The heart is extremely simple and there are no true blood vessels. A reduced radula may be present (major evidence that these animals *are* molluscs) and the gut is straight with only salivary glands opening into it. The nervous system is archaic as in the polyplacophorans and monoplacophorans. The

apparent renal system consists of a pair of ducts which have a common opening into the mantle cavity but which may not be excretory. Through them pass the gametes which are formed in a pair of reproductive organs which open separately into the pericardium (the most primitive condition). The majority of species are hermaphrodite and the ducts possess glands for secreting an egg case and storage vesicles for sperm.

As indicated by the reduction of the foot, the aplacophorans are excessively sluggish animals. They occur from shallow water to great depths, usually on muddy substrates. They are carnivorous, members of the order Neomeniomorpha feeding on coelenterates, and those of the order Chaetodermorpha on protozoans and other minute inhabitants of bottom muds. In shallow waters they occur twined around the stems of hydroids.

Gastropods (Class Gastropoda)

This great group of molluscs, containing perhaps 105,000 species, represents one of the most varied assemblages of animals and includes snails, slugs and limpets. Adaptive radiation has permitted effective exploitation of every environment in the sea and the invasion of freshwater and land. A few gastropods have become parasites.

In contrast to that of the Amphineura, evolution of the gastropods involved greater concentration of the viscera and a consequent increase in the height of the shell. This was followed by coiling (which also occurs in larval *Neopilina* and in certain living

and many extinct cephalopods) so that the elongated viscera were more economically disposed. Coiling was initially in a plano-spiral, that is bilateral symmetry was retained, as in the primitive cephalopod *Nautilus*. The foot, and after it the head, could be withdrawn into a deepened mantle cavity. Such coiling probably occurred in early molluscs. Existing gastropods are also characterised by another phenomenon—the remarkable and totally distinctive process of torsion.

Torsion involves an anticlockwise swing in the horizontal plane of the visceropallium in relation to the head-foot, a process made possible by the thin 'neck' which connects these two parts of the animal. The major consequences of torsion will be seen by comparing the diagrams on page 86. (where coiling in a plano-spiral is assumed to have preceded torsion). The shell muscles which must already have been reduced to one pair were further reduced to the one on the right which became the columellar muscle. The mantle cavity became anterior while the coils of the viscera rested on the posterior upper surface of the foot. Previously weight must have tended to press on the mantle cavity, which now assumes a commanding position, just above the head, and tends in the further process of evolution to assume greater sensory and exploratory importance. But the immediate problem presented by torsion involved sanitation: the anal and renal products previously voided posteriorly were now voided over the head. The

immediate solution was the appearance of a slit in the mid-line of the roof of the cavity through which the exhalant current, carrying faeces and excrement, was ejected upwards and well clear of the head. Within the body the major effects of torsion were to twist the alimentary canal so that the anus lay above the mouth, and also the nervous system so that the primitive loop between the anterior cerebral and pleural ganglia, and the posterior visceral ganglia was twisted into a figure of eight.

The process of torsion can be followed during development in a number of relatively primitive gastropods with free-swimming larvae, e.g. the topshell *Trochus*, or the limpets, *Patella* and *Acmaea*. As no intermediate stage is known, it probably originally occurred as a result of a mutation involving asymmetry of the two larval shell muscles. The immediate consequences are of value to the larva, which can now pull the head into the mantle cavity and follow this with the foot, which then or later carried an operculum. The adult was faced with the problems of sanitation noted above and only further evolution enables these to be fully solved.

Still further evolution involved asymmetrical coiling with consequent effects on the organs in the mantle cavity, and so on the auricles, kidneys and eventually the reproductive system. The shell became asymmetrical by a pulling out of the spire, usually to the right (dextral) and rarely to the left (sinistral). The coiling was rearranged above the foot, so that it lay obliquely with the spire skewed upwards. The process is indicated in the accompanying diagram, which also shows how the right side of the mantle cavity becomes reduced with the slit no longer in the midline. This condition persists in the most primitive living gastropods, the Pleurotomariidae, topshells with a slit living in very deep water. The right ctenidium, osphradium and hypobranchial gland are all small. This is true of all gastropods with paired ctenidia (zygobranchous) except where secondary symmetry has been attained as in the keyhole limpets.

The eventual loss of the organs of the right side of the mantle cavity had far-reaching consequences. Circulation of water was now from left to right (*see* bottom diagrams), the anus being displaced to the right side. The solitary ctenidium retained the two rows of filaments, that is, it was aspidobranch. But such a gill requires attachment to the roof as well as the floor of the cavity (*see* bottom diagram B) and sediment tends to collect in the small pocket on the left of this. Complete solution of respiratory problems came with the fusion of the gill axis to the wall of the cavity and the loss of the filaments on the left side. This final condition, with pectinibranch ctenidium, (shown in the bottom diagram C) is found in the majority of gastropods which have ctenidia.

Loss of the right ctenidium was followed by that of the auricle it had supplied: the diotocardiate was followed by the monotocardiate condition. The next changes involved kidneys and gonads. Possibly before torsion the latter fused (or one was lost) with the solitary opening by way of the right (post-torsional) kidney. Reduction of the kidneys involved either one or other remaining functional and this had a profound effect on further evolution through its influence on the reproductive system.

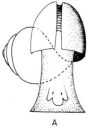

Diagrams showing change in posture of gastropod shell following asymmetrical coiling. A, dextrally coiled shell, unbalanced on head-foot; B, axis of coiling directed posteriorly; C, spire of directed upward, so restoring balance.

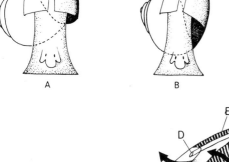

A

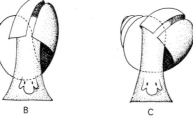

B   C

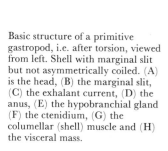

Basic structure of a primitive gastropod, i.e. after torsion, viewed from left. Shell with marginal slit but not asymmetrically coiled. (A) is the head, (B) the marginal slit, (C) the exhalant current, (D) the anus, (E) the hypobranchial gland (F) the ctenidium, (G) the columellar (shell) muscle and (H) the visceral mass.

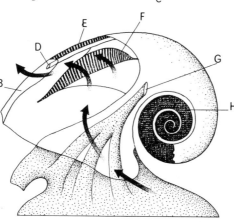

Diagrams (from posterior) of disposition of organs and currents in A, zygobranchous gastropod with slit; B, archaeogastropod with single aspidobranch ctenidium; C, mesogastropod with pectinibranch ctenidium. The osphradium is in each case seen as a dark circle or circles, the hypobranchial gland as a dark scalloped region on the upper surface and the gut as a thick black ring.

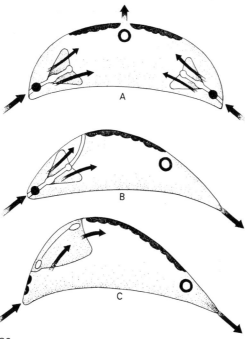

Where the right kidney remains functional it also serves as a reproductive duct but its function in this respect is necessarily limited to the outward passage of egg or sperm for later union in the sea. But where the left kidney is functional, the former right ureter becomes solely concerned with reproduction. It also extends forward by enclosure of a former groove along the right wall of the mantle cavity. Internal fertilisation now becomes possible. Glands are developed in the female for the formation of yolk and of protective capsules, and cavities for the reception of sperm. In the male a penis develops on the right side of the head. At copulation sperm is conveyed into the female genital system and after fertilisation albumen is laid down around the egg and a protective capsule formed around one or more eggs before these are laid. The fertilised eggs utilise the albumen to develop into miniatures of the adult. Internal fertilisation permits the invasion of new habitats, notably freshwaters and land. This is a consequence of having the functional kidney on the left side. Primitively gastropods are of separate sexes although there is a tendency towards protandry.

There is great variation in the form of the shelled gastropods. This is due to differences in growth gradients around the generative curve around the mantle margin where the shell is formed. An opercular plug is present except where the limpet form is assumed, a return to a primitive form (judging from *Neopilina*) which occurs repeatedly. The conical shell represents the last and greatly exaggerated whorl. The early coils soon disappear. All limpets hold tightly with the sucker-like foot pulling the shell tightly down for protection against adverse conditions. The radula with the jaws remains the usual feeding apparatus. The former may be broad with many teeth for scraping or narrower with fewer and larger teeth for seizing flesh. In the highly specialised Toxiglossa (*see* page 89) it is reduced to a single tooth. Some gastropods collect finely divided food, primarily plant plankton, by ciliary means. The pectinibranch gill is enlarged and the cilia which primitively were used to collect and dispose of sediment become concerned with feeding. This occurs in the Slipper Limpet or Slipper Shell (*Crepidula fornicata*), a North American species which has become very common in England following its introduction with relaid American oysters. The cemented vermetids with partly uncoiled or even straight shells feed either by cilia or by production of entangling mucous threads from glands which normally lubricate the foot.

Subclass Prosobranchea

These are typical shelled snails almost entirely marine and showing the full effects of torsion. They are the most numerous and varied of the gastropods. With the exception of the order Neritoidea (*see* page 88) few have penetrated into freshwater and fewer still have invaded land. With few exceptions they are of separate sexes and there is usually a free-swimming veliger larva.

Topshells, limpets
(Order Archaeogastropoda)

These are the most primitive gastropods, beginning with those (the Pleurotomariidae) which retain paired ctenidia, the big genus *Haliotis* which includes the large abalones of the Californian coast in which the flattened shell is perforated with a series of holes, the slit-limpets, genus *Puncturella*, and the larger keyhole limpets with a solitary apical opening which include the smaller genera *Fissurella* and *Diodora* and the larger *Megathura* (again from California) with a black mantle covering the shell.

The remaining archaeogastropods have lost the right ctenidium. They include the Trochacea or topshells common on all rocky shores. The largest species occur on coral reefs and include the great *Trochus niloticus* and the impressive Green Snail (*Turbo marmoreus*) which has a massive calcareous operculum. The smaller species of *Calliostoma* are common in temperate seas in both Atlantic and Pacific with *Gibbula* also on British and *Tegula* on American shores. Species of *Astraea*, allied to *Turbo*, occur on both American coasts.

Even more common are the limpets of the superfamily Patellacea or Docoglossa. Although there are many other types of limpets (including the keyhole species just mentioned), these are the commonest of all and few rocky shores free from the action of winter ice are without them. Particularly in the southern hemisphere they may be accompanied by the externally very similar pulmonate *Siphonaria* (*see* page 90). The Patellacea are of three types. There are those (family Acmaeidae) which possess a single aspidobranch ctenidium disposed sideways in the small mantle cavity. Such limpets are widespread but are particularly common in the Pacific. In North America there are some twenty species along the north Pacific coast and only two on the Atlantic side. In Great

Common Limpet (*Patella vulgata*) viewed from underside. The circular shell is normally held closely against the rock surface by the round sucker-like foot with which the animal also slowly moves. Between foot and shell is a pallial groove containing numerous secondary gills. The head with the single pair of tentacles denotes the anterior end.

A large conch moving over the sand on a Caribbean shore with its fleshy tongue-like foot extruded to perform the locomotion. This is the kind of shell which, with the end of the spiral cut off to blow through, has traditionally been used as a trumpet, as in the Tritons of mythology.

Britain there are only two small species of *Acmaea*. The common limpets on the east coast of the Atlantic are species of *Patella*, with *P. vulgaris* almost the commonest intertidal gastropod. In the Patellacea the ctenidium is lost and replaced functionally by a ring of respiratory leaflets (secondary gills) around the margin of the pallial groove. The third family, Lepetidae, is confined to deeper water and in this neither ctenidia nor secondary gills occur.

All of these archaeogastropods have a functional right kidney so that the reproductive system is not emancipated from dependence on the excretory system. The heart has two auricles even where one ctenidium is lost.

Order Neritoidea

Usually included within the archaeogastropods, these animals are very distinct. The left kidney is functional, the right kidney duct incorporated in the reproductive system. A penis is acquired in the male and a glandular genital tract in the female.

Internal fertilisation occurs and, in consequence, invasion of freshwaters and land. Largely a tropical group, species of the genera *Nerita* and *Neritina* occur on both oceanic shores of the United States but none in Britain. Neritacea only occur on rocky shores. In Great Britain there is a solitary freshwater species, *Theodoxus fluviatilis*, but there are many tropical freshwater and terrestrial species.

Periwinkles, slipper limpets (Order Mesogastropoda)

With almost negligible exceptions, these animals have a pectinibranch ctenidium and are all monotocardiate. They penetrate soft and often muddy substrates. Some have a siphonate extension on the left side of the mantle cavity, enabling them to draw in water from above the substrate in which they burrow. There is usually a corresponding siphonate extension of the shell. Internal fertilisation (except where secondarily lost) is universal. Egg capsules are often elaborate with young emerging as freely swimming veligers or with the adult form. Of very mixed feeding habits, there is some tendency towards change to a carnivorous habit with the mouth at the end of an everted

proboscis. The nervous system is somewhat more concentrated.

So varied are the mesogastropods that only a selection of the many diverse types occupying a variety of habitats can be mentioned. Among the least specialised are the ubiquitous periwinkles, species of *Littorina* which are absolutely characteristic of rocky shores the world over. The Common Periwinkle (*L. littorea*) together with *L. obtusata* which lives on fucoid weeds, and the northern Rough Periwinkle (*L. saxatilis*), which is viviparous, occur on both sides of the north Atlantic. The small *L. neritoides* lives so high that it is barely touched with spray except at spring tides. Related are the apple snails (genus *Pomatias*) and other terrestrial snails. The freshwater *Viviparus* is viviparous; in the freshwater genus, *Valvata*, the aspidobranch ctenidium is retained. All the terrestrial and freshwater prosobranchs have an operculum.

Returning to the sea, in which all other prosobranchs live, the superfamily Cerithiacea contains animals which have lost internal fertilisation. The turret shells, genus *Turritella*, with species on relatively shallow, muddy bottoms in all seas, feed by cilia. They draw in sperm by the same means as the cemented vermetids already mentioned. The beautiful species of *Janthina* have the opposite habit, living in surface waters supported by a float of air entrapped in mucus formed by the pedal glands. They are carnivorous. Unrelated prosobranchs found near the surface are heteropods such as *Atlanta*, which retains a complete although very delicate transparent shell, and others such as *Pterotrachea* without a shell. These are very active animals which swim upside down with the laterally compressed foot acting as a fin. The heteropods are carnivorous. In *Pterotrachea* one sees the complete dominance of the head-foot, just as in *Vermetus* the visceropallium entirely controls form.

Mesogastropod limpets include the Slipper Limpet (*Crepidula fornicata*) which forms chains, the lowest of which are females and the highest (and so youngest) are males which fertilise the females beneath. The cap-of-liberty shells (genus *Capulus*) are related but solitary; related to these are *Thyca*, small blue limpets parasitic on tropical starfishes. Unrelated snails such as *Enteroxenos* live within the body cavity of sea cucumbers (Holothuria) and, except as larvae, have no resemblance to molluscs.

The tropical conches such as the Great Green Conch (*Strombus gigas*) of the West Indies and the impressive Indo-Pacific spider shells (genus *Pterocera*) are browsing herbivores protected by a massive shell. The elongated operculum digs into the sand to give periodic purchase as the animal lurches along. The burrowing pelican's foot shell (genus *Aporrhais*) of moderate depths in north temperate seas is also a strombid or conch. The rounded moonshells (genera *Natica* and *Polynices*, the latter exclusively American) live under sand, seizing and boring into bivalves. The numerous, largely tropical cowries (family Cypraeidae) crawl over and feed on selected animals such as sea squirts and soft corals. Certain slug-like mesogastropods (genera *Velutina* and *Lamellaria*) have similar feeding habits. Unlike the 'true' sea slugs (*see* page 90) they have only one pair of tentacles.

Whelks, oysterdrills and conches
(Order Neogastropoda)

Here evolution in the prosobranchs culminates. The nervous system is more concentrated and sense-organs better developed. All are carnivorous with an eversible proboscis. The genera *Buccinum* and *Busycon* are examples of large scavenging whelks. The smaller but ubiquitous dogwhelks, largely species of *Thais* (or *Nucella*), are intertidal, living on acorn barnacles, mussels and so on. The American oysterdrills (genus *Urosalpinx*), now also a pest on British oyster beds, and the European *Ocinebra* bore through the shells of bivalves. The smooth-shelled olive and pencil shells (genera *Oliva* and *Terebra* move just below the surface of sand, as do the rounded 'cameo-shells', (genus *Cassis*), which include the great helmet shells. A small group occupies rounded cavities within the calcareous skeletons of living corals. Finally, there are the poisonous toxiglossids, species of the tropical genus *Conus*, which pounce on their prey which they then poison and swallow whole.

Sea slugs (Subclass Opisthobranchia)

In these exclusively marine gastropods, the shell is reduced, internal or lost; this permits detorsion, the mantle cavity moving back to the right, opening out and finally disappearing. A secondary—purely external—bilateral symmetry is attained in the sea slugs. The visceral nerve loop becomes untwisted and shortened. With loss of the shell comes a striking adaptive range in form, colour, feeding habit and locomotion. All opisthobranchs are hermaphrodite, usually with reduced free-swimming larvae. Where the shell is lost the animals are difficult to preserve with any indication of their often bizarre form and striking colours. They should be studied alive.

Canoe and bubble shells
(Order Cephalaspidea = Bullomorpha)

These inhabit sandy or muddy bottoms and retain a sizeable shell (notably demonstrated by the barrel shells—genus *Actaeon*) into which the animal can completely withdraw. The shell is often scroll-like, as in the canoe shells (genus *Scaphander*), the bubble shells (genera *Bulla* and *Haminaea*) and in *Philine*. The head may occupy over half the length of the body, serving as a shield in burrowing. The large foot has lateral parapodia which extend upwards around mantle and shell. These animals are carnivorous, often with calcareous crushing plates in the stomach.

Sea hares
(Order Aplysiacea = Anaspidea)

Here are included the widely distributed sea hares (genus *Aplysia*). The thin shell is completely enclosed; the animals are effectively 'slugs' but with large parapodia which may be used in swimming. The mantle cavity is on the right side and contains a large gill as well as a conspicuous 'purple gland' which produces a copious, probably protective, secretion. Green weed is cropped with jaws and there is a large crop for its storage and initial digestion.

Sea butterflies
(Order Thecosomata)

These are shelled pteropods with a mantle cavity and a transparent shell, spirally wound or pointed or else replaced by a remarkable gelatinous 'pseudoconch'. All are planktonic and often—as *Limacina*—extremely abundant. The parapodia become 'wings' for swimming and plant plankton is collected by their ciliated 'fields'.

Order Gymnosomata

These are 'naked' pteropods in which the small, elongated body has parapodial fins. There is no mantle cavity. They move relatively quickly after their animal prey, often thecomatous pteropods. Food is seized by tentacles which are sometimes armed with suckers.

Order Notaspidea
(= Pleurobranchomorpha)

These are larger, flattened animals with a reduced internal shell but without a mantle cavity, the large plume-like gill on the right being overhung

Sea hares (the species shown here is *Aplysia punctata*, of Europe) look like slugs but they have a shell, which is inside the body.

Sea-slugs (formerly known as Nudibranchia, or naked gills) are often brightly coloured and the dorsal surface is ornamented with fleshy processes known as cerata. Some sea-slugs feed on hydroids and the nematocysts from these migrate from the sea-slug's stomach into the cerata and are used by the sea-slug to sting its enemies. This remarkable process is not understood.

by the mantle. The common genus *Pleurobranchus* (*Oscanius*) swims with the parapodia; it is carnivorous, feeding on large sea squirts.

Order Acochlidiacea
These are minute animals which live in the intertidal spaces between sand grains on a saturated sea beach. They have only a few external features, and are without shells, however, they do have protective spicules.

Order Sacoglossa
An interesting group of small opisthobranchs with much the same habit as the plant bugs on land. Although ranging in form from shelled, spirally coiled animals to naked 'slugs', all feed on green weeds, penetrating the cells with a piercing radula and sucking out the contents with a pump-like pharynx. They conform in colour with their host plant, e.g. the common European *Elysia viridis*,

named for its green colour, is often found feeding on green algae of the genus *Codium*.

True sea slugs
(Order Acoela = Nudibranchia)
Except in larval life there is no shell or mantle cavity and secondary gills are produced in a ring round the median anus. The dorsal surface often has processes known as cerata in which nematocysts (sting cells) from coelenterate prey may be stored for protection, or again as branching lateral processes in the larger species of the genera *Tritonia* and *Dendronotus*. All are externally symmetrical with two pairs of tentacles. They undergo annual migrations, coming inshore to spawn. Feeding habits are most diverse, almost every genus having its particular food organism including sponges, hydroids, fish eggs, etc. Sea slugs are often strikingly coloured and most beautiful animals.

The Great Pond Snail (*Limnaea stagnalis*) is omnivorous but feeds largely on animal matter. It may even kill a newt or a small fish. It eats the larvae of the carnivorous water beetle (*Dytiscus*) but is in turn eaten by the adult beetle. *Limnaea* also eats the young of its own species.

The Great Black Slug (*Arion ater*), of Europe, will try to eat almost anything plant or animal, even newspaper. Despite its vernacular name it is by no means always black. It may be white, yellow, red or brown.

Subclass Pulmonata

The mantle cavity is vascularised, forming a lung with a small contractile aperture, the pneumostome; anus and ureter open outside this. The coiled shell may be rounded, flattened or elongate; the limpet form may be assumed or the shell reduced or lost. But even in the last there is no complete detorsion. The visceral nerve cord is lost owing to the concentration round the oesophagus of all nerve ganglia, i.e. the visceral ganglia move forward. There is a complicated hermaphrodite reproductive system. There is no operculum. With far less structural modification than in the opisthobranchs, this subclass includes the extremely numerous and highly successful land snails and slugs, with many others in freshwaters and some on the seashore.

Order Basommatophora
These are largely aquatic snails such as the Common Spired Pond Snail (genus *Lymnaea*) or the discoidal genus *Planorbis*. There is one pair of non-invaginable tentacles with eyes at the base. Air usually enters the lung but occasionally water; secondary gills occur outside the cavity (as in the genera *Planorbis* and *Physa*), or within it in the marine family Siphonariidae, the common shore limpets in much of the southern hemisphere. The freshwater limpets such as species of the genus *Ancylus* respire through the body surface. All are probably herbivorous.

Order Geophila (= Stylommatophora)
The hosts of land snails, for example, the ubiquitous Helicinidae, and the slugs, species of the genera *Limax*, *Arion*, etc., are here included. The immediate difference is possession of two pairs of tentacles with eyes on the tips of the hind pair. The major adaptations concern resistance to desiccation and to cold. They may hibernate and they may aestivate. The lung functions but in the tropical family Vaginulidae respiration is through the moist integument. The great majority are herbivorous but slugs of the family Testacellidae, with a small shell at the posterior end and suitably modified radula, are carnivorous and feed off earthworms.

Tooth or tusk shells (Class Scaphopoda)

This is the smallest molluscan class with the mantle fused ventrally to form the characteristic tapering, tubular 'tusk' shell. Exclusively marine, they burrow in sand with the three-lobed foot which issues from the wide end; a respiratory current enters and leaves the other end which projects above the surface. The reduced head bears paired clusters of food-collecting captacula. There are no ctenidia. Sexes are separate with external fertilisation. The few genera live in deep water.

Bivalves (Class Bivalvia = Lamellibranchia = Pelecypoda)

This great group consists of symmetrical, laterally compressed molluscs with mantle lobes enclosing the body and forming a shell of two calcareous valves with a connecting, uncalcified ligament. Interlocking valve teeth form the hinge. The valves 'gape' except when drawn together by contraction of the two primitive adductors which have evolved by enlargement of pallial muscles; paired shell muscles withdraw the laterally compressed foot. The head is lost, contact with the environment being via the mantle margin which, in the region where water enters, carries tentacles and sometimes eyes. There is no radula but the ctenidia are greatly enlarged and strain finely divided food from the increased water current. Between them and the mouth on each side is a pair of ciliated labial palps which control what passes into the gut. Sexes are usually separate although protandry is not uncommon and sex may alternate. Fertilisation is always external but may occur in the mantle cavity or in chambers in the ctenidia where the larvae are then incubated (e.g. in the flat oysters—genus *Ostrea*—and freshwater mussels). There is usually a free-swimming larva.

The whole form is adapted for life within and progress through soft substrates, and bivalves are the most numerous and successful of 'infaunal' invertebrates. They have successfully invaded freshwaters. In contrast to gastropods, the bivalves appear very homogeneous, and only a very few, notably the shipworms, are not obviously bivalves. They have exploited every possibility of life on the sea bottom and freshwater and may occur in populations of astronomic proportions.

Subclass Protobranchia

These bivalves display a mixture of primitive and very specialised characters. The basic structure is shown in the genus *Nucula* (nut shells) which go back to the Palaeozoic era. The ctenidia retain the primitive structure although the filaments increase in number extending further forward. As in all the bivalves, they are suspended from the roof of a mantle cavity that surrounds the body. The anterior inhalant current is filtered through the ctenidia and leaves posteriorly. Feeding is here primarily the concern of extensions of the outer palp folds, of the proboscides which extend beyond the shell and collect organic deposits, passing them along a ciliated groove for selection between the ridged palp lamellae. Only minor food supplies come from the ctenidia. The large foot has four pairs of retractor muscles. Movement is horizontal and just below the surface. The reproductive organs open through the kidney ducts.

Other genera such as *Yoldia* feed in the same way but have remarkably elaborate 'pumping' ctenidia, drawing in water largely by muscular means. Species of *Yoldia* live vertically disposed with the inhalant current entering posteriorly through a short siphon ventral to the exhalant current. This condition prevails in most bivalves, enabling them to burrow deeply for protection while drawing in water for feeding and respiration.

The other protobranchs have enlarged ctenidia and excessively small palps without proboscides.

Subclass Lamellibranchia

Included here are the great majority of bivalves. The ctenidial filaments are elongated and reflected, forming lamellae, and the two arms are united by interlamellar junctions. Adjacent filaments are united by cilia (filibranch condition) or more often by tissue junctions (eulamellibranch condition). The number of filaments greatly increases so that the mantle cavity on either side is largely occupied by two downward-descending lamellae. These enlarged ctenidia constitute animated sieves of the greatest efficiency. They are the sole feeding organs, the palps being concerned with selection of the finely divided food, suspended plant plankton or deposited organic matter. The pedal (i.e. shell) muscles are reduced to two pairs, anterior and posterior.

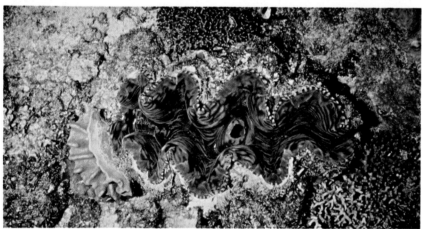

Part of a mussel bed on the coast of Wales. The Common or Edible Mussel (*Mytilus edulis*) is widespread, extremely numerous, used as food or for bait and, by the extensive clusters it forms on them, protects pier piles, sea walls and the like from erosion by waves.

Giant Clam (*Tridacna gigas*) on an Indo-Pacific coral reef. This is the largest bivalve ever evolved and may reach 1.5 metres in length. The thickened mantle margins (seen within the shell valves) contain microscopic plant cells (zooxanthellae) on which it feeds.

The typical lamellibranch has a rounded or elliptical shell as in the cockles (genus *Cardium*) or the American Hard-shell Clam or Quahaug (*Mercenaria mercenaria = Venus mercenaria*) the animals living close under the surface and having very short siphons. By appropriate changes in the growth gradients around the mantle margins, the shell alters in form. It may elongate as in the razor shells (genera *Solen* or *Ensis*) which, with the aid of the plunger-like foot, move vertically up and down; or it may become oval with accompanying development of very long siphons. The foot is reduced and the fused siphons are mobile. A typical deep burrower is the American Soft-shell Clam (*Mya arenaria*) also common round Great Britain. The deposit-feeding superfamily Tellinacea (genera *Tellina*, *Macoma*, *Abra*, *Scrobicularia*) have long, separate inhalant and exhalant siphons but are also very mobile with a large foot. Burrowing and also 'nestling' in crevices has led to boring in rock and wood. The majority of rock borers, for example, the common piddocks and species of the genus *Rocellaria*, bore by abrasion with the shell valves. The date mussels (genus *Lithophaga*), which are confined to calcareous rocks, penetrate by chemical means. Always the food consists of suspended matter entering through the inhalant siphon.

The shipworms (family Teredinidae) bore into wood. Allied to the pholads, the shell is reduced to a small but highly efficient wood-cutting tool which is held against the head of the boring by the foot which is a sucker. Some part of the energy used in boring comes from the wood fragments which pass through the gut where the cellulose is digested.

Bivalves have also established themselves on hard substrates that is from 'infaunal' they have become 'epifaunal'. When the larvae settle after planktonic life they attach temporarily by horny 'byssal' threads produced by a gland in the foot. In some bivalves this byssus persists and the adult is attached, as in the widely distributed mussels (genus *Mytilus*), beds of which are illustrated. Attachment leads to major reorganisation. The anterior adductor is first reduced (as in *Mytilus*) and the posterior end of the animal enlarged, and then the anterior adductor is lost with consequent reorganisation around the solitary, centrally placed, posterior adductor. This is so in the scallops (family Pectinidae), all of which are initially byssally attached, the majority becoming free as adults when they swim, holding the valves horizontally. The rock scallops (genus *Hinnites*) and the 'thorny oysters' (genus *Spondylus*) become cemented by the right valve. The edible oysters (family Ostreidae) are also cemented but by the left valve: they have lost the foot. This last family contains flat oysters such as the European *Ostrea edulis* and the elongate, cupped American, Portuguese and Japanese oysters (*Crassostrea virginica*, *C. angulata* and *C. gigas*). These are the most numerous and important of commercial bivalves. In genus *Ostrea* the larvae are incubated but not in the genus *Crassostrea*. There is alternation of sexes.

The largest bivalves ever evolved belong to the tropical family Tridacnidae. *Tridacna gigas* may be over 120 centimetres long. These animals literally farm immense populations of single-celled plants (zooxanthellae) in siphonal tissues which are directed upwards and greatly extended in length and breadth to form richly coloured, scalloped margins. The form of the animal has been profoundly modified by this association, the mantle and shell having in effect swung round the body in the vertical plane, and the hinge finally beside the foot on the underside.

The final group of the Lamellibranchia is known as the Anomalodesmata on account of the anomalous or unusual appearance and habits of many of its members. Some are confined to outlying parts of the world such as southeast Australia, others occur in the abyssal seas. These are the septibranchs with ctenidia modified to form a muscular, perforated septum periodically lifted to draw in a sudden current containing dead or moribund animals through the inhalant siphon. The reduced but muscular palps push this food into the large mouth; the stomach is a crushing gizzard. Although the great majority of such animals live in profound depths, species of the genus *Cuspidaria* with a characteristic siphonal shell extension occur in moderate depths in muddy gravel. In addition there is the extraordinary 'watering-can shell', *Penicillus*, which occurs in sand on some tropical shores. It consists of a sometimes sizable tube, open at the upper end but closed by a rounded perforated palate, like a watering-can rose, at the other. A pair of small flattened valves on one side near the base is the only external indication that this is a bivalve.

Squids, cuttlefishes, octopuses (Class Cephalopoda)

Much of the most elaborately constructed and active molluscs are the cephalopods. All are predacious carnivores with a highly concentrated central nervous system within a protective cartilaginous cranium and with sense-organs, notably image-forming eyes, equivalent to those of vertebrates. They must have evolved from primitive crawling molluscs by formation of a chambered, gas-filled shell which lowered specific gravity and permitted life in mid waters where they became the dominant organisms. There was a major tendency for coiling, as in the extinct ammonites, but without loss of bilateral symmetry. The mantle cavity, while remaining the respiratory chamber, became modified as an organ of jet propulsion with the foot converted into a funnel directing the propulsive stream. Circulation within the cavity was controlled by muscular contraction. The head became surrounded by highly mobile tentacles now armed with suckers and sometimes hooks. In the course of evolution the shell became internal (except in *Nautilus*) or was effectively lost. Cleared of this encumbrance, cephalopods gained speed, made further possible by a heightened metabolic rate due to a more efficient circulatory system. Modifications involve a more powerful ventricle, an arterial system leading to capillaries, recollection of blood into veins and appearance of branchial hearts which drive blood through a second set of capillaries within the extended surface offered by the ctenidia. The kidneys are enlarged and the 'pancreas' is also excretory. The gut is adapted for dealing with animal food. There are powerful 'jaws' and a small radula, and digestion is entirely extracellular, within the lumen of the stomach

The Common Octopus (*Octopus vulgaris*) of the Atlantic and Pacific, showing the double row of suckers on the underside of each of the eight arms. The usual food is crabs: the octopus covering the crab with its arms as with a tent and attacking the crustacean with its parrot-like beak, which is at the centre of the complex of arms.

and that of either the large caecum or the 'liver'. Sexes are separate, with the functions of the penis performed by one of the tentacles which conveys packets of spermatazoa (spermatophores) into the female mantle cavity. Here nidamental glands produce protective capsules with yolky eggs from which the young hatch as miniature parents.

As finally evolved the cephalopod form represents an extension of the dorso-ventral axis but with the head moved round to the ventral side (former underside) which now goes in front while the posterior mantle cavity lies on the topographical underside. The former conflicting antero-posterior and dorso-ventral axes become merged.

Subclass Nautiloidea

This once abundant class with a straight or coiled external shell is now represented by three species of *Nautilus* in the west Pacific and eastern Indian oceans. The coiled shell has many gas-filled chambers with mantle tissues extending through a central siphuncle. The head-foot can be completely withdrawn into the shell with the opening closed by a fleshy hood. Respiration being then impossible, this occurs only as an emergency reaction to danger. The head also carries many tentacular retractile appendages which have no suckers. The flexible pallial funnel consists of two curled, applied surfaces which by their movements produce

the pallial water flow for respiration and for jet propulsion.

Nautilus is tetrabranchiate with two pairs of ctenidia, auricles and kidneys, a duplication possibly associated with a primitive circulation without branchial hearts. The nervous system although elaborate is simpler than in other cephalopods. The eyes have no lens. These are carnivorous molluscs, although their mode of feeding has never been observed. They have nearly neutral buoyancy and appear to rest on the bottom by day, rising above this by night. They inhabit depths down to 200 metres.

Subclass Coleoidea

These dibranchiate animals constitute the remainder of the living cephalopods. The mantle is external and the wall of the pallial cavity extremely muscular. This, instead of the funnel in the tetrabranchiate *Nautilus*, provides the force for propulsion. The jet is directed by the funnel which

A Squid (*Sepioteuthis sepioidea*) hovering in mid-water. Unlike the octopus, squid have two long arms in addition to the usual eight arms. These are normally held drawn in but can be shot out like a pair of tongs, at lightning-speed, to seize prey.

Squids (Order Teuthoidea)

The squids which have torpedo-shaped, streamlined bodies with terminal fins are highly adapted inhabitants of surface waters and include the fastest marine invertebrates. The various species of *Loligo* and allied genera are extremely numerous. Although themselves amongst the most efficient of predators, they are a major source of food for other animals such as fishes and seals. They collect in great numbers on the bottom for reproduction and produce enormous masses of gelatinous spawn. The adults then die.

Squids of deeper waters have blunter and wider bodies and include the Giant Squid (genus *Architeuthis*), the largest invertebrate whose fully extended tentacular arms are five times the four-metre length of the body. These squids are preyed upon by sperm whales. Oceanic squids of the family Cranchiidae, which hang almost motionless in the sea, have an unusual buoyancy mechanism consisting of an enlarged coelomic (body) cavity filled with ammonium chloride.

Octopuses (Order Octopoda)

There are here no long tentacular arms. The common octopods (family Polypoidea) have a sac-like body without fins or skeleton. Although they do employ jet propulsion, they frequently crawl with the tentacles. They usually inhabit crevices in rocks from which they dart out on their prey. The egg masses resemble bunches of small, blackish grapes. The related family Argonautidae is pelagic with the sexes strikingly dissimilar. By means of membranes on a pair of modified arms the female forms an adventitious shell, the well-known 'paper nautilus', in which she lives and in which the eggs are deposited. The male is very small and, as in some other octopods, at copulation the modified arm which carries the spermatophores becomes detached after insertion in the mantle cavity of the female. Originally thought to be a parasite, the detached arm continues to bear the name hectocotylus.

The deep-sea octopods or Cirroteuthoidae probably live near, rather than on, the bottom at great depths. They have greatly modified, short bodies which are soft and gelatinous and bear fins. They probably swim primarily by the action of the deeply webbed arms.

Flying squid (Order Vampyromorpha)

The small, purplish-black 'Vampire Squid' (*Vampyromorpha infernalis*) was formerly classified with the octopods. But in addition to eight arms united by a swimming web, it also possesses two long sensory filaments which can be retracted into special pockets. They are totally different from the long, tentacular arms of the decapods. The body is covered with small light organs, and at the base of each fin there is a larger organ from which the light can be admitted or excluded by the action of an 'eye-lid'. The animals inhabit depths between 1,000 and 2,000 metres in the subtropical and tropical oceans. Since young stages are also taken from these depths it appears that all their life is spent there.

is here an open-ended cylinder and highly mobile so that the animal—proceeding in the opposite direction to the jet—can move with ease in any direction. Associated with a circulatory system involving capillaries and branchial hearts there is one pair of auricles and one of kidneys. There are always at least four pairs of sucker-bearing arms. A pouch from the gut near the anus forms an ink-sac, the product of which, expelled through the anus and funnel, forms a concealing smoke screen or else a 'dummy' to distract the attention of an enemy. The camera eye, with lens and highly developed retina, is comparable to that of vertebrates. Pigment cells, under the direct control of the nervous system, permit rapid colour change. Light organs or photophores are particularly numerous and elaborate in deep-sea species. With the possession of a complex brain, *Octopus*, as shown experimentally, has the capacity to learn by experience. It is probably not so well endowed as the more active squids which, however, cannot be so easily kept in captivity.

Cuttlefishes (Order Sepioidea)

In these cephalopods the eight normal arms are supplemented by a pair of long retractile arms, with suckers confined to the ends which are clubbed. The arms are shot out with great precision to seize prey. The order comprises the cuttlefishes. Species of the genus *Sepia* are common and very characteristic cuttlefishes. The broad body is fringed on each side by a long undulating fin. The animals live in shallow water on a sandy bottom, rising above this by buoyancy adjustment within the internal shell or cuttlebone which consists of thin chambers laid down one below the other during growth. The oldest chambers contain gas. As in *Nautilus*, these cuttlefishes swim and hunt at night; during the day they bury themselves in the sand. The smaller species of the genus *Sepiola*, with rounded bodies and small fins, also live on the bottom but *Spirula spirula* which has a coiled internal shell with a siphuncle, is an inhabitant of oceanic depths; it is bathypelagic.

PEANUT WORMS OR SIPUNCULIDS
(Phylum Sipuncula)

The sipunculids comprise a distinct group of exclusively marine animals, the members of which may be easily recognised. There are about 250 described species. They are worm-like, with a long, cylindrical body, but this is unsegmented and is formed from two regions. The anterior one is a more or less slender 'introvert' which is constantly run in and out of the plumper main part of the body. The body cavity is a continuous coelomic space containing the gut, excretory organ or organs, and the gonads which produce the eggs or sperm according to sex. The coelomic fluid contains large numbers of free cells, some of which are red from the respiratory pigment, haemery-thrin, which they contain. This pigment is functionally like haemoglobin, but is chemically quite different. It is known to occur elsewhere in the animal kingdom only in the polychaete worm *Magelona*. The mouth of sipunculoids opens at the tip of the introvert, and leads to a coiled gut which loops forward to open in the mid-dorsal line at a conspicuous anus near the base of the introvert. The tip of the introvert around the mouth may be simply lobed or extended into branched tentacles used for feeding.

In older books the sipunculids may be found classed as annelids or 'appended' to the annelids. They are certainly no more closely related to them than are the molluscs, but sipunculids do show two structural features reminiscent of annelids: the nephridia, of which there may be a pair or only a single one, and the nervous system. The nervous system consists of a dorsal brain related to a ventral nerve cord by two connectives forming a ring round the gut. The ventral nerve cord, however, shows no sign of segmentation.

The most noticeable feature of sipunculids is the introvert. The turgid state of the body of the 'peanut worms' which belong here, is also notable, but this is not characteristic of all sipunculids.

Sipunculids are sedentary in habit, living in permanent or semi-permanent burrows in mud or muddy sand, in fissures in rocks, under stones or amongst algal holdfasts. Many may be found intertidally, but some occur in depths up to 5,000 metres. They are typical, nevertheless, of the littoral and of shallow coastal seas. Various species of *Golfingia*, *Phascolosoma* and *Dendrostoma*—the latter with bushy tentacles round the rim of the introvert—are the most likely to be seen between tidemarks.

The sexes are separate. There is a heavy preponderance of females in many species, but the sex of the individual cannot be distinguished externally. The eggs and sperm are discharged into the sea through the excretory nephridia. A trochophore type of larva develops which, after a time (variable from one day to a month according to species), transforms and eventually sinks into the sea floor.

ECHIUROID WORMS
(Phylum Echiuroidea)

Echiuroid worms are bulbous marine animals of uncertain classification that live in rock crevices or burrow in sand. They have a proboscis for feeding and strain small particles from the surrounding water.

In the last century naturalists united the Echiuroidea and the Sipuncula into a heterogeneous group known as the Gophyrea and placed them near the annelids. The sipunculoids are certainly very distinct and have no close relationship either to the annelids or to the echiuroids. While the echiuroids may be somewhat nearer the annelids, the two groups must have diverged from a common stock at an early stage in their evolution. Adult echiuroids show no signs of segmentation but they do have a pair of annelid-like bristles near the anterior end of their bodies and some have several at the hind end as well.

Most echiuroids are found in mud or under stones and fissures in rocks, and the most noticeable feature is the grooved, often gutter-like proboscis which extends from the plump and commonly rather short body. It was this division of the body into an anterior 'proboscis' and a posterior 'trunk' region which led the earlier naturalists to group the echiuroids and sipunculids together. But even this resemblance is superficial, since the echiuroid proboscis, unlike the sipunculid introvert, cannot be retracted. It is, nevertheless, a highly mobile and sensitive organ. It is used for feeding, and while in some forms such as *Thalassema* it may be short, funnel-like or shovel-like, in others, such as *Bonellia*, it may be very long and bifurcated at the tip.

Some echiuroids may be large. *Urechis caupo* in central California looks like a large, uncooked sausage. It may be twenty-five centimetres long and 2·5 centimetres across; *Ikeda taeniodes* in Japan can be over thirty centimetres in length and has a proboscis which may be extended for over a metre when searching for food.

These large mud-dwelling echiuroids live in U-shaped burrows which are often used as refuges by other invertebrates such as small crabs and scaleworms, or even by small fishes. The mobile proboscis is normally extended from the burrow to suck up the debris and rich surface mud. *Urechis* has a relatively short proboscis and feeds in a rather different manner. It secretes a sack-shaped membrane of mucus across the burrow. Water is driven through the burrow by vigorous pumping movements of the body, and particles suspended in the water are caught on the mucous sack. This is then eaten and a new sack secreted. The mucus forms a highly efficient net, straining from the water virtually all particles larger than four millimicrons.

The sexes are separate and the gametes are shed into the sea where fertilisation occurs. The larva which develops usually remains free-swimming for a relatively long time, a month or more according to the species. *Bonellia viridis* found in the Mediterranean is unusual and very specialised in that the male is a minute creature which lives as a parasite in the much larger female.

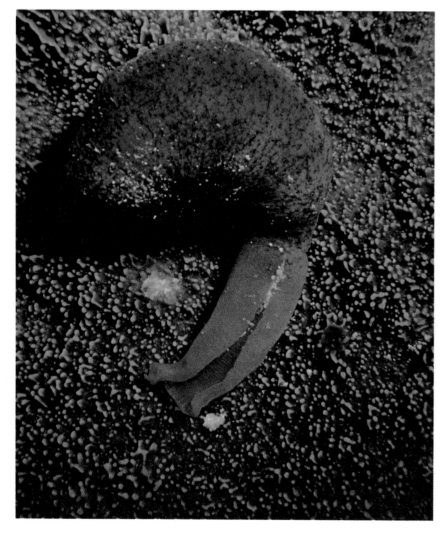

SEGMENTED WORMS
(Phylum Annelida)

The annelids include the Polychaeta, the Oligochaeta and the leeches or Hirudinea. The polychaetes are almost exclusively marine. The oligochaetes include the earthworms and several types of freshwater worms. The leeches are also mainly characteristic of freshwater, but some are found on marine animals and in wet places on land.

Structure

Annelids are all soft-bodied creatures without hard skeletons. The epidermis secretes a thin cuticle, but this is pliant. Chitinous bristles or chaetae are also secreted and these help in movement, but they have been lost in leeches. The cuticle of the gullet in some annelids forms thickened projections called teeth or 'jaws' which function in food capture and in defence.

The annelid body is essentially a cylinder of muscle arranged in segmental units enclosing a fluid-filled (coelomic) cavity. Beneath the epidermis is a layer of circular muscle and beneath this a layer of longitudinal muscles. These are antagonistic because the fluid in the coelom is incompressible, so that contraction of one causes deformation of the other. The coelom thus acts as a kind of 'hydrostatic' skeleton.

Each segment is related to the outside by a pair of excretory nephridia and a pair of ducts which bear the sex cells or gametes to the exterior. These two kinds of duct are variously related and in some species one may serve both purposes. In most annelids this plan is modified in relation to their excretory and reproductive needs.

The whole series of segments is bounded by an anterior prostomium and by a posterior pygidium. In polychaetes the prostomium contains the brain and bears special sense-organs—tentacles, eyes, palps and such. In oligochaetes and leeches the brain is farther back and the prostomium is simple. In polychaetes the pygidium may also bear sensory tentacles.

Three systems unite the segments into a functional whole: the gut which passes from the mouth at the base of the prostomium through every segment to open at the anus on the pygidium; the vascular system; and the nervous system.

There are often more internal differences to this basic pattern than one would expect. The segmen-

tal arrangement of the body is related to locomotion and movement. It is generally worms which have become sedentary or which have changed their mode of movement that have modified this plan most obviously. The prostomium, untrammelled by these considerations, is particularly variable in development. At one end of the scale it may be expanded into an elaborate feeding crown of tentacles, as in sedentary tube-dwellers such as the feather-duster worms; at the other, reduced to an insignificant cone, as in forms which burrow actively.

The marine bristle worms, the polychaetes, show the most variety, and the various kinds of earthworms and leeches are, by comparison, little different one from another. Consequently, the main families of polychaetes are described separately here while the main families of the other two classes are described together.

Feeding

Many worms live in the silt or mud of estuaries, in sand on the seashore, or at the bottom of ponds and ditches. They all live on the organic matter in the mud—other and smaller organisms or their remains. Such worms are generally cylindrical, with a simple conical prostomium fitting them for burrowing. Often they have some kind of proboscis which can be protruded, or a pharynx adapted to suck in the food. Special sense-organs

A marine bristle worm, *Spirobranchus gigantea*, that lives on coral heads and builds itself a calcareous tube into which it can withdraw for protection. To feed and breed the worm pushes its head out from the top of the tube and unfolds two spiral systems of tentacles. The species is the most common reef polychaete in the Caribbean and the Indo-Pacific.

such as tentacles and eyes are generally reduced but various sense receptors in the skin are, nevertheless, present. Even earthworms are far more selective in feeding than is supposed, and turn away from light.

The most nutritious mud is on the surface, for not only does it receive matter from the water above, it also supports a population of micro-organisms. The habit of selecting the organic detritus in the mud has led to the evolution of many ways of doing this by means of tentacles. There are many families of polychaetes described below which show these developments. The terebellids and spionids are two examples. A further transition from feeding on surface particles to particles suspended in the water may be seen in the sabellid and serpulid feather-duster worms. Here the prostomial crown is held expanded above the opening of the tube or burrow and cilia on each filament cause water to pass through it. Particles in suspension are caught in mucus and conveyed along ciliary gutters to the mouth in the centre of the crown.

More active worms generally have well-developed eyes and tentacles and, in the Polychaeta, well-developed paddle-like parapodia to help in crawling or swimming. Many seashore worms such as *Phyllodoce*, crawl among the weeds in search of food, and some are actively carnivorous. They often have an eversible proboscis armed with jaws and teeth, but many—the amphinomids and eunicids, for example—may use these for rasping off algae, hydroids and sponges growing on rocks. The leeches are perhaps the most specialised annelid predators, some being really parasites and confined to a single host which they seldom leave. The mouth and gut are adapted for taking meals of blood; and often to taking large meals at long intervals.

Respiration

Small worms usually have no difficulty in meeting their respiratory requirements by diffusion through the skin, but larger worms commonly have gills of some kind. Earthworms, some of which may be very long, are never thicker than one's finger. They have a particularly well-vascularised skin. Worms which live either in freshwater or in the sea often live in burrows or tubes which are irrigated by the worm in order to respire. Water is thereby drawn over the general body surface and the gills. Most tubes and burrows have an inhalant and an exhalant aperture

for this reason and may be simply U-shaped. In polychaetes gills are often filamentous or arborescent extensions from the parapodia, but they are sometimes extensions of the body wall, unrelated to parapodia though still segmental in arrangement. In either case they are commonly paired. The sabellids and serpulids use their crown for respiration as well as for feeding.

Living in silts and mud where the organic matter is high, many worms are faced with conditions of poor oxygen supply. These difficulties are met either by irrigation of the burrow or by gills which are exposed on the surface. Most worms have the red blood pigment haemoglobin dissolved in the blood plasma and a few have an allied greenish pigment, chlorocruorin.

The development in the earthworms and leeches of a good capillary blood supply to the skin, kept moist with fluid, enables them to respire in air with the skin acting as a lung. They are, of course, restricted to places with a high humidity because of the dangers of water loss: in soil, in rotting vegetation and in tropical forests.

Reproduction and development

It is well known that an earthworm which loses a few of the most posterior segments can regenerate those that are lost. Many other worms have an even better ability to regenerate missing parts and may even reproduce themselves in his way, the anterior part regenerating a new tail, and forming a new head on the part which breaks away. Many syllid polychaetes develop new heads at definite intervals along the body, each part eventually breaking off as a separate individual. Some small freshwater oligochaetes habitually reproduce themselves vegetatively and rarely, if ever, reproduce sexually.

In most polychaete annelids the sexes are separate, the eggs or sperm maturing in the coelom to be released into the sea where fertilisation occurs. While there is much variety of behaviour, the actual time of spawning is commonly related to the lunar or tidal cycle and may occur on only one or two days or nights in the whole year. Nereids metamorphose in the months preceding this spawning period into the heteronereid form which is better able to swim to the surface, congregating to spawn. The common *Nereis diversicolor* of western Europe is exceptional in not undergoing metamorphosis and spawning in the mud. In the eunicid 'palolo' worms the gametes develop in the hinder segments of the body and these break away to writhe, headless, to the surface, the anterior end remaining to regenerate and spawn another time. All these processes of metamorphosis, regeneration and the onset of sexual maturity are delicately balanced and under hormonal control.

While most polychaetes are dioecious, that is with separate sexes, some are hermaphrodite, with testes producing sperm and ovaries producing eggs being found in the same individual. Usually only one or other is functional at one time, the sex of the worm changing with age. Both the oligochaetes and the leeches are exclusively hermaphrodite and have developed mechanisms for transforming sperm to each other without fertilising themselves. The sperm are generally received into special spermathecae in which they are stored

Earthworms are hermaphrodite and mating entails the exchange of sperms. Two worms in adjacent burrows reach out to each other over the intervening ground and become joined in a temporary union for this purpose. Sperms from the partner are stored in special receptacles, known as spermathecae. These are later used to fertilise the worm's own eggs as these are being laid.

and nourished until the eggs are later laid and fertilised. Such precautions have led to quite complex behaviour patterns. In the leeches the exchange of sperm is not always simultaneous as it usually is in earthworms, and in some leeches, such as the medicinal leech, the eggs may not be fertilised and laid for many months after reception of the sperm. Gnathobdellid (jawed) leeches have a small penis (normally retracted) for introducing the sperm, but rhynchobdellids and pharyngobdellids produce spermatophores which are implanted into the aperture of the female duct. Some leeches implant the spermatophore in a special area of skin, from which the sperm make their way into the coelom.

Both oligochaetes and leeches have an area of skin called the clitellum which secretes the cocoon in which the eggs are laid. The clitellum is not always obvious and may be developed only in the breeding season. The cocoon is secreted as a belt, and as the worm slides out of it the eggs are laid and fertilised, the two ends of the cocoon closing together as the head is withdrawn. Leech cocoons are quite variable in appearance and may be attached to stones or carried about on the body.

These developments of hermaphroditism and of a clitellum secreting a protective cocoon in which the relatively large eggs are laid, may have evolved in adaptation to life in freshwater, swamps and soil. The young worms emerge sufficiently advanced in development to cope with the rigorous physiological conditions of their environment. In the marine polychaetes the eggs are often very small, often only a tenth of a millimetre across, but they are released in enormous numbers into the

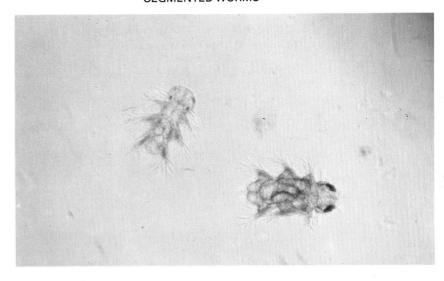

sea. Development is correspondingly rapid, the young larva, which is of the trochophore (trochosphere) type, often swimming and fending for itself within a few days.

Polychaete larvae are very variable in appearance though recognisable by their numerous bristles, and those of many families are quite distinctive. Most develop several segments before settling down on the bottom to continue life as miniature adults; others have a longer larval life drifting through the water and are quite unlike the adult worm in appearance. A particularly elegant larva is that of *Owenia*, the so-called Mitraria. It undergoes a cataclysmic metamorphosis into a worm-like form on leaving the plankton.

The Ragworm (*Nereis* sp.), one of the marine bristle worms, sheds its ova and sperms into the sea where the eggs are fertilised and develop into free-swimming larvae with rings of bristles.

Polychaetes (Class Polychaeta)

This elegant polychaete worm is probably a species of *Pontodoras*. It is probably planktonic as indicated by the elongated parapodia and has a worldwide distribution.

The polychaetes are distinguished by the chaetae which arise in bundles from more or less prominent paddle-like extensions of the body wall, the parapodia. They are almost exclusively marine, although a few have penetrated estuaries or are even found in freshwater.

In older books the various families are usually placed in one or other of two groups, the Errantia, comprising mainly worms which move about actively, and the Sedentaria which include worms living permanently or semi-permanently in tubes or burrows. The division is not a natural one and really serves no useful purpose. The main families are briefly described below without reference to these old divisions.

Phyllodocids (Family Phyllodocidae)
The phyllodocids comprise a large family of worms distinguished by the dorsal leaf-like extensions of the parapodia. They may be green or brown or have speckled markings, with relatively long, slender bodies composed of a large number of segments. They occur in a variety of habitats: in sand, mud, under boulders and in crevices on rocky shores. *Eulalia viridis* is a common European example which lives in crevices on rocky shores.

SEGMENTED WORMS

When the tide is out it may be seen making its way amongst the tangled weeds on the rocks. It is commonly five to seven centimetres long but barely three millimetres across and has a brilliant green colour. Two species of *Eulalia* occur on the New England coast. Some phyllodocids are common among algal holdfasts, whilst others have adapted themselves to a pelagic life in the open ocean. Eyes are often well developed as are the sensory tentacles arising anteriorly. Unlike the smaller nereids with which they might be confused on first acquaintance, they have a proboscis that is simple, balloon-like, with a granular papillate surface but without the pair of jaws characteristic of nereids.

Tomopterids (Family Tomopteridae)

These almost transparent creatures, mostly placed in the one genus, *Tomopteris*, swim in the open sea. They are often only one centimetre or so in length but have a series of well-developed parapodia acting as paddles and are without chaetae save for a single long trailing aciculum on each side just behind the head. They are never very numerous near the shore but often occur in numbers in the open ocean.

Family Nephtyidae

Nephtys may be found in sandy beaches and species of the genus are often common in the relatively 'clean' sand of seaside resorts which is not muddy enough for most worms. There are many species, all much alike to the casual observer. They may be recognised by the creamy colour and rather iridescent sheen of the body cuticle. It is difficult at first to tell which end is which, for the prostomium is small and though they have short tentacles it is difficult to see them. There are no eyes. The parapodia on the other hand are well developed and foliaceous. If a *Nephtys* is dug up and dropped into the sea, it will be seen to swim well, the body being thrown into a series of waves. As soon as the head touches the bottom swimming stops and the worm digs itself into the sand by means of the proboscis, and the body rapidly disappears in a series of jerks. The burrows they make are temporary. When buried, respiratory currents are passed over the gills which lie between the main lobes of the parapodia. These are carnivorous and scavenging worms.

Glycerids (Family Glyceridae)

Glycerids are long worms with cylindrical bodies, usually without colour apart from the red blood pigment, and found in mud or muddy sand. When dug up they writhe about, lashing their bodies from side to side. Many are small, but some are quite large and may be thirty centimetres or more in length, though this is exceptional. The prostomium tapers to a point and appendages and parapodia are inconspicuous.

Glycerids are carnivorous and notable for the enormous balloon-like proboscis which can be everted from the mouth. The proboscis is armed with four short teeth or jaws at the tip. Glycerids have no blood vessels and the pink or reddish colour of many species is due to the red blood pigment, haemoglobin, in corpuscles circulating in the coelom. Species of the genus *Glycera* occur on both sides of the Atlantic Ocean and on the American west coast.

Sea mice (Family Aphroditidae)

The sea mice owe their name to the numerous slender, hair-like chaetae which form a felt over the back. Other, stouter, black or golden chaetae project from the sides of the body and help the animals to crawl about in the surface sands in which they live. Underneath the felt there is a series of paired and overlapping scales developed from alternate parapodia.

Aphroditids may be found only below low water mark, but may be seen brought up in a trawl or washed ashore after gales. They are then usually covered with mud or sand and the golden hue of their chaetae will not be appreciated unless they are cleaned or allowed to clean themselves by burrowing through sand in an aquarium. They are rather lethargic animals, moving slowly about just beneath the surface with the tip of the abdomen curled up to allow respiratory currents to pass in and out over the back under the felt.

Some sea mice are quite large and may be fifteen centimetres or more in length. They are cosmopolitan.

Scaleworms (Family Polynoidae)

The scaleworms are quite closely related to the sea mice and used to be included in the same family. They differ, however, in having no felt over the back, so that the pairs of scales are revealed. The scales are rounded, often overlap and may extend from one end of the body to the other or from the head backwards for only part of the total length. Their bodies are somewhat flattened and this fits them for their life under boulders and in rock

Polychaete means 'many bristles' (chaetae or setae = bristles). Among marine bristle worms the multiplicity of bristles reaches its peak in the Sea Mouse, *Aphrodite aculeata*, the body of which is broad and flattened and covered with a felt of bristles. *Aphrodite* creeps over sandy seabeds with an almost mouse-like action, except that it moves slowly.

Hermodice sp., an amphinomid polychaete worm found in the warm temperate and tropical seas. It feeds on hydroids and corals and gains immunity from attack through the long white bristles on its parapodia. It is sometimes called a 'fire worm' because of the burning sensation experienced when the bristles enter the skin of fingers and hands.

crevices. Many species are quite common, and may be seen clinging to the underside of upturned, large boulders or stones on rocky shores. Some live in the burrows of other invertebrates, including those of other worms—or even in the mantle cavity of molluscs. *Gattyana cirrosa*, for example, may be found in the burrow of the large terebellid, *Neoamphitrite figulus*, on muddy shores in the English Channel, and similar associations may be found elsewhere. *Arctonoë vittata* lives under the mantle of the Keyhole Limpet (*Diodora aspera*) on the American west coast.

Nereids (Family Nereidae)

A large family of worms, many of which live in sand or mud on the seashore—often in vast numbers—and known to bait-diggers as rag-worms or clam worms. The large species *Nereis virens* is often called by them the 'King Rag'. They are usually reddish or orange, sometimes green in colour, rather limp, and the well-developed para-podia down each side of the body give the worm the appearance of a tattered strip of rag. The larger species, however, are more muscular. One of the commonest species (*Nereis diversicolor*) in western Europe has adapted itself to living in estuaries and has penetrated the Baltic as far as Finnish waters. Four North American species are restricted to freshwater in California. Nereids have small eyes on the prostomium, which has two very short tentacles, but there are four pairs of longer tentacles immediately behind the prostomium. The body is apparently undifferentiated, each segment being much like the others.

Most ragworms live in burrows in mud and sand but others live under stones or amongst the holdfasts of big seaweeds. The fore part of the gut can be everted as a kind of proboscis and this is provided with a single pair of jaws which help to pull the food into the mouth as the proboscis is retracted. The food consists of dead or dying animals, weed or mud according to the species.

Some species metamorphose on the approach of sexual maturity: their eyes enlarge and the para-podia are expanded to serve as efficient paddle-like structures for swimming. Very often the metamor-phosed region is restricted to the hinder part of the body, so that the first few segments remain unchanged. Both male and female heteronereids, as they are called, swim to the surface of the sea discharging their eggs and sperm into the water, where fertilisation occurs. This is no haphazard process; the spawning period is restricted to a few nights and the spawning itself occurs during a 'nuptial dance'. The adult worms usually die soon after. Some species spawn in the sandy mud in which they live and do not metamorphose in this way. In both cases the larvae which develop spend little time in the open water and soon crawl about on the bottom.

Syllids (Family Syllidae)

Most of the syllids are very small and unlikely to be noticed by the casual observer. Nevertheless, they are quite common and may be found by placing hydroids and weed in a bowl of sea water. If there are any syllids present these will eventu-ally collect along the edge of the bowl nearest the light.

Most syllids have numerous long cirri on the head and along the sides of the body, though some, such as those in the genus *Exogone*, have quite short appendages. Some syllids metamorphose when breeding, or bud off new individuals differ-ent from themselves which, like the heteronereids described above, are better adapted for swimming and spawning. They may be seen in spring and summer at night by hanging a light over the side of a small boat, for most of these forms are attracted to light. Some species reproduce themselves vegetatively, new heads developing at regular intervals down the body and each section eventu-ally breaking away to become a new individual. *Syllis* and *Autolytus* have species on both sides of the Atlantic.

Eunicids or rockworms (Family Eunicidae)

This is a large family and includes a wide variety of worms found in muddy sand, under boulders on rocky shores and on the level sea bottom below tide level. Nowadays systematists subdivide this group into a series of families, but they are all united by a similar proboscis structure. This takes the form of a ventral shovel-like structure which can be protruded from the mouth and bears a series of replaceable jaws. Some of the 'rock worms' may at first be confused with nereids, but they may be distinguished by their greater number of head tentacles, brighter colours and frequent possession of simple or feathery gills arched over the back. They are, in fact, quite unrelated to the nereids.

Of the various groups now regarded as distinct families may be mentioned the onuphids which live in muddy thick-walled or shelly tubes with particularly long tentacles and feathery gills, and (in contrast) the lumbrinereids which, as their name implies, are remarkably earthworm-like in appearance. They are found on muddy shores and among the roots of eelgrass.

Amphinomids (Family Amphinomidae)

The amphinomids comprise a very distinct group of marine worms mainly confined to warmer waters. They may be recognised by the bunches of slender, often golden chaetae. They are worms to be handled with caution when they are alive, for the tips of their bristles tend to break off and cause irritation to the skin. Some amphinomids may be mistaken for aphroditid sea mice, but they may be distinguished by the lack of scales or 'felt' over the back and by the presence of the distinct sense-organ known as the caruncle. The caruncle may be quite small but is unlike anything found in other polychaetes. It commonly takes the form of frilly-edged lobes extending back over the top of the head.

The body of amphinomids may be short or long and more eunicid-like. Amphinomids are mainly browsers, scraping off sedentary or encrusting animals such as bryozoans, sponges or coelenter-ates from the rocks and algal holdfasts on which they are commonly found.

Ariciids (Family Ariciidae)

The ariciids are superficially rather like capitel-lids: long, thin and tapering towards both ends. They are also found in muddy sand but ariciids

Usually all that is seen of the Lugworm (*Arenicola marina*) is the coils or strings of sand it ejects onto the surface on a sandy beach. The worm itself lives in a tube below the surface of the sand. This one has been dug out and lies exposed on the surface.

are generally larger than capitellids and have gills along the back, at least towards the hinder end. *Scoloplos armiger* is a common form on European coasts and it is usually this species which is responsible for the brown blobs of jelly about a centimetre across found on the surface of the sand in spring. They are the egg capsules in which the young at first develop.

Ariciids subsist on organic material in the mud and sand and are usually found on the beach where such material collects.

Cirratulids (Family Cirratulidae)

Cirratulids are often common in rather foul mud full of rotting vegetation or amongst the roots of eelgrass. The body is long, tapered at both ends, without easily recognisable parapodia and with abundant tentacle-like gills scattered over the body but most abundant towards the anterior end. These gills are extended to the surface and may be seen even when the tide is out, but they can be quickly withdrawn. Other, superficially similar tentacles are used for feeding. The genus *Dodecaceria* is rather different. These are small, black worms with very few tentacles grouped at the anterior end. Some live in great numbers in limestone near low water mark; others apparently build up calcareous tubes on the rocks on which they are found. One species has remarkable powers of regeneration, for at times the body breaks up spontaneously into fragments, each becoming a new individual. *Cirratulus cirratus* occurs on both sides of the Atlantic Ocean, replaced by *C. grandis* south of Cape Cod, Massachusetts.

Magelonids (Family Magelonidae)

The family created to include the curious worms belonging to the genus *Magelona* has a wide distribution, but the various species are sporadic in occurrence. They may be seen on somewhat muddy sand at extreme low-water mark or below tide level. Though small they are distinctive. They have a flattened extension in front of the head shaped rather like the point of a broad spear. Immediately behind this there is a single pair of long, slender and highly mobile tentacles, simple at the base but with many short papillae towards the tip. The tentacles are ciliated and are used for feeding. If the worm is removed from the sandy

sheath-like tube in which it lives, it will be seen to have a pale pink pigment. This is haemerythrin, a pigment rather like haemoglobin in function, but quite unlike it chemically. It is found in corpuscles in the worm's body cavity and is something of a biochemical curiosity for it is known to occur elsewhere in the animal kingdom only in the sipunculids.

Lugworms or lobworms (Family Arenicolidae)

The lugworms, used by fishermen as bait, are probably the most familiar of all seashore worms. There are many species, some reaching a large size. Most live in sand or muddy sand between tidemarks. Their burrows may be recognised when the tide is out by the large, coiled castings and by the funnel-shaped depressions in the sand caused by the worm's activities beneath. They are sand eaters. *Arenicola marina*, the Common European Lugworm, lives in an L-shaped burrow, the castings being made from the vertical shaft and the head of the worm being directed towards the toe of the 'L'. As the worm feeds, sand caves in from the surface above. The worm, while feeding well below the surface and gaining protection from predators thereby, is thus able to feed on the richer material from the surface. Water for respiration is pumped through the burrow and is drawn through the sand in front of the head. In this way more food is obtained, for the sand which is eaten in the head shaft of the burrow filters out particles in the water pumped through it.

Most lugworms have a coarsely annulated body and a narrower tail. The middle part of the body is provided with a number of pairs of arborescent gills, each of which corresponds to a parapodium. The parapodia are reduced.

Arenicola marina, found in Europe and eastern America, spawns on the surface of the sand, the times of spawning being related to particular tides at one time of the year.

Capitellids (Family Capitellidae)

The capitellids are found in rather foul mud or muddy sand and in such places they are often extremely abundant. They are mostly small worms with cylindrical bodies and when dug up it is very difficult not to break them into fragments for they are extremely fragile. They are bright red in colour due to the haemoglobin in the blood which may well help them to live in an environment in which the oxygen content is often very low.

Bamboo worms (Family Maldanidae)

The maldanids have a very distinctive appearance but, except in parts of the world where they happen to be abundant, are probably less familiar to most naturalists than many worms. They have long and narrow segments rather like the joints of a bamboo cane. Most of them lie buried vertically in the mud or sand within a tube and with the head downwards. The posterior end generally has a crown-like rim or collar and this can easily be mistaken for the head. The head end is often obliquely truncated and, indeed, the head may on first inspection appear to have been lost. Maldanids commonly live surrounded by a thin gritty tube. *Clymenella torquata* is common near Woods Hole, Massachusetts.

Spionids (Family Spionidae)

With few exceptions these are all very small worms living in the sand between tidemarks, in old mollusc shells or rocks. Various species of *Polydora* are perhaps the most common and widespread. They may be distinguished by the single pair of flexible tentacles just behind the head which are continually lashed about in search of food. They may best be seen by placing some colonised shells or rock fragments in a glass jar or aquarium. Spionids are often common in soft limestone or chalk and in old oyster shells, and their presence can be detected by the small holes (two milli-metres or so across) arranged in pairs like two keyholes placed stem to stem. Each of the tentacles has a ciliated gutter along which the tiny particles on which they feed are conveyed to the mouth. Sand grains too large to be ingested may be cemented around the worm to form a tube. If the worm is in limestone and protected from wave action a short chimney may form.

Spionids are notable for their powers of repro-duction and dispersal. Eggs are often fertilised after their release but still within the parental tube from which the larvae later escape. Some species pass as long as three months in the plankton before settling and adopting the adult mode of life.

Chaetopterids (Family Chaetopteridae)

Chaetopterus variopedatus is found all over the world. It is one of the most remarkable of all annelids by virtue of the extreme differentiation of the body segments and by its specialised feeding mechan-ism. It may be found intertidally only at extreme low water of spring tides; more usually the open-ings of its tubes or the tubes themselves may be seen below low water mark or amongst the hold-fasts of large seaweeds tossed ashore after gales. The tubes in which they live are easily recognised; extremely tough, yellowish and coarse outside, smooth and translucent inside, one centimetre or more across and roughly U-shaped, the openings being somewhat restricted. The worm within is extremely delicate and almost colourless.

Chaetopterus feeds by filtering the particles sus-pended in the water by means of a mucous net secreted and held between two anterior parapodial 'arms'. As the net becomes loaded it is rolled up into a ball within a special cup-shaped structure and is then passed forward along a mid-dorsal ciliary gutter to the mouth. The water is pumped through the tube by three pairs of muscular 'fans' which work in a most beautifully co-ordinated manner. The current serves to bring food and also for respiration.

If a *Chaetopterus* is removed from its tube and gently swirled round in a bowl of sea water in the dark, the worm will be seen to luminesce. Several in a bowl will emit enough light to read a watch.

Sabellariids (Family Sabellariidae)

These are most numerous on exposed rocky coasts. Their tubes are made of compacted sand and shell fragments and are found massed on rocks and boulders, the openings giving a honeycomb ap-pearance to the whole colony. In less favourable places they may be found in twos and threes or in small clumps, but in parts of Central America they are so numerous as to form prominent reefs.

Individual tubes may be broken open to reveal the worm within. When fully grown most species are 2·5 centimetres or more in length and have a heavy anterior end capped by a crown of flattened chaetae. At the hind end there is a slender reflexed 'tail'. Simple parapodial gills may be seen curved over the back. When filled with ripe eggs they may have a pink or purple colour by transparency of the body wall.

The crown of chaetae and the enlarged anterior segments act as a stopper to the tube when the worm retracts. Immediately behind the stopper is a mass of short tentacles which are used for feeding. This may be seen by placing part of a colony in a glass jar or aquarium, when the worms will extend sufficiently from their tubes to spread out the tentacle mass in the water.

Eggs and sperm are discharged into the sea. The larvae which develop are at first quite unlike the adults. They live in the open sea for some time; later, when a suitable substratum is encountered, they settle down and metamorphose. The larvae tend to be gregarious on settling so that a new colony is formed or an old one extended.

Owenids (Family Oweniidae)

Owenia is a curious little worm found throughout the world in relatively clean sand. Though indi-vidual species vary in size they are mostly about five centimetres in length and three millimetres across. They are easily recognised by the long, flexible tubes they build from sand grains or shell fragments laid one on the other like the tiles on a roof. The worm is much shorter than the tube it builds, the body being cylindrical and terminating in a short, frilly crown used for feeding.

Eggs and sperm are shed into the water where fertilisation takes place. The larva which develops is known as a Mitraria, a tiny transparent creature shaped somewhat like a bishop's mitre and with long, slender chaetae trailing beneath. It is so unlike the adult that when the larva metamor-phoses into the adult worm much of the larval structure is remodelled or discarded.

Pectinarids (Family Pectinariidae = Amphictenidae)

Pectinaria and *Cistenides* may be seen towards low-water mark of spring tides on clean, sandy beaches, but the beautifully regular tubes which they build are probably more familiar than the

Portion of a reef formed by tubes of the honeycomb worm (*Sabellaria* sp.) on exposed surface of rock on a sandy beach near low-tide mark. The worms cannot leave their tubes. They protrude their heads and tentacles when the tide is in to catch particles of food and also sand-grains to repair their tubes.

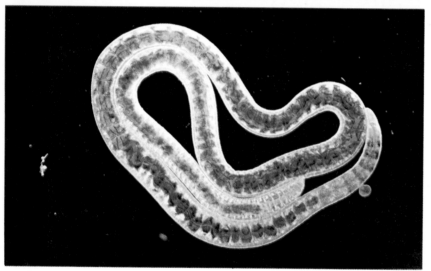

Peacock worms, *Sabella pavonina*, live in shallow seas in long narrow muddy tubes of their own making. To feed and breathe they push their heads out of the tubes, so allowing the ring of richly-coloured tentacles to collect particles of food. These are passed to the mouth by the cilia on the surfaces of the tentacles.

A tubifex worm, small, bright red and writhing, of the kind found in clusters in foul water such as duck ponds, polluted rivers and neglected horse troughs. In a badly polluted river they may be sufficiently abundant in the mud to appear as irregular red bands at or near the water's edge.

terebellids and they can be wholly retracted within the mouth. Perhaps the most noticeable feature differentiating them from other worms is the gills. These are often rather flattened and pointed structures arranged in a transverse row across the back of the head. *Melinna palmata* is found in long, slender tubes built vertically in the mud which usually project slightly as short chimneys from the surface. Species of the genus *Melinna* have red blood, but some other ampharetids have blood of a greenish hue due to the presence of chloro-cruorin—the same pigment found in sabellids and serpulids.

Terebellids (Family Terebellidae)

This is a large family of worms of very characteristic appearance. Many are small, but some are several centimetres long and as fat as a man's thumb. They may be recognised by their medusa-like head of writhing tentacles. Some terebellids make tubes of shell fragments or other débris; others live in burrows in the mud, in mud-filled crevices in rocks, or under boulders. The burrows or tubes are irrigated for respiratory purposes by piston-like swellings passing down the body. In addition to the head tentacles, which are used for food gathering, there are also at the head end one to three pairs of bright red gills.

These worms glean a wide area for the débris and surface mud on which they subsist; each tentacle is highly extensible and largely independent in activity. Species of *Polycirrus* do not live in a tube or burrow. They may be found among algal holdfasts or under stones near low-water mark. They are a bright orange colour and commonly withdraw the body completely under the writhing mass of tentacles. In Europe, perhaps one of the most familiar terebellids is *Lanice conchilega*, the 'Sand Mason' which constructs shelly tubes with frilly tops which project several centimetres out of the sand. *Amphitrite figulus* (also known as *A. brunnea*) occurs on both sides of the Atlantic Ocean.

Sabellids (Family Sabellidae)

The sabellid fan, or feather-duster worms are perhaps the most elegant of all the annelids. Few layment would recognise them for the worms that they are. Their annelid nature will only be realised by removing the tubes in which they live by carefully slitting these open with scissors. The anterior end of the worm has an array of flexible, sometimes branched and usually highly coloured tentacles which spread out whenever the worm expands from the tube. This crown is primarily a feeding organ but it serves also for respiration. Water is passed through the crown by the activity of the cilia on the crown's rays, and particles caught in mucus are conveyed to the mouth in the centre along ciliary gutters passing down each ray. *Schizobranchia insignis*, a species common on parts of the United States north-west coast, has highly coloured, densely branched crowns of deep purple, claret or grey-black hue—all varieties of the same species. *Sabella penicillus*, the common sabellid of English estuaries and occurring also along the Atlantic coast of Canada and New England, has a simple, delicate but widely spreading crown with bars of purple and pink giving a concentric effect

worms within. The tubes are narrowly conical and open at both ends. The tip of the tubes projects like a chimney just above the surface of the sand. The worm lives head downward, eating the sand and ejecting its castings through the chimney. The tube is built up from pieces of shell and sand, all carefully cemented together with mucus so that the sides are perfectly smooth. The body is thin-walled and transparent and the sand within the gut is clearly visible through the body wall. The body of the worm is as delicate as the tube is relatively strong. At the anterior end of the body there is a series of stout, golden chaetae arranged as two comb-like or pectinated structures, one on each side, from which they take their name.

Ampharetids (Family Ampharetidae)

Some species of ampharetid are important members of the faunas in the mud of shallow seas, but some are found intertidally in great numbers where conditions suit their needs. They are relatively small worms living in the mud or in fragile, sandy tubes. They are not unlike terebellids to which they are distantly related and, like them, have numerous tentacles with which they feed, but these tentacles are not as extensible as those of

when the crown is open. The crown is a vulnerable part of the worm which can contract within its tube with startling rapidity. In many species withdrawal can be evoked by a shadow, but some respond only to vibration. *Megalomma vesiculosum* has a separate eye on each ray of the crown and its perception of shadow is particularly keen.

Chlorocruorin pigmentation gives the blood of sabellids a greenish colour.

Serpulids (Family Serpulidae)

These are very like sabellids in many ways, but most of them are much smaller and they secrete hard limey tubes, usually attached to stones, but some small species of *Spirorbis* may be found on seaweeds. Another difference is that most have one of the rays of the crown modified as an operculum which acts as a stopper to the tube when the worm retracts. As in the sabellids, the crown is brightly coloured. *Pomatoceros triqueter*, a common species found on stones in western Europe, has several colour varieties, the crown appearing orange, brown or blue according to different combinations of several distinct pigments. These differences are genetically determined. Like sabellids, serpulids are filter-feeders.

The sex cells may be shed freely into the water or the eggs may be fertilised in the parent tube and develop there as young larvae. The common *Spirorbis* of Europe and eastern North America, secretes flat, white, spiral tubes one or two millimetres in diameter on rocks and seaweed. They sometimes 'brood' their larvae in a special chamber within the opercular stalk; in other species they develop within the tube. The genus *Manayunkia*, containing two species, occurs in North America in freshwater in Pennsylvania, New Jersey and the Great Lakes.

Oligochaetes (Class Oligochaeta)

The Oligochaeta includes the familiar earthworms. The body is typically long, cylindrical and annulated, each annulus bearing several stout chaetae, each emerging separately from the skin. There are no parapodia as in the polychaetes, and, as befits burrowers, the prostomium is small, conical and without appendages. There are some exceptions; many of those that live in freshwater, for example, have bundles of chaetae rather like polychaetes and may have various appendages. Nevertheless, their internal structure is much more varied. They are hermaphrodite, that is, every worm is both male and female, and both types of sex cell are produced at the same time. As a concomitant of this the gonads are restricted to certain segments and an elaborate behaviour pattern has evolved to prevent self-fertilisation when pairing. The belt- or saddle-like clitellum round the middle of the body characteristic of breeding worms is a specialised area which secretes the cocoon in which the fertilised eggs are laid.

The actual arrangement of the genital segments and of the ducts from them are of prime importance in the classification of the group. While this provides a 'natural' division, it often makes practical identification difficult. Typical members of the main families can, nevertheless, be recognised by other characters.

Before these true relationships had been worked out naturalists divided the Oligochaeta into two series of families, one characteristic of freshwater (Microdrili or Limicoles), the others including all the earthworms (Megadrili or Terricoles). All the families of true earthworms in fact agree in having the ducts bearing the male cells (vasa deferentia) opening well behind the segments in which the cells are produced. This arrangement has presumably evolved with the need to prevent self-fertilisation during simultaneous exchange of sperm. The families characteristic of freshwater are more distantly related.

Members of three families of truly freshwater oligochaetes are likely to be encountered: these are the Aelosomatidae, the Naididae and the Tubificidae. Two other families, the Lumbriculidae and the Enchytraeidae are also found along the edges of ditches and ponds or in wet places along their margins. The tubificids are small, cylindrical, bright red worms found under foul conditions with a low oxygen content, as in duck ponds, and along the banks of polluted streams and estuaries. The mud banks of the Thames in central London can appear blood red at low tides from countless millions of these worms. They are sold in aquarist's shops as 'blood worms' as food for tropical fish. Their bright red colour is the result of the large amount of haemoglobin in the blood. When covered by water the hind part of the body protrudes from the mud and shows an incessant corkscrew-like writhing motion. This serves to pass water over the body surface where respiratory exchange takes place.

Aelosomatids and naidids are different. Both groups may be found in the silt at the bottom of ponds, lakes and quiet streams. They are generally minute, semi-transparent creatures. One species of *Aelosoma* reproduces vegetatively and may be found in short chains of two or three individuals. They live on diatoms and unicellular algae. Naidids also reproduce vegetatively and are often larger than aelosomatids. *Chaetogaster* and *Stylaria* are two typical genera found all over the world. The only certain way of distinguishing these two families is to examine the bristles under a microscope. In naidids, those on the ventral side of the body are cleft at the tip; those of aelosomatids from a similar position are simple.

Lumbriculids, enchytraeids and tubificids all have cylindrical bodies and typical species can usually be distinguished with a little experience. They may certainly be distinguished by the character of their bristles. Those of tubificids and enchytraeids arise in bundles; those of lumbriculids arise in pairs as in earthworms. Tubificids are red and writhing, as already mentioned; enchytraeids are whitish and often hold the body rigidly. Most enchytraeids are half the size of tubificids and they are found in rotting vegetation and the roots of aquatic or semi-aquatic plants. Lumbriculids are much larger, and like tubificids are red from the haemoglobin in the blood. They live in ditches and ponds and like the other freshwater oligochaetes reproduce vegetatively.

The true earthworms are externally much alike although ranging in length from a few centimetres to over three metres. Most earthworms fall in one of four families, one of which—the Eudrilidae—is a small family found in Africa. Of the other three, the Megascolecidae are typically southern in distribution, extending into southwestern Asia and the warmer parts of North America. The southeast Asian genus *Pheretima* belongs to this group too.

Many megascolecids can be recognised by the almost complete ring of chaetae which protrude from each segment. The Glossoscolecidae are difficult to distinguish externally from the Lumbricidae, which include all the common earthworms of the northern hemisphere: the genera *Lumbricus*, *Allolobophora* and *Eisenia*. The Giant Australian Earthworm of the genus *Drawida* belongs in a family of its own, Moniligastridae. The most significant differences are internal ones affecting the arrangement of the gut and excretory organs. This is especially so in those that live in soils subject to periods of heavy rain or periodic drought.

Some tropical earthworms and other oligochaetes are arboreal, living in the dirt or water which accumulates in the axils of branches or leaves. The beneficial effects of earthworms on soil were reported in a classic treatise by Charles Darwin. One family of oligochaetes, the Branchiobdellidae, is commensal-parasitic on crayfishes. The individuals superficially resemble minute leeches.

Leeches (Class Hirudinea)

The leeches are easily recognised. Most of them are found in ponds and streams where they live off the blood of other invertebrates, amphibians, or reptiles. All have a more or less prominent sucker at the posterior end. There is another sucker around the mouth but this is more variable in development and is often less easily recognised. Behind the anterior sucker there is usually a series of eyespots arranged in pairs on the dorsal side; these are often difficult to distinguish when there is much dark pigment in the skin. Unlike other annelids, leeches have no chaetae.

When leeches swim they throw the body into undulations in the vertical—not horizontal—plane. They also move about by 'looping', rather like geometrid moth caterpillars, or using the suckers at each end as feet.

The Hirudinea may be divided into four groups based on the structures around the mouth and certain other features. Of these four groups, the Acanthobdellae include a single genus of fish parasites found in Russia. They are curious creatures, in many ways linking the leeches with the oligochaetes. The other three groups all have common and widespread representatives: the Rhynchobdellae which include most of the fish leeches, the Pharyngobdellae which also include common freshwater leeches, and the Gnathobdellae which include various leeches found in ditches and horse ponds. The medicinal leech, once used for blood-letting, belongs to this last group.

The Rhynchobdellae have no jaws but are equipped with a kind of proboscis. They include two families: the Glossiphoniidae which are dorso-ventrally flattened leeches found in freshwater, and the Piscicolidae (= Ichthyobdellidae) with cylindrical bodies and a prominent anterior sucker. The anterior sucker in glossiphoniids is no wider than the head. Piscicolids are found not only on freshwater fishes, but also on marine fishes.

Many Gnathobdellae, the jawed leeches, spend some of their lives out of water. They suck the blood of various invertebrates or vertebrate animals, piercing the skin with their lancet-like jaws and covering the wound with the anterior sucker.

Macrobdella decora is a common North American species belonging to this group. In warm countries leeches may be a hazard in swamps and paddy fields. These are all Gnathobdellae belonging either to the Hirudidae, the family to which the medicinal leech belongs, or to the Haemadipsidae which are especially well adapted to life out of water. In tropical forests they may be found hanging by the posterior sucker from foliage, ready to attach themselves to any animal, including man, which brushes past them. In such leeches the jaws are well developed, but in others including the various species of *Haemopis* (the so-called horse leeches) the jaws are much weaker structures. The horse leeches are found in ditches throughout Europe and North America. They feed on the blood of various soft-bodied vertebrates.

The tendency for jaw reduction seen in the Gnathobdellae is taken further in the fourth and last group, the Pharynchobdellae. The leeches included in this group have entirely lost the power of piercing the tissues of other animals and of sucking their blood. They feed instead on whole insect larvae, small earthworms and so forth. *Trocheta* is quite a large leech, sometimes several centimetres long, found occasionally in gardens. It feeds on earthworms. Pharyngobdellae may also be found in freshwater. In Europe, *Erpobdella octoculata* is a common species, whilst *Erpobdella punctata* is perhaps one of the commonest and most widespread in North America.

The main families of leeches can be distinguished after a little experience, but individual species are often difficult to determine and may have to be dissected to name them precisely. The Rhynchobdellae may be recognised by the mouth forming a small pore in the oral sucker. The pharynx is protruded through this. The other leeches all have larger mouths really confluent with the rim of the anterior or oral sucker. The Gnathobdellae are distinguishable from the Pharyngobdellae by their jaws and by the number of eyes: Gnathobdellae have five pairs arranged in a pair of backwardly projecting rows, the Pharyngobdellae (Erpobdellidae) only three or four pairs.

ARTHROPODS
(Phylum Arthropoda)

Arthropods are the most numerous and widespread group of animals and include such diverse forms as insects, crustaceans, spiders, millipedes and centipedes, which with one exception (Onychophora) are characterised by an external skeleton and paired, jointed limbs.

They show clear affinities with annelids or segmented worms and have doubtless evolved from annelid-like ancestors. *Peripatus* (class Onychophora) has the appearance of being half-annelid, half-arthropod and has even been called a worm-insect. Although onychophorans are considered here under the Arthropoda, some authors do not consider them to be true arthropods.

Arthropods have a much thicker cuticle than annelids and it usually forms a stout case known as the exoskeleton, which has soft joints at intervals to give the body and limbs flexibility. Fundamentally, each segment of the body has one pair of swimming or walking limbs, but some limb pairs may disappear as others become specialised for other purposes and no longer function exclusively as locomotory organs. One pair may function as protective pincers, and one or two pairs, the antennae, which have come to lie in front of the mouth, have a sensory function. Others may serve to capture, hold or break up food; still others may serve for sperm transfers or respiration.

The evolution of a rigid exoskeleton has been correlated with changes in the musculature. Instead of the continuous muscle layer found in annelids, there is a system of separate muscles giving greater flexibility of movement. Another feature linked with the possession of an exoskeleton is that the extensive perivisceral coelom characteristic of annelids, which by the turgidity of its fluid holds the body of the worm sufficiently rigid for locomotion to be possible, is replaced by a reduced haemocoelic space filled with blood. This in turn has resulted in the loss of the numerous paired excretory organs, the nephridia, which are a characteristic of annelids. Instead, there are one or more pairs of coelomoducts which often function as excretory organs as well as forming ducts for the reproductive organs. Cilia occur but rarely. Finally, arthropods have numerous hair-like bristles, known as setae, arranged in groups on the exoskeleton. These are hollow outgrowths of the cuticle which contain an epidermal cell, or part of one and which fulfil a variety of functions.

The first true arthropods, the extinct trilobites, were aquatic, and the hard exoskeleton has been an important factor in the adaptation of modern arthropods to a terrestrial habit, as it reduces loss of water from the body by evaporation.

The cuticle covering the body continues into the alimentary canal through the mouth, forming the stomodaeum or fore gut, and through the anus, forming the proctodaeum or hind gut. These involutions of the cuticle may be short or may form almost the whole lining of the digestive canal, as in the higher crustaceans and insects. The rigid exoskeleton, together with the cuticular linings of the alimentary canal, is shed periodically during a moult or eodysis. The base of the old cuticle is separated by enzymatic action from the underlying cell layers. The secretion of the new cuticle then begins and when sufficiently thick to be protective, the animal ruptures the old cuticle along predetermined lines and crawls free. When the outer layer is shed, the soft and distensible new cuticle already formed beneath it expands to allow the body to grow, and then soon hardens.

The nervous system of arthropods is very like that of annelids. There is a brain composed of nerve ganglia lying above the alimentary canal in the head region, a nerve ring encircling the canal and joining the brain to ventral head ganglia from which a paired nerve cord runs ventrally through the body with a pair of ganglia in each segment. Sense-organs include ocelli or simple eyes, compound eyes, antennae and various others more specialised still, but these vary from group to group.

The early developmental stages of the embryo are determined by the ova being heavily laden with yolk. Cleavage is of the type known as centrolecithal, in which the parts of the divided nucleus are arranged in a protoplasmic layer on the yolk surface.

In species arthropods outnumber the rest of the animal kingdom. The number of known species of insects is usually estimated to be a million, and it is possible that as many more have yet to be described. Crustaceans are also numerous and mites, related to spiders, may prove to be as abundant. Mites have only in the last two decades received much attention, but it is becoming clear that they are economically important and embrace many species.

Velvet worms (Class Onychophora)

Velvet worms, considered by some authors as a separate phylum, may be described as primitive terrestrial arthropods with a caterpillar-like body. They are classed as arthropods largely on the basis of their internal structure which includes a perivisceral haemocoel, tracheae, chitinous cuticle and a pair of feeding appendages. They also have affinities with annelid worms in possessing nonjointed appendages and a thin cuticle and in the structure of body wall and nephridia. The primitive nature of their arthropod characters indicates that they diverged from the main lines of arthropod evolution at an early date.

There are about eighty known species with a wide but discontinuous distribution in the southern hemisphere and parts of Asia. *Peripatus*, the type genus, measures between 2·5 and 7·5 centimetres long but a Central American species, *Macroperipatus geayi*, reaches 12·5 centimetres in length. They are always found in moist habitats, under stones or the bark and rotten wood of fallen trees, as they are highly susceptible to desiccation. In an ordinarily dry room *Peripatus* can lose a third of its body weight in four hours. The colour of the body varies according to species, the upper parts being dark grey, green, brown or red and the underparts light or whitish.

The defence mechanism consists of two slime glands at the sides of the mouth which secrete a milk fluid when the animal is disturbed. This substance shoots out for a distance of about eight to thirty centimetres, congealing on contact with air and forming sticky threads which entangle the enemy.

Velvet worms are nocturnal and carnivorous, feeding on small insects such as termites and on such crustaceans as woodlice as well as the carcasses of large insects like grasshoppers. Carrion seems to be taken and species which live in termites' nests eat only dead termites.

Structure

Onychophorans lack the hard exoskeleton of typical arthropods. The thin, flexible cuticle shows no external segmentation and the body wall consists of layers of circular and longitudinal muscle as in annelid worms.

There is a variable number of paired, unjointed limbs, which are hollow, cone-shaped structures, each bearing a retractile foot with hooked claws and containing excretory tubules. The reproductive aperture lies ventrally between the last pair of limbs, and the anus is at the posterior end.

The head is continuous with the body and bears three pairs of appendages: long extensible antennae, blunt oral papillae associated with slime glands and jaws which lie within the oral cavity. The jaws are atypical in that there is only one pair and they bite with the tips instead of the base as in other arthropods.

The body cavity is a blood-filled space known as a haemocoel. It extends the whole length of the body and contains the gut, reproductive organs and a pair of slime glands. Two lateral spaces contain the nerve cords and salivary glands and the heart lies in a shallow cavity above the haemocoel.

Digestive system

Prey is captured by means of a suctorial lip on the mouth cavity which contains the jaws and the common duct of the two salivary glands. From the mouth a muscular pharynx joins a short oesophagus leading into the gut which is a simple straight tube extending to the anus. Pairs of excretory organs or nephridia connect with the pairs of limbs and open on the ventral surface by tubules.

Circulation and respiration

The circulatory system is more primitive than in other arthropods, consisting of a long tubular heart with pairs of ostia or lateral slits in most of the segments. There are no other blood vessels.

Velvet worms breathe by means of tracheae or air tubes and this characteristic is for some authors justification for their inclusion in the phylum.

Nervous system and sense-organs

The nervous system is primitive, consisting of two large ganglia lying above the oesophagus and occupying most of the head, and a pair of ventral nerve cords which give off strands to the segments. The eyes are comparatively undeveloped and are probably capable only of perceiving changes in light intensity. In addition to the antennae, there are numerous minute papillae covering the surface of the body. They are regarded as tactile organs but may also be sensitive to taste and humidity.

Reproduction

The sexes are separate and have paired gonads with ciliated ducts leading to the genital aperture. In the female the ducts are differentiated to form a uterus. Internal fertilisation is usual but in *Peripatus capensis* the male deposits a capsule containing spermatozoa on the body of the female. White blood corpuscles in the female's body puncture the skin and the lower wall of the capsule ruptures, releasing the spermatozoa which reach the ovaries by way of the bloodstream and fertilise the eggs. Fertilisation is not a simple process, however, for in a female just sexually mature the young egg cells use the sperms as nourishment and grow for a year. At the next coupling they are fertilised, and superflous sperms are used to feed the next generation of egg cells. There is a further overlap in many species in that, although young are born every year, the period of pregnancy is thirteen months, so that for one month in every year the mature female carries two sets of embryos, one in the early stages of development and the other near the end of their development.

In most species of *Peripatus* the young are born alive. One Australian species lays eggs with a large yolk, but in most others the embryos are nourished through the uterine wall, and in one South American species there is a placenta resembling that of mammals. The genus as a whole therefore has a remarkable mixture of primitive and highly specialised characters, especially those concerned with reproduction.

Pauropods (Class Pauropoda)

All the members of the Pauropoda are small, none being more than one millimetre long. They are widespread in both temperate and tropical regions where they live in damp locations among dead leaves, rotten wood and under bark and feed mainly on decaying vegetable matter. Two common genera are *Pauropus* and *Eurypauropus*. About sixty species have been described.

Their affinities with other arthropods are uncertain because of the simplicity of their structure and lack of information about the early stages of their development.

The body consists of a head followed by eleven, rarely twelve, segments and a tail segment or pygidium. The segments are partially fused in pairs, each pair having a dorsal shield known as the diplotergite. There are nine pairs of functional legs and an almost vestigial pair on the first segment. Each leg consists of five joints and ends in several setae or bristles.

There are no eyes, but a sensory organ of unknown function occurs on each side of the head. The sides of the body are provided with long, tactile setae and the branched antennae bear setae.

The respiratory and vascular systems are much reduced, but the nervous system is similar to that of millipedes.

The sexes are separate. The gonads are ventral and the gonopore or genital opening is situated on the third segment behind the head. Hatching larvae have only three pairs of legs and pass through four larval stages before becoming adults.

Millipedes (Class Diplopoda)

Millipedes and centipedes were formerly grouped together in the class Myriapoda, but about the only features they have in common are an elongated body and numerous legs, and they are now placed in separate classes, Diplopoda (millipedes) and Chilopoda (centipedes).

Although millipedes are noted for their large number of legs, even the longest ones have only 200 legs and most species have fewer. A typical millipede has an elongated worm-like body divided into segments. Most species are cylindrical in section but lateral extension of the segments gives some species a flattened appearance. The head bears a pair of antennae, a pair of jaws and a group of ocelli or simple eyes on each side. Except for the first four segments and one or two of the posterior ones, the segments are double and each bears two pairs of jointed legs, whereas centipedes have only one pair on each segment.

There are about 6,500 species. The smallest are only two millimetres in length, while the largest measure about thirty centimetres. When disturbed, most species coil into a spiral. One British species, the Pill Millipede (*Glomeris marginata*), rolls itself into a ball the size of a pea, in the manner of a Woodlouse. It differs from the Woodlouse in having seventeen to nineteen pairs of legs, acording to sex, and the last segment bears only one plate instead of several narrow strips as in a Woodlouse. Tropical species are usually black but may be brightly coloured, and may reach the size of a golf ball when rolled up. In some smaller forms the body is soft, but most species have a chitinous integument strengthened with lime salts. Growth is by successive moults of the integument, which leaves the body soft and vulnerable until the new integument that has grown beneath the old one has hardened. Most millipedes have two rows of stink glands along the sides of the body which secrete a noxious substance in colour, capable of killing or repelling insects. One constituent of the secretion is hydrocyanic acid.

All millipedes are vegetarian, feeding mainly on decaying plant matter. Sometimes they attack living plants and larger species may eat dead animal matter. They normally live among leaf litter, under bark or in rotting logs, but may burrow into the earth, going especially deep in dry weather. Their main role is therefore as scavengers. Respiration is by tracheae, and there is a well-developed system of blood vessels.

The sexes are separate. The reproductive organs

A velvet worm, *Macroperipatus trinitatis*, of Trinidad. Velvet worms are primitive arthropods with specialized anatomy, that live under rotten logs and move with a caterpillar-like motion.

The serrated millipede (*Lophostreptus*) of East Africa on an aloe leaf. Millipedes do not have anything like a thousand legs, as their name suggests. They live in damp soil feeding mainly on rotting vegetation.

are in the front part of the body, the genital ducts opening behind the second pair of legs. The eggs hatch into larvae which usually have three pairs of legs. The life-span may be only one or two years or as many as seven in some species, and during this time millipedes grow in length by adding in groups of up to three or more fresh segments each moult. One of the commonest genera is *Julus*, and *Julus terrestris*, a burrowing millipede often mistaken for a Wireworm, shows a form of parental care. The female constructs a dome-shaped nest of earth mixed with saliva and lays her eggs through a hole in the top, sealing the nest with the same material.

She may make several such nests, and it is not uncommon to find her coiled around one of them. Other species lay their eggs in the ground in batches of twenty-five to fifty. A Californian species, *Luminodesmus sequoiae*, is luminous.

An important feature of behaviour which distinguishes millipedes from centipedes lies in their locomotion. Whereas centipedes have a wriggling movement, the legs opposite each other moving alternately, millipedes glide slowly over the ground, successive waves of movement passing along the row of legs, which alternately contract in groups and then spread out.

Centipedes (Class Chilopoda)

Centipedes, of which there are about 1,500 species, are active and predacious, with fangs and a poisonous bite, their prey including insects, slugs, earthworms and even other centipedes. They are worldwide in distribution and vary in length from a few millimetres to ten or more centimetres. The largest species, *Scolopendra gigantea* of Central America is twenty-six centimetres long and 2·5 centimetres wide. It can catch lizards, mice and large insects.

The head is distinct and bears a pair of antennae, three pairs of jaws (mandibles and two pairs of maxillae) and groups of ocelli (except in the large order Geophilomorpha). The body is divided into a number of similar segments most of which bear only one pair of jointed walking legs, in contrast to millipedes which have two pairs. There are usually fifteen to twenty pairs of legs. The first pair of legs is modified into fangs used as organs of attack. The House Centipede (*Scutigera forceps* or *S. coleoptrata*) which is a cosmopolitan species about five centimetres long has a bite as severe as a wasp sting. This centipede is light brown, marked with three dark stripes, and its fifteen pairs of banded legs are long so that the body is carried like that of a spider when the centipede is running.

The body, which is usually flattened and in some species long and almost thread-like, has a smooth, elastic integument which is never strengthened with lime salts.

Respiration is by tracheae or air tubes, opening by means of spiracles along the sides of the body, but in the order Scutigeromorpha they are situated along the midline of the back. Whereas in millipedes the tracheae are simple and unbranched, in the centipedes they are branched and anastomosing as in insects. The nervous system is typical of the arthropods, and the alimentary canal is a straight tube with salivary glands opening into the fore part and the excretory Malpighian tubules at the rear end.

The reproductive organs lie above the gut and the genital pores are located on the genital segment towards the rear of the body. Centipedes are divided here into the subclasses Epimorpha and Anamorpha based on differences in development. Another scheme divides the class directly into four orders. In the Epimorpha the eggs are laid in clusters and the larvae have a full complement of segments and legs, whereas in the Anamorpha single eggs are laid and the larvae hatch with only seven pairs of legs, others being acquired after successive moults. In the Epimorpha the female excavates a chamber in the earth, usually under a stone, using her head and mouth-parts. She wraps her body around the eggs in a tight coil, with the legs pointing inwards, so that they are not visible from the outside and not in contact with the soil. From time to time the female uncoils, and licks an egg, holding it with the fangs and first pair of walking legs, presumably to remove spores of moulds, since eggs become infected with fungi in a few days. If an egg falls from the mass she will retrieve it and she will attack fiercely anything that seeks to molest the eggs.

Centipedes are nocturnal, usually hiding by day in damp places under leaf litter, stones or logs. A few species are luminescent at night, but the function of this light is still unknown. The best-known luminous species is the long, thread-like *Geophilus electricus*, this species is found in many parts of Europe.

The bite of large tropical species can be very painful but is seldom fatal to human beings.

Class Symphyla

Relatively little work has been done on the Symphyla, but there are probably more than the hundred described species in this cosmopolitan group. The genus *Scolopendrella* has received attention in the United States because of its importance in agriculture. Symphyla live under stones, logs and in leaf litter, their white bodies showing up against the dark earth. The integument entirely lacks pigment and is not strengthened by the deposition of lime salts. They feed on decaying vegetable matter and occasionally the dead bodies of insects. They also attack the roots and other tissues of live plants, at times causing extensive damage to celery, lettuce, asparagus and beet.

Scutigerella immaculata is particularly notorious.

The largest of them does not exceed eight millimetres in length. Typically, the head is distinct from the body which consists of fourteen segments protected by overlapping dorsal plates and twelve pairs of jointed legs. The head has a Y-shaped suture like insects and bears a pair of long, segmented antennae. The respiratory spiracles open near the bases of the antennae. There are no eyes. The mouth-parts include a pair of mandibles, a pair of maxillulae and two pairs of maxillae. In several respects the Symphyla resemble the insect order Thysanura (the bristle-tails). One resemblance is that the first pair of legs have long, slender processes known as parapodia. The remaining legs have five joints, the outer joint bearing a pair of claws.

The reproductive organs are paired and open by a single pore lying beneath the third and fourth pairs of legs. The females lay their eggs in the soil, the larvae hatching with six or seven segments bearing legs, additional pairs being added with each moult. There are six larval stages.

Insects (Class Insecta)

The insects are by far the largest and most successful class of arthropods, with nearly a million known species. In this respect they outnumber all the other animals by about four to one, and their great biological diversity is correlated with the very large number of habitats which they have exploited. Except for the sea practically every kind of environment, no matter how small and how exacting its demands, supports a flourishing insect fauna. The insects' most distinctive anatomical features are the subdivision of the body into head, thorax and abdomen, the presence of three pairs of thoracic legs, and a head which bears one pair of antennae and three pairs of feeding appendages. Most insects have two pairs of wings but these have not been evolved in certain primitive forms and have been lost secondarily in some other groups. The abdomen has no walking legs in the adult stage though genital appendages are often present. The insects are primarily terrestrial and almost all respire through a system of internal air-tubes or tracheae. Insect development generally involves some degree of metamorphosis and in the more specialised forms this entails profound external and internal changes. The earliest known fossil insects date back to Devonian times; the class almost certainly arose from some myriapod-like ancestor, but we have little detailed knowledge.

THE EXOSKELETON: The outer surface of an insect is covered with a layer of cuticle which varies in thickness from one part of the body to another and from one species to another. In large beetles, for example, it provides a thick protective armour—brown, jet-black or brightly coloured—while in the delicate larva of a midge it forms a thin, flexible and transparent investment. In all insects, however, this cuticular exoskeleton is a continuous non-cellular layer secreted by a thin sheet of underlying epidermal cells. It is composed of a carbohydrate called chitin associated with various proteins and it not only encloses the outer surface of the insect but is even infolded to line or support some of the internal organs. The cuticle is a surprisingly elaborate structure usually composed of three main sub-layers, the epicuticle, exocuticle and endocuticle, and it is a system of enormous functional importance. Many of the insect's most characteristic features reflect the properties of the cuticle. cop.1

To begin with, the cuticle defines the insect's size, shape and appearance, equipping it with a variety of external organs used in feeding, locomotion, defence and reproduction, and conferring on the insect its distinctive colours and surface texture—whether smooth or sculptured, hairy, bristly or covered with tiny scales. Secondly, the cuticle protects its owner, combining mechanical strength with lightness and withstanding normal strains and stresses with a high margin of safety. It is also characteristic of the cuticle that it may be relatively soft and flexible or hard and rigid, depending on whether or not some of the cuticular proteins have undergone a process of sclerotisation, analogous to the tanning of leather. Hard plates or sclerites separated by soft membranes combine rigidity and flexibility, thus ensuring protection while permitting movement. To this end, the cuticle provides sites on which are attached most of the insect's muscles, the two working together harmoniously as the skeleto-muscular system. Where the greatest flexibility is needed, as at the joints near the base of the wings, a specially elastic, rubber-like protein known as resilin is incorporated into the cuticle. Less obvious, though of vital importance, is the way in which the cuticle acts as a waterproof covering, enabling the insect to conserve the water in its blood and tissues and so saving it from desiccation—always a danger to members of this essentially terrestrial group. The water-conserving function is performed mainly by specially arranged wax molecules in the outermost cuticular

A green lacewing. The green lacewings or 'golden-eyes' are attractive neuropteran insects of the family Chrysopidae (p. 137). The female lays each egg at the end of a long, slender, vertical stalk and the larvae feed mainly on aphids, whose body contents they suck out through their long, curved, piercing mouthparts.

Common wasp (*Vespula vulgaris*, queen). The wasps, known in North America as yellow-jackets, have large, kidney-shaped compound eyes and conspicuous antennae. The central part of the 'face' is the clypeus, while the area above and between the antennae is the frons. Below each eye a large mandible is hinged to the head-capsule.

layer, the epicuticle, and it is interesting to speculate on the extent to which the success of the whole class of insects depends on this thin film of wax.

So efficient a solution to many of the insect's problems is, of course, not without its drawbacks. A cuticle impermeable to water is also one through which oxygen cannot readily diffuse and a respiratory system of delicate cuticular tubes transports air to the innermost tissues. This in turn imposes limits on the maximum size which insects can attain. Further, the very rigidity of the cuticle which provides such effective protection also entails complications in the growing insect. Its cuticle can stretch only to a limited extent and at intervals, therefore, it must shed the constricting exoskeleton and secrete a larger one. During the process of moulting the insect is relatively inactive and unusually vulnerable. But even this unpleasant necessity has its advantages, for the shape and structure of the cuticle can be varied at certain moults, and the insect may thus pass through a metamorphic sequence of distinct forms, each adapted for the exploitation of different habitats, food sources, activities or functions.

THE HEAD: In most insects the head is a well-developed feeding and sensory centre. It is composed of six segments which undergo amalgamation during their early development in the egg. The head of the newly hatched insect and its subsequent growth stages is therefore usually a more or less globular, capsule-like structure. The cuticular walls of this capsule have to withstand the stresses caused by muscular movement when the insect feeds and they are therefore braced by an internal skeleton or tentorium—essentially an H-shaped or X-shaped system of struts formed by infoldings of the cuticle. Further reinforcement of the head wall occurs through the development of ridge-like folds of cuticle (appearing on the surface as sulci) which run over the surface of the head in a more or less constant pattern. They thus divide the head into a number of anatomical regions— the vertex dorsally, the frons and clypeus forming the 'face', the labrum or upper lip, genae (cheeks) and so on.

At each side of the head, most insects have a large compound eye consisting of a great number of closely packed visual elements. Between the compound eyes many insects possess two or three much smaller, spot-like simple eyes or ocelli,

sensitive to light but probably unable to form a proper visual image. The sensory equipment of the head is largely completed by a pair of antennae— segmented appendages, moved by basal muscles and differing greatly in length and shape from one group of insects to another. The antennae are densely covered with microscopic sense-organs, usually in the form of bristles or cone-like structures formed of thin, hollow outgrowths of cuticle. Through these the insect perceives odours, changes in the temperature or humidity of the air, and sometimes other stimuli as well. Finally, towards the lower side of the head are attached the mouth-parts which, because they exhibit a bewildering diversity, require separate treatment.

MOUTH-PARTS AND FEEDING MECHANISMS: The mouth-parts of insects are formed typically from three pairs of segmented appendages, attached to the head and surrounding the mouth. The most anterior of these are the mandibles, behind which are the maxillae and then the third pair, fused in the midline to form the labium or lower lip. In omnivorous chewing insects such as the cockroaches the mandibles are hard, massive structures whose biting surface is armed with tooth-like projections. The maxillae bear lobes, teeth or hooks to help in manipulating the food and each also carries a short, segmented palp supplied with microscopic sense-organs. Another pair of palps is borne by the labium, on the inner surface of which lies a tongue-like hypopharynx. Saliva is poured out between the labium and hypopharynx and the latter helps in swallowing the masticated food.

Mandibulate mouth-parts of this pattern occur also in many carnivorous and herbivorous insects, though with slight modifications enabling them to deal more effectively with their characteristic foods. When the choice of food is more restricted, however, the mouth-parts are more highly modified and often bear little resemblance to the primitive mandibulate type from which they must have evolved. In the Hemiptera, for example, that suck the sap of plants or the body fluids of animal prey, the mandibles and maxillae consist of very long, bristle-like stylets protected at rest by a long proboscis, the labium. When such insects feed the stylets, held closely together, are protruded from the labium and penetrate the plant or animal under attack. Between the stylets lie two microscopic channels; down one of these saliva is pumped while the sap or blood is sucked up the other. Bed bugs feed in this way, for example, but many other blood-sucking insects have evolved feeding mechanisms which achieve the same results by different anatomical means. Female horseflies, to take one example, pierce the skin of their victims with powerful sword-like mandibles and then drink from the pool of exuded blood via a complicated system of capillary tubes on the highly modified labial palps. In the nectar-feeding butterflies and moths the mandibles are absent and the maxillae form a hollow proboscis. This is spirally coiled beneath the head at rest but it can be extended for feeding through the complicated action of its muscles and inflation by blood pressure. Many such examples of specialised feeding mechanisms could be mentioned; the evolutionary plasticity of their mouth-parts has clearly been an important cause of the insects' success.

THE THORAX AND LOCOMOTION: The insect thorax consists of three body segments, the pro-, meso- and metathorax. Each consists externally of a dorsal cuticular plate or tergum, a ventral region or sternum and a pair of lateral areas or pleura. The tergal, sternal and pleural sclerites are subdivided by various cuticular ridges or grooves while infoldings of the cuticle form a stiff internal framework which braces the thoracic exoskeleton so that it can resist the strains imposed on it when the muscles of the legs and wings contract repeatedly.

Insects have three pairs of legs which move in a definite sequence when they walk, while special adhesive pads and claws near the end of the leg help it to grip the surface. Walking is not the only means of insect locomotion, however, and the characteristic jumping of grasshoppers or fleas takes place through specially enlarged hind legs equipped with unusually powerful muscles. Aquatic insects and soil-burrowing forms have legs specially adapted for movement in these unusual media while in many insect larvae, such as caterpillars or fly-maggots, movement is effected partly or entirely through the muscles of the body-wall acting on the fluid-filled visceral cavity. In these cases the legs are reduced or even lost altogether in the course of evolution.

The capacity for flight is one of the most striking characteristics of adult insects, though some species—fleas, lice and worker ants, for example—lack all traces of wings and are unable to fly. Generally, however, the insects possess two pairs of wings. The mesothorax bears the fore wings and the metathorax carries the hind pair. Typically a wing is a stiff, light, transparent or coloured cuticular plate supported by a more or less extensively developed strengthening network of rib-like thickenings, the wing veins. In the Coleoptera and Orthoptera the fore wings form thick covers protecting the more delicate, membranous hind wings, and a variety of special modifications occur in certain other insect groups. Usually, however, both pairs of wings are used for flight, the insect moving them up and down and twisting them slightly in the process so as to produce a propeller-like effect. A region of relatively low air pressure is

A harvester ant, *Messor*, showing characteristic modifications of the thorax and abdomen found in all higher Hymenoptera. Worker ants are wingless, so that the three thoracic segments are relatively small. The first abdominal segment is fused with the metathorax, the second (and in some, the third as well) forms a small, constricted node, while the remaining abdominal segments make up the large gaster.

A robber-fly (Asilidae). The members of this family are active predators on other insects, provided with a horny, piercing proboscis and long, powerful prehensile legs. At the end of each leg is a pair of well-developed pulvilli which in this specimen show up as conspicuous yellow lobes beyond the black tarsal segments.

Larva of a Stag Beetle, *Lucanus cervus*. Stag Beetle larvae live in rotting trees and are inactive, C-shaped creatures with a soft, fleshy body, a strong, sclerotized head-capsule, and three pairs of legs (the last two of which can be stridulated). The larval stage lasts nearly four years and the pupa inhabits a cell constructed from segments of chewed wood.

Top

A hover-fly (Syrphidae) taking off. Like all Diptera, the Syrphidae fly by movements of the fore wings, which they use skilfully to hover motionless above flowers. The hind wings are modified into tiny structures shaped like a drumstick and called a haltere. These vibrate at the same frequency as the fore wing but they act as gyroscopes to control the flight movements of the insect.

Above

A cockchafer, *Melolontha melolontha*, in flight. The cockchafers or June-bugs are beetles, with the fore wings modified into hard, sclerotized, protective elytra. These meet along the back when the insect is not flying and conceal the softer, membranous hind wings. Flight takes place through vibration of the hind wings alone, the elytra being held still and outstretched.

thereby created above and ahead of the insect and a zone of high pressure below and behind it. The forces which thus support the insect and propel it forward are derived ultimately from contractions of the elaborate thoracic musculature, contractions which may be repeated more than a hundred times a second. These contractions cause small, temporary distortions of the thoracic exoskeleton which are eventually converted into movements of the wings by a complicated system of cuticular levers near the wing base. Variations in these flight mechanisms create the variety of insect movements: the clumsy, fluttering flight of a heavy moth, the rapid darting of a dragonfly or the controlled hovering of a hawk moth or syrphid fly.

THE ABDOMEN AND ITS APPENDAGES: In the abdomen the segmented nature of the insect body is most clearly visible. Most insects have eleven abdominal segments and in the embryonic stages these usually each bear a pair of rudimentary appendages. The adult insect, however, often has the terminal segments of the abdomen reduced and as a rule the only appendages which it bears are the ones on the eighth, ninth and eleventh segments. In male insects these include the copulatory organs which usually consist of a protrusible aedeagus or penis and a pair of clasper-like structures which grip the female during mating. The female, on the other hand, often possesses an ovipositor formed from two pairs of abdominal appendages, between which the eggs slip when being laid. By means of variously constructed ovipositors, different species can lay their eggs in a great variety of situations—in cracks or crevices, embedded in the soil, in plant tissues or within the body of another insect. The ovipositor of bees and wasps is well developed but has lost its original function and been transformed into a sting. In the Lepidoptera and some Diptera an anatomically quite different type of ovipositor is formed from the last few abdominal segments which can be extended or retracted in telescopic fashion. At the very end of the abdomen, many insects retain a pair of cerci, the appendages of the eleventh segment. These may be long and feeler-like, as in the mayflies (Ephemeroptera) and most stoneflies (Plecoptera), they may show various degrees of reduction to stumpy, inconspicuous structures, or, as in the earwigs (Dermaptera), they may form the conspicuous forceps in which the body ends.

DIGESTIVE SYSTEM: The tubular alimentary canal of insects is differentiated into a number of successive regions, each with its own special functions. The most anterior region, the fore gut, is lined with cuticle and normally comprises a narrow oesophagus, a capacious crop (in which the food is stored temporarily) and often also a gizzard which grinds the food into fine particles. These then pass into the mid gut, which is the main digestive region. The cells lining its wall secrete a variety of digestive enzymes and the products of digestion are absorbed through the same cells into the blood. In many insects the mid gut is produced into tubular or pocket-like extensions, the gastric caeca. These increase the area of the surface over which digestive secretion and absorption occur and in some insects they also harbour micro-organisms which are essential to the life of the insect—probably because they supply it with certain vitamins. While passing through the mid gut the food is often enclosed in a delicate tube, the peritrophic membrane, which protects the gut from abrasion by hard particles. The most posterior region of the alimentary canal is the hind gut which, like the fore gut, is lined with cuticle. It has two main functions: the excretory organs discharge their contents into it anteriorly, and in most insects it helps to conserve water by absorbing it from the excretory material and the undigested remains of the food. For this reason the hind gut is often lined by special groups of water-resorbing cells, the rectal papillae, and in some insects there is a close association between the wall of the rectum and the excretory tubules, so permitting recirculation of the absorbed water.

EXCRETION: In most insects the excretory functions are performed by a set of delicate Malpighian tubules, so named after the Italian anatomist Marcello Malpighi, who discovered them in 1669. They vary in number from less than four to over a hundred and open into the alimentary canal near the junction of the mid gut and hind gut. Their walls consist of a single layer of cells which extract waste products from the blood and deposit them in the central cavity of the tubule, usually as solid spherules of uric acid or its salts. These substances are insoluble and therefore enable the insect to withstand dry conditions since, unlike some other excretory substances, they do not require large volumes of water to be lost with them when they pass out of the body. Their insolubility also enables them to be deposited as harmless crystalline residues in various parts of the body of some insects. This occurs notably in the special urate cells of the so-called fat-body—a diffuse organ composed of large masses of whitish adipose tissue packed between the other viscera in the body cavity.

RESPIRATION: Insects respire by means of a system of branching cuticular tubes or tracheae. These generally open on the surface of the body through small paired apertures, the spiracles, on some of the thoracic and abdominal segments. The oxygen entering through the spiracles diffuses along the tracheal system until it reaches the finest intracellular branches, where it passes directly into the respiring tissues. This method of respiration has several interesting consequences. The physical process of diffusion, for example, tends to limit the size of an insect; the larger the body the less efficiently can oxygen reach the tissues in sufficient quantity, though some large, active insects supplement diffusion by pumping air through the tracheal system, using bellows-like ventilation movements of special tracheal air sacs. Again, the spiracles represent sites through which water will evaporate and spiracular closing mechanisms have evolved in most insects to limit the water-loss. These in turn entail complications in the methods by which the cuticular lining of the tracheal system is shed at the moult. As might be expected, aquatic insects and those living as internal parasites have special respiratory problems and their tracheal systems show many adaptations to these unusual habitats.

BLOOD AND CIRCULATORY SYSTEM: Because of the efficiency of tracheal respiration, insect blood is

A stonefly, *Perla bipunctata*. The abdomen of this insect is covered dorsally by the folded wings, but a pair of thin, antenna-like structures can be seen projecting beyond them to the left of the photograph. These are the cerci, appendages of the last abdominal segment. They are usually feeler-like in the stoneflies, but they assume very different forms in some other insects or they may have been lost altogether in the course of evolution.

not required to transport oxygen and with rare exceptions it contains no respiratory pigments. It does, however, help to remove the carbon dioxide formed in respiring tissues, it conveys food materials and hormones, and it also exerts an hydraulic effect in expanding structures like the male copulatory organ or the wings of a newly emerged insect. The blood also contains corpuscles (haemocytes) which dispose of invading bacteria, engulf fragments of disintegrating tissues and enable the blood to clot on injury. As in other arthropods, the circulatory system is an open one. Blood is pumped forwards along a tubular dorsal heart and carried into the head by the only major blood vessel, the aorta. Here it escapes into the general body cavity or haemocoel, moving through poorly defined channels in this space and also circulating in the extensions of the haemocoel which form the cavities of the appendages and wing-veins. Movement of the blood in this way may be assisted by pulsatile 'accessory hearts'. Finally the circulating blood returns to the dorsal region of the haemocoel and re-enters the heart through valved apertures, the ostia. Although well-defined blood vessels are few in number, the blood circulation of many insects is probably more efficient than was once thought likely. The blood of the Alder Fly (*Sialis lutaria*), for example, completes one circuit of the body every minute or so, and definite patterns of flow occur in the wing-veins of many species.

NERVOUS SYSTEM AND INSECT SENSES: The insect nervous system consists of a series of segmental ganglia linked into a longitudinal chain by bundles of nerve fibres and connected by peripheral nerves with the various regions of the body. The brain lies in the head, receiving nerve tracts from the eyes, antennae and ocelli, and connected below to the suboesophageal ganglion. This centre controls the mouth-parts and is in turn connected with further ganglia forming a ventral chain in the thorax and abdomen. Each ganglion has a certain independence in governing the activities of the body segment to which it belongs, but connections between the various ganglia ensure the co-ordination necessary for many activities.

Much of the complicated behaviour of insects depends on their possessing elaborate sense-organs which mediate vision, hearing, smell, taste and touch. The compound eyes consist of large numbers of separate visual elements or ommatidia, each with its own lenses and light-sensitive cells. Through them the insect forms more or less distinct images of surrounding objects

Opposite bottom
An ichneumon fly. The Ichneumonidae are one of the major families of parasitic Hymenoptera, most of which have larvae that develop as endoparasites of Lepidopteran larvae. The adults of many species frequent flowers, especially Umbelliferae, in warm, sunny weather. The long ovipositor of the female is used to insert its eggs into the host-insect within which the larva develops.

A male Saturniid moth, *Bunaea alcinoe*. The conspicuous structures on each side of the head are the strongly pectinate antennae, each with many paired processes resembling the teeth of a comb. In related species it has been shown that the antennae are covered with microscopic olfactory sensilla which enable the male to detect minute amounts of a sex-attractant pheromone released by the female.

Side view of a locust, showing the opening of the auditory organ. On each side of the first abdominal segment, locusts have a well-developed auditory organ which can be clearly seen here above the base of the hind leg.

Mating in a cave-dwelling beetle, *Stenocara phalangium*. The male is about half the size of the female.

and detects their movement. Many insects are also able to distinguish between different colours, though the hues they recognise do not correspond exactly with those perceived by human beings. They can, for example, often appreciate ultra-violet radiation—to which we are blind—and some possess the ability to discriminate between light polarised in different planes. The Honey Bee (*Apis mellifera*) actually employs this unusual faculty in locating sources of nectar. As might be expected, the visual powers of insects vary considerably; those relying on sight to find their mates, to hunt their prey, or to identify the flowers they frequent, are best equipped, whereas parasitic insects and those living mainly in dark situations may be almost blind. Insect larvae also have reduced visual organs, usually in the form of one or more simple eyes (lateral ocelli) on each side of the head.

Not all insects can hear, but there are some in which this sense is important and in which complex auditory organs are present. The short-horned grasshoppers (Acrididae) have drum-like tympanal organs, one on each side near the base of the abdomen, and rather similarly situated organs are found in the cicadas and such moths as the Geometridae and Arctiidae. On the other hand, in the long-horned grasshoppers and crickets (Tettigoniidae and Gryllidae), the hearing organs are found in the fourth segment (tibia) of each fore leg. Despite great differences in appearance, all these organs operate by the same basic mechanism—an area of thin, membranous cuticle vibrates when sound waves impinge on it and the movements of the membrane are then translated into nervous impulses by special sensory structures, the chordotonal sensilla. In this way insects perceive a wide range of sound vibrations, including those far above the highest pitch audible to man. Responses to the sounds made by other insects of the same species play a rôle in the mating behaviour of grasshoppers and crickets and help to keep the members of a population together. Some moths, however, employ their auditory senses to perceive the supersonic cries of the bats which prey on them and which may thus be avoided.

Related to the mechanisms employed in hearing are a range of tactile and similar sensory devices. These depend on innervated hairs, bristles and other microscopic sensilla which are situated in the cuticle and respond to the stresses set up there when parts of the body are moved. In this way they mediate the sense of touch and provide the insect with information about its own movements, thus enabling it to change or maintain its orientation. Flight movements, for example, are controlled in this way. Also present in the cuticle are minute hair-like or peg-like sense-organs which are stimulated by volatile substances in the atmosphere or by aqueous solutions of other materials. These chemoreceptors, analogous to our own organs of taste and smell, are particularly numerous on the antennae and mouth-parts but may also occur elsewhere, as in the butterflies and blowflies which can perceive sugary solutions through the terminal segment of the leg. The chemical senses are of great biological importance. Through them an insect may find its food, its mate, and a site where its eggs can be laid, and in some cases the

sensitivity of the organs is quite remarkable. A few molecules only of the sex-attractant produced by the female Gipsy Moth (*Lymantria dispar*) are enough to stimulate the male to fly in her direction.

Reproduction

Male and female insects often differ in size or coloration and are sometimes even more strikingly distinct. The female Winter Moth (*Operophtera brumata*), for example, is a spidery, almost wingless creature while the male is a normal winged moth. The primary sex differences in insects, however, are found in the internal reproductive organs. In males the testes are paired structures, the cells of which differentiate to form the spermatozoa. When mature, these pass along a tube, the vas deferens, on each side of the body, to be stored temporarily in pouch-like seminal vesicles. From here the sperms eventually move to the external copulatory organ through a single ejaculatory duct. Accessory glands open into the reproductive tract and their secretion often forms a proteinaceous envelope—the spermatophore—enclosing the sperms. In the female the paired ovaries each consist of one or more tubular ovarioles containing the developing eggs. Yolk is gradually deposited in these, sometimes through the agency of distinctive nurse-cells, sometimes via the unspecialised lining of the ovarioles. The process of yolk deposition is under the control of hormones produced by endocrine centres in the head and depends also on an adequate diet. It is the high protein content of a female mosquito's blood-meal which is necessary for her eggs to develop; male mosquitoes have not the same need for protein and live on sugary plant secretions alone. The eggs are discharged from the ovary when fully ripe and pass along the oviducts into the vagina before they are laid.

The courtship behaviour of insects varies greatly in complexity, but seems always to consist of a linked series of reflexes forming a kind of stereotyped ritual which culminates in the transfer of semen. Small deviations from the events which normally make up the chain prevent its completion and such differences therefore tend to isolate closely related species by preventing cross-breeding. The sexes are attracted to each other in a variety of ways. The male Grayling Butterfly (*Eumenis semele*) follows a potential mate which he has located visually, males of some other Lepidoptera respond to attractant scents emitted by the other sex, and male mosquitoes are attracted by the characteristic buzz of the female. In some fireflies, males are attracted by the female's light, while in the crickets (Gryllidae) it is the female that is attracted by the song of a stridulating male. Further courtship behaviour may involve the stimulation of the female; the male Grayling Butterfly, for instance, seizes her antennae between his wings, releasing a sexual scent from special scales there. Many insects mate on the ground or on vegetation, but dragonflies and others do so in flight and in the mayflies (Ephemeroptera) and also some midges a female will invade a swarm of hovering males of her species in order to mate.

In the great majority of insects the spermatophore or free semen is transferred directly to the female by the male genitalia, though a few groups have evolved unusual indirect mating techniques. In the primitive Thysanura, for example, the male deposits droplets of semen on a thread attached to the ground and the female then moves over them and takes them into her reproductive tract. In the Bed Bug (*Cimex lectularius*) the male deposits the spermatozoa not in the female reproductive ducts but in a special pouch at one side of her abdomen. The spermatozoa then penetrate the delicate cuticular lining of the pouch and undertake a remarkable migration through the body cavity until they finally reach and invade the ovaries, where they fertilise the eggs. In the vast majority of insects, however, once the sperms have entered the female reproductive system they are retained there in a special storage organ, the spermatheca. Then, when an egg has been discharged from the ovary and is passing along the oviduct to be laid, the sperms leave the spermatheca, enter the egg through a special aperture (the micropyle) and a single sperm fuses with the nucleus of the egg cell.

The normal pattern of insect reproduction—mating followed by the deposition of fertilised eggs—is not found in all species. The best-known exceptions are the parthenogenetic forms, in which males are sometimes or always wanting and the females lay eggs which, though unfertilised, can develop into normal progeny. Aphids reproduce

A damselfly, *Coenagrion*, mating. The damselflies and dragonflies (order Odonata) have a unique method of copulation. Before mating the male transfers sperm from his genital aperture to a secondary copulatory organ near the front of the abdomen. When the sexes pair the male uses processes at the back of his abdomen to grasp the female by the neck or prothorax. She, in turn, bends her abdomen forward to receive sperm from his secondary copulatory organ. Mating may occur in flight or on vegetation.

A viviparous parthenogenetic aphid giving birth to young. The aphids have very complicated life cycles including bisexual and parthenogenetic forms, which may lay eggs or produce living young. Commonly the females migrate to herbaceous host plants in the spring and there produce several generations of living young by parthenogenesis. In some species the newly born females may already contain the embryos to which they will give birth when fully mature.

An adult cicada, *Tibicen*, with the cast skin from which it has just emerged. Cicadas lay their eggs in the stems of trees or shrubs. The newly emerged nymph falls to the ground and leads a subterranean existence for months or years, feeding on the roots of plants and moulting several times. Eventually the fully grown nymph emerges from the soil and moults into the adult insect which lives entirely above ground. The cuticle of the last nymphal stage splits dorsally and is cast off from the entire surface of the body, the cuticular lining of the gut and tracheae being shed with it.

which, in many insects, undergoes characteristic rotational displacements (blastokinesis) as it develops. It also sinks into the yolk somewhat and becomes enclosed in a cellular amniotic membrane. As the embryo continues its development it undergoes segmentation and most of the segments develop small appendages. Many or all of the abdominal appendages later disappear, but the more anterior rudiments differentiate into antennae, mouth-parts and legs, and the embryo gradually assumes the form in which the young insect will emerge from the egg. When this is about to happen the embryo shows obvious signs of activity and swallows some of the amniotic liquid. Air passes through the shell and begins to enter the tracheal system. In some insects the egg shell is softened by a specially secreted hatching enzyme. The emerging insect then breaks through the shell and associated membranes, its head often bearing special cuticular spines or a sharp process—the egg-burster—to accomplish this.

The young insect which finally leaves the shell is not only much smaller than the adult but also differs from it in shape and appearance to a greater or lesser extent. The ensuing period of post-embryonic development involves more or less extensive changes of form which constitute the metamorphosis. The relatively inelastic cuticle requires periodic moulting during insect growth. At each moult the old cuticle becomes detached from the underlying epidermis and is partially digested by enzymes. Its remains are then shed as a complete cast 'skin', a thin, new cuticle having been first laid down beneath the old one. The emerging insect distends itself and the new cuticle grows harder and thicker. The successive growth stages are known as instars and the number of instars in the life-cycle varies from one group of insects to another. Some have five or even fewer, others have more than twenty; most lie between these limits. In apterygote insects such as the Thysanura and Collembola, the adult, sexually mature insect continues to moult at intervals throughout its life, but other insects never moult after the adult stage has been reached.

In insects which display an incomplete or hemimetabolous metamorphosis (the apterygote and exopterygote orders), the successive instars gradually become more like the adult. Wings appear as minute, fleshy, external pads which gradually increase in size with each moult, the external genitalia grow by similar small increments, and development involves no very abrupt transitions (though the final moult into the adult is often accompanied by more extensive changes than any earlier one). In the endopterygote insects, on the other hand, metamorphosis is holometabolous. That is, there are first a series of very similar larval instars, then an abrupt and extensive metamorphosis into a quiescent pupal instar followed by the adult stage. The transformation of a caterpillar to the chrysalis and then to the butterfly indicates the magnitude of the changes involved. In extreme cases most of the larval tissues die and undergo breakdown or histolysis while a new set of adult organs develops from special persistently embryonic zones of tissue, the so-called imaginal discs or histoblasts. The main significance of the pupal stage, therefore, is that it

parthenogenetically during the summer and a special form of parthenogenesis occurs in the Hymenoptera such as the Honey Bee, the female progeny developing from fertilised eggs and the males from unfertilised ones. Another deviation from normal reproductive habits takes the form of viviparity, in which the eggs develop within the mother's body and are produced as active larvae or nymphs. Aphids provide the most familiar example of this, but it occurs in a few exceptional species from many groups of insects.

Development and metamorphosis
Insect development begins with the growth of the young embryo within the egg shell. The nucleus of the fertilised egg divides repeatedly to form a superficial layer of cells, the blastoderm, around the yolk. Further differentiation of parts of the blastoderm gives rise to a superficial germ-band

makes possible the transition from a larval phase, in which the insect exploits one set of environmental conditions, to an adult phase in which a totally different set of habitats may be utilised. All types of insect metamorphosis, however, are controlled by the same hormones, produced in endocrine glands in or just behind the head. Secretions from specially modified brain cells stimulate a pair of thoracic glands to secrete a hormone called ecdysone, which is needed for growth and moulting. Other glands, the so-called corpora allata, secrete a juvenile hormone and while this is being produced the insect cannot develop adult characteristics. As the life-cycle proceeds, however, the secretion of juvenile hormone declines, either gradually or more abruptly, thus inducing either a gradual, hemimetabolous metamorphosis or the rather more abrupt holometabolous mode of development.

Aspects of insect biology

ATTACK AND DEFENCE: Many insects behave aggressively, attacking and capturing their prey or defending themselves against their enemies, large and small. Predacious insects commonly employ their mouth-parts, and the more highly evolved predators usually have well-developed raptorial legs, as in the praying mantids and the very similar Mantispidae (Neuroptera). The earwigs (Dermaptera) and the rather primitive Japygidae use their forcep-like cerci in dealing with other insects, while even the relatively inert pupae of some beetles and Lepidoptera bear structures resembling miniature snares.

Perhaps more remarkable than these mechanical devices, however, is the extraordinary variety of glands which secrete venoms and other defensive liquids in so many insects. These substances range from the merely nauseous to the acutely

Stages in the life cycle of the Citrus Swallowtail Butterfly *Papilio demodocus*. The first illustration shows the newly emerged larva beside the empty egg-shell, from which it has gnawed its way out. The next photograph shows the fully-grown caterpillar beside the skin of the previous larval instar. There follows a photograph of the same instar in its prepupal phase, hanging up and about to pupate. The pupa or chrysalis is suspended by a fine silken thread around its middle and in the next illustration the pupal integument is splitting dorsally to allow the adult butterfly to emerge. In the last photograph we see the recently emerged adult, with its wings now expanded and hardening.

A praying mantid in the act of devouring a grasshopper. Mantids are exclusively carnivorous, both as adults and nymphs. Their well-developed eyes, mobile head, long prothorax and powerful, spiny front legs are all parts of a complex adaptation to the predatory habit. When a small insect approaches, the mantid strikes rapidly and seizes its prey between the femur and tibia of the front leg, drawing it back towards the head, where the powerful mouthparts chew it up.

toxic and they may ooze out gently or be expelled forcibly in a well-aimed spray. The beetle-like cockroach *Diploptera punctata*, for example, blows a defensive secretion out through the second pair of spiracles, and in the Bombardier Beetle *Brachinus* it is the pressure of free oxygen, produced chemically in the defensive gland, which forces out the secretion. Some caterpillars, for example those of the Yellow Tail Moth (*Euproctis chrysorrhoea*), have fragile hairs which release an urticating substance on being broken; many Hymenoptera inject poisonous secretions into their victims with a sting, while some Diptera and Hemiptera do the same with their mouth-parts. It is probably a protein fraction—melittin—which is the most toxic of the several substances injected by the Honey Bee (*Apis mellifera*) when it stings, though in general the defensive secretions are a chemically miscellaneous group, each usually a mixture of several substances. The venom of the wasp *Vespula vulgaris* contains, among other things, the pharmacologically active substance serotonin, many ants rely on a spray of formic acid, while complex

quinones and higher aldehydes occur in the defensive secretions of many groups of insects.

One remarkable but chemically still unidentified set of substances is the venoms used by some Hymenoptera to paralyse their prey, which is then stored to provide fresh food for their offspring. Some of these have a highly specific paralysing effect and are very active in minute concentrations. One part of the venom of the parasitic wasp *Bracon hebetor*, for instance, induces permanent paralysis of a caterpillar even when diluted with 200 million parts of the caterpillar's blood.

PROTECTIVE COLORATION AND MIMICRY: Many insects safeguard themselves from their vertebrate enemies by protective colour patterns which fall into the three categories of cryptic coloration, warning coloration and mimicry. Cryptic coloration ensures concealment and takes many forms, the simplest being a general similarity to the colour of the background. Green caterpillars and green Heteroptera or Orthoptera occurring on fresh grass or foliage are examples, as are the darker colours of those found on the surface of soil and rocks or among dead leaves. In recent years the pollution of the atmosphere in some industrial areas has led to the evolution of races of moths whose dark (melanic) colouring protects them from predatory birds when they rest on the bark of soot-covered trees. Another simple method of concealment employs the principle of countershading: a more or less cylindrical caterpillar coloured dark above and light below will, when illuminated from above, appear flat and blend more effectively with its background. The larva of the Eyed Hawk Moth (*Smerinthus ocellata*) is an instance, all the more interesting because its countershading is related to its habit of resting in an inverted position, suspended below a twig by its abdominal legs. Disruptive coloration is another protective device; the familiar outlines of the body are broken up and therefore concealed by a pattern of more irregular and conspicuous patches, as on the wings of many Lepidoptera. Perhaps the most remarkable examples of camouflage, however, are those in which the insect resembles in considerable detail some feature of its natural environment. The Pine Hawk Moth (*Hyloicus pinastri*) and others imitate the bark on which they rest; many geometrid caterpillars and phasmids bear a close resemblance to twigs, while other insects simulate lichens or the excrement of birds. Perhaps the most intriguing, however, are the strikingly close resemblances to leaves found in the phasmid *Phyllium crurifolium* or the orthopteran *Cycloptera*, where colour, shape and the pattern of leaf veins are closely imitated. Other examples of leaf-simulators are the Oriental butterflies of the genus *Kallima*, whose markings even extend to imitation fungus-spots and in which dry- and wet-season forms of the same species differ so as to be in harmony with the condition of the fallen leaves at these times.

Insects which are distasteful to vertebrates in some way are often marked with warning colours and thus advertise their unpleasant character. Their enemies learn to recognise them more quickly. They employ a few bold colour schemes such as the black and yellow pattern of a wasp or the caterpillar of the Cinnabar Moth (*Tyria*

jacobaeae). Related to such warning patterns are others that are an empty threat—such as the intimidating eye-spots on some insect wings—or those in which conspicuous shapes or colours deflect an attack to an unimportant part of the body or misrepresent the position of the insect. The brightly coloured hind wings of some grasshoppers and Noctuid moths, visible only when the inconspicuous resting insect suddenly takes to flight, are 'flash colours' of a related kind.

Finally there is mimicry, the close resemblance in shape or colour between different species. Such resemblances are usually superficial, affecting only the readily visible characters, and similar appearances can be produced in the most diverse ways, yet among some insects there are complex mimetic associations involving many forms of several species. In some cases the mimic is an innocuous species which evidently gains from its resemblance to a distasteful model. Females of the African Swallow-tail Butterfly (*Papilio dardanus*) exist in several forms which mimic distasteful butterflies from other genera. In America the Viceroy (*Limenitis archippus*) mimics the much more common Monarch (*Danaus plexippus*); should the mimic outnumber the 'distasteful' model the advantage might possibly be lost. In a rather different and probably commoner form of mimicry, several distasteful species have adopted very similar patterns of warning coloration. Each species therefore benefits, since they share the losses sustained while their enemies are learning to associate the colours with distastefulness. The black and yellow colours of many wasps and the red and black colours of the burnet moths (*Zygaena*) and the Cinnabar Moth (*Tyria jacobaeae*) are examples.

SOUND AND LIGHT PRODUCTION: Some insects can produce biologically important sounds without the aid of special structures, but the most effective stridulators have elaborate organs enabling each species to create its own characteristic sound patterns. Thus, among the grasshoppers, many male Acrididae have on the inside of each hind leg a row of minute pegs which are drawn, in quick succession, across a ridge on each of the closed fore wings. More complex are the tymbals lying near the base of the abdomen in male cicadas. Each consists essentially of a convex area of cuticle which can be moved in and out very quickly and repeatedly by powerful muscles, the individual clicks almost merging in a stream of sound. Generally the songs of the best-known stridulators are produced by the males, which may have a varied repertoire of songs. In the short-horned grasshoppers, one of these brings the sexes together and others stimulate the female or challenge a rival male. Not all insect songs have a sexual significance, however; the many inconspicuous stridulatory devices of Coleoptera and Heteroptera often occur in both sexes and are perhaps defensive.

The relatively few insects that produce light have long attracted attention. Fireflies and glowworms are mostly beetles of the families Lampyridae and Cantharidae, and according to the species their light varies from a feeble glow to spectacular displays by thousands of males, all flashing in unison night after night for weeks on end. The European Glow-worm (*Lampyris noc-*

tiluca) has wingless, larva-like females whose sixth and seventh abdominal segments bear luminous organs which attract the winged (and only feebly luminous) male. In the American Firefly (*Photinus pyralis*), however, both sexes can flash regularly, the female responding to the male flash and thus enabling him to find her. The light emitted by the various glow-worms and fireflies may be bluish, greenish, yellow, orange or red; it may be produced by larvae or adults; and the luminous organs vary in number, position and complexity. The most elaborate ones consist of masses of photogenic cells arranged around tracheae beneath an area of transparent cuticle. Light is produced when an organic substance, luciferin, is oxidised within the photogenic cells with the aid of an enzyme, luciferase. This mechanism is remarkably efficient, for about ninety per cent of the energy radiated by the luminous organ of a firefly takes the form of visible light, compared with a mere five per cent for an electric light blub.

SWARMING AND MIGRATION: Large numbers of insects, all of a single species, occur sufficiently often to be a familiar sight, though the circumstances in which these aggregations develop are quite diverse. Some are casual, passive accumulations due to waves, winds or tides, but others are more actively formed in the course of some special

A leaf-insect. The leaf-insects and their close relatives, the stick-insects, belong to the order Phasmida. In leaf-insects the body is flattened, the legs bear flat expansions and the forewings closely resemble leaves. Even the wing venation is modified to resemble the pattern of veins found on a leaf. The close protective resemblance to foliage finds a parallel in some long-horned grasshoppers.

The Wasp Beetle, *Clytus arietis*, is sometimes seen on wooden fences and posts within which its larva develops. Its black and yellow banded body mimics wasps of the genus *Vespula*, and it resembles them not only in colour but also in its jerky movements and quivering antennae.

behaviour. The mass emergence of a species under favourable environmental conditions is one such cause, as in the caterpillars of the Antler Moth (*Cerapteryx graminis*) which occasionally form plagues on grassy mountain slopes in the north of the British Isles. In some ladybird beetles, mass hibernation may take place and thousands of specimens of, say, the American *Hippodamia convergens* may be found together. The enormous swarms of flying or marching locusts—Acrididae such as *Locusta*, *Schistocerca* or *Nomadacris*—have long been proverbial, but a real understanding of this behaviour is much more recent. Locusts are close relatives of the common meadow grasshoppers, differing in that locust populations can, when overcrowded pass from a 'solitary phase' into the gregarious, swarming condition, reverting to solitary status again when conditions alter. Mating swarms of insects, composed of hundreds or thousands of individuals dancing in the air, are familiar sights in calm weather. They occur in the mayflies (Ephemeroptera) and among the more primitive Diptera—mosquitoes, midges and blackflies. Such swarms consist normally of males of a single species and in the Diptera the swarm develops and maintains itself above some natural marker characteristic of the species—a pool, a road, a patch of lichen or something similar. Females enter the swarm separately to mate.

Sometimes connected with swarming, the habit of insect migration is especially characteristic of species that occupy one temporary habitat after another and it may vary from spectacular mass flights to inconspicuous periods of enhanced mobility. The powerful flight of some of the larger dragonflies enables them to migrate over hundreds of kilometres, sometimes in considerable numbers. In the Middle East, a pentatomid bug, *Eurygaster integriceps*, migrates each summer from its breeding areas in the plains up into the mountains. Later it moves down several hundred metres to hibernate through the winter, and then returns again to the plains in the following spring. Not all migrating insects depend on their own exertions, however. Weak-flying aphids and thrips are carried on winds in the so-called 'aerial plankton' but such movements are nevertheless entitled to be called migratory when the insect moves to a more favourable habitat or from one species of host plant to another. Even strong fliers like the locusts are ultimately at the mercy of large-scale air movements, and swarms of the Desert Locust (*Schistocerca gregaria*) tend to accumulate across tropical Africa and Asia in a belt where northerly and southerly winds meet. It is, however, the butterflies whose migratory behaviour has been studied longest and which include some of the best-known examples. During the winter the Painted Lady (*Vanessa cardui*) breeds in North Africa and when the spring comes it flies north across the Mediterranean and Europe. Though it breeds again in the summer in these more northern latitudes, the species cannot survive the cold winter there and the occurrence of *Vanessa cardui* in Britain, for example, depends entirely on its migratory flights. In North America the Monarch Butterfly (*Cynthia plexippus*) is perhaps the most famous migrant, overwintering in semi-hibernation on selected 'butterfly trees' in Florida and California, then dispersing to the north again when the spring comes.

SOCIAL INSECTS: Colonies of the Honey Bee and other social insects are quite different from aggregations of ladybirds or migrating locusts. The social insects live in integrated communities which include parental generations and the developing young, and the origins of this kind of organisation must be sought in some form of maternal care, such as occurs sporadically in many groups of insects. Prolongation of the adult life enables the parents to tend their young and from this subsocial stage it is not a far step to the fully social mode of life, in which some members of the colony care for the offspring of others. The termites (Isoptera), the ants and some groups of bees and wasps are social insects in this sense. These differ appreciably from one another and there are many variations within each main social group, but their

Glow-worms, *Lampyris noctiluca*. The wingless female emits light from the underside of the last two abdominal segments and is often conspicuous in hedges or grassy places on summer nights. The male has wings and is only slightly luminous. Both adults and larvae live as predators on snails, the female laying her eggs on the ground they frequent.

Termite nests, Australia. The nests of termites (order Isoptera) vary greatly in size and complexity, but some species produce large, elaborate structures with complicated systems of internal cavities and galleries, allowing control of the temperature and carbon dioxide content of the atmosphere. The nest is constructed and maintained by the worker termites and contains a royal cell for the primary reproductives. It may be constructed of a material formed after soil is mixed with the termite's saliva and allowed to dry and harden.

great similarity is the division of the species into castes. These normally include the sexual forms and the more numerous sterile individuals—the workers and, in some ants and termites, the soldiers. Each caste is adapted to perform its own special set of functions; the sexuals are responsible for reproduction, the workers tend the developing young, collect food and maintain the nest, while the soldiers defend the colony. In termites the workers and soldiers are sterile males and females; in the Hymenoptera they are sterile females only. The division of labour found in social insects may be accompanied by more or less marked differences in the appearance of the castes; worker ants and termites are small, wingless and often almost blind while the soldiers—also wingless— have large heads and powerful mandibles or other defensive structures.

The exact make-up of the colony varies from group to group and is best understood in terms of its origins. Termite colonies are usually founded by a royal pair (male and female) that remains in the colony for years, surrounded by their offspring, some of which have developed into soldiers or workers while others are still immature. Each colony of the wasp *Vespula* is founded in the spring by a queen which mated during the previous year and survived the winter hibernation. Her earliest offspring are sterile females—the workers—which extend the nest and enable more workers to be reared. Towards the end of the summer males and a new generation of queens are produced. These mate and the young queens scatter to hibernate under dead leaves or bark, eventually to found new colonies in the following year. All the others—the old queen, males, workers and developing brood—die off in the autumn.

The bumble bees—species of *Bombus*—have a rather similar annual cycle but in the Honey Bee (*Apis mellifera*) the queen lives for many years. She may leave the hive with a swarm of older workers, allowing a new queen to develop among those left behind, or when old and failing she is superseded without swarming. In either case the production of new queens takes place in special queen cells and the colony is potentially immortal. Males—the drones—are produced throughout the summer and fertilise queens from their own or other colonies during a nuptial flight. Towards the end of the summer they are driven out of the hive by workers to die of hunger and cold.

A striking characteristic of many social insects is the more or less elaborate nest in which they live. This is largely constructed and maintained by the workers. It varies considerably in size and structure from one species to another and the largest nests are very impressive habitations. Termite nests are sometimes built from a cement-like mixture of soil and saliva and may be six metres high and 4·5 across, with a complicated system of internal corridors and chambers. Social wasps build with 'carton'—a papery substance made of chewed-up wood—and Honey Bees do so with the wax secreted by special abdominal glands, while ants use soil or carton, sew leaves together with silk, or live in various natural cavities or crevices. Special accommodation may be provided for the developing brood and for food storage, the temperature of the nest may be regulated in various ways,

Worker Honey Bees (*Apis mellifera*) on wild comb. The worker bees are sterile females and on them devolves all the work of maintaining the colony. They construct the wax combs, clean and repair them, tend the developing brood, store honey and pollen, and forage for nectar, pollen and water. During its adult life the worker performs these and other duties in a fairly well defined manner.

Wood ants (*Formica rufa*) dragging a butterfly to their nest. The wood ant and its allies, build large mound nests out of pine-needles, twigs, leaves, dead grass and other similar material, on and near which large numbers of workers can be seen hurrying about. They take plant and animal food and it has been estimated that a large colony may bring home nearly a hundred thousand insects daily.

and the whole structure forms a complex habitat in which a variety of other insects may also live in harmony with the primary occupants.

It is not surprising that many analogies have been drawn between the social insects and human societies. Fundamentally, however, these are misleading or meaningless.

PHEROMONES: One of the most striking results of research into insects' behaviour has been the realisation that many of their activities are controlled by specific volatile chemical substances called pheromones. These are secreted in small quantities by special glands and released into the insect's surroundings or on to the surfaces it frequents. They are then perceived, usually through the olfactory sensilla, by other members of the species, whose behaviour they subsequently modify. Among the most intensively studied pheromones are the sex-attractants which a virgin female insect releases down-wind, where they are perceived by males that then assemble in her vicinity. The silkworm moth *Bombyx mori* produces such a substance known as bombykol, now isolated and identified chemically, while others have been obtained from such insects as the gypsy moth, *Porthetria dispar*, and the housefly, *Musca domestica*. Less often it is the male insect which produces a pheromone that attracts females. The large hibernation aggregations of some ladybird beetles (Coccinellidae) are also thought to be formed in response to a pheromone, though here the substance affects all members of the species and is not based on sexual attraction. A particularly complicated set of pheromones has been identified as controlling the behaviour patterns shown by some species of bark beetles (Scolytidae) when they are attracted to trees where other members of the species are already present. Yet a further group of these interesting substances is the alarm pheromones found in many ants and a few other species. Insects which perceive these are induced to run or fly more actively and may also behave more aggressively to their natural enemies. Some insects also produce pheromones exerting various effects on the development of other members of the species—the so-called morphogenetic pheromones. Perhaps the best known of these is the 'queen substance' which the Honey Bee queen secretes from her mandibular glands. Worker bees receive the substance from the queen and it inhibits the growth of their ovaries so that they remain sterile. It also prevents the workers from constructing 'queen cells' in the comb and so stops the colony from rearing a new queen. Some

termites, too, produce pheromones which control the development of the various castes, while in locusts the sexual maturation of the male is promoted by a pheromone secreted by the other males present. There is little doubt that further investigation will reveal more fully the important role that pheromones play in the lives of insects.

AQUATIC INSECTS: The insects are primarily a terrestrial group, but many species have successfully invaded aquatic environments. The immature stages of virtually all Odonata, Ephemeroptera, Plecoptera and Trichoptera are aquatic, as well as those of many Diptera and some Neuroptera. To these may be added all stages of such Heteroptera as the pond-skaters (Gerridae), the water-boatmen (Corixidae) and the back-swimmers (Notonectidae), together with the Dytiscidae, Gyrinidae, Hydrophilidae and some other families of beetles. These insects have exploited all the main freshwater environments—fast-flowing stony streams, slow rivers with lush vegetation, shallow ponds, deep lakes and a number of more temporary habitats. Brackish waters have also acquired their complement of insects and only the seas have remained almost closed to them—perhaps because marine habitats were already fully colonised by other invertebrate groups before insects appeared on the evolutionary scene. With such a diversity of habitats it is not surprising that many aquatic insects display intriguing adaptive modifications. The inhabitants of fast–flowing streams are particularly interesting in this connection: the larvae of some Diptera—the Blephariceridae and Deuterophlebiidae—are provided with a row of suckers for clinging to stones in the fast currents, while nymphs of the mayflies *Ecdyonurus* and *Heptagenia* are flat and streamlined so as to creep into crevices and avoid the full force of the water. In general, however, the main problems confronting aquatic insects are those connected with locomotion and respiration. Both in turn are often related to the station occupied by the insect—whether it dwells on the surface, is closely associated with the surface film, swims freely in the main body of water, crawls among vegetation or burrows in the bottom sediments. Among the commoner surface-dwellers are the pond-skaters (Gerridae) whose long middle and hind legs rest on the surface and move in a sculling fashion to propel the insect. The whirligig beetles (Gyrinidae) swim half-submerged, using broad, flat legs as efficient oars. A similar principle is adopted by most species which swim below the surface—the Corixidae, Notonectidae and Dytiscidae, for example. Such insects usually propel themselves by rowing movements of the hind legs which are effectively broadened by fringes of long hairs. These offer resistance to the water when the leg sweeps back on its propulsive stroke, but then collapse so that the return stroke is made with the minimum of effort.

As might be expected, insects living on the water-surface have no special respiratory problems; they breathe atmospheric air just as terrestrial species do. The simplest respiratory adaptations to aquatic life occur in species which live submerged but come to the surface periodically for a supply of air. In some dipteran larvae and pupae and in the larvae of dytiscid beetles, for instance,

The lesser water boatman, *Corixa*. The corixids are a successful group of fully aquatic Heteroptera, mainly found in ponds and lakes, where they swim actively by rowing movements of the hair-fringed hind legs. The middle legs are used mainly for holding on to submerged vegetation while the front legs are used in feeding. Corixids are unusual among Hemiptera in that their food consists of microscopic diatoms and algae which are swept towards the short blunt proboscis by movements of the paddle-like front legs. They carry an air store on top of the abdomen, beneath the wings, and renew it periodically by coming up to the surface of the water.

the spiracles at one end of the body are borne on funnel-like processes which project through the surface film and so conduct air into the tracheal system. Other insects like the adult *Dytiscus*, or such Heteroptera as *Notonecta* and *Corixa*, visit the surface to renew a bubble of air which is trapped beneath the wings or among hairs on the body. Air from this bubble passes into the tracheal system and by an ingenious mechanism the insect can also use it for a time to extract further oxygen from the supply dissolved in the surrounding water. The most highly adapted aquatic insects, however, are those which remain submerged, obtaining all their oxygen from the water. A few do this by means of a very specialised air-film or plastron in communication with open spiracles, but in the majority the tracheal system is a closed one, into which the oxygen simply diffuses through areas of thin cuticle. Sometimes these areas are specially developed as plate-like or tufted gills—seen along the sides of the body in mayfly nymphs and some trichopteran larvae, for example. But such structures are by no means general in aquatic insects and even the species with gills may depend on them only during conditions of oxygen shortage.

PARASITIC INSECTS: There are two main kinds of insect parasites—ectoparasites, living and feeding on the outer surface of their hosts, and endoparasites which spend their life within the host's body. The best-known ectoparasitic insects are those found on birds and mammals, including all members of the insect orders Mallophaga (biting lice), Siphunculata (sucking lice) and Siphonaptera (fleas), together with a few from other orders.

One of the most obvious features of all these insects is the reduction in their sensory and locomotor organs; the eyes are vestigial or absent, the wings usually lost and the legs adapted for clinging rather than walking. The body is flattened and often provided with rows of bristles which help to resist dislodgement from the fur or feathers of the host. The parasite's behaviour is usually directed towards securing or retaining a place on the host and the feeding habits are specialised: adult fleas, Siphunculata and the pupiparan Diptera all suck blood with their highly modified mouth-parts. All ectoparasites show some degree of host specificity—living mainly or entirely on a comparatively small selection of closely related hosts.

Insect endoparasites are of two main kinds. One small group is made up largely of Diptera whose larvae parasitise vertebrates: a few calliphorid flies such as *Dermatobia*, a group of oestrid flies living in the nasal cavities of ungulates or as 'warbles' beneath the skin of cattle or rodents, and the Gasterophilidae whose larvae live attached to the stomach lining of horses, elephants or rhinoceroses. The great majority of endoparasitic insects, however, belong to a rather special group sometimes known as parasitoids. These consist of the parasitic Hymenoptera (ichneumonids, braconids, many chalcids and so on) and some Diptera, notably the family Tachinidae. They are unusual in three ways: they parasitise hosts which are not much larger than themselves (usually other insects), the habit is confined to the larval stages while the adults are free-living, and unlike most parasites they almost always end by killing the host. When this is another insect it is usually attacked in the egg, larval or pupal stage and the parasitoids exercise considerable specificity in their choice of host. The parasitic Hymenoptera usually deposit their eggs within the host, whereas the tachinids usually lay theirs externally. In the latter case, either the young parasitoid larva finds the host and bores through its cuticle, or the parasitoid's eggs are eaten by the host, the larvae hatch out in its gut and penetrate into its body cavity. The developing larvae then proceed to attack the tissues of the host, eventually devouring almost everything. A single host may support one or many parasite larvae and in some cases the parasite larva is itself attacked by further parasites of its own.

Living within the host's tissues the parasitic larva needs special respiratory mechanisms. In some it merely punctures one of the host's tracheal trunks and is thus assured of an air supply. In others, gill-like structures are produced and the parasite obtains its oxygen rather as though it were an aquatic insect. When fully grown the larvae pupate either within or outside the remains of the host and the adult parasitoid eventually emerges to complete the cycle. Virtually all insects have their complement of these parasitoids; they often exert an important influence in controlling the numbers of the host, and when this is a pest it may be deliberately controlled through the artificial introduction of parasitoids.

INSECTS AND PLANTS: Very many insects depend directly for their food on green plants, so that close and sometimes remarkable relationships have grown up between the two groups. A large number of plant-feeding insects simply devour large quantities of foliage, as do the locusts, grasshoppers, many caterpillars, some sawfly larvae, Coleoptera and other groups. Many species are specialists, however, confining their attentions to restricted parts of a particular species or genus of plant. The scolytid beetles and their larvae, for example, construct complicated galleries between the bark and the wood of trees, feeding there in the process. The woody tissues of plants are also attacked by a great variety of purely wood-boring insects: the larvae of cerambycid and buprestid beetles, of Lepidoptera like the Goat Moth (*Cossus cossus*) and of siricid sawflies. Some such insects attack healthy, growing trees, and some decaying wood, while others concentrate on newly felled or structural timber. More delicate feeding habits are found in the aphids, leaf-hopper, plant bugs and their allies, whose needle-like mouth-parts enable them to pierce the leaves and stems to draw their

Pupae of a Hymenopteran parasitoid around a caterpillar. The Ichneumonidae and their allies are a very numerous group of parasitic Hymenoptera, the larvae of which are mostly endoparasites of other insects such as Lepidopteran larvae; they often emerge from the host to pupate after their larvae have devoured its internal organs.

A leaf-rolling weevil, *Attelabus nitens*. This insect belongs to a family (Attelabidae), closely related to the true weevils (Curculionidae). It provides for its young by partially cutting a segment of leaf (often oak or sweet chestnut) and rolling it into a kind of tube within which an egg is laid. The young weevil larva hatches from the egg and feeds on the rolled leaf, which also gives it protection, before falling to the ground to pupate in the soil.

sustenance direct from the phloem vessels or mesophyll tissue.

Three kinds of plant-inhabiting insects are particularly interesting: leaf-rollers, leaf-miners and gall-making species. The leaf-rolling habit is well developed in the Lepidoptera, where many caterpillars use their silk for tying the rolled leaf together to provide protective cases for feeding and pupation. Adult weevils of the subfamily Attelabinae roll compact, thimble-like structures from part of the leaf then lay an egg within it; the larvae hatch and feed on the rolled leaf tissue. The leaf-mining habit is confined to larvae—mainly of the dipteran family Agromyzidae and the lepidopteran Gracillariidae, though it also occurs in sawflies and beetles. The larvae are small and highly specialised, with their appendages reduced or altogether absent, and they feed on the soft tissue between the upper and lower epidermis of the leaf. Galls are formed through the hypertrophy of the plant tissue in response to the presence of the insect. They are often conspicuous and very characteristic in appearance and the majority are caused by the hymenopteran gall wasps (Cynipidae), the dipteran gall midges (Cecidomyiidae) and a few aphids. The gall not only offers the developing insect shelter and food, but also provides a habitation for parasites of the gall-forming species and other insects which it tolerates as guests or temporary visitors.

Very many insects are especially associated with flowers, feeding on the pollen or nectar and in the process transferring pollen from one flower to another. Connected with these habits are a great variety of mutual adaptations between flower and insect. The insect mouth-parts may be elongate, as in most butterflies and some moths and bees, so as to reach deep-seated nectaries. Pollen-collecting hairs are distributed over the bodies of some bees and others have special brush-like or basket-like contrivances to hold pollen for transfer to the nest. The visual and chemical senses of insects, too, enable them to detect the flowers they frequent. On the other hand, the bright colours and scents of the flowers will attract insects, special floral markings—the honey guides—help them to find the nectaries, and in some flowers various spring-like mechanisms dust the insect visitors with pollen. Other plants specialise in attracting pollen-feeders and produce an over-abundance of pollen (some of it sterile). In many cases the adaptive relationship between the plant and its pollinator is quite complicated. The separate male and female flowers of the Cuckoo Pint (*Arum maculatum*), for example, are enclosed in a chamber formed from the lower part of the spathe. Small psychodid flies and other insects are attracted to the flowers and trapped temporarily in the chamber, where they pick up pollen and later transfer it to other flowers. The North American Yucca Moth (*Tegeticula yuccasella*) has evolved a mutually beneficial association with the flowers of the yucca plant. The female moth has a special tentacle-like process of the maxilla on which pollen can collect. It visits an unfertilised flowers, lays an egg in the ovary, and then deposits some of its pollen store on the pistil. It thus fertilises the flower and at the same time provides for one of its own offspring which, when it hatches, feeds on some of the ripening seeds of the yucca plant.

Classification

In the classification of Linnaeus—with whom modern taxonomy begins—seven orders of insects were recognised. Today, although the limits of a few groups are still controversial, it is possible to distinguish some twenty-nine orders of living insects, together with a dozen or so less well defined orders known only as fossils. Progress in the sub-division of the class has been accompanied by a vast increase in the number of described species of insects. Nearly a million are now known, more are being discovered at the rate of several thousand a year, and the total number of species in the class may well prove eventually to exceed three million. In this respect the insects far outnumber all the other groups of animals combined.

In the following systematic survey, the insect orders are grouped into three main sections, the Apterygota. Exopterygota and Endopterygota. Other more elaborate arrangements probably reflect the evolutionary relationships of the various orders more accurately, however, and some of these are briefly mentioned where necessary.

Apterygote insects

These are primitively wingless insects which retain several pairs of abdominal appendages and in which the adult insect usually moults at intervals until it dies. In other respects, however, the four living orders of apterygote insects are not very closely related to one another.

Silverfish and bristletails (Order Thysanura)

The Thysanura are small or medium-sized insects with an elongate body, normal biting mouth-parts, and three long, tail-like processes at the end of the abdomen. The most primitive living thysanuran is

Tricholepidion gertschii, found under bark and rotting wood in California. Much more familiar, however, are the domestic silverfish, of the family Lepismatidae. Of these *Lepisma saccharina* and *Thermobia domestica* are widely distributed, *Lepisma* preferring cool, damp situations and *Thermobia* living in warm, dry places such as restaurants or centrally heated premises. These and a few other domestic species—such as the Australian *Ctenolepisma longicaudata*—are occasionally minor pests, but the majority of lepismatids are harmless, outdoor species. *Trichotruria nigeriensis*, an African form, is found in termite nests and some are similarly associated with ants. The members of the remaining family, the Machilidae, live under bark or stones, among leaves or dead wood, and some—including species of *Petrobius*—are found on the seashore. The Thysanura feed on dry or decaying material of plant origin and have unusual mating habits.

Order Diplura

These unfamiliar insects are structurally rather like the Thysanura, but they have no eyes, their mouth-parts are sunk into the head in special pouches, and the abdomen ends in only two terminal processes, the cerci. The Campodeidae are widely represented by species of *Campodea*—small, fragile, whitish insects living in the soil or plant débris, with long, filamentous cerci. The Japygidae are larger and mainly tropical or subtropical; their forcep-shaped cerci resemble superficially the pincers of earwigs and are used for catching their prey. The most striking representatives of the family are the Australian species of *Heterojapyx* which may reach five centimetres in length and are the largest known apterygote insects. Newly hatched japygids cluster together and are tended by their mother. The family Projapygidae includes a few species with short, tubular cerci.

Order Protura

The Protura are slender, whitish insects about a millimetre long, living mainly in soil, humus and decomposing organic matter. They are blind, without antennae, with unusual piercing mouth-parts and with small, paired appendages on the first three abdominal segments. They have five immature instars and unlike other apterygotes the adults probably do not moult. Their most unusual feature—unique among insects—is the way in which the abdominal segments increase in number from eight to eleven during development. Species of *Eosentomon*, *Protentomon* and *Acerentomon* are widely distributed and represent three of the families into which the order is divided.

Springtails (Order Collembola)

The Collembola are by far the largest order of apterygote insects with over 2,000 species, some having a very wide geographical range. They have several very distinctive anatomical features: the highly modified mouth-parts sunk into pouches within the head, the presence of only six abdominal segments, and the unique abdominal appendages. These last include a ventral tube, used for gripping smooth surfaces, and a forked jumping organ, by means of which the Collembola can leap

actively. The suborder Arthropleona includes the more elongate, normally segmented forms, while the Symphypleona are almost globular or pear-shaped, with the body segmentation obliterated. Many Collembola are common and extremely abundant but they are usually small and therefore inconspicuous. They occur mostly in damp situations—in soil or leaf–mould, under bark, and in rotting wood or fungi, with a few aquatic and seashore species. They feed mainly on fungal hyphae or organic débris and a few are pests of field crops or mushroom beds. *Bourletiella hortensis* is a common symphypleonan in Europe and North America, while *Sminthurus viridis* is a pest of clover in Europe and Australia; both belong to the family Sminthuridae. The Arthropleona is by far the larger section and includes two main groups. The Poduroidea are usually dark-coloured, with a rough, warty integument and short appendages; *Onychiurus armatus* and the freshwater *Podura aquatica* occur in both the New and the Old Worlds, while *Anurida maritima* and its allies are found on the seashore in Europe and elsewhere. Perhaps the most remarkable poduroid is a New Zealand species, *Holacanthella spinosa*, which measures up to a centimetre in length and is the giant of the order. The members of the other main section of Arthropleona—the Entomobryoidea—are brownish, white or mottled with a smooth, sometimes scaly, integument; *Orchesella*, *Entomobrya*, *Isotoma* and *Tomocerus* are some of the important genera.

A silverfish, *Lepisma saccharina*. These insects are familiar inhabitants of houses, usually occurring in relatively cool, damp places where they quickly conceal themselves in cracks and crevices when disturbed. They feed on various animal and vegetable products including sugar, floury materials, paper and book-bindings, but are rarely a serious nuisance.

The springtail, *Podura aquatica* (Collembola), is a minute insect about a millimetre long. It is unusual for a Collembolan in living on the surface of fresh water (lakes or ponds) where it sometimes occurs in very large numbers, all supported on the surface film.

Exopterygote insects

These make up the first of the two large groups of pterygote insects. Such insects are either winged or, if apterous, then clearly derived from winged ancestors. They do not moult as adults and have no abdominal appendages other than the cerci and external genitalia. The exopterygotes normally have a simple hemimetabolous metamorphosis (p. 118) without a pupal stage. The first two exopterygote orders listed below—the Ephemeroptera and the Odonata—are unusual in that they cannot fold their wings back flat over the abdomen when at rest; instead they are held out sideways or above the body. In this they resemble some extinct groups of primitive pterygotes with which they can be grouped as the Palaeoptera, in contrast to all the remaining winged insects or Neoptera.

Mayflies (Order Ephemeroptera)

The mayflies are fragile insects with membranous wings supported by numerous veins, with inconspicuous antennae and the abdomen ending in long cerci, with or without a median filament. The mouth-parts of the adult are vestigial; they cannot feed and their short aerial life is largely occupied with reproduction. The sexes mate in flight, each female entering a swarm of flying males for this purpose, after which she lays hundreds or thousands of eggs, scattering them on the surface of the lake or stream or even submerging to lay them under water. The nymphal stages are entirely aquatic, breathing with the aid of gills and adapted to life in a variety of freshwater habitats. Nymphs of some mayflies, such as *Ephemera*, live in the mud or sand at the bottom of lakes or rivers, being provided with strong, burrowing fore legs and long, tusk-like mandibles. Species of *Cloeon* (Baetidae) or *Siphlonurus* (Siphlonuridae) swim actively in mid-water with their hair-fringed cerci. The Caenidae have nymphs that live in muddy or sandy environments with the second pair of gills modified into plates which protect the more posterior ones, while the Ecdyonuridae inhabit fast-flowing streams or wave-washed lake shores and have a flattened, streamlined body. These nymphs sometimes have sucker-like holdfasts which enable them to adhere firmly to stones despite the turbulent water.

Ephemeropteran nymphs are mainly herbivorous and moult twenty times or more during their development. When full-grown they float to the surface and moult once more into a peculiar winged stage, the subimago, which is very like the adult in appearance but not yet capable of reproduction. The subimago flies to the side of the water and there transforms by a final moult into the fully functional adult. A subimaginal moult is found in no other order of living insects, but it may well be a relic of the early days of pterygote evolution, when the adult moulted repeatedly, as do most apterygote insects. In this respect, as in many structural features, the mayflies seem to have retained some of the archaic characteristics of the most primitive winged insects. All stages of the mayflies—nymphs, subimagines and adults—are readily eaten by fishes and many of the angler's artificial flies are intended to imitate them.

Dragonflies (Order Odonata)

These are large, powerful flyers with two pairs of glassy, membranous wings, a specialised venation and strongly developed predatory habits. The flying dragonfly seizes the smaller insects on which it preys with its strong, spiny, forwardly directed legs and consumes them with its well-developed biting mouth-parts. The eyes are large—as befits an active predator—the antennae are inconspicuous and the abdomen is often long and almost thread-like, though broader-bodied forms are found in the family Libellulidae. There are two main groups of dragonflies; the larger, more powerful ones form the suborder Anisoptera, while the smaller, more delicate damsel-flies belong to the Zygoptera. Both are widely distributed with many species, but a third suborder, the Anisozygoptera, is today represented only by the Oriental genus *Epiophlebia*. Adult dragonflies mate in flight, the male flying ahead of the female and gripping her head with his terminal abdominal claspers. The female then bends her abdomen forward and receives the spermatozoa from a special copulatory organ which lies at the front of the male abdomen and which he fills with semen from the true reproductive aperture before the start of the mating flight. After mating the female lays her eggs, either embedding them in aquatic plants with her serrated ovipositor or washing them off the abdomen so that they sink to the bottom or adhere to submerged vegetation. Like the adults, dragonfly nymphs are actively predacious, catching small aquatic animals with the highly specialised labium. This is a jointed structure covering the mouth like a mask when not in use, but capable of being extended rapidly to seize the prey with a pair of pointed terminal hooks. Small Crustacea, insects (including other dragonfly nymphs), worms, and even tadpoles and small fishes, are captured and devoured in this way. Zygopteran nymphs have three long, pointed gills at the hind end of the body, but the Anisoptera lack these and respire by drawing water into the rectum, the walls of which are lined with gills.

A mayfly (*Ephemera*). The large fore wings have a complete set of veins and the wing has a slightly pleated appearance recalling a partly folded fan. In this and other ways the mayflies recall the archaic forms of an early phase in insect evolution.

This rectal respiratory chamber has another subsidiary function, for by expelling water abruptly from it through the anus the nymph can make rapid, jet-propelled movements. Dragonfly nymphs moult about a dozen times and when mature they climb out of the water and undergo a last moult into the adult. Among the many families of Zygoptera the Agriidae are represented in Europe and North America by species of *Agrion* and the Coenagriidae by *Enallagma* and *Coenagrion*. The Anisoptera include such families as the powerful Aeshnidae (e.g. *Aeshna* and *Anax*), the broad-bodied Libellulidae and the club-tailed Gomphidae. Allied to these are the Petaluridae, a family of very large dragonflies whose larvae live in burrows in mud or peat; the Australian *Petalura ingentissima* is one of the largest members of the order, with a wing expanse of up to 16·5 centimetres.

Stoneflies (Order Plecoptera)

Like the mayflies and dragonflies, these insects are aquatic in their early stages. Structurally, however, the stoneflies are neopteran insects which, with the next eight orders listed below, form a complex of orthopteroid forms. The adults are sombre-coloured, soft-bodied, weak-flying insects, usually found near running water. They have two pairs of membranous wings, biting mouth-parts, long, slender antennae and cerci which are usually also long and thread-like. Some eat lichens or unicellular algae but others probably do not feed as adults. They mate on the ground or on vegetation and the female lays her eggs in the water, either while flying over its surface or, more rarely, by submerging herself. The nymphs of most species live in well-oxygenated streams and rivers, but some are found in standing water. They feed on algae and mosses or, in the large family Perlidae, on smaller insects—especially the young stages of mayflies or chironomid flies. Development takes from one to four years and there are over twenty moults. The full-grown nymph crawls out on to the land and there moults into the adult stage. The most primitive stoneflies are the Eustheniidae from Australasia and Chile, but the unusually large North American Pteronarcidae also retain some archaic features. The Leuctridae, Capniidae and Nemouridae are widely distributed in the northern hemisphere while the Perlidae is by far the largest family represented in many parts of the world.

Order Grylloblattodea

This order contains only sixteen species, the first-known of which (*Grylloblatta campodeiformis*) was discovered as recently as 1914 in the Canadian Rockies; other species are also found in North America, as well as in Japan and Russia. The order is interesting mainly because its members combine some characteristics of the cockroaches with others found in the Orthoptera. They are therefore 'living fossils'—relics of an early stage in orthopteroid evolution. *Grylloblatta campodeiformis* is a pale yellowish, wingless insect, fifteen to thirty millimetres long, found under stones at elevations of 450 to 1,950 metres, where the temperature is often near freezing point. It lays eggs in the soil or among moss and it has been found that it takes about five years to develop to adulthood.

Grasshoppers, crickets and allies (Order Orthoptera)

In the restricted sense employed here, the Orthoptera includes the grasshoppers, crickets and their close allies. They have thickened, protective fore wings, simple antennae and biting mouth-parts and most of the species are equipped with stridulatory and auditory organs and can jump actively with their powerful hind legs. The Orthoptera are best represented in the warmer regions and there are over 20,000 species divided into four main sections: the Tettigonioidea (long-horned grasshoppers), the Grylloidea or crickets, the Acridoidea (short-horned grasshoppers) and a small group, the Tridactyloidea. Each of these comprises several families, and some species are agricultural pests.

The Tettigoniidae—bush-crickets or katydids—number over 5,000 species. Both sexes have auditory organs in the front tibiae and the males stridulate by rubbing the wings together. The females have long, pointed or scimitar-shaped

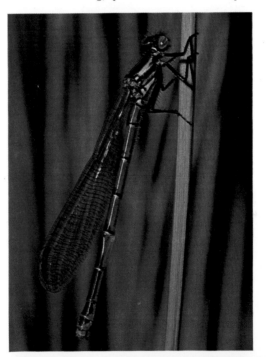

A damselfly, *Pyrrhosoma nymphula*, resting on vegetation. This species occurs throughout Europe and in Asia Minor. It lays its eggs on the underside of the floating leaves of water-plants. The nymphal stages may be found among the dead leaves and debris on the bottoms of ponds, streams and ditches.

A dragonfly, *Neurothemis stigmatizans*, from New Guinea. This Australasian species belongs to the family Libellulidae. Males are provided with densely veined wings, but the females may be of two kinds, one with a dense venation, the other where it is more open and the wing is less highly pigmented.

The Bog Bush-cricket (*Metrioptera brachyptera*). This species is generally found in marshy or boggy places, usually in heath or moorland and associated with the cross-leaved heath, *Erica tetralix*. Almost always the insect's hind wings are absent and the fore wings are reduced to short lobes, but the fully winged form does occur as a great rarity. The illustration shows a female, with a conspicuous, pointed ovipositor visible at the end of the abdomen.

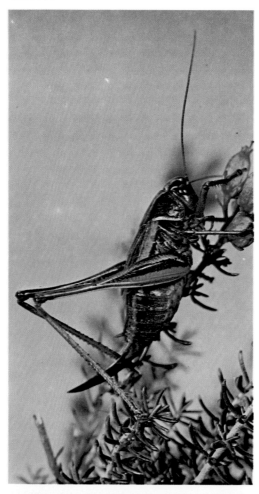

A cricket, stridulating near the entrance to its burrow. Males of the Orthoptera stridulate in various ways. In the crickets and their allies, sounds are produced by the edge of one fore wing being drawn across a set of ridges (the file) on the other fore wing. This causes the latter wing to vibrate and produce a complex pattern of sound, characteristic of the species. Several different types of song may be produced, each with its own role in courtship.

ovipositors and lay their eggs in the soil or embedded in plant tissues. *Tettigonia viridissima* is a large, bright green species found in Europe, though less spectacular forms such as *Leptophyes punctatissima* or the marsh-loving *Metrioptera brachyptera* are commoner. In North America the wingless Mormon Cricket (*Anabrus simplex*) can be a serious pest of crops in the Great Plains. *Saga* and its allies are carnivorous, but most tettigoniids are plant-feeders. Closely related to them are the Stenopelmatidae which include such North American forms as the camel crickets (e.g. *Ceuthophilus*) and the wingless sand crickets (*Stenopelmatus*). The 'wetas' and king crickets of the Australasian region also belong to this family; the New Zealand species *Hemideina megacephala* lives in rotten logs or old trees and the male has an enormous head with huge mandibles. The Gryllidae or true crickets are a large and widely distributed family differing from the tettigonioids in having only three tarsal segments, in the detailed structure of the ovipositor, and in the wing venation. The European House Cricket (*Acheta domesticus*), which has also been introduced into the United States, has many common relatives in meadows, woods and sandy or bushy places. *Nemobius* and its allies are the ground crickets, while *Oecanthus* includes the tree crickets—delicate, nocturnal, arboreal insects that lay their eggs in the pith of plant stems and so differ from most gryllids, which deposit them in the ground. More unusual are the species of *Myrmecophila*—small, oval, wingless crickets associated with ants in America, Europe and Asia. Related to the Gryllidae are the Gryllotalpidae or mole-crickets, large species armed with powerful, spade-like front legs which they use to burrow through the soil like moles (though some species can also fly). They feed on insects, worms and plant material and *Gryllotalpa* is a cosmopolitan genus.

The Acrididae are the largest, most familiar, and most notorious family of Orthoptera, for they include the short-horned grasshoppers of meadows and prairie country as well as the locusts which periodically devastate the crops and natural vegetation of warmer regions. Unlike the Tettigoniidae and Gryllidae they have short antennae and auditory organs at the base of the abdomen. The males of most species stridulate by rubbing the hind legs against the wings and the females have short, stout ovipositors with which eggs are laid in the soil. Species of *Chorthippus* are common in Europe, while the lubber grasshoppers of the United States include such large species as *Romalea microptera*. *Dissosteira* and *Melanoplus* are also important North American genera, the latter including the Rocky Mountain Locust which in the last century destroyed crops over a wide area, later to disappear from the scene. Today the most injurious locusts occur in the Old World—species such as the Desert Locust (*Schistocerca gregaria*), the Red Locust (*Nomadacris septemfasciata*) and the widely distributed Migratory Locust (*Locusta migratoria*). *Chortoicetes* includes the plague locusts found in the dry interior regions of Australia. Closely related to the Acrididae is a distinctive African family, the Pneumoridae or bladder-locusts, so called from the inflated abdomen of the male. The relatively small family Tetrigidae (grouse locusts) are harmless insects with a very characteristic prothorax produced backwards so as to cover most of the abdomen. The Tridactylidae or pigmy mole-crickets comprise some fifty species of small insects, often living near water and able to burrow into sandy ground. *Tridactylus variegatus* occurs from southern Europe to the East Indies and *Ellipes minuta* is sometimes abundant in California. The only close relatives of this family are the peculiar Cylindrachetidae, soil-burrowing insects from Australia, New Guinea and Patagonia which have independently evolved a very close resemblance to the true mole-crickets (Gryllotalpidae).

Stick insects and leaf insects (Order Phasmida)

The Phasmida are a predominantly tropical group, allied to the Orthoptera but with a much smaller prothorax, rather different external genitalia and five-segmented tarsi. They also lack specialised stridulatory and auditory organs and are unable to jump. The phasmids are all herbivorous and their eggs are large, hard-shelled objects which often bear a striking resemblance to seeds and sometimes remain dormant for long periods. Perhaps the most remarkable members of the order are the African and Oriental Phylliidae, in which the body and legs are flattened into leaf-like shapes and the wing-venation imitates the leaf veins. More numerous, however, are the elongate, usually wingless, twig-like species such as the North American Walking Stick (*Diapheromera femorata*). The Australian species, *Palophus titan*, is a giant stick insect of similar form, measuring up to twenty-five centimetres in length. The order also includes more normal-looking, thick-set species, however, such as *Timema californica* of the western United States. A few genera of phasmids are parthenogenetic and lack true males, though sterile intersexual forms of a male-like appearance are sometimes encountered. The nymphs of many species are able, when attacked or injured, to break off a leg near the base, subsequently regenerating a new one. *Carausius morosus*, an Oriental species reared by children or as a laboratory animal in many parts of the world, exhibits both parthenogenesis and regeneration and is also able to adjust its colour fairly rapidly to that of its background.

Earwigs (Order Dermaptera)

The Dermaptera include about a thousand species of medium-sized insects, most of which have very short fore wings (beneath which the large hind wings can be folded in neat parcels) and bear conspicuous defensive forceps—the cerci—at the end of the abdomen. The great majority fall into the suborder Forficulina, exemplified by the common European Earwig (*Forficula auricularia*). This species has been introduced into the Americas, South Africa and Australasia and, like most earwigs, is an omnivorous and nocturnal insect. The female lays a mass of white, oval eggs in the soil, carefully tending them and the young nymphs which hatch out in the spring. These moult four times before becoming adult and in temperate climates the whole life-cycle lasts a

Desert locusts (*Schistocerca gregaria*) about to mate. *Schistocerca* is a locust of major economic importance, whose swarms occur over a wide area of the Old World from Africa through Arabia to Pakistan. As in other locusts, mating is not preceded by any special courtship behaviour; the male clings to the female's back and the spermatozoa are passed to her enclosed in a proteinaceous sac, the spermatophore.

A short-horned grasshopper (Acrididae) from Ethiopia. Two characteristic features of these insects are the relatively short antennae (much shorter than those of crickets or bush-crickets, for example) and the greatly enlarged femur of the hind leg. This accommodates the powerful tibial levator muscles which enable the grasshopper to jump.

131

A stick-insect, *Trachythorax maculicollis*, mating. The stick-insects (order Phasmida) include long, thin, twig-like species, flat green leaf-simulators (p. 121), and a smaller number of more normal looking insects.

The common European Earwig, (*Forficula auricularia*). This is a male specimen, as shown by the large, strongly curved, forcep-like cerci at the hind end; in females the cerci are somewhat smaller and almost straight. *Forficula* females display a simple form of maternal care; they lay a clump of eggs in a cavity in the soil and watch over the eggs and newly hatched young.

year. Most of the Forficulina are structurally very similar to each other, though they are divided into some six families; the Forficulidae, Labiidae and Labiduridae are represented in Europe and North America, but the majority of the species are tropical. Differing in many respects from these are the other two suborders of Dermaptera, the Hemimerina and Arixeniina, each with only a single genus. *Hemimerus* is a blind ectoparasite of bamboo-rats (*Cricetomys*) in Africa, while *Arixenia* lives in bat-inhabited caves in south-east Asia. Both are wingless, viviparous, rather bristly insects whose cerci are soft, flexible structures not modified into forceps.

Web-spinners (Order Embioptera)

These are a group of about 300 species which live gregariously in silken tunnels that they spin in the soil, beneath stones, or under the bark of trees. The silk is secreted by glands in the first tarsal segment of each fore leg, the movements of which weave the threads into the characteristic webbing. The males are usually equipped with two pairs of soft, membranous wings but the females are always apterous. The Embioptera feed on dead vegetable matter and eggs are laid in the silken tunnels, where the females also tend the newly hatched young. They occur in all the warmer parts of the world and are divided into seven families. Of these the Clothodidae, from South America, are the most primitive, but the Embiidae include most species.

Cockroaches and praying mantids (Order Dictyoptera)

At first sight it seems strange to include in one order the cockroaches (suborder Blattodea) and the praying mantids (suborder Mantodea). Cockroaches are generally flat, thick-set, omnivorous insects, able to run rapidly, while the slower-moving mantids are more elongate and live entirely on smaller insects which they capture with their highly specialised front legs. Nevertheless the two groups agree in many details of thoracic and abdominal structure, in wing venation, and in their habit of laying batches of eggs enclosed in a hard-walled capsule or ootheca. Of the two the Blattodea are the more generalised and have persisted with relatively little fundamental change since Upper Carboniferous times, a period of about 250 million years. The best-known cockroaches are the cosmopolitan domestic species such as the dark brown *Blatta orientalis* with its reduced wings or the smaller *Blattella germanica*, a light brown species with dark thoracic stripes. Most of the 4,000 species live wild, however, mainly in warm regions and a few have unusual habits. *Nocticola*, for example, is a pale, blind, wingless, cave-dwelling species, *Attaphila* is associated with ants, and *Cryptocercus punctulatus* is a North American species feeding on dead wood, which it digests with the aid of symbiotic protozoans inhabiting its gut. The Australian species of *Panesthia* burrow in the soil, where they live in family groups consisting of an adult male and female and ten to twenty of their offspring. A few species are viviparous, but most cockroaches lay their eggs in a hard, brown, purse-shaped ootheca, sometimes carried about by the mother for several days, projecting from her body. The young hatch within this after it has been deposited and the ootheca then splits open to release them. They moult between six and twelve times according to species, gradually metamorphosing into the adult cockroach.

The mantids comprise about 2,000 species from the warmer regions, all predacious and armed with a pair of very powerful, spiny fore legs which they hold raised in an attitude of supplication. They are sometimes protectively coloured, resembling the leaves or flowers on which they lie in wait for their prey, seizing it between the femur and tibia of the front leg by a sudden movement. A pale green species, *Mantis religiosa*, is one of the few found in Western Europe and occurs also in the eastern United States since its introduction there early this century. The north American fauna also includes *Tenodera aridifolia*, a large species introduced from China, as well as a southern species, *Stagmomantis carolina*. The voracious habits of mantids sometimes make mating a hazardous operation for the male; if not recognised in time he is liable to be treated as the legitimate prey of the female, who may devour him (starting at the head end) even while copulation is in progress. Mantid oothecae are very variable in shape, laid attached to twigs, bark, or stones and they accommodate the eggs in a single, central cavity. The young mantids are as predacious as, and similar in shape to, their parents. These young will undergo up to a dozen moults in the course of their development to the adult mantid.

Termites (Order Isoptera)

The termites are often known as 'white ants' but they are in no way closely related to the true ants and such biological similarities as there are between the two groups have been evolved independently. The termites are, in fact, near relatives of the cockroaches, from which they differ structurally in having two pairs of entirely membranous wings and in lacking the ovipositor and external male genitalia. Biologically, they are remarkable for their highly developed social organisation. They live in large colonies that inhabit a system of galleries in the soil or wood or they construct nests which are sometimes very large and elaborate structures. This mode of life is associated with differentiation into as many as four anatomically and functionally distinct castes. These are: the primary reproductives, fully winged forms which swarm out from established colonies and mate, each pair (king and queen) founding a new colony; the supplementary reproductives, smaller, pale forms with reduced eyes and fleshy, non-functional wings (these develop in colonies which have lost one or both of the primary founders and they take over the latter's reproductive functions); the workers, which are small, wingless, sterile forms responsible for building and maintaining the nest, foraging and feeding the reproductives and the young progeny; and finally the soldiers, which are also wingless and sterile and are responsible for defending the colony. The soldiers have large heads with powerful mandibles or, in a few species, with a snout-like projection from which they discharge a sticky secretion that immobilises enemies (usually ants).

The worker termites feed on plant material of one sort or another: trees, dead stumps, logs or wooden buildings may be attacked, some species favouring dry wood, some living in damp structures. Other species feed on dry grass or leaves while *Macrotermes* and its allies supplement their diet with the fructifications of specially cultivated 'fungus gardens' within their nests. The food is broken into small fragments and fed to those members of the colony that do not forage for themselves. A newly founded colony gradually grows in size as more and more eggs are laid and in some species it may ultimately number over a million individuals and endure for scores of years. In these large colonies the queen is virtually an egg-laying machine; the growth of her ovaries causes the body to swell into a large, sausage-shaped structure and she lies inert in a special royal cell attended by crowds of workers.

The 1,700 species of termites are essentially tropical and fall into six families. The most primitive is the Mastotermitidae, containing only the Australian *Mastotermes darwiniensis*. The Kalotermitidae include species like *Kalotermes snyderi*, the dry-wood termite of the south-east United States, while to the Hodotermitidae belongs *Zootermopsis*, the rotten-wood termite of the Pacific coast. The first two of these families lack a true worker caste, as do some Hodotermitidae, but one is present in the Rhinotermitidae (which includes *Reticulitermes flavipes*, a destructive subterranean species from the northeastern United States) and in the Termitidae. This last family is the largest of all, containing about two-thirds of all the species, and its representatives occur in all the warmer regions. Among the commonest termites in Africa are species of *Trinervitermes*, which feed on grass and build domes or conical mound nests. *Amitermes meridionalis* is the celebrated 'Magnetic Termite' of Northern Australia, whose huge mound-like nests always point north and south with broad faces to east and west, apparently for maximum warmth from the sun.

Order Zoraptera

This order comprises only sixteen species of *Zorotypus*, two found in the United States, but none in Europe. They are minute insects living under bark, rotten wood or associated with termite nests. The adults exist as both winged and apterous forms, but very little is known about them.

Booklice (Order Psocoptera)

This order includes about a thousand species of small, inconspicuous, soft-bodied insects with very characteristically modified biting mouth-parts. Some of its members are apterous, but the majority of species have two pairs of membranous wings held roof-like over the abdomen in repose and bearing a characteristic system of venation. Most Psocoptera live on trees and shrubs or under bark and stones but some, such as *Trogium pulsatorium* and species of *Liposcelis*, occur in houses, barns or granaries, in dusty places or among old papers and other débris; for this reason they are often known as booklice. The Psocoptera feed on fungi, lichens,

An Australian cockroach, *Balta bicolor*. This species is closely related to the cosmopolitan German cockroach, *Blattella*. It flies at night and is often attracted to lights.

The fully winged primary reproductives from a termite colony shown here, are swarming. Each pair, if successful will mate to form a new colony.

Pediculus humanus, the common louse of man. These wingless insects occur in two forms, perhaps to be regarded as separate species, the head and body lice. Lice cement their eggs to the hairs of the host and the three nymphal stages and the adults all feed on the host's blood, which they suck up through their specialized piercing mouthparts. *Pediculus humanus* can transmit epidemic typhus and was also responsible for conveying the 'trench fever' that occurred among combatants in the First World War.

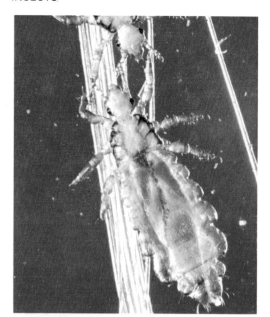

A Pentatomid bug, *Edessa rufomarginata*. The Pentatomidae and their allies form one of the largest sections of terrestrial Heteroptera. Their name is derived from the division of the antenna into five segments, otherwise unusual among Heteroptera. Pentatomoids are also distinguished by the large and conspicuous scutellum of the mesothorax which may extend back to cover most of the abdomen, so giving them the common name of 'shield bugs'.

A pond skater, *Gerris*. These are commonly found sculling over the surface of still or slow-flowing water by means of their long middle and hind legs and helped to float by the unwettable hairpile over the ventral surface of their bodies. They feed mainly on dead floating insects and lay their eggs on submerged vegetation, the young stages having habits similar to the adult.

pollen and other vegetable materials and have a simple life-cycle with about six immature stages. The majority of species belong to the suborder Eupsocida, which includes such families as the Psocidae, Mesopsocidae and Pseudocaeciliidae. Two smaller suborders, the Trogiomorpha and Troctomorpha, are also recognised.

Biting lice (Order Mallophaga)

The Mallophaga consist of over 2,800 species, all ectoparasites of birds or, to a lesser extent, of mammals. They are wingless, rather flat insects with bristly bodies and without compound eyes. They have reduced biting mouth-parts and feed on the feathers or hair of their hosts, though some species occasionally take blood. The eggs are cemented to the fur or plumage and the three immature instars also live as ectoparasites. The suborder Amblycera includes a large family of bird-parasites, the Menoponidae, of which *Menacanthus stramineus* and *Menopon gallinae* are pests of domestic poultry. The other main suborder, the Ischnocera, includes a large bird-infesting family, the Philopteridae, as well as the Trichodectidae from mammals. The last-mentioned family includes the common Dog Louse (*Trichodectes canis*), and species of *Damalinia* from horses, goats and cattle. A third suborder, the Rhynchophthirina, is represented only by the peculiar *Haematomyzus* found on elephants and wart-hogs.

Sucking lice (Order Siphunculata)

Like the Mallophaga, with which they are sometimes united, this order is exclusively ectoparasitic, though its 300 or so species are all associated with mammalian hosts, especially the carnivores, rodents and ungulates. The sucking lice are blood-feeders with mouth-parts radically re-organised into three stylets accommodated in a cephalic sac. Like other insect ectoparasites they are wingless, flat, almost blind insects with legs that end in well-developed claws, enabling them to cling to the hairs of the host. The eggs are normally cemented individually to the hairs and the three immature stages resemble the adult in most features. The most notorious siphunculate is *Pediculus humanus*, the Head and Body Louse of man, which can transmit the micro-organism causing epidemic typhus. The Echinophthiriidae are a distinctive family of scaly lice infesting seals and sea-lions, while the Hoplopleuridae include species from rodents and the Linognathidae some pests of cattle.

Order Hemiptera

The Hemiptera are by far the largest exopterygote order with over 50,000 species. They vary greatly in appearance and biology, the suborder Heteroptera including such insects as the plant bugs, bed bugs, pond-skaters and water boatmen, while the even more diverse suborder Homoptera contains the leaf-hoppers, frog-hoppers, cicadas, aphids and scale-insects. The one unifying characteristic of this great assemblage is a piercing and sucking proboscis in which the mandibles and maxillae have been transformed into thread-like stylets capable of penetrating deeply into the plant or animal tissue on which they feed. The Homoptera all live on the juices of plants but the Heteroptera include plant-feeders, predators and blood-sucking species. Many Hemiptera are injurious to man or his crops, either through the direct injury caused when they feed or through transmitting pathogenic micro-organisms.

The Heteroptera—so-called because their fore wings are divided into a tough basal part and a membranous apical region—fall into three main sections: the Geocorisae or terrestrial bugs, the Amphibicorisae living on the surface of water, and the Hydrocorisae, which swim beneath the surface. Among the Geocorisae, the shield-bugs (Pentatomidae) include many relatively large and conspicuous species, mostly phytophagous but with some predators among them. The Harlequin Bug (*Murgantia histrionica*) attacks cabbages in North America, while *Eurygaster integriceps* is an injurious Old World species; *Antestia variegata* attacks fruit and coffee in Africa while the bright green *Nezara viridula* is a widely distributed pest. Another predominantly phytophagous family is the Coreidae, to which belongs the North American Squash Bug (*Anasa tristis*); some coreids have striking leaf-like expansions on their legs and many produce a nauseous defensive scent. Probably allied to them are the brightly coloured Pyrrhocoridae, including various species of the red, white and black *Dysdercus* which convey a fungal disease of cotton in Africa and elsewhere. The members of the large, cosmopolitan family Lygaeidae are also mostly plant-feeders, found in moss, surface litter or low vegetation; the Chinch Bug (*Blissus leucopterus*) is a pest of cereal crops in North America. In the family Tingidae, much of the body and fore wings is covered with a lace-like pattern of sculptured reticulation; though plant-feeders they are now thought to be related to a very large predacious family, the Reduviidae or assassin bugs. Most of these feed on other insects, but *Triatoma* sucks the blood of mammals (including man) and transmits the trypanosome causing Chagas' disease in South America. Two other predacious families are the Nabidae and the Anthocoridae, both commonly found on vegetation where they feed on various small arthropods and lay their eggs in the plant tissues. The related Cimicidae are the bed bugs, of which *Cimex lectularius* is the species found in temperate regions. The largest family of Heteroptera is the Miridae, which includes phytophagous and predatory species as well as some which can feed in both these ways. They are rather delicately built, usually elongate-oval insects. The Apple Capsid (*Plesiocoris rugicollis*) is a pest of apples in Britain, whereas *Blepharidopterus angulatus* is a beneficial orchard insect feeding on the injurious red-spider mites. Lastly among the Geocorisae come the Saldidae—dark, oval-shaped predators, some of which can endure immersion in water for quite long periods and are perhaps related to the stock from which some aquatic Heteroptera evolved.

The Amphibicorisae live on the surface of water and are partly covered with a dense, unwettable hair-pile which helps them to float. The narrow pondskaters (Gerridae) catch insects with their fore legs while the long middle and hind legs enable them to scull quickly over the water-surface. *Halobates* is a peculiar marine gerrid found far from land on the larger oceans. The stream-dwelling Veliidae (water crickets) are stouter, with shorter legs, while the Hydrometridae are delicate, stick-like insects which walk slowly on still or sluggish waters. The Hydrocorisae live below the surface of the water; they have evolved various methods of obtaining the air supply they need for respiration and many of them swim actively with their hair-fringed legs. The Naucoridae are broad, flat insects with raptorial fore legs. *Aphelocheirus* has adopted plastron respiration (p. 125) and therefore does not need to visit the surface to obtain oxygen. The Belostomatidae are large species, feeding on tadpoles, young fishes, molluscs and insects. There are several North American species, *Lethocerus americanus* being over five centimetres long. The Nepidae or water scorpions are also actively predacious. They breathe through a long tube at the end of the abdomen; *Nepa* is a flat, oval insect, while *Ranatra* has a long, cylindrical body. The Notonectidae or backswimmers move upside-down with powerful strokes of the hind legs and carry an air store on the underside of the abdomen and beneath the wings. Many species lay their eggs in or on aquatic plants and *Notonecta* has species in all parts of the world. Last come the water boatmen or Corixidae. They are structurally rather distinct and differ from other Hemiptera in feeding on diatoms and other microscopic algae. They swim by rowing movements of the hind legs and the males of some species can stridulate.

The suborder Homoptera contains two main sections: the Auchenorrhyncha, in which the proboscis arises directly from the back of the head, and the Sternorrhyncha, where its base is enclosed by parts of the prothorax. A small third group, the Coleorrhyncha, consists of a single peculiar family (the Peloridiidae) occurring mainly in forests of the southern beech (*Nothofagus*) in Australasia and South America. Among the Auchenorrhyncha, the cicadas (family Cicadidae) are mainly tropical and subtropical, living in bushes and trees, where the males sing loudly (though the primitive Australasian *Tettigarcta* is voiceless). Eggs are laid in the plant stems and the newly hatched insects fall to the ground. They complete their development in the soil, burrowing with their strong fore legs and feeding on the roots of plants. Development is slow and in some North American species of *Magicicada* it may be seventeen years before the adults

A water scorpion, *Nepa cinerea*. *Nepa* and its allies live below the water surface in weedy places, breathing through a long respiratory tube that conducts air from the atmosphere into the tracheal system. They are predacious, catching small invertebrates with their powerful fore legs and sucking out their body contents. The eggs are laid in chain-like clusters.

emerge. The Cicadellidae or leaf-hoppers are medium or small, somewhat long-bodied forms, of which over 8,000 species are known from all regions of the world. Many injure their host-plants seriously and a few transmit virus diseases, e.g. *Circulifer tenellus*, a pest of sugar beet in the United States. A closely allied group is the Membracidae, in which the dorsal side of the prothorax is extended into a spine or some other bizarre-shaped process. The Cercopidae are the frog-hoppers, cuckoo-spit insects and American spittle bugs, in which the nymphs develop inside a mass of froth which they create by blowing bubbles with the posterior abdominal segments; *Philaenus spumarius* is a common European and North American species, remarkable for the many colour varieties in which the adult occurs. Some twenty other families of Auchenorrhyncha make up the Fulgoroidea, of which the best known in temperate countries are probably the Delphacidae. They are small insects with a large spur on each hind tibia and they lay their eggs in plant stems. The many tropical fulgoroids include species in which the head has a rather large anterior projection; in the South American *Laternaria* this process is shaped

like a peanut, coloured to resemble the jaws of a crocodile.

Four groups of insects make up the section Sternorrhyncha. Of these the best known are the aphids or greenfly in the Aphidoidea, most species of which are polymorphic, existing as a series of different forms: winged or wingless, parthenogenetic or bisexual, viviparous or egg-laying. Several different generations may succeed one another and the life-history is often further complicated by the habit of migration from a woody winter host (where sexual reproduction takes place) to an herbaceous summer host on which rapid parthenogenetic multiplication takes place. Aphids often secrete a sugary liquid (honeydew) which is attractive to ants and in some cases mutually beneficial associations have been evolved between the two groups. Many species are pests: *Eriosoma lanigerum* is the woolly aphis of apple trees, *Adelges abietis* forms pineapple-shaped galls on spruce, and *Viteus vitifoliae* once devastated the vineyards of France. *Myzus persicae* attacks many hosts and like some other aphids it transmits a number of plant virus diseases. A less familiar group of Homoptera is the Psyllidae, whose members look like miniature cicadas and have curious flat nymphs, the various species of which are often more distinctive than are the corresponding adults. *Psylla mali* is found on neglected apple trees in Europe and has been introduced into North America, but the psyllids reach their greatest abundance in the Australasian region, where they have taken the place of the aphids. The scale-insects or Coccoidea are an economically important Sternorrhynchan group of great biological interest. Male Coccoidea are delicate, midge-like insects, whereas the better-known females are wingless, flat and more or less degenerate. They secrete a waxy substance which in some species covers their body like a hard scale, beneath which they live and lay their eggs. Males develop by an elaborate metamorphosis involving two quiescent, pupa-like instars, but these are absent from the female life-cycle. *Quadraspidiotus perniciosus* is the notorious San José Scale, and various mealybugs (Pseudococcidae) attack citrus fruits and greenhouse plants. On the other hand, the Indian Lac Insect (*Laccifer lacca*) provides the waxy materials from which shellac is made and the Mexican species *Dactylopius coccus* yields the dyestuff cochineal. The white-flies or Aleyrodidae are the last of the main groups of sternorrhynchan Homoptera. They are very small, usually white, moth-like insects whose immature stages are flat, immobile, limpet-shaped creatures often decorated with tufts or radiating threads of wax. The last instar nymph undergoes a complex transformation into the adult and is often inaccurately known as a pupa. *Trialeurodes vaporariorum* is a cosmopolitan pest of tomatoes and other plants, often found in greenhouses.

Thrips (Order Thysanoptera)

These are very small insects often found on flowers or grasses in large numbers. They have peculiar piercing mouth-parts and feed on plant juices or on small arthropods. Some are apterous, but most have very narrow, strap-like wings fringed with long hairs. In one suborder, the Terebrantia, the female lays her eggs in plant tissues; members of

A Costa Rican tree-hopper (Membracidae). At first sight this photograph suggests a formidably spined plant. In fact each 'spine' is the pointed dorsal process on the prothorax of a Membracid, several of which are clustered one behind the other, with their young. These structural and behavioural features presumably protect both the insects and the plant on which they feed, but some Membracids have quite improbably elaborate thoracic processes, the adaptive significance of which is far less obvious.

Feeding aphids clustered along a plant stem. Many aphid species are especially abundant on the softer, more succulent parts of their host-plants, where their powers of parthenogenetic reproduction (p. 118) enable large colonies to build up quickly. There is reason to believe that the initial distribution of the aphids is a random process, but that they remain feeding, and therefore congregate, at places where the plant sap contains nutrients that they prefer.

the other suborder (Tubulifera) have no ovipositor and their eggs are laid superficially. The first two instars are pale, soft-skinned, wingless forms with more strongly sclerotised head and legs. The next two or three stages are quiescent and entirely pale; they bear wing-pads and resemble the pupae of endopterygote insects. These pupa-like stages do not feed, they commonly shelter in the soil or among surface débris, and the last one moults into the adult. Some Thysanoptera damage cultivated plants directly or, in a very few species only, by transmitting virus diseases. *Heliothrips haemorrhoidalis* is a widespread greenhouse pest and species of *Taeniothrips* damage fruit trees.

Endopterygote insects

These, the second major group of winged insects, are distinguished from the others by their complete metamorphosis or holometabolous life-cycle (p. 118). The larval stages are succeeded by a quiescent pupal instar, during which many larval organs and tissues are destroyed and the new adult ones are formed. The name Endopterygota denotes that the wing-pads begin their development within the larval body and only come to project externally in the pupa.

Alder-flies, lacewings, ant lions and allies (Order Neuroptera)

These vary considerably in size and are usually predacious. The adults have biting mouth-parts and membranous wings, often with a profuse venation; the larvae are almost always active, long-legged forms and many bear powerful jaws. In the suborder Megaloptera, species of the family Sialidae (alder-flies) are commonly found on vegetation near water, the larvae being aquatic with long, segmented gills arranged along each side of the abdomen. The Corydalidae (dobson-flies) have similar habits but are usually larger: the New Zealand *Archichauliodes dubitatus* may reach a span of ten centimetres and *Corydalus cornutus* from North America is even larger, with very powerful mandibles in the male. The snakeflies (Raphidiidae) have an unusually long prothorax, a long ovipositor, and the larvae live under bark; *Raphidia*, *Agulla* and *Inocellia* are important genera. The remaining Neuroptera form the suborder Plannipennia, all of which have suctorial larval mouth-parts formed from the modified mandibles and maxillae. The Sisyridae, such as *Sisyra* and *Climacia*, are small, brownish insects whose larvae feed on freshwater sponges. More familiar are the brown lacewings and green lacewings (Hemerobiidae and Chrysopidae respectively) whose larvae prey on aphids. Chrysopid larvae are sometimes decorated with the dry skins of their victims, whose body contents have been sucked out. The Mantispidae have a remarkably close resemblance to praying mantids, feeding in the same way with similarly modified fore legs. Their larvae are specialised predators, entering the egg-sacs of spiders and feeding on the young ones. An intriguing group is the Myrmeleontidae or ant lions. The adults resemble slender dragonflies but the larvae are squat, bristly forms with long, powerful, piercing jaws. They conceal themselves at the bottom of a conical pit in dry soil and attack ants and other insects which fall into the pit. Closely related to them are the Ascalaphidae whose otherwise similar larvae do not construct pits but catch their prey on the surface of the ground. Neither family occurs in Britain but both are represented in all the continents.

Scorpion-flies (Order Mecoptera)

The Mecoptera comprise some 300 species of essentially terrestrial, carnivorous insects, though species of the genus *Boreus* apparently feed on moss. The best-known families are the Panorpidae and Bittacidae, both with a beak-like head, two pairs of membranous wings and terrestrial, caterpillar-like larvae. *Panorpa* seems to feed mainly on dead or dying insects. The male has bulbous genitalia, held like a scorpion's sting. The Bittacids have more normal genitalia and capture small insects with their powerful hind legs, hanging upside-down.

Butterflies and moths (Order Lepidoptera)

The butterflies and moths, of which there are about 100,000 known species, include some of the most familiar and easily recognised insects. One of their main characteristics is the possession of cuticular scales which are really flattened, hollow hairs ornamented by longitudinal ridges and attached to the body by a small socket. The scales clothe the body, wings and appendages and are the basis of the bright and distinctive colour patterns found in many species. In almost all adult Lepidoptera the mandibles are vestigial or absent and the maxillae are modified into a proboscis. This is coiled spirally beneath the head in repose but may be extended through the combined action of blood-pressure and muscular activity, thus enabling the insect to suck up the nectar and other liquids on which it feeds. Lepidopterous larvae are caterpillars, with a well-developed head bearing powerful mandibles, minute antennae and up to six ocelli each side. Three pairs of short thoracic legs are usually present and usually five pairs of abdominal prolegs—stumpy protruberances armed with rows of microscopic hooks. With very

A snake-fly, *Raphidia*. The Raphidiidae derive their common name from the long prothorax and well-developed head, which give them a distinctly snake-like appearance. The female has a long ovipositor which it uses to lay eggs in crevices in the bark of dead or decaying trees. The larvae (which closely resemble beetle larvae) live predaciously within the dead or decaying wood and pupate in a cell in the bark or at the foot of the tree.

137

few exceptions the larvae are phytophagous, devouring the leaves, stem, root or fruit according to species and feeding in exposed situations or burrowing into the plant. It is not surprising that many species are pests of cultivated plants. When fully grown the larvae cease feeding and often spin a silken cocoon in which they pupate. A few primitive Lepidoptera have pupae with functional mandibles and with the wings, legs and other appendages projecting freely from the body. In the majority, however, the pupa is of a characteristic obtect type—sometimes referred to as a chry-

A scorpion fly, *Panorpa*. The scorpion flies derive their name from the bulbous genital segment of the male abdomen, which recalls a scorpion's sting, but the female has a more normal abdomen. *Panorpa* larvae are similar to caterpillars in general appearance, with small abdominal pro-legs and unusual visual organs not unlike the compound eyes of adult insects.

A strikingly decorative Lepidopteran larva from central America. The larvae of Lepidoptera sometimes bear various horn-like or wart-like processes on their body or are provided with tufts of bristles or eversible repugnatorial glands called osmeteria.

salis—in which the appendages are closely stuck down against the body.

The Lepidoptera have been subdivided in several different ways, three suborders being recognised. Of these, the most primitive is the Zeugloptera, containing only the family Micropterigidae, a group of small moths so distinct that they have sometimes been given the status of a separate order of insects. The adults have well-developed mandibles and the maxillae do not form a proboscis. *Micropterix* feeds on pollen as an adult and large numbers can be found on buttercups in the spring. The larvae of the New Zealand *Sabatinca* feed on mosses and liverworts, but in Britain *Micropterix* larvae occur in grass tussocks from which these lowly plants are absent.

The second suborder is the Monotrysia, so-called because, unlike the higher Lepidoptera, the female usually has only a single reproductive aperture, situated on the sternum of the ninth abdominal segment. The Eriocraniidae are small species, often with legless leaf-mining larvae and with pupae whose long mandibles are used to break out of the silken cocoon before the adult moth emerges. A better-known group of monotrysian Lepidoptera are the ghost moths or swifts (Hepialidae). They are large, fast-flying, crepuscular species whose larvae are either soil inhabitants, sometimes injuring grass and crops, or woodborers. Some hepialids are unusually large and handsome moths; the Australian *Leto stayci*, for example, has a wingspan of up to twenty-three centimetres and very large larvae which feed in the trunks of eucalyptus trees. Another monotrysian family is the Incurvariidae; *Adela* includes the small metallic fairy moths with long antennae, often seen flying in bright sunshine, while the yucca moths of the southern United States (p. 126) are species of *Tegeticula*.

The great majority of Lepidoptera are placed in the third suborder, the Ditrysia, in which the female reproductive system has two apertures: a copulatory pore on the eighth abdominal segment and an egg-laying aperture on the following segment. It contains over seventy families, only a selection of which can be mentioned here. The Sesiidae or clearwings are day-flying moths with scale-less transparent wings and the body often coloured so as to resemble wasps and bees. The larvae are wood-borers, and *Synanthedon salmachus* damages currant and gooseberry bushes in Europe, North America and New Zealand. The American Peach Tree Borer (*Sanninoidea exititiosa*) is another injurious species. The related family Tinaeidae is much more widely known since among its two thousand or more species are the clothes moths whose larvae feed on woollen materials, especially when somewhat soiled and left undisturbed. The commonest of these is *Tineola bisselliella*, but larvae of another clothes moth, *Tinaea pellionella*, have the more interesting habit of occupying tubular, silken cases, open at each end, in which they also pupate. Several other groups of small moths are related to the Tinaeidae. The Gracillariidae, for example, comprise about a thousand species with leaf-mining larvae, of which *Phyllonorycter* is widely distributed. The Plutellidae include the cosmopolitan *Plutella xylostella* (the Diamond-back Moth), an important pest of *Brass-*

ica crops (cabbage and its relatives), while the Orneodidae have most unusual wings, each cleft into six narrow, plume-like branches.

The Cossidae, a somewhat isolated family, are moderate or large-sized moths typified by *Cossus cossus*, the European Goat Moth, whose very large, long-lived, pinkish-brown larvae burrow in the wood of oak, elm and ash. *Prionoxystus robiniae* is a common North American species with similar habits, and a remarkable Australian cossid, *Xyleutes boisduvali*, has a wingspan of twenty-five centimetres and an abdomen as large as a small banana.

Another striking family of Lepidoptera is the Psychidae or bagworms, whose larvae build and inhabit portable cases of leaves, twigs or grass, spun together with silk. The adult males are normal moths, but the females are wingless, degenerate creatures that never leave the larval case in which they have developed. Related to them but quite different in habits and appearance are the Zygaenidae. *Zygaena* includes the attractive red and black burnet moths and *Ino*, the brilliant metallic green foresters, both characteristic of the Palaearctic region. An important group of small species are the Tortricidae, sometimes known as bell moths from the outline of their folded wings. The caterpillars are often leaf-rollers and several species are capable of considerable damage. *Tortrix viridana* sometimes defoliates oaks in Europe, while the Spruce Budworm (*Choristoneura fumiferana*) has devastated Canadian conifer forests. A related family, the Eucosmidae or Olethreutidae, also has its complement of injurious species: the European Codling Moth (*Cyclia pomonella*), a serious pest of apples and other fruit, is now widely distributed in North America, South Africa, Australia and New Zealand, and the Oriental Fruit Moth (*Grapholitha molesta*) damages peaches in the United States. A more entertaining member of the same family is *Laspeyresia saltitans* whose larvae live in 'jumping beans'—actually the seeds of a Mexican plant, *Sebastiana*—causing them to move in a most curious fashion.

The pyralid moths are a large assemblage of small or medium-sized species including the Galleriinae (some of whose larvae feed on the combs of bee hives and in wasps' nests), the Crambinae or grass moths and the Phycitinae, with such pests of stored foodstuffs as the Mediterranean Flour Moth (*Ephestia kuehniella*). To redress the balance, however, one might point out that the Cactus Moth (*Cactoblastis cactorum*) was deliberately introduced into Australia to destroy the dense growth of prickly pear in New South Wales and Queensland. The Pyralidae is a largely tropical group but the very many species of Pyraustinae have a wide distribution and the family includes some unusual genera with aquatic larvae. The larvae and pupae of *Acentropus* live in tubes composed of fragments of the leaves of water plants and the larvae of some species of *Nymphula* are equipped with well-developed gills. A more normal species is the notorious European Corn Borer (*Ostrinia nubilalis*) which was introduced into the United States about 1917 and has since spread over many eastern and central states, causing great harm to the maize crops, as the larvae of the Corn Borer live in the stems of the plant.

Most of the preceding families make up what the older collectors classified as the Microlepidoptera. The ones now to be mentioned are generally larger and better known and form the so-called Macrolepidoptera. First among them are the Lasiocampidae (eggars and lappet moths) with stout, hairy caterpillars which, in European and North American species of *Malacosoma*, live gregariously in large, silken, tent-like nests. The larva of *Pachypasa otus* spins a bulky, white cocoon which provided the ancient Greeks and Romans with silk, but a larger number of wild or semi-domesticated silkworms occur in the related family Saturniidae. This latter is mainly a tropical group containing some large and handsome moths with prominent, bipectinate antennae and often with scale-less 'windows' on the wings. *Saturnia pyri*, a close relative of the commoner Emperor Moth, is the largest European lepidopteran and the Cecropia Moth (*Hyalophora cecropia*) is the largest in North America, while the Australian *Coscinoscera hercules* and the Asiatic Atlas Moth (*Attacus atlas*) are among the largest moths in the world. The last-mentioned species produces silk in usable quantities, as do several species of *Antheraea*, *Philosamia cynthia*, *Theophilus religiosae* and others. The Luna Moth (*Actias luna*) from North America is a beautiful, pale green species equipped with purple-brown markings, eyespots, and long tails on its hind wings. It is not surprising that the Saturniidae are reared enthusiastically by many amateur entomologists. By comparison with them the creamy white Silkworm Moth (*Bombyx mori*) of

Threat display by the caterpillar of the puss moth, *Cerura vinula*. The striking features of this larva (see p. 142) contrast with the more sober, cryptically coloured adult. The pupa is enclosed in a hard, woody cocoon, found on tree-trunks; the adult emerges within this and breaks out by softening it with a secretion from the mouth and then using two sharply pointed teeth on the front of the head.

Opposite top
A pair of Common Blue
Butterflies (*Polyommatus icarus*). This
attractive species is distributed
from the Canary Islands through
North Africa into Europe and the
cooler parts of Asia. The larvae
feed at night on various species of
Leguminosae and pupate in a
loose wispy cocoon near the base
of the host-plant.

Opposite middle
Small Pearl-bordered Fritillary
(*Clossiana selene*). This butterfly is
found in Europe, the temperate
parts of Asia and also in North
America, where it is represented
by several subspecies. It occurs in
woodland clearings and damp
places, where its larva feeds on
wild violets.

Opposite bottom
The Broad-bordered Bee
Hawkmoth (*Hemaris fuciformis*)
feeding. This hawkmoth flies
during the daytime and visits
honeysuckle and *Rhododendron* in
search of nectar. The wings have
transparent areas, formed through
the loss of scales, and this feature,
together with its habits of flight,
causes the moth to resemble a
bumble-bee.

the family Bombycidae is uninteresting in appearance. But it is the species which, from its original home in China, has been introduced to many other countries and is cultivated on a large scale in commercial silk production. Each cocoon consists of a single thread of silk which, when unravelled, is about 900 metres long. Many varieties of this insect are known and the species has been so thoroughly domesticated that it no longer occurs wild.

The butterflies, which are not a single natural group of Lepidoptera, include some six families. The dominant one is the Nymphalidae, a diverse group of about 5,000 species containing a variety of well-known forms. The Painted Lady (*Cynthia cardui*), for example, is probably the most widely distributed butterfly in the world, while the Red Admiral (*Vanessa atalanta*) and the Mourning Cloak or Camberwell Beauty (*Nymphalis antiopa*) are equally familiar in Europe and North America. The Satyrine butterflies of the same family are brown or greyish species with a number of distinctive spots, often arranged in a row, near the margins of the wings. One large species, *Melanitis leda*, ranges from South Africa to Japan (where its larva is a pest of bamboo and sugar-cane) and is unusual for a butterfly in flying only in the evening and at dawn. The milkweed butterflies or monarchs (*Danaus*) are large, apparently distasteful, orange-brown species with black markings, found in both the New and the Old World, but two other sub-families of nauseous, protectively flavoured butterflies have characteristically restricted distributions: the Acraeinae are essentially African and the Heliconiinae come from South America. As might be expected, many species of these groups are mimicked by other Lepidoptera without distasteful properties. The last of the nymphalid butterflies to be mentioned here are *Morpho* and its allies: large and brilliantly metallic in colour—often an iridescent blue—they soar among the trees of tropical forests in Central and South America. The smaller though not unnattractive 'blues' so well-known in Europe and North America belong to a wide-ranging family, the Lycaenidae, which also includes copper-coloured and dark brown species. The larvae of some lycaenids prey on aphids and similar insects, while others are associated with ants.

Among the commonest butterflies are some of the white, yellow, or orange-coloured Pieridae, such as the cabbage whites (species of *Pieris*) or the clouded yellows (*Colias*) and brimstones (*Gonepteryx*). *Pieris rapae*, the small Cabbage White Butterfly, is a cosmopolitan species and the activities of its larva make it probably the most injurious of all butterflies. A much more spectacular family is the Papilionidae or swallowtail butterflies, mostly large, iridescent black, dark blue or green species with yellow, orange, red, green or blue markings and one, two or three 'tails' on each wing. In Britain, the solitary species *Papilio machaon* is a rarity of the East Anglian fens, but the genus to which it belongs has representative species in the Americas, India, Australia and elsewhere. An African species, *Papilio dardanus*, has been described as the most interesting butterfly in the world: it has numerous colour varieties in both

sexes and enters into complex mimetic associations with other distasteful Lepidoptera. Also belonging to the Papilionidae are the Apollo butterflies (*Parnassius*) from mountainous parts of the northern hemisphere and the large, magnificently coloured, bird-winged or Ornithoptera butterflies (*Troides*) of which a number of species have been described from the forests of south-east Asia. After such a remarkable family it seems an anticlimax to turn to the last group of butterflies, the Hesperiidae or skippers: a large family of small or medium-sized species with a characteristic darting, erratic flight. Perhaps their greatest claim to fame lies in the black and yellow Australian Regent Skipper, *Euschemon rafflesia*, which is probably the most archaic butterfly existing today.

One of the largest families of moths is the Geometridae, slender, large-winged species with larvae that have prolegs on only the sixth and tenth abdominal segments. They progress with characteristic looping movements and are variously known as measuring worms, inchworms, loopers or earth-measurers. Some of them resemble twigs in shape and coloration when they rest with the long, cylindrical body projecting at an angle from the stem which they grip with the prolegs. The family includes a few serious defoliators such as the European Winter Moth (*Operophtera brumata*) and the American Fall Cankerworm (*Alsophila pometaria*), both incidentally with wingless females. The hawk moths or Sphingidae include many large and striking species capable of strong flight around dusk, hovering over the flowers from which they feed with their long probosces—known in the Central American genus *Coccytius* to measure up to 25 centimetres when unrolled. The larvae are robust, often brightly marked with spots or stripes, and sometimes bear a curved horn-shaped process on the back of the eighth abdominal segment, whence their American name of 'hornworms'. Species of *Protoparce* do considerable damage to tomatoes, tobacco and other crops in the United States but otherwise the group does not include many important pests. The Death's Head Hawk Moth (*Acherontia atropos*) is a large, black, brown and yellow species whose thorax is marked dorsally so as to resemble a human skull. Its range extends from Britain to the Cape of Good Hope and the adult has two unusual features: it robs bee hives of honey and it can emit a shrill, chirping sound, probably by blowing air through its proboscis.

The Noctuidae, sometimes known as owlet moths, are heavily built, dull-coloured nocturnal species, commonly attracted to lights. They are usually of moderate size, but the Black Witch (*Erebus odora*) which regularly migrates northward from tropical America may have a wingspan of 12·5 centimetres and the Agrippina Moth (*E. agrippina*) from South America may have a wingspan of twenty-five centimetres. There are over 20,000 species of noctuids and the smooth-skinned larvae include some of the most serious pests of cultivated plants. Those usually known as cutworms are soil-dwellers which feed on the surface at night, biting through the stems of young plants near the base and destroying far more than they consume. The larvae of other species are the armyworms, so-called because they sometimes invade

crops in large numbers. Such a species is *Spodoptera exempta* which feeds on maize, sugar-cane and other graminaceous crops in Africa and exists in solitary or gregarious phases like those of locusts. Other injurious noctuids are the Red Bollworm of cotton (*Diparopsis castanea*) from Africa and the New World Corn Earworm (*Heliothis zea*) which also attacks cotton, tomatoes and other plants. As a diversion from the usual theme of plant injury by larval rather than adult Lepidoptera, it is worth mentioning that a few noctuid moths have strong proboscies with saw-like cutting edges which they use to pierce holes in various fruits and then suck out the juice. Another family of nocturnal moths, related to the Noctuidae, is the prominents (Notodontidae) whose larvae feed on shrubs and trees. *Stauropus fagi* is the European Lobster Moth, so-called because of the unusual appearance of the long-legged larva. Equally odd is the appearance of the larva of another European species, the Puss Moth (*Cerura vinula*). It is green and purple with a prominent fleshy protruberance on top of the metathorax, two long, red, filamentous append-ages at the hind end and a thoracic gland which produces formic acid. Sometimes included in the Notodontidae is a small group of species allied to *Thaumetopoea processionea* whose larvae are the European Processionary Caterpillars. These march about in columns and can be induced to follow their leader in a circle, each larva maintain-ing head and tail contact with the ones in front and behind. Also related to the Noctuidae are the Lymantriidae or tussock moths whose larvae are provided with conspicuous dorsal hair-tufts. The Gipsy Moth (*Lymantria dispar*) is a serious pest of North American forests, having been introduced accidentally into Massachusetts about 1866. *Lymantria monacha*, the Nun Moth, plays a similar destructive rôle in Central Europe. Finally there is the family Arctiidae, which includes the tiger moths and ermine moths, with brightly spotted or banded wings and 'woolly bear' caterpillars, as well as the narrow, dull-coloured 'footmen' whose larvae feed mainly on lichens. *Arctia caja*, the Common Garden Tiger of Britain, extends right round the northern part of the northern hemi-sphere, while the Crimson Speckled Moth (*Utetheisa pulchella*) occurs in most of the Old World, including Australia. The family has few injurious species but the larvae of *Hyphantria cunea*, the Fall Webworm of the United States, build large webs within which they feed gregariously on the foliage of various shrubs and trees, while *Earias insulana* is the Egyptian Bollworm so destructive to cotton in some tropical areas.

Caddis-flies (Order Trichoptera)

The Trichoptera or caddis-flies include some 5,000 species of medium-sized, weakly flying, moth-like insects, usually dull brownish in colour. Their mandibles are vestigial and the wings are held roof-like over the abdomen when in repose. They are commonly encountered on vegetation, tree-trunks and stones near the edges of still or running water and with a single exception (*Enoicyla*) they have aquatic immature stages (which are usually more interesting than the adults). The larvae are unusual in that many spin and inhabit a portable tube of silk, strengthened and adorned with a

variety of materials—sand grains, small pebbles, leaves, stalks, or even empty mollusc shells. Other species live in silken, net-like retreats, often several larvae to each habitation. The case-bearing larvae are usually plant-feeders; the others are predacious. The mature larvae pupate either in the larval cases—which are previously anchored down with silken threads—or in specially constructed pupal cases which may themselves enclose a cocoon. The pupae have strong mandibles enabling them to bite their way out of the case, after which they crawl or swim to the surface or to some dry support, where the adult emerges. Among the thirty or so families of Trichoptera are the Rhyacophilidae, whose larvae occur in running water, the small Hydroptilidae (in which only the last larval instar constructs a case) and the net-spinning Hydropsychidae. The Phryganeidae are large caddis-flies, usually from lakes or marshes, the Limnephilidae are one of the largest families, and the Leptoceridae have long antennae and often slender, larval cases.

Flies (Order Diptera)

The Diptera or true flies form one of the largest orders of insects with over 85,000 species, including a number of very common ones. Some, like the mosquitoes and tsetse flies, are of great economic importance because they suck blood and thereby may transmit disease-causing micro-organisms among men and domestic animals. Apart from a few wingless species, the adult Diptera fly with only the front pairs of wings, the hind ones having been reduced to small club-shaped halteres which control the equilibrium of the flying insect but do not propel it. Dipteran larvae are mostly soft-skinned maggots or worm-like creatures adapted to life in a great variety of environments, especially in water or wet organic matter. The group may be divided into three suborders. The Nematocera are the most primitive, with many-segmented antennae and larvae provided with a relatively well-developed head. The Brachycera have shorter, three- to five-segmented antennae and larvae with a reduced head. In many ways they form a link

The Mulberry Silk Moths (*Bombyx mori*) newly emerged from their cocoons, with pair in centre mating. This is the silk moth of commerce, now completely dependent for its survival on the various domesticated races. Silk is produced as a secretion of the labial glands of the larva and is drawn out into a delicate thread through a spinneret on the labium. It is used by the insect to form the cocoon. The silken thread has to be unravelled before it can be spun by man.

A day-flying Uraniid moth, *Alcides agathyrsus*. This handsome species from New Guinea is strikingly similar in coloration to a swallowtail butterfly, *Papilio laglaizei*, which it also resembles in its high, circling flight. It is quite probable that *agathyrsus* is a distasteful species and that *laglaizei* is a harmless insect which gains protection by mimicking it.

between the Nematocera and the most specialised suborder, the Cyclorrhapha. The members of this group have characteristically three-segmented antennae and larvae which are virtually headless maggots pupating within a puparium (a brown, egg-shaped structure formed from the hardened skin of the mature larva).

A large and familiar group of the Nematocera is the Tipulidae (craneflies or daddy-long-legs). The adults are harmless, long-legged, often big insects, whose fleshy, grub-like larvae are usually either aquatic or live in decaying vegetation. The larvae of some species, the so-called leatherjackets, can do considerable damage to lawns and grassland and in Europe *Tipula paludosa* is a common species of this kind. The craneflies are surprisingly well-represented in New Zealand and in species of *Elephantomyia* from this part of the world the mouth-parts of the adult are borne on a proboscis as long as the abdomen, well-adapted for probing into deep flowers for nectar. Very different insects are the Psychodidae: minute, fragile, moth-like flies, often encountered in damp, dark situations. *Phlebotomus* and its allies are the blood-sucking sandflies which spread a variety of tropical diseases—pappataci fever in the Mediterranean region, kala azar and Oriental sore in North Africa and South America. The species from temperate regions are harmless, however, and the larvae of species of *Psychoda* play a useful role in sewage purification. They occur in large numbers on filter beds, where they feed on the rich growth of bacteria, algae and other microscopic organisms which otherwise would quickly increase and clog the filters.

The Culicidae or mosquitoes are a large group of great medical importance. Species of *Anopheles* transmit malaria, *Aedes aegypti* is the Yellow Fever Mosquito, while other species of *Aedes*, together with *Culex* and *Mansonia*, spread infection by parasitic filarial worms. Culicid larvae occur in a wide variety of aquatic habitats, each characteristic of particular species—ponds, streams, salt marshes or the water collecting in hollow trees are only a few of the places which harbour them. The

Top
Larvae and pupae of a mosquito, *Culex*, hanging from the water surface film. Larvae and pupae of the Culicidae are aquatic, but breathe air, which they obtain from the atmosphere by pushing a respiratory tube through the surface film. The larvae have such a tube at the posterior end of the abdomen and in *Culex* they hang down in the water at an angle to the surface. The pupae are the stouter comma-shaped individuals in this picture and their respiratory tubes are paired structures developed from the thorax.

Middle
Adult mosquito, *Culex pipiens*. Females of the true *Culex pipiens* feed on birds and do not bite man, though they hibernate indoors during the winter. Females need a blood meal to lay their eggs, which form a compact mass or egg-raft that floats on the water surface. A closely related form, sometimes treated as a distinct species, *Culex molestus*, bites man viciously, though it can mature its eggs without a blood meal.

Bottom left
Larval cases of a caddis-fly, *Sericostoma*. The larvae live in streams and are caterpillar-like creatures which construct conical, somewhat curved cases out of sand grains. The adults are a favourite food of trout and are imitated by the 'Welshman's Button' of the fly fisherman.

Bottom right
Head of a deerfly, *Chrysops*. This is a member of the family Tabanidae, with species mainly in north temperate regions, parts of Africa, and the Far East. The females suck blood and visit flowers for nectar, but the males lack mandibles and are flower feeders. Some African species of *Chrysops* act as intermediate hosts of a nematode worm that parasitises man.

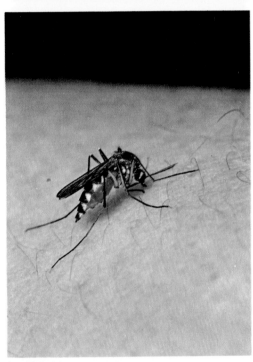

143

A daddy-long-legs or cranefly (*Tipula*). Some members of this rather primitive group of Diptera are quite large insects, with long spidery legs. *Tipula* larvae occur in a variety of habitats, depending on the species, and can be found in moss, turf, mud or water.

Larva of the Phantom Midge (*Chaoborus crystallinus*). This species is a member of the Culicidae, but unlike mosquitoes, the adult female does not suck blood. The aquatic larva is a remarkable, almost transparent form with two pairs of air-sacs, which control its buoyancy and enable it to float at various levels in the water. The larva has a closed tracheal system, breathing through the cuticle, and uses its prehensile antennae to feed on small aquatic insects and crustaceans.

larvae of most species feed on micro-organisms which are swept into the insect's mouth by water currents set up through the activity of its 'mouth-brushes'. They breathe through a posterior respiratory siphon which is pushed through the water surface to obtain air. The comma-shaped pupa respires in a similar way, but its paired respiratory funnels lead into the thorax. When adult, the females of most species require a blood meal in order to ripen their eggs. Each species of mosquito shows characteristic preferences for particular vertebrate hosts and has a characteristic cycle of biting activity during the twenty-four hours of the day. Factors such as these help to determine which species are important transmitters of human disease and decide the methods which can be used to control them. As in most other blood-sucking Diptera, it is only the females which feed in this way; male mosquitoes are harmless, do not bite, and live on the sugary secretions of plants.

The Cecidomyiidae or gall midges are so named because in some species the phytophagous larvae produce characteristic galls on their host-plants. The adults are minute, delicate midges but because of the activities of the larvae some species are of considerable economic importance. One of these is the Hessian Fly (*Mayetiola destructor*), a pest

of wheat which was carried from Europe to North America, allegedly through the forage accompanying mercenary troops in the eighteenth century. The larvae of a few other species are remarkable for their ability to produce daughter-larvae without completing their development. This very unusual process of reproduction by an immature stage is known as paedogenesis and the young are naturally parthenogenetically produced. Larger, stouter insects with short, thick-set antennae make up the family Bibionidae. St Mark's Fly (*Bibio marci*) is a heavy, slow-flying, black species common in Europe in the spring. The adults of smaller species are often associated with flowers and can act as orchard pollinators; the primitively constructed larvae are terrestrial vegetable feeders, often occurring gregariously.

The Mycetophilidae or fungus gnats are another group with essentially terrestrial larvae. They number about 2,000 species of delicate, small or medium-sized flies whose larvae usually feed on fungi or rotting vegetation. Some species are pests of commercial mushroom beds and *Sciara* attacks decaying fruit, vegetables and seedlings. The larvae of a few mycetophilids can produce light and the glow-worm cave at Waitomo, in New Zealand, is celebrated for the luminous activities of *Arachnocampa luminosa*.

The blackflies or Simuliidae are small, stoutly built flies with short antennae and in some species the blood-sucking females can transmit parasitic nematodes and other micro-organisms. Perhaps the most serious of these is a filarial worm, *Onchocerca volvulus*, which is spread in Africa by *Simulium damnosum* and *S. neavei* and which is believed to cause 'river blindness'. The larvae are entirely aquatic, usually living in rather swift-flowing water, trapping food particles with well-developed mouth brushes. They have a circle of hooks at the posterior end, by which they attach themselves to submerged stones or vegetation, though *Simulium neavei* larvae are carried about on the carapace of a freshwater crab, *Potamon niloticus*. When full-grown, simuliid larvae spin a silken cocoon and the pupa formed within this attached case has long, branching respiratory filaments. The last of the commoner nematoceran families, the Chironomidae or non-biting midges, are also well known for their aquatic larvae, though in some species the immature stages are terrestrial. Adult chironomids are short-lived, rather delicate, mosquito-like insects, the males with bushy antennae and given to forming mating swarms in the afternoon and evening. The aquatic species lay their eggs in long, gelatinous strings and the worm-like larvae often live in tubular cases or freely in the bottom sediments, though a variety of larval habits and habitats are encountered. The larvae of *Chironomus* contain haemoglobin which is used for respiratory purposes when the oxygen supply is rather low; from their red colour these larvae are often known as bloodworms. Two other chironomids have achieved fame from their unusual habits: *Pontomyia natans* is a marine insect from Samoa in which the adults spend part or all of their time submerged, while the larvae of *Polypedilum vanderplanki* can enter a state of suspended animation during which they will withstand remarkable extremes of temperature.

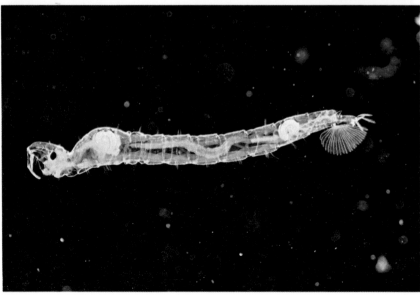

Among the Brachycera, the Stratiomyidae or soldier flies are sometimes handsome, coloured or metallic insects, often found on vegetation in damp places. The larvae of some species are carnivorous, but others feed on decaying material or rotten wood; they include terrestrial and aquatic forms, some of the latter, such as *Odontomyia*, provided with a long respiratory tube by which they hang suspended from the water surface. The Rhagionidae or snipe flies are predacious, with carnivorous larvae found in the soil or leaf-mould. Much better known, however, are the horseflies or deerflies (Tabanidae)—medium or large, stout insects whose females suck blood and have long, cylindrical larvae that inhabit damp soil, mud and similar moist habitats. *Tabanus* includes the larger, heavier species while *Haematopota* and *Chrysops* are smaller, with spotted or banded wings. Most species confine their injurious nature to sucking blood, but two West African species of *Chrysops* can transmit a parasitic filarial worm injurious to man. The Asilidae or robber flies tend also to be large and are bristly, powerful fliers, actively predacious on other insects. They have large bulging eyes, a bearded face and a stout proboscis. Their larvae live in the soil, leaf-mould or wood and are predacious or scavengers. The giant of the family is an Australian species, *Phellus glaucus*, with a body up to five centimetres long. *Asilus crab-roniformis* is a large, yellow and black robber fly found in Europe and other species of the genus occur in most parts of the world. Another interesting Brachyceran family is the Bombyliidae, densely hairy bee-like or wasp-like insects often found on flowers in sunny places. Their larvae are parasitic, those of *Bombylius*, for example, attacking the larvae of solitary bees. The Empididae comprise over 3,000 species of dark, greyish or yellowish insects with a long, horny proboscis used for preying on smaller insects. The males of some species have the curious habit of presenting their prey to the female before mating and in *Hilara*—with species in North America, Europe and Australia—the offering is wrapped up in silk spun from glands in the front legs. Also predacious are the long-legged Dolichopodidae, a large family of small, bristly, metallic green or blue flies often found on flowers, foliage or grass. Their larvae, like those of the Empididae, live in the soil, leaf-mould, rotten wood and other habitats.

The Syrphidae or hover-flies are one of the more familiar groups of cyclorrhaphan Diptera. They are mostly medium-sized, flower-haunting insects, often banded with yellow on a dark background and therefore superficially resembling wasps, e.g. *Syrphus ribesii* from Europe and North America. Other species, such as the Drone Fly (*Eristalis tenax*), resemble bees, while species of *Volucella* not only resemble wasps or hornets but actually breed in their nests. The larvae of the Syrphidae vary considerably in habits and appearance. Many of the commoner garden syrphids have larvae which prey on aphids and the slug-like larvae or their pupae can often be found among aphid colonies. The larvae of the bulb flies *Merodon* and *Eumerus* eat out the centre of narcissus bulbs and have been introduced from Europe into North America. *Eristalis* larvae are aquatic scavengers, characteristic of heavily polluted water and provided with an unusually long respiratory siphon which extends to the surface from deep within the liquid. *Microdon* larvae are also scavengers, found in ants' nests and so slug-like in appearance that they were originally described as a new species of mollusc. Not far removed from the hover-flies are the Phoridae— small, active, bristly flies found among decaying vegetation or associated with the nests of termites or ants. The larvae are often scavengers or feed on the dead bodies of snails or larger animals and at least one species has a predilection for pupating in empty milk bottles. *Termitoxenia* is one of the very few hermaphrodite insects, the adult passing first through a male phase and ending up as a female.

Many Cyclorrhaphan flies have been placed in the section Acalyptratae, with other thirty families. Most of these are best left to the specialist, though a few acalyptrates have attained wider fame. *Drosophila* is one of these. Under natural conditions its species are associated with fermenting fruit or tree-sap; in the laboratory they have been the subject of a vast amount of genetical research. The larvae of the Agromyzidae are one of the major groups of leaf-miners, usually forming long, serpentine mines: *Agromyza* and *Phytomyza* are widely distributed genera with some common species. Among other acalyptrates are some very serious pests of cultivated plants. The Carrot Fly (*Psila rosae*—family Psilidae) is an example, its larvae feeding superficially in the large taproot. In the eastern United States the Apple Maggot (*Rhagoletis pomonella*) infests several kinds of fruit and the same family (Tephritidae) also includes the notorious and widespread Mediterranean Fruit Fly (*Ceratitis capitata*), the Queensland Fruit Fly (*Dacus tryoni*) and the Olive Fly (*Dacus oleae*) from the Mediterranean countries and South Africa. The Fruit Fly (*Oscinella frit*) is the last name to be mentioned in this catalogue; like other members of the family Chloropidae its larvae are injurious to graminaceous plants, in this case especially to oats.

Most of the remaining Cyclorrhapha are placed in the section Calyptratae, of which four families may be recognised, typified by the House Fly, Bluebottle and allies. The Oestridae have larvae which live in the tissues and body spaces of

A fruit-fly (Tephritidae). The patterned wings and horny 'ovipositor' are characteristic of this successful family, the larvae of which feed internally on living plants. Some form galls on the inflorescences of Compositae, others burrow into fruits, mine leaves or bore into the stems or roots of various host species; a few are serious pests (p. 146).

145

Opposite
Monarch Butterflies (*Danaus plexippus*) overwintering. The Monarch Butterfly is a celebrated migrant. During the summer it occurs over the whole of the United States and southern Canada. In September it migrates southwards in great swarms which spend the winter on trees, half asleep, over an area extending from Florida to California. About March the same insects fly north, the females laying eggs on milkweed plants before dying. The new generation of butterflies then repeats the southward migration in the autumn.

mammals and include a few pests of domestic animals. *Oestrus ovis*, for example, deposits its larvae in the nostrils of sheep, from where they move into the nasal and frontal sinuses, where they may cause obstructions, before being sneezed out to pupate in the soil. Better known members of the same family are the warble flies of cattle (*Hypoderma bovis* and *H. lineata*). These lay eggs on the flanks and legs of their hosts and the larvae migrate through the body, eventually reaching the back, where they perforate the skin and form swellings ('warbles'). The mature larvae escape through the holes—which reduce the value of the hides—and pupate in the soil. The Calliphoridae is a large family exemplified by the bluebottles (*Calliphora*) and many species of blowfly, whose larvae feed on carrion or even on living tissues. *Lucilia sericata* and *L. cuprina* are the sheep blowflies which lay their eggs in the soiled fleece around the hindquarters, the larvae then boring into the flesh and sometimes killing the sheep; the problem is a major concern of Australian sheepfarmers, but is also important in Britain and elsewhere. *Cochliomyia hominivorax*, the Screw-worm Fly of North and South America, is a wound-infesting calliphorid injurious to cattle. It has recently been exterminated in some areas by an ingenious method: artificially sterilised males are liberated in large numbers and as the females mate only once the reproductive capacity of the population is thereby reduced below the level necessary for survival. Other members of the Calliphoridae breed in decaying vegetable or animal matter or have larvae that parasitise earthworms, woodlice or insects. In this respect they resemble another large family, the Tachinidae, whose larvae are almost all parasites of other insects, especially of lepidopterous larvae. Their reproductive biology shows many interesting variations, all devoted to one end: that of ensuring that the larvae develop in the host insect. Some Tachinidae cement their eggs to the host and the larvae immediately bore through its skin, other species lay small eggs which are swallowed by the host and hatch in its gut, while in many the young larvae are thick-skinned

migratory forms which actively seek out a host. Once inside the body of the host, the tachinid larvae consume its tissues and eventually leave the remains of the host and pupate in the soil.

The family Muscidae includes the House Fly (*Musca domestica*), whose larvae develop in all kinds of rotting plant or animal matter, including animal and human excrement. Not unnaturally the adults transmit a variety of more or less undesirable bacteria. Other members of the family have a wide range of habits and some of the species with phytophagous larvae are agricultural pests—the Onion Fly (*Hylemyia antiqua*), the Cabbage Maggot (*Erioischia brassicae*) and the Spinach or Beet Leaf Miner (*Pegomyia hyoscyami*) are three which occur in both Europe and North America. The so-called Biting House Fly or Stable Fly (*Stomoxys calcitrans*) breeds in stable refuse and horse manure and the adults—both male and female—use their long proboscis to suck the blood of man, horse and cattle. Similar adult habits are characteristic of the tsetse flies—various species of *Glossina* living in Africa south of the Sahara. They are of very great medical and veterinary importance since they transmit the trypanosomes which cause sleeping sickness in man and 'nagana' in cattle. Female tsetse flies are viviparous, depositing their fully grown larvae one at a time. In this and other respects they resemble a peculiar group of blood-sucking, sometimes wingless and more or less ectoparasitic insects, the Hippoboscidae. One of these *Melophagus ovinus* is a minor pest of sheep wherever they are reared; others are associated with different mammalian and bird hosts including bats.

Fleas (Order Siphonaptera)

The fleas are a well-defined and homogeneous group of over 1,500 species which, in the adult stage, are usually regarded as ectoparasites of birds and mammals. They are wingless with a brown, bristly, strongly sclerotised body compressed from side to side. Their eyes are greatly reduced and the antennae are short but the legs are well developed and in many species the hind pair is used for jumping. Adult fleas of both sexes feed on the blood of their host, which they suck up after piercing the skin with their specialised mouth-parts. For this reason several species can transmit disease-causing micro-organisms from one host to another, the most serious instance being the spread of bubonic plague—the 'black death' of mediaeval times and a major tropical disease long after it had died out in Europe. This disease, due to a bacterium, *Pasteurella pestis*, is primarily an infection of rodents and exists in two forms: sylvatic plague, affecting wild field rodents, and urban plague affecting rats and therefore more closely associated with large human populations. Any flea which can feed on man as well as on the rodent hosts will transmit the disease but the most important species is the Rat Flea (*Xenopsylla cheopis*). The fleas involved in the spread of the sylvatic plague are less well known, but a squirrel flea *Diamanus montanus* plays some part in this in the western United States. Rats also act as reservoirs of another disease, endemic typhus, which can be transmitted to man by *Xenopsylla cheopis* and by another rat flea, *Nosopsyllus fasciatus*.

A green-bottle fly, *Lucilia*. Different species of *Lucilia* differ in their habits and larval food-preferences. *L. caesar* breeds in carrion and excrement, while *L. cuprina* and *L. sericata* are sheep blowflies, the eggs being laid on the fleece and the larvae feeding in the skin and causing serious injury.

Fleas lay their eggs in the fur or plumage of the host, a single female producing 300–500 eggs. These collect in the nest where the larval stage emerges by splitting open the egg shell with a spine on its head. The larvae are small, whitish, worm-like creatures quite unlike the adult and they are not parasitic. Instead they live on various kinds of organic débris in the nest, including the faeces of the host. When full-grown—about ten millimetres long—the larva spins a silken cocoon, the outer surface of which is covered with sand grains or fragments of débris. Within this it pupates, but the emergence of the adult is often long delayed if the pupal case is left undisturbed. Once it emerges, the adult is attracted to the host, on which it resumes its rather temporary form of ectoparasitism.

Pulex irritans is the so-called Human Flea, but under hygienic conditions it is much more likely to be encountered on one of its other hosts, especially on pigs. On the other hand, *Ctenocephalides felis*, a species commonly found on the Domestic Cat, readily bites man. This species, together with the Dog Flea (*Ctenocephalides canis*) and other species, is capable of transmitting certain animal tapeworms, but these latter are only very rarely the cause of human disease. To the layman, the most noteworthy feature of *Pulex irritans* and the two species of *Ctenocephalides* is that over most of the world they are the species whose 'bite' produces such irritation and discomfort. Perhaps the most unusual flea is the Jigger or Chigoe Flea (*Tunga penetrans*), originally from South America but now established as a pest of man over much of Africa. When unfed, *Tunga* is a minute flea, about a millimetre long; males leave the host after feeding in the normal way, but the fed females burrow into the soft skin of the feet and swell to the size of a pea, laying eggs which fall to the ground and then develop in the same way as other species.

Ants, wasps, bees (Order Hymenoptera)

This large group of over 100,000 species includes the ants, bees and wasps as well as the more primitive sawflies and a large array of parasitic forms such as the ichneumon flies. Its members exhibit a wide range of interesting biological phenomena, including several types of highly developed social organisation. The Hymenoptera receive their name from the two pairs of glassy, membranous wings, the fore and hind wing of each side being coupled together in flight by a row of small hooks. The female usually has a well-developed ovipositor which in some species is used to insert eggs into plant tissue or the body of a host insect, while in others it is employed as a defensive sting rather than for egg-laying. The larvae vary a good deal in appearance, especially in some parasitic groups. In general the head capsule is well developed, but whereas most sawfly larvae have thoracic and abdominal legs, these are not found in the other groups. The Hymenoptera are divided into two suborders, the Symphata or sawflies and a much larger section, the Apocrita. The latter may in turn be divided into the so-called Parasitica (not all of which are actually parasitic) and the Aculeata, to which belong the ants, bees, wasps and some others. The distinction between Parasitica and Aculeata is not very clear.

The sawflies are easily recognised because their abdomen is not constricted into the 'wasp waist' found in other Hymenoptera and their ovipositor is used for sawing or boring into the plants in which their eggs are inserted. The larvae are virtually all phytophagous, some feeding externally on the foliage or flowers, others burrowing into tree-trunks, stems or fruits. Most sawfly larvae look very much like lepidopteran caterpillars, but in several families the abdominal appendages are absent and some have even lost the thoracic legs as well. The Xyelidae are the most primitive sawflies; they occur in the northern hemisphere and their larvae are associated with conifers and catkin-bearing trees. The Siricidae (wood wasps or horntails) are large sawflies whose white, grub-like larvae bore in wood. The larvae of the North American *Tremex columba* bore in hardwoods while *Urocerus gigas* is a striking black and yellow insect found in the coniferous forests of Europe and Asia. Also attached to Coniferae are the Diprionidae, whose larvae feed externally on the needles; species of *Diprion* and *Neodiprion* are serious defoliators in Canadian forests. Several other small families of sawflies can be mentioned only in passing—the Pergidae, for example, are a characteristically southern hemisphere group from Australia and South America while representatives of the Orussidae occur widely scattered over the globe and have larvae which are perhaps parasites of wood-boring beetles. About three-quarters of all sawfly species, however belong to the Tenthredinidae, the larvae of which are usually external feeders on a great variety of trees, shrubs and herbaceous flowering plants as well as some on ferns. *Pristiphora erichsonii* is a destructive pest of larch in Europe and North America and the Gooseberry Sawfly (*Nematus ribesii*) is injurious to gooseberries and currants in the same parts of the world. The Apple Sawfly (*Hoplocampa testudinea*) is a serious pest of European orchards, the larvae burrowing into the young fruitlets and feeding inside them. Species of *Pontania* are best known from the characteristic smooth, bean-shaped galls which their larvae produce on the leaves of willow,

Opposite
A hover-fly (*Syrphus ribesii*) feeding on Michaelmas daisy. Like many of the higher Diptera, the Syrphidae have mouthparts that are well adapted for feeding on the sugary secretions of flowers, and they may also take up pollen at the same time.

A flea on the fur of an East African grass rat (*Rhabdomys*). Adult fleas are well adapted as ectoparasites of mammals or birds; they feed on the host's blood, and their smooth, laterally compressed bodies allow them to move through the fur or plumage, while the backwardly directed spines and teeth on the body prevent them from being dislodged when the host grooms itself. Flea larvae, however, are free-living in the host's nest or lair, where they feed mainly on organic debris.

An Australian sawfly. Sawflies are the more primitive Hymenopteran insects, and fossilised sawfly wings are among the earliest known remains of this order. The majority of living species lay eggs in woody or herbaceous plants, on, or in, which their larvae feed.

some other sawflies have leaf-mining larvae, while those of *Caliroa* are peculiar, slug-like creatures covered with a dark, slimy secretion and feeding externally on the leaves of deciduous trees.

Most of the so-called parasitic Hymenoptera have larvae which feed on the body of the host insect, either internally or sometimes as external parasites. They are therefore of great importance as agents in the natural limitation of insect populations and many species have been artificially reared and introduced into various parts of the world in order to effect the control of insect pests. The Parasitica also include species with plant-feeding larvae, however, such as the gall-forming Cynipidae and those chalcid wasps that live on seeds. In all cases the adult Parasitica are free-living and feed on nectar and sometimes on the body-fluids exuding from the larval host when it is punctured with the ovipositor. The Ichneumonidae are one of the largest parasitic families with thousands of species, the vast majority having lepidopterous caterpillars as their hosts, though some develop on sawfly larvae, Coleoptera, other insects, and even spiders. The adults are commonly found on umbellifers and other flowers on sunny days and a few are very large insects with ovipositors up to fifteen centimetres long; pride of place goes to forms like *Thalessa* and *Megarhyssa* which lay their eggs in the wood-boring larvae of the Siricidae and are able to drill through solid wood in order to reach their hosts. The slender reddish-brown species of *Ophion* are commonly

attracted to light and a very unusual habit is found in *Agriotypus*, where the adults swim beneath water to find their hosts (the larvae of caddis-flies). Closely related to the Ichneumonidae are the Braconidae, smallish insects which also commonly parasitise lepidopterous larvae, each caterpillar sometimes nourishing more than a hundred individual parasites. *Apanteles glomeratus* is a common parasite of Cabbage White caterpillars and its numerous sulphur-yellow cocoons can often be seen among the remains of the larvae they have killed. A few braconids indulge in polyembryony—a kind of multiple twinning in which each fertilised egg may give rise to dozens of larvae.

The Cynipidae include some parasites of other insects, but the majority of cynipid larvae develop in plant galls. These structures are induced to form through the presence of a living larva in the plant tissues and they have a great variety of characteristic forms and colours. Oaks are especially susceptible and among the many cynipid galls found on them in Europe are the hard spherical marble galls formed by *Andricus kollari*, the flattish, button-shaped galls on the undersides of the leaves (*Neuroterus*) and the large, spongy, pinkish-yellow oak-apples due to *Biorhiza pallida*. Roses are also commonly hosts to gall-forming Cynipidae and *Rhodites rosae* gives rise to the striking pin-cushion or bedeguar galls, consisting of a dense mass of scarlet filaments as big as an egg. Comparable galls occur on North American oaks and roses and in California *Neuroterus sal-*

tatorius galls fall from the leaves and jump about on the ground through the activities of the larvae inside them. Australia, incidentally, has a very poor cynipid fauna and most of the plant galls there are due to scale-insects. The majority of cynipids show a remarkable alternation of bisexual and parthenogenetic generations, both the adults and galls of the two successive generations differing considerably. It is also worth noting that the galls offer food and shelter to many other species, so that a miniature insect community may be established through the activities of a single primary gall-forming species.

The group Chalcidoidea comprises twenty or so families, mostly parasites of other insects, including some which are hyperparasites, that is, they parasitise insects which are themselves parasitic on an original host insect. The chalcidoids include some of the smallest Hymenoptera, especially in the Trichogrammatidae and Mymaridae (fairy flies) which develop in the eggs of the host species. Of the non-parasitic chalcids the most remarkable are the fig insects or Agaontidae, in which the males are wingless and never leave the inside of the fig fruit, while the females are more normal insects. Agaontids develop in galls within wild figs, the female insect mating before she leaves the gall. In escaping from the fig she becomes dusted with pollen and so is able to fertilise the other figs which she enters to lay her eggs. *Blastophaga psenes*, the best-known fig insect, was specially introduced into California to make possible there the cultivation of Smyrna figs. Last among the Parasitica, the Proctotrupoidea and allies consist of some ten families concerning whose biology much further research is needed. The Scelionidae are all egg-parasites and the Platygasteridae develop in gall-midge larvae.

A number of families commonly treated as aculeate Hymenoptera are actually parasitic and represent a kind of half-way stage towards the typical aculeates. Among them are the small, ant-like Dryinidae which parasitise various Homoptera and in which the female has long, claw-like front legs with which it captures and holds its prey. The allied Chrysididae or ruby wasps are striking insects with brilliant metallically coloured bodies and larvae that develop as external parasites of bee or wasp larvae. The Scoliidae and Tiphiidae are medium or large, hairy, wasp-like insects and seem to be primitive aculeates, yet they too have larvae which are parasitic (usually on scarabaeid beetle larvae). In the ants or Formicidae, however, one sees a large, successful and biologically diverse family of undoubted aculeates, all 4,500 species of which are social. There are normally two castes, the sexual forms and the workers. The male and female reproductive forms are the 'flying ants', which are fully winged and usually swarm out of their colonies over a short period of time to undertake a nuptial flight. When this is over, the female excavates a small chamber in which she eventually starts to lay eggs, being nourished during this period by food materials stored in her fat-body and by the products of her disintegrating wing muscles. The first larvae of the new colony develop into workers which forage for themselves and also supply the queen with food. The worker ants are always wingless, sterile females and in some species they may include forms with larger heads and mandibles that are known as soldiers and defend the colony or have other special functions. The workers are often very numerous in large colonies such as those of the European wood ants (*Formica rufa* and its allies) and their various activities are often very characteristic of certain groups of ants. The driver ants of Africa and the legionary or army ants of South America, for example, inhabit only temporary nests or 'bivouacs' from which they may wander in large armies that capture and consume all the insects and other small animals in their path.

Another group, the harvesting ants especially characteristic of drier Mediterranean countries, live on seeds which they store in underground chambers as a food reserve in times of drought. It was these to which the sluggard was directed in *Proverbs*, vi:6. The parasol ants *Atta* and their relatives from Central America have large nests with special chambers in which they cultivate fungus gardens, the 'soil' of which is formed of chewed-up leaf fragments brought in from the foraging expeditions. The food-storage problems of the honeypot ants, such as *Myrmecocystus* of the south-west United States, are solved in an ingenious way: certain workers are gorged with honey-dew and their grossly distended bodies hang almost immobile from the roof of the nest. Two or three hundred of these 'repletes' may be found in a nest and in Australia, where certain species of *Camponotus* have this habit, the aborigines value them as a source of food. Many species of ants have established symbiotic relations with aphids, coccids, membracids and the larvae of lycaenid butterflies, while ant-nests usually contain a variety of insect and other arthropod guests. A few ants are slavemakers, capturing the workers of other species, on whose labour they are partly or wholly dependent.

The Pompilidae or spider-wasps are a very large group of active, long-legged insects which prey on spiders. They usually construct underground burrows to which the spider is brought after being paralysed by a sting. An egg is then laid on each spider which serves as fresh food for the developing pompilid larva. The most striking members of the family are the large 'tarantula hawks' such as *Pepsis formosa* of the southern United States and Central America, with a body about 37 millimetres long. The members of the family Vespidae are, however, much more familiar to the layman for they include the common black and yellow wasps of the genus *Vespula* (known in America as yellowjackets or hornets) as well as the larger European Hornet (*Vespa crabro*), now introduced into the United States. Such insects live on nectar, ripe fruit and sugary liquids, but they are also predacious and feed their larvae with masticated insects. They have a highly devloped social organisation (p. 123) and inhabit elaborate, papery nests composed of several tiers enclosed in an outer envelope and built in the ground, or suspended from trees, or in other situations according to the species concerned. In most areas a successful nest may contain five thousand or so workers by the late summer, but in New Zealand *Vespula germanica*, introduced there from Europe, makes gigantic colonies over four metres across

149

A digger wasp carrying its prey, a long-horned grasshopper, to its nest. The digger wasps or Sphecidae are solitary species which provision their nests with various species of insects, the exact nature of their prey, nest-construction and other habits varying from one group to another. In general the female wasp paralyses its prey by stinging it, transports it to its nest and then lays an egg on it. The resulting wasp larva feeds on the prey and completes its development in the nest.

A paper-wasp, *Polistes canadensis*. *Polistes* and its allies are widely distributed insects, closely related to the more familiar wasps or yellow-jackets (*Vespula*). Their nest, however, is a single papery comb suspended from the underside of a surface such as the eaves or ceiling of a building and it lacks the outer protective covering found in *Vespula* nests.

and apparently containing several queens. Not all Vespidae have such elaborate forms of social organisation, however. In *Polistes*, for example, which occurs in most parts of the world (though not in Britain) the nest consists of a single small tier of cells, not surrounded by an envelope. The workers are hardly distinguishable from the queens in appearance, though her presence in the colony prevents them from laying eggs; should she die they soon begin to do so. The polybiine wasps are also social. They form a large tropical group, mostly from South America, though *Belonogaster junceus* is a common species in Africa, forming small colonies in which there is little differentiation of caste: the older females are egg-layers and the younger ones are foragers. The family Vespidae also includes a large number of purely solitary species. In temperate regions these are mostly members of the Eumeninae which usually prey on small caterpillars that are then stored in the nests, of which a considerable variety is found. The potter wasps, *Eumenes*, for example, construct vase-shaped nests of mud attached to plant stems, while *Odynerus* usually makes burrows in the soil.

Another group of solitary wasps are the members of the family Sphecidae, typified by *Sphex* and its allies—large, graceful, long-legged species with a greatly attenuated waist. They usually build burrows in the soil and stock them with lepidopterous larvae, Hemiptera, Orthoptera or other insects and arachnids which are first paralysed by being stung. An egg is then laid in each cell and the resulting larva feeds on the prey provided by the parent. As a rule the cell is sealed once it has been provisioned and an egg has been laid, but some species continue to supply insects to the developing young and the European *Ammophila pubescens*, for example, may maintain two or three nests, each in a different stage of development.

Related to the sphecoids are the bees, both solitary and social, which make up the group Apoidea. Most of these, like the primitive family Prosopidae and the Andrenidae, are solitary species, nesting in the soil, in hollow stems, and in other such places, while some Megachilidae line their cells with specially cut circular pieces of leaf and are hence known as leaf-cutter bees. Of the social species from the family Apidae, *Bombus* includes the various bumble bees which form annual colonies in the ground, often in deserted mouse nests. They include some valuable pollinators but attempts to domesticate them on this account have not yet been successful. The very similar-looking cuckoo bees (*Psithyrus*) are social parasites without a worker caste; their females invade *Bombus* nests to lay eggs which are then reared by the *Bombus* workers. The very small, tropical, stingless bees—*Melipona* and its allies—are interesting because the well-defined castes are perhaps genetically determined. Stingless bees were domesticated as a source of honey by the Maya Indians of Central America, but the familiar Honey Bee is a quite different species, *Apis mellifera*, which exists in several races. Under wild conditions this insect nests in caves or hollow trees but it is usually seen only in artificially housed colonies which may each contain over 50,000 workers with a queen and a variable number of males (the drones). The latter are ejected at the

A solitary bee, *Andrena*, emerging from its nest. *Andrena* contains very many species from north temperate areas of the Old and New World. Their nest consists of a vertical tunnel in the soil, with lateral branches off it. Many individuals commonly nest close together in areas where the vegetation is sparse.

end of the summer and die, a new generation being reared each year. They function only in the nuptial flight when a newly emerged queen, having previously disposed of any rivals, mates—usually for the only time in her life. This she does with a single drone out of the many that follow her and she subsequently returns to the hive to begin her reproductive life. The worker Honey Bees undertake a variety of duties in a more or less well-defined sequence according to their age—tending the brood, comb-building, guarding the hive, and foraging for nectar, pollen or water. It is the foraging bees which, on returning to the hive from a successful sortie, indulge in remarkable dances which indicate to other foragers the location of food supplies in the field.

Beetles (Order Coleoptera)

The beetles form the largest order of insects with over 330,000 known species. They vary greatly in size, detailed structure and biology, but are usually easily recognisable because their fore wings are transformed into a pair of hard, thick, protective elytra. These meet down the middle of the back when the insect is not flying, but are held forwards and out of the way of the beating hind wings during flight. Beetle larvae are very diverse in appearance but commonly have a well-developed head, biting mouth-parts and thoracic

Nest of the Common Wasp (*Vespula vulgaris*) in a garden shed. The nest is built of carton, a cardboard-like material composed mainly of wood fibres mixed with saliva to form a pulp that is applied in strips with the mandibles and allowed to dry. Each nest consists of about six horizontal combs (in cells of which the larvae are reared), joined by vertical pillars and enclosed in an outer envelope. *Vespula vulgaris* usually builds subterranean nests but they are sometimes also found in enclosed spaces in buildings.

legs, though they lack abdominal prolegs. Some have a strong, sclerotised cuticle; others are soft, fleshy grubs which may have no legs at all. Both adults and larvae inhabit a great variety of situations and display many modes of life. According to the group to which they belong, beetles may be aquatic, terrestrial, or subterranean soil-burrowers; they (or their larvae) may burrow in wood, mine leaves, or live in the nests of birds or of social insects; many are phytophagous or predacious, some are scavengers or feed on fungi, carrion, woollen materials or stored foodstuffs; but they include few parasites and hardly any are truly marine. A large number of beetles injure cultivated plants, stored grain, or timber and some of the most serious pests belong to the order Coleoptera.

This great assemblage is accommodated in four suborders: the relatively primitive Adephaga, two small groups of Archostemata and Myxophaga, and the enormous section Polyphaga. The most familiar adephagan beetles are the Carabidae or ground beetles, comprising over 25,000 species, mainly nocturnal and dark or metallic in colour. They are usually the beetles which scuttle away when a stone is overturned and the larvae live in the soil, in débris or under bark. Both larvae and adults are generally predacious, feeding on other insects or on slugs or snails. *Calosoma sycophanta*, one of a widespread genus of handsome iridescent beetles, was introduced into the United States from Europe to combat the caterpillars of the Gipsy Moth. Another widely distributed genus is *Brachinus*, the so-called bombardier beetles, which defend themselves by audibly emitting puffs of a volatile irritant secretion from glands near the posterior end of the body. The family includes many quite large species, some up to five centimetres long, but it also has a few dwarfs, such as the peculiar, minute, blind Australian species of *Illaphanus* that live under stones and are associated with ants. Often included in the Carabidae are the tiger beetles or Cicindelidae, active predators with prominent eyes and long, pointed mandibles. The larvae are mostly ground-dwellers, living in burrows which may go down into the soil thirty centimetres or more. Each larva has a pair of dorsal hooks that can anchor it in its burrow and a broad head used to plug the entrance while it lies in wait for its prey. This consists of other insects wandering near the opening of the burrow; they are perceived by the well-developed ocelli of the larva, seized by its mandibles, and dragged down into the burrow to be devoured. The medium-sized species of *Cicindela* are found in sandy localities all over the world; *Tricondyla* includes wingless, tree-haunting forms, while the very large, black species of *Mantichora* from Africa have unusually fearsome mandibles in the male sex. Another intriguing group of carabid beetles is the Paussinae, all from warm countries and mostly associated with ants, which sometimes carry them about in the nest by gripping the beetles' inflated antennae. Many paussids produce an aromatic secretion which collects on special hair-tufts on their body, from which it is avidly licked off by the ants.

The remaining adephagan families are aquatic and three of them are sufficiently widespread to be mentioned here. The Haliplidae are small beetles found among aquatic vegetation or under submerged stones, in still or running water. They have unusual larvae which bear segmentally arranged groups of fleshy processes along the body. A more familiar family of water beetles is the Dytiscidae, which include the large species of *Dytiscus* found over much of the northern hemisphere as well as many other genera of varying sizes. The adults are smooth, streamlined, oval-shaped insects which swim by rapid, simultaneous movements of the long, hair-fringed hind legs. The males of some species have sucker-like structures (actually modified hairs) on the front legs which are used to grip the female while mating. Both sexes respire through a renewable air-store beneath the elytra and are actively predacious on other aquatic insects. The larvae are also predators and have unusually specialised mouth-parts: the long, sickle-shaped mandibles are channelled along their inner faces and can be plunged into the prey, whose body fluids are then sucked out along the channels. Last among the aquatic Adephaga are the whirligig beetles or Gyrinidae—some 700 species of dark, shiny, convex insects which can dive to the bottoms of ponds, but are more usually found gyrating endlessly on the surface, often in some numbers. To live in this way they are provided with unusually broad swimming legs fringed with flattened hairs and their eyes are divided each into an upper part for aerial vision and a lower one for use beneath the water. The predacious larvae carry a pair of projecting, feathery gill filaments on most of the abdominal segments.

The small suborder Archostemata includes one small family, the Cupedidae. This comprises some twenty-five species that are scattered widely over the globe, though none of them occurs in Europe. The larvae are specialised wood-feeders and the main interest of the family is that it has numerous fossil representatives as far back as the Permian and is probably a survival from archaic coleopteran stock.

Of the very many families of polyphagan beetles, only the better known can be mentioned here. The first of these is the Hydrophilidae, some of which live in damp or marshy places while others are fully aquatic and have a superficial resemblance to dytiscids. They differ, however, in carrying their air-film on the ventral side of the body, in swimming with alternate movements of the legs and in having long, feeler-like maxillary palps. The antennae are correspondingly short and in the fully aquatic species they bear unwettable hair-tracts which can be used to convey air to the ventral bubble, the submerged beetle simply pushing the antennae through the water-surface to establish communication with the atmosphere. *Hydrophilus piceus* is one of the largest British beetles and in this and some other genera the eggs are laid in a remarkable cocoon-like structure which may be attached to floating grass and other objects. The Histeridae are usually compact, shining, predacious beetles frequenting dung, carrion and ants' nests or living beneath bark and in the tunnels of wood-boring insects. The very flat species of *Hololepta*, measuring up to eighteen millimetres long, are the largest representatives of the family. An almost purely carrion-feeding

group is the Silphidae, which includes the black or black and orange burying beetles—species of *Nicrophorus* which excavate soil beneath the dead bodies of small vertebrates, so covering them. Eggs are then laid on the corpse and the larvae feed on it. *Aclypea opaca* and some other species differ from most members of the family in being plant-feeders, sometimes injuring cultivated plants in Europe and North America. Allied to the Silphidae are the predacious rove-beetles or Staphylinidae, a very large family easily recognised by the very short elytra which cover the folded hind wings but leave most of the abdomen exposed. The largest, like the Devil's Coach Horse (*Staphylinus olens*), are over 2·5 centimetres long, but most staphylinids are relatively small. They and their larvae are normally predacious, often on insects associated with decaying animal or vegetable matter. More than three hundred species are found in ants' nests, some of them being tended by the ants.

One of the most distinctive groups of Polyphaga is the lamellicorn beetles, so-called because their antennae each bear a club composed of more or less flat, leaf-like plates. They include first the tropical Passalidae: large, flat, black stridulating insects, all rather similar in appearance and living in rotten wood, apparently in small family groups. They are sometimes known as bessbugs or, from their shiny surface, as 'patent-leather beetles'; none occurs in Europe and only three species are found in North America. The Lucanidae also have larvae which inhabit decaying trees. The adults are stag-beetles, in which the males have enormous antler-like mandibles, sometimes longer than the rest of the body. *Lucanus cervus* is the large European species and *L. elephas* from the southern United States runs it close in size. Most of the species are tropical, however, and some of them are particularly large and striking insects: *Chiasognathus grantii* from Chile and *Cladognathus giraffa* from India and Java both have mandibles of fearsome dimensions. The convex, shining 'dor beetles' of the family Geotrupidae are also lamellicorns. They are mostly dung-feeders, and *Geotrupes* constructs burrows down to forty-five centimetres deep in the soil. At the end of the burrow an egg is laid on a plug of dung, which serves as food for the larva. This group is sometimes included in the largest of the lamellicorn families, the Scarabaeidae, of which about 20,000 species are known. It includes cockchafers like the brilliant metallic green *Cetonia* or the duller-coloured maybugs and June beetles (*Melolontha* in Europe and *Phyllophaga* in North America). Some of the most unusual scarabaeids, however, are the large rhinoceros or elephant beetles, in which the males (and, very rarely, the females) have conspicuous horns on the head of pronotum or both. One of them, *Dynastes tityus*, about six centimetres long, occurs in the eastern United States, but is far outshone by the Hercules Beetle (*Dynastes herculeus*) from Central and South America, which measures about thirteen centimetres long, nearly two-thirds of this being accounted for by the prothoracic horn. Australia has large elephant beetles, *Xylotrupes australicus* and *Haploscapanes barbarossa*. In many tropical countries species of *Oryctes* attack coconut palms, the female boring into the trunk to lay her eggs and the larvae feeding on the decaying

Opposite top
The Great Water-beetle (*Dytiscus marginalis*) feeding on a Three-spined Stickleback (*Gasterosteus aculeatus*). This is an intensively investigated beetle, a monograph of over 1,000 pages having once been devoted to it alone. *Dytiscus* lays its eggs in the stems of aquatic plants. The larva, like the adult, is an active predator and it pupates in a cell in damp soil near the water's edge. The adult beetle can fly from one pond to another.

Opposite middle
Stag Beetles (*Lucanus cervus*) mating. The male beetle, here seen above the female, has unusually large, antler-like mandibles which he uses in wrestling matches with other males. The mandibles of the female are more normal in size. The larvae develop in rotting wood (see p. 113).

Opposite bottom
A tiger beetle (*Cicindelidae*) with its prey. These medium-sized beetles are active predators with prominent eyes and long, pointed mandibles.

top
Hercules Beetle, *Dynastes tityus*, from Arizona. The Dynastine beetles—closely related to the cockchafers—include some remarkable horned species in which the males (and in a few species the female as well) have long pointed processes on the head and pronotum.

A dung-beetle (Scarabaeidae). The dung-beetles are related to cockchafers but differ in that the larvae and adults of many species are dung-feeders, showing a variety of interesting habits and often forming underground chambers or tunnels in which their young develop.

tissues. The larvae of the Scarabaeidae are usually whitish, fleshy grubs and in many species they are injurious to grassland, feeding among the roots of the turf. The family also includes the notorious Japanese Beetle (*Popillia japonica*), so destructive in the United States since about 1918. To many, however, the most interesting members of the group are the sacred scarab beetles which attained great significance as talismans and as part of the religious mythology in ancient Egypt. The species concerned seem to have belonged to the genera *Scarabaeus*, *Copris* and *Catharsius*, all feeding on dung which they roll into balls and bury beneath the ground. In some of these balls the female lays an egg and the resulting larva completes its development without leaving the ball.

A family of some agricultural importance in temperate regions is the Elateridae or click-beetles, so-called because they can jump with a sudden, sharp noise, using a peculiar peg-and-socket contrivance on the underside of the thorax. The larvae of many species are wireworms—slender, hard, cylindrical forms feeding underground on grass, cereals and root-crops, though other species have wood-feeding larvae. Adult elaterids are found on flowers or other vegetation and the genus *Pyrophorus* contains brightly luminous fireflies from the southern United States and

South America. Related to the elaterids are the Buprestidae, a very large and mainly tropical family of hard-bodied, metallic green, blue or coppery insects, some of which—like the Australian species of *Stigmodera*—are mounted as jewelry. The blind, legless larvae usually bore under bark or in wood and a few are injurious to cultivated plants. The Cantharidae or soldier beetles are rather soft-bodied insects often found on flowers in sunny weather. They and their flat, velvety, soil- and moss-dwelling larvae are predacious and the family is allied to the Lampyridae (fireflies and glow-worms). These are nocturnal insects with luminous organs (p. 122) usually best developed in the female, which in many species is a degenerate, wingless creature. Species of *Photinus* and *Photuris* are the usual fireflies in the eastern United States, *Lampyris noctiluca* is the Common European Glow-worm. Lampyrid larvae and adults are predacious on small animals—insects, slugs and earthworms.

The Dermestidae are smallish, oval beetles whose larvae act as scavengers, feeding on leather, fur, skins, wool, carrion and some stored foods such as bacon, cheese and grain. Species of *Dermestes* and the larvae of *Anthrenus* are the most important domestic pests; the adults of *Anthrenus* leave the house to feed on the pollen and nectar of garden flowers. Equally troublesome to the house-holder and to those caring for old buildings are several members of the Anobiidae whose larvae bore into wood and eventually reduce it to powder. *Anobium punctatum* is destructive to furniture and flooring (especially when made of softwoods). On the other hand the Deathwatch Beetle (*Xestobium rufovillosum*) attacks old, seasoned wood such as the structural timbers and roofs of churches.

The Cleridae are a mainly tropical group of brightly coloured, chequered, hairy, predacious beetles found on foliage, flowers and tree-trunks. Some Nitidulidae—small, dark beetles—also inhabit flowers, but others occur around sap-flows or in decaying fruit, fungi, carrion or stored grain. They are one of the many families of clavicorn beetles, the best known of which are the ladybirds or Coccinellidae. Both as adults and larvae, most ladybirds prey on aphids or other small, soft insects but the family also includes a group of plant-feeding species, of which the Mexican Bean Beetle (*Epilachna varivestis*) attacks a variety of crops in the southern United States. A very different-looking family is the Tenebrionidae, dark brown or black beetles superficially like carabids in appearance. Many occur in deserts or arid regions but *Tenebrio* is a cosmopolitan insect found in granaries and flour-stores along with its larvae (known as mealworms and often bred for feeding to pet animals). The Meloidae are the oil beetles or blister beetles, known as such because they contain the vesicant cantharidin (which is extracted commercially from the elytra of the European 'Spanish Fly', *Lytta vesicatoria*). Their main interest lies in the unusual life-cycle which involves a succession of different larval forms. The first instar is a minute, hard-skinned insect, the triungulin, which seeks out a host—the solitary bee *Andrena*, for instance in *Meloe*. It is then transported to the bee's nest, where it moults to a scarabaeoid-like larva that feeds on the stored honey and then transforms into a legless grub.

The Cerambycidae or longicorn beetles are a large family, varying greatly in size and appearance but nearly all with unusually long antennae. Their wood-boring larvae may take several years to complete their development and sometimes damage trees used for timber. *Prionus* includes some large, dark brown species but these are easily exceeded in size and decorative appearance by various species from Central and South America: the Harlequin Beetle (*Acrocinus longimanus*) with its brown, grey and reddish markings, the black and brown *Macrodontia cervicornis* or the metallic green *Psalidognathus superbus*. The common British black and yellow *Clytus arietis* is strikingly like a wasp and the family includes a number of other mimics such as the Australian species of *Hesthesis*, which closely resemble thynnid wasps in appearance and movements. A related and even larger family is the Chrysomelidae or leaf beetles, with shorter antennae and a shiny, sometimes metallic apperance. The adults feed mainly on foliage and flowers, as do the larvae of some species, though other larvae are stem-borers, root-feeders or leaf-miners. The Chrysomelidae include many important pests such as the flea-beetles (*Phyllotreta* and other genera) and the notorious Colorado Potato Beetle (*Leptinotarsa decemlineata*). This brown and yellow, striped insect with plump, orange and black larvae, was originally restricted to wild solanaceous plants in western North America. With the increasing cultivation of the potato it spread east and was eventually transported to Europe, dispersing rapidly eastwards across France and Germany into Russia. Another chrysomelid genus, *Donacia*, has unusual aquatic larvae which obtain oxygen by puncturing the air-spaces of submerged aquatic plants, while *Cassida* and its allies are the curiously shaped tortoise beetles, whose flat, spiny larvae adorn themselves with their cast skins and excrement.

The weevils or Curculionidae are by far the largest family of Coleoptera and are usually recognised by their head projecting into a snout-like proboscis of varying length. This bears the mouthparts terminally and in many species it is used by the female to drill holes in which the eggs are then laid. In forms like *Balaninus* the proboscis is greatly attenuated, while *Otiorhynchus* and its relations have a very short, broad snout. Curculionid larvae are legless, whitish grubs, most of which feed internally on various parts of their host plants— stems, roots, fruits, seeds or leaves are all liable to attack by one species or another. The Grain Weevil (*Sitophilus granarius*), is a widely distributed pest of stored grain, while the larvae of *Anthonomus pomorum* feed inside the young flower-buds of apple, preventing them from opening. Its close relative is the Cotton Boll Weevil (*Anthonomus grandis*), a native of Central America which crossed the Rio Grande in 1892 and thereafter became an extremely serious pest in the southern states. The bark-beetles or Scolytidae are sometimes included in the previous family. They bore out elaborate systems of radiating galleries between the bark and wood of many trees and shrubs and *Xyleborus* has an organised pattern of polygamy, with one male to about sixty females. It and other genera are the so-called ambrosia beetles which cultivate special fungi on which the larvae are nourished.

Seven-spot Ladybirds (*Coccinella septempunctata*) hibernating in a cluster on hawthorn. *Coccinella* is a common garden insect, beneficial in that the larva and adult feed on aphids. Unlike most beetle pupae, those of Coccinellidae are hard, coloured forms freely exposed above ground. The adults overwinter, sometimes in large aggregations, and emerge the following spring to lay eggs on plants frequented by aphids.

Two African weevils mating. The weevils or Curculionidae are a most successful group of beetles usually recognisable by their elbowed antennae and a snout or rostrum of variable length. In some species this is a very long, delicate process, but in others it may be only a short, blunt extension of the head, as in the species illustrated here.

Galleries of the Elm Bark Beetle (*Scolytus scolytus*). This species forms a more or less oval system of galleries beneath the bark of the main trunk and larger branches of elm trees; there are two generations of beetles a year. *Scolytus scolytus* and *S. multistriatus* carry the fungus *Ceratostomella ulmi*, the cause of the very destructive Dutch elm disease.

Order Strepsiptera

These unusual and little-known insects are related to the beetles, with which they are sometimes classified. Male Strepsiptera are curious little creatures with branched antennae, large eyes, fan-like hind wings and the forewings reduced to small, club-shaped halteres. The females, on the other hand, are almost invariably degenerate forms whose sac-like body is devoid of eyes, wings and legs and protrudes only a little from the body of the insect which it parasitises (usually some species of leaf-hopper or bee). The Strepsiptera are viviparous and the young larvae, known as triungulins, escape from the body of the mother through a special brood canal. They are microscopic, free-living, six-legged forms and soon attach themselves to a host insect, penetrating the latter's skin and completing their development as internal parasites. The male life-cycle includes a pupal stage, from which the free-living insect eventually emerges, but this is not present in the permanently parasitic females. Species of *Stylops* parasitise solitary bees of the genus *Andrena*, *Elenchus* attacks delphacid leaf-hoppers, while *Eoxenos* is exceptional with free-living adult females.

Conclusion

A group of animals so numerous and diverse as the insects allows of very few generalisations, but one fact which stands out clearly is their very great biological success. This is undeniable, whether judged by the number of insect species, the density of their populations, the variety of habitats they have entered, their wide distribution in space and time, or the impact they have made on man's economy and well-being. To analyse the causes of this unique achievement is inevitably to speculate, but it is interesting to consider a few of the factors that were probably involved. Three are of a quite general nature: the immense evolutionary plasticity of the cuticle, the highly efficient method of tracheal respiration, and the insect's well-developed ability to resist desiccation. Together these made possible the conquest of a variety of terrestrial habitats and permitted the evolution of wings and of a sufficiently intense metabolism to support active locomotion by flight. The importance of this is illustrated by the immense success of the Pterygota, which vastly outnumber the primitively wingless insects. Within the Pterygota the most important advance seems to have been the evolution of a holometabolous mode of development with the resulting dominance of the endopterygote orders and the extensive exploitation by their larval stages of many habitats hardly penetrated by the exopterygotes. Finally one must recall the many special adaptations which have promoted the success of individual groups of insects. The suctorial mouth-parts and feeding mechanism of the Hemiptera, for example, are fundamentally identical throughout the group. The adults of the Lepidoptera and cyclorrhaphan Diptera show equally how the potentialities of characteristic feeding habits have been realised to the full, while the parasitic Hymenoptera illustrate how the distinctive nutritional requirements of the larva can underlie another great adaptive radiation. Many other examples could be cited testifying to the evolutionary achievement of the insects and the conditions of their success. From dimly perceived beginnings in the Devonian period they have reached and maintained a position in which they participate in virtually every ecological system on the land or in freshwater. It is difficult to imagine a world without insects, and if this were so it would be a very different world indeed.

Crustaceans (Class Crustacea)

With about 26,000 described species, crustaceans are the third largest group of arthropods and include such diverse forms as crabs, lobsters, shrimps, woodlice, scuds, barnacles, fairy shrimps, fish-lice and water-fleas. Predominantly aquatic, they occur in both marine and freshwater habitats throughout the world and many forms are partly or wholly parasitic. They also vary greatly in size. Some water-fleas measure only 0·25 millimetres in total length, while the largest crabs have a body width of about thirty centimetres and a leg-span of some three metres.

Structure

Like other arthropods, crustaceans have a segmented body, an exoskeleton and paired, jointed limbs, but in addition they are characterised by two pairs of appendages in front of the mouth, the antennules or first antennae and the antennae or second antennae. In most crustaceans both are used as feelers, but in some species such as water-fleas (order Cladocera) the antennules are reduced in size and the antennae are branched and used for swimming. In others, such as some of the parasites, one or both pairs may be absent from the adult, though present in the young.

The exoskeleton varies from a thin, transparent layer in some of the small water-fleas to the thick, heavily calcified and pigmented structure found in crabs and lobsters. The surface of the exoskeleton may be smooth or have various kinds of projections, one of the commonest being a hair-like process called a seta, which is articulated at its base with a small pit. Some are simple, thin and flexible while others are complex feather-like structures of varying degrees of rigidity. They are often arranged in definite groups and rows on limbs used for feeding or cleaning, and they may prevent foreign particles from entering the respiratory chamber.

Each segment articulates with the next by means of a flexible membrane, but several segments may be fused together and covered by a single large plate of exoskeleton. Several groups of crustaceans have a carapace, which is basically a protective flap extending backwards from the head and covering most of the trunk. In species like lobsters and crabs the carapace is fused to the thoracic segments.

The limbs differ greatly in number, form and function in the various groups and are modified to perform particular functions in different parts of the body. Behind the antennae or 'feelers' lie the mandibles which function as jaws for either biting and crushing or merely squeezing and pushing food into the oesophagus. The maxillules and maxillae, which lie in sequence behind the mandibles, are variously developed but are usually associated with feeding. Three additional pairs of appendages are modified for feeding in the decapods: these are known as the first, second and third maxillipeds. In the crabs the third maxillipeds close over the other mouth-parts like doors.

When the body is clearly divided into a thorax and an abdomen, as in the shrimps, the thoracic limbs are called pereiopods, and the abdominal limbs are called pleopods. These two sets of limbs are often modified to serve different functions which are described in the accounts of the groups.

All the variations are thought to have been derived originally from a three-branched plan similar to the trunk limbs of the Cephalocarida. These small crustaceans have limbs with a six- or seven-jointed inner branch or endopodite, a flat two-jointed outer branch or exopodite, and a flap or epipodite on the outer side at the base of the exopodite. The walking legs of shrimps could develop from this three-branched type by elongation of the jointed endopod and suppression of the other two branches; the flattened trunk limbs of the fairy shrimps could develop from the basic type by elimination of the joints in the endopodite and enlargement of the base of the limb, etc.

Digestive system

In the smaller crustaceans such as water-fleas and copepods the gut is often a simple tube with a pair of outpushings or diverticula. In the larger crustaceans the gut develops a complex internal filter mechanism. The gut wall becomes thickened and the lining develops patches which may become hard and calcified, forming ossicles which are moved by muscles running from the gut to the exoskeleton. In crayfishes and their allies these ossicles form a gastric mill in which food can be ground. Large particles are prevented from travelling down the gut by a filter separating the gastric mill from the mid gut. Opening into the mid gut there are one or more pairs of glandular organs, which reach a large size in crabs. These organs are collectively known as the hepatopancreas and perform some of the functions of the liver and pancreas of the vertebrates. Various digestive enzymes are produced in these glands, and a large amount of glycogen, fats and other materials can be stored. The hind gut is usually simple in structure and lined with a thin layer of chitin.

Respiratory and circulatory systems

In crabs, shrimps and crayfishes the gills are attached to the bases of the thoracic limbs and to the wall of the thorax near the limb bases. The carapace overhangs the gills, enclosing them in a branchial chamber through which water can be pumped by means of a flap on the maxilla. In other crustaceans the gills are located differently, or may be absent if the animal is small and uses the whole body surface for respiratory exchange.

In isopods the abdominal limbs are flattened for respiratory purposes, and are well supplied with blood vessels. In some mysidaceans (opossumshrimps) the gills at the bases of the legs are lost and the whole carapace becomes highly vascularised. Currents of water for respiratory purposes can be created in various ways. Fairy shrimps (order Anostraca) produce combined feeding, respiratory and locomotory currents by means of their leaf-like trunk limbs. Barnacles pump water in and out of their mantles by their feeding movements or by reduced forms of these.

Blood circulates through the gills and travels by more or less well-defined channels to the pericardial cavity which surrounds the heart and is separated from the rest of the body cavity by a membranous pericardium. The heart of a crab lies dorsally just underneath the exoskeleton, and its shape is almost square, but in many crustaceans the heart is long and tubular, resembling that of an insect. Blood enters the heart through valves or ostia which allow an inflow of blood when the heart dilates, but close when the heart contracts and the blood is forced to leave the heart by the arteries. The number of arteries leaving the heart varies in different groups, but the main direction of flow is usually forwards. In general the arterial system is well developed in the Malacostraca and poorly developed in the other groups. Some of the smaller crustaceans lack a heart: this applies to many ostracods and copepods.

The oxygen-carrying capacity of the blood may be increased by the presence of a respiratory pigment which combines reversibly with oxygen. Two such pigments are known in crustaceans but no species has both. Haemocyanin, which contains copper, is blue when combined with oxygen and is found in isopods (woodlice), amphipods (scuds), decapods (e.g. lobster, crabs) and stomatopods (mantis shrimps). Haemoglobin, which contains iron, is red and is found in various small crustaceans, particularly the subclass Branchiopoda (fairy shrimps and water-fleas), but not in any of the malacostracans (crabs, scuds and woodlice). These pigments are not contained in corpuscles as

Some animals gain a living by cleaning the small external parasites and pieces of skin from the bodies of other animals. There are cleaner fishes that do this to other fishes and there are cleaner shrimps that perform the same service to fishes. Here, a cleaner shrimp (*Hippolysmata grabhami*) is cleaning a Copper Band Butterfly-fish (*Chelmon rostratus*).

Female *Cyclops*. The two egg sacs are attached to the posterior end of the thorax and do not hinder the swimming movements of the thoracic limbs.

The eyes are usually compound like those of the insects but simpler eyes are also found, particularly in the smaller crustaceans such as copepods. Cave-dwelling and deep-sea crustaceans are often blind.

Receptor organs for the sense of touch take the form of setae provided with nerve cells which relay signals to the central nervous system when the setae touch an object. The antennules and antennae are usually well provided with such tactile setae, and in some shrimps one or more branches of these appendages may bend backwards and extend beyond the tail so that the shrimp can receive warning of approach from behind.

Balance is maintained in many crustaceans by means of two globular structures, known as statocysts, which contain small particles resting on delicate setae. When the body is on an even keel the particles in both statocysts emit similar stimuli and different stimuli when the body is tilted. Experiments show that some shrimps can retain balance with only one statocyst and that the statocyst also sends stimuli to the brain when the body is turned in a horizontal plane.

Crustaceans also have chemical senses akin to our senses of taste and smell. Special thin-walled setae containing a projection from a nerve cell are thought to be one type of chemoreceptor. Another receptor is in the form of a small pit in the cuticle connected with a nerve cell. Such receptors are most abundant on antennae and mouth-parts.

haemoglobin is in the vertebrates, but are dissolved in the blood plasma. The blood does contain some cells which function in a manner similar to the white blood cells of vertebrates. They help to resist infection by ingesting foreign bodies in the blood, and they can plug small wounds.

Excretory system

The two main organs concerned with excretion are the antennal and maxillary glands. Both are well developed in a few crustaceans (e.g. *Hutchinsoniella* and *Nebalia*) but usually one is reduced or absent. In most malacostracans the antennal gland persists and in decapods this gland is known as the green gland as it is often that colour. In other groups the antennal gland may be present in the young, but degenerates in adults as the maxillary gland becomes functional. Both glands are similar in basic structure. There is an internal end sac, a canal and an exit duct, which may be expanded into a bladder. The main end product of nitrogen metabolism in crustaceans is ammonia, but the urine also contains amounts of uric acid and urea.

In addition, the gills are highly permeable and the gut wall is capable of secretion, and it is probable that some waste products are eliminated by these routes. Experiments in which coloured substances are injected into the blood show that they can be moved from the blood into the lumen of the gut.

Nervous system and sense-organs

The nervous system is centred on a brain lying above the anterior end of the gut and a chain of ganglia lying below the gut. The brain supplies nerves to most of the sense-organs in the head. The first ganglion, the suboesophageal ganglion, supplies nerves to the mandibles and other mouth-parts, and the other ganglia are usually spaced so that one lies in each segment. This arrangement is modified in species with short bodies. For instance, crabs have a concentration of nervous tissue in the thorax where a number of ganglia are joined together.

The eyes, often stalked and movable, are usually the most conspicuous sense-organs and in most crustaceans the optic nerves are particularly large.

Growth and reproduction

In common with other arthropods, crustaceans can increase in size only when the exoskeleton is soft and distensible. This is normally so only after the moult or ecdysis, when the exoskeleton is shed and the new one, which has been formed underneath, allows the crustacean to absorb water and swell. The whole process is controlled by hormones secreted by endocrine organs in the eyestalks. Maturation is also under hormonal control, but is governed to some extent by the size of the individual. For most species there is a minimum size below which they do not reproduce.

The sexes are usually separate, but hermaphrodites are found among barnacles, some notostracans and the cephalocarids. Some shrimps normally change sex during their lifetime. Similarly, the isopod *Rhyscotoides* starts life as a male and later changes to a female.

The transfer of sperms from male to female is often aided by specially modified appendages. In most male decapods one or more pairs of abdominal limbs, the pleopods, are tubular and close to the genital opening so that they can conduct the seminal fluid. The sperms are frequently enclosed in a case or spermatophore, which is placed on the body of the female near the genital orifice; sometimes in an exoskeletal pocket, the seminal receptacle. The eggs may be shed freely into the water or carried by the female in a variety of ways. They may be attached to the pleopods, as in crabs, shrimps and crayfishes, or carried in a brood-pouch. In peracarids the brood-pouch is formed by plates at the bases of the legs, but in water-fleas the brood-pouch lies between the trunk and the carapace, and in the notostracans a pouch is formed on the eleventh pair of legs. Anostracans have a brood-pouch on the ventral side behind the last pair of limbs, while many copepods carry their eggs in a similar position in thin-walled sacs.

The young crustaceans emerging from the eggs show a great variety of form. Sometimes they are miniature adults, but frequently they are larvae which differ greatly from the parents. The most important larval form is the nauplius, characterised by the possession of three pairs of appendages of which the antennae are the largest and are used for swimming. The importance of this larva lies in its widespread occurrence in different groups of crustaceans. Nauplii are found in branchiopods, copepods, cirripedes, euphausiaceans and a few decapods. The cephalocarids and mystacocarids have larvae which resemble nauplii in some respects, and the ostracods hatch in a form resembling a nauplius with a bivalved carapace. This distribution among the different groups adds to the idea that crustaceans are a natural group.

Subclass Cephalocarida

The discovery of this new group, which was announced in 1955, was a most exciting advance in the study of crustaceans. They have many primitive features and their trunk limbs throw a new light on the ways in which the limbs of other crustaceans may have arisen (see p. 157).

All the species so far described are small, only two or three millimetres long, and without any trace of eyes. The head bears a short horseshoe-shaped carapace which covers only one segment of the trunk. The body is elongated with twenty segments lying behind the head. *Hutchinsoniella* and *Sandersiella* have eight well-developed limbs on the trunk, and *Lightiella* has seven. In all three genera there is a small rudimentary appendage on the ninth trunk segment. At the tail end of the body there are two rami, each bearing a seta which is half the length of the body.

The four species described are from Japan, North America and the Caribbean, and are included in the family Hutchinsoniellidae. They live in soft marine sediments where they feed on organic débris. The débris is gathered in the midline between the two rows of limbs and is pushed forwards to the mouth by the bases of the limbs. Each individual of *Hutchinsoniella* lays only two eggs at a time and during the breeding season from June to September, an individual can produce three broods of young. The annual production of only six offspring per individual is a remarkably low rate of reproduction compared with the cladocerans (p. 161). *Hutchinsoniella* passes through eighteen stages before it matures but the duration of these stages is unknown.

Subclass Branchiopoda

It is difficult to characterise this subclass concisely because there is such a variety of form, but each of the four living orders (Anostraca, Notostraca, Conchostraca and Cladocera) has features in common with at least one of the others so that the Branchiopoda appear to form a valid unit. Most of the group have flattened trunk limbs which form the basis of an elaborate filter feeding mechanism. The antennule is generally small and not subdivided. The number of body segments is variable, being low in cladocerans and high in the notostracans. The number of limbs is even more variable, because in the notostracans and conchostracans there are more pairs of limbs than segments.

The whole group is basically of freshwater origin, but a few cladocerans are marine and the Brine Shrimp (*Artemia salina*) lives in waters which can contain several times as much salt as the sea.

Order Anostraca

This order is the only one in the subclass Branchiopoda which is characterised by having stalked eyes. There is no carapace and the trunk is elongated. In most forms there are eleven pairs of flattened, paddle-like limbs which serve for locomotion, respiration and feeding. Most species swim with the limbs uppermost. Feeding involves all the limbs which by their movements suck water into the median space between the two rows of limbs, which are fringed by fine feather-like setae.

These setae form a filter which retains small food particles in the median space and another series of setae comb the particles free into the median space so that they can be washed forwards by small subsidiary currents at the bases of the limbs. On reaching the region of the mouth the particles are first of all entangled in a sticky secretion and then subsequently pushed into the oesophagus by the mandibles.

The eggs are laid into the brood-pouch behind the last pair of limbs. They may be carried for a day or two before being released in a tough shell. In common with the eggs of many other branchiopods they can withstand severe conditions. Eggs of the Brine Shrimp (*Artemia salina*) have been dried and subjected to high vacuum, heated to 103°C. for over an hour, and cooled to the temperature of liquid air for several hours. In spite of such treatment some of the eggs still hatch when immersed in salt water. *Artemia* can also produce another type of egg which does not develop a tough coat. These eggs are kept in the brood-pouch until they hatch as nauplius larvae. Eggs of most Anostraca must be dried or frozen or both before they will hatch. A resting period is also required, and the eggs hatch at different intervals.

Most anostracans live in temporary pools. *Branchinecta paludosa* is a common circum-arctic species of which there are relict populations left behind after the Ice Ages. One such population is found in

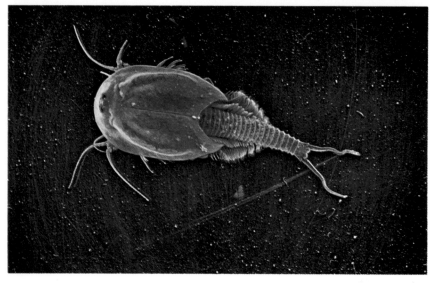

The brine shrimp, *Artemia salina*, has the distinction of being able to live in water several times as salty as the sea. The other outstanding feature is the paddle-like legs that serve not only for locomotion and respiration but also for feeding. The movement of the legs not only carry the animal around but also draw water towards the mouth which takes in the small particles of food.

Tadpole shrimps are freshwater shrimps of unusual appearance that live mainly in temporary pools, as a result of which they are irregular and erratic in their occurrence. *Triops cancriformis*, shown here, is rare in Britain but abundant in certain parts of Europe, especially in the ricefields of southern France and in Spain where it sometimes causes damage by uprooting rice seedlings.

the Tatra Mountains of Czechoslovakia, and another is found on Medicine Bow Mountains, Wyoming, in the United States.

Order Notostraca

Members of this order have a large shield-shaped carapace and numerous trunk limbs, some segments bearing three or more pairs. The eyes are not stalked but are grouped together on the dorsal surface. Notostracans are omnivorous, eating both animals and plants, and are capable of feeding on large and small particles. The small particles are collected by a complicated mechanism involving all the trunk limbs. The particles are gathered in the midline between the two rows of limbs and are pushed forwards to the mouth by limb bases.

The eleventh limbs bear pouches into which the eggs are laid. The eggs are resistant to freezing and drying, and apparently require such treatment before hatching. Resistance to drought has enabled the eggs to become efficient agents of

dispersal; when dry they can be blown about by the wind, and this may account for isolated populations on oceanic islands.

The two genera *Triops* and *Lepidurus* are grouped together in a single family. Both are found in temporary pools of freshwater. *Triops* is most common in the drier parts of the world. *Lepidurus* is particularly common all round the Arctic, where *L. arcticus* lives in permanent lakes and in small pools which freeze solid for several months during the winter. Other species of *Lepidurus* live in warmer parts of the world. The temporary flooding of rice fields makes them an ideal habitat for *Triops*, which sometimes becomes a pest by uprooting rice seedlings. In deserts pools may form only once in several years, and may last for only a week or two. *Triops granarius* can develop in such pools and grow from egg to adult in a week, so that it can lay eggs before the pool dries up.

Some populations of *Triops* consist entirely of hermaphrodites. In *T. cancriformis* the populations near the northern limit of the species are predominantly hermaphrodite, while the southern populations are generally bisexual.

Order Conchostraca

The bivalved carapace of a conchostracan extends forwards and backwards to enclose both the head and the trunk. Enclosing the trunk limbs prevents their use in locomotion, and swimming is effected by the large, branched antennae. The numerous trunk limbs are used to create a current of water between the valves of the carapace, and fine setae on the inner borders of the limbs filter out any particles which may be used as food. Most species produce eggs which can withstand being dried. When these eggs are wetted a nauplius larva emerges. *Cyclestheria hislopi*, a circum-tropical species, is exceptional in producing a second type of egg which will develop quickly in the brood-pouch of the mother and give rise to a miniature of the adult without first having to pass through a nauplius stage.

Most conchostracans live in temporary pools, but they are not confined to these situations. *Limnadia lenticularis* is widespread in North America and Europe, living mainly in lakes bordering the Arctic Ocean, and *Cyclestheria hislopi* has been found in permanent waters in Africa. There are probably about 200 species scattered throughout the world.

Water-fleas (Order Cladocera)

Many species of this order are about the size of a flea and swim by jerky movements of their branched antennae. They have a bivalved carapace similar to that of conchostracans, but it does not cover the head. The trunk limbs are less numerous than in conchostracans, varying from four to six pairs.

Cladoceran reproduction is prolific. Females can produce eggs which do not need to be fertilised and in good conditions a large species such as *Daphnia magna* can produce broods of 100 eggs at intervals of three days. Each egg can give rise to a female which becomes mature in eight days when the water is warm. The eggs are carried by the females in a pouch between the trunk and the carapace. Egg-laying is closely related to moulting, the young being released from the brood-pouch several hours before the mother moults, and the new eggs are laid a few hours after moulting. This regular cycle will continue throughout the adult life of a female as long as the temperature and supply of food are favourable. In unfavourable conditions, such as low temperatures or shortage of food, some of the eggs develop into males, and some females then produce another type of egg which needs fertilisation. The fertilised eggs are usually enclosed in a modified brood-pouch shaped like a saddle (*ephippium*), which breaks loose when the female moults. Ephippial eggs are resistant to severe environmental conditions such as freezing and drying, and hatch when conditions improve. Some Arctic populations produce ephippial eggs which do not need to be fertilised, so that males have become unnecessary.

The blood of cladocerans has a remarkable similarity to human blood in that it contains a red respiratory pigment, haemoglobin, which combines reversibly with oxygen and transports it to the tissues of the body. When a cladoceran lives in well-aerated water it has little need of such a pigment, and under such conditions the blood is pale. When the oxygen content of the water is low the water-flea can compensate by increasing the haemoglobin content of the blood, so that in poorly aerated water the blood may be bright red. This is similar to the increase in haemoglobin in the blood of man when he goes to live high on a mountain where the air is rarefied. The increase in man is only of the order of ten per cent, but in water-fleas the increase can be over twelvefold. The process is reversible, so that if red water-fleas are placed in well-aerated water they become pale by losing their haemoglobin. The change from red to pale takes about ten days.

There are over 400 species of Cladocera, arranged in eight families. The family Daphniidae comprises typical water-fleas which feed by filtering microscopic-sized plants from the water. Other cladocerans have lost the filterng mechansim. *Leptodora* is such a form which has become a

predator, living in the plankton of lakes in the northern hemisphere, and feeding on smaller crustaceans. *Leptodora* is also remarkable for being the only cladoceran with a nauplius larva which hatches from the fertilised egg.

Water fleas (*Daphnia*) are so-named for their method of swimming, which is a 'hop and a drop', using their branched antennae. To maintain its position in the water a *Daphnia* must swim continuously. A flick of the antennae lifts it up after which it begins to sink until another flick lifts it up again.

Subclass Mystacocarida

The first mystacocarid was described in 1943 from specimens collected from beaches in Massachusetts and Connecticut. Since then allied species have been found on South American, African and European coasts.

The general form of the body is worm-like, both the head and the eleven-segmented trunk are elongated. The anterior region of the head bears antennules, and the posterior region bears antennae, mandibles, maxillules and maxillae. All these appendages are well developed with branches projecting sideways from the body. These projections are used in locomotion. The use of the antennae in particular is essentially similar to the locomotion of a nauplius larva, but the mystacocarid does not swim freely, and lives in the water-filled spaces in sand. The first trunk limb is

also fairly well developed, and is modified to assist in feeding. The remaining four trunk limbs are small, being formed from a single segment with a few setae; they do not appear to play any part in locomotion. There are no other appendages on the trunk, but the caudal furca is well developed, and is equipped with strong terminal spines.

At present there are three known species of the single genus *Derocheilocaris*, all of which are blind and feed by filtering small particles from the water between sand grains. The sexes are separate, and the females do not carry the eggs. The first stage in development is essentially similar to a nauplius larva, but the trunk has three segments clearly developed. Subsequent development consists in the gradual addition of segments and appendages over the course of ten stages.

Copepods (Subclass Copepoda)

No one knows how many species of copepods exist, but there are well over 4,500 and new species are being described at a rate of over 100 a year. They live almost anywhere there is water and many parasitic species are known. It is difficult to give a general description of the copepods because they exhibit such a variety of form and the parasites are often so bizarre that they can be identified as copepods only by studying the life-history. They never have a carapace, although some of the thoracic segments may fuse with the head. They have up to six pairs of trunk limbs, but this number is frequently reduced. The number of body segments is always low, typically nine. A single median eye formed from three ocelli is present in most of the non-parasitic species. Sometimes two of the ocelli develop large lenses so that a copepod like *Corycaeus* appears to have two enormous eyes. The eggs normally give rise to nauplius larvae.

Order Calanoida

There are over twenty families in this order, characterised by long antennules which are usually held stiffly at right angles to the long axis of the body. The males have one or both of the antennules modified for grasping the females. A feature of their internal anatomy is the possession of a heart which is absent from other copepods.

Most species of this group live in the sea, but the family Diaptomidae, with over two hundred species, dwells almost entirely in freshwater. Some representatives of other families, particularly the Centropagidae, are also found in freshwater. One member of the latter family, *Limnocalanus macrurus*, is regarded as a marine glacial relict left behind when rising land cut off arms of the sea as the ice retreated at the end of the Ice Ages. This species is distributed from the Great Lakes of North America to the Baltic and Caspian seas. It prefers cold deep lakes and breeds in the winter. In Britain it has been found only in Ennerdale Water.

Calanus finmarchicus is important as the main food of the Herring. It has a very wide range, extending from the Arctic to New Zealand, but it is particularly abundant in northern seas. *Calanus* sheds its eggs freely into the sea, but most of the freshwater

calanoids carry their eggs in a transparent sac at the base of the abdomen. The eggs give rise to nauplius larvae which moult five times before changing to forms similar to the adult but lacking the full complement of limbs. This stage is called a copepodid, and it moults yet another five times before becoming fully adult.

Order Cyclopoida

The free-living cyclopoids are almost monotonously alike in general appearance. The body is clearly divided into two regions: an anterior part formed by the head and thorax, and a posterior part formed by the last thoracic segment together with the abdomen. Females normally carry two egg sacs.

The numerous species of the family Cyclopidae abound in freshwater throughout the world. There are also marine and brackish water species. Some of the larger species are carnivorous, eating other crustaceans or insects, sometimes even attacking small fishes. Other species are herbivorous, feeding on diatoms and filamentous algae. Some freshwater species are important as intermediate hosts for worms parasitic in man, particularly in the tropics.

In addition to the free-living cyclopoids there are twelve or more families associated in various ways with other animals. The precise nature of the association is not always known, and the term semi-parasitic is often applied to cloak our ignorance. *Paranthesius rostratus* lives in the mantle cavities of marine bivalved molluscs, and other species of *Paranthesius* are found associating with sea anemones and polychaete worms. *Paranthesius* is still easily recognisable as a cyclopoid, but others become greatly modified. *Mytilicola* for instance looks like a maggot and lives in the intestine of the Common Mussel (*Mytilus edulis*).

Within the family Notodelphyidae a series of genera can be used to trace the transition from a fairly normal cyclopoid to a highly modified, distorted parasite. All the members of this family are parasites of sea-squirts (class Ascidiacea), and the females have an internal brood-pouch which may be distended into a globular shape. They cling to the host by means of a hook at the end of the antenna. Females of *Notodelphys* look like a *Cyclops* with a swelling in the middle of the body. The legs are fairly well developed and several species have been seen to swim when sufficiently provoked. The genus *Demoixys*, shows a considerable reduction of the abdomen, and the segments of the thorax are not very clearly separated. The legs of *Demoixys* show varying degrees of development in different species. In some they are recognisable as legs with two branches and in others they are reduced to simple projections bearing a single seta. Further reduction of the appendages is found in *Ooneides*, which has a grossly inflated body without any external signs of segmentation. The mouth-parts are minute.

Order Harpacticoida

The body of a harpacticoid is not obviously divided into regions, and the antennule is gener-

The copepod, *Rhincalanus gigas*, is a common planktonic crustacean in the southern oceans. It has been estimated that there are more copepods in the world than all other multicellular animals put together. Indeed, they form the staple food for many marine animals, such as the herring, and are therefore of great economic importance.

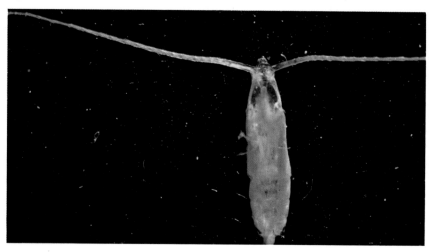

ally much shorter than in cyclopoids and calanoids. The general form of the body varies considerably. Some species are long and tubular, almost worm-shaped, and often live between the grains of marine sands. Other species are flattened and like tiny woodlice.

The feeding habits of these small copepods have not been studied but it is usually assumed that they feed on organic débris. Several species, such as *Thalestris rhodymeniae*, make tunnels in fronds of seaweeds, a habit which is reminiscent of the leaf-mining insects in terrestrial plants and others tunnel in wood. Some species live among the gills of crabs, and one remarkable species, *Balaenophilus unisetus*, is found in large numbers on the fringed edges of whalebone in the mouths of whales, where it is thought to feed by scraping off algae which grow on the surface of the whalebone.

There are over thirty families of harpacticoids, with numerous species living in the sea, brackish water and freshwater. *Canthocamptus staphylinus*, one of the commonest freshwater species, becomes abundant in winter but during summer it makes a gelatinous cyst in which it remains inactive when temperatures are high and the oxygen content of the water is low. Most marine harpacticoids live on or in the substratum, but a few species have become planktonic. *Microsetella norvegica* is one such species with a wide distribution in all the major oceans of the world.

Order Caligoida

In general form the body of a caligoid is reminiscent of a flattened cyclopoid but the abdomen is reduced and the head enlarged. The appendages, particularly the antennae and maxillae, are modified for clinging to fishes. The eggs are usually disc-shaped in a single row in long tubular egg sacs. The hatching nauplii are free-living, but the later stages are mostly parasitic on fishes, although the ability to swim is frequently retained and adult females with eggs are sometimes caught in the plankton.

Most members of this group are strictly marine, but some are carried into freshwater by their hosts. *Lepeophtheirus salmonis* is a parasite of salmon when in the sea. The presence of this copepod on a salmon caught in freshwater is usually taken as an indication that the fish has recently returned from the sea. There is evidence that copepods can live for about two weeks in freshwater, but the eggs are said to drop from the females within two days of leaving the sea.

Several of the largest members of this group are parasites on the Ocean Sunfish (*Mola mola*). Both *Cecrops latreillii* and *Orthagoriscicola muricata* are over three centimetres long and relatively broad. They live gregariously in pits which they excavate in the skin of the Sunfish.

Order Monstrilloida

In the adult stage these copepods are free-swimming, but they have neither mouth-parts nor a gut. The nauplius larva also lacks a gut and becomes parasitic in a marine worm or in a mollusc. On the host the nauplius loses its limbs and develops two long processes which seem to be concerned with food absorption. The adult develops within the larval skin and eventually

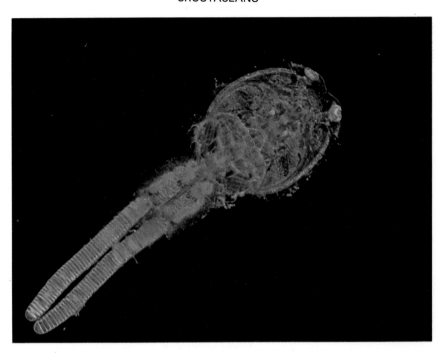

Caligus sp., is one of the copepods that is known as the fish louse. Although it spends much of its time as an ectoparasite on marine fishes it is often found in plankton, when it is swimming from one host to another. The individual shown here, a female, is carrying a pair of long egg-sacs.

breaks out of the host and swims away equipped with a single pair of antennae projecting forwards and four pairs of swimming legs. The females are thought to liberate their young near a prospective host because their swimming appendages are not well developed.

Order Lernaeoida

Some of the most spectactular parasitic copepods belong to this group. The largest species, *Penella balaenoptera*, over thirty centimetres long, parasitises whales. Other species are not so long, but have swollen bodies and long egg sacs. The best known species is *Lernaeocera branchialis*, a common parasite of the Whiting and Cod. When adult the female is only recognisable as a copepod by the presence of two egg sacs. The head is inserted into a gill bar of the fish host, and the swollen twisted body lying in the gill chamber loses its appendages. The eggs hatch as free-swimming nauplii which quickly change into small copepodids and attach themselves to the gills of flounders. The attached copepodids feed and grow, moulting four times before the males become mature. The males die after mating and transferring sperms to females which then search for the final host, a member of the cod family. When a host is located the female buries her head in the tissues of a gill bar. The head develops three horns which pass out at right angles to the long axis of the body and anchor firmly in the host tissues. The horns are simple at first but later become branched like antlers. The genital segment then elongates and swells until the characteristic form of the adult female is achieved.

A considerable number of freshwater species are known in this order. *Salmincola* occurs on members of the salmon and whitefish families. The genus *Lernaea* is particularly well-represented in the freshwaters of tropical Africa, but species of the same genus are known from Asia, Europe and both North and South America. Most species of *Lernaea* are parasites of fishes, but a North American species, *Lernaea ranae*, parasitises tadpoles of the Green Frog.

163

Fish lice (Subclass Branchiura)

Argulus sp., a true fish louse, swimming freely in the water of Lake Baringo, Central Kenya. Species of *Argulus* are found on freshwater and marine fishes. These crustaceans of the subclass Branchiura have a pair of suckers on the maxillae (subsidiary jaws) for attachment to their host. They also have spines on the underside of the head, pointing backwards. As the fish louse always aligns itself on its host with its head directed towards the fish's head, passage through water merely drives the spines in more firmly.

base. There are four pairs of swimming legs, and most species can swim actively, except for the genus *Chonopeltis*.

About eighty species of Branchiura are known from all over the world. The freshwaters of Africa are particularly rich in species. Marine species are also widespread. All the species are parasites, mainly on fishes. *Argulus nobilis* reaches a length of twenty-five millimetres and is a parasite of the Alligator Gar in the southern states of North America. *Argulus foliaceus* is common in Europe and is often found swimming freely, feeding as an external parasite on freshwater fishes. The female lays her eggs on water plants or sticks them on to stones. Up to 250 eggs may be laid at a time and take three to five weeks to hatch. The young resemble the parent except that the maxillules bear claws and not suckers. About seven stages, possibly more in some species, are passed before the adult stage is reached.

In the genus *Chonopeltis* neither adults nor larvae can swim, and they die in a day or two if removed from their host. The larva of *Chonopeltis* has an exceptionally well-developed pair of maxillules with hooked spines for attaching itself to its fish host. It is not known how *Chonopeltis* transfers from one host to another. It may drop off one host and wait on the bottom until a new host comes near enough for it to reattach itself.

The general appearance of a branchiuran is dominated by the large flat rounded carapace which extends over the thorax and sometimes covers the short abdomen as well. A pair of stalkless compound eyes is present near the front of the head. The maxillules are modified to form a pair of large suckers, except in the genus *Dolops* where they have strong claws. The second maxilla is usually leg-like, but has a number of stout spines at the

Ostracods or seed shrimps (Subclass Ostracoda)

Ostracods have a bivalved carapace into which they can withdraw all their limbs. The two valves can be drawn tightly together by means of an adductor muscle. The body is short with few limbs. In addition to the usual sequence of antennules, antennae, mandibles and two pairs of maxillae, there are only two pairs of trunk limbs. Some specialists maintain that the second maxillae are missing, so that there are three pairs of trunk limbs. Whichever view is correct the fact remains that ostracods have only four pairs of limbs behind

Ostracods, or seed shrimps, are small crustaceans with the body enclosed in a bivalve shell. They have the smallest number of appendages of all crustaceans and in the order Myodocopa the last appendage, looking like a miniature elephant's trunk, ends in a group of bristles which are said to be used for cleaning the inside of the shell.

the mandibles. The caudal rami are often well developed and mobile, bearing claws which can be brought forward to clear the space between the trunk limbs and maxillae.

The largest ostracod is about the size of a cherry and swims actively in the deeper parts of the sea. Many ostracods do not swim, but scuttle along the bottom of the sea or of lakes and ponds. Their feeding habits are diverse and incompletely known. Some are filter feeders, using filters on the maxillae to collect minute algae. Others eat organic débris or filamentous algae, and some are predators on other small animals.

Reproductive habits are also varied. Some species carry their eggs inside the valves of the carapace, while others stick the eggs to the surface of aquatic plants or to stones at the water's edge. The larva emerging from the egg has a bivalved carapace, but only three pairs of limbs which are added to as the young ostracod moults and grows. Eight larval stages are passed before reaching the adult stage.

Wherever there is water it is usually possible to find ostracods, and there are also a few terrestrial species which live in the leaf litter of forest floors: *Mesocypris terrestris* is found in Africa, and *M. audax* in New Zealand. The latter species has been observed to walk among the leaf litter with some agility, having somewhat stronger limbs than is usual in aquatic ostracods.

A few ostracods are confined to special situations or special relationships with other animals. In North America there are about nineteen species of the genus *Entocythere*, all of which live among the gills of crayfishes.

There are four orders containing approximately 200 species. Ostracods have been abundant in times past and about 2,000 fossil species have been described, going back to the Lower Ordovician (425 million years ago). The fossil forms are useful in correlating formations in wells drilled for petroleum, especially in non-marine beds.

Order Myodocopa

This group includes a number of marine species, most of which are planktonic. The branched antennae can be protruded through notches in the carapace and used in locomotion while the shell is tightly closed. These are the only ostracods possessing a heart. *Gigantocypris*, the largest known ostracod, belongs to this group.

Order Cladocopa

These ostracods have no antennal notches in the carapace, the antennae have two branches, and there are only two pairs of appendages behind the mandibles. Both eyes and heart are absent. The best-known members of this group belong to the genus *Polycope* which lives in the sea and skims the surface of thin layers of mud covering sandy areas.

Order Platycopa

Although they are similar to the Cladocopa in having branched antennae and in lacking heart and eyes, the Platycopa have an extra pair of appendages behind the mandibles. The best-known genus, *Cytherella*, lives in deep water and has a heavy shell which probably leaves it unable to swim.

Order Podocopa

In this group the antennae have only one branch, the other being reduced to a vestige, and there are four pairs of appendages behind the mandibles. The caudal rami are rod-shaped or vestigial, while in the other orders they are flat with a curved border bearing claws or strong setae. All the freshwater species belong to this group, as well as a large number of marine species and the few known terrestrial species.

Cirripedes or barnacles and allies. (Subclass Cirripedia)

An adult cirripede lives attached to some solid object or parasitises another animal. The non-parasitic forms include the common barnacles of the seashore. These are strikingly unlike other crustaceans, but when the body is removed from the outer shell it is seen to have a thin exoskeleton and six pairs of jointed limbs with fine setae. These limbs are used to catch food floating in the sea close to the barnacle. The abdomen of a barnacle is reduced to a vestige.

The tough outer shell or mantle is really a modified carapace which encloses the rest of the body. The larval barnacle attaches itself to a rock by means of cement formed in a gland opening on the antennule. The body is then rotated so that the limbs point upwards and the mouth opens upwards in a position such that it can receive food when the limbs sweep through the water. The limbs or cirri sweep forwards through the water in unison, but in some species each cirrus is capable of independent contraction. If all the cirri are held out in the water and one comes into contact with food it can grasp the food and bend over to carry it to the mouth.

Some barnacles, such as the Goose Barnacle (*Lepas*), have long stalks but the most abundant forms are the acorn barnacles which lack stalks. The arrangement of the calcareous plates on the mantle is variable and is used as an aid in classification. The opening for the limbs is normally guarded by two pairs of plates, the scuta and the terga, which can be closed tightly together when the limbs are withdrawn into the mantle. This gives protection against desiccation to those barnacles living in the intertidal zone. In some of the stalked barnacles the scuta and terga are surrounded by a large number of plates which show all stages in transition to small scales on the stalk. Most acorn barnacles have a definite pattern of plates surrounding the central two pairs. The basic number of plates is eight, but these may be

Barnacles can be roughly divided into stalked barnacles and sessile barnacles. The first of these include the goose barnacles. The second include the acorn barnacles that are found in such vast numbers everywhere in the shallow seas and on the shores. The photograph shows the carapace of a shore crab encrusted with acorn barnacles.

fused or modified in various ways to give six as in *Balanus*, four as in *Elminius*, or all may be joined together as in *Pyrgoma*. The mantle with its plates forms a turret inside which the animal can move up and down, causing a flow of water through the mantle cavity which serves as a respiratory current.

The eggs usually hatch as nauplius larvae in the mantle cavity which are liberated into the plankton and moult several times before changing into a cypris larva. The cypris, which looks like an ostracod, has a bivalved carapace enclosing the rest of the body and the limbs. It can be distinguished from an ostracod by the possession of six pairs of trunk limbs which are all similar in appearance. Selection of the site for attachment is an important step in the life-history since the barnacle cannot detach itself and move to a new site. Many barnacles are gregarious settlers, thus ensuring cross fertilisation. The sperms are transferred by means of a penis which is capable of considerable elongation. Most barnacles are hermaphrodite so that self-fertilisation is possible if another barnacle is not near enough. A few barnacles have separate sexes, and in some of these there are complemental males, which are dwarf forms settling on the margins of the mantle of the larger females. These dwarf males are an additional mechanism for ensuring cross fertilisation.

The order Thoracica contains mostly non-parasitic forms, including a few commensal species which attach themselves to other animals. Some of these, such as *Coronula*, attached to the surface of whales, are not parasites, but others show the beginnings of true parasitism. *Rhizolepas annelidicola* is a stalked barnacle which lacks both mouth and anus and is completely parasitic. The stalk has roots which penetrate the body of a marine polychaete worm, from which *Rhizolepas* must obtain its food.

Profound modifications to a parasitic mode of life are found in the order Rhizocephala, *Sacculina* being the best-known example. *Sacculina carcini* is a parasite of the Shore Crab (*Carcinus maenas*) and several other crabs. The adult appears as an orange bulge between the crab's thorax and the abdomen and rooting processes spread throughout its body. The adult *Sacculina* lays eggs which hatch as nauplii, resembling other barnacle nauplii. These change to cyprids which seek out new hosts, penetrating through the base of a seta. The parasite enters the crab as a small mass of cells, having lost its appendages, and comes to rest under the intestine. From this small mass roots grow in all directions, and the mass enlarges, finally bursting through infection. A crab afflicted in this way is incapable of moulting.

Another order of cirripedes, the Ascothoracica, are also parasites. The eggs give rise to a cypris larva which seeks out a sea anemone or a sea urchin and there becomes so grossly distorted that recognition of the adult as a crustacean is extremely difficult. The outline of the body is sometimes broken by numerous projections, and all that is visible externally is a small tufted mass.

The Acrothoracica are a small order with about eleven species. In general form they resemble the stalked barnacles, but the cirri are reduced and the animal burrows into the calcareous shells of molluscs and corals. *Trypetesa lampas* burrows into the columella of empty whelk shells which are occupied by the Hermit Crab (*Eupagurus*).

Malacostracans or higher crustaceans (Subclass Malacostraca)

This group includes the largest and most familiar crustaceans, such as lobsters, crabs, shrimps, scuds and woodlice, and all the orders have a common basic body plan. The thorax is composed of eight segments and the abdomen of seven, although the last two often fuse together. The oviduct of the female opens on the sixth thoracic segment and the genital duct of the male opens on the eighth thoracic segment. The thoracic limbs are often modified for various functions. When one or more pairs are highly modified to aid in feeding they are called maxillipeds, crabs having three pairs and woodlice one pair. The abdomen usually bears pleopods and the last segment bears a pair of uropods which are often flattened to form a fan.

Malacostracans are divided into five superorders, each of which contains one or more orders.

Superorder Phyllocarida
The living members of this group are placed in the single order Leptostraca, which contains a single family with nine species. The best known species is *Nebalia bipes*, first described by Fabricius in 1780 from Greenland, but now known to extend from Europe to Chile and Japan. This species lives on the lower parts of the seashore, under stones and among weeds. It seems to be tolerant of quite foul conditions and is often found near decaying seaweed.

The thoracic limbs are distinctive, being all alike and flattened with a lage flap or epipodite on the outer edge. The inner edges of these limbs bear setae which form part of a filter feeding mechanism. A well-developed carapace covers the thorax and part of the abdomen. A muscle runs across the body and can draw the two sides of the carapace together, giving a bivalved appearance. The eyes are on short stalks, and in *N. bipes* are bright red, but the related *N. typhlops* which lives in deeper water is blind.

The eggs are carried by the female *Nebalia* between the thoracic limbs. They hatch at a late stage of development when they have the same basic structure as the adults. The planktonic *Nebaliopsis* appears to lay its eggs freely into the sea where they float as they develop.

Superorder Hoplocarida
This division, like the last, contains a single order, the Stomatopoda or mantis shrimps. The second

thoracic limb is very large and has the last segment flexed so that its sharp point is directed forwards, the whole limb resembling the front leg of a Praying Mantis.

The abdomen is long and bears well-developed, flattened pleopods bearing branchial filaments for respiration. At the end of the abdomen there is a well-developed tail fan of characteristic design in which each uropod appears to have three branches. The carapace is short and does not cover the whole of the thorax. A most remarkable feature is found in the head where there are two movable segments bearing the eyes and the antennules. These movable segments are unique among crustaceans.

All the stomatopods are marine, inhabiting burrows in the sea bottom. They live particularly in the warmer oceans, but a few species extend into the temperate zones. In North America, for example, the northern limits are Massachusetts and California. The largest species is a little over thirty centimetres in length. They feed voraciously, capturing smaller crustaceans with their large second thoracic limbs. They are pugnacious and difficult to capture, the mantis-like limbs effecting such damage that they are called 'split-thumb' in Bermuda and the West Indies. The eggs are retained in the burrow by the female. In the Mediterranean species, *Squilla mantis*, the duration of embryonic development is ten or eleven weeks. The first two larval stages are believed to live on the bottom of the sea, but the later stages are planktonic and have a large carapace which usually bears a long anterior spine and two posterior spines. Nine or ten larval stages are passed before the adult form is assumed.

Superorder Syncarida

The Syncarida do not have a carapace and there is no brood-pouch under the thorax. The thoracic limbs usually have two well-developed branches. If abdominal appendages are present they have a reduced inner branch. The other characteristics are somewhat variable and are best dealt with under the three orders.

Order Anaspidacea

There are only four known living species in this order, three species in Tasmania and one in South Australia. The body is elongated with all the segments distinct, except the first which joins with the head. The abdomen bears well-developed pleopods with a large exopod and small endopod. The eyes are variable. In *Anaspides* and *Paranaspides* the eyes are set on short movable stalks, while in *Koonunga* they are very small and set immovably on the side of the head. *Micraspides* is a colourless subterranean form lacking eyes. All the species live in freshwater.

The eggs are not carried by the females, and as far as is known development is direct, so that there are no larval stages and the creature hatching from the egg is a miniature of its parents. The largest species, *Anaspides tasmaniae*, reaches a length of about five centimetres.

Order Stygocaridacea

The first specimens of this group were described in 1963. Four species are now known from Chile and the Argentine. In some respects this group is intermediate between the Anaspidacea and the Bathynellacea. The body is elongated and flexible and the thoracic limbs are well developed, but the pleopods are reduced or absent. The uropods are well developed, with flat branches, the outer branch having two segments. The telson bears distinct rudiments of a caudal furca; this feature is absent from the Anaspidacea, but well-developed in the Bathynellacea. A small rostrum projects forwards between the antennules. A statocyst is present in the antennules. This is a feature in common with the Anaspidacea, but lacking in the Bathynellacea.

The stygocarids are blind and colourless, living in the spaces between sand grains in freshwater. Their biology is unknown.

Order Bathynellacea

Members of the order, which comprises over fifty species, have been found in Japan, Malaya, Africa, South America and Australia.

The body is elongated and cylindrical in form. All the thoracic limbs have a similar two-branched structure, except the last which may be reduced to a small projection. Pleopods may be present on the abdomen in a reduced form, but they are absent from many species. The uropods are always well developed, usually narrow and rounded with a

Odontodactylus scyllarus, from the seas around Thailand. It is one of the mantis shrimps, so called because in feeding on other crustaceans they capture their prey with the second pair of legs each of which is flexed like the legs of the insect, the Praying Mantis.

series of conspicuous spines. Caudal rami are also present and armed with a few spines.

These creatures spend their lives in the spaces between sand grains, immersed in water, often at considerable depths below the surface of the earth. All are blind and generally colourless. *Thermobathynella adami* has been found in a hot spring where the temperature reaches 55°C. The young hatch in a form similar to the adult.

Superorder Peracarida

When the world has been thoroughly explored this may prove to be one of the largest groups of crustaceans. There are marine, brackish water, freshwater, subterranean and terrestrial peracaridans. They extend from the greatest depths of the oceans to the line of permanent snow on mountainsides.

Females have a brood-pouch which is usually in the form of plates at the bases of the thoracic limbs, but some isopods (family Sphaeromatidae) have internal pouches opening on the ventral surface, and in the Thermosbaenacea there is a dorsal brood-pouch formed by the carapace. The mandibles normally have an additional process, the lacinia mobilis, which lies on the medial edge and aids in pushing food upwards towards the oesophagus. There are seven orders in this superorder.

Order Spelaeogriphacea

The single known member of this order, *Spelaeogriphus lepidops*, was described in 1957 from specimens collected in a cave on Table Mountain, South Africa. The largest specimens are about seven millimetres long. The body is elongated and the head bears no eyes. A small carapace joins with the first thoracic segment and overlaps the sides of the head, hiding the mouth-parts in side view. There are seven pairs of walking legs, the first three pairs bear well-developed exopods with numerous setae which may aid in swimming. The abdomen bears four well-developed pairs of pleopods and a reduced fifth pair. The uropods are relatively large and have an unsegmented endopod and a two-segmented exopod.

The adult females carry ten to twelve eggs in a brood-pouch at the bases of the thoracic limbs. the

duration of development, the form of the young stages and the general biology of this species are unknown. They are said to swim swiftly with rapid undulations of the body.

Order Thermosbaenacea

This order comprises two genera: *Thermosbaena* with one species and *Monodella* with five. *Thermosbaena mirabilis* lives in hot springs in Tunisia where the water temperature reaches 48°C. Four species of *Monodella* have been found in subterranean water, both fresh and brackish, around the Mediterranean Sea, and a fifth species has been found in freshwater in a cave in Texas. All are less than five millimetres in length. The eyes are reduced or absent, but the antennules are large and well equipped with sensory setae. A small carapace covers the anterior part of the thorax. In mature females the carapace enlarges to form a brood-pouch. *Thermosbaena* has five and *Monodella* seven pairs of walking legs. A pair of uropods forms a tail fan which is larger in *Monodella* than in *Thermosbaena*.

As far as is known these crustaceans feed on organic débris. Their mouth-parts are capable of both biting into large particles and scraping up numerous small particles. The sexes are separate, and the females carry four to ten eggs at a time in the brood-pouch. The newly hatched young resemble their parents, but lack the last pair of legs.

Opossum shrimps (Order Mysidacea)

Opossum shrimps are shrimp-like in appearance and carry their developing young in a pouch under the thorax. The shrimp-like appearance is given by the presence of a carapace covering most of the thorax, a pair of stalked eyes, and an elongated abdomen with a tail fan. The brood-pouch is formed by plates at the bases of the thoracic limbs. These limbs have an inner endopod which can be used for walking, and an outer exopod which is used to create a respiratory current. In some mysids the exopod also creates feeding and swimming currents. The pleopods on the abdomen vary in development in different groups of mysids. In the primitive mysids, such as the Lophogastridae, the pleopods are well developed with two branches, and are used for swimming. In the more advanced mysids the pleopods become rudimentary in the females, and one or more pairs may be modified for sexual purposes in the males. The uropods form a well-developed tail fan. In the more advanced mysids there is a clear vesicle at the base of the inner branch of each uropod. Within each vesicle is a statolith resting on a group of small setae. These organs help the mysid to maintain its balance. The antennal gland is well developed as an excretory organ. The heart is long and tubular having both an anterior and a posterior artery.

Suborder Lophogastrida

These differ from other mysidaceans in having well-developed pleopods and in having gills at the bases of the thoracic limbs. There is no statocyst at the base of the inner branch of the uropod.

All the Lophogastrida are marine and live in fairly deep water. Most are deep red in colour. The largest known mysidacean is of this group; a

Female opossum shrimp, *Mysis* sp., with eggs in her brood pouch. This genus lives in the brackish waters of Europe. All opossum shrimps are marine or estuarine except one, *M. relicta*, which lives in freshwater. They live on sandy seabeds or among seaweeds and migrate to the surface at night. In India and other parts of Asia they are netted for human consumption.

specimen of *Gnathophausia ingens* about thirty-five centimetres long was caught in the eastern Pacific in 1961.

Suborder Mysida

The Mysida have no gills, the gill function being taken over by the carapace which is very well supplied with blood vessels. The pleopods of the females are rudimentary, and a statocyst is usually present at the base of the inner branch of the uropod. Most of this group are marine, but there are a few notable freshwater species. *Mysis relicta* is the best-known of these, being found in lakes in North America and Europe. It is usually considered to have been isolated in these lakes when they were cut off from the sea by rising land at the end of the Ice Ages. In Britain it is known from several loughs in Northern Ireland and from Ennerdale Water in England. This species is also known from brackish water such as the Baltic Sea and near the mouths of some of the large Siberian rivers. The glacial origin of this species is reflected in its breeding, which occurs in winter, and in its occurrence only in lakes with cool water in the deeper areas to which *Mysis* migrates in summer.

Order Tanaidacea

In general form the Tanaidacea resemble small isopods, but the carapace is fused with the first two thoracic segments and overhangs on each side to enclose a small branchial cavity. There are seven pairs of walking legs, the first bearing pincers.

There are about 250 species arranged in five families, most of which are marine and extend down to depths of over 6,000 metres. The deep-sea species are often much larger than those living in shallow water. *Herpotanais kirkegaardi* reaches a length of twenty-five millimetres, while few shallow water species reach ten millimetres and many are one millimetre long.

The tanaidaceans burrow in crevices or build tubes in muddy sand, and seem to feed mainly on organic débris. The breeding biology is known for few species; *Heterotanais oerstedi* is probably the best known. Females lay between ten and twenty eggs into the brood-pouch, which lies between the thoracic legs. The eggs hatch as miniature adults in fourteen to nineteen days but lack the last walking legs and pleopods. Each female probably produces only two broods in a year.

Isopods, sowbugs, woodlice and allies (Order Isopoda)

This group, containing approximately 4,000 species, includes the water slaters, woodlice and various isopod parasites. There is no carapace and the eyes are not stalked. The body is usually but not always flattened and the appendages on the abdomen are broad and flattened for use in respiration. This is an important means of distinguishing isopods from amphipods which do not have flattened abdominal appendages. The first walking leg is usually shorter than the others and the claw modified for grasping. This leg is used to hold food.

Suborder Asellota

This group is often regarded as containing the most primitive isopods. The legs have a free basal segment which in other isopods is incoporated into the body wall.

There are twenty-three families in this group, many of which live in the deep sea down to the deepest regions. All known members of the family Asellidae are confined to freshwaters in the northern hemisphere, although *Asellus aquaticus* penetrates into brackish water in the Baltic Sea. The family differs from other members of the Asellota in having the first and second abdominal appendages free and not joined together by spines. *Asellus* is the most widespread genus in the family, extending across the whole of Europe, Lake Baikal, Eastern Asia, North Africa, and both the eastern and western sides of North America. *Asellus cavaticus* lives in caves in Europe and lacks eyes.

These freshwater slaters commonly feed on leaves which fall into the water and *Asellus* is very abundant in pools surrounded by trees. Diatoms and other algae are also eaten.

A female *Asellus* can produce four or five broods during a summer, each containing up to 100 eggs. Each brood is carried by the female for two or

Isopods are crustaceans related to shrimps and lobsters but are distinguished from them and their many relatives in having no carapace and in having the abdominal appendages broad and flattened and used in respiration. They include woodlice and water skaters and more unusual animals such as *Antarcturus* sp., shown here from shallow water off South Georgia.

Isopods have compound eyes which, are not stalked, as in so many crustaceans but, as in insects, are made up of ommatidia. In a typical sowbug these may number twenty to twenty-five but in the deep-sea isopod *Bathynomus*, from the Gulf of Mexico, living where light is dim at best, each eye has 3000 ommatidia.

Large woodlice from East Africa. The individual on the left has rolled up defensively as if to demonstrate why these land isopods are sometimes called 'pill bugs'.

The Common Sandhopper (*Talitrus saltator*) is a small crustacean that burrows into sand on European shores. It can walk and swim well but excels in jumping. It is most commonly met with when piles of rotting seaweed on the drift line on the seashore are disturbed. These small crustaceans are then seen jumping in all directions like fleas. The sandhopper can jump a distance of one metre and a height of thirty centimetres. This is a greater distance than any other animal of similar size.

three weeks. In good conditions a female is mature fifty days after leaving the parental brood-pouch.

Suborder Flabellifera

There are about ten families in this suborder which is characterised by having the uropods lateral in position so that they form a tail fan. Most species are marine, but there are a considerable number of brackish water species and a few freshwater forms, particularly in subterranean waters.

In this group is found the largest isopod, *Bathynomus giganteus*, reaching a length of twenty-seven centimetres, pale lilac in colour and living at considerable depths in the oceans.

The family Limnoriidae contains a number of species known as gribbles, which burrow in wood and cause damage to wooden pier piles.

Many species of the family Sphaeromidae live in brackish water. They have the ability to contract into a ball, a development parallel to the ability of the pill woodlice of the family Armadillidiidae.

In the family Anthuridae the body is elongated and there is often a pair of statocysts in the telson. Most anthurids are marine, but some species, particularly of the genus *Cyathura*, extend into

brackish water or even freshwater, where they may become exceedingly abundant. *Cyathura polita* has been found in densities up to 4,000 per square metre in the Pocasset River, Massachusetts.

Suborder Gnathiidea

The larvae of this group suck the blood of fishes, and take such enormous meals that the adults never need to feed. *Paragnathia formica* lives as an adult in holes in mud banks at the edge of salt marshes on European estuaries, and *Gnathia oxyuraea* lives in crevices on rocky shores. The basic structure is similar to that of the Flabellifera, but when the larva has gorged itself on blood the thorax is distended. The females brood their young internally until they hatch as small isopods which swim away to attack fishes.

Suborder Valvifera

The members of this suborder have large uropods which can close like a pair of doors over the respiratory limbs. Most species live in the sea, a few species live in brackish water and fewer in freshwater. The most notable freshwater species is *Saduria* (= *Mesidotea*) *entomon*, which is another example of a glacial relict (*see* pp. 160 and 162). It is found in brackish water and in freshwater in lakes in North America and Europe. Specimens from a lake in Sweden have the ability to survive in full strength sea water; this ability is very unusual in a freshwater crustacean.

Suborder Phreatoicidea

At first sight one might confuse this group with amphipods. They have cylindrical or laterally compressed bodies with a well-marked downward curve of the tail, so that the general aspect is that of a gammarid amphipod. The abdominal appendages, however, are flat and typically isopodan in structure. Most species of this group live in the freshwaters of New Zealand and Australia, but *Mesamphisopus capensis* under moss on stones in swift mountain streams in South Africa. Several species are blind and live in subterranean habitats. The Australian species include a terrestrial form, *Phreatoicopsis terricola*, which burrows in damp earth in the forests of Victoria.

Woodlice, sowbugs and pill bugs (Suborder Oniscoidea)

This is the most successful group of terrestrial crustaceans. Woodlice live in damp places from the polar circles to the Equator. The respiratory appendages of the most terrestrial species have fine tubes which resemble the tracheae of insects, and are thought to perform a similar function. Most woodlice have well-developed glands along the sides of the body. When woodlice are attacked these glands discharge a sticky repugnant fluid, which can repel predators such as spiders. This is a factor in the success of woodlice as land animals.

The family Ligiidae contains semi-aquatic forms such as the large sea slaters of the genus *Ligia*, which scavenge on seashores.

Among the other six families of woodlice the Armadillidiidae or pill woodlice are notable for their ability to roll into a ball, which protects them from small predators and desiccation. In general the members of this family are much more resis-

tant to desiccation than other woodlice, and may be seen in bright sunlight when others are hidden.

Suborder Epicaridea
Many of this parasitic group are so distorted when adult that they can be identified as crustaceans only by studying their life-histories. A typical life-history begins with the emergence from the egg of a small isopod with large, hooked claws at the ends of its legs. This first stage can swim, and it seeks out a planktonic copepod to which it clings by means of the clawed legs and its mouth-parts. These mouth-parts are modified for piercing and sucking, so that blood can be obtained from the copepod. After moulting on the copepod the young isopod leaves to find another host, which is usually a decapod.

The most highly modified epicarideans belong to the family Entoniscidae which are internal parasites of crabs. The young isopod enters a crab via the gill chamber. Once inside the limbs are discarded and the parasite looks like a legless fly maggot. Later the body enlarges and develops numerous bulges so that any resemblance to an isopod is lost. This applies only to females; the males remain small and do not lose their shape.

Other epicaridians, belonging to the family Bopyridae, are not so highly modified, so that even the females are recognisable as isopods. Bopyrids live particularly in the gill chambers of shrimps and prawns, causing a large swelling on the side of the host. The first parasite to arrive in the gill chamber develops into a female, and the next arrival settles on the edge of the brood-pouch of this female and develops into a male. This peculiar method of sex determination can be reversed if a transfer is made at an early stage. If a young male is transferred to a new host not previously infected then the male will develop into a female and will cause any later arrival to develop into a male.

Amphipods, scuds and sideswimmers (Order Amphipoda)
Amphipods share several features with isopods; they have no carapace and the eyes are not stalked. They differ from isopods in being laterally compressed and in having rounded rather than flattened pleopods. The heart is located more anteriorly than in isopods, and the chief excretory organ is the antennal gland, which is vestigial in isopods. There are four suborders.

Suborder Hyperiidea
Members of this group are very similar to the gammarideans (*see* below), but they can usually be distinguished by their enormous eyes and small coxal plates. There are about a dozen families in this group. Most species are active marine plankton dwellers. Some feed on copepods and others associate with jellyfishes and salps. *Hyperia galba* is common in the subgenital pits of jellyfishes (Scyphozoa) and it has been shown to feed on their tissues. *Phronima sedentaria* is usually found enclosed in a transparent barrel-shaped house made from the empty test or outer coat of a salp.

Suborder Gammaridea
This is a large and important group with over 2,500 species grouped into over fifty families in modern classifications. The chief distinguishing feature is the enlargement of the first segment of each leg to form a coxal plate. There are normally seven walking legs and the females carry their young in brood-pouches between the legs. The eggs are laid into the brood-pouch a short time after moulting. In many species the female is carried by the male for a day or two before she moults, and soon after she moults the male places sperms on her ventral surface. When first laid the eggs are enclosed in a gelatinous case. This gradually dissolves, and it is believed that this permits fertilisation to take place. The duration of incubation varies with temperature. In summer the young may leave the brood-pouch after sixteen days, but in winter the time may be as long as three months. A typical female *Gammarus* in a temperate climate will produce four to six broods varying in size from seven to forty in her life.

The largest family is the Gammaridae, which has species living in the sea, brackish water and freshwater. Lake Baikal in Siberia is remarkable for its gammarids; about 300 species are endemic to this ancient lake. This family also includes the blind well shrimps of the genus *Niphargus* which has about eighty-five species living in wells and caves.

The Talitridae resemble the Gammaridae in general form, but the abdomen has become modified for springing. The Common Sand Hopper (*Talitrus saltator*) can hurl itself several times its own length by suddenly jerking its tail. Some of the talitrids have become terrestrial and live in the damp leaf litter on forest floors. One such species, *Talitrus sylvaticus*, has been found in great abundance in rainforests near Sydney, Australia. In some areas 4,000 were recorded in a square metre.

Suborder Caprellidea
Caprellids have slender bodies, few limbs and are incapable of swimming. The two families differ greatly in form and habits. The Caprellidae have very long bodies and limbs. The first free body

Krill is the name given to a number of species of small prawn-like crustaceans that abound in incredible numbers in the plankton, especially of the polar seas. They form the staple food of large baleen whales. One of the most common is *Euphausia superba*, a group of which is shown here.

segment carries a well-developed pair of pincers which can be used to catch small animals as they swim by. The caprellids move about on hydroids and seaweed in a slow, deliberate manner.

The Cyamidae are all parasites of whales and dolphins. Very little is known of their biology, except that they cling to the skin of their host and presumably eat the surface layers. The body is shorter and more flattened than in the caprellids and the legs carry strong, hooked claws. There are about fifteen species from the oceans of the world.

Suborder Ingolfiellida

There is a single genus, *Ingolfiella*, in this group. The seven known species are blind and the adults range in length from one to fifteen millimetres. The body is narrow and elongated and the first two legs have a characteristic two-segmented claw which bends back against a larger segment.

The remarkable feature of this genus is its wide range. Separate species have been recorded in the depths of the ocean, in cave pools in the Congo, in coral sands in the Gulf of Siam, in ground waters of Yugoslavia, and in gravels off the Eddystone lighthouse in the English Channel. This distribution has led to the concept of a hypogean fauna living in ground water under continents and seas.

Cumaceans (Order Cumacea)

In general form cumaceans resemble tadpoles, with a large, rounded head and thorax and a long, narrow abdomen. The largest species is about thirty-five millimetres long. A small carapace is present and fuses with the first three or four thoracic segments. On each side the carapace overhangs to enclose a branchial chamber which houses a gill attached to the base of the first thoracic limb.

Cumaceans are mostly marine with a few estuarine species. They burrow in the surface layers of sand or mud, and often project the head slightly above the surface. In this position they can respire and feed. A current of water is drawn in at the front of the head by movement of the first thoracic limb. The maxilla bears a filter of setae which strain off any food particles in the water, and the current then flows over the gills and out from under the carapace in front of the head, over the top of the inflowing current.

There are about 500 known species arranged in seven families. Of these families the Pseudo-cumidae is of particular interest because it has in the Caspian Sea about twenty species which have adopted body shapes similar to members of other families which are not represented in the Caspian. It appears that in their absence the pseudocumids have radiated to fill the niches that would otherwise be filled by these other families.

The species which appears to have penetrated furthest from the sea into brackish water is *Almyracuma proximoculi* which has been found in shallow water near the mouth of a river on Cape Cod, Massachusetts.

Order Euphausiacea

The Euphausiacea are shrimp-like but differ from true decapod shrimps in not having the first three pairs of thoracic limbs modified as mouth-parts. The last thoracic limb is often reduced so that it does not function as a leg, but a large gill usually remains at the base. The thoracic limbs are otherwise all similar in structure, with well-developed outer branches, but in a few genera one pair of legs may be greatly enlarged. In *Stylocheiron* the third legs are very elongated and equipped with pincers, which are used to catch prey. The abdomen bears five pairs of well-developed pleopods which are used in swimming.

Luminous organs or photophores are found in most Euphausiacea at the bases of the second and seventh legs and in a row along the underside of the abdomen. These organs have a complex structure involving a light-producing region, a reflecting surface and a lens. The function is unknown but it is usually assumed that the light may be used to attract members of the opposite sex.

All the ninety species of euphausiids are marine, and some genera, such as *Bentheuphausia*, extend down to depths of well over 1,000 metres. Other genera live nearer the surface and may perform considerable vertical migrations. Their eggs are usually small, and hatch as nauplius larvae. Several larval stages are passed before the adult stage is reached.

Some euphausiids occur in great swarms and constitute the main item in the diet of baleen (whalebone) whales which may consume as much as three tonnes of euphausiids at one feeding.

Decapods (Order Decapoda)

The largest and most familiar crustaceans belong to this group. As in all malacostracans the thorax is formed by eight segments, each bearing a pair of appendages. The first three pairs of appendages are modified to serve as additional mouth-parts, so that the oral complex has six pairs of appendages in the following sequence: mandibles, maxillules, maxillae and first, second and third maxillipeds. In the crabs the third maxillipeds close over the other mouth-parts like a pair of doors. This leaves the last five pairs of thoracic appendages to function as locomotory limbs. The name Decapoda implies that they all have ten legs, but these are not always in evidence. For instance, in the porcelain crabs the last leg is reduced and tucked between the thorax and abdomen.

The carapace is fused dorsally to all the thoracic segments and overhangs on each side to enclose

A Common Prawn (*Palaemon serratus*) of European seas cleaning itself. The term 'prawn' has no scientific validity and is often used interchangeably with the word 'shrimp'. Almost any large shrimp is likely to be called a prawn. If any distinction is to be made it is that a shrimp lacks the pointed rostrum which projects forwards in front of the eyes.

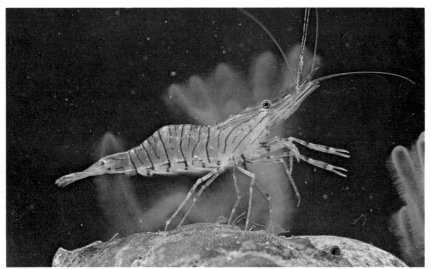

the gills in a branchial chamber through which water is caused to flow by the movements of a flap attached to the maxilla. This flap, the gill bailer (scaphognathite), produces a current which flows from the rear forwards, although in some crabs the direction can be reversed. Outflowing water usually passes on either side of the mouth and past the bases of the antennae and antennules. In land crabs the gills are often reduced and the branchial cavity spongy and well stocked with blood vessels.

Suborder Natantia

In these shrimps and prawns the abdominal limbs or pleopods are well developed and used for swimming. The suborder is divided into three sections: Penaeidea, Caridea and Stenopodidea.

Section Penaeidea

In this section there are pincers on the first three pairs of legs, but the third legs are not larger than the first two pairs. Some species of the family Penaeidae reach thirty centimetres in length and form the basis of profitable fisheries in the tropics and subtropics. Most of the shrimps taken by the Texas Shrimp Fishery belong to this family. Some of these species live in brackish water as adults but return to the sea to breed. Females do not carry the eggs but shed them freely into the sea. The eggs give rise to a nauplius larva, which has three pairs of limbs. When the nauplius develops trunk segments it is called a metanauplius. This changes into a protozoea, which has seven pairs of limbs but still swims like a nauplius by means of its antennae. The next stage, called a zoea, develops movable eyes and swims by means of its thoracic limbs. When the thoracic limbs are better developed, each with two branches, and the abdomen has increased in size the larva is said to be in the schizopod or mysis stage, because it resembles a mysidacean. Later, when the abdomen has developed its pleopods for swimming, as in the adult, the post-larval stage is entered.

The Sergestidae, which dwell mainly in the deep sea, differ from the Penaeidae in having rudimentary fifth legs and sometimes the fourth legs are also reduced. The eggs give rise to a protozoea so the number of free-living larval stages is reduced.

The family Leuciferidae contains only the remarkable genus *Leucifer*, which has about six species living in the plankton of the warmer oceans. This shrimp has a very long head, no gills, and lacks the fourth and fifth pairs of legs. The eggs are carried by the female, at least for a short time, and give rise to a metanauplius larva.

Section Caridea

The third pair of legs never has pincers in this group, which is also characterised by a bend in the abdomen and by the sides of the second abdominal segment overlapping the first and third segments. Females carry their eggs attached to pleopods. The earliest larval stage is a zoea, but some species emerge at a much later stage, particularly those living in freshwater such as the Atyidae.

Twenty-two families and about 1,600 species belong in this section.

The Common Brown Shrimp of Europe (*Crangon vulgaris*), migrates into estuaries in the summer, and feeds on a mixed diet of worms,

crustaceans and plants. In summer the eggs take about four weeks to hatch, and the young shrimp takes about three years to become mature.

The pistol shrimps (family Alpheidae) have one very large pincer (it may be left or right) which is constructed in such a way that the movable joint can be snapped violently to produce sharp shock waves in the water which are violent enough to stun the small fishes on which the shrimp feeds.

Another unusual habit is shown by *Periclimenes pedersoni* which often lives in close association with a sea anemone and is visited by fishes. The shrimp attracts attention by waving its antennae. The fishes draw close and remain still while the shrimp walks over the skin and removes parasites and cleans wounds. Fishes will also open their gill covers to allow the shrimp inside.

Section Stenopodidea

The outstanding characteristic of this entirely marine group is that the third leg is larger and stronger than the first two, which are often small and weak. All three pairs of legs carry pincers. There is only one family, the Stenopodidae.

Stenopus hispidus is the largest known 'cleaner shrimp', with a body about seven-and-a-half centimetres long. The body and legs are conspicuously striped with white and red. These shrimps live in pairs in shallow water in tropical seas, and are visited by fishes which allow the shrimps to clean parasites from the skin.

Another species, *Spongicola venusta*, lives in pairs in the internal cavity of the Venus's Flower Basket sponges. The larval shrimps enter the sponge and are unable to leave after they have grown.

Suborder Reptantia

The development of the exoskeleton reaches a climax in the reptant decapods, which are crawlers and do not use the pleopods for swimming, but for the attachment of eggs. The first pair of walking legs is often more powerful than the others and frequently armed with strong pincers. There are over 6,000 species arranged in four sections.

Section Palinura

The langouste or spiny lobsters belong to this group. They can be distinguished from the true lobsters as the outer branches of the uropods on the tail fan are not divided into two parts. Pincers, when present, on the front legs, are weakly developed. The European species belong to the genus *Palinurus* and the American species to the genus *Panulirus*. Specimens of the latter genus from California have been recorded with a weight of 14·4 kilograms.

The eggs give rise to a flat transparent larva with long legs. This is called a phyllosoma, because the body is leaf-like. This larva lives in the marine plankton, and moults eleven times before changing into a form more like that of the adult.

Section Astacura

This group comprises lobsters and freshwater crayfishes. They differ from the Palinura in having stout pincers on the front legs, and have the outer branch of the uropod subdivided.

The family Homaridae includes lobsters and a number of smaller forms, the largest species being

North American freshwater crayfish are divided between two subfamilies. The five species to the west of the Rocky Mountains belong to the Astacinae, the same as the European crayfishes. Paradoxically, the more than 200 species to the east are placed in a different family, the Cambarinae. Crayfishes burrow into banks of rivers and sometimes become even semi-terrestrial. There is a record from North America of crayfishes entering the hibernaculum of snakes and devouring the torpid reptiles.

A spiny lobster on a mudflat at Udjong Kulon, Java. Spiny lobsters are characterised by their long and heavy antennae often with saw-tooth edges. These can be used against enemies and can be used independently of each other. A spiny lobster has been seen warding off two fishes at once, attacking from opposite sides.

Homarus americanus which reaches a weight of sixteen kilograms and a length of almost one metre. The European Lobster (*Homarus vulgaris*) rarely reaches half the size of its American counterpart, while the South African Cape Lobster (*H. capensis*) is usually only ten to twelve centimetres long. A large female of *H. vulgaris* can carry up to 32,000 eggs on the pleopods. These eggs may take eleven or twelve months before they hatch. The larvae which emerge are in the mysis stage.

The Norwegian Lobster, Scampi, or Dublin Bay Prawn (*Nephrops norvegicus*) is much smaller than the Common Lobster, and ranges from the Norwegian coast to the Adriatic. There is an allied species off the coast of Brazil, and six other species of *Nephrops* in the Indo-Pacific area.

In the temperate northern hemisphere crayfishes of the family Astacidae are the dominant freshwater decapods. They feed on freshwater molluscs, worms and other small animals, but frequently take plant food as well. Many species are scavengers. The Common European Crayfish (*Astacus = Potamobius astacus*) lays its eggs towards the end of November. Development to the hatching stage takes six months. The young resemble the parents in general structure, but have a more globular carapace and not all the limbs are fully developed. Three or four years pass before the

crayfish becomes mature, and total longevity may exceed twenty years.

The American crayfishes can be divided into two subfamilies. Those to the west of the Rocky Mountains are members of the same subfamily as the European species (Astacinae), while those to the east of the Rockies and in Mexico and the Caribbean are sufficiently different to be placed in their own subfamily Cambarinae. One species of this group, *Cambarus affinis* (= *Orconectes limosus*), has been introduced into Europe and Japan. The breeding cycle of this species in Europe shows an interesting contrast with that of the native species. The eggs are laid in April or May and hatch in five to eight weeks.

The eastern North American crayfishes have undergone an extensive differentiation to form over 250 species, more than all those in the rest of the world. They occupy a wide variety of habitats ranging from caves and ponds where some species are blind and without pigment, to semi-terrestrial forms which burrow to the water table, emerging at night to feed, in some instances causing damage to newly planted crops. These cambarine crayfishes vary considerably in size. Carapace length measurements of populations of *Procambarus clarkii* in Louisiana show that it matures at about thirty-one to thirty-two millimetres and averages about forty-five millimetres with an extreme of seventy-four millimetres. The diminutive *Cambarellus shufeldtii*, however, matures at about nine millimetres, the adults rarely reaching a carapace length of twenty-five millimetres. The total length is about double that of the carapace.

In the southern temperate zone the families Parastacidae and Austroastacidae assume the ecological role played by the Astacidae in the northern hemisphere. These southern crayfishes are similar in appearance to their northern relatives, but lack appendages on the first abdominal segment. They are found in Australia, New Zealand, Fiji, South America and Madagascar, but not in Africa. The largest species, *Astacopsis franklini* of Tasmania, reaches a weight of about 3·5 kilograms. *Engaeus fossor*, another Tasmanian species, has become semi-terrestrial and burrows in damp soil.

The crayfishes in general are important elements in the natural web of food relationships, many species eating vegetation, dead animals and detritus, themselves to be eaten by a wide range of fishes, amphibians, reptiles, birds, and mammals.

Section Anomura

This section comprises a wide variety of crab-like and lobster-like forms. They differ from the true crabs in possessing a tail fan, and differ from the lobsters in that the abdomen either bends forwards under the thorax or is soft and often asymmetrical with a reduction of the pleopods on the right side. The last leg is often reduced in size and hidden under the thorax. There are about twelve families in this group: the most important ones are mentioned below.

The hermit crabs (family Paguridae) are well known for their habit of keeping the large soft abdomen, which is usually coiled round to the right, within the shells of gastropod molluscs. The uropods at the end have special anti-skid surfaces

which can be applied closely to the inside of the mollusc shell to give a good grip which will allow the hermits to retreat inside the shell when danger threatens. The appendages on the right side of the abdomen are lost, but those on the left are retained and used by the females for attachment of eggs. Some hermits live in the straight tubes of *Dentalium* and allied genera, and have a straight abdomen, but the appendages on the right side are missing, indicating that they have descended from ancestors which inhabited coiled shells. Other pagurids do not carry shells, and have short symmetrical abdomens lacking appendages on the right side. In such species the upper side of the abdomen is more heavily armoured than in 'shelled' species.

Members of the family Coenobitidae are known as land hermit crabs. The most interesting species is the Robber Crab (*Birgus latro*) which when full grown does not carry a shell. The hard symmetrical abdomen lacks appendages on the right side. Young individuals are sometimes found carrying shells, and in captivity they have been induced to persist in this habit for about four years. In nature they drop the habit early in life and assume the adult form. The females return from land to the sea to liberate their young, which hatch in the form of zoea larvae. This planktonic larva explains the wide distribution of this land crab on isolated islands in the Indo-Pacific area. The adults have become so adapted to a terrestrial life that they can be drowned if kept forcibly submerged for long periods.

Stone crabs (family Lithodidae) look superficially like spider crabs. The carapace is triangular and heavily beset with spines, and the legs are relatively long. The abdomen is tucked forwards underneath the thorax. The most conspicuous difference from spider crabs is found in the last leg, which is very small and is normally carried between the thorax and abdomen. Most species are found only in the cooler waters of the northern hemisphere. The North American and European Stone Crab (*Lithodes maia*) reaches its southern limit in Britain. Some of the Arctic species reach a large size: the King Crab (*Paralithodes camtschatica*) has a legspan of over a metre. This species is found off the coast of Alaska and extends across the northern Pacific to the coasts of Japan and Siberia. The larva is similar in many respects to the larvae of hermit crabs.

Squat lobsters (family Galatheidae) form a substantial family with over 200 species. They resemble lobsters, but carry the abdomen flexed forwards under the thorax and have a small last leg which can be tucked into the branchial chamber and used for cleaning purposes. *Galathea* feeds by brushing up organic débris from the surface of sand or mud, using a series of setae at the end of the long third maxilliped. These setae are cleaned by other-setae on the second maxilliped, and these in turn pass the food to the other mouth-parts. All the galatheids are marine, but the closely related Aeglaeidae has about twenty freshwater species in South America.

The family Porcellanidae are the most crab-like of the Anomura, but they have a small tail fan, and the last leg is very small and hidden beneath the thorax. Feeding is by alternate movements of the third maxillipeds which are first extended into the

water and then swept back towards the mouth. Long setae on the maxillipeds trap small organisms and other edible particles and transfer them to the other mouth-parts. Porcelain crabs are found throughout the tropical and temperate seas. There are well over 200 species living in the shallower parts of the oceans or on the seashore. Their colours often match their backgrounds to provide very effective camouflage. The common *Porcellana platycheles* of Europe resembles the encrusting growths of animals and plants found on the undersides of stones on the shore, while the main colour of *Orthochela pumila*, from the Gulf of California, is bright yellow matching the fan corals (Gorgonacea) on which it spends most of its time.

Section Brachyura

There are well over 4,000 living species of true crabs belonging to this section. The most obvious characteristics of a crab are the wide carapace covering the whole of the dorsal surface, the small abdomen tucked forwards under the thorax and the well-developed pincers on the front legs. There is an immense range in size from minute species which are the size of a pea when adult, to the giant spider crabs with legs spanning over 2·4 metres. There are twenty-six families of crabs, the most notable of which are mentioned below.

A female of the hermit crab, *Coenobita hilgendorphi*, leaving the shell of the Giant Land Snail (*Achatina fulica*), to lay her eggs in the sea. Hermits of this genus are semi-terrestrial, often wandering far from the sea. Their gills are reduced in size but this is counterbalanced by a network of fine blood-vessels under the skin of the abdomen which acts as a gill.

The female of the Robber Crab or Coconut Crab (*Birgus latro*) in berry, the egg-mass being visible between the large claw and the first leg. Robber Crabs are diurnal and terrestrial, with the ability to climb trees. They are prized not only for their flesh but for the edible oil extracted from it.

Two male fiddler crabs, *Uca lactea*, from Thailand, fighting. The enormously large claw on one side is, however, more than a weapon. It is used also to signal possession of a territory, to threaten a rival and to court a female. Of the two males pictured here, one has the right claw much enlarged, the other has the left.

A ghost crab, *Ocypode albicans*, of tropical beaches. Ghost crabs run at great speed and are coloured like the sand, their shadow being more conspicuous than they are themselves.

Some members of the family Dromiidae still have traces of a tail fan. This is taken to indicate that they are primitive crabs, and this idea is supported by the fact that they were among the earliest crabs to appear in the fossil record. They also have some specialisations: the last legs are modified so that they bend upwards and can be used to hold mollusc shells or pieces of sponge on the back. *Dromia vulgaris* holds pieces of sponge on its back and lets them grow there. This habit has been shown to give some protection from *Octopus* which will eat *Dromia* if it has no sponge, but leaves it alone if it has a good growth on its back. All the dromiids are marine and many of the 156 species extend into deep water.

Shame-faced crabs of the family Calappidae have large flat chelae which can be held together in front of the head so that there is a narrow opening between the carapace and the chelae. The inflowing respiratory current passes through this opening and is strained free of sand or silt by means of numerous fine setae on the border of the carapace. The outflowing respiratory current passes out in the midline through two small tube-like extensions near the bases of the antennae.

The family Portunidae includes nearly 300 species, most of which are capable of swimming to some extent. *Carcinus maenas*, the Green Crab of North America, or Common Shore Crab of northern Europe, has a very limited ability to swim, and this is reflected in the slight widening of the last leg. In *Polybius henslowi*, which is an excellent swimmer, the hind legs are broad with a flat round paddle at the end. Various species of *Portunus* have a reputation for pugnacity, which derives from their technique of leaping upwards with pincers raised and snapping. This is their normal hunting behaviour, and is very effective with small passing prey, but they will also apply it to a human finger or toe. Most portunids are marine, but some extend into estuaries, like the edible Blue Crab (*Callinectes sapidus*) which has a wide distribution on the North Atlantic coast of the North American Continent.

In the family Potamonidae are included the river crabs of the Old World. They spend their whole lives in freshwater and lay large eggs which develop directly into small crabs. The number of species is uncertain, but runs into hundreds.

Over 900 species belong to the family Xanthidae, which is the largest family of decapods. These crabs are non-swimmers, heavily armoured and particularly abundant on tropical reefs and rocky shores exposed to heavy wave action. Several species of this family carry small sea anemones in their pincers; members of the genus *Lybia* are particularly noted for this habit.

The pea crabs (family Pinnotheridae) receive their common name for their shape and size, although some of them reach a much larger size than the average pea. They live in association with other animals, particularly in the mantle cavities of bivalved molluscs. Over two hundred species have been described. *Pinnotheres pisum* is common in mussels in Europe, and *P. ostreum* is widespread in oysters on the Atlantic coast of north America.

The family Grapsidae contains over 300 species which inhabit a wide range of habitats. Most are marine, but some extend into estuaries and some on to land. They have a characteristic square carapace, and the claws are usually equal in size. *Pachygrapsus marmoratus* is common on rocky shores in southern Europe, while another species of the genus (*P. crassipes*) is abundant on rocky shores from Oregon to the Gulf of California. The Chinese Woolly-handed Crab (*Eriocheir sinensis*) has been transported to Europe, presumably in ballast tanks, and has become abundant in some rivers. It lives in freshwater as an adult, and can penetrate far upstream, but it must return to the sea to breed.

The family Oxypodidae includes the fiddler crab (genus *Uca*) which abound in mangrove swamps and mud flats throughout the warmer parts of the world. The male *Uca* has one claw very much larger than the other. This claw is often brightly coloured and is used in display to attract females and to defend a territory around a burrow. Ghost crabs (genus *Ocypode*) also belong to this family. They are also called racing crabs, because they can run sideways at high speeds across tropical beaches.

Spider crabs (family Majidae) form the second largest family of crabs, with over 600 species. They have a triangular carapace and long thin legs. In the largest species, *Macrocheira kaempferi*, from the deep sea off Japan, the legs span over 2·4 metres. Many members of this family decorate themselves with seaweed and pieces of sponge, so that they are difficult to detect among natural shore growths.

Spiders and allies (Class Arachnida)

Arachnids attract the layman's attention mainly on account of the venomous propensities of certain spiders and scorpions and the parasitic and disease carrying activities of ticks and mites, but to zoologists they have a deeper significance. The fact that they represent an independent and highly successful invasion of the terrestrial habitat gives a particular interest to their morphology, their physiology and their behaviour. Although arachnids have inherited from their annelid ancestors many features in common with the insects—for example a tough external skeleton, a dorsal blood vessel and a ventral nerve cord—they differ from the latter group in certain important aspects.

External structure

The body is divided into two main portions: the cephalothorax or prosoma and the abdomen or opisthosoma. The latter may be connected to the prosoma across the whole width of the body as in scorpions or there may be a narrow pedicel or waist as in spiders. Arachnids do not possess antennae. The first pair of appendages, the chelicerae, belong to the mouth-parts and in many orders they are chelate or pincer-like, but in others, notably the spiders, they terminate in a fang used for piercing prey. Directly behind the chelicerae lie a second pair of appendages, the pedipalps. These may be simple leg-like structures or, as in scorpions, terminate as chelae or pincers like those of crabs and lobsters. All arachnids, with the exception of some of the mites, possess four pairs of legs and these lie directly behind the pedipalps, although the last pair of legs may not be present in the youngest stages of some orders. In most orders the prosoma is protected by a single sclerotised plate, the carapace, but in some, such as the solifugids and the schizomids, it may be subdivided into a number of separate tergites. Eyes are present in most but not all arachnid orders, and they are always simple ocelli, never compound as in insects.

The abdomen is a distensible sac, frequently showing signs of external segmentation in the form of dorsal and ventral plates. The ventral surface of the second abdominal segment usually bears the genital aperture whilst the last true abdominal segment bears the anus. A few orders, for example the whip scorpions (order Uropygi), possess a telson or tail composed of post-abdominal segments which project beyond the anus. The abdomen bears no appendages except for the pectines of scorpions and the spinnerets of spiders.

Nutrition and excretion

Most arachnids are carnivorous and prey on a variety of small arthropods. These are killed either by crushing or, in the case of spiders and pseudoscorpions, by the injection of venom. With the sole exception of some mites and harvestmen which ingest solid food particles, the small mouth lying behind the chelicerae admits only liquid food, which is drawn into the digestive tract by means of a sucking stomach or muscular pharynx in the prosoma. This means that the first part of the digestive process takes place outside the body and involves the secretion of digestive enzymes which reduce the edible parts of the prey to a fluid consistency. Further digestion takes place within the gut diverticula of the prosoma and abdomen.

Coxal glands and Malpighian tubules are the main excretory organs. The former, lying in the prosoma, open through pores lying just behind the basal segments of the legs whilst the latter are abdominal structures and open into the posterior part of the gut where they discharge guanine crystals and sometimes uric acid. In addition excretion is assisted by nephrocytes in the blood sinuses.

Nervous system

In most arcachnids the nervous system is highly concentrated into a distinctive anterior 'brain'. In scorpions, however, although the prosomal ganglia are fused to form a single 'brain', the abdominal ganglia remain distinct, a character which is considered primitive.

The sense-organs include eyes, slit sensilla and sensory hairs or setae. Within the two latter categories considerable diversity of structure is found but very little is known about the function of these organs. The slit sensilla or lyriform organs include structures of differing function, but are sensitive to changes in cuticular stress and respond to both air and ground vibrations. The eyes usually comprise a median pair mounted in the midline with smaller eyes, generally six in number, arranged along the antero-lateral margin of the carapace. In addition special sensory structures of unknown function, such as the pectines of scorpions, and the malleoli of solifugids are also found in some orders.

Respiration

Respiration in the smallest arachnids such as mites and palpigrades takes place over the whole body surface but amongst the rest two principal types of respiratory structure are found. The first of these, not found in any other group of animals, are the book-lungs which occur in scorpions, whip scorpions and amblypygids. These are gill-like structures lying in paired abdominal cavities and opening to the exterior by spiracular slits. The second type of respiratory structure, apparently in some cases derived from the book-lungs, is the tracheal system found in solifugids, ricinuleids, harvestmen and some mites. This network of air-filled tubes, penetrating deeply to all parts of the body, is superficially similar to the system found in insects but independently evolved. Spiders may combine both book-lung and tracheal respiration.

Circulation and respiration

The heart is a muscular tube lying dorsally within the abdomen. It is surrounded by a pericardial chamber from which the blood is drained through lateral slits or ostia. An arterial system, which tends to be reduced in animals with a well-developed tracheal system, then carries the blood from the heart to all parts of the body. Blood drains back to the heart through a system of ill-defined sinuses.

Little is known of the respiratory function of the blood, although a pale blue copper-containing pigment has been described in spider blood. Better understood is the hydrostatic role of the blood. Spider legs lack direct extensor muscles and, in jumping spiders (Salticidae) at least, the jump is brought about by a straightening of the legs caused by a sudden increase in blood pressure.

Reproduction
The sexes are always separate and the gonads consist of paired organs lying ventrally within the abdomen. Except in some ticks and mites the genital aperture always opens ventrally on the second abdominal segment (or eighth body somite). The diverse and complex methods of copulation are described separately for each order.

Parthenogenesis has been reported in a number of species of mites, scorpions and spiders, but this type of reproduction is very rare in arachnids.

Growth and life-history
All arachnids grow by periodically moulting the cuticle or exoskeleton, a process known as ecdysis. In the early stages the young, although incompletely formed, resemble the adults in essentials and there is no complete metamorphosis as in higher insects. There are never true larvae in the entomological sense in the life-history of arachnids.

Except for some harvestmen and mites, arachnids are generally aggressive, carnivorous creatures and therefore tend to lead solitary lives. Nevertheless a degree of maternal care is found in some species and a few spiders actually feed their young with semi-digested food. Social behaviour is likewise rare but occurs, for example, amongst spiders of the genus *Stegodyphus*, and small silver spiders of the genus *Argyrodes* may often be found living commensally in the webs of the much larger *Nephila*.

Scorpions (Order Scorpiones)
Fossil scorpions are found as far back as the Silurian (400 million years ago), which makes them the most ancient of all terrestrial arthropods. Approximately 700 species have been described, ranging in length from thirteen millimetres to more than eighteen centimetres. They are found throughout the warmer parts of the world, extending into southern Europe and as far north as British Columbia on the western seaboard and North Dakota in central North America. Contrary to popular belief scorpions are by no means restricted to desert regions and are sometimes abundant in tropical rainforest and even occur near the snow-line in the Himalayas. However, as they are active only at night and spend the day hiding beneath stones or rotten logs, they are seldom encountered.

The prosoma is covered by a single carapace, broadly joined to an abdominal region comprising seven wide segments and five constricted segments, the latter forming a 'tail' and terminating in a post-anal sting. The pedipalps are large pincer-like structures but the chelicerae are small and project only slightly in front of the carapace. The ventral abdominal surface bears a pair of comb-like organs called pectines, which project from just behind the genital aperture and have an unknown sensory function. They are found in no other order.

Although many scorpions can inflict painful stings, very few species are known to be dangerous to man. The most notorious species belong to the genera *Tityus* in Brazil, *Centruroides* in Mexico and the southwestern United States, and *Androctonus* in North Africa. The venom, a neurotoxin produced by two glands lying in the base of the sting, causes paralysis of the cardiac and respiratory muscles and can be fatal in children and elderly people.

Insemination is by means of a spermatophore which is deposited on the ground by the male during a nuptial dance. The female is then manoeuvred on to the spermatophore which enters her genital orifice. Development takes several months, perhaps even a year, and is interesting because throughout the order the young are produced viviparously or ovoviviparously. The eggs of viviparous species possess no yolk but develop in special ovarian diverticula that put out tubules to absorb nutriment from the maternal digestive caeca. This uterine feeding of scorpions is a remarkable parallel of the placental system of mammals. As soon as the young are born they climb on to the mother's back where they remain for a week or more before leaving to take up an independent existence. Most scorpions take about a year to reach maturity.

Pseudoscorpions (Order Pseudoscorpiones)

These tiny animals occur throughout the world with the exception of the polar regions, but they are seldom encountered even by naturalists. More than 1,500 species have been described, very few exceeding eight millimetres in length. They occur in a wide variety of cryptic habitats, for example, under bark or stones and amongst vegetable débris, but they are not readily noticed because they do not usually move when disturbed. A cosmopolitan species, *Chelifer cancroides* is found in houses. They are also encountered on occasions clinging to the legs of flies, a dispersal activity known as phoresy. The name of this order indicates a superficial resemblance to scorpions, but this is confined to the possession of large grasping pedipalps. There is no 'tail' or terminal sting. Instead the pseudoscorpions possess venom glands in the pedipalps whilst the glands of the chelicerae analogous to the poison glands of spiders, are used in this order for the production of silk. This silk is employed in the making of small nests in which the eggs are laid. After laying, the eggs remain attached to the ventral surface of the female where they are carried until hatching within a membranous sac where they feed on 'milk' secreted by the mother.

Harvestmen (Order Opiliones or Phalangida)

The Opiliones, also known as Phalangida, include the familiar daddy-long-legs or harvestmen. There are about 3,200 species distributed throughout the world, usually in moist environments. Although most harvestmen possess disproportionately long legs (some have a legspan of twenty centimetres) a few genera comprise squat, heavily built species.

The body appears a single globular or triangular unit, the prosoma and abdomen being broadly united. In most species the paired eyes are mounted on ornate tubercles projecting from the centre of the carapace. The chelicerae are small and chelate whilst the pedipalps are small leg-like appendages. There are no poison glands but many species of the order possess repugnatorial glands along the anterolateral margins of the carapace. Harvestmen are more omnivorous than other arachnids with the exception of mites and ticks and will consume not only small invertebrates which they capture and kill, but also dead animal and vegetable remains.

The reproductive system of opilionids is somewhat anomalous. Apart from certain mites, harvestmen are the only arachnids in which the male possesses an intromittent organ or penis. Mating takes place frequently and without elaborate courtship. The female is also unusual in possessing a long protrusible ovipositor with which she lays her eggs in crevices in humus, moss or rotten wood.

Opposite top
Scorpions command no affection by either their habits or appearance. There is, nevertheless, one thing to their credit: the females make good mothers. For the early part of their lives the babies are carried around on the mother's back until they are able to fend for themselves.

Opposite bottom
A Hairy Desert Scorpion (*Hadrurus hirsutus*), of North America, in the typical defensive attitude. The claws are held well apart ready to grasp. The tail is poised over the back with the sting, in the last segment of the tail (the telson), positioned to be thrust forward.

A harvestman, more often called daddy-long-legs, for obvious reasons, with a burden of mites on its legs. Apart from the greater length of their legs, harvestmen differ from their close relatives, the spiders, in having a less pronounced waist between thorax and abdomen and in the abdomen being segmented. Harvestmen are most numerous in late summer and the legend has it that large numbers of them suddenly appearing presage a good harvest.

Giant red velvet mites of the deserts of the United States. Most American mites are some shade of red. Mites generally are world-wide. Half the species are parasitic on other animals and on man. They are found wherever there is the slightest amount of vegetable or animal food for them.

A whip scorpion or vinegaroon, *Mastigoproctus giganteus*, of Mexico and the south western United States. Its second vernacular name derives from its habit of squirting defensively a fluid made up mainly of acetic acid, so that the animal smells like vinegar.

Ticks and mites (Order Acari)
The Acari (sometimes called Acarina) are by far the most numerous and diversified of all the arachnid orders. More than 25,000 species are now known, and this probably represents only a fraction of the world fauna. They are to be found throughout the world and in an incredibly wide range of habitats. They include both terrestrial and aquatic forms, and a large number are parasitic on plants and animals. It is the parasitic mode of life, coupled with the fact that they are disease carriers, that makes mites and ticks of economic importance, and the most intensively studied of all arachnids.

The great burst of adaptive radiation, resulting in the production of an abundance of species, is associated with a departure from the rather rigid ancestral arachnid body plan. Few traces of external segmentation remain and it is seldom possible to recognise the division into prosoma and opisthosoma. The mouth-parts have undergone extensive modification in response to specialised modes of feeding and this is particularly apparent in

parasitic species. Likewise the limbs have frequently become modified. In hair or feather mites, for example *Analges*, they have become attachment organs whilst in burrowing forms such as the mammal parasite *Demodex* and plant parasites (family Eriophyidae) they are reduced to stumps.

As one might expect in a group occupying so many different types of environment, mating behaviour is varied. Sperm may be transferred to the female by an intromittent penis, by the use of a spermatophore, or by means of specially modified structures on the legs or chelicerae. The majority of mites lay eggs, which are deposited in soil or humus, and some possess an ovipositor similar to that found in harvestmen. Viviparity occurs amongst parasitic mites and a few species are ovoviviparous. The young stages of mites are distinguished by the possession of only three pairs of legs and are known as larvae.

The mites of economic importance are very numerous and include such forms as the Itch Mite (*Sarcoptes*), and *Psoroptes* which causes mange in a variety of domestic animals, *Tetranychus* which attacks many fruit trees in America, and *Eriophyes* which infests many cultivated plants in both Europe and America. A large number of blood-sucking ticks are of particular importance as transmitters of disease: *Margaropus* transmits Texan fever, *Dermocentor* spotted fever and tularemia, and *Ornithodoros* relapsing fever in Africa.

Micro-whip scorpions (Order Palpigradi)
Palpigrades or micro-whip scorpions are an obscure order of minute arachnids less than two millimetres in length, about which very little is known. Some fifty species have been described and these are widely scattered throughout the world, including Europe, the southern United States, South America, West Africa, Madagascar, Thailand and Australia. The body consists of a prosoma covered by a large anterior carapace and a much smaller posterior carapace and joined by a slight constriction to a segmented abdomen terminating in a long flagellum or tail. The chelicerae are fairly large and chelate, the pedipalps are simple leg-like structures and the anterior pair of legs bear a number of long fine sensory hairs. Almost nothing is known of the biology of these secretive creatures. The main genus is *Koenenia*.

Whip scorpions (Order Uropygi)
The whip scorpions are comparatively large arachnids occurring in some of the warmer parts of the world. They are found in the northeastern part of South America, in the southern United States and Central America, on the Indian subcontinent and throughout eastern Asia and much of Indonesia. However, they are conspicuously absent from Africa, Madagascar and the Middle East although at least two introduced species appear to have become established in West Africa. They are retiring nocturnal creatures and are usually found hiding beneath stones and logs or amongst vegetable débris. The great majority of species are found in humid habitats although a few species also occur in more arid regions. About eighty species have been described, the largest having a body length of approximately eight centimetres.

The prosoma is covered by a single large carapace and is united by a slight constriction to an obviously-segmented abdomen. The abdomen terminates in a long flagellum or tail and it is from this that the group takes its popular name. The chelicerae are non-chelate and resemble those of spiders except that they lack venom glands. The pedipalps are comparatively short but very massively built, bearing numerous spurs and terminating in a pair of pincers. The first pair of legs are longer and thinner than the remaining pairs and are not used in walking, but are held out in front as sensory appendages. At the base of the flagellum, on either side of the anus, lie a pair of large glands. These produce a secretion consisting largely of acetic acid mixed with wetting agent, which can be squirted in a well-directed stream to a range of several centimetres.

Mating in whip scorpions has only recently been observed, although a courtship dance in which the male grasped the front pair of the female's legs in his chelicerae had previously been described. The eggs are laid in a mass suspended beneath the female and even after hatching the young remain for a considerable period attached to their mother. The female dies soon after the young have dispersed and up to three years are required for them to reach maturity. The principal genera include *Thelyphonus*, *Hypoctonus*, and *Mastigoproctus*.

Schizomids (Order Schizomida)

Schizomids or tartarides were previously united with the whip scorpions in a single order. They are widely dispersed throughout the tropical regions, although they not infrequently get carried to colder climates where they become established in hot-houses and other heated buildings. About fifty species have been described, the main genera being *Schizomus* and *Trithyrens*. All are small and the largest does not exceed seven millimetres.

The prosoma is covered by three plates or tergites and united by a pedicel to a segmented abdomen, which terminates in a small telson. The chelicerae are somewhat chelate but otherwise resemble those of spiders except that they lack poison glands. The pedipalps, although large, differ from those of whip scorpions in that they move vertically instead of horizontally and do not terminate in a pair of pincers.

Almost nothing is known of the biology of the schizomids thought they have been found, like the Uropygi, in subterranean cells with a mass of eggs adhering to the ventral surface of the abdomen.

Tail-less whip scorpions (Order Amblypygi)

Tail-less whip scorpions or whip spiders are another small order of predominantly tropical arachnids and were at one time united with schizomids and uropygids in the order Pedipalpi. They are secretive nocturnal animals ranging in body length from about four millimetres to forty-five millimetres and are characteristically found in damp dark habitats, beneath logs or in caves and sewers. They occur in the northern half of South America, Central America and the West Indies, Florida and southwestern United States. They are widespread in Africa south of the Sahara, India, Burma, Borneo and New Guinea. One species has recently been found in Iran. There are about sixty species.

The body consists of a broad prosoma covered by a single carapace and joined by a narrow pedicel to a soft segmented abdomen. The abdomen does not possess a terminal flagellum or telson. The chelicerae are similar to those of whip scorpions and like them have no poison glands. The pedipalps are large, formidable structures. Although they terminate in a simple claw they bear long sharp spikes on their inner surface reminiscent of the front legs of the Praying Mantis, and they are used in a similar manner for seizing and holding prey. The front pair of legs are long and thin and are held out in front and around the animal like antennae.

The courtship and mating of these bizarre flattened animals has only recently been observed. After pacifying the female by tapping and stroking her with his legs, the male deposits a spermatophore on the ground, subsequently adding two sperm masses. The female advances forward of her own volition and takes up the sperm masses under her genital operculum and the animals then separate. The eggs are laid into a thin sac which is carried by the female beneath her abdomen until the young have hatched and passed their first moult.

Spiders (Order Araneae)

Spiders, with more than 40,000 described species, are the largest of all the arachnid orders. They occur widely throughout the world and with the

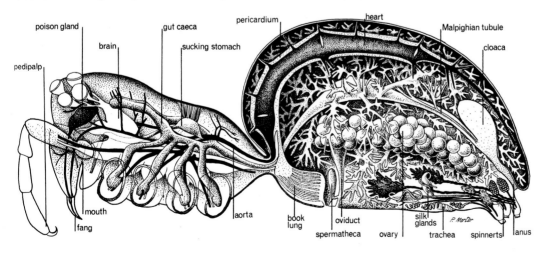

Internal anatomy (semi-diagrammatic) of a typical labidognath (higher) spider.

181

Tailless whip scorpions are not easily seen because they live in caves or deep crevices in rocky cliffs. Their legs are longer than those of whip scorpions. One recorded for Peru was five centimetres long in the body but its front legs measured twenty-two centimetres.

A red-kneed bird-eating spider of the rain forests of Costa Rica. Large hairy, tropical spiders of this sort are now popularly called tarantulas although the original tarantula is a small European spider, far less fearsome-looking. Despite being called 'bird-eating' they feed mainly on insects but will eat small birds and mammals the size of mice.

exception of mites and ticks have radiated more widely than any other group. Spiders range in body length from less than a half millimetre to nearly ten centimetres, although the legspan of the largest species may be more than twice this.

The prosoma is covered by a carapace and is connected by a narrow pedicel to the abdomen which in most forms is a soft elastic bag usually showing no external trace of segmentation although this may be reflected in the colour pattern. The chelicerae end in a hollow fang which is connected to a poison gland. The pedipalps are simple leg-like structures but in the male are modified into complex organs of copulation.

The anterior ventral surface of the abdomen, in common with all arachnids, bears the genital openings and in the female these may be associated with a complex sclerotised structure called the epigyne. The male palp and female epigyne are the main characters used for identifying different species of spider. On either side of the genital

aperture are the main openings to the respiratory system which may consist of two pairs of book-lungs, a combination of book-lungs and tracheal tubes or, in a few cases, tracheal tubes only. The posterior end of the abdomen bears the anal tubercle and spinnerets which are finger-like organs, usually six in number, from which various types of silk are discharged through spigots.

Venom

With the exception of a single small family all spiders possess 'venom' glands. For the most part this venom is effective only against the animals which constitute the spiders' normal prey and in some species it may only contain accessory digestive juices. However, a few spiders possess venom of extreme toxicity that affects domestic animals and, on occasion, man himself.

The most notorious of all venomous spiders is the Black Widow (*Latrodectus mactans*). This species is widely distributed throughout the warmer parts of the world, being known by a variety of local names, although it is the North American sub-species which has acquired the worst reputation. *Latrodectus* produces a neurotoxin causing severe pain, muscular cramp, paralysis and hypertension. Although fatalities are recorded, particularly amongst young children, most patients recover in a few days without permanent injury. Other spiders with dangerous venom include *Phoneutria* and *Loxosceles* in South America and *Atrax* in Australia.

Not all spider venoms are neurotoxic like that of *Latrodectus*. In some species such as *Lycosa raptoria* in South America and *Loxosceles* the effect is haemolytic and produces widespread ulceration, whilst other spiders, for example *Phormictopus*, possess a combination of both types of venom.

Silk

Silk is a scleroprotein secreted as a liquid by several large glands lying ventrally in the abdomen. These glands are of several different sorts, each producing a special kind of silk for particular purposes, for example in different parts of the web or cocoon. The glands open through numerous small spigots on the spinnerets, and as the silk strands are drawn out, tension causes the component crystallites to become orientated and it is this, rather than evaporation, which hardens the silk into a strong, elastic solid.

Although the construction of orb-webs as snares for capturing flying prey is perhaps the most conspicuous use to which silk is put by spiders, many species construct no snare at all, but hunt freely over the ground or on the foliage of shrubs and trees. These forms usually trail a 'safety-line' of silk behind them wherever they go. Others construct snares quite different from the orb-web, for example large sheets, subterranean tubes or asymmetrical tangles in addition to many highly individual and more specialised devices.

Another very important use to which silk is put is the construction of the cocoon. This usually consists of a tough, water-resistant outer layer with an inner flocculent silk mass in which the eggs are cushioned. Many specialised and elaborate types of cocoon protect and conceal the eggs in particular habitats.

Reproduction and life-history

Soon after reaching maturity the male spider spins a rudimentary web on which he deposits a droplet of sperm. This is then sucked up into the special organs at the end of his palps, which may be likened to the reservoir of a fountain pen. Having charged his palps he goes in search of a female and after some form of courtship, which may be either swift and tactile or prolonged and visual, proceeds to mate. This involves the insertion of the palpal organ into the female genital aperture on the abdomen. Discharge of the palpal organ is brought about either mechanically by increased blood pressure or by endocrine stimulation of glands within the palp, whose secretions drive the semen out. The female can store the sperm she receives from her mate for long periods, up to eighteen months in some cases, and use it to fertilise several batches of eggs. These may number over 1,000 per cocoon in some species although 20–100 is more usual. The eggs hatch within a few weeks of being laid and the young spiders stay in the cocoon until after their first moult. There is no true larval stage in the development of spiders, although the term is sometimes applied to the earliest, semi-embryonic instars.

Moulting takes place at intervals, the frequency depending on the species and on the rate at which the individual has fed. The fresh cuticle is pale and soft, and the spider usually retires to a secluded spot in which it is safe from attacks by predators and where the cuticle may harden without the danger of distortion, which might result from undue movement. Most spiders undergo six to ten moults before reaching maturity with the males probably requiring fewer moults than the female.

The life-cycle is usually completed within a single year, but primitive spiders, some of which grow to considerable size, of the suborder Orthognatha (= Mygalomorpha) the females may live more than twenty years and continue to moult even when mature. This does not apply to males, which tend to survive for a year or less after maturing at about three years of age. Amongst other spiders, many of which complete their life-cycle in a single year, the adult males may survive for only a few weeks.

Spring and autumn are the seasons when most spiders reach maturity in temperate regions. In September and October an acre of rough grassland may contain a population of over two million spiders. This is also the season for gossamer, which consists of accumulated masses of silk produced during the dispersal activity known as 'ballooning'. Dispersal is brought about by spiders, both young and adults, climbing up plant stems and releasing strands of silk into up-currents of air until they become airborne. By this means spiders may be carried considerable distances over land and sea.

Main types of spider

The term 'tarantula', although widely used by laymen, has little meaning zoologically since it has been applied indiscriminately to many different sorts of spider (and indeed other animals). Today it is most frequently used to refer to any of the large, hairy spiders belonging to the suborder Orthognatha (= Mygalomorpha). These are more

primitive than most spiders and the majority construct subterranean burrows. The trapdoor spiders (families Ctenizidae and Barychelidae) build elaborate tunnels with hinged lids.

The second suborder, Labidognatha (= Araneomorpha), includes spiders such as the Common Garden Spider (family Araneidae = Argiopidae) which construct orb-webs, comb-footed spiders such as the Black Widow (family Theridiidae) which construct a loosely tangled web, and funnel-web spiders (family Agelenidae) which construct a large sheet with a tubular retreat at one corner.

Spiders that do not construct snares include the crab spiders (family Thomisidae) which sit for example on flower heads and catch their prey by stealth, wolf spiders (family Lycosidae) which chase their prey over the ground and jumping spiders (family Salticidae) which are amongst the very few with well-developed sight and stalk their victims slowly over considerable distances. It is amongst the jumping spiders that the most colourful and elaborate courtship displays are found. The male, often brightly coloured and with a metallic sheen, performs a 'dance' in front of the female which reduces her to a passive state during which he can mate without fear of attack.

Garden spider courtship is in many respects an unequal affair, the male being so very much smaller than the female and standing the risk of being eaten by her once mating has taken place. However, the statement, often repeated, that the female always eats the male is an exaggeration.

A crab spider, *Misumena* sp., of North America, has just captured a hoverfly. Crab spiders are so named for the way they walk. Their habit is to crouch motionless on a flower, the colour of their body changing to match the flower, and wait for insects to alight.

The Ricinulei are not only among the rarest members of the animal kingdom, but are also secretive in habits and very small, and so are seldom seen. They look like tiny spiders but one feature that marks them off from other Arachnida is the movable flap on the front of the carapace that can be lowered like a visor over the head to protect the mouthparts.

Wind scorpions (Order Solifugae or Solpugida)

These formidable creatures, also known as camel spiders and sun spiders, are characteristic of the warmer and more arid parts of the world. They are absent from Europe except for south-east Spain, but occur throughout Africa and the Middle East, extending into Turkestan and India. In the New World they are restricted to Florida and the south-western United States extending as far northwards as southwestern Canada (around hot springs) and throughout Central America, and in a narrow coastal belt extending along the northern and western coasts of South America into southern Chile. They are conspicuously absent from Australia. About six hundred species are known.

Anatomically solifugids are distinctive. The prosoma bears a number of tergites and is connected by a somewhat constricted waist to a large, soft and distinctly segmented abdomen. The prosoma bears a pair of enormously large and strong chelicerae which, for their size, are probably the strongest biting jaws in the animal kingdom. This impressive armament compensates solifugids for their lack of venom. The pedipalps are simple leg-like appendages bearing numerous long fine hairs of apparent sensory function and terminate in suckers, used in climbing smooth surfaces. The legs themselves are likewise long and hairy in most species. Ventrally the basal segments of the last pair of legs bear a number of very peculiar structures known as racket organs (malleoli) found

nowhere else in the animal kingdom and believed to be sense-organs.

Most solifugids are active, fast-moving hunters, many of them being diurnal. The need for speed, coupled with the comparatively large size of these creatures has resulted in the evolution of a well-developed tracheal system and no traces of the ancestral book-lungs remain.

Courtship has seldom been seen. The female becomes cataleptic in response to tapping and stroking by the male, who then opens the female genital orifice with his chelicerae. Having emitted a spherical globule of semen, the male picks it up in his chelicerae and inserts it into the female. The whole process takes only a short time, and he then departs rapidly. The female lays her eggs in a deep burrow in which she continues to live. After hatching, the young are apparently fed on prey brought back to them by the mother, and this continues until they eventually leave the maternal burrow to take up an independent existence.

Ricinuleids (Order Ricinulei)

The Ricinulei, with only about forty described species, is the smallest and least known of all the arachnid orders. They have been found in tropical West Africa (*Ricinoides*), and in Texas, Central America and several parts of tropical South America (*Cryptocellus*). They occur in the moist litter of dense rainforests or in caves. These strange secretive animals are all less than one centimetre long and have an extraordinarily thick cuticle. The prosoma is covered by a single carapace in front of which there hangs a hood or cucullus which covers the chelate chelicerae. The narrow pedicel connecting the prosoma with the opisthosoma is concealed giving the appearance of the abdomen being broadly joined to the carapace. There is a small anal tubercle projecting from the rear of the abdomen but no telson. The pedipalps are small and chelate and the legs are comparatively short and simple.

During the 1970's much work was done on the ecology and behaviour of cave-dwelling ricinuleids in Mexico and several new species have been described from this region. Courtship and mating have been observed and the young successfully reared in captivity. The eggs hatch into a six-legged larva which eventually moults and acquires a fourth pair of legs.

For many years ricinuleids enjoyed the distinction of being probably the rarest order of animals in the world. For many years the entire order was known by only thirty-two specimens. Recently, however, several large collections have been made.

Horseshoe crabs (Class Merostomata)

Horseshoe crabs (sometimes erroneously called king crabs) are a small but important group of marine animals once united with the arachnids but today placed in a separate class. However, horseshoe crabs, arachnids and sea spiders, all of which have chelicerae rather than mandibles, are often united in the subphylum Chelicerata. They are represented by five living species, one of which,

Limulus polyphemus, occurs commonly along the eastern seaboard of the United States and around the shores of the Gulf of Mexico. The remaining four species are found in the waters of the East Indies northwards as far as Japan and Korea, and also around India and Ceylon. They are the sole representatives of a group which was abundant in the Palaeozoic seas. Fossil merostomes are found in the Lower Cambrian deposits and the horseshoe crabs themselves have survived almost unaltered since the Silurian.

The flattened, horseshoe-shaped prosoma is covered in a tough leathery cuticle and bears a pair of compound eyes. The opisthosoma is hexagonal and shows very little trace of segmentation. It fits neatly into the posterior recess of the prosoma and bears six short movable spines along each lateral margin. The body terminates in a long stout spine which the animal uses to push itself into the mud and also to right itself.

The somewhat featureless dorsal armour conceals a fairly elaborate ventral surface. Beneath the prosoma there are six pairs of chelate limbs. The first pair, which are very much smaller than the others are the chelicerae and the second pair represent the pedipalps but do not differ in structure from the three following pairs of legs except in males, where they are modified for clasping the female. The last pair of limbs is modified for shifting mud and bears special paddles in addition to minute chelae. The opisthosoma or abdomen bears six pairs of appendages, the first modified to form a genital operculum and the remaining five to serve as gills.

Adult horseshoe crabs are bottom-living organisms and feed on a wide variety of both animal and plant material. Food is picked up by the chelate appendages and passed to the gnathobases (the basal segments of the limbs, bearing numerous sharp spines) which macerate the food which is then passed forward to the mouth.

The sexes are separate and the female lays her eggs in a shallow depression scooped out of the

sand. Fertilisation is external and takes place during egg deposition, after which the eggs are covered and left. They hatch into a small swimming 'trilobite' larva about one centimetre long, which has a superficial resemblance to the extinct class of animals called trilobites. Growth is slow and maturity is not reached for about three years during which time over a dozen moults occur.

Horseshoe crabs are of little economic importance although attempts have been made to grind them up on a commercial scale for fertiliser, and in the Far East the eggs are regarded as a delicacy.

A group of horseshoe crabs or king crabs on a sandy beach on the eastern seaboard of the United States. Females have scraped depressions in the sand and are laying their eggs. Most members of the group are males and they are fertilising the eggs. Finally sand will be scraped back over the eggs.

Sea spiders (Class Pycnogonida)

Sea spiders are an abundant group of bizarre marine organisms clearly derived from a common stock but sufficiently aberrant to be placed by some authors in a separate subphylum. Pycnogonids occur in all seas both in the littoral zone and at great depths. Nevertheless, they have remained a poorly-known group of animals. Although most are small, the polar oceans contain individuals with a legspan of over sixty centimetres. The most characteristic feature of sea spiders is their legs which may number from four to six pairs. The body to which they are attached is greatly reduced and the abdomen is present only as a small tubercle projecting from the trunk. The extreme reduction of the trunk and abdomen has resulted in organs such as the gut diverticula and ovaries being forced out into the legs. Anteriorly the sea spiders have a large muscular proboscis bearing the mouth at its tip. The proboscis is inserted into the sea anemones and other sessile marine organisms on which pycnogonids feed and sucks out their fluids.

Appendages, apparently homologous with the chelicerae and pedipalps of arachnids, are usually present whilst a pair of small legs, usually found in front of the walking legs and known as ovigerous legs, are used by the male for carrying the egg masses. They may be entirely absent in the female.

These egg masses consist of fertilised eggs gathered by the male after being laid by the female and brooded by him until hatching. Hatching results in the formation of a 'protonymphon' larva in which there is no trace of walking legs. The larvae may either remain attached to the male or more often become parasitic, particularly on hydroids. There are about five hundred species. Common genera include *Nymphon*, *Pycnogonum* and *Colossendeis*.

A sea spider, *Pseudopallene ambigua*, living at a depth of seven metres in Adventure Bay, Tasmania. The sea spider's body is remarkably reduced in size and the vital organs are mainly housed in the long slender legs.

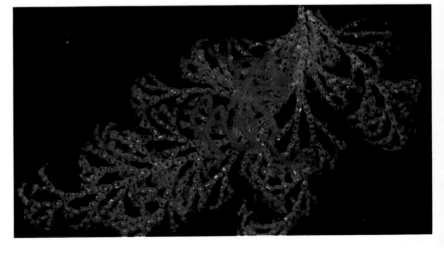

PENTASTOMIDS
(Phylum Pentastomida)

Pentastomids comprise about 65 species of worm-like parasitic animals possessing apparent arthropod affinities but now placed in a separate phylum. They infect the respiratory passages of a number of vertebrates, particularly reptiles, but also some mammals. They are particularly abundant in the tropics but also occur in temperate regions although none is known from North America. The life-cycle involves an intermediate vertebrate host in which larval development takes place. Although pentastomids may parasitise man occasionally, they have little economic importance.

The worm-like body is covered in a thick cuticle that is periodically moulted in the course of development. The musculature of the body wall resembles that of the annelids and is arranged in layers. There are no true appendages although the four anterior hooks by means of which the animal attaches itself to its host may often be borne on projections resembling rudimentary legs. It is from these four projections and the short anterior proboscis bearing the mouth that the name of the group is derived. There are no respiratory, circulatory or excretory organs.

WATER BEARS
(Phylum Tardigrada)

Tardigrades or bear animalcules are minute organisms that are widely distributed throughout the world but most are less than 0·5 millimetres long and therefore seldom seen. There are about 340 described species, but many more probably await discovery. Some of the known species are members of the marine littoral fauna and others occur in freshwater habitats. However, the great majority live in the water film surrounding terrestrial mosses and lichens and are thus characteristic of habitats that become periodically desiccated. The survival and also the wide distribution of tardigrades depends on their ability to withstand such desiccation, and this is done by shrivelling into a small anabiotic granule in which metabolism effectively ceases. In this highly resistant condition they are immune to immersion in liquid helium ($-272°$ C.), ether, absolute alcohol and other noxious substances, but revival may be brought about, even after an interval of several years, by immersion in water. Within only a few hours the animals swell and start to feed and reproduce.

The body is squat, plump, cylindrical and segmented and may bear a variety of cuticular plates or other ornamentation. The legs are stubby outpushings of the body wall terminating in claws, but are not jointed like arthropods. Some tardigrades may be carnivorous but the vast majority feed on the juices of lower plants, which they obtain by piercing individual cells with special sylets.

The sexes are separate and fertilisation is internal although this is achieved in a number of different ways. Eggs are laid and may be extremely resistant to desiccation although in favourable conditions they are thin shelled. They hatch in about two weeks into diminutive tardigrades.

The relationships of the tardigrades are particularly unclear and although they possess some distinctive arthropodan characteristics, they cannot be closely linked with any of the known groups.

ARROW WORMS
(Phylum Chaetognatha)

The Chaetognatha, or arrow worms, are among the most abundant animals in the marine plankton. There are some forty species, with elongated bodies divided into head, trunk and tail regions. Length varies from six to a hundred millimetres, the usual being about twenty millimetres. There are one or two pairs of horizontal fins and a horizontal tail fin. On either side of the mouth is a row of chitinous hooks or teeth (hence the name Chaetognatha, 'bristle jaw') which are covered by a sort of hood while the animal is swimming. The internal anatomy is simple, with no specialised respiratory, circulatory or excretory system. There are nerve-ganglia in the head, and a large ventral ganglion and four longitudinal muscles in the trunk. Although called arrow worms, they are not closely related to other so-called 'worms', nor to any other phylum, although certain details of their anatomy and development suggest an affinity with the echinoderms and the vertebrates. They are an ancient group and their remains are found in rocks of the Middle Cambrian.

Except for two bright orange-red species living at depths of 1,000 to 2,000 metres in the Atlantic, the arrow worms are transparent, so although present in most oceanic plankton hauls, they are not readily seen. A slight difference in refractive index, a pair of small black eyes and food in the straight digestive tract alone serve to reveal them. Each eye is divided into five separate retinas so placed as to cover the field of view in all directions, including downwards through the transparent head.

Although one genus is benthic and some occur at depths of more than 6,000 metres, arrow worms are most abundant in the upper 200 to 300 metres, where they are outnumbered, among the larger forms, only by the copepods on which they feed. Like many other planktonic animals, some species move daily up and down in response to changes in light intensity. For much of the time arrow worms hover in the water, sometimes with a quivering of the body, then suddenly alternate contraction of the upper and lower pairs of longitudinal muscles sends the tail up and down and the body flashes arrow-like through the water for a distance perhaps six times the arrow worm's own length. The product of this exercise may be the capture of a copepod, a small fish such as a young herring, or even another arrow worm. The prey is gripped by the curved teeth and devoured.

The Chaetognatha are hermaphrodite, with paired ovaries in the hind end of the trunk and male organs in the tail. Mating has been observed only in the benthic genus *Spadella* (two mature individuals exchanged sperm masses). The fertilised eggs are laid singly or in clumps in the sea. There may be several broods in a year.

Off the British coasts two species, *Sagitta setosa* and *S. elegans*, are found, the first characteristic of coastal waters, which are less saline and poorer in plankton, the other characteristic of more oceanic water. It is possible to distinguish between the two masses of water simply by identifying which species is present.

Eighty-five per cent of the described species of chaetognaths occur in the Indo-West Pacific region. *Sagitta enflata* is the most common species. Some species of *Spadella* are peculiar to Australian coasts.

Sagitta elegans is characteristic also of the northeastern and northwestern shores of North America, although other species of *Sagitta* are abundant.

A sample of plankton under the microscope consisting mainly of arrow worms. These small marine animals have achieved a great importance in oceanography. Species of arrow worms are so characteristic of different water masses that they are used as indicators of the movements of water in the sea therefore dispensing with lengthy chemical analyses.

POGONOPHORES
(Phylum Pogonophora)

The first specimens of Pogonophora, thread-like animals living in tubes, in the manner of some marine bristle worms, were dragged from the sea bed around Indonesia in the closing years of the past century and lay for years neglected on the shelves in museums. Their structure was so puzzling that no attempt was made to fit them into the scheme of classification. In 1934 another species was found at 3,500 metres in the Sea of Okhotsk and placed among the bristle worms. In 1937 the Swedish zoologist, E. Johansson, established for this species the class Pogonophora (beard-bearers). Subsequently abundant discoveries established the existence over a hundred species. These have since been elevated to a phylum, supposedly related to the echinoderms and the protochordates.

Typically, the body is long and thread-like, made up of three regions. The first region, the proboscis, is short and bears a crown of one to two hundred or more tentacles. The second region has a pair of body cavities which do not communicate with the outside world at any point. The hind region occupies most of the length of the body. It is segmented and equipped with toothed platelets called girdles that may serve to anchor the animal in the chitinous tube, secreted by glands in the hind region, in which it spends the whole of its post-larval life. The whole body may be thirty centimetres long and only two millimetres in diameter.

The animal is without a gut. It lacks special sense-organs. Its nervous system consists of a brain and a simple dorsal nerve-tract. There are longitudinal muscles in the body wall, a muscular heart and blood vessels containing red blood with haemoglobin. The sexes are separate, although externally male and female look alike. The tentacles, lined with minute feather-like pinnules richly supplied with capillaries which are almost certainly respiratory in function. Water, drawn in by ciliary action, enters a pore at the distal end of each tentacle and leaves by another pore at the inner end.

Feeding may be by absorption of substances dissolved in the sea or by the tentacles trapping small particles which are then digested and absorbed.

Pogonophores live mainly at depths of 2,000 to 10,000 metres and are widespread over the world. Following a brief period of embryonic development within the parent body they escape and become sedentary on the sea bed with the base of the tubes they construct around themselves buried in the mud. Like bristle worms they withdraw into their tubes when disturbed.

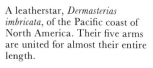

A leatherstar, *Dermasterias imbricata*, of the Pacific coast of North America. Their five arms are united for almost their entire length.

STARFISHES, SEA-URCHINS AND ALLIES (Phylum Echinodermata)

Although the free-swimming larvae are bilaterally symmetrical, adult echinoderms ('spiny-skinned' animals) are superficially radially symmetrical, most commonly pentagonal, with five rays or arms. All are marine or—rarely—live in brackish water. One characteristic feature is an external skeleton of calcareous rods and plates embedded just under the skin surface, often joined at their edges to form a shell and usually covered with tubercles or spines. In one class, the holothurians, the skeleton takes the form of scattered spicules. There is a spacious body cavity, or coelom, and a water vascular system of canals used in respiration or locomotion, or both. Perhaps the most distinc-

tive feature of the Echinodermata is the presence of branches or tube feet attached to the canals.

The (more than five thousand) species of the phylum living today fall into five classes: Asteroidea (starfishes), Ophiuroidea (brittle-stars), Echinoidea (sea-urchins), Holothuroidea (sea-cucumbers), and Crinoidea (sea-lilies). Although there are marked differences in appearance, the members of these classes have so much in common that to begin with a detailed description of a starfish, as a typical representative, and then to examine how the others differ from it, may save unnecessary repetition.

Starfishes (Class Asteroidea)

A typical starfish has five arms radiating from a central disc. It has no head. With its relatives it was originally classed with sea anemones and jelly-fishes as a member of the Radiata, distinguished from more familiar bilaterally symmetrical animals.

The smallest starfishes (genus *Marginaster*) are less than a centimetre in diameter when fully grown. The largest (genus *Marthasterias*) may be a metre across. Most are ten to thirteen centimetres across. The number of arms is usually five or multiples of five, but there are species in which the number varies from one individual to another. The circumboreal Sun-star (*Solaster papposus*) usually has twelve arms, but the number may vary from eight to fifteen. *Heliaster*, of the Pacific coast of North America, may have forty arms, and *Labidiaster*, from the Southern Ocean, may have up to fifty.

The arms may be short or long, cylindrical or flattened. In some species they are so short that the body is no more than a pentagonal disc. The body may be thin and flattened, or so thick that the centre of it rises almost in a cone. The surface may be smooth—either because it is covered with small plates fitting evenly together or because it is covered with a thick skin—or it may be very rough or spiny. Spininess is more a characteristic of deep-sea starfishes, but one shallow-water form, of the genus *Acanthaster*, that lives on coral reefs, is

covered with short spikes. Many starfishes are an uninteresting pale yellow, but some are a brilliant crimson or blue, while others may show more than one colour in pleasing patterns.

On the oral side or underside of a starfish are five grooves, each running down the centre of one of the arms. The point at which the grooves meet is a small opening, the mouth. Running the length of each arm on both sides of the groove are rows of very small, finger-like processes, known as tube feet. These are slowly but constantly moving. As some are withdrawn to the surface of the arm until they almost disappear, others are extended, and as they extend the free end expands into a flattened disc, and the whole of the tube foot is waved about in a slow, searching movement, except when the starfish is moving rapidly in one direction. The tube feet are the starfish's organs of locomotion, and are unlike anything found in any other group of animals than the echinoderms. If a finger is placed against them, each flattened disc becomes a sucker taking hold of the skin. If the starfish is turned on its back it recovers its normal position by turning the tip of one arm over so that the tube feet grip the rock or the surface of the sand. With this initial leverage the arm slowly turns more and more, enabling more tube feet to get a grip. With the other arms co-operating in a similar manner, the whole body continues the movement until in a slow somersault the starfish has regained its

Some starfishes reproduce by splitting in two and re-growing the lost half. In the course of this some end up with eight or more arms, due to over-generous regeneration, while others have only four arms instead of the normal five.

branch off. This whole system of tubes forms a simple but effective hydraulic apparatus.

When it is necessary to extend the tube feet a small ampulla at the top of each contracts and pumps water into the tube foot which is thereby extended. Muscular contraction shortens the tube foot and pulls the starfish forward. The tube feet are actuated by an intricate system of nerve-fibres, and each tube foot tends to work independently of the rest. This series of delicate tubes is capable of exerting a pressure of one kilogramme per 1·5 square centimetres, a force that is obviously unnecessary to enable so light an animal to move about, but, like all animals living in shallow seas, a starfish needs to find a way of combating the tremendous action of the waves, especially during gales, when the inshore seas are lashed to a fury. During such times crabs and others find shelter under rocks, or in their crevices, or bury themselves in the sand; the starfish clings to the rocks, flattening itself against the surface with all the power its tube feet can exert.

Respiration

On the surface of the starfish's body are two sets of structures best seen with a hand-lens. Between the plates or rods studding the surface are many small tufts of skin which are really irregular bladders. These are the gills. Through them oxygen is taken from the water to aerate the fluid filling the internal body cavities. Also scattered among the plates are areas covered with minute pincers, known as pedicellariae, each composed of two or three jaws, set on slender stalks and moving at their lower ends on ball and socket joints. Their function is to keep the surface clean so that the gills do not become overlaid with débris, or the surface coated with other animals. For at certain seasons the sea swarms with eggs or larvae of all kinds. Only a percentage of these survive but the larvae of sponges, hydroids, barnacles and other sessile organisms settle on the bottom after their brief free-swimming existence, metamorphose and fix themselves to any solid object on which they come to rest. In this way stones, rocks, seaweeds, and the shells of mussels, oysters and other shellfishes often bear an accumulation of fixed organisms on their surfaces. All stationary or slow-moving animals are liable to suffer from this rain of larvae. It is not uncommon to see a crab with several small barnacles on its back, as well as a growth of hydroid, a few tube-worms and other sessile animals. This has no harmful effect on a crab. In fact some crabs deliberately plant such things on their backs. But to a starfish depending for its respiration on the tufts of skin distributed over the middle of its upper surface, such an accretion would be a serious handicap, and the pedicellariae keep the surface clean by picking off and crushing any organisms that come within their reach.

Nutrition

Many starfishes are carnivorous, feeding mainly on shellfishes, and anyone who has tried to force open an oyster shell will know how the animal will resist. Having selected an oyster, a starfish wraps itself around the shell and fastens its tube feet securely on the two shell valves. Then it begins to

normal position. The tube feet at the end of one of the arms then release their hold and stretch out to their full extent to take hold of the surface once again. They begin to contract, exerting a force that draws the starfish an almost imperceptible distance over the sand. Slowly the movement quickens as, unseen, the tube feet all along the undersides of the arms co-operate and the starfish, gathering speed, moves away. Despite its shape, a starfish does not move like a wheel, and especially when going at its greatest rate moves in a straight line with one arm in advance.

A starfish moving with apparent purpose in one direction on a firm even surface may appear to be travelling fast, but experiments show the surprisingly slow speed of fifteen centimetres a minute. Even the pentagonal forms can climb vertical surfaces, such as pier piles, and there are also starfish that burrow, using their arms to shovel aside the sand, sinking into it quickly.

The back of a starfish is covered with calcareous plates or ossicles of irregular outline embedded in the skin. Some of the larger ones bear short spines, and whereas some appear to be scattered irregularly over the surface, others are arranged in a definite pattern, a few forming a ring round the outer edge of the central part of the body. From the ring a line of plates runs down to the tip of each arm. At one point on the central ring there is a plate that is larger than the rest. This is the madreporite or sieve plate, and through minute openings in its centre, hardly visible to the naked eye, water is drawn through a tube, the stone canal, into the ring canal and finally into the radial canals. It is from these that the rows of tube feet

pull. The oyster resists. The power in its muscles is approximately equal to that exerted by the starfish, but the staying power of the latter is greater and the oyster gives way and its shell opens. Starfishes require a shell gape of as little as 0·1 millimetres for the process to proceed. Holding the shell apart, the starfish extrudes its stomach and wraps it around the soft body of the oyster, at the same time sending out a stream of gastric juices that slowly digest it. Having neither teeth nor jaws, the starfish must wait until the oyster's body is reduced to a soft, semi-fluid mass before relaxing its hold and withdrawing its stomach.

A starfish has no obvious sense-organs but at the tip of each arm is one tube foot that cannot be retracted. This functions as a tactile organ. Just above it there is a small red spot, a light sensitive area called an optic cushion. But in its search for food the starfish relies less on touch or sight than on chemoreception, a combined sense of taste and smell. If, for example, meat juices are poured into a tank containing starfishes, they become very active. The searching movements initiated indicate how a starfish would behave in the presence of food.

Mention has been made of the struggle between a starfish and a bivalve mollusc, which the starfish wins by sheer endurance and the ability to insert its stomach through extremely thin fissures. It may take up to fifteen hours before the task is completed and experiments with dummy bivalves showed that a starfish may persist in its efforts to open a shell for two nights and a day. In bivalves such as certain mussels which have a permanent opening between the shells, near the hinge, a starfish is able to insert its stomach and start digesting the soft body inside. There is some evidence that the digestive juices may be toxic to the bivalve's heart, and may lower its powers of resistance.

Some starfishes swallow smaller molluscs whole, others ingest sea-urchins, hermit crabs, shrimps or crabs. *Acanthaster*, living on coral reefs, feeds on the coral polyps, leaving behind a bare patch of limy coral cups. This, the Crown-of-Thorns starfish has been reported as ravaging coral reefs in Australian waters.

All starfishes have some cilia on the surface of the body. In species whose surface is covered with cilia small organisms are trapped by the cilia and passed down grooves to the mouth. A few starfishes ingest mud and find their nourishment in whatever organic material it may contain.

Reproduction

In general reproduction is by eggs shed into the sea where they are fertilised. An interesting feature of this is that when one female starts to shed her eggs all other females in the area are stimulated to do likewise and the males are stimulated to shed their milt. This 'breeding crisis' can be touched off by a ripe starfish being accidentally crushed. The number of eggs released may be two-and-a-half million from each female, as in the case of *Asterias*, a common genus. The eggs develop into bipinnaria larvae, which may swim about for some three weeks before settling and metamorphosing.

Some starfishes produce a few heavily yolked eggs which do not have a planktonic larval life.

They are laid in sheltered places on the sea bed, where the female then covers them with her body. Or the eggs may be attached to the female's mouth. A few starfishes have brood-pouches on the upper surface of the disc in which the young remain for a period.

Reproduction can also be the result of fission and in many starfishes there is a high degree of regeneration. Usually this involves replacing a lost arm, but a starfish can lose all but one arm and, provided the central disc is attached to it, regenerate the other four. Species of *Linckia* can regenerate even from a piece of arm, and while the new disc and arm are re-growing it assumes what has been called the comet form, like a star with a long tail, the tail being the arm from which regeneration is proceeding. *Linckia columbiae*, of the Californian coast, will break off one of its arms, holding fast with this one arm while the rest of the body pulls away. The jettisoned arm then grows into a new starfish. This is so common that in any community of this species there are all sizes, from comets beginning regeneration to complete individuals.

A starfish that a week before had one arm bitten off by a painted prawn. The wound on the stump healed and the growth of a new arm began. Soon the starfish will have its complement of five arms.

The Common Starfish (*Asterias rubens*), of Europe, climbing the glass wall of an aquarium and ingesting the cast claw of a crab. This unusual view gives the opportunity to see the tube feet in action.

Brittle-stars and basket stars (Class Ophiuroidea)

Brittle-stars are found in all seas, on all types of sea bed and at all depths. Some have been brought up from depths of about six kilometres. A few occur in shallow waters, however, and if one of them should by chance be left stranded by the receding tide it will bury itself in the sand or, if disturbed, will immediately make for the edge of the water.

Brittle-stars do not reach the large sizes attained by the biggest starfishes. Very small individuals, less than five centimetres in diameter, may sometimes be found on rocky reefs exposed at low tide, but the underwater camera has revealed that in the shallow seas they occur in patches covering several square metres on the sea bed. In such a patch many individuals will be closely crowded together, often with their arms interlaced. The patches are isolated, with large areas of sea bed in between that are more or less devoid of brittle-stars. This had long been suspected from the way successive hauls with the trawl would bring up no brittle-stars, and then in one haul the trawl would be almost filled with them.

Form

The arms, which are solid, slender and cylindrical, do not merge gradually into the body, as in a starfish, but are clearly marked off from the central disc of the body. Turned on its back, it displays further differences. The grooves so conspicuously present in a starfish are covered in by a series of calcareous plates, through which protrude short tentacles, or modified tube feet. The absence of functional tube feet alters the whole behaviour. Without tube feet another method of locomotion is used, and a brittle-star moves with wriggling movements of the arms, which are flexible each arm being made up of a series of sections or joints so loosely held together that portions of an arm can be readily thrown off in order to escape from an enemy, a new arm being regenerated in due course. Instead of clinging to a rock surface during storms, a brittlestar creeps into crevices.

The change of habit resulting from the loss of the tube feet is carried a step further in the Euryalae, or Gorgon-headed starfishes, whose arms branch again and again until the end-branches often number tens of thousands, so that the creatures come to resemble a dense coil of snakes. Their habit is to climb up the stems of sea-pens and certain tree-corals and, while holding on with some of the branches of their arms, to spread the others out like a net in order to catch any small organisms floating by. To climb, the arms and their branches must move in a vertical direction, winding and coiling upwards or downwards. This is made possible by the ossicles supporting the arms.

Respiration

The heavily ossified arms preclude the use of breathing tufts like those of the starfishes, so on the lower surface at the junction of each arm with the central disc there is a pair of slits leading into a respiratory pouch. By the alternate expansion and contraction of the central disc, which is not solid as in a starfish but soft with either a bare skin or a thin layer of scales covering it, water is drawn into and pumped from the pouches.

Digestive system

Instead of pulling open shellfishes by sheer force, the brittle-star must feed on smaller prey, often (especially in the case of those living in deep waters) on the organic débris littering the sea-bottom. The mouth is provided with five 'jaws', often with serrated edges (the so-called 'teeth'), not to crush food but to strain out indigestible matter. And since the stomach is not protrusible a larger mouth is necessary.

There are other differences between brittle-stars and starfishes, although in general there is a close similarity in their organisation. First, whereas the starfish has extensions of the digestive system known as pyloric caeca into the arms, the stomach of a brittle-star is confined to the disc. Secondly, there is no anus in brittle-stars, the excreta being voided through the mouth. Thirdly, there are no large extensions of the body cavity into the arms.

Nutrition

Most brittle-stars feed on microscopic plankton (plant and animal) and on organic particles. As in many starfishes, there are cilia that set up currents towards the mouth. Food is trapped by mucus secreted by glands along the arms, the mucus being carried by the ciliary currents to the mouth. There are, however, some brittle-stars that feed on bristle-worms and small crustaceans caught with the tips of their arms, which are flexible.

Brittle-stars are so named because they so readily cast portions of their arms if disturbed. They can replace the lost portions. Snake-stars is another name for them and refers to the sinuous movements of the arms in locomotion.

Movement

Although the movements of the arms are lateral, so that a brittle-star squirms with serpentine movements of the arms, it will also move in a direct line. This may be done in one of two ways. By the first method one arm is leading, two are trailing, and the two in between carry out rowing movements. The second method is for four of the arms to carry out rowing movements in pairs, with the fifth arm trailing. High speeds are achieved by starfish standards: as much as two metres a minute, or ten times faster than a starfish. This is surprising in view of the way they are found crowded together.

Another surprise is that whereas the species of starfish tend to be localised or have a relatively circumscribed geographical range, there is one brittle-star (*Amphipholis squamata*) that is almost cosmopolitan. It is found between tide-marks, and is remarkable in being able to make its arms luminescent, and in brooding its young.

Regeneration and reproduction

Regeneration is a feature of brittle-star behaviour. As the name of this class of echinoderms implies, the arms are very fragile. This is particularly noticeable in a common shallow water species, *Ophiothrix fragilis*, which seems to fall to pieces almost as soon as it is touched. Regeneration is associated with asexual reproduction. Some species of brittle-stars commonly tear themselves in two, each half regenerating the part lost. It has been reported that a reef in the West Indies is populated with great numbers of a self-dividing brittle-star, *Ophiactis savignyi*, but all collected were males. The place had evidently been colonised by a single male specimen that had arrived there as a pelagic larva. It continuously divided, eventually forming the whole population.

Reproduction is similar to that in starfishes but the planktonic larva is known as an ophiopluteus. Many brittle-stars, however, are ovoviviparous, the eggs being hatched within the bursae—the pouches at the bases of the arms which serve for respiration. In an Antarctic species, *Ophionotus hexactis*, the eggs are hatched in the ovaries themselves, which are attached to the inner walls of the bursae. Of the number of eggs found in each ovary only one develops, and it uses the other eggs as food. The young brittle-star developing from this egg grows to a considerable size within the ovary, which becomes dilated into a thin-walled sac. The remarkable feature is that the young brittle-star, despite its size, eventually makes its way to the exterior through the slit-like opening of the bursa. There are other species in which the young burst the walls of the bursae to make their escape. The ruptured parts then regenerate. In several other species the young developing within the ovary are numerous and tightly packed together.

Sexual dimorphism

Although it is not possible to tell the sexes apart, there are species of brittle-star in which something very like coupling takes place, the male lying across the female with arms entwined. There are, moreover, two species in Indo-Pacific waters that go further. One of these is *Ophiodaphne materna*. The French scientist who first described the species, and gave it this name, noticed that his specimen carried a much smaller one across its mouth, and that the arms of the two were entwined. He assumed that the small individual was a baby brittle-star being carried around by the mother. Later it was established that the small individual was a male, and that eggs and sperms are shed in the usual way, but the parents continue in a constant embrace.

Sea-urchins, sand dollars and allies (Class Echinoidea)

Sea-urchins are most common in shallow waters, and in some places they can be found in large numbers on the shore. The vital organs are enclosed in a shell made up of rows of plates closely fitting together, forming a rigid hollow box which may be almost spherical, heart-shaped or flattened and discoidal. The surface is typically covered with bristling spines. The mouth is on the underside of the box and from it protrude five white teeth. These are only a part of an elaborate chewing mechanism called Aristotle's lantern because of its resemblance to old-fashioned oil lanterns. The greater part of this is inside the shell.

At first sight there appears little resemblance between a sea-urchin and a starfish, but both have tube feet and pedicellariae, and if the spines are removed from the shell—or test—of a sea-urchin, the same five-part radial pattern can be seen. In fact if one of the more bulky starfishes could have its arms further shortened, turned upward, fused and then coated with spines there would be little difference between it and a sea-urchin, except that

the calcareous plates in the skin of the sea-urchin form a more continuous coat.

A sea-urchin from the Mediterranean, its rounded, box-like body beset with spines. The spines vary in shape from species to species, from long and slender to short and stubby or even club-shaped.

193

The Sand Dollar of the American coasts has a flattened shell covered with very minute spines. Because of its lack of flesh and the considerable amount of calcareous matter in its shell few animals except starfishes feed on it.

The Common or Edible Sea-urchin (*Echinus esculentus*), of Europe, on the move with tube feet extended. The tube feet of sea-urchins can be extended well beyond the spines to take hold of the substratum and their subsequent contraction pulls the animal along.

Some sea-urchins are only six millimetres across, and even the largest, *Sperosoma giganteum*, of Japan, of which only one specimen has been found, is little over thirty centimetres across. The average size, however, is five to eight centimetres across.

Some sea-urchins either bury themselves in the sand or carve cavities in rock. The habit of burrowing into a rock is seen in several species living in situations where they are liable to be dislodged by violent wave-action. This is done by the abrading action of the spines, and a species of *Strongylocentrotus* living on the coast of California illustrates not only this but also climbing ability. This urchin, as was shown some years ago, climbs the steel pier-piles, which are about one centimetre thick. After twenty years there were holes in the steel where the urchins had rubbed it with their spines. This removed the anti-corrosive layer, exposing the steel to the action of sea-water; but although some of the wear was due to leaching by salt water, some of the further damage was undoubtedly caused by urchin spines rubbing into the metal.

Echinostrephus molaris, of the Indo-Pacific, burrows several centimetres into rock. It spends much of its time near the entrance to the burrow and drops into it when disturbed, wedging itself tightly inside with its spines so that it cannot be removed.

A few species, by burrowing when young and then enlarging the burrows when they are older and bigger, are imprisoned within their excavations, but are able to survive on food washed into the cavities.

The Heart-urchin (*Echinocardium cordatum*) of the coasts of Britain burrows in sand, and although the dead and empty heart-shaped shells are a common feature, especially on the south–west coasts, the live animal is seen only by digging it out of the sand. It lies buried up to twenty centimetres deep, with a vertical shaft to the water above for breathing purposes.

The Indo-Pacific species is noted for its needle-sharp spines with a so-called poison bag at the tip. Penetration of the skin by these spines is a very painful experience.

Another use to which the spines are put (in addition to this and protection from enemies) is for resuming the normal position. A sea-urchin thrown on to its back pushes into the sand with some of its spines, throwing those on the other side over so as to displace the centre of gravity, and then it rolls over into the normal position. In the Clypeastroidea or cake-urchins, the spines are furnished with vibratile hairs which cause a continuous flow of water over the respiratory tube feet.

The pedicellariae are used not only for keeping the shell clean but, in some species, for seizing small pieces of seaweed and holding them over the shell for camouflage. Their other, probably most important, function is as organs of defence, and some are provided with poison glands.

Some species of sea-urchin appear to be without spines because these are so small. The test is flattened and may even be flexible. A good example of a flattened form is the Sand Dollar (*Dendraster excentricus*) of the Pacific coast of North America, and its habits show that spines would be an encumbrance. When the tide is in the Sand Dollar assumes a vertical position, half-buried in the sand, but oriented so that it is cross-wise to the flow of the water. When exposed at low tide it drops flat and quickly covers itself with sand. Moreover, when in the normal feeding position it will quickly bury itself at the approach of a starfish that feeds on it. It reappears at the surface about half-an-hour after the starfish has passed.

In some sea-urchins the spines are numerous and short, looking almost like a coat of short fur, as in the heart-urchins (genus *Echinocardium*) or they may be long, slender and numerous, as in the genus *Diadema*, or long, stout and few, as in the genus *Histocidaris*, or they may be thickened, some of them being as thick as pencils. These urchins are commonly called slate-pencil urchins. Many sea-urchins, those with the very thick spines especially, use them as legs in walking. The speed attained is not great, but it is strange to see the spines being moved like stilts, carrying the sea-urchin along, with the tube feet reaching out as if investigating the surroundings as the animal progresses.

Indeed this is what is happening, because the tactile sense must be the main means by which a sea-urchin communicates with its environment, although there must also be some chemical sense (a combined taste and smell), and some species show a sensitivity to light. This we see in the genus *Diadema*, the spines of which move in relation to changes in the intensity of light. When a shadow falls across *Diadema antillarum*, a shallow-water species in West Indian waters, its spines move to point in the direction of whatever has caused the shadow. The spines are poisonous, and this behaviour can be seen as a direct use of the spines as a means of defence.

Species of *Diadema* are highly sensitive to changes in the intensity of light, and young individuals actually change colour from day to night. *D. antillarum* also seeks shady places when the sun is strong at midday, while *Paracentrotus lividus*, living on rocky shores in the Mediterranean, reverses the process and in the daytime moves into a few centimetres of water, into the glare of the sun, but often it shades itself with pieces of seaweed held by the tube feet on the upper parts of the shell.

Nutrition

The food is both animal and vegetable matter, which is masticated by the teeth already mentioned, but in the cake-urchins the teeth are used as shovels to scoop up sand, their food being the decaying matter mixed with sand.

Movement

Neither the rounded nor the flattened shape of sea-urchins seems promising from the point of view of animal locomotion. Yet sea-urchins can move as rapidly as starfishes and can climb vertical surfaces just as well. In the rounded sea-urchins the tube feet on the lower surface can readily reach the ground, but those higher up on the shell can be enormously extended to reach out either to the ground or to nearby solid objects to take hold by their suckers. So the sea-urchin moves along by pulling with its tube feet, like so many ropes, and to some extent by levering with its spines.

The climbing abilities of some sea-urchins can readily be seen when they are in sea-water aquaria. Even a bulky animal like the edible Mediterranean urchin, *Echinus esculentus*, which is more or less spherical and may be ten to thirteen centimetres in diameter, can climb readily up the glass wall of the aquarium using only its tube feet. The green sea-urchin of the New England coast has similar ability. The *Colobocentrotus*, of tropical seas, will cling successfully to surf-battered rocks by its tube feet.

Sometimes the spines are used in conjunction with the tube feet, and even the teeth may occasionally be brought into play in locomotion.

Reproduction

Reproduction is usually by the shedding of eggs and sperms into the water, the resulting larva being known as echinopluteus. The rigid shell of the sea-urchin gives little opportunity for the formation of brood-pouches, yet there are species in which the young are not free-swimming but are brooded in clusters around the parental mouth, or in a brood-pouch formed by spines, usually spines modified in shape, arching over to form a sort of basket containing small but fully formed sea-urchins.

A 'breeding epidemic' of sea-urchins similar to that noted in the starfishes has been observed. Indeed it can happen more frequently, since the accidental injury can more readily occur, as when a ripe sea-urchin is squashed and its ova or sperms are shed into the water. One view explaining this is that the stimulus which sets off the neighbouring individuals to breed is a hormone liberated into the water with the germ-cells from the sea-urchins.

Damaged sea-urchins show less tendency to regeneration than starfishes. They will grow again lost spines, pedicellariae and tube feet, and have even been known, under adverse conditions, to shed all their spines and later to grow a new set. Otherwise regeneration seems to be restricted to repairing holes in the shell.

A common sea-urchin on the Great Barrier Reef, *Echinometra mathaei* is frequently found in spherical hollows in the rock in which the animal just fits. The rocks may be completely honeycombed with these holes, scraped out by the sea-urchins using their spines.

The sea-urchin, *Diadema* sp., is extremely sensitive to light and moves its spines towards a shadow passing over it. In this way it presents its armature effectively to an enemy.

A sea-cucumber from the Red Sea. Sea-cucumbers appear sufficiently unlike starfishes and sea-urchins that their relationship to them is not obvious, yet these elongated soft-bodied marine animals have basically the same structure.

Sea-cucumbers (Class Holothuroidea)

The sea-cucumbers show yet another variation in the range of form exhibited by the Echinodermata. As the name suggests they are elongated, and have a skeleton of microscopic spicules embedded in the skin. These spicules may be simple or branched rods, perforated plates, wheels, anchors or variants on these shapes. Each species possesses spicules of two types. Those in the deeper layers of the body wall are flattened, while those nearer the surface are thicker, more elongate, and project through the skin, making it rough. The latter assist in locomotion. In one group, the Psolids, the spicules are modified into large overlapping scales. The mouth is at one end of the body and is surrounded by tube feet that are much enlarged and converted into definite feelers. Nevertheless, even in sea-cucumbers the radial pattern is evident in five longitudinal double rows of tube feet.

In most species the three rows of tube feet on the lower surface of the body are modified for locomotion. A few species are without tube feet, however, and these move by contraction of the muscles. In addition they grip when necessary with the ring of tentacles around the mouth.

Nutrition

Food consists either of decaying matter mixed with sand—in which case the feelers round the mouth are short and stout to shovel the sand into the mouth—or of small floating organisms, when the feelers are long and branched and covered with slime in which the prey becomes entangled.

The typical holothurian has an elongated body which is slightly flattened. The tube feet on the dorsal side are usually simplified, fewer in number and smaller, and those on the ventral side are correspondingly more numerous and larger, and modified for a more strictly locomotory function. Those in which all the tube feet are small or absent altogether are usually burrowers.

Extreme modifications from the typical form occur, especially in deep-sea holothurians. The body may be slug-like, with or without a tail, or ornamented with lobes and finger-like processes. The species of *Pelagothuria* have a central body with a ring of long tentacles around the mouth, and are probably wholly pelagic. *Scotoplanes globosa*, a deep-sea holothurian, has a rounded oval body with a ring of short tentacles around the mouth, a dozen or so finger-like processes on the ventral surface and four long finger-like processes on the dorsal surface. Holothurians of similar shapes, which depart radically from the typical, are a conspicuous feature of the bottom fauna at great depths of the ocean.

Some years ago it was found that a number of holothurians contain a poison in their body walls, known as holothurin, which is poisonous to fishes. The poison seems to have no effect on human beings, however, whether taken in when fishes are eaten that have fed on holothurians, or directly by eating holothurians known as trepang.

Most sea-cucumbers are dull in colour, monochrome, with grey, brown, purple and black predominating, though a few show simple colour patterns. Burrowing species tend to be pink and violet, and a few sea-cucumbers are red or orange.

Regeneration

The holothurians have even greater powers of regeneration than starfishes. If irritated they eject their viscera through the anus as a protective device and grow a new set in a few weeks. A few species constrict themselves midway along the body, then by twisting the two halves of the body and pulling antagonistically two fragments, sometimes more, are formed, each of which is capable of growing into a complete individual by regenerating the lost parts. This seems not so much a process of asexual reproduction as a response to adverse conditions.

Regenerative processes are involved in active defence, following ejection of all the viscera. When molested, *Holothuria forskali* (known as the Cottonspinner) bends the hind part of the body round in

The sea-cucumber, *Pentacta tuberculosa*, from three metres depth, off the coast of Western Australia, creeping over a rock with its slender, branching tentacles extended to catch plankton as with a drag-net.

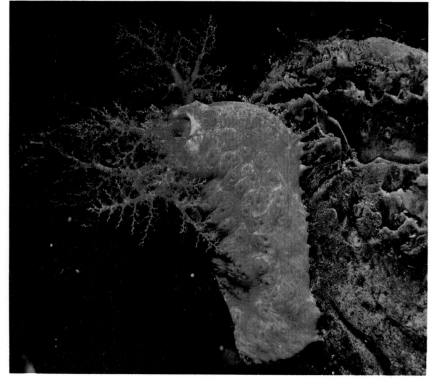

196

the direction of the threat and ejects white threads of the respiratory system, known as the Cuvierian tubules, through the anus. In the water the threads swell and form a sticky mass, which may entangle the attacker. These tubules are later regenerated.

Reproduction

Reproduction is mainly by the method, usual in other echinoderms, of shedding ova and sperms into the sea. The free-swimming larva is known as an auricularia. There are species, however, that show some degree of parental care. In some species the fertilised eggs find their way into individual pockets in the parental skin, presumably pushed in there by the tentacles or the tube feet of the mother. In other species there are larger pouches capable of accommodating several eggs and also the embryos developing from them. A few species retain the eggs in the body cavity, but in these instances the manner in which fertilisation is effected is so far undiscovered.

Sea-lilies and feather-stars (Class Crinoidea)

A sea-lily differs from the other classes of echinoderm so far discussed in having its mouth on its upper surface. It consists of a stalk of pentagonal joints with whorls of appendages (called cirri) at intervals, surmounted by an inverted cup strengthened on its outer side by regularly arranged plates. From the sides of the cup spring five arms, which are directed upwards and which may branch once or many times, each branch bearing a number of side-branches, or pinnules. The arms usually number ten or so but may be as many as one hundred or as few as five. Down the centre of each pinnule and each branch runs a central groove lined with vibratile cilia. Food particles dropping from above are caught in these grooves and passed on to the mouth by the action of the cilia. The tube feet also lie in the grooves but their function is solely respiratory. Most sea-lilies are sessile, the base of the stalk ending in a flattened plate for attachment to a rock, or in a rooting process embedded in mud. The cirri are capable of catching hold of solid objects for support, and if the stalk breaks the cirri are capable of carrying the rest of the body to a new resting place. Sea-lilies are of great antiquity and many fossils have been found. Today they are found in great abundance on the sea floor from a few metres to about 4,000 metres. Unfortunately virtually nothing is known of large aspects of their biology.

In the shallow offshore waters their place is taken by an unstalked relative, the feather-star. This is mobile, and while clinging to a solid support with a circlet of cirri on the undersurface of the cup, is able to pull itself along by its arms. Few of the feather-stars move about, though some can swim in short bursts by flapping their arms. The Rosy Feather-star (Antedon bifida) is sometimes found between tide-marks on the coasts of Britain, but its usual habitat is on the muddy patches just offshore, where it is sometimes found in abundance. Orange or red in colour, it has ten arms, each feathered with many side branches, and it rests on twenty-five short stalks, or cirri, on the underside of the central disc. It moves about by gently undulating movements of the cirri. Its food consists of minute particles caught in the currents created by cilia lining the arms and passed down to the mouth.

The smallest feather-star is only 2·5 centimetres across, the largest (Heliometra glacialis), living in the Okhotsk Sea, is ninety centimetres across. Feather-stars are found at all depths down to 1,800 metres, and the greatest concentration of species is in the seas between New Guinea and Borneo northeastwards to the Philippines. The circumboral species, Antedon dentata, living at depths below thirty metres, extends into the western Atlantic as far south as New York.

Perhaps the greatest interest lies in the life-history of the feather-stars. Their close resemblance to the sea-lilies is obvious, and in the early stages of their post-larval life they are stalked. This is only a transitory phase, but it is enough to suggest that they are descended from stalked ancestors, and therefore must be regarded as specialised sea-lilies. The other important feature of the development is that the free-swimming larva looks very like one of the salps—to be discussed later—of the genus Doliolum. As a consequence it is called a doliolaria. It is irregularly barrel-shaped, with a tuft of cilia at one end and four bands of cilia encircling the body, which look superficially like the muscle-bands of the species of Doliolum. After swimming about for two to three days the doliolaria settles on the bottom, or on seaweed, and begins to elongate. Eventually a stalked animal, known as a pentacrinoid or miniature sea-lily, is formed.

A feather-star on the hydrocoralline (Millepora). Feather-stars could be described as being like starfish turned upside-down, with ten feathery arms that are waved in the water to catch small particles of edible material. By flexing and extending these arms they can swim.

CHORDATES
(Phylum Chordata)

The chordates form a large and highly diverse animal group which comprises vertebrates or animals with backbones (subphylum Vertebrata) as well as three subphyla of animals which lack vertebrae but which resemble vertebrates in certain important respects. These three subphyla (Hemichordata, Tunicata and Cephalochordata) are often referred to collectively as protochordates or lower chordates, in contrast to the vertebrates or higher chordates. At some stage in their life-history both higher and lower forms possess gills, a dorsal nerve cord and a supporting skeletal rod known as the notochord.

The protochordates are primitive marine creatures with a mixture of invertebrate and vertebrate characteristics and they indicate the successive stages by which vertebrate animals may have evolved from invertebrate stock.

In the higher chordates the notochord is a stout but flexible rod of tissue lying above the alimentary canal and around it the backbone is laid down. In the developing embryo a longitudinal groove in the ectoderm sinks inwards above the notochord, closing to form a tube as it becomes detached from the ectoderm. This forms the main nerve trunk, which is hollow, unlike the main nerve trunk of higher invertebrates, which is solid and situated ventrally.

Although gills of some form are the means of respiration in so many aquatic animals, chordates are unique in having gill slits opening from the sides of the pharynx. These are such a feature of chordate anatomy that even in terrestrial vertebrates they appear as transitory embryonic structures.

Although there are numerous species in the groups, very few of them are familiar enough to have earned common names. Indeed, what serves as the common name for most of the groups is really only a descriptive phrase based on the scientific names. The genera (groups of related species) are more familiar even to the zoologists than are any of the component species. Only the best-known or most noteworthy groups could even be mentioned on the following pages. The lure of the unknown still beckons in zoological oceanography.

HEMICHORDATES
(Subphylum Hemichordata)

This subphylum consists of two classes of marine animals: Enteropneusta and Pterobranchia, most of which feed on minute organic particles. The Enteropneusta sift them from the mud they swallow, or trap them in a current of mucus which flows over their body surface towards the mouth, where it is ingested. The Pterobranchia trap particles and small plankton with their tentacles, passing them to the mouth in a mucus stream directed by the cilia clothing the tentacles.

Larval hemichordates also have significant features. The sexes are separate, ova and sperms are shed into the water and the fertilised egg develops into a banded tornaria larva, similar to that of the echinoderms. In due course the larva settles and metamorphoses. Development too is remarkably like that of echinoderms. Consequently the similarity of their larvae and the details of their development has focused attention on a possible close relationship between echinoderms and protochordates, which suggests a common ancestry for both these and vertebrates. At first this link with the echinoderms amounted to no more than a tentative suggestion, but then came the discovery that all three contain a phosphagen in the muscle, which includes a compound of creatin, whereas the phosphagen or phosphate of all other invertebrates is a compound of arginin (an amino acid).

Acorn worms (Class Enteropneusta)

These have a worm-shaped body and an acorn-shaped proboscis. They range from five to fifty centimetres in length. They occur in all seas and live in mud or sand from hightide mark down to great depths of the ocean. Some make complicated burrows. Others live in tubes made of grains of mud or sand glued together with mucus, whilst others move freely on the deep-sea bed. Several genera are recognised: *Protoglossus, Saccoglossus, Harrimania, Glossobalanus, Balanoglossus, Ptychodera, Schizocardium* and *Glandiceps*.

The elongated oval (acorn-shaped) proboscis is followed by a fleshy collar that overlaps the base of the proboscis. The rear margin of the collar also overlaps the front end of the long worm-like trunk. The trunk bears a groove, into which the numerous gill slits open. Acorn worms burrow with the proboscis, which is made turgid by water drawn in by ciliary action through pores on its surface. To deflate the proboscis the water is expelled by contraction of the muscular walls.

The acorn worm is one of several groups of animals that collectively form the lower chordates and afford a link between the invertebrates and the vertebrates. Until their discovery a wide gulf separated these two major groupings of the animal kingdom, and it was difficult to see how the vertebrates had evolved from invertebrate ancestors. The fundamental difference between the two groups is that in the invertebrates the main blood vessels are dorsal to the gut and the main nerve cord is ventral to it. In vertebrates this is reversed.

In acorn worms the main part of the central nervous system arises in the ectoderm of the larva, but does not then become separated from it, as in the vertebrates. Yet it shows how the typical nerve cord of vertebrates may well have developed.

The coelom of the acorn worm arises as pouches of the cavity known as the archenteron, as it does in vertebrates, and forms three segments: in the proboscis there is a single coelomic cavity which communicates with the exterior by two ducts, the second coelom, in the collar region, consists of two cavities, and the third, in the trunk, is also paired and contains the reproductive organs. The coelom of acorn worms, like their nervous system, appears to foreshadow the development of parts which are carried to a more advanced stage in vertebrates.

There is no notochord as such in acorn worms but there is an outgrowth from the gut which lies in the collar and helps to support it, and this was interpreted as the beginnings of a notochord. It is now thought to be a diverticulum of the gut and to be in no sense a notochord.

Pterobranchids (Class Pterobranchia)

This includes a number of marine animals of small size which have in common with the acorn worms many of the features so far discussed. They differ, however, in some details of anatomy and behaviour: they have two tentacled arms, arising from the region of the body corresponding to the collar region of an acorn worm. They live in tubes of their own secretion (e.g. *Rhabdopleura*); some species are colonial new individuals budding and sharing a common chitinous investment.

TUNICATES (Subphylum Urochordata)

Tunicates, also known as urochordates, comprise two thousand species of marine chordate animals and are divided into three classes: the sedentary Ascidiacea or sea-squirts, the pelagic Thaliacea and the Larvacea. As the name would suggest all have a tunic or test. They feed by ciliary currents, have gill slits, a reduced nervous system, but no notochord, except in the Larvacea.

These chordates have no coelom or body cavity, but in the adult form there is a dorsal atrium. The tunic or test is generally composed of a substance called tunicin, related to cellulose and therefore somewhat unusual in animals. In the Larvacea, however, the test is not composed of tunicin. This will be described later. In fact, there is a growing tendency to regard Larvacea as examples of neoteny, where a larval stage of development persists, as in certain crustaceans and amphibians.

A group of sea-squirts on a coral reef off Heron Island. They are bags of jelly with two openings, water being drawn in through one and driven out through the other. The water passes across a branchial basket, clearly seen in several of these individuals, which extracts oxygen and traps food particles.

Class Ascidiacea

A sea-squirt is a sedentary animal clothed in a tunic or test composed of a matrix of tunicin—a substance chemically related to cellulose—in which are scattered cells as well as nerves and blood vessels, the whole reinforced in some species by calcareous or organic spicules. The general form of the animal, when fully expanded, is of a vase with a vertical tube, with a terminal mouth or branchial opening at its apex, and a lateral tube a little way down from the mouth, its opening being called the atrial opening. Water is drawn in at the branchial opening, circulates over the large gill basket inside and is ejected through the atrial opening. During this circuit oxygen and food particles are taken from the water and waste products are carried away with the exhalant current. When at rest the sea-squirt withdraws these siphons; and shore-living forms, at rest when the tide is out, will further contract when touched, squirting out a long thin jet of water.

The gill basket or branchial chamber is part of the pharynx. This begins with a small tube, the inner part of which is guarded by a ring of tentacles that prevents the entry of large objects. Beyond this the pharynx enlarges and its walls are pierced by numerous gill slits lined with cilia, whose action sets up the current circulating through the pharynx and from there through the rest of the alimentary canal and out again to the exterior. On the floor of the branchial chamber is an organ known as the endostyle, secreting mucus in which food particles are trapped. Cilia lining the endostyle pass the mucus upwards and over to the dorsal midline of the pharynx, where it is rolled into a mucus rope by a row of tentacles, or a ciliated membrane in some species, the rope being passed backwards to the oesophagus, thence to the stomach and the intestine. Faecal pellets are passed from the anus to the atrial opening to be discharged.

One of the special features of urochordates is that the tubular heart has pacemakers at each end, which periodically reverse the flow of the blood. Otherwise there are few blood vessels, the circulatory system being mainly made up of haemocoelic cavities. There are no capillaries.

Although the viscera are relatively simple, apart from the branchial chamber, there are a few features which seem to be the homologues of organs found in vertebrates. The endostyle, for example, is believed to be the forerunner of the thyroid gland. Then there is a neural gland, containing gonadotropic substances believed to correspond to the vertebrate pituitary. It is situated near the brain, or dorsal ganglion, which sends out nerves to various parts of the body.

Urochordates are mainly hermaphrodite and fertilisation usually takes place in the sea, some species showing a marked self-sterility. Some species are oviparous, others viviparous, but in most species, e.g. the genus *Clavelina*, there is a

Tubular sea-squirts, *Ciona intestinalis*, of European seas, showing the inhalant and exhalant syphons for dealing with a current of water. Sea-squirts are common fouling organisms on buoys, pier-piles and ships' bottoms.

Sea-squirts are also known as tunicates because the body is bounded by an obvious coat or tunic. This may be cartilaginous and translucent, as in *Ciona* (above) or thick and seemingly leathery as in *Halocynthia papillosa*, shown here, of European seas.

tadpole-like larva with a well-developed notochord in the muscular tail. This is lost at metamorphosis. The larva also has a dorsal nerve cord but there is differentiation to produce something that could pass as a brain. The tubular nerve cord contains a sense-organ, or eye-spot. In its life-history the tunicate shows a degenerate evolution, the larva showing much more the features that might have led on to the evolution of the vertebrates.

Adult sea-squirts may be sessile or stalked, the stalked forms being more characteristic of the deep-seas, where the lower part of their stalks are embedded in mud or ooze. Sea-squirts are mainly solitary (*Ciona*), but there are colonial forms (*Botryllus, Amaroucium*) in which numerous small individuals are invested by a common tunic. In some species groups of individuals, while not forming a true colony, develop a common stolon or root stalk upon which new individuals are budded as, for example, in *Clavelina*.

One of the most attractive of the many unobtrusive organisms encrusting rocks around the coasts of Europe is the Golden-stars Sea-squirt (*Botryllus schlosseri*). This consists of jelly-like, shapeless masses in which groups of individual sea-squirts are set, each group forming a golden star the constituent members of which share a common exhalant opening.

Class Thaliacea

These are pelagic, and although very numerous do not show as high a total of species as the Ascidiacea. The Thaliacea are similar to the sea-squirts in structure except that the mouth and the atrial opening are at opposite ends of the body and the animals swim and feed by means of conspicuous muscle bands which pump water through the digestive canal. By the contraction and relaxation of these bands the barrel-like body pulsates as water is drawn in at the front and forcibly ejected at the rear. Most of them are translucent, some are luminescent, and since they tend to occur in large shoals they are one of the commoner causes of phosphorescence on the sea's surface at night. There are three orders in the class Thaliacea: Pyrosomida, Doliolida and Salpida.

Although the body of the Thaliacea is relatively simple in construction it has a complex method of asexual reproduction. In one of the best-known forms, *Doliolum*, buds appear on the underside of the body and creep up the sides of the barrel in a constant procession. They make their way to a small fin at the rear of the parent body, and thence to a long tail that is continually growing longer, making room for the never-ending stream of buds. These settle down in three rows along the tail, one on top and one each side. Each bud in the top row grows a stalk, and other buds settle on the stalks. Concurrently, the buds on the side rows take on the task of feeding the whole colony while the original parent body becomes a producer of new buds.

A change now takes place in which the top buds break away and each starts another budding process. The buds that settled on their stalks increase in number, but these now break away, become sexually mature, produce ova and sperms, fertilised eggs and, finally, larvae, which are tadpole-like initially but subsequently metamorphose into the barrel-shaped *Doliolum*. There is, therefore, an alternation of generations, the asexual budding individuals giving rise to sexual individuals whose larvae develop into asexual forms.

A planktonic salp showing the transparent barrel-like body with muscle bands arranged like hoops. Pulsations by the hoops draw water in at the mouth and drive it out at the rear, propelling the animal through the water.

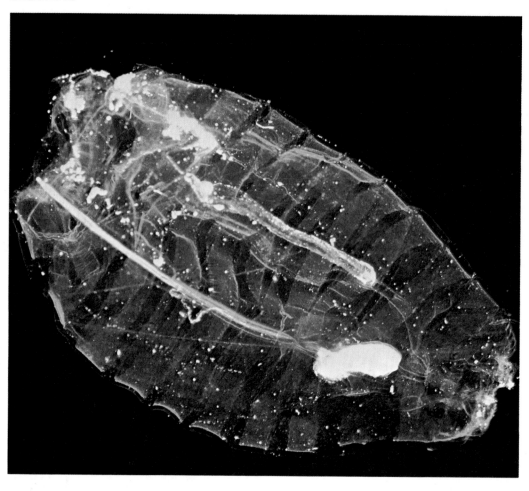

Class Larvacea

In some respects the Larvacea resemble the larvae of *Doliolum*, but they are pelagic larvae that become sexually mature without losing the tail or the notochord. There is, however, a change in that a tunic is formed, but not of tunicin. This tunic constitutes an elaborate apparatus for concentrating nanoplankton for food. Movements of the animal's tail cause a current of water to flow through the tunic, where the nanoplankton is filtered from it. The tunic does not adhere to the animal, however, and from time to time the animal may abandon it and secrete a new one elsewhere.

LANCELET (Subphylum Cephalochordata)

The lancelet, formerly known as species in the genus *Amphioxus*, is now, through adherence to the strict rules of scientific nomenclature, named *Branchiostoma*. There are some two dozen species, widely distributed over the world, but tending to be localised. Small, fish-like, usually about five to eight centimetres long, the lancelet is found close inshore on sandy beaches. The largest of all, fifteen centimetres long, is found in shallow waters around the coast of Amoy in southern China.

The *Branchiostoma* burrow into sand head first by a wriggling action of the body, then when they have buried themselves they turn about and come to rest with only the head end, including the mouth, exposed above the surface. At night and during the breeding season they come out of the sand and swim about, returning to the resting place at dawn. There they feed on organic particles and small plankton drawn into the mouth on an inhalant current.

The body is laterally compressed and pointed at each end. There is no distinct head but there is a low fin running down the back, becoming leaf-shaped around the tail and continuing along the under-surface to about one-third of the length of the body. The mouth is a short way back from the front end of the body and is sunk in a funnel-shaped cavity, the margin of the funnel being fringed with tentacle-like processes called cirri. The lower surface of the body, behind the mouth, bears two metapleural folds extending back to the atriopore, which is two-thirds of the way back, and just in front of where the ventral fin ends, giving a definite tail.

A marked feature of the surface of the body are the myotomes or muscle segments, which are visible externally. They are V-shaped, with the apex of the V directed forwards. Their number ranges from fifty-eight to sixty-nine, according to the species. The myomeres on the two sides of the body alternate with each other.

Internally the lancelets have several well-marked features supporting their identity with the primitive vertebrate stock. They also show features so obviously similar to those seen in such animals as the sea-squirts that they may well be the evolutionary link between the vertebrates and invertebrates.

The alimentary canal in the lancelets extends in a more or less straight line through the body, from the mouth in front to the anus lying near the front ventral edge of the tail fin. Immediately above it and extending from one end to the other is a rigid rod formed of vacuolated cells filled with fluid which renders the whole rod turgid. This is the notochord, and it is clearly a skeletal rod occupying the same relative position as the backbone in vertebrates. It projects beyond the myotomes.

Lying above the notochord and extending to almost the same length is a main nerve cord, and at its centre is a narrow canal, the neurocoele. From the main nerve cord, or spinal cord, sensory nerves run to the skin and motor nerves go out to the myomeres.

In the development of the embryo the notochord arises from the endoderm and the spinal cord sinks in from the ectoderm, as in true vertebrates.

The system of blood vessels includes a main ventral vessel, with arteries going to the gills, branching into capillaries which re-form into veins that leave the gills and join up to form a dorsal aorta. Although there is no heart (the blood is forced through the circulatory system by peristaltic or wave-like contractions of the vessels themselves) the disposition of the circulatory system bears very close comparison with that of fishes.

By way of contrast feeding, respiration and excretion are closely similar to those found in hemichordates and urochordates, and the excretory system especially recalls that of some of the higher invertebrates.

In feeding, the cilia lining the oral funnel create an inhalant current. Water is drawn into the mouth through a membraneous velum bearing twelve short tentacles that hold back larger particles in the water but allow small organic particles through. The current then passes into a large branchial chamber formed by the pharynx, closely comparable to that of urochordates. This is barrel-shaped and its walls bear up to ninety gill slits. Oxygen is taken from the water for breathing, and the particles are caught and passed by cilia lining the gill slits to a groove in the floor of the branchial chamber known as the endostyle. This groove is

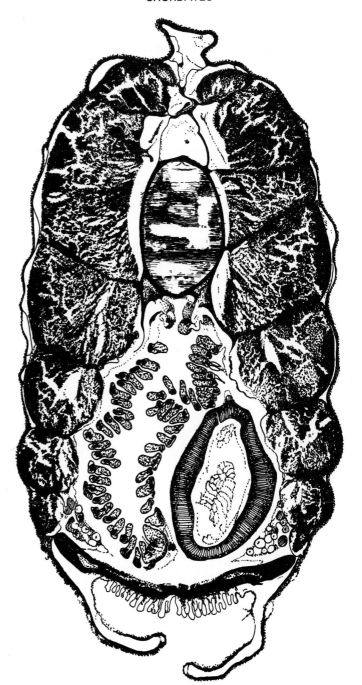

lined with cilia and with glands secreting a mucus. The particles are trapped on the mucus and with it are carried forward by ciliary action to the front end of the endostyle. There the mucus travels along two ciliated grooves up the sides of the pharynx to another groove on the dorsal surface of the pharynx, to be passed backwards and into a straight intestine to be digested. The only other organ in the alimentary canal is a liver, and there is a blind caecum leading off from the intestine. Excretion is by ninety pairs of nephridia, very like those found in annelid worms and not usual in chordates.

In lancelets the sexes are separate. The reproductive organs lie beneath the front part of the intestine, and eggs or sperms are passed out through the atriopore. Fertilisation takes place in the sand where the adults live, on warm days in late spring or early summer.

The Lancelet (*Branchiostoma* sp.), seen here in cross-section, is the most fish-like of the chordates. It spends most of its life buried in the sand with only the head protruding. It has no skull nor a proper heart. The spinal cord is well developed, however, and can be seen in the cross-section situated centrally with the main nerve cord above it. The muscles which surround it are also fish-like, particularly when seen from the side, where they are visible externally and appear as V-shaped segments.

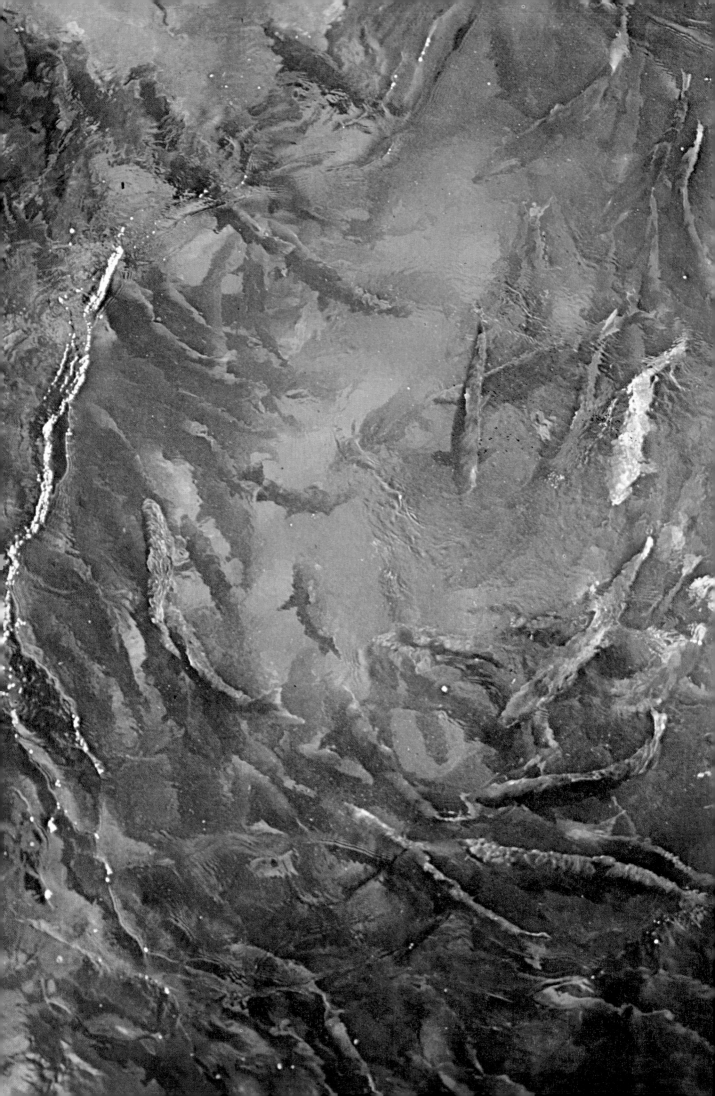

VERTEBRATES
(Subphylum Vertebrata)

Although it is customary to accept the Hemichordata, Tunicata and Cephalochordata as successfully bridging the gap between invertebrates and vertebrates, in fact they do no more than indicate some of the possible features of early vertebrate evolution, as there is still a gulf between them and even the most primitive of modern backboned animals which the fossil evidence does little to bridge. The oldest remains of undoubted vertebrate animals consist of fragments of the shields of the fish-like ostracoderms found in Ordovician sandstones in the United States. These are usually described as 'bony'. The only fossil clue to anything earlier than this is contained in an impression on a piece of Silurian shale from Scotland that has been named *Jamoytius*. It shows a body similar to, but somewhat larger than, that of *Amphioxus*, and is more markedly barrel-shaped in the middle, with a lateral horizontal fin running along each flank. Nothing is known of the internal structure and it is assumed that the skeleton was wholly of cartilage and that the first vertebrates had skeletons of the same material. This, together with the evidence obtained from the protochordates living today, suggests that the vertebrates arose from the same stock as the echinoderms, possibly in pre-Cambrian times, and that their further evolution is sketched in from what can be gleaned in studies of acorn worms, salps, *Amphioxus* and *Jamoytius*. All the present-day vertebrates agree in their fundamental characters, and the evolution from fishes to amphibians, to reptiles and then to birds and mammals is easy to trace, and such gaps as exist between these various groups can be reasonably and satisfactorily bridged.

Even the most lowly of the true vertebrates are far more advanced and more complicated in structure than anything found in the protochordates. The notochord is a prominent feature of the early embryo, but this is later replaced by a cartilaginous skeleton, and in most vertebrates the cartilage is later replaced largely by bone. This is an innovation of prime importance in evolutionary terms. Cartilage and, more particularly, bone represent a malleable material capable of extensive modification to give the shapes and parts needed for an elaborate skeletal framework affording rigidity with flexibility. The flexibility of the notochord of *Amphioxus* is shown by the animal's wriggling into sand, but these movements are limited as are its swimming abilities. When the notochord is replaced by cartilage and bone, divided into vertebrae, not only is more play allowed to the muscle segments but strength in the axial rod is not lost while the freedom of movement in the body is increased.

Further developments are associated mainly with this freedom of movement and the increased potential for locomotion it brings. Limb girdles are possible, a pectoral girdle and a pelvic girdle, to support two pairs of limbs with their independent skeletons. This sequence is illustrated by the Agnatha (lampreys and hagfishes) with an axial skeleton that is little better than a reinforced notochord; the cartilaginous fishes (sharks and rays) with an axial rod (backbone) of cartilage and limb girdles of cartilage with pectoral and pelvic fins supported by cartilaginous units; bony fishes with a skeleton similar to that of cartilaginous fishes but of bone, the limbs being used for swimming but in some species already serving for walking over the sea bed or on land; and the bony skeletons of all the higher vertebrates with their toed limbs, endlessly modified for walking, running, jumping, climbing, flying, swimming and grasping.

Concurrently with these progressions the front part of the axial rod pursues its independent evolution. In the lampreys cartilages appear partially enclosing and protecting the brain, and this rigid box becomes elaborated as a cranium in the cartilaginous fishes to the skull characteristic of all other vertebrates. Not the least important development in this connection is the addition of jaws, so important not only in increasing the range of feeding but for use in defence and attack. The lampreys have no biting jaws although they have sharp horny teeth on their protrusible tongue, but from the cartilaginous fishes onwards hinged jaws armed with teeth (secondarily lost in birds and some other higher vertebrates) play a significant role in their habits and behaviour.

As the scope of their activities increases there comes the need for a more complex nervous system and with it an amplification of the seat of control, the brain. In lampreys it is still simple yet shows the specialisations seen in the rest of the

Opposite
The Adams River run of the Fraser River, British Columbia stock of Sockeye Salmon, *Oncorhynchus nerka*, is of immense importance to Canadian fisheries. After a period of two to three years in the sea the adult fish gather in the mouth of the river during the summer and begin their mass migration towards the spawning grounds which lie as much as 1,000 kilometres up-river.

vertebrates. There are the hind brain with its medulla oblongata and cerebellum, largely concerned with muscular activity, and the mid and fore brains, with prominent optic and olfactory lobes, dealing with sight and the sense of smell respectively, but with small cerebral hemispheres. It is virtually impossible to summarise briefly the changes that take place in the brain as we progress upwards along the line of vertebrate evolution, except to say that the brain itself becomes more complicated in its internal organisation, and that there is a steady increase in the size and organisation of the cerebral hemispheres. This trend reaches its highest point in the enormous size of the heavily convoluted cerebrum (or cerebral hemispheres) in man which has overgrown the rest of the brain. The cerebrum is the seat of voluntary or conscious processes, and its size and development give a rough guide to intelligence.

The degree of development of the brain determines the shape of the skull and its size relative to the rest of the body. This has an important if subsidiary bearing on the shape of the head.

It follows naturally that the increasing organisation of the brain demands a higher form of sensory receptors or special sense-organs and, conversely, the better the sense-organs the more specialised must be the part of the brain dealing with them. In the lowest vertebrates smell (chemical perception in air or water media) plays a larger part than sight or hearing and this position is largely reversed as we approach the higher vertebrates, but again there is not a steady sequence. In general the ear and the eye become more efficient, but the development of the olfactory sense does not follow a clear line. A dog, for example, has as acute a sense of smell as a shark, while frogs and birds have little sense of smell.

The digestive system of vertebrates is a long way from the simple tubular gut of *Amphioxus*, and the excretory system includes kidneys which are very different from the nephridia of *Amphioxus*.

In vertebrates the sexes are always separate. Even when individuals are described as hermaphrodite or intersexed they function either as male or as female, or not at all. There is not the hermaphroditism seen in invertebrates, in which the same individual can be functionally male as well as functionally female. Nor is there asexual reproduction, although this figures so prominently in the life-histories of some of the protochordates. The reproductive processes, as a consequence, show the same increasing specialisation as the other systems, with elaborate courtships, special forms of nesting and nest building, increased parental care and with it a reduction of the number of young at one time, monogamy (or at least a selective polygamy), sexual dimorphism often linked with elaborate secondary sexual characters, and arising out of these come distinct social structures quite unlike any found in even the highest social insects. The social tendencies are further emphasised by an increasing territorial instinct. In general terms, all these become more emphasised as we pass from the lower vertebrates to the higher, and the tempo of these changes quickened as soon as vertebrates had become established in a terrestrial mode of life.

Although the first vertebrates came into being.

more than 600 million years ago, they were all aquatic until just over 350 million years ago. Until then respiration was by gills, but they were gills of a special kind, being formed as openings in the walls of the pharynx. If the deductions we draw from the protochordates are correct, the pharynx was at first large and cavernous and the gill slits numerous. Later the pharynx became reduced in size and the gill slits fewer in number, usually not more than six. Respiration was by swallowing water and having it pass through the gill slits when the oxygen was extracted. Early in the evolution of fishes there arose, as an outgrowth from the gut, an organ with hydrostatic functions, the swim bladder, which controlled the specific gravity of its possessors, enabling them to rise or sink in their fluid medium. In a few species of fishes this became an accessory breathing organ, and when species arose capable of taking air into the swim bladder, and at the same time possessing fins that could also function as legs, the way was clear for emergence on to land. This was no doubt limited at first, and necessitated a periodic return to water, and so the first Amphibia came into being.

The Amphibia gave rise to the Reptilia, some of which were poikilothermic (cold-blooded), while others were homoeothermic or warm-blooded or, to be more precise, could exercise control of the body temperature so that it remained steady despite changes in the temperature of the surrounding air. (When so-called warm-blooded animals hibernate they are said to relinquish their temperature control.) The first important factor in the transition from poikilothermy to homoeothermy is an efficient system of blood vessels, and particularly an efficient heart. The basic pattern of the circulatory system in all groups of vertebrates, except the Agnatha (lampreys and hagfishes), is essentially similar. The differences are largely in matters of detail. The main change is in the heart.

In the Agnatha there is no heart. Instead there is a ventral aorta which is contractile and drives the blood forward to arteries crossing the gills where it is oxygenated; the direction governed by rather primitive membranous valves. In cartilaginous and bony fishes there is a muscular heart with a single auricle and a single ventricle. In the Amphibia there are two auricles and one ventricle, so that there is an incomplete separation of pure and impure blood in the heart, and in reptiles there is an improvement on this in that the ventricle is incompletely divided. The reptile heart is, therefore, on the way to the condition found in birds and mammals, in which the heart is completely four-chambered, with a right and a left auricle and a right and a left ventricle.

This survey of the vertebrates, being brief, necessarily omits many details that are important to a full understanding of the subphylum. Its aim has been to emphasise two points more especially. One is that as we pass from the lowest to the highest vertebrates there is a steady, almost orderly, increase in the specialisation and complexity of all the bodily organs and systems. The other is to underline the fact that the vertebrates are a closely knit group, which is why they constitute no more than a subphylum in our scheme of classification, despite the diversity of animal forms they contain.

Fishes (Superclasses Agnatha, Gnathostomata)

Fishes are the most ancient form of vertebrate life and from them evolved all other vertebrates including man. They are cold-blooded animals ranging from a centimetre to twelve metres in length and are adapted to an aquatic existence with gills and fins, although a few species can move on land and breathe air. Some fishes such as the jawless lampreys and hagfishes have not changed much for millions of years, but most species show a great diversity of form, habit and behaviour in adaptation to a wide range of environment. With 20,000 species, fishes account for over forty per cent of all living vertebrate species.

Basic anatomy

Generally the body is torpedo-shaped or fusiform, and oval in cross-section. In free-swimming forms the body is streamlined, as in the tunny or mackerel. This is nearly circular in cross-section for about a third of its length from the snout, and from this point its contours decrease gently to the tail. This has been called a double wedge, a thick one forwards to the head and a thin one backwards to the tail. There is no neck, projections are reduced and the whole body is shaped to move with the greatest economy of effort.

Nearly all fishes have bilateral symmetry, the right and left sides of the body being mirror images of each other, and there is usually a well-developed head region, which generally tapers smoothly into the tail. The appendages are called fins.

A fish is usually covered with a tough skin continuous with that of the mouth and other body openings. This skin also covers the eyes, carries colour pigments and may contain slime glands. Scales, which are often present in the skin, form a protective exoskeleton.

The fins are either paired, or single and median. The paired fins are the pectorals and the pelvics or ventrals. Both vary greatly in shape and position. The pectorals, attached to the pectoral girdle, are usually nearer the eyes than the pelvics, which are generally ventral. The fins in the midline of the back are known as the dorsal fins, while those in the midline ventrally are the anal fins.

The fin rays of bony fishes are either hard and spiny or soft. Spiny rays are unsegmented and uniserial. Soft rays are typically segmented, usually branched, and always biserial. Fin rays are used in fin formulae when describing fish species. Roman numerals denote the number of spiny rays, and arabic figures indicate the number of soft rays, branched or not. Thus, DIII/5 signifies that the fish has a dorsal fin in which there are three spiny rays followed by five soft rays; and D2/6 denotes a fin with two unbranched soft rays followed by six branched soft rays.

The bold colouring of the dragon fishes is a warning of the long, dangerous dorsal fin spines which are equipped with venom-producing tissue. Here two species, the Turkeyfish or Red Firefish (*Pterois volitans*) on the right, and *Pterois antennata* on the left, display their long fins; both live in the Indian Ocean.

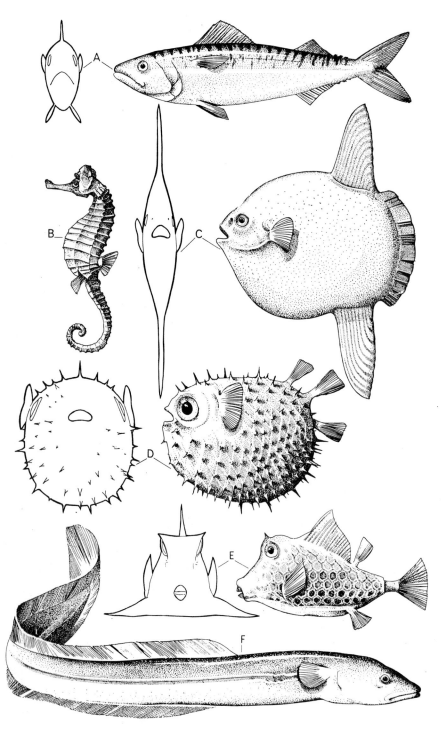

position varies greatly in different forms. All over the body there may be small openings of sensory organs located in the skin. Generally on either side of the body there is a row of pores called the lateral line and frequently this is readily visible.

Body form

Divergences from the body form of a truly pelagic fish such as the mackerel or tunny can be related to adaptations in swimming movements made to suit a particular environment or behaviour pattern. Speedy movement is useful for capturing food and escaping from enemies. Where speed is sacrificed some compensatory changes are necessary. Examples include heavy armour, protective coloration, venomous spines, electric organs, or an adaptation to a habitat where enemies are scarce. Amongst the cartilaginous fishes the fast-moving Blue Shark retains a streamlined shape and powerful muscular tail. Other sharks are sluggish with thick-set bodies, rounded mouths and flattened heads. The Carpet Shark, for example, does not hunt its prey but lies in wait, camouflaged as a weed-covered rock. Skates and rays have broad flat bodies in which the pectoral fins are continuous with the head, and the tail is very weak. These bottom-living types with a depressed body form tend to be sluggish. The compressed body, which is flattened from side to side, is common amongst the bony fishes. The Anglerfish, a well-known flattened bony fish, has a depressed body like the rays. A large group, the Pleuronectiformes, which includes soles, plaice and halibut, is also flat, but is so shaped because early on in life the laterally compressed young fish falls over on its side and the lower eye travels to the uppermost side. Laterally compressed fishes are found in many orders, some of which are extremely familiar. The angelfishes, for example, which inhabit South American freshwater, have very compressed circular bodies. They are slow swimmers but have long and filamentous fin rays and escape their enemies by darting into clumps of weeds, which they closely resemble. Many coral fishes have similar shapes but they rarely stray far from the protection of the coral and they are partly concealed by their coloration. Poor swimmers with short squat bodies have developed bony armour, as in the trunkfishes (Ostraciontidae), or spines as in the porcupinefishes (Diodontidae). Porcupinefishes and puffers, when alarmed, inflate their bodies by taking water into their stomachs. Sunfishes also have rounded flattened bodies and some have a protective leathery skin.

Many fishes, the best known of which are the eels, have elongated bodies. The body is also rounded, which is admirably suited to their way of life, living as they often do in rivers and lakes with soft muddy bottoms. They move easily through weeds, and are equally adept at hiding in holes under bridges or in walls alongside rivers. Many elongated forms are very compressed, for example, the ribbonfishes. Others resemble a piece of rope as do the snipe-eels, and the pipefishes. Symbranchid eels, though not related to the true eels, have also evolved an eel-like body.

Of all the many shapes to be found amongst fishes, one of the most peculiar is that of the seahorses. They swim in an upright position, propel-

The wide variety of forms found in fishes is well demonstrated by comparing (A) the Mackerel (*Scomber scombrus*), (B) the Seahorse (*Hippocampus punctulatus*), (C) the Sunfish (*Mola mola*), (D) the Globefish (*Chilomycterus antennatus*), (E) the Trunkfish (*Ostracion gibbosus*) and (F) the Common Eel (*Anguilla anguilla*).

The openings on the body are the mouth, the gill apertures which may be covered by an operculum or bony flap, the spiracle in primitive forms, and the vent or anus through which waste matter is passed out of the body. In some forms the anus and the openings for the urinary and genital products open into a depression or cloaca. In some fishes two small openings near the vent, the abdominal pores, allow communication between the body cavity and the outside world. They are usually lost in the more highly evolved species. Other openings are those of the sense-organs. There may be one or two nostrils, sometimes called nares, on either side of the snout. Lampreys have only one opening and in other species the openings may be ventral. The paired eyes are usually on either side of the head, but their

led by their pectoral and dorsal fins, and hold their heads at right angles to their bodies—a most unusual feature in fishes. In addition they can use their tails to hang on to weeds or rocks. The body is protected by plates, and these, in some species, are drawn out into filaments which closely resemble the weeds amongst which the fishes live.

From this one can see that an infinite variety of body forms is to be found amongst fishes, gradually evolved over millions of years to suit the environment in which each form lives.

Fins

The basic fin plan of paired and unpaired fins has already been described, but the origin of fins and their adaptation as locomotor, balancing and other organs is still a controversial subject. It is likely that the unpaired fins arose from a primitive median fold of skin, which in time became strengthened by skeletal structures. Parts of the fold disappeared to give eventually the infinite variety of unpaired fins found in modern fishes. The origin of the paired fins may have been continuous lateral body folds, which again broke up to give the broad-based primitive paired fins. As fish fins evolved it is likely that their skeletal elements became more complex. Assuming that fins in present day lampreys are primitive, then the early fins were supported by cartilage (or bone) rods which were in two parts; the basals inside the muscle of the body and the radials in the fin. In the Selachii (sharks etc.) the radials are further subdivided, and often extend almost to the edge of the fin. Outside the radials, horny rays

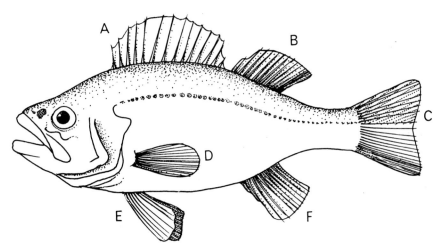

The fins of fishes are designated as follows: (A) spinous dorsal, (B) soft dorsal, (C) caudal, (D) pectoral, (E) pelvics, (F) anal.

may extend to the edge of the fin and thus provide extra support. Though some primitive fossil forms have fins with narrow bases, the embryological development of the pectoral fin, for example, in a modern fish shows that there is a concentration of segments at the fin base.

The 'lobe fins' of the Coelacanth and some of the lungfishes are today taken to be primitive. These have a fleshy lobe at their base and internally a definite central skeletal axis, formed of basals with radials projecting on either side. The dorsal and anal fins of the sturgeons, another ancient group, are also lobed. Though nowadays the cartilaginous fishes are not thought to be more primitive than the bony fishes, the latter show a much greater variation in the form and uses made

The Butterfly Gurnard (*Paratrigla vanessa*), one of the many marine bottom-living fishes with strongly armoured heads. Its most obvious characteristic is the large pectoral fins the first few rays of which are separated and can be used like fingers to support the body and detect buried food as the fish moves slowly along the bottom.

An ideal scale from a two-year old salmon smolt. The wide rings represent periods of rapid growth and the narrow ones less rapid growth. (A) first summer rings, (B) first winter rings, (C) second summer wide rings, (D) second summer narrow rings, (E) second winter rings and (F) third summer (plus) growth rings.

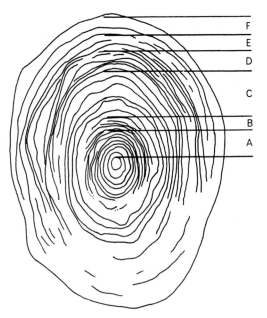

of their fins. It is outside the scope of this book to try to list the changes that have taken place in the internal structure of the paired fins.

The primitive types of tail fin may well have been supported by a straight vertebral column with equal lobes on either side. Even though tails look symmetrical in some adult fishes nowadays, they are not so formed internally.

The heterocercal tail found in most selachians and primitive bony fishes has the vertebral column bent upwards, the upper lobe being elongated and the lower having the larger area, as in the dogfishes. In some the upturned lobe is greatly reduced, so that the lower lobe of the tail fin lies at the end of the fish, and the tail appears symmetrical, e.g. species in the genera *Lepisosteus*, *Amia*, and *Polypterus*—all of which are archaic forms.

In most higher fishes the tail appears outwardly symmetrical (homocercal), but this type of tail has been developed by the reduction of the upper lobe into a minute vestige, and the enlargement of the lower lobe to form the greater part of the fin. Some tails become greatly elongated into whip-like structures (as in the rat-tails), and other tails (as in the cods), formed from the anal and dorsal fins.

Two interesting modifications are seen in the cartilaginous fishes. In the Thresher Shark (*Alopias vulpinus*) the upper lobe is greatly elongated. These fishes hunt systematically, several working together to beat the water to drive fishes into compact shoals and thus make them easier prey. In the stingrays the tail is much reduced but bears on it a strong spine which has a defensive function. Amongst the unusual tail fins of bony fishes may be mentioned the filament-like extension of the upper lobe in the Mailed Catfish (*Loricaria filamentosa*), and the very reduced diminutive tail of some pipefishes.

The dorsal fin is generally a stabilising fin, yet it shows remarkable diversity in size and function. In primitive fishes it remains as a long fringe extending the length of the body, and may serve as an organ of locomotion. Some of the front rays may be prolonged into long filaments and be useless except as ornament. The dorsal fin may be a single small fin as in the herrings (*Clupea*), or a

series of three separate fins as in the cod (*Gadus morhua*), or several finlets as in the Bichir (*Polypterus bichir*), or large and long as in the sailfishes (Istiophoridae). The dorsal fin may also be modified to transfer venom through its spines, as it is in the weevers (Trachinidae) and the stonefishes (*Synanceia*). In many fishes the front rays are spiny and are erected in defence. The front ray of the dorsal of the Anglerfish (*Lophius*) is prolonged with a fleshy tip which is used as bait to attract prey to its cavernous mouth. Among the oceanic anglerfishes, the ceratioids, the bait takes the form of a blob which can be made luminous at will. In the Echeneidae, the suckerfishes or remoras, the dorsal has become an efficient sucker by means of which the fishes can attach themselves to any flat surface, such as other fishes, ships, turtles etc. They can detach themselves quickly when they want to move off to feed. In several families one of the dorsal fins has no rays in it and is a fleshy structure called the adipose fin.

The anal fin also varies greatly; it may be long and serve as a locomotor organ, a rudder or a balancer, it may be absent, or may be modified as a copulatory organ.

The pectorals are usually behind the gill openings and in the sharks they are large and used for steering, but in the rays they are used for locomotion. In the bony fishes they are mainly used for steering, though in some instances they are used for propulsion. Like the dorsal fin spines in some forms, the pectoral fin spines are occasionally associated with venom glands. In the Exocoetidae, the flying-fishes, the pectoral fins are enlarged and used for gliding through air. In some South American freshwater forms these fins are flapped and thus used as wings. In others some of the rays are long and form finger-like processes which are used as legs, to search for food, and also as sensory organs.

The pelvics, which may be very reduced or absent, are situated far back in primitive fishes, or may be forward below the pectorals or even in front of the pectorals in some bony fishes. They are generally used as accessories in swimming, but in fast movement they are often folded back out of the way. Their main modification is to form a sucker; in the gobies the pelvics are united into a deep sucker. In other fishes the pelvics become part of a complex copulatory organ.

Skin

As in other vertebrates, the skin is a covering of the whole body affording protection against disease and is often a means of perceiving changes in the environment through various sensory receptors contained in it. It also has, to varying degrees, respiratory, excretory and body water balance (osmoregulatory) control functions. In addition it has chromatophores and reflecting granules which enable some fishes to change colour to suit their environment. Some skins contain venom glands and nearly all have mucus (slime) glands. The skin is two-layered, consisting of the outer epidermis, often thin and formed of flattened cells, and the inner dermis, which contains nerves, blood vessels, sense-organs and connective tissue. The dermis forms the scales which are absent from some fishes, for example the lampreys, the paddlefishes and the sticklebacks. In some the scales are minute and sunk in the skin so that the fish seems naked, e.g. the freshwater eels.

Scales vary enormously. The placoid scales of sharks are plate-like with a small cusp, while thick rhombic scales are found in primitive fishes (sturgeons, paddlefishes, garpikes). Cycloid scales are smooth and often circular; ctenoid scales are of similar shape with exposed spiny posterior margins.

Placoid scales are called dermal denticles, and are covered with an enamel-like substance beneath which is a dentine-like substance with a pulp cavity inside—very like a human tooth in structure. The teeth of sharks and higher vertebrates evolved from such scales, as well as various spines, skull bones, and bony plates on the body. The scales of many fishes are used to estimate age (*see* fig. of salmon scale on previous page).

Scale patterns in fishes are often used taxonomically, especially in the cyprinids where scale counts along the lateral line, from the origin of the dorsal fin to the lateral line and from this to the base of the pelvic fin, are used as specific characters.

From the skin have developed barbels and flaps, which are either sensory organs or accessory feeding mechanisms. Those around the mouth of sturgeons and catfishes locate food; the flaps serve as camouflage and protective devices as in the seahorses, or the sargassumfishes. Fishes display a large variety of colours, yet one can generalise on a pattern related to habit. Free-swimming open water fishes are coloured plainly with a whitish belly and silvery sides merging into a greeny-blue upper side. Fishes that live on the bottom or amongst weed are usually well marked above and pale below. The brightly coloured forms are often coral reef dwellers. Many young pelagic fishes are transparent, whilst many deep-sea forms are a uniform black.

The colour producers are of two kinds, the chromatophores and iridocytes. Chromatophores are found in the dermis outside or beneath the scales, and in these cells are the colour producers or pigment granules. These granules can disperse

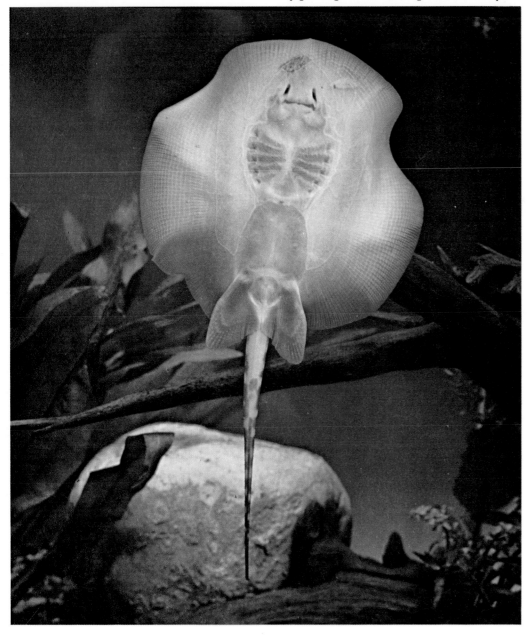

A young ray, in atypical pose, shows the adaptations to bottom-dwelling which are characteristic of the group. The five gill slits each side of the pharynx which occupies the centre of the disc are exhalent apertures for water drawn in through the dorsal spiracle; the mouth, connected to the nostrils by grooves is not used for respiration.

This Indo-Pacific sea horse, *Hippocampus kuda*, shows the typical upright swimming posture of sea horses with the dorsal fin gently undulating to move the fish forwards. The body has a bony exoskeleton with little flexibility except in the tail which is prehensile and can anchor the fish to coral or algae.

or concentrate within the cell; some absorbing wavelengths of light and reflecting others, Chromatophore granules are of three kinds, red and orange, yellow, and black, and an association of these produces other hues. For example, black and yellow give green. The iridocytes are small bodies which reflect the colours outside the fish; white, silver and some other colours are thus produced.

Colour is used to camouflage or to reveal. Colour changes to represent the background are protective, but some fishes with very bright colours, such as the darters of North America, the sticklebacks, and the cichlid fishes of Africa, use them for sexual recognition. Disruptive coloration is a means of concealment whereby the shape of the fish is broken. There are many examples of fishes that look like logs, leaves or weeds.

In the skin of some fishes are developed light organs which produce light in two ways; either by photophores, which are cells in glands capable of producing light under glandular (endocrine) or nervous control, or by means of luminous bacteria which live on the fishes in definitive pits in the skin. These luminous organs are of use in mutual recognition or sexual recognition, in keeping a school together, and in some cases attract prey.

Finally there are venom glands, derived from the mucus glands of the skin. The venom is injected by means of hollow spines on the back in stonefishes (*Scynanceia*), and in grooves along spines in sting-rays (Dasyatidae), weevers, and spurdogs. In the former species wounds can be fatal.

Digestive system

Jawed fishes are thought to be more advanced than jawless forms. Lampreys and hagfishes have a jawless suctorial mouth by means of which they attach themselves to their hosts. Inside the sucker are rasping teeth which break down the flesh and allow the parasite to suck the blood. Sharks usually have a ventral mouth with sharp teeth, the backward position of the mouth resulting from the prolongation of the upper jaw to form a snout. Rays have a straight mouth under the head, but in the manta rays that live in open waters the mouth

is terminal and forward prolongations from the pectoral fins form the 'horns'. These are formed into a funnel as the ray attacks a shoal of fishes, thereby guiding the prey into the mouth. The prey is sieved out of the water.

Fishes which suck in their food have a ventral mouth often fringed with barbels developed from the flesh of the lips. Notable examples with this type of mouth are the sturgeons, the loaches, the suckers (family Catastomidae) of North America and Asia, and the Loricariidae of South America. Suctorial mouths are often used as anchoring devices in fishes that live in fast flowing streams, for example *Gyrinocheilus* (family Gyrinocheilidae) of South-East Asia which, when attached by the mouth, takes in water for breathing through a second opening above the gill cover.

The shape of the mouth and jaws can vary enormously to suit specialised diets. The African elephant mormyrids have long down-turned trunks to probe into mud; butterfly-fishes have slender snouts, small mouths and fine teeth to feed in the interstices of the coral. John dories have jaws that swing forward to engulf prey, and many deep-sea fish can virtually dislocate their jaws to accommodate large prey.

Teeth are adaptations for feeding probably derived from placoid scales, and this can be seen in sharks where the body scales closely resemble the teeth on the jaws. In the bony fishes teeth are found on the jaws, in the mouth cavity, and in the pharynx. Upper jaw teeth are found on the premaxillary and maxillary bones and lower jaw teeth on the dentary. On the roof of the mouth teeth may be found on the vomer, palatine, and on the side on the ectopterygoids, and often they are found on the tongue. Pharyngeal teeth are found in some parts of the gill skeleton, especially the last gill arch. The teeth vary greatly in carps and minnows, for example, and are useful specific characters. Some teeth are crushers and are robust and flattened; others used for grasping are long and narrow; others may be fang-like, and of these some so-called canine teeth are hinged and lock in position as the mouth opens, as for example in the morays (family Muraenidae) and species of the

The suckerdisc on the head of this Brook Lampern (*Lampetra planeri*) is a feature of the superclass Agnatha – the jawless fishes. Seven separate gill openings on each side, each communicate with an internal gill pouch. The large eye of this fish shows that it has finished metamorphosis from the amocoete stage and is sexually mature.

genus *Alipisaurus*. Other teeth are fused into beak-like structures. Many fishes have weak teeth, and those that feed on plankton often have no teeth at all. Such fishes, e.g. coregonids and shads, have projections from the gill skeleton which are elongated and serve to filter the plankton from the water passed out over the gills. These rakers, as they are called, are useful taxonomic characters.

The mouth leads to the pharynx, and this into the oesophagus, which many fishes are able to enlarge. The stomach shows adaptation to the feeding habit of the fishes. Pikes, gars and other fish-eating fishes have elongated stomachs; the sturgeons, gizzard shads, and grey mullets have greatly thickened muscular stomach walls which grind the food which usually comprises hard shelled organisms. Some fishes can fill their stomachs with water and thereby greatly distend their bodies in defence, in others the stomach is reduced or absent. The intestine in carnivores is shortened, but most plant-eating fishes have long intestines. Some sharks and other fishes have folds in their stomachs to increase the absorptive area.

Digestion and digestive juice show great variation. Most prominent are the mucus glands. Some fish stomachs have gastric glands which secrete protein-digesting juices. The liver is a storage organ with a bile-secreting gall bladder, and the pancreas secretes a digestive juice which sometimes has a component capable of digesting carbohydrate. However, we still have a great deal to learn about the digestive tract, digestion and absorption of digested food in fishes.

Respiration and circulation

Fishes take in oxygen and pass out carbon dioxide, a waste product of the breakdown of materials that takes place in the cells.

Gaseous exchange takes place in the gills and other accessory respiratory structures. In the lam-preys and hagfishes there is a ventral respiratory tube in the pharynx, which is separated from the upper food tract. The respiratory tube leads to the gill pouches, which are seven in number in the lampreys, five to fourteen in *Eptatretus* and six in *Myxine*, the hagfish. Each pouch in the lamprey has an inner opening from the pharynx and an external one from the pouch to the outside. In the hagfishes the six pouches open into a common duct near the sixth pouch, and each pouch is covered with gill filaments which are well supplied with blood from the afferent branchial arteries, and the oxygenated blood is collected into the dorsal aorta which conveys it all over the body. Water usually flows into the gill pouches and is expelled by muscle contraction. In hagfishes water is also helped in and out by expansion and contraction of the nasal sac, which opens on top of the head in a single nostril, and at the other end of the roof of the mouth.

In the Gnathostomes, or jawed fishes, gills are also the main organs of respiration, although many supplementary methods have evolved. Gills are carried on branchial arches. In sharks and their allies these are not unlike the pouches of the lampreys, but in the bony fishes the separate chambers are reduced and the gills are closer to each other.

Gas bladders which apparently evolved from the last pair of embryonic gill pouches in primitive fishes sometimes form lungs. The lungs of the lungfishes (Dipneusti) are paired in the African species (genus *Protopterus*) and South American lungfish (genus *Lepidosiren*) and open by a single duct on to the floor of the mouth, but that of the Australian lungfish (genus *Neoceratodus*) is single. These lungs have folded walls and are well supplied with blood. In the genus *Polypterus*, archaic fishes found in Africa and commonly called bichirs or lobefins, the gas bladder is laterally bilobed with a duct opening in the floor of the mouth. Dorsal 'lungs' are present in the living 'fossils' the bowfin (genus *Amia*) and the reedfish (genus *Calamoichthys*) and in the North American gars (genus *Lepisosteus*). In the more modern fishes a single gas bladder is found which usually lies in the midline above the gut; in some it is subdivided and may or may not retain its connection with the gut. In some it retains a connection with the outside by a pore near the anus. In some bottom-living fish the gas bladder is lost.

Where the gas bladder is used for respiration it is richly supplied with blood either from the dorsal aorta or the blood vessels that run to the gills. In most fishes, however, the blood comes from the coeliaco-mesenteric artery that also carries blood to the gut. Oxygenated blood from the 'lungs' returns eventually to the heart. The lampreys and hagfishes, sharks and allies, and the coelacanth (genus *Latimeria*) do not have gas bladders, nor is it likely that their ancestors had one. In the bony fishes the gas bladder functions as a hydrostatic organ by means of which the density of the fish is adjusted to suit the environment. In other words it regulates buoyancy. In those fishes (physostomes) that retain a connection between gut and gas bladder, the bladder is first filled when the fish is very young. Many fishes (physoclists) have this connection in early life, fill up their gas bladder by

The external gill openings of (A) the Spotted Dogfish (*Scyliorhinus* sp.) are clearly seen between the mouth and the pectoral fin, whilst the spiracle appears as a black orifice behind the eye. In (B) the Rabbitfish (*Chimaera monstrosa*) there is a gill opening in front of the pectoral fin, whilst in (C) the Trout (*Salmo trutta*) this is above the pectoral, but still between the fin and the mouth. In (D) the Thornback Ray (*Raja clavata*), however, the gill clefts are on the underside of the fish, with the nostrils anterior to them and the spiracles are on the upper surface behind the eyes (E).

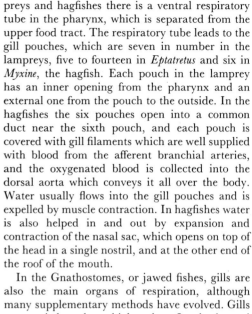

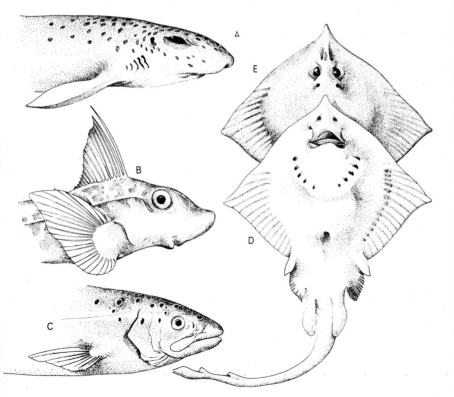

gulping air and then the duct is closed. In adults gas is secreted into the bladder with a change in hydrostatic conditions, for example when a fish moves from deep into shallow water. Gas secretion and absorption is not a very fast process, thus a fish netted at eighteen metres, if hauled quickly upwards through the water, arrives with a greatly distended gas bladder. The reason for this is that the gas-absorbing mechanism was not able to absorb the gas quickly enough, and under reduced pressure the gas expanded.

The gas in the gas bladder is secreted from the blood vessels concentrated in regions of the bladder. This secretory mechanism is the so-called gas gland, where the small blood vessels of the many capillaries that form the rete mirabile reach the surface of the bladder. The blood to these capillaries comes from the aorta through a branch of the coeliaco-mesenteric artery, which also supplies oxygenated blood to part of the gut. The gas is usually oxygen, though sometimes nitrogen may be present in some fishes. It is resorbed again by diffusion, but into groups of blood vessels other than the secreting ones, or into a very specialised network of blood vessels connected with the secretory blood vessels, or in special thin-walled chambers usually at the rear of the gas bladder. The blood vessels in these so-called oval organs open into the venous system.

It appears that the secretion of gas is under nervous control, the stimulus being perceived either by skin sense-organs or the eyes. In some fishes the gas bladder is associated with sound reception and may extend into the inner ear. In others three pairs of little bones derived from vertebrae, collectively called the Weberian apparatus, connect the front of the bladder to an extended section of the inner ear. Thus pressure changes are transmitted from the bladder through the malleus, incus and stapes on either side to the ear, and it seems that the carps, which have well-developed Weberian ossicles, perceive sound better than other fishes. Some fishes use the gas bladder to produce sound by vibrating the bladder wall using specially developed muscles. Other means of breathing air are found in many tropical fishes. In some African spiny eels (genus *Mastacembelus*) the gills secrete a slime which allows atmospheric oxygen to enter. In the snakeheads (genus *Ophiocephalus*) extensions develop from the pharynx and the mouth. These are highly vascularised, and gas exchange can take place from the air. Similarly the gill chamber of the mudskippers (genus *Periophthalmus*) is folded and highly vascularised and in some of the loaches (family Cobitidae) part of the intestine can absorb oxygen from air taken in through the mouth. In an African catfish the branchial cavity is extended to the tail and the gills are fused to form a valve at the opening of the sac. A respiratory labyrinth is formed from the first gill arch in the climbing-perches.

Many of these air-breathing fishes can stay out of water for several hours and some move overland by pushing themselves with their pectoral fins.

Nervous system and sense-organs

The nervous system of fishes is extremely elaborate and consists of the brain, the spinal cord, the nerves and the sense organs.

The brain is protected by the cranium or skull and can be divided into fore, mid and hind brain. The fore brain is mainly concerned with smell and the olfactory nerve carries the stimuli from the olfactory sense-organs to the olfactory lobes. These are large in sharks and other fishes that hunt by smell. Many fishes have another pair of outgrowths behind the olfactory lobes. These are the cerebral hemispheres, which may be in two lobes or may be joined to form a single body. These hemispheres are very small in the lampreys and hagfishes, and usually small in the bony fishes; this region is also mainly concerned with smell.

The upper surface of the lamprey's brain is covered by a vascular choroid plexus which helps in nourishing the brain. The lower part of the mid and hind brain in lampreys is the source of all the cranial nerves except the olfactory (smell) and optic (sight). Special sense centres are small in this primitive brain, but the medulla oblongata of the hind brain is well developed by virtue of its control of the sucker. The pineal eyes, well-developed in lampreys, will be discussed later (*see* p. 216). The lower part of the brain between the fore and mid brain forms a pair of sacs which end as the infundibulum, and this connects with a sac-like upgrowth from the buccal ectoderm—the tissue of the mouth cavity—which becomes folded and forms the fore and mid part of the pituitary body, an endocrine organ. In lampreys the cavity retains its connection with the outside opening through the nostril on top of the head.

In sharks and rays the brain is better developed than in lampreys, but retains its basic primitive structure. The fore brain is large, with a thick roof and floor to the cerebral hemispheres which deal with the well-developed sense of smell. Just behind is the ventral hypothalamus of unknown function, and attached to the end of this is the sacculus vasculosus which, it is believed, is a pressure receptor enabling the fish to perceive changes of pressure in its environment. The mid brain, as in the lampreys, is very large and is probably the most important part of the brain. It deals with sight, some smell, part of the lateral line system, and taste. Behind this is the cerebellum which deals with balance, receiving stimuli from the ears and the lateral line. The medulla oblongata lies behind the cerebellum, and from this part arise most of the cranial nerves, especially those that deal with respiration and various visceral functions.

The brain extends backwards into the spinal cord from which metamerically arranged paired nerves are given off, i.e. their number is the same as that of the vertebrae between which they pass. These nerves deal mainly with swimming and some peripheral sense-organs.

The brain of bony fishes has the same plan as that of lampreys and sharks. The fore brain deals mainly with smell, but most of the optic fibres end in the mid brain. The roof forms a pineal body, but not an eye-like structure. Experiments have shown that the fish brain is capable of association and that the fish has a capacity for learning which is unaffected if the fore brain is removed, but cannot take place if the mid brain is removed. These powers of association are probably centred in the optic lobes. The cerebellum is large and governs the sense of balance.

The organ of smell is a pouch that opens to the outside world through the nares. The pouch is a blind sac, except in a few bottom-living bony fishes and the lungfishes. The nasal sac is lined by sensory epithelium which transmits olfactory sensations to the brain. The sense of smell is extremely acute and is used for shoaling, hunting, and homing. Fishes which have their nares plugged cannot find their food, and some fishes, e.g. of the genus *Lepomis*, if moved from their home are able to find it again by their sense of smell. Salmonids returning from the sea to spawn are said to find the stream in which they were born by detecting the smell of their natal waters. If their nostrils are plugged they are then unable to find their way.

Many fishes are able to detect very minute quantities of some substances. For example, the freshwater eels can detect pure organic substances at a dilution of one in one million, million, million (1×10^{-18}).

Allied to smell are the 'skin' senses whereby the fishes can detect temperature changes by means of fine nerve endings in the skin, especially at the front end of the body. In sharks and rays part of the lateral line system responds to a rise and fall in temperature. The sense of touch is exceptionally well developed in some catfishes (Siluridae) but in general this sense is not as well developed as in higher animals, except possibly in the barbels around the mouth. The sense of taste is mainly located on the lips, mouth, pharynx and on the snout, but some fishes that do not feed by sight have taste buds, innervated by branches of the ninth and tenth cranial nerves, on other parts of the body. Carps are apparently capable of tasting salty, bitter, sweet and acid stimuli.

Generally fish eyes have a large dense round lens which is usually moved towards the retina by a muscle to enable the fish to focus. The amount of light reaching the retina is controlled by an iris which in lampreys, some shark-like and primitive bony fishes cannot be opened or closed. Focusing or accommodation (change of vision from near to

A catfish's barbels are its main means of contact with prey and its surroundings. They are covered in sensory cells which serve both as organs of detection and taste; in contrast, their eyes are small and play a minor role in everyday life.

far) is limited, and in some sharks and rays is achieved by slight changes in the shape of the lens. In others the lens can be moved by muscles, and the Brown Trout, which feeds by sight, has a well-developed muscle. It is said that trouts can focus at the same time on distant and near objects by using different parts of the retina, since the lens is ellipse-shaped and consequently has two focal lengths.

Many deep-sea fishes have tubular lenses used for viewing things above them. Fishes that live in the shallower waters have colour vision and are said to respond to twenty-four hues very close to each other. Where binocular vision is important for food catching, as in the pikes, there seem to be sighting grooves on the snout in front of the eyes. Other fishes, like the plaice, can move their eyes independently so that one can look forwards and the other backwards. In the four-eyed fishes (Anablepidae) the lens is so shaped that the fishes can see upwards into the air and at the same time downwards into the water. Some sharks, e.g. tope (genus *Galeorhinus*), have a third eyelid which can be moved to cover the eye, and in the bottom-living flatfishes and rays the upper part of the pupil is covered by a thick lobe which effectively shades the eyes from light shining from above. Many fishes that live in caves are blind, and their eyes have disappeared completely or are mere vestiges hidden under the skin, as in the Kentucky Blind-fish (*Amblyopsis spelaea*) and the Cuban Blind-fish (*Stigicola dentatus*).

The pineal eye or organ in the lampreys has a retina, pigment cells and a lens-like structure, and in the skull above it is an orifice covered by unpigmented skin allowing light to penetrate. Some sharks also have unpigmented skin above the pineal organ, but this organ is not so well developed as in the lampreys and hagfishes and some bony fishes.

The inner ear of fishes is divided into a pars superior in which are the semi-circular canals and ampullae and a sac-like structure, the utriculus, which deals with equilibrium and a pars inferior, which deals with hearing, composed of two vesicles, the lagena and sacculus.

In the ampullae are sensory hairs and cells which respond to a movement of the body. In the bony fishes the uticulus, sacculus and lagena each contain a bone called the otolith. Movement of these against the sensory hairs enables the fish to determine its position automatically. The size and shape of the canals and vesicles differs greatly; they are particularly large in some cavefishes. The sense of hearing is seated mainly in the utriculus and the range of sound perception shows wide variation.

The lateral line sense-organs are found only in fishes and larval stages of amphibians. The lateral line canals extend variously along either side of the body or in bands crossing the ventral surface of the body and on the head in three main, branched canals. In some the canals alongside the body may be short, as in the bitterlings (genus *Rhodeus*) and smelt (genus *Osmerus*), or long, as in cods (genus *Gadus*). In some there may be several parallel rows. Different parts of each canal are innervated by the eighth, ninth and tenth cranial nerves, which end in the medulla. The receptor in the lines is a neuromast which, when stimulated, gives off electric discharges, but the exact functioning of this sense-organ is not fully understood. Experiments have shown it to respond to pressure waves and low-frequency vibrations.It may be that the line conveys localised disturbances to the fish along the length of its body, or maybe it can pick up moving objects such as predators.

Fishes are the only animals that can generate and discharge electricity. Voltage varies, and there are two types of electricity generated, one in which a strong current is produced and is capable of stunning, as in the electric eels (genus *Electrophorus*), electric rays (genus *Torpedo*), and electric catfishes (genus *Malapterurus*); and the other weak currents of low voltage. These weak currents produce a continuous field around the fish which, when broken, enables the fish to locate enemies and obstacles, even in very muddy water. The reflected electric impulses are picked up by special electric receptors, as in some of the South American gymnotids and the African mormyrids.

Skeleton and movement

The skeleton includes the primitive backbone (the notochord), bone, cartilage, fin rays and can be divided into the external skeleton—scales, spines, scutes and fin rays—and the internal skeleton, some of which can be seen through the skin. There is a membranous skeleton which sheaths nerves, cartilage, bone, muscles, body cavity lining, tendons, and ligaments. The notochord is an elongated rod of tissue, present in all embryos, which may persist as in the sturgeons, or be reduced to small pieces between the vertebrae.

The skull is cartilaginous in lampreys and consists of a series of box-like structures around the brain and the sense capsules for smell, sight and hearing (olfactory, optic and otic capsules), and a branchial basket supporting the gills, pharynx and sucker. The shark skull is in one piece—the chondrocranium—and covers the brain. It includes two capsules for eyes and ears. There were probably eight visceral arches originally, the first was probably lost, the second became the upper jaw, the third now forms the support for the tongue and jaws, and the rest are now the first to fifth gill arches. In the bony fishes the skull is more complex and consists of inner bones and outer bones (dermal) formed from skin elements, which give the shape of the face with its countless variations.

The vertebral column is generally composed of vertebrae—usually one for each body segment—which have side processes along the length of the body, and these may bear dorsal or ventral ribs. The vertebrae also protect the spinal cord.

In many bony fishes there are small needle-like bones in between the muscles, as for example in the herrings, pikes, and some salmon.

The muscles of fishes are of three main types, smooth muscle (mainly the involuntary muscles of the gut), heart muscle, and the voluntary or skeletal muscle which forms the main part of the body. These are generally found in segmental blocks, the myomeres, which are joined by the connective tissue myosepta.

Locomotion may be passive, whereby the fishes, usually as eggs or young forms, are carried by currents. Otherwise they may adhere to other fishes, as do the lampreys and remoras (family Echeneidae). But the more usual method is swimming, and body form can be related to this method of locomotion.

Fins are used in many ways for propelling the fishes. For example the bowfin (genus *Amia*) undulates its dorsal fin and so propels itself forward. One of the electric eels (genus *Gymnotus*) undulates its long anal fin, or a dorsal and ventral may be undulated as in the filefishes (genus *Monacanthus*, and the skates and rays undulate their enlarged pectorals. Where there is a rigid body as in the trunkfishes (family Ostraciontidae), the caudal fin propels the body, and in many bony fishes the pectorals can be used as scullers.

Generally the paired median fins serve as stabilisers and often enable the fish to move up or down. They are also used as keels to keep the body upright.

The main organ of propulsion is the body itself, and its action is one of three types. First there is the serpentine motion, as in the eel, brought about by alternate contractions of the muscle blocks on either side of the body starting from the head end. Then there is a wagging motion, which is caused by alternate contractions of all the muscles on one side so that the tail lashes like a paddle, the trunk being rigid. Finally the fish may propel itself forward by sweeping the last third or so of the body from side to side. This is effected by alternate contractions of the myomeres, first on one side of the body and then the other, so that the body is thrown into a series of curves ending in wide sweeps of the tail region. This last method is used by most actively swimming fishes.

There are often much exaggerated reports of the speed at which fishes swim; generally the larger the fish the greater the speed. The Swordfish (genus *Xiphias*) is probably the fastest fish, reaching one hundred kilometres per hour. The marlins (genus *Makaira*), tunas (genus *Thunnus*), and bonitos (genus *Sarda*) reach about eighty, and the mackerels (genus *Scomber*) twenty. A salmon leaping may reach twenty-five kilometres per hour.

This picture shows Spotted Eagle Rays (*Aetobatus narinari*) off the San Blas Islands. Characteristically when swimming they move through the water with an even greater grace than a bird or a bat.

FISHES

Urogenital system and osmoregulation

The kidneys of fishes are paired elongated structures which lie above the gut just below the vertebral column. Each opens to the exterior through a duct, and these may fuse to form a single duct or urogenital sinus (as in the sharks and their relatives), or a so-called urinary bladder (as in some of the bony fishes). Most fishes have a mesonephric kidney made up of a large number of tubules, each enlarged at its end to form what is known as the Bowman's capsule.

In each capsule lies a mass of capillaries (the glomerulus) from the renal artery which conveys blood to the kidney and the renal vein which conveys blood from the kidney. Waste matter to be excreted enters the kidney in the arterial blood and then passes out of the capillaries in the Bowman's capsule. From here it is collected in the kidney ducts and eventually leaves the body through the urinary duct.

The male gonads are the testes, in which the milt or spermatozoa develop, and these are usually paired. In the sharks these products pass out via a temporary storage organ called the seminal vesicle, from here to the urogenital papilla or projection and so ultimately out of the body.

In the bony fishes seminal vesicles are rarely found, and true sperm ducts are not found in some forms, e.g. some salmon and trouts, in which the testis narrows into the so-called testicular duct.

In many fishes the sperm pass to the exterior through modified kidney tubules. In higher forms the sperm do not pass through the kidney at all because the duct which carries the sperm is a more recent development, and originates from the testes.

The female organs, the ovaries, are usually elongated and paired, but may fuse or become much shortened. They are held in place by mesenteries (folds of membrane) which sling them from the roof of the body cavity. When the eggs are ripe the ovaries are enlarged and may fill most of the body cavity. In lampreys and hagfishes the eggs pass into the body cavity and out through the abdominal pores. In the egg-laying sharks some of the oviduct tissue secretes a shell, and in those sharks that give birth to living young the oviduct is subsequently enlarged to form a uterus where the young develop. Many bony fishes pass their eggs from the ovary directly into the oviduct, though in some forms, e.g. the salmon and trouts, the ovaries rupture and the eggs pass into the body cavity and finally out of the body through pores near the anus, the so-called vent.

Many waste products pass out of the body through the anus and skin, but most pass through the kidneys. An aquatic environment makes it difficult to balance body fluids and their salts with those of the environment. The gills and mouth membranes are permeable, that is they allow both water and some salts to pass through them. In the sea the salts in the surrounding water are more concentrated than in the fluids in the body of the fish, so the water is 'drawn out' of the body and the salts of the sea-water move in, according to the principles of osmoregulation. To counter this imbibition of salt the marine fish drinks sea-water. In freshwater, on the other hand, the salts move out of the fish and the fish takes in water through the gill filaments, but not through the mouth. In fact in freshwater special devices are adopted to prevent the intake of water and the loss of salts. For example, a great deal of mucus is secreted to make the skin fully waterproof, and the skin has less blood vessels in it.

The kidney apparatus is a filter system where salts from the renal blood are absorbed in the glomeruli of the Bowman's capsule. This system was developed for life in freshwater and is still used as such in freshwater forms. But in the sea, as it is a problem to keep the water in, the kidney mechanism is ill-suited, and glomeruli are reduced or absent. This reduces the water loss, and in addition water is taken in and salts passed out through the gill tissue.

Some fishes can pass from salt into freshwater, and freshwater into salt water with no apparent discomfort, e.g. eels and salmon; their kidneys and gill mechanisms are adaptable. In the eels the chloride cells of the gills can apparently serve either as salt-secreting or an salt-absorbing cells when necessary. These changes are usually preceded by, or happen at the same time as, changes in the secretory activity of the pituitary, thyroid, and the gonads.

Reproduction

This is usually bisexual in that the eggs develop in the females and the sperm in the males. Some fishes have hermaphrodite organs capable of forming both eggs and sperm in the same individual and self fertilisation takes place, but this is rare. Hermaphrodite glands are found in some perches, darters, and black basses. Other basses start off their lives as males and eventually become female. Many wrasses, parrot fishes, damsel-fishes, and sea-breams also undergo sex reversal usually from female to male. In the live-bearing (viviparous) Amazon Molly (*Poecilia formosa*) sperm enters the body of the female and incites the egg to develop, but does not pass on to offspring any of the male characteristics. As a result only females are produced. The eggs are chemically stimulated to growth by the sperm from males of other related species but no genetic combination occurs.

The sperm is produced in the testis and is used to fertilise the eggs, which vary greatly in size according to the species. The smallest are half a millimetre and the largest ninety millimetres in diameter. The numbers produced by females of different species vary from over fifty million eggs in an Ocean Sunfish (*Mola mola*) to just one or two in each ovary as in some topminnows. A female Atlantic Salmon produces about 340 to 360 eggs per kilogram of body weight. Most females that lay millions of eggs do not bother to protect eggs or young but some, like the salmon, prepare nests in the gravel of the river bed. The sticklebacks make nests of plant material and take great care in looking after the eggs laid in them. Others that give birth to live young may look after their progeny most assiduously.

Fish eggs usually have a 'shell' around them which may be only a very thin membrane or quite a tough skin (as in the salmonids where the eggs are laid in gravel). Or where fertilised eggs are laid, a thick shell is formed around the egg as it lies in the oviduct, e.g. sharks and rays. Eggs may float as do those laid by oceanic fishes, or may sink as do those of the salmon. Some adhere to plants, or are only sticky for a time like those of salmon and trouts. Most eggs are spherical in shape, some are pear-drop shaped, others oval. Some have string-like processes to serve as anchors, and some have sticky stalks for attaching the eggs to the substratum. Eggs can take several weeks, or even months, to hatch according to the species.

Sexual dimorphism

Often it is impossible to tell male from female except when the fishes are running ripe, at which time pressure on the flanks of a fish will, if female, result in eggs being extruded, or sperm if the fish is a male. Sometimes the male can be distinguished by small whitish tubercules which disappear after spawning (called pearl organs) on the head, as in some carps, or by the very humped back and hooked jaws of the Pacific Pink Salmon (*Oncorhynchus gorbuscha*).

The male may have an elongated genital papilla which in some instances is used as a penis for transmitting sperm into the female. At spawning time the male Brown Trout and Atlantic Salmon develop a hook on the elongated lower jaw which fits into a hole on the upper jaw. This kype, as it is called, may already be present if the fishes move into the river just before spawning time, or will develop in the river if the fishes run up in spring or early summer. At spawning time small male trouts have a brilliant white front edge and tip to the dorsal fin and the front edge of the pelvic and anal fins, whilst the male charrs (genus *Salvelinus*) become very red, especially on the belly. The fin structure may change, as for example in the North American Fantail Darter (*Etheostoma flabellare*), in which the tips of the spines become knobbly in the breeding male. The caudal fin of the male of a favourite aquarium fish, the Swordtail (*Xiphophorus helleri*), has a greatly elongated lower lobe. In several species the anal fin becomes enlarged and is used to pass the sperm into the female, e.g. guppies and some top-minnows (family Poeciliidae). In others (e.g. genus *Xenodexia*) the pectorals are enlarged and used to clasp the female as the sperm is transferred from the male.

In sharks and rays the pelvic fins are modified to produce elongated claspers which are placed inside the femal cloaca and keep it open to allow the sperm to enter. The difference in colour between some male and female salmonids has already been mentioned; usually the males are much brighter in colour than the females. This is also true of many other fishes, for example, in dragonets (genus *Callionymus*), wrasses (family Labridae) cichlids, cyprinodonts. The beautiful colours of the male Threespine Stickback (*Gasterosteus aculeatus*) and the male Minnow (*Phoxinus phoxinus*) at spawning time compare favourably with the colour of any fish. In the South American Lungfish (*Lepidosiren paradoxa*) the pelvic fins are covered with bright scarlet processes at breeding time.

One of the most unusual developments is to be found in the Asiatic cyprinodonts (family Phallostethidae) where a fleshy organ, the priapum, is developed below the head and chest of the male. It

The Swordtails (*Xiphophorus helleri*) from the rivers of Central America are popular aquarium fishes and, as usual many new forms have been produced by selective breeding. The fish gets its name from the male having an elongated lower lobe to the tailfin.

has its own specialised skeleton and the ducts from the testes, kidneys and intestine open on it.

In some deep-sea fishes, the ceratioid anglerfishes, there is a most unusual relationship between the sexes. The male is parasitic on the female and early on in its life holds on to the female by its mouth. The site selected appears to be haphazard, and sometimes more than one male becomes attached to a female. Having bitten on to the female, the lips and tongue of the male become one with the flesh of the host. Nearly all the organs of the dwarf male degenerate, except the reproductive organs. The vascular systems of the two fishes coalesce and the dwarf male is nourished from the blood of the female. It has been suggested that this unusual relationship has evolved because these fishes are sluggish, live in near darkness and are solitary, so that their chances of meeting a mate would otherwise be remote. Yet many other sluggish, solitary deep-sea fishes manage to mate without taking such severe measures.

Many fishes mature during the first year of their life, yet others, like the female eels for example, may not mature until they are over twenty years of age. The male Atlantic Salmon may mature in the river when two years old or less, and about five inches in length, and some take part in the spawning of the large fishes which have been down to the sea feeding grounds. Female salmon parr do not mature until they have spent at least a year-and-a-half, often three, in the sea. The female salmon scoops a nest in the bed of the river by turning over on her side and flapping her tail —a process called cutting. By this action she sweeps the gravel off the bottom and eventually makes a hole called a redd, or nest. Here where there is little or no current she lays her eggs, 800 or so at a time, and the male passes out his sperm simultaneously. Immediately afterwards the female moves upstream, cuts vigorously and covers the eggs with gravel; this protects them and at the same time starts her next nest.

Many fishes (salmon, trouts and charrs) have intricate courtship patterns in which the male may swim alongside the female quivering his body violently; in others such as the carps the ritualistic behaviour of the males serves to assemble the sexes and possibly stimulate the female to lay eggs. The behavioural significance of various aspects of the courtship of the Brown Trout and sticklebacks has been analysed at great length. By nodding their heads some females, like the bullheads (genus *Cottus*), attract the males into crevices under stones; when the male enters, the female turns upside down and lays a clump of sticky eggs on the underside of the stone. Often all that happens at spawning is that fishes of two sexes swim alongside each other to shed their genital products.

Some fishes move from the sea to spawn in freshwater (salmon, trouts, smelts), others leave freshwater to spawn in the sea (eels). Sites for spawning are chosen carefully and are defended, often until death: a good example of this is shown by the Siamese Fighting Fish (*Betta splendens*).

Nest building varies from the scooping of holes in gravel or sand to making a nest of weed. Some fishes even lay their eggs in other animals. The bitterlings (genus *Rhodeus*), lay their eggs by means of a long ovipositor into the mantle cavity of the freshwater mussel, and lumpsucker (genus *Careproctus*) lays its eggs under the shell of a crab. Bubble nests may be made by the males of the labyrinth fishes (family Belontiidae) who blow bubbles of air in mucus. After this nest-making there follows an elaborate courtship in which the female approaches her mate, he turns her on her side and then tightens his body around her and turns her upside down. She is released, and the male moves below her. The female passes out eggs and the male some sperm, so that the eggs are fertilised as they sink towards the bottom. The male catches the eggs in his mouth, where they are covered with mucus. He then swims up and sticks them to the underside of the bubble nest, which is floating on the surface. Three to seven eggs are passed out at a time, and the process is repeated until about 150 eggs are laid. The male protects them, for the female will eat her own eggs. When they are hatched, any young straying from the nest are caught by the male and blown back to the nest. One of the paradise-fishes (genus *Macropodus*) has

A mermaid's purse, the egg-case of a ray or skate (family Rajidae). All rays of this family, and some small sharks, lay their eggs in horny cases which are often tangled in algae. When the young are fully developed they slip out through a slit in the case – which is then often cast up in shoreline jetsam.

similar breeding habits, but here the eggs (which are lighter than water) are laid by the female as she turned upside down below the mass of bubbles, and the eggs float into the bubbles. If they miss they are put in place by one or both of the parent fishes.

At a higher level of parental care some fishes incubate the eggs inside the body. Male seahorses (genus *Hippocampus*) and pipefishes (genus *Syngnathus*) have brood-pouches into which the female lays the eggs. In the Brazilian Catfish (*Loricaria typus*) the lower lip of the male parent becomes enlarged to form a brood-pouch where the eggs are incubated. Some marine catfishes (family Ariidae) incubate their eggs in their mouth, as do some cardinalfishes (family Apogonidae).

Some fishes are viviparous. In ovoviviparous sharks, living young in an advanced stage of development are passed out of the female in egg capsules. Others have living young in the oviduct, and these are fed from the blood stream of the mother (e.g. the genera *Mustelus*, the smooth-

hounds and *Sphyrna*, the hammerheads).

Many bony fishes from different families have developed viviparous habits, the guppies (genus *Poecilia*), the foureyed fishes (family Anablepidae), the halfbeaks (family Hemiramphidae), perch-like fishes (order Percomorphi) and many others that will be mentioned later in the section.

Development

As soon as the egg is fertilised by the entry of a sperm the pronuclei of the egg and sperm fuse. Thus the chromosomes that carry the character of each parent (genes) come together and a complicated development starts. Division of the fertilised egg into smaller units takes place until large numbers of cells are formed, and these eventually differentiate and form the different parts of the young fish. Once out of the shell the fish is called a larva, or fry. The larval period in some fishes may last only a few hours; in others e.g. the sea lampreys, it lasts for as long as five years. On the average it is a matter of weeks. Many fishes in early larval stages feed on a yolk-sac, and whilst

The Worm Pipefish (*Nerophis lumbriciformis*) is a coastal European species which greatly resembles the algae amongst which it lives. This species does not have a pouch for its eggs as do some other pipefishes and all sea horses, and the eggs are laid in a groove on the male's belly by the female. The male will carry them until they hatch.

Opposite bottom
Pacific salmon, *Oncorhynchus* sp., larvae within the gravel of the redd. Salmon eggs are large and yolky; after hatching the larvae stay buried in the gravel for two to three months sustained by the large yolk sac, before emerging as active free-swimming alevins.

this persists the fishes are sometimes called prolarvae. When the yolk is used up the young fish is called an advanced fry or alevin.

The larvae of the freshwater eels, called Leptocephali, are colourless and flattened and metamorphose into rounded eel-like forms just before entering freshwater (*see* p. 240). The larvae of the flatfishes at first swim in a vertical upright position, but after metamorphosis adopt the bottom-living habit, the flattened body turning over and lying parallel to the bottom, and the lower eye moving to the upper side. The larvae of many herrings are transparent because of the presence of a large amount of mucus in the muscles. Other larvae start off life with enlarged fins which disappear in the adult (genus *Lophius*—the Angler).

Some fishes, like the Fifteenspine Stickleback (*Spinachia spinachia*), may live for only one year; others, like female eels, live for twenty-five years. Some carps have lived in captivity for fifty years.

Distribution and migration

On land, physical barriers such as mountain ranges and deserts impede the movement of animals and explain the restricted habitat of some and the wide distribution of others. Similar physical features restrict the distribution of many freshwater fishes. In the oceans the barriers seem to be such factors as temperature, light, and salinity, other chemical characteristics, ocean currents, submerged ridges, deeps and, on a smaller scale, the configuration of the coast line. Some of these barriers may no longer exist; the present distribution of many species can be related to conditions only as they were millions of years ago.

Temperature affects the food, growth and development of a fish. Any one species of fish has a temperature tolerance, i.e. the degree of cold and heat it can stand, and sudden changes of temperature can be as lethal as an excess. Because of their reaction to temperature some fishes are called cold water forms, for example the trouts and salmon (family Salmonidae). In summer, in lakes, such fishes tend to stay in the deeper colder waters, e.g. the charrs (genus *Salvelinus*) and the whitefishes (coregonids). Clearly many fishes choose the temperature to which they are best suited.

Fishes can be divided into groups dependent on their tolerance to environmental factors. Thus fishes that can live in greatly different salinity conditions are called euryhaline; if restricted in movement by the salinity of their environment they are called stenohaline. The Threespine Stickleback (*Gasterosteus aculeatus*), equally at home in fresh or salt water, is an example of a euryhaline type, whereas the Minnow (genus *Phoxinus*) is a stenohaline type.

Another way of classifying fishes is based on their habitat, the main division being into marine fishes, freshwater fishes and a smaller division, the estuarine fishes. These can further be divided into benthic if they live on the bottom, pelagic if they swim about freely, or planktonic if they are carried about by currents.

Freshwater fishes that live in shallow waters are often called littoral, those that live in the darker, deeper waters are termed profundal, and those that inhabit the zone in between are called limnetic; in this zone there are no rooted plants, but there is enough light to permit the growth of minute plants in the deeper water.

In the sea there are numerous ecological zones. The main division is into pelagic and benthic, each of which is further subdivided. The pelagic is divided into two main zones; the neritic (which is the zone above the continental shelf), and the oceanic (which includes all other waters). Fishes to be found in the neritic zone include the herrings (family Clupeidae), some mackerels (family Scombridae), barracudas (family Sphyraenidae), tunnies (genus *Thunnus*), sailfishes (genus *Istiophorus*), grunts (family Pomadasyidae), as well as many sharks. In the oceanic zone are four divisions. Down to about 200 metres live such fishes as dolphins (*Coryphaena*)—not to be confused with the true dolphins, which are mammals—flyingfishes (family Exocoetidae) and mantas (family Mobulidae). In the zone below 200 metres, where the water is always cold and the light dim, the fishes are either predators or can feed on the dead food that drops from above. Many of the fishes move up from this zone at night to feed in the zone above, and these include such fishes as the hatchetfishes (family Sternoptychidae), lanternfishes (family Myctophidae) and some of the fishes with exceptionally large mouths, e.g. species of the genus *Stomias*. The third zone is completely dark and the waters very cold. The inhabitants are widely dispersed and many have luminous organs. Here are found ceratioid anglerfishers, deep water eels, and gulpers (genus *Eurypharynx*). Finally, of the fishes living in the great deeps of the oceans we know very little. Specimens are scarce, and only occasionally are some caught at great depths, like a deep-sea angler that was caught at a depth of about 3,352 metres off West Africa.

The benthic fishes can also be classified by zones. Those that live in the splash zone above hightide mark are not numerous and include such forms as the gobies (family Gobiidae). In the littoral zone live a vast variety of fishes that move in and out with the tide, and only a few of them need be listed, e.g. flatfishes, stingrays, eels, morays, blennies, pipefishes and gobies. Below, in the inner sub-littoral zone where the light is still good, live such fishes as skates and rays, cod and pollack (family Gadidae), trunkfishes (family Ostraciontidae), filefishes (family Balistidae), dogfishes (family Squalidae), parrotfishes (family Scaridae), and searobins or gurnards (family Triglidae), to name but a few. Somewhat deeper is the outer sub-littoral zone, where the light is poorer. Haddock, rat-tails and hakes are found as well as halibuts and the chimaeras. Below this is a zone into which some of the fishes from the zone above descend where they join a sparse fauna of brotulids, deep-sea eels, and sea snails.

The geographical distribution of fishes, a branch of zoogeography, is threehold; local distribution; regional distribution (which deals with groups in selected parts of the world); and worldwide distribution, which deals with broad concepts of distribution.

To understand fully the present-day distribution of fishes a knowledge of their past history is essential, as well as that of any past geologic or geographic changes. The present-day distribution of any one form may well produce valuable clues to its evolution. Many are still moving into new territories, others seem to be dying out; unfortunately there seem to be more of the latter. Man-made pollution, unsurmountable obstacles which keep the fishes from their spawning grounds and overfishing are often the cause.

Zoogeography is a vast subject and only a broad sketch can be given here. Patterns of distribution differ from one continent to another. The fishes of Africa, for example, show great diversity and include a number of archaic forms such as the lung-fishes (genus *Protopterus*) and the bichirs (genus *Polypterus*). The cichlids of the Great Rift Valley occur nowhere else. There is a large cyprinoid (carps and relatives) fauna which is probably a branch of the Asian cyprinoids, while in the north-west live forms which are closer to the European forms than those of Africa.

In Eurasia, where there is a vast number of closely related cyprinoids, they are the dominant fish group. There are only two relict archaic fishes, the paddlefish and the sucker *Myxocyprinus* of China.

In Europe itself the Ice Ages reduced the fish population greatly, leaving only six families of fishes consisting of about 120 species. All are fairly widespread and two of the families have only a single species, the pike and the mud-minnow. The carps (family Cyprinidae) and loaches (family Cobitidae) form the greater part of the fauna. There are only two catfishes (family Siluridae) but quite a few other forms which spend part of their lives in the sea, e.g. salmon, sturgeons, lampreys, shads and gobies.

The oriental region consisting of tropical Asia and stretching from India to South China and Indonesia has a great variety of cyprinoid fishes and catfishes. A single archaic fish (*Scleropages*) occurs here and freshwater herrings are rarer than in Africa. There are, however, some specialised fishes which have developed anchoring suckers so that they can live in very fast running mountain streams; these will be described later.

Australia is peculiar in that it has no indigenous freshwater fishes except the lungfish (genus *Neoceratodus*) and a fish called Bonytongue (genus *Scleropages*) of the family Osteoglossidae which is also represented by different genera in Africa and South America. All its other fishes are either of marine origin or have been introduced from other countries.

In North America there are about 600 species of freshwater fishes in twenty-one families. The richest and most diverse representation is found in the Mississippi basin, south-east America and the Great Lakes. On other parts of the continent the fish fauna is thin in variety, especially in Canada, Alaska and Mexico. There are no true freshwater fishes in the West Indies.

It is said that about a third of the North American fishes originated where they now live, this includes such forms as the darters (family Percidae), cavefishes (family Amblyopsidae), and mooneyes (family Hiodontidae). But more than half of the North American fishes are of Eurasian origin, for example the carps (family Cyprinidae), perches (family Percidae), pikes (family Esocidae), mudminnows (family Umbridae) and

about a sixth probably came from such South American forms as the characins (family Characidae), the cichlids and some of the catfish families. It should be mentioned that the darters are considered a subfamily of the perches and descended in isolation from common ancestors.

There are over 2,000 species of fishes to be found in South America, all derived from a few ancestors. Most numerous are the characins, catfishes and cichlids. There is an archaic lungfish (family Lepidosirenidae), two species of Bonytongue (family Osteoglossidae) and two species of a family Nandidae of spiny-rayed fishes. All these three families are represented in Africa as are the characins. Most of the South American fauna, however, developed when the North and South American continents were separated in the past. It is argued that the affinities between the African and South American fishes suggest a land connection between the two continents.

The distribution of marine fishes will not be dealt with in such detail for the picture is not so clear, but there is little doubt that temperature plays an important part in distribution. For example, the 12°C. isotherm divides the North Temperate Zone into the subtropical and subarctic regions. Along this line such warm water loving forms as the pilchards (genus *Sardina*), anchovies (family Engraulidae), and red mullets (genus *Mullus*) give way to more northerly forms like the herrings, cods and plaice. Many Mediterranean species are not found north of this line, which also marks the southern limit at which salmon and trouts (genus *Salmo*) migrate into the sea. At the northern end of the Temperate Zone is the northern limit of many of the British sea fishes and the southern limit at which the charrs (genus *Salvelinus*) migrate into the sea.

Most fishes stay near home, but some are renowned travellers. A great many of them are always, or nearly always, on the move—even though the distance covered may only vary from around a metre to a few hundred metres from home. Such short distance movements must be distinguished from the long distance migrations

Rainbow Trout (*Salmo gairdneri*) at Fairy Springs, New Zealand. This is one of several North American species of trout and the one that has been widely distributed to other parts of the world, just as the European Brown Trout has been distributed. The Rainbow has a faster growth rate than the Brown Trout under similar conditions, and consequently is better adapted for culture in fish farms and later release.

from one locality to another. These migrations are rarely sporadic, but take place with regularity at set times of the year.

Migrations are made either for the purpose of spawning or for feeding. The migrations of the Mediterranean tunnies (genus *Thunnus*) were well known to the Romans, but even at the present day they are not fully understood. Year after year they enter the Mediterranean in large shoals and appear in certain localities with regularity; as these habits are known to the fishermen, the tunnies are caught in large numbers. However, it is reasonably certain that the migrations are for feeding and are dependent on the movement of the prey of tunnies—pilchards, herrings and mackerels. The migration of the mackerel, which starts as the sea begins to get much warmer in early summer, is a spawning journey. The fishes move into shallow waters near the coast where they spawn and then move into bays and estuaries to feed on young fishes. Also in warmer weather the pilchards (genus *Sardina*) approach the southernmost coasts of Britain and leave as the seas get colder. This is a feeding migration.

The great economic importance of herrings has made their movements of especial interest, and it is now possible to recognise many different races of the most economically important species the Atlantic Herring (*Clupea harengus*), each of which has different feeding and migratory patterns.

Though experts differ, it is probable that fishes originated in sea water, and that many forms found today in freshwater came from ancestors of marine origin. As they became more numerous it

is probable that competition for food and space resulted in some forms emigrating into other territories. Some may have moved into estuaries and eventually freshwater. At first these were transient excursions, but in time some forms became established and stayed there. Even today some move into freshwater from the sea for only a short period of their lives. The result is that almost all orders of fishes have freshwater representatives. A large group, the Ostariophysi, has evolved completely in freshwater, and some of its members have now become secondarily marine.

Two extremes in migrations to and from sea to freshwater are the anadromous type as carried out by the salmon (genera *Salmo* and *Oncorhynchus*), which move into freshwater to spawn having spent most of their feeding life in the sea, and the opposite migration of the freshwater eels (genus *Anguilla*). In this, the so-called catadromous habit, the eels spend most of their feeding life in freshwater and return to the sea to spawn. This habit is also seen in some of the galaxids; one species of this family from Patagonia, Australia and New Zealand moves from freshwater to spawn in the sea. It is of interest that other galaxids move from the sea to freshwater to spawn, as do their distant relatives the salmon.

Amongst fishes with an anadromous habit are the sturgeons (genus *Acipenser*), shads (genus *Alosa*), Striped Bass (*Roccus saxatilis*), and sea and river lampreys (genera *Petromyzon* and *Lampetra*).

Movements up and down stream and confined to their water-sheds are called anadromous. An example is seen in the Amazon where the

In fishes as in all other animals some species are solitary and some are gregarious. The latter live in schools. That is large numbers move about together, each member of the school following the same direction as its fellows and all evenly spaced from each other. This is a picture of schooling fishes passing under a pier in the Caribbean.

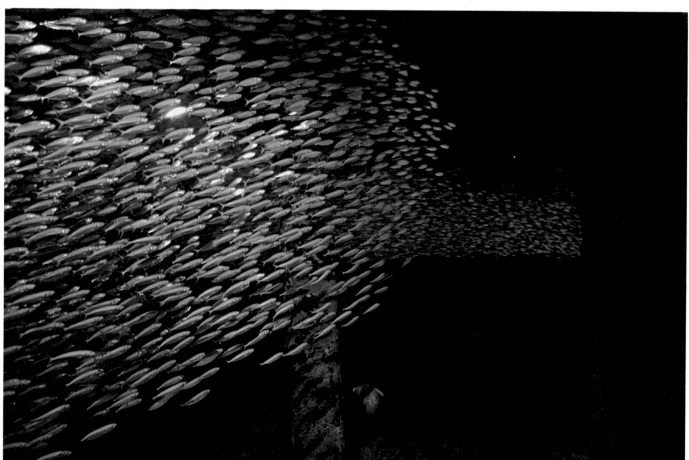

bocachicas in the wet season travel great distances upstream. Less spectacular journeys are made by the trouts that often move upstream to spawn in the shallower waters. In lakes, the charrs or lake trouts (genus *Salvelinus*) in North America and coregonids (genus *Coregonus*) move into the shallows at spawning time. In the more northerly parts of North America and Europe these two forms are anadromous.

Often the movement between fresh and sea water is not related to spawning. In Europe the Brown Trout (*Salmo trutta*) will move out into estuaries presumably to feed, and the European Common Flounder (*Platichthys flesus*) moves considerable distance into freshwater and some gobies (genus *Sicydium*) drop down to the sea as larvae, but do not stay long. The Threespine Stickleback (*Gasterosteus aculeatus*) may be marine in habit in such northerly regions as Greenland, Alaska, and Kamchatka; and in Britain it is common in estuaries and in freshwater, but in Spain and Italy it is almost entirely freshwater in habit.

Two migrations merit fuller description. Firstly, the salmon (genera *Salmo* and *Oncorhynchus*). The Atlantic Salmon (*Salmo salar*) spawns in freshwater where the young feed for periods ranging from just over a year to seven or eight years; the further north the longer the stay. Just before their seaward migration the young become silvery as a result of the deposition in the skin of an excretory product called guanin. Once in the sea they migrate to food-rich areas, none returns in less than a year, and some may spend four or more years in the sea before returning. After spawning most males die, but about five per cent of the females return to spawn again, and a very few for a third spawning. All Pacific salmon (genus *Oncorhynchus*) die after spawning. The young of some species start migrating seawards shortly after hatching: *Oncorhynchus gorbuscha* (Pink Salmon), *O. keta* (the Chum Salmon) and some *O. tschawytscha* (Chinook Salmon or Sockeye). The migratory journey of the Sockeye may be 3,218 kilometres or more. It is believed that once they reach coastal waters the sense of smell enables the salmon to identify their parent stream and so return to spawn in the river in which they were born. Proof of this is fairly conclusively shown by tagging experiments whereby the young are tagged as they leave the rivers and identified on their return.

Secondly the migration of the freshwater eels (genus *Anguilla*). This is equally spectacular, and both they and the salmon show unique powers of navigation. The European and eastern North American eels spawn in a region of the Atlantic near the Sargasso Sea. The young drift back to their respective coasts, the journey of the European *Leptocephalus* (pre-metamorphosis eel larva) taking about three years. Upon nearing the coasts in late autumn they are about seven centimetres in length, flattened, leaf-like, and colourless. A metamorphosis follows, the larvae stop feeding, become shorter in length and cylindrical in shape but remain transparent. The sharp needle-like teeth of the *Leptocephalus* are also lost. Early the following spring, as they start ascending the rivers, colour starts to appear in the skin. Thus the transparent glass eels change into elvers. Their migration may extend into late spring, and in any one river the migration time and migration path are very similar year after year. Countless millions reach the rivers, where they will stay for five to twelve years if they are males, and from ten to twenty-four years if they are females. Before leaving the adults stop feeding, become silvery, and their eyes get bigger. The fishes are in excellent condition, with large food reserves in the flesh and are thus fitted for their long fast as they migrate to spawn in the deep warm waters of the western Atlantic. Fishery biologists do not believe the very tenuous theory that all European eels die before they reach their spawning grounds. It is of interest to note that the spawning journey of the salmon is also a fasting one. The spawning grounds of the European Eel (*A. anguilla*) and the American Eel (*A. rostrata*) overlap to a considerable extent but there is apparently little or no interbreeding, despite very similar appearance and life-history.

The factors which cause and influence the many different types of migrations found in fishes are varied. Salmon have a homing instinct probably guided by smell and oceanic currents, the drive being provided by the spawning urge. Similarly the spawning urge sends the eel off on its long journey, which often starts on dark windy moonless nights. It has been suggested that eels can perceive microseismic vibrations produced by Atlantic storms and so pick up and anticipate the sort of weather conditions that are most favourable for them and assist in their down-river migration.

Classification

As noted in the previous section the classification of fishes is not easy. Many experts differ on matters of detail, and sometimes of substance. The aim of classification is to arrange all fishes, both living and fossil, into some sort of order which shows the relationship between the groups and which also gives some clues to their evolutionary history. A classification should also take into account aspects of the embryological development and genetics of each group. However, gaps in knowledge, especially in the fossil record cause any classification adopted to be a synthesis. Trends in classifications tend also to be affected by currently fashionable theories—regrettable as this must appear to the non-systematist. The classification adopted here is that published by J. S. Nelson (1976) in his *Fishes of the World*, an approach which is refreshingly free from the influence of any cult.

Jawless fishes (Superclass Agnatha)

These fish-like vertebrates lack jaws and pelvic fins, and have only two semi-circular canals in the inner ear. Vertebral centra are not developed but the notochord is unconstricted. The gill arch skeleton is fused with the neurocranium. Two classes with about sixty living species.

Lampreys and cephalaspids (Class Cephalaspidomorphi)

These have a single nostril opening between the eyes not connecting to the pharynx and gills opening from the pharynx through a series of separate pouches each with an external opening. There is one living order.

Lampreys (Order Petromyzoniformes)

These eel-like animals have a sucker disc on the head, with teeth on the sucker and tongue most conspicuously developed in adults. There are seven paired gill openings along the sides just behind the eyes, which are large in adults, a single nostril in mid-line and just behind this an unpigmented patch of skin beneath which lies the pineal organ, with a retina and lens-like structure; this acts as a third eye.

Lampreys are restricted to the cooler waters of both northern and southern hemispheres. They occur both in the sea and in freshwater but all species breed in freshwater. Only six or so are migratory the remaining twenty-four species spending their entire lives in freshwater. The eggs are laid in a nest excavated in coarse gravel by the female who removes the stones with her sucker and clears fine débris by vigorous tail flapping. The male also uses his sucker to keep station by the nest but in the act of spawning fastens on to the female's head and loops his body around hers. The fertilised eggs fall into the interstices of the nest gravel. Frequently, several pairs will spawn in the one gravel bank. After hatching, the young drift downstream into a muddy part of the stream, burrow into the mud, filtering micro-organisms from it by pumping water over the gills. At this larval stage they are known as ammocoetes and the eyes are poorly developed.

The ammocoete stage may last for up to six years depending on temperature and species. It is ended by a metamorphosis in which the eyes, vertical fins, and teeth become better developed. Some species breed within the next few months and these do not feed during this period, the gut becoming atrophied as the gonads develop. Several species, however, develop pointed teeth in the sucker disc and adopt a parasitic life-style, sucking the blood from bony fishes and while doing this injecting the host with an anti-coagulant produced in the salivary glands.

The north Atlantic species, *Petromyzon marinus*, is a parasitic, migratory species found both in Europe and North America, which entered the Great Lakes through canals and seriously affected their fisheries. The Lampern, *Lampetra fluviatilis*, although found only in Europe is a parasitic migratory species, as is the Pouched Lamprey, *Geotria australis*, of the southern hemisphere. The American Brook Lamprey, *Lampetra lamottei*, of the Great Lakes and the Mississippi River drainage, and the European *Lampetra planeri* are examples of non-parasitic species.

Hagfishes and pteraspids (Class Pteraspidomorpha)

These have no pectoral fins; bone, when present, is of a cellular nature. Living representatives, the hagfishes, lack bone.

Hagfishes (Order Myxiniformes)

These eel-like animals have poorly developed vertical fins, degenerate eyes, thick fleshy barbels around the mouth slit and teeth on the tongue. They have a single mid-line nasal opening on the top of the head which connects through to the pharynx. One family (Myxinidae) divided into the subfamilies Myxininae with a single external gill opening each side and the Eptatretinae with five to sixteen gill openings.

The hagfishes are entirely marine and are widely distributed in relatively shallow water in the temperate zones but at considerable depths in the tropics. They do not pass through a protracted larval (ammocoete) period or a metamorphosis. The eggs are laid on the seabed and are large and yolky. About thirty are produced per individual. Both ovaries and testes are developed in each specimen but only one organ is functional at a time.

Well-developed mucus pores form a series along the lower sides and all hagfishes are remarkably slimy. They feed largely on dead or dying fishes and invertebrates and are notorious for their attacks on fishes caught on long lines. They bore into them and consume everything but skin and bone. The North Atlantic Hagfish, *Myxine glutinosa*, has for a long time been regarded as a pest on parts of the Norwegian and the New England coasts. It eats considerable quantities of shrimp-like crustaceans. In the North Pacific there are several species of *Eptatretus*, which have several gill openings along each side. *E. burgeri* lives in shallow water along the coasts of Japan and Korea, while *E. stouti* is found from California to southern Alaska at depths of twenty to 1,100 metres.

Jawed fishes (Superclass Gnathostomata)

This group, which includes all the living fishes, is distinguished by having jaws which are derived from modified gill arches; paired limbs are usually present and there are three semi-circular canals in the inner ear. The gill arches are not fused to the neurocranium. Vertebral centra are usually well developed. There are two classes of living fishes, the Chondrichthyes—the sharks, rays and chimaeras, and the Osteichthyes—the lungfishes, coelacanth, bichirs, sturgeons and bony fishes.

Sharks, rays and chimaeras (Class Chondrichthyes)

The skeleton is cartilaginous although often calcified and thus hard. Fin rays are horny and unsegmented (ceratotrichia). The teeth are fused to the jaws and replaced serially; the biting edge of the upper jaw formed by the palatoquadrate. Swimbladder and lung absent; a spiral valve present in the lower gut. Fertilisation of the egg is internal; males have pelvic intromittent organs (claspers). The blood contains high levels of urea which maintains water balance in the body. Most chondrichthyans are marine fish, only a few species live in freshwater.

There are two main evolutionary lines (subclasses), the Elasmobranchii (sharks and rays) with about 600 species, and the Holocephali (chimaeras and ratfishes) with about twenty-five species.

Sharks (Superorder Selachimorpha)
With five to seven gill slits on the sides of the head; the anterior edge of the pectoral fin not fused to the head. The upper jaw not fused to the cranium, the jaw suspension is amphistylic or hypostylic (that is it is suspended by the hyomandibulars and ligaments) this demonstrating its derivation from a gill arch. The anal fin may be present or absent (order Squaliformes). The pectoral girdle fused ventrally but not jointed dorsally. Four orders are recognised.

Horn Shark or Port Jackson Shark (Order Heterodontiformes)
This archaic type of shark is similar to those which were dominant in the Triassic. They have two large dorsal fins, each with a stout spine in front. The head is heavy and deep with broad ridges over the eyes. In the front of the jaws the teeth are small and sharply pointed but at the sides they are large and flattened or rounded.

The Port Jackson Shark, *Heterodontus philippi*, is common in southern Australian seas in shallow water down to about 160 metres. On the Pacific coast of Mexico and California as well as in the Gulf of California the Horn Shark, *H. francisci*, is found from surf level to twenty-five metres. Both feed on hard-shelled animals and grow to about one and a half metres; they are quite harmless. Heterodontids lay their eggs in dark brown horny cases, with a spirally twisted edge; they are usually wedged between rocks and hatch in eight to nine months, the young fish being only ten to thirteen centimetres at hatching. They are found in the warm temperate Indo-Pacific oceans.

Cow and frilled sharks (Order Hexanchiformes)
The cow sharks belong to the family Hexanchidae and all have six or seven wide gill slits although the first is not continuous under the throat. They also have a single dorsal fin.

The Six-gilled Shark, *Hexanchus griseus*, is widely distributed in the cool, temperate Atlantic, off the North American and European coasts. It is very similar to, if not identical with the Six-gill Shark of the north Pacific and of the southern hemisphere. Sharks with seven gill slits are *Heptranchias perlo*, found in deep water mainly in the tropics although also in the Mediterranean, and *Notorynchus maculatus* which lives in the warm waters of the Indo-Pacific. All are oceanic species which occur rarely in shallow inshore water, although *N. maculatus* has shallow nursery areas.

The Frilled Shark, *Chlamydoselachus anguineus*, is the only member of the Chlamydoselachidae

There is a wide variety of caudal fins in sharks. Shown here are those of (A) cowsharks or sixgill sharks (genus *Hexanchus*), (B) porbeagle or mackerel sharks (genus *Lamna*), (C) thresher sharks (genus *Alopias*), (D) dogfish sharks (genus *Squalus*), (E) sand sharks (genus *Carcharinus*) and (F) angel sharks (genus *Squatina*).

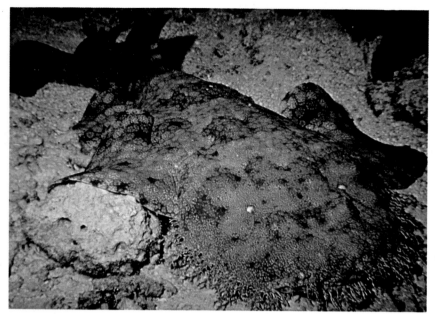

the surface of the sea. It lays its eggs in thirty centimetre long horny egg cases which are left on the shallow sea bed to hatch unattended, but much of its biology is virtually unknown.

Carpet sharks (Family Orectolobidae)
A family of rather small bottom-living sharks, rarely growing longer than four metres all with the nostril connected to the mouth by a deep groove and with a fleshy barbel on the edge of the nostril. They are most common in the tropical Indo-Pacific, but one of the largest is the Atlantic Nurse Shark, *Ginglymostoma cirratum*, found off the African coast and from Brazil to Rhode Island. It is common in shallow water and lies close to the seabed beside reefs; it is only dangerous to man when provoked. Almost as large is the Indian Ocean Zebra Shark, *Stegostoma fasciatum*, which is boldly marked with dark bars on a light brown background. It lays eggs in egg cases, while the Nurse Shark gives birth to living young. Bold marking, in this case with dark-edged light spots and bars, is a feature of the Wobbegong, *Orectolobus maculatus*, found along the Australian coast.

Sand sharks (Family Odontaspidae)
Characterised by their long curved slender teeth the sand sharks are widely distributed in warm oceans. Their five gill slits are placed forward of the pectoral fin, which is broad as are all the fins of these sharks. Heavy-bodied, they have the appearance of sluggish sharks, and yet their diet is composed of fishes, often fast-swimming species. The Mediterranean and tropical eastern Atlantic Ragged-tooth Shark, *Odontaspis ferox* grows to four metres in length, a little smaller than the Sand Tiger, *O. taurus*, which occurs on both sides of the tropical Atlantic and which is found in inshore waters. These and the Australian Grey Nurse, *O. arenarius*, are potentially dangerous to man, especially in the process of capture, but they impinge on man's activities chiefly by taking fish from nets and as predator on fishes.

In deep water the family is represented by the Goblin Shark, *Mitsukurina owstoni*, which grows to about three and a half metres. It has been reported from off the Portuguese, South African and Japanese coasts in depths around 500 metres. Its jaws are protrusible but its more remarkable feature is the prolongation of the snout into a flattened beak.

Mackerel sharks (Family Lamnidae)
An assemblage of active open sea sharks which include the Porbeagle, Mako and Great White Shark, the Threshers, and the Basking Shark, which groups are accorded family status by some scientists.

The Great White Shark, *Carcharodon carcharias*, is the most aggressive and dangerous of all sharks. It grows to a length of at least six and a half metres and possibly to eight metres, and is found in the open ocean in tropical waters, although occasionally it comes into coastal waters. Like its relatives, the Porbeagle, *Lamna nasus*, and the Mako Shark, *Isurus oxyrinchus*, it has a broad lunate tail fin which helps make these the fastest swimming sharks known. Their body temperatures are also somewhat higher than the surrounding water temperature. The Mako is a large shark found in all oceans

This Wobbegong Shark (*Orectolobus ogilbyi*) of Heron Island, Queensland, shows the wonderful combination of mottled or marbled colours and fleshy appendages that conceal it as it lies on the seabed. Most of the thirty species of carpet sharks are found in the Indo–Pacific region, where they tend to be known by the Australian name of Wobbegong. In spite of their sometimes large size, carpet sharks are not aggressive but have been known to use their teeth in defence.

The Sand Tiger Shark (*Odontaspis taurus*) is one of the commoner of the slender-toothed sharks and ranges over the eastern Atlantic from the Mediterranean to South Africa, and in the western Atlantic. It is a moderate-sized shark, voracious in feeding on fishes and squid.

family. Its gill slits are enormously wide and the first rings the head like a frill; its teeth have three pointed cusps. It is widely distributed in deep water in temperate oceans off northern Europe, Japan, western North America, South Africa, and New Zealand. Little is known of its biology, but like its closest relatives it gives birth to fully formed young. It grows to two metres in length. The Six- and Seven-gilled Sharks are rather larger.

True sharks (Order Lamniformes)
This order contains most of the well-known sharks. They are typified by having two dorsal fins, neither of which has spines in it, a single anal fin, and five gill slits. There are about 200 species.

Whale Shark (Family Rhincodontidae)
Rhincodon typus, the Whale Shark, is the largest known fish reaching a certain length of over fifteen metres, and possibly eighteen metres. It is widely distributed in tropical seas and feeds on planktonic organisms and fish. It is most frequently seen at

but mainly in tropical and warm temperate zones. Its food is composed of surface-living fish and squids, as is that of the Porbeagle, which lives in cooler water such as off the British Isles. Both species grow to about three and a half metres in length.

The Basking Shark, *Cetorhinus maximus*, is also a cool temperate species, but in contrast to its relatives it feeds on plankton in the surface waters of the sea. As a consequence its teeth are minute but its gillrakers, which filter the plankton from the water are well developed. It is found in both northern and southern hemispheres.

The Thresher Shark, *Alopias vulpinus*, is distinguished by the extreme length of its tail fin, which is said to be used to herd prey fish into compact schools before the shark attacks. Mostly oceanic in distribution it is occasionally found inshore. It lives in the north Atlantic and in Australian waters is represented by a similar species. All members of this family give birth to a few well-formed pups after a long gestation period.

Dogfishes (Family Scyliorhinidae)
Some sixty species of small sharks belong to this family. Most are bottom-living shallow-water sharks with the dorsal fins placed well down the tail.

One deep-water species is the False Cat-shark, *Pseudotriakis microdon*, which is found in the north Atlantic at depths of 305 to 1,525 metres and which has long-based dorsal fins and minute teeth. It grows to three metres in length.

Most dogfishes, however, grow to less than one metre. Several are common in European seas including the Dogfish, *Scyliorhinus canicula*, and the Nursehound, *S. stellaris*, while in deep water (200 to 500 metres) the Black-mouthed Dogfish, *Galeus melastomus*, is common. The Swell Shark, *Cephaloscyllium ventriosum*, lives on the Californian coast among kelp beds; as a defence mechanism it inflates its belly with water so that it doubles in size. In general, the shallow water dogfishes are conspicuously and often beautifully patterned. All lay their eggs in slender egg cases, which are anchored often in algae.

Requiem sharks (Family Carcharinidae)
Many of the well-known and dangerous tropical sharks belong to this family, members of which are generally slender-bodied with two dorsal fins, a long upper tail fin lobe, and five gill slits. Most have sharply-pointed, serrated triangular teeth.

One of the most widely distributed is the Bull Shark, *Carcharinus leucas*, which lives in the tropical Atlantic and Indo-Pacific, usually in inshore waters and in fresh water as in the Zambezi, Euphrates and Ganges Rivers, and Lake Nicaragua. It grows to about three and a half metres in length and although it mainly eats fishes and squids, it frequently attacks man. Other members of this large genus are oceanic in habit like the Whitetip Shark, *C. longimanus*, probably the most common oceanic shark, growing to around three and a half metres it is found in all tropical seas. The equally large Blue Shark, *Prionace glauca*, has a similar distribution and in summer migrates north as far as western British coasts, although it is not found inshore.

A common European member of the family is the Tope, *Galeorhinus galeus*, which grows to two metres in length. Like its Australian relative, the School Shark, *G. australis*, and the Soupfin or Oil Shark, *G. zyopterus*, of the Pacific coast of North America, it feeds on small fishes and squids. The last species, as its name suggests was heavily exploited for liver oil, and its fins used for soup by the Chinese community of North America.

In contrast to these fish-eaters the Smooth Hound, *Mustelus asterias*, of Europe, and the Californian Leopard Shark, *Triakis semifasciata*, have flattened teeth and feed on crustaceans and shellfish which they crush with these specialised teeth.

Hammerhead sharks (Family Sphyrnidae)
Sharks with the sides of the head greatly expanded, the eyes and nostrils placed far apart on the edges of the 'hammer'. This curious development may be a hydrofoil to enhance swimming or may confer advantages in detecting scents in the water. In many ways they are similar to the Requiem Sharks, but they are confined to tropical seas. One of the largest is the Great Hammerhead, *Sphyrna mokkaran*, growing to six metres and found in all three warm oceans. It feeds mainly on fishes including stingrays and like several of its relatives has been known to attack man.

Spiny-finned sharks (Order Squaliformes)
Many of the members of this order have a prominent spine in each dorsal fin; the anal fin is always absent. There are about seventy-five species known. Most appear to be live-bearers.

The Epaulette Shark (*Hemiscyllium ocellatum*), a shallow-water shark of northern Australia and the West Pacific. Possibly the big spots on the sides are eye-spots which make the fish look bigger than it is, for it lies so still on the sea bed that it can be picked up by hand by divers; it is quite harmless and grows to one metre in length.

The Blacktip Shark (*Carcharhinus limbatus*) is worldwide in tropical seas. It swims with languid grace by means of side to side sweeps of its tail. It grows to about 2.5 metres in length.

Spurdogs and sleeper sharks (Family Squalidae)

This group of sharks have colonised the deep sea very effectively and possibly form the major part of the biomass on the lower continental shelf. Among these are the Velvet-belly, *Etmopterus spinax*, of the eastern north Atlantic, common at 200 to 700 metres and growing to fifty-three centimetres in length. This is one of the very few sharks to possess luminous organs. Another deep water species is the smallest known shark, the Dwarf Shark, *Squaliolus laticaudus*, which is found in the Pacific Ocean between 300 and 900 metres. It grows to a length of fifteen centimetres. Much larger are the deep water species of *Centrophorus* which grow to around one and a half metres and are very abundant between 400 and 1,500 metres in all but polar seas. The shallow-water spurdogs, like the North Atlantic *Squalus acanthias*, are smaller but extremely abundant, forming huge, often single-sex schools. These are widely exploited as food fish and for fish meal, but as their growth rate is slow and fecundity low they may be quickly overfished.

The Bramble Shark, *Echinorhinus brucus*, is a large relatively deep water species, as is the Greenland or Sleeper Shark, *Somniosus microcephalus*, which is one of the few sharks to be found in polar waters.

Saw sharks (Family Pristiophoridae)

The snout is produced into a long flat blade with teeth, which are alternately long and short, embedded in each side. A pair of long barbels on the underside of the snout assist it in finding its food, largely burrowing invertebrates. Possibly as few as four living species exist, all in the tropical Indo-Pacific. One of the better known species is the Common Saw Shark, *Pristiophorus cirratus*, an inhabitant of southern Australian seas which grows to about one and a quarter metres long.

Angel sharks (Family Squatinidae)

The angel sharks appear to be intermediate between the sharks and the rays, but the lateral position of the gill slits and the pectoral fins, which are not fused with the body anteriorly, place them with the sharks. They are found worldwide in warm temperate oceans, living mostly inshore on the seabed. On the Pacific coast of North America, the Californian Monkfish, *Squatina californica*, is common; it is said to feed on invertebrates and to lay egg capsules. The European Monkfish, *S. squatina*, however, is a live-bearer and mainly eats bottom-living fishes; similar reproduction is recorded for the Australian Ornate Angelshark, *S. tergocellata*.

Rays, guitarfishes and sawfishes (Superorder Batoidimorpha)

The gill slits are ventral; the pectoral fins fused to the sides of the head anterior to the gill slits; eyes and spiracle always dorsal. The spiracle is well developed and acts as an inhalent opening for respiration, important for a group which are largely bottom dwellers. The anal fin is absent, and the pectoral girdle is fused dorsally as well as ventrally. All living forms belong to the order Rajiformes; there are about 320 known species.

Sawfishes (Family Pristidae)

The snout is produced to form a long blade about one third of the total length, with equal sized teeth along the edges; no barbels beneath snout; teeth minute in jaws. There are two dorsal fins and a well-developed caudal fin which is the main propulsive element. Their evolution from the primitive ray-like fishes has an interesting parallel in the saw sharks which are similar in form but derive from sharks. Sawfishes are common in tropical seas, mainly in shallow inshore areas and especially in estuaries, ascending even into fresh water as in the Zambezi River and Lake Nicaragua. The Greater Sawfish, *Pristis pectinata*, grows to about ten metres in length, and lives in all tropical oceans, while *P. pristis* is rather smaller, and occurs in the eastern Atlantic from Portugal to West Africa. All sawfishes use their saws primarily for rooting in the sea bed to expose buried invertebrates; they are also said to attack schooling fish lashing their toothed snouts from side to side and then to return to pick up dead and injured fish. All sawfishes give birth to well developed young, but the teeth of the baby are soft and covered by a gristly membrane until after birth.

Guitarfishes (Family Rhinobatidae)

The body form of the guitarfishes is flattened anteriorly, but the tail is fleshy and supports large dorsal and caudal fins. Most of them have the characteristic guitar or fiddle shape, and are bottom-living fishes which forage in shallow water on the sea bed for crustaceans and other invertebrates. The Spotted Guitarfish, *Rhinobatus lentiginosus*, is a common species on the North American coast from Mexico to North Carolina; *R. rhinobatus* occurs from southern Portugal to Angola as well as in the Mediterranean, it attains a length of one metre. The giant guitarfish or Sand Shark, *Rhynchobatus djeddensis*, grows to three metres, and is widespread in the tropical Indo-West Pacific. The guitarfishes are ovoviviparous.

Electric rays (Family Torpedinidae)

The body is flattened, soft, with smooth naked skins; mouth small; dorsal fins relatively small with two in some species none in others; caudal fin broad and paddle-like. Their notable feature is the large electric organ, derived from branchial muscles in the head and anterior body. All electric rays are ovoviviparous.

The largest species is the Atlantic Torpedo, *Torpedo nobiliana*, which occurs off both European and North American coasts, as well as off South Africa, it is nearly two metres in length. Its electric shock can attain 170 to 220 volts. Although it is found in shallow inshore waters it is rarely in conflict with man, rather its electric ability is used to stun active swimming fishes (by enfolding them within its 'wings') which are then eaten at leisure. The Lesser Electric Ray, *Narcine brasiliensis*, is common between Argentina and North Carolina, it is much smaller, and is said to feed mainly on invertebrates although it has weak electrical properties. In deeper water of 300 to 900 metres off the Florida coast and in the Caribbean, *Benthobatis marcida* is found. The eyes are totally covered with skin and it is effectively blind.

Skates and rays (Family Rajidae)

In this large family the body and pectoral fins form a lozenge shaped disc and the tail is thin with very small dorsal fins (which are sometimes absent) and caudal fin reduced or absent. Small electric organs are developed, derived from the caudal musculature, these produce electric fields probably used for species recognition. Swimming is by means of undulations of the pectoral fins. All rays lay their eggs in horny capsules with prominent corners.

They are worldwide in distribution although in the tropics they are found mainly in deep water. Most are bottom-living species with relatively unspecialised diets of invertebrates, although some like the Arctic Skate, *Raja hyperborea*, found in the northern Atlantic eat substantial quantities of fish. Some species, like the Barndoor Skate, *R. laevis*, of eastern North America, and the Skate, *R. batis*, of European seas are very large (one and a half and two and a half metres long respectively), but many others are small and live in inshore waters.

In deep water there are also relatives of the

Guitarfishes (family Rhinobatidae) are found worldwide in tropical and warm temperate seas. They are well adapted for life on the sea bed but are quite active and hunt for food which is mainly crustaceans. Although they look like sharks their ventral gill openings show them to be rays.

231

The Blue-spotted or Ribbontail Ray (*Taeniura lymma*) grows to 2.4 metres in length and is a common inhabitant of shallow water and reef lagoons through the tropical Indo–West Pacific. Its tail spines are long and capable of inflicting dangerous envenomed wounds.

skates, like the Leafsnout Ray, *Springeria folirostris*, found in 300 to 512 metres in the Gulf of Mexico. The snout is produced to form a needle-like point with two leaf-like flaps below its tip. This species, with several species of *Anacanthobatis* from the same area and off South Africa are sometimes placed in the family Anacanthobatidae.

Stingrays (Family Dasyatidae)

Degeneration of the tail has proceeded further in this group and the dorsal fins are absent in most, while none have a caudal fin. The tail is long, whip-like and has one or more long serrated-edged spines on its dorsal surface. These spines have venom-producing tissue along grooves on their underside and stab wounds are excruciatingly painful and occasionally fatal to humans. Most stingrays are relatively sluggish, lying partly buried under sand on the sea bed; a few species enter river mouths and may be found in fresh water. Mostly they eat bottom-living invertebrates and they are usually found in inshore waters over soft bottoms.

The largest species is the tropical Indo-West Pacific *Dasyatis brevicaudata*, which grows to about four and a quarter metres in length and weighs about 430 kilograms. It has caused deaths in Australia and the Pacific Islands. In European waters the Stingray, *D. pastinaca*, migrates north to Britain in summer, but occurs in the Mediterranean all year round; it grows to a width of more than two and a half metres. Of similar size is the western Atlantic species *D. americana* which ranges from New Jersey to Brazil.

In tropical seas butterfly rays are widely distributed. These are broad across the wings, with very short tails; in some species a spine is developed others have a single dorsal fin. One of the better known species is the Smooth Butterfly Ray, *Gymnura micrura*, of the western Atlantic from Brazil to Chesapeake Bay. It grows to eighty-six centimetres in length, and forages over the tide-covered sand flats in search of crabs, shrimps and molluscs. The butterfly rays are more active than the stingrays. All members of the family are viviparous.

River stingrays (Family Potamotrygonidae)

These are the only elasmobranchs to have become adapted to life in fresh water and they are found only in the rivers and lakes of northern South America which flow into the Atlantic and Caribbean. They are small fish, rarely more than thirty centimetres in diameter, which burrow in the mud of the river or lake bed. The body is almost circular and the tail rather thick with a stout serrated spine on its dorsal surface. The spine has venom-producing tissue on the underside and can inflict serious, even fatal and always painful wounds, if trodden upon or handled incautiously. One of the better known species is the River Ray, *Potamotrygon motoro*, of the Paraguay River.

Eagle rays (Family Myliobatidae)

In these rays the head is elevated and clear of the pectoral fins; the tail is long and whip-like with a small dorsal fin and one or more spines. They are widespread in all tropical and warm temperate seas. The Eagle Ray, *Myliobatis aquila*, which is found in the eastern Atlantic from Britain to Senegal, grows to nearly two metres in length, and feeds on molluscs. In areas where mussels, oysters, or clams are farmed the eagle ray can become a pest. It swims gracefully by powerful downstrokes of its long pectoral fins. Like the river stingray it is ovoviviparous.

Manta rays (Family Mobulidae)

A small family containing about ten species of active swimming, mainly pelagic rays which have long pectoral fins, by means of which they 'fly' through the water. The mouth is terminal and there are a pair of movable fins on each side (modified from the anterior pectoral rays) which act as funnels to direct plankton into the mouth. These plankton eating rays are all large, even the Pygmy Devil Ray, *Mobula diabolus*, is nearly two metres in width. This is an Indo-Pacific species, represented in the tropical Atlantic by *M. mobular*. The Atlantic Manta, *Manta birostris*, attains a width of more than six and a half metres and a weight of more than 1,360 kilograms, a similar if not identical fish occurs in the Indo-Pacific. Despite their size they are harmless, although they have been known to overturn a small boat when harpooned. They are viviparous, the young being nourished by maternal uterine secretions.

Chimaeras (Subclass Holocephali)

The only living members of this group are the chimaeras or ratfishes, distinguished by the fusion of the upper jaw (palatoquadrate) with the cranium (hence holocephali meaning whole head).

Chimaeras and ratfishes (Order Chimaeriformes)

A gill cover overlies the four gill openings on each side. There is no spiracle. There is a conspicuous spine in the front of the dorsal fin. The backbone is incomplete and comprises calcareous rings around the primitive notochord, and the tail is heterocercal or diphycercal, if the latter then prolonged as a filament. The skin is naked. Males have elaborate pelvic claspers and a spiny hook on the forehead with which they are believed to grasp the female. Fertilisation is internal, the eggs are laid in a tough, brown capsule with a long spike which anchors it in the mud. Three families and about twenty-five species are recognised.

Chimaeras (Family Chimaeridae)

The snout is bluntly rounded, the eye large, and mouth small with incisor-like teeth in front of the jaws (thus they are also called rat-fish or rabbit-fish). Two genera are recognised, *Chimaera* and *Hydrolagus*, the latter being found in rather deeper water; they occur in the cool regions of the major oceans. One of the best known species is the Atlantic Ratfish, *Chimaera monstrosa*, which ranges from northern Norway to Morocco, and the Mediterranean in depths of 300 to 500 metres. Its food consists of bottom-living invertebrates principally brittle-stars and crustaceans.

Longnose chimaeras (Family Rhinochimaeridae)

Similar in body form to the chimaeras, all members of this family have greatly elongated snouts. In *Rhinochimaera atlantica*, which occurs in the north Atlantic at depths of 1,220 to 1,400 metres, the snout is a smoothly rounded and has a heavily innervated proboscis, but in the rather deeper water genus *Harriota* the snout is flattened dorso-ventrally and has a retroussé tip. Members of the family are found in both Atlantic and Pacific Oceans.

Ploughnose chimaeras (Family Callorhynchidae)

Similar to the chimaeras but with a heterocercal tail, and the snout lengthened and turned downwards, forming a ploughshare-like tip. All four species occur in the southern hemisphere, off southern South America, New Zealand, southern Australia and Africa. In general they live in shallow water, like the Elephant or Ghost Shark, *Callorhinchus milii*, of Australia and New Zealand which ranges from five to fifty metres. It grows to a length of one metre.

Bony Fishes (Class Osteichthyes)

This large grouping embraces all the living fishes other than those already discussed. The skeleton is composed at least partly of true bone and the skull has sutures. The fin rays which are not spiny are segmented and dermal in origin (lepidotrichia). The biting edge of the upper jaws is usually formed by the premaxillae and maxillae. There are three semi-circular canals present in the inner ear;

a swim bladder (or lung) is usually present; spiral valve is present in the lower intestine in only a few primitive species.

The 18,000 or so species comprising this group are divided into four subclasses, Dipneusti, Crossopterygii, Brachiopterygii, and Actinopterygii, of which the last subclass contains the overwhelming majority of species.

Lungfishes (Subclass Dipneusti)

External nostrils lie on edge of upper jaw, internal nostrils (now thought to be a migrated external nostril—see Crossopterygii) on the anterior palate. Palatoquadrate fused to the lower neurocranium; maxillae and premaxillae absent; branchiostegal rays and gular plates absent. Swim bladder replaced by a functional lung. Two orders containing six species of freshwater fish.

Australian Lungfish
(Order Ceratodiformes)
The single species, *Neoceratodus forsteri*, is the only recognised member of the family Ceratodidae. It differs from other lungfishes fundamentally in having the body compressed and covered with very large scales. The pectoral and pelvic fins are broad and paddle-like while internally there is a single lung in the body mid-line above the gut.

This lungfish, found in the Mary and Burnett Rivers of south-east Queensland is the only one found in Australia. It has been introduced into other Australian rivers. It grows to a length of one and a half metres. These rivers are generally permanent watercourses with dense vegetation and do not dry out, although in summer they become slow-flowing and often stagnant with little dissolved oxygen. In these circumstances, the lungfish breathes air at the surface, filling its lung by using its nostrils. It does not aestivate as do the African lungfishes. It is carnivorous, and spawns from August to October in shallow water, the eggs adhering to vegetation; the young fish do not have external gills.

South American and African lungfishes
(Order Lepidosireniformes)
These lungfishes are more closely related to each other than they are to the Australian species; all have a cylindrical body and elongated, rather narrow pectoral and pelvic fins. They also have small scales, a swimbladder with two lobes, and their larvae have external gills. There are two families with five species.

South American Lungfish
(Family Lepidosirenidae)
An eel-like fish with elongated pectoral and pelvic fins (the latter in the breeding male becomes much branched and richly supplied with blood vessels). *Lepidosiren paradoxus* lives in the Paraná and Amazon river systems and is particularly common in the Gran Chaco region, living in shallow swamplands and stagnant backwaters of the river courses. In such areas dissolved oxygen is sparse and the fish depends on air-breathing for survival. The gills are poorly developed and probably insufficient to obtain oxygen from the water even in good conditions. The greater part of this region is liable to seasonal droughts and as the water recedes the fish lives in a burrow in the mud of the swamp; inside this burrow it breathes air and lies inactive until the rains return. In extreme drought the burrow may be plugged with mud and the fish curls into a ball at the foot of the tunnel.

Spawning takes place in the burrow soon after it is flooded, the male guarding the eggs during incubation and hatching. The young have four pairs of feathery external gills just behind the head but by the time it has reached a length of four centimetres these are lost, and the young fish can breathe air. The elaborate, blood rich pelvic tree of the brooding male fish is thought to supply oxygen to the larvae in the burrow.

This species grows to one and a quarter metres.

The Australian Lungfish (*Neoceratodus forsteri*) also known as the Burnett Salmon is found in a few rivers in Queensland. It is the rarest of modern lungfishes and the one that has changed least in outward appearance in the passage of time. It uses its gills more than most lungfishes, is less tolerant of foul conditions of water and it cannot aestivate in a cocoon of mud and thus survive droughts as the African lungfishes can.

African lungfishes (Family Protopteridae)

These lungfishes have paired lungs lying ventral to the gut. They live in tropical African fresh water. Four species are recognised. Each has a rather elongated body with a blunt head and pointed tail, and very long, thin pectoral and pelvic fins.

The largest species is *Protopterus aethiopicus*, which grows to two metres in length and ranges from the Nile southwards through east and central Africa. This species tends to live in permanent standing water and rarely aestivates as other members of the genus do, however, it can do so if necessary. It breeds in a pit excavated in the river or lake bed, and the male guards the eggs driving away other fishes and even attacking intruding humans. The young have long, feathery external gills, which they do not lose until they reach about fifteen centimetres in length, when they move into the shallow reed beds and papyrus root swamps.

The rather smaller *P. annectens*, found in central Africa from Senegal and Nigeria to the Zambezi system, lives in more marginal waters, swamps, small creeks and the edges of rivers. These areas dry out in hot weather and the fish burrows into the mud, forming a hollow at the end of the tunnel in which it curls up with its tail over its head and secretes a mucous coccoon. The lungfish stays like this throughout the drought, and can survive for as long as four years, although longer than a year is rarely necessary. They breed soon after the swamps they inhabit become flooded after the rains return.

Tasselfins (Subclass Crossopterygii)

A group of fishes which are well-known as fossils, first appearing in the Lower Devonian period. Although some of these early forms were markedly similar to the lungfishes (they have often been placed in the same class) the two lines had diverged by the mid-Devonian. The tasselfins have two dorsal fins and lobe-like pectoral and pelvic fins. The body is covered with heavy cosmoid scales. A single order of living fishes.

Coelacanth (Order Coelacanthiformes)

An order of mainly fossil fishes (five families and thirty or so genera) found mainly in freshwater environments in the earliest forms but in marine situations after the Triassic period. They were a successful group throughout the Cretaceous, but after that with one exception became extinct. A single living species remains.

Gombessa (Family Latimeriidae)

The Gombessa is a stout-bodied fish with two dorsal fins, the first composed of spines and the second, like the anal, pectoral, and pelvic fins on a stubby muscular limb. The fin rays emerge from the musculature of this lobe in characteristic fashion. The tail fin is diphycercal, consisting of three lobes. There are no branchiostegal rays but there are two flat gular plates under the throat. It grows to a length of nearly two metres.

The Gombessa or Coelacanth lives in the tropical western Indian Ocean, and apparently only around the Comoro Archipelago to the north of Madagascar, although the first one to be recognised by scientists was caught off East London, South Africa, in December 1938. After that an intensive search of the East African coast eventually led to the discovery of the Comoro population, which live in the much creviced, nearly vertical rock and coral slopes of the islands' coasts. Regretably little is known about Coelacanth biology but they are caught on fish-baited hooks in depths of 150 to 400 metres.

They give birth to well-formed young fish, with possibly no more than twenty per litter in the largest females, but the method by which internal fertilisation is effected is not known, for the male has no intromittent organ. The Coelacanth swims slowly by means of gentle sculling movements of the pectoral, pelvic, second dorsal and anal fins, all highly mobile on their limb-like bases. No doubt by swinging its broad tail it can make rapid progress through the water. Its body is excessively oily and must be close to neutrally buoyant.

The fish that shook the scientific world, as well as a large part of the non-scientific world, in December 1938, was the Coelacanth (*Latimeria chalumnae*), seen here in the East London Museum in South Africa to which the carcase was taken for study. One reason why its discovery was so important is that it represents a group of fishes long thought to have been extinct.

Bichirs and Reedfish (Subclass Brachiopterygii)

These primitive fishes have a fan-shaped axis to the pectoral fin the rays being supported by numerous radials attached to a cartilaginous plate and two rods which are attached to the scapula and the coracoid. The body scales are ganoid, rhomboid in shape and shiny. The first dorsal fin

consists of separate finlets each with a spine to which is attached one or more rays; there are no branchiostegal rays but a pair of gular plates cover the underside of the head. A spiracle is present, as is a spiral valve in the gut; the swimbladder is bilobed with a duct into the pharynx ventrally. There is a single order Polypteriformes with one family.

Bichirs and reedfish (Family Polypteridae)

A small family of African freshwater fishes all rather eel-like with hard, shiny scales. Numerous fossil forms are grouped with the eleven living species. The Nile Bichir, *Polypterus bichir*, which grows to seventy centimetres in length, is found in the Nile and Lakes Rudolf and Chad in the densely weeded margins of the lakes as well as in river backwaters. In these often oxygen deficient waters it relies heavily on its lungs and air-breathing to survive. It feeds mainly on fishes and amphibians when adult, on aquatic insect larvae and crustaceans when young. It breeds during the rainy season; the larvae have an external gill each side of the head and hang on submerged plants by means of an adhesive gland on top of the head. Ten species of bichir are found in tropical African fresh water; all are distinguished by having pelvic fins.

The Reedfish, *Calamoichthys calabaricus*, is a slender snake-like relative found in stagnant waters of the Niger delta and the Cameroons. It lives in dense vegetation and relies heavily on air breathing to survive. It lacks pelvic fins and grows to ninety centimetres in length.

One of a number of primitive freshwater fishes which breathe atmospheric oxygen by means of a lung-like swim bladder, the Reedfish (*Calamoichthys calabaricus*) grows to ninety centimetres in length. It lives in stagnant waters of West Africa.

Ray-finned Fishes (Subclass Actinopterygii)

The pectoral fin ray supports are attached to the scapulo-coracoid complex. Branchiostegal rays are usually present and gular plates absent. The dorsal fin rays are attached directly to the body not to the fin spines. Spiracle usually absent; most groups without a spiral valve in the gut. This group is divided into three subordinate groups (infraclasses), the Chondrostei (living representatives—the sturgeons, but which also includes the numerous palaeonisciform fossil fishes), the Holostei (living representatives—the gars and bowfins), and the Teleostei (which comprise all other bony fishes in thirty-one orders).

Sturgeons and paddlefishes (Order Acipenseriformes)

These large freshwater and anadromous fishes live in the northern hemisphere. Their skeletons are largely cartilaginous; fin rays more numerous than their internal supports; tail fin heterocercal; a single branchiostegal ray; intestine with a spiral valve. Two families with twenty-five species.

Sturgeons (Family Acipenseridae)

Rather stout body with a well developed snout and toothless ventral jaws; the back and sides of the body with large bony scutes. Most sturgeons belong to the genus *Acipenser* which is found in both Europe and North America. The European Sturgeon, *Acipenser sturio*, is widely distributed on the Atlantic coast and in the Mediterranean and Black Seas, but overfishing, together with pollution of river mouths and dammed rivers have made it a relatively rare fish. Most other anadromous sturgeons are similarly depleted. It breeds during spring and early summer on pebbly bottoms in moderate currents in large rivers, the very numerous eggs (up to 2.5 million) being shed in the gravel. Young fish stay in the river for up to three years before migrating to sea where they feed mainly on bottom-living invertebrates. Sturgeons grow to a length of three metres and a weight of 214 kilograms, and are valued food fish both for their flesh and for the yield of caviar. The major caviar industry is now in the USSR although the Iranian coasts of the Caspian Sea also produce it; most comes from the Sevruga, *Acipenser stellatus*, and the Beluga, *Huso huso*, which unlike the *Acipenser* sturgeons which have small, protrusible mouths, has a large crescent shaped mouth. The Shovelnose Sturgeon, *Scaphirhynchus platorynchus*, represents a distinct group in which the snout is curved and the spiracle absent. It lives in the Mississippi River system and migrates only in that system.

Paddlefishes (Family Polyodontidae)
A family of sturgeon-like fishes which have the snout greatly elongated into a beak and the skin without scutes. The North American Paddlefish, *Polyodon spathula*, lives in the Mississippi system but is becoming rare. It grows to around two metres in length and is a plankton feeder with a huge mouth and well-developed gill rakers. Its only relative the Chinese Paddlefish, *Psephurus gladius*, has a protrusible mouth, few and smaller gill rakers and eats fishes. It lives in the Yangtze Kiang and attains a length of seven metres.

Gars (Order Semionotiformes)
Living representatives of the order are the gars or garpikes of North America, all elongate fishes with long, heavily toothed jaws. The tail fin is heterocercal, but only slightly asymmetrical; the scales are heavy and ganoid and are hinged to the underlying scale with a peg and groove. The vertebrae are opisthocoelous (convex anteriorly, concave posteriorly) a condition found in no other fish. There are three branchiostegal rays; no gular plates. Numerous fossils are assigned to this order but it contains only seven living species.

Gars (Family Lepisosteidae)
The gars have a highly vascular swim bladder and a large pneumatic duct which connects to the throat so they can breathe air when deoxygenated water conditions require it. Therefore they can inhabit heavily vegetated and swampy areas in oxbow lakes and backwaters where dissolved oxygen is sparse, as well as more open water. Normally they lie motionless in the water, usually partially hidden by vegetation, and wait for prey to come close. The gar makes a sudden charge, frequently taking its prey crosswise in its heavily toothed jaws. Their food is mainly fishes and crustaceans. They spawn in spring in shallow water, loose schools forming there; the eggs are laid in vegetation and the newly hatched young attach themselves to plants by an adhesive sucker on the underside of the snout.

The Alligator Gar, *Lepisosteus spatula*, lives in the Mississippi River and along the coast of Florida and the Gulf of Mexico, often in salt water. It grows to a length of three metres, and is said to attack wildfowl. A rather smaller species, the Longnose Gar, *Lepisosteus osseus*, ranges from Mexico to Quebec and also lives partly in estuarine water.

Bowfin (Order Amiiformes)
This group contains numerous fossil forms in seven families but only one living species. It is characterised by its smooth, rounded cycloid scales, single median gular plate and numerous branchiostegal rays. The tail fin is slightly heterocercal, and the long dorsal fin of uniform height. The swim bladder connects to the pharynx and can function as a lung.

Bowfin (Family Amiidae)
Confined to the freshwaters of eastern North America, the Bowfin, *Amia calva*, ranges from the Great Lakes through the Mississippi system, and along the Atlantic coastal states from Florida to the Carolinas. It grows to a length of ninety centimetres. It lives in quiet waters often backwaters overgrown with vegetation which are frequently poor in dissolved oxygen; in such waters it breathes air by means of its swim bladder. In spring males construct a shallow nest on the bottom in which the eggs are laid; the young have a cement gland on the head by which they fasten themselves to plants or the edge of the nest in early life. They are guarded by the male until they reach a length of ten centimetres.

Bony tongues (Order Osteoglossiformes)
One of the larger groups of primitive fishes. The caudal fin skeleton usually has a large first ural centrum and no urodermals, and has sixteen or fewer branched rays. The tongue is bony and has well-developed teeth. There are six families and over one hundred species of freshwater fishes, in four families.

The Mooneyes (family Hiodontidae) are freshwater fishes found in eastern North America; only two species are known. They are silvery fishes with large eyes, the retina of which has rods but no

A small sturgeon species the Sterlet (*Acipenser rutheneus*) lives in the basins of the Black and Caspian Seas and in Siberia; it grows to eighty centimetres in length. Spending all its life in freshwater, it migrates upstream to spawn in spring on gravel shallows.

The Arapaima (*Arapaima gigas*) is the largest of all freshwater fishes. It lives in murky waters of the Amazon Basin and its swimbladder is adapted for breathing atmospheric oxygen, adult Arapaima come to the surface every twelve minutes or so to breathe.

Opposite bottom
Moray eels (family Muraenidae) are principally tropical eels which live amongst rocks, coral reefs, and wrecks. Most have long, very sharp teeth and some species are highly aggressive and have to be handled with great care.

cones and reflects light from a tapetum lucidum; they are crepuscular and nocturnal fishes. The Mooneye, *Hiodon tergisus*, lives in clear water of large lakes and rivers in the Great Lakes region; it grows to forty-three centimetres. The Goldeye, *H. alosoides*, is more widely distributed, somewhat larger and favours turbid waters.

The Featherbacks (family Notopteridae) live in the freshwaters of tropical Africa and South-east Asia; they are laterally compressed with a small dorsal fin, and a long-based anal fin which runs from the pelvics to the tail fin. They swim by gentle undulations of the anal fin. The Featherback, *Notopterus chitala*, an important food fish in South-east Asia, lives in swamps, rivers and canals; it breathes air at the surface. The False Featherback, *Xenomystus nigri*, is widely distributed in tropical West Africa.

The members of the family Osteoglossidae include the Arapaima, *Arapaima gigas* of tropical South America, *Heterotis niloticus* of tropical Africa, the Arawana, *Osteoglossum bicirrhosum* of South America, and the Barramundi, *Scleropages leichardti*, of tropical Australia. Another *Scleropages* lives in South-east Asia. All live in slow-flowing rivers, oxbow lakes and swamps, and all can breathe air. The Arapaima is one of the largest known entirely freshwater fishes, reputedly growing to four and a half metres in length and 200 kilograms. It makes a nest in sand on the river bed; the eggs and young fish are guarded by an adult.

The freshwater Butterflyfish, *Pantodon buchholzi*, is the only member of the family Pantodontidae. It grows to ten centimetres in length, lives in still waters, weedy ditches, ponds and backwaters of rivers in West Africa, usually hanging motionless just below the surface of the water. It feeds mainly on insects which alight or fall on the water's surface. It also uses its long pelvic rays as 'stilts' in shallow water, propping itself up on the bottom. It is reputed to be able to catch slow-flying insects by leaping out of the water.

Elephant fishes (Order Mormyriformes)
The elephant fishes (family Mormyridae) derive this name from the long, trunk-like snout that some possess. All are African freshwater fishes; there are about 100 species known. *Mormyrus kannume*, which grows to eighty centimetres, and lives in the Nile system and some of the Great Lakes is a typical long-snouted species. It is mainly active at night and is able to set up a weak electrical field around itself (with organs derived from the caudal muscles). This enables it to navigate in the dark and to detect food and predators. A consequence of this electrical sensitivity is that the hind brain is extremely well developed.

The only member of the family Gymnarchidae is *Gymnarchus niloticus*, which is widely distributed in tropical Africa including the Nile. It lives in turbid water and generates a considerable electric field, disturbances to which can be detected very rapidly. It is eel-like in shape with a long dorsal fin but with a finger-like, fin-less tail.

Herrings and anchovies (Order Clupeiformes)
A large and economically important order of mainly marine fishes distributed worldwide except in polar seas. Most have an elongate, compressed body, with the pectoral fins low down, pelvic fins far back on the belly, and frequently with sharp scutes along the belly. The swim bladder opens into the gut and anteriorly into the region of the inner ear where the diverticulae are encased in bony capsules. Lateral line canals are developed on the head only and communicate with the *recessus lateralis* chamber in the neurocranium. There are four families and about 300 species; one family (Denticipidae) is represented only by a West African freshwater fish, about five centimetres in length, called *Denticeps clupeoides*.

Herrings (Family Clupeidae)
Mostly abundant as surface-living fishes in coastal waters of tropical, subtropical and temperate seas. Many species are anadromous; others live in estuarine water, while some are purely freshwater fishes. Generally, they are rather small (few species attain one metre in length), silvery sided, plankton-eating fish which have well developed gill rakers.

An important commercial species is the Atlantic Herring, *Clupea harengus*, which is found both on the North American coast as well as the European, and in the north Pacific is replaced by *C. pallasi*. The Alewife, *Alosa pseudoharengus*, is an important fish on the North American seaboard and enters rivers to spawn. Although still common the migrating schools are greatly diminished. There are several other shads on the North American coast, as well as off Europe, where the Twaite Shad,

Alosa fallax, is still moderately abundant. Sardines, such as *Sardinops ocellata*, of southern Africa, and related species in the Pacific Ocean are enormously valuable food fish, as well as for reduction to fish meal. They are also important to the food chains of the sea.

Anchovies (Family Engraulidae)

Anchovies are well distributed in tropical and subtropical seas but they are most abundant in the Indo-Pacific. They are usually smaller than the related herrings, have a prominent snout and large jaws framing a huge mouth. Their bodies are slender and rounded in cross-section. Anchovies comprise important fisheries, such as that for the European Anchovy, *Engraulis encrasicolus*, which is mainly caught for food, and the Anchoveta, *E. ringens*, of Peru which forms huge fisheries mainly used for reduction to fish meal.

Tarpons, tenpounders, and bonefishes (Order Elopiformes)

Superficially these are herring-like fishes with slender bodies, low set pectoral fins and posteriorly placed pelvics, cycloid scales, and a deeply forked caudal fin. Their larvae are long flattened, transparent, *Leptocephalus* larvae (see p. 231). There are five genera in three families with perhaps ten species.

Possibly the best known member of the order is the Atlantic Tarpon, *Tarpon atlanticus* (family Megalopidae), a fish which is most common on the American coast between North Carolina and Brazil. It attains a length of nearly two and a half metres and a weight of 159 kilograms and is a famous game fish. Although spawning takes place in the ocean the larvae drift inshore, and young Tarpon are abundant in low salinity coastal lagoons and mangrove swamps. The Pacific Tarpon, *Megalops cyprinoides*, is a smaller fish, which like the Bonefish, *Albula vulpes*, (family Albulidae) and the Tenpounder, *Elops saurus*, (family Elopidae), is often found in shallow water.

Eels and gulper eels (Order Anguilliformes)

Slender serpent-like fishes which lack spines in the fins and have no pelvic fins. In some the pectoral fins are also absent. Gill openings are restricted and the opercular bones are entirely covered by skin. The skin is smooth and slimy, the scales are often absent and when present are small and embedded. The larvae are transparent and a flattened, willow-leaf shape, known as *Leptocephalus* larvae. About nineteen families and 600 species of mainly marine fishes.

The freshwater eels of the family Anguillidae are catadromous, breeding in the sea but spending the major part of their lives in fresh water; all have pectoral fins and minute embedded scales in the skin. They are widely distributed mainly in temperate regions, although in the Indo-West Pacific they are found in tropical conditions. The American Eel, *Anguilla rostrata*, is found from Newfoundland to Panama; it is a close relative of its European counterpart, *A. anguilla*, and both attain a length of more than one metre. An even larger species, the Longfinned Eel, *A. dieffenbachii*, occurs in New Zealand, sometimes reaching a length of two metres and a weight of fifty kilograms.

Moray Eels represent one of the largest eel families (Muraenidae), containing about 100 species. In this group the pectoral fins are absent and the gill openings are restricted to a small pore each side; they have no scales and the posterior nostril is usually close to the eye while the anterior nostril is often on the lip. Morays are most abundant in tropical seas, living in crevices in rocks and coral. Most have long, sharp teeth and are active fish-eating predators. They bite very

The Ribbon Eel (*Rhinomuraena amboinensis*) is one of over a hundred species of morays or painted eels that are nearly all coastal fishes and abundant in the region of coral reefs. Voracious, they have the habit of coiling themselves into crevices and striking out on their prey in the manner of snakes.

savagely when threatened and have inflicted severe wounds when handled; some species attain a length of three metres. Most, however, are smaller, and some like the Zebra Eel, *Echidna zebra*, of the Indo-Pacific have blunt rounded teeth and feed exclusively on crustaceans.

The Conger Eels (family Congridae) are marine, possess pectoral fins, but have scaleless skins; the family contains about 100 species. The European Conger, *Conger conger*, attains a length of more than two and a half metres, and inhabits rocky shores, reefs and wrecks. It feeds mainly on crustaceans and cephalopods but also eats fishes. The American Conger, *C. oceanica*, is a rather smaller species living on the continental shelf from Cape Cod southwards to Brazil. The Garden Eels, such as *Nystactichthys halis*, which is common in the Caribbean, live in clusters in the ocean bed in shallow water, each eel in its own burrow and evenly spaced so that they resemble a regularly planted garden. Normally, they extend the front two-thirds of the body out of their burrow and swaying with the water movement snap up planktonic organisms as they drift by; if disturbed they retreat into their burrows. The fins in these eels are greatly reduced.

Closely related to the Congers are the Pike Eels (family Muraenesocidae), which also lack scales, and have pectoral fins, and thick, muscular bodies. Pike Eels, however, have long jaws with large, very sharp pointed teeth. They are best represented in the Indo-Pacific but are confined to tropical seas. Several species are large, like the widespread Indian Ocean *Muraenesox arabicus* which grows to two metres in length; these large specimens can be very aggressive when captured.

Several families of eels are found in the deep oceans, either with bathypelagic or benthic lifestyles. One of the latter is the monotypic family Simenchelyidae, the Snub-nosed Parasitic Eel, *Simenchelys parasiticus*, which grows to sixty centimetres in length and has been reported in many temperate seas. It lives at depths of 700 to 2,500 metres and is parasitic in habit, burrowing into the body of larger fishes, such as halibut. Its skin produces copious mucus. Among the bathypelagic

species of eel, are the Snipe-eels (family Nemichthyidae) of which the *Nemichthys scolopaceus* is probably the best known species. It is extremely long and slender, with elongate, bird beak-like jaws, and large eyes; it is widely distributed in the Atlantic Ocean at depths of 500 to 1,000 metres. At sexual maturity the male Snipe-eel's long jaws degenerate into a short snout and the eye increases in size; it is believed that the males, at least, die soon after spawning. A similar beak shape is found in the Bobtailed Snipe-eel, *Cyema atrum*, which lives in tropical oceans at 1,000 to 3,000 metres, and which belongs to the family Cyemidae. Its eyes are minute, but its body is short and resembles a dart.

The Gulper Eels are regarded as highly aberrant eels, although they were formerly placed in a separate order (Lyomeri). Three families are recognised containing about eight species, but the biology of none is well known and the relationships and status of some are in dispute. All are bathypelagic fishes with very long jaws and mouthparts, but with the eye close to the end of the snout. They lack pelvic and pectoral fins, opercular bones, branchiostegal rays and scales. One of the better known species, *Eurypharynx pelecanoides*, occurs in all tropical and warm temperate oceans, most commonly at depths of 1,400 to 2,800 metres.

Spiny-eels and halosaurs (Order Notacanthiformes)
An order of eel-like fishes which have *Leptocephalus* larvae. All have pectoral fins placed high on the side, pelvic fins abdominal in position, the anal fin long and merged with the tail fin. All are deep water benthic fishes and the order has a worldwide distribution. The Spiny Eel, *Notacanthus chemnitzii*, grows to more than a metre in length and inhabits the north Atlantic ocean. It has a series of short, stout spines on the back and the anal fin commences with about twenty slender spines. It occurs at depths of 200 metres, and feeds on bottomliving sea-anemones. The halosaurs (family Halosauridae) have a small dorsal fin, prominent snout and ventral mouth; they live at depths of 800 to 2,000 metres.

Trouts and allies (Order Salmoniformes)
A large order of fishes which show relatively primitive features. The taxonomic placement of many of its groups is still debatable and as recognised here it includes parts of the Isopondyli, and Iniomi of earlier classifications (as well as the Haplomi). The present classification includes some twenty-four families (including the salmons, trouts, pikes, mudminnows, smelts, smooth-heads, hatchet-fishes, and numerous deep sea fishes), placed in five suborders.

Pikes and mudminnows (Suborder Esocoidei)
A group which is widely distributed in the cool temperate freshwater of the northern hemisphere, all having posteriorly placed dorsal and anal fins, pectoral fins sited low on the sides and abdominal pelvic fins. The pikes (family Esocidae) are generally large fishes of elongate shape. The largest species is the Muskellunge, *Esox masquinongy*, of the Great Lakes region and the Ohio river in North

Milkfish (*Chanos chanos*) are active, swift-swimming Indo–Pacific Ocean fish which come close inshore to spawn in low salinity lagoons and estuaries. An important food fish in Asia, it is cultivated in freshwater and brackish pools from fry caught in the sea (*see* page 242).

America, which grows to a length of nearly two and a half metres and a weight of forty-five kilograms (although such large specimens are exceptional today). The European Pike, *E. lucius* (known in North America as the Northern Pike) is circumpolar in distribution, but only attains a length of one and a half metres and thirty-four kilograms, but again such big fish are rare. Like the North American Grass Pickerel, *E. americanus*, and the Chain Pickerel, *E. niger*, these fish have few but large teeth in the dentary (lower jaw), toothless maxillae which form the edge of the upper jaw, and dense masses of small, sharp, backward-pointing teeth on the vomer and palatines. As this dentition suggests they are active predators feeding on invertebrates and small fishes when young, and becoming wholly piscivorous as they grow larger. The largest species eat fishes, aquatic birds and mammals. All rely mainly on vision to detect prey, and lie in cover waiting the chance to attack.

The mudminnows (family Umbridae) are small fishes, attaining at most twenty centimetres. Most are found in North American freshwaters, but one species, the European Mudminnow, *Umbra krameri*, lives in the Danube and Dniester rivers. Like the Central Mudminnow, *U. limi*, which is widely distributed in the Great Lakes region and the Mississippi, and the Eastern Mudminnow, *U. pygmaea*, which lives on the eastern seaboard of the United States, it inhabits slowly flowing rivers and swamps and can survive in conditions of low dissolved oxygen and long periods of ice. However, the Alaska Blackfish, *Dallia pectoralis*, lives in the tundra region often in sphagnum bogs and survives being frozen into the ice for periods of several weeks at a time.

Trouts and salmons
(Suborder Salmonoidea)

An important group of food and sporting fishes although a number of small, less valued species are included. Some seven families are placed in this suborder. In the northern hemisphere the family Salmonidae is widely distributed, most are large freshwater or anadromous fishes which have an adipose fin, a swim bladder connected to the gut,

and incomplete oviducts so that the eggs lie in the body cavity. One of the best known species is the Atlantic Salmon, *Salmo salar*, which occurs on both sides of the North Atlantic. It breeds in gravel beds often in the headwaters of streams and after a period of one to three years the young fish migrate to the sea to feed. This marine phase again lasts for from one to three years before the adults return to the rivers to spawn; during their sea life the salmon range far across to Greenland waters as well as in the Norwegian Sea. Pacific Ocean salmons belong to the genus *Oncorhynchus*, which is characterised by having a long-based anal fin. Seven species are recognised, five of which occur in North America. Essentially they have the same life-style as the Atlantic Salmon but each species differs in the distance it spawns upstream and in the length of time it spends in the sea and river.

Another North American fish is the Rainbow Trout, *Salmo gairdneri*, but this has proved so suitable for artificial rearing and culture that it has been widely redistributed around the temperate parts of the world. The Brook Charr, *Salvelinus fontinalis*, is another species which is popular in this way, although in both northern Europe and Atlantic North America there is a native charr, *Salvelinus alpinus*, which grows to a large size in the north where it is anadromous. The Brown Trout, *Salmo trutta*, a European salmonid is also partly an anadromous species, the sea-going form being known as the Sea Trout. The Graylings (*Thymallus*) and the Whitefishes (genera *Coregonus, Leucichthys*, and *Prosopium*) are all widely distributed across North America and northern Eurasia; both groups have been placed in separate families in the past.

The Smelts (family Osmeridae) have a similar distribution but are mainly marine fishes which breed in rivers, although some populations are land-locked in freshwater lakes. The European Smelt, *Osmerus eperlanus*, smells strongly of cucumber and is delicious to eat.

In the southern hemisphere the place of the salmons and trouts is taken by fishes of the families Galaxiidae, Aplochitonidae and Retropinnidae, which live in New Zealand, southern Australia

The European Pike (*Esox lucius*), with its long head and mouth filled with sharp teeth, could almost be accepted as the archetype of sinister menace. The Pike lurks among weeds until prey is sighted. It turns slowly to face the prey with only the slightest motion of the fins. Then, with an incredibly swift lunge, the prey is seized, juggled into position and swallowed.

Juvenile Brown Trout (*Salmo trutta*) possess the line of dusky parr marks on their sides. Originally native only to Europe, it has been widely introduced elsewhere for sport fishing. The trout is very sensitive to water quality and is one of the first fish to disappear in polluted rivers.

and, in the galaxiids, the tip of South Africa as well as South America. A number of species are catadromous, but others live entirely in fresh water. One of the most widespread, the Jollytail, *Galaxias maculatus*, spawns among vegetation flooded by high spring tides and the eggs are stranded until the next tidal cycle before they are moistened and hatch. Most members of these families are small fishes, twenty centimetres being more or less the maximum length.

The Ayu, *Plecoglossus altivelis*, lives from Manchuria to Japan and Formosa, is a fish which looks like a salmon but is placed in the family Plecoglossidae. Its teeth are characteristic being small and broad and lie in a fold of skin in the jaws. It grows to thirty centimetres and is a valued food fish.

Argentines and smooth-heads (Suborder Argentinoidei)

A large group of salmoniform fishes of which the argentines (family Argentinidae) are the best known. Marine fishes found in the Atlantic and Pacific, they have rather small mouths, large eyes, large scales, and an adipose fin. *Argentina silus*, which lives in the north Atlantic at depths of 90 to 900 metres, and is about fifty-six centimetres in length is one of the largest species. The smooth-heads or slickheads (family Alepocephalidae) are mostly small, mid-water fishes found in all the oceans. Generally their bodies are covered by thin, large scales which are easily detached, but their heads are naked and have shiny black skin. One of the large species, *Alepocephalus rostratus*, which grows to seventy centimetres in length, is common

in the north Atlantic; most, however, are between ten and twenty centimetres in length.

Dragonfishes and hatchet-fishes (Suborder Stomiatoidei)

Mainly confined to the deep sea this group contains many specialised fishes. Some retain the adipose fin, most do not. Light organs are widespread throughout, as are large teeth and distensible jaws—well suited to the capture of large, active prey on rare occasions. Several members of the group exhibit this feature such as the Viperfish, *Chauliodus sloanei*, from the Atlantic Ocean, and the Black Loose-jaw, *Malacosteus niger*. The hatchet-fishes, family Sternoptychidae, live in the upper water masses of the world's oceans and have large eyes, well developed light organs, as well as the deep, compressed body and narrow tail which makes them resemble a hatchet.

Milkfish and Beaked Salmon (Order Gonorynchiformes)

An order containing about sixteen species of soft rayed fishes with rather slender bodies, single, short-based dorsal and anal fins but with no adipose fin. There are no pharyngeal teeth, nor intercranial diverticula of the swim bladder, but there are structural modifications to the base of the cranium and the anterior vertebrae which suggest that these fish are close to the evolutionary line of the Cypriniformes and Siluriformes rather than the Clupeiformes with which they were at one time placed. Four families are recognised.

The Milkfish, *Chanos chanos*, sole member of the

family Chanidae, is a large fish of herring-like appearance (it grows to nearly two metres) of the tropical Indo-Pacific. It is particularly abundant in estuaries and lagoons and in South-east Asia is cultivated in low salinity pools from larvae caught in the wild. It is a very important food fish. The Beaked Salmon, *Gonorynchus gonorynchus*, only member of the family Gonorynchidae, is long and slender, grows to forty-six centimetres, is pinkish in colour and lives partially buried in sand in the temperate Indo-Pacific. The only other members of the order belong to the families Kneriidae and Phractolaemidae which are small elongate fishes living in fresh water in tropical Africa.

Carp-like fishes and characins (Order Cypriniformes)

An order which contains many of the world's freshwater fishes and which is possibly the second largest order of fishes with some 3,500 species. Their external features are abdominal pelvic fins, cycloid scales, lack of true spines in the fins (although some species have spines derived from consolidated soft rays). Internally, the single most important feature is the modification of the first four or five vertebrae to enclose a series of bony ossicles linking the swim bladder to the inner ear—the so-called Weberian apparatus. Two major groups are recognised, the characins and the carps.

Characins (Suborder Characoidei)

The characins are a very diverse group of freshwater fishes mainly found in South America and

Africa (with a few species in Mexico and Central America which are relatively recent arrivals). They have the anal fin usually short but occasionally moderately long, scaled bodies, and usually an adipose fin. Most have well developed teeth, often very specialised in form.

Possibly the best known in temperate areas are the aquarist's tetras (family Characidae), small brightly-coloured fishes from tropical South America, which are ideal for the heated aquarium. Many of these, like the Jewel Tetra, *Hyphessobrycon callistius*, the Serpa Tetra, *H. serpae*, and the Rosy Tetra, *H. rosaceus*, are closely related inhabitants of the backwaters of the middle Amazon basin and Guyana. The Neon Tetra, *Paracheirodon innesi*, is another popular aquarium fish which originated from the Brazilian-Peruvian borders on the upper Amazon. All these tetras are carnivorous and have sharp-edged teeth. This specialisation is most highly developed in the piranhas, examples of which are Natterer's Piranha, *Serrasalmus nattereri*, and the White Piranha, *S. rhombeus*, both inhabitants of the Amazon basin, which have razor-edged, interlocking teeth, which are regularly replaced. Although they are fierce predators, attacking other fishes and wounded or dead animals in the water, their alleged hunting in packs and devouring of swimmers is much exaggerated. In contrast to the sharp-toothed, carnivorous piranhas, some South American characins, like *Myleus rubripinnis*, have flattened, molariform teeth in the sides of the jaws, and feed solely on fruits and leaves of trees.

Other characoid fishes are elongate predators,

The South American characins of the genus *Metynnis* are usually called Silver Dollars because of the shape and colouring. They have the dorsal adipose fin characteristic of the family. Despite their similarity to the carnivorous piranhas, Silver Dollars have flattened teeth and eat only water plants.

whose body-shape closely resembles that of the Pike. In Central and South America the Pike-characins (family Ctenoluciidae) have long jaws, dorsal and anal fins set far back down the body, and have a small adipose fin. The Hujeta, *Ctenolucius hujeta*, grows to thirty centimetres in length and is widely distributed in rivers in Panama, Colombia and Venezuela. In tropical Africa a similar looking family is present (family Hepsetidae) with one species, the Kafue Pike, *Hepsetus odoe*, found from Senegal and the Congo basin to the Upper Zambezi. It grows to thirty-six centimetres in length and is a fierce predator.

The Freshwater Hatchet-fishes (family Gasteropelecidae) are deep-bodied, strongly compressed fishes with a well-developed pectoral musculature; they live in tropical South America and Panama. The Common Hatchet-fish, *Gasteropelecus sternicla*, grows to six and a half centimetres, and lives in the Amazon region. These fishes leap out of the water and fly by rapid movements of the pectoral fins.

Four distinct families of characoid fishes are separated into the superfamily Gymnotidae and comprise the knife eels (families Gymnotidae, Apteronotidae, and Rhamphichthidae) and the electric eel (family Electrophoridae). All are found in tropical South America and Central America. In all the body is elongate, anal fin very long and providing the main propulsive power, the dorsal fin absent or small, and pelvic fins are absent. In the Electric Eel, *Electrophorus electricus*, about half the bulk of the body is comprised of the electric organs which can produce a shock of 500 volts at one ampere. This fish, which grows to nearly two and

a half metres in length, uses this electrical power to stun active-swimming fishes on which it feeds, and also surrounds itself with an electrical field which helps it to navigate in the deeply shaded and turbid water in which it lives. The members of the other families have weaker electrical abilities with which they detect predators and navigate; most are crepuscular or nocturnally active.

Carps and loaches (Suborder Cyprinoidei)

A large group of freshwater fishes which usually have protractile, toothless mouths, and lack an adipose fin. Members of the suborder are found in Africa, Europe, Asia, and North America, and comprise six families and at least 2,000 species.

The carp family (Cyprinidae) contains the great majority of these species and is found throughout the above range. Its members have the upper jaw bordered by the premaxillae, usually have thin, narrow lips, and possess pharyngeal teeth in from one to three rows, but with no more than eight teeth in the outer row. The body is usually covered with scales and the head naked, the fin rays are all branched and soft, except that in some species the anterior dorsal, anal, or pectoral rays may be thickened and spine-like. Male cyprinids develop spawning tubercles (pearl organs) especially on the head and anterior body when breeding. This family is also well-known for the development of cells in the skin which, when damaged in an injured fish, release an alarm substance (Schreckstoff) into the water which is detectable by conspecific fishes.

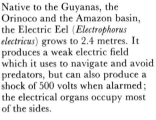

Native to the Guyanas, the Orinoco and the Amazon basin, the Electric Eel (*Electrophorus electricus*) grows to 2.4 metres. It produces a weak electric field which it uses to navigate and avoid predators, but can also produce a shock of 500 volts when alarmed; the electrical organs occupy most of the sides.

North America has some 200 native species many of them small minnow-like fishes. Typical of this group is the Emerald Shiner, *Notropis atherinoides*, a ten centimetre long, pelagic schooling fish found in rivers and lakes and widely distributed from the Mackenzie River system southwards to Alabama and Texas. Some one hundred species of *Notropis* are recognised. The Colorado Squawfish, *Ptychocheilus lucius*, however, is a large species, growing to one and a half metres in length and a weight of thirty-six kilometres. It lives in the Colorado River, but is now reduced in numbers due to the building of dams; *P. oregonensis* is found in Pacific coastal rivers.

In Eurasia there are very many cyprinid fishes. The Carp, *Cyprinus carpio*, a native of the Danube basin and central Asia is well-known as a food and sporting fish, and has been widely distributed in Europe, North America, southern Africa and Australia. It is a large fish, attaining one metre in length and twenty-five kilograms in weight, which lives in deep, slow-flowing rivers and lakes among heavy vegetation. It feeds on invertebrates and plant material which are crushed by the flattened pharyngeal teeth. Like many other cyprinids it has pairs of barbels on the lips. The principal European members of the family are the breams, *Abramis*, barbels, *Barbus*, Dace, Chub and Ide, *Leuciscus*, Roach, *Rutilus rutilus*, Rudd, *Scardinius erythrophthalmus*, Tench, *Tinca tinca*, gudgeons, *Gobio* and the Minnow, *Phoxinus phoxinus*.

The genus *Barbus* is widely distributed across Europe, Asia and Africa. Many of the species are small, such as the aquarist's barbs, for example the Tiger Barb, *B. pentazona*, a five centimetre inhabitant of the Malay Peninsula, Sumatra and Borneo, which is brightly coloured and boldly striped. Others are large, for example the European Barbel, *B. barbus* which attains one metre in length and lives in large, generally fast flowing rivers. In the southern rivers of the Himalayas live the Mahseers, *B. putitora* and *B. tor*, the former of which grows to over two and a half metres in length. Both are long-bodied, torpedo-shaped fishes, with two pairs of barbels and well developed lips; they live in fast-flowing rivers and are among the most famous freshwater game fishes. Other barbels live in Africa, many are small fishes like the west African *B. macrops* which grows to ten centimetres, but others, such as the Large-scaled Yellow-fish, *B. marequensis*, of the Limpopo and Zambezi Rivers grow to sixty centimetres.

The variety of life-styles among the cyprinid fishes is almost infinite. *Engraulicypris argenteus*, of the African Great Lakes and Victoria Nile is a small surface-living, plankton-eating fish found in large schools; the Silver Carp, *Hypophthalmichthys molitrix*, grows to one metre in length, is native to the Amur basin and China, and feeds on phytoplankton; the Ziege, *Pelecus cultratus*, which lives in eastern Baltic, Black and Caspian Sea rivers, is an active fish-eating predator which grows to fifty centimetres in length. In contrast, the Gudgeon, *Gobio gobio*, grows to fourteen centimetres and is a bottom-living, invertebrate-eating, European fish, while the Blind Cave Barb, *Caecobarbus geertsi*, is a small cave-dwelling species from the Congo system, the eyes of which are completely regressed.

The Mirror Carp (*Cyprinus carpio*) is one of several varieties of carp developed after centuries of selective breeding. The body has a few large scales as opposed to the fully scaled wild carp and the scaleless Leather Carp. All have the prominent barbels characteristic of the species.

245

The Suckerbelly Loaches (family Gyrinocheilidae) differ from the carps in lacking pharyngeal teeth, having the lips well developed with thickened rasp-like surfaces, and having each gill opening divided into two, an upper and a lower opening. These fish live in South-east Asia in running water, rasping algae off rocks with their lips; as a result, the mouth cannot be used in respiration and the upper part of the divided gill opening acts as an inhalent aperture, while the water expelled from the gills emerges from the lower portion. One species, *Gyrinocheilus aymonieri*, a twenty-five centimetre fish from Thailand, is commonly kept by aquarists.

The suckers (family Catostomidae) are carp-like fishes which usually have thick fleshy lips, the upper jaws bounded by both premaxillae and maxillae, and a single row of sixteen or more closely packed pharyngeal teeth. Of the sixty or so species most are found in North America, although a few live in China and north eastern Siberia. One of the most widely distributed species, as well as the most northerly, is the Longnose Sucker, *Catostomus catostomus*, a sixty-three centimetre long species which ranges from Labrador westwards to Alaska and the Yana River in Siberia. It is a slender-bodied fish which inhabits rivers and lakes, but breeds in swiftly flowing rivers over gravel bottoms; it eats bottom-living invertebrates. The Quillback, *Carpiodes cyprinus*, is widely distributed in the central and eastern parts of the United States and lives mainly in large rivers and big lakes. It grows to a weight of five and a half kilogrammes, and was at one time commercially exploited. It is deep-bodied with long anterior rays in the dorsal fin, similar in this respect to the Chinese species, *Myxocyprinus asiaticus*, found in the Yangtze Kiang.

The hillstream loaches (family Homalopteridae) are found only in India, the Malay Peninsula, Borneo, Formosa, and south-west China and live in rivers where the current is swift to torrential. All are small fishes with the front part of the body flattened and the pectoral and pelvic fins expanded laterally so that the underside of the belly forms a flat sucker disc. The body form is an adaptation to life in fast-flowing water, as is the mode of respiration, water being drawn in at the sides of the mouth and expelled through the gill openings. *Homaloptera smithi* is a seven centimetre fish found in waterfalls in Thailand. *Gastromyzon borneensis*, is only a little larger and lives in central and north-west Borneo.

The true loaches belong to the family Cobitidae, and are found in Asia, Europe, and northern Africa. Most are elongate, often worm-like fishes which live close to the bottom; all bury themselves under rocks, plants, or in the mud and are often cryptically coloured. The swim bladder is enclosed in a bony capsule and the mouth fringed with numerous barbels. Some, like the Weatherfish, *Misgurnus fossilis*, live in stagnant ponds and breathe air, gaseous exchange taking place in the lower gut; this is a European species but a similar fish lives in eastern Asia. The most common European loach is the Stone Loach, *Noemacheilus barbatulus*, an inhabitant of clean running water. The Clown Loach, *Botia macracantha*, grows to

Clown Loaches (*Botia macracantha*) are popular aquarium fishes which originate in Sumatra and Borneo. They are unusual members of the loach family being brightly-coloured and active. The Tiger Barbs (*Barbus tetrazona*), in the background, come from the same region.

thirty centimetres, lives in Sumatra and Borneo and is a brightly coloured aquarium fish.

Catfishes (Order Siluriformes)

A group of fishes in which the body is usually slender and either scaleless or covered with hard bony armour. The upper jaw is bounded by the premaxillae, which have fine teeth, but the maxillae are reduced and support the usually large barbels. An adipose fin is often present, and in some groups is supported by a spiny ray; a spine is also present in the dorsal and pectoral fins. The Weberian apparatus, involving the modification of the anterior vertebrae and the auditory capsules, is more complex than in the Cypriniformes but indicates the close affinities of the two groups. Catfishes are mainly freshwater, although two families (Ariidae and Plotosidae) live in the sea; they total perhaps 2,000 species of which the majority are South American but the order is found throughout the tropical and warm temperate world, and is least well represented in Europe.

There are about forty species of catfish endemic to North America which belong to the family Ictaluridae. Their bodies are smooth and scaleless, they have a strong spine in the dorsal and pectoral fins and a well developed adipose fin. Some, like the Blue Catfish, *Ictalurus furcatus*, are large, growing to one and a half metres in length and up to sixty-eight kilograms in weight. This species is slender with a forked tail and is found throughout the Mississippi river system and in rivers of the Gulf of Mexico. It is an important commercial and angling fish. Most ictalurids are, however, smaller and the Brown Bullhead, *I. nebulosus*, grows only to forty-six centimetres. It is widely distributed in eastern and central North America and has been introduced to Europe, New Zealand and elsewhere. The madtoms, *Noturus* spp. are common species in still waters; they have a long-based adipose fin and venom glands on the pectoral spines which can give a painful wound. Two ictalurid catfishes are blind and subterranean.

Bagrid catfishes (family Bagridae) are flat-headed, long-bodied and found in tropical Africa and South-east Asia. They have large adipose fins and spines in both dorsal and pectoral fins; barbels are well developed. *Bagrus docmac*, a one metre long fish living in the Nile basin, the Great Lakes and westwards to Nigeria is a typical African species of commercial importance. The only native catfishes in Europe are members of the family Siluridae, and the wels, *Silurus glanis*, originally a Danubian species has been widely redistributed by man. It is a large fish, reputedly attaining a length of three metres and a weight of 300 kilograms. Other members of the family such as the Mulley, *Wallagonia attu*, of India and South-west Asia are almost as large. The Mekong Catfish, *Pangasianodon gigas*, is another huge catfish growing to two and a half metres, but belongs to the family Pangasiidae, which is confined to Asia. It lives in the Mekong river but although famous as a Food fish and celebrated in ethnological literature its biology is little known.

In South America several endemic catfish families are numerous. Best known are the Callichthyidae of which several members are aquarium fishes, such as the Dwarf Corydoras,

Corydoras hastatus, found in the Amazon basin and like all the family having large overlapping rows of tile-like scales on the back and sides. It also has a spine in its adipose fin. The Cascarudo, *Callichthys callichthys*, which ranges from the Guianas to Paraguay, and the Hassar, *Hoplosternum thoracatum*, of the coastal area of the same region all have these heavy scales. Both these species make bubble-nests in which the eggs are shed, a defence against the frequent low oxygen levels of the waters in which they live. Another large family of South American catfishes are the Loricariidae, and these too have bony plates on the back and sides, some also have an adipose fin. Many of these fish are algae eaters, their thick, fleshy lips and fine teeth enabling them to scrape encrusting algae from rocks, fallen branches or other plants.

Among the numerous catfishes in Africa the Electric Catfish, *Malapterurus electricus*, belongs to the family Malapteruridae. It is a thickset, heavy-bodied species which lacks a dorsal fin but has a large adipose fin. It is widely distributed in the Nile system, West African rivers and the Zambezi, living in swamps and reed beds. The electrical organs lie in the muscles either side of the body. It can grow to more than a metre in length and a weight of fifteen kilograms. Another common family in Africa is the Clariidae (they are also found in Syria and South-east Asia); its members are long and slender with a long-based dorsal fin. They have an air-breathing organ connected to the gill cavity which allows them to survive out of water for a long time.

The family Ariidae mainly live in the sea and are worldwide in distribution in tropical areas. The Sea Catfish, *Arius felis*, which grows to thirty centimetres, lives between Virginia and Panama especially in shallow sandy-bottomed areas. Like most ariid catfishes the males incubate the eggs in their mouths for a period of up to six weeks. The other sea-going catfish family, the Plotosidae, is Indo-Pacific in distribution, and contains the Barber-eel, *Plotosus lineatus*, a thirty centimetre long, striped fish of the shallow inshore waters. Its dorsal and pectoral spines have venom glands at their bases which can inflict exceedingly painful wounds. The native Australian catfishes, like the Freshwater Catfish, *Tandanus tandanus*, belong to this family and colonised this continent by their ability to tolerate salt water, although this species is now confined to fresh water.

Lanternfishes and relatives
(Order Myctophiformes)

In this group the edge of the upper jaw is formed from the premaxillae and the maxillae are not included. An adipose fin is usually present; the pelvic fins are usually abdominal; photophores are well developed. All the group are marine fishes, mostly found in the open ocean.

The Lizardfishes (family Synodontidae) are rather slender bodied with a broad head, large jaws with numerous teeth and heavily scaled bodies. They live in tropical to warm temperate seas in all the oceans, usually lying close to the bottom propped up on the pelvic fins or, in some species, partially buried in sand. Most are small, one of the largest species being the California Lizardfish, *Synodus lucioceps*, a sixty centimetre

Lizardfish (*Synodus variegatus*) showing by its stance how its vernacular name suggested itself. Its body is cylindrical, its head is large and its mouth wide. The fish waits on the sea bottom with its head tilted upwards ready to dart out at passing prey, then gulping it down and returning to the sea bottom. In parts of the Indo-Pacific lizardfishes are known as grinners.

long, almost two kilogram inhabitant of the Pacific coast of California. It lives at depths of about eighteen to forty-six metres. A rather similar looking fish is the Bombay Duck or Bummalo, *Harpadon nehereus* (family Harpadontidae), which lives in the northern Indian Ocean. It is particularly abundant in estuaries and areas of low salinity where it is caught in large nets fixed to posts in the seabed. It forms an important commercial fishery.

The Lanternfish family (Myctophidae) derive their name from the numerous photophores which form regular species-characteristic patterns on the belly and sides. In some species the males have a different light organ pattern to the females which clearly is used for recognition. Lanternfishes live in the middle layers of the world oceans, coming nearer to the surface at night. They live in schools and are extremely common if rarely seen on account of their habitat. Some 200 species are known, most are around ten centimetres in length. Other deep sea members of the order Myctophiformes are the bottom-living tripod fishes (family Bathypteroidae) which perch just above the seabed on their elongate pelvic and tail fin rays, and the lancetfishes (family Alepisauridae) which are large (up to two metres) active, predatory mid-water fishes.

Beardfishes (Order Polymixiiformes)

A single family of living fishes (Polymixiidae) represents this order which has only three species. They are fairly deep-bodied, large-eyed fishes with a pair of long barbels beneath the throat. They occur in the warm Atlantic, Pacific, and parts of the Indian Oceans at depths of 183 to 640 metres. The Atlantic species, *Polymixia nobilis*, grows to twenty-five centimetres and is brownish on the back, with a rosy tint on the head, golden green on the sides.

Trout-perches (Order Percopsiformes)

A small group of North American freshwater fishes which are represented by eight species in three separate families. The trout-perches (family Percopsidae) are slender fish with ctenoid and cycloid

scales, head scaleless, dorsal fin with both spines and rays and an adipose fin. The Sandroller, *Percopsis transmontana*, is a ten centimetre long fish found only in the Columbia River in sandy or weedy lagoons and backwaters. The Pirate Perch, *Aphredoderus sayanus*, the only member of the family Aphredoderidae lives in the Great Lakes and southwards through the Mississippi basin. It has a short based but long-rayed dorsal fin, but has no adipose fin; it lives among dense plants and mud in lakes and quiet reaches of rivers. The third, and largest family with five species, is the Amblyopsidae, most members of which are cave fishes. The Northern Cavefish, *Amblyopsis spelaea*, lives in limestone caves in Indiana and Kentucky, has a long slender body, minute eyes which are covered by skin and abundant small sensory papillae on the head. It lacks pigmentation and is pale pink in colour. The female broods her eggs in the gill chamber.

Cod-fishes (Order Gadiformes)

A large order of mainly marine fishes of great commercial importance. They generally have an elongate body, with long-based dorsal and anal fins, and the pelvics, when present, are placed far forward beneath or in front of the pectoral fins. There are about 700 species.

The deep-water cods (family Moridae) are found mostly in the deep sea either close to the seabed or in mid-water. They closely resemble the true cods in appearance often having a chin barbel and two or three dorsal fins. The swimbladder has an internal connection to the auditory capsules. They are found in all oceans and although most are small, some, like the European species *Mora mora*, grow to fifty centimetres in length.

In the true cods (family Gadidae) the swimbladder is not connected to the auditory capsules; there are two groups in the family, those with three dorsal and two anal fins and those with two dorsal and a single anal fin. Most cods are found in the cool seas of the northern hemisphere and some are found in cool, temperate seas in the south. Many have great commercial importance and these include the Atlantic Cod, *Gadus morhua*, Haddock, *Melanogrammus aeglefinus*, and Saithe (or Pollock in North America), *Pollachius virens*, all three fish being found off the European as well as the North American Atlantic coasts. The Polar Cod, *Boreogadus saida*, a small species (up to forty-six centimetres) is found close to the edge of the polar ice cap in both the Atlantic and the Pacific oceans. The Navaga, *Eleginus navaga*, is another Arctic species of the Atlantic living in shallow coastal waters. In the north Pacific the Wall-eyed Pollock, *Theragra chalcogramma* is very abundant, widely distributed and now heavily exploited by Korean and Japanese fishing boats. Some gadoids are mesopelagic schooling fishes, among them the Blue Whiting, *Micromesistius poutassou*, an extremely abundant fish in the north Atlantic and one which offers considerable commercial promise. In near Antarctic water it is replaced by *M. australis*, which is equally abundant. Numerous small codfishes live on the shallow continental shelf, among them are the Whiting, *Merlangius merlangus*, and several species of pout, *Trisopterus* sp., fish which are mainly exploited for fish meal.

The second group of cod-fishes, which have two dorsal and a single anal fin include the lings. The best known is the Ling, *Molva molva*, a two metre long inhabitant of the temperate eastern Atlantic. The Torsk, *Brosme brosme*, is found on both sides of the north Atlantic in water of ninety to 914 metres, while on the North American coast there are several so-called 'hakes', such as the White Hake, *Urophycis tenuis*, which like the others mentioned is a moderately important commercial fish. To this group also belong the rocklings, such as the Five-bearded Rockling, *Ciliata mustela*, which are abundant on European shores. They are related to the burbot, *Lota lota*, the only member of the cod family to live in fresh water, which grows to a length of one metre and is distributed in large lakes and rivers from eastern England (now possibly extinct) eastwards through northern Europe, Asia and North America.

The true hakes (family Merlucciidae) are elongate fishes with two dorsal and one anal fin, a terminal mouth and no chin barbel. There are possibly ten species found mainly in temperate waters in the Atlantic and Pacific Oceans, although in tropical waters they occur at depths of 100 to 900 metres. Important fisheries exploit the Stockfish, *Merluccius capensis*, off southern Africa, *M. hubbsi* off South America, and the European species *M. merluccius*. Hakes all live at considerable depths, close to but above the seabed, and migrate towards the surface at night.

Another family of cod-like fishes found in the open sea at considerable depths are the rat-tails (family Macrouridae). In the deep sea the rat-tails probably comprise the greatest biomass of bony fishes and they are found at all levels except the shallowest and possibly abyssal depths. Most have two dorsal fins and a single long anal fin (which provides the main propulsion in swimming), the tail is drawn out into a long thread—hence the name rat-tail. Many species have a chin barbel; some have an organ on the belly close to the vent which contains luminous bacteria. The Round-head Rat-tail, *Coryphaenoides rupestris*, which occurs at depths of 400 to 1,200 metres on both sides of the North Atlantic, grows to one metre in length. It has been fished quite extensively in recent years (mainly by USSR trawlers) and has some potential as a commercial fish. The Rough Rat-tail, *Macrourus berglax*, is another large North Atlantic species which is found in shallow Arctic waters.

The cusk-eels and brotulas (family Ophidiidae) are now recognised as another group of gadiform fishes. They are slender-bodied fishes, which often have the vertical fins united, and have the anus just behind the throat. Most are marine fishes although some are freshwater, such as *Lucifuga dentatus*, a cave fish in Cuba, which is oviparous. Some of the largest cusk-eels belong to the genus *Genypterus*, and may grow to one and a half metres; they live off New Zealand, South Africa and southern Australia. The deepest living fishes are brotulids found in the Sunda and Puerto Rico trenches at a depth of about 7,000 metres.

The family Carapidae includes the pearlfishes which are found in all tropical and warm temperate oceans. They are extremely slender with pelvic fins absent and the anus placed on the throat.

Many pearlfishes are parasites or commensals on marine invertebrates and live inside the body cavities of sea cucumbers, clams, sea urchins, starfishes, and tunicates. In some cases they eat the internal organs of the invertebrate host; one example of this is the Mediterranean *Carapus acus*, which lives inside sea cucumbers.

Eelpouts (family Zoarcidae) are marine fishes found mainly in cool temperate to cold seas and living on the shore down to considerable depths in the sea. They are particularly abundant in polar seas. The body is elongate with dorsal and anal fins joined to the tail fin, the pelvic fins are small. Most are bottom-living fishes but the genus *Melanostigma* contains several species with a flabby gelatinous body adapted to life in mid-water. More familiar are the Viviparous Blenny, *Zoarces viviparus*, of the eastern North Atlantic and the Ocean Pout, *Macrozoarces americanus*, of the North American Atlantic coast, both of which live in shallow water. The eelpouts of the genus *Lycodes* are very common in the cooler bottom water of the North Atlantic.

Toad-fishes (Order Batrachoidiformes)

A group of fishes which are short-bodied and flat-headed with the eyes almost dorsal. Two dorsal fins, the first spiny; pelvic fins placed anterior to the pectorals. Some fifty-five species are recognised (all in the family Batrachoididae), most being found in warm or tropical seas. In general, they are inconspicuously coloured fishes but some, like *Sanopus splendidus*, which lives in the Gulf of Mexico, is boldy striped with light blue and has yellow margins to its fins; it lives close to underwater caves into which it retreats if disturbed. A number of toad-fishes make loud sounds by muscular vibration of the swimbladder; a notable sonic performer is the Atlantic Midshipman, *Porichthys porosissimus*, of the American Atlantic and Gulf coasts, which also has rows of photophores along the sides. The Venomous Toadfish, *Thalassophryne maculosa* which is found on both coasts of Central America has hollow spines on the gill covers with venom glands—wounds from these spines are intensely painful.

All members of the cod family are marine except the Burbot (*Lota lota*), the only freshwater member of the family. In England, in recent years, the Burbot has been adversely affected by works such as land drainage. So it has become rare. This coupled with its secretive habits of hiding among weeds during the day near the bottom, coming out at night to feed on frogs and small fishes, has meant that it is extremely seldom seen.

A frogfish (family Antennariidae), so called because the broad head and apparently jointed pectoral fins make them look like frogs. Members of the family are usually cryptically coloured to match their background and entice small fishes to within striking distance by means of a small lure on the end of a fin ray on the snout.

Anglerfishes (Order Lophiiformes)

These marine fishes have a fascinating body form and highly specialised life-style. Almost all members of the order have the first ray of the dorsal fin far forward on the snout to form a fishing rod (illicium) with a lure at its tip (the esca) with which they attract prey towards the mouth. Most have the pelvic fins forward of the pectorals, although the deep-sea anglers have no pelvics at all. There are some 200 species divided into fifteen families.

The anglers or goosefishes (family Lophiidae) are large, broad-headed fish with a narrower tail; the mouth is huge and heavily toothed. Skin flaps around the outline of the body help to conceal it when it lies on the seabed, and the illicium is long with a flap-like esca. The common European Angler fish, *Lophius piscatorius*, ranges from the Black Sea to the Barents Sea in depths of eighteen to 550 metres; it grows to two metres in length. The American Goosefish, *L. americanus*, is closely related. Both produce ribbons of floating spawn.

The frogfishes (family Antennariidae) live in all

tropical and subtropical seas and are mostly benthic fish crawling around the branched corals or reef faces or living among algae; some are pelagic. They are cryptically coloured and their skins have numerous warty projections or flaps which assist in concealment. The illicium is pronounced and is very variable from species to species. One pelagic species is the Sargassofish, *Histrio histrio*, which grows to nineteen centimetres and lives among the floating *Sargassum* weed of tropical oceans; it sheds its eggs as a floating mass in the weed.

The Longlure Frogfish, *Antennarius multiocellatus*, lives in the tropical western Atlantic and has a long illicium; it is often seen crawling over the open seabed and is thought to mimic a gastropod mollusc. The batfishes (family Ogcocephalidae) live in all the tropical oceans and pull themselves across the bottom with their arm-like pectoral fins. They are flattened from above with a rounded or triangular body, and have a small worm-like lure beneath the snout. The Long-nosed Batfish, *Ogcocephalus vespertilio*, is a western Atlantic species which ranges from the Bahamas to New York.

The deep-sea anglers (Suborder Ceratioidei) are represented by ten families of generally round-bodied, large-toothed fishes found in the middle waters of all the oceans. Some are large, like *Ceratias holboelli*, the females of which reach more than a metre in length; they are found in the Atlantic. Others, such as *Linophryne arborifera* are only seven centimetres long; this species has a long luminous fishing lure on the snout and a much branched barbel on the throat. In both species the small males become sexually mature once they have attached themselves virtually as parasites to a female fish.

Indostomus (Order Indostomiformes)

A single species, *Indostomus paradoxus*, which lives in freshwater lakes in Burma and Thailand and grows to three centimetres. Its body is slender with a series of spines on the back and small dorsal fin, similar and opposite to the anal fin. There are a series of bony plates on the back and sides and the snout is long. Originally this fish was seen as a link between the pipefishes and the sticklebacks but it is now placed in a separate order its affinities being uncertain.

Flyingfishes, toothcarps, and silversides (Order Atheriniformes)

A group containing some 850 species divided into three main lines (suborders Exocoetoidei, Cyprinodontoidei, and Atherinoidei), groups which have been moved more than once in earlier classifications.

Flyingfishes, halfbeaks, and garfishes (Suborder Exocoetoidei)

Although some live in freshwater these are mostly marine fishes, with the dorsal, anal, and pelvic fins placed towards the tail, and the lateral line, when present, on the underside of the body. In the family Exocoetidae there are two major lines, the flyingfishes which have enlarged pectoral fins and the halfbeaks with the elongate lower jaw; all members of the family are surface-living fishes. Some flyingfishes, such as the Atlantic Flyingfish,

Cypselurus heterurus, have enlarged pelvic fins as well as big pectorals and are typical of the 'four-winged' flyingfishes which are capable of more sustained 'flight' than the 'two-winged' flying-fishes. In fact, no flyingfish flies, they glide over the surface of the water with outstretched fins and all their propulsive power comes from a burst of underwater swimming assisted by sculling of the long lower tailfin lobe in the surface of the water. An example of the two-winged flyingfishes is *Exocoetus volitans*, a thirty centimetre fish which lives in all tropical seas. All flying-fishes lay eggs with long adhesive filaments which act as floata-tion devices and tangle in flotsam. Halfbeaks are also tropical fishes and most live in the sea. A well-known Atlantic species is the Ballyhoo, *Hemiram-phus brasiliensis*, which lives between Brazil and New England; it feeds mainly on plant matter and small fishes and is eaten by a wide range of sea-birds and fishes. Among the freshwater halfbeaks is *Dermogenys pusillus*, a seven-centimetre inhabit-ant of South-east Asia. The males have modified anterior anal rays which act as an intromittent organ and the female gives birth to from twelve to twenty young fish each about one centimetre long.

Garfishes or needlefishes (family Belonidae) are long, slender-bodied fishes with long, heavily-toothed snouts. Most are marine tropical and warm temperate species, but some like the Euro-pean Garfish, *Belone belone*, occur in temperate waters in summer: a few species live in freshwater, such as *Belonion apodion* of South America. This species is sexually mature at five centimetres length. In contrast, the Houndfish, *Tylosaurus crocodilus*, grows to one and a half metres and lives in shallow water between Brazil and Bermuda including the Gulf of Mexico.

Killifishes, toothcarps, livebearers (Suborder Cyprinodontoidei)
This group contains possibly 500 species of mainly freshwater fishes although many are found in brackish water. Most are small, lack a lateral line (although it is developed on the head), have pelvic fins near the middle of the body, and have a protrusible mouth. Eight families are recognised; only the largest are discussed below.

The killifishes or toothcarps (family Cyp-rinodontidae) are widely distributed in tropical and warm temperate areas except for Australia. All are egg layers, although one species, *Rivulus marmoratus*, is a functional hermaphrodite. The Mummichog, *Fundulus heteroclitus*, ranges along the North American Atlantic coast from Newfound-land to Texas. It lives in fresh water and estuaries as well as in the shallow coastal sea, and can survive in conditions of low dissolved oxygen, high temperatures and varied salinity. It grows to about thirteen centimetres. Another American species the Desert Pupfish, *Cyprinodon macularius*, lives in hot springs where the temperature may be 50°C, while *Cyprinodon milleri* from Death Valley in California and Nevada lives in pools which in summer partially dry out, increasing the salinity of the water to twice that of the sea's. On the Mediterranean coast of Europe species of *Aphanius* inhabit shallow, low salinity pools and ditches, and eastern Spain has an endemic toothcarp, *Valencia hispanica*. Similar species of *Aphanius* are

found in the Middle East and Red Sea basin. The lyretails of Africa (genus *Aphyosemion*) are common and beautiful aquarium fishes, some of which like *A. walkeri* of Ghana live in temporary rainpools, laying their eggs at the end of the rainy season in the humus of the pool bottom where they survive through the dry season to hatch out with the next rains.

The four-eyed fishes (family Anablepidae) live in coastal and estuarine waters of Central and northern South America. Each eye is divided horizontally by a band of opaque tissue which gives the eye an upper and a lower part. These fishes lie at the surface of the water with the eye division at the air-water interface, and can thus see to detect prey or predators in the air or below in the water. The males have a modified anal fin and all three known species are livebearers.

The best known livebearers, however, are the members of the family Poeciliidae which are found from the southern United States to Argentina. To this family belong popular aquarium fishes like the Guppy, *Poecilia reticulata*, the Sailfin Molly, *P. latipinna*, the Platy, *Xiphophorus maculatus*, and the Swordtail, *X. helleri*. All males have modified anterior rays in the anal fin forming an intromit-tent organ to convey a spermatophore to the female. Several litters of young fish may result from a single mating. The Mosquito-fish, *Gambusia affinis*, has been widely introduced around the world in attempts to control the malaria-carrying mosquito, often to the detriment of native eaters of mosquito larvae.

Silversides and rainbowfishes (Suborder Atherinoidei)
The silversides (family Atherinidae) are mostly small, marine fishes with two well-separated dorsal fins, and a bright silver stripe down their sides. They have no lateral line. A number of species live in freshwater, among them the Lake Eyre Hardyhead, *Craterocephalus eyresii*, of South Australia, and several species of *Chirostoma* in Mexico. The Hardhead Silverside, *Atherinomorus stipes*, is an abundant fish in the Caribbean region and grows to twelve centimetres, while the Sand Smelt, *Atherina presbyter*, is a common European species. Most silversides lay eggs with long threads by which they are attached to littoral algae or flotsam. An exception to this general rule is the Grunion, *Leuresthes tenuis*, which lives on the California coast and spawns at night high on beaches during the spring tides, burying its eggs in the sand where they remain until hatching with the next spring tide.

Rainbowfishes (family Melanotaeniidae) are found in fresh and brackish water in Australia and New Guinea. They are deep-bodied compared with silversides, but have two dorsal fins, the first comprising weak spines. The Crimson-spotted Rainbowfish, *Melanotaenia fluviatilis*, is a brightly-coloured, nine centimetre long inhabitant of South Australia, New South Wales and Queensland. The rainbowfishes are egg layers, and the eggs have fine filaments which fasten to water plants.

Two remarkable families of fishes (Phallos-tethidae and Neostethidae) from South-east Asia are relatives of the silversides, but the first dorsal fin is reduced to a single small spine. All nineteen

Opposite
The Mandarinfish (*Synchiropus splendidus*), a dragonet from the tropical Pacific Ocean which lives in shallow water amongst rocks and corals. The brilliant colouring is associated with the copious, bad tasting, possibly mildly toxic, mucus on the skin, a warning to predators.

species are small (two to four centimetres) transparent and live in freshwater pools and ditches. The males have a long organ formed from the pelvic fins and anterior ribs just below the head which are used to clasp the female during spawning; all the species are believed to be egg layers.

Opahs, dealfishes and oarfishes (Order Lampridiformes)

An order which has been expanded in recent classifications to include a diversity of fishes. The fins contain soft rays only, the pelvic fins, when present, are placed well forward, and scales are small if present.

The Opah, *Lampris guttatus*, (family Lampridae) is worldwide in tropical and warm temperate seas, living in mid-water at depths of 100 to 400 metres. It is a deep-bodied fish attaining a length of one and a half metres and a weight of fifty kilograms, but must swim swiftly as it eats a range of mid-water fishes and squids. It is brilliantly coloured, deep blue on the back shading to silvery sides and with crimson fins. The dealfishes (family Trachipteridae) are slender-bodied sea fishes, with a highly protrusible mouth, the dorsal fin is long-based, the anal fin is absent while the tail-fin is turned up vertically to form a fan-like tail. There are probably only about seven species but the considerable changes in body form with growth make certain species allocation difficult. The common North Atlantic species is *Trachipterus arcticus*, which grows to two and a half metres in length and ranges from Greenland to Madeira; a smaller species which lives in warm temperate to tropical seas is the narrow-tailed deep-headed *Zu cristatus*.

The oarfishes (family Regalecidae) are also long and slender and highly compressed. The dorsal fin runs the length of the body, but the first rays are thickened and elongate, and the pelvic fins are long. Only two species are recognised both being open ocean mesopelagic fishes which are rarely seen except when stranded. *Regalecus glesne* is probably worldwide in distribution but its biology is little known.

The family Atelopidae contains about ten species all of which occur in tropical and warm temperate oceans at depths of 183 to 550 metres. They are slender-bodied with a long anal fin, jugular pelvic fins, and a small dorsal fin. One species, *Atelopus japonicus*, found in the Indo-Pacific Ocean grows to sixty centimetres; it is probably a bottom-living fish but its biology is not well-known. The same can be said for the fishes of the family Mirapinnidae, the single species, *Mirapinna esau*, could be called the Hairyfish as its body is covered with a hair-like pile. The pectoral and tail fins are very large but the fish itself is only five centimetres long. Its systematic placement is doubtful.

Squirrelfishes, pineconefishes and others (Order Beryciformes)

An order which contains fishes of varied shape which have in the past been placed in separate orders. The precise relationships of some groups is still arguable. Some fifteen families are represented containing about 150 species.

Pricklefishes (family Stephanoberycidae) are a small family of deep-sea fishes which live in the tropical Indian, Pacific and Atlantic Oceans.

Their bodies are covered with small, toothed scales. One Atlantic species is *Acanthochaenus luetkeni*, a twelve centimetre inhabitant of depths of 2,200 to 5,300 metres. The bigscale fishes (family Melamphaeidae) have large, paper-thin rounded scales which are easily detached, stout bodies and rounded heads. There are at least twenty species. The Crested Bigscale, *Poromitra crassiceps*, lives in the eastern Pacific from Alaska to Chile at depths of 550 to 1,830 metres; it grows to fifteen centimetres in length. The family Trachichthyidae are deep-bodied fishes with a large head which is ridged and has deep cavities which contain copious mucus. One of the best known species is the Slime Head, *Hoplostethus mediterraneus*, found at depths of 350 to 900 metres in the Atlantic Ocean. The belly of this fish (and its relatives) has sharply pointed scales.

Berycoid fishes, sometimes called Alfonsinos, (family Berycidae) form a small family of about ten species. They are rather deep-bodied with a large eye, and the pelvic fins have one spine and seven to thirteen rays. Most live at depths of 300 to 500 metres and are orange-red in colour. One of the two European species is *Beryx decadactylus*, sixty-one centimetres inhabitant of deep water from the west of Ireland to the North African coast.

Pineconefishes (family Monocentridae) are represented by two Indo-Pacific species. In both the dorsal spines are relatively large as are the single pelvic spines. The body is short and deep and is covered with roughened heavy scales. Both species are small, *Monocentris japonicus* grows to thirteen centimetres in length and is found from South Africa to Japan; it has two small sacs under the lower jaw which are filled with luminous bacteria. Similar light organs are found in the Lanterneye fishes (family Anomalopidae) which occur widely in the Indo-Pacific and in the Caribbean. These fish live around reefs and are nocturnally active; the light organ is blinked continuously (presumably a means of keeping the school together). As a bacteria filled organ cannot be voluntarily extinguished the whole organ is revolved in *Anomalops kaptoptron* so that the dense black tissue on its back cuts out the light.

The squirrelfishes (family Holocentridae) are widely distributed in tropical and warm temperate seas especially in rocky or coral reef areas. They live in relatively shallow water, down to 100 metres but are mainly nocturnally active, hiding in caves, among crevices and under shelter by day. They are often brightly coloured with reds predominating, and striped. They also make a considerable variety of grunting or clicking noises. A common western Atlantic species is the Longjaw Squirrelfish *Holocentrus ascensionis*, which ranges from Brazil to Bermuda and attains sixty-one centimetres in length. Other squirrelfish genera are *Adioryx*, *Flammeo*, and the soldierfish genus *Myripristis*.

Three families of whalefishes also belong to the Beryciformes, the redmouth whalefish (Rondeletiidae), flabby whalefishes (Cetomimidae) and the Barbourisiidae. Some have small pelvic fins and numerous sensory pores on the head but the last family lacks pelvics, the skin is smooth, and the eyes are minute. About fifteen species are known; all deep-sea fishes found in all the oceans.

Dories and boar-fishes (Order Zeiformes)

A small group of fishes comprising possibly fifty species, which have the pelvic fin abdominal in position, with one spine and five to nine rays, and the anal fin with four spines distinct from the remainder of the fin. All are marine fishes, many of them deep-sea species like the members of the families Oreosomatidae and Grammicolepididae, but some, like the John Dory, *Zeus faber*, of the eastern Atlantic lives in relatively shallow water (down to 200 metres). It is highly compressed from side to side and the mouth is large and forms a long extensible tube when capturing prey. Despite its apparent clumsy appearance it is an effective predator on fishes. The American John Dory, *Zenopsis ocellata*, has a shallower head profile and grows to around sixty centimetres.

The boar-fishes (family Caproidae) are found in moderate depths (100 to 400 metres) in all oceans but are not often seen; there are about six species. The Boar-fish, *Capros aper*, lives in the Mediterranean and the Atlantic from Ireland to North Africa. Mostly it lives close to the red and yellow encrusting growths on rocks and in crevices on the edges of the continental shelf, but occasionally it occurs in shallow water. It is straw to red coloured and attains sixteen centimetres in length.

Pipefishes, seahorses and cornetfishes (Order Syngnathiformes)

An order containing possibly 200 species of fishes which have the mouth at the end of a long tubular snout and tufted lobe-like gills. In some classifications they are grouped with the sticklebacks. Trumpetfishes (family Aulostomidae) are found in tropical seas, usually close to coral or reefs and sometimes hanging motionless in the water. The body is covered with scales, and there is an underlying network of fine bones beneath the skin and a series of dorsal spines. The cornetfishes (family Fistulariidae) also occur in tropical seas but are scaleless, have no dorsal spines, and have a long filament from the tail. They are active predators, living near the surface and in sea grass beds; the Blue-spotted Cornetfish, *Fistularia tabacaria*, common from New England to Brazil, grows to one and a half metres in length.

Snipefishes (family Macroramphosidae) are deep-bodied with a long dorsal fin spine and are common in mid-waters of all the oceans. The Snipefish, *Macroramphosus scolopax*, is best known in the eastern Atlantic at depths of 100 to 300 metres. The related Razorfish, *Centriscus scutatus*, also has a dorsal spine but it is displaced to the end of the body, which is covered with thin bony plates, and is sharp edged. It is usually seen in a vertical posture, and may live commensally with long-spined sea urchins.

The pipefishes (family Syngnathidae) are mainly marine fishes which are most common in tropical and warm temperate seas. Some like the Snake Pipefish, *Entelurus aequoreus*, live at the sea's surface, but most are cryptic animals living among algae or over sandy shores. A common European species is the Greater Pipefish, *Syngnathus acus*, which attains thirty centimetres in length. The male has a double fold of skin on the tail in which the eggs are deposited and develop. In other species, like the Indo-Pacific *Syngnathoides*

biaculeatus, and the freshwater Asiatic *Doryichthys deokhatoides*, the male's brood pouch is on the belly. The best known of all the family are the seahorses (genus *Hippocampus*) of which there are about twenty-five species, all lacking tail fins, having a prehensile tail, and a hard exoskeleton. Males of all seahorses have a brood pouch on the tail.

The sea-moths (family Pegasidae) are also Indo-Pacific fishes, but they are small (up to fourteen centimetres long). Species such as *Pegasus volitans*, are flattened with broad lateral pectoral fins, and flutter across the sea bed in shallow water. Their systematic position has been uncertain; they were placed with the scorpaenids.

Sticklebacks and tubesnouts (Order Gasterosteiformes)

Slender-bodied small fishes found in both the sea and fresh water; the upper jaw is protractile, a series of free spines on the back. Two families are recognised within the order which at various times has been placed with the Scorpaeniformes and the Syngnathiformes.

The tubesnouts (family Aulorhynchidae) are very slender fishes with about twenty-five free spines on the back, which live in the North Pacific. *Aulorhynchus flavidus* lives from Alaska to California in dense schools near the surface but close to algal cover. It grows to sixteen centimetres. The true sticklebacks (family Gasterosteidae) are closely related and found in both freshwater and marine habitats. The Sea Stickleback, *Spinachia spinachia*, is a European marine fish growing to nineteen centimetres; it is most common in algae rich areas

Opposite
This Squirrelfish (*Adioryx caudimaculatus*) is one of a number of fishes given this vernacular name. They are usually bright red and being nocturnal have large eyes, the colour and the size of the eyes being enough to suggest the familiar rodent.

Two Sticklebacks (*Gasterosteus aculeatus*); both males are approaching breeding condition as shown by their blue eyes and reddened throats. The bright colours help in distinguishing between the sexes, and play a major role in territorial and courtship display as the male builds a nest on the bottom which he defends against other males.

The Zebra Firefish (*Dendrochirus zebra*) swimming. It spends much of its time on the seabed where its many spines are a menace. It is one of many scorpaenid fishes. Its distinctive colouring and habit of boldly swimming in plain view are clearly an advertisement of the fact that it is well protected by its spines.

in shallow water. The Three-spined Stickleback, *Gasterosteus aculeatus*, lives mainly in fresh water but to the north of its range increasingly lives in the sea (it has been caught in the mid-Atlantic). It is distributed across the whole of the northern part of the northern hemisphere. In contrast to this wide range, the Four-spine Stickleback, *Apeltes quadracus*, lives only on the Atlantic fringe of North America from Newfoundland to Virginia. All the sticklebacks and tubesnouts build a nest of plant material welded together with mucus, in which the eggs are laid. The males devote much energy to defending the nest and the young fish, territorial defence, and courtship of the females, behaviour that makes them much studied animals.

Swamp-eels (Order Synbranchiformes)

Superficially eel-like but unrelated to eels, the swamp-eels are slender, lack pectoral fins, the dorsal and anal fins are mere ridges on the tail and the pelvics are minute; gill slits open ventrally into a single restricted opening. Most live in stagnant fresh water or brackish water; one lives in the sea. They breathe air at the surface and absorb it in the pharynx or hind gut; some species can aestivate in droughts. They are found in Central and South America (*Synbranchus marmoratus* is widely distributed), Africa (*Monopterus boutei* which is a blind, cave-dwelling form), and Asia. The Rice Eel, *Monopterus alba*, is found in China, Japan and Thailand and grows to ninety-one centimetres. It produces a bubble nest into which the eggs are spat to develop and hatch. The Cuchia, *M. cuchia*, is found in India and South-east Asia living in swamps, backwaters of rivers, and ditches, and is generally nocturnal. Both species breathe air continuously and are valuable local food fishes.

Scorpionfishes, gurnards and sculpins (Order Scorpaeniformes)

A large order of fishes containing some 1,000 species and including what were formerly known as the 'mail-checked fishes' distinguished by the presence of a bony stay across the cheek. Some twenty-one families are included and only a selection of these is discussed.

Scorpionfishes and gurnards (Suborder Scorpaenoidei)

The scorpionfishes (family Scorpaenidae) are distributed worldwide except in the Antarctic. They are stout-bodied fishes with strong dorsal fin spines and numerous spines on the head. Many, like the Redfish, *Sebastes marinus*, of the eastern North Atlantic and the Rock Cod, *S. levis*, of the Californian coast are viviparous. Others, like the Cabezon, *Scorpaenichthys marmoratus*, of the American Pacific coast lay eggs, in this case on the shore and they are violently poisonous. Venom glands are well developed and a number of scorpion fishes can inflict painful wounds, among them the butterflyfishes or turkeyfishes of the genus *Pterois*, an Indo-Pacific group with long spines and bright colours. Members of the family Synanceiidae, usually called stone-fishes, which are distributed in the Indo-Pacific including the Red Sea, also have venom glands. These are sited at the base of the very sharp dorsal fin spines and wounds from them can be fatal; they produce the most deadly of all fish venoms. They lie among corals perfectly concealed by their colouring and rough skins.

The gurnards or sea robins (family Triglidae) are worldwide in tropical and temperate seas. They are all bottom-dwelling species which have the lower pectoral rays free from the membrane and used for probing the seabed for food. They are formidable sound producers, the swimbladder being vibrated by drumming muscles. The Tub Gurnard, *Trigla lucerna*, is a common European species which grows to sixty-one centimetres; the Northern Sea Robin, *Prionotus carolinus*, is smaller and lives on the American Atlantic coast. The family Hexagrammidae or the greenlings are North Pacific fishes of considerable commercial importance on the Asian coast. The Kelp Greenling, *Hexagrammos decagrammus*, is common in shallow water along the North American coast, while the Ainame, *H. otakii*, lives around Japan and Korea.

The flatheads (family Platycephalidae) are marine fishes of the Atlantic and Indo-Pacific; as their name suggests the head is flattened although the body is rounded. Their normal life-style is to lie buried in sandy or muddy bottoms; the Dusky

Flathead, *Platycephalus fuscus*, is a large (up to fourteen kilograms) southern Australian species of commercial importance.

The poachers (family Agonidae) occur in the North Atlantic, North Pacific, and off southern South America. Their bodies are encased in a rigid armour and the pectoral fin is large. The most abundant European species is the Pogge or Hooknose, *Agonus cataphractus*, which ranges from northern Norway to England; the Sturgeon Poacher, *A. acipenserinus*, is a Pacific coast species in North America. Totally different in shape because their bodies are rather soft and unarmoured are the lumpfishes and sea snails (family Cyclopteridae). These fish are found in both Arctic and Antarctic conditions as well as in the temperate Atlantic and Pacific Oceans. Most are benthic fishes but some have adopted a bathypelagic life. In most the pelvic fins have been modified to form an efficient sucker disc. The Lumpsucker, *Cyclopterus lumpus*, is widely distributed in the northern Atlantic.

The sculpins (family Cottidae) are common in the sea in the northern hemisphere, possibly most abundant in the North Pacific, but they are also found off southern America, New Zealand and southern Australia. Their broad heads with sharp preopercular spines are characteristic. In North America particularly and less so in Eurasia they are found in fresh water. The European Miller's Thumb, *Cottus gobio*, is a ten centimetres long inhabitant of clean rivers and stony-bottomed lakes. In Lake Baikal in the USSR the family Cottocomephoridae are represented by some twenty species which have evolved in geographical isolation and now inhabit all habitats offered by the lake. Some live on the lake's deep bottom or in the shallows, while some have become pelagic.

Flying gurnards (Order Dactylopteriformes)

A small group of tropical and warm temperate marine fishes (family Dactylopteridae) which have heavily armoured heads and bodies with large scute-like scales. Their pectoral fins are enormously large, and of brilliant colouring. They are benthic fishes which 'walk' over the seabed on their short pelvic rays, but when alarmed spread out their pectoral fins in a startling and unnerving display of colour. *Dactylopterus volitans* is a thirty-two centimetre long inhabitant of both sides of the tropical and subtropical Atlantic Ocean.

Spiny-finned fishes (Order Perciformes)

The largest and most diverse of all fish orders containing some 7,000 species and said to be the largest vertebrate order. Typically, its members have spines in dorsal and anal fins, ctenoid scales, pelvic fins anterior in position with a spine and not more than five soft rays, and the upper jaws bordered by the premaxillae. Eighteen suborders are recognised; representative families of all except three (Schindleroidei, Kurtoidei, and Luciocephaloidei) of these are discussed below.

Basses, perches, sea breams, and others (Suborder Percoidei)

A large group of spiny-finned fishes which is probably polyphyletic in origin; many of the best

The Coral Trout or Blue-spot Rock Cod, *Cephalopholis miniatus*, is widely distributed through the Indo–West Pacific region. It is abundant on coral reefs and grows to forty-six centimetres in length.

FISHES

The European Perch (*Perca fluviatilis*) is a great favourite with the angler because of the ease with which it will take bait. Its prey is smaller fishes and small invertebrates. Its favoured habitat is slow sluggish waters and lakes and it tends to form loose schools after the first weeks of life.

known fishes belong to this group including the croakers, jacks, grunts, butterflyfishes, cichlids and damselfishes.

The snooks belong to the family Centropomidae and are mainly marine fishes although some live in estuaries: other family members are freshwater, such as the Nile Perch, *Lates niloticus*, and the glassfishes (*Chanda* spp.). The Caribbean Snook, *Centropomus undecimalis* grows to twenty-four kilograms. The family Percichthyidae also contains marine, estuarine and freshwater species including the European Bass, *Dicentrarchus labrax*, a sea fish primarily, the Striped Bass, *Roccus saxatilis*, of North America, both fine sporting fishes, the Stone Bass, *Polyprion americanus*, which grows to two metres, but when young is often found accompanying flotsam in the open sea, and the Giant Sea Bass, *Stereolepis gigas* of the warm North Pacific which grows to more then two metres and weighs up to 270 kilograms. It lives just below the kelp beds at thirty to forty-six metres depth. The Australian Murray Cod, *Maccullochella macquariensis*, is almost as large but lives in the rivers of Queensland and New South Wales.

The family Serranidae contains other sea basses, the groupers, hamlets and kelp basses. Like the previous family they are spiny-finned with ctenoid scales, with three flat spines on the preoperculum. The Jewfish, *Epinephelus itajara*, is a giant member of the family growing to nearly two and a half metres and a weight of 318 kilograms. It occurs on the tropical Atlantic and Pacific coasts of America; the Groper, *E. lanceolatus*, of the Indo-Pacific is possibly even larger. Many serranids are hermaphrodite, but it is rare for both sexes to develop simultaneously, although in the Belted Sandfish, *Serranus subligarius*, a fifteen centimetre inhabitant of Florida's seas, self-fertilisation is possible. Several serranids live in European seas but only the Comber, *S. cabrilla*, reaches as far north as Britain; most are warmer-water fishes.

Soapfishes (family Grammistidae) are similar to the serranids but their skin produces copious mucus which contains an irritant poison; they live in the tropical Atlantic and Indo-Pacific. The sunfishes (family Centrarchidae) are freshwater fishes endemic to North America (although introduced to Europe and southern Africa). The family members are distinguished as nest builders, the male excavating a depression in the lake bottom in which the eggs are laid and guarded. Several species belong to the genus *Lepomis*, among them the Pumpkinseed, *L. gibbosus*, a brightly coloured inhabitant of quiet clear water both in brooks and lakes. It grows to twenty centimetres. The Longear Sunfish, *L. megalotis*, lives in similar habitats and has an 'ear flap' on the gillcover which is jet black with a golden-green edge. The Smallmouth Bass, *Micropterus dolomieui*, is larger, growing to sixty-eight centimetres length, and is a popular sporting fish which has been widely distributed both in North America and elsewhere in temperate freshwaters. *M. salmoides*, the Largemouth Bass, is larger still, attaining a weight of eleven kilograms, and is popular with anglers. Both are voracious predators, eating fishes, amphibians and a wide range of invertebrates.

Cardinal fishes belong to the Apogonidae a large family of mostly marine fishes in shallow tropical and subtropical seas. They are very common on coral reefs, brightly coloured often with red predominating, and mainly active at night. Many species mouth-brood their eggs.

The perches (family Percidae) are freshwater fishes of the northern hemisphere, but are most numerous in North America. The Eurasian Perch, *Perca fluviatilis*, is naturally distributed from Britain to Siberia; it grows to about fifty-one centimetres in length and is well-known to anglers for its bold

bite, conspicuous dark stripes, reddish orange ventral fins and its sharp spines. Across North America it is replaced by the Yellow Perch, *P. flavescens*, a similar species, which also inhabits lakes and slow-flowing rivers. Larger members of the family exist in the genus *Stizostedion*: in North America the Walleye, *S. vitreum*, and in Europe the Zander, *S. lucioperca*, both slender-bodied and attaining ten kilograms in weight. Both are crepuscular predators, their diet being almost entirely fishes, and both species have a tapetum lucidum in the retina, acting as a mirror to double the light falling on the sensitive cells. The Zander has been introduced to western Europe and Britain with serious effects on native fish stocks. In Europe there are a number of small percid fishes including the Ruffe, *Gymnocephalus cernuus*, a twenty-five centimetres long inhabitant of lowland rivers, the Zingel, *Aspro zingel*, which is confined to the River Danube, and *Romanichthys valsanicola*, which lives in the fast-flowing headwaters of the Danube in Romania. North American rivers support a large number of darters, most belonging to the genus *Etheostoma*, all slender-bodied fishes. The Orange-throat Darter, *E. spectabile*, grows to eight centimetres and is widely distributed in the Mississippi-Missouri system in small to moderate sized streams, mainly in shallow riffles. The Iowa Darter, *E. exile*, lives in southern Canada and northern United States but inhabits slow-flowing rivers and lakes. All darters become brilliantly coloured in the breeding season.

The Bluefish, *Pomatomus saltatrix* (family Pomatomidae), is found in subtropical parts of all three oceans. It forms large schools offshore and in the open ocean and is a voracious predator on schooling fishes. It grows to ten kilograms in weight and is a noted sporting fish. The remoras or shark suckers (family Echeneidae) are similar to the Bluefish in their slender form but are distinguished by the greatly modified first dorsal fin above the head and back which forms a flattened, oval disc with slatted struts. This exerts a powerful suction pressure and the remora attaches itself by it to sharks, large fishes, turtles, cetaceans and even ships. The Suckerfish, *Echeneis naucrates*, is worldwide in tropical seas and attaches itself briefly to a number of larger animals but it is an active predator, eating fishes and crustaceans which it captures free swimming. It grows to ninety centimetres. The Slender Suckerfish, *Phtheirichthys lineatus*, is usually found attached to groupers or barracudas, while the Whalesucker, *Remora australis*, attaches itself to various cetaceans, and the Sharksucker, *R. remora*, to many species of offshore tropical sharks. Many of the remoras which are group specific feed on the parasites of their hosts, but some also range close by the host feeding independently of it.

Jacks and scads (family Carangidae) form a large and economically important group of marine fishes found in the Atlantic, Indian and Pacific Oceans most abundantly in tropical regions but also in temperate seas. Most have a series of large, spiky scales along the sides of the tail. The Great Trevally, *Caranx sexfasciatus*, is an Indo-Pacific species weighing up to eighteen kilograms and a fine sporting and to a less extent food fish. The Crevalle Jack, *C. hippos*, is found in the tropical

Atlantic as far north as Nova Scotia, and the Caribbean; its flesh is sometimes toxic due to the uptake of toxic plant substances through the food chains. Many young carangids have the habit of accumulating under the bell of jellyfishes; the European Scad or Horse Mackerel, *Trachurus trachurus*, shows this behaviour. The Pilot-fish, *Naucrates ductor*, similarly accompanies large sharks, turtles and even ships.

The Dolphinfish, *Coryphaena hippurus*, belongs to the family Coryphaenidae. It is an open sea inhabitant of tropical and warm temperate zones feeding on surface-living fishes, especially flying-fishes. Its coloration is brilliant. Like the dolphinfish family the Australian family Arripidae contains only two species, the Australian Salmon, *Arripis trutta*, and the Ruff, *A. georgianus*. Both are inshore fishes, the former being common in estuaries; this species grows to a large size (nine kilograms) and is a good sporting fish for anglers. Snappers (family Lutjanidae) occur in the Indian, West Pacific, and Atlantic Oceans and are marine fishes rarely found in estuaries. They are very numerous and in tropical seas important food fishes. However, in some areas their flesh is toxic, causing ciguatera poisoning due to plant toxins in the food chains. The Mutton Snapper, *Lutjanus analis*, ranges from New England through the Caribbean to Brazil, and is an important food fish. The most common Caribbean reef fish, however, is the Schoolmaster, *L. apodus*, which lives among coral and, when young, in mangrove swamps and turtle grass beds. The Red Snapper, *L. sebae*, is an Indo-Pacific species also found over reefs; it grows

Opposite bottom
Slender Suckerfish (*Echeneis naucrates*) in Australian waters. With its first dorsal fin modified to form an efficient sucker, this kind of fish has been able to spread round the world, hitchhiking on larger fishes, such as sharks. It has no economic value.

Two Yellowfin Mojarras (*Gerres cinereus*) and a Smallmouth Grunt (*Haemulon chrysargyreum*), both common fishes on the edges of Caribbean reefs. The mojarras eat benthic invertebrates feeding on sandy patches by thrusting their mouths into the bottom and puffing out sand through the gill openings. Grunts form small schools by day on the reef.

FISHES

to a large size (twenty-two kilograms) and is a reddish colour with three broad red stripes.

Grunts (family Pomadasyidae) are equally widely distributed and look similar to the snappers but have weaker dentition. They get their name from the audible grunting noises made by grinding together their pharyngeal teeth, the sound being amplified by the swimbladder. Also closely related to them are the emperors or scavengers (family Lethrinidae), but they have long snouts and deep scaleless cheeks. They live mainly in the Indo-Pacific where they are important food fishes.

The seabreams and porgies (family Sparidae) are marine fishes of the Atlantic, Indian and Pacific Oceans although some like the European Gilthead Bream, *Sparus auratus*, are common in estuaries. Many of them feed mostly on molluscs and have large, rounded crushing teeth in the sides of the jaws. Others like the Mediterranean Saupe, *Sarpa salpa*, graze on fine algae and have incisiform teeth. Some like the South African Mussel Cracker, *Sparodon durbanensis*, grow large, in this case up to eighteen kilograms. The drums or croakers (family Sciaenidae) are mostly marine fishes but they are common in estuaries and one species, the North American Freshwater Drum, *Aplodinotus grunnieus*, lives entirely in freshwater. Some are very large, the Black Drum, *Pogonias cromis*, of the Atlantic American coast may grow as heavy as sixty-five kilograms and nearly two metres in length, similar to the length of the Australian Mulloway, *Johnius antarctica*, and the European Maigre, *Argyrososmus regius*. Drums owe this name

to their capacity for making sounds by special drumming muscles attached to the elaborate swimbladder; in part at least this has a navigational function and keeps members of the school in touch in the often heavily silted estuaries in which they live.

Red mullets or goatfishes (family Mullidae) derive this name from the long paired barbels beneath the chin. These are highly sensitive organs which seek out buried food in the bottom mud or sand. Many species are reddish but the coloration changes rapidly and some have a different colour at night. They are most common in tropical seas but occur in temperate waters as well, for example the European Red Mullet, *Mullus surmuletus*, off the British coast. The sweepers (family Pempheridae) are mainly Indian and Pacific Ocean tropical species, abundant on coral reefs in large schools. They are deep-bodied, large-eyed fishes growing to about fifteen centimetres, and with a long anal fin; they are mainly nocturnally active. The Copper Sweeper, *Pempheris schomburgki*, is one of the few Caribbean and western Atlantic species.

The family Toxotidae or the archer fishes contains three to four species of Asiatic freshwater and estuarine fish which are well known for their ability to spit a series of drops of water at insects near the water's edge. They are accurate shots at three metres and feed on insects and arthropods dislodged in this way. *Toxotes jaculator*, which grows to twenty-three centimetres in length, is very widely distributed. In their deep body shape and long snouts the butterflyfishes resemble the

Butterflyfishes are small, highly-coloured marine fishes found generally on coral reefs. The deep body allows for considerable agility so that the butterflyfishes flutter around coral reefs, diving into cracks and crevices at the first sign of disturbance. Their habits suggest that their colours are used to advertise their territories, which they defend with vigour, not for camouflage.

The Zebra Angelfish (*Pomacanthus semicirculatus*) is widely distributed on coral reefs in the tropical Indo–West Pacific Ocean. The heavy spine on the lower edge of the gill cover is a feature of the marine angelfishes. As with other angelfishes the young and adult coloration differs, in this species the body has alternate light stripes on a dark blue background.

The cichlid *Sarotherodon burtoni* of Lake Tanganyika, one of the most specialized mouth-brooding species. The male has dummy egg spots on its anal fin which attract the female to attempt to collect them in her mouth, in doing so she collects sperm which fertilise the eggs already held in the mouth.

Grey mullets (family Mugilidae) are active schooling fishes of shallow, well-lit waters, most common in tropical and temperate seas. They feed on algae encrusting rocks, pier pilings and harbour walls, and also on bottom mud; they have a gizzard-like stomach and long intestine which helps in digesting this nourishment-poor food.

Barracudas are fierce predators of the warmer seas. In some areas such as the Caribbean they are more feared than sharks. There are records of these fishes attacking swimmers but most barracuda species are small and not dangerous. Their normal food is other fishes and they have been seen to herd these into shoals after the manner of sheepdogs, and then to attack.

archerfishes, but they belong to the family Chaetodontidae. Their fine teeth and prominent mouths are perfectly equipped for picking out minute animals from coral reefs (including the coral polyp itself). They are brightly coloured inhabitants of all tropical seas and have evolved to fill many of the available niches in shallow waters. The marine angelfishes are sometimes placed in a distinct family (Pomacanthidae); they have a strong spine on each preopercle.

The leaffishes (family Nandidae) are freshwater fishes of tropical South America, Africa and Asia, although opinions differ about the inclusion of *Badis*, the Asian genus, with the others. The best known of the family is the Leaffish, *Monocirrhus polyacanthus*, a ten centimetre South American species which perfectly imitates a floating leaf in colouring and body form.

On the Pacific coast of North America the surfperches (family Embiotocidae) are represented by some twenty species living mainly in coastal waters. They are all viviparous and the anterior rays of the anal fin of males is adapted to aid impregnation. They range in size from seven to forty-five centimetres; a few species are regarded as sporting fish. The cichlids (family Cichlidae) mostly have a similar deep body shape but these are freshwater fishes of southern America and Africa, with a few species in South-west Asia. Body shapes are, however, variable from the deep, flattened body of the angelfishes, *Pterophyllum* sp. to the slender body of the pike cichlids, *Crenicichla* sp., both South American forms. In the Great Lakes of Africa intense speciation has produced larger numbers of endemic species in each lake, and cichlids have evolved to exploit most of the available living spaces and food resources. Many of the African species are mouthbrooders. There are possibly as many as 700 cichlid species.

Damselfishes (family Pomacentridae) are colourful small marine fishes of all tropical and warm seas which superficially resemble the deep-bodied cichlids. They are particularly common on coral reefs and many spawn on discrete patches of coral or rock, the eggs being guarded by the male. The family includes the anemonefishes or clownfishes (genus *Amphiprion*) which have a commensal relationship with the large tropical sea anemones. Anemonefishes change sex as they grow older, so that the 'senior' fish is always a functional female; they lay their eggs close by the sea anemone for protection.

Grey Mullets (Suborder Mugiloidei)

A group which contains the single family Mugilidae, although other classifications include the next two suborders as well. The grey mullets are coastal marine, brackish and freshwater inhabitants of tropical and temperate seas. Their mouths are moderately small with teeth on the lips and protrusible jaws. The stomach is muscular and gizzard-like and the gut very long; this allows digestion of the high proportion of plant material and organic mud they ingest.

Barracudas (Suborder Sphyraenoidei)

A family (Sphyraenidae) of predatory marine fishes found throughout the tropical and temperate seas. They are long and slender with a pointed head, large jaws and long teeth. Their diet is almost entirely fishes and in places their flesh becomes toxic due to the build up of plant toxins in the food chain, elsewhere they are always free from toxin. The Great Barracuda, *Sphyraena barracuda*, of the western Atlantic and Caribbean, which grows to nearly two metres, is a rather formidable fish and has been known to attack bathers especially in clouded water.

Threadfins (Suborder Polynemoidei)

A single family (Polynemidae) of marine and brackish water fishes distinguished by their complex pectoral fins, the lower section of which comprises long separate rays. Much of their bottom-living invertebrate prey is detected by these rays. One of the best-known species and also the largest is the Gucchia, *Eleutheronema tetradactylum*, which grows to almost two metres. It is a common fish in Indian estuaries and is widely distributed in the Indo-West Pacific; it has considerable economic importance.

Wrasses and parrotfishes (Suborder Labroidei)

A large group of mainly tropical and warm temperate marine fishes found in all oceans, many have bright colours and diverse living strategies. Three families are included, the wrasses (Labridae), the Australian Odacidae, and the parrotfishes (Scaridae). Many wrasses and parrotfishes change sex with age, usually from active female to male, with associated changes in coloration; this led particularly in the parrotfishes to gross overestimates of the number of species, as initial phase and terminal phase males looked so unlike the females. Parrotfishes have strong beak-like fused teeth in the jaws and powerful pharyngeal teeth; they can crush most hard shelled animals and are particularly destructive to coral reefs. Wrasses also have strong jaw and pharyngeal teeth. Some parrotfishes secrete a mucus coccoon around themselves at night in which they sleep; others, like some wrasses, burrow in sand or wedge themselves in crevices to sleep.

Blennies, weevers, stargazers, and Antarctic cods (Suborder Blennioidei)

A large group of diverse fishes which in earlier classifications were placed in several categories. Some thirty-five familes and about 1,000 species are included; only a selection are discussed.

The weevers (family Trachinidae) are marine fishes of the eastern Atlantic ranging south to West Africa. The spiny first dorsal fin and the opercular spines have venom glands and wounds cause severe pain. The largest species is the Greater Weever, *Trachinus draco*, a forty-one centimetre long inhabitant of European seas. The stargazers (family Uranoscopidae) also have venom glands on spines above the pectoral fin and, in addition, electric organs behind the eyes. They live buried in the seabed and occur in all subtropical and tropical oceans.

In contrast, the Antarctic 'cods' (family Nototheniidae) are found only in this polar ocean and in sub-Antarctic regions, comprising nearly seventy percent of the fish there. Most are bottom-living fishes, some live close to the sea ice, and a few are pelagic. Many live in temperatures below 0°C and some have a glycoprotein which lowers their blood freezing temperature. Like the ice fishes (family Channichthyidae) of the same region some have no red blood cells.

Extremely abundant in tropical and warm temperate seas the clinids (family Clinidae) and the blennies (family Blenniidae) are mainly shallow water and littoral sea fishes. A few blennies live in fresh water. The two groups look superficially similar but the clinids have fully scaled bodies and the blennies are scaleless. Both families have slender two-rayed pelvic fins placed in front of the pectorals. Many of the clinids are viviparous but most are egg-layers; they are particularly abundant on the southern African coast and the Pacific coast of middle America. Many are specialised for living in crevices in rocks, coral and sponges, and the weedfish, *Fucomimus mus*, of South Africa mimics the algae in which it lives. Some of the tropical blennies are involved in interesting

Some fishes render toilet services to other fishes, especially fishes larger than themselves. They have become known as cleanerfishes. They derive their nourishment from the parasites and skin detritus which they remove and swallow in the process of manicuring their customers. The Blue-streak Wrasse, *Labroides*, attending to the larger *Platax* Batfish shows a typical cleaner fish at work.

An elongated and blenny-like fish commonly found hiding under stones along the coasts of Europe and North America, while the tide is out, is known as the Gunnel or Butterfish (*Pholis gunnellus*). Its body is very slimy, making the fish as slippery as butter. The female lays her eggs in small clumps, about 2.5 centimetres diameter, which she then compacts into a ball by curling her body into a loop containing the eggs as they are laid. She thrusts the eggs into a hole in the rocks or into an empty shell and for about a month both parents take turns in guarding the eggs.

mimetic relationships, some harmless species resembling heavily toothed aggressive species. One widespread Indo-Pacific species, *Aspidontus taeniatus*, mimics the Cleaner Wrasse, *Labroides dimidiatus*, which generally goes unmolested by fish predators. *Aspidontus*, however, employs this immunity to attack the larger fish biting off chunks of skin and scales. The wolffishes (family Anarhichadidae) are large blennioids which live in the North Atlantic and North Pacific; their teeth are very large and well suited to a diet of hard-shelled animals. The Wolffish or Sea Cat, *Anarhichas lupus*, is a European species which is exploited for food. Other blennioid families are the quillfishes (Ptilichthyidae), prowfish (Zaproridae), butterfishes (Pholidae), and the pricklebacks (Stichaeidae).

Ragfish (Suborder Icosteoidei)

A suborder containing the single species *Icosteus aenigmaticus*, which grows to a length of more than two metres and inhabits the North Pacific from California to Alaska and thence to Japan. Young fish live in inshore waters near the surface but the adults are pelagic or bathypelagic. The calcification of the skeleton is slight and fresh specimens are floppy and soft—hence ragfish.

Sandeels (Suborder Ammodytoidei)

Long slender-bodied fishes with pointed chins which can burrow into sandy seabeds, although when not alarmed they swim in dense schools in mid-water. Most species occur in the eastern Atlantic but sandeels are also found in the North

Pacific and Indian Oceans. Sandeels (family Ammodytidae) are mostly small, like the ten centimetre long *Ammodytes tobianus* of European seas. They are important as food for many larger fishes and sea birds.

Gobies and sleepers (Suborder Gobioidei)

A large and successful group of fishes which contains over 1,000 species in seven families. Most are small fishes living in the sea, brackish or fresh water, they have colonised many benthic living spaces in these general habitats. Gobies (family Gobiidae) typically have the pelvic fins fused together to form a disc-like fin which has weak powers of adhesion. They are most abundant in tropical seas and include what is regarded as the world's smallest fish, *Pandaka pygmaea*, of eleven millimetres found around the Philippine Islands. They are also common in temperate areas, such as the British coast where eighteen species occur, including the Giant Goby, *Gobius cobitis*, which grows to twenty-seven centimetres in length. Most gobies lay eggs on hard surfaces, including dead bivalve shells, and guard them until hatching. The pelagic European Crystal Goby, *Crystallogobius linearis*, however, lays its eggs in the empty tube of a marine worm. A number of gobies have commensal relations with burrowing crustaceans. The sleepers (family Eleotridae) are goby-like fishes whose pelvic fins are not modified into a disc. They are closely related to the gobies (some authorities place them in the same family) but are more tropical in habitat. They live in fresh water, estuaries and the sea. The Mudskipper, *Periophthamodon schlosseri*, is an Indo-Pacific species which lives on mud flats and in mangrove swamps; the eyes are placed high on the head and they can see in the air even when the body is wholly submerged, they can also stay out of water for hours absorbing oxygen through the mouth and pharynx. The Loach Goby, *Rhyacichthys aspro*, is a hill stream inhabitant of the Indo-Australian archipelago which is adapted for this life-style by its flat undersurface and perfectly streamlined body shape.

Surgeonfishes and rabbitfishes (Suborder Acanthuroidei)

Surgeonfishes (family Acanthuridae) are so called because of the very sharp knife-like spines on the caudal peduncle; in most species these spines retract into a sheath. They live mainly in the Indo-Pacific and less numerously in the Atlantic Ocean, and are deep-bodied compressed fishes which are brightly coloured. All have specialised teeth with which they graze algae growing on coral and rocks; they also have long intestines. The Convict Tang, *Acanthurus triostegus*, is widely distributed in the Indo-Pacific Ocean; the Blue Tang, *A. coeruleus* is a common species ranging from Bermuda to Brazil; both grow to about twenty-five centimetres in length. The rabbitfishes (family Siganidae) are found only in the Indo-Pacific, although two species have penetrated the Suez Canal into the Mediterranean. Most are reef fishes which eat algae and live in shallow water. The dorsal fin spines are sharp, the first one pointing forward. They also have venom tissue at their bases. The Coral Spinefoot, *Siganus corallinus*, ranges from the

Seychelles to the Philippine Islands; like most members of this family it is around thirty centimetres long.

Tunnies and billfishes
(Suborder Scombroidei)

A group of large marine fishes which includes many valuable food fishes and some of the most powerful, fast swimming fishes known. The snake mackerels (family Gempylidae) and the Cutlass fishes (family Trichiuridae) are slender-bodied with long continuous dorsal fins and most have a distinct small tail fin. All have formidable, large fang-like teeth. They are pelagic and bathypelagic fishes of tropical and subtropical seas. Some have considerable economic importance like the Black Scabbardfish, *Aphanopus carbo*, the staple food fish of Madeira, and the silvery Scabbardfish, *Lepidopus caudatus*, of Portugal. The tunas and mackerels (family Scombridae) are also worldwide in range, and many species are warm season migrants into cool temperate seas. One of the best-known species is the Atlantic Mackerel, *Scomber scombrus*, a fish found in offshore waters on both sides of the North Atlantic. It attains a weight of only one kilogram and is thus small when compared with the giant Bluefin Tuna, *Thunnus thynnus*, which grows to 907 kilograms. The Bluefin is also a North Atlantic species and specimens have been known to migrate from the American to the European coast. There is also regular warm season migration northwards on both sides of the North Atlantic. In temperate regions of the southern hemisphere a closely similar species, the Southern

Bluefin Tuna, *T. maccoyii*, occurs, and is much the same size. The Yellowfin Tuna, *T. albacares*, is another large tunny but has a more oceanic distribution, as has the Big-eye Tuna, *T. obesus*. These, with the Albacore, *T. alalunga*, which only attains a weight of forty-three kilograms, the Skipjack, *Katsuwonus pelamis*, and the Bonito, *Sarda australis*, are heavily exploited (often overexploited) by high-seas fisheries. These powerful and fast swimming fishes have been found to have body temperatures higher than that of the surrounding water, partly on account of their high metabolic rate and partly as a result of an internal heat exchange system which retains heat produced by muscle action.

The Swordfish, *Xiphias gladius*, belongs to the family Xiphiidae and is characterised by its long, flattened bill. It also lacks pelvic fins. It is a marine fish of cosmopolitan distribution in temperate and warm temperate seas from the surface to about 600 metres. It feeds on a wide range of smaller fishes and squids: but it is exploited by man both as food and for sport, as are the billfishes (family Istiophoridae), which are more common in tropical and subtropical seas. They all have a long bill but it is rounded in cross-section; they also have long pelvic fins and two keels on each side of the caudal peduncle. There are about ten species, all well-known as sporting fishes and they include the Sailfish, *Istiophorus platypterus*, the spearfishes, *Tetrapturus* sp., and the marlins, *Makaira* sp. The Blue Marlin, *M. nigricans*, feeds on a wide range of fishes and squids and grows to a weight over 500 kilograms.

Mudskippers leave the water as the tide ebbs and during this time they seem to become strongly territorial. That is the only logical explanation for the way a mudskipper periodically raises its dorsal fin as if signalling to other mudskippers nearby to keep away.

FISHES

Medusafishes, butterfishes and blackfishes (Suborder Stromateoidei)

A fascinating group of about sixty species of mainly oceanic fishes which have toothed pouches either side of the pharynx. Most are tropical species but some live in temperate seas; all have lightly calcified skeletons. Many are known to feed on medusae, ctenophores and salps, and several species including the Man-of-war Fish, *Nomeus gronovii*, which lives in association with the siphonophore Portuguese Man-of-war, *Physalia*, are found with medusae. The butterfishes (family Stromateidae) are excellent food fishes mainly living on the American coast.

Gouramis and climbing perches (Suborder Anabantoidei)

Members of this group have a suprabranchial respiratory organ formed by modification of the first gill arch which is labyrinthine in form. This is an adaptation for air breathing as many species live in still, oxygen-poor water. They are most abundant in Asia with a few in Africa. A number of species lay their eggs in bubble nests at the surface, such as the Siamese Fighting fish, *Betta splendens*, of the family Belontiidae. The Gourami, *Osphronemus goramy*, (family Osphronemidae) lives in South-east Asia, grows to sixty-one centimetres and is widely cultured in fish ponds where its air-breathing ability allows it to survive less than excellent conditions. Another member of the group is the Climbing Perch, *Anabas testudineus*, (family Anabantidae) which can move itself overland using the spiny gill covers and pectoral fins to keep a grip on the surface while flexing its tail for propulsion.

Snakeheads (Suborder Channoidei)

This small group contains about ten species of the family Channidae. All have long slender bodies and long-based dorsal and anal fins; the head is broad and heavily scaled. They live in fresh water in both tropical Africa and Asia, and all have an accessory breathing organ in the gill chamber which allows them to breathe atmospheric oxygen. *Channa asiatica* grows to thirty centimetres in length and lives in South-east Asia, but although *Ophicephalus micropeltes* lives in the same region it grows much larger and may weigh up to twenty kilograms. It is a valued food fish. Many of the snakeheads live in stagnant water, canals and even paddy field drainage ditches. They are an important food resource.

Spiny eels (Suborder Mastacembeloidei)

The group of freshwater spiny eels (family Mastacembelidae) which have a series of isolated short spines along the back, and a long fleshy snout with tubular nostrils at the front and sides. There are about fifty known species distributed in tropical Africa, Asia and the Euphrates region. They mostly live in dense weed beds or on soft muddy bottoms in which they burrow. *Mastacembelus armatus* grows to seventy-five centimetres in length and is an important food fish in India, Burma and South-east Asia where it lives in heavily vegetated swamps. Another Asiatic species is *Macrognathus aculeatus*, a genus distinguished by its very long snout. A second family (Chaudhuriidae) is found only in Lake Inle, Burma; it has no dorsal spines.

Clingfishes and dragonets (Order Gobiesociformes)

A small order of shallow-water, bottom-living fishes with flattened undersides and scaleless skins. They are found mainly in the sea in tropical and temperate regions of the Atlantic, Indian and Pacific Oceans. A few clingfishes (family Gobiesocidae) live in fresh water in Central America and the Galapagos Islands. The clingfishes have an elaborate and powerful ventral sucker formed mainly by modification of the pelvic fins. They cling to rocks and resist dislodgement by waves or running water. Many live in the intertidal zone, including the Pacific coast species, found in North America from British Columbia to California, the Flathead Clingfish, *Gobiesox maeandricus*, which grows to fifteen centimetres, and the Short Clingfish, *Lepadogaster lepadogaster*, which is common on rocky shores in Britain.

The dragonets (family Callionymidae) have in earlier classifications been placed close to the blennies. They are marine fishes found in all temperate and tropical seas but most abundantly in the Indo-Pacific. In general they are shallow-water fishes which burrow in sandy bottoms, but some like the European Spotted Dragonet, *Callionymus maculatus*, extend as deeply as 300 metres. Adult males are usually more brightly coloured than the females and spawning is preceded by an elaborate courtship display. The most common European species is the Dragonet, *C. lyra*, which grows to thirty centimetres; the rather smaller Lancer Dragonet, *C. bairdi*, lives on the American Atlantic coast. The Mandarinfish, *Synchiropus splendidus*, is a brilliantly coloured species from the Philippine Islands. All dragonets have a spur on the preoperculum which is often heavily spined. Some species have toxic mucus on their bodies; possibly their brilliant colouring acts as a warning of this. Members of the family Draconettidae have lateral line canals only on the head.

Flatfishes (Order Pleuronectiformes)

Flatfishes are highly adapted to life on the ocean bottom and as adults they have both eyes on one side of the head and lie with the blind side downwards. Yet, as larvae and postlarvae they resemble other bony fishes with an eye each side of the head. During metamorphosis late in their development one eye migrates from its normal position to lie beside the other resulting in a complex crossing of the optic nerves and considerable changes in cranial osteology and musculature. The blind side is unpigmented in most species, the side with the eyes is coloured; there are often discrepancies in dentition and the development of the pectoral and pelvic fins between the two sides. Six families are recognised and there are about 500 species; they are mostly marine fishes.

Psettodids (Family Psettodidae)

These are primitive flatfishes close to the basic perch-like stem, with the anterior dorsal ray spiny, jaws large, similar in size and dentition each side, and with the eyes together on right or left side of the head indifferently. Two species only are recognised, *Psettodes belcheri* of the West African coast, and *P. erumei* an Indo-Pacific species which grows to about sixty-four centimetres.

Opposite bottom
The Leopard Flounder (*Bothus pantherinus*) a flatfish which lives in the Indo–West Pacific. This is a male fish with the pectoral fin rays very elongate and the eyes spaced far apart.

264

Citharids (Family Citharidae)

A small family of flatfishes living in the Atlantic, Indian and west Pacific Oceans. The family is composed of four genera, *Brachypleura* and *Lepidoblepharon*, which have their eyes on the right side of the head (dextral) and *Citharus* and *Citharoides*, which are sinistral (eyes on the left side of the head). *Citharus macrolepidotus* is a twenty-five centimetre long inhabitant of the Mediterranean and tropical eastern Atlantic, living in depths of 100 to 300 metres on fine sand and mud bottoms.

Scaldfishes and lefteye flounders (Family Bothidae)

A large family of flatfishes in which the eyes lie on the left side of the head, the pelvic fins have no spines and the dorsal fin begins far round in front of the eyes. Three major subdivisions exist: the subfamily Bothinae in which the base of the pelvic fins on the blind side is shorter than that on the eyed side and with the pectoral and pelvic fin rays not branched; the subfamily Paralichthyinae in which the pelvic fin bases are of almost equal length and both pelvic and pectoral rays are branched; and the subfamily Scophthalminae in which both pelvic fin bases are elongate. A number of species of the Bothinae are well-known including the Peacock Flounder, *Bothus lunatus*, of the tropical western Atlantic from Bermuda and Florida southwards to Brazil. In this genus the eyes are widely spaced, and the male's eyes are more widely separated than those of the female. It lives in relatively shallow water among turtle grass patches and on sheltered sand patches and grows to about forty-five centimetres in length. This is almost double the length of its European relative, the Scaldfish, *Arnoglossus laterna*, a common fish off the British coast, which gets its name Scaldfish from the way the large scales become detached in the trawl giving it a scalded appearance. Two North American members of this family are large and important food fishes, the California Halibut, *Paralichthys californicus*, and the Summer Flounder, *P. dentatus*, a fish which ranges from Maine to South Carolina. These are approximately the same size as the European Turbot, *Scophthalmus maximus*, which is also a valuable food fish.

Plaice and flounder (Family Pleuronectidae)

These are often called the Right-eyed Flounders describing their most important feature. It is a large family of flatfishes with nearly 100 species including some of the largest fish known. The Atlantic Halibut, *Hippoglossus hippoglossus*, attains a length of nearly two metres and weight of 300 kilograms and more; it is widely distributed in deep water (109 to 1,000 metres) right across the cool temperate region of the North Atlantic. A closely similar species, *H. stenolepis*, occurs in the North Pacific, from California to Alaska and from Japan to Siberia, and is even larger than the Atlantic species. In both the body is thickset and the jaws large and heavily toothed. These fishes are not confined to the ocean floor but are active mid-water predators on fishes and squids. In the colder parts of their ranges these halibuts overlap with the Greenland or Black Halibut, *Reinhardtius hippoglossoides*, which is an Arctic species. It too is a

mid-water fish which eats fish, squids and prawns. Its upper eye is placed on the edge of the head giving it much better all round vision than most flatfishes. The Arrow-tooth Flounder, *Atheresthes stomias*, is another large, active flatfish from the North Pacific.

Many members of the family are smaller but highly valued as food fishes. In European seas the Plaice, *Pleuronectes platessa*, is an especially valued fish. It ranges from the Barents Sea to Spain and the Mediterranean and is abundant on sandy and

This head-on view of a plaice (*Pleuronectes platessa*) shows how well it is adapted for life on the sea bed. Its eyes protrude to give it all-round vision above and to the sides, but its jaws are close to the sea bed to enable it to seize the buried invertebrates on which it feeds.

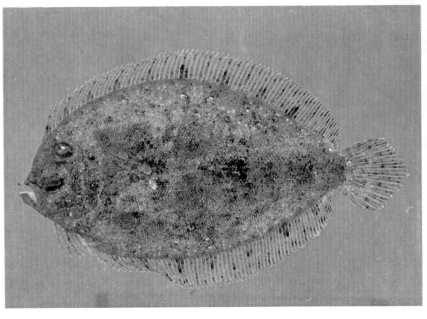

The Beaked Leatherjacket (*Oxymonacanthus longirostris*) lives amongst corals on the edges of reefs close to deep water. It ranges through the tropical eastern Indian Ocean and western Pacific, and grows to only eight centimetres long.

muddy bottoms in twenty-seven to seventy-three metres depth, although juvenile Plaice are common on sandy beaches in a few centimetres of water. The Flounder, *Platichthys flesus*, is another common fish in Europe and has much the same range, although it penetrates into estuaries and is common as a juvenile in many freshwater rivers and lakes with connection to the sea in northern Europe. It is distinguished from the plaice by possessing small spiny scales along the bases of the dorsal and anal fins. A similar feature distinguishes the North Pacific Starry Flounder, *P. stellatus*, but in this case the whole body is covered with small spines. Both members of this genus shows high frequencies of reversal, the eyes being on the left side of the head (even though the family as a whole is dextral). In the European Flounder as many as thirty per cent of some populations are sinistral, but sixty per cent of the American and almost all the Japanese Starry Flounders are sinistral. Other members of the family include the Smooth Flounder, *Liopsetta putnami*, of the American North Atlantic coast, the Lemon Sole, *Microstomus kitt*, and the Dab, *Limanda limanda* of European seas.

Soles (Family Soleidae)
Soles are worldwide in tropical and warm temperate seas but are most abundant in the eastern Atlantic and the Pacific. A number of species are found in fresh water in tropical America. In all soles the eyes are on the right side of the head and the preopercular margin is covered by skin. Possibly one of the best known species is the Sole, *Solea solea*, which is distributed from Norway to the Mediterranean. Like many other soles it is a shallow water fish which buries in the seabed and is mainly active at night.

Tongue-soles (Family Cynoglossidae)
The tongue-soles are sinistral, very elongate, with the mouth placed far to one side, eyes minute, and pectoral fins absent. They are tropical marine fishes, particularly numerous in the Indian Ocean where they are valuable food fishes. The Long Tongue-sole, *Cynoglossus lingua*, ranges from East

Africa to Sri Lanka and the West Pacific, grows to forty-three centimetres in length, and is especially common in muddy estuaries. Some tongue-soles are found in freshwater rivers.

Triggerfishes, pufferfishes and allies (Order Tetraodontiformes)
A fascinating group of fishes which show many highly specialised characteristics. Normal scales are absent but the body may be covered with heavy bony scales, as armour-plate covering or spines. The spiny dorsal fin is absent (except in the triggerfishes and their relatives), gill openings are greatly reduced and pelvic fins generally absent. There is also considerable specialisation in tooth structure. Five main groups are considered here.

Triggerfishes (Family Balistidae)
The body is deep and compressed and the first dorsal fin has a strong first spine which is locked into place by the small second spine. Teeth in the jaws are strong but separate and suitable for crushing hard-shelled organisms. The Grey Triggerfish, *Balistes carolinensis*, is found on both sides of the Atlantic Ocean, occasionally in autumn penetrating as far north as the British Isles. The Queen Triggerfish, *B. vetula*, is confined to the tropical western Atlantic; it feeds on the heavily spined *Diadema* sea urchin. These triggerfishes have thick bony plate-like scales on the body, but the file fishes, which are regarded by some authors as belonging to the family Monacanthidae are covered with finely spined minute scales.

Boxfishes (Family Ostraciontidae)
Members of this family are encased in a stout bony 'shell' which is only incomplete round the mouth, eyes, gill-opening, and where the dorsal, anal and caudal fins protrude. They are worldwide in distribution in tropical seas. They swim slowly, moving with gentle sculling movements of the posterior fins, but derive some protection from toxic secretions of the skin which are distasteful to other fish and even toxic to fishes confined in the same aquarium. Many are brightly coloured and live near coral reefs.

Pufferfishes (Family Tetraodontidae)

The pufferfishes have four fused teeth in the jaws, separated by a median suture, which gives them a beak-like appearance. The skin is naked or covered, especially ventrally, with small prickles. Most pufferfishes are tropical marine fishes but a number of species occur in the freshwaters of tropical Africa and Asia. The blood, liver, gut, and gonads contain a virulent toxin which is capable of killing a human if eaten in quantity, and produces severe gastric disorder if allowed to contaminate the flesh. Despite this, pufferfishes are eaten and esteemed in Japan where they are known as Fuju.

Porcupinefishes (Family Diodontidae)

A small family of tropical marine fishes which are characterised by the long sharp spines in the skin, and by having two fused strong teeth in the jaws. Porcupinefishes can inflate themselves with water or air causing the skin spines to stand erect. One of the better known species is *Diodon hystrix*, which grows to ninety-one centimetres, and is found in all seas in shallow water over turtle grass beds and sandy flats. It feeds on molluscs, crabs and sea urchins.

Ocean sunfishes (Family Molidae)

A group of surface-living open ocean fishes which include several huge and little known species. In these fishes the teeth are fused into a single unit in each jaw making a strong, sharp beak. The body is almost circular in outline with the dorsal and anal fins at one end and a short-based tail fin which occupies the rear end of the circle; they are literally all head and no body. Their food consists of soft bodied oceanic animals, jellyfishes, salps, ctenophores, and siphonophores. Considering the sparse nourishment of such a diet it is surprising that they reach the huge size that they do; *Mola mola* apparently attains a weight of 1,500 kilograms. Other species may be larger. The slender Sunfish, *Ranzania laevis*, has a rather more elongate body and is bright silver on the sides and deep blue on the back; it is a comparatively rare fish.

Pufferfishes or fugus can inflate themselves with water so as to increase their size to make them more formidable to potential predators. Their internal organs and blood are highly toxic to man, but despite this they are esteemed a delicacy in Japan where specially prepared, the fugu is widely eaten.

Amphibians (Class Amphibia)

As the amphibians developed and adapted to various situations on land, so a great diversity of types evolved. Over the millennia many of these have become extinct, and only three orders remain of the eleven or so which are known to have existed. These are the newts and salamanders (Caudata or Urodela), frogs and toads (Salientia or Anura), and caecilians (Gymnophiona or Apoda). Considered broadly, the tailed caudates spend much of their life in water, the frogs and toads are terrestrial, coming to the water only to breed, and the caecilians have adapted for life in moist soil.

The newts and salamanders have retained the ancestral type of elongated body and tail, which are used effectually in water, though in particular species they are modified to fit such specialised habitats as mountain streams or deeper, still waters. Most have four legs, but in some forms, as in the Amphiuma Lamper Eel (*Amphiuma means*) of the United States, these are vestigial or have even been lost altogether, as befits their habitat.

Some tailed amphibians occur on land and may even move actively there, but the loss of the tail by adult frogs and toads has given them extra mobility on land. Not only have they lost the tail, but their bodies are broader in proportion, and the strong and elongated hind legs found in many species account for the order being named the Salientia (*saliens*, leaping). There is no neck, and the head, in marked contrast to that of the newt, cannot turn easily on the body.

The caecilians have lost their limbs and are more eel- or worm-shaped, though with a fin-like membrane round the exceptionally short tail. These burrowing species have only vestigial eyes, but a small protrusible tentacle lies between eye and mouth and has a sensory function.

Locomotion

Many of the toads and some other salientians walk on land in a typical tetrapod manner, and salamanders can progress in the same way, though the shape of body and tail and their shorter legs impose modifications. Specialised forms of walking occur as part of the mating pattern in some species. Frogs use their hind legs for leaping, and some toads may do this on occasion. Treefrogs are often extremely expert jumpers, as well as being able to cling to almost any surface on which they land: in this they are aided by sucker discs on their feet, which also assist them to clamber on near-vertical surfaces. Some salamanders also leap when frightened, but their feet are not adapted to clinging.

In the water, amphibians can both walk and swim. When undisturbed or during courtship, newts often walk slowly along the bottom, but when swimming they keep their legs pressed to their sides and use only the tail for propulsion. Frogs and toads in general use the hind legs when swimming, either solo or when paired during amplexus. Caecilians swim in eel-like fashion.

A number of tail-less amphibians habitually dig in soft earth. Spadefoots of American and European genera use the special digging shovels on their hind feet and so sink into the soil, as do the small South African species of the genus *Breviceps*. The Australian *Myobatrachus gouldii* uses all four feet for digging, while *Hemisus marmoratus* employs its shovel-shaped nose for this purpose.

Skin

The skin is soft and moist, free of scales, but having a number of glands which open externally. In addition to those glands scattered throughout the skin, aggregations occur in particular parts of its surface: toads and salamanders have large parotid glands which are defensive in function and occur behind and above the eyes, while in newts and salamanders groups of hedonic glands (which have an erotic function) are found particularly around the face, skin, cloaca and tail, their exact location varying with the species.

The skin serves a number of functions. It prevents excessive loss of body fluid, provides a

The long hind legs of the treefrog are particularly developed for jumping, while the spatulate ends of the digits conceal adhesive discs which enable it to cling to a variety of surfaces. This picture of the European Treefrog (*Hyla arborea*) illustrates these characteristics.

medium for exchange of gases with the exterior (comparable to the function of the lungs), contains sensory nerve-endings which warn of adverse changes in the environment, as well as the glands mentioned above. Its colour varies enormously from one species to the next, and may provide camouflage or warning coloration—sometimes both are found in the same species. It is possible that the distinctive odours emitted by certain frogs are also defensive in purpose.

Unlike the skin of mammals, that of amphibians is permeable to water in both directions. The rate at which water passes in or out varies with the moisture of the environment, the degree of dehydration of the animal, and the particular species, genus or family concerned. Thus, toads have a particularly dry skin through which water is not readily lost, and they can therefore inhabit more arid areas than frogs. Species which live under desert conditions are especially rapid in taking up water when there is a shower.

Gas exchange can be an important function of the skin. It has been suggested that because amphibians on land cannot obtain enough oxygen through their lungs alone, cutaneous respiration is vital to them. On the other hand, when hibernating under water, the animal's oxygen needs at low temperature can be wholly met by cutaneous respiration, so that there is no need to surface in order to use the lungs. Further extremes are reached in certain completely lungless salamanders occurring in mountain brooks, their skin alone sufficing for the intake of oxygen from these highly aerated waters.

The colour of the skin depends on three different types of pigment-containing cells, the melanophores containing black or brownish melanins, guanophores containing the uric acid derivative guanin, and the lipophores yellowish globules of fat and possibly also granules of red pigment. The colour displayed by any amphibian depends on the proportions of these various cells and on their degree of expansion or contraction, varying with the proportion of incident light absorbed by each type of cell. Any individual frog or treefrog may show major changes in its basic colouring within a few minutes, and many normally blend magnificently with their background and change colour as it does. Injection of mammalian melanotrophic hormone into bright green treefrogs can cause rapid alteration of colour through olive-green to brown in a few minutes. When treefrogs are sick; they sometimes show this change to a dark brown colour, presumably as a result of changes in the hormone balance. The mechanism of the colour change relates to changes in the state of the pigment cells: variations on the normal theme may occur if one or other of these chromatophore types is wholly missing. This occurs on rare occasions in certain treefrogs, the ground-colour of the affected individuals being blue instead of the normal green.

As well as cryptic camouflage, some animals show bright warning coloration, associated with defensive mechanisms which make them distasteful to predators. In the case of amphibians, these are frequently the skin secretions. Warning colours are usually bright reds, yellows or even white, often contrasted sharply with black patches, so making the animal very conspicuous. In some cases—as in the European Fire-bellied Toad (*Bombina bombina*)—the upper surface is darkly camouflaged, but the warning coloration on belly and sides of the legs is exposed when the creature is attacked. One other colour mechanism used against predators is the bright 'flash colours', normally hidden when the animal is at rest but exposed momentarily on the thighs when it leaps: this is found in certain South American and Australian treefrogs, and is believed to be startling enough to make an attacker lose sight of the camouflaged treefrog as it lands.

Teeth and alimentary canal

A number of salientians have no teeth at all, but others have small ones used for gripping prey. The simple teeth are not employed to break up the food, as in the mammals, and only one or two species bite with them. Some caecilians have teeth in the larval stage but lose them when adult.

The tongue is completely missing from the group of anurans known as the Aglossa, which are

The Spotted Salamander (*Ambystoma maculatum*) is a forest-living species from eastern North America. In early spring dozens, or even hundreds, of these salamanders congregate at their breeding ponds to mate and lay their clusters of eggs. The rest of the year they are secretive and stay hidden during the day.

Opposite top
The Common Bullfrog (*Rana catesbeiana*), a large frog found in the United States, characteristically rests in the water with its eyes and nostrils just breaking the surface. In this position air can be taken into the lungs, through the nostrils, yet at the same time the frog is alert for danger from above. It is, however, not wholly dependent on the nostrils for breathing because the skin plays a large part in respiration.

The highly-coloured Arrow-poison Frogs are restricted to South America. They are small smooth-skinned frogs characteristically wearing warning colours. They get their common name from the poison produced by small glands in the skin. The South American indians use the poison for their arrow tips.

completely aquatic and use their hands to cram food into their mouth. Many urodeles have fixed tongues incapable of active motion. In contrast, frogs and toads have mobile tongues, fixed at the fore end and free at the back, which they can project at their prey. While not comparable in size or efficiency with the tongue of chameleons, the anuran's tongue plays an important part in aiding it to feed on active prey, which sticks to the tongue which is coated with sticky secretions from glands situated in the tongue and in surrounding parts of the mouth. Some salamanders have this sticky tongue too.

The food passes from the mouth into the amphibian's oesophagus, its passage in many anurans being assisted by a muscular contraction that pulls the eyeballs down into the roof of the mouth, making the frog or toad give a convulsive blink as it swallows. The food goes through a straight oesophagus where it is coated with mucus. Ciliated epithelium may help to pass it on its way to the distensible stomach, where hydrochloric acid is secreted with the enzyme pepsin to start the digestion of proteins in this acid medium.

In the next part of the gut, the duodenum, further mucus is secreted, while alkaline pancreatic juice containing other enzymes which break down protein and carbohydrate derivatives are poured in from the adjacent pancreas. Near the entry of the pancreatic duct into the duodenum lies that of the bile duct, coming from the gall-bladder, into which the bile is secreted from the liver. The bile assists in the process of the emulsification of fat, and so helps to prepare fatty material for absorption from the gut. This takes place in the small intestine and the absorbed products of digestion pass via the blood vessels to the liver, some being stored there, while others travel to other depots about the body.

Waste products pass on into the wide rectum

and so to the cloaca ('drain') which is the joint receptacle for faeces and urine, whence they are expelled to the exterior. The cloaca, thus, is comparable to a combination of rectum and bladder in the mammals.

Venom and poison mechanisms

Unlike the poisonous snakes, few amphibians have any means of injecting venoms into either attackers or prey. Tailed or tail-less species alike, however, possess strong venoms which in emergency are exuded from the skin glands. Sometimes these are produced when the animal is seriously sick. They have an extremely unpleasant taste—human observers can testify to the burning sensation produced in a predator's mouth—and a number of toxins have been isolated from them. Several glucosides which act on the heart have been isolated from the skin secretions of toads, while those from the South American treefrogs of the genus *Dendrobates* are used by local Indians to tip their arrows with poison, apparently rapidly producing in their victim a curare-like paralysis and death. One of the strongest animal toxins known is said to be batrachotoxin, derived from the skin secretions of the South and Central American treefrog *Phyllobates bicolor*.

Respiratory and circulatory systems

As already stated, respiration in amphibians is not solely a function of the lungs. The skin also plays a part—whether greater or lesser depends on the species—and the lungs may even be entirely absent. In amphibians such as the Axolotl, the larval gills are retained, the degree of their development varying inversely with the oxygen level of the water where the animal is living.

In lungs, gills and skin the same basic mechanism is employed for interchange of gases between the amphibian's blood and the outside. The larger arteries break down into arterioles, and these lesser vessels in turn split up into more, this time the thin-walled capillaries. The capillaries gather together again into venules and so into veins. The capillary walls are only a single cell thick, and oxygen and other gases easily penetrate them and the thin surrounding tissue. With gills, easy interchange occurs between the surrounding water and the blood within the capillaries. In the skin capillaries the situation is similar, though the surrounding medium in this case may be either air or water. Lungs are an advance on the other two mechanisms: they are paired elastic sacs within the chest, linked by the two bronchi with the unpaired trachea, along which air is drawn. Within the lungs the bronchi subdivide into lesser bronchioles, and these in turn have terminal dilations or alveoli. The alveoli themselves have walls only a single cell thick, and their walls are intimately covered with the blood capillaries. There is therefore only a double layer of cells between the blood in the capillaries and the inspired air in the alveoli: at the same time, the surface area between the alveoli and the capillaries is extremely great, so that a large surface is available for passage both of oxygen into the blood and carbon dioxide and other waste gases from it.

Unlike the mammals, whose respiration results from muscular movements of the chest wall, the amphibians breathe by moving the floor of the mouth, first drawing air into the buccal cavity and then (after closing the nostrils) forcing it onwards to the lungs. At the same time, oxygen can enter the capillaries of the roof of the mouth by a mechanism corresponding to that of cutaneous respiration.

The heart comprises two auricles and one ventricle, which receives both the oxygenated arterial blood from the left auricle and the stale blood which has come from the body via the right auricle. Among the salamanders, the septum between the two auricles fails to separate the two chambers, as it contains small perforations: in some of the tailed amphibians from mountain streams these holes are especially large.

The arterial system varies from tadpole to adult, and also between anurans and tailed amphibians. In the tadpole a series of four arterial arcades comes off the aorta on each side, to form a series of four paired aortic arches which join again at the back to form the dorsal aorta. The first three of these arches pass through the external gills. From the anterior pair come the carotids, while when the lungs develop, the pulmonary artery comes from the fourth arch. What happens subsequently depends on the fate of the gills. Where these are retained, then the aortic arches remain. In urodeles which lose their gills, there is a corresponding reduction in the aortic arches: the first one no longer connects with the dorsal aorta, but serves the carotid only. The second one forms the main aortic channel, with a lesser one in the third; the importance of the fourth arch now lies in the pulmonary artery, which the tiny ductus Botalli connects with the dorsal aorta. The development of the adult anuran continues further, with the third arch disappearing and the pulmonary artery losing its connection with the dorsal aorta.

The venous system likewise undergoes modifications during the transition from larva to adult. The paired cardinal veins which continue forward from the larval kidney in the adult become united posteriorly to form the inferior vena cava, while their anterior portions degenerate into the small azygos veins.

Skeleton

In a few amphibians there are exoskeletal remnants, e.g. scales occurring in some apodans, and claws on the digits of the clawed frogs (*Xenopus* spp.) and the salamander *Onychodactylus*.

The endoskeleton is partly cartilaginous, even in the adult. The number of vertebrae varies enormously, from nine in the salientians to as many as 250 in the urodeles and apodans. Generally, there is a single cervical vertebra, a variable number of thoracolumbar ones (associated in some species with ribs), a single sacral vertebra, and others which form the skeleton of the tail. Here the anurans have a long rod known as the urostyle, while the apodans (which have no sacrum) are practically tail-less and have few vertebrae. The tailed amphibians may have many more. The vertebral bodies in the axolotls (*Ambystoma*) and the caecilians are biconcave, but in other urodeles and the salientians are concavoconvex, so that they can be closely fitted to one another. In the

salientians the concave surface is forward, in the urodeles the convex one.

The skull is lightly built, but ranges through a variety of form. In the tail-less amphibians alone the range is very wide: a large amount of cartilage is present in the cranial wall, in contrast to the caecilians, where this is absent from the adult though the bones are heavier. The urodele cranium is floored and roofed only at the back, though the apertures above and below are covered by other skull bones.

Bottom
A Common Frog of Europe (*Rana temporaria*) swimming to the surface of the water. The webbed hind feet at the end of the long legs provide the propulsive power. All *Rana* species are true, typical frogs: slim and agile with a pointed head and protruding eyes.

AMPHIBIANS

The limbs of frogs and toads have five digits each, the fourth toe from the inside of the hind foot being the longest. The paired main bones of their limbs form radio-ulna and tibio-fibula. Tailed amphibians usually have only four digits on the front limbs and five on the hind ones.

Nervous system and sense-organs

The relative proportions of the brain vary with the habits of the different amphibians. Where the eyes are of importance, as in the frogs and toads, the optic lobes are large. In urodeles they are relatively small. The olfactory bulbs are fused together in the former, unfused in the latter.

A special sensory organ, the organ of Jacobsen, formed as a sensory pit in the nasopharynx, enables the animal to smell food which is in the mouth. Its development is taken further among snakes and lizards.

Apart from some of the anurans, amphibians

A pair of European Common Frogs (*Rana temporaria*) in a breeding embrace or amplexus. The males call from the banks of streams or ponds to attract the females. The male then enters the water, climbs on the back of a female and clasps her around the chest. He fertilises the eggs as they are ejected by the female.

have no tympanic membrane: it has been suggested that where this is the case, vibrations reaching the fore legs may be conveyed to the inner ear by a mechanism involving the supra-scapular bone, the cartilaginous operculum and its muscle as this lies under tension. The operculum is only found in amphibians, where it occurs in the fenestra ovalis of the ear: it is present in some anurans and urodeles in association with a greatly reduced stapes.

Reproduction

The kidney of the amphibian receives its blood supply from two different sources, oxygenated blood coming along the renal artery and blood returning from the rear end of the body via the renal portal vein. Urine passes by the mesonephric duct to the cloaca, and thence to the bladder which forms a dilatation in its anterior wall. In the anurans, fluid can be re-absorbed through the bladder wall.

The ovaries are paired bodies, each comprising a number of lobes which are covered by the mesovarium. Literally thousands of ova may be produced from them in twenty-four hours by some anurans, while in contrast the little *Sminthillus limbatus* only lays a single egg at a time. The eggs are shed into the coelomic cavity, and ciliary movement passes them into the openings of the oviducts. As the eggs go down these, the jelly-like coat of albumen is added from the secretions of the oviducal glands.

The testes of the male lie in front of the kidneys: from them the vas efferentia carry the sperms into the kidney itself and subsequently via its tubules to the mesonephric duct.

In two families of anurans, the Bufonidae and the Atelopodidae, there are paired structures known as Bidder's organ. These normally contain some rudimentary gonadal tissue, but if the ovaries or testes are removed from a toad, Bidder's organ develops to form a functional ovary.

Fertilisation is usually external among amphibians, but there are exceptions to this rule. The primitive frog *Ascaphus truei* has a prolongation of the cloaca which is used by the male as an intromittent organ with which it effects fertilisation of the female, who in turn uses hers as an ovipositor. Some caecilian males can use their cloacae similarly.

Sexual dimorphism

Some species of anurans show marked differences between the sexes, but in others they may be hard to tell apart by external characteristics. Thus in *Xenopus* the only certain external distinction lies in the degree of development of the slight folds about the vent. In many species one sex grows more than the other: frequently the female is the larger, but in the American Bullfrog the male is bigger. Males of some species show external vocal sacs in the throat region. Discoloration here often gives a clue to their presence, but in the African Toad (*Bufo regularis*) the male has a blackish throat without trace of such a sac. In the female the throat is perfectly white.

During the breeding season many males develop pigmented callosities known as nuptial pads on their fingers or fore arm. In the Hairy Frog

(*Astylosternus robustus*) the flanks at this time develop hair-like processes of skin.

The female may posses attributes lacking in the male. These range from the pearly granulations which can be detected by touch on the flanks of the European Common Frog during the breeding season to the pouch in treefrogs of the genus *Gastrotheca*, inside which the eggs and young develop.

Among tailed amphibians, the male of many newts has a crest which develops during the breeding season, and at this time he is brightly coloured, in contrast to the somewhat drab female. There is also an associated swelling of the cloacal glands at this time.

Breeding habits

While amphibians commonly breed in the water, this is not always the case. In the majority of species, however, the two sexes congregate at one particular breeding place at the appropriate season. This may be diffuse, such as a large body of water, or they may be closely confined to a very small area. How they find their way there has not been determined, but probably actual knowledge of the terrain plays some part. In some cases the song of the firstcomers may help to draw together others of both sexes. In at least two species, celestial navigation has been shown to play a part.

Male anurans characteristically sing, different species having a very wide variety of types of call. The song appears to attract the females, while the males remain spaced a short distance apart. In some cases the male grabs at any moving thing which might be a female, in others she comes up and touches him first. The males of those few species which are voiceless search more widely for the females, probably of necessity.

In mating, the male anuran sits on the back of the female, with his fore arms clasped round her. In this embrace or amplexus they swim together, the female being the more active partner. Other males which attempt to clasp are kicked away by the one *in situ*. When the female is ready to lay her eggs she stretches in a particular way, and the eggs emerge at the same time as the male emits seminal fluid. Movements of the hind legs of the male at this time are characteristic for each species, and distribute the eggs.

Newts and salamanders have a completely different mating pattern. In the first place, they are voiceless, so there is no song. Display of the male to the female employs other senses, visual and olfactory. A male newt in the full glory of its breeding colours may first attract a female by swimming in front of her, but it subsequently stimulates her by rubbing its hedonic glands (which may be on the chin or around the flanks and cloaca) on her snout. Alternatively, males of some species stand in the water in front of the female and waft the secretions of their glands to her by lashing the water with their tail. When the interest of the female has been sufficiently roused, she walks towards the male. Among some of the plethodontid salamanders of the United States, the pair undertake a particular 'tail-walk', during which the snout of the female is pressed against the base of the male's tail. The tail-walk may be carried out in water or on land. At some stage in the courting pattern the male emits from his cloaca a bundle of sperms in a gelatinous capsule, the spermatophore. This is taken up into the cloaca of the female as she passes over it, sometimes by the cloaca being pressed on to it and sometimes with the assistance of her hind feet. In some species the male swims while clasping the female with his legs or even wraps himself round her, and this may be associated with deposition of the spermatophore near the female's cloaca or even between its lips. Once the spermatophore has been taken into the cloaca, it dissolves and the sperms are stored in the spermatheca, a sac in the roof of the cloaca. Subsequently a sperm is liberated from this as each egg is laid. This storage of sperms has made it possible for the females of some species to lay eggs months after mating, so that in one or two cases the mating and spawning seasons are totally distinct. The mating behaviour of caecilians remains obscure.

A male Spring Peeper Treefrog (*Hyla crucifer*), of North America, 'singing', with its vocal sac inflated. The air going across the vocal chords produces the call, which is greatly amplified in the sac. In the early spring the chorus from many Spring Peepers is said to sound like sleigh bells at a distance.

A male Caucasus Newt (*Triturus vittatus ophryticus*) shown displaying to a female. At the start of the breeding season the male develops a prominent crest on the back and tail. He then stages an elaborate nuptial display for the female's benefit.

In spring the female European Common Frog (*Rana temporaria*) lays a mass of spawn of many hundreds of eggs in still, shallow water. On hatching the tadpoles at first hang on to the old spawn feeding on the remains of their yolk-sacs (top right). After a few weeks (top left) the forelimbs appear and then the hindlimbs. The tail is then absorbed and, after the lungs have developed, the gills disappear. At the beginning of summer the metamorphosis is complete and the tadpole has changed into a froglet which emerges from the water onto land.

Nest building

The eggs may be deposited singly or in clusters, and there may or may not be any vestiges of a nest. Some of the common species of frog lay eggs in clumps which float, others in small numbers which sink amongst aquatic vegetation. The eggs of some frogs are laid even in the surface film of the water. Special breeding ponds have evolved, in the form of small pools in tree-boles or in the tropical bromeliad plants. Some anurans have taken things further and lay in special nests. One or two treefrogs (e.g. *Hyla faber*) build individual clay pools in which the eggs are laid, while other frogs have become foam-nesters: in the genus *Rhacophorus* the male uses his hind feet to whip up a froth from the albumen exuded with the eggs, and this hardens round them in a sort of meringue. The nest is suspended in vegetation over the water and later liquefies after the tadpoles have hatched, so that they drop into the water. Leaf-nesters of the genus *Phyllomedusa* make nests in foliage above water, laying their eggs between two leaves which they stick together, or even in a single folded one.

Other nests are made in burrows in the ground or in damp sphagnum, both by anurans and by a number of American species of newt. One parent, often the female, is frequently found remaining with the eggs, and appears to provide both moisture and some fungicidal properties which protect the eggs until they hatch. A number of caecilians also coil round their eggs in burrows.

Viviparity and oviparity

The ultimate form of the nest occurs when the eggs are attached to the parent. The male Midwife Toad (*Alytes obstetricans*) bears the eggs tangled round his thighs and cares for them till they hatch.

The Surinam Toad (*Pipa pipa*) goes even further, and the eggs are taken on the back of the female, sinking into this so that the young develop in pits in the mother's skin. Among treefrogs of the genus *Gastrotheca*, the eggs are packed by the male into a pouch in the back of the female, from which tadpoles or baby froglets emerge in due course. The final examples come from Darwin's Frog (*Rhinoderma darwinii*) where the male swallows the eggs, which develop in his vocal sacs, and from the little-known African genus *Nectophrynoides*, where the young develop within the oviducts of the female. Fertilisation of the eggs within the female occurs after the male sperms are emitted directly into her cloaca.

THE TADPOLE: Amphibian eggs hatch to produce a larval form which in the anurans is quite different from the adult. This difference is less marked in the tailed amphibians, and even less in the caecilians. At hatching the tadpole can do little more than wriggle, and it spends much of its time hanging from the water-weeds, using up the remains of its yolk-sac. It starts with external gills, but in the anuran these soon go and are replaced by internal gills as the opercular plate grows over the gill arches. Water is taken in at the mouth and passed out over the gills. Limbs develop gradually, the fore limbs of the newt larva being present within a few weeks of hatching, though in anurans they are hidden by the tissues covering the gill arches.

With the appearance of the limbs the anuran tadpole starts to reabsorb its tail, and soon metamorphosis is complete. In tailed amphibians only the gills disappear, and in caecilians also this is the sole change occurring at metamorphosis. A few minor changes are not so noticeable: thus larval forms have no eyelids, and this is also the case in some adult salamanders which are noted for retaining some of their larval characteristics.

Before metamorphosis the lungs develop and are functional by the time the gills disappear. The circulatory system changes completely into a new pattern of blood vessels. With the growth of the limbs, these become more capable of sustaining the creature's weight on land. All this requires an increased intake of food, and in particular protein. Larval caudata are carnivorous from an early age but anuran tadpoles are in many cases herbivores at first: these change their habits and become scavengers on protein, or even openly predacious on other tadpoles before their legs appear. If kept on a purely vegetarian diet, tadpoles will grow slowly but no legs will develop. This may perhaps account for the occasional giant tadpoles found in the Edible Frog (*Rana esculenta*).

NEOTENY: From time to time newts are found which have reached adulthood without losing their gills or other larval characters. At the same time they may be sexually mature. Neoteny, as this state is called, has been recorded among a number of species, usually as part of a population occurring in cold and deep water. Sometimes it is also associated with albinism. Some subspecies of European newts from mountain lakes are completely neotenous, as is the Mexican Axolotl (*Ambystoma mexicanum*); other species of the genus show occasional neoteny.

Classification

Any consideration of the classification of amphibians has to include both extinct and existing species, and it must be remembered that by far the greater number are now extinct. Normal classification techniques use a number of lines of approach which consider various anatomical, physiological, ecological and genetical facts relating to each species. While it is possible to utilise all these to clarify the degrees of affinity of existing species, the fossil remnants of extinct ones may allow comparisons of bony anatomy only, while perhaps the fossil strata themselves may give some clue to the ecology and behaviour of the various species. Even the bony anatomy may be misleading, since the skeleton of vestigial limbs may be easily overlooked or even missing, or (as perhaps with *Protobatrachus*) a metamorphosing larva may be mistaken for the usual adult form of a species.

The most important means of separation of the various subclasses is based on the origin of the vertebral centra. Development of the vertebrae progressed with adaptation to life on land. The centrum had a dual origin, from the original hypocentrum which hung below the notochord and the newer pleurocentrum behind this. These appear as separate entities in the Temnospondyli and the Anthracosauria, with shapes which are characteristically different in the various orders. The shape and character of the centrum is also important in the classification of frogs.

Other diagnostic characters may be found in the skull; for example, the exact situation of teeth in the roof of the mouth, or the presence or absence of certain of the bones or cartilages. The degree of fusion of some of the bones of the jaw may also be of importance. In the salientians, the thigh

The Striped Pyxie Toad (*Pyxicephalus delalandii*), of East Africa, lays its eggs in rain puddles. As the water will evaporate quickly, the eggs are adapted to hatch in two or three days. The tadpoles develop very rapidly and the metamorphosed toadlets are ready to leave their rapidly shrinking puddle in about three weeks.

A male Midwife Toad (*Alytes obstetricans*), of western Europe, carrying a string of eggs around his thighs. Three or four times a year the female lays about a hundred eggs in a string which the male immediately wraps around himself. He enters water periodically to moisten the eggs and finally, on one such visit, the tadpoles hatch and swim off.

275

One of the Mole Salamanders (*Ambystoma tigrinum*) of North America spends most of its life in water but does come out on land at times especially on rainy nights to hunt small invertebrates. Some larvae never develop into this form. They grow to a larger size, eventually become sexually mature but still retain their gills, a condition known as neoteny.

The Rough-skinned or Pacific Newt (*Taricha granulosa*) of the coniferous forests of the Pacific coasts of North America. One remarkable observation of this species is that when molested it adopts a defensive posture, depressing its back and bending its head and tail upwards until they nearly touch one another. At the same time the tip of the tail goes into a tight coil with the orange undersurface turned uppermost. The limbs are extended stiffly from the sides and the eyes are depressed in their sockets, with the lids closed.

muscles and the cranial morphology may be used for comparison, but particular importance is laid upon the form of the pectoral girdle. In the earliest known cases, the epicoracoids are fused together, but in other frogs they may be separated or fused at either end. To a lesser extent the pelvic girdle may be of use, particularly in connection with the shape of the sacral vertebra.

Breeding behaviour may sometimes be so characteristic as to warrant the removal of a small number of amphibia from one genus and their separation into a new one. On the other hand, some well-defined genera show remarkable variation in breeding behaviour; e.g. *Crinia*, where the eggs may be laid on land or in the water, or *Hyla*, where there is great variety of breeding sites, even to the individual breeding ponds constructed by *H. faber*.

Caecilians (Order Apoda) (=Order Gymnophiona)
Family Caeciliidae
Within a single family the relatively small number of about fifty species is divided into sixteen genera.

Caecilians occur in a number of tropical countries, but are seldom seen even when being deliberately sought. Their worm-like form is particularly adapted for burrowing in the earth, but they may sometimes be found under boulders, and they have occasionally been taken when swimming in streams. Probably they feed on worms and termites. Although some larvae are aquatic, others develop completely to metamorphosis within the egg, while those of *Ichthyophis glutinosus* from Sri Lanka develop within it until they have their external gills. In some cases the mother produces living young.

The species *Chthonerpeton indistinctum* is said to be capable of using its cloaca as a sucker, to enable the animal to remain in one place against the pull of a strong current of water.

Newts and salamanders (Order Caudata or Urodela)
The order is divided into eight families distributed among five suborders.

Suborder Cryptobranchoidea
Family Hynobiidae
Five genera of primitive salamanders belong to this. All are species from Asia. In the genus *Hynobius* the female enters the water only to lay her egg sacs, but the male spends the winter there as he guards them. In cold surroundings, such as the mountain brooks it inhabits in Siberia, *Ranodon sibiricus* delays metamorphosis until the age of three years.

Family Cryptobranchidae
This family is probably derived from the Hynobiidae, and retains some larval characteristics. Only two genera occur, each represented by one or two species of large salamander. The first is *Cryptobranchus*, the Hellbender, found in the eastern parts of the United States, where it lives in mountain rivers. A heavily built newt, up to forty-five centimetres long, it has no external gills, but a single gill slit remains open, often only on one side of the neck.

Megalobatrachus, the other half of the family, occurs in China and Japan. The Japanese Giant Salamander (*M. japonicus*) grows to a length of 150 centimetres. This is a species found in mountain streams, where it hides in holes. It has a capillary network of blood vessels beneath the skin and probably uses these in respiration. The gill slits are all closed in the adult, and there are no external gills.

Suborder Ambystomoidea
Family Ambystomatidae
Four genera are included in this. The best-known species are the tiger salamanders of the United States and Mexico. Some of the numerous species are particularly prone to neoteny, the Mexican Axolotl (*Ambystoma mexicanum*) being the best-known example. The salamanders live in a variety of swampy or damp areas, hiding by day but active after dark. Some occur in desert areas, while one or two are known from brackish lakes or even highly saline ones, e.g. the Devil's Lake Tiger Salamander (*A. tigrinum diaboli*).

Dicamptodon is represented by the single species *ensatus*, the Pacific Giant Salamander, which is found from British Columbia to California and is up to thirty centimetres long. On land it occurs under logs in moist places, and probably lays its eggs in similar situations and near water. Neoteny is known, and it has been suggested that the species only metamorphoses when local conditions make aquatic life impossible for the larvae.

Rhyacosiredon and *Rhyacotriton* are monotypic genera of small newts from the United States and Mexico which live in mountain streams.

Suborder Salamandroidea
Family Salamandridae
This includes an assemblage of nine genera which cover many of the newts. Distribution of *Cynops* ranges from China to the United States and Europe. *Triturus* comprises the majority of the European newts, with *Pleurodeles* for the western Mediterranean pleurodele, the small genus *Euproctus* of mountain newts, and *Salamandra* to cover two European terrestrial species. *Triturus* extends as far as Japan, and corresponding to it in the United States are the genera *Diemictylus* and *Taricha* (which were formerly included in it). The land and water phases of *Diemictylus* are so dissimilar that at one time they were considered as different creatures. Newts of the genera *Triturus*, *Diemictylus* and *Taricha* are found in the water during the breeding season, but seldom otherwise, though the female may spend weeks depositing her eggs. The adults of *Diemictylus* spend the first two or three years of their life on land when they are known as efts, and as full adults are completely aquatic newts. The European Fire Salamander (*Salamandra salamandra*) spends only an hour or two doing this, while in the other species of the genus (*S. atra*) mating occurs on the melting snow of its alpine haunts, and the young develop within the mother.

In *Salamandra*, *Euproctus* and *Pleurodeles* the males clasp the females during mating, using their tails as nooses to hold their mates, so that their cloacae are very close together. *Pleurodeles* is noted also for the fact that the sharp ribs often pierce the body-wall and their ends reach the exterior.

Family Amphiumidae
The single genus *Amphiuma* contains two species, both from the United States, and known colloquially as the Congo Eel or Lamper Eel. Eel-like in form, they still have rudimentary limbs and lungs, though the gill cleft remains open in the adult. The Two-toed Amphiuma or Lamper Eel (*Amphiuma means*) may grow to a metre in length, and lives in still waters such as swamps. The male constructs a nest in which it induces females to lay. There is no spermatophore, and the eggs are fertilised by the emission of sperms over them.

Family Plethodontidae
The plethodontid salamanders comprise about twenty-five genera from north America and Europe. They are lungless and include both terrestrial and aquatic species. The genera *Bolitoglossa* and *Chiropterotriton* extend from Mexico through Central to South America, where some species may occur at heights up to 3,300 metres. *Hydromantes* is represented by several species in mountainous areas of Europe and the High Sierras of California.

While some of the newts are fairly short and tubby, variation extends to the extremely long and thin worm salamanders (*Batrachoseps*), which occur under rotten wood or burrow deep into the ground in various parts of the United States. Some genera (as in the North American *Desmognathus*) include both terrestrial and aquatic species; some species or subspecies (as in the genera *Eurycea* and *Gyrinophilus*) from the United States are entirely neotenic.

Most of the species of the type genus *Plethodon* are nocturnal, and found by day under or within old logs, though rock crevices may also be used as shelter. One of the most abundant species in the eastern United States is the Red-backed Salamander (*P. cinereus*) which occurs in two phases once considered two separate species; the lead-backed form is, as the name implies, grey-coloured. There are three genera each consisting of a single, blind cave species. These are the Ozark or Grotto Salamander (*Typhlotriton spelaeus*); genus *Haideotriton*, which was described from a single specimen

The Fire Salamander (*Salamandra salamandra*), of central to southern Europe, is reputed to be able to pass unharmed through fire. One explanation offered for this story is that Aristotle, to impress on his pupils the coldness of the amphibian skin, told them it was so cold that the salamander would be able to pass through fire unharmed.

An unusual photograph of a salamander, *Bolitoglossa*, exposed at night in the rain-forest of Costa Rica.

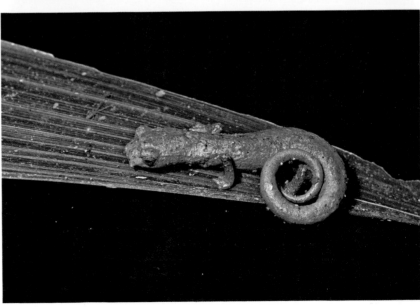

Hamilton's Frog (*Leiopelma Hamiltoni*) which has been found only in the Stephens and Maud Islands of New Zealand. Members of this genus live in the mountains where the air is moist and cool and where there is little standing water. The larvae develop within the egg-capsule and hatch as froglets; there is no free-swimming tadpole stage.

The Asiatic Horned Frog (*Megophrys nasuta*) is really a toad belonging to the same family as the spadefoot toads. Its specific name is derived from the long projection of skin on the end of its snout. It also has a horn of skin on each upper eyelid. It has a very wide mouth and strong jaws.

found in a sixty-metre deep well in Georgia; and the Texas Blind Salamander (genus *Typhlomolge*) from deep caves and wells of Texas.

Suborder Proteida
Family Proteidae
Two genera only occur, *Proteus* in Europe and *Necturus* in North America. A single species, the Olm (*P. anguineus*) is found in the underground rivers of certain Yugoslavian caves, and after spates is occasionally found outside the caves. This is a permanently larval form though it has lungs: in shape it is eel-like, but with rudimentary limbs. Although unpigmented, the skin will gradually darken if kept in the light.

The mudpuppy (*Necturus*) contains seven species and is found in streams in Canada and the United States. Again, they have both lungs and permanent gill tufts, with two pairs of gill slits remaining open. The limbs are well developed. Living in a

more open habitat than *Proteus*, the skin is pigmented and the eyes function adequately. Mudpuppies grow to thirty centimetres in length.

Suborder Sirendoidea
Family Sirenidae
Here again there are only two genera, both from the United States: *Siren* and *Pseudobranchus*. The Greater Siren (*Siren lacertina*) and Lesser Siren (*S. intermedia*) are further eel-shaped species, but have external gills and well-developed fore limbs. The hind limbs are missing. The Greater Siren grows to between sixty and a hundred centimetres long. The Striped Dwarf Siren (*Pseudobranchus striatus*) is considerably smaller, with primitive and function-less gills. They are found particularly in the weedy parts of shallow rivers where the current is not strong.

Frogs and toads (Order Salientia)
The anurans are now classified in the order Salientia, which is subdivided into fifteen families.

Suborder Amphicoela
Family Ascaphidae
These are primitive frogs, divided into the two genera *Liopelma* and *Ascaphus*. *Liopelma* comprises two species occurring in the montane uplands of New Zealand, where they are the only native frogs, and a third which has been found only in the Stephens and Maud Islands. In their haunts there is no standing water and the eggs are laid on the damp ground, the froglets developing wholly within the egg.

Ascaphus occurs as a single species found in the cold mountain streams of western North America. Under these circumstances the larva takes three years to reach metamorphosis. In the adult the cloaca has a mobile skin extension, used by the male in insemination of the female. She in her turn uses hers as an ovipositor, placing the eggs on the under-surface of rocks in the rapidly flowing water, to which surface they are adherent. The frogs can only survive in this cold environment, and can be transported alive from it only in insulated flasks.

Suborder Opisthocoela
Family Pipidae
All the members of this family are tongueless. They are also wholly aquatic, somewhat flattened in form, and seek their prey by scent. In the muddy waters which they inhabit, the lateral line organs of *Xenopus* serve to indicate if live food is present.

The family contains four small genera. The first is *Pipa* from South America, comprising five species. They have a rugose skin, with sensory tentacles at the tips of fingers and toes. Spawning takes place as the pair 'loop the loop', and the fertilised eggs (which are sticky) land on the back of the female and adhere to it. They then sink into pits in the mother's back, where the froglets develop.

Xenopus is another genus with half a dozen species, this time found in parts of Africa south of the Sahara. This is the toad that was used in the diagnosis of human pregnancy; following the injection of the patient's urine, the female frog will respond to the hormones secreted during pregnancy by spawning within a few hours. These eggs are simply dropped among the water plants.

The two remaining genera *Hymenochirus* and *Pseudhymenochirus* are somewhat similar, containing five tropical African species between them. The eggs are emitted singly by the female when her cloaca is held out of the water, so that they are projected on to the surface film.

Family Discoglossidae
Another family which contains four small genera. The first of these, *Alytes*, holds two species, of which the best known is the Midwife Toad (*Alytes obstetricans*) from Europe. At spawning and shortly afterwards, the movements of the male result in the ropes of spawn becoming tangled round his thighs, where they remain until the tadpoles hatch. By day the eggs remain moist. Eventually the tadpoles hatch and swim off on one of the occasions when the father is in the water.

Barbourula is a wholly aquatic monospecific genus found in the Philippines, floating on the surface of streams when undisturbed.

The genus *Bombina* contains four surviving species, European and Asiatic in distribution, the best-known being the Fire-bellied and Yellow-bellied toads of Europe. They are minute blackish species which occur in pools and streams. When attacked by predators they expose their bellies and the under-surface of the limbs, which bear bright warning colours.

The final genus, *Discoglossus*, contains two species of Mediterranean distribution. Of these, the better-known Painted Frog (*D. pictus*) occurs in two distinctly marked forms. Their colour difference is determined by a single genetic character, on which some research has been carried out. The species only occurs near water, in which the females may spawn several times during the year.

Family Rhinophrynidae
This is the third family of the suborder Opisthocoela and contains the single monotypic genus *Rhinophrynus*, the Mexican Digger Toad. It withstands extreme desiccation over long periods and spawns after heavy rain. The tadpoles are filter-feeders, eating algae, diatoms and the like.

Suborder Anomocoela
Family Pelobatidae
In this are some ten genera, including the European and American spadefoots (*Pelobates* and *Scaphiopus*) and the horned frogs (*Megophrys*). The spadefoots are adapted for life in dry habitats, living in burrows which they excavate in soft soil with the digging tubercules on their hind feet. They appear on the surface of the ground only in damp weather, often remaining in their burrows for days on end. Spawning takes place only after heavy rain, when breeding choruses are heard from temporary pools. Development of the tadpoles is rapid, and cannibalism occurs from time to time. Even non-cannibalistic tadpoles will devour their fully metamorphosed fellows if these return from land to water. On occasion large shoals of *Scaphiopus* tadpoles are found forming a feeding aggregation.

The genus *Megophrys* comprises about twenty species, distributed from the Himalayas through south-east Asia to the Philippines. While some occur at sea level, many are montane species, found only above 1,000 metres. Other genera from the high Himalayas and Tibet are included in this family.

Family Pelodytidae
The genus *Pelodytes* with its two species is the sole representative of this family. Some taxonomists claim that it is really not separable from the family Pelobatidae. The species occur in western Europe.

Suborder Diplasiocoela
Family Ranidae
Some three dozen genera occur in this family, which includes the true frogs (genus *Rana*). Also in it is the large Goliath Frog (*Gigantorana*), sometimes classified under *Rana*. Frogs vary in their habits, some, like the Edible and Marsh Frogs (*R. esculenta* and *R. ridibunda*), seldom being found more than one jump from water, while others, like the Common Frog (*R. temporaria*) and the American Woodfrog (*R. sylvatica*), wander more widely. The genus *Rana* ranges from the Arctic Circle to the Cape of Good Hope and occurs in all the continents except Australia: none is found naturally in New Zealand. Parental care of the young is normally lacking, but the male American Bullfrog (*R. catesbeiana*) will sit surrounded by its own tadpoles, which it protects against predators. This is an actively aggressive species, and one of the few where the male is larger than the female.

The South American arrow-poison frogs of the genus *Dendrobates* are brightly patterned with warning coloration, and live both on the forest floor and in the trees, moving actively and fearlessly by day. The male of various species carries the tadpoles on his back from pool to pool, for the water they live in is present in minute quantities in the tree hollows and similar places that are their habitats. Males of the genera *Prostherapis*, *Hyloxalus* and *phyllobates* also carry tadpoles about on their backs.

There are about 200 species of true frogs in the genus *Rana*. This one, *Rana chalconota*, is found in Thailand. In most species of *Rana* the skin is smooth and usually green or brown although there may be considerable variation in shade or pattern. Although the genus is found throughout the world its origin was almost certainly African.

Another genus of interest is *Astylosternus*, to which the 'hairy frogs' (*A. robustus*) belong. The males develop hair-like projections on the skin of their flanks during the breeding season.

The genus *Cornufer*, found from New Guinea to the Philippines, includes several small species which live wholly in forest plants, where its eggs are also deposited, the tadpole developing completely to metamorphosis within the egg. Other species live on the forest floor, their eggs being laid there and direct development of the tadpoles ensuing.

Several of the genera of this family are small and little known. *Ooeidozyga* comprises seven or eight aquatic frogs occurring from south-east Asia to the Philippines, though the adults do emerge on to the adjacent bank at night. Rattray's Frog (*Anhydrophryne rattrayi*) is a species living on the forest floor in South Africa whose eggs develop in a hole in the ground and whose tadpoles are so helpless that they drown if placed in water.

Family Rhacophoridae
There are about eighteen genera in this family, which includes various tropical treefrogs. Numbers of these are found in Africa, where they breed in the minute quantities of water found in the leaf axils of plants. Others occur from here to eastern Asia. The genus *Rhacophorus* in particular specialises in making foam nests, sometimes placed in vegetation over water so that the hatching tadpoles can drop from them, and sometimes in shallow burrows in moist ground. Other species of the genus are known as 'flying frogs', since they have been recorded as making long slanting glides from tall trees, apparently using the membrane of their large webbed feet as gliding surfaces.

Many of the other genera in the family are at present little known.

Family Microhylidae
Roughly sixty genera have been described, many of them rather obscure ones, and several comprising species found at high level in the New Guinea rainforests. *Microhyla* itself ranges from Florida (*M. carolinensis*) to south-east Asia. Several genera comprise species which feed on ants: the oriental *Kaloula* and the narrowmouth toads *Gastrophryne* and *Hypopachus*. Species of the three genera show adhesive properties during amplexus, the male and female during this time adhering to one another by means of their sticky skin secretions, which is also highly irritant.

Family Phrynomeridae
The last family of the suborder Displasiocoela contains the single genus *Phrynomerus*, a small group of African species. One of the best-known is *P. bifasciatus* (which apparently has no common name), found in the southern half of Africa. It hides in burrows, from which it emerges to breed after heavy rain. The skin secretions are remarkably irritant, even to the undamaged human hand.

Suborder Procoela
Family Pseudidae
Two small genera, *Pseudis* and *Lysapsus*, make up this family, each containing only a few aquatic frogs. *Pseudis* is found in certain high-altitude lakes in South America. The contrast between the very large tadpoles and the much smaller adult is so marked that one species has been named *P. paradoxus*.

Lysapsus comprises a small group of three species which occur in Brazil and adjacent countries.

Family Bufonidae
Seventeen genera have been described. They include the toads of the extensive genus *Bufo*, which occurs in all the continents except Antarctica and Australia; though the Giant Toad (*Bufo marinus*) now flourishes in the last, introduced by man. This genus has developed a warty skin with a particularly noxious secretion and is generally less tied to water than other anurans. The various species are found in drier habitats than frogs, though there are one or two that cannot survive under these conditions: the South American Giant Toad (*B. ictericus*) which lives along streams, and some of those occurring in montane valleys of the United States, such as the Deep Springs or Black Toad (*B. exsul*), the Yosemite Toad (*B. canorus*) and the Dakota Toad (*B. hemiophrys*).

Toads are usually brown or blackish in colour, sometimes patterned with green and in some cases having a yellow dorsal stripe. One bright yellow species has recently been described from India (*B. koynayensis*).

The other genera are less well-known but include the interesting *Nectophrynoides*, a genus made up of a few small species from the mountains of West Africa: the male at fertilisation applies his semen directly to the female's cloaca and the tadpoles develop within the oviducts of the mother.

Family Atelopidae
This contains only two small Central American genera of treefrogs, *Atelopus* and *Brachycephalus*.

The Giant or Marine Toad (*Bufo marinus*) is one of the largest species of toad, reaching a length of over twenty centimetres. It is a native of southern U.S.A. and South America but has been introduced into several parts of the world to control sugar cane beetles. In Australia, where it has few natural predators, it is becoming a pest.

Some members of the first are very brightly coloured, moving by day under the protection of this warning coloration. Zetek's Toad (*A. zeteki*) is particularly known to tourists in Panama.

Typical treefrogs (Family Hylidae)

Just over thirty genera have been allocated to this family. The type genus *Hyla* is a large one comprising the typical treefrogs widely distributed through the tropical and temperate parts of the world, but conspicuously absent from much of Africa and from India. Treefrogs have several specialisations for their arboreal life: their digits have expanded discs at the tips, which assist gripping so effectively that a treefrog can cling to a vertical sheet of glass. They are often strong jumpers which can launch themselves at a sedentary insect accurately enough to engulf it as they land. Despite their particular adaptation to arboreal life, most species spawn in water and have tadpoles of the usual type. There is, however, one genus showing a modification here: the Blacksmith Frog (*H. faber*) and the allied *H. rosenbergi* who model their private breeding ponds out of clayey earth. The female *H. goeldii* carries the small clutch of eggs on her back, while another genus (*Gastrotheca*) has developed an enclosed pouch on the back of the female into which the male pushes the fertilised eggs as soon as they are laid, singly or in pairs. Here they develop and the larvae later emerge as tadpoles or even as baby froglets, according to the species. The Spring Peeper (*H. crucifer*), abundant in the eastern United States and south-eastern Canada is familiar to most Americans because of its long springtime chorus from ponds and marshes during the early breeding season which is said to sound like sleigh bells at a distance.

The family also includes the cricket frogs (*Acris*) and chorus frogs (*Pseudacris*) of the United States, where the second group is particularly common. The genus *Phyllomedusa* contains a number of leaf-nesting species from Mexico and Central America, and even as far south as Uruguay.

Family Leptodactylidae

In this are swept up approximately sixty genera. The family is centred on the Australasian region and a number of the genera are confined to Australia itself. The nominate genus *Leptodactylus* contains a number of foam-nesters found in Central and South America, Mexico and even in Texas (*L. labialis*).

Something like two hundred species make up the genus *Eleutherodactylus*, which has its headquarters in the West Indies and Central America. The eggs are normally laid in or on the soil and the female remains with them; metamorphosis is completed within the egg, and only after this does hatching occur.

The small genus *Batrachuperus* contains two purely aquatic species from high-altitude South American lakes. *Telmatobius* likewise comprises a few totally aquatic species from the high Andes and the Brazilian Chaco. The genus *Ceratophrys* from South America contains another group of so-called 'horned frogs'.

Several genera from the more arid parts of Australia have special adaptations for survival in their particular environment. During the dry season they retire deep into the ground. Water is taken up rapidly, both into the peritoneal space and the bladder, and for this reason they are known as 'water-holding frogs' and are dug up by the aborigines for their water content in times of drought. With the coming of the rains, the frogs rapidly reappear and spawn in the temporary floodwaters. Metamorphosis of the tadpoles is very rapid, enabling them to leave the pools before they evaporate. A number of species lay their eggs in burrows in the earth. The isolation of colonies in species of such genera as *Crinia* is leading to the production of races so different from one another that they can be considered as virtually separate species.

Family Centrolenidae

This contains four small genera with about forty species between them, ranging from Mexico through to South America and occurring from sea level into the high mountains. In the genus *Centrolenella* the eggs are laid in situations where they are kept moist by the spray from waterfalls and other natural agencies. In some species of the genus, the eggs are fastened to the under-surfaces of leaves for the duration of incubation. The Centrolenidae is now usually included in the family Hylidae.

This treefrog (*Hyperolius marmoratus*) is small and long-bodied with adhesive discs on its digits. It is widespread in Africa and is not a true treefrog as it lives in reeds and sedges around pools or in swamps. The species shown here is sometimes called the Marbled Rush Frog because of its striped or variegated patterning.

The Horned Frog (*Ceratophrys ornata*), living in the Argentine, has an exaggerated reputation for evil. It is believed that if this frog bites the lip of a grazing horse that horse will die. This is clearly wrong since the frog has no poison in its mouth and this reputation probably rests on its unusual aggressiveness even to the point of attacking another animal many times its own size and inflicting a painful wound with its long teeth.

Opposite
An Arrow-poison Frog (*Dendrobates pumilio*), of the rain forests of Costa Rica, is associated with an unpleasant characteristic, in this instance the poison glands in the skin, and the colouring is therefore regarded as a warning to would-be predators.

Fossil amphibians

There are still large gaps in the fossil record. The major differentiation of the extinct species is into two subclasses, the Apsispondyli and the Lepospondyli, based on the differences in the centra of the vertebrae. In the former, the centra were ossified from cartilage and in the latter from the notochord, it is believed.

The Apsispondyli divide into two superorders, the Labyrinthodontidae and the Salientia (which includes the modern forms). The labyrinthodonts are named on account of the labyrinthine folding of the enamel of their teeth, and comprise five orders. The Ichthyostegalia are the earliest, starting in the Upper Devonian and Carboniferous. Mainly aquatic, they were succeeded by the next order, the Rhacitomi, which continued to the end of the Permian and even into the Triassic. Species such as *Eryops* were up to 1·5 metres long. By the end of the Permian they had evolved from an almost entirely aquatic existence to one which was mainly terrestrial. The Stereospondyli succeeded the Rhacitomi during the Triassic, degenerating from the rhacitome type with a return to a wholly aquatic existence. They ranged up to 3·3 metres long, and before their extinction towards the end of the Triassic such species as *Trematosaurus* had apparently re-colonised the sea.

The Embolomeri appeared in the Carboniferous and died out in the early part of the Permian. The earlier forms had fish-like characteristics and were mainly aquatic, later species being adapted for terrestrial life, while later again there was re-adaptation for a freshwater habitat. These were an offshoot from the main stem, with some reptilian characteristics, being known up to six metres long. The Seymouriamorpha, which are confined to the Permian, showed a number of reptilian characters, though the earliest reptiles had certainly preceded them in chronological sequence.

The subclass Lepospondyli comprised a number of small species, up to 0.6 metres long. The order Aistopoda occurred in the Palaeozoic coal-swamps of Europe and North America. They developed from tetrapod ancestors, but had snake-like bodies with ventral armour, and had returned to an aquatic existence. Their relationships are obscure. The order Nectridia contained two separate groups, classified together on account of the characteristics of their caudal veretebrae. The limbs in both groups were small or vestigial, but while one remained externally similar to the aistopods, the other contained animals with extreme developments in the shape of their heads. The remaining order is the Microsauria, comprised of small salamander-like amphibians probably adapted for life in muddy water, which had died out before the end of the Permian.

Despite their incompleteness, these amphibian fossil forms help us to reconstruct the most important stages of the evolutionary process, and in so doing two completely opposite tendencies are detected. The first is to full terrestrial status and the second is a return to aquatic life. The terrestrial forms gradually reduced their body length and evolved stronger limbs, whereas the aquatic forms either became snake-like or evolved flattened bodies, with accompanying reduction of limbs and a return to a longer body. To some extent this is what can be observed in modern amphibians also. However, this is not to suggest that amphibians as a group are merely a precarious survival, as was pointed out at the end of the previous chapter when discussing their relationship to fishes. Certainly the division between amphibians and fishes is much more clearly drawn than the division between amphibians and the reptiles that follow. But the eventual appearance of the reptile does not represent a vertical line in development—if one takes the analogy of a tree of evolution—but rather a layer of development, a level of organisation that has progressed beyond that achieved by the amphibians, but which is not as far advanced as that of either the birds or the mammals. The succeeding chapter of this book illustrates this path of development.

Reptiles (Class Reptilia)

Reptiles are vertebrates, terrestrial or aquatic but always breathing atmospheric air by means of lungs from hatching or birth onwards. In addition to this, which does not distinguish them from birds or mammals, they have a skin covered with horny scales, sometimes supported by bony scutes. Paired limbs, when present, are generally short and, typically, so inserted into the sides of the body that the animal is compelled to crawl. Once they were the dominant animal group on the earth, but now the dinosaurs, flying pterodactyls, pelyosaurs, ichthyosaurs and others have disappeared. Only four of the sixteen orders survive: the rhynchocephalians (primitive lizard-like relatives of the dinosaurs), the crocodilians, the chelonians and the squamatines.

In the heart there is incomplete separation of arterial and venous blood. The cerebellum is relatively little developed; the main area of the brain controlling the animal is the medulla. Reptiles can be either oviparous (egg-laying) or ovoviviparous (egg hatching when about to be laid). The embryo has an amnion and allantois in its fluid-filled sac.

They have a variable body temperature, which is always slightly above that of the atmosphere or of the surrounding water. That is, a reptile is poikilothermic (unable to regulate its temperature), like fishes and amphibians.

Physiology, reproductive features, nervous system and anatomy all show that reptiles are transitional between the lower vertebrates (fishes and amphibians) and the higher vertebrates (birds and mammals).

Structure
Body form and locomotion
The body form of present-day reptiles can be reduced to three fundamental types: the most primitive with a long body and a long tail, as in crocodiles and lizards; those with a long body with a tail not clearly marked, as in snakes; and those

Rear-fanged Tree Snakes (*Oxybelis acuminatus*), of tropical America, are brightly coloured and of slender build. They move fast through the trees preying on lizards and hummingbirds.

Opposite
The Scarlet Snake (*Cemophora coccinea*) is one of a group of snakes peculiar to the southeastern United States. They are all small, the largest of them being no more than forty-five centimetres long. The Scarlet Snake is secretive, non-poisonous and feeds mainly on the Brown-backed Skink (*Lygosoma laterale*).

The Starred Agama or Hardun (*Agama stellio*) is one of the commonest lizards around the Nile delta. It resembles the true agamas with its broad, short head, thick body and strong legs but differs from them by having rings of pointed scales covering the tail.

One of the commonest colubrine snakes is the European Grass Snake (*Natrix natrix*). Although non-venomous its size alone (average a metre long) tends to intimidate. Its yellowish-white collar has earned it the alternative name of Ringed Snake and because it is found near water it is sometimes called the Water Snake.

A Red-eared Terrapin (*Pseudemys scripta*) breaks the surface of the water to take in air. This common freshwater turtle of North America gets its name from the bright red band behind the eye of the female and young. When courting, the male places his forefeet together and vibrates their long claws against the female's head.

with a short body encased in a shell, as in tortoises and turtles. The last two types have evolved from the first.

Crocodiles and lizards have an elongated body, though in some the body is shorter than the tail. The limbs of crocodiles are strongly built, while those of lizards are relatively weak. The fore limbs in some lizards are so reduced in size that they are little more than stumps. When present they are in all instances inserted laterally as paired organs at right angles to the body, so that the body can be kept permanently raised off the ground. In practice many reptiles rest on the belly and progress by lateral undulations of the body and tail.

In snake-like reptiles the absence of limbs is correlated with an elongated body and a relatively shortened tail. An elongated body is more suited than any other for crawling or swimming by undulations. Locomotion in snakes is not entirely comparable with that in eels or worms. The ribs play no part in it, the usual type of locomotion being effected by the pressure of the undulating sides of the animal and its projecting scales against the irregularities of the ground, coupled with muscular contraction on one side and relaxation on the other side. Boas, pythons and some of the heavier vipers have a method of rectilinear movement in which waves of muscular contraction pass from head to tail along the belly. The enlarged ventral scales are projected at each forward movement and dig into the ground. Another method of ground movement, called side-winding, is used by the desert vipers and rattlesnakes. In this rapid and complicated movement the body of the snake is thrown into a series of loops, which touch the ground for a fraction of a second at regular intervals, and progress is made by a succession of leaps. Movement is made in an oblique direction and not that in which the head is pointing.

Finally, the chelonians (tortoises and turtles) have a short, squat body form, and the tail is usually short. Only a few of the larger chelonians can walk and most of them have retained the primitive method of locomotion, creeping. Aquatic chelonians have modified limbs which enable them to swim as well as walk; the more completely aquatic species have flipper-shaped limbs and move about on land only with great difficulty.

When considering the reptiles, the fossil forms cannot be ignored. Each displayed adaptations to a particular way of life. *Diplodocus*, a long-necked type with long limbs raising the body off the ground, bore only a remote resemblance to crocodiles and large lizards. *Ceratosaurus* was a bipedal running type with weak fore limbs, as in the present-day kangaroo. Ichthyosaurs were fish-like in form and habits, showing a striking convergence with the mammalian dolphin. Pterodactyls, which were flying reptiles with fore limbs modified to form wings, probably resembled bats. These four types became extinct.

One of the most interesting phenomena is the transition from a lizard-like to a snake-like form. Lizards belonging to the families Cordylidae, Scincidae, Anguidae and Amphisbaenidae show between them all stages in the elongation of the body and the reduction of the limbs. The digits become progressively fewer and the limbs shortened until they are reduced to stumps and then disappear. In snakes the limb girdles have atrophied and disappeared, although there are vestigial traces in some snakes such as the pythons and boas.

Scales and pigmentation

The skin of reptiles, unlike that of fishes and amphibians, has a horny surface layer with glands only in certain parts of the body, such as the thighs, throat and around the cloaca. In consequence reptiles have a completely dry skin which prevents desiccation. They are not slippery and moist like eels and frogs, and they rely on their muscular strength, agility and bite as means of escape from captors.

In lizards and snakes the horny layer of the epidermis forms a continuous covering of small scales. These are unlike the scales of fishes, which originate in the dermis and are separated from one another. As reptile scales typically form a hard, unbroken sheet and lie below the outer layer of the epidermis, the animal must moult to permit body growth.

Crocodiles, alligators, gavials and some lizards have bony dermal scales upon which the horny epidermal covering is moulded. Some hard layers are collectively known as the exoskeleton. This is highly developed in the chelonians (turtles and tortoises), forming a dorsal carapace and a ventral plastron. The carapace is in part fused with the vertebral column and with the ribs, and over its surface is a mosaic of horny plates.

Unlike snakes, most tortoises do not moult the scales, which increase in area and thickness as the animal grows. Each year a new epidermal scale is formed on the under surface of the old one, overlapping it around the edges. As one 'ring' is added each year, the age of a young tortoise can be estimated by counting the rings formed around the margins of the original scales. The age of older tortoises cannot be estimated in this way because the centres of the scales become worn and the ring obliterated, and in many species there is an irregular moult of the surface layer of scales.

The coloration of reptiles is caused by pigment, either diffused or contained within chromatophores (pigment cells), or by physical effects such as light-interference patterns or by varying combinations of these three causes. The main pigments do not differ from those of fishes and amphibians and, like them, can be varied in some species to harmonise with the background. The pigments of a chameleon, for instance, are orange-red (carotenoids), black (melanins) and silvery white (guanins). They are contained in branching chromatophores and become dispersed or concentrated as the chromatophore itself changes its surface area in response to nervous excitations. Very few other lizards are able to change colour in this way, and turtles, snakes and crocodiles cannot change their colour even by moulting.

Teeth and alimentary canal

Lizards and snakes have the teeth fused to the jaws and sometimes also to the palatine bones. In some snakes and in two lizards there are hollow fangs connected with poison glands. Crocodile teeth are strikingly different from those of other reptiles. They are set in sockets, more like the teeth of

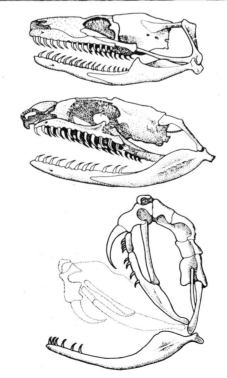

A young skink of the subspecies *Eumeces schneideri princeps* which lives in rocky areas of the Caucasus in western Asia. Members of this genus have elongated bodies and long flexible tails and are sometimes mistaken for snakes. They have flaps for closing the ear-holes so that, when burrowing, sand cannot injure their ear-drums.

The epidermal layer of scales typical of the surface of a reptile takes on an extreme form in the thorn-like protrusions of the Thorny Devil or Moloch (*Moloch horridus*). An agamid lizard found in Australia, the Moloch is, despite its fearsome armour, an inoffensive creature, living in sandy places and feeding on ants flicked out of the air with the tongue.

Types of dentition in snakes. *Top*: non-venomous snakes. *Centre*: back-fanged poisonous (opisthoglyphous) snake. *Bottom*: front-fanged poisonous (proteroglyphous).

mammals. Tortoises have teeth only in the embryo and these are subsequently replaced by a horny beak analogous to that of birds. The reptile tongue varies greatly in form and in its mode of operation. It may be short, fleshy and relatively immobile as in some lizards, or long and forked with a wide range of movement as in other lizards and all snakes. The alimentary tract is divided into well-defined sections and ends in a cloaca, where the genital and urinary tracts join the digestive tube. The opening of the cloaca may be transverse or longitudinal, according to whether the body is short or long.

Reptiles have varied diets. Some are herbivores, other carnivores, piscivores, insectivores, and even egg-eaters. Ophiophagous reptiles, as the name implies, are those that eat snakes.

Venom and poison mechanisms

Among the higher vertebrates a venomous or toxic physiology is a feature peculiar to the reptiles, the Duckbilled Platypus and some shrews. Reptile venom leaves the gland as a clear, viscous, yellowish-amber liquid without particular odour or taste. Venoms are proteins related to the albumen in the white of an egg and they contain both toxic and antitoxic substances. Among the former a coagulin, a haemolysin, a haemorrhagin and a neurotoxin have been isolated. Coagulin is a diastase, or related enzyme, which comes from the white blood corpuscles and causes coagulation of the blood. Acting within the blood vessels it induces clots which may lead to death through embolism. Its action is transient, since it is offset by that of the haemolysin which breaks down the red corpuscles and liberates haemoglobin. Haemorrhagin acts on the walls of the blood capillaries, changing their permeability and allowing blood to pass into the

tissues, especially in the skin, lungs, intestine and bladder. Neurotoxin has a selective action on the nervous system. By affecting the brain it brings about stupor and a dazed condition; by attacking the spinal cord it causes first paralysis and, after reaching the medulla, nausea, sickness and profuse sweating. Finally, the heart and respiration cease functioning. Beside these toxic components venom contains antigens which moderate each of the toxic actions; it is a cause and cure combined. There is an anticoagulin, an antihaemolysin, an antihaemorrhagin, and so on. In other words the venom contains its own antivenin, but not in sufficient quantity to neutralise its own action entirely.

Not all venoms have the same composition or the same action. The poison of adders and rattlesnakes mainly affects the blood, while that of cobras acts principally on the nervous system. Venoms can exist in some animals without any inoculating mechanism, the classic example being provided by frogs and toads, whose skin contains substances as toxic as those of the most poisonous snakes. Instances of this occur from the coelenterates to the mammals.

The wounding mechanism in snakes and the Gila Monster (the only venomous lizard) is formed by the teeth, some of which have become modified into fangs and have a furrow or canal down which the poison flows. Vipers, rattlesnakes and allies are the most highly developed in this respect.

Respiration and circulation

Respiration is entirely pulmonary and never by means of gills as in larval amphibians. The breathing tract, consisting of a trachea and bronchi, is well developed and kept open by cartilaginous rings. The lungs are simple sac-like organs,

Lizard heart (*left*) and crocodile heart (*right*). *LA* and *RA* are the left and right auricles (*see opposite*).

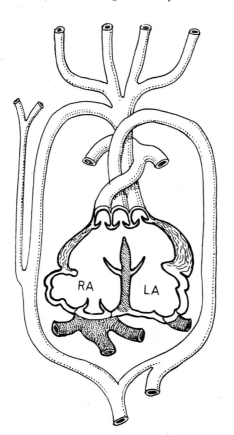
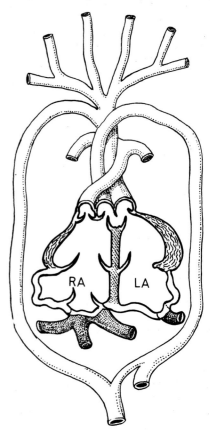

their walls folded inwards into ridges, forming numerous small compartments which greatly increase the respiratory surface. The lungs of most lizards are similar in size, but in snakes and some snake-like lizards the left lung is reduced, often vestigial, while the right lung is very long and lies between the other internal organs. In the lungs of tortoises and crocodiles the partitions are more extensive, the spongy structure so formed allowing a more rapid oxygenation of the blood. All reptiles possess a three-chambered heart. There are two auricles but only one ventricle, which is incompletely divided by a septum and controls the extent to which the arterial and venous blood mix. There are always three pairs of aortic arches modified to perform certain functions. The carotid arteries branch from the right systematic arch, which originates in the left part of the ventricle and contains mostly oxygenated blood. The pulmonary artery, originating in the right part of the ventricle, contains mostly non-oxygenated blood.

The ventricle in the crocodile heart has only a small gap in the septum, so that arterial and venous blood do not completely mix within the heart. There is therefore an almost perfect circulation. But there are two aortic arches, one coming from the right side of the ventricle and the other from the left. Any advantage from this almost complete division of the ventricle would be lost but for two things: first, the left arch, which contains deoxygenated blood, is narrower than the other; secondly, there is a communication through the foramen of Panizza between the two arches, allowing the oxygenated blood to pass from the right arch to the left, but not the other way. Thus the aorta contains mainly oxygenated blood.

Because of the imperfections in their respiratory and circulatory systems, reptiles have only enough oxygen to supply their tissues and maintain the processes of food combustion. Therefore their temperature can be raised only a few degrees above the ambient temperature, except during incubation of the eggs in ovoviviparous forms. This explains why reptiles flourish best in warm climates where they are able to remain active throughout the year, and why they are sparsely represented in temperate regions where they must undergo alternating periods of activity in summer and torpor in winter. This is the natural result of a slow metabolic rate.

Skeleton

The reptile skeleton is largely composed of bone. There is very little cartilage and often a bony exoskeleton in addition to the skeleton proper. The skull also is completely ossified.

The vertebrae of the Rhynchocephalia (Tuatara) are biconcave and pierced by the notochord. In all other reptiles the vertebrae have one convex face and one concave, allowing progressively better articulation in the higher reptiles. The number of vertebrae varies from sixty in crocodiles to 300 or 400 in snakes. There is much variation in rib structure. They are fused together in tortoises, extend from end to end in snakes and are limited to the trunk region in crocodiles.

The skull structure differs from group to group. The Tuatara, tortoises and crocodiles have a strongly built skull. Their lower jaw articulates directly with the cranium by two condyles which fit into the articular depressions. A hard palate separates the nasal and mouth cavities.

Lizard and snake skulls show similarities. They are lightly built and embody a system of levers. Slender and movable bony rods extend backwards from the rear of the skull to articulate with the two parts of the lower jaw and, as the front ends of the lower jaw are not fused together, this permits a wider opening. In snakes the two parts of the lower jaw can be moved apart. The maxillae (upper jaws) of vipers have a rocking movement and are pushed forward by levers to direct the poison fangs outwards. Few animals have such an elaborate jaw mechanism.

The reptile limb has typically five digits, but these have been modified to form paddles in turtles, wings in the extinct pterodactyls, or have become more and more rudimentary in certain lizards. They are completely absent in snakes.

Nervous system and sense-organs

The reptile brain shows an advance on that of the lower vertebrates, especially in its size. The Tuatara of New Zealand and several lizards have an eye-like structure lodged in an opening in the roof of the skull, known as the parietal foramen. This unpaired pineal or median eye is just under the skin. The function of this 'third eye' is not fully understood. It may function as a gland, as well as being sensitive to light. The large size of the parietal foramen in many fossil reptiles, amphibians and fishes suggests that the pineal eye of these animals once played an important sensory role and that it has degenerated in the course of evolution.

The cerebellum of reptiles is poorly developed, this being related to the slowness and simplicity of their movements. The presence of a middle ear with a Eustachian tube, ossicles and tympanum is a feature of all reptiles except snakes. Crocodiles have an external auditory meatus as well. The eye does not differ much from that of most higher vertebrates, except that in tortoises and crocodiles the front of the eyeball is supported by a ring of bony plates (sclerotic ring), which is a conspicuous feature in extinct reptiles and in birds, and has therefore evolutionary significance. The eyelids are free and movable or are fused together and transparent as in snakes. When they are movable there is always a third inner eyelid, or nictitating membrane, which moves in a horizontal plane in crocodiles and tortoises. This not only protects the eye but, being transparent, enables a crocodile to see while underwater.

In snakes and some lizards the tongue is highly developed as a sensory organ and is used to detect scent particles in the air when hunting prey.

Reproduction

UROGENITAL SYSTEM: The reptile kidney is the first in the vertebrate series to possess a metanephros succeeding the mesonephros and pronephros in the course of embryonic development. Reptiles have thus a more advanced urinary system than that of fishes and amphibians, urine being taken from the kidneys to a bladder by ureters. A bladder is present in tortoises and lizards.

In the female the ovaries are paired, thin-walled

A Puff Adder (*Bitis arietans*) scenting out its prey, a grass rat, after striking at it. This snake draws its prey into its mouth with its fangs until the powerful swallowing muscles are able to take over. The Puff Adder is easily identified by the crescentic yellow markings along its back.

Anole lizards are highly territorial and males have a most striking display with which they warn off other males or try to attract females. Two males will sidle round each other with their bodies and necks puffed out, nodding their heads. The climax comes when both open out a brilliant yellow throat flap and wag their tails slowly up and down. By putting a mirror in front of this Caribbean anole lizard the photographer was able to trigger off the same display.

sacs within which eggs may be seen in different stages of development. The mature eggs enter the oviducts from the body cavity through ciliated funnels at the upper ends of the oviducts. After mating, the spermatozoa ascend as far as these funnels, where they fertilise the descending eggs. These are then surrounded by albumen and a shell and are ready for laying when they reach the cloaca.

The male system is more complex because of the linking of the testes by the ureters of the embryonic mesonephros, which form sperm ducts carrying the sperm to the copulatory organs. In all reptiles except the Tuatara the cloaca is modified to form a penis. In tortoises and crocodiles it is simple, but in lizards and snakes it is double, forming two hemipenes which may be used together or singly. The penis often bears recurved spines which serve to maintain a firm hold on the female during the act of copulation. In the resting state the penes are retracted into the cloaca.

Diverse glands are attached to the genital organs or are linked to them physiologically. There are musk glands in crocodiles, femoral glands in lizards and cloacal glands in most other reptiles. The strong and (to humans) offensive odour emanating from these glands appears to play some role in bringing the sexes together.

Sexual dimorphism

There are usually no appreciable external differences between male and female crocodiles and tortoises. In snakes the sexes differ in a number of characteristics, such as the relative proportions of the tail and body, in the scales, the coloration and the power of emitting odoriferous liquids. The males are generally smaller than the females and have a relatively longer tail, which is more distended at its base owing to the presence of the hemipenes. The males also have more numerous caudal scales and better developed cloacal glands.

It is in lizards particularly that sexual dimorphism reaches a degree comparable to that in amphibians and birds. Iguanas, anoles and flying dragons have dorsal crests, dewlaps, neck lappets and brilliant colours, all of which are either better developed in the male than in the female or belong exclusively to the male.

Contrary to one of Darwin's hypotheses, the special organs and colours of the male seem to have no bearing on the female's choice, and the females generally appear indifferent to these features.

Breeding habits

There are few species of reptile in which the male and female remain peaceably together for any length of time. One of the exceptions is found in certain lizards of southern Asia, in which the pairs live in burrows and there raise their offspring.

In snakes the sexes associate only during the breeding period and mating is generally peaceable. Davis, an American naturalist, has distinguished two main modes of sexual union. The first is shown by the boas and pythons, most of which are large and have spurs of a kind on some part of the cloacal region, these being vestiges of hind limbs. When the male glides along the female's body in mating, he scratches her back and sides with these spurs and in this way incites her to offer him the opening of her cloaca. The grating produced can be heard at some distance. When the two cloacae have been brought together, the male introduces one of his hemipenes into the female's cloaca and injects his sperm.

The second method of copulation is characterised by an intertwining of the two bodies which may bring together only the anterior parts or the tails. Before this happens the male must follow the tract of the female and glide along her body until his head is level with hers. The intertwining facilitates the apposition of the cloacae and insertion of the copulatory organs. Often there is a preliminary dance by the two individuals, whose bodies are already partly entwined. It may last for several hours and may be accompanied by apparently intense physical excitation. Such a method of copulation has been observed in colubrine snakes, vipers, small European species, cobras and rattlesnakes.

There are three essential features in the breeding habits of lizards: fierce fighting among the males for the possession of the females, brief and vigorous copulation, and frequent homosexuality. Fights between males have been observed in most species and even in inoffensive-looking geckos and chameleons. Those with a rigid casque armed with spines use it for attack and as a shield. If one of the adversaries loses his tail the other immediately swallows it. The victor of the fight then turns to the female and, seizing her roughly by the neck with his powerful jaws, he forces her to be still. His hind limbs hold her as he inserts one of the hemipenes, which work alternately, into her cloaca. Copulation lasts only a few seconds, but may be repeated several times in the space of a few hours. Males may often try to mate with other males. This aberrant behaviour may be due to the fact that sexual recognition depends on the reaction of the partner: acquiescence indicates a female, resistance a male.

Crocodilians have breeding habits similar to those of lizards. Males in rut often undertake long journeys to seek females. They may be seen playing in groups, lashing their tails, puffing themseleves up and bellowing loudly. The groups of males emit a strong odour of musk. Copulation is rough and always takes place in water.

Freshwater and marine tortoises and turtles also copulate in water. In the European Pond Turtle (*Emys orbicularis*) the male climbs on to the female and does everything to induce her to keep still. He bites her head and neck, even pulling out the head scales, and holds her head underwater at the risk of drowning her. Some females are blinded during this ordeal. Even more vicious attacks have been noted in the Iberian Terrapin of Andalusia and Morocco.

In general the sexual act in tortoises is made difficult by the presence of the carapace and their clumsy and lengthy manoeuvres attain their end only with difficulty. Riding on the hind part of the back of his mate, on which he has little grasp, the male must take advantage of the moment when she becomes still to rear up almost vertically in an unstable position and insert his penis into her cloaca. In many species the males, in probable evolutionary reaction to these difficulties, have developed longer claws on the fore feet, a longer tail, and a more concave plastron than their female partners.

Nest-building

Nest-building does not reach the level attained by some fishes and amphibians, much less the variety and perfection found in birds. Most reptiles lay their eggs on the ground or in a scooped-out hollow which is afterwards filled in. Other than these there is only the rudimentary nest-building of crocodiles and alligators, which lay their eggs in layers in sand or conceal them under decaying vegetation.

Below left
A pair of Slow-worms (*Anguis fragilis*) pictured in the act of mating. The male (grey) is gripping the female (brown) with his jaws. In Britain, pairing takes place soon after emergence from hibernation. The slow-worms then disperse and the young are not born until late in the summer. They are independent from birth.

Below
A female Leathery Turtle (*Dermochelys coriacea*) digging in the sand preparatory to laying her eggs. Like other marine turtles, the Leathery Turtle mates in the shallow seas and the female then comes ashore to deposit her eggs, although most of its breeding places are unknown. The Leathery Turtle, itself the largest of the marine turtles, is found in all the tropical seas.

Unlike most lizards of the family Lacertidae, the female of the Common or Viviparous Lizard (*Lacerta vivipara*) appears to give birth to living young, as in mammals. In fact, the eggs hatch at or about the moment they are laid, the young emerging immediately, so that they appear to have been born alive. This is called ovoviviparity. Sometimes the hatching is delayed and an intact egg is laid, the animal then appearing to be truly egg-laying or oviparous.

The crocodilians are among the truly oviparous or egg-laying reptiles. They lay hard-shelled eggs in large clutches ranging from ten to sixty in a clutch. This young crocodile has just broken through the tough shell with the aid of an egg-tooth on its snout, the egg-tooth being shed soon after hatching.

A female Puff Adder (*Bitis arietans*), of Africa, coiled around her numerous young. Like most poisonous snakes Puff Adders give birth to live young, that is, they are ovoviviparous like the Common Lizard (above). This species of Puff Adder has been known to give birth to seventy young ones.

The eggs are always laid on land, even in the most markedly aquatic species such as marine turtles. The eggs are usually left to be incubated by heat from the sun. Some lizards and snakes aid the incubation, while female pythons coil up round their eggs to keep them relatively warm during the several weeks of the incubating period or at least protect them in this way from some predators.

Oviparity and ovoviviparity

Tortoises, crocodiles and many lizards and snakes are oviparous, laying eggs like those of birds. The shell is membranous, or only slightly calcareous, and overlays a yolk surrounded by albumen. On the surface of the yolk is the germinal disc, which becomes the embryo. The size of the egg varies from that of a hazelnut in lizards to that of a goose egg in crocodiles and other large reptiles. A clutch contains from ten to sixty according to the species. The incubation period depends on the temperature and can last up to twelve or thirteen months in the Tuatara. As an aid to breaking out of the egg, the young reptile has an 'egg-tooth' at the end of its snout. This tooth, like the similar tooth in most birds, is shed soon after hatching.

Besides the oviparous species there are others, sometimes of the same genus, which retain their eggs instead of laying them, the young undergoing all or part of their development in their oviducts. These species are called ovoviviparous and include the European Common or Viviparous Lizard (*Lacerta vivipara*), Seps (*Tetradactylus*), the Slow-worm (*Anguis fragilis*), various European vipers and most poisonous snakes. There are varying degrees of ovoviviparity, for the times of laying and hatching can be out of phase with each other. If laying precedes hatching the animal is oviparous, but individuals of the same species may 'hatch' eggs in the oviduct and be ovoviviparous. Many eggs are laid, but these already have embryos and are not long in hatching. On the other hand, if hatching precedes laying the young are born as active individuals, as in vipers. When laying and hatching coincide, as in some of the common lizards, the female lays the almost completely incubated eggs from which the young immediately emerge.

The second of these three types is the most interesting because it raises a problem of nutrition. If hatching occurs within the oviducts, it is essential that the newborn should find food there, in the absence of the egg yolk that has already been consumed and before they can catch their own food. It appears that a secretion from the walls of the oviducts meets this requirement. In some instances there is a placenta.

The advantages of ovoviviparity over oviparity are obvious. An egg laid a long time before it hatches is in danger of being destroyed, climatic conditions and predators alike presenting considerable hazards. An egg kept within the mother has a greater degree of safety. The European Grass Snake (*Natrix natrix*) lays from twelve to twenty eggs, while the ovoviviparous adder (*Vipera* sp.) bears from six to twenty young. The Green Lizard (*Lacerta viridis*) lays about ten eggs, while the Viviparous Lizard (*L. vivipara*) gives birth to about ten young. In certain ovoviviparous lizards the brood may be reduced to a single individual.

Tuatara (Order Rhynchocephalia)

The Tuatara (*Sphenodon punctatus*) is the only surviving member of a group of reptiles common during the Mesozoic era, the Age of the Reptiles. This remarkable animal survives naturally only on certain small islands in Cook Strait, New Zealand, where it is rigorously protected by government regulations.

The Tuatara has a typically lizard-like appearance. It is olive green or grey and reaches a total length of over sixty centimetres. Very little has been recorded about its ability to change colour. The underparts are covered with large epidermal scales, while those of the back are granular in appearance. A row of spines extends down the middle line of the head, back and tail. Both limbs and body are strongly built and the teeth are inserted on the edges of the jaws. Each digit bears a strong claw and is flattened at the base.

There is nothing unusual about this reptile at first glance and only its anatomy indicates that *Sphenodon* is a separate and archaic type of reptile. In particular, the skull is much stronger and firmer than that of lizards and snakes, its parts being joined together by bony arches. The vertebral column is primitive in structure, while extending back from the sternum is a series of ventral abdominal ribs (chevron bones) that are reminiscent of the chelonian plastron. The Tuatara generally becomes active at night. Under natural conditions its food consists of insects, especially beetles and grass-hoppers, but it sometimes hunts lizards, earthworms and snails. It lives in the burrows of various species of petrel and lays about ten eggs, measuring just under three centimetres in length, in holes in the sand. The incubation period is a lengthy one, lasting some thirteen months. Nothing is known of its breeding habits or the way in which it pairs. Fertilisation is accomplished without the aid of a penis.

Tortoises, terrapins and turtles (Order Testudines=Chelonia)

The terms tortoise, terrapin and turtle have caused much confusion. In Britain it is usual to call land-living chelonians tortoises and marine chelonians turtles, using the term pond tortoise or terrapin for those which are at home both on land and in freshwater. In the United States the term turtle is used as a general name for all the chelonians, though sometimes the strictly terrestrial ones are called tortoises, while the aquatic ones are referred to as turtles. The name 'terrapin' was used by early settlers for a variety of edible saltwater and brackish water chelonians of North America.

These animals are closer to crocodiles than to lizards and snakes. Their body is entirely covered by a firm shell from which only the head, limbs and tail emerge. The upper shell (carapace) and the underpart (plastron) are formed by the welding together of polygonal dermal plates. On the underpart these plates may be extensive as in the box terrapin, or few and small as in the Snapping Turtle. Chelonians have horny jaws resembling those of birds. The carapace is fused to the axial skeleton and is formed of polygonal plates usually covered by scales and not visible from the outside.

The Leathery Turtle (Leatherback in United States) (*Dermochelys coriacea*) differs from other chelonians in that its carapace is relatively thin, and is not fused to the underlying skeleton but has a covering of heavy skin. Some place this turtle in a separate suborder.

Like most reptiles, chelonians lay eggs, the shells of which are slightly calcareous in land-dwelling specimens and parchment-like in aquatic forms. In certain species several hundred eggs are laid in separate batches in the course of the year. They are laid in holes in the ground, then covered with sand and left to eventually incubate in the heat from the sun.

Tortoises live to a great age. For example, a Giant Tortoise (*Testudo gigantea*) kept in captivity on Mauritius lived to a known age of 152 years, and such a life-span is not exceptional. In temperate climates their active life is interrupted by hibernation, but in warm lands this does not occur. Chelonians may be herbivorous or carnivorous but rarely both. There are twelve extinct and twelve living families.

The Tuatara (*Sphenodon punctatus*), of New Zealand, is the only surviving member of the order Rhynchocephalia, all the other species having become extinct 100 million years ago. It has a primitive vertebral column. It also has a series of ventral abdominal ribs and a well-developed pineal eye, both being features found in the early reptiles that lived over a 100 million years ago.

The Indian Starred Tortoise (*Testudo elegans*), of the jungles of India and Sri Lanka, is characterised by a high shell marked with radiating yellow streaks on a black background. Starred tortoises habitually lie up under shrubs or grass tussocks by day and feed at night, except in the rainy season, when they are also active by day.

A subspecies of the Giant Tortoise (*Testudo elephantopus vandenberghi*) which is still fairly numerous on Albemarle Island in the Galapagos. At one time fifteen species or subspecies inhabited the Galapagos Islands but many today have become extinct at the hand of man.

Opposite
The Wood Turtle (*Clemmys insculpta*), sometimes called the Wood Terrapin, lives mainly near woodland streams but it has also been seen wandering far from water to feed. The young Wood Turtle is remarkable in having a very long tail, which may be as long as its shell.

Land tortoises (Family Testudinidae)

Most species of tortoises belong to this family and to the genus *Testudo*, which consists of about fifty species distributed over much of the warm parts of the earth, except Australia and Polynesia.

The Algerian or Spur-thighed Tortoise (*T. graeca*) is the commonest and one of the smallest species in the genus, its overall length being no more than thirty centimetres and its weight about two kilograms. It is most abundant around the shores of the Mediterranean and North Africa, but is also found in Spain, the Balkans and Asia Minor. Hermann's or the Greek Tortoise (*T. hermanni*) is another Mediterranean species, generally found only on coasts, although a few isolated colonies inhabit parts of France. It is absent from North Africa. The Margined Tortoise (*T. marginata*), which appears to be confined to Greece, is similar to *T. graeca* in the number of its shields but differs in that the posterior part of its carapace is greatly expanded and has a toothed edge. A most important distinguishing feature of *T. graeca* is the presence on each thigh of a horny tubercle or spur, which on large specimens can be almost one centimetre long. *T. hermanni* and *T. marginata* do not possess this tubercle.

These are the three European species of tortoise, and though all are commonly called 'Greek tortoises' only one of them, *T. marginata*, is properly to be regarded as such. All have the same features and habits. Males generally have a longer and thicker tail than females. It extends through a sizable notch in the plastron and a curve in the corresponding part of the carapace.

Tortoises are generally vegetarians, but food selection may vary. In gardens they forage among melons, gourds, cabbages and other vegetables, particularly dandelion and clover flowers.

Copulation takes place in summer, preceded in the wild state by fighting amongst the males. Females lay between ten and twelve eggs, which are buried and left to hatch. The egg is white, almost spherical and has a partly calcareous shell. It measures between 2·5 and 3·5 centimetres and weighs twenty grams.

The Madagascan Radiated Tortoise (*T. radiata*) is a handsome animal, each plate of its carapace having a yellow spot with yellow bands radiating from it. This Tortoise is now confined to the far south of Madagascar. The region is almost waterless but is plentifully supplied with prickly pears, which provide the Tortoise with sustenance and shelter.

The Ploughshare Tortoise (*T. yniphora*) of Africa is a close relative of the Radiated Tortoise. The foremost plate of the plastron is curved and extends under the throat, giving it the appearance of a ploughshare. Nothing definite is known about its function, though it is probably used for digging.

The Gopher Tortoise (*Gopherus polyphemus*) of the south-eastern United States (in a genus closely related to *Testudo*) has a similar plate which it uses extensively for burrowing, for it spends much of its life in burrows. This species and the Desert Tortoise (*G. agassizi*) and Berlandier's or Texas Gopher Tortoise (*G. berlandieri*) are the only members of the family found in the United States.

The handsome South American Tortoise (*T. denticulata*), which is about sixty centimetres long, is marked by a yellow or orange spot on the black plates of the carapace. The Starred Tortoise (*T. elegans*) belongs to the jungles of India and Ceylon and its striking colour pattern rivals that of the Madagascan Radiated Tortoise.

Giant tortoises are larger than Greek tortoises and there are certain differences in the arrangement of the plates on their carapace. However, naturalists agree in placing these tortoises in the genus *Testudo*. There are two species of giant tortoise: *T. gigantea* which inhabits the Seychelles and Aldabras, and *T. elephantopus* found on the Galapagos Islands. The carapace of *T. gigantea* has a small nuchal plate (neck plate) which is absent in the other species.

Like their smaller relatives giant tortoises are strictly herbivorous. In captivity they feed on enormous quantities of cabbage leaves and other greenstuffs, but they can go without food for several weeks without suffering. Their moderate habits and resistance to starvation explain how they manage to live on the most desolate islands.

Each female apparently lays a maximum of twenty eggs in a year. They are about the same size as a hen's egg. The newborn tortoise is very small. Eighteen months later it is still no bigger than a man's fist and weighs about eighty grams. At first the carapace is soft, giving little protection. Growth continues for forty years and then either becomes extremely slow or stops altogether. The largest individuals may have a carapace 150 centimetres long and may weigh about a quarter of a tonne on completion of growth.

A century or two ago these tremendous animals were common on many of the islands in the Indian Ocean (Seychelles, Aldabras, Comoros, Reunion, Mauritius and Rodriguez), but today the only localities where they exist in a wild state are the coral islands or atolls of the Aldabra group. Under government protection a small number live in a partly domesticated state in the Seychelles, Reunion, Mauritius and Rodriguez. Because they were an important survival food to the mariners in the age of sail, sailors often transported them from one island to another in attempts to establish them on more barren islands. Today it is almost impossible to reconstruct the former natural distribution. The tortoises from the Galapagos, however, are in an unmixed wild state and are of the greatest importance to the zoogeographer interested in their distribution.

Freshwater tortoises or turtles
(Family Emydidae)

These might well be called amphibious tortoises, for much of their life is spent on the banks of rivers and ponds, and they enter the water only to hunt fishes and amphibians.

Members of the family Emydidae are the common freshwater turtles of almost world-wide distribution, missing only from Australia, Antarctica, central and southern Africa and central and southern South America. They include the American Box Turtle (*Terrapene carolina*) which has an efficent hinged plastron with which it can close itself up almost completely in its shell with only the tough, scaled feet exposed. It is terrestrial in habits, and seldom enters the water. The Diamond-back Terrapin (*Malaclemys terrapin*), another member of the family, is almost completely aquatic and is found commonly in brackish and tidal waters.

The European Pond Tortoise (*Emys orbicularis*) was common in prehistoric times throughout northern Europe, including the British Isles, but is now confined to southern Europe, North Africa and south-west Asia. It has a flattened shell and limbs which, though bearing claws, are web-footed and serve as swimming organs. It often grows to an overall length of about thirty centimetres, and it has a dark brown carapace marked with yellow lines.

Strictly carnivorous, the Pond Tortoise feeds on fishes, frogs, insects, worms, molluscs and crustraceans as well as on small rodents and young birds. It retires into the mud in October and does not resume activity until the following spring.

Mating takes place during the summer in water. The male mounts the female and wounds or even drowns her if she resists. The eggs are about 3·5 centimetres long by two centimetres across. A clutch consists of about ten eggs which are laid in the soil. Incubation takes three or four months. Males mature at twelve or thirteen years and

Even such large tortoises as this Spurred Tortoise (*Testudo sulcata*) disappear during the dry season in Africa, presumably hidden among rocks where their boulder-like carapaces escape notice. With the coming of the rains, they come out to feed on the new green vegetation and to breed.

A Desert Tortoise of Arizona, U.S.A. During the heat of the day desert tortoises hide in holes they have dug in the ground, each hole leading by a long passage to a spacious chamber. The tortoises remain in this cool hideout until dusk, when the air is cooled sufficiently for them to emerge in comfort and feed, as often as not, on cacti.

The Diamond-back Terrapin (*Malaclemys terrapin*) lives in the tidal waters and in salt and brackish water lakes along the Atlantic coast of North America from Massachusetts to Florida. It feeds mainly on crustaceans and molluscs. The flesh of this terrapin has long been a table delicacy, especially during the end of the nineteenth century.

The Common Snapping Turtle (*Chelydra serpentina*) is the most widespread and one of the most numerous of the turtles in the United States. On land this snapper is aggressive when disturbed, lunging and biting savagely at an intruder. In the water, however, it is a poor swimmer and lies in wait for its prey on the bottom.

females at fifteen to twenty years. The life-span is a long one, and some individuals have occasionally been reported as reaching an age of more than a hundred years.

Painted terrapins (*Chrysemys picta*), called painted turtles in the United States, where they are native and one of the most widespread turtles in the country, are barely fifteen centimetres long. They are greenish brown with prominent yellow bands and plastron. The marginal plates around the edge of the carapace are usually scattered with red. The back plates are edged with red and the soft parts of the body carry red and yellow lines.

The Spanish Terrapin (*Clemmys leprosa*) is very common in ponds and rivers in south-west Europe, the Iberian peninsula and north-west Africa. It frequently suffers from a skin disease inside the carapace caused by freshwater algae. The secretions of its cloacal glands give it an unpleasant odour. Copulation in this terrapin is even more brutal than in the Pond Tortoise. Other species of the same genus are found in the Balkan peninsula, Asia Minor and the United States.

The Diamond-back Terrapin (*Malaclemys terra-pin*) is economically an important species as it is a popular dish in the United States. Its carapace is greenish brown with concentric dark lines, while the sides and plastron are yellow. It lives in coastal brackish and marine waters of the southern and eastern United States. It feeds mainly on fishes, molluscs and crabs. Hibernation takes place in the mud and lasts from October to March.

Mud and musk turtles (Family Kinosternidae)
This small family of American terrapins consists of about twenty species which frequent the ponds and marshes of Canada, the United States, Mexico, Central America and north-west South America. Some of these, the mud terrapins, are peculiar in having the anterior and posterior parts of the plastron hinged and movable, and some species are thus able to enclose themelves entirely in their shells. The Common Musk Turtle or Stinkpot (*Sternotherus odoratus*) is the most widespread species and owes its specific name to the unpleasant odour from its cloacal glands. It feeds on amphibians and fishes. When handled it first withdraws into its shell, leaving only its eyes visible, keeping a watch on its adversary. It then suddenly shoots out its head and tries to bite.

Big-headed turtles (Family Platysternidae)
This family consists of a single species, *Platysternon megacephalum*. It is about thirty-seven centimetres long and has strong jaws provided with marginal serrations. The head is too big to be retracted into the shell. The tail is longer than the carapace and is protected by whorls of small bony plates. *Platysternon* lives in mountain torrents and is found in southern China, Thailand, southern Burma and Indo-China. It can scale rocks and climb trees.

Snapping turtles (Family Chelydridae)
Snapping turtles have reduced shells, lateral spines and a long tail. There are two species in the United States: the American Common Snapping Turtle (*Chelydra serpentina*) and the Alligator Snapping Turtle (*Macroclemys temmincki*), which have similar habits. They spend much time in water, coming to the surface occasionally to breathe. They are very aggressive and have powerful hooked jaws which can inflict severe injuries. On land they move slowly, raising themselves on their limbs as alligators are usually seen to do.

Snake-necked turtles (Family Chelidae)
The Matamata (*Chelys fimbriata*), found in the rivers of Brazil, the Guianas and Venezuela is a mass of bumps, warts and cutaneous flaps and an accretion of mosses and other aquatic plants. When motionless on the bottom of a stream it resembles a stone. The head is flattened and triangular and is extended to form a proboscis. It has a soft beak. The Matamata does not pursue its prey but lies in wait using the cutaneous projections on its head as bait. Little is known of its habits. It rarely leaves the water, the female laying her eggs in the mud on the river bank.

The Australian Snake-necked Turtle (*Chelodina longicollis*) is characterised by its extremely long neck. It is glossy brown on the back and glossy brown mixed with yellow below. It feeds mainly on small fishes and is diurnal.

Soft-shelled turtles (Family Trionychidae)

Members of the Trionychidae have only three claws on each limb and the carapace has no scale investment but consists simply of bony plates covered with skin. The horny beak is covered by soft lips and the snout ends in a small proboscis. The family comprises some twenty species divided into seven genera, the largest and most widespread being *Trionyx*, which is found in both the Old and New Worlds. The Nile Soft-shelled Turtle (*T. triunguis*) is one of the commoner and is also to be found in the Congo, Senegal and Syria. It is greenish with scattered white spots. The Indian Soft-shelled Turtle (*T. gangeticus*) lives in Indian rivers, while the Florida or Southern Soft-shelled Turtle (*T. ferox*) inhabits the rivers of the south-eastern-most United States. All these turtles are between fifty and seventy-five centimetres long. They are strictly aquatic and feed on fishes, frogs and molluscs. The female lays about twenty spherical eggs, and then takes care to bury them in sand some distance from the water.

Marine turtles (Family Chelonidae)

In common with all aquatic chelonians, marine turtles have a depressed carapace and limbs adapted for swimming. The bones of their limbs are flatttened, widened and even extended laterally in the form of spurs and thus recall those of the Mesozoic ichthyosaurs and plesiosaurs and the modern cetaceans (dolphins, porpoises and whales). The carpal and tarsal bones are fused together and the digits are contained within clawless flippers. These turtles normally live in warm waters, but may be carried by currents into the Mediterranean and to the European and American shores of the North Atlantic.

The Green Turtle (*Chelonia mydas*), an edible species in danger of extinction, may reach a length of 120 centimetres and weight between 120 and 160 kilograms. It feeds on algae and other marine plants. The eggs are laid at night on the beaches of remote islands and buried in the sand. The same female will return two or three times at intervals of about a fortnight before the entire clutch of 100 to 200 eggs is laid.

The Common Loggerhead Turtle (*Caretta caretta*) is only ninety centimetres long and is brown in colour. It is carnivorous, feeding on fishes, molluscs and crustaceans.

The Hawksbill Turtle (*Eretmochelys imbricata*) has a hooked beak and is the smallest of the species, its carapace being no more than eighty-three centimetres long. In the young the plates of the carapace overlap, but in the adult they merely adjoin and are the characteristic brown colour with yellow markings of genuine tortoiseshell. The Hawksbill Turtle has much the same diet as the Loggerhead. The eggs are laid either by day or by night on beaches along sheltered bays.

Leathery turtle (Family Dermochelidae)

The carapace of the Leathery Turtle or Luth (*Dermochelys coriacea*)—known in the United States as the Leatherback—looks heart-shaped from above and is formed simply of dermal ossicles which are not fused to the vertebrae and ribs. The skin has the appearance of brown leather and bears seven longitudinal ridges. The Leathery

The Australian Snake-necked Turtle (*Chelodina longicollis*), a small freshwater turtle with a shell only twelve centimetres in length, catches fish by darting out its very long neck in a snake-like movement.

The unusual looking Matamata (*Chelys fimbriata*) is a snake-necked turtle from the rivers of South America. Its eyes are small and the nostrils are elongated to form a narrow proboscis. It captures small fish by suddenly opening its mouth and at the same time expanding its throat so that water containing its prey is sucked in.

The Soft-shelled Turtles of the family Trionychidae include species in Africa, South and East Asia and North America. The carapace is covered with a leathery skin which overlaps the bony shield beneath. The legs have become modified to paddle-shaped flippers. Most species live in freshwater.

295

The Hawksbill Turtle
(*Eretmochelys imbricata*) is found
in all tropical and some subtropical seas. Its common name
is descriptive of its hooked and
elongated jaws. Apart from being
hunted for its valuable tortoiseshell
it is also caught in the Caribbean
for its flesh which is highly
esteemed there as food.

The Pacific or Olive Ridley
(*Lepidochelys olivacea*) is a small
marine turtle found in most warm
waters and also wandering into
some temperate seas. The picture
shows a pair mating in water but
afterwards the female must come
ashore to lay her eggs. Well-known
nesting beaches are on the Pacific
coast of Mexico and in the
Guianas.

A female Loggerhead Turtle
(*Caretta caretta*) dropping her eggs
in a hole she has dug in the sand.
This marine turtle is common to
all tropical and subtropical seas.
The picture shows clearly the
barnacles attached to the shell.

Turtle is the largest marine turtle, reaching a
length of 180 centimetres and a weight of about
400 kilograms. The lining of the mouth and gullet
is entirely covered with long pointd papillae which
form an excellent filter for food. The fore and hind
flippers differ greatly in length. The tear glands
exude an albuminous substance which probably
protects the eyes against salt water.

Hidden-necked turtles (Family Pelomedusidae)
The most important of the hidden-necked turtles is
the Amazon Tortoise or Arrau Turtle (*Podocnemis
expansa*), distributed throughout the tropical regions of South America. The Amazon Tortoise is
olive-coloured above and yellow below. It is the
largest and commonest tortoise in the Amazon
region.

Another species, *Pelusios derbianus*, found in West
Africa from Gambia down to Angola, is unusual in
that it is the only species in this family which has a
movable front lobe to its plastron.

Plateless turtles (Family Carrettochelyidae)
Very little is known of these rare turtles found only
in New Guinea except that, like the soft-shelled
turtles, they are almost completely aquatic and
strong swimmers and lack the horny plates or the
shell. This makes them something of a 'missing
link' between most of the other turtles and the soft-
shelled turtles (family Trionychidae).

Crocodilians (Order Crocodylia=Loricata)
Although similar to large lizards in appearance
crocodiles, gavials, alligators and caimans have
distinctive structural features. In some respects
they are the most highly developed of present-day
reptiles as well as being the closest living relatives
of the large Mesozoic reptiles. As a group they
possess a number of striking features, including a
four-chambered heart, socketed teeth, a palate
separating the mouth from the nasal channels and
spongy lungs. The dorsal part of the body has a
protective covering of bony plates which are
neither fused together nor joined to the underlying
skeleton. This covering enables them to move with
surprising speed. The underparts and sides also
have scales and some species have bony shields
under the throat.

Many anatomical features indicate that crocodilians are essentially amphibious. They are web-
footed in various degrees. Eyes, nostrils and ears
are placed in the upper part of the head, thus
enabling the animal to use these organs while
almost completely submerged. When the crocodile
dives, each eye is covered by a nictitating membrane and the auditory openings and nostrils are
closed by valves.

Crocodiles are well equipped for a predatory
life. Their jaws are large, strong and provided with
powerful teeth. The tail is compressed laterally
and bears a dorsal crest of erect scales. It is an
excellent weapon, as well as being used for swimming. The tongue is thick and attached to the floor
of the mouth. The cloacal opening is tansverse and
there is a single copulatory organ. Crocodiles do
not moult the epidermis.

All crocodiles are oviparous. The eggs are oval
and have a partially calcareous shell. The female
lays about thirty eggs at the water's edge or in

The American Alligator (*Alligator mississipiensis*), one of the two species of alligators, is found only in the southern United States. The broad, short head seen clearly here contrasts with the narrower longer head of the crocodile. The lower row of teeth project upwards into pockets in the upper jaw when the mouth is closed so that only the upper teeth then show.

nests of vegetation. The heat of the decomposing materials of the nest aids incubation. At the end of the snout the young crocodile has a special 'egg-tooth' for breaking through the shell.

Crocodilians are divided into three families: the Gavialidae, represented by a single genus (*Gavialis*), the Gavial or Gharial of India, in which the snout is extremely long and slender; the Alligatoridae, comprising four genera, including the alligators and caimans; and the Crocodylidae, the true crocodiles and False Gavial (*Tomistoma*). The differences between crocodiles and alligators are not very great, the most marked being the position of the teeth. In crocodiles the fourth tooth of the lower jaw projects when the jaws are closed, whereas in alligators this tooth fits into a pit in the upper jaw and cannot be seen.

Gavials (Family Gavialidae)
The Indian Gavial or Gharial (*Gavialis gangeticus*), which lives in the waters of the Ganges, Mahanadi, Brahmaputra and Indus basins, has a long, rod-like snout that widens at the nostrils. It is not dangerous to man, though the males sometimes grow to a length of 608 centimetres. It feeds almost entirely on fishes.

The female lays about forty eggs in a nest on the river bank. They are about nine centimetres long and seven centimetres across, and are arranged in the nest in layers with sand between each layer. The newly hatched young are about thirty-five centimetres long and are extremely active.

Crocodiles (Family Crocodylidae)
This family of true crocodiles consists of about sixteen species, distributed principally in tropical areas. The snout is broader than in the Gavial, and the genus *Crocodylus* has nasal bones dividing the nasal aperture. Although their main food is fishes, crocodiles will eat other animals and are occasionally given to becoming man-eaters.

Crocodiles live in lairs dug out of the banks of

The Indian Gavial or Gharial (*Gavialis gangeticus*) feeds mainly on fishes which it catches by a sideways sweep of the head and jaws, made easier by the extreme slenderness of the snout. The gavial is not known to attack man but it may feed on the human corpses put into the Ganges at the end of burial ceremonies

297

rivers and lakes. The opening is below water-level and a sloping tunnel several metres long leads from it into the dwelling space.

The typical representative of this family is the Nile Crocodile (*Crocodylus niloticus*). It measures up to 4·5 metres long and was once very common in Africa but is becoming rare because of unrestricted hunting. It is still found in South and Central Africa and Madagascar, but has completely disappeared from many of its former habitats, particularly in North Africa.

During September the female lays twenty to thirty eggs about eight centimetres long, and hollows out a nest where she arranges the eggs in layers, flicking a covering of sand between each layer with her tail. She then covers the whole nest over thoroughly, making it completely invisible to man. Hatching takes place after about two months.

In Asia the principal species is the Mugger or Swamp or Marsh Crocodile (*C. palustris*), which lives in marshes and pools in India and Ceylon, but undertakes long journeys overland in times of drought.

The Estuarine or Salt-water Crocodile (*C. porosus*) occurs in coastal regions of southern Asia and northern Australia. An immense creature some six metres long, it is the most marine of crocodiles and individuals have been seen well out to sea. It is dangerous to man, being fierce and easily aroused.

The American Crocodile (*C. acutus*) also ventures out to sea. It is found in the southern United States, Central America, Columbia and Ecuador and reaches a length of some 4·5 to six metres. It should not be confused with the caiman which is an inhabitant of the same parts of Central and South America.

A West African crocodile (*Osteolaemus tetraspis*) resembles the caiman in having a broad, short snout and ossified ventral scales. It does not normally exceed two metres in length.

The False Gavial (*Tomistoma schlegeli*) possesses a long, slender snout but it is smaller than the gavial, not exceeding 4·5 metres in length, and has a more easterly distribution, extending into Malaya.

Alligators and caimans (Family Alligatoridae)
This family, comprising seven species, is similar to the Crocodylidae but the head is broader and shorter, and the snout more obtuse. In the genus *Alligator* there are nasal bones dividing the nasal aperture and the ventral scales are not ossified.

The American Alligator (*A. mississipiensis*), which grows to a length of 3·6 metres, occurs only in the southern United States, reaching as far north as latitude 35°.

The Chinese Alligator (*A. sinensis*) inhabits the Yangtse–Kiang river-basins and is smaller than the American species, being only about two metres in length. It has no webs between its digits.

Alligators spend much time lying on the banks of streams in the sun or floating underwater with only the top of the head showing. They feed on all kinds of aquatic animals and on any terrestrial animals caught at the water's edge. Some twenty to thirty eggs are laid in summer, each between five and eight centimetres long, and they are

The American Crocodile (*Crocodylus acutus*) is characterised by its long narrow snout. There is reliable evidence for it reaching seven metres but large specimens have become very rare.

The Nile Crocodile (*Crocodylus niloticus*) is the typical representative of the true crocodiles. The average adult is about four and a half metres long. The young crocodiles feed on insects and later on fish.

The American Alligator (*Alligator mississipiensis*) in its typical habitat in the Aransas National Wildlife Refuge in Texas. A bare decade ago the species was dangerously near extinction. At the present time well over a million are living in the swamps and lakes of the United States, having been brought back spectacularly almost from the brink of oblivion by wise conservation measures.

incubated in a nest, by the heat of the decaying matter.

During summer droughts, particularly in the breeding season, alligators move up and down a river in search of a more suitable location. During the breeding season the males utter loud calls as they fight amongst themselves, and often wound each other. The females build nests at the water's edge using branches and decaying vegetation. After laying the eggs the female remains nearby to guard them throughout the incubation period. The shell is hard. The white has a jelly-like consistency and is concentrated at each end of the egg, while the yolk occupies the middle part, filling out almost to the shell.

Young alligators feed on frogs, tadpoles and insects. Their rate of growth is rapid and at the end of their first year they are 0·5 metres long, twice their length at birth. They reach 1·2 metres at the age of two and become adult at the age of five or six years. A specimen hatched in the London Zoological Gardens was nearly three metres long and weighed eighty kilograms when twelve years old. Older individuals may reach about five metres. in length.

Caimans differ from alligators in having ventral scaling composed of overlapping scutes, and a nasal aperture not divided by bone. There are several species, all of which live in Central and South America. The Black Caiman (*Melanosuchus niger*) is the largest, growing to a length of about five metres. The Broad-nosed Caiman (*Caiman latirostris*) inhabits the rivers of eastern Brazil and is generally about two metres long.

Lizards and snakes (Order Squamata)
Lizards (Suborder Sauria=Lacertilia)

The term 'lizard' also includes geckos, iguanas, chameleons, slow-worms and monitors. Twenty existing families make up the order; four others are known only from fossils. There are about 3,000 species, the largest of which may grow to a length of three metres. Lizards may be adapted for walking, running, climbing, gliding, swimming, creeping or burrowing. The tongue may be thick and joined to the floor of the mouth, or extensile and even prehensile. The teeth are inserted on the ridge or the inner face of the jaws and the cloacal groove is transverse. Their diet is diverse, consisting of insects, small animals and vegetable matter. The epidermal scales may be modified to horny tubercles or reinforced with bony plates. Reproduction is sometimes oviparous and sometimes ovoviviparous.

Some lizards have an elongated body and reduced limbs, thus closely resembling snakes. The only unmistakable lizard feature, besides the movable eyelids, is that the parts of the lower jaw are fused, whereas in snakes these are linked only by ligament. Therefore lizards cannot open the mouth wide or swallow large prey. Only a few lizards have a forked tongue.

Geckos, agamas and iguanas may be grouped loosely as 'lizards with thick tongues' and they account for about a third of the total number of species. The tongue is wide, thick, fleshy and fixed to the floor of the mouth. Only the anterior edge of the tongue is free and this can be extended to catch their prey, such as insects.

In contrast, the lacertids, tegus, monitors and Gila Monster have a forked and sometimes very slender tongue. It is cylindrical, deeply cleft and flickers ceaselessly in and out between tightly closed lips. The lizard's tongue is a very sensitive tactile organ and is not poisonous. All lizards with forked tongues have movable eyelids and teeth fixed to the inner edges of the jaws.

Geckos (Family Gekkonidae)

Geckos are represented by 675 species in all the warm regions of the world. They have a flattened body and most species have pentadactyl limbs, although some have only four digits. They do not exceed an overall length of thirty-five centimetres. Apart from some desert species, geckos have transverse rows of supple laminae on the undersides of their digits and these act as adhesive pads which enable them to walk upside down and on vertical surfaces.

Plate-like scales are restricted mainly to the underparts, the soft skin of the back being covered only with sparse horny tubercles. Geckos are therefore particularly vulnerable to attack and are

A young Spectacled Caiman (*Caiman crocodylus*) seen basking on a log. This species of caiman lives in the Amazon and Orinoco regions but has been introduced into the swamps of the southern United States. Many young ones have been imported into the United States as pets.

A Day Gecko of the genus *Phelsuma* that lives on the island of Mauritius. Unlike most geckos, the day geckos are active during the day and are very brightly coloured, making them very conspicuous in the sunlight and easily recognisable by other members of their species.

active only at night. Spontaneous contraction of the tail muscles allows the tail to break off when seized. A new tail grows quickly but in most cases this is usually not as well shaped nor as symmetrical as the original tail.

Geckos feed on very small animals, particularly insects. When several species of gecko live together, they occupy different niches during the day, although they may exploit the same feeding place at night.

The sound made by most geckos is a kind of repeated clicking of the tongue. In certain species the sound 'gecko' or similar syllables is repeated several times. The common name is thus an onomatopoeic word, which first served to indicate one animal, then all those closely resembling it. Most geckos are oviparous but take no care of the eggs, which are merely laid in some sheltered spot.

The Wall Gecko (*Tarentola mauritanica*) is one of the most widespread in Mediterranean countries, particularly Spain and North Africa. Its usual habitat is on old walls and coastal rocks, where it remains motionless in the sun during the hottest part of the day. Its colour harmonises with that of the background, making it inconspicuous. At night it hunts flies, mosquitoes, nocturnal butterflies and spiders. The digits widen from the base and only two on each foot have claws. It is ashen grey with a variety of marblings, and has a total length of no more than fifteen centimetres.

The Turkish Gecko or Mediterranean Gecko (*Hemidactylus turcicus*) is smaller than the Wall Gecko but has similar habits and distribution. All its digits end in a claw. It is now found also in the United States, Cuba and India where it was accidentally transported in ship cargos.

The European Gecko (*Phyllodactylus europaeus*) is found in Italy, Corsica, Sardinia and the coastal islands of southern France. It is one of the smallest geckos, abut seven centimetres long. Its digits are flattened only at the tips and each ends in a retractile claw.

The Tokay (*Gecko gecko*) often reaches a length of nearly thirty-five centimetres. It is one of the commonest species in Bengal, southern China and Indonesia, where it lives among the trees in the jungle as well as in houses, feeding on insects and mice. It is also said to be very partial to fledglings taken from the nest, and even to lizards and small snakes. Its common name is based on its call, *to-kay, to-kay*, which is repeated several times, and with such volume that it can be heard at a distance of more than 100 metres. The Tokay is a strong, aggressive animal, which will bite as soon as molested.

The Leaf-tailed Gecko (*Uroplatus fimbriatus*) of Madagascar was at one time regarded as the sole representative of the family Uroplatidae, but is now considered only a rather 'different' member of the gecko family. It is also called the Flat-tailed or Bark Gecko because of its appearance and its ability to change colour in imitation of the bark of the trees on which it lives. The tail, limbs and sides are edged with thin flaps which adhere closely to the surface, thus reducing the shadow cast by the animal and contributing to its concealment. Its digits are markedly flattened and cling tightly. This gecko reaches almost thirty centimetres in length.

Opposite top
The Banded Gecko (*Coleonyx variegatus*), of the deserts of the southern United States, is seven to ten centimetres long with a slender, tapering tail. Although it does not have adhesive foot pads, it can climb over rocks with the use of its claws.

Opposite bottom
The Web-footed Gecko (*Palmatogecko rangei*), of South-west Africa, has evolved a type of foot unique among sand-loving reptiles. Its almost clawless digits are connected by broad webs which allow the gecko to move easily over loose sand.

The Leopard Gecko (*Eublepharis macumilaris*), of southern Asia, has normal eyelids as well as a nictitating membrane, which is usually spoken of as a third eyelid. This is remarkable only because most geckos have lidless eyes, the surface of their eyes being constantly cleaned by the nictitating membrane.

The Tokay Gecko (*Gecko gecko*), of south-eastern Asia, is a large and aggressive gecko, up to thirty-five centimetres long. The photograph shows a male in threat display. The call it makes, *to-kay*, is as loud as a dog's bark, and it also has a bite as powerful as that of a small dog.

A Wall Gecko (*Tarentola mauritanica*) showing the distinctive pads on the underside of its toes. Widespread along both shores of the Mediterranean, it spends much time basking on rocks, but can move with great speed to catch insects. As in many other geckos, its eyes are modified to let in the minimum of bright light. The edges of the iris are serrated and when brought together leave only a vertical line of tiny holes.

The Flying Gecko (*Ptychozoon homalocephalum*) has an overall length of about twenty centimetres and is essentially tree-dwelling. It is well adapted for leaping and gliding, having folds of skin on each side of the body that can open out to form a sort of parachute. When the animal is at rest its purple-brown colouring blends with the surroundings. It has flattened, adhesive digits.

The Naked-toed Gecko (*Gymnodactylus miluisi*) which lives in the Australian deserts has slender, pointed digits. It runs well up on its feet in a cat-like fashion. Its body and head are very dark, with a sprinkling of light-coloured spots. Its tail becomes distended after a period of extensive feeding, afterwards shrinking as the fatty reserves within it are used up.

Other species of gecko are found in parts of South America and in the United States. The Leaf-fingered Gecko . (*Phyllodactylus tuberculosus*) inhabits southern California, while the Banded Gecko (*Coleonyx variegatus*) lives in the deserts of California and southern Texas. The Banded Gecko is among the few gecko species with free eyelids. It does not have adhesive foot pads.

Agamids (Family Agamidae)

The agamids consist of about 300 species peculiar to the warm parts of Asia, Africa, Australia and southern Europe, but not Madagascar or New Zealand. They closely resemble the iguanas of America.

The teeth are inserted in the outer edge of the jaws and are differentiated into what look like incisors, canines and molars. The dentition can be correlated with habit: cutting incisors in the vegetarians, pointed incisors in insectivorous species, and so on.

The skin is covered with overlapping, epidermal, keeled scales, often shaped into spines. Scales with crests and lappets often occur in the males.

The tail is long but does not break easily as in other lizards. The eyes have movable eyelids and the pupil is always circular. The ability to change colour is often highly developed.

Apart from these common characters, agamids differ markedly from one another in their adaptation to diverse modes of life. Terrestrial species have a flattened body, while the tree-dwelling species are narrower. A few have loose folds of skin along the sides of the body which are used in gliding.

The agamas proper (genus *Agama*) are terrestrial and live in stony, rocky or even mountainous regions up to heights of 3,000 metres and, exceptionally, higher. The Starred Agama or Hardun (*Agama stellio*) lives in Greece, Asia Minor and Egypt. It hunts insects and can move at a great speed. The Starred Agama remains wild, and therefore difficult to approach even when living near human habitations. Some reach a length of nearly forty centimetres. The colour is a dull brown set off with dark spots. The sides of the neck and tail have spines.

The Common Agama (*A. agama*) of Africa is much the same size but is distinguished by two fundamental features: it can change colour rapidly and it is polygamous. The male has a sky-blue head and the back is bluish brown with light blue marking and brilliant yellow dots. The throat is orange-coloured with blue stripes, and the sides and tail are bright yellow. The underparts of the body are straw-coloured. During the breeding season the male may be seen surrounded by six or seven females, and he guards them fiercely. Being less wild than *A. stellio*, the Common Agama often finds its way into houses and may become partially domesticated. Some will even gather up the crumbs round the table.

The southern Asiatic genera *Phrynocephalus* and *Leiolepis* are strictly monogamous. *Phrynocephalus*

Agama lizards make up a large family living exclusively in the Old World. They are small to medium-sized with powerful claws and live on the ground, or among rocks or in trees. Their ability to change colour, depending on temperature and emotional changes is well developed. It seems that they originated in the Oriental Region and spread to Africa in one direction and Australia in the other.

lives a sedentary existence in a burrow concealed under a stone. The male and female live together. The female gives birth to active young which feed on ants and other insects along with the parents.

In India and Malaya there are many species of the genus *Calotes*. These animals have a jagged crest that starts above the head and continues down the back. They have powerful claws which enable them to be true tree-dwellers and they change colour readily.

The Harlequin Lizard (*C. versicolor*) is also called the Bloodsucker because its throat changes immediately from pale yellow to scarlet when it is excited. The Harlequin Lizard lives near human habitations, hunting insects and larvae in the hedges and trees. Its habits are usually gentle and agreeable, and during the breeding period the male may be seen dancing before the female. He holds himself upright on his hind feet and sways his head to and fro several times, opening and shutting his mouth and changing colour rapidly. After these lengthy preliminaries he turns to a mimetic display, aping the postures assumed when fighting another male, which no doubt plays as important a part as the changes of colour. About a month after pairing the female lays her eggs in the ground and two months later the young *Calotes* are hatched.

The Lesueuri's Lizard (*Physignathus lesueuri*) is found in southern Asia and Australia and is semi-aquatic. The body and tail measure fifty centimetres and are compressed from side to side, enabling it to swim rapidly.

The mastigures or spiny-tailed lizards (genus *Uromastix*) inhabit the desert regions extending from the Sahara to north-west India. Their bodies are covered with smooth, delicate scales and their tails have many spines. Some mastigures reach a length of about forty-five centimetres. They avoid the sun during the hottest part of the day by retiring into a burrow hollowed out with their powerful claws. The burrows may reach 2·4 metres long and are also used during hibernation. As soon as the atmospheric temperature drops below 15°C., the mastigures begin to become sluggish and their bodies stiffen. They have a varied diet: various types of insects, flowers, plants and dates. They defend themselves by lashing out with their tails. If pursued by a small mammal or a snake, they seek refuge in a burrow, blocking up the entrance with their tails.

The species which lives in the Sahara and in North Africa (*U. acanthinurus*) is remarkable for its capacity to change colour according to the temperature. At low temperatures its back is blackish brown, while its belly is a dirty white. In hot weather the colours are yellowish orange and green. In Algeria it is called the Date-palm Lizard because it feeds on dates.

The Spiny Lizard, Moloch or Thorny Devil (*Moloch horridus*) of the Australian deserts is completely covered with spines, the largest of which are on the head and neck, above the eyes, behind the nostrils and in front of the ears. It feeds mainly on ants caught with its tongue and can consume over a thousand in one meal.

The Australian Bearded Lizard (*Amphibolurus barbatus*) inhabits the dry parts of Australia. When it opens its mouth a collar of scales at the sides of its throat bristles out like stiff hairs.

The Australian Frilled Lizard (*Chlamydosaurus kingi*) is ninety centimetres long and has a fold of skin that can be spread out like a ruff when the mouth is opened in aggressive display. The frill, which measures twenty centimetres in diameter and is supported by cartilage, has serrated edges and red, blue and brown spots. In its native Australia the Frilled Lizard is arboreal and insectivorous. The natural gait on land is bipedal and it leaves the prints of only the three median digits of

The Australian Bearded Dragon (*Amphibolurus barbatus*) in threat display with its mouth open and its spiny throat pouch inflated. At the same time it changes colour from a dark olive-brown to a bright yellow with orange bars.

The Australian Frilled Lizard (*Chlamydosaurus kingi*) putting on a seemingly fearsome threat display with its mouth wide open and with its neck frill raised and spread out like a ruff. In this way the Frilled Lizard confronts an enemy with a head suddenly appearing much larger than it was a second before, using the element of surprise as a means of intimidation.

its hind feet. These tracks are particularly interesting in resembling those of birds and certain dinosaurs of the Mesozoic era.

The flying dragons or flying lizards (*Draco*) of south-east Asia and Indonesia (there are about fifteen species) are twenty to thirty centimetres long and on each side of the body have an extensible fold of skin supported by five to seven ribs. These membranes look like wings when extended but act only as parachutes that help in leaping from tree to tree. This is an extreme development of the gliding ability found also in the Flying Gecko *Ptychozoon* (*see* p. 302). The brilliant colouring of these lizards, several of which also have dewlaps, can be seen when they are in flight. In one species the 'wings' are bright orange-yellow with longitudinal lines, but when the lizard settles in a tree they fold and assume the colour of the bark. The body in some species has a metallic

brilliance with dots and wavy transverse bands on a brown background. The belly is usually pale yellow and sometimes spotted. The throat sac of the male is orange-yellow with a blue spot at the base, and that of the female is different and sky-blue.

Iguanas (Family Iguanidae)

Iguanas are the New World counterpart of the agamids and closely resemble them except that the teeth of iguanas are inserted on the inner edges of the jaws. They are generally larger and have dorsal and caudal crests, lappets and spines. There are about 400 species adapted to widely different modes of life: terrestrial, arboreal, burrowing, semi-aquatic or even semi-marine. They are mainly insectivorous but some are omnivorous and herbivorous. Many have the ability to change colour. The anoles of the Carolinas, Florida, the Bahamas and Cuba, of which the best-known

The Common or Green Iguana (*Iguana iguana*), an arboreal lizard found in the tropical forests of South America usually along river banks. Although a good climber it will readily take to water if alarmed. The iguana's flesh and eggs are highly esteemed locally as food and in some areas it has become very scarce.

species is the Green Anole (*Anolis carolinensis*), have several features normally associated with chameleons. They are small tree-dwelling lizards, feeding mainly on flies, spiders and similar prey, and they have flattened, adhesive digits. The outer toe is opposed to the other digits and is prehensile. The males have a throat sac or dewlap which distends when the lizard is excited. The changes of colour largely depend on temperature and on the intensity of sunlight. When it is very hot or cold the animal becomes dark brown and at moderate temperatures a rich green. In shady conditions the predominant colour is grey, turning to brown in sunlight. The dewlap is vermilion when the animal is excited and yellowish when relaxed, sometimes with red spots or lines. During fights between males the adversaries are greyish until the duel is ended, when the defeated animal becomes dark yellow and the victor a brilliant green.

Colour in lizards depends on pigments and the blood in the blood vessels. The pigments of anoles are of two colours and kinds only: a brown pigment contained within pigment cells, and a green pigment distributed throughout the skin as scattered granules. The lizard is green when the pigment cells contract, and becomes brown as they expand. When the pigment cells expand the brown pigment conceals the green, producing the grey to brown coloration. The change from green to brown is due to impulses conveyed through the nervous system. The colour of the dewlap is produced mostly by the contraction of the pigment cells exposing the colour of the blood in the capillaries.

The Fence Lizard (*Sceloporus undulatus*) of the eastern United States is almost legendary because of its speed as it runs along a fence or a tree. Its food consists of insects. It is sometimes called the

305

Marine Iguanas (*Amblyrhynchus cristatus*), found only on the Galapagos Islands, are seen basking on the rocks. Different subspecies are found on different islands but some are becoming scarce, menaced particularly by domestic animals that have run wild. They are inoffensive creatures feeding mainly on seaweeds.

The Texas Horned Lizard (*Phrynosoma cornutum*), popularly called a horned 'toad' in the United States, has a short flattened body covered with scales and spines and in appearance is somewhat toad-like. The ejection of blood from the eyes of horned lizards is something of a mystery as not every individual performs and its function is a matter of speculation.

Pine Lizard as it usually dwells in open pine forests.

The Basilisk (*Basiliscus basiliscus*) inhabits riverbanks in the lowlands of Mexico and through Central America to north-west South America. Its head, back and tail are surmounted by a crest carrying about forty rays. The erectile head crest is particularly well developed in the male. There are several species of basilisk, and these lizards can leap among the branches of trees and shrubs with great agility. They are essentially semi-aquatic, usually living near streams or ponds, and can run on their hind legs over the surface of the water for short distances. Their food consists exclusively of plants and insects.

There are two species of true iguanas, *Iguana iguana* and *I. delicatissima*, which attain a total length of ninety centimetres and a weight of over twelve kilograms. They have a serrated dewlap under the throat and a crest of soft spines running from one end of the body to the other. These animals live in the forests of tropical America, generally on river banks, and jump into the water when disturbed. Their burrows are deep hollows in the banks and they leave them only to feed or to lay their eggs in holes made in the bases of trees.

The Marine Iguana (*Amblyrhynchus cristatus*) and the Galapagos Land Iguana (*Conolophus subcristatus*), both found only on the Galapagos Islands, are in danger of extinction because of domestic dogs and cats released on the islands.

Amblyrhynchus is a large lizard about 135 centimetres in length and weighing up to ten kilograms. Groups of several hundred bask in the sun on the rocks by the seashore, waiting for low tide in order to browse on seaweed and other marine plants. They spend the night in fissures in the rocks. From time to time they make for the sea and proceed from one islet to another, moving by undulations of the body and tail. Despite their large size and tricuspid teeth they are harmless animals, showing no fear when approached.

Conolophus has quite different habits and is somewhat smaller (up to 120 centimetres long). It lives in sandy burrows far from the sea and is extremely aggressive. It feeds on plants and grasshoppers.

The black iguanas (*Ctenosaura*), which are peculiar to Central America, show some similarities to the mastigures in that only the tail has rows of spines. They have vicious natures and will bite or wound an aggressor with their spines. More terrestrial than arboreal, they can run in a bipedal fashion. They feed on mice, birds and plants and may reach a length of over sixty centimetres.

Iguanids of the genus *Phrynosoma* resemble agamids of the genus *Moloch*. The entire body is covered with spines. However, the Texas Horned Lizard (*Phrynosoma cornutum*) and closely related species have head spines like horns and a bony armour not found in *Moloch*. Most species of *Phrynosoma* are popularly called horned 'toads'.

Phrynosoma means 'toad body'. These lizards have indeed some resemblances to toads, but are not so bulky and reach a length of about fifteen centimetres. They start moving with a series of small hops reminiscent of batrachians, afterwards running with speed. Like toads, they use the tongue to catch insects. At nightfall or when being

European Green Lizards (*Lacerta viridis*) basking on the branch of a tree but alert to dart away at the slightest disturbance. The young Green Lizards are a brownish colour, the adult males yellow-green and the females grass green, all colours providing excellent camouflage among grass and leaves.

watched they bury themselves in the sand. The horned lizards have also been seen to shoot tears of blood at an adversary. When the animals are very excited and 'angry' it appears that their blood pressure rises rapidly, rupturing the capillaries in the conjunctiva of the eyes.

The horned lizards live in the deserts of Mexico and the south-western United States, where their coloration matches that of the terrain. On sand they are yellow, in pine and cedar woods their backs are decked with spots of colour that look like lichens, on basaltic outflows they turn black. In the Grand Canyon in Colorado where the ground is strewn with pebbles varying in colour from white to brick red, the spots on the body exhibit the same range of colours.

One species inhabits the high plateaus of Mexico up to altitudes of 3,000 metres, withstanding the very low night temperatures. Like the black salamander of the Alps, it is ovoviviparous and gives birth to young that have almost completed their development and are miniature adults.

Typical lizards (Family Lacertidae)

Members of the Lacertidae are very numerous in Europe, Asia and Africa, but are absent from Madagascar, the Americas, and Australia. The family consists of about 180 species, two being found in England.

All are slender with long pointed tails and are extremely agile. They move so quickly that the eye can hardly follow them.

Lizards often appear during the hottest part of the day and bask on rocks and old walls. If approached they immediately seek refuge in a crevice. The furthest limit of their habitat is a line running from Norway and Sweden to the north of China and Japan. They pass the entire winter in a hole, sheltered from the cold.

Lizards are great eaters of insects, spiders, worms and small molluscs. They are preyed upon by snakes, weasels, shrews and even by birds, and have little defence except to retreat. If they lose part of the tail it grows again, often forming a double or triple structure. The scaling of the new tail is always uneven and not like that of the original tail.

In the breeding season the males fight for possession of the females. The sexual act is always brief during which the male holds the female in his powerful jaws, and a glutinous secretion from the femoral glands helps to maintain a hold.

Lizards are either oviparous or ovoviviparous. The eggs have a hard or parchment-like shell and are laid in a hole in the ground. On hatching, the young lizard breaks open the shell by means of a small egg-tooth which is afterwards shed. Young lizards are strong and agile and hunt greenflies and ants. From the first year of its life, the lizard

A juvenile Eyed or Jewelled Lizard (*Lacerta lepida*) basking on a rock. It is a large and particularly beautiful lizard, with the colours varying with age. It lives among rocks or on hillsides, sometimes at high altitudes. It is a good climber and very agile. Although its bite can be painful it is not dangerous.

The Sand Lizard (*Lacerta agilis*), like the green and eyed lizards, and, indeed, all reptiles, is fond of basking in the sun. It lives in dry sandy areas. The female digs a shallow hole in the sand in June or July in which she lays up to thirteen eggs. Incubation takes two to three months, according to the temperature.

periodically moults, shreds of skin becoming detached one after another.

The Wall Lizard (*Lacerta muralis*) is distributed from central Europe to the northern parts of Africa and Asia Minor. The typical form is not more than twenty centimetres long. It is to be seen in summer on old walls, debris and ruins, where it finds both shelter and food. Its grey colouring is variegated with lines and light-coloured spots which harmonise with its surroundings.

The handsome European Green Lizard (*L. viridis*), found in the Channel Islands, southern and central Europe and Asia Minor, is less common than the Wall Lizard and chooses less arid spots. It prefers grassy plains, hedges or the edges of woods, often keeping to the banks of ditches and rivers, and is always ready to dive to the bottom of the water. Vivid green coloration, sometimes spotted with black, is excellent camouflage among grasses and leaves. The biggest males can attain a length of nearly forty centimetres.

The European Sand Lizard (*L. agilis*) which measures about twenty centimetres long is found in western and central Europe and in some parts of England. The female is light brown or greyish above with three longitudinal series of irregularly shaped dark brown or black spots each with a central white spot. The flanks and underparts of the mature male are bright emerald green.

The European Common or Viviparous Lizard (*L. vivipara*) is midway between the oviparous and ovoviviparous forms. The eggs are retained in the mother's body and are generally laid at the moment of hatching. Sometimes, however, hatching is retarded and the birth is not ovoviviparous but oviparous.

It is the most northerly of all the lizards and also the one that occurs at the highest altitudes in Europe, being found in the Alps at heights of 2,400 metres. It is widespread in the British Isles including parts of Ireland.

The Eyed or Jewelled Lizard (*L. lepida*) is found in the south of France, north-west Italy, Spain and north-west Africa. It is both large and handsome and may attain a length of over sixty centimetres. In addition to marblings along the back it has a series of blue eye-spots circled with black along each side. Unlike the Viviparous Lizard the Eyed Lizard has a marked southerly distribution. Because of its size the Eyed Lizard makes a formidable opponent and attacks prey as large as mice, other lizards and snakes. Its fierce habits are also revealed during the mating period, when the male bites the female so savagely that she is often in danger of being killed.

Sandracers (genus *Psammodromus*) have overlapping scales like fishes. They are small, extremely agile and inhabit barren, sandy regions in south-

The Viviparous Lizard (*Lacerta vivipara*) is the only lizard to be found in the tropics as well as within the Arctic Circle. It is also the only reptile in Ireland. It prefers dry areas of heather and bracken, mountain slopes and woodland glades. As the photograph shows it also is fond of basking.

ern Europe and North Africa. They are replaced in the islands of Corsica and Sardinia by a species of *Algyroïdes*, the smallest of the lacertids.

Species of the genus *Acanthodactylus* have digits fringed with scales. There are several species distributed in southern Europe, North Africa and southern Asia.

Tegus (Family Teiidae)

Tegus are the American counterpart of lacertids; they are especially varied, abundant and widespread in South America. The dentition of the Teiidae consists of canines and molars. The tongue is long, slender and forked. It is a wonderful instrument for exploring the ground and detecting food. The members of this family vary greatly in size and form, some being very small and skink-like, others elongate and practically limbless, while a few, by way of contrast, are large and powerful.

The Racerunners (genus *Cnemidophorus*) are found in the United States, Mexico, Central America and northern South America. Their choice of habitat is varied and they feed largely on insects and snails. The Six-lined Racerunner (*C. sexlineatus*) is found throughout the south-eastern

The Whiptail Lizard (*Cnemidophorus lacertoides*) of South America is one of several species known as racerunners. This second vernacular name could to a varying extent be applied to a large number of the world's lizards which tend to remain still for long periods, usually basking, and then to race off at top speed either because they are disturbed or in pursuit of prey.

The Gila Monster (*Heloderma suspectum*), of the southwestern United States and Mexico, has a large, blunt head and stout body and all its movements are slow and sluggish. It is carnivorous but does not depend on rapid movements to catch its prey, merely scenting out nestling birds and baby animals that cannot run away, or feeding on the eggs of birds and reptiles.

United States and into the mid-western States. It is very active and conspicuous, feeding on insects of open, well-drained areas where, because of their great speed, they are called 'Fieldstreaks'.

The Common Tegu (*Tupinambis teguixin*) of tropical America is the largest representative of the family, and some individuals reach a length of 120 centimetres.

The back is covered with small square scales arranged in regular longitudinal and transverse rows, bluish black, set off by white flecks and dots.

The Common Tegu feeds on worms, insects and rodents but also devours fowls and their eggs. On the approach of a rattlesnake it begins to hiss.

Gila Monster and Beaded Lizards (Family Helodermatidae)

The heloderms inhabit the deserts of Arizona, Nevada, Utah and Mexico. The family comprises one genus with two species: Gila Monster (*Heloderma suspectum*) and the Beaded Lizard (*H. horridum*).

The body has a rounded appearance and is entirely covered with coarse, bead-like tubercles. These tubercles are many-coloured and form designs of orange-red or salmon-coloured spots on a dark brown background. Heloderms feed on birds' eggs, nestlings, helpless young mammals and slow-moving invertebrates. The tail becomes distended when it is well fed and thin in times of food shortage. The Beaded Lizard reaches a length of eighty centimetres but the Gila Monster rarely exceeds fifty centimetres.

Heloderms are the only known poisonous lizards, but they differ from snakes in that the venom is secreted by a gland in the lower jaw. There are about ten long, pointed and grooved teeth in each jaw. The bite is not usually lethal to man.

Monitors (Family Varanidae)

Monitors range in length from two to three metres and are as powerful as small crocodiles. They live in the hotter parts of Africa, Asia, Australia and Malaya, where some are aquatic and others terrestrial. According to habitat, their food consists of fishes, amphibians, snakes, lizards, birds and mammals. They are particularly fond of eggs and are skilful in putting them into their mouths, cracking the shells and swallowing the contents. In the course of one year an Indian monitor kept in captivity ate sixty rats, four Cutler's cavies, six eggs and eleven pounds of meat.

All monitors have a very long, forked tongue, which closely resembles that of a snake, particularly as it can be withdrawn into a sheath at its base to protect what is in fact a very sensitive

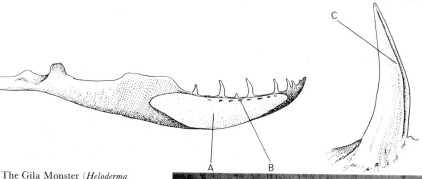

The Gila Monster (*Heloderma suspectum*) has a rather primitive venom mechanism. There is a gland (A) on either side of the jaw, with a number of ducts (B) adjacent to the points where the teeth emerge from the jaw. There is no apparatus for transmitting the venom, however. This is expelled from the gland when the animal bites and is carried up the groove (C) on the front surface of the tooth. This is why a Gila Monster bite, though potentially dangerous, is rarely effective.

The Nile Monitor (*Varanus niloticus*), of Africa, is adapted to living in many habitats. It can climb trees well, run fast, dig burrows, swim and dive expertly and stay underwater for at least an hour. It feeds on lizards, small mammals and birds and is noted for its ability to find the nests of crocodiles and swallow the eggs. It is also able to crush crab and mollusc shells with its cone-shaped teeth.

tactile organ from damage while the prey is being swallowed. Monitors have small rounded scales with pointed granulations, only the underparts being covered with large scales. The head on the long neck is very mobile and can be turned in all directions, a faculty not possessed by other lizards, nor by snakes and crocodiles. The long tail is rounded in terrestrial species and compressed in aquatic ones. It is a powerful weapon and is used by the monitor in preference to teeth as a means of defence.

The Desert Monitor (*V. griseus*) is the only varanid living in the desert regions of the Sahara, Arabia and south-west Asia where its range extends to the north of India. The tail, which is almost 1·5 metres long, is greyish yellow in colour, harmonising well with the sand.

The Nile Monitor (*V. niloticus*) grows to over two metres in length and is dark with yellow spots. The tail is crested and compressed, so forming a swimming organ. It lives by African rivers, notably the upper Nile, and can remain underwater for long periods, being able to seal its mouth and nostrils.

The Malayan Monitor or Kabaragoya (*V. salvator*) inhabits southern China, Burma, Sri Lanka and Malaya and reaches a length of from two to three metres. There are two stripes on its back. Its compressed tail enables it to swim with ease several kilometres out to sea, but it is equally at home on land and in the branches of trees. It feeds on crabs, birds, molluscs and squirrels and carrion. A Kabaragoya can swallow eggs without breaking the shells, the whole being digested in the stomach by the powerful action of the gastric juices.

The Komodo Dragon (*V. komodoensis*), the largest known monitor, was not discovered until 1912. It is now confined to certain small islands in the Sunda archipelago, particularly Komodo Island. This giant grows to over three metres in length. It feeds on young deer and wild pigs and occasionally attacks wild horses. The Komodo Dragon is so voracious that it attacks and devours its own kind as well as the dead bodies of all other animals.

A forerunner of the Komodo Dragon was *V. priscus* from the Quaternary deposits of Australia, a giant measuring seven metres in length. From all points of view the Komodo Dragon can be considered as a relic of giant reptiles long since extinct, and an animal of such scientific interest deserves to be protected from more imminent destruction. Strict measures have now been adopted to prevent hunting it without permission.

Chameleons (Family Chamaeleonidae)

There are over eighty species of chameleons occurring mainly in Africa and Madagascar.

The Common Chameleon (*Chamaeleo chamaeleon*) is typical of the family. The body is characteristically flattened from side to side and has a long prehensile tail which is usually neatly coiled while the animal is at rest. The head is triangular in profile, ending in a pointed crest. The limbs are slender and wonderfully precise mechanisms. Both fore and hind feet have two digits opposed to the other three, forming a gripping device. With its feet and prehensile tail the chameleon is an excellent tree-climber but it moves cautiously.

The eyes can move in all directions and work independently of each other, giving separate views but coordinated in the chameleon's brain into an all-round picture. Binocular vision enables the animal to estimate distances more accurately. The eyelids are fused and have a small circular hole as a pupil.

The club-shaped tongue is prehensile and can be extended about the length of the animal itself. When at rest it forms a fleshy, spirally coiled mass lodged on the floor of the mouth. There are two large blood vessels and ligamentous bands extending from base to tip. The tongue is extended by a

The Komodo Dragon (*Varanus komodoensis*) inhabits the Indonesian islands of Komodo and Flores. It is the largest of the monitors, reaching a length of three metres. A striking feature of monitors is the slender, forked tongue which can be protruded well beyond the mouth.

The Three-horned or Jackson's Chameleon (*Chamaeleo jacksoni*) shooting out its very long tongue to catch a cricket. The tail is prehensile and curls round the branch, as shown in the picture, to give the animal additional support to that afforded by the vice-like grip of the forcep-shaped feet.

The Two-lined or High-casqued
Chameleon (*Chamaeleo bitaeniatus*),
of East Africa, is an ovoviviparous
species which bears its young
alive. As soon as the tiny young
are born they are independent and
swiftly make off through the
bushes or trees.

The Common Chameleon
(*Chamaeleo chamaeleon*) lives mainly
in bushes and trees in woods or
orchards. It moves slowly and
precisely along the branches and
sometimes stays motionless for
hours, relying on camouflage for
protection. Like most chameleons
it feeds on insects and other small
invertebrates.

sudden rush of blood and the release of the ligamentous bands, and is retracted by means of a muscular contraction. As a result, a chameleon less than thirty centimetres long by extending its tongue can catch an insect some twenty centimetres away. The insect is caught by the split tip of the tongue and is brought back to the mouth by the action described above.

In the chameleons colour change reaches its highest development among the vertebrates. The granular skin contains black, yellow and red colour cells, together with others that have a whitish, pearly appearance. The colour cells are star-shaped and contain pigment granules which expand and contract under nervous stimuli. In expanding, the cell branches increase in size, thus distributing the granules and making their colours visible. Contraction of the colour cells concentrates the granules so that they form indefinite points of colour. If the yellow cells are expanded when the red and black ones are contracted, the skin becomes a yellowish colour. When both red and yellow cells are dilated the colour is orange. The pearly white cells impart an iridescent effect to the colours.

In the mating season the males have brilliant colouring, while the females are darker. The males fight among themselves, and eventually copulation takes place, during which the female is securely held by the feet of her mate. In the autumn the female scoops out a hole in the ground, sometimes as much as twenty centimetres deep and ten centimetres across. The front legs do the scraping while the back ones throw out the soil. Several dozen eggs are laid, which the female carefully covers. The period of incubation varies with the temperature and may last four to ten months.

Besides the Common Chameleon which is oviparous, there is an ovoviviparous species, *C. bitaeniatus*, which inhabits the mountainous regions of East Africa. After the normal processes of development about six young are born, measuring about four centimetres in total length.

Chameleons sometimes have one or more horns on the snout in place of a point or crest on the head. The most highly developed in this respect is the horned chameleon, known as the Armoured Chameleon (*Leandria perarmata*). At present it is known from only one specimen from Madagascar. This animal has a serrated crest down to eye level, a bony hood on the nape of the neck, a spiny crest along the back, and rows of spines arranged in rosettes along either side of the body.

Skinks (Family Scincidae)

In a number of lizard families there are pronounced genetic trends towards reduction of limbs and elongation of the body, and these lizards look so much like snakes that they are often mistaken for them. Only certain characters, such as the fusion of the lower jaw, confirm that they derived from lizards. Such similarities to true snakes are the result of convergence due to similar modes of life. In the family Scincidae the tongue, used for both eating and drinking, is thick and fleshy like that of toads and frogs, except that its entire surface is covered with scaly papillae. The more generalised types of skinks look like heavily built

The Blue-tongued Skink (*Tiliqua scincoides*), of Australia and Tasmania, is one of the best known skinks as it is so often kept as a pet. When this skink is on the alert or moving about it slowly flicks its long blue tongue in and out, as shown in the picture. It is ovoviviparous and gives birth to about ten young at a time.

The Weasel Skink (*Leiolopisma mustelinum*), as its common name implies, is a very long-bodied, slender member of the Scincidae. Although its limbs and digits are well-defined it has such a long flexible tail that it may sometimes be mistaken for a snake.

313

and inelegant lizards, but in the specialised types the body becomes longer and every possible stage in the reduction of the digits and then of the limbs can be found.

Many skinks live in sandy desert regions and are remarkably adapted for digging in loose sand and do so with an ease of movement which gives them the appearance of swimming. Most species are ovoviviparous, laying eggs that have reached an advanced stage of embryonic development. They are the commonest lizards in the world with over 600 species and a cosmopolitan distribution, although relatively few species occur in the western hemisphere. Most of those found in the United States belong to the genus *Eumeces* along with a single species each of two other genera, *Lygosoma* and *Neoseps*. About forty species inhabit South America. Both *Eumeces* and *Lygosoma* are widely distributed in the Old World.

Common skinks in the United States are the Five-lined Skink (*Eumeces fasciatus*) in which the young have five distinct light stripes down the back and a bright blue tail (the stripes are very indistinct in the adults and the tail becomes brownish like the rest of the lizard); the Broadheaded Skink (*E. laticeps*) in which the adults are large and olive brown but the young have red heads and are called 'red-headed scorpions'; the Coal Skink (*E. anthracinus*) of the mountains of the eastern United States; the almost legless Sand Skink (*Neoseps reynoldsi*) of central and southern Florida, and the Little Brown Skink (*Lygosoma laterale*) of the woodlands of southeastern and midwestern United States.

The Blue-tongued Skink (*Tiliqua scincoides*) which inhabits Australia and Tasmania reaches an overall length of sixty centimetres. The limbs are short but still have five digits and the smooth skin is yellowish brown in colour with dark transverse bands. The tongue has a bluish coloration. The Blue-tongued Skink can withstand a wide range of temperatures and feeds on vegetables, fruit or earthworms. It is related to the genus *Mabuya*, belonging to the warmer regions of the Old and New Worlds, and to *Macroscincus coctaei*, now confined to the Cape Verde Islands.

The Common Skink (*Scincus Scincus*) is abundant in North Africa, Egypt and the Sahara. It is yellowish with transverse purple stripes and reaches a length of about twenty centimetres. The Arabs call it 'sand fish' because it moves so easily through the sand owing to certain structural

The Stump-tailed Skink (*Trachysaurus rugosus*), of Australia, has a short tail and large arched scales, making it look somewhat like a fir-cone. Like the Blue-tongued Skink, also of Australia, it is ovoviviparous but usually only gives birth to two young at a time, which is not surprising as each is more than half the size of the mother.

The Giant Girdle-tail Lizard or Sungazer (*Cordylus giganteus*), of South Africa, resembles the Stump-tailed Skink (above) but it is a member of a different family, the Cordylidae. When attacked the sungazer lies flat on its belly and stretches its limbs back by its sides. In this way only its hard, spiny surface is exposed to the enemy and its soft belly is protected.

characteristics such as smooth skin, streamlined sides, wedge-shaped head, powerful limbs, and fringed, flattened digits. It requires a constantly high temperature.

The genus *Chalcides* includes species with well-developed limbs and five digits on each foot, species with four digits, and others with short and widely separated limbs with no more than three digits on each.

The Seps or Three-toed Sand Skink (*C. striatus*) is common to southern France, Spain and Portugal. The body and tail carry between nine and eleven longitudinal black stripes which stand out against the greenish-bronze background colour. The limbs are not used in locomotion and the body is decidedly snake-like, the tail taking up over half the total length of about forty centimetres. The limbs are less than a centimetre long and both pairs are well separated from each other. When the animal starts to move, it folds its limbs back into depressions along the sides of the body and crawls like a snake. The Seps prefers sunny places and feeds on spiders and insects. It is ovoviviparous and gives birth to about fifteen well-developed young.

In the skink genus *Lygosoma*, which inhabits Eurasia, Africa, Australia, the eastern United States and Polynesia, there is far greater limb reduction than in the others. As in the Seps, one species has short limbs, each with three digits, while in another species they are reduced to minute stumps.

The Stump-tailed Skink (*Trachysaurus rugosus*) of Australia has enlarged scales and a short tail. It reaches a length of from thirty to thirty-five centimetres, has slow, placid movements and is partly carnivorous, eating the smaller kinds of lizards. It is markedly ovoviviparous and after a gestation period of about three months gives birth to one or two young, already a third the length of adults.

Girdle-tailed lizards (Family Cordylidae)
There are about twenty species of girdle-tailed lizards. The Giant Girdle-tail or Zonure (*Cordylus giganteus*) bears some resemblance to the Stump-tailed Skink. It grows to a length of nearly sixty centimetres and lives in rocky districts in South Africa. It feeds mainly on grasshoppers. The scales are ossified, those of the back and tail being developed into spines. These spiky scales are also found in the snake lizards *Chamaesaura*, but in that genus the limbs are much reduced.

Slow-worms and glass snakes (Family Anguidae)
Anguid lizards have a forked tongue, but otherwise they resemble skinks in having an elongated body and reduced limbs. Specimens of one species of the genus *Gerrhonotus*, the Alligator Lizard (*G. liocephalus*) found in western and southern North America and Central America, measure up to forty centimetres long and have four fairly well-developed limbs, each with five digits. A lateral fold extends down each side of the body. The animal behaves like a typical lizard with an extra long tail.

In the genus *Sauresia* there are only four digits on each limb and in *Panolopus* this number is reduced to two or even one. *Ophisaurus* has only hind limbs and genera such as *Anguis*, which includes the Slow Worm, have no external limbs.

The Glass Snake, known as the Scheltopusik (*Ophisaurus apodus*), has a cylindrical body with a lateral fold of skin as in *Gerrhonotus*, and there are rudimentary limbs at the sides of the cloaca. This Glass Snake reaches a length of 120 centimetres and has a brown back and light underparts. It feeds on mice, worms, insects and molluscs and is found in southern Russia, the Balkans and Asia Minor.

The genus *Ophisaurus* is represented in the United States, where they are called glass lizards, by three species. Their food includes insects, spiders, eggs, small snakes, other lizards and snails. Large specimens may reach a total length of ninety centimetres.

The Slow-worm (*Anguis fragilis*) is the only completely limbless anguid lizard, but it has vestiges of shoulder and pelvic girdles within the body and is certainly derived from four-footed lizards. It is also called the blindworm because the eyelids close after death instead of remaining open as in snakes. It reaches a maximum length of fifty centimetres, lives in Europe, western Asia and

The European Glass Snake (*Ophisaurus apodus*) is the largest of the Anguidae and as well as reaching a length of 120 centimetres has also a thick body. It feeds on lizards and mice and other small vertebrates that are numerous in the rocky areas in which it lives. Mice are crushed with one snap of its jaws.

315

Algeria. In the British Isles it occurs over much of England, Scotland and Wales but is not found in Ireland. It inhabits humid places such as woods and grasslands. Although mainly nocturnal it will appear during daytime if the sky is overcast or if it is raining. It hunts worms, woodlice, caterpillars and slugs.

Several times during the summer the Slow-worm sheds its outer epidermis, which comes off in shreds and not in a single piece as in snakes. In autumn it retires into a deep burrow where up to thirty individuals may sometimes be found twisted round one another. They emerge in the spring and mate soon afterwards. The male seizes the nape of the female in his jaws and entwines his body closely round hers, bringing the two cloacae into contact. The two hemipenes function in turn.

From six to twenty eggs are laid in August or September and immediately hatch into young, four to five centimetres long. Young Slow-worms are silvery above and dark below, only acquiring the adult colouring (brown or grey above, whitish below) several months later.

The legless lizards (formerly family Anniellidae)—two species found in California and Baja California—are burrowing, snake-like relatives of the anguid lizards.

Worm lizards (Family Amphisbaenidae)

This lizard family has greatly reduced structural features. Not only are the hind limbs absent, but in most species the fore limbs also have disappeared. The body and tail have a uniformly cylindrical appearance, the eyes and ears being completely hidden under the skin. Worm lizards occur mainly in Africa and South America, but they are also found in Mexico, Florida, the southwestern United States and the Mediterranean areas of Europe. They remain underground nearly all their lives and look remarkably like earthworms. Food is mainly earthworms, spiders and insects.

The Two-handed Worm Lizard (*Bipes canaliculatus*) is one of the few species having fore limbs, but even these are very small. It is found in western Mexico and Lower California. The Worm Lizard (*Rhineura floridana*) is found only in northern and central Florida where few people recognise it as a lizard even when turned up by a plough.

The White Amphisbaena (*Amphisbaena alba*) of tropical America is the largest of the worm lizards, reaching a length of about sixty centimetres, and is as thick as a man's finger. It is essentially a burrower and looks like a large white earthworm, the eyes appearing merely as black dots through the skin. It is often found in manure heaps and feeds on ants and termites.

The remaining eight families are generally small and restricted geographically. The flap-footed lizards (family Pygopodidae) of about twenty species restricted to Australia, New Guinea and Tasmania, are very snake-like, even to possessing immovable eyelids. They have no fore legs and the hind legs are represented by a flap or fold of skin seldom more than half a centimetre wide. They are believed to be related most closely to the geckos.

The night lizards (family Xantusidae) are represented by about eleven species found in Central America, Mexico, the southwestern United States and Cuba. They secrete themselves in rock fissures by day and search out insects and other small invertebrates at night. They resemble somewhat the iguanids.

Relatives of the skinks are flap-legged skinks (family Dibamidae) of southeastern Asia (about three species) and the rather rare limbless skinks (family Feyliniidae) of four species from tropical Africa.

The gerrhosaurids (family Gerrhosauridae) include more than twenty species found in Africa south of the Sahara, but not including the tropical rain forests, and Madagascar. They seem to be a link between the skinks and the lacertid lizards.

The last family, Xenosauridae, consists of four

The Common Worm Lizard or White Amphisbaena (*Amphisbaena alba*), of South America, is often found in ants' nests, leading local people to believe it is reared by ants. It does feed on ants, however, as well as on termites and crickets. Worm lizards have remained virtually unchanged since they first appeared on earth many millions of years ago.

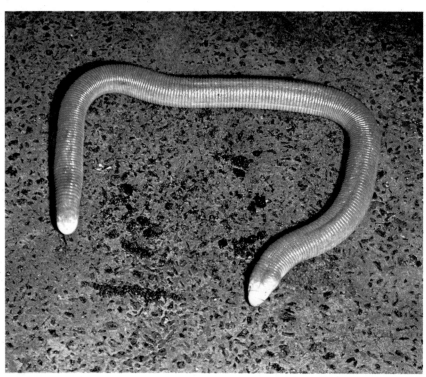

The Slow-worm (*Anguis fragilis*) has a snake-like appearance but is in fact closer to the lizards by virtue of its vestigial limbs which are invisible externally but anatomical examination reveals traces of a pelvic girdle on either side of the body and scarcely ossified bones (A) just anterior to the vent (B) of the animal.

Unlike the Slow-worm, certain primitive boas and pythons have external traces of vestigial limbs which can be moved, and it seems that the claw or spur (A) which is situated just above the anterior to the vent (B) plays a part in the copulatory act to excite the female. The claw mechanism (C) is unusual in that it lies within the rib cage. (D) is ventral cross-section.

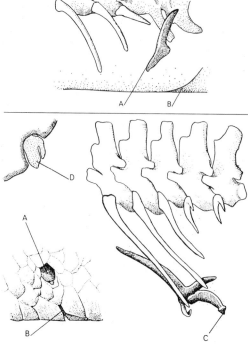

little-known, very rare species. One, the Chinese Lizard (*Shinisaurus crocodilurus*), is found only in China and the remaining species in the genus *Xenosaurus* are found in Central America, particularly in central Guatemala and Mexico.

Snakes (Suborder Serpentes=Ophidia)

The eleven living families of snakes or ophidians are related to the lizards with which they are grouped under the name Squamata (scaly reptiles). The character that clearly distinguishes snakes is the ligamentous connection which permits the two parts of the lower jaw to move apart during swallowing. The tongue is slender, deeply forked and retracts into a basal sheath. Except in one genus, the teeth are pointed and recurved. The body is always slender, elongated and cylindrical. The scales are invariably smooth and slightly overlap one another. In most cases there is a series of transversely enlarged plates beneath the belly. There are usually two rows of scales under the tail. There are no external limbs, but some primitive forms such as boas and pythons have vestiges of a hind pair. Snakes have none of the spines, tubercles, horns, crests, dewlaps, collarets or parachute membranes found in many lizards. The eyelids are always fused together and form a transparent membrane over the eye, while lack of mobility in the eyeball results in a fixed stare. The brain case is closed in front. There is no external ear opening. The left lung is generally reduced in size or entirely absent, and the right lung has become greatly enlarged and elongated.

The ribs are not used in locomotion, which is predominantly undulatory, but rectilinear and sidewinding methods of locomotion are found in certain species. The cloacal opening extending across the body ventrally marks the dividing line between trunk and tail.

The snake's remarkable powers of swallowing enable it to engulf whole animals several times its own diameter. The mechanism for this is most ingenious. The two parts of lower jaw are articulated to the cranium by a pair of lever-like bones which enable the mouth to be widely opened. The two parts of the lower jaw also have some degree of independence in movement and work rather like the two arms of a man hauling on a rope. After the prey has been gripped between the teeth it is gradually forced towards the oesophagus, which is also very distensible owing to the absence of a sternum and the suppleness of the skin. The gastric juices are powerful enough to digest bones, teeth, spines and egg shells. The faeces are fluid and are ejected with the urine and the bile, the whole forming a whitish paste on contact with air.

Snakes are as well equipped for capturing their prey as they are for swallowing and digesting it. Less than one third of them are venomous and of these perhaps a third can kill on injecting their poison. Other species kill by constriction or biting and swallowing.

The teeth are fused to the jawbones and are shed periodically, being replaced by new ones present on the inner sides of the jaws. There are three main types: solid, grooved and canaliculate. Primitive snakes such as boas, pythons and most colubrids have solid teeth. These snakes are aglyphous, that is, they have no poison-injecting mechanism and use the teeth only to grip the prey as it is swallowed. In addition to solid teeth the remainder of the colubrids have two teeth at the rear of the upper jaw which are enlarged and grooved to form poison-conducting fangs. In these back-fanged (opisthoglyphous) snakes the venom is primarily used to paralyse the prey as it is being swallowed. All true poisonous snakes, however, have front fangs, either deeply grooved as in the elapids (cobras, sea-snakes) or canaliculate as in the viperids (vipers, rattlesnakes). In front-fanged (proteroglyphous) snakes the upper jawbones can be moved forwards and the fangs erected, so that they stab rather than bite.

Three stages in the consumption of a grass rat by the African Puff Adder which has a very wide head relative to the neck which enables it to accommodate large venom glands. In the first picture (top) the rat has been struck with a lightning like stab of the large erected fangs. The puff adder then uses its large fangs to hook the prey into its mouth until it is far enough down for the throat muscles to begin their powerful swallowing action (middle). Finally (bottom) the swallowing of the prey is almost complete.

The forked tongue is sometimes called a sting but has nothing to do with the injection of the venom; it is not firm enough nor sharp enough to penetrate human skin. This tongue is continually flickering in and out through a groove in the upper lip. It is a very sensitive tactile and gustatory organ and may also have an olfactory function. During the process of swallowing, it is carefully sheathed along the floor of the mouth so that it cannot be injured.

Although their modes of life are less diverse than those of lizards, snakes may be terrestrial, arboreal, fossorial or aquatic (freshwater or marine) in habit. Generally speaking, they have a fairly restricted diet, some feeding on rodents, others on birds or frogs, fishes or insects.. The Dasypeltinae, a subfamily of the Colubridae have become highly specialised as egg-eaters.

In their modes of reproduction, snakes range from oviparous species that lay their eggs soon after fertilisation to ovoviviparous species that give birth to well-formed young. The eggs are usually elliptical and enclosed in a parchment-like shell. The mother leaves them in a hole in the ground, where the temperature and humidity conditions are generally sufficient for their development. Nest building has not been observed.

Most of the 2,600 species of snakes now known are confined to the tropics, although a large number are common in the temperate zones as far north as 67° in Europe and 60° in Asia. *Vipera berus* has been found 282 kilometres inside the Arctic Circle. In North America the northern limit recorded is 52° in British Columbia, and the South American limit is probably Santa Cruz in Argentina. All the species recorded from these zones are thought to be viviparous. The number of species diminishes progressively towards the polar regions: Spain and Italy, fourteen; France, eleven; Holland, Belgium, Great Britain and Scandinavia, three. There are no snakes in Iceland, Ireland or New Zealand.

Boas and pythons (Family Boidae)

These are the most primitive of living snakes and they kill their prey by constriction. The initial attack is remarkably quick and is usually made with the mouth open. A coil is simultaneously thrown around the victim and is then strengthened by other coils.

Although boas and pythons are similar in appearance, they were formerly divided into separate families because of differences in skull and in methods of reproduction. In the boas the supraorbital bone is absent and there are no premaxillary teeth. These snakes produce living young. The pythons all lay eggs, and the supraorbital bone is present. In most pythons, but not all, the pre-maxillary bone bears teeth. The boas are mostly inhabitants of the New World, although some are found in temperate Asia and North and East Africa, Madagascar, Round Island near Mauritius, and one genus inhabits New Guinea and other islands of the eastern Indo-Australian archipelago. Boas are most numerous in the West Indies and Central and South America. The pythons are inhabitants of the Old World, including Australia, but with the exception of Madagascar. Both are represented in New Guinea and various other Pacific islands.

The Timber or Banded Rattlesnake (*Crotalus horridus*) with the mouth prised open exposing the fangs hanging from the upper jaw. Understandably the snake is dead and the fangs only partially bared.

The pythons share with the boas the coil-suffocation method of attack. Unlike the boas they are viviparous. They are often found near water but their almost prehensile tail allows them to climb trees with ease. The Royal Python (*Python regius*), of West Africa, is also known as the Ball Python because when molested it coils itself into a tight ball.

Boas and pythons are among the largest of snakes. The Reticulated Python (*Python reticulatus*) reaches up to nearly ten metres total length and the Anaconda nine metres. Although there is an authenticated report of a Reticulated Python eating a full-sized bear (perhaps weighing about eighty kilograms), records show that they prefer comparatively small animals. As the snake's stomach becomes distended, the skin of the body stretches. After the meal the snake lies quite motionless for several days as though asleep, and at the end of this period of digestion it disgorges a ball of fur, the only part that cannot be digested. It is readily able to regurgitate food, however, before this, particularly if it is in a situation where danger threatens.

The ancestral forms of the constrictors occur in the Cretaceous period, and nearly all existing species have a pelvic girdle, together with vestigial hind limbs in the form of claws or spurs set close to the cloacal opening.

Members of this family have 'labial pits' or sense organs in their upper lips. These can be seen externally as depressions and are comparable to the 'facial pits' in some vipers. These organs are primarily used as heat receptors and probably help in locating warm-blooded prey.

One of the best-known species is the Boa Constrictor (*Boa constrictor*) which lives over much of tropical America from western Mexico to northern Argentina and in the West Indies and grows to about four metres in length. It is not dangerous to man and in fact is inclined to make its escape when anyone disturbs it. The Boa Constrictor is easily reared in captivity and can be fed on rabbits, rats and pigeons. Cannibalism has been reported on a number of occasions: for instance, if two boas are in a cage together one of them will stifle the prey, but sometimes both will seize it, one at each end. In swallowing the prey they move towards each other, since their recurved teeth do not allow them to let go of the prey easily. When the two snouts

The reputation of the Boa Constrictor (*Boa constrictor*) is in part built up on exaggerated reports of vast length and appetite. This South American species is no giant and rarely exceeds three metres in length. A series of tight coils thrown round its prey kills it by constriction.

The Giant Anaconda (*Eunectes murinus*), an aquatic and arboreal member of the boa family living in the northern parts of South America, is said to be the largest living snake. Authenticated records quote seven and a half metres but some unconfirmed reports claim nine metres or more.

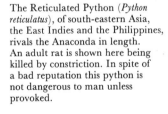

The Reticulated Python (*Python reticulatus*), of south-eastern Asia, the East Indies and the Philippines, rivals the Anaconda in length. An adult rat is shown here being killed by constriction. In spite of a bad reputation this python is not dangerous to man unless provoked.

touch, the larger snake is bound to swallow the other.

Unlike the Boa Constrictor, the Giant Anaconda (*Eunectes murinus*) is largely aquatic. It usually lives along the banks of pools and rivers and preys on mammals and birds that come there to drink. Having dragged them under the water it then kills and swallows them. It may often be seen allowing itself to be carried downstream by the current. It climbs as well as it swims and often uses the trees along the bank as a refuge. The Anaconda may reach a length of about nine metres, but no authentic record of one this size is known. Its colour pattern consists of black spots and rings against an olive-green background. The female gives birth to a brood of over thirty young.

The Emerald Boa (*Boa canina*) of South America is one of the most magnificent boas. The adult is a handsome greenish yellow with white rings, while the young are yellowish with a delicate pattern of darker bandings. Arboreal in habit, this snake destroys many birds (particularly parrots) and monkeys. It grows to a length of two metres or more.

The Rainbow Boa (*Epicrates cenchris*) has a red background colour marked with bluish rings. Its opalescent sheen seems to be caused by the reflection of ultra-violet light from its scales. It tends to live in hollows in the ground and is a little shorter than the preceding species.

The Sand Boa (*Eryx jaculus*) is found in arid desert regions in southeastern Europe, Asia Minor, Egypt and Algeria. Its prey is small animals.

The Reticulated Python (*Python reticulatus*) is much the same size as the Anaconda, the largest individuals reportedly reaching a length of over nine metres and a weight of some one hundred kilograms at an estimated age of seventy. The largest reasonably authentic record is of one 8·4 metres long and weighing a hundred kilograms. The Reticulated Python comes from the Indo-Malayan region. It grows rapidly during the early years of its life, but as it gets older the growth rate decreases. At the age of four it may have already reached a length of three metres, but it requires over twenty more years for this size to be doubled.

The Indian Python (*P. molurus*) comes from the same regions as the preceding species, except that there have been no authenticated records from Thailand or the Malay peninsula. It has been recorded from Java, and is distinguished from the Reticulated Python by its smaller size and the spearhead markings on the head and neck. Some remarkable observations of this species were made in the Paris Botanical Gardens. Copulation took place in February and in May the female laid fifteen eggs, each measuring about 12·8 centimetres in lengh and seven centimetres in width. She then coiled herself around them in the form of a bell, her head at the top. Incubation proceeded uninterruptedly for two months. Within the coils of the animal a temperature of from 32° to 42°C was recorded, some eight degrees higher than that of the cage. This is particularly remarkable in a reptile whose temperature is normally close to that of its environment. While incubating the eggs the female was not behaving as a cold-blooded animal but appeared in a feverish state, as shown by her intense thirst and complete lack of appetite. On hatching, the young measured from fifty to sixty centimetres in length.

The common African Python (*P. sebae*) for which no good, widely used common name seems to exist, reaches a length of almost six metres. It has alternating periods of no appetite and ravenous hunger. Individuals have been known to go without food for two and a half years.

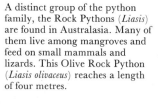

A distinct group of the python family, the Rock Pythons (*Liasis*) are found in Australasia. Many of them live among mangroves and feed on small mammals and lizards. This Olive Rock Python (*Liasis olivaceus*) reaches a length of four metres.

The Royal Python or Ball Python (*P. regius*) from West Africa, the Diamond Python or Australian Python (*Movelia spilotes*), and the Malayan Python (*P. curtus*) are all small snakes with attractive patterns composed of many-coloured spots.

There are also burrowing pythons. *Calabaria reinhardti* from West Africa measures about one metre in length and is so active that when it is placed on sand it burrows out of sight in a few seconds.

Blind burrowing snakes (Family Typhlopidae)

There are several families of snakes whose habit is to burrow in the ground, the main one being the Typhlopidae. Because of their essentially burrowing nature the Typhlopidae have a perfectly round body, smooth slippery scales and rudimentary eyes, which are scarcely visible under the skin. There are no broad ventral plates across the belly. Apart from their dark brown coloration, they could be taken for large earthworms. The length of the largest species does not exceed a metre.

The Typhlopidae are usually known as blind snakes or worm snakes. They are harmless and feed on ants and termites in whose nests they are often found. Their scales evidently protect them from the bites.

The family consists of more than 200 species distributed over the warmer parts of the earth. The species of *Typhlops* have teeth only in the upper jaw, while those of *Leptotyphlops* (family Leptotyphlopidae) have them only in the lower jaw. The teeth are few in number, small and not particularly strong. There is an extraordinary convergence between the characters of Typhlopidae and those of the caecilians, which are limbless burrowing amphibians. Similar modes of life are linked with parallel structural features in these two groups.

Other burrowing snakes have the bones of the skull fused to a greater or lesser degree and thus have unusual power of penetration into the ground. The tail is generally very short and the eyes small. One of these, the False Coral Snake (*Anilius scytale*)—family Aniliidae—from northern South America is superbly marked with alternating bands of black and pink. Another species of the same family, the Pipe Snake (*Cylindrophis rufus*) from Thailand and Indo-China south of latitude 17°N. and the Malay peninsula and archipelago, is completely cylindrical, but can flatten itself against the ground when disturbed. Tail and head look so alike that it is not always easy to distinguish between them; and when faced with an enemy it rears its tail up like the head of a snake about to strike. In *Uropeltis grandis* from southern India the tail ends in two short spines which are often mistaken for poisonous stings. *Xenopeltis unicolor*, a snake with iridescent scales, is found in southern Asia and feeds on lizards and rats.

Another similar genus of blind snakes is *Leptotyphlops*. These snakes differ from those of *Typhlops* mainly in their dentition. They are also burrowing snakes feeding on ants and termites. Most blind snakes lay eggs but a few species have been found to bear live young.

Blind snakes of the family Typhlopidae are among the most primitive of snakes. Most belong to the genus *Typhlops*. Their eyes are vestigal and the head is adapted for burrowing. A spine at the tip of the tail has earned these snakes an undeserved reputation for being poisonous but they are quite harmless.

Colubrid snakes (Family Colubridae)

A clear distinction must be made between colubrid snakes and vipers. Coloration is not a completely reliable feature, since a species exists with the same colour pattern as that of a viper. The arrangement of the large scales on the head is a somewhat safer indication, the colubrine snakes generally having only three large scales between the eyes. The only unmistakable feature of a viper is its enlarged fangs, but even in this detail a young snake can confuse identification. In some countries the shape of the pupil or the head might be used for the purpose and in other instances, a short, abruptly narrowing tail.

First to be considered are the European colubrine snakes, of which one of the commonest is the Grass Snake (*Natrix natrix*), distributed from North Africa to Central Asia and Scandinavia. It is found in England and Wales and was probably at one time an inhabitant of the lowlands of Scotland. It is easily identified by the yellowish-white collar round the nape. The colour pattern of the body is highly variable and there are several varieties, one being entirely black and another completely white (albino). Usually the back is greenish brown, while the underparts are speckled black and white. The Grass Snake also has a pronounced keeling of the scales. In England the maximum recorded length of this snake is 1·7 metres, but in southern Europe its reaches about two metres.

This snake is a good swimmer and lives in dry as well as damp habitats. Its prey includes mice, fishes and a large quantity of frogs and newts. In early autumn it crawls into burrows and sometimes into heaps of straw or manure, remaining there until March or April. Mating and copulation take place in spring. The eggs are laid in August, in numbers of ten to forty-five. These are placed as they are laid under heaps of vegetable matter, the heat of decomposition incubating the eggs. The

newly hatched young are about fifteen centimetres long.

The Viperine Grass Snake (*N. maura*) is a close relative of the Grass Snake. Its brownish coloration and zigzag markings are like those of the Common Viper. It is less widely distributed than the Grass Snake and is usually seen near water. Being a good swimmer it preys on amphibians and on fishes and their young. It does not exceed a metre in length.

The Smooth Snake (*Coronella austriaca*) is even smaller, growing to no more than seventy-five centimetres in length. Its scales are not keeled but smooth and reddish in colour, another feature shared with the viper. It is a common European species and is found in southern England. It usually lives in dry, rocky places where it catches insects and lizards. When picked up it will try to bite. The smooth snake is particularly interesting for its ovoviviparous method of reproduction. From four to fifteen eggs are laid and hatch

Opposite top
The Corn Snake (*Elaphe guttata*), of the United States, climbs trees by wedging its body between the ridges of the bark and edging upwards by means of its keeled ventral plates. It feeds on nestling birds and rodents, which it kills by constriction, and also on birds' eggs.

Opposite bottom
The water snakes of the genus *Natrix* are one of the most widespread and abundant groups of non-venomous snakes in the world. This Red-necked Keelback (*Natrix subminiata*) lives in Thailand and like all Old World species of water snakes lays eggs.

The Grass Snake (*Natrix natrix*) is a common European species. Although more or less harmless, if cornered it will inflate its body, flatten its head and strike viciously but harmlessly. It will also emit a foul-smelling secretion from the anal glands. The European Grass Snake also shams dead as a last resort.

The Smooth Snake (*Coronella austriaca*) is a common European colubrid snake. At the start of the breeding season males have been seen fighting, with the front part of the body raised as in vipers or rattlesnakes. Mating takes place in spring and again in the autumn and the young are born alive.

immediately. The young are active and about twenty centimetres long.

The magnificent colubrine species, the Dark Green Snake (*Coluber viridiflavus*), is fairly common in southern Europe. It grows to a length of more than two metres and is one of the largest of the European snakes. Its specific name comes from the contrasting yellow spots and lines on its dark green body. In France it is sometimes called the 'whip snake' because it has a long and slender tail that lashes as it runs. It is an aggressive animal and can rarely be tamed. It lives alone in bushes, hedges and undergrowth, where it feeds on rodents, nestlings, lizards and other snakes. Its eggs are cylindrical and have calcareous shells.

Species of the colubrine genus *Elaphe* have a large number of vertebrae and ribs, and consequently of ventral scales. The Aesculapian Snake (*E. longissima*), of southeastern Europe and Asia Minor, is a magnificent bronze-coloured species generally between 135 and 200 centimetres long. It is most often found in bushes and hedges, where it preys on all kinds of rodents. Though savage and aggressive, it soon becomes tame and domesticated in captivity. This is thought to have been the snake which, in classical times, was dedicated to Aesculapius, the god of medicine, although there is no conclusive proof of this.

The Ladder Snake (*E. scalaris*) has a prominent, pointed snout and the pattern of the black spots along its back resembles a ladder. It is especially fond of the sun and invariably comes out in the open at the hottest time of the day. Found in France in vineyards, hedges and on heaps of stones, it hunts rodents, birds and lizards. It is 120 centimetres long and is ill-tempered and vicious.

The Corn Snake, also the subspecies known as the Rosy Rat Snake and the Great Plains Rat Snake, (*E. guttata*) lives in the United States and has scarlet spots on an orange or grey background. The Blue Racer (*Coluber constrictor*) also inhabits

the United States and is related to the European Dark Green or Angry Snake (*C. viridiflavus*). The Coachwhip Snake (*C. flagellum*) also lives in the agricultural areas of the United States. It is long and slender, particularly in the lash-like tail region. The counterpart in Asia is the Oriental Rat Snake (*Ptyas mucosus*), one of the few snakes to rear straight up in front of an aggressor and leap off the ground at him.

In India and Sri Lanka the Wolf Snake (*Lycodon aulicus*) often enters houses and even stays there. Though no more than sixty centimetres in length, it catches many of the mice which infest granaries. The Domestic Snake of tropical Africa, *Boaedon lineatum*, is one of the best ratters.

The best known of egg-eating snakes is *Dasypeltis scaber*, which lives in tropical and southern Africa. Although no thicker than a man's finger, it can swallow an egg three or four times the size of its own head. Only when the egg is inside the mouth and this has been closed do processes in the throat formed from projections of the vertebrae come into play. These processes act like a saw to break the egg-shell, the entire contents of the egg then flowing into the stomach, while the shell is rejected. In other egg-eating snakes the whole egg passes into the stomach and both shell and contents are digested. This applies especially to the Madagascan colubrine snake *Licheterodon madagascariensis*, which swallows the entire egg without breaking it, the egg first being held between coils of the body so that the jaws can seize it.

There are also snake-eating colubrids (subfamily Boiginae) such as *Clelia clelia*, which was once believed to constrict like the boas. This species lives in Mexico, Central America and northern South America and appears to be completely immune to the venom of the snakes that form its food.

Colubrine snakes as a whole are rarely dangerous to man, but there is a large non-venomous

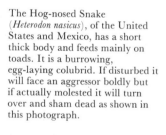

The Hog-nosed Snake (*Heterodon nasicus*), of the United States and Mexico, has a short thick body and feeds mainly on toads. It is a burrowing, egg-laying colubrid. If disturbed it will face an aggressor boldly but if actually molested it will turn over and sham dead as shown in this photograph.

species in Madagascar (*Natrix sexlineatus*) that drops from trees on to people or animals passing below, biting them savagely. The Hog-nosed Snake (genus *Heterodon*) found in the United States is a relative of this Madagascan species. Its snout has a hard, trowel-shaped projection which enables it to burrow in loose soil. Its fearsome appearance suggests a poisonous species and anyone who does not know its habits can be badly frightened by it. When disturbed, it assumes a menacing attitude, inflating itself in an astonishing fashion and flattening its neck like a cobra. If the bluff succeeds, the animal deflates itself and escapes, but if the adversary remains unaffected by this acting the snake rolls over on to its back, feigning death. Unfortunately it overacts its part. If put the right way up it turns over on to its back again, as though this was the only possible position for a dead snake.

Poisonous colubrid snakes

All these bear poisonous fangs at the back of the mouth and are thus known as rear-fanged snakes. Consequently they are opisthoglyphous. The poison is used to paralyse the prey before it is swallowed.

The Mediterranean representative of this subfamily, the Montpellier Snake (*Malpolon monspesulanus*), can attain a length of roughly two metres. It lives in arid, rocky regions, where it preys on field mice, voles, birds, lizards and other snakes.

In tropical regions many of the back-fanged colubrids are arboreal and so closely resemble tree branches that they are difficult to see. When disturbed, they glide away into the foliage with incredible speed. They feed on birds and lizards.

The Vine Snake (*Thelotornis kirtlandi*) is an arboreal snake inhabiting the African forests. Its green and brown shades are a perfect camouflage in the foliage. It has two peculiarities: it is one of the rare colubrine snakes with a horizontal pupil, and it inflates its neck when annoyed.

The Boomslang (*Dispholidus typus*) is another arboreal species. It lives in South Africa, particularly in the Cape area, and was long regarded as harmless to man. We now know that its venom is a potential danger, but it rarely bites human beings because its fangs are so far in the rear of its mouth.

The Afrikaans name 'boomslang' means tree snake, and this snake is certainly well adapted to arboreal life with its long, slim body and protective green and brown coloration. It can stay motionless for hours, patiently waiting for some prey to approach. When disturbed, the Boomslang can distend its neck and even its entire body, a characteristic it shares with the Vine Snake (*Thelotornis*).

The Mangrove Snake (*Boiga dendrophila*) is another tree-dwelling snake of about the same length as the Boomslang. It measures about 1·5 metres and lives in Asia among the long, outside roots of mangrove trees near coasts and estuaries. Its colours are unlike those of the surroundings, the glossy black of its body being broken at intervals by gold bands which give it a most handsome appearance. It has an aggressive nature and is sometimes called the 'cat snake'.

Stories of flying snakes are scarcely credible, but some tree-dwelling colubrids such as the Indo-Malayan Golden Tree Snake (*Chrysopelea ornata*) take off from the top branches of trees and glide to a landing at an angle of about forty-five degrees. As the snake takes off it spreads its body to create air resistance and during the descent it holds itself quite rigid. The non-venomous colubrids of the genus *Ahaetulla* behave in the same way.

There are aquatic colubrids such as the Tentacled Water Snake (*Herpeton tentaculatum*) of Indo-China and Thailand. The head of this small snake has two small appendages which possibly attract the snake's prey and earn it its common name.

The Blunt-headed Tree Snake (*Imantodes cenchoa*) from the rain forests of Central and South America, has a slender elongate body and tail with very wide ventral and dorsal scales. When climbing, the slender body is strongly compressed by muscular action.

325

The Forest Cobra (*Naja melanoleuca*), of the rain forests of Africa, is the longest of the cobras, up to two and a half metres in length. It is often found in or near water and feeds on fishes and amphibians, as well as on lizards and small mammals.

The Banded Krait (*Bungarus fasciatus*), of southern India, eastwards to south China and Indonesia, is strikingly coloured with black and yellow bands, and has a ridged back. It lives on the ground feeding on other snakes, and is nocturnal. Although its venom is potent it is inoffensive and seldom dangerous to humans.

The Green Mamba of which there are two kinds, leads a quiet existence in the trees, feeding on birds and chameleons, and rarely showing aggression towards man.

The Proboscis Snake or Long-nosed Tree Snake (*Dryophis nasutus*) of India has an elongated snout bearing a soft outgrowth. In Madagascar there are two species of the genus *Langaha*, called 'cockscomb' and 'swordknot' because of the shapes of their head appendages.

Cobras, kraits and mambas (Family Elapidae)

These snakes are front-fanged and extremely poisonous. They attack and kill their prey by biting it with long fangs. The ejected venom flows down a groove at the back of each fang.

There are two species in India: the Indian Cobra and the King Cobra. The Indian Cobra (*Naja naja*) grows to a length of about two metres. There is undoubtedly some justification for the cobra's reputation, as it is responsible for about a quarter of the snake-bite deaths recorded in India. The attacks generally occur at night as people walk barefoot along footpaths where a cobra lies hidden in the dust. A cobra preparing to attack first erects the front part of the body, at the same time flattening the neck. The cobra's characteristic marking, which is like a pair of spectacles, appears on the neck as it is flattened. Once in this partially erect position the cobra sways from side to side, probably measuring the distance to its target. Suddenly the head darts forwards and downwards as it strikes.

It is because the cobra gives good warning that snake-charmers can handle it easily. Similarly when being attacked by a mongoose, the cobra is at a disadvantage because it cannot cope with the quick and instinctive action of this small mammal. In general the Indian Cobra is not aggressive and will move away.

The King Cobra or Hamadryad (*Ophiophagus hannah*) is the largest and most dangerous of all poisonous snakes. It may exceed 4·8 metres in length and will attack a man or even an elephant without hesitation.

Africa has seven species of cobra which are smaller and less dangerous than the Indian forms. The Egyptian Cobra (*Naja haje*) is perhaps the snake Cleopatra used to take her life. The Black-necked Cobra (*N. nigricollis*) is another widely distributed species and has the habit of ejecting its poison towards its enemy's eyes. It is sometimes called the spitting cobra.

All spitting snakes, it is believed, take visual aim and then eject their venom to a distance of up to two metres by means of powerful muscles surrounding the poison glands. If the venom hits the eyes it can momentarily blind and confuse an enemy, allowing the snake to escape. This venom is dangerous only if it penetrates an abrasion on the skin, but burns and irritates the eyes and prompt washing with clean water may be necessary to save the sight.

The kraits of south-east Asia are closely related to cobras, but a clear distinction must be made between the Blue Krait or Common Indian Krait (*Bungarus caeruleus*) and the Banded Krait (*B. fasciatus*), the former being dangerous and responsible for as many deaths as the Indian Cobra, while the latter is much less poisonous. Alternating black and yellow bands give the Banded Krait a handsome appearance. Both species reach a length of 1·2 metres and occasionally exceed this.

Mambas (genus *Dendroaspis*) are tree-dwellers and confined to equatorial and southern Africa. They are extremely poisonous and attack with unbelievable speed and ferocity. Their venom can kill a man within ten minutes.

The front-fanged Elapidae are represented in America by a number of species. The best known is the Harlequin Coral Snake (*Micrurus fulvius*), the most poisonous (but not the most dangerous) of American snakes. This is not to be confused with the rear-fanged False Coral Snake which has an identical colour pattern of alternating black, red and yellow bands (the red may vary to pink). The Harlequin Snake is a magnificent creature, never more than a metre in length. It bites slowly and deliberately, gradually sinking its fangs into its enemy. It is one of the few venomous snakes which do not leave go of the victim after biting.

Vipers (Family Viperidae)

Vipers and rattlesnakes might belong to the same family, characterised by the structure of the fangs and the way they are used. The bones bearing the fangs can be swung forwards and upwards, moving the fangs with them as the head is lengthened. Vipers have only to strike and not bite, as the tips of the fangs are bevel-edged and the venom runs down a canal in each fang. In the vipers proper the fangs are almost as long as the head.

Typical vipers are found in Europe, Asia and Africa, reaching high latitudes and high altitudes. The young are fully developed when the eggs are laid. They can break through the shell and from the first resemble their parents in form. At hatching, they have sufficient venom to kill four mice.

The Common European Viper or Adder (*Vipera berus*) is the most widely distributed species, being found throughout Europe and central and northern Asia. In Scandinavia it extends beyond the Arctic Circle and in Asia reaches eastwards as far as Siberia. It is the only viper found in Great Britain. It tends to live in dry places such as heaths and moorlands but it may be found in marshes. Its habit is to bask in the sun. It hunts principally at night for rodents, birds, lizards, amphibians, earthworms and slugs. It is savage and is always ready to strike, its bite being dangerous and requiring immediate attention.

This viper usually has a number of large scales or plates between the eyes. The colour pattern is very variable, but there is usually a long zigzag band edged with a double row of dark spots along its back. The tail narrows rapidly and forms only a small part of the total length, which exceeds sixty centimetres in the largest individuals.

The Asp Viper (*V. aspis*) differs from the Common Viper in that the tip of the snout is upturned. The scales covering the top of the head are normally small, but there is much variation. This snake tends to be brownish red with dark spots. Sometimes, though rarely, these spots unite to form a zigzag dorsal band. The distribution of the Asp Viper is more southerly than that of the Common Viper, extending over much of southern Europe.

The Asp Viper is more prone than the Common European Viper to frequent warm, dry spots such as rocks, scrub, waste land, hedges and bushes,

and it always stays near its chosen refuge. Its diet is similar to the Common Viper's. It is an aggressive animal, invariably biting if disturbed. The Asp Viper is a little larger than the Common Viper, females reaching a length of about seventy-five centimetres and males about seventy.

Orsini's Viper (*V. ursinii*) may be found in parts of France and in the mountainous regions of Italy, Yugoslavia, Austria and Hungary.

In India the genus *Vipera* is represented by Russell's Viper (*V. russelli*) which has particularly slender and venomous fangs and is as much feared as the cobra. It is a very handsome snake, being pale brown in colour with black bands edged with white or gold. It is nocturnal and preys on rodents, and will even pursue rats and mice into houses. Its maximum length is about 165 centimetres.

True vipers, however, are at their commonest and most diverse in Africa, typical genera being *Cerastes*, *Bitis* and *Causus*. Some specimens of the Horned Viper (*Cerastes cerastes*) have a pair of horn-shaped protuberances above the eyes, giving

The Eastern or Harlequin Coral Snake (*Micrurus fulvius*), with its brilliant warning colours, is the most poisonous of the North American snakes. During the day it hides under stones or mossy tussocks and in the evening comes out to hunt other snakes, lizards and frogs. It never grows to more than a metre in length.

The Asp Viper (*Vipera aspis*), of southern Europe, is similar in appearance and habits to the Adder but prefers a drier, warmer habitat. It is slow-moving but aggressive and more dangerous to man than the Adder. In winter asps hibernate, sometimes several individuals coiling together. In the breeding season males indulge in ritual battles. Like adders, asps are ovoviviparous.

South American Pit Viper (*Bothrops* sp.), of the lance-headed type, is long-fanged and very poisonous. Lance-heads are mainly green but the colour is very variable. A feature of so many Pit Vipers is the horns over the eyes, which are no more than raised scales.

this, these snakes are not especially aggressive and incidents are uncommon. Like most vipers the species of *Bitis* are ovoviviparous. The young measure about twenty centimetres long at birth and already have fangs capable of killing a prey as large as a rat. The most important species are: the Puff Adder (*B. arietans*) found throughout Africa, the Gaboon Viper (*B. gabonica*) and the Rhinoceros Viper (*B. nasicornis*). The last mentioned species takes its name from the two raised scales at the tip of its snout. Some species are extremely handsome with brilliant colour patterns. (In the United States several species of harmless snakes are erroneously called puff adders).

Species of the African genus *Causus* are known as night adders. A peculiarity is the great size of their venom glands, which extend beyond the head down the front part of the body. One species, *C. rhombeatus*, has a chain of lozenge-shaped markings on its body and is very commonly found in piles of rubbish near human dwellings. *C. resimus* has a more savage disposition and is a fine olive-green colour. The species of *Causus* are exceptional in being oviparous.

The species of *Atractaspis* belong to Africa and are burrowing and oviparous snakes of an aggressive disposition. In proportion to their length (seventy-five centimetres at most) they have the longest fangs of any snake and make formidable adversaries.

Pit vipers (Family Crotalidae)

The rattlesnake genus *Crotalus* contains some twenty-six species distributed from North America to South America. The rattle at the end of the tail is formed by a series of loosely connected horny segments. When the animal moves these segments make a noise like that of a hand-rattle. A rattlesnake sheds its epidermis periodically, except at the tip of the tail where the horny segments add a 'button' each year. There should be as many 'buttons' as moults, but their formation is irregular and the terminal ones may not occur or break off. So the number of segments is no true indication of age or of the number of times the shedding occurred. Before the dead epidermis is shed it has already been replaced by a new epidermis.

Obviously closely related to the true vipers, the pit vipers have developed, in the enforced isolation of the group in the New World, heat-sensory pits in the head just behind the nostrils. These apparently help the animal sense the approach of warm-blooded prey even in complete darkness. There may be other reasons for the development of these organs, but as yet man has been unable to discover them.

The Timber Rattlesnake (*C. horridus*) of northeastern America and extreme southern Ontario is one of the more common species. It varies in length from one to two metres and its colour pattern is highly variable, consisting of transverse brown bands on a yellowish background. The more northerly the habitat, the more these bands obscure the background colour. A peculiarity of this species is that in winter it congregates by the hundred.

The Eastern Diamond-back Rattlesnake (*C. adamanteus*) inhabits Florida and Georgia. Like *Causus rhombeatus* it has lozenge or diamond-shaped

them an appearance of ferocity in keeping with the virulence of their poison. Living in desert regions, the Horned Viper buries itself in the sand and lies in wait for its prey.

Snakes of the genus *Bitis* are short and thick in form, sometimes as thick as a man's arm though no longer than one to 1·5 metres, of which less than a tenth is tail. The head is widened to lodge the enormous venom glands, and the fangs are sometimes about four centimetres long, the dose of poison they inject being quickly fatal. In spite of

markings on its back. It can reach a length of over two metres and is the largest and most dangerous species of its genus. In the southwestern states, from central Arkansas to southeastern California, it is replaced by a greyish-coloured rattlesnake (*C. atrox* which is scarcely less aggressive in behaviour and whose venom is almost as virulent. There are several other species of this unattractive animal.

The only rattlesnake found in South America is the Cascabel (*C. durissus*). Its venom contains an unusual quantity of neurotoxins which paralyse the victim's neck.

One difference between rattlesnakes of the genus *Crotalus* and those of the closely related genus *Sistrurus* lies in the scales on the top of the heads. These are small in the former genus, while with *Sistrurus* they are large and symmetrically arranged. The members of this genus are also smaller, rarely more than a metre in length. The Pygmy Rattler (*S. miliarius*) is particularly common in Florida and is so small that it is hardly able to inflict serious bites. The Massasauga or Swamp Rattler (*S. catenatus*) feeds on frogs and toads and was prolific in the marshy lands of the United States and Canada before they dried out or were drained through agricultural practices, but its distribution is now more local and restricted.

The genus *Ancistrodon* (or *Agkistrodon*) is represented in both New and Old Worlds. The Copperhead (*A. contortrix*) is found in the eastern United States and Canada and the Water Moccasin or Cottonmouth (*A. piscivorus*) inhabits the southern part of the same area. The name 'cottonmouth' refers to the colour of the inside of the mouth. This is one of the largest of the venomous snakes in the United States, sometimes reaching a length of nearly two metres. Other species of these rattleless pit vipers are to be found in eastern Europe, Asia and Malaysia. Both the Cottonmouth and the Water Moccasin are ovoviviparous, but some of the other species lay eggs.

Next to the King Cobra the largest poisonous snake is the Bushmaster (*Lachesis muta*). It is an oviparous species, the female protecting the eggs by coiling round them until they hatch. The Bushmaster is about three metres long and lives in the scrub and forest regions of tropical and Central America, where it is made nearly invisible by its dead-leaf colour and spotted markings.

The Fer-de-lance (*Bothrops atrox*) is a well-known species from southern Mexico, through Central America and into northern South America as well as in the West Indies, where it is common in the sugar plantations of Martinique. It kills rats in large quantities and also attacks workers gathering the canes, although it is mainly a forest-dwelling species. This crotalid is only found on St Lucia and Martinique and is entirely absent from Guadeloupe.

Bothrops waits in its lair until twilight before coming out to hunt. It glides noiselessly, feeling the ground with its forked tongue. Then raising its head, it silently coils itself. This is the position from which it attacks, darting its head out to strike at a rat, bird or lizard that has come within reach. *Bothrops* is never much more than 2·4 metres long and most specimens are between 1·2 and 1·5 metres. The female pit viper may lay as many as sixty eggs at a time.

The history of this pit viper is closely connected with the introduction of the mongoose, a small Indian carnivore. This mammal was brought to Martinique in 1850 to kill off the viper, but became a considerable pest itself. When the mongoose challenges *Bothrops* in combat it invariably wins. Its tactics are always the same. It moves round the viper, worrying it incessantly but never actually attacking. It is only after it has dodged the snake's striking by leaping sideways or upwards that it pounces upon the snake and bites repeatedly behind the head until the snake is killed.

Sea-snakes (Family Hydrophidae)

Certain of the front-fanged snakes are marine in habit. Their natural habitat is the tropical parts of the Indian and Pacific oceans, the open sea, coastal waters and even estuaries. Some occasionally pass through the Panama Canal and enter the Atlantic Ocean. Those that live in the open sea but near the shore settle on outlying reefs when not swimming. With their long flexible bodies and laterally compressed tails sea-snakes are well

The Sidewinder Adder (*Bitis peringueyi*) is one of the puff adders of South Africa. It gets its common name from its peculiar sidways looping action when moving rapidly across loose sand. The photograph, taken in the Namib Desert, shows the track the snake makes.

The Western Diamondback Rattlesnake (*Crotalus atrox*), of southwestern United States, is slightly smaller than the Eastern Diamondback but just as dangerous. If provoked, it will actually pursue an aggressor, repeatedly lunging at it. The purpose of the 'rattle' in the tail is still not known for certain.

The Banded Slender-necked Sea Snake (*Hydrophis fasciatus*) has an abdomen four or five times the diameter of the neck, almost like a small plesiosaur without flippers. Members of the *Hydrophis* genus very seldom come on land and when they do they have difficulty in moving about. They are mainly fish-eaters and some live almost exclusively on eels.

adapted to swimming. Reliable investigations indicate that owing to their lung structure and tight sealing of the nostrils, they can stay underwater for about eight hours. The curvature of their bodies, due to the mid-ventral lines being shorter than the mid-dorsal one, and their peculiar scaling make them helpless on land. Unlike terrestrial snakes, which have large ventral scales corresponding to the ribs, sea-snakes have small ventral scales which are useless for locomotion on land. In other words the better adapted they are to an aquatic existence the more they are handicapped for life on land.

Sea-snakes display two types of colour pattern, being dark above and light below, or ringed overall with black and greyish green. Both patterns provide good camouflage against seaweed, but this does not save them from sea-birds, sharks and other large fish. Their own prey consists of smaller fishes and eels, which they kill with a venom, more powerful than that of a cobra.

Sea-snakes would seem to be particularly dangerous to bathers in stormy weather and during the rainy monsoons which blow onshore, since they sometimes gather in great numbers among the roots of mangrove trees. Actually they are apparently very mild tempered and very few fatalities occur, even among fishermen bitten by these snakes.

Among the more primitive of the sea-snakes is *Laticauda colubrina*, an Asiatic species distributed from India to Japan and Australia. An unusual feature of this snake is the large scales on its underparts. The females are oviparous and come on land to reproduce. Often during this land invasion these snakes enter villages and take fishes that have been put out to dry. Females reach a length of 1·3 metres, or twice the size of the males.

Unlike this partly terrestrial sea-snake, *Pelamis platurus* is entirely marine in habit, and has a very wide distribution. The females are ovoviviparous and bear from two to eighteen young, usually giving birth among rocky inlets in small islands. They are said to protect their offspring during their early life by coiling themselves round them.

In addition to the sea-snakes just described, the existence of giant sea-serpents has often been

maintained. Although many people claim to have seen such creatures, scientific investigation has failed to secure any specimens, and large animals thought to be sea-serpents have always proved to be species of known fauna. Marine reptiles measuring twelve metres long were common in the Mesozoic era, but it is generally accepted that these large forms became extinct about seventy million years ago. The four orders of reptiles described in this book are the only existing representatives of the highly diverse group which, having evolved from the same ancestral stock as birds, became the dominant animals for a million years. There is unfortunately no evidence—certainly no detailed evidence—to show how cold-blooded terrestrial reptiles became warm-blooded flying birds. There is, however, the fossil form *Archaeopteryx* which, though undoubtedly a bird, has marked reptilian characteristics. The body is much more reptile-like than bird-like, and there is a long tail. There are teeth in both jaws and the bones are not pneumatised. Even more significant, perhaps, are the three clawed digits on the fore limb. In some way these can be said to survive on the first and second digits of the young hoatzins of northeastern South America, and although the claws become smaller as the birds mature, the call of the hoatzins is much more reptilian than avian and their musky odour is very similar to that of crocodiles.

As an indication of their reptilian ancestry most birds have scales on their legs and feet, and the bill and claws are in fact specialised scale-like structures, too. But the progression from scales to feathers is not so easy to explain. Keratin, a fibrous protein with high sulphur content present in the epidermis of vertebrates, is responsible for the formation of both hair and feathers and scales and claws, and one can speculate that heat regulation was one of the factors most responsible for the appearance of feathers. Other aspects, such as colour for protection and sexual display, are probably subsequent functions. But in the quest as to how the progression from reptiles to birds took place the clues are few. One can deduce the progress logically, but the finding of *Archaeopteryx* is only the beginning.

Birds (Class Aves)

A single feature—feathers—marks every bird for what it is. Other principal features characteristic of the class are wings and beaks. Together these make birds the most easily classifiable and the most easily identifiable of all animal classes. Even flightless orders like the kiwis and the penguins display structural characteristics so obviously avian that the possibility of alternative classification does not arise. If flight were the only factor distinguishing birds from other vertebrates, then the systematic position of the one mammalian order capable of flight, the bats, would have to be reconsidered. But fur instead of feathers places the bats unquestionably among the mammals. Teeth (not found in living birds) and the absence of a beak simply confirm that they have no place in the avian order.

To date almost nine thousand living bird species have been identified and placed in twenty-eight orders according to their many and varied degrees of anatomical differences and similarities. Their distribution is universal and diversity marked. This very diversity makes it impossible to do more than consider birds at familial level within the framework of this text. But from group to group are traced the structural and behavioural adaptions imposed by environment and other extraneous circumstances. As the text progresses from the more primitive orders to the most highly specialised, an almost unbelievable variation will be apparent within the class as a whole. Size, colour, feeding patterns, flight characteristics, all have aspects unknown in the other animal classes. Superior to the reptiles but inferior to the mammals in the evolutionary scheme, birds display at least one outward sign of their reptilian ancestry: scales on feet and legs, and of course the feathers that are the later modifications of their ancestors' body scales. Some systems of classification even group the two classes together as sauropoids (lizard-like animals), for studies of fossils and comparative anatomy show that birds have descended from reptiles through forms like the extinct *Archaeopteryx*, a primitive bird of the Jurassic period with some reptilian features (teeth, a long tail and free digits on the fore limbs) on which avian features (feathers and a capacity for flight) were superimposed.

A fine study of a European Common Starling (*Sturnus vulgaris*), taking off to fly away from its nest in a cavity in a tree trunk in search of food for its nestlings.

Structure

Birds are warm-blooded, bipedal, air-breathing vertebrates with fore limbs modified into wings or wing-like structures, and non-glandular skin covered with feathers.

The alimentary canal, with well-differentiated sections, begins with the beak and ends in the cloaca. The respiratory system consists of two spongy lungs and a number of air sacs. There is a four-chambered heart and a single aortic arch inclining to the right. The kidneys are metanephric in type. The brain, particularly the cerebellum, is well developed. The method of reproduction is oviparous, with an amnion and an allantois. The eggs are typically laid in a nest, where they are usually incubated by one or both parents. Some nests are mere hollows in the ground.

Feathers and pigmentation

Birds have a thin skin, consisting of two layers, the epidermis or outer layer, and the dermis or inner layer. Although the skin is thin, it produces feathers, beaks, claws and thin scales, but no cutaneous glands, except the uropygial gland at the base of the tail (Gk. *oura*, tail; *pyge*, rump), and not all birds have it. The form of the claws and beak can usually be correlated with habits and closely linked with diet. Scales are present only on the feet and legs.

Except in a few groups of birds such as the ostriches, penguins, tinamous, etc, feathers do not grow evenly over the entire surface of the body. When chickens and other fowl are ready for roasting one may see the areas from which the feathers were plucked forming well-defined tracts. In the higher orders, such as the perching birds, these tracts are even more sharply defined and follow patterns so uniform that they are given standard names. Preening birds are not only repairing individual feathers, but rearranging the plumage just as humans readjust their clothing after physical activity. Actually the feathers which cover the entire body so well grow from less than two-thirds of the skin area.

Usually there are several kinds of feathers making up the plumage of birds: the remiges, or large flight feathers of the wing; the rectrices, or large flight feathers of the tail, used for maintaining stability and for steering and braking; the tectrices, or contour feathers, which cover the body and coverts, which cover the bases of the flight feathers; the small, fine feathers which form the down; the filoplumes, or hair-like feathers, which occur on the body; and other modified feathers, such as the bristles fringing the mouth opening of most insectivorous birds.

The remiges, rectrices and contour feathers are all quill or vane feathers. The number and arrangement of the remiges and rectrices seldom vary within a species. The remiges are of three kinds; primary, attached to the 'hand' and forming the point of the wing; secondary, on the fore arm; and tertiary, or scapular, from the fore arm to the shoulder (*see* diagram on p. 336).

Quill feathers consist of a shaft or stem bearing a long vane down each side.

The shaft has a hollow basal part, or calamus, embedded in the dermis, and a solid distal part, or rachis, supporting the vanes. Until the feather completes its growth the calamus contains blood vessels, which enter through the narrow basal opening, the inferior umbilicus. The blood flows only as far as the superior umbilicus, at the junction of the calamus and the rachis. The vanes extend along opposite sides of the rachis. Each consists of a row of small branches, or barbs, which bear lateral branches, or barbules. The barbules of adjacent barbs overlap; those projecting towards the base of the feather lie on top and have a few small hooks, or barbicels, on their undersides. These lock on to corresponding notches on the underlying barbules of the previous barb, giving the feather cohesion as a unit and enabling the bird to fly. If the cohesion is disturbed it is rearranged by the bird preening the feather with its beak, using the oily secretion from the uropygial gland.

The tectrices have the same structure as the quills but are usually less rigid. In some species there is a miniature feather, or aftershaft, on the tectrices, which grows from the top of the calamus. It is almost identical in structure with the main part of the feather but lacks barbicels. In emus and cassowaries the aftershaft is as large as the main feather.

The down-feathers, which form the down of young birds and also persist in the adult under cover of the contour feathers, have at most a very short shaft from which spring long and fragile barbs, almost devoid of barbules. The filoplume grows on most parts of the body. It is small and superficially resembles the hairs of a mammal, consisting mainly of the axial part.

Full-grown feathers, which are mainly dead material, are shed and renewed during the moult, usually once a year, but in some species there are two or more moults a year or one full moult in which all feathers are replaced and a partial moult. While this replacement is in progress some

Albatrosses spend their lives gliding over the oceans, coming to land only for breeding. Their magnificent wings are of paramount importance to them. It is not surprising therefore that the wings are used to the full in courtship displays whether these take place on the ground or, as with this Royal Albatross (*Diomedea epomophora*), in a display flight.

birds may become temporarily flightless.

The coloration of the feather is without doubt its most striking feature and is the result of structural (physical) or chemical (pigmentary) factors, or both. Structural colours are produced by the diffraction, reflection and refraction of light by systems of fine laminae, reticulations and prismatic formations in the feathers. They can always be distinguished from chemical colours because they disappear when the structures producing them are destroyed or altered, but remain unaffected by chemical solvents. Pigmentary colours, on the other hand, are produced by the presence of biochemical substances in the feathers, such as melanins, which are buff, red, brown or, more often, black; carotins which are yellow; and guanins which are white. Some birds appear to have black in the plumage which, as in the European Magpie, because of structural layering becomes iridescent green, blue or purple.

The feathers of a parrot of the genus *Ara* provide an example of structural and chemical colourings. If one of the red feathers is compressed it will retain its colour, because this is produced by pigments. Similar treatment, however, will turn one of the blue feathers brown, and a green feather yellow, because a structural colour is superimposed on the brown and yellow pigments. In this case the structural colour results from a superficial reflecting layer overlying a deeper prismatic layer.

There is usually a change of colour or shade of colour during the moult. So during its lifetime and through a single year a bird may show a succession of distinct plumages. First comes a simple pattern of the down in the young bird. This will be followed by the juvenile colour pattern, which may later give way to a winter dress. Next comes the summer or breeding coloration, followed by a new winter plumage, then again a breeding plumage, and so on. When male and female have different plumages, the young may resemble one or other of the parents (usually the female) or they may be intermediate between them, or unlike either for part of their early life.

Changes in colour through moult are gradual, for the feathers are replaced gradually, never all at one time. So there may be an almost imperceptible transition from winter to summer dress and vice versa. A good example of a gradual seasonal change is seen in the Ptarmigan and Willow Hen of northern latitudes. Both are white as snow in winter, white with brownish markings in spring, brownish in summer, and brown flecked with white in autumn. Some colour changes are not due to moult, but to feather wear. The tips of the feathers frequently differ in colour from the centre and when the tips are worn off the bird changes colour.

Beak and alimentary canal

The bird's beak is formed by hard epidermal coverings, or rhamphothecae, over both the upper and lower jaws, and has a pair of nostrils often fringed with bristles. It serves many purposes, one of the most important being to obtain and grasp food. In consequence the form of the beak is to a large degree related to diet. Insectivorous birds may have small beaks for picking up their prey one at a time, or, as in swallows and swifts, widely gaping beaks to catch insects in flight. Others have stout beaks with which they bore holes in tree-trunks to secure their prey. Seed-eaters use their beaks to crack or remove husks from seeds, and consequently these are short, thick and strong. Birds of prey have a hook-tipped beak, often with a toothed edge. Wading birds are well adapted with long bills. Ducks and geese have broad, flat bills with transverse lamellae for straining food from water. Other highly specialised bills are seen in pelicans with their remarkable pouched beaks,

All curlews have long bills but it is especially long in the Long-billed Curlew (*Numenius americanus*), which lives in the western half of the United States and winters in Mexico. The length of the bill does, however, vary greatly. In other respects this is a typical curlew living on marshes and mudflats and nesting in meadows and pastureland.

The American Avocet (*Recurvirostra americana*) breeds on the shores of marshes and lakes in the western half of the United States. It feeds in the usual manner of avocets by skimming the surface of water with its slender upturned bill and can be readily recognised by its brown neck and white bar on the wing.

Probably the most grotesque bird in the world is the Shoebill (*Balaeniceps rex*). It feeds on a variety of marsh animals in the papyrus swamps of the White Nile.

The Hawfinch (*Coccothraustes coccothraustes*), of Europe, is an extraordinarily shy bird and consequently seldom noticed by the casual observer. Its beak represents an extreme example of the cone-shaped beak typical of the finches and used for cracking hard seeds. A Hawfinch can even crack cherry stones.

A Golden Eagle (*Aquila chrysaetos*) calling. This bird shows the large, strong, sharply-hooked beak needed by all the raptors and which, with the aid of their talons, they use to kill and dismember their prey.

crossbills with the tips of the beak crossed, and the hornbills and the toucans with their outsize bills.

The beak, then, is a useful identifying feature, but not necessarily a reliable guide to relationships. Where the several related species in a single group have adopted different diets their beaks differ in shape, as in the Darwin finches of the Galapagos. Conversely, unrelated species with the same type of diet have the same kind of beak, as in herons and storks. The tongue, also, is related to diet. There is the thick, fleshy tongue of the parrot, used in manipulating food in the beak, the long, extensile tongue of the woodpecker, and the grooved tongue of the hummingbird, which is forked near the tip.

The alimentary tract of a bird consists of a number of clearly distinct parts. The base of the gullet, or oesophagus, is often enlarged into a crop for food storage. In pigeons and turtle-doves the crop secretes a milky substance used in feeding the young. The oesophagus ends at the glandular stomach, known as the proventriculus, which secretes the gastric juices. Beyond this is the heavy muscular gizzard, which crushes and grinds the food. Birds often swallow grit, which remains in the gizzard for a time and helps to grind up the food. Beyond the gizzard lies the small intestine, an organ of fairly uniform diameter, ending in the cloaca, as in reptiles and amphibians. The pancreas and the gall-bladder discharge digestive fluids into the forepart of the small intestine. The cloaca receives the discharge from the intestine as well as from the genital and urinary organs.

Modifications of parts of the alimentary tract can be correlated with the bird's diet. In seed-eaters the crop, gizzard and rectal caecae are more extensively developed than in flesh-eaters, possibly because vegetable matter, particularly seeds, takes longer to digest. Exceptions in this respect are pigeons which have short caecae and owls which have long ones, but this may perhaps be explained by a relatively recent change in diet.

Wings and flight

The exceptional feature of the bird skeleton is the modification of the fore limbs for flight. There are other adaptations also connected with flight. The shoulder girdle is particularly well developed and forms a rigid support for the wings. It also serves for the insertion of some of the wing muscles. The sternum or breastbone, which extends not only along the length of the thorax but most of the trunk as well, forms a wide plate with a substantial median projection, or keel. This keel gives anchorage to the large flight muscles. Extending laterally from the front of the sternum are two short and strong bones, the coracoids, which, along with the light but strong clavicles, form the pectoral girdle. In a sense, birds have two pairs of 'collarbones', the true collarbones, or clavicles, in front, and the coracoids lying behind them. From the top of each coracoid a scapula or shoulder-blade extends to the rear along the rib cage, further strengthening the whole structure to the stresses of winged flight. The shoulder socket, or glenoid cavity, is formed at the junction of the coracoid and scapula.

The wing is a modified arm, the three parts of which (upper arm, fore arm, and hand) carry the remiges. The bases of these feathers are overlaid

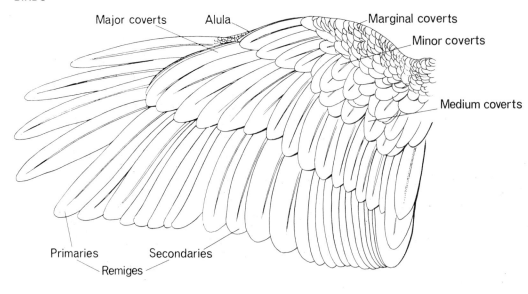

The upper surface of an extended wing of a Sparrowhawk (*Accipiter* sp.) showing the position of the various types of feathers. The primary and secondary remiges or flight feathers, attached to the 'hand' and forearm respectively, point backwards and partly overlap each other. The major coverts or tectrices overlap the remiges and are in turn overlapped by the alula or bastard wing and the marginal, minor and median coverts.

Previous page
Puffins are seabirds that roost and nest on cliffs and spend most of the day feeding on the sea. Their wings are relatively small but sufficient to carry the bird seemingly awkwardly and laboriously from cliff to sea and back again.

by rows of smaller feathers called wing coverts. The hand is considerably reduced and consists merely of three digits fused together in varying degrees. The first digit is reduced to two bones, the second to three, and the third to one. The bony structure of the bird's wing is therefore different from that of the bat with its four, elongated fingers, and from that of the flying reptiles of the Mesozoic era, which was supported by the arm-bones and one much elongated digit.

The movements of the wings of most birds are so rapid that they cannot be properly analysed or explained without the help of slow-motion film. This is particularly true of hummingbirds, so named from the humming sound produced by an exceptionally rapid motion of the wings. Analysis of wing movements of the hummingbirds shows that the wings first extend upwards, are then brought forward (the feathers opening fanwise at the same time) and finish with a strong backward and downward beat. It is with this last movement that they obtain their thrust on the air and drive the bird forwards and upwards against the direction of the beat. Put another way, the bird loses height during the first phase and regains it during the third phase of wing action. The wing tips actually trace out figures of eight, the lower loop of the figure being smaller than the upper one. There are other patterns of wing movements during flight of different species groups. In general, when the wing is raised during flight each feather rotates on a plane like Venetian blinds, allowing the air to pass through and rotate closed for the down beat.

The speed, nature and type of flight of any bird depend on the form of the wing and the proportions of its various parts. In pointed wings the leading primary feather is usually longer than the others, which are progressively shorter. A pointed wing in which the 'arm' is short, as in swifts, is best adapted for speed and manœuvrability. A pointed wing coupled with a long 'arm', as in a goose, usually means a slow, powerful and sustained flight. Rounded wings, those with the middle primary feathers longer than the others, indicates slower but less sustained flight, as in the partridge. The unusually wide wingspan of eagles, albatrosses and frigate-birds enables them to make maximum use of winds and other air currents and

glide for long periods of time without actually beating their wings. Vultures with their long but broad wings are able to ride rising air currents effortlessly. This is an example of economy of effort brought to an extremely high level of perfection.

In order to support the wing movements and to give the forward part of the body sufficient stability, the thorax has to be supple as well as strong. This is ensured by a number of special features. Some of the vertebrae (thoracic and lumbar) are fused (ankylosed) at their transverse and neural processes. The ribs are held firm and yet remain flexible by being braced at both the upper vertebral part and a lower sternal part. They are additionally strengthened by uncinate or hooked processes projecting backwards from each rib to overlap the rib immediately behind.

Legs

Birds, being winged, are necessarily bipedal, and consequently peculiar structural features are to be found in the legs. The first is that the pelvic girdle, which supports the entire weight of the body and must stand the stresses of landing from relatively high speed flight, is elongated and fused with some of the vertebrae.

Secondly, the femora or thighbones are held in a nearly horizontal plane to bring the feet nearer the bird's centre of gravity while perching so that the bird does not fall forwards. The loss of height caused by the horizontal position of the thighbones is compensated for by the tibia or shinbone being elongated and fused with the fibula and some tarsal bones to form a long tibiotarsus, and yet a third segment is formed by the tarsometatarsus (commonly called the tarsus). The tarsus and metatarsus are distinct in the embryo but then fuse together to form this third section, on which there are scales instead of feathers.

A bird is digitigrade, that is, it stands only on its digits, heels raised off the ground. Normally there are four digits to the foot, three in front and one behind for most walking and perching birds, and two in front and two behind in many climbing birds. The toes of some species are adapted for walking on mud or floating aquatic vegetation; those of the Jacana, for example, are very long. The Grebe's toes are edged with membranes, and in the Coot each toe is lobe-webbed, but most swimming birds have webs either between the three front digits, as in ducks, or even between all four, as in pelicans. Many running birds have only three toes on each foot, or two as in the Ostrich.

The claws at the end of the digits are also subject to modification. They are, for example, wide and flat in birds which scratch the soil, and serrated and sharply pointed in birds of prey.

A peculiar feature of birds is that they are able to cling to a branch without muscle fatigue. This is because the muscles which curl the toes and cause the feet to grasp the perch have long tendons; these run behind the tarsus, round the heel, and then close against the forward surface of the leg bones. So the more the bird bends its legs, as when it perches, the greater the pull of the tendons on the toes and the firmer their grip on the branch (*see* diagram on page 338).

Respiration and circulation

The trachea begins with a glottis without an epiglottis, and it has no larynx. Instead of a larynx near the upper end of the trachea, birds have a syrinx near the lower end. The syrinx serves the same general purpose as the larynx and is particularly well developed in singing birds. It is situated at the point where the trachea branches into two bronchi. Each main bronchus, the mesobronchus, runs through the lung and sends branches separately to the anterior and posterior airsacs. The airsacs also connect directly with the lungs and some connect with the airspaces in the pneumatic bones. The functioning of this complicated system serves to cause air to flow through the lungs in one direction during both inspiration and expiration. On inspiration, air passes through the lungs and posterior airsacs from the mesobronchi and through the lungs to the anterior airsacs. On exhalation, air passes from posterior airsacs through the lungs and back into the mesobronchus, where it mixes with air flowing out of the anterior airsacs. The hinged ribs allow large volume changes in the thorax. This system enables birds to extract oxygen more efficiently from thin air at great altitudes.

The avian heart and associated arteries could be derived from one similar to that of the crocodile by the loss of the left aortic arch, which leads from the right ventricle and contains mixed blood. Birds have only the right aortic arch, which carries oxygenated blood from the left ventricle to the organs of the body. This is therefore a perfectly developed blood system and as it is linked with the airsac respiratory system it enables a bird to maintain a constant body temperature of between 43°C. and 44·5°C., a great advance in comparison with reptiles and higher than that of mammals.

Nervous system and sense-organs

The bird brain is considerably more advanced than that of reptiles. The fore brain and the cerebellum are particularly well developed. They co-ordinate the 'instinctive' actions and the precise movements of the body. The fore brain is large but smooth, while the cerebellum has folds which increase the surface area of the cortex.

The ear consists of an inner part with a simple cochlea, a middle part with a single ossicle, the

The long scythe-like wings and short tail of the Spine-tailed or Needle-tailed Swift (*Hirundapus caudacutus*), give it the high-speed flight for which all swifts are well-known. Short broad wings reduce the speed and are a characteristic of woodland species for which manoeuvrability rather than speed is the first essential.

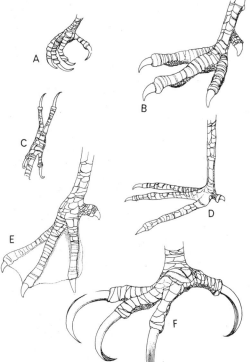

Birds' feet reflect adaptation to particular habits. The opposable hind toe of perching birds (A) is adapted for gripping a slender branch or twig, while climbing birds (C) have zygodactyl or yoke-shaped feet with sharp claws for clinging to the bark of trees. Predatory birds (F) have a wide grasp and curved talons. Walking birds (B) have heavy tarsi and toes with short, blunt claws. The elongated digits and claws of wading birds (D) give support on soft mud, but have little grasping power. In swimming birds (E) the feet are webbed and function like paddles.

The special muscular arrangement that allows birds to cling to the branch of a tree for long periods without fatigue. The more sharply the bird bends its leg, the greater the pull on the long tendons controlling the toes.

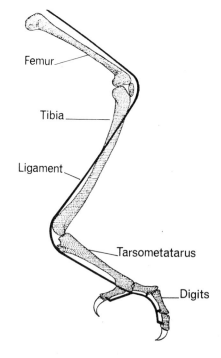

Femur

Tibia

Ligament

Tarsometatarus

Digits

The woodpecker family, represented here by Lewis' Woodpecker (*Asyndesmus lewis*), of California, are adapted to clinging to vertical surfaces of tree-trunks and for this they have two structural modifications. The feet are zygodactylus, that is two toes point forward and two are directed backwards as they cling to the surface. The other main modification is the wedge-shaped tail with its strong quills which protrude beyond the tip. This tail can be pressed against the trunk branch to act as a prop.

columella, and an outer part reduced to a small auditory meatus opening behind the eye. In this anatomical detail then birds show little advance on the reptiles. The owls have an extremely acute sense of hearing.

The olfactory organs consist of a pair of nasal cavities opening externally through nostrils on top of the beak, and into the mouth through posterior nostrils (choanae) at the rear of the palate. This enables birds to breathe and eat at the same time—a superior arrangement possessed by chelo-

nians and crocodiles, among reptiles, and also by mammals, and this has obvious advantages.

The sense of taste and touch in birds may be better developed than is commonly believed. The tongue, particularly of some species, has gustatory and tactile sensory endings, and these occur also on the beak. However, most birds will eat their usual foods even after these endings have been coated with repellant tasting chemicals.

Of all the senses possessed by birds, vision is undoubtedly the most fully developed. The eye is normally rather flattened and the walls are strengthened by a ring of ossicles. Within the eye is a crystalline lens, a comb-like projection into the vitreous humour chamber from the choroid (known as the pecten), and on the outside is a third eyelid (the nictitating membrane), which moves horizontally across the front of the eye. The functions of these curious structures have been variously interpreted, but the fact remains that most birds have a visual acuity not less than our own, some possibly better, and all serve the birds well in their modes of life.

A possible interpretation is as follows. Binocular vision gives an impression of relief and thus of distance, and is obtained when two different images, one from each eye, are superimposed upon each other. Man's eyes are so placed that the visual field common to both subtends an angle of 140°. In owls, however, the binocular field is reduced to 60°, in birds of prey to 50°, and in most other birds to 30°. According to these figures, birds ought to have a very poor perception of relief and distance, but this is by no means true. A Sparrowhawk gliding through the air can suddenly drop on a mouse seen on the gound and never fail to seize it, and a fast-moving swallow can catch a fly in the air with unerring accuracy.

The fact is that the eye of a bird has a number of special features. Instead of a single yellow spot or fovea in each eye there are two, one central and one lateral. In other words there are two spots of maximum sensitivity instead of one, as in the usual vertebrate eye. The central foveae are for lateral vision, while the lateral foveae give accurate forward vision within the binocular field. Owls have only one fovea, but as this is central their forward-directed eyes are specially adapted to forward binocular vision.

The single human fovea has about twenty visual cells to a square measuring ten microns across. The same area of the fovea of a bird has one hundred. Therefore one would expect visual acuity to be much greater.

For efficient nocturnal vision, as in the owl, the retina is associated with a very large number of visual cells carrying visual purple, a sensitive red substance which is lacking, or almost lacking, in other birds and which the human eye has in only a relatively small amount. The retinae of other species have oil droplets, which may be coloured yellow, orange or red. Light passes through the droplets before reaching the visual cells, modifying the colours of the images perceived. They seem to act either as filters to cut down glare from sky or water or, in the case of yellow droplets, to enhance hues in the green vegetation. It can now be assumed with a reasonable degree of certainty that most birds have at least fair colour vision.

Although the lateral position of the eyes reduces the binocular field, this loss is compensated for by increased fields of lateral vision. Apart from owls, whose eyes are in the front of the head, most birds can see through 300° without moving their eyes, leaving a blind angle of only 60° behind them. In man the blind angle is 160°.

Reproduction

UROGENITAL SYSTEM: The excretory and reproductive organs of birds are very similar to those of some reptiles. For example, the kidneys are metanephric and the ureters lead into the cloaca. Birds have no urinary bladder and excrete nitrogenous waste products as a concentrated uric acid solution of thick consistency. This excretion becomes part of the faeces. The accumulated droppings of certain seabirds, rich in nitrogen, are used as fertilisers under the name of guano.

In the male the testes discharge their product through ducts derived from the embryonic (mesonephric) excretory tubules, which have lost their urinary functions and are quite independent of the adult excretory system. The sperm is evacuated through the cloaca.

In most birds the male has no copulatory organ, and to enable the sperms to penetrate the genital canals of the female, the cloaca of the two partners must be everted and brought into contact. A few birds, (ducks, ostriches, rheas, emus and cassowaries) have a copulatory organ or penis.

Female birds usually have two ovaries and two oviducts when very young, but later only the left ovary and the left oviduct become functional; the right ovary persists only as a bare rudiment. In a laying bird the ovary is very prominent, looking like a small bunch of grapes. It contains ovules, or ovarian eggs, at all stages of development, some still very small and no more than a cell with a nucleus, while the older ones are large and full of yolk. Each ovule is enclosed in a sac with a rich supply of blood vessels, so arranged as to prevent bleeding when the sac is ruptured and the ovule discharged into the oviduct. Here fertilisation takes place, provided sperms are present. At the beginning of its passage down the oviduct the egg becomes surrounded by albumen; in the next stage it is enveloped by a double membrane; and finally it acquires a shell and in many species colouring. As the egg descends it rotates, producing two spiral bands called chalazae which hold the yolk suspended in the albumen, which is eventually absorbed by the embryo, and the egg is 'laid' through the cloaca.

Sexual dimorphism

In some species the cock and hen are outwardly alike. In others there are marked differences, and in some of these the secondary sexual characters are so great that male and female look as if they belong to different species. This difference in outward appearance between the sexes is known as sexual dimorphism.

Sexual dimorphism may be expressed in differences of body size, of plumage, shape of beak or claws, wattles, comb and song. The male is usually larger than female, but in birds of prey the female is the bigger of the two. Combs, wattles and ear lobes are mainly found in the order Galliformes, and if not peculiar to males they are at least more highly developed in them than in females. Song is also more prevalent and variable in the male, whose syrinx shows greater development.

The commonest manifestation of sexual dimorphism occurs in the plumage, and all gradations are to be found. At one extreme is the European Blackbird, the male being black with a yellow bill, while the female is dull brown with a brownish bill. At the other extreme are peacocks, fowls, pheasants and birds of paradise, in which the males have significant plumage modifications and the females have dull-coloured plumage.

In Darwin's view dimorphism could be explained by sexual selection. The female would presumably select the handsomest and strongest male, and the chosen male would then transmit his special features to his descendants, and so on. There are certain objections to this hypothesis, and it may have to be rejected in favour of one based on physiological considerations. The secondary sexual characters which distinguish a cock from a hen fowl may be taken as a convenient example. These are: the spur; the plumage, consisting of particularly long and brilliantly coloured feathers (hackles on the forepart of the breast, lancet-feathers on the sides and sickle-feathers at the rear of the body); the comb and wattles, which are firmer and redder; the crowing call; the sexual and fighting instincts.

When a young cock is castrated he becomes a capon, characterised by a greater development of adipose tissues and by the absence of a comb, of the power to crow, and of the sexual and fighting instincts. These characteristics can be restored, however, by grafting on pieces of testis; alternatively if an ovary is grafted, the bird quickly loses

The face of the Barn Owl (*Tyto alba*) shows the forwardly directed eyes typical of birds of prey which need pronounced acuity of vision if they are to catch their prey. The frontal set of the eyes gives an owl binocular vision over a restricted field and for lateral vision the head has to be turned to compensate. As a consequence owls are able to turn the head through one hundred and eighty degrees to compensate for this.

its brilliantly coloured feathers and spurs, and comes to resemble a hen. On the other hand, if the ovaries are removed from a young hen and a piece of testis grafted in, the pullet then outwardly becomes a cock. In other words, the secretion of hormones by the testis has a determining influence on the comb, the crowing and the instincts, while the ovary inhibits the development of the spurs and the plumage. Actually then, the brighter coloured cocks, governed by the hormone secretions, are more 'virile' and 'win' the hens because of this and not because they look more handsome to the female.

So great is the sensitivity of these biochemical actions that fowls can be bred with the base and tip of the feathers showing the colour of one sex and the middle section that of the other. All that is necessary to produce this is the removal of the ovaries from a hen, followed later by a graft of a new ovary. That part of the feather which was formed in the interval between the two operations will be a brilliant black, like that of a cock.

SONG: One of the finest expressions of sexual dimorphism is observable in bird song. In this, however, a clear distinction must be made between call and song. A call consists of a brief sound of relatively simple acoustic structure. Most species have a variety of calls, each with a definite purpose. The female Mallard uses a soft call to keep together her straggling ducklings. Young birds frequently make begging calls to solicit food from the parent birds or from other adult birds. And there are many kinds of alarm calls; a Jay alighting near a Blackbird's nest containing eggs will cause the owner to utter an alarm call that will usually bring other birds to the scene to drive off the marauder. Flocks of starlings roosting on public buildings can be sent swirling into the air in response to the alarm call of one individual. Most species have a series of calls that enable individuals to communicate with one another, calls associated with pain, fear, threat and intimidation or possibly greeting between mated birds.

In the Far East swiftlets use their calls in a form of echo-location to guide them through the total darkness of the caves in which they breed. The sound they utter is near the upper limit of the audible range of the human ear and lasts for only a fraction of a second, yet by perceiving and making use of these sound waves reflected from the cave walls the birds are able to orientate themselves.

True song, such as that of the Nightingale or the Canary, is almost exclusively confined to the 'song-birds' that form the majority of the group known as passerines or perching birds.

A song consists of a series or pattern of notes and like the calls may perform a variety of functions. The commonest kind of song is that which serves to proclaim territory and to warn off another bird of the same sex. Where this kind of song is employed sometimes the female also sings, as in the European Robin and Mockingbird. Usually territorial song has a dual function, for it serves also to attract a mate. In the Brown Towhee, however, it seems to be solely for the purpose of attracting a breeding partner, since mated males do not sing. Song may have yet another function; to co-ordinate the activities of individuals; a singing male is advertising his physiological readiness to mate and thus attracting most readily the females in the same condition. A mated pair often sing during courtship. Other songs may be to produce a gaping of the young nestlings. It is possible that some songs are sung in the absence of other stimuli; that is, when the bird has nothing much to do. Finally, the elaboration of song among birds such as some of the thrushes and Old World warblers is so great, often beyond what biological necessity seems to require, that the possibility of birds singing for pleasure cannot be ruled out.

Another kind of song known as subsong is frequently heard in winter or is sung by females or immature birds. It is a quiet almost inward rendering often of an imperfect or simplified version of the true song. The significance of subsong is uncertain but it appears to represent a condition of reduced intensity. Evidence on the development of song in young birds shows that in some, such as the Canary, the song is entirely inherited, while in others, such as the Skylark, the song has to be learnt from other birds of the same species. In the European Blackbird the subsong is inherited but the true song is learnt partly from other birds. Song is also learned by mimicry, which reaches its fullest development among forest-dwelling species or birds with strong territorial instincts. Many birds such as the European Marsh Warbler, the American Mockingbird freely imitate the songs of other birds.

The Australian Lyrebird goes even further, and reproduces sounds made by mammals, the whistling of a workman, a train whistle, and even the whine of a circular saw. The ability to imitate other sounds may be no more than evidence of a plasticity of behaviour and may not endow the bird with any special advantage. Parrots, however, are something of an enigma. In the wild state their calls are usually restricted to those that co-ordinate flock behaviour and consequently give no clue to the range of mimicry of which they are capable when they are in captivity.

Breeding habits

Some birds are polygamous and a few polyandrous but in most species a male and female will pair for a time, and there is reason to believe that a few mate for life. The onset of pairing invariably leads to a reversal of normal habits. Normally sociable birds may become quite pugnacious, with males fighting among themselves, apparently for the possession of the female or for the right to preen and parade before her. Breeding habits vary with given circumstances, and captivity can have a profoundly modifying influence.

POLYGAMY AND MONOGAMY: It is not possible to draw firm conclusions about forms of behaviour. An example of polygamy is seen in the farmyard cock which, like the cock pheasant and cock turkey, protects his harem of hens and mates with each in turn. Every aspect of his behaviour shows a marked sexual dimorphism, with his almost complete lack of interest in nest building and incubation, or in the care of the young. On the other hand, he shows the greatest interest in the welfare of the hens, calling them when he has found food and letting them feed first. He also chooses the roosting place if there is no hen-house.

The plumage of the male Mandarin Duck (*Aix galericulata*) is the most ornate of the duck family. In its breeding display the drake Mandarin makes much use of its plumage, a noticeable feature being the way the chestnut back feathers are depressed as part of the courtship pattern. The female's dull plumage helps to conceal her from predators, which biologically is the most desirable since she carries the burden of producing the next generation.

Ostriches are polygamous. The male mates with several females who lay their eggs in a communal nest but only the male and one of the females incubate the eggs and guard the chicks.

In the painted snipes (genus *Rostratula*), small wading birds from the humid regions of Africa, Australia, southern South America and tropical Asia, in the button-quail (family Turnicidae) of India, Malaysia, southern Europe and China, and the jacana (*Jacana spinosa*) of Central America, there is a remarkable reversal of normal sexual behaviour. In these, the female is polyandrous and courts the males, leaving them thereafter to brood the eggs and care for the young.

Many seabirds, geese, swans and birds of prey mate for life. Courtship in these species may be prolonged but, once a bond has been formed, the pair is usually parted only by death and only the minimum of courtship is needed after the first breeding season. There may be instances of birds mating for life in species other than those mentioned but it is difficult to be sure without intensive study of individual species. Certainly pairs are known to have remained together for several years and parrots, which have reached a high level of social development, probably pair for life.

More commonly, birds come together for one breeding season only. It is usual to find all members of a species taking their partners more or less at the same time. At the end of the breeding season the pairs break up. The following year each bird probably takes a different partner.

In fact, neither monogamy nor polygamy, nor any intermediate condition, is likely to prove invariable in any species. Just as in a monogamous human society there is bigamy, occasional polygamy, desertion, divorce and broken marriage, so in avian affairs there are departures from normal.

This has been proved in certain instances of ringed wild birds kept under constant observation, and these precise records are backed by numerous instances of circumstantial evidence. It is not even true that conjugal infidelity results when the physiological condition of a pair fails to coincide because one of the pair is at a higher state of sexual activity than another. A typical, well-authenticated instance is of a cock starling that mated with three hens in succession. He shared the incubation with one, and at the same time fed all three hens at their nests. When the first brood was off he gave his main attention to the second hen but continued to feed the third hen, and he gave the third all his attention when the second brood was off the nest. Yet monogamy is the rule in starlings.

Where monogamy occurs it will survive long migrations, from breeding place to winter quarters and back again. It has been shown in the case of Montagu's Harrier that the male arrives at the previous year's nesting site several days before the female, taking possession of the hunting grounds where the brood will be reared. He will then establish his territory and prepare the breeding site before the arrival of his mate. It is invariably his mate of the previous year that appears ten days or so later. The plumage of the female, though normally brown with certain colour variations within the species, is now a deep black. There is no conclusive evidence that the two have wintered together. All that is certain is that every year they find each other again and then mate, build a nest and bring up their young.

FIGHTING BETWEEN MALES: It has always been assumed that the males fight for possession of the females, that in a polygamous species the male fights to keep unsuccessful males from the harem, and that in a monogamous species two males will fight for the lady's favours. This idea is wrong. Careful study has shown that most of the fighting—if not all—is over a territory. The female may happen to be near, but it would be wrong to assume that the two males are fighting for her. In one of the few instances in which a definitive study has been made of this—a study of blackbirds—it was seen that males fight not only for territory but whenever they meet during the days preceding the actual breeding season. In all instances where breeding behaviour has been closely studied, whether among birds or mammals, it has been shown or suggested that fighting between males is for territory, not for a female, or for dominance in a hierarchy.

The fiercest fights are those of the gallinaceous birds, particularly the Phasianidae, the domestic cock, pheasant cock and Peacock. The fighting instinct is a secondary sexual character of the male, closely linked with the secretion of a hormone by the testes and accompanied by a striking splendour of plumage. The males of the Javan Peacock and of various pheasants (Silver, Reeves's

The Spruce Grouse (*Dendrophagus canadensis*) is fairly common across Canada and into Alaska, a very tame and non-social grouse living in coniferous forests. It is monogamous.

and Copper) fight so ferociously, almost like fighting cocks, in fact. Fighting and courtship are closely allied, and it is not uncommon to find that the male's first approach to a female, a prospective mate, entering his territory is aggressive. But as the female's response is one of submissiveness his aggressive display quickly dies down.

Fights between males are not always a matter of actual physical combat. Sexual rivalry more often expresses itself in a threat display, a mock attack accompanied by the erection of the crest and other feathers, all of which is governed by an innate and inflexible code of behaviour. The male hoopoes, with their wings a dazzling contrast of black and white, will display in flight for hours while exhibiting little more than a virtuosity in their flying skill. Two partridge cocks meeting in a furrow will alternately pursue and withdraw, carefully leaving a space between them so that there is no risk of their actually coming to blows. Male blackcaps will chase one another furiously in and out of bushes, but in fact they go no further than uttering a full-throated song punctuated by sharp cries of anger. When two male Green Woodpeckers meet they go into a head-shaking display, though they have beaks as sharp as chisels and can chip the bark off an oak tree. Birds of prey will often do no more than make a show of coming to grips in mid-air, though they are well equipped to kill. Other species will stage a kind of tournament. On the plains where the Little Bustard lives innumerable narrow paths lead across the fields to a small corner where all the young shoots will be trampled down. This is the arena where all the males in the immediate neighbourhood meet, often staying for hours at a time, strutting and threatening, and bounding up and down in the air. Finally all return to their favourite haunts, leaving only a few feathers to mark the scene of their rivalry.

COURTSHIP: The songs and displays which are used to repel other males are also used to attract and court females. Unattached females seek out males who are advertising their availability and the rituals of courtship continue through the breeding season to help maintain a bond between the pair. The display of some male birds is quite spectacular. That of the Peacock is relatively simple compared with that of a related species, the Argus Pheasant. The male of this bird clears a small arena in the depths of the Malaysian forests where he calls and then waits for a female. When she appears he performs a complicated and lengthy dance which culminates in his spreading his enormous wing feathers to form a saucer with a constellation of 'eye-spots'. This highly specialised display stimulates the female to a comparable degree of sexual activity and mating follows.

The display grounds of male manakins, a family of South American birds, are all close together and actively protected. Whenever a female comes into sight each of the males starts a form of acrobatic display. The victorious male then dances with the female whereupon mating follows immediately.

The Cock-of-the-rock, which inhabits Guyana and Brazil, has well-defined display grounds where each male displays in turn, in a form of acrobatics, which lasts until he is exhausted. As each performance ends and the next begins the females make a loud noise, as if applauding.

The birds-of-paradise of New Guinea, the most spectacular of all birds, participate in group-dancing displays in the trees, each species having its own individual pattern of behaviour. The display includes dances, the spreading of gorgeous plumes, whistles and calls, all combining to give a most spectacular effect. In some instances the display ends with the male hanging upside-down from a branch with all his plumes spread. In all species the movements and postures of the males result in the brilliant plumage being shown to produce the maximum effect.

In the Ruff, a bird related to the plovers, courtship takes place on a small stretch of high ground in marshy grassland, where the males await the females. When one appears the males erect their ruff feathers and lower their heads, displaying to the full their splendidly coloured 'ruffs'. This type of performance by a number of rather highly ornamented males in a small area of court is known as a lek display, but the area is called a hill. The females then choose their mates from among the males on display.

Lesser Black-backed Gull (*Larus fuscus*) giving the 'mew call'. This is a long-drawn note made with the neck stretched forward, usually with the bill directed downwards and widely opened. It is a plaintive call and is associated with breeding activity, indicating a friendly attitude towards mate and, later, young, and is in no sense aggressive.

Albatrosses breed colonially on remote islands. Here Waved Albatrosses (*Diomedea irrorata*), are engaged in courtship display on Hood Island in the Galapagos. The courtship display consists of calling to each other, rubbing bills and also displaying their magnificent wings.

Nest of an Eider Duck (*Somateria mollissima*) on the seashore. Eiders are usually birds of the sea coasts or freshwater near the sea. They live in the Far North and the only remarkable thing about the species is that the female plucks down from her own breast to line her nest, in such quantities that man has been able to exploit this commercially.

The African Fish Eagle (*Haliaeetus vocifer*) builds its nest in a large tree taking two to three months to construct it, in the first place, and adding to it year by year, until it may be as much as one and a half metres across and thirty centimetres high. The nest is made of sticks and lined with grass or green leaves, even with the nests of weaver birds.

344

Another feature of bird courtship is concerned with the special coloration of the mouth; orange-yellow in the Kittiwake, bluish mauve in the Fulmar and so on. When face to face male and female will open their beaks to display these colours. The beak is also used to caress the feathers of the mate, and at times to impart a beak-to-beak 'kiss'. Some birds, such as cassowaries, have brightly coloured throat pouches, and when a male Frigate-bird displays his inflated pouch the female becomes submissive. In this display the male also spreads his wings.

NEST BUILDING: A bird's nest is more than just a shelter for eggs and young. Birds are almost the only oviparous vertebrates with a constant and relatively high body temperature. The nest therefore enables them to provide the vital physiological requirement of a fairly uniform temperature in which their eggs will hatch and their young thrive. Birds must incubate their eggs and this can be done most efficiently in a nest. Nearly every species specialises in some form of nest construction, some elaborate, some simple. King and Emperor penguins, however, do not build a nest,

but keep the egg warm by resting it on their feet and covering it with a fold of skin developed specially on the lower abdomen.

CASUAL NESTS: Certain owls, such as the Little Owl and the Long-eared Owl, together with parrots, doves and hoopoes, simply choose a ready-made cavity to use as a nest: a hollow in a tree or a rock, the underside of a stone, or the eaves of a roof all give suitable shelter.

In extreme cases the nest of another bird may be appropriated. The sparrow, for example, is known to use the House Martin's nest; the Nutcracker takes over from a squirrel after driving the indignant owner out; and swifts will persist in worrying starlings and sparrows, driving them away and taking the abandoned nest. Parasitic birds, some cuckoos, honey-guides and cowbirds, for example, go much further and lay their eggs among those of other birds, and then leave the foster-parents to rear the young.

CONVERTED NESTS: These are nests located in the hollow of a tree or of a rock, sometimes even on an overhanging rock or the fork of a branch. Some birds add only some branches to improvise a nest

Not all birds seek isolation when nesting. Communal nesting is common among seabirds and this colony of Elegant Terns (*Sterna elegans*) illustrates this gregarious behaviour. Here scores of terns are gathered in their nesting colony on the beach of the Sea of Cortez, Mexico.

345

The outstanding feature of plovers is the way their eggs resemble the pebbles among which they are laid. The young plovers also are cryptically coloured and linked with that is their habit of freezing at the slightest sign of disturbance or danger so that they take on the cloak of invisibility as illustrated by this group of two chicks and two eggs of the Little Ringed Plover (*Charadrius dubius*).

The House Martin (*Delichon urbica*) traditionally nested under cliffs. With the advent of houses came a suitable substitution for this natural habitat and now the majority of House Martins make their cup-shaped nests of pellets of mud under the eaves of houses.

346

in one of these places. The eyries of some eagles are typical of the simplest form of converted nest. Other types are better fitted out, such as those of wood pigeons, sparrowhawks, storks, magpies and crows. Here the bird gathers together branches, twigs, strips of bark, leaves, lichens, a little clay, hair and feathers, and then builds a strong nest which sometimes lasts for several years and may even attract the attention of the 'nest stealers'. From a distance a Crow's nest looks like a bundle of sticks perched on a tree-top. Though it seems crude enough from below, it is surprisingly strong and snug, and if dismantled will be found to contain something like almost a kilogram of twigs, bark strips and roots as well as strands of wool, hair, moss and other soft lining materials. There is nothing careless in the construction either. The cock Crow, who alone builds the nest, spends a great deal of energy choosing the sticks and working them into the nest.

HOLLOWED-OUT NESTS: These are made by digging and range from a simple shallow depression in the surface of the ground to a tunnel dug in a bank or cliff. The Skylark nests in the fields in a hollow dug by the female alone and lined with blades of grass, dry stalks and pieces of root. Partridges, quail and all similar ground-nesting birds do much the same. Ostriches and other ratites, such as rheas, emus and cassowaries, also lay their eggs in bare hollows in the ground dug by the males.

The Kingfisher's nest consists of a tunnel, a metre long and about six centimetres in diameter, cut in a river bank. At the far end it widens out into a dry nest-chamber, the floor of which becomes strewn with fish bones and other remains of food. A Kingfisher often uses the same nest year after year, so that when the heads and wings of dragonflies are found strewn on the floor, with the fish bones, it may safely be concluded that this nest has already been used once before for rearing young. Bee-eaters are also skilful miners, the nest tunnels being as much as two metres long.

Woodpeckers, parrots, hornbills and similar birds make hollows in trees, though they sometimes save themselves effort by taking over a ready-made hole. A Green Woodpecker's nest has an opening some eight centimetres in diameter and is about forty centimetres deep. The maximum diameter of the nesting chamber is twelve centimetres, leaving the female only enough room for herself and her eggs during the incubation period. The inner surface of the chamber is perfectly smooth and the bottom is covered with small chips of wood.

Some hornbills have the strange habit of imprisoning the female and her eggs by blocking up the nest opening with mud, which not only protects the eggs but prevents the female leaving during the incubation period. The male brings her food and then goes on to feed the young. He is greatly emaciated by the time his laborious task is completed. While in her prison the female undergoes a moult.

PLASTER NESTS: Some swallows and some martins make their nests in or close to human habitation, preferring eaves, stables and barns, window recesses or chimneys. Whatever the site, it is invariably sheltered from rain, which would soon reduce the mud nest to a sodden and shapeless mass. Some

500 journeys over a period of eight days or so are needed to fetch and carry material for the construction of the swallow's nest.

The Red-rumped Swallow makes a nest of mud plastered to a vertical rock face, terminating in a spout, which hangs down and looks rather like the neck of a bottle with its opening on the underside.

The Brazilian Ovenbird's nest is spherical or muff-shaped, made of clay, completely smooth inside and out, and attached to a branch of a tree. A side opening leads to the brood chamber, which is concealed from the outside by a partition.

WOVEN NESTS: These are perhaps the most complex of all nests, and the behaviour patterns attending their construction are equally complex. They are remarkable achievements when it is remembered that the bird's only tool is its beak. Nests have to be strongly built and firmly secured if they are to hold a family of restless chicks and survive the wind, the swaying of the bough on which they are built, and the rain. A variety of materials is used: blades of grass, dry leaves, lichens, mosses, fur, feathers, horsehair, strands of wool and even spiders' webs. These are all skilfully

The Common Kingfisher (*Alcedo atthis*) flying away from its nest in a sandy bank. The parents dig the tunnel with their beaks. This goes back half a metre to a nesting chamber where the chicks remain until they are ready to leave the nest altogether. The floor of the tunnel becomes fouled with the remains of fishes and their own droppings which steadily flow to the entrance and down over the face of the vertical bank. The odour from this liquid mass is a characteristic of the nesting site.

347

woven together and held in position with a mixture of mud and saliva. The thickness of the walls appears to be correlated with the weight of the chicks to be reared; it would seem that there is even an adjustment according to the position of the supports. Some nest walls may be more than two centimetres thick, while others are sometimes as fine as a hairnet, with the eggs plainly visible inside.

The wall is generally made up of three layers, the outer layer being the thickest, while the inner one is made of the finest materials which may help to conserve the heat from the female's body. A typical nest is a small, hemispherical basket; there are others shaped like a hammock, a muff, or a bottle, or moulded to fit their surroundings. The nests of the Red-backed Shrike and the Blackcap are basket-shaped and made entirely of grass. Those of the European Blackbird and the American Robin are much the same, though the blades of grass are often bound together with mud, always so in the American Robin. The Chaffinch and the European Goldfinch use a wider range of materials and their nests are of the most intricate construction. The Wren's nest hangs in a bush and is muff-shaped and made mostly of moss. The Old World Oriole's nest is more like a hammock, hangs from a branch, and is made of all kinds of materials welded together with saliva. The Sedge-warbler's basket-like nest is built in the rushes above water-level. Those of the Coot, the Grebe and other species float on the water. The Water Hen's nest may be any one of these types according to particular circumstances.

The nests of the Weaver-bird, the Baltimore Oriole and the Penduline Tit are different from

Moorhen (*Gallinula chloropus*), working at its nest. An interesting feature of Moorhen behaviour is the way the birds contrive to keep the top of the nest and its contents above water level. In the event of flooding a pair will quickly gather more nesting material to build up the nest.

A communal nest of the Social Weaver (*Philetairus socius*) is one of the most complex of all avian structures. Many pairs of weavers combine to build a huge thatch in a tall tree. After this each pair builds its own nest under this canopy, cheek-by-jowl with the nests of its neighbours.

others, being completely closed and slung from a branch. The opening is at the outer end of a sleeve-like extension at the bottom or the side of the nest. The walls, which surround an inner chamber sheltering the eggs, are made of intricately inter-woven vegetable fibres. Some species add pieces of clay as stabilisers at suitable points to prevent the nest swinging too much in the wind. There may be as many as a hundred nests hanging together in one tree, giving the appearance of a gigantic hive, particularly of some of the African Weaver-birds.

OTHER TYPES OF NESTS: The Tailor-bird, which lives in Asia, southern Europe and North Africa, builds the walls of its nest from leaves cleverly sewn together. It is usually the male bird that undertakes this labourious work, first making a series of holes in the leaves with his beak and then threading vegetable fibres through them, finally overcasting the seams exactly.

The Edible-nest Swiftlets of the Indo-Australa-sian archipelago make their nests out of mosses, agar-rich seaweeds, and a few of their own feath-ers. They cement these materials together with their own saliva, which is both copious and gluti-nous, solidifying on contact with the air. A few species build their nests solely of saliva. These are sold in the Far East under the inappropriate name 'swallow's nests' and are used as a basis for soup.

SOCIAL NESTS: The Weaver-birds, as we have seen, often build their nests close together in a tree. The Sociable Weavers of South Africa go much further and have a collective nesting structure built around a tree trunk, the individual nests being part of a large formation built by a group of birds. From the outside this collective nest, which houses many hundreds of birds, looks like a conical roof

The hen Goldfinch (*Carduelis carduelis*) builds the nest, watched by her mate. The materials used are diverse: roots, grass, lichens, moss and wool forming a cup. This is lined with vegetable down and wool, hair sometimes being added. The result is a neat, soft but durable, camouflaged nest.

Golden Oriole (*Oriolus oriolus*), of Europe, feeding its nestlings. The hen builds the nest almost unaided, her mate assisting only in the early stages. She carries the main burden of incubation the cock relieving in the middle of the day only, but both parents feed the fledglings.

several metres in circumference. The entrances to the individual nests are under the edge of the roof.

Some birds seem to be quite casual in their choice of a nesting site, building in the first suitable place, in spite of the fact that they could have chosen another which was less exposed and where the nest would have been more durable.

It is often claimed that birds adapt themselves to circumstances and use whatever nest building materials are near at hand, even though this means abandoning ways of construction inherited from their parents. Instinct would here seem to be tempered by expediency, but little is known of the reasons why unusual materials are selected by birds when those more normal for the species could be used. Many strange cases have been recorded. A Heron's nest found in England was built almost entirely of thin iron wire mixed with a few twigs. A curious Golden Oriole's nest was found attached to the end of a forked branch of a beech tree. Part of it was made of pieces of ribbon and red string, and the rest of tram tickets, string and paper streamers. The Spotted Flycatcher's nest usually consists of blades of grass, small roots, moss, horsehair and down-feathers, but one found in Hyde Park, London, was made of spent matches and cigarette packets. A sparrow's nest observed in Switzerland was made entirely of watch springs.

Sparrows have been found nesting in the most unexpected places; in a railway station clock, in an old cannon, even in the throat of a stone lion. Tits have been found nesting in old coffee pots, biscuit boxes, jam pots, baskets, cartwheel hubs, street lamps, letter-boxes, disused pumps, spare wheels on trucks, and so on. The Wren (known in America as the Winter Wren) also chooses strange places to nest. One nested in a crown of thorns on an old statue and another in the pocket of a jacket hung up daily in a yard. The nest was not interfered with and the brood successfully reared.

Eggs and development

Usually the size of the egg is proportional to the size of the bird producing it. That of a Hummingbird is little more than 0·8 centimetres long, while an Ostrich, the largest of modern birds, lays an egg measuring as much as thirteen by fifteen centimetres and with a volume equal to that of about two dozen hen's eggs. The average size of a hen's egg is six by four centimetres and weighs fifty-five grams. Generally the eggs of precocial species are larger than those of altricial ones.

As for shape, eggs may be grouped into four main categories: almost spherical (some penguins, owls and the Honey-buzzard); oval or ellipsoidal (Peregrine Falcon, gulls, Grebe and Golden Oriole); slightly enlarged at one end (most birds); and pyriform or pointed at one end and rounded at the other (auks, puffins, plovers).

Shells may be porcellaneous and highly glossy (tinamous), smooth and glossy (passerine and galliform birds), smooth and matt (birds of prey and waders), coarse and granular (ostriches), oily-looking (ducks), or covered with a chalky layer (pelicans). There is also wide variety in the coloration. About a quarter of all bird species lay white eggs; the rest lay coloured eggs, which may be spotted to a varying degree. The spots may be no more than simple dots or they may form lines, scrawls, blotches or marblings, which are often grouped into a kind of cap or crown at one end of the egg. A fowl's egg is whitish, a Starling's sky blue, a sparrow's brown spotted, a Wren's and a tit's red spotted, and so on.

Form and coloration are apt to vary within a species, if not within a clutch. Individual females of the Meadow-pipit, for example, lay such dissimilar eggs that they could be mistaken for the eggs of separate species. The last eggs to be laid in a clutch are often paler and have fewer spots than the first. Food, too, may have some influence upon colour and spots, since this is the source from which the female draws the materials for egg pigments.

Coloration is sometimes said to be mimetic. This is true in some cases though not in others. The eggs of birds nesting in dark places are white; but so too are many others which lie in open nests or in nests on the ground, but they are usually close-brooded, as by the pigeons. The Magpie and the Starling, in contrast, have closed nests and lay coloured eggs. Cuckoo's eggs show some degree of mimicry, the colour and appearance often resembling those in the nest in which they are laid. Little is known about this phenomenon, but as it seems that an individual will parasitise one species more than another, it is not a question of the eggs of one individual varying. For example, a species commonly parasitised in Scotland is the Meadow-pipit, in Hungary the Great Reed-warbler, in North Germany the Grey Wagtail, and its choice of host is constant.

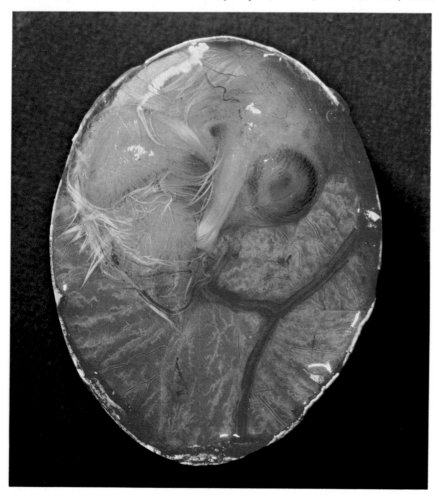

A hen's egg opened up to reveal a fifteen-day-old embryo chick. The yolk-sac still occupies most of the cavity of the egg and the system of blood-vessels which transfer nutrients from it to the developing chick can be seen clearly.

The number of eggs varies considerably from one species to another and is very probably related to the availability of food for rearing the brood after hatching, to the mortality rate of the species, and to the size of the brood patch. Many birds lay only one egg in a clutch, most pigeons lay two, herons three to five, the Great Tit five to ten, many charadriiform birds four, and the European Partridge ten to sixteen. The number also varies with the physical condition and age of the individual female. A non-migratory bird, weakened by the rigours of a prolonged winter, will lay fewer eggs in the first clutch than in the second. Fecundity can be increased by removing eggs from the nest as they are laid, a practice that is general among poultry farmers and also followed in Holland, where the nests of the Sheldrake and the Plover are regularly emptied.

STRUCTURE AND CHEMICAL COMPOSITION: The egg of a bird is contained within a calcareous shell which may vary from thin and fragile if the nest is downy to thick and robust if the nest is either on the ground or crudely constructed. The shell of a hen's egg is between two- and three-tenths of a millimetre thick and consists of ninety-eight per cent calcium carbonate and phosphate and two per cent organic matter. In the latter are certain pigments, particularly porphyrins, which are present in considerable quantities when the egg is laid, but which change rapidly on exposure to light. The shell is pierced by countless small pores through which the embryo obtains the air it needs.

Lining the inner surface of the shell is the shell-membrane which consists of an inner and an outer layer, between which air is accumulated at one end, this air-filled cavity being known as the air cell. Its extent, which may be seen by holding the egg up to the light, is a rough indication of the age of the egg.

Immediately inside the shell-membrane lies the albumen or white of the egg, which makes up nearly half the total weight. It is a watery, viscous solution of albuminous substances containing mineral salts as well as amino-acids, two of which (lysine and tryptophane) are especially important as growth factors.

The yolk is suspended within the albumen and is, strictly speaking, the egg or ovum, that is, the part which enters the oviduct from the ovary. It is enclosed in a thin membrane and is held in position in the centre of the egg by two twisted threads of albumen, the chalazae. It is made up of two parts: the germinal disc, which is the only living part and which gives rise to the embryo; and the yolk or vitellus, a collection of protein substances destined to nourish the embryo. The yolk also contains the yellow colouring matter which varies according to the amount of herbage the hen eats. Among wild birds the colour of the yolk varies from very pale yellow to a dark red, almost a maroon; as far as a panel of experts could tell the eggs of all bird species were edible.

An egg which comes from the ovary of a diseased hen may contain disease germs; it is also possible for germs to be introduced into the oviduct during copulation or to pass through the pores of the shell. As long as the egg is fresh and viable these germs are destroyed by antibodies in the albumen, but when this starts to lose its

Wild birds and their eggs

Species	Number of eggs per clutch	Number of clutches per year	Mean size: length × greatest width (mm)	Usual colour of the eggs	Length of incubation (days)
Albatross, Royal	1–2	1	103 × 65	White	77–80
Auk	1–2	1	75 × 47	Brown with dark spots	30
Avocet, European	3–5	1	50 × 35	Speckled grey	24
Blackbird, European	4–5	2–3	29 × 21	Greenish	15
Bustard, Little	3–4	1–2	52 × 38	Pale, spotted	21
Buzzard, Common	2–4	1	57 × 45	White with brown spots	30
Coot	6–9	2–3	52 × 36	Speckled grey	23
Cormorant, Great	3–4	1–2	65 × 40	Pale blue, chalky	28
Corncrake	6–14	1–2	37 × 27	Grey with brown spots	15
Dove, Turtle	1–3	2	31 × 23	White	14
Duck, Common Eider	4–10	1	77 × 51	Greyish green	28
Eagle, Golden	1–3	1	77 × 60	White with red spots	42
Falcon, Peregrine	3–4	1	52 × 40	White with brown spots	29
Flamingo, Greater	2	1	90 × 54	Chalky white	32
Gannet, Northern	1–2	1	78 × 49	Bluish, chalky	44
Goldfinch, European	5–6	2–3	17 × 13	White with brown spots	14
Goose, Greylag	3–7	1	85 × 58	Whitish	28
Grebe, Great Crested	3–4	1–2	55 × 37	Whitish, chalky	28
Grouse, Black	5–8	1	57 × 41	Yellowish with brown spots	26
Grouse, Hazel	8–10	1	40 × 35	Reddish	21
Guillemot (Common Murre)	1	1	81 × 50	Spotted, colour variable	29
Gull, Herring	2–4	1	70 × 48	Olive green with brown spots	26
Heron, Grey	3–5	1–2	60 × 43	Bluish green	28
Jackdaw	4–6	1	36 × 25	Greenish with brown spots	18
Kingfisher, European	2–7	2	22 × 19	Lustrous white	20
Lapwing, European	3–5	1	47 × 34	Yellowish with black spots	28
Lark	3–4	2–3	24 × 17	Yellowish with brown spots	12
Magpie, European	5–8	1	34 × 24	Greenish with brown spots	18
Mallard	7–14	1–2	57 × 40	Greenish	26
Moorhen	5–10	2–3	44 × 31	Reddish with brown spots	21
Nightingale	4–5	1	21 × 16	Brownish green	14
Nightjar	2	2	32 × 22	White with brown spots	18
Ostrich	12–15	1	150 × 130	Ivory white	45
Owl, Barn	4–6	1–2	40 × 32	White	32
Owl, Brown	2–4	1	47 × 39	White	30
Owl, Eagle	2–3	1	60 × 50	White	35
Owl, Little	4–5	1–2	35 × 29	White	28
Owl, Long-eared	4–5	1–2	40 × 32	White	28
Oystercatcher	2–4	1	57 × 40	Light brown with dark spots	27
Partridge, Red-legged	10–16	1	41 × 31	Yellowish and spotted	24
Pheasant, Ring-necked	8–15	1	46 × 36	Olive green	25
Plover, Golden	3–4	1	52 × 36	Yellowish with brown spots	28
Puffin, Common	1–2	1	61 × 42	White, frequently spotted	42
Quail, European	7–12	1–2	30 × 13	Brown with dark spots	20
Robin, European	5–6	2	19 × 15	Yellowish with brown spots	14
Ruff	3–4	1	44 × 31	Greenish with black spots	21
Snipe, Common	3–5	1–2	40 × 28	Yellowish with brown spots	20
Sparrowhawk, European	4–5	1	40 × 32	White with red spots	35
Starling, European	6–7	1–2	30 × 21	Bluish	13
Stork, European Common	3–5	1	73 × 52	White	30
Swallow, Barn	4–5	2–3	20 × 14	White, with or without spots	15
Swift, European Common	2–4	1	31 × 19	White	20
Thrush, Song	4–5	2–3	28 × 21	Greenish white	14
Tree-creeper (Brown Creeper)	5–7	1–2	15 × 12	White with brown spots	15
Vulture, Griffon	1	1	90 × 70	White	51
Woodcock, European	3–5	2	44 × 33	Brown with red spots	21
Woodpecker, Green	5–7	1	32 × 23	White	18
Wood Pigeon	1–3	3	41 × 30	White	17

vitality the germs are able to multiply and become a possible source of infection for the consumer.

ABNORMAL EGGS: Eggs are sometimes soft-shelled, that is, they are surrounded merely by the elastic shell-membrane and are without the calcium carbonate and phosphates. This abnormality results from some physiological malfunction such as a secretionary upset or a nutritional deficiency such as lack of calcium in the diet. Often all that is needed for captive birds to return to normal shell formation is the addition of ground-up oyster-shells to their food.

Double or triple-yolked eggs are another abnormality, caused by two or three ovarian eggs entering the oviduct together and then becoming surrounded by a single coat of albumen and a single shell. Such eggs are, however, extremely rare; statistics show that in poultry only one out of every 500,000 eggs has two yolks, while only one out of every 25,000,000 eggs has three yolks.

Yolkless eggs are also recorded, but very rarely. These are much smaller than normal eggs; in the case of the Domestic Hen, for example, they are about the size of a Pigeon's egg. There was once a widespread belief that these eggs were laid by cocks, and it was also said that the twisted

chalazae inside were snake embryos. The explanation is that the hen is suffering from a constriction of the oviduct which prevents the entry of the ovarian egg or yolk, with the result that only the white and the shell can be formed. An extremely rare abnormality is an egg with another smaller but quite complete egg inside it. The variations and abnormalities described above for the Domestic Chicken are equally likely to occur among the eggs of other birds.

INCUBATION AND EMBRYONIC DEVELOPMENT: There are two aspects to incubation: sitting and the development of the egg. Both go on until the egg is hatched, and in general the former is essential to the latter because the egg must be kept at a fairly constant temperature to allow the embryo to develop normally.

Sitting may begin immediately after the first egg is laid or it may be delayed until the last one is laid (as in most passerines). Usually it is the female that incubates the eggs, but the male may relieve her or even be responsible for most of the incubation. In some of the sea-birds, such as penguins and albatrosses, each parent may incubate the egg continuously for two weeks or longer, while the other parent returns to the sea to feed. In some species (phalaropes, rheas, cassowaries, painted snipes, button-quails) the male assumes the tasks of the female and not only builds the nest, but also sits on the eggs and guards the young.

The period of incubation varies largely with the size of the bird, the European Cuckoo taking about eleven days, the Linnet twelve days, the Bullfinch fourteen days, the Barn Swallow fifteen days, the Wren about fifteen days, the Domestic Fowl twenty-one days, swans about thirty-three days, the California Condor fifty-five days, and the Emu fifty-eight days. The Royal Albatross requires particularly long incubation: seventy-seven to eighty days. By contrast, the Ostrich, the largest living bird, takes only forty-five days.

The first stage in the development of an embryo is the division of the fertilised ovum into two cells, then into four, eight, sixteen and so on, until they become quite numerous. In eggs not heavily laden with yolk the division is complete. In a heavily yolked bird's egg, cell division is confined to the germinal disc which then spreads across a part of the yolk to form a blastoderm. As viewed at low magnification, it has the appearance of the cracked glazing on old pottery. In section the blastoderm is seen to consist of three superimposed layers, which are no more than the embryonic layers (ectoderm, mesoderm and endoderm) found in most animals.

The endoderm, the innermost layer, continues to spread round the yolk until it has encircled it completely. This forms the vitelline sac which resembles that in the embryos of fishes. This sac hangs below the ventral part of the embryo, ultimately to become a part of the belly of the young. Yolk is gradually transferred to the body of the embryo by way of blood vessels, through enzymatic processes acting upon this yolk to reduce the size of its molecules (to amino-acids) which can be assimilated in the embryo body.

Simultaneously, two other embryonic organs are formed. There is a second sac, the allantois, which communicates with the hind end of the gut and comes to lie close to the shell. Like the vitelline

Unlike altricial young precocial species, like the Mallard shown here, are born open-eyed, with a covering of fine down and are fully active. They are nidifugous, leaving the parental nest immediately or soon after hatching.

Garden Warbler (*Sylvia borin*) chicks in their nest. They are three days old, their eyes are not yet opened, and at this stage, at the slightest vibration of the nest, they automatically thrust their heads upwards at the same time gaping wide. The action is innate and assists the parents when bringing food.

sac, the allantois is provided with numerous blood vessels which have important functions. The allantois is, in fact, both a respiratory organ and part of the excretory system of the embryo. Then there is a third sac, the amnion, which surrounds the embryo. This sac is derived from the ectoderm, not from the endoderm, and forms a protective covering. It is filled with amniotic fluid, which both supports the body of the embryo and prevents its desiccation.

While these membranous organs are developing, many other changes are taking place within the embryo. First, a groove develops along the dorsal surface. Its edges fold inwards and eventually join to form a neural tube, which later gives rise to the brain and to the spinal nerve cord. Below this (ectodermal) neural groove lies the notochord, which is an axial rod derived mostly from the endoderm; in later development it becomes a part of the vertebrae. Along this axis appear the muscle segments and the remainder of the vertebrae. The eyes, which are always formed at an early embryonic stage from the three germ layers, appear in the head, and the gill pouches appear on the sides of the neck, like those in young fishes. The foremost pair develops into the auditory capsules, while the others eventually close up and disappear. One of the first organs to appear is the heart. Later the limbs form.

As the nutrient materials are used up, the form of a bird gradually begins to emerge. When embryonic development is complete the young bird breaks the shell, sometimes having an egg-tooth on its beak to facilitate this process. This tooth is subsequently shed.

DEVELOPMENT OF THE CHICK: There are two kinds of hatchlings, one born in an advanced state and the other in a retarded state of development. The first are born with their eyes open and can run about almost as soon as they hatch. Such chicks are said to be precocial. They may also be nidifugous, that is, able to leave the nest at once. Their bodies are covered with down feathers and their reserves of fat are sufficient to sustain them until they can find their own food. The second type are born blind and helpless, and have neither feathers nor food reserves. These altricial chicks, as they are called, consequently must remain in the nest for a time. They are nidicolous, unable to leave the nest and dependent on parental care and feeding. Pigeons are fed with a milky secretion from the parent's crop. Birds with precocial chicks are fowls, ducks, gulls, ostriches and others. Those with altricial chicks include pigeons, birds of prey, passerine and piciform birds.

Bird migration

Among the familiar sights of autumn in the northern hemisphere are the swallows preparing to fly south and the formations of wild ducks, geese, cranes, storks and other large migrant birds passing overhead. Few other living creatures make such long and regular migratory journeys. Recent scientific studies are beginning to reveal convincingly why birds migrate, how their journeys are made, how far they go, and what routes they take.

Snow Geese (*Anser caerulescens*) in their winter quarters in New Mexico having spent the summer in Canada and Alaska.

353

The information on which these conclusions have been based has been obtained in a number of ways, one of them being bird ringing. Bird ringing, or banding as it is known in North America, provides information about the movements of birds, the routes used by migrants, and, on occasion, the approximate time they have been travelling, as well as the duration of their visits. The bird is either taken from the nest or is trapped, care being taken not to harm it, and a numbered band of monel or aluminium alloy is fixed round one of its legs.

Thousands of birds are ringed in this way each year and all those concerned with shooting or trapping birds—or anyone finding a dead ringed bird—are asked to report the finding. If the bird is captured unharmed the information on the ring should be recorded and the bird released. The authority concerned should then be notified. If a foreign ring is found the authority in the country where it is recovered will forward the information.

FACTORS DETERMINING MIGRATION: Two of the best-known European migrant birds are the Swallow (*Hirundo rustica*) and the related House Martin (*Delichon urbica*), both of which nest in the temperate parts of Europe from April to September. As they arrive in small groups at the beginning of spring they start to build their nests, the Swallows on rafters in barns or stables, the Martins typically under the eaves, but both may nest anywhere else that is sheltered from the wind and rain. The male and female share in building the nest of mud, which they line with down. In it the eggs are laid, brooded and hatched, and the young reared. Bringing up the brood and feeding them on insects caught in flight keep the parents busy until the time comes for the young to learn to fly and to be capable of fending for themselves.

Spring and summer slip by while all this is going on, and with the last days of September, the shorter days, the birds become restless. They tend to fly around in small parties, but mainly they gather in groups on roofs and on telegraph wires. This is a characteristic sight which warns the countryman that he will awaken one morning soon to find the Swallows and the Martins gone. After a journey of several thousand kilometres they arrive from October onwards in the Sudan, in West Africa and in many parts of southern Africa, even at the Cape of Good Hope. Here they spend the non-breeding part of their year.

If a bird's homeland is where it nests and rears its young, then Europe is the homeland of the Swallow. It would be therefore emigrating when flying from Europe to Africa, and immigrating when it comes back; the complete migration is the outward and the return journey between breeding place and winter (or non-breeding) residence. Fundamentally, the immediate cause of migration is related to the secretory activity of the birds' sexual organs but initially, it is supposed, the migratory habit evolved because of the need for food. These two determining factors are also found in fish migrations—eels, salmon, and tunny—where the migrants travel each year to spawning areas (breeding migration) and feeding grounds (feeding migration).

Swallows complete the outward journey in a single flight. There may, of course, be short rests on the way, but there will be no long stops along the migratory route. Swallows are able to make this long trip because they moult before they leave. In this they are unlike several species of wild ducks, which nest in the far north of Asia and leave early for the Caspian and certain of the Tibetan lakes, where the summer moult occurs. Only in autumn do they move on into India and Africa and complete the second phase of their emigration after moulting. There is thus a breeding place, a moulting place, and a non-breeding place. Since there is no moulting on a return trip, there is no long stop.

In countries in the middle latitudes, and with temperate climates, there are three kinds of migratory birds: summer residents that breed in a particular area (e.g. in European species, swallows, and in American species, the Red-eyed Vireo); winter visitors that nest further north in summer (e.g. greylag geese in Great Britain and the American Wigeon or Baldpate in the United States); birds that pass over the country during their outward and return journeys (e.g. in Europe, cranes, and in America, the Sanderling that breeds in Alaska but stays in southern Argentina during the northern winter).

In all three types of migration breeding grounds are distinct from winter quarters. In tropical areas, however, there is no such distinction, as reproduction is not so restricted by factors of time and place. Migrations do occur here, but these are probably caused by the need to find food; the Sulphur-bellied Flycatcher (*Myiodynastes luteiventris*) of Central America, for example, flies further south.

Birds are normally selective in their food, and with their high degree of mobility they can fly to where the kind of food they require is available. Locust-eating birds will follow swarms of these insects, while birds of prey will appear in large numbers during the dry season when bush fires drive small animals out of their hiding places and make them easy victims. Intertropical hummingbirds can hardly be said to migrate, but they regularly fly several hundred kilometres in search of the nectar they require.

One of the most curious patterns of bird movement is that of the Pennant-winged Nightjar (*Macrodipteryx vexillarius*), which is insectivorous and catches flies while on the wing. The insects on which it feeds are particularly abundant during the rainy season, and the Nightjar follows a strict schedule of migration determined by these flies. This bird lives in the savanna regions of southern Africa during the spring rains, from September to December. Then from January to March it migrates northwards, passing over the equatorial forest and settling in the savanna country of northern Africa (Sudan), again during the season of spring rains from April to June. In July and August it crosses back over the forest zone and returns to its point of departure. Nesting takes place south of the equator and moulting occurs north of it.

As a general rule, species whose range of food is limited make the longest journeys. Of European migratory birds, the great majority are aquatic or insectivorous in habit. Aquatic birds leave shortly before the lower temperatures reduce the food supply in their normal habitats; similarly, insectivorous birds do not winter in regions where insect food is scarce. Grain-eating and omnivorous birds migrate only to a limited extent, while woodpeckers and similar birds which find their prey, winter and summer alike, in the trunks of trees are among the few that do not migrate.

However, the European Quail (*Coturnix coturnix*), which winters on the shores of the Mediterranean and even further south in Egypt and tropical Africa, is the only gallinaceous bird with a granivorous diet to undertake such lengthy migrations. It may be that whereas most species of quail are intertropical, the European one has extended its breeding grounds far to the north only to return each year to its ancestral feeding area.

A knowledge of the history of each species of bird during the glacial periods would be of great help in explaining bird migrations. Changes of habitat would follow changes in climate and the extensions or reductions of a territory might well explain the present behaviour of the species. It is likely, for example, that during the retreat of the glaciers in the late Cainozoic era in northern Europe and in America a number of birds were able to extend their range northwards. They might thus have been led into regions where the winter conditions force them to go southwards each year. Many present-day bird species had evolved long before the Ice Age, but the conditions of that time have probably influenced the pattern of their distribution.

In other words the present-day migrations of many birds may well be related to those they made in the past. It could be concluded that the migratory habit is merely a form of adaptation to changing conditions on the earth's surface, and one which has become modified according to time and place. Thus birds appear to have become highly successful in withstanding such changes.

Very different are those migrations which are usually called irruptions. These can hardly be explained by any of the foregoing hypotheses. They may occur at intervals of years, or of decades, and have no relation to breeding behaviour, for those birds subject to them breed at any time and anywhere. Such irruptions bring certain European birds to Great Britain, such as the Crossbill (*Loxia curvirostra*), and the Waxwing (*Bombycilla garrulus*), and of an Asian species, Pallas's Sandgrouse (*Syrrhaptes paradoxus*).

Crossbills appear irregularly over a large part of western Europe, though normally they are seen only occasionally in certain mountain woods, their true habitat extending over the great coniferous forests of northern Europe. There they nest and feed on conifer seeds. During some years these birds have roamed as far afield as Great Britain and southwestern France. What is remarkable is the Crossbill's ability to adapt itself to local foods quite different from those of its northern habitat. It has been observed feeding on grapes, sunflower seeds, apple pips and damaged fruit. Often many birds die in migration, but by the beginning of winter the survivors return to their habitual surroundings.

METHODS OF MIGRATION: Migratory birds do not all make their journeys in the same manner. Social birds, such as swallows, bee-eaters, and others which normally live together in flocks, retain their social instincts during migration, departing and travelling together. Similar social migratory tendencies are also exhibited by some birds that are solitary and aggressive during the breeding season; for example, most of the small singing birds of Europe, such as warblers, finches, robins, wrens, old-world fly-catchers, and so on. When they migrate their aggressive instincts wane and they become gregarious, individuals of different species often congregating in one flock. There are also other solitary birds, the Golden Oriole and many birds of prey among them, which not only live alone during the non-migratory period but also travel alone. Their movements are, more often than not, so isolated that they pass unnoticed, little more being observed than that they are here at one time of year and absent at another.

The method of flying may also vary a great deal with the species. Most of the small passerine birds travel in dense groups without any particular formation, but ducks, geese, cranes, storks and others fly high in skein, line or V-formations. There is a double advantage in this kind of formation flying; visibility is increased and flying made easier for the individual because there is continuous flight in a single direction. These flight patterns have the advantage of each participant being able to 'see' where he is going.

Passerine birds usually travel at night and rest by day, which tends to give them better protection against birds of prey. It is these night flyers that are sometimes attracted to lighthouses or beacons where many are killed as they dash themselves against the glass of the light. Wading birds and web-footed birds will travel by night or by day, and often cover long distances without a rest. Birds generally take off into the wind and, like gliders, take advantage of the air currents at different altitudes. They usually avoid severe atmospheric disturbances, although they may be caught up in cyclones or violent storms. Otherwise birds tend to keep the same compass course regardless of weather conditions. This may explain the presence each year in Great Britain of many American stragglers and vice versa.

Direct observation and radar tracking have both recently provided some detailed and exact information on the height and speed of bird flight. Flocks of geese, for example, have been seen flying at a height of 2,500 metres above the North Sea during a storm, while others have been plotted by radar at a height of 1,500 metres and over a distance of 128 kilometres. The flight of small passerine birds is influenced by the force and direction of the wind and altitude is usually less than 90 metres. The intensity of light, visibility, rain and the presence of trees will also influence the height. The average speed of flight during a migration may be high: radar plotting has shown that some geese fly at an average speed of thirty-eight kilometres an hour. As for length of flight, a Finch has flown 600 kilometres in a day and a Shrike 200 kilometres.

Flying is not the only means of locomotion during migration. Penguins from the antarctic regions may occasionally swim long distances.

MIGRATORY ROUTES: There are two interesting features of migratory routes: direction and distance.

The view that birds fly along straight lines, linking the equatorial regions with temperate and cold areas is an oversimplification

Information provided by bird ringing or banding has proved that our knowledge of migration is still far from complete. The first factors to be taken into account are the great natural barriers which birds seek to avoid: oceans, seas, deserts and mountain chains. European passerine birds migrating to Africa tend to avoid long passages over the Mediteranean, preferring one of the shorter sea-routes from Spain to Morocco, from Italy and Sicily to Tunisia, and from Asia Minor to Egypt. North American migratory birds heading for South America fly either to Venezuela by way of the Isthmus of Panama or across Florida, Cuba and Yucatan, but seldom over the West Indies. The importance of natural barriers can be overstressed, since there are striking instances of birds crossing the most formidable of such obstacles. Deserts, for example, are often crossed and oases are used as stopping places, and there are instances of the Sahara being used as a winter retreat. The Himalayas are crossed in both directions by geese (*Anser indicus*) and cranes (*Grus grus*) as they fly between their nesting grounds on the high plateaus of Asia and their winter quarters in India. The Alps and the Caucasus Mountains are also crossed by high-flying migrants.

In the Mediterranean, migrating European robins, swallows, wagtails and starlings are quite commonly seen from ships and they will sometimes perch on board, even on rare occasions remaining for the entire crossing.

When passerines have a long sea crossing ahead, they might be expected to fly high. In fact this is seldom so. Individuals of all species often fly low over the water, zigzagging along with frequent changes of course, twisting and turning above the waves as they utilise up-currents of air.

Waterbirds, of course, do not appear to be deterred by the vast stretches of ocean to be crossed in the course of their migrations. The Tahitian or Bristle-thighed Curlew (*Numenius tahitiensis*) is a particularly good example, as it travels for thousands of kilometres across the Pacific between the various islands where it winters and Alaska where it nests.

Arctic Terns make some of the longest migratory journeys of all. They nest in northern Europe, Asia and Alaska, and then travel far down into the southern hemisphere to the Antarctic where they spend the southern summer. Often they will fly between 12,000 and 15,200 kilometres each way along the coasts or over the sea. Their migrations are thus the reverse of those of Wilson's Storm Petrel (*Oceanites oceanicus*), which nests in the southern hemisphere.

The migrations of the Arctic Tern (*Sterna paradisea*) provide an interesting comparison with those of the Great Shearwater (*Puffinus gravis*). From June to August, the northern summer, the Tern nests and the Petrel resides without nesting in northern Europe. Between September and November both species migrate to the southern hemisphere, and during the southern summer from December to March it is the Tern that is the resident and the Shearwater that nests in southern Africa. Both then return north in April and May.

The reversal of the seasons in the two hemispheres leads to even more remarkable results. During the cold Asian winter between October and March, the Malayan archipelago is the refuge of many birds: wagtails, cuckoos, plovers and herons. From April to September, on the other hand, a number of very different species settle

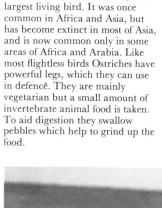

The Ostrich (*Struthio camelus*) is the largest living bird. It was once common in Africa and Asia, but has become extinct in most of Asia, and is now common only in some areas of Africa and Arabia. Like most flightless birds Ostriches have powerful legs, which they can use in defence. They are mainly vegetarian but a small amount of invertebrate animal food is taken. To aid digestion they swallow pebbles which help to grind up the food.

there to escape their own winter. These include bee-eaters, kingfishers, cuckoos and pratincoles from Australia. The Malayan archipelago forms therefore a vast reception area for migrants coming alternately from north and south.

Considered generally, bird migrations appear to be periodic movements made necessary in the first place by food requirements, especially of the young, but initiated by hormone stimulation of the reproductive organs. But all the records, studies and attempts at explanation still leave us unable to understand this remarkable phenomenon. We do not know why birds begin their flight as large groups, why they pass over the same regions each year, or how young birds that have never flown over the area before can stay on course. Of one thing we are sure: migration is a dynamic response in every sense of the term. For a discussion of navigation see p. 420.

Running birds

The Ostrich and its allies are for convenience often grouped together as ratites (from the flat or 'raft-like' sternum) or running birds. Their principal identifying characteristics are flightlessness and anatomical modifications such as a flat sternum and the heavy legs associated with a terrestrial mode of life. All other birds are known as carinate birds because, unlike the flightless ratites, they have a keeled sternum or carina. The carina is a ridge of bone that increases the surface area of the sternum and so provides a greater area for the paired flight muscles, which are larger and more powerful than in the ratites. Other differences include the reduction of the clavicles and a wide angle between the scapula and coracoid, immovably articulated with each other to form the glenoid cavity which receives the head of the humerus, the bone of the upper wing. The clavicles brace the upper ribs and strengthen the glenoid fossa in carinate birds. The ribs of the ratites are without the uncinate processes which ordinarily lend suppleness and solidity to the thorax. Their bones have no air cavities and are therefore heavier than those in other orders. Externally the wings are considerably reduced in size or absent altogether. The wing feathers are modified either as soft plumes or as spike-like shafts. They are not air-resistant. All these features appear to be adaptive and associated with loss of flight; their occurrence throughout the different families of ratites therefore does not indicate any affinities between them. It seems more likely that the ratites come from different groups of flying birds where these modifications have arisen independently.

The ratites are very well adapted to running in the desert and the savannas of the Old and New Worlds; the cassowaries, however, are forest dwellers. Feet are long and strong, usually with a small number of toes, as in the ungulate mammals. They are palaeognathous birds, that is, they have a primitive palate, a taxonomic feature of some importance. They include the cassowaries, rheas, emus and a large number of fossil forms or species that have recently become extinct. The order Tinamiformes, which contains many species of South American partridge-like birds with weak flight, and the Apterygiformes, now represented by the flightless Kiwi, share certain ratite features.

Starting with the Ostriches there are twenty-eight orders of birds divided into 161 families, totalling about 8,700 species.

Ostriches (Order Struthioniformes)

Ostriches are the largest of living birds, some males weighing as much as 155 kilograms and standing 244 centimetres. Weight, small wing area, and inadequate wing feathers and flight muscles combine to make them flightless. It is not unusual, however, for Ostriches to run at speeds of forty to sixty kilometres an hour. Normally they run with folded wings, but these can be used to help the birds to turn or brake.

The Ostrich's wings are very small, and the feathers soft, with pendant barbs and short barbules that have no interlocking mechanism. A line of wing quills of this composition runs along the margins of the wings and there are three superimposed layers of wing coverts. A singular feature is that two of the wing fingers end in claws or spurs that can be used in attack. The rest of the plumage exhibits the same softness and structure as the wings. There are no rectrices, their place being taken by elongated tail coverts. The legs are long, strong and almost without feathers. There are only two toes, of unequal length, and the larger one ends in a nail. This is the greatest reduction in the number of toes exhibited by any bird. The Ostrich has a long neck, much of it bare of feathers, and a small, flat head terminating in a rounded beak with a huge gape. The eyes are large, and the upper lid has lashes.

Only one species of Ostrich survives and this is found in Africa and Arabia. Its great stature, its gait and the fact that it lives in the desert, explain why in ancient times it was compared to that other desert animal, the camel. Hence its specific name *Struthio camelus* (ostrich camel).

There are several races of Ostrich which interbreed in captivity and produce fertile crosses. In Africa there is a Northern and a Southern Ostrich, the first is found in Algeria, Tunisia and the Sudan, the second in the Transvaal, Natal and Cape Province. The differences between them are pronounced. The Northern Ostrich is larger and has a bare patch on the top of its head, which appears when the chicks are two months old. The skin of the hen bird is bright yellow and that of the cock scarlet, while the skin of the Southern Ostrich is light grey and dark blue in hen and cock respectively.

The plumage of these two races is very similar. Young birds and hens have grey-brown body plumage, turning to black at the tail and near the wings; the tail and wing feathers are a dirty white. The cocks have magnificent plumage, ebony black on the body, with pure white wing quills and huge tail coverts.

The Ostrich inhabits desert and savanna, though never straying very far from water, of which it needs about seven litres a day. It is omnivorous, but mainly vegetarian. In captivity its stomach sometimes contains an extraordinary variety of objects, because of its habit of picking up and swallowing bright or metallic objects. It is gregarious and lives in large flocks, often in company with antelopes and zebras.

The Double-wattled Cassowary (*Casuarius casuarius*) of Australia and New Guinea. The female lays two to three eggs and leaves the male to incubate them and care for the young. Living in the jungle, the prominent growth of bone may help to protect the Cassowary's head as it moves swiftly through the dense thorny undergrowth.

Opposite
The Gentoo Penguin (*Pygoscelis papua*) breeds in large colonies on the South Shetlands and other antarctic islands. This picture shows the ease with which a penguin moves in water emphasising its complete adaptation to swimming. Two eggs are usually laid in a nest on the ground and hatch after an incubation of seventy-two days.

Ostriches breed in the spring and are polygamous. Mating takes place after an elaborate courtship display. The cock makes the nest, a mere scrape in the sand about ninety centimetres across and thirty centimetres deep. The hens lay their eggs in the shared nest and both cock and the senior hen sit in turn until the eggs hatch. The eggs are about fifteen centimetres long and twelve centimetres in diameter. Each weighs about 1,200 grams and has a thick, tough, ivory coloured shell. Incubation takes from forty-two to forty-eight days. The baby Ostrich is precocial and at birth is about the size of a Domestic Hen. The cock and hen look after and protect the chicks.

Rheas (Order Rheiformes)
There are two species in this order, the Commom Rhea (*Rhea americana*) and Darwin's Rhea (*Pterocnemia pennata*).

The Common Rhea lives in flocks on the pampas and savannas, feeding on vegetable matter or small mammals, according to the season. Sometimes it joins a herd of cattle, feeding

with them on clover and lucerne. It is neither as large as the Ostrich (the cock's maximum height is 170 centimetres) nor so striking. The plumage of both cock and hen is blackish on the head and on the top of the neck, yellow and ashen grey on the body, and dirty white on the belly. The neck is partly feathered, and in this respect it differs from that of the Ostrich. Each foot has three clawed toes webbed at the base.

In spring the cocks become very aggressive as they select and segregate their harems of three to seven hens. Courtship is brief. The cock digs the nest and sits on the eggs. There may be as many as fifty eggs laid by several females, lemon yellow when first laid and weighing as much as 800 grams. Incubation takes forty days.

Emus and cassowaries (Order Casuariformes)
Two families make up the order, the emu (family Dromaiidae) and the cassowary (family Casuariidae). The Common Emu (*Dromaius novaehollandiae*) is the second largest living bird, the cock often standing over 200 centimetres high. It is very like the Common Rhea in that its neck is partly feathered and it has three toes. The plumage of both cock and hen is deep brown, the feathers have two shafts diverging from the base.

Emus are found throughout mainland Australia and their habits are similar to those of other ratites, except that they are monogamous and their courtship is more prolonged. The cock bird makes the nest and hatches the brood. The eggs number fifteen or more and are a fine green colour. Each weighs about 270 grams. Incubation takes two months.

The Common Cassowary (*Casuarius casuarius*) differs from the other ratites: its plumage has the look of fur rather than feathers and it has a helmet or bony crest on its head (*see* p. 343). The wing quills are reduced to stiff rods which hang over its flanks. Head and neck are partly bare and brightly coloured: yellow, green, blue, violet and red. Some individuals have similarly coloured neck wattles. The rest of the body is all brown or black. Males and females are alike and stand some 140 centimetres high. There are three toes on each foot.

Cassowaries are found in northern Australia, New Guinea and parts of Polynesia. Geographical isolation has led to the evolution of several species distinguished from one another by the presence or absence of wattles, as well as the colouring of the neck. Unlike the Ostrich, rheas and emus, the cassowaries are solitary and usually timid. Their normal habitat is the forests.

Kiwi (Order Apterygiformes)
The kiwis of New Zealand are now rare survivors of this diminished ratite order. There is a single family, Apterygidae, made up of three species: the Common Brown Kiwi (*Apteryx australis*), the Greater Spotted Kiwi (*Apteryx haasti*) and the Little Spotted Kiwi (*Apteryx oweni*). No larger than a Hen, the Common Brown Kiwi has four toes and a long, pointed and curved bill with nostrils near the tip. Its wings are so short that they are hidden beneath its body plumage, which is more like hair than feathers. It has no tail. Both male and female are iron brown.

Kiwis are nocturnal, remaining hidden in the forest during the day and emerging at night to feed on earthworms, insects, larvae, soft fruits and leaves. It is then that they utter the cries of *ki-i-wi*. The scientific name, *Apteryx*, means 'without wings'. They can run and jump with surprising speed and are lively, graceful creatures. The hens lay a single egg in a hollow roughly lined with moss. The egg is white and relatively large for the size of the birds.

Tinamous (Order Tinamiformes)

The neotropical tinamous look remarkably like game birds, and the smallest is the size of a Quail. Size apart, there is a close uniformity of appearance throughout the group. Although they are carinate birds, palate structure has determined classification of the fifty species with the palaeognathous birds. But unlike other palaeognathous orders the tinamous can fly, although not very strongly. The tails of some species retain the down feathers.

Most of the tinamous inhabit the dense rainforests of South America and colouring is cryptic to afford protection. Two of the commonest species are the Variegated Tinamou (*Crypturellus variegatus*) and the Crested Tinamou (*Eudromia elegans*), a species of the open pampas.

The eggs, which are laid on the ground, their shiny surfaces blending into the wet, glistening moss and leaves of the forest floor, are the most strikingly beautiful found among birds. Some have the look of burnished metal, but most have the appearance of glazed porcelain in pale pastel grey, lilac and primrose, or olive and dark reds, purples and even blacks. These are incubated by the male.

Penguins (Order Sphenisciformes)

Confined to the southern hemisphere, penguins

form a separate order of flightless birds comprising six genera: *Aptenodytes*, *Pygoscelis*, *Eudyptes*, *Megadyptes*, *Eudyptula* and *Spheniscus*. They are the most completely marine of all birds and are able to swim underwater as fast as seals. Webbed toes and wings reduced to form strong flippers that cannot be folded mark their adaptation to their environment.

Ashore they are, of course, bipedal, with an awkward gait. Their diet is mixed, consisting mainly of fish, crustaceans and small squids. They are a gregarious and monogamous order, nesting in large colonies. The male takes an active part in rearing the young.

The Kiwi (*Apteryx australis*) lives in the dense evergreen forests of New Zealand and as the symbol of the country it has appeared on stamps and coins. The bill is long and flexible and unique in having the nostrils at the tip, indicating that the bird finds its food more by smell than sight.

Aptenodytes is a genus which includes the two largest species of this order: the Emperor Penguin (*Aptenodytes forsteri*) and the King Penguin (*A. patagonica*), 120 and 150 centimetres long respectively.

Pygoscelis, also an Antarctic genus, includes the Adélie Penguin (*Pygoscelis adeliae*) and the Gentoo Penguin (*P. papua*). Both are about sixty centimetres long.

The Rockhopper Penguin (*Eudyptes crestatus*) and the Macaroni Penguin (*E. chrysolophus*) belong to the genus *Eudyptes*, common in New Zealand and subantarctic islands. The Yellow-eyed Penguin (*Megadyptes antipodes*) is the only species of its genus.

Eudyptula, a genus of small species, includes the Fairy Penguin (*Eudyptula minor*) and the White-flippered Penguin (*E. albosignata*).

The sixth genus, *Spheniscus*, includes the African Jackass Penguin (*Spheniscus demersus*) and several South American species of medium size.

Divers and loons (Order Gaviiformes)

These are web-footed birds well adapted to swimming and diving, but with short wings that restrict flight. They spend their lives on or in the water, yet occasionally make long flights. Once in the air, they fly strongly. The position of the legs, well back on the body, is indicative of their aquatic habits. Divers are the only birds with legs completely encased in skin. Only the tarsi are exposed, protruding at the rear of the body like twin propellors. Like grebes, they are fast surface swimmers, and partly because their bones are relatively solid and not fully pneumatic they can, by expelling the air from body and plumage, also submerge themselves with barely a ripple to reveal

A King Penguin (*Aptenodytes patagonica*) incubating its single egg. Male and female share the task. They build no nest but carry the egg in turn on their feet, covered with a fold of abdominal skin. The chick hatches in summer when food is plentiful and lays down a good supply of fat to last it over the winter. The following spring brings sufficient food to complete its development.

A vast rookery of Adélie Penguins (*Pygoscelis adeliae*). Adélies return to the rookery in October when the sea is still frozen. The nests are sited at the foot of icy slopes. Some birds return to the same nest site year after year. The two eggs are incubated in turns by the male and female while the other is away feeding at sea. The young chicks congregate in creches and leave to go to sea in February.

Top left
The Magellanic Penguin (*Spheniscus magellanicus*) with its chick. It has a striking piebald plumage, even its bill sometimes being sprinkled with white. It lives on islands off the South American coast nesting in burrows. Usually two eggs are laid. During the breeding season it feeds on cuttlefish found around the inshore kelp beds.

Top right
A nesting colony of the Rockhopper Penguin (*Eudyptes crestatus*). The rookery is usually sited on rocky islands where there is plenty of tussock grass, sometimes several hundred metres away from the sea. The Rockhopper is distinguished by the black feathers of the crown which are elongated into a crest and by narrow yellow lines from the forehead above the eye which fall in five plumes.

Bottom
The Black-throated Liver or Arctic Loon (*Gavia arctica*) is distributed round the North Pole, being absent only from Greenland and Iceland. It prefers to breed on large inland waters from which it can obtain plenty of food. The two olive-brown eggs with dark spots are laid in a scrape near the water's edge.

The Little Grebe (*Podiceps ruficollis*), also known as the Dabchick, is widespread across Europe and races are found throughout Asia and Africa, Australia and New Zealand. It nests on semi-floating vegetation on ponds and lakes, but is seldom found on open sea. Its food consists of aquatic insects, fishes and frogs.

The Great Crested Grebe (*Podiceps cristatus*). The crest which usually lies flat on the head is raised during a display that incorporates much head shaking. The nest is floating and composed of rotting vegetation. At the slightest alarm the bird covers the eggs with weeds and dives to safety so the pure white eggs soon become well stained and camouflaged.

their presence. Underwater propulsion is by the legs alone. Buoyancy can be increased by trapping pockets of air within the plumage.

Divers seldom leave the water, as they walk with difficulty on land. They prefer freshwater habitats in summer but in winter frequent salt water rather than fresh. They are found only in the northern hemisphere, mainly but not exclusively along the sea coasts of northern Europe and North America, with winter migration southwards. There are four species. The Red-throated Diver or Loon (*Gavia stellata*) is the smallest and the commonest. It nests in northern Asia, America and Europe. The Black-throated Diver or Arctic Loon (*G. arctica*) has an arctic-boreal distribution. The Great Northern Diver or Common Loon (*G. immer*) is a species found in the northern United States, Canada, Greenland and Iceland. The White-billed Diver or

Yellow-billed Loon (*G. adamsi*), on the other hand, is found in North America and Eurasia.

Adult plumage is similar in both sexes, with strong, bold contrasts of black and white in summer, and somewhat duller plumage in winter. Except during the breeding season the species are rather similar. Flight feathers are moulted simultaneously and during the ensuing flightless period the birds withdraw into protective solitude. Two eggs are laid by the water's edge. The main food is fish.

Grebes (Order Podicipediformes)

Although formerly placed in the same family and order as divers, grebes are now classified separately. The webbing is reduced to lobed fringeing membranes outlining only the three front toes, as it is in members of the coot family. The tail is reduced to a downy stump and the rectrices are atrophied.

Grebes usually prefer freshwater to salt and are often found on reed-fringed lakes and ponds, nesting in masses of floating vegetation. Distribution is world-wide. *Podiceps* is the largest, most widespread genus, with thirteen species. The other three genera are found only in the New World: the large Western Grebe (*Aechmophorus occidentalis*) of North America, the Pied-billed Grebe (*Podilymbus podiceps*), and the flightless Short-winged Grebe (*Centropelma micropterum*) of South America are representative species.

Plumage in all genera is striking. A short tail with a sheared-off look is also typical of the order. Short wings impose weak flight. Elaborate courtship and a curious habit of eating their own feathers is also common to them all. This last feature is still unexplained. Like the divers the grebes are able to expel the air from body and feathers and sink below the surface to safety.

The large genus *Podiceps* includes the dabchicks and the typical ornamented grebes. The commonest dabchicks are: the Least Grebe (*P. dominicus*) found in the southern United States and South America; the Little Grebe (*P. ruficollis*) about twenty-five centimetres, with bright red neck patches, found in the Arctic regions of the Old World and the eastern hemisphere; and Australia's Black-throated Little Grebe (*P. novaehollandiae*). It is usual to include among the dabchicks the Hoary-headed Grebe (*P. poliocephalus*) of Australia and the New Zealand Dabchick (*P. rufopectus*).

The ornamented forms include the Old World Great Crested Grebe (*P. cristatus*); three South American species, the Lesser Golden Grebe (*P. chilensis*), the Great Grebe (*P. major*) and the Silver Grebe (*P. occipitalis*); and the Horned Grebe (*P. auritus*), the Red-necked Grebe (*P. grisegena*) and Black-necked Grebe (*P. nigricollis*). The last three are common in North America and occur in the Old World too.

The Great Crested Grebe (*P. cristatus*), the largest and an inhabitant of the Old World, is about the size of a gull. It is identifiable by its long white neck and white front, which are in contrast to the brown upper parts. Two stiff tufts of black feathers project backwards from the head. In the breeding season the head of both male and female is framed by a fringe of rufous and black feathers.

As a prelude to nesting and breeding the pair indulge in an elaborate courtship behaviour of head-shaking, displaying, the presentation of nesting materials to each other, loud and excited vocal display, preening and, most characteristic, hard rushes towards each other until they meet and rise neck to neck and breast to breast. The hen lays three or four whitish eggs. The chicks leave the nest shortly after they are hatched and seek protection from time to time beneath the parental wings. It is quite common for the male or the female to carry the young on its back.

The Black-necked Grebe (*P. nigricollis*) differs from the Great Crested Grebe in its plumage. The upper parts are black, except for the red wings and a fan of yellow feathers behind each eye.

Albatrosses, shearwaters and petrels (Order Procellariiformes)

The essentially oceanic birds of this order seldom come to land except during the breeding season. The main characteristics are the hooked bill sheathed in horny plates and the long tubular nostrils. A variety of aquatic creatures make up their diet. They nest in a burrow, a depression in the ground or on a pile of soil and vegetation and lay only one egg. The chicks are altricial and are fed by regurgitation.

Albatrosses (Family Diomedeidae)

These large, long-winged birds have a strong, easy gliding flight that can be maintained over long distances. For the most part they belong to the southern hemisphere. There are two genera: *Diomedea* and *Phoebetria*. A few species occur regularly and breed in the North Pacific, none in the North Atlantic.

One of the most striking of the fourteen species is the Wandering Albatross (*Diomedea exulans*) of the southern oceans. It is the largest of this family, with a wingspan of 330 centimetres or more and a weight of nine kilograms.

In flight the Albatross glides without effort, sailing in wide sweeps over the waves, neck withdrawn, so that the head lies along the axis of the body, which itself is spindle-shaped. The legs are extended tailwards and the webbed feet, often protruding beyond the tips of the tail feathers, move only to act as a rudder. The long wings, their tips slightly inflected, are similarly motionless. An occasional twist of the widespread tail and a turn of the head are the only visible movements as the bird exploits the force of the wind currents. In strong gusts the wing tips curve inwards and come closer together and the bird lets itself be borne along at a dizzy speed, describing a vast circle across the sea before resuming its former position, perhaps in the wake of a ship.

The take-off of an Albatross is aerodynamically similar to that of a seaplane. Stretching out its neck and spreading its wings, it paddles at full speed into the wind with its webbed feet. Soon the bird's breast is out of the water with only the feet beating the surface. The moment it is airborne the Albatross resumes its aerodynamic shape, neck retracted and undercarriage drawn up.

The gliding feats of the Albatross have been the subject of speculation. Although it has not been possible to make precise tests to prove how these feats are performed, it seems that the Albatross normally flies no higher than fourteen metres. It uses the slight increase in wind speed at this height to remain airborne. The bird glides downwind, gathering speed, then turns upwind and climbs with the increased wind speed providing lift to bring it back to the original height. The Albatross also makes use of the slight air currents generated by the movement of waves.

These birds have a protracted and complicated courtship involving display, dancing, squawking and bill fencing. Both mates collaborate in building the nest, usually in colonies. Incubation of the single egg takes about eight weeks, and up to ten months more are needed to rear the fledgling until it is able to take care of itself. As it takes a whole year to rear a single Royal Albatross or Wandering Albatross chick these species breed once every

The Wandering Albatross (*Diomedea exulans*) on its nest on the ground. Like others of the family, it breeds in colonies on remote islands in the southern hemisphere. The single chick is at first covered with white fluffy down, changing after a few weeks to buff-grey. It develops rapidly, its only enemy at this time being the marauding skua.

The White-tailed Tropic Bird (*Phaethon lepturus*) in flight. Tropic birds fly with rapid wing-beats and feed by plunging on their prey of fish and squid from a height of about fifteen metres, catching it just below the surface. Although they breed in colonies, at sea outside the breeding season they are seen only in ones and twos.

species include the Short-tailed Shearwater or Slender-tailed Shearwater (*P. tenuirostris*) of Australia, the Greater Shearwater (*P. gravis*) found throughout the Atlantic, and the Sooty Shearwater (*P. griseus*) of the southern hemisphere.

The fulmars or foul-gulls are typically represented in the northern hemisphere by the Northern Fulmar (*Fulmar glacialis*) and in the southern hemisphere by the smaller Silver-grey Fulmar (*F. glacialoides*). An ill-smelling oil that is spat out at intruders at the nest has earned the fulmar its alternative common name. Also included in this group are the polymorphic Giant Fulmars (*Macronectes giganteus* and *M. halli*) of southern oceans, the black and and white Cape Pigeon or Cape Petrel (*Daption capensis*), and the pure white Snow Petrel (*Pagodroma nivea*) of the Antarctic ice fields.

The typical petrels include the gadfly petrels, *Bulweria* and *Pterodroma* (which includes the Cahow (*P. hasitata* of Bermuda) species. Little is known about many of them due to their pelagic haunts and rather secretive breeding habits.

And finally there are the prions, a small genus of only four species of *Pachyptila* found in Antarctic waters.

Storm petrels (Family Hydrabatidae)

This is a family of tube-nosed birds about the size of the swallow. They are strong in flight, skimming the waves on long, pointed wings and pattering over the surface on their long legs. The commonest southern species is Wilson's Storm Petrel (*Oceanites oceanicus*) also known as Mother Carey's chickens. The common northern species is simply known as the Storm Petrel (*Hydrobates pelagicus*). Leach's Storm Petrel (*Oceanodroma leucorhoa*) is abundant in the northern oceans; it and Wilson's Storm Petrel are among the most abundant of birds. The storm petrels also breed on islets in dense colonies.

Diving petrels (Family Pelecanoididae)

Black and white on the underparts, with small beaks and feet, the five species of the single genus *Pelecanoides* are found in the waters of the Antarctic and radiate northwards to Peru, New Zealand, Australia and other parts of the South Atlantic and Pacific. Unlike other tube-nosed birds their flight is very direct and they dive into the water where they swim with their wings. A single egg is laid in a burrow in soft soil.

other year. The breeding cycle for the smaller albatrosses is shorter.

In the North Pacific the best known and most common are the Black-footed Albatross (*Diomedea nigripes*), and the Laysan Albatross (*D. immutabilis*), the Black Gooney and White Gooney respectively, particularly on or near the Hawaiian Islands where both species breed. At Midway Island, western-most of the Hawaiian chain, they have created safety problems through their persistent attempts to land and nest on or near the aircraft runways. Their courtship performances, performed heedless of the hazards of ships and aircraft led to their being dubbed 'Gooney Birds'.

Shearwaters and fulmars (Family Procellariidae)

This is a migratory and wholly marine family with certain common characteristics: thick plumage, hooked bill, long tubular nostrils and webbed feet. Genera are distributed throughout the oceans of both hemispheres. There are four main groups: the true shearwaters, the fulmars, the typical petrels and the prions.

The shearwaters nest in vast colonies, each pair digging a deep burrow that ends in an incubation chamber where one of the parents sits on the egg while the other brings it food. Once hatched, the chick is left alone and fed at intervals. Later it is abandoned altogether until it takes wing and fends for itself. The Manx Shearwater (*Puffinus puffinus*) is a typical species found in the Mediterranean and eastern North Atlantic areas. Other typical

Pelicans and allies (Order Pelecaniformes)

The major characteristic common to this group of large, aquatic birds is that they are totipalmate, that is, all four toes are joined by a web. Such complete webbing of the foot is found only in the Pelecaniformes. The families of the group have an extensible beak pouch. Nesting is usually colonial, and the chicks are altricial, fed by regurgitation. Distribution is world-wide.

Tropic birds (Family Phaethontidae)

A single genus contains the three species and is found only in the tropics. The Red-billed Tropicbird (*Phaëthon aethereus*) is a native of the Atlantic, eastern Pacific and northern Indian oceans. It looks rather like a large tern. Plumage is white or pinkish white on the underparts, and white finely barred with black on the back. Its most charac-

teristic feature is a much elongated, central pair of tail feathers. Its shrill, piercing call has earned it the name Bosun Bird from sailors. With its grace and agility the Tropic-bird is master of the air, and an expert fisherman. Courtship behaviour is excited and often violent. It breeds on rocky and desolate islands. Each pair produces a single egg, laid on a cliff ledge without a nest of any kind. The globular chick is thickly covered in white down and looks more like a powder-puff than a bird.

The other two species of the single genus are the smaller White-tailed or Yellow-billed Tropic-bird (*P. lepturus*) of the Atlantic, Indian and Pacific oceans and the Caribbean and the Red-tailed Tropic-bird (*P. rubricauda*) of the Indian and western and central pacific oceans.

Pelicans (Family Pelecanidae)

Pelicans, among the largest of birds, have extremely large bills with great distensible pouches suspended below the lower mandibles, which they use as scoops in their fishing operations. They never fly with fishes in the pouch. There are six species, four of them from the Old World, and two from the New. Generally the beak is blue edged with red, and the pouch and the area round the eyes are ochre yellow. The plumage in both sexes is mainly white, though variations occur—white tinged with grey in the Dalmatian Pelican (*Pelecanus crispus*), which has curly feathers on its nape, and white tinged with rose in the Old World White Pelican (*P. onocrotalus*). The Dalmatian Pelican is also found over a wide area in southern Asia, the White Pelican throughout

Africa and Asia and occasionally in some parts of south-east Europe.

The American White Pelican (*P. erythrorhynchos*), of North and Central America, has a wingspan of 300 centimetres. The Brown Pelican (*P. occidentalis*) which is one of the few non-white species, ranging from Canada to southern South America, does its fishing in salt water, diving from a great height and with an enormous splash.

Though clumsy looking, pelicans swim and fly extremely well. Only the Brown Pelican dives underwater. The others employ a variety of tactics to catch their fishes. Sometimes they capture them by dropping on to them from a considerable height, at other times they act as 'beaters', forming a semi-circle and driving the fishes together so they can take them at their ease.

Pelicans nest near water, choosing places covered by high vegetation. They lay three or four pure white eggs. The chicks are quite helpless and are fed large quantities of food by the parents. In two months the young are able to fly.

Gannets and boobies
(Family Sulidae)

The Sulidae fall into two groups, the gannets of temperate seas, and the more tropical boobies. The gannets are colonial cliff-nesters. Here both birds incubate the single egg, covering it with their overlapped feet before settling down to brood as they lack a brood patch. When the chick develops flight feathers it flutters down to the sea. Hunting tactics are spectacular, often involving straight-as-a-plummet dives from a height of thirty metres.

The Old World or Great White Pelican (*Pelecanus onocrotalus*) breeds in large colonies building a simple nest on the ground. Up to 40,000 pairs of birds have been seen in one colony in Africa. The same nesting colonies are used year after year and in the tropics breeding may continue throughout the year.

365

The fishes are swallowed before the bird resurfaces. The commonest species are the Northern Gannet (*Sula bassana*), the Cape Gannet (*S. capensis*) of South Africa, and the Australian Gannet (*S. serrator*) although these may be but subspecies of the Northern Gannet. Adult plumage is white with a black tip to the wings.

There are six species of booby. Three are well distributed throughout the tropical world: the Masked or Blue-faced Booby (*Sula dactylatra*), the Red-footed Booby (*S. sula*) and the Brown Booby (*S. leucogaster*). The masked species is the largest and the brown the commonest. The other three species are more limited in range. The Peruvian

The King Shag (*Phalacrocorax albiventer*) of the Falkland Islands, one of the white-breasted cormorants which are found exclusively in the southern hemisphere. Like all cormorants it is highly gregarious both in the water and on the breeding and roosting grounds.

A male Anhinga or Snakebird (*Anhinga anhinga*), also called the Darter, from its habit of darting its long, slender bill forward from its coiled neck, before it dives. As it hunts through the water it spears its prey, surfaces, then throws the fish into the air and swallows it as it falls.

Booby (*S. variegata*) and the Blue-footed Booby (*S. nebouxii*) are restricted to the western coast of the American continent, and Abbott's Booby (*S. abbotti*) is confined in its distribution to only two islands, Assumption Island and Christmas Island, in the Indian Ocean.

Cormorants and shags
(Family Phalacrocoracidae)

These are sombre-looking birds with long bodies, long necks, long beaks with a hooked upper mandible, completely webbed feet, short legs and wedge-shaped tails. Plumage is predominantly black with a greenish or bronze sheen in both sexes. The wings are short and do not permit long flights out to sea. One species is known to be flightless. They are, like the seagulls, birds of the coast. They hunt by diving and picking up their prey underwater. When a cormorant meets resistance from its victim it beats it on the water, submerges it, shakes it, and somehow manages to keep it away from the unwanted interest of its comrades brought to the spot by the commotion. After diving, the cormorant always seeks out an elevated spot, where it perches with wings outspread. It is commonly supposed that this is to dry the feathers, which are not as 'waterproof' as those of other birds, but it is interesting to note that even captive species in zoos, who do not have to dive for food, persist in spreading their wings after feeding.

The mating habits of the Great Cormorant (*Phalacrocorax carbo*) are unusual. Both female and male take an active role in the courtship.

The nests are built of twigs or seaweed and are set close together on the ground in crowded colonial sites, and sometimes in trees. Eggs usually number two to six and are white. The young are covered in black down. Their appetites are apparently insatiable and their beaks remain permanently agape for food regurgitated by the parents. The enormous shaggy chicks jostle continuously to keep their place in a nest much too small for them. Incongruity is heightened when the parent arrives, sits down on the heap, and tramples over its huge children as it distributes the fishes into their ravenous beaks. One of the eager chicks will stimulate the parent to disgorge by putting its head into the adult's throat.

There are thirty cormorant species, eleven of which are white-breasted cormorants (black above and white below) found exclusively in the southern hemisphere. The Common or Great Cormorant (*Phalacrocorax carbo*), the largest and most widely distributed species, breeds on the coasts of northern Europe, Iceland, western Greenland and around the mouth of the St Lawrence River. It is also extensively distributed over Asia, Australia and New Zealand and is the species trained by Japanese fisherman to catch fishes for them. The Green Cormorant (*P. aristotelis*), known as the Shag in the British Isles, is crested for a few months during the spring and breeds along the coasts of northern Europe and the Mediterranean. The commonest cormorant of North America, the Double-crested Cormorant (*P. auritus*), breeds in large colonies from Alaska to Central America. During the breeding season it has an orange and yellow face and tufts of curly black and white feathers on each side of its head.

The Blue-footed Booby (*Sula nebouxii*) of the Galapagos and Seymour Island is large to medium in size with proportionally long bill and tail. It is a coastal fisher, the male especially being able to plunge dive into very shallow inland water from the air for food. They take mainly fish, but they also take squid.

Most of the species belong to the southern hemisphere and are typically represented by the King Cormorant (*P. albiventer*) of the Falkland Islands, and Pied Cormorant (*P. varius*) of Australia and New Zealand. The Pygmy Cormorant (*P. pygmaeus*) ranges throughout the eastern hemisphere, and the flightless Galapagos Cormorant (*Nannopterum harrisi*) is found only in the Galapagos Islands.

Darters and anhingas (Family Anhingidae)

A close relative of the cormorants, the darters or anhingas—sometimes called the snakebirds—are distinguished by their long and slender necks, which terminate in long, straight, pointed bills. They are a little like herons, with raven-black bodies and webbed feet. Inhabitants of the inland tropical rivers, lakes and swamps, they perch and nest in trees and feed on fishes speared with their beaks. Nesting is colonial. Both parent birds incubate the eggs and care for the young.

The New World Anhinga or Darter (*Anhinga anhinga*) is found from the southern United States to Argentina. The African Darter (*A. rufa*) is widely distributed in Africa, Madagascar and Iraq. There is also an Indian Darter (*A. melanogaster*) and an Australian Darter (*A. novaehollandiae*). The last two may be subspecies of the African Darter.

Frigate-birds (Family Fregatidae)

A peculiarity of these birds is that the tips of both lower and upper mandible are hooked downwards. They also have feathered tarsi, and a web that extends only halfway along the toes. The wings are long, like the tails, which are deeply forked. They are clearly adapted to flying best.

An extraordinary feature is the 210 centimetre wingspan to the 1.5 kilograms body weight. This

The male Magnificent Frigate-bird (*Fregata magnificens*) inflates its red throat pouch to an enormous size and spreads its wings when displaying to the females. These Frigate-birds breed in colonies on tropical and sub-tropical American islands. They are spectacular fliers but very ungainly on land.

The Grey or European Common Heron (*Ardea cinerea*) is common throughout most of Europe and Palearctic Asia, and also parts of Africa. In Britain it is unpopular around trout farms, where it is often seen perched close by watching motionless or stepping slowly through the water, waiting for a fish to come within reach, when it spears it in one swift jab. Even so, it often damages more fish than it eats.

ratio gives unequalled powers of effortless flight that can be transformed into a swift and accurate attack on another bird, causing it to give up its food. This aggressive piece of behaviour has earned it the name Man-o'-war Bird. If the Frigate-bird is a successful pirate, it is also a most efficient fisher in its own right. It has been seen to dive from a great height with deadly accuracy to pluck small fishes from the water without so much as brushing its feathers on the surface. It usually nests near gannet or cormorant colonies and preys on their young.

Frigate-birds are indigenous to the tropical waters of the south Atlantic, the Pacific and the Indian oceans. The Ascension Frigate-bird (*Fregata aquila*), found only on Ascension Island, is believed to be one of the swiftest of large birds. Its body is black with a metallic sheen. The male has a bright red pouch of naked skin under the throat which he inflates during courtship and before mating. The young have a white head and neck.

Other species are the New World's Magnificent Frigate-bird (*F. magnificens*), the Great Frigate-bird (*F. minor*), and the Lesser or Least Frigate-bird (*F. ariel*), the smallest of them all.

Herons, storks and allies
(Order Ciconiiformes)

This order, which includes six families, herons, hammerhead, shoebill, storks, ibises and spoonbills, is characterised by long, featherless legs adapted to a wading mode of life. All are capable of strong flight, and each foot has four toes. The shape of the beak varies, but in all it has sharp cutting edges and appears to be hafted to the long neck. The Circoniiformes are not adapted for speedy movement. Herons generally have a slow and formal gait as they stride along on the edges of marshes, ponds and sluggish rivers, marking the exact position of their prey and then seizing it with a swift and precise movement.

Herons, egrets, bitterns (Family Ardeidae)

While individual species differ in size, length of feet, size and shape of head, and beak, and in nesting habits, there are common family characteristics.

The structure of the neck vertebrae allows the neck to bend only in the vertical plane. It cannot move laterally. In repose the neck is curved in the shape of an 'S' and the head is drawn between the shoulders. The neck is extended only to seize prey by a strong and rapid muscular action which carries the beak to its target. Herons and their relatives are the only birds that fly with neck tucked back and head between the shoulders. This makes it impossible to confuse them, even at a distance, with storks and cranes. There is only a rudimentary uropygial gland but under the breast and flank feathers there are thick patches of powder down which reduces to a very fine dust that is used when preening soiled feathers. The down soaks up the slime and is removed when the feathers are combed with the pectinated comb-like inside of the middle claw and also acts somewhat as a water repellant.

The Ardeidae are widely distributed waterbirds, living only in marshy areas and on the seashore. Their food consists mainly of fishes, but includes frogs, reptiles, crustaceans, molluscs and even insects. With the exception of the bitterns, which live alone, they are sociable and live in colonies or heronries, built in trees or among reeds. The family includes the typical or day herons, night herons, egrets, and bitterns and is represented in all but the very cold regions of the world.

TYPICAL HERONS: One of the most widely distributed of the typical herons is the Grey or European Common Heron (*Ardea cinerea*), more than a metre in height with a wingspan of 150 to 180 centimetres. Its plumage is ashy grey above, with white underparts and slaty blue to black quill feathers. It has a black pendent crest, a band of white feathers spotted with black on the front of the neck, a long yellow beak and greyish-brown legs. The iris of the eye is yellow, a characteristic that gives an almost fierce appearance. It is, however, a wary and timid bird. It will readily take to flight, but will defend itself with its beak, as will most members of the family.

The heron goes hunting mainly at dawn and at dusk, stepping slowly and cautiously along the water's edge, and sometimes remaining immobile for long periods, intently watching the water at its feet. When it sees a fish or a frog it takes careful aim, then with a swift forward movement of the head and neck seizes it, and usually swallows it whole if it is small enough. The heron is not, however, a selective feeder and will catch what it can when it can. Although a skilful fisherman, it will, like all the Ardeidae, consume large quantities of other animals, even river mussels, the shells of which it will crack with one stab of its beak. Its daily intake of food is estimated at about 340 grams, little enough for a bird weighing over two kilograms.

Heronries are not always situated near the fishing grounds. They may be some distance away and the birds will then visit them several times a day in heavy, almost leisurely, flight. The nests are generally built in the tops of tall trees, occasionally among reeds, or even on the ground. They may be bulky, more than a metre in diameter and about sixty centimetres deep, with walls made of interlaced twigs and branches. As many as a hundred nests have been seen in a single tree.

From the end of February until May there is great activity in the heronries, which resound with raucous cries, some of fear, threat or anger, and some used only in courtship and mating.

The courtship display consists of bowing with neck extended, or with beak pointed towards the sky and feathers raised. Bill snapping or rattling forms part of the prenuptial display. The male holds out a branch in his beak and the female takes it, possibly as a token of acquiescence. This branch is the first used in building the new nest or in repairing an old one. The male assumes the task of bringing the materials, while the female builds.

The period of sexual display is, in many species, marked by colour changes of the 'soft' parts, such as bill, legs and feet. However, the brighter colours do not last for very long. The iris of the Green Heron (*Butorides virescens*) turns from its usual yellow to orange, and its legs and feet from their normal near-yellow to bright orange, almost coral. The colours may even fade during the egg-laying period, though it has been observed that if either

The Purple Heron (*Ardea purpurea*) is widespread over the Old World, but a rare vagrant to the British Isles. It resembles the Grey Heron in appearance and habits but is smaller. It breeds in reed-covered swamps, the nests usually consisting of dead reeds, built on a platform of reed debris just above the water level. The nests are not usually built close together.

The Little Egret (*Egretta garzetta*) is distributed throughout the Old World. It grows specially adapted feathers on its mantles for use during displays. These plumes are called aigrettes. They are moulted at the end of each breeding season. In the early 1900s immense numbers of egrets were slaughtered for their plumes which were used in millinery.

369

the first nest or clutch is destroyed the colour change occurs again.

The nest is usually finished towards the middle of March, when four or five eggs are laid in the course of a week. They are bluish green and without spots, usually six centimetres long and about two centimetres across. Both parents share the incubation period of a little less than a month. When hatched, each chick is covered with a shaggy down. The young birds eat voraciously. At first the parent will thrust regurgitated food into the mouth of the young; later it is placed on the edge of the nest. The chicks fight and jostle for the food, and often the latest to hatch are smothered by the others, while the parents, lacking instinctive behaviour to deal with the situation, look on undisturbed. For several weeks the young birds are unable to fly or to fend for themselves. After about two months they leave the nest, in May or June. Four or five months later comes the great migration which precedes the winter.

The Grey Heron is most widely distributed over Europe and across central Asia, but its breeding area extends into southern and south-east Asia, with sporadic areas of distribution in Africa. Those breeding in the more northerly parts of the range migrate south for the winter. Some of the herons from other parts also migrate.

The Purple Heron (*Ardea purpurea*) is smaller and, as its name implies, has feathers of a fiery magenta on head, neck and breast. The wings are grey all over, instead of grey and black like those of the Grey Heron. The habits of the two species are very similar, but the Purple Heron does not live in the temperate regions of Europe, Asia and Africa; it is found nearer the Equator. It never nests in tree tops.

Common New World species include the Great Blue Heron (*A. herodias*) and the Little Blue Heron (*Egretta caerulea*).

The egrets are more slender and distinguished looking than the herons. Their plumage is usually a brilliant white. The Common or Great Egret (*Egretta alba*) is almost the same shape as the Grey Heron and has much the same habits. Sometimes it nests in trees and sometimes among reeds. It is rarely found in Europe, except near the Danube and in southern Russia. One sub-species is distributed over Australia, Africa, Asia and the parts of Europe; another subspecies ranges from the central United States as far south as Argentina.

The Little Egret (*Egretta garzetta*), distributed throughout the Old World, is barely sixty centimetres high and has a wingspan of a metre. With its black bill and feet, yellow eyes, and dazzling white plumage, it is, together with the Flamingo, one of the most beautiful birds found in Europe. It breeds in large colonies in river marshes, building its nest in elms, ash trees, poplars, tamarisks, and even among reeds and rushes. Colonies are found all over southern Europe and North Africa, and in suitable areas in the Far East. Every winter these migrate further south.

The Cattle Egret (*Bulbulcus ibis*) is a common heron found in Asia and Africa, where it associates with cattle. Its plumage is white like that of the egret, but its plume is of long, single feathers of a reddish brown colour. It is thickset and has a short, strong bill and short feet. One of the ornithological surprises of recent times has been the arrival of the Cattle Egret in America, probably through Guyana, whence it has spread into South America and northwards into Canada.

Three species of egret in North America were being rapidly destroyed a few years ago to supply milliners with plumes for women's hats. Protective laws put an end to what threatened the species with extinction, and the Snowy Egret (*Egretta thula*) and large Common Egret (*E. alba*) are common again.

The Squacco Heron (*Ardeola ralloides*) is another white heron, distinguished by a crest of long, yellowish feathers streaked with black, and a

The Squacco Heron (*Ardeola ralloides*) on its nest with young. It is distributed over southern Europe, Asia and Africa. It breeds in mixed colonies with other egrets and herons. The nests may be built in trees, bushes or among reeds, and are usually no more than loosely-woven reeds. A more elaborate structure is needed in trees, however, when sticks and grass may be added.

The Night Heron (*Nycticorax nycticorax*) is found throughout North and South America, Europe and southern Asia. It lives in a wide variety of habitats, including salt and fresh water. Towards dusk, Night Herons gather and fly to the feeding grounds. They feed on a wide variety of animals including fish, crustaceans, insects and amphibians.

dozen or so white feathers edged with black falling in a tuft over the back of its head. It is no bigger than a gull, but its silhouette closely resembles that of a heron or egret. It nests in the heronries of other species of herons, ibises and egrets in southern Europe, Asia, Africa and Madagascar. It feeds on fishes, frogs, crustaceans and insects.

BITTERNS: There are twelve species of bittern, four large bitterns of the genus *Botaurus* and eight small bitterns of the genus *Ixobrychus*. Distribution of the first group is throughout America, Eurasia, South Africa, Australia and New Zealand. The small bitterns are found throughout the tropical and temperate regions. Both genera have marked cryptic colouring and similar concealment posture.

The Little Bittern (*Ixobrychus minutus*) is little known because it is nocturnal, spending the day squatting in solitude in places where its brown, black, yellow and white plumage gives perfect camouflage. Sitting quite still, neck upstretched, it is easily taken for a dry reed. Maximum length is thirty-eight centimetres. The very similar Least Bittern (*I. exilis*) of North and South America is, however, not nocturnal.

The genus *Botaurus*, which includes the Australian Bittern (*Botaurus poiciloptilus*), the American Bittern (*B. lentignosus*) and the South American Bittern (*B. pinnatus*), is typically represented by the Eurasian Bittern (*B. stellaris*), another nocturnal species easily identified by three longitudinal black stripes on a chestnut breast and by the curious posture it adopts. When at rest it leans slightly forward and pulls back its long neck so that the head appears to rest on the nape. When alarmed it ruffles its plumage, the feathers on the neck bristling, and opens its beak ready to attack. In its concealment attitude the feathers are compressed, the body rigid, and neck, head and beak pointed obliquely upwards in an unbroken line.

The booming cry of the male bittern, audible from five kilometres, is unforgettable. The sound is made by a protracted and noisy inhalation of a large quantity of air, which is then exhaled in explosive bursts. The booming is most frequent during the mating season, since this is the way in which the bittern lays claim to its territory and attracts the female—or females, for it is reputedly polygamous. It nests solitarily, not in colonies like the other Ardeidae. It is a partial migrant in Britain, now breeding in parts of Norfolk, and is well distributed over Europe, central Asia, and the extreme south of Africa.

NIGHT HERONS: The genera, *Gorsachius* and *Nycticorax* contain nine species of night heron. Typical of the first is the Japanese Night Heron (*Gorsachius goisagi*), a timid forest bird, rather like a bittern in appearance. The most widely distributed of the second genus is the Black-crowned Night Heron (*Nycticorax nycticorax*), breeding in both Americas, Eurasia, Africa and the East Indies. Nesting is colonial, in stick nests set high up in trees. The Yellow-crowned Night Heron (*Nycticorax violaceus*) which is found in North and South America is also a colonial nester.

Boatbilled heron or boatbill (Family Cochleariidae)

Considered by many experts as an aberrant member of the heron family Ardeidae, the Boat-

The African Little Bittern (*Ixobrychus minutus*) lives among reed-beds and is widespread throughout the Old World. At thirty-five centimetres, it is one of the smaller herons. The Little Bittern feeds on all manner of prey, including fish, frogs, eggs of other reed-bed birds and also other heron chicks. It is a fast and agile climber of bushes and trees. Nests are usually built at the water's edge, but nests in trees are not unusual up to a height of three metres.

At eighty centimetres long the European Bittern (*Botaurus stellaris*) is larger and less agile than the Little Bittern. In spring, and chiefly at night, the male utters a characteristic deep 'booming' call that can be heard as far as five kilometres away. The nest, built among the reeds, on mud or floating, is constructed from dead reeds with finer material for lining. Nest-building, incubation and feeding the young are carried out by the female. Although it looks passive, a Bittern readily shows aggression. It does not wait to be attacked but advances menacingly on an intruder.

371

The European White Stork (*Ciconia ciconia*) of Europe and Africa is traditionally the bearer of good luck and babies. Here a White Stork is making a submissive gesture on landing at the nest already occupied by its mate. Although large birds, they often look quite small against their massive nests.

bill's (*Cochlearius cochlearius*) bill sometimes resembles that of the Shoebill, except that the upper mandible is not hooked. Except for the remarkable bill it is very much like the Black-crowned Night Heron. It inhibits the mangrove swamps of Guyana and Brazil, and is a night-feeder. Both sexes incubate the eggs in a shallow stick nest.

Shoebill (Family Balaenicipitidae)
The Shoebill, or Whale-headed Stork (*Balaeniceps rex*), looks remarkably stork-like, with long, strong legs and unwebbed toes. The tip of its large, broad bill is hooked. Its plumage is dark bluish-brown and the back of the head is ornamented with an occipital crest. Shoebills live mainly in the marshes along the banks of the White Nile and its tributaries and are ground-nesters. It is the only species of the family.

Hammerhead or hammerkop (Family Scopidae)
The single species of this family, *Scopus umbretta*, is peculiar to Arabia, tropical Africa and Madagascar. It takes its common name from the heavy bill and the crest at the back of the head, which, with the neck, resembles the top of a hammer. Its habits are those of the stork and heron. Its nest, placed in the fork of a tree, is a stout dome built of sticks and mud and lined with grass. Each nest is made by a single pair who use it and repair it annually. According to an African legend the nest is built for the Hammerhead by the labour of other birds.

Storks and jabiru (Family Ciconiidae)
There are seventeen species, all with stout bodies, long, slender legs, and short toes only slightly webbed. The claws are blunt and nail-like. In their strong, easy flight the relatively short neck is stretched forward. Unlike the herons, they are almost voiceless. The only sound they make is a clattering of the beak. Their young have two successive coats of down.

Although protected almost everywhere, storks are diminishing in all countries where once they nested in great numbers. This decrease has been variously attributed to the draining of marshy regions, and to the increased dangers from lighthouses, beacons and high-tension cables encountered during migration. On the other hand, the reduction may be merely a normal fluctuation.

The White Stork (*Ciconia ciconia*) is the type bird of the group. It has a strong body, a long, straight, conical bill with cutting edges, white plumage with black wing coverts and flight feathers, and long, pointed feathers directed downwards under the neck. It attains a length of 120 centimetres, has a wingspan of nearly 210 centimetres, and the males may weigh up to four kilograms. Everyone is so familiar with the picture of the stork perched on its chimney-top nest that one is almost surprised to find these storks sedately walking across a marshy meadow in postures similar to the heron. This is its hunting ground and here, mainly in the morning and evening, it will catch and eat great quantities of frogs, snakes, lizards, small rodents and insects.

Since ancient times this bird has enjoyed a kind of veneration, which has served to protect it. It has little fear of man and has become sociable and almost domesticated in regions where feeding conditions allow it to nest, as in Alsace, Germany, Holland and Scandinavia. Elsewhere in Europe it is mainly a summer visitor, passing through on its spring and autumn migration. It winters in Africa, especially in the region of the great lakes. Owing to its wide range and the regularity of its movements, the stork has always been regarded as the typical migratory bird. Like the swallow it is a harbinger of spring to the peoples of the lands it visits.

Ringing has made it possible to identify quite accurately the routes followed by the migrating storks. Those that nest in western Europe cross France, Spain, Morocco, Tibesti, and Lake Chad before reaching the great African lakes where they winter. Those that nest east of the Weser, on the other hand, fly across Hungary, Turkey, Asia Minor, Syria and Egypt by way of the Nile Valley before finally arriving at the same destination. The distance covered by both groups is more than 9,500 kilometres.

In February or March the male stork arrives at his old nest and takes up his station to await the return of his mate, for storks are monogamous. Having once paired, each couple remains paired for life. As soon as they are together again after migration they begin to rebuild their old nest. The male bird brings branches, reeds, straw, rags, paper, lumps of earth and turf. The female assembles them. With the passing of years nests reach enormous dimensions. Some have been known to be over 240 centimetres in diameter, 240 centimetres deep, and over forty-five kilograms in weight. As a foundation, the ridge of a roof, the top of a chimney or a church tower are favourite sites.

During the last fortnight in April or at the beginning of May (a month earlier in the Mediterranean region) the female lays four white, finely grained eggs, each measuring at least eight by five centimetres. Incubation is shared by both parents and generally lasts about a month.

When hatched, the chicks are covered with short, white down, which is replaced eight days later by a second coat of the same colour. Far from being silent like their parents, they can be heard whining, croaking and whistling. They also begin bill clattering, throwing their heads back and then bringing them forward, making their beaks clap. This is the way in which they greet their parents when they return with food. This food is laid on the edge of the nest, but water is given to the young birds by regurgitation.

Not until they are two months old are the young storks able to make their first flight, accompanied by their parents, who still watch over them. Soon after the 'teaching flight' the bond is broken. From August onwards the young birds disperse. A month later all the storks fly to their winter quarters in East Africa.

The Black Stork (*Ciconia nigra*) is slightly smaller than the White Stork and its only white part is on its belly. It is much shyer and builds solitarily in wild forest. It nests in Spain and eastern Europe, in south-west and central Asia, and has recently started to breed in parts of southern Africa. It disappeared from western Europe in the nineteenth century, probably retreating before increasing human settlement, and the remnant in Spain may have been part of a much wider range.

A common American species (the only true stork in the United States) found from Florida swamps to Argentina is the Wood Stork (*Mycteria americana*), once misleadingly known as the Wood Ibis. It is similar in general colouring to the White Stork, but is distinctive in having a black tail and pink legs.

A species found in Africa might be called a giant

The Marabou or Adjutant Stork (*Leptoptilos crumeniferus*), is often referred to as 'a stork with the habits of a vulture'. Marabous often congregate in large flocks in marshes or on the fringes of inland waters, feeding mainly on carrion. The pouch hanging down from the front of the neck can be inflated and contains a system of air sacs connected with the left nostril. What use this is to the bird is not yet clear.

stork because it reaches a height of 150 centimetres and has a wingspan of 300 centimetres. Its bill is turned slightly upwards and generally covered at the base by a thick skin, or cere, in the shape of a saddle. This has earned the name Saddlebill Stork and the generic name *Ephippiorhynchus* ('beak covered with a horse's saddle'). The Saddlebill Stork (*Ephippiorhynchus senegalensis*) has brilliant black head, neck, wings and tail, while the rest of the plumage is pure white. The iris and cere are golden yellow, the bill red with a black median band, and the feet greyish brown marked with red at the root of the toes.

The related Maguari Stork (*Euxenura maguari*), of South America, is 100 centimetres long, white with black in the wings and upper tail coverts and red feet. Its tail is slightly forked.

The 140 centimetres long Jabiru (*Jabiru mycteria*), ranging from Mexico to Argentina, is white with naked and blue-black head and upper neck, and orange and scarlet lower neck. It is one of the largest flying birds in America.

The ugliest of all the Ciconiidae are undoubtedly the vulture-like Marabou or Adjutant Stork (*Leptoptilos crumeniferus*) of Africa and the Lesser Adjutant (*L. dubius*) of southern Asia. Its stiff strut has earned it its military name. It has a pouch hanging on the front of its featherless neck. Its head too is bald, except for a few bristles. The back plumage is dark green with metallic tints. The wing quills and rectrices are black, while the back of the neck and the underparts of the body are white.

The carrion-eating marabous are found scavenging in towns, especially near slaughterhouses. The protection given the Marabou is not entirely disinterested, for as well as being a first-class scavenger it has long, white tail feathers

The European or White Spoonbill (*Platalea leucorodia*) is found in the marshy areas of Europe. It nests solitarily, more rarely in colonies of mixed species. Usually four eggs are laid in a nest which is built either in a tree or on the ground and constructed from sticks or reeds. Incubation takes twenty-one days.

Opposite
The Sacred Ibis (*Threskiornis aethiopica*) is common now only in subsaharan Africa. It was held sacred by the Ancient Egyptians but is now extinct in Egypt. It feeds by probing for crustaceans and molluscs in soft mud with its long decurved bill, but also eats locusts, grasshoppers, frogs, small reptiles and fish. It nests in colonies on the tops of thorn trees or in rushes in swamps.

which are highly prized in India as ornaments.

The open-bills or shell-storks (*Anastomus*) have mandibles which, when shut, are in contact only at the ends, leaving an open space in the middle, adapted for the capture of the shell fish which form their food. Two kinds are known, one in Asia and the other in Africa. In the African Open-bill (*Anastomus lamelligerus*) plumage is dark and the feathers of the neck, belly and thigh end in a long, narrow plaque with a horny appearance.

Spoonbills and ibises
(Family Threskiornithidae)

A highly specialised bill is also seen in the European or White Spoonbill (*Platalea leucorodia*) and the closely related American Roseate Spoonbill (*P. ajaja*). The beak tip is flat and wide, like that of a duck, but more markedly so. The bird sweeps this spoon-shaped bill back and forth, filtering crustaceans from the water.

This feature apart, the White Spoonbill resembles the Little Egret, but is somewhat larger. It has the same white colour and is found in the marshy regions of Europe as well as on the seashore, lagoons and estuaries. There are nesting colonies in Holland, the south of Spain, and especially in the lands bordering the Danube. Elsewhere they

are vagrant. The only New World species, the Roseate Spoonbill (*A. ajaja*), is found in Florida, although it is commoner in South America.

The ibises, with their long down-curving beaks, are familiar among the hieroglyphics on ancient Egyptian monuments. The Sacred or Tantalus Ibis (*Threskiornis aethiopica*) has white plumage except for the wings which are partly black. The head and neck are naked and covered with black skin.

The Scarlet Ibis (*Eudocimus ruber*) inhabits tropical South America. Two more species of medium height are found throughout the tropics: the Glossy Ibis (*Plegadis falcinellus*) and the Hadeda Ibis (*Bostrychia hagedash*) of Africa. The Glossy Ibis inhabits both Old and New Worlds. It sometimes strays into southern Europe and is an autumn visitor to southern Britain and breeds as far north as the southern United States. It was once thought to be a courser on account of its size and shape, but it has the gait and the habits of the herons and storks. Its plumage is red-brown and black with a magnificent metallic gloss of purple and green. The lower Danube valley is the only region in Europe where the Glossy Ibis nests. From there it tends to wander to a number of places before reaching Africa for the winter season.

Flamingo (Family Phoenicopteridae)

The three flamingo genera used to be grouped in a separate order Phoenicopteriformes since the three front toes are completely webbed. They have some habits and a raucous and resounding cry similar to those of the Goose. Yet their very long legs and other aspects of their behaviour are more stork-like, their gait and stance especially resembling those of the Heron, Crane and Stork. Both in water and on land they assume unusual postures and are able to stand for hours on one leg, the other folded under the belly, and the head laid on the back. When swimming they look rather like swans. They breed in large colonies on lakes, sometimes numbering several thousands of individuals.

In the breeding season the lakes look as though surrounded by a dam of red bricks, or as though masses of red leaves are floating on the surface.

A flight of these birds is itself an unforgettable sight. When something disturbs them, one of them gives the alarm and the rest straighten their necks, and march in Indian file, uttering their unpleasant cries as their pace quickens, develops into a trot, and then into a gallop. At the same time the wings start beating and at last they take off with a display of rose and red, broken by the ebony black of the wing-feather tips. In flight the birds' necks are outstretched and their legs fully extended behind.

The flamingo's beak is as highly specialised as that of the Boatbill. The upper part of the mandible is smaller than the lower and forms a kind of lid. The inside edges have transverse lamellae, as in the bills of ducks and geese. Through these the flamingo sieves out small crustaceans, worms and other small animals by pressing its tongue against the lamellae to drive out the water and hold back all the edible matter. Flamingo bills maybe of two kinds; shallow-keeled as in the Greater Flamingo (*Phoenicopterus ruber*) and deep-keeled as in the Lesser Flamingo (*Phoenicomaias minor*). The latter filters the surface water, extracting diatoms and fine blue-green algae. The former feeds in the mud, taking insect larvae, crustaceans and seeds. The two flamingos can therefore feed side by side without competing.

The nest is a low cone-shaped mound of mud. Usually two white eggs are laid, measuring nine by five centimetres. Incubation lasts a month.

The Greater Flamingo sometimes called the Rose-coloured Flamingo, lives in temperate and tropical regions throughout the world. Colonies can be found in southern France, East Africa, the Bahamas, the Greater Antilles, northern South America and India. The great centres of nest building in the Old World, however, appear to be in the Rann of Kutch, in north-west India. In the New World the same species is common on tropical mud-flats, although some are found as far north as Florida.

Ducks, geese and swans (Order Anseriformes)

This is a group of aquatic birds made up of two families, the widely distributed Anatidae, which contains all the familiar ducks, geese and swans, and the tropical Anhimidae or screamers that are inhabitants of the New World.

Screamers (Family Anhimidae)

Although screamers of South America do not look much like ducks or geese, anatomically they are very similar. They have very little webbing between the front toes and a bill like that of a Moorhen. The Horned Screamer (*Anhima cornuta*) lives in the rain-forests of tropical South America. It is about the size of a turkey, almost uniform greyish black above and white below, with white rings around the eyes and neck. It is remarkable for the eight-centimetre 'horn' or caruncle on its forehead and for the two sharp spurs on its wing. A related but hornless species, the Crested Screamer (*Chauna torquata*), lives in the lagoons, swamps and pampas in Paraguay, southern Brazil, Uraguay and northeastern Argentina. Its nest, lightly built

The Scarlet Ibis (*Eudocimus ruber*) with its magnificent scarlet plumage lives in the coastal areas of tropical South America. It roosts and nests in large colonies in mangrove swamps and feeds on the beaches and mudflats, picking up small marine creatures. Birds kept in captivity often lose their brilliant scarlet colour possibly due to deficient diet.

The Crested Screamer (*Chauna torquata*) is one of three species of screamers confined to tropical and subtropical South America. Screamers are large, ungainly birds rather like turkeys but related to ducks and geese. They are wading and swimming birds and their long toes, which are only slightly webbed, enable the birds to walk over vegetation mats floating on the lakes.

A pair of Mute Swans (*Cygnus olor*) which, like most swans, mate for life. In the wild the Mute Swan breeds across northern Europe and Asia, migrating southwards in winter from the colder parts of its range. In most parts of Europe it has been introduced to lakes and rivers and lives a resident, semi-domestic life.

of rushes, stands in the water. About six buffish-white eggs are usually laid, and from these hatch out yellowish-brown, down-covered chicks. There is one other species, the Black-necked Screamer (*C. chavaria*) of northern Columbia and Venezuela.

Swans, Geese and Ducks (Family Anatidae)

There are forty-three genera in this family, grouped in three subfamilies and ten tribes: the subfamily Anseranatinae contains only the tribe Anseranatini; the Anserinae contains the tribes Anserini, Dendrocygnini; the Anatinae contains the Tadornini, Anatini, Aythyini, Cairinini, Somateriini, Mergini and Oxyurini. All are known as ducks except for the Magpie Goose of the Anseranatini and the geese and swans of the Anserini.

Certain characteristics are common to all ten. Bills are long and flat, and soft except for a hard 'nail' at the tip. Necks are long. Eggs are pale without spots, and the young are nidifugous and covered with soft, fluffy down. Flight feathers are, exept in the Magpie Goose, moulted all together leaving the bird flightless for a short period.

The edges of the bill bear rows of fine serrations or lamellae. In geese, these are used for cutting grass and in the mergansers they are sharp teeth for holding fish. The dabbling ducks have many fine lamellae which serve as filters. The tongue is particularly fleshy and muscular and it acts like a piston, sucking water into the mouth and expelling it again. The transverse plates allow only certain particles into the mouth and these are retained and swallowed. Presumably there is also some selection of edible from inedible particles, since the tongue and bill are lined with taste buds.

Most ducks are poor walkers because their feet are set far back on the body. The feet, webbed across the three front toes, are not suitable for locomotion on land. Ducks, swans and geese are essentially aquatic, excellent swimmers and many are good divers. Many, like the Mallard, are able to remain upended in order to rummage in the mud at the bottom, with only the tail showing, while the feet paddle to maintain equilibrium. The divers use their feet to swim underwater. Ducks are as expert in flight as in swimming. They have no difficulty in taking off from the water.

The swans and geese usually mate for life. They have no sexual dimorphism in their plumage; their courtship is simple and the male helps to care for the brood. In most ducks there is a marked dimorphism, with elaborate courtship displays and the pair bond is temporary. In common with other aquatic birds, ducks make their plumage waterproof with the oily secretion of the uropygial gland situated at the base of the tail.

MAGPIE GOOSE: This is the only species of the tribe Anseranatini. The Magpie Goose (*Anseranas semipalmata*) is an Australian bird. Unlike the other Anatidae it moults its flight feathers gradually.

WHISTLING DUCKS OR TREE DUCKS: These, the

Dendrocygnini, are found mostly in the tropics. Unlike the typical ducks they show no sexual dimorphism. The commonest of the eight species is the Fulvous Tree Duck (*Dendrocygna bicolor*) of the New World and Africa.

SWANS: The Anserini can be reviewed in two convenient groups, the swans and the geese. Swans, the largest of the Anseriformes, have long flexible necks,and are able to swim and paddle but unable to dive. The species are grouped into two genera, *Coscoroba* and *Cygnus*.

The Coscoroba Swan (*Coscoroba coscoroba*) is a small species found in South America. The others include three all-white European swans—the Whooper or Wild Swan (*Cygnus cygnus*), Bewick's Swan (*C. bewickii*) and the Mute Swan (*C. olor*)—two all-white North American species, the Whistling Swan (*C. columbianus*) and the rare Trumpeter Swan (*C. buccinator*); and to conclude the list, two southern hemisphere species, the Australian Black Swan (*C. atratus*) and the Black-necked Swan (*C. melanocoryphus*) of South America.

The Whooper Swan and Berwick's Swan breed in the Arctic tundra of Europe and Asia and migrate southwards in winter. Bewick's Swan can be found as far north as northern Siberia, where it blends with its snow-covered surroundings. From October to April it migratres to more southerly countries. The Mute Swan is particularly well known in Britain, where it now lives as a partially domesticated species. During the breeding season its behaviour is aggressive, driving off all other ducks and even drowning their young. It is recognisable by a knob at the base of the beak.

The Whistling Swan is nearctic, breeding from Alaska to Hudson Bay and migrating south. The Trumpeter Swan, the largest swan of all, does not appear to migrate far from its breeding grounds.

Swans are strictly monogamous, the male remaining attached to its mate for life. During part of the courtship display he caresses her head and neck uttering soft and gentle cries. Both birds collaborate in building the nest, although the female does the actual building. During incubation the male watches over his companion and sits on the eggs while she is away feeding. When the cygnets are hatched he helps to feed and protect them. The family remains thus united until the following year when the cygnets separate from their parents. If alarmed while swimming, young cygnets take refuge between the uplifted wings on the back of the father (cob) or mother (pen).

TRUE GEESE: The true geese are less markedly aquatic than the swans. Two genera, the grey *Anser* and the 'black' *Branta*, both of the northern hemisphere, make up most of the group. Both are strongly migratory. Wild geese breed mainly on the vast swamps and cold lake-dotted tundra regions. In winter they fly south to temperate parts of Europe and Asia, or—in the New World—to the southern states of North America.

The type bird of the genus *Anser* is the Wild or Greylag Goose (*Anser anser*). From this species the Domestic Goose was derived. Yet there is strong contrast between the mobility of the one and the ponderousness of the other. The Wild Goose is the largest and strongest of the geese. Extremely long flights during migration are quite common.

Other species are the White-fronted Goose (*A.*

albifrons), the Bean Goose (*A. fabilis*), the Pink-footed Goose (*A. brachyrhynchus*), the Snow Goose (*A. caerulescens*) and the Emperor Goose (*A. canagicus*). Both the Bean Goose and the White-fronted Goose are regular formation flyers. Family parties stay together during migration and they gather on traditional wintering grounds where they become a pest because of the way they damage crops and pasture.

The common species of the genus *Branta* are the Canada Goose (*Branta canadensis*), the Barnacle Goose (*B. leucopsis*), the Brant or Brent Goose (*B. bernicla*) and the Nene or Hawaiian Goose (*B. sandvicensis*).

The Black-billed or Cuban Tree Duck (*Dendrocygna arborea*), the largest of the tree ducks, is confined to the West Indies. It lives in swamps and pools of tropical forests feeding on tree fruits and other vegetation. For most of the year these tree ducks live in flocks and are active mainly at night.

The Lesser White-fronted Goose (*Anser erythropus*) is distinguished from the larger White-fronted Goose (*A. albifrons*) by its larger white facial patch which extends onto the forehead and by the wing tips which extend beyond the tail.

The Ruddy Shelduck (*Tadorna ferruginea*) used to have a much larger breeding range in Europe but marsh drainage and shooting has taken its toll and breeding is now restricted to northeast Greece, Turkey and the Black Sea coast. It is still common in Asia ranging as far as southwest China. It is a large handsome duck with orange-brown plumage and in the breeding season the males have a black collar.

Barnacle geese are sturdier, have shorter bills and are more pronouncedly black and white than the so-called grey geese. Except that they frequent the sea coasts and rarely penetrate far inland, their habits are much the same. Their food consists of marine plants, molluscs, crustaceans and insects. Like other wild geese, the Barnacle is an Arctic bird, moving south only in winter.

The Brant or Brent Goose is black and brown with a white breast. The Canada Goose has white throat and cheek patches, a black head and neck.

SHELDUCKS AND SHELDGEESE: The Tadornini is the most primitive tribe of the subfamily Anatinae and includes the typical shelducks or sheldgeese of the Old World: the Common Shelduck (*Tadorna tadorna*), the Ruddy Shelduck (*Casarca ferruginea*), the Egyptian Goose (*Alopochen aegyptiacus*), the New Zealand Shelduck (*Tadorna variegata*), and the Cape Barren Goose (*Cereopsis novaehollandiae*).

DABBLING DUCKS: Perhaps the most attractive and certainly the largest tribe is the Anatini, the dabbling or dipping ducks. In the very large genus *Anas* are grouped the colourful European Common Teal (*Anas crecca*), Mallard (*A. platyrhynchos*), Pintail (*A. acuta*), Shoveler (*A. clypeata*), Gadwall (*A. strepera*), European Wigeon (*A. penelope*) and the Black Duck (*A. rubripes*).

The dabblers are so called because they feed by dipping their heads, necks, and bills underwater for food on the bottom, not by diving. Usually classified with them are the three steamer ducks, two of which are completely flightless, of the genus *Tachyeres* of South America, which propel themselves along the surface by paddling with both their feet and wings.

Generally the breeding plumage of the male is bright and conspicuous, whereas that of the female is dull. Greens, russets, blues and yellows occur in patterns characteristic of each species. Only in summer do the two sexes look alike, when the male goes into eclipse plumage. This coincides with the renewal of his body feathers and with a period when he moults all his wing quills and becomes temporarily incapable of flight. Many species have a patch of bright coloured feathers (the speculum) on the wing, which plays a big part in species-recognition and in courtship display.

The favourite haunts of wild ducks are ponds, marshes and flooded meadows, the borders of lakes and watercourses. But the nest is built on land, lined with down plucked from the breast of the female, who builds the nest and sits on the eggs. The ducklings are covered with a thick coat of down when hatched. They are essentially precocial and, led by their mother, enter the water immediately after hatching.

Dabbling ducks of all species—mallards, gadwalls, shovelers, pintails, teals—are the favourite game birds and so many are taken annually that in recent years several countries have had to take legal measures for their preservation.

The commonest is that known as the Wild Duck, the Mallard (*A. platyrhynchos*), from which the Domestic Duck originates and with which it still interbreeds occasionally. In mating plumage the drake's head and neck are a beautiful glossy green, separated by a white band from the brown nape and breast. The wings are brown with a superb violet-blue speculum, framed with black and white. The rest of the body is a greyish white. The beak is yellow, the feet orange-red. The four middle tail coverts are longer than the others and are turned upwards. By contrast the male in eclipse resembles the female, both being brown marked with black, but retaining the speculum that is characteristic of the species.

The annual cycle of the Mallard Duck may be taken as typical of all northern species of duck. It begins in September or October, when the drakes have regained their brilliant plumage and have already paired off, though the mating season is still a long way off. On expanses of fresh water, and even in estuaries and salt-water lagoons, ducks gather by the hundreds, dabbling in search of food. They are forever foraging and will eat almost any living thing in the water, from leaves and seeds of water plants to molluscs, worms, larvae, insects, frogs and small fishes. According to statistics compiled in the United States their stomach contents consist of ninety per cent vegetable matter and ten per cent animal matter. As the mating season approaches, their feeding activity becomes even greater and their appetites insatiable.

After the end of the winter, to the ordinary call are added the many variations of voice that accompany the courtship. Mating usually takes place on the water. The male and female then choose a site for the nest, usually a tussock of grass on the shore or on an islet.

There are a dozen eggs in a clutch, looking very like those of the Domestic Duck. The female broods alone for twenty-four to twenty-eight days, at the end of which time the ducklings hatch, and the protective duck can be seen at the head of her bustling family. It is two full months before the ducklings, then half-grown, can fly and look after themselves. The drake meanwhile often goes after other females, promiscuity being common.

June comes and suddenly neither duck nor drake is anywhere to be seen. This is the period of the eclipse, when the drakes lose their flight quills and are unable to fly. They hide, silent, in the reed beds, males and females together. Here they remain until the end of August, when the males have regrown their full plumage and are able to fly again.

Whereas Mallards that nest in western or southern Europe also winter there, those breeding farther north, in Scandinavia or Canada, for instance, migrate southwards at the approach of the cold season.

Many species, such as the Gadwall and the Wigeon (sometimes Widgeon), are winter visitors to Britain and other parts of Europe. The males of these two species can be distinguished from each other by their plumage; the first has a grey head and body with a white speculum, the second a chestnut head and green speculum. Their cries are quite different. The quacking Gadwall is answered by the whistling cry of the Wigeon. The Gadwalls like dabbling, while the Wigeons prefer probing in mud and grass for their food. The Wigeon and Pintail are often seen in small groups in North America. The second of the two is a most elegant duck, with a sombre plumage in which black and white dominate. It has a swan-like neck and pointed tail.

The teals are the smallest of the European and American ducks. No bigger than pigeons, they are livelier, more alert, and stronger in flight than other ducks. In Europe there are the Garganey Teal (*A. querquedula*) and the Common or European Teal (*A. crecca*), while in America and Canada there are the Green-winged Teal (*A. carolinensis*) and the Blue-winged Teal (*A. discors*). The Garganey's speculum is green with a white

margin, and the Common Teal's black with a white margin. The males can be distinguished even more easily in nuptial plumage, when the male Garganey has a brown head and enormous white 'eyebrows', and the Common Teal a head plumage that is of glowing red with a broad green band extending from the eye to the nape.

POCHARDS: These are the Aythyini, the diving or 'bay' ducks. Primarily birds of the northern hemisphere, their distribution is world-wide. The specific gravity of the group is higher than that of the dabblers, making diving easier. Under water they propel themselves with their feet. They are poor walkers and fly with a quick wing beat.

The best-known pochard is the Canvasback (*Aythya vallisneria*), of North America. Its back is finely barred with black and white, and its head and neck are reddish brown.

The Red-crested Pochard (*Netta rufina*) is a very handsome European duck, about the same size as the Mallard. The drake can be recognised by its big reddish head and vivid red beak, its black

The Mallard or Wild Duck (*Anas platyrhynchos*). The female duck is less colourful than the drake, although in summer he goes into an eclipse plumage that is little different from his mate's. The Mallard ranges across the whole of North America, Europe and Asia, from the Arctic Circle southwards. It is one of the most adaptable species in the world.

The male Red-crested Pochard (*Netta rufina*) can be recognised by its striking bright ginger head and scarlet bill. The female lacks these distinctive markings. Being a diving duck it prefers fairly deep water, although its best-known breeding area in Europe, the Camargue, consists of fairly shallow saline lagoons.

breast and belly, grey-brown back, and grey wings. Today it is found only on large, open expanses of water. It approaches the banks only at nesting time, in search of reeds amongst which to build its nest.

Other species are the Ferruginous Duck or White-eyed Pochard (*Aythya ferina*) and the Tufted Duck (*A. fuligula*), both resident in and winter visitors to Britain and Europe. In nuptial plumage the first has a shining chestnut-red head and a very light grey body, bordered with black on breast and tail. The Tufted Duck's head, back and chest are dominated by a brilliant black with iridescent lights, contrasting with the pure white of its flanks. It has a crest which drops gracefully on to its nape.

PERCHING DUCKS AND GEESE: The tribe Cairinini are the brightest coloured ducks of all. Two interesting species are the Barbary Duck and the Mandarin Duck. The perching ducks are forest birds that nest in trees. In addition to the webbed feet of the more aquatic tribes they have claws, and a sturdy hind toe well adapted to clinging to tree branches.

The Barbary Duck (*Cairina moschata*), also called the Muscovy Duck, originally came from South America. Freed slaves introduced it to Africa whence it ultimately spread to Europe finding popularity where there was no pond on which to keep ordinary ducks. Its habitual colouring is a metallic dark green with white spots, which may be more or less extensive (mixed variety), or dominant (white variety). Fleshy excrescences appear at the base of the beak. This is a polygamous species.

The Mandarin Duck (*Aix galericulata*) of China, is a popular ornamental bird. Its vivid and varied colours almost defy description. Reds, greens, blues, yellows and browns contrast with the pure white of its front. The mutual affection shown by each pair explains why the Chinese make this bird the symbol of conjugal fidelity.

EIDER DUCKS: The marine tribe Somateriini has four species: the Common Eider (*Somateria mollissima*), the King Eider (*S. spectabilis*), the Spectacled Eider (*S. fischeri*) and Steller's Eider (*Polysticta stelleri*). The first, the Common Eider, is highly prized for its excellent and abundant down, commercially exploited as eiderdown. The female plucks the down from her breast to line the nest.

MERGANSERS OR SEA DUCKS: The Mergini is a northern hemisphere tribe with marked diving ability. Most are sea birds. The mergansers or sawbills, the goldeneyes and the black, velvet and surf scoters make up the tribe. Two mergansers are common in Europe, the Goosander (*Mergus merganser*) and the Red-breasted Merganser (*M. serrator*). Both are common in North America too. Both have the same long silhouette on the water and in flight, the same thin, hooked beak, the same green head, black back, and white breast when in breeding plumage. The distinguishing marks are a crest and reddish hood in the red-breasted species and white neck and body of the Goosander. Both breed in northern latitudes and come south only during extreme cold. In America the Red-breasted Merganser rarely flies farther south than the northern United States. The Hooded Merganser (*Lophodytes cucullatus*) is found only in North America. Mergansers feed mainly on fish caught

The King Vulture (*Sarcorhampus papa*) is a scavenger of the tropical forests of Central and South America. With its keen sense of smell it seeks out carrion but it has been known to kill newly-born calves and small reptiles. Unlike most other vultures it will not scavenge human refuse.

in the saw-toothed bill. They roost in holes in trees, except for the Red-breasted Merganser.

STIFF-TAILED DUCKS: With the Oxyurini the catalogue of the Anatidae tribes is complete. These are small, chubby ducks distributed through all five continents. Their name is earned by the rigid rectrices of most species. The type bird is the Ruddy Duck (*Oxyura jamaicensis*) of North America.

Birds of prey (Order Falconiformes)

Eagles, buzzards, sparrowhawks, falcons and vultures are sometimes called diurnal birds of prey to distinguish them from the unrelated nocturnal birds of prey, as owls used to be known. All are admirably built for a predatory life. Many are strong, fierce, and most of them are large. Sight and rarely sense of smell are well developed. The wings may be broad or narrow but they are always long, to give powerful sustained flight. Legs are short and strong, with four digits, three forward and one in opposition except in the Osprey which can reverse one toe so that it has two pointed in each direction. The digits end in curved, pointed

claws or talons. Prominent identifying features are the powerful hooked beak, and the cere, a fleshy protuberance, on the upper mandible. The head is fairly large and carried on a short, robust neck. The overall impression is one of great physical power. The lower mandible is shorter than the upper and partly enclosed within it when the beak is shut. The upper mandible sometimes has a pointed, tooth-like projection on each side, the sharp edges forming a double pair of cutters. The cere is pierced by the nostrils and is usually coloured yellow, red or green. The same colours are often repeated on digits and tarsus.

Prey is normally warm-blooded vertebrates, though some hunt fishes, reptiles, amphibians, or insects, and some are carrion-feeders. Victims are held in the talons while the bird plucks out tufts of feathers or fur and then dismembers them. Powers of digestion are considerable, and the few indigestible parts are regurgitated as pellets. Analysis of these seems to indicate that birds of prey eat many small animals harmful to man and his crops.

The raptors are strong flyers and the stiff feathers covering wing and body produce a

Opposite top
The Goosander or Common Merganser (*Mergus merganser*) is sometimes called a 'saw-bill' because its long, narrow bill has backward-pointing serrations in both mandibles which prevents slippery fish escaping. Goosanders have been persecuted for preying on salmon and trout but they are beneficial in so far as they also take predatory fish such as pike and eels.

Opposite bottom
The male King Eider Duck (*Somateria spectabilis*) as shown here is an impressively coloured bird; the female is a more sober brown colour and easily camouflaged when on her nest. The species is found throughout the Arctic and north temperate marine waters. The King Eider is believed to feed at greater depths than the Common Eider (*S. mollissima*), taking animals such as sea urchins and crabs.

The Andean Condor (*Vultur gryphus*) is the largest bird of prey in the world. Although now fairly rare it has suffered less persecution than the Californian Condor (*V. californianus*) of North America. Although feeding mainly on carrion it will also take eggs from the large colonies of seabirds on the Peruvian coast.

Opposite
Flamingos are a family of large, beautifully-coloured aquatic birds living on alkaline or saline lakes in America, Asia, Europe and Africa. They have specialised bills for filtering out small animals or microscopic plants from the mud or water. They are gregarious birds and colonies of the Lesser Flamingo (*Phoeniconaias minor*) sometimes number over a million pairs.

characteristic noise during flight. Feathers cover all or part of each tarus, giving the bird a trousered look, an effect seen in most species. Only the digits are always bare. The beak is clearly outlined in profile along the whole of its length. The eyes are laterally placed in the head.

The birds of prey live singly or in pairs, except when migrating. All are monogamous. Mating occurs in the spring, preceded by fighting and display, which the female appears to watch with a measure of interest. The eggs are few in number (in some species there is only one) and these are brooded by the female alone, the male feeding her as she sits.

The nests or eyries are built in high, inaccessible situations, a necessary precaution for a bird whose young remain helpless longer than most.

New World vultures (Family Cathartidae)
The American vultures are distinguished from the Old World species by several anatomical features. The nostrils are not completely separated internally and are elongated, not round, in section. The hind toe is set slightly higher than the three front

ones, which are slightly webbed at the base. They are voiceless birds.

The best-known member of this group is the Andean Condor (*Vultur gryphus*), more than ninety centimetres in length and with a wingspan of about three metres. It is easily recognised by its shining black plumage, embellished with a white band on each wing and a white collaret at the base of the neck. The red colour of the fleshy comb and wattles contrasts with the grey head, neck and crop region. It is an impressive bird. In the Andean Cordilleras it is said to soar to a height of 4,800 to 6,000 metres.

The Andean Condor is found northwards from the Magellan Straits to the Equator on the west coast of South America, but only to the Rio Negro (Argentina) on the east. In Chile and Peru it is the most widespread bird of prey. Its habits are much like those of other vultures and it forms flocks that disperse only in the breeding season. A crude nest is built on a rocky ledge and during. November to December (the southern summer) two eggs are laid, whitish yellow with small brown spots. The young birds remain with their parents for a long

time before flying away to fend for themselves.

The California Condor (*Vultur californianus*), the largest North American bird, was numerous until the westward trek in the middle of last century, when it fell victim to poison put down for wolves and coyotes, and doubtless many were shot also. Estimates put its present number at about sixty individuals. It incubates a single egg.

The King Vulture (*Sarcorhamphus papa*) has a wingspan of two metres. It is a richly coloured bird, with black wings and tail, white underparts, flesh-coloured head and front and red-tipped black beak. Unlike the condor, the King Vulture is a forest bird, found in South America.

The Black Vulture (*Coragyps atratus*), also known as the Urubu or Gallinazo, is smaller than the King Vulture and is entirely black. It inhabits the central United States and South America, where it acts as a scavenger and in certain towns has become quite domesticated.

The Turkey Vulture (*Cathartes aura*) is the most widespread and common member of the family. It is found from southern Canada to the Straits of Magellan. Particularly in the southeastern United

States, it is known as the Turkey Buzzard as its almost naked red head and neck does remind one of a turkey and its soaring flight is similar to that of the birds known in England as buzzards. Its value as a scavenger has afforded it the protection of law in some of the United States.

Old World vultures, hawks, harriers (Family Accipitridae)

Nine subfamilies of large raptorial birds make up the Accipitridae: the Old World vultures (Aegypiinae), the kites (Elaninae, Milvinae and Perninae), the lammergeier (Gypaetinae), the true hawks and eagles (Accipitrinae), the harriers (Circinae), and bat-hawk (Machaerhamphinae), and the serpent eagles (Circaetinae). All have powerful beaks and the female is in every case larger than the male, as in raptorial birds generally.

In some classifications, particularly in America, the Gypaetinae are placed under the Aegypiinae; the Machaerhamphinae are considered members of the Elaninae; the eagles and soaring hawks are placed in a separate subfamily the Buteoninae;

A group of vultures feeding off a carcase in Africa. Vultures soar all day in their search for food. The large powerful vultures, such as the African Lappet-faced Vulture (*Torgos tracheliotus*), are able to tear the hide of a large animal with their strong beaks. Smaller vultures have to wait their turn and pick over the remains.

Opposite
The Secretary Bird (*Sagittarius serpentarius*), the sole living species of the family, is found only on the plains and grasslands of subsaharan Africa and is completely absent from the equatorial rainforests. It usually walks or runs and only takes to the wing when seriously disturbed. It covers long distances on foot looking for food; mainly insects, small mammals, snakes and occasionally birds.

The Black Kite (*Milvus migrans*), with its wide distribution in the Old World, is one of the most numerous birds of prey. A pair may mate for life and in the spring indulge in spectacular courtship flights. They are more sociable breeders than most birds of prey, sometimes two or three pairs nesting in one tree. In Africa and Asia nests are sometimes found on buildings.

and in the ospreys become a subfamily, Pandioninae.

Old World vultures (Subfamily Aegypiinae)

These birds have nostrils separated by a median partition. They feed almost exclusively on carrion and faecal matter and, because of this, certain species are tolerated scavengers in hot climates, for without them hygiene would be a more difficult problem. Their appearance and odour are as repellent as their food. They are adapted neither for hunting at high speed nor for fighting. Their feet are strong, the toes armed with sharp curved claws. The hooked beak is strong and built for shearing and dismembering dead animals. Most have unfeathered but vividly coloured head or neck. The long neck enables them to get the whole head into the corpse that is being dismembered. They have an enormous, protruding crop, which becomes gorged with food. The digestive juices of the stomach are powerful enough to break down even bones, and only remnants of these are regurgitated in the small pellet.

Like the New World vultures they have remarkable powers of gliding and soaring. On immense wings they plane effortlessly for hours, using rising convection currents. High up out of sight, at a height of several thousand metres, they scan the land below with keen eyes, and on sighting food plummet to the ground and run towards the corpse with outstretched neck, tail erect, and wings half open.

One of the largest species is the Hooded Vulture (*Neophron monachus*), 100 to 106 centimetres long, with a wingspan of nearly 200 centimetres. The plumage is a uniform dark brown, and the bare parts of the head a bluish coloration. There is a collaret of feathers at the base of the neck. This vulture ranges across central Asia, the countries bordering the Mediterranean and North Africa. It nests in mountainous and wooded regions.

The Griffon Vulture (*Gyps fulvus*) is only slightly smaller than the Black Vulture, has a lighter coloration and has no collaret at the base of the neck. It has much the same range and habitat, however, and is also found in South Africa. It used to nest extensively along the Mediterranean coast, but has now disappeared from much of it, driven out by the march of civilisation, which has deprived it of the carrion and excreta that form its food. It may occasionally find its way into the northern parts of Europe.

The Griffon Vulture lays a single white egg, just over nine centimetres long by seven centimetres wide, which may be spotted with brown. Both sexes share the long incubation, which lasts for about fifty days, and the long fledgling period. The chick is ravenous from the moment it is hatched. One observer relates that a young bird taken from the nest soon devoured two thrushes and a cuckoo. The next day it ate a kite, a carp, and the entrails of several birds. Three weeks afterwards it could scarcely be satisfied. In one day it swallowed the viscera of two calves and devoured all else it could find, even pieces of wood and soil in an attempt to satisfy its large appetite.

The Egyptian White Vulture, or Pharaoh's Chicken (*Neophron percnopterus*), is smaller. It was among the sacred birds of ancient Egypt and

figures in stylised form in Egyptian sculpture and reliefs. Its wings span no more than 165 centimetres. The plumage is white, tinged with brown to a varying degree on the underparts, particularly on the edges of the wings. Its range covers southwest Asia, including peninsular India, the Mediterranean countries and North Africa. It is found in large numbers in Africa and India, where it is accepted for its scavenging activities. Flocks of these birds swoop down on town squares and streets and quickly remove refuse. Others follow desert caravans, seeking some beast that has had to be abandoned. It also has the habit of opening Ostrich eggs by hurling stones at them.

KITES: There are three subfamilies: the white-tailed Elaninae, the swallow-tailed Perninae and the true kites or Milvinae. All are characterised by slim form, long narrow wings, and an elongated tail. They are fast in flight but not fast enough to catch other birds on the wing. Often they take dead prey or steal the prey from falcons and ospreys by harrassing them continually.

The European species, the Red Kite (*Milvus milvus*) and the Black Kite (*M. migrans*), of Eurasia, Africa and Australia, are both migratory, those nesting in Europe appearing in March and leaving for Africa in September. They live in plains, meadows and marshes, and less commonly in hilly or mountainous country. The first species was once abundant in the British Isles, but is now found only in Wales, where it is resident. Kites have been known to enter farmyards and seize chicks, but generally they are scavengers and even line their nests with rags and papers collected in the vicinity of human habitations. Urban cleanliness is the main reason for their rarity in Europe today. The Brahminy Kite (*Haliastur indus*) is a common species in Australasia.

Some North American species are less inclined to scavenge, and usually hunt their food. One, a true kite of the subfamily Milvinae is the Mississippi Kite (*Ictinia mississippiensis*) and another the Swallow-tailed Kite (*Elanoides forficatus*) a member of the subfamily Perninae, the fork-tailed kites. Both are great destroyers of insects. The second species is rather like a swallow or swift in form; with wings that cross over each other when at rest, and a forked tail. It is sixty centimetres long, with two deeply sunk eyes, a hooked beak, and claws shaped into talons. The plumage on head, neck, breast and underparts is snow white, while the rest of the body is black, with a metallic sheen. This species is social in habit, and flights of forty to fifty soaring and gliding individuals are not uncommon. Another American species is the Everglade Kite (*Rostrhamus sociabilis*), a true kite (Milvinae), which feeds on freshwater snails.

The Honey-buzzard (*Pernis apivorus*) which, despite the English name, is a kite of the subfamily Perninae, is insectivorous and feeds mainly on wasps, bumblebees and wild-honey bees. It is the only bird of prey in which the area between the eyes and the beak is covered with small, scale-like feathers instead of stiff, bristle-like feathers. It is identifiable by three transverse, unevenly spaced brown bands on the tail. In other details the plumage coloration varies greatly, but the dominant colour is a coppery brown. The wingspan may reach almost 150 centimetres.

The Lammergeier (*Gypaetus barbatus*) in flight. With a wingspan of up to three metres, when circling high above its rocky habitat, its flight is most distinctive. Its long pointed wings are swept back in a gentle curve and with the long wedge-shaped tail give an impression of power and grace.

This species lives in Europe, Asia and Africa, being fairly common throughout north-west Europe, although it stays only to breed, arriving in May and leaving for equatorial Africa in September. During this five-month period pairing, nesting, egg-laying, incubation and the rearing of the young take place. The birds are therefore fully occupied, and while at work they seem to take delight in aerial displays, uttering their incessant cries as they wheel through the air. The two egges are usually rounded, and white with brown spots. As in the buzzard, incubation takes a month.

The American White-tailed Kite (*Elanus leucurus*) is a representative of the subfamily Elaninae which is resident from southern Europe, central Asia and the south-western United States to Australia and southern South America. It is a white and grey kite found flying over marshes, river valleys, and well-watered foothills where it preys on rodents, lizards and large insects.

LAMMERGEIER: The Lammergeier or Bearded Vulture (*Gypaëtus barbatus*), the single species of the subfamily Gypaetinae, is unlike other vultures in having feathers on head and neck, and in its eagle-like bearing. The name *Gypaëtus* means both vulture (*gyps*) and eagle (*aëtos*), which emphasises that it is an eagle that has taken to eating carrion.

The Lammergeier is found mainly in high mountainous regions, but is gradually disappearing from Europe through persecution by man. It lives alone or in pairs, builds its nest in remote rocky regions and produces its eggs early (February to March) despite the high altitude. The young have a thick covering of down, which protects them against the cold.

Eagles and sea-eagles (Subfamily Accipitrinae)

Some authors call this subfamily the Buteoninae. Of all the birds of prey the eagle holds pride of place. It has figured in mythology, literature and art, and has been widely used as a symbol of greatness. Length of beak and of wing make the numerous genera easy to recognise. The beak is straight and ungrooved over the greater part of its length, with the tip of the upper mandible curved and brought to a point. The wings, when spread, are roughly quadrangular in shape and have a scalloped appearance at the tips. The feet are feathered down to the toes. The principal genera are *Aquila, Hieraëtus, Spizaetus, Haliaeetus*. All are aggressive predators and some are carrion feeders.

The most majestic species is the Golden Eagle (*Aquila chrysaëtos*), found as a rare species in mountain and forest areas of Europe, Asia and North America. The female, as in most birds of prey, is a little larger than the male, about a metre long, with a wingspan of over two metres. The plumage is dark brown, although it looks almost black when the bird is seen in flight.

The Golden Eagle has great muscular strength and can carry in its talons prey as large as the young of a chamois, a goat or a sheepdog. Exaggerations are only too common, and there is no truth in the stories of these eagles carrying off human beings. It is very unlikely that even the largest could fly off with any weight exceeding nine kilograms.

It invariably nests in a tall tree or on a steep rock ledge. The main structure consists of dried

385

The Tawny Eagle (*Aquila rapax*), distributed widely in open country in Asia and Africa, is the most common of the world's large eagles. There are many sub-species, all with brown plumage, which makes identification difficult. It feeds on small mammals and carrion and will chase other birds to steal their prey.

branches, some as thick as a man's arm, lined with twigs, bark and dried grass. To start with it is only about twenty-five centimetres deep, but over the years, with the constant addition of new materials, it may become as much as 120 centimetres deep.

The female lays a single egg or two eggs in March or April, each measuring about 7.5 centimetres long by six centimetres wide, and having an average weight of just over 150 grams. The shell is white with red spots and rough to the touch. Incubation lasts a month-and-a-half, the male taking no part except to bring food.

The two or three eaglets hatch at intervals of two or three days. The first to hatch usually survives the others, either by killing them or by taking their share of the food. The mother provides food of a suitable size for her brood and prepares it with care. The eaglet's plumage is first white. This gradually turns grey and then brown, and by the end of four or five years has assumed its typical coloration and appearance.

A closely related species is the Imperial Eagle (*A. heliaca*), a little smaller and distinguished by its square-cut tail, the cleft in its beak extending behind the eyes, and by the white or partially white feathers on its shoulders. It breeds from south-eastern Europe to central Asia, and also in Spain and north-west Africa, but winters in parts of Africa and southern and eastern Asia. Unlike the Golden Eagle, it prefers the plain and the steppe to mountainous country, building its nest in trees or even on the ground. It has a cry rather like the cackling of fowl, and it destroys many rodents.

The smaller Spotted Eagle (*A. clanga*), almost black in colour, is found particularly in marshy regions or near rivers over the same area as the Imperial Eagle, but it is not so magnificent, and its prey is seldom larger than small rodents, lizards, snakes, frogs and insects.

The Booted Eagle (*Hieraëtus pennatus*), no bigger than a Buzzard Red-tailed Hawk, is more or less pure white on the front of the body and dark brown on the back and ear regions. It has a tuft of white feathers projecting from the point where the wings join the body. It was once a summer migrant common in the wooded areas of western Europe, but today it is found mainly in central Europe, Asia Minor and Africa. It can fly at heights as great as the other members of its family, but it will also take cover in trees and perch on a branch to watch for its prey, small mammals, birds, reptiles and insects. Spotted and Booted Eagles are easily reared in captivity—another indication of the great difference between them and the Golden and Imperial Eagles.

The Harpy Eagle (*Harpia harpyja*) of South America is the largest and most powerful eagle.

At certain times of the year migrating bands of sea-eagles or fish-eagles appear off the coasts of Europe, northern Asia and North America. Their aquatic habits set them apart from other eagles. Their food consists almost entirely of fishes, aquatic birds, and a diversity of carrion. The European Sea-eagle or White-tailed Eagle (*Haliaëtus albicilla*) is brown with a white tail. The Bald Eagle (*H. leucocephalus*), a species resident in America, has a white head and neck. This is the species that is the national emblem of the United States. It lays two eggs in a tree-top nest and enjoys a diet almost wholly consisting of fish. Another species (*H. vocifer*), named for the loud cries it utters, lives on the banks of the great African rivers and lakes.

SERPENT EAGLES: These birds are so slow and indolent in movement that they fall easy prey to human hunters. They are not prolific, the female laying only a single, relatively large egg in a tree-top nest where the parents take turns sitting on the egg. Both help to feed the chick, which is said to have such an enormous appetite that it requires two or three snakes a day.

Visitors to southern France, particularly the Camargue, will be familiar with the Short-toed Eagle (*Circaëtus gallicus*). The underparts of the body are white with brown spots, while the back and upper sides of the wings are brownish grey. There are three dark bands across the rear part of the tail.

The migrations of these fine-looking birds extend over southern Europe, North Africa and parts of Asia. They arrive in France in May and

The Red-tailed Hawk (*Buteo jamaicensis*), of North America, with two young in its nest. It is not a true hawk, but a large buzzard with a wing-span of up to 130 centimetres. It is widespread from the deserts of the south up to the Yukon and Alaska in the north, feeding mainly on small rodents and birds.

leave in September, and are most commonly found in the Vosges, the Alps and the Pyrenees, and sometimes in lowland regions. Forest clearings and ponds are particularly favoured sites. They stalk all kinds of rodents, reptiles, amphibians and insects. As they destroy vipers, they are protected in most countries.

One curious species the Bateleur (*Terathopius ecaudatus*) is fairly often seen in zoological gardens. Its specific name refers to its short tail, the feathers of which barely extend beyond the rump. The bird is somewhat variable in colour, with a black breast and underparts, a brownish-red back, and wings ranging from cream to black or dark blue, but the underparts are almost entirely of a silvery sheen. When at rest it has a curious appearance, for it fluffs out its feathers, particularly those on the head and neck. It preys mainly on snakes, and has also been reported to attack young gazelles, lambs and young ostriches. It is found through much of Africa.

BUZZARDS: (The word buzzard is used in America to refer to New World vultures (*see* p. 382). In this text it refers to members of the subfamily Buteoninae, which is considered by some a part of the Accipitrinae). These birds resemble the typical eagles in their massive form and long, quadrangular wings with rounded tips. But here the resemblance stops, for the beak is curved to the base, and the lower legs are without feathers. They are slow-moving, somewhat wary birds, preferring to stalk terrestrial prey rather than to attack other birds. They sometimes eat carrion or vegetable matter.

While an adult Short-toed Eagle has a wingspan of nearly 200 centimetres, the Common Buzzard's (*Buteo buteo*) is no more than 150 centimetres. Both have a short beak, curved over its whole length, and bare, rather slender tarsi. But the Common Buzzard's short wings make it less able in the air. Plumage and coloration vary so much from locality to locality that a number of district geographic races or even species have been recognised.

The Common Buzzard is one of the commonest European birds of prey, widely distributed over Europe, Asia and Africa, resident in some areas and migratory in others. Individuals nesting in the summer in Scandinavia and Germany pass over or spend the winter in western Europe. In the British Isles the bird breeds in Scotland, Wales and western England. It tends to inhabit hedged and tree-lined fields. Here it sits unseen and watches for its prey. For long periods it will remain motionless, perched on one foot with the other hidden beneath its feathers. As soon as it spots a mouse or some other small rodent it glides quickly towards it, seizes it and devours it on the spot. Its diet also includes moles, shrews, reptiles, amphibians and insects. The buzzard is thus a useful animal and deserves protection.

Great care goes into building the nest, placed high in the fork of a tree. It is lined with fine twigs, which are covered with moss, fur and other small pieces of material. The bird will often refurnish an earlier nest or even take over an old rook's nest and adapt it to its needs. The same nest, repaired year after year, may be used by buzzards, goshawks, kites and crows in turn, the former owner rarely seeking to evict the current occupant.

Pairing takes place during March to April and is accompanied by flight displays, during which the birds make mewing sounds. Two to four near-spherical eggs are laid at intervals of several days. They are white with brown spots and take about a month to hatch, the male and female taking turns to brood them, one sitting while the other catches the food needed by both. The young are reared over a period of several months. When they are big enough, they fly away to fend for themselves in some other area.

HARRIERS OR MARSH HAWKS: These are small-sized birds of prey with a wingspan of no more than 140 centimetres. They are slender in form with long, slim legs and an elongated tail, while the ruff of feathers around the front part of the head gives them an owl-like look. They prefer flat terrain, particularly near water, and take a wide range of food. Their habit of harrying or flying to and fro over an area in search of prey gives them their common name. The nest is built on the ground

A female Hen Harrier (*Circus cyaneus*). This slender, long-legged bird of prey has an unusually large ear-opening hidden by a ruff of feathers, giving it an owlish appearance. This adaptation presumably enables it to locate mice and other small animals rustling in the leaf litter, for it hunts always by flying low over the ground.

and shelters the four or five white, rounded eggs.

All harriers are at least partially migratory, spending the summer in the temperate parts of Europe, Asia and North America and moving somewhat southwards in winter. The Hen Harrier (*Circus cyaneus*) is found over much of Europe, North Africa, Asia and North America, where it is known as the Marsh Hawk. It breeds in the northern parts of its range. The habits of the related Montagu's Harrier (*C. pygargus*) gives a good general idea of the life of birds of prey.

Montagu's Harrier arrives from Africa or Asia towards the end of March and during the early days of April. At the end of its long journey it heads for its old nesting area. In many regions suitable nesting sites are rare and it must therefore take possession of favourable territory as soon as possible. The male appears alone and as he flies over the site his flight is on leisurely wing-beats broken by gliding movements. In round wide circles, he describes interlacing curves, as if surveying the land where the nest will be built.

The female, which arrives about ten days after the male, is the mate of previous years, for many birds of prey are not only monogamous, but mate for life. Almost immediately the two birds begin their courtship, swirling together in a spiralling flight interrupted by downward glides and turns, which demonstrate their remarkable agility in the air. Then comes the mating flight, when the male displays to his watching mate. His usual circling movements cease and he begins to glide slowly towards the female and hovers before her with outspread wings. With ever-increasing speed he flies straight at her until he makes a short and sudden dive, his wings swinging over her. During this lordly, almost aggressive display he seems about to collide with her, but soars upwards, expending the impetus gained in the dive. He passes so close to the female that she gives an uncertain flap of her wings as though momentarily thrown off balance, and is forced to fly out of his way. There is a magnificent rhythm in the flight during which the male displays his light-coloured breast and then the silvery underparts of his wings to his mate. The rush of air through his feathers produces a whistling sound, and his plumage glistens in the light. This display is repeated several times, almost without pause. The male may even fly high into the air, to repeat his aerobatics with elaborate rolls and spins.

These manoeuvres become more and more frequent and before long are reinforced with a new and most curious form of display, which can be watched only through binoculars as it takes place high in the sky. As the male utters shrill cries like those he usually makes when returning with prey, the female turns to meet him and then flies below her mate, keeping to his rhythm. When she is a suitable distance, the male lets fall his prey. With a sudden beat of her wings the female brakes in the air and begins to fall. Then she stretches out her feet and in one of them seizes the food. By now the male has resumed his circling and gliding flight, in which the female takes part after she has eaten his offering. Soon she will leave all the foraging to the male and for ten weeks remain at the nesting site.

As the female is relieved from regular hunting for food, she devotes herself to building the nest. This is laid in the heather and is made of interwoven roots and twigs. The first egg is laid towards the end of May and is soon followed by several others. Incubation is undertaken by the female alone, while the male continues to provide the food. Prey is handed over in full flight, away from the nest.

A ground nest is particularly vulnerable, and the female will use any diversionary behaviour when leaving or returning to her nest to distract the unwanted attention of potential predators.

As with the Common Buzzard, incubation lasts for about a month. The chicks hatch at intervals of two days, following the order in which the eggs were laid. To begin with the chicks are mere balls of down, but they soon become more active. They have enormous appetites, and at two hourly intervals the male can be heard calling as he returns from hunting. The female takes the prey from him, kills it, dismembers it at the nest and distributes the pieces to her hungry chicks.

At this stage more than ever, attention must be diverted from the nest with its three or four white balls of feathers, an easy prey for high-flying marauders, and the parents show fight to any buzzard or crow which might make off with the chicks. And at the slightest alarm the chicks hide.

One month after hatching, the young harrier has its first lesson in flight, when it is rewarded with a piece of food. Little by little it is forced to fly higher and higher in pursuit of the parent birds and the prey that they drop for it in full flight. Their most difficult task is to make the young bird leave the nest altogether, and then they must urge it to hunt. But this is not entirely a matter of training. At the appropriate time instinct begins to take over.

True hawks (Subfamily Accipitrinae)

These are perhaps best described as forest hawks, broad-winged and long-tailed. The commonest genus is *Accipiter*, to which both the Goshawk and the European Common Sparrowhawk belong. (The Sparrowhawk described here is the European hawk and should not be confused with the American Sparrowhawk, which is an unrelated falcon (*Falco sparverius*), (see p. 391).

The Goshawk and the European Sparrowhawk are so similar in appearance that they are often confused with each other. However, the Goshawk is larger than the Sparrowhawk and has shorter and stouter toes. Both have a long tail and broad, rounded wings, and are good flyers. The plumage, which varies slightly according to age and sex, is slate blue above and white barred with reddish brown below. There are characteristic reddish crescent-shaped markings on the underparts.

The Goshawk (*Accipiter gentilis*) reaches a length of sixty centimetres from head to tail and has a wingspan of nearly 120 centimetres. It can be recognised in flight from the breadth of the wings, which is more than half the bird's length, and by the three black bands across the tail. The flight is rapid and the wings are nearly always in motion. Although the Goshawk usually takes its prey on the wing, it will also seize an animal that is resting on the ground, running or swimming. In a forest it can rapidly pursue its victim through trees and bushes by closing its wings and steering itself with its outspread tail, even following the victim into a burrow or a hole in a tree.

In short the Goshawk is a first-class hunter that takes all manner of prey. And for this reason it has been hunted and destroyed without compunction, with the result that in many places, including North America, it has become very rare.

The Goshawk builds its nest high in a forked beech, oak, pine or fir. One nest may be used for several years, being repaired with new twigs before each brood is reared. The eggs, which number three or four, are bluish, sometimes spotted with brown. Incubation requires about three weeks. The female feeds the young with food caught by the male and left in a place set well away from the nest for her to collect.

The European Sparrowhawk (*A. nisus*), which is smaller than the Goshawk and has longer and more slender digits, ranges throughout Europe, North Africa and much of Asia. It is one of the smaller birds of prey, being little bigger than a pigeon. Its habits are rather like those of the Goshawk except that it attacks smaller prey. Small birds seem to be aware of its threatening presence and will unite in flocks to harry it and put it to flight. Wagtails and swallows will hotly mob and pursue a stray individual within their territory.

The breeding habits of the European Sparrowhawk and the Goshawk are very similar. The nest is built at a medium height and contains whitish yellow eggs with reddish spots, which often form a circle round the broader end of the egg. During the incubation period and the first week after the young are hatched, the Sparrowhawk follows the same precautionary measures as the Goshawk. The male bird never brings food direct to the nest.

Newly hatched Sparrowhawks are completely white, except for the beak and feet. The crescent-shaped markings on the underparts first appear at the end of about three weeks.

The Goshawk and Sparrowhawk were formerly used in the chase, but as they are 'birds of low flight' as opposed to the falcons, 'birds of high flight', they were used to hunt only hares, rabbits and partridges. This practice still exists in certain parts of Asia and India.

Osprey (Family Pandionidae)

The single species *Pandion haliaëtus* is a handsome, medium-sized bird of prey, easily recognised by its whitish underparts and the absence of 'trousered'

The Dark Chanting Goshawk (*Melierax metabates*) together with its near relative the Pale Chanting Goshawk (*M. canorus*) are large grey hawks common and widespread in open country in Africa, with little to distinguish between them. They are called Chanting Goshawks from their habit of perching on trees in the breeding season and whistling for long periods in a monotonous way reminiscent of monks chanting. They feed mainly on lizards.

A female Osprey (*Pandion haliaetus*) seen on the nest with her two chicks. The Osprey breeds on all continents except South America where it occurs as a winter visitor only. It has recently returned to Scotland where it breeds only by freshwater lochs. In other parts of the world it is also found along sea coasts.

feathering on the legs. The head is also white, and there is a brown band running downwards from each eye to the nape. The rest of the body plumage is dark brown.

Pandion haliaëtus is a 'fishing eagle' and always lives near water. Flying at a height of ten to thirty metres, alternately flapping and gliding, it watches for fishes in the water below. As soon as it sees one within reach, it plummets down to seize it, sometimes submerging for a second or two. Then it emerges and flies off, holding its prey horizontally with its feet. The prey is eaten in the nest, which is generally at the top of a tree or on some inaccessible rock. The Osprey's eggs are elliptical in outline, and white with slate-grey and brownish-red spots.

Throughout Europe, Asia and North America the Osprey is keenly hunted by fisherman, who lure it into traps baited with fish and set on the surface of the water.

Falcons (Family Falconidae)

The true falcons, perhaps not so regal in their bearing as the Golden Eagle, are still imposing birds, and are perhaps the most specialised of all birds of prey. The long, narrow pointed wings, slender tail, and rapid flight are reminiscent of swallows or martins. The beak is short, powerful and curved down to the base, and differs from an eagle's beak in having a pair of teeth on the upper mandible corresponding to a pair of notches on the lower mandible.

Falcons are merciless and unerring hunters, destroying great numbers of animal pests. At the same time they are highly discriminating, never killing for killing's sake and eating only what they themselves have taken while in flight. Such restraint has led to their being trained for use in hunting.

Their usual habitat is the forest, where they build their large nests, but several species range the prairies and other practically treeless regions. Although they are usually migratory, if a region suits them well they stay on permanently. There are numerous species, including the well-known Peregrine Falcon.

The Peregrine Falcon (*Falco peregrinus*) is the species commonly found over most of Europe, Asia and also in America, where it is also known as the Duck-hawk. The European birds migrate to equatorial Africa each winter and return north in the summer, and are sometimes even seen in towns. It is a curious fact, however, that this fearless hunter does not defend itself against attacks from other birds, and kites, for example, will lie in wait for it and take away its food.

The Gyrfalcon (*F. rusticolus*) is the largest, strongest and handsomest of the falcons. There are three major phases; one completely white apart from a black spot on each feather; another very dark grey; and one in between the other two. It is found in Arctic America, Greenland, Iceland and Scandinavia, and in days when falconry was popular the Danish government used to send a special ship each year to search for specimens. It is a bird that has always been held in the highest esteem and is easily handled and trained.

The Saker (*F. cherrug*) is an eastern species, whose commonest wintering places are in the Balkans, Asia Minor and Egypt. In habits and coloration it resembles the Peregrine Falcon, and has, as one description puts it, 'a crow's breast, a kite's head, a beak between that of an eagle and a crow, and a hand between that of a crow and a falcon'. It is not completely black, the upper parts being merely darker than in most falcons.

The hobbies are small, fast-flying insectivorous falcons. The European species (*F. subbuteo*) is often said to be the most graceful and agile of European falcons. The upper parts are slate grey and the underparts white with crescent-shaped markings. It lives and breeds in Europe during the summer. Its normal prey is the lark, caught in flight, but at times it will also take dragonflies, butterflies, grasshoppers and other insects.

The Merlin (*F. columbarius*), called the Pigeonhawk in America, is a small falcon with a wingspan of no more than sixty centimetres. Its flight is like that of a Swallow: fast, zigzagging, skimming across the ground, soaring into the air, and going wherever the chase may lead. It breeds in northern Europe, Asia and North America, and in winter migrates to southern Europe, North Africa, India and South America.

The Kestrel (*F. tinnunculus*)—closely related to the confusingly named Sparrowhawk (*F. sparverius*) of America—is one of the commonest European falcons. Its colouring resembles that of the Red-legged Partridge, the upper parts being reddish brown with small blackspots, and the underparts rather lighter in colour. The most characteristic feature of this hawk is its manner of hovering, as though held on the end of a string, while exploring its hunting grounds. This habit has earned it the name of Wind-hover. It does this repeatedly throughout the day. Together with its high-pitched cry, this makes it easily recognised. The Kestrel seldom takes birds in flight, and it

A Kestrel (*Falco tinnunculus*) with prey: it occupies a wide variety of habitats from mountains and wooded valleys to open moorland and farmlands, even breeding successfully in suburbs and city centres. A common and widespread falcon of the Old World, its numbers fluctuate in relation to that of its main prey, the Short-tailed Vole. In England it was highly susceptible to certain agricultural chemicals until these were banned.

A male American Kestrel (*Falco sparverius*), known as the Sparrowhawk in America, although it is, in fact, a falcon and nearly identical to the European Kestrel (*F. tinnunculus*). In North America many other species, such as buzzards and harriers, are also called hawks making identification confusing.

feeds mainly on rodents and insects, a characteristic which makes it unsuitable for falconry but an asset to farmers. The American Sparrowhawk (*F. sparverius*) is very similar in size, appearance, and habits, to the Kestrel, as mentioned already.

The Red-legged Falcon (*F. vespertinus*) is handsomely marked, the plumage being slate grey, variegated with white in the female, while the beak, feet and leg feathers are reddish orange. It is rarely seen in western Europe, except in southern France, but it is very common in eastern Europe and Asia, where flocks of a hundred or so are not unusual. It has the habit of flying to and fro, rather like a bat, over what seems to be a carefully marked out area, taking in insects as it goes. Its cry is like the Kestrel's but uttered more slowly and less often. This little falcon is also useful to man.

FALCONRY: The art of training hawks, especially peregrine falcons, or duck-hawks as they are known in America, for hunting was practised in India several centuries before the Christian era. The sport spread to Europe and North Africa. At the French court falconry was particularly favoured under the Valois and in England it was a favourite sport of kings and noblemen, from the Norman conquest to the seventeenth century.

Falcon training was something of an art, with its own rules and rituals. The falcon was held in captivity, starved, and kept in a disturbed condition to weaken it and make it more tractable. The bird's head was covered by a leather 'hood' during training so that it should not be disturbed or frightened by the sight of men, dogs and horses. After much care it eventually became accustomed to its master and would perch quietly on his arm. Falconry is still practised in many parts of the world and virtually all species of hawks, eagles and falcons have been trained at some time.

Opposite
The Bald Eagle (*Haliaeetus leucocephalus*), so-called because of its snow-white head feathers, is the national emblem of the United States. Because of its depredations on the Blue Fox and on salmon it was persecuted for many years and is now almost extinct except in Alaska and Florida. Now that the eagle is protected throughout North America its population may improve.

The Brush Turkey or Brush Megapode (*Alectura lathami*) mainly inhabits the dense rain-forests of eastern Australia. It feeds on the ground during the day, raking over the vegetation with its strong feet to find insects and grubs. It also takes fruits. If disturbed it prefers to run away from danger although it can fly quite well.

Caracaras (Subfamily Polyborinae)

These include nine species of Falconidae in South America, one of which (*Caracara cheriway*) finds its way north to Mexico and the extreme south of the United States and has been adopted as the national bird of Mexico. Caracaras have strong legs and are primarily ground birds, scavenging anything from carcases on which vultures are feeding to insects and snails and birds.

Secretary-bird (Family Sagittariidae)

The scientific name for the lone member of the family is *Sagittarius serpentarius*, the common name referring to the head crest which looks like the quill pens clerks used to stick in their wigs.

Unlike the other raptors, the Secretary-bird has long legs, and long wings and tail. The plumage is ash grey, except on the upper legs and the rear part of the back, which are black. It lives in Africa, south of the Sahara to the Cape.

Groups of secretary-birds may be seen moving rapidly over the ground on their long legs or flying like swans, neck outstretched and legs extended. During the breeding season there is considerable aggression between the males. Both sexes work together to build the nest, which is generally placed low in the fork of a tree.

Like many birds of prey the Secretary-bird has a special partiality for snakes. Using one of its wings as a shield against counter-attack, it batters the reptile with its feet, at the same time retreating and jumping out of reach of the venomous bite with incredible speed. Finally, it seizes its prey and hurls it into the air several times in order to stun it.

The species can be kept in captivity, in South Africa they are kept to destroy snakes and rats.

Gallinaceous birds (Order Galliformes)

The cosmopolitan order Galliformes includes the domestic fowls, turkeys, guinea-fowls, pheasants, partridges, grouse and quail, and less well-known species such as brush-turkeys and curassows. All have thick-set bodies and small heads. The smallest species is about thirteen centimetres long and the longest, the Peafowl, may reach 230 centimetres counting its tremendous tail. The legs are moderately long and strongly built, and the strong feet are adapted for scratching the soil in search of food. They run well, but short, rounded wings are not adapted to long flight, and most species are essentially terrestrial and non-migratory in habit.

A stout arched bill and strong claws stamp the galliform birds as graminivorous, finding seeds either on or under the soil. On each foot there are three toes pointing forwards and one backwards, the latter generally being set higher than the others. The males often have spurs for fighting.

Most of the galliform birds are sexually dimorphic, with differences in size, plumage, spurs and various integumentary organs such as the comb and wattles. The males are usually polygamous and take no part in the building of the nest or in the rearing of the young. They are fierce and aggressive. The females lay numerous eggs in a crudely made nest. The young are precocial.

The Galliformes are divided into seven families. In Tetraonidae (ptarmigan, grouse, capercaillies), which live in cold and temperate parts of the northern hemisphere, the tarsi and toes are more or less feathered and the males have no spurs. The Phasianidae (pheasants, jungle and domestic fowls, partridges, quail, bobwhites, francolins, peacocks and argus pheasants) live in warm and temperate regions and are particularly numerous in Asia. They have naked tarsi, while the males have one or two spurs on each leg. The nostrils are not covered with feathers. The other families are: Numididae (guinea-fowls), Meleagrididae (turkeys), Megapodidae (brush turkeys), Cracidae (curassows, guans, chachalacas), and Opisthocomidae (hoatzin).

Megapodes (Family Megapodiidae)

Also known as brush-turkeys, incubator birds or moundbuilders, these have the stout, arched beak typical of the galliform birds. They have short, rounded wings, large tails and stout legs with strong claws, and are not unlike the turkeys of the New World. Native to Australia and New Guinea, they were carried to South Pacific islands.

Unlike the other galliform species, the megapodes do not brood their eggs but lay them in enormous mounds of sand and earth mixed with sticks and leaves, scraped together by pairs or groups of birds. Some of these mounds are the work of generations of birds and may reach a height of five metres and a diameter of sixteen metres. Each egg is laid in a separate hole, which is then carefully filled up. Heat from the decomposing vegetable matter hatches the eggs by a form of artificial incubation. When hatched the chicks are strong enough to fend for themselves and can usually fly within twenty-four hours of hatching. Some species lay the eggs in fissures in rocks allowing the heat of the sun, retained by the rock at night, to incubate the eggs.

One of the genera is *Leipoa*, meaning a 'deserter of eggs'. This expresses an earlier belief that, having built the mound and laid their eggs, the megapodes took no further interest in them. Far from deserting their eggs, they provide them with optimum conditions of temperature and humidity and have merely relieved themselves of the personal contacts of incubation. The territory of each male contains a mound. In many species the cocks are polygamous and the hens of each harem lay their eggs in the mound made or defended by their mate. It is now known that the cock not only stays in the vicinity of the mound, calling and displaying thoughout the breeding season, but regulates the temperature of the mound, thus justifying yet another name given to the megapodes: thermometer birds. He appears to know, with the accuracy of a thermometer, when the mound is getting too warm, and he scrapes away some of the mound material to increase ventilation. If the temperature drops below the optimum he adds rotting material to raise it.

Curassows (Family Cracidae)

Curassows, guans and chachalacas are all confined to the Americas, between Texas in the north and the Argentine in the south. They are arboreal roosters but ground-feeders, scratching among dead leaves for food in much the same way as domestic fowls, with which they readily associate. Curassows have a fine crest of recurved feathers and the beak is stout at the base, which is provided in many species with a fleshy cere or a frontal protuberance. The males are usually black with white underparts, and the females brown. The male of the Great Curassow (*Crax rubra*) is a metre long, and black with a yellow knob on top of the beak. The female is reddish brown, and her head and neck are black spotted with white; she has no beak knob. Ornamentation of the beak is a feature of other male curassows: the Black Curassow (*C. alector*) has a pendent wattle on the beak, and the Great Razor-billed Curassow (*C. mitu*) has a blade-like casque.

In the guans, which are smaller than curassows about sixty centimetres long, the sexes are alike and both are brown to olive with a metallic sheen. The Horned Guan (*Oreophasis derbianus*) has a long, red spike growing up between the eyes. Guans of the genus *Penelope* seem to be irresistibly attracted to fire, and a method of luring them is to light fires in the branches of a tree.

Chachalacas are smaller than guans. They are slender, with long tails, brownish green to olive. They are named after their cackling calls.

Ptarmigan or grouse (Family Tetraonidae)

The ptarmigan's generic name, *Lagopus*, refers to the hair-like feathers that cover its feet in winter, enabling it to walk in its snow-covered environment. There are three species: the Rock Ptarmigan, the White-tailed Ptarmigan of North America and the Willow Ptarmigan with its British subspecies, the Red Grouse. The wings are short and rounded in outline. The end of the tail is also rounded. Nostrils are feathered. The males are larger than the females.

The Rock Ptarmigan (*L. mutus*) and Willow Ptarmigan (*L. lagopus*) are circumpolar in distribu-

tion. The northerly part of their range covers Scotland, Sweden, Norway, Lapland, Siberia and Canada. In summer distribution is just below the snow-line, and they nest close to fern-covered and glacial regions. During the winter they may descend to the valleys, where they are confined to rocky areas close to forest.

The winter plumage of most species is white, only the beak and tail being black (the males also have a black band running from the beak to just behind the eyes). It is thus well camouflaged against the snow. The Red Grouse alone does not assume this winter plumage.

About February, red and black-barred feathers of the breeding plumage appear on the wings and the upper parts of the body. With this comes a change in the bird's behaviour. The flocks split up into pairs, which then look for nesting sites. The male engages in a vigorous leaping display and utters raucous calls which are answered by the softer cries of the female.

The shallow scrape in the ground that serves as a nest may be placed in the shelter of a rock, under a bush, or in a clump of heather, and is lined with leaves and plants. There are from six to ten eggs, which vary in colour from reddish yellow to whitish yellow with brown specks. They are incubated for three weeks. As soon as they are hatched, the chicks leave the nest and follow the mother. If disturbed with her family by a predator, she seeks to escape, while the young scatter and hide among

The cock Willow Ptarmigan (*Lagopus lagopus*) showing his white winter plumage against a background of snow. In spring, after the thaw, the cock dons his breeding plumage and starts his spectacular courtship displays. Favourite hillocks or boulders are used as look-out posts, from which he defends his territory against other males. The hens move from one territory to another to choose their mates.

Opposite
The African Jacana (*Actophilornis africana*), sometimes called the Lilytrotter, has exceedingly long toes and long straight claws, which enable it to walk over floating vegetation on tropical and subtropical pools and lakes. It is a good swimmer and will often dive under water to escape a predator. It feeds on small aquatic animals, seeds and sometimes fish.

the stones and plants. When the alarm is over she returns and re-musters her brood with a particular call, which plays much the same part as the clucking of the Domestic Hen.

During the summer the family stays together, feeding on bilberries, wild strawberries, buds and shoots of shrubs, together with insects, worms and snails. The plumage has now taken on brown, grey, yellow and black mottlings, which render the birds practically invisible as they crouch against the ground. When they take wing they display the white undersurface of their wings and their black tails, leaving no doubt as to their identity. When on the ground, ptarmigan run and walk partridge-like. Less highly prized as game birds than related species, they are hunted in some northern areas.

The summer plumage of the Willow Ptarmigan or Grouse (*L. lagopus*) is redder and browner than that of the Rock Ptarmigan, and during winter there is no black band in the eye region. Their habits are very similar, except that the Willow Grouse is found in the birch forests, peat bogs, and frozen plains of northern Europe and America, but not in the more southerly mountainous regions. Its flesh is regarded as a great delicacy, and the bird is hunted by British and Scandinavian sportsmen.

The subspecies, Red Grouse, is peculiar to the British Isles, where it lives on moorlands in Scotland, northern England, Wales and Ireland. The plumage is mainly reddish brown without any trace of white, although the hen is paler than the cock. The plumage maintains this coloration throughout the year. The Red Grouse feeds mainly on heather shoots and other moorland plants, but the young take insects also. The hen lays from five to fifteen eggs, which take twenty-four days to hatch. It is only within recent years that the Red Grouse has become recognised as an aberrant form of the Willow Ptarmigan.

Capercaillie and Black Grouse differ from those of the genus *Lagopus*. They have a wider tail, in which the rectrices and contour feathers may be erected and spread like those of a peacock. The tarsal part of each leg is feathered, and the toes are bare. The eyes of both sexes are surrounded by a ring of bare bright red skin. They are polygamous, too, a habit related to the more marked dimorphism between the sexes. The cocks are more agressive and take no part in rearing the young.

The Wood-grouse or Capercaillie (*Tetrao urogallus*), the largest grouse, is one of the larger European birds, with a wingspan up to 150 centimetres and a weight of six to eight kilograms. Although not brilliantly coloured, the cock is a handsome bird with bluish-black upper parts and greyis, zigzag stripes. The breast feathers have a metallic sheen. The tail is dark blue and can be erected and fanned to display its white crescent-shaped markings. The hen, smaller and with duller plumage, is mainly reddish with brown stripes on the upper parts.

This bird was once widespread in central Europe, but it has been so heavily hunted and so ravaged by epizootic diseases (e.g. coccidiosis, to which most galliform birds are prone) that it now occurs only over a much more restricted area. In the British Isles it became extinct about 1770, but was reintroduced into Perthshire in 1838, and is now locally quite common. In France it is almost entirely confined to the Vosges, Jura and Pyrenees, where it occurs between heights of about 1,000 and 1,500 metres. It is still fairly or locally common in Scandinavia, Russia, and central and northwestern Siberia. It is a vegetarian feeder.

The Capercaillie is a shy bird and leads a solitary existence. Outside the breeding season the cock lives apart from his harem. Even at the height of winter, with thick snow on the ground, it may spend weeks on the same conifer, stripping it of its needles and shoots. When seeking food on the ground, it is a fair runner, but its flight is both clumsy and noisy.

The breeding season begins in April, when the cocks assemble on display grounds, and fierce combats may ensue to establish breeding territories. Young males have to fight for a place, and the combats often end in the death of one of the protagonists. This is a season of great activity. Just before sunrise the cock leaves the top of his favoured fir-tree where he has spent the night, crows a little during a noisy flight from tree to tree, and then descends to the ground where, rain, snow or frost, he begins to call. With head erect, throat feathers bristling, tail fan outspread, and wings half-open and dropping, he struts along, lifting his feet high at each step. His first calls consist of a series of isolated notes, which rapidly fall in pitch and lead finally to a full-throated song like the noise of a bottle being opened suddenly, followed by grating and low whispering sounds. The song lasts for no more than a few seconds. During this brief time the cock is quite unaware of anything going on around him and may be easily caught off guard by hunters. (The bird is also rather unwary during his courtship display, but does not close his eyes as is often supposed.) From time to time he leaps high into the air, noisily beating his wings. His calls are feeble and are barely audible a hundred metres away, the range being particularly short when the ground is uneven. But the noise of his wings as he jumps and the 'bottle-opening' sound are louder. During the entire display the cock maintains the same posture, sometimes trailing his wings as he runs across the forest floor or the short grass in clearings.

This ceremony continues until nine or ten in the morning and may be resumed briefly in the evening. As the cock calls, struts and displays his fan-like tail, the hens watch intently and respond with raucous cries. After mating the cock leaves the hens to their nest building, egg-laying, and chick-rearing. As early as the end of May he withdraws from his harem and returns to his solitary life until the following year.

The hen makes a simple bowl-shaped hollow in the ground under a clump of heather or a bush, and lines it with dried grass. The five to eight eggs are about the size of those of a Domestic Hen and are reddish yellow with innumerable brown spots. The incubation period is rather less than a month. The young can run as soon as they are hatched, but are accompanied by their mother, who may still continue to live with them during the winter. Their food consists of ant pupae, small insects, soft berries, young shoots and so on. As the stomach gradually becomes stronger, the young birds are able to ingest conifer needles and buds, which form the bulk of their food in winter.

The Black Grouse (*Lyrurus tetrix*) is placed in another genus, mainly because of its lyre-shaped tail. It should not, however, be confused with the Lyrebird, which belongs to the order of perching birds (*see* page 443). The male is about the size of a fowl cock, his plumage a bluish black with a metallic sheen. There is a broad white bar set obliquely on the wings, and the under-surface of the tail also is pure white. The lyre-shaped tail is due to the outer rectrices being longer than those in the middle and turned outwards. This arrangement is particularly noticeable when the bird spreads its tail and at the same time moves the feathers downwards and backwards. Another characteristic of the Black Grouse is that the upper part of the bare red ring round the eyes is swollen and has something of the appearance of an eyebrow ridge. The hen, which is smaller than the cock, has a brownish-red plumage with brown stripes and a white band across the wings.

The Black Grouse is found in the wooded regions and mountain areas of northern Asia and Europe, where it may occur up to a height of over 1,800 metres. A few small trees are sufficient as perching places. Most of the time the bird spends running quickly over the ground in search of berries, shoots and insects, or flying off in its cumbersome and noisy fashion at the least sign of alarm. It is quieter in its habits than the Wood-grouse, less wild and more sociable. Although sedentary, it moves about in search of sun and food.

Courtship takes place from April to May, when from twenty to thirty males gather in a particular place to call, display and fight, with the females as spectators. The first mating call, usually heard half an hour before sunrise, is so loud and clear that it can sometimes be heard over half a kilometre away. It begins with mewing sounds, followed by rising and falling hissing noises. Then come sonorous, rolling sounds, a little like the gobbling of a turkey. These calls are accompanied by a dance recalling that of the Wood-grouse. The bird circles around, prancing with outstretched neck, wings drooping and tail erect. The movements are quick and jerky.

Each cock has a harem of three or four hens, which remain with him during the breeding season. Afterwards the sexes separate and the hens rear the young. Like that of the Wood-grouse, the nest is a simple depression in the ground lined with dry leaves. The six to ten eggs of the clutch, about the same size as those of the Domestic Hen, are yellowish red with brown spots. Incubation lasts four weeks. The chicks are like those of the Wood-grouse and are reared in the same way.

Hybrids between Black Grouse and Capercaillie and the Red Grouse and Capercaillie have been known to occur occasionally.

The Hazel Hen (*Tetrastes bonasia*) has only the upper two-thirds of the tarsi covered with feathers. The beak is partly hidden by the adjacent feathers and the cocks have an erectile crest on the head. But sexual dimorphism is less marked than in the Wood-grouse and Black Grouse. Both are brownish red in colour with grey and white markings, while the male also has a black throat. The tail is short and non-erectile.

This species lives in mountainous regions of central Europe and northern Asia. It is found most often in mixed deciduous and coniferous woods and has a particular liking for oak, birch, walnut and hazel trees. During the summer months it finds much of its food on the ground and, being a fast and powerful flyer, is able to change its feeding grounds. In winter, when the ground is covered with snow, it becomes almost entirely arboreal. Except during the breeding season when the birds break up into pairs, for they are monogamous, the Hazel Hen lives in coveys.

Unlike most of the galliform birds, both sexes work together building the nest, which is as roughly constructed as that of other grouse. The cock calls loudly as they work, while the hen at his side responds with softer notes. The eggs are reddish in colour with brown spots. They measure four by three centimetres and there are eight to ten in a clutch. Incubation lasts three weeks. The plumage of newly hatched chicks provides good camouflage against the soil. Accompanied by the parent birds, they spend the summer months looking for insects, worms and ant pupae. Later on they take more and more vegetable food, and eventually on the approach of winter become entirely herbivorous.

Three North American grouse are the Greater Prairie Chicken (*Tympanuchus cupido*), the Lesser Prairie Chicken (*T. pallidicinctus*) and the Sage Grouse (*Centrocercus urophasianus*). All lead the same kind of life as the Partridge. All inhabit the grasslands. The prairie chickens can be recognised by the two tufts of feathers on the neck. These are

The Sage Grouse (*Centrocercus urophasianus*) is the largest and most colourful of the American gamebirds and best known for its spectacular mating dance. The cock is here seen in display which is accompanied by a loud booming mating call. The Sage Grouse is found only in the western half of the United States where sage-brush grows. Its plumage blends perfectly with this vegetation.

The Chukar Partridge was once thought to belong to the same species as the Rock Partridge (*Alectoris graeca*), but is now regarded as a separate species (*A. chukar*). The Chukar is found on barren hillsides in Asia, Asia Minor and the Middle East. It has been successfully introduced into New Zealand and the United States.

inserted above air sacs in the skin and stand erect when the cock inflates the air sac during his dancing display in the breeding season. Accompanying the display is the unmistakable booming mating call.

Prairie chickens are polygamous like the Capercaillie and Black Grouse. The cocks are very aggressive. They perform a vigorous dance displaying to one another at a special place, called a booming ground, from the calls they make there. This popular game bird is being rapidly decimated in the United States and will ultimately become extinct if not given protection. The subspecies known as the Heath Hen, which formerly occupied much of the northeastern United States, became extinct only in 1932.

A resident forest species of most of Canada and the United States is the Ruffed Grouse (*Bonasa umbellus*). It is fairly common in mixed and deciduous woodlands where it is a popular game bird known to hunters as the partridge. Its 'drumming', heard particularly during spring, is part of its courtship-territorial procedure. It perches firmly on a log or stump and beats its wings in a vertical position making a noise much like that made by shaking a heavy piece of cardboard or paperboard. The beats start slowly and rapidly increase before abruptly terminating.

Pheasants and allies (Family Phasianidae)

The game birds of the pheasant family include the partridges, quails, true pheasants and peafowls. The tarsi are bare, and there are no feathers round the nostrils or inflatable air sacs in the neck. Some species are heavily spurred. They are ground feeders and tree roosters. Plumage is copious. Sexual dimorphism is exhibited by some members of the family, and for the most part these are the species that are polygamous. The rest are monogamous. The family is more widely represented in the Old World; the American quails are the sole representatives in the New World.

European partridges belong to two genera, the typical representatives of which are the Red-legged Partridge and the Common Partridge.

The Red-legged Partridge lives in southern Europe and North Africa. In about 1770 it was introduced into England, where it is now quite common in the southern and eastern parts.

The birds live together in groups and are most commonly found in open and hilly country. They run quickly but are poor flyers, taking off only when disturbed. Opinion is divided as to whether they perch or not. Their calls are by no means harmonious, the female responding to the male with loud cacklings.

Red is the dominant plumage colour of the Red-legged Partridge (*Alectoris rufa*), while bill, legs and toes are also red. A black band borders the throat, and the feathers along the sides have red and brown markings.

This species is about the size of a large pigeon. The hen is a little smaller than the cock and has no spurs, but otherwise looks quite similar.

The Red-legged Partridge appears to be monogamous. Pairing occurs in spring, and in April and May the female lays ten to sixteen eggs in a simple depression in the ground. On leaving the nest (after a month's incubation) the young move around with one or both parents. The family does not break up until the height of summer, when both the adults and the young birds join groups of their own age.

In southern Europe the Red-legged Partridge is often confused with the Rock Partridge (*A. graeca*), a species which also occurs in the French Alps above about 1,500 metres. It is also found further south in the most arid areas of the Carpathian, Balkan and Apennine regions in the Near East, and central Asia. But the two species can be readily distinguished. In the Rock Partridge the black throat band has no pendant feathers such as are found on the breast of the Red-legged Partridge. And there are two black bands along the sides of *graeca* and only one in *rufa*. They are also dissimilar in habitat, since the Rock Partridge favours high altitudes in arid and rocky areas, coming down to the valleys only in winter.

The breeding habits of both species are similar. For most of the year the birds live in groups, which break up into pairs in spring and summer and then reform in autumn when the young have been reared. The nest is hollowed out in the ground and, as in the Red-legged Partridge, the female lays about fifteen eggs, which take a little over three weeks to hatch.

The Common Partridge (*Perdix perdix*) differs from the preceding species in a number of characteristics. The beak is shorter; cocks have no spurs; colour is mostly greyish; there is no black band round the neck; the plumage below the throat and around the eyes is reddish and wings and sides bear reddish bands; the legs and feet are grey. There is also a chestnut, horseshoe-shaped marking on the breast, which is not always very distinct.

The Common Partridge is found over most of Europe and in North Africa and western Asia. As the species has a wide area of distribution and is of sedentary habits, it is not surprising that it is divided into numerous subspecies or geographical races distinguished in slight details of plumage.

Frequenting open country, the Common Partridge always lives in groups, except during the breeding season. They are thus able to exploit fully the food resources of their territory.

Like the Red-legged Partridge, the common species has behaviour characteristics that are well known to sportsmen. When undisturbed, it walks with neck withdrawn into the shoulder region and back curved, pecking from one side to the other. When hurrying, it runs quickly on its small feet, with neck outstretched. If it is disturbed, it immediately crouches against the ground, preferably in a furrow, where its colour helps to conceal it. The flight is cumbersome and relatively short in extent, and they take off at the last moment with a whirring of wings and soon plane down to earth again. They rarely perch.

Pairing takes place in early spring and is accompanied by considerable restlessness. Each pair selects a definite territory suitable for feeding the brood. The nest is a makeshift hollow in the ground, lined with dead leaves. The hen lays up to twenty pear-shaped eggs, of a uniform yellowish green. As in the Red-legged Partridge, the eggs are brooded for rather more than three weeks. During this time the cock stays close to the nest, and after the eggs have hatched he accompanies the brood.

In caring for the young, the cock runs hither and thither, looking in all directions for possible danger. A low warning call from the hen is a sign for the young to gather around her, and she then leads them to some hiding place among the crops, trees, bushes, furrows or ruts. As soon as the chicks are safe the hen and her mate indulge in a distraction display, facing the enemy and striving to draw him away from their young. If they succeed, the hen is the first to fly away, rejoining the young in their hiding place and leading them further away.

Partridges rest during the middle of the day, and feed mostly during the morning and in the early evening. They eat a good many insects, worms and molluscs, as well as seeds, berries, shoots and weeds. They are consequently more of a help than a pest to agriculture.

The Common Partridge is one of the most abundant European game birds. In parts of the Continent, however, it has become rare locally and requires frequent restocking. This is usually without much success, however, since birds raised in captivity are not adapted to a free-living existence and are easily taken by foxes and birds of prey. Even worse, they may be carrying parasites common among captive birds, particularly of the coccidial variety, which cause much damage.

QUAIL: Old World quail differ from partridges in structure and habits. They have a shorter beak—always less than half the length of the head. The tarsi are slender and without spurs or horny tubercles. The primary wing feathers are longer than the secondaries, and the eye areas are feathered, not bare.

They are also less social in habit than partridges, forming flocks only when they migrate. They are among the few gallinaceous birds that fly south in winter and they may range as far as Africa. Although monogamous, the males pay little attention to the young. Quail are more insectivorous than granivorous. They have a tendency to plumpness, which makes them choice game birds.

The Common Quail (*Coturnix coturnix*) is the only species of this group inhabiting Europe. It is also the smallest of the European galliform birds, being something like a miniature partridge, and about the size of the European Blackbird or an American Robin. The head is striped, the body greyish brown variegated with black, white and yellow spots on the back and sides which merge with the more uniformly coloured underparts. The black speckling on the breast of the female is the main feature distinguishing her from the male.

The species has wide distribution in Europe, Asia and Africa, and has been introduced into New Zealand and the United States. Throughout its range it lives in lowland plains offering good grass cover. A few birds visit the British Isles.

Quail appear to be poor flyers, yet they manage to travel thousands of kilometres between their nesting and winter quarters. In a single night they may fly from Rome to Tunis, covering 600 kilometres at a speed of about sixty kilometres per hour. After this long trip they are exhausted and on landing fall easy prey to hunters. Only the remarkable rate of reproduction has kept this species from extinction.

The Common Quail breeds during its short stay in the northern countries, when each male takes charge of a territory and fiercely defends it against rival birds. If there are enough females the males are polygamous, but if not, they are monogamous. In any event they play no part in nest building, brooding or rearing the young. The female broods seven to fifteen pear-shaped eggs, which are yellowish with brown spots. Incubation takes three weeks and the young quail are precocial, lively and alert as soon as they are hatched. They grow rapidly and at the end of five or six weeks are already strong enough to join the parent birds in their annual migration.

It often happens that quail miss the northward migration in early spring, having already nested in Africa. In this event they arrive in western Europe in July and August when they may produce a second clutch. These late broods are easily attributed to spring-nesting birds.

The characteristic call notes of the Common Quail are heard mainly during the breeding season. The three short-syllabled notes of the male sound something like the words 'wet my lips'.

The Chinese Quail (*Coturnix chinensis*) is related to the Common Quail. The Chinese are said to have used these birds to warm their hands, and there are several old tapestries that show them doing this.

The type bird of the New World quails is the Bobwhite (*Colinus virginianus*), although in the southern United States it is often called a partridge. In Virgina and California it is among the commonest of the game birds. Like the Common Quail, some groups in northern regions migrate south at the beginning of winter, although ordinarily the Bobwhite is not a migrant. It is monogamous, the males staying with the females to take part in brooding the eggs.

Attempts to introduce the Bobwhite into Europe to increase the supply of game birds have never been successful.

Other New World quails are the Scaled Quail (*Callipepla squamata*) of Mexico and the southwestern United States, the California Quail (*Lophortyx californicus*) and its close relative Gambell's Quail (*L. gambelii*) of western America, the Mountain Quail (*Oreortyx pictus*), and the Harlequin Quail (*Cyrtonyx montezumae*). Many species have picturesque plumes arising from the crown of the heads. Other species range through Mexico, Central and South America.

The francolins (*Francolinus*) are partridge-like birds found in Africa and Asia. As in pheasants, the cocks have two pairs of spurs on the upper parts of the strong tarsi. One species (*Francolinus francolinus*) was formerly found farther north to the Mediterranean basin, particularly in Sicily, the Aegean area and Turkey.

TRUE PHEASANTS: These form an extremely striking group of birds, in which the males have a brilliant plumage and the females look plain and modest in contrast. Pheasants have little defence against their numerous enemies, and the males, belligerent among themselves, fall an easy prey to foxes and other predators. They can be kept in semi-captivity only when they are guarded with care.

All pheasants have a long tapering tail, which in certain species reaches a length of over two metres. The head is often ornamented with a crest or ruff, and the cocks have spurs. They are sedentary, passing the time in fields, heaths, thickets or even in forests in search of seeds, grain, fruit, leaves, roots, insects, earthworms and slugs. They have a quick way of walking and running, and they may occasionally perch, particularly at night. The flight is noisy and of short duration.

The males have a harsh cry, something between that of a Peafowl and a Guinea-fowl, and it is heard particularly during the breeding season, when their calls may attract the females or perhaps provoke other males. Being essentially polygamous, they assist in neither nest building nor brooding, and they exhibit no evidence of parental care towards the chicks. The nest, built by the female alone, is a depression hollowed out in the ground in the shelter of a hedge or a bush. There are usually about ten green or olive-brown eggs in a clutch. The young hatch after twenty-five days and are almost ready to fly about twelve days later. The hen stays with them until autumn.

The principal game bird is the Common Ring-necked Pheasant (*Phasianus colchicus*). Its plumage is predominantly brown, enhanced with a beautiful pattern of spots and metallic glints. The feathers of the head and neck are a brilliant greenish gold merging with blue and violet. The cheeks and the margins of the eyes are vivid red, while the long tail feathers are coppery red with purple highlights. The specific name indicates its origin in Colchis, the ancient name of a province in what is now the Soviet Republic of Georgia.

The Ring-neck has been introduced into the plains region of the United States, where it had never lived before. It has successfully established itself in this new environment and has increased to an amazing number and is a popular game bird.

Reeve's Pheasant (*Syrmaticus reevesii*) is named after the English traveller who brought it from China during the first half of the nineteenth century. This species has a white head and a golden throat and neck, while the feathers over the rest of the body have yellow, white, black and chestnut mottlings.

Other cock pheasants are no less striking. The Golden Pheasant (*Chrysolophus pictus*), a native of China and Tibet, has a crest of golden hair-like feathers and an orange ruff with black markings.

The Silver Pheasant (*Lophura nycthemera*) has a shining black crest and silver back marked with zigzag black lines. The underparts are black with metallic glints. The beak is white and the feet pink.

Lady Amherst's Pheasant (*Chrysolophus amherstiae*), a particularly handsome bird was introduced into England by Lady Amherst. The crest of the cock is red and the collaret is silvery. The back is green and the underparts white, while the wings and tail are black and white.

The short-tailed pheasants, or monals, have wings like partridges and a glittering plumage. The Impeyan Pheasant (*Lophophorus impejanus*) is typical. This has an iridescent plumage of blues, greens and bronze, like burnished metal. The Blood-pheasant (*Ithaginis cruentus*) of the Himalayas is grey and green with splashes of red on head, throat and tail. In the Crimson or Satyr Tragopan (*Tragopan satyra*) the cocks have erectile feathers on each side of the head, like horns. Tragopans are the only Phasianidae to build large nests of twigs and leaves in trees. In the Brown-eared Pheasant (*Crossoptilon mantchuricum*) both sexes have cheek feathers which project like ears.

Fowls of the genus *Gallus* form a well-defined group within the family Phasianidae. Whether wild or domesticated, all have the following distinguishing features: a fleshy crest or comb on the head, sometimes associated with a tuft of feathers; fleshy ear-lobes below the eyes and wattles hanging below the beak; long drooping feathers on the neck and breast that form the hackles of the cock; wing coverts developed as pendent, lancet-shaped feathers; a tail usually projecting upwards and bearing a number of curved sickle feathers; pointed spurs on the cock's legs. Sexual dimorphism is well marked and polygamy is the rule. The eggs are uniformly white or brown, according to the bird's food.

The wild fowls include Sonnerat's Fowl (India), Stanley's Fowl (Ceylon), the Javan Fowl and the Red Jungle Fowl, which is found in India, Malaya, Indo-China and the Philippine Islands.

The most important of these is the Red Jungle Fowl (*Gallus gallus*) which, apart from its wide distribution, is rightly considered to be the source of all domestic breeds. The head and neck are a brilliant yellow. The feathers of the back are purple-brown, being bright red in the middle and brownish-yellow round the edges. The long, drooping upper covert feathers of the tail are the same colour as those of the neck. The medium-sized wing coverts are a vivid chestnut brown, while the larger feathers have greenish-black tints. The breast feathers are black and greenish-golden glints. The primary feathers of the wing are a dark greyish black with lighter edgings, while the secondaries are red outside and black in the middle. The tail feathers are black. The eye is orange-red, the comb red, the bill brownish, and the feet a dark slate colour. The hen is smaller in size and duller in colour, and the comb and wattles are little developed.

Opposite
The Golden Pheasant (*Chrysolophus pictus*), one of the most brightly-coloured of all pheasants. In the wild in China it inhabits areas of low scrub and bamboo thickets on the higher rocky slopes of mountains. Although little is known of its habits in the wild it breeds readily in captivity and is popular in zoos and ornamental collections.

The Red Jungle Fowl prefers high mountainous regions and rarely comes below a height of 1,000 metres. It is usually found in thickly wooded country, where it lives in flocks, feeding on seeds, fruit, buds and insects, particularly termites. The ringing calls of the cock and his aggressive instincts are like those of game cocks. He is polygamous and takes no part in rearing the brood.

It was Darwin who showed that the present-day varieties of domestic fowls were bred from the Red Jungle Fowl by long-term selection of chance variations. In the first place, of all wild species the Red Jungle Fowl is the closest to certain domestic races. And it is the only wild species to give fertile hybrids with domestic breeds. Lastly, domestic fowls, even though very specialised, are always liable to revert to the ancestral type, when the characters of the plumage resemble closely those of the Red Jungle Fowl.

According to Darwin, the wild species was first introduced into Europe in the sixth century B.C. At the beginning of that century the Romans already had six or seven distinct breeds. There were barely as many in England and France in the fifteenth century, but since then the numbers have increased. Present-day breeders now recognise nearly seventy kinds, difficult to classify, but with differences in the number of toes on each foot (usually four but sometimes five), the shape of the comb, the presence or absence of a ruff of curly feathers on the sides of the head or below the beak, the presence or absence of feathers on the feet, the colour of the ear-lobes and tarsi, fecundity (measured by the number and weight of the eggs laid each year), brooding capacity, hardiness of the chicks, capacity for putting on fat, and the delicacy of the flesh.

In practive five large groups of domestic breeds may be distinguished: four-toed with a single dentated comb, four-toed with a flattened type of comb (e.g. Pea or Rose Fowl), four-toed with a crest of curly feathers, four-toed with feathered legs and five-toed.

The Game Cock, the closest to the ancestral species, is large with an upright and stately carriage, a strong hooked beak, and fearsome spurs. The comb is single and dentate, while the tarsi are bare and end in four digits. Its plumage is quite like that of the Red Jungle Fowl.

What may be called the common breed of fowl is reared on many small farms. It is like the Red Jungle Fowl with a single dentate comb, white or red ear lobes, well-developed wattles, grey unfeathered legs, plumage with metallic glints, and a tail with gracefully curving sickle feathers.

The Red Jungle Fowl (*Gallus gallus*), regarded as the ancestor of all domestic poultry. In the wild, it is extremely wary and still survives in fair numbers in spite of centuries of persecution by man. During the breeding season jungle fowl are found in family parties of one cock and several hens. In winter they congregate in larger flocks.

The Peacock is the male of the Common or Blue Peafowl (*Pavo cristatus*). Here it is displaying the magnificent plumes of its tail-coverts, decorated with colourful eyespots. Although a native of India and Sri Lanka, the peacock has been kept in captivity in Europe and many other parts of the world for over 2,000 years.

The Leghorn Fowl is rather similar to the common breed, but is distinguished by a comb that is erect in the cock and drooping in the hen.

The giant of the pheasant group, and also one of the most remarkable, is the Argus Pheasant (*Argusianus argus*), a forest bird of Malaya, Sumatra and Borneo. The secondary feathers of the wing and those in the middle of the tail are extremely long and are decorated with eye-spots with brilliantly coloured centres. When these feathers are spread the bird is transformed and well deserves the name Argus, a reference to the mythical Argus with a hundred eyes. The bird is more than 180 centimetres long, over 120 centimetres of which is tail.

At the beginning of the breeding season each male Argus Pheasant prepares a large display ground in the heart of the forest, stripping it of its vegetation and afterwards keeping it completely cleared. When females come into breeding condition a number of them are likely to respond to his calls and visit the display ground.

The cock displaying to a hen is a magnificent sight. First he dances around her in ever smaller circles, smartly striking the ground at each step. Having come close to his partner, he stops suddenly and spreads one of his wings sideways. If the female appears to accept this display and makes no show of flight, the male then positions himself in front of her and suddenly displays the full splendour of his wings, an immense screen starred with delicately coloured eye-spots. The primary wing feathers touch the ground on each side, while the extremely long secondary feathers rise almost vertically above the back. The long tail feathers are also raised, undulating with the swaying of the body. The trembling of all these quill feathers makes a noise like that of a Peafowl spreading. Meanwhile the bird bends his neck back to bring the head behind one of the wings. From there he keeps watch, peering through a fold of the wing. This display usually causes the hen to take up a submissive attitude, whereupon mating follows immediately.

The Argus Pheasant and the Peacock, or more properly the Peafowl species, could be confused, as both have feathers with eyespots, but those of the Peafowl are the tail coverts (the feathers that lie over the true tail quills) not the wing feathers. These, too, can be erected in a fan, by the strong muscles under the skin of the rump.

The long train makes it easy to identify the Peafowl. Other characteristics are a long neck, a stout hooked bill, a crest on the head, fairly long legs and small spurs. Peafowl live in the forests and jungles of northern Asia, remaining on the ground by day and perching at night. In common with most galliform birds they are omnivorous. They live in groups which split up when pairing takes place during the breeding season. It is then that the Peacock fully displays his fan. His harsh scream is quite unearthly, and heard at daybreak it can be most startling. There are two shrill notes. The first seems to pierce the last traces of the dawn twilight. The second is a fifth lower in pitch and ends so abruptly it can be heard only at close quarters. Then follows a harsher cry, and this may be repeated as many as seven times at intervals of three or four seconds. After pairing the cock leaves the Peahen to build the nest, normally under a bush. The clutch consists of about ten eggs that are closely brooded by the female, which also takes great care of the young, though they are not difficult to rear in the Peafowl's native land.

The genus *Pavo* includes two species with much the same habits: the Common Peafowl (*P. cristatus*) of India and Ceylon, and the Green Peafowl (*P. muticus*), found in Indo-China and Java. The head, neck and breast are blue in the first and green in the second. The crest feathers of the Common Peacock have barbs at the tips, while those of the Javan species are barbed over most of their length.

The so-called Black Peacock, with dark blue wings, and the White Peacock appear to be varieties of *P. cristatus*. The precise date at which the Peafowl was introduced to Europe is not known, and in the fifteenth century it was still a rarity. The Congo Peafowl (*Afropavo congensis*), a fairly close relative of *Pavo*, was first described in 1936. It is very rare, which explains why such a large bird was unknown for so long.

Guinea-fowl (Family Numididae)
The various guinea-fowl species of Africa, Arabia, Madagascar and the Mascarene Islands have few or no feathers on neck or head. The head bears a crest of feathers or, in some species, a bony casque. There are also fleshy appendages, such as ear-lobes and wattles, and horny tubercles. The naked skin is variously coloured, but usually is blue. The plumage is dark with a white mottling. The cocks of some species have spurs.

These birds dwell in large groups in forest clearings, steppes and savannas, uttering their harsh cries. They scatter at the slightest alarm, coming together again later when called by one of the old cocks. They feed on insects or plants according to season. During breeding they break up into pairs, which later return to the group. The hen builds the nest on the ground and lays about ten eggs.

The Vulturine Guinea-fowl (*Acryllium vulturinum*) of East Africa, so named because its head and neck are almost bare, has a feathered fringe extending at ear-level round the back of the head. It can also be recognised by the long white band running down each hackle. The Crested Guinea-

fowl (*Guttera cristata*), also of East Africa, has spurs and a crest of feathers on the head.

Lastly, there are two species with blue or red wattles hanging below the bill. Both were domesticated in Greek and Roman times, when they were known as African fowls, but were later allowed to revert to the wild state. Today only the species with red wattles, the Common or Domestic Guinea-fowl (*Numida meleagris*), is found in captivity. It comes originally from West Africa and the Cape Verde Islands and is recognisable by its pearly-green plumage. The same species exists in a wild state in Central America, where it became established from domesticated stock originally brought from Europe.

Guinea-fowls are easy to rear, and the hen produces a yearly average of eighty eggs, small, yellowish or brown with various mottlings, each weighing about fifty grams. The eggs make good eating, and the flesh has the same taste as pheasant meat.

Turkeys (Family Meleagrididae)
Two species of wild turkey are found in North and Central America. The neck and head are bare. A fleshy, pendent wattle, which can be distended and erected, springs from the base of the bill and hangs down on one side. The cocks also have a tuft of stiff, hair-like feathers on the breast and, like the Peafowl, are able to raise and spread the tail. The tarsi are spurred and the plumage has a metallic sheen.

The Vulturine Guinea-fowl (*Acryllium vulturinum*) is one of the most beautiful of African gamebirds. It is particularly numerous in northern Kenya where it inhabits regions of semi-desert and acacia scrub and also wild mountainous areas. When the flock is feeding two birds usually act as sentinels to keep watch for predators. The African Hawk-eagle, the Martial Eagle, the Caracal and Serval all prey on it.

401

The Common Turkey (*Meleagris gallopavo*) still occurs in the wild in North America. After years of persecution it has become exceedingly wary. It is a very strong flier over short distances. The hen nests on the ground laying between eight and fifteen eggs. Sometimes more than one female will lay in the same nest.

In the wild state turkeys live in small groups in open forests, feeding on insects, seeds and fallen fruit. The males make gobbling noises like those of the Domestic Turkey. During the breeding season fights occur between the cocks, which may wound or even kill each other. Then come the courtship displays during which the cocks, which are polygamous, make grating sounds, revolving and spreading their tails. The nest, built by the hen, is a simple depression lined with dry leaves, in which about twelve cream-coloured eggs with reddish spots are laid.

The Common Turkey (*Meleagris gallopavo*) extends from southern Canada by way of the eastern and southern United States to Mexico. The Domestic Turkey has been bred from this. The most valued of the breeds is a bronze-coloured variety in which the cock may weigh over eighteen kilograms and the hen seven to ten kilograms.

This turkey was introduced into Europe after the Spanish conquest of Mexico and by 1541 was known in England. As a domestic bird it was taken back to North America by the first settlers. When they first settled in the eastern states the wild turkey was abundant there. Its numbers were decimated by encroaching settlement. Conservation measures in recent years have resulted in the original wild bird becoming more numerous and it is now beginning to spread into areas from which it has been absent for generations. The Domestic Turkey is descended from the Mexican species introduced from Europe. The one other species is the Ocellated Turkey (*Agriocharis ocellata*) of Mexico and northern Central America.

Hoatzin (Family Opisthocomidae)

The single species (*Opisthocomus hoazin*), of northeastern South America, has so many curious features that it is placed in a separate family. The adults are crow-sized, and brown with pale streaks on the breast. They have a long tail of ten loosely arranged feathers and an untidy crest on a very small head. The nest, built by both male and female, is an untidy collection of sticks in a treefork by a river bank.

Young Hoatzins have claws on the first and second digits of the wings. With the bill and feet these are used to climb about the nest or among the branches of the tree. As the Hoatzin grows and is able to fly the digits and claws grow smaller. These 'quadrupedal' birds recall the fossil *Archaeopteryx*.

It is interesting that the Hoatzin has a musky odour like a crocodile and that its call sounds more like a reptile than a bird. For reasons that are obvious it is sometimes known as the Reptile-bird.

Cranes and rails (Order Gruiformes)

This primarily aquatic order is divided into several families whose similarities are mainly anatomical and skeletal. Most species of cranes and their allies have a raised hind toe and only the extremity rests on the ground. Feet are not webbed, but are sometimes lobed. The young are nidifugous, and nests are built on the ground. Diet is vegetarian rather than insectivorous.

Mesites (Family Mesitornithidae)

There are three species of these rail-like birds found only in Madagascar, alternatively called mesites, roatelos, or monias. All are near flightless (they even climb to their nests). They measure just under thirty centimetres in length and have more powder-down patches than any other bird. At least one species, Bensch's Monia or Rail (*Monias benschi*) is polyandrous, and the males build the nest, a loose platform of sticks several feet from the ground, and incubate the eggs.

Hemipodes and button-quails (Family Turnicidae)

This is another odd family of quail-like birds whose behaviour is more like that of the bustards (page 408). They are small birds found from southern Spain eastwards to the Philippines and the Solomon Islands and southwards to South Africa and Australia, in flat grasslands. They seldom take wing but are speedy swimmers. They lack a fourth, backwardly directed toe (whence hemipode or half-foot). Hemipodes are polyandrous and the female does the courting. The males build the nests and incubate the eggs. The incubation period is very short (a mere thirteen days in some species) and the chicks precocial.

The Striped Button-quail (*Turnix sylvatica*) is a rather widespread species of Africa, which just reaches southern Spain. Like all fourteen other species of button-quail, it is mainly sedentary with little or no true migration. Its behaviour and feeding habits are more like those of the quail, which it resembles in appearance, than those of the cranes, to which it is more closely related. The Quail-plover (*Ortyxelos meiffrenii*) of Africa is the only species of its genus; all other members of the family are in the genus *Turnix* except for the Collared Hemipode.

Plains-wanderer (Family Pedionomidae)

The Collard Hemipode (*Pedionomus torquatus*), or Plains-wanderer, closely resembles the button-quail but has a well-developed hind toe, paired carotid arteries and pear-shaped rather than oval eggs. It is thought to be nearer the ancestral button-quails. The Collared Hemipode looks like a quail with orange-yellow legs. It rarely flies but tends to run or crouch in the grass if disturbed. The female, about twelve centimetres long, is greyish brown with a vivid chestnut patch on the chest and a black and white collar. The male is smaller, more uniformly coloured, and he makes the grass-lined scrape in which the female lays three or four grey blotched eggs. He incubates the eggs and feeds the precocial young.

Cranes (Family Gruidae)

Shy and wary when alone, the cranes are watchful and always on the alert; but for the most part they are gregarious creatures, and in flocks a few birds detach themselves from the main group as sentinels to give warning of danger. Driven from a particular place, the flocks never return *en masse* but straggle back one at a time until they have been reformed. A powerful call keeps individuals in constant touch. When nesting, cranes are particularly shy. They are seen usually only when they emerge in search of grain and occasionally insects, worms, molluscs, frogs and small rodents.

They are gregarious except during the breeding season which, in northern countries, is in the spring and early summer. The males are monogamous and help in hatching and rearing the chicks, which leave the nest shortly after hatching.

The most widely distributed species in Europe is the Common Crane (*Grus grus*), 120 centimetres high, with a wingspan of over 240 centimetres, and

A young Hoatzin (*Opisthocomus hoazin*) using its wing claws to move along a branch. It can also swim well and when coming out of the water clambers back into the trees using feet, wing claws and bill. Although the wing claws disappear as the young develop, adults often use their wings to help in climbing over branches.

One of the most striking of all cranes, the Crowned Crane (*Balearica pavonina*) is found over much of Africa from the Sudan and Ethiopia southwards. In the breeding season it indulges in spectacular courtship dancing, when the crown is displayed to full effect. Some of the dances of local tribes in West Africa are based on these courtship displays.

A group of Sandhill Cranes (*Grus canadensis*) feeding. Their breeding range extends from the Canadian, United States and Russian arctic southwards. Several sub-species occur in the American population, some resident and some migratory. The Sandhill Crane is similar in size and colour to the Common Crane (*G. grus*) except that the forehead is red instead of the crown.

weighing over four kilograms. Its plumage is ashen grey, except for the forehead, nape, throat, remiges and rectrices, which are black. On the top of the head is a bald red patch. The bill is straight and longer than the head. A particular feature of the adult is a tuft of long feathers, curved and separated to form a plume over the tail.

Migration begins in August or September and reaches its peak in Europe in October or November, when squadrons flying in V-formation at an estimated thirty kilometres an hour attract attention with their resounding cries. The return takes place in February or March. The flocks winter in India and in Africa, from Morocco and Tunisia to Ethiopia and the Sudan, and from Israel to the delta of the Congo.

The beautiful Crowned Crane (*Balearica pavonina*) of tropical Africa was once known as the Balearic Crane, for it could then be found as far north as the Mediterranean islands of that name. It is a striking bird with head doubly decorated with a black velvet cap and an occipital tuft of bristle-shaped feathers.

One American species is particularly well known, the Whooping Crane (*Grus americana*), a large white bird with red face and black primary wing feathers. Every individual is known, for the species is on the verge of extinction, and on the only wintering grounds at Aransas Refuge in

Texas, the entire population (thirty-eight in 1965) may be counted. In 1952 numbers had dropped to only twenty-three birds. By 1956 they had increased to thirty, by 1960 the census showed thirty-six in the wild and six in captivity. In the breeding season the birds gather in one area of the prairies of northwestern Canada. The 1977 census gave a total of seventy. All migrate south in the non-breeding season, spending the winter in the Texas area. The species is rigorously protected and every encouragement is given to increase its numbers.

The Demoiselle Crane (*Anthropoides virgo*), of central Asia, North Africa, and south-east Europe, is distinguished by dazzling white tufts of feathers on each side of its head. It is smaller than the other cranes (about a metre tall), but even more graceful.

The non-European cranes have much the same habits as their European relatives.

Limpkin (Family Aramidae)

The Limpkin or Courlan (*Aramus guarauna*), the sole member of the family, a sedentary wader of tropical America, has the build of a crane. Its eggs are similar to those of the rail and its chicks dark brown. Its melancholy call has earned it a variety of names: Clucking Hen, Courlan, Lamenting Bird and Crazy Widow. It frequents marshes and waterways, hunting large snails. It swims well although its feet are not webbed. It is found as far north as the states of Georgia and Florida.

Trumpeters (Family Psophiidae)

This is a small family of three South American species. The Common Trumpeter (*Psophia crepitans*) looks rather like a long-legged guinea-fowl and is about the size of a pheasant. It has a magnificent, gaudy plumage: black, purple shot with blue and green, ice-blue shot with bronze, silver grey, and other tints. With the other two species, it makes its home in the humid forests of South America, where it feeds on seeds and fruit. The strange cries (from which it takes its common name) are strongly ventriloquial, deep reverberating sounds from within the bodies, uttered with a closed beak.

Rails, moorhens and coots (Family Rallidae)

Four very long toes, sometimes with membranous lobes, and eminently suited to walking on the wet mud of ponds and lakes or swimming, mark the largest family of the group. Nearly all can swim and dive. But wings are so short as to make prolonged flight impossible. Many species found on remote islands are flightless. The chicks are quite strong at birth, covered with down, and able to leave the nest after a very short time. On each wing the chick has a horny spur enabling it to creep about among the grass. In some species this spur is retained in the adult. The food of most species is mixed animal and vegetable.

The type bird of the Rallidae is the Water-rail (*Rallus aquaticus*), common in all the marshy regions of northern Europe and Asia. Its favourite haunts are among the tangle of water-plants, where it moves easily, because it has flat sides. Since it is solitary and very cautious, a great deal of patience is needed to observe it in its natural surroundings. It is easier to hear than to see. Its cry is repeated several times and on a lower note at each repetition, the whole ending in a grunt.

The Water-rail is little bigger than a Turtle-dove, with a long, slightly down-curved red bill which alone is sufficient to distinguish it from other species of the genus. Plumage is russet-coloured with black streaks on the upper parts, grey on the rest of the body, with transverse black stripes on its flanks.

The nest is bowl-shaped, well hidden among reeds. The female lays six to ten eggs, creamy white with some greyish-mauve spots. The male shares the three-week incubation. When hatched the chicks have a black down with metallic tints, which they moult between July and November. This is also the time when the adult birds lose their summer plumage, including the flight feathers, before acquiring their winter plumage. For some weeks they are highly sensitive to cold and are flightless. This phenomenon is known as the eclipse plumage and also occurs in many of the ducks. Although a poor flyer the European Water-rail migrates south for the winter.

Other typical rails include the Clapper Rail (*R. longirostris*), the Virginia Rail (*R. limicola*), and the King Rail (*R. elegans*) of America, the Slate-breasted Water Rail (*R. pectoralis*) of Australia and South Africa's Cape Rail (*R. caerulescens*).

Rails with shorter bills are known as crakes in Europe. The Corncrake (*Crex crex*) resembles the European Water-rail in size and colouring, but its wings are redder and its belly yellower or dun-coloured. Its bill is much shorter and brownish. Also known as the Land Rail, the Corncrake is essentially a land bird. In company with quails it frequents meadows, fields and moorland. It is timid and not particularly sociable. Its cry, like the sound of a stick being drawn across a comb, is heard chiefly in the evening. When approached it will run swiftly away and is soon lost in the vegetation. It rarely takes refuge in flight.

The Corncrake seldom begins its nest before May or June, when the grass is highest. It builds in a dry place, making a depression in the ground lined with twigs and leaves. Its laying and breeding habits are like those of the Water-rail.

The Corncrake is migratory, leaving Europe each September or October for Africa and returning in April or May. And each year its numbers diminish, partly because it is favoured as game in some countries, and partly because machine-mowing takes a heavy toll of the young.

The Spotted Crake (*Porzana porzana*) has a speckled plumage streaked and dotted with white. Its bill is short and yellow. Its green feet match the grass on which it walks. In habits it differs little from the Water-rail. Its cry is more distinct,

There are eight species of Wood Rail in Central and South America of which the Grey-necked Wood Rail (*Aramides cajanea*) is figured here. All are large rails with stout bills, generally olive-brown upper parts, a grey breast and black hind parts. When flushed they take wing but with obvious reluctance. Otherwise they rely on their legs.

405

however, and is repeated with clockwork regularity. It lays from eight to fifteen eggs, considerably more than the Water-rail. It breeds throughout most of Europe and into central Asia and winters in Africa and southern Asia.

There is a smaller version of the Spotted Crake, the Little Crake (*P. parva*), an active species hardly bigger than a Blackbird.

The most widely distributed, and probably the most common short-billed rail of North America is the Sora (*P. carolina*), sometimes known as the Carolina Rail. It is similar in size and habits to the Spotted Crake but is brownish above with a black cap, mask, and bib; bluish grey face, neck, and breast; and grey-and-white barred flanks.

Forbes Rail (*Rallicula forbesi*), one of four species found in New Guinea, is remarkable for the special nest it builds for sleeping, whereas most birds use a nest only for the reception of the eggs and the rearing of the young.

The smallest rail is the American Black Rail (*Laterallus jamaicensis*) of temperate North America, twelve centimetres long, black with reddish nape and white bars on the back. It is so secretive that it is rarely seen, although its calls can be heard.

One of the largest rails is the Ypecaha Wood-rail (*Aramides ypecaha*), of Brazil to Argentina, forty-five centimetres long, brown with a grey head and throat, blackish tail and chestnut breast. The Flightless Wood-rail or Weka (*Gallirallus australis*), of New Zealand, is as large as a domestic hen. It not only manages to survive near human habitations but will even enter houses and steal bright objects. It is nocturnal and will eat almost anything. It is able to run down rats and mice as well as birds the size of a duck.

The moorhens or gallinules fall, anatomically, between the rails and the coots.

The Moorhen (*Gallinula chloropus*), known in America as the Common Gallinule, has a conical bill, red with a yellow tip and a red frontal shield (that part of the upper bill which flares out into a broad shield-like structure on the forehead). Its plumage is olive green; the rest of the body is slate grey, with white under tail-coverts divided by a black line. Its feet are green.

Resident in the southern parts of its range, migratory in the north, it can be found near pools, ponds and marshes, and any stretch of river where reeds and rushes abound. It prefers small areas of open water, but also needs cover for its nest. It is less timid than the rail and commonly settles near villages and sometimes among waterfowl in public parks. It can often be seen climbing a sloping tree-trunk. When swimming, its head and tail jerk in a characteristic rocking movement. It can dive below the surface, and in shallow water will squat on the bottom, with only its beak breaking the surface. It seldom flies, except when migrating, and seemingly with reluctance. It breeds on all continents but Australia and is the most widespread of the rails.

In the spring, after pairing, the cock and hen jointly build the nest, sometimes on a mud shelf, among water-plants, suspended between the reeds, or even afloat. Some pairs build in trees overhanging the water, and some occupy the old nests of tree-building birds. Five or six eggs are laid in April or May, varying from grey to red with red-brown spots and blotches. Incubation takes three weeks and brooding is by both male and female. At first the chicks are black. They leave the nest on the second day and begin to swim under the supervision of their parents. The families break up at the end of the summer.

The European Purple Gallinule (*Porphyrio porphyrio*) breeds in southern Spain, Sardinia, Sicily, and occasionally in the south of France as well as in Africa, southern and southeastern Asia, Australia, Indonesia, the Philippines, Madagascar, and New Zealand. Twice as big as the Moorhen, it is also distinguished from it by its colouring, which ranges from purple to sky blue, by its more extensive frontal shield and its longer front toes. Its habits are much the same as those of the Moorhen. It is easily kept in captivity.

The American Purple Gallinule (*Porphyrula martinica*) ranges from the southern United States and the West Indies to southern central South America. It resembles the Moorhen or Common Gallinule in size and habits, but its plumage is predominantly a rich purple.

Gallinules are found all over the world, typically on large areas of semi-stagnant water, among clumps of water-plants, their bright plumage harmonising with the colours of the bright green vegetation and its flowers. They feed on vegetation as well as insects, frogs and lizards. One of the most remarkable is the Takahe or Notornis (*Notornis mantelli*), known from only three specimens since 1855 and believed to be extinct, until in 1948 a small group was found living in South Island, New Zealand, in a valley 600 metres above sea-level and a week's journey from the nearest human habitation. The Takahe, now numbering about a hundred, is rigidly protected by law. It is the size of a large domestic hen and has an almost parrot-like beak. Its plumage is purple-blue with a green sheen, and the frontal shield a brilliant red.

The genus *Fulica* contains species of coot, which have toes edged with scalloped membranes, or lobed-webbing very much like a web. The Common Coot of Europe (*Fulica atra*) can be found wherever there is a sizeable expanse of water and is resident and numerous in many districts of the British Isles. Its range extends across Europe, except for the far north, central and southern Asia, northwestern Africa, and Australia. Its dark plumage is broken by its white bill and frontal shield. Unlike rails and moorhens, coots are sociable, and are gregarious outside the breeding period. They remain underwater just long enough to snatch up the plants which form their food.

Floating, or fixed among the weeds, the nest contains six to nine light grey eggs finely speckled and spotted. These are brooded by each parent in turn for a period of three weeks. Often there are two broods, one in May and another in August. The female will brood the second clutch on her own, while the male continues to bring up the young hatched three months earlier. Sometimes the chicks hatched in the first brood will help feed those hatched in the second.

Although the coots of Britain and France are mainly sedentary, those living in northern Europe migrate south as soon as the weather turns cold. They always travel by night and at great speed. Daily distances of 300 to 400 kilometres are not unusual. A ringed coot has been known to cover the 720 kilometres from Hamburg to Cayeux-sur-Mer (Normandy) in thirty-six hours.

The very similar American Coot (*F. americana*) is found from northern North America to north-western South America and in Hawaii.

Finfoot or sun-grebe (Family Heliornithidae)

There are three species in this family: one in tropical Africa, one in Central and South America, and one in Bengal, Malaya and Sumatra. This scattered distribution suggests that sun-grebes were once more widely distributed and had many more species. Now the birds are not common in any area. In addition, they are shy and live singly or in pairs by densely wooded streams, so that their habits are not well-known.

Sun-grebes are similar to grebes in appearance but are probably more closely related to coots, and, like both of these, their feet have scalloped, lobate webs. Bodies, necks, tails and bills are elongate. Bills are grebe-like and bear perforate nostrils. Sun-grebes swim partly submerged or hunt from low perches, feeding on fishes, shrimps, beetles, snails as well as vegetable matter.

The African Finfoot (*Podica senegalensis*) is the best-known species. The male is forty centimetres long, dark brown spotted black and white above, flanks barred and underparts white. A white line runs from the eye along the side of the neck. The throat is sooty grey. The female is smaller and has a white throat. The call is a low booming, heard especially during courtship as the seasonal flood-waters rise. Three to five eggs, white with red and buff streaks, are laid in platform-like nests built of grass and reeds in the forest, away from water.

The American Sun-grebe (*Heliornis fulica*) is the smallest of the family, about thirty centimetres long, olive-brown above and whitish below, with a white stripe behind the eye. The bill is scarlet and the feet are banded with yellow and black.

The Asian Sun-grebe (*Heliopais personata*), fifty centimetres long, is brown above, with black head and throat, yellow bill and green legs. It has the same white stripe behind the eye.

Kagu (Family Rhynochetidae)

The Kagu (*Rhynochetos jubatus*) of New Caledonia, was once common enough but is now close to extinction. It is long-legged, greyish and heron-like, with bright orange-red bill and legs, and a large head with a pronounced crest. The single species of the genus, it is much reduced in number. By day the Kagu sleeps among rocks or under tree roots, emerging only at night in search of insects and snails. Its piercing, rattling scream is audible a distance away.

The breeding habits of the Kagu have been studied in captivity. The courship dance of the male is a remarkable performance, half-running, half-skipping, with the participant tumbling about. A single pale-brown egg, dotted and streaked with reddish brown, is laid in a ground nest of leaves and twigs. Both parents share the incubation.

Sunbittern (Family Eurypygidae)

This family consists of one species, the Sunbittern (*Eurypyga helias*) of Central and South America. It is superficially like a bittern, but seems to be more closely related to the Kagu, and is forty-five to fifty-four centimetres long. It flies very little but walks slowly and deliberately on its orange-coloured heron-like legs, its long, snake-like neck held parallel to the ground. It lives alone or with its mate in dense tropical forests and swamps, usually near water, where it hunts insects or small fishes speared with a quick stroke of the sharp bill. Two eggs are laid in a nest of sticks, grass and mud, in low trees or on the ground. The parents share nest building, incubating and feeding the precocial young.

Cariamas or seriemas (Family Cariamidae)

These large birds have long neck and legs, short broad bill, erectile crest and long tail. They live in pairs or small groups and if pursued run with lowered head, flying only if hard pressed. They feed mainly on insects, especially ants, but also eat fruit and berries, and sometimes snakes and lizards. They breed and tame easily in captivity, and the young are often taken from the nest and raised with domestic fowls, which they protect. The first egg of many birds often differs from the rest of the clutch. This is especially so in cariamas, for one of the two eggs laid is glossier, more heavily pigmented and more pear-shaped than the other.

There are two species, the Crested Seriema (*Cariama cristata*) ranging from central Brazil to Paraguay and northern Argentina, and Burmeis-ter's Seriema (*Chunga burmeisteri*), restricted to

The Crested or Red-knobbed Coot (*Fulica cristata*) of south and central Africa, Morocco and south Spain. It gets its name from the two brownish-red knobs on top of the white plate on the front of its head. Otherwise it is very similar in appearance and habits to the Common Coot (*F. atra*).

The Kori Bustard (*Ardeotis kori*), the largest of the bustards, may weigh over thirteen kilograms which is close to the size limit above which flight is impossible. It flies reluctantly and only for short distances but is a swift runner. Mainly dark brown in colour it lives in dry, open country in South and East Africa. The male is here displaying.

and tail feathers that can be erected in a fan. A tuft of long white bristly feathers hangs below the bill. The female, smaller and without the 'beard', is more drab than the male. It still breeds in discrete areas in Europe and central Asia.

During the breeding season the males develop a throat pouch, which disappears at the end of the season. For a long time there was controversy whether such an organ existed or not, but this was finally settled by dissection of an adult male which died in captivity.

The Little Bustard (*O. tetrax*) is more common but less widespread. It is half the size of the Great Bustard and never has a beard, but on the throat of the male is a curious white V-shaped mark on a black ground, below this a white collar, and below that a black one. The Bustard is extremely shy. At mating time the male bird erects his black throat feathers into a sort of ruff and dances, alone or with other males. When a female draws near he leaps into the air in odd, contorted postures.

The Australian Bustard (*Ardeotis australis*), up to fourteen kilograms in weight and with a wingspan of 210 centimetres, is probably the heaviest extant flying bird. Its plumage is of varying shades of brown, white below and with a dark band on the chest. In courtship display the male, which is much bigger than the female, inflates his throat pouch until, when fully distended, it brushes the ground. The single egg is laid on bare ground in the cover of a bush. The chick is cryptically coloured and freezes motionless if alarmed.

In Africa, the stronghold of the bustards, one widely distributed species is the Black-bellied Bustard (*Eupodolis melanogaster*), which lives in high grass and seems to prefer burnt areas. It feeds mainly on insects and flower buds.

Waders and gulls (Order Charadriiformes)

This order includes a diverse collection of plovers, snipe, curlew, redshanks, woodcock, sandpipers, oystercatchers, jacanas, gulls, avocets and auks. Most of the family are small to medium size waders, or shore birds, found on or near water. Their habitats are as varied as the structure of their feet: some webbed, some unwebbed, some with four toes, some with three, some with short toes, others long.

northern Argentina and parts of Paraquay. The first lives on open grasslands and pampas, the second in sparse bushy forest. Both are omnivorous.

Bustards (Family Otididae)

The family comprises several genera of running birds—about thirty species distributed through the dry regions of the Old World. Like the related trumpeters (Psophiidae), bustards look ostrich-like. They have heavy bodies and fly clumsily, but are able to run with great speed; they lack a hind toe. They associate in companies and inhabit grassy plains and arid steppes. The males are polygamous and fight fiercely in the breeding season. They feed off leaves, buds and seeds, with some insects (beetles especially) and voles. The females nest on the ground and alone brood and rear the chicks.

The Great Bustard (*Otis tarda*) looks somewhat like a tan, black-spotted turkey, but has longer legs and a more pointed beak. In breeding plumage the male has a chestnut back with black margins, white underparts, white wings with dark grey tips,

Jacanas or lily-trotters (Family Jacanidae)

The jacanas resemble the Moorhen in size and habits and are found in both Old and New World on tropical marshy shores of lakes and streams. The most outstanding feature of the six genera is the extraordinary length of the legs, toes, and flat, straight claws, which enable them to walk on water-lilies and the floating leaves of other aquatic plants in lakes and rivers. Some have a long, flowing tail and in some species the plumage of the upperparts is iridescent. Male and female are similar, but the hen is usually larger than the male. The male does most of the incubating and looks after the chicks.

The American Jacana (*Jacana spinosa*) ranges from Texas southwards to Argentina. In courtship it displays its wings to reveal bright yellow patches of feathers, but its general colour is maroon and black. The Pheasant-tailed Jacana (*Hydrophasianus chirurgus*) of the Himalayas to Ceylon and eastwards to Java and the Philippines lays its eggs on floating vegetation, sometimes half-submerged. It is believed that the female of this species does the incubation. The thirty centimetres African Jacana (*Actophilornis africanus*), brown with a blue forehead, is found in mountain regions, walking on moss-covered rocks, or in swamps. In Australia and Indonesia the family is represented by the Bronze-coloured Lotus-bird (*Irediparra gallinacea*), a species with an erect comb.

Painted snipe (Family Rostratulidae)
These are so named for their snipe-like build and their bright colours. There are only two species: the Old World Painted Snipe (*Rostratula benghalensis*), of the tropical and subtropical regions of Africa, southern Asia and Australia, and the smaller, American Painted Snipe (*Nycticryphes semicollaris*) of South America. The female is larger and more brilliantly coloured than the male and at mating time it is the females who fight for possession of the males. Both species leave nest building and breeding to the males. Pairing is not permanent.

Oystercatchers (Family Haematopodidae)
The single genus is made up of six species very similar physically and in habits. The European Oystercatcher, or Sea-pie (*Haematopus ostralegus*), is forty to fifty-four centimetres long, black and white with an orange-red bill two-and-a-half times the length of the head, and pink legs and feet. Its striking colours and loud, shrill cry are unmistakable. It is a coastal bird, feeding on shellfish such as mussels, limpets and, more rarely, oysters. In some parts of England it is known as the Musselpecker. The American Oystercatcher (*H. palliatus*), of the temperate and tropical coasts of North and South America, is almost identical and is treated by some authorities as the same species. The Black Oystercatcher (*H. bachmani*) of North America and the Sooty Oystercatcher (*H. fuliginosus*) of Australia, are both sooty black with flesh-coloured legs.

During the oystercatchers' nuptial ceremonies the male dances before the female. There may be two males present, in which event one mimics the actions of the other, as if trying to out-dance him. The contest ends with one of the contestants admitting defeat and departing.

Plovers and lapwings (Family Charadriidae)
Plovers are gregarious, disruptively coloured birds fifteen to forty centimetres long, with large eyes in a round head, and a usually straight beak, sometimes slightly enlarged at its extremity. The wings are fairly large, straight and pointed, giving rapid and prolonged flight. On the ground they are always on the move in search of food: worms, insects, molluscs and other small animals. Some frequent the fields, and others river-banks and beaches.

TRUE PLOVERS: There are two principal genera, *Charadrius* and *Pluvialis*, respectively known as the sand or winged plovers, and the golden plovers.

There are four species of *Pluvialis*: the Eurasian Golden Plover (*P. apricaria*) which breeds in northern Europe and north-west Asia; the American Golden Plover (*P. dominica*) found in the

northern parts of North America and Russia; the Grey or Black-bellied Plover (*P. squatarola*) with circumpolar distribution; and, last, the New Zealand Dotterel (*P. obscurus*).

Each autumn the Eurasian Golden Plover and the Grey Plover fly south from their breeding grounds. The golden species is the more striking of the two. In its breeding plumage the male's crown, neck and upper parts are brilliant black, spotted with golden yellow. A white line starting above the eyes borders the face and throat and extends right along the flanks. Throat, breast, belly, bill and feet are black.

The breeding plumage of the Grey Plover is a duller, greyish black, with white or silver spots instead of golden ones. It breeds in high latitudes throughout the northern hemisphere. It is, however, one of the most strongly migratory of all birds and in winter is found on virtually every coast in the world.

Charadrius, a large genus of smaller and less colourful species than *Pluvialis*, includes the plovers, so called because they have a black collar on a pure white neck and front. They are also called

The American or Lesser Golden Plover (*Pluvialis dominica*) with its outline broken up by its bold black and white and gold plumage which blends into the background. It breeds in arctic North America and much of arctic Russia. In the Yenisei River area it overlaps slightly with the range of the Eurasian Golden Plover and apparently sometimes interbreeds with it.

The Banded Plover (*Vanellus tricolor*) near its nest. It is confined to Australia, particularly the south and west, and Tasmania. It frequents cultivated areas, swamps, edges of rivers and flood plains, feeding generally in small parties although sometimes large flocks of over 200 birds may build up before breeding.

sand larks or stone-runners, probably because of their preference for sandy or pebbly beaches. The Little Ringed Plover (*Charadrius dubius*) and the Kentish or Snowy Plover (*C. alexandrinus*) are no biger than a lark. The Ringed Plover (*C. hiaticula*) is the size of a blackbird. Its breeding range covers northern Europe, including the British Isles, and the northernmost parts of Asia. That of the Little Ringed Plover lies further south and is overlapped by the range of the Kentish Plover which breeds on every continent and in America is known as the Snowy Plover. These plovers are active little birds, ceaselessly running about, uttering the little cries by which they probably maintain contact among themselves.

The North American Killdeer (*C. vociferus*) is similar to these in appearance and habits, but is somewhat larger and is graced with bright tawny orange patterns of the tail. Outside the breeding season it ranges south to Peru.

LAPWINGS: Crests, wattles and spurs distinguish the various lapwings (genus *Vanellus*) from the true plovers. Plumage of all species shares some common characteristics: white-tipped tail with black distal bar, and black primaries. They are rather aggressive, found regularly everywhere except North America where they have been known to stray on occasion.

Generically the word lapwing includes numerous species. In a more restricted use it refers to *the* Lapwing, sometimes called the Green Plover or Peewit (*Vanellus vanellus*), found throughout most of Europe and central Asia. This species lives in marshy plains, flat meadows and cultivated land, on the shores of ponds and lakes, and on the sea coast. Its migrations are local and scattered, some birds being sedentary, others migratory, irrespective of age. Breeding plumage consists of a mantle of coppery green with glossy tints of purple; cheeks, tail coverts and underparts are white, skullcap, throat and 'whiskers' a metallic black. It is a timid bird and the slightest disturbance puts it to flight.

At the onset of the breeding season the male Lapwing indulges in an aerial courtship display during which flight is punctuated with rapid ascents, turns and wheeling. It is a whirling, tossing, tumbling flight, with a loud intermittent drumming from the wings, a sound that can be heard some distance away. The nest is a depression in the ground made by the Peewit pivoting on its breast. Usually four pear-shaped eggs are laid, with their more sharply pointed ends directed to the centre of the nest. They are stone-coloured with dark blotches, harmonising with the ground on which they lie. Although afforded some protection by this natural camouflage, they are not difficult to find and the eggs are taken by other birds, notably by jackdaws, and by man in countries where plovers' eggs are considered a delicacy. The female may lay as many as five fresh clutches to replace lost eggs.

In Africa the lapwings are typically represented by the African Blacksmith Plover (*V. armatus*), and in Australia by the Banded Plover (*V. tricolor*).

The Spur-winged Plover (*V. spinosus*) has a disputed place in the family. Some authorities prefer to place it among the coursers. Equally controversial was its alleged habit of entering the open mouths of crocodiles. The bird may remove leeches from the crocodile's teeth and gums on occasion, but it has never been seen walking inside the mouth and only very rarely has been seen leaning near or within the jaw area. It makes a somewhat reciprocal gesture by uttering a ready cry at the approach of intruders, thereby alerting the crocodile.

OTHER GENERA: These include the Wrybill or Crooked-billed Plover of New Zealand, the turnstones and the Surfbird. The Wrybill (*Anarhynchus fontalis*) is a shore bird with a unique feature: a right-hand lateral twist to its beak. This is supposed to be an adaptation to its habit of seeking out insects and other invertebrates from under stones. A similar habit—though not the bill adaptation—is found in the two species of turnstone. The Black Turnstone (*Arenaria melanocephala*) breeds only in Alaska, and the Ruddy Turnstone (*A. interpres*), the commoner of the two, is a ground-nester in the Arctic tundra. Both species migrate south, the first as far as Cape Horn, the second even further, to Australia and New Zealand. The Surfbird (*Aphriza virgata*) also breeds in Alaska. Mottled grey and white, it has a black tail with a white band at the base. It feeds on small marine creatures along the coasts from Alaska to Chile where it has earned its common name by appearing to be quite at ease in the wild surf region.

Woodcocks, sandpipers, curlews (Family Scolopacidae)

The numerous species of these ground-dwelling waders form a heterogeneous group difficult to classify precisely. Although all have multicoloured plumage (predominantly of chestnut and brown), the size and shape of their bills and their feet vary widely. Plumage is cryptic, so that individuals on the ground are difficult to see, whether on the seashore, in grass or among dead leaves. This is a family largely native to the northern hemisphere.

The European Woodcock (*Scolopax rusticola*), one of the best known of the Scolopacidae, can be recognised by its autumn-leaf tints and its long, straight, pointed beak. It has a preference for moist woodland, where all day long it searches for food among the leaf mould, only leaving in the evening to fly to marshy meadow or moor. The innumerable holes which it digs in dung to extract insect larvae suggest that it is particularly attracted to grazing land. It digs in mud too, slowly and circumspectly trampling the ground, seemingly to bring the grubs to the surface.

The nest is built in a rough hollow in the ground, deep in the woods. The clutch generally consists of four light brown eggs with reddish spots, incubated by the female alone, her mate being essentially polygamous and without paternal instinct. A wood where woodcocks nest can be identified during the breeding season by the males' regular evening courtship flight song, called 'roding'. In this they follow certain well-marked 'airlanes', until the females call with a soft whistle from the ground.

The species has wide distribution in the Arctic region of the Old World and in the higher regions of Indonesia. Some are resident in northern Europe, others are migratory in habit, leaving in November to return in March. In the United States there is a smaller, monotypic species, the American Woodcock (*Philohela minor*), which lives in alder slashes and other low vegetation. It makes a good game bird because it responds to any disturbance, sitting motionless and quiet until a hunter is upon it, then rising almost vertically with a noisy whistling flurry of its wings before levelling off in swift flight. The hunter must be quick to aim and fire, because the bird will quickly drop back into cover. It also performs a courtship flight similar to that of the European Woodcock.

Snipe are distinguished from woodcock by their more slender build, more delicate beaks, featherless legs, longitudinally striped plumage, and preference for more open terrain. There are several species, the most abundant being the Common Snipe (*Gallinago gallinago*), a form of which (formerly called Wilson's Snipe) is found in America. It is resident in North America, the British Isles and France. Its habits are similar to those of the woodcock.

Another Old World snipe, the European Jacksnipe (*Lymnocryptes minima*), is much smaller. This bird will usually sit until intruders are almost on top of it, as if it were deaf to the approaching steps.

The Short-billed Dowitcher (*Limnodromus griseus*) of North America is the only snipe of that country to be found on open shores. It can be readily identified by the white lower back, rump and tail, and by the straight snipe-like bill. In spring the underparts, especially on the breast, lose their light grey colour and become more rufous. The method of feeding is characteristic: the bird jabs its long bill vertically into the mud with rapid movements rather like the action of a sewing-machine needle.

SANDPIPERS: The true sandpipers, unlike the woodcock and snipe, are predominantly coastal rather than inland birds. The smaller species are known in Britain as stints. All breed in the high latitudes and all undertake long migrations. The most widely distributed species is the Dunlin (*Calidris alpina*), which can be recognised, in its summer plumage, by a black patch on the lower breast. It arrives in April and goes north again in November. The Little Stint (*C. minuta*) is a smaller version of the Dunlin, no bigger than a European Robin or American Bluebird. Temminck's Stint (*C. temminckii*) is even smaller, and the smallest of all is the Least Sandpiper or American Stint (*C. minutilla*) which American ornithologists used to place in the genus *Erolia*. The Knot (*C. canutus*), the largest of the sandpipers, is about the size of a European Song Thrush or American Robin.

The closely related Old World species, the Ruff (*Philomachus pugnax*), owes its specific name to the male's beautiful breeding plumage which is set off by a 'ruff' or frill of long, erectile feathers. The colour of the plumage varies considerably from individual to individual, and may be any pattern of chestnut, white and black on a blue ground. Such an attire is unique among birds. The female, or reeve, lacks the long neck feathers or ruff. At the beginning of the breeding season the males assemble at a stamping ground, or lek, where they indulge in a great deal of display and mock fighting. The females select their mates from among the assembled males.

Also closely related are the sandpipers of the genus *Tringa*. They are most familiarly represented in Europe by the Redshank (*Tringa totanus*), a graceful, long red-legged species, markedly sociable. Slightly less common is the Spotted Redshank (*T. erythropus*), larger than the common Redshank and, in its summer plumage, spotted white on black, unlike any other wader. The Greenshank (*T. nebularia*), larger and greyer than the Redshank, has green legs and a long recurved bill. The Lesser Yellowlegs or Yellowshank (*T. flavipes*) of North America, smaller than the Redshank, has—as its common name suggests— bright yellow legs. It is distinguishable from the Greater Yellowlegs (*T. melanoleuca*) only by its smaller size and its call. Its summer plumage is black-brown mottled and spotted with white like that of the Wood Sandpiper (*T. glareola*), which breeds in northern Europe. The Green Sandpiper (*T. ochropus*), also of northern Europe, has green legs but in flight looks black with strongly contrasting white underside, rump and tail. The

The European Woodcock (*Scolopax rusticola*) showing how its plumage camouflages it against the woodland undergrowth. Both sexes have the same coloration. The Woodcock's bill is sensitive at the tip and slightly mobile, enabling it to find earthworms and insect larvae by touch, when probing for them in soft soil.

The Green Sandpiper (*Tringa ochropus*) and Marsh Sandpiper (*T. stagnatilis*) wading in shallow water. The Marsh Sandpiper is the larger of the two and breeds in marshy areas across northern Europe and as far east as Mongolia and Manchuria. The Green Sandpiper is unique among Palearctic wading birds in nesting in wooded areas.

Common Sandpiper (*T. hypoleucos*) is smaller and frequents the banks of rivers and streams. It swims well, dives with ease and has a characteristic tail-bobbing action. It breeds throughout North America, where it is called the Spotted Sandpiper (*T. macularia*), and Eurasia, and winters in the southern hemisphere. The male is strictly monogamous and participates in the brooding and rearing of the chicks. There are two monotypic American genera, the Upland Sandpiper (*Bartramia longicauda*) and the Willet (*Catoptrophorus semipalmatus*). The four species of godwit (genus *Limosa*) and the Tattler (*Tringa incana*) are also closely related to the sandpipers.

CURLEWS: This survey of the Scolopacidae ends with the curlews, which are fairly large birds, averaging about the size of a Jackdaw, with long down-curved bills. They are birds of seashores and river banks, where their cry—an exact onomatopoeic rendering of their name—cannot pass unnoticed. Their plumage varies little, either at mating time or between young birds and adults.

Curlews of the genus *Numenius* are the largest representatives of the family. The Long-billed Curlew of North America (*N. americanus*) is the biggest with a length of sixty centimetres. Its Old World counterpart is the Curlew (*N. arquata*). A third species, the holarctic Whimbrel or Hudsonian Curlew (*N. phaeopus*) shares with the rest of the genus the pattern of high latitude breeding and long migrations. The extent of some of the migrations is best illustrated by that of the Bristle-thighed Curlew (*N. tahitiensis*), which breeds in the mountains of Alaska and winters in the islands of Polynesia. The nearly extinct Eskimo Curlew (*N.*

borealis) of North America was brought to its present low ebb by hunting pressure during its migration through the United States and Canada.

Stilts and avocets (Family Recurvirostridae)
Although two groups are included in this single family, only the avocets have a recurved or uptilted bill. There are four genera in this cosmopolitan family of long-legged waders. Black and white plumage patterns are common to all four and there is little sexual dimorphism.

The Common or Black-winged Stilt (*Himantopus himantopus*) is resident in southern Europe, Africa and Asia. It occasionally wanders farther north, even reaching into the British Isles. This monotypic species is easily recognised by its black and white colouring, long pink legs, very long, pointed bill and pointed wings longer than the body (like those of a Swallow). The stilt is equally at home in sea water or freshwater. In flight it looks like a miniature stork. Races are found in Asia, Africa, America, Australia and New Zealand.

The Banded Stilt (*Cladorhynchus leucocephalus*) is an Australian monotypic species. The Ibis-bill (*Ibidorhyncha struthersii*) is a central Asian species with an uncharacteristic feature: a down-curved beak.

The Eurasian Avocet (*Recurvirostra avosetta*) is black and white too, but its legs are shorter than those of the stilt and its beak is typically recurved. It sweeps shallow waters with side-to-side movements of its beak to sweep up many different kinds of small invertebrates.

The American Avocet (*R. americana*), the Chilean Avocet (*R. andina*) and the Australian Avocet

(*R. novaehollandiae*) have brown touches in both their head and neck plumage.

Phalaropes (Family Phalaropidae)

The three phalaropes are similar: all are swimmers rather than waders, usually preferring freshwater to salt only during the breeding seasons. All have lobe-webbed feet, like the coot. They rarely venture on land except to nest and feed. The male is smaller than the female, and has less resplendent plumage. Sexual roles are reversed, with the female doing the courting and the male incubating the eggs and caring for the young. Distribution is holarctic.

The Grey Phalarope (*Phalaropus fulicarius*)— called the Red Phalarope in North America—is a circumpolar breeder. The Red-necked or Northern Phalarope (*P. lobatus*) nests in subarctic tundra regions. Wilson's Phalarope (*P. tricolor*) belongs to the prairies of Canada and the United States. Even outside the breeding season it prefers a freshwater habitat; the other two species feed off plankton at sea. All three species habitually undertake long migrations to winter in the seas, principally of the southern hemisphere.

Crab-plover (Family Dromadidae)

The noisy Crab-plover (*Dromas ardeola*), which lives on the coasts of East Africa and the northern and western shores of the Indian Ocean, is the sole member of the family. It is large, with mainly white plumage (primaries and back are black), long greenish-blue legs and a bill like that of a tern. It feeds mainly on crabs, swallowed whole if small enough. Its haunts are coral reefs exposed at low tide, but it nests colonially in the sandy banks on the shore, tunnelling in 120 to 150 centimetres to a nesting chamber. The clutch consists of a single pure white egg, and the chick is mottled grey and white. The Crab-plover is a flock-feeder, and they will try to protect an injured bird.

Stone-curlews or thick-knees (Family Burhinidae)

The several species of this family share a common physical trait: swollen heels. The type bird is the Stone-curlew or Thick-knee (*Burhinus oedicnemus*), which has a wide breeding range that includes western Europe and parts of Asia and Africa. Plumage is reddish brown with black spots. The beak is shorter than the head and, since it is a nocturnal bird, its eyes are large. Its hind toe is atrophied, as in many other terrestrial species. It has a harsh cry, somewhat like that of the Curlew, but not so melodious. Usually solitary, the Stone-curlew readily takes wing when approached. It feeds on insects, worms, snails, lizards and voles, and occasionally it attacks other birds. It nests, as its common name suggests, on bare stony ground. Other species are found in Africa, southern Asia, Australia and South America.

Pratincoles and coursers (Family Glareolidae)

The pratincoles are a subfamily of brownish shore birds with long wings and an easy flight that often leads to wrong identification as terns. They are, however, waders and not swimmers. Their common names, sea-partridge and sea-swallow, demonstrate the unreliability of observers. Pratin-coles hunt on the wing, skimming across the grass to catch dragonflies and grasshoppers, and rising into the air to survey their hunting grounds. In South Africa they are known as locust birds. Their true domain is the sky, where they circle tirelessly. The Common Pratincole (*Glareola pratincola*) ranges mainly over southern Europe, Africa, and southern Asia and occasionally wanders farther north.

The coursers are a subfamily of long-legged, terrestrial birds that live in arid or semi-arid regions and generally lack the hallux or hind toe. They are insectivorous, like the related pratincoles. Plumage is cryptic. The colouring of the Cream-coloured Courser (*Cursorius cursor*) of Africa, for example, is a perfect camouflage in the sandy and desert-like terrain which is its favourite habitat. The male and female of this species run with incredible speed, about fifteen paces apart. Its commonest nickname is 'Desert Runner'. It also flies well and takes advantage of this to range from district to district. It is sometimes found on the sand dunes of southern France and other European coasts as well as south-west Asia.

Seedsnipe (Family Thinocoridae)

This family of short-legged little shore birds includes only four species, all confined to South America. Plump, with short bills and pointed wings, seedsnipes live on stony ground at all altitudes, feeding on buds and seeds.

Sheathbills (Family Chionididae)

The two species of sheathbill (*Chionis alba* and *C. minor*) are primarily terrestrial in habit, though they fly and swim fairly well considering the small size of the wings and the unwebbed feet. They are confined to Antarctic and subantarctic shores, and

The Black-winged Stilt (*Himantopus himantopus*) has a worldwide distribution with five distinct subspecies being recognised. Its extraordinary long legs enable it to feed in fairly deep water where it picks water bugs and insects off the surface. On dry land, however, its long legs sometimes compel it to bend its knees when feeding.

Yellow-billed Sheathbills (*Chionis alba*) with a group of Chinstrap Penguins (*Pygoscelis antarctica*). These Sheathbills breed on islands in the north-west of Antarctica. They build their nests in crevices in the rocks around colonies of Adélies and Chinstraps.

The Stone-curlew (*Burhinus oedicnemus*) at its nest. In Europe its numbers have been considerably reduced owing to changes in its habitat induced by agriculture. Each pair of birds needs a fairly large, isolated breeding territory well away from human disturbance.

The Great Skua (*Stercorarius skua*) is unique in that races breed in the north, mainly on Iceland, the Faeroes and Scottish islands, and in the south, around the coasts of Antarctica, subantarctic islands and southern South America. The skuas are fish eaters which have also taken to piracy.

are the only bird without webbed feet to be found in southern seas. Plumage is unbroken white, and the bill has a horny case. They feed on eggs and chicks of sea birds, seaweed, molluscs and small crustaceans.

Skuas and jaegers (Family Stercorariidae)

Their strongly hooked bills distinguish the four species of the family from the closely related gulls and terns. Outside the breeding season they are solitary and oceanic. During this period they probably eat mainly fish which they catch for themselves or steal from other birds. During the summer they prey on small birds and mammals and also eat carrion. There has been much misunderstanding of the feeding habits of skuas in the past.

The commonest species, the Arctic Skua or, in America, the Parasitic Jaeger (*Stercorarius parasiticus*), is a pirate that will suddenly appear in the middle of a flock of terns and harass them until they disgorge. The species is found on coasts and islands throughout the Arctic.

The Great Skua (*S. skua*), sixty centimetres long, is found in both polar regions, off Scotland, the Faroes and Iceland, and most abundantly, in the Antarctic and subantarctic regions, where it preys on the penguins' eggs and chicks. This is the species known simply as the Skua in North America.

Two other species are the Pomarine Skua (*Stercorarius pomarinus*), known in America as the Pomarine Jaeger, and the Long-tailed Skua or Jaeger (*S. longicaudus*), both of the northern hemisphere.

Gulls and terns (Family Laridae)

Like the plovers and curlews these web-footed hook-billed or pointed-billed birds have green, speckled eggs and more or less nidifugous chicks similarly speckled. Their flight is superbly effortless. In a stiff breeze they make economic use of their long, supple wings. A few slow measured beats and wings become rigid again and the birds soar and glide almost at will, maintaining height by using the force of the winds.

Gulls swim well but they never dive. They are rarely found far out at sea. Many come inland, where they walk without difficulty in a hurried gait. Sometimes they rob the nests of other birds. Distribution of more than forty species is cosmopolitan, with a marked concentration in the northern hemisphere.

Gulls live in noisy colonies even during the breeding season, when they nest side by side on ledges or in hollows in rock or sand dunes. Two to three heavily spotted brownish eggs are laid in a seaweed nest. The chicks are only semi-altricial. They are fed by their parents until, at five or six weeks, they are strong enough to fly and fend for themselves. Adult plumage, which in some species may take three years to acquire, is typically white with grey or dark wing and back variations between species.

There are more than a dozen species of European and American gulls. The commonest are the white-headed gulls which include the Herring Gull (*Larus argentatus*), the Lesser Black-backed Gull (*L. fuscus*), and in Europe only, the Common or Mew

A mixed flock of gulls following a fishing boat in the North Sea. Although their main food is fish, many European gulls come inland each day during the winter months, feeding on waste food on rubbish dumps around the towns or searching for insects on playing-fields and farmland.

The Arctic Tern (*Sterna paradisaea*) in flight. It breeds in the Arctic and then crosses the equator to spend the southern summer in the Antarctic, a migration of some 17,500 kilometres. By making this long migration the Arctic Tern enjoys continuous summer for eight months of the year.

The Black Skimmer (*Rynchops nigra*) skimming along the surface of the water hunting for small fishes swimming just below the surface. It is the largest of the skimmers, about fifty centimetres long. The plumage is distinctively black and white with orange legs and a bright red bill. Although skimmers are related to gulls and terns they do not form such tightly-packed breeding colonies but come together loosely as pairs.

many and Denmark mostly migrate to Gibraltar and Morocco following the coasts of Holland, Belgium, France and Spain. The gulls of central Europe separate strangely and inexplicably: some head straight for the south-east to reach the Adriatic and continue via Italy, Sicily and Tunisia, while the rest, for no clear reason, first fly north to the Baltic and then take one of the routes taken by the gulls of Denmark and northern Germany.

Terns (sometimes called sea-swallows for their forked tails) are markedly different from gulls, though general colouring patterns are similar. They are slightly smaller. Their bills are pointed, not hooked; their pointed wings are very long and narrow; and their legs are very short. They seldom alight on water and walk with dificulty on land. Small feet make them poor swimmers, but they are tireless, wonderful flyers, skimming the surface of the waves, seizing prey from the water as they pass, or soaring high, cleaving the air like arrows. In a flash they will dive headlong towards the sea, stopping just short of the surface to inspect the water, then wheeling and climbing again to repeat the manoeuvre. Some species settle on the surface to feed, others make a noisy dive below surface to catch their prey. The gregarious terns are ground-nesters, laying two or three eggs in an unlined scrape or among small heaps of plant stems.

Three groups make up the subfamily: the black-capped terns, the noddies and the monotypic Inca Tern (*Larosterna inca*) of South America.

Possibly the most widely distributed is the Common Tern (*Sterna hirundo*), which has a white body, a light grey mantle, a black cap, red bill and red feet. Its shrill incessant cry is easily identifiable. The Little or Least Tern (*S. albifrons*), almost cosmopolitan, is the smallest. It is scarcely larger than a Swift but no bird is more active. Its bill and legs are yellow and it has a white patch on its forehead. Otherwise its habits are those of other terns, as are those of the inland nesting Black Tern (*Chlidonias nigra*) which used to breed in parts of England, but now does so only occasionally. It breeds fairly commonly in eastern North America.

The noddies are tropical species, of which the dark-plumed Common Noddy or, in America, the Noddy Tern (*Anous stolidus*) is the commonest, and the white Fairy Tern (*Gygis alba*) the smallest.

Skimmers (Family Rynchopidae)

This is principally a tropical family of three species, larger than the terns but smaller than the gulls. There is the African Skimmer (*Rynchops flavirostris*), the Indian Skimmer (*R. albicollis*), and the Black Skimmer (*R. nigra*) of America. The main peculiarity of the adult birds is a lower mandible much longer than the upper which is flattened laterally to almost knife-blade thinness at the tip. Skimmers fish in the estuaries, mainly in the evening and at night, flying close to the water—as the common name suggests—with the lower mandible dipped below the surface to flip fishes into the mouth, and the short upper mandible ready to close on them. By day they roost by open beaches, lakes and rivers, their vertical slit pupils protecting the eyes from the sun's glare. The American species is confined to coastland and the shore itself.

Gull (*L. canus*). Other gulls found only in America include the Californian Gull (*L. californicus*) and the Ringbilled Gull (*L. delawarensis*). There are also the hooded and masked gulls, those that acquire dark-coloured heads in the mating season, among them the Black-headed Gull (*L. ridibundus*), the Laughing Gull (*L. atricilla*), the Red-billed or Silver Gull (*L. novaehollandiae*) of Australia and the Mediterranean Black-headed Gull (*L. melanocephalus*).

The Black-headed Gull (*L. ridibundus*), about thirty-eight centimetres long, is a small gull. In the spring it assumes a hood of black feathers. The Common or Mew Gull (*L. canus*), which can be used as the type bird, has an ashen-grey back and white front and lower parts. The tail is rounded when spread, whereas in other species it is very slightly forked. The bill is generally shorter than the head, but strong and hooked at the tip. Both sexes are exactly identical.

The two extremes in size are found in the Great Black-backed Gull (*L. marinus*) and the Little Gull (*L. minutus*), which are about the size of a small Golden Eagle and a Domestic Pigeon respectively. There are two exceptional types: the Kittiwake (*Rissa tridactyla*), in which the hind toe is atrophied, and Sabine's Gull (*Xema sabini*), which has a forked tail.

Most gulls are sedentary round the northern European coasts, but their numbers are increased in winter by migrants from the north. Through ringing, the migration routes of some, such as the Black-headed Gull, are well known. We know, for example, that in Europe the gulls of north Ger-

Auks, guillemots, puffins (Family Alcidae)

The Alcidae are the northern counterparts of the southern hemisphere's penguins. These short-winged birds of northern seas have several features reminiscent of grebes and superficially resemble the penguins: legs at the back of the body, short wings, indifferent flight and great skill at swimming and diving. They use wings rather than feet to propel them while swimming underwater. On land they stand upright and walk rather quickly. Flightlessness accompanies simultaneous moulting of the flight feathers in most species. As in the gulls, black, white and grey are the predominant colours.

The northern seas would be depressingly bare if their great wealth of fishes and plankton did not support huge colonies of terns, gulls, kittiwakes, fulmars, gannets, razorbills, guillemots and puffins in hundreds and thousands on rocky islets. At a distance a vague murmur tells of their presence and at closer quarters it becomes a deafening uproar of raucous, strident cries from clouds of birds wheeling round the cliffs.

The Little Auk or Dovekie (*Plautus alle*) is a bird with black upper parts, white underparts, and a very short beak. It feeds on plankton which it scoops up from the water as it swims along, beak open. It seldom goes on land except in the breeding season. Its main breeding grounds are in Greenland and Spitzbergen.

The Guillemot or Common Murre (*Uria aalge*) also has a black back and white belly, but its bill is longer than that of the auks. Though it has bred in Europe as far south as France and Spain, it is essentially an inhabitant of arctic waters. Immense breeding colonies are found in Iceland, the Faroes, Greenland and Labrador. The birds nest on every possible ledge of the cliffs, sitting with their black backs towards the sea. At the slightest noise all turn around, as if to plan, showing their contrasting white front.

Only one egg is laid and both parents share the incubation. When newly hatched, the chick is a little ball of black down quite incapable of looking after itself. It is fed by its parents and flies down to the sea before its wing feathers have fully grown. It then swims out to sea accompanied by its parents.

The Common Puffin (*Fratercula arctica*) has a parrot-like bill laterally compressed, slate-grey at the base and ornamented during the breeding season with vivid red, yellow and black plates. The button-like eyes are red and white and the hood is black. Although its gait is clownish, the Puffin is a good, strong flyer and walks well. But it is at swimming and diving that it excels. In the rookeries of northern Europe the puffins inhabit burrows in which they lay and hatch their single egg. The mouths of these burrows are so close together that the nesting area looks like a honeycomb.

There is a certain similarity in attitude and habit between the Razorbill or Razor-billed Auk (*Alca torda*) of the Arctic and the unrelated penguins of the southern hemisphere. On land, both stand erect on short legs which are placed well back on the body. The gait of both is clumsy and in quick retreat turns rapidly to a slide or crawl. Both swim with consummate ease and are skilled divers, being able to remain submerged up to two

minutes and to penetrate ten metres deep, propelling themselves with their wings. Such similarities illustrate common adaptations to environment in unrelated birds.

The Razorbill also has a highly developed social instinct. It normally lives in flocks, and during the breeding season gathers in thousands on cliffs and islets. Its food is mainly fishes, supplemented by aquatic animals. The Razorbill is found all over the North Atlantic and the Arctic Ocean during the summer. In Europe it breeds as far south as Brittany and the Channel Isles. In winter it goes even farther south and has been seen on the shores of the Mediterranean. In North America it seldom breeds south of Canadian shores but usually large flocks can be seen wintering off Long Island. Head

The Razorbill (*Alca torda*), a seagoing auk related to puffins and guillemots. Like the puffin its bill is deep and laterally compressed. In adults the bill is marked by a white line which extends on both sides back to the eye. More than any other auk the Razorbill most nearly resembles the extinct Great Auk.

The Rhinoceros Auklet (*Cerorhinca monocerata*), the largest of the auklets, has a curious short horn projecting upwards from the base of the upper mandible. It is also distinguished by a pair of white plumes on each side of the head, one from above the eye, the other from the corner of the mouth.

and upperparts are black, breast and belly white. The bill is laterally compressed, arched and marked with a prominent white stripe on each side in winter. The cry is low and distinctly raucous.

The Razorbills' courtship is rather grotesque. Male and females rub bills and nibble each other's head and neck, or sit with bills held vertical, rattling their mandibles like castanets. The couples select nesting places on a ledge of rock or in an old burrow or a mere depression in the ground. The female then lays one large brown, pear-shaped egg, six by five centimetres, which both birds take turns to sit on. When hatched, the chick is a mere ball of black down. The parent birds bring it fishes until, at about three weeks, the young bird is strong enough to dive into the sea from its tall cliff.

Although numerous murrelets and auklets throng the northern coasts the ill-fated Great Auk (*Plautus impennis*), was a common, flightless member of the Alcidae until the middle of the century when hunting brought extinction.

Sandgrouse and pigeons (Order Columbiformes)

The columbiform birds, which once included the extinct dodos and solitaires, are mostly of moderate size, the largest being as big as a Swan, but most are about the size of the Wood-pigeon and Stock Dove. The thick-set body is carried on short legs, giving a slow and rather clumsy gait. Long, pointed wings give rapid and sustained flight. The head is small and the neck rather short. Pigeons and doves also have a characteristic bill structure; the basal part is covered with soft skin, and the terminal part is horny. The nostrils open through longitudinal slits in the soft part of the beak. Three toes on each foot are directed forwards; the fourth points backwards. All four toes are set at the same level. The males have no spurs and the claws are short and straight.

Their food is almost entirely seeds and fruit, but unlike other grain-eating birds they have very short rectal caeca which is quite unusual.

The sexes are similar in appearance and, though tending to live in groups columbiform birds are monogamous, the males taking part in nest building and in brooding and caring for the chicks, which are quite helpless when hatched and are fed on 'pigeon's milk' formed in the crop of the adult. The birds of this order produce few eggs, usually two in pigeons and doves, and three in the sandgrouse.

Sandgrouse (Family Pteroclidae)

This family includes about sixteen species which differ from the pigeons in some respects: the newly hatched young are covered with down and they leave the nest soon after hatching. But like pigeon nestlings the young are fed with a milky substance from the adult's crop. The wings are long and pointed, and the first digit on the foot is missing. These birds inhabit desert and steppe, and their plumage is cryptically coloured to blend with the ground on which they spend most of their life. Those living on sand are fawn-coloured, and those from the steppes are striped. When motionless they are almost invisible. The nest is built on the ground at the foot of a bush, or simply hollowed out in the sand. The adults bring water to their chicks by soaking their breast feathers.

The Pin-tailed or White-bellied Sandgrouse (*Pterocles alchata*) is the only species resident in Europe, but it also ranges into Asia as far east as India, and southwards into northern Africa. It breeds regularly in France, Spain and Portugal.

Pallas's Sandgrouse (*Syrrhaptes paradoxus*), a species that looks rather like a turtle-dove, but with wings much longer than the tail, is found from south-east Russia to Mongolia, but occasionally migrates to Europe, sometimes in large numbers.

The extinct dodos and solitaires of the family Raphidae also formed part of the Columbiformes.

Pigeons and doves (Family Columbidae)

Pigeons proper are thick-set and have a relatively small head, the front of which bulges forward over the bill. The bill is somewhat constricted in the middle and membranous at the base. Only the upper parts of the legs are feathered, and the feet are usually quite bare. When folded, the wings border the tail, which may be rounded or straight at the tip.

Distribution is world-wide in tropical and temperate zones, with the greatest number of species in the Far East and Australasia. Apart from certain tropical species, they feed on grain and seeds, which are swallowed whole. Unlike other birds they do not sip when drinking but take long draughts.

The wild variety of the Domestic Pigeon is known as the Rock Dove (*Columba livia*). Whether wild or domesticated pigeons have definite social habits. They move about in flocks during the day and roost together at night. Fighting seldom occurs during the breeding season and when it does it is more of a mock combat. These birds also have regular habits. They begin the morning with a chorus of calls. Then the flock sets out to feed

A male Pin-tailed Sandgrouse (*Pterocles alchata*) showing the pattern of white on its underparts which gives it the alternative name of White-bellied Sandgrouse. Over much of its range it is the commonest sandgrouse, sometimes being seen in flocks of many thousands. It is typically a desert bird but also frequents cultivated areas and marshes feeding on seeds of grasses and wild plants.

and drink, returning to their perching place, where they stay during the hottest part of the day. In the afternoon they again go off to feed and drink, and finally retire at night to the cover of trees or rocks. Such regular habits make them adapt to captivity.

Courtship takes place during the spring and summer, and in Europe breeding continues from April to late autumn. During courtship the males coo loudly, display before the females, and indulge in display flights. They are monogamous and tend to mate for life, a feature remarkable in birds so strongly gregarious.

For about five or six months before it is fully adult, the cooings of the male have a dull and melancholy sound, these having replaced the feeble and rather nasal calls of the adolescent. The cooings eventually take on a richer quality when the bird is mated. When displaying to the female a sort of bubbling sound seems to come from its crop. At a more advanced stage of courtship the display movements seem more like a bowing to the female and the cooing sounds almost like speech. During the display the female bows her head and points her beak downwards in response to similar movements by the male, which without stopping its song nuzzles her with its beak. When the female submits she crouches by the side of her mate.

A pair of courting pigeons may be silent for hours on end, while one of the pair, usually the male but sometimes the female, gently runs its beak through the head feathers of its mate. Similarly, the intertwining of the beak mandibles is clearly an important part of the courtship displays. At this stage the male regurgitates some of the 'milk', which is swallowed by the female. It was once thought that some of the hormones contained in this secretion stimulated the sex glands of the female and brought her into a comparable breeding condition.

These displays go on for several days and are followed by nest building, in which the male once more plays the leading part. He chooses the nesting site in a tree or gap in the rocks and gathers twigs, roots and other materials, which are then set in place by the female. The nest is a crudely constructed, openwork platform. Although it seems an unlikely structure to withstand wind and rain, it is in fact quite robust.

There are two eggs in each clutch, elliptical in profile and pure white, with a faint bluish tinge. They are brooded by the male and female in turn, but neither seems particularly attached to them. If driven off the nest they may abandon the eggs.

Incubation begins as soon as the second egg is laid and lasts an average of seventeen days. There is an interval of one or two days between the hatching of the two chicks. They are born practically naked, blind and helpless. They are first fed with the 'milk' from the crop, and then with softened seeds and grain. The parents keep them as warm as possible until, after about ten days, their feathers begin to grow. In less than a month the young pigeons can fend for themselves, but they stay on in the nest a little longer with their parents.

The above description of habits and life history are specifically those of the Domestic Pigeon, but in general may be applied to most species of pigeons or doves except for details such as times of breeding and so forth. Many species in the temperate regions are at least partially migratory though the Domestic Pigeon is sedentary.

The Wood-pigeon or Ring-dove (*Columba palumbus*) is the largest of the European pigeons, with a maximum length of nearly forty-five centimetres. The general colour of the plumage is greyish. The breast is wine-red with a metallic sheen, and there are patches of white on the wings and the sides of the neck. Those on the neck form a ring or collar (whence 'Ring-dove'). This species is found throughout Europe and migrates from the northerly parts to winter in northern Africa. It also occurs in western and central Asia. It is called the Wood-pigeon because in the wild state it lives and nests in wooded areas, descending to the ground only to feed.

The Stock Dove (*C. oenas*) is a smaller bird, about thirty cenimetres long. It is bluer than the Wood-pigeon and has no white patches on neck and wings, though the latter have black markings. The two species have much the same habitat and habits. The Stock Dove is found in Europe, North Africa, and western Asia, and is fairly common throughout the British Isles.

The Rock Dove (*C. livia*), the source of domestic breeds, is about the same size as the Stock Dove, but is more varied in colour. The lower part of the back is white or pale grey, there are two black bars across the wings, and the tip of the tail is black. It nests on cliffs on the coast or in mountainous regions and is found in Europe, India, western and central Asia, and northern and western Africa.

Feral pigeons, that is birds descended from domesticated pigeons that have to some extent reverted to the wild state can be seen in many towns, particularly in public squares, as the Europeans have carried them wherever they have gone.

DOMESTIC PIGEONS: Darwin was very interested in evidence that domestic pigeons furnished in sup-

The Wood Pigeon or Ring Dove (*Columba palumbus*) usually only lays two white eggs, but the breeding season is long and several broods may be raised. The unfledged nestling, known as a squab, is fed with pigeon's milk, a curd-like substance produced from the parent's crop.

The Collared Dove (*Streptopelia decaocto*) originated in Asia but since the 18th Century has been steadily spreading across Asia and into Europe. reaching Britain in 1955, and since then spreading as far as the Outer Hebrides and Iceland. In Britain the population built up to a phenomenal 19,000 birds by 1964. The spread results from the dove's association with man, feeding on grain put down for poultry or spilt in railway sidings.

port of his famous theory of evolution. He showed that the races were derived from the Rock Dove by artificial selection of natural variations or of those appearing from breeding. Their common origin was shown by the ease with which the races bred, not only among themselves but also with the wild Rock Dove. That the crosses were fertile, and that the races also showed some tendency to revert to ancestral type, particularly in the characteristic black bands on the wings that are found in the wild Rock Dove, added further support to his theory. In addition, it was unlikely that the various races had come from distinct wild stocks and that the Rock Dove could be the only survivor.

The domestic races differ among themselves and from the Rock Dove in certain features of form, plumage, bill and behaviour.

The Roman pigeons are one of the races closest to the ancestral stock. With a maximum length of nearly fifty centimetres and a wingspan of over a metre, they are the largest of the domestic pigeons and are readily identifiable by the red ring circling the eyes. They are slow breeders and, because they are rather heavy and clumsy, fall a ready prey to cats and raptorial birds.

The tumblers are not a pure race, but a mixture of breeds, with one curious mode of behaviour in common: all are able to turn backward somersaults in flight and on the ground. Such acrobatic behaviour may well be attributable to some deformation of the semicircular canals in the ear or of the cerebellum, the centre for the co-ordination of such movements.

The Jacobin pigeons have a distinctive form of plumage, the feathers of head and neck turn forward in the form of a hood. The necktie pigeons have a tuft of feathers at the base of the bill and their cooing resembles drum beats.

Fantail pigeons have a large tail consisting of as many as forty-two feathers. It can be raised and spread like a fan. At the same time the head is bent backwards until it touches the fan.

Pouter pigeons, particularly the males, have a very large gullet which they can inflate with air. When they do this the head is almost completely lost behind the great swelling of the breast, and in this position they strut about, their long wings and tail trailing the ground. This is a difficult breed to rear since the special structure of the gullet makes it impossible to feed the young on 'milk' regurgitated from the crop.

CARRIER-PIGEONS: These do not constitute an independent race, but are more an assemblage of breeds obtained by various crosses and have little in common except a highly developed sense of direction, which enables them to return unerringly to the nests.

A carrier-pigeon usually flies at somewhere between 180 and 300 metres depending on atmospheric conditions, though in a head wind it may fly close to the ground. Speed varies, but is usually between fifty and 100 kilometres an hour. A fully trained carrier-pigeon taken to a point up to several hundred kilometres from its loft will fly home in a direct line in the shortest possible time. A successful homing flight can be made even on a moonless night. Wind, rain or fog may slow the bird but will not stop it. There is a record of a carrier-pigeon that flew from Ution to its original home in New York City (about 500 kilometres away) after being kept in captivity for two years.

The way in which pigeons and other birds navigate over long distance is not fully understood. Experiments indicate that birds can orientate and fly on a compass course by reference to the position of the sun and stars. It can also calculate its geographical location by reference to the height and movement of celestial bodies and, by comparing these with the equivalent data for its destination, lay off a course for home. This is essentially how a human navigator operates. Recent experiments have shown that some birds can orientate with a magnetic sense by reference to the earth's magnetic field.

Over short distances carrier-pigeons learn to recognise local landmarks and so improve with training. One can only speculate that something similar occurs when birds migrating over long distances year by year return to precisely the same spot to nest, as when a swallow not only arrives at the same stable door in spring but perches nearby waiting for the door to be opened for it to enter.

The whole process of bird navigation is remarkable enough but hardly more so than the feat of memory implied by the behaviour of such birds as swallows.

The Passenger Pigeon (*Ectopistes migratorius*) is now extinct, but was once very numerous. The famous naturalist Audubon relates that flights of these migrating birds used to darken the sky for hours and make a sound like the distant rumbling of thunder. There were millions of individuals. Entire forests were spoiled by their droppings, and the branches of trees were broken as the birds moved among them. While it is true that the pigeon was slaughtered in vast numbers, the survivors appear to have been wiped out in the wild by an epidemic almost within a single year. The species became totally extinct in 1914 with the death of the last known individual in the Cincinatti Zoo.

The Turtle-dove (*Streptopelia turtur*) breeds in the more southerly parts of Europe and also in western Asia and North Africa. In the British Isles it is commonest in southern and eastern England, where the first pairs appear towards the end of April or in May, and are in the habit of nesting on the verges of woods, in bushes and hedges.

This bird is the smallest European member of the family Columbidae. It is also more slender in form and more graceful in appearance than the pigeons, and has a smaller head and longer neck. The bill is straight and slender, and the plumage tends towards a brownish red. On the sides of the neck are three or four black bands on a white background. The remiges and contour feathers of the wings are dark brown with a reddish border. It is attractive in appearance and in its gentle habits.

In September the Turtle-dove leaves Europe for its winter quarters in Africa, returning the following year. If taken when young, turtle-doves soon get used to captivity in aviaries and become remarkably tame. Another species known as the Collared Turtle-dove (*S. decaocto*)) is even more readily tamed it is almost pure cream in colour, with a black collar.

While the turtle-doves, like most pigeons, are tree-dwellers, the ground-doves and the bronze-wings are more terrestrial in habit, and form a transition between the columbiform and galli-naceous birds. They spend most of the time on the ground searching for seed, and sometimes even nest on the ground. The small, sparrow-like Ground Dove (*Columbina passerina*) is peculiar to the Americas. The several genera of pigeons known as bronze-wings are native to Australia.

Closer still in appearance to the gallinaceous birds, the Nicobar Pigeon (*Caleonas nicobarica*) is almost entirely greenish-bronze in colour and is one of the most beautiful birds of the south-east Asian forests, particularly of the Nicobar Islands and New Guinea.

MORE BIZARRE MEMBERS OF THE FAMILY: These include the parrot pigeons, the crowned pigeons, and the Tooth-billed Pigeon. A species of the first group, *Treron abyssinica*, is a pigeon with a heavy, squat body, short wings and tail, and legs almost entirely covered with feathers. The tip of the bill is expanded to form a solid, pincer-like arrangement. The plumage is predominantly green with a brilliant metallic sheen. The name given to them in Africa, parrot pigeons, is rather apt for, like the parrots, they take up curious positions when climbing branches, feed on fruit and nest in holes in trees. There are many species in the genus.

The three crowned pigeons (*Coura* spp.), which occur in New Guinea, are quite different. They are essentially terrestrial in habit, wandering in forests in small groups and gathering up seeds and fruits fallen from the trees. A conspicuous feature is the fanlike crest of feathers on the head, which can be erected or lowered at will. They are large, up to eighty-three centimetres long.

To conclude this survey of the Columbiformes, some mention must be made of the Manumea or Tooth-billed Pigeon (*Didunculus strigirostris*), an almost extinct native of the islands of Samoa. It is about the same size as a Domestic Pigeon and the plumage is a dark shining green. This bird is terrestrial in habit and feeds on roots and bulbs.

Parrots and parakeets (Order Psittaciformes; Family Psittacidae)

This distinctive family Psittacidae includes par-rots, cockatoos, macaws and lories. All show a high degree of specialisation to arboreal life, using both beak and feet to climb. The feet also serve as 'hands' to husk and hold seeds. These two habits distinguish them from all other birds. Another characteristic is the bill, the two mandibles of which are curved and opposed, so that the lower fits into the larger upper one when the beak is closed. One curious character of the group is that the upper mandible usually articulates (with a movable joint) on the cranium. Being essentially fruit- and seed-eating birds, they have well-developed crops, in which the food is stored before entering the stomach. Lastly, plumage is nearly always very brightly coloured. Green is the predo-minant colour, and red, yellow and violet are quite common and can occur in the same individual.

Distribution is world wide through the tropics, with the main concentrations in Australasia and South America. The tropical forests in which they live gregariously are brightened with their gay colours and resound with the incessant clamour of their chattering, shrieking calls. In the morning and evening they set out in great flocks to planta-tions of fruit trees, which are soon despoiled by their raids. During these excursions they prove to be both cautious and wily, displaying remarkable intelligence.

Although parrots never live alone, but move about tropical forests in noisy groups, they are strictly monogamous. In most species the male and female build the nest in a hollow tree, where the young are fed until they are able to fend for themselves.

Longevity is quite common. Some individuals may live to an age of seventy to eighty years, at least in captivity.

The classification of the various members of the order presents certain difficulties. It is sufficient

Gregarious and brightly coloured, macaws are the largest members of the parrot family, up to a metre long, including the long tail. They live in the tropical forests of South America. This group of Scarlet Macaws (*Ara macao*) and Red-and-green Macaws (*A. chloroptera*) shows up their bright colours, long tails and massive beaks characteristic of the genus.

The Philippine or Red-vented Cockatoo (*Cacatua haematuropygia*), of the Philippines, is only one of numerous kinds of birds of the parrot family found in the Australasian region and the East Indian islands. The name is from the Malay *Kakatua*, which was adopted by the Dutch traders. Its English spelling is influenced by the word 'cock', although this has no relevance.

here to point out the distinction between the typical parrots, the kaka, kea, kakapo, lories and lorikeets, pygmy parrots and cockatoos.

The typical parrots include the macaws, the amazons, parakeets, lovebirds, budgerigars and conures. One of the best known is the African Grey Parrot (*Psittacus erithacus*) particularly prized for its highly developed powers of mimicry.

Almost as well known are the colourful macaws of the New World, strikingly coloured, long-tailed birds with bare cheek patches. Native to the tropical rainforests of Central and South America, they are most commonly represented by the metre long Scarlet Macaw (*Ara macao*), the slightly smaller Gold and Blue Macaw (*A. ararauna*) and the greenish-blue Military Macaw (*A. militaris*).

The numerous species of amazons constitute another familiar South American genus. Commonest and most widespread is the large green Mealy Parrot (*Amazona farinosa*). The best talker is the Yellow-headed Amazon (*A. ochrocephala*). A third New World group are the conures, which are smaller than the amazons.

The cockatoos are quickly recognised by the crest of erectile feathers on the head. They are fairly large birds and are generally light-coloured. The most widespread species, the Sulphur-crested Cockatoo (*Cacatua galerita*), is completely white except for its crest of long yellow feathers. Cock-

atoos are found in Australia, Tasmania, New Guinea, the Philippines and neighbouring islands. Being easily domesticated and trained, they are popular as pets for the home or the aviaries of public zoos.

Small-tongued parrots are represented by a single black-coloured species found in Australia and New Guinea, where its native name is *kasmalos*. Like the cockatoos, the bird is crested, and also has bare cheek patches like the macaws. Its characteristic feature is the shape of its tongue, which is long and cylindrical and ends in a spoonshaped swelling. When the bird has reduced its food to a pulp with its beak, it gathers it up with its tongue. A projection from the roof of the mouth enables it to empty the 'spoon' in one operation.

The three main species of cage parrots are the African Grey Parrot (*Psittacus erithacus*), the Youyou (*Poicephalus senegalus*), and the Orange-winged Parrot (*Amazona amazonica*). The first two live in West Africa, while the third comes from South America. The African Grey Parrot is not entirely grey, for its tail is blood red. the You-you's head is grey, and the rest of the body green and yellow. The South American species is predominantly green. All three parrots are splendid talkers, have good memories, a marked intelligence, and are readily tamed in captivity.

The common name 'parakeet' is applied to small parrots with a long tail. The Carolina Parakeet (*Conuropsis carolinensis*) was one of the more northerly species, since it occurred in the United States, until it became extinct. The Budgerigar (*Melopsittacus undulatus*), which is found in Australia, is another. In the wild state the Budgerigar's plumage is predominantly green with some yellow, and there are small wavy black markings on the head. Several varieties have been produced by selective breeding. In one of the most popular the green coloration is replaced by a skyblue shade. These birds are quite the most delightful of all parrots.

Their breeding behaviour is also particularly interesting. While the male is always in breeding condition, he never forces his attentions on his mate, as many other birds do. He continues his courtship until she is ready to mate. When they copulate the female lowers her head to the male, who takes her beak in his own and enfolds her in his long wings. When the time comes to feed his mate, he is tireless.

The female builds in a hollow tree. She works away at the opening until it is just the size required. Then she chips off pieces of wood from the sides of the cavity and with these she covers the floor. Over a period of two days she lays from four to eight white, rounded eggs, which she broods for eighteen to twenty days. During the incubation period she is fed by the male, and leaves her nest only in cases of necessity. The young remain in the nest for thirty to thirty-five days and are not left by the parents until they are fully feathered.

The small, short-tailed parrots, particularly those of the genera *Agapornis* and *Psittacula*, are commonly known as lovebirds. The first is found in Africa, the second in India and Ceylon. Schomburgk, an explorer and naturalist of the early nineteenth century, remarked: 'In choosing the Turtle-dove as the symbol of idyllic love, the poets have been quite unaware of the greater affection displayed by a pair of lovebirds. There is complete harmony between male and female. When one eats or takes a bath, the other does the same. If the male calls, the female will join him in song. When one is sick, the other will care for it and feed it. Even when a flock of these birds gathers in a tree, the members of each pair are always together'.

The Blue-winged Parrotlet (*Forpus passerinus*), not much bigger than a sparrow, is the smallest of the Brazilian parrots. Its plumage is a handsome green, variegated with blue and yellow. The smallest of all parrots, however, is a species from New Guinea, the Pygmy Parrot (*Nasiterna pygmaea*), which is no bigger than a Canary. Little is known of its habits.

Certain small parrots found in Australia. New Guinea, Malaya and Polynesia are known as lories. These have a feebly developed beak and the tongue usually has a papillose or brush-like tip. (The name of one genus, *Trichoglossus*, is Greek for 'hair tongue'.) As might be supposed, these birds use the tongue for gathering nectar and pollen from flowers. Their mode of life is rather like that of butterflies and humming-birds, but they also feed on fruit and insects. There are about a hundred species, which differ markedly in colour pattern. They include the Black Lory, the Red Lory, the Green Lory and so on. But there is little chance of seeing these attractive birds except in museums as they do not thrive in captivity.

The Kea (*Nestor notabilis*), of the mountainous regions of the South Island of New Zealand, is a large bird measuring about fifty-five centimetres in length. General plumage colour is brownish green; the tail is green with a black bar near the tip, the rump is reddish, and there is some blue on the wings. The upper mandible of the bill is long and sickle-shaped. Its food consists of carrion, insects, berries, buds, and honey. The Kea also feeds on any blowfly larvae living in the wool of sheep, and on occasion inflicts fatal injuries on the sheep themselves with its pecking.

The genus *Strigops* has only one species, the Kakapo (*S. habroptilus*), a curious nocturnal parrot found in New Zealand. It was formerly classified among the owls since its eyes are partly turned forwards and its beak, like that of a typical owl, is hidden in its feathers. Much of its life is spent on the ground, where it hunts for food by night, and during the day retires into a burrow made among the tree roots. The ravages of wild dogs threaten the species with extinction.

Cuckoos and turacos
(Order Cuculiformes)

This arboreal order, the most closely related to the parrots, includes cuckoos and road-runners, turacos or plantain-eaters. Cuckoos are sometimes called 'climbing birds that cannot climb', for although the toe arrangement is that of climbing birds, two in front and two behind, they are quite unable to climb. They are perchers which fly from tree to tree, often alighting in a climbing manner and steadying themselves with the wings and elevated tail. Having long wings, they fly well with the direct flight of a Falcon or Sparrowhawk. Their white, dusky-barred underparts also give them the appearance of a Sparrowhawk.

Turacos or plantain-eaters
(Family Musophagidae)

These members of the cuckoo order look rather like small game birds. They are peculiar in that the outer toe can be turned either forwards or backwards. There are about twenty species, all of which live in small groups in the African forests and, like parrots, are both noisy and frugivorous. Their scientific and common names are both derived from the mistaken belief that they feed on wild bananas (*Musa*, a species of plantain). The plumage is unusual in containing a water-soluble red pigment which may be washed out by rain.

Cuckoos and road-runners
(Family Cuculidae)

This is a primarily arboreal group, mainly insectivorous. Some species are social parasites laying their eggs in the nests of other birds, others—like the coucals—build their own nests and brood their own eggs. The American anis even build communal nests.

The widely distributed Old World typical cuckoos of the subfamily Cuculinae are wholly parasitic. The commonest genera are *Cuculus*, breeding throughout the palaearctic region, *Chalcites* found in the Far East and Australasia, *Chrysococcyx* of Africa, and several, including the Koel (*Eudynamys scolopacea*), that used to be placed in separate genera.

This Black-capped Lory (*Lorius lory*) of the Aru Islands, Indonesia, is seen feeding off tree fruits in the tropical forests. All parrots are gregarious and usually brightly-coloured, moving through the trees with noisy chattering.

The Kea (*Nestor notabilis*) belongs to a small family of parrots found only in New Zealand. Having evolved in isolation for so long they now bear little relationship to other parrots. Outside the breeding season Keas forage in flocks usually in low-level forests but also above the bush-line amongst scree and bare rock.

The Common or Eurasian Cuckoo (*Cuculus canorus*), famous for laying its eggs in other birds' nests. Here a young cuckoo is being fed by a Reed Warbler (*Acrocephalus scirpaceus*). The young Cuckoo has an enormous appetite and consumes all the food its foster-parents can provide, so it grows rapidly and soon becomes far too large for the Reed Warbler's nest.

The Common Cuckoo (*Cuculus canorus*), a lively, agile bird, is a summer visitor to Europe and northern Asia. Its characteristic call is generally first heard about the middle of April in the British Isles, but the bird is very difficult to see because it conceals itself among the foliage of trees. The head and upper parts are ashy grey, becoming darker over the shoulder region. The underparts are lighter in colour, with dusky transverse bars like those of sparrowhawks. This feature, shared with one of the raptorial birds, may help it to assert itself in its chosen territory.

Much has been written on the Cuckoo's parasitic habits, but there is considerable disagreement, even between observers. The female appears to lay an egg directly in the selected nest, then removes one of the host's eggs with her beak, so that the total number of eggs remains the same. Yet it has been reported that, if the nest is too small or to fragile she lays her egg on the ground and then carries it to the selected nest. She then removes one of the host bird's eggs in her beak or crop. She lays four or five eggs in all, each in a different nest.

The choice of host is not a random choice. It is usually a small insectivorous bird, such as a

Willow Warbler, a Pipit, a Wheatear, a Sedge-warbler, a Robin or a Wren. If the protective host is a seed-eating bird, a Linnet or a Bullfinch for example, it will be one that feeds its young mainly on insects, which is the only diet suitable for a young Cuckoo. And a Cuckoo that lays brownish eggs, for example will always choose a host that lays a similar colour.

Whatever the nest in which it is laid, the Cuckoo's egg is usually the first to hatch, or at least hatches very soon after the eggs of the host. Although the young Cuckoo is blind, naked and feeble when hatched, it is soon the only occupant of the nest, for it is extremely active, particularly in its efforts to get rid of the host's eggs and chicks. If other eggs are in the nest it wriggles until it gets the offending egg on its back and slowly heaves itself upwards until it topples it over the edge and on to the ground. It repeats this exercise until it is the sole occupant. When it is not the first to hatch it treats the nestlings in the same way as the eggs, though not always with success. This aggressive behaviour is determined by the rapid growth of the young Cuckoo, which is so much bigger than its host's offspring and bigger than the host too. It is a voracious bird and begs for food with greater intensity than its foster-brothers and sisters, and so stimulates the foster-parents to give more food to it than to their own chicks. Within a few days the young Cuckoo thrives while they starve. With this advantage it pushes the weakened chicks out.

Egg mimicry is one of the Cuckoo's remarkable adaptations to parasitism. It is the only bird to match the size and colour of its eggs to those of the host species with varying degrees of success. The most plausible explanation is that an individual Cuckoo always chooses the same species of bird to parasitise. It is therefore not surprising that a young Cuckoo brought up by foster-parents of this species should, when adult, lay its eggs in another nest of the same species.

A female Cuckoo may lay about twenty times during the breeding season, on each occasion placing a single egg in a different nest. Thus in a brief breeding season it is possible to rear a larger number of young than a pair of cuckoos could manage alone. Although the female Cuckoo never leaves her territory she shows no interest in the hatching of her young.

Why these intruders are tolerated by their foster-parents is problematic, except that no special behaviour pattern has been evolved to deal with parasitisation. The instinctive urge to feed a young chick within the nest is so great that the foster-parents continue to feed the parasite even when weakened by their constant search for food to sate its appetite. Even more remarkable is that other birds as well as the foster-parents may feed it with food intended for their own young.

The Common Cuckoo has been blamed for destroying the young of useful insectivorous birds, but it largely makes up for this by the enormous number of caterpillars it eats. Certain of the Asian and African cuckoos have also been similarly accused. But as some of these lay their eggs in the nests of crows the charges are less serious.

The Bronzed or Shining Cuckoo (*Chrysococcyx lucidus*) breeds on islands off New Zealand. It lays its eggs in the nests of flycatchers, and after laying the adults depart. The young brought up by the foster-parents follow a month later, making a non-stop flight of 1,900 kilometres to Australia, and then head northwards, following the path already taken by their parents, another thousand kilometres to the Bismarck and Solomon Islands.

The Yellow-billed and Black-billed Cuckoos (*Coccyzus americanus* and *C. erythrophthalmus*) of North America are non-parasitic and build their own nests of twigs. They winter in South and Central America. The malkohas of tropical Asia, which are related to them, not only build their own nests but are largely non-migratory.

The anis (genus *Crotophaga*), ranging from Mexico to Argentina, with glossy black plumage, long tails and laterally compressed bills, present the antithesis of what is expected of members of the cuckoo family. Although a pair of anis may sometimes build a nest on their own, usually a group builds one large communal nest of sticks, in which all the hens lay their eggs and share the incubating and rearing of the young.

Road-runners are another group of non-parasitic cuckoos which live in the more arid parts of North America; there is one genus found in southeast Asia. The Road-runner or Chaparral Cock (*Geococcyx californianus*) is as large as a Bantam, which it resembles somewhat in having long, powerful legs and a long tail. As the name implies it is chiefly a ground bird and lives among desert scrub, where it feeds on lizards and small snakes. It runs very fast for a small bird and can keep pace with a car travelling at twenty-four kilometres per hour along a rutted desert track.

Another non parasitic genus of ten species of ground-dwelling cuckoos is found only in Madagascar. These are the couas. They build their own nests, feed on insects and fallen fruit on the forest floor, and seek safety by running instead of flying. The Crested Coua (*Coua cristata*) is a large conspicuous bird that moves about in noisy parties.

Other ground cuckoos, ranging from Africa, Australia and southern Asia, are the twenty-eight species of coucals. They are large, slow-flying birds, mainly dark in plumage, with short down-curved bills, rounded wings, long tails and long, strong legs. They build bulky nests of green leaves and grasses. Their call is a deep bubbling note.

Owls (Order Strigiformes)

Despite similarities in the bill and strong claws, owls are very different from the diurnal birds of prey. Apart from their nocturnal habits their distinguishing characters are soft feathers and silent flight, feet feathered down to the digits, and a rather large head with the beak almost hidden in fluffed-out feathers. Their eyes, frontally set as in man, are surrounded by very small feathers which fan out to form a disc-shaped mask. There are small earflaps, positioned asymmetrically, which help to focus sound waves into the ears. The ears themselves are very sensitive and supplement the vision, which is very sensitive in dim light. The eyes face forward so that the visual fields overlap to give stereoscopic vision. As the eyes cannot move in their sockets, the owl has to turn its head.

The owl's well-known silent flight gives it a great advantage as it swoops on its prey. The

The Roadrunner (*Geococcyx californiana*) is a non-parasitic ground cuckoo of the southwestern United States, shown here with a lizard in its beak. A bird of desert and semi-desert regions it feeds mainly on lizards, two of its other vernacular names being Lizard-bird and Snake-killer. A distinctive feature is its habit of running fast with its short wings outstretched. It seldom flies and then poorly.

The Smooth-billed Ani (*Crotophaga ani*) of Central and South America inhabits hillsides, plantations and wet pasturelands where cattle graze. Small flocks feed on the ground or more usually on the backs of cattle stripping off the ticks. The generic name means tick-eater.

noiseless approach is partly due to the owl's light wing loading. On its broad wings it can glide down, so avoiding the winnowing rush of wing-beats. The sound of its arrival is further deadened by the softness of the plumage and, in particular, by the flexibility of the flight feathers which effectively muffle the sound of the air rushing past them. It has been suggested that this is chiefly achieved by the special construction of the outer vane of the outermost flight feathers of the wing which forms a loose fringe. These form the leading edge which in other orders cuts through the still air when the wing is flapped, producing most of the flapping, whirring sound that is typical of a bird in flight. The modification of these outer feathers causes a thin, slower-moving cushion of air to separate the fast-moving and the stationary air and prevents the noisy shearing effect. Close examination of the outer vanes of these two feathers reveals that the vanes are extremely narrow.

The owl's digestive powers appear to be more limited than those of the diurnal birds of prey, for the pellets they regurgitate consist of bones as well as hairs and feathers. Another difference between the two types is that owls do not build proper nests, but lay their eggs in a hole in a tree, in old crows' or hawks' nests, or in a cleft in a rock. The eggs are always white and usually nearly spherical.

These and other differences have led modern ornithologists to separate the two families making up the order Strigiformes from the Falconiformes. Through anatomical similarities they seem fairly closely related to the nightjars.

Barn Owl (Family Tytonidae)

The Common Barn Owl (*Tyto alba*), otherwise known as the White or Screech-owl, but not to be confused with the American Screech-owl (*Otus asio*), is one of the commonest and most handsome of European birds, and has an almost world-wide distribution. In some countries it is called the 'Monkey Owl' as its face looks much like that of a monkey. It differs from other owls in having a complete ruff-like ring of feathers around the head. The feet are bare or covered with only a few soft feathers. The plumage is truly magnificent, golden or reddish above, with brown, grey or white markings. The underparts are whitish with black spots. Its breeding habits are similar to those of other owls, except that it prefers to nest in ruined houses, barns, granaries, pigeon-cotes and so on. It returns to the same nesting place year after year.

Typical owls (Family Strigidae)

The largest species in the order is the Eagle-owl (*Bubo bubo*), whose thick, fluffy plumage makes it look larger than it really is. It is about sixty centimetres in length and has a wingspan of some 170 centimetres. Plumage varies from yellow to red according to age and sex, and there are wavy transverse brown stripes and brown markings running along the body. Above each ear there is a horn-like tuft of black feathers, which usually stick out at an angle from the head. It is a magnificent bird, which, seen in its natural state, cannot be confused with any other owl. It is found in Europe from Spain to northern Scandinavia and also extends over Russia and Asia and in Africa. It has even been recorded as an occasional visitor to the British Isles. In France it is almost entirely confined to rocky and mountainous regions.

The Eagle-owl tends to live in wooded regions with rocky escarpments, where it builds its nest in spring. This usually consists of dried leaves placed in a rocky crevice and here the female lays two or three white rounded eggs. While she is sitting on them the male provides the food. After this both birds share in feeding and bringing up the young.

By day the Eagle-owl perches motionless on rocks and trees, camouflaged by its plumage. With its eyes almost closed, it seems to be half asleep, but the slightest noise will arouse it. It hunts at twilight, at intervals uttering its hooting cry. At times it seems as though it is laughing, howling or moaning, and these sounds are so similar to those made by human beings as to frighten anyone unfamiliar with them.

The Eagle-owl feeds on all manner of mammals, birds, reptiles and amphibians, and it does undoubted service in eating small rodents, hares, rabbits, weasels and stoats.

The Eagle-owl is replaced in America by the Great Horned Owl (*B. virginianus*) which ranges from the tree limit of North America to the Straits of Magellan. The habits and general appearance of the two species are very similar.

The North African Desert-owl is a subspecies of the Eagle-owl. Its biscuit colour blends with that of the surrounding sand.

The Long-eared Owl (*Asio otus*) is about half the size of the Eagle-owl. The greys and browns of its plumage closely resemble bark and thus give camouflage against the background of trees among

A Barn Owl (*Tyto alba*) landing on its nest in a hayloft with prey for its five chicks. It is distinguished by its heart-shaped facial disc and large dark eyes. At night it hunts low over the ground to take small mammals, or snatch small birds roosting in bushes or ivy. Its exceptionally acute hearing enables it to locate prey in total darkness.

The Great Horned Owl (*Bubo virginianus*), one of the largest and most powerful of owls, fifty centimetres long, it is found from Canada right through to southern South America. It sleeps during the day in dense coniferous woods, forests and mountainous areas, hunting by night. It preys on small mammals, birds and snakes. It will take domestic poultry and cats when other food is scarce, earning its name of 'night tiger'.

The Spotted Eagle Owl (*Bubo africanus*), the smallest and most common and widespread Eagle Owl over most of Africa. It usually lives in rocky areas of bush and savannah or forested areas. In the Kalahari, however, it has adapted to desert conditions. Although it may kill quite large prey it depends to a large extent on insects.

The Long-eared Owl (*Asio otus*) lives mainly in woods and forests and is strictly nocturnal. As it roosts by day in dense cover it is seldom seen. Although owls cannot move their eyes independently like other birds they have good nocturnal vision and their restricted angle of vision is compensated by having a very mobile neck. The Long-eared Owl, for example, can turn its head through 270 degrees.

which it lives. This is the species often heard at night in woodlands, parks and orchards. It is widely distributed through Europe, including the British Isles, northern Asia, North America and North Africa, nesting in some parts and invading others in the summer in flocks of about ten individuals. In years when voles are locally abundant there may be real invasions by the species.

Like most owls, the Long-eared Owl is essentially useful to man and in country districts should be protected. Analyses of its pellets show them to be formed almost exclusively of the bones of rodents. It is only when mice are lacking that the Long-eared Owl will satisfy its hunger at the expense of various small birds.

The breeding season is in spring. The cry of the male may first be heard in February or March, when the female will answer with higher-pitched sounds. From time to time they make a clapping noise with their wings. The nest is a roughly built affair, and is often the abandoned nest of a Rook, Magpie, Jay or Squirrel. The eggs, about six in number, are white and rounded, three to four centimetres in diameter. They are incubated for rather less than a month. When hatched the young are covered in white down and are still blind, but they soon become brown, and when they are five days old their eyes open. Within several weeks their wing feathers are large enough to enable them to flit from bough to bough.

The Short-eared Owl (*A. flammeus*) has much the same powers and general coloration as the Long-eared Owl, but its plumage is marbled rather than barred. It has longer wings and, as its common name suggests, shorter horn-like tufts of feathers than its congener. This owl lives in open country, including marshy areas, where it captures frogs, small rodents and insects. It is essentially a wandering, migratory bird, flocks of twenty to thirty individuals moving from one part of Europe (including the British Isles) to another. It winters in Africa and is also found in North and South America and in northern and central Asia.

Scops or screech owls of the genus *Otus* are also found in Europe and occasionally in the British Isles. In the United States they are the commonest owls. The Scops Owl (*Otus scops*), a useful insectivorous species, is a good deal smaller than the Short-eared Owl, averaging about twenty centimetres in length and fifty centimetres in wingspan. This miniature owl lives in small groups, which appear in Europe in spring and migrate in autumn to the African interior. In the south of France it is a familiar resident in gardens and parks, where its somewhat melancholy but not unpleasing song may frequently be heard at night.

The Screech Owl (*O. asio*) is not, as its scientific specific name might indicate, found in Asia, but only in North America. The Latin meaning of *asio* is 'a kind of horned owl' which is exactly what the little Screech Owl is. Oddly enough its common call is a quavering whistle, not a screech.

Owls without ear-like head tufts include the Tawny Owl and the Pygmy Owl, in addition to the barn-owls, which form a separate family, the Tytonidae. Their habits are much the same as those of the eared or horned owls.

The Little Owl (*Athene noctua*) is a small, handsome-looking bird with greyish-brown plumage. The underparts are lighter in colour and marked here and there with white spots. The legs carry relatively few feathers, and the face or mask is not strongly marked.

The Little Owl is found over Europe and much of Asia and Africa. It is a common resident in England and Wales, mostly in copses, parks, gardens and orchards.

Being much less nocturnal than the other owls, the Little Owl ventures out during the day, but hunts only at night and during the early morning. It destroys an incredible number of rats, mice, voles, field mice and insects. The brood of four or five hungry owlets keeps the parents continually at work providing food. The cries of the Little Owl, and of owls in general, are much more varied than is commonly supposed. The most frequent calls of the Little Owl are sharp, quick cries or shrill whistling sounds, which it utters whenever it is aroused or disturbed.

The Sparrow Owl or Pygmy Owl (*Glaucidium passerinum*) is one of the smaller species. It flies by day and has a flight recalling that of a Swallow. In the ease and rapidity with which it moves it is more like a diurnal bird of prey. But it can also climb trees like a Parrot and may hunt on the ground or in the air. It feeds on small animals such as mice, shrews and insects. It lives in a broad belt from Scandinavia and south-east France across to China.

Some of the small North American owls have a curious habit of living in rabbits' burrows. One such is the Burrowing Owl (*Speotyto cunicularia*). In soft ground it can excavate its own burrow but elsewhere it relies on using the abandoned tunnels of prairie dogs, viscachas, armadillos and others. This commensalism is to the advantage of the owl.

These small, burrow-dwelling species have become so terrestrial in habit that they are practi-

The Burrowing Owl (*Speotyto cunicularia*) seen with its young. It lives on the open plains of western North America and Florida, through Central and South America and the West Indies. It is a small owl with spotted plumage and relatively long slender legs. Although it can fly when danger threatens, it usually runs into its burrow with remarkable speed.

cally flightless and will flatten themselves against the ground rather than fly when disturbed. Their legs are relatively long and adapted for running. About six eggs are laid, which look like those of a pigeon and take about three weeks to hatch.

The Tawny or Wood Owl (*Strix aluco*) is found in forests and wooded regions over much of Europe, western Asia and north-west Africa. It is the commonest of owls in the British Isles. It is difficult to describe the plumage as it varies with age and sex, passing from greys to reds and browns. The characteristic features are the breast markings, which look something like an inverted fir-tree, and the white spots on the shoulder regions. This species is much the same size as the Long-eared Owl.

The Tawny Owl has a number of different calls, the best known being a kind of *kouwitt*. The pitch varies and the cry has a creaking, mewing or shrill quality, and consists of one, two, three or even four syllables. As these calls are made they fall in pitch until the last syllable, which is made on a rising note. Sometimes the cries follow one another in rapid succession, and certain observers believe that this form of cry is peculiar to the female. The male begins calling as early as the end of December and goes on until June. It may begin calling again in the autumn, even in the middle of August, and it may also be heard, less frequently, at other times. The well-known *oo-oo* cries of the Tawny Owl usually consist of two or three syllables, a signal audible a long way off. After listening for about five seconds it utters a short call followed by a brief silence. Then comes a series of discreet sounds, dying away in a trill. After this there is a further silence of five to seven seconds and the whole sequence is repeated.

The Tawny Owl builds in a tree hollow or takes over the old nest of a rook, woodpecker or squirrel. The female lays several white, rounded eggs just over four centimetres in diameter. These she broods for about a month, during which time she is fed by the male. Both birds help to rear the young in common with most birds of prey.

In North America the Tawny Owl is replaced ecologically by the rather similar Barred Owl (*S. varia*). Another member of the genus is the Great Grey Owl (*S. nebulosa*) which is found in the forests of the Arctic regions of America and Eurasia. Its plumage is so thick that it appears larger than the Eagle-owl or Great Horned Owl, but actually weighs much less than either of these.

The handsome Snowy Owl (*Nyctea scandiaca*) of the Arctic sometimes winters in Scandinavia, Canada, the United States and Russia. The plumage is pure white in the male but the female has a varying number of dark barred markings; the younger individuals are more heavily barred. The species feeds on hares, lemmings and ptarmigans, hunting on the ground or in flight according to circumstance. It is skilled in catching fishes, lying in wait on the banks of rivers or lakes to seize one in its claws.

Nightjars and allies
(Order Caprimulgiformes)

This order includes the Oilbird, frogmouths, potoos, owlet-frogmouths and the nightjars: all are brownish, mottled, birds with nocturnal or crepus-

The Ferruginous Pygmy Owl (*Glaucidium brasilianum*) of America occurs in two distinct subspecies. One group lives in North America, the other in South America. The picture shows a member of the southern subspecies from Tierra del Fuego. It is a very small owl, little more than fifteen centimetres long, but is a fierce hunter sometimes taking prey larger than itself.

The Tawny Owl (*Strix aluco*) is one of the commonest owls in Eurasia and northwest Africa. It is strictly nocturnal preying on small mammals, and birds up to the size of a Mallard. It will also take earthworms, beetles, snails and slugs. This wide diet together with its tolerance of man has enabled the Tawny Owl to maintain or even increase its numbers over much of its range.

A female Great Grey Owl (*Strix nebulosa*) seen with her chicks. A very imposing owl, its massive head may be fifty centimetres in circumference and its large, heavily-barred facial disc, bordered with a dark ruff, makes an almost perfect circle. It has a wide breeding range on both sides of the Atlantic but its numbers vary enormously with the population of its prey, which are mainly voles.

The Common Potoo (*Nyctibius griseus*), of tropical America, is related to the nightjars. Its distinctive far-carrying call, sad and beautiful, can often be heard on moonlit nights, but during the day it is seldom seen as its plumage blends in so well with the trees on which it roosts.

cular habits. All except the Oilbird are insectivorous in their feeding habits.

Oilbird or guacharo (Family Steatornithidae)

This family has only one species: the Oilbird (*Steatornis caripensis*) or Guacharo of northern South America and the island of Trinidad. Although only thirty-three centimetres long, it has a wingspan of about a metre. It spends the day deep in caves, finding its way through the darkness by using an echo-location mechanism similar to that used by bats. In colouring and form the Oilbird is similar to the nightjars. It nests in colonies on rocky ledges high above the cave floor. From the two to four eggs in each nest are hatched the naked young, which in two to three weeks pass through two downy stages, during which they attain a weight that is half as much again as the parents. As flight feathers form, the excess weight is lost. Probably because its food is mainly the very oily fruit of palm trees, its flesh is very fatty and the natives use impaled carcasses as torches.

Frogmouths (Family Podargidae)

These also resemble the nightjars in appearance. There are a dozen species confined to south-east Asia and Australia. During the day frogmouths roost lengthwise on a tree branch, with head up and eyes closed, their cryptically coloured plumage matching the bark. There is virtually no sexual dimorphism. The nest is a platform of twigs or a wad of their own feathers camouflaged with plants. The one or two eggs are incubated by both parents, the male sitting by day and the female by night. They are terrestrial feeders: insects are not taken in flight but as they rest on the ground.

Potoos or wood-nightjars (Family Nyctibiidae)

There are five species (genus *Nyctibius*) in this family, distributed from southern Mexico to Brazil. Like true nightjars they hunt insects at night, not in uninterrupted flight but in forays from a branch, taking an insect on the wing and returning to the same perch. By day they rest in a vertical posture on a broken branch, with head up, tail down, and eyes closed. They are solitary birds. The single white egg is laid on the top of a broken-off branch or precariously on a ledge of bark. Both parents taking turns at incubating.

Owlet-frogmouths (Family Aegothelidae)

Very little is known about the seven species from Australia and New Guinea known as owlet-frogmouths, owlet-nightjars, or moth owls. They resemble small nightjars but have something of the habits of owls. They perch crosswise on branches, sit upright, and when flying for insects at night pursue a straighter course than nightjars. Like owls they can turn their heads through 180 degrees, and their calls are owl-like. They lay four to five white eggs in tree hollows.

Nightjars (Family Caprimulgidae)

This is the largest family of the order, comprising the subfamilies Caprimulginae, the typical nightjars or goatsuckers, and Chordeilinae, the nighthawks. Large eyes, wide gape for taking insects on the wing, quiet flight, long pointed wings and slight sexual dimorphism are typical.

The European Nightjar (*Caprimulgus europaeus*) of Europe and central Asia is a large bird mottled with brown, red and black, simulating the colouring of dead leaves. This is excellent camouflage, since it lives in woods and forests. During the day it remains perched lengthwise along a branch and is scarcely visible. As evening falls it starts hunting in the clearings, along the forest ridges, or high up in the air. It is then that the penetrating song, a monotonous churring from which the bird gets its name, can be heard. The mouth is huge, wide and deep, and prolonged into a sticky throat that acts as a trap for insects. It makes no nest, merely laying its eggs in a hollow in the ground under a bush where the hen alone sits on them. It is migratory and winters mainly in tropical Africa.

The North American species include the Whip-poor-will (*Caprimulgus vociferus*), very similar to the Nightjar, and the Poor-will (*Phalaenoptilus nuttallii*). The Poor-will is curious for its habit of hibernating in the winter when insects, the principal item of its diet, are scarce. During this period body temperature drops from about 40°C. to 18°C.

Farther south the White-necked Nighthawk (*Nyctidromus albicollis*) inhabits Middle and South America. In Africa the commonest species are the small Pennant-winged Nightjar (*Macrodipteryx vexillarius*) which has several of the inner flight feathers of the wing lengthened into long streamers, and the Long-tailed Nightjar (*Caprimulgus climacurus*).

The subfamily Chordeilinae is confined to the New World and is typically represented by the Common Nighthawk (*Chordeiles minor*) in North America. The Lesser Nighthawk (*Chordeiles*

A female Tawny Frogmouth (*Podargus strigoides*) with its young. It is widely distributed throughout the whole of Australia, common even in the suburbs of large towns. Although a rapid flier it feeds mostly on ground-living insects, grasshoppers, snails and slugs and occasionally mice. This highly-camouflaged species is related to the nightjars.

The European Nightjar (*Caprimulgus europaeus*), of Europe and central Asia, spends the winter in tropical Africa. When nesting the hen lays her eggs on the ground and incubates them there being extremely well-camouflaged by her mottled brown and grey plumage. The male is distinguished by white markings on the wings and tail.

acutipennis) is represented in both north and tropical South America.

Swifts and humming-birds
(Order Apodiformes)
True swifts and crested or tree swifts, together with the superficially dissimilar humming-birds, are fast-flying, short-legged, weak-footed, insectivorous birds. They are principally birds of the tropics and subtropics, though one or two nest in the northern hemisphere.

Swifts (Family Apodidae)
This family is unique in two features: individuals of the species belonging to it sometimes spend a whole night on the wing, and frequently copulate in the air. A familiar representative of the genus *Chaetura* is the Chimney Swift (*C. pelagica*) of North America, while the Old World genus *Apus* includes several African species and one—the Common Swift—that reaches the British Isles.

The Common Swift (*Apus apus*) is all black with a light-coloured patch on the throat. It is on the wing from morning to evening, twisting and turning with incredible agility. If it alights, it clings to the face of a wall or trunk of a tree. Its feet are so small and its legs so short that it has difficulty in taking off again if it falls to the ground. Like the other wide-billed birds, it catches insects while in flight. It reaches Europe from Africa later in spring than the apparently similar swallows, and leaves earlier. It is unmistakable because it is

The Common Swift (*Apus apus*) breeds in Europe and part of Asia and winters in Africa. It is unique in spending virtually all its life on the wing except when incubating. It feeds only on flying insects caught on the wing but this may be a disadvantage in bad weather when the swift may find it difficult to find food.

one of the noisiest of birds, and all the time it is on the wing it repeats its shrill cry. Its nest is a hole in a tree or crack in a rock, an old tower, belfry, or the roofspace of a house. It usually lays two eggs, but sometimes three or four. The hen sits and the cock brings her food.

All swifts have large salivary glands, but the swiftlets (genus *Collocalia*), of Asia and Oceania, produce saliva in such quantities that they can use it as the principal material for nest building. They nest in colonies on the face of tall sea cliffs or in dark caves. Their cup-shaped nests are made wholly of saliva, or of saliva mixed with moss or feathers, according to the species. When a swiftlet starts to build, it flies to the place selected and literally spits saliva on to the rock. It repeats this ten or twenty times, drawing a semicircle or horseshoe shape in saliva. This dries quickly and provides a solid formation for the nest. Some species use various vegetable substances bound together with saliva; the tiny Edible-nest Swiftlet (*Collocalia inexpectata*) uses saliva only. Once the frame has been laid down, it alights on it and, turning its head alternately to the right and left, builds up the nest wall which, when finished, is marked with undulating stratified lines.

The saliva, which dries very rapidly, is like a strong solution of gum Arabic. A thread of it drawn from the bird's mouth can be wound round a stick until all the saliva in the bird's mouth and in the ducts of the salivary glands has been extracted.

These are the 'swallow's nests' that are considered a delicacy, and the caves of Karang-Kallong in Java yield more than 300,000 a year.

The American Chimney Swift also uses saliva in the construction of its nest, but only to glue small twigs together and to the vertical surface of the interior of chimneys. The nest thus formed is a neat, surprisingly sturdy shelf on which the white eggs are laid. There is no doubt but that the nests were built inside tree hollows or in caves before European man introduced his chimneys though it is very rare to find a Chimney Swift's nest in such a situation today. These birds winter in South America where recently some have been found 'roosting' inside tree hollows in Peru.

Swifts are well-named as their flight speed is faster than that of almost any other bird; some say the fastest.

Crested swifts (Family Hemiprocnidae)
A group of three species related to the true swifts is assigned to this family. All inhabit the forests of south-east Asia (India to the Philippines and Solomons), but they are not as continually on the wing as the true swifts. They feed on insects taken in flight mainly at dawn and dusk, and spend much time perched on bare branches. They have forked tails, strong legs and toes, a pronounced crest, a distinctive white marking above the eye and another well below it. The nest is minute, a few layers of bark on a dead tree limb with the single egg cemented to the floor of the nest.

Humming-birds (Family Trochilidae)
Although they feed on nectar and small insects found in flowers these birds are not related to the sunbirds or the honey-eaters. They are related to

the swifts and have the same short legs, which leave them almost helpless on the ground. In some of their habits humming-birds resemble Old World flycatchers, while the structure of their tongue is in some ways comparable to that of woodpeckers. Nevertheless they are very specialised birds and there is no risk of confusing them with any other species in the Americas where they occur. In general, they are tiny birds and their minute legs are almost hidden among their feathers. They have tubular, pointed bills; tubular, fringe-tipped tongues, slightly forked at the tip, and squamous plumage which refracts light.

Over 300 known species and subspecies have been identified, distributed through the western hemisphere from the Magellan Strait to Canada, and from the humid low country and forests of the Amazon to the highest peaks of the Andes. This wide distribution embracing so many different habitats, is perhaps one of the most remarkable things about humming-birds. They seem to be so weak and so specialised in their way of life, yet they are amazingly adaptable and can live as well in a desert as in an equatorial climate, or even among the snows and ice of high mountains.

The northernmost species migrate annually from the confines of North America, where they nest, to Mexico and Central America, where they pass the winter. The greatest migrants are the Ruby-throated Humming-bird (*Archilochus colubris*) and the Rufous Humming-bird (*Selasphorus rufus*), which breed farthest north, the latter going as far as Alaska. When migrating, some follow a Mexican route, while others go by way of Florida, Cuba and the Yucatan peninsula. Almost all avoid the direct route involving the hazardous crossing of the Gulf of Mexico. In addition to these migrations in latitude, there are many others of fairly limited range which take the humming-birds to different places according to the season. The general impression is that these frail-looking birds are really continuously on the move in search of favourable conditions and more varied sources of food.

The largest of the family is the Giant Humming-bird of the Andes (*Patagona gigas*), which is up to twenty-one centimetres long; the smallest is the Bee Humming-bird (*Mellisuga helenae*), of Cuba and the Isle of Pines, no longer than five centimetres including tail and long bill.

For colourful plumage the humming-bird has no rivals. There are species with crests, collarets, plumes and other ornamental accessories, and in adition their plumage is iridescent, changing tone with the incidence of the light on the structural colour of the feathers and showing rich metallic effects. This is reflected in the popular names given them by travellers: emerald, garnet, ruby, topaz, bluebeard, golden belly, rainbow.

But for all their fine plumes most humming-birds do not have a pleasing song. All are exceedingly pugnacious, however, and even the smallest are so aggressive that they often succeed in driving away much larger birds.

The wings are marvellous structures. The keel of the breastbone, to which the flight muscles are attached, is better developed than in other birds and the humerus is short. Their beat is vibrant and humming and the rate of movement comparable to that of insects. In the tiny *Pygmornis rubra* of Brazil there may be as many as fifty beats per second. The characteristic attitude of the humming-bird is its hovering as it gathers nectar from a flower without alighting. It is amazing that they can stay so still, hanging in the air, yet in continuous flight. They are so expert in this that they are able to visit a large number of flowers in a relatively short time, flitting from one to the other at lightning speed, their wings never for a moment ceasing to vibrate. They are the only birds that can fly backwards.

Humming-birds use only the beak and tongue for feeding. Their bills vary in length and in degree of curve towards the tip, but they are always slender and pointed. The longest bill is that of *Docimestes* where it is the length of the bird's body, and the shortest is that of *Opisthoprora*.

Inside the bill is a cylindrical tongue, seemingly forked but actually with the outer edges rolled upwards and inwards in two half-cylinders joined over most of their length. Together they form a pair of tubes well adapted for sucking up nectar, pollen and tiny insects, for humming-birds are not solely nectar-eaters. Although nectar itself provides them with sufficient food to replace the energy they expend, it is insufficient for growth and repair of tissues, and so insects and spiders are taken as a source of protein. They find these inside the flowers and hunt them in the air like flycatchers, and they will also rob spiders' webs of flies that have been caught in them and even take the spiders themselves.

The Broad-billed Hummingbird (*Cyanthus latirostris*), one of only two species in the genus, is characterised by a long, straight bill broadened at the base. The male, shown here, is perhaps the most attractive of all hummingbirds, with a brilliant viridescent green back and a bright blue throat and upper chest. It breeds in the southwestern United States and Mexico.

433

The mating habits of the male humming-birds are simple. They usually live apart from the female, except for a brief courtship followed by a swift mating. In most species courtship display consists of the males performing intricate aerial dances and displays before the perching female. The cock gives no help to the hen in building the nest, incubating, and rearing the young. In this respect the male humming-birds generally resemble the gallinaceous birds more than they resemble the related swifts.

The strangest of all the humming-birds, Loddige's Racket-tailed Humming-bird (*Loddigesia mirabilis*), known from a single valley 2,200 to 3,000 metres above sea-level in Peru, has only four tail feathers instead of the usual ten. The two outer tail feathers are long, supple and sinuous, and with these it displays before the female, making first one then the other undulate, or striking them one against the other like whiplashes. The males of the Long-tailed Hermit (*Phaethornis superciliosa*) forgather at the mating season and, far from fighting, embark on a protracted series of displays.

By contrast, the females of these two species have no comparable claims to distinction. They build their nests and bring up their young in a straight-forward manner. The typical nest is a small cup of regular shape set at the intersection of two branches or astride a branch. It is made of the finest fibres from the vegetable and animal kingdoms, including spiders' webs, and saliva is usually used to hold it in position. Sometimes coarser materials are added, but the inside of the nest is always fine and delicate.

There are two eggs in each clutch and the hen may lay two or three clutches a season, especially in tropical regions. They are the smallest of all birds' eggs, and always a uniform matt white. The chicks are very weak when hatched and remain in the nest for several weeks, fed with insects by the mother, or with nectar from her gizzard, as she thrusts her beak into the chick's oesophagus before regurgitating. Female humming-birds are most attentive and seldom abandon their eggs or young.

Colies (Order Coliiformes)

The colies or mouse-birds are small birds (twenty-eight to thirty-five centimetres) of southern Africa. Anatomically the six species of the single family (Coliidae) seem to resemble the woodpeckers (Piciformes) and the kingfishers and hornbills (Coraciiformes). They have short legs, strong curved claws and a reversible outer toe on each foot. This is an adaptation to climbing trees. The bill is rather like the finch's but fleshy around the nostrils. The body plumage, including a crest on the head, is soft and hair-like, but the tail feathers are long and stiff. They creep about trees and bushes rather like mice, feeding on berries and fruits and move in bands of twenty to thirty, keeping in contact with one another by whistling. Their mouse-like appearance is exaggerated by the dun colours of their feathers, but there is blue and white in the plumage of some species.

Trogons (Order Trogoniformes)

These birds have a unique foot structure: the first and second toes are turned backwards, while the third and fourth point forwards, an arrangement described as heterodactylous. Because of this marked difference from all other birds they are placed in a separate order, which consists of a single family, Trogonidae.

The trogons are essentially forest-dwelling birds and are rarely seen, even in the districts of Africa, Asia and America where they are most common. They lead solitary lives, making little noise and apparently concealing themselves in the densest and darkest places. They feed mainly on insects, which are taken in flight during the morning and evening. Their soft and downy plumage makes very little noise in flight. The songs are both monotonous and weak in quality. The short, strong beak bears stiff bristly feathers at the base, is hook-tipped, and sometimes denticulated. Like

The Narina Trogon (*Apaloderma narina*) is the commonest and most widespread of the African Trogons, living in forests up to 1800 metres, but it is not often seen except in the rainy season. Then the male displays, inflating a blue-green bladder in its throat and calling with a deep cooing. Little is known about its nesting behaviour.

The Lesser Pied Kingfisher (*Ceryle rudis*), of Africa and southwest Asia, is a sturdy, short-tailed bird with entirely black-and-white plumage. It lives in open country near lakes, estuaries, tidal creeks and slow-moving rivers or canals. When hunting it hovers over the water, with fast-beating wings, then plunges to take its prey. As well as fish it also takes insects, shrimps, frogs and crayfish.

many arboreal birds, some species have a long, rather stiff tail which serves as a counterpoise and as a brace when digging their nest in soft rotting-wood, termite or ants' nests.

Species of *Harpactes*, in which the male and female are distinctly and beautifully coloured, live in Malaysia. Sexual dimorphism is also found in the African genus *Hapalodermes*, and is even more marked in the species of *Calures* from America; most species are sexually dimorphic.

One American species is particularly well-known, the Quetzal (*Pharomachrus mocinno*) which extends from Nicaragua to Mexico. It is a beautiful bird, nearly 120 centimetres long. The male in particular is brilliantly coloured, with greenish-gold tints on the head, back and breast, with carmine shades on the underparts. The eye is encircled with black feathers, the bill and feet are yellow, and there is a rounded crest of hair-like feathers on the head. The tail bears extremely long, flowing feathers. The Quetzal is the national bird of Guatemala.

Kingfishers, hoopoes, hornbills and allies (Order Coraciiformes)

Most members of this cosmopolitan order are tropical Old World species. Long bills, short legs, short wings, bright plumage and hole-nesting are the characteristic features shared by many of the order. Most groups have two or more of the forwardly directed toes fused along the sides for parts of their length and one group is able to reverse one of its toes to the rear, becoming zygodactylous. The fusion of toes is referred to as syndactyly.

Kingfishers (Family Alcedinidae)

This is a particularly bright-plumed group of three subfamilies, the Alcedininae, the Daceloninae and the Cerylinae. The typical kingfishers, the Alcedininae, have their most commonly known European representative in the Common Kingfisher (*Alcedo atthis*), a small solitary bird frequenting peaceful streams in Europe and the East. Perched on an overhanging willow branch it waits, motionless, until it plunges headlong to take its fish. The catch is then taken back to the bough, where it is always swallowed head first.

The Common Kingfisher has brilliant plumage of metallic green combined with azure blue and coppery red. It is squat and its extremely short tail contrasts with its long, wedge-shaped bill.

Like many other members of the family, the Kingfisher's nest is a burrow in the river bank and consists of a long entrance passage terminating in a roomy chamber, usually strewn with fishbones. The eggs are incubated by both parents. When the eggs are hatched the parent birds share the task of feeding and otherwise caring for the young. The nestling's feathers develop in waxy sheaths which protect them from the filth which gathers in the nest.

There are several related insectivorous species in the same family, including the Pygmy Kingfisher (*Ceyx picta*) of Africa and the numerous brightly coloured three-toed kingfishers of south-east Asia.

The Daceloninae, the tree, forest or wood kingfishers, are arboreal species of Australasia and Africa that eat insects, reptiles and even small birds or mammals. They have slightly longer tails than the typical kingfishers. The lower mandible is enlarged and the bill hooked at the end. The best-known species is the Laughing Jackass or Kookaburra (*Dacelo novaeguineae*), which owes its popular name to its cry. It is the largest representative of the family, attaining the size of a Raven. This species is often seen in towns, where it scavenges and eats snails and slugs. It makes its burrow in termite nests. The Racket-tailed Kingfisher (*Tanysiptera galatea*) of the Moluccas and New Guinea is a magnificent bird with elongated median tail feathers ending in rackets.

The Cerylinae are fishing kingfishers and the only members of the family found in the New World. The commonest is the Belted Kingfisher (*Ceryle alcyon*) with blue-grey back and white underparts with a blue-grey band across the breast of both sexes and a tawny band below this on the female, and a penetrating rattle of a call. The largest of the New World tropical genus *Chloroceryle* is the Crested Amazon Kingfisher (*C. amazona*). The Green Kingfisher (*C. americana*) is a small species found from the south-western United States to southern South America. One of the smallest is the Least Kingfisher (*C. aenea*), found through Mexico, Central America, and northern South America, which is only about twelve to fifteen centimetres long. A less colourful species in the Old World is the black and white Pied Kingfisher (*Ceryle rudis*) of Africa and south-west Asia. This species is particularly fond of crayfishes.

Todies (Family Todidae)

The five species of tody are confined to West Indian islands: one each in Jamaica, Puerto Rico and Cuba, and two on Hispaniola. They are wren-sized with broad, flattened beaks, finely serrated at the edges, facial bristles, short tails, and quill-like tongues. All are bright green above and pale below, with bright red bibs (the Jamaican Tody is known as a 'robin'). They sit in pairs on a branch, flying out to catch passing insects with a loud whirring of wings. Their nests are in tunnels in the ground where three to four white eggs are laid.

Motmots (Family Momotidae)

Eight species of this family are distributed from Mexico to northern Argentina. They range from eighteen to forty-six centimetres in length, much of which is tail. The plumage is mainly brownish green, with turquoise blue on the head. The bill is serrated as in the todies, and like them motmots fly out from a branch to take passing insects. They also eat snails, lizards and fruit. The elongated, median feathers of the tail are trimmed as the bird preens until only the racket-shaped ends are left. The nest is in a long tunnel in a bank, where three to four eggs are laid. General nesting habits are similar to those of the kingfishers.

Bee-eaters (Family Meropidae)

The twenty-five species of bee-eater can be typified by the Common Bee-eater (*Merops apiaster*), which usually nests in large colonies, burrowing into a sandy river bank or a cutting in a road. The horizontal passage may be one to two metres long

435

BIRDS

Two Common Bee-eaters (*Merops apiaster*) perch on a sun-bleached skull in Spain. One of the most brightly-coloured birds in Europe the Bee-eater has pointed wings, long forked tail feathers and a very long beak. It is usually seen in noisy flocks catching insects, particularly bees and wasps, on the wing. It has the rapid circling flight of a swallow.

and ends in a chamber. Sometimes the pair is assisted by non-breeding 'helpers'. The Bee-eater's favourite food is wasps and bees. With its blues, yellows, orange, reds and black, it is as lovely and colourful a bird as the Roller. The family occurs in the Old World from southern Europe and central Asia to South Africa, Madagascar, and Australia.

Cuckoo-roller (Family Leptosomatidae)
The single species is sufficiently different to justify its being placed in a separate family: although it has colours as bright as the true rollers and performs similar aerial acrobatics, it has a reversible fourth toe, powder-down patches on the sides of the rump and a bill overhung by large tufts of feathers.

Rollers (Family Coraciidae)
Sedentary in southern Europe and the northern shores of the Mediterranean, but venturing much

The European Roller (*Coracius garrulus*) breeds in Europe, northwest Africa and northwest India and winters in the East African savannah regions. Its flight is strong and graceful but on the ground it moves clumsily. The name 'roller' comes from the male's beautiful courtship display when he tumbles and rolls down through the air from a great height, often continuing the rolling in level flight.

farther north in summer, the Eurasian Common Roller (*Coracias garrulus*) is jay-like, has a greenish-blue or aquamarine head and front, yellow back, purplish-blue wing tips and greyish-brown tail. It has a long, straight beak, hooked at the tip, is solitary, flies strongly, and sits waiting for its prey, which it seizes on the wing. It makes its nest in a tree hollow or in a rock, at most adding a meagre amount of grass, straw or feathers.

Ten other species, distributed over Africa, Asia and Australia, make up the family, all noted for their acrobatics in the air, rolling, zigzagging, rocketing up with closed wings and diving.

Ground rollers (Subfamily Brachypteraciinae)
The five species making up this subfamily are confined to Madagascar. They are similar to rollers except that they hunt insects and other small terrestrial animals in the forests, continuing to do so from dusk well into the night. Correlated with this, their legs are stouter and longer and the wings more rounded and shorter.

Hoopoes (Family Upupidae)
The Hoopoe (*Upupa epops*), the only species in the family, has a pinkish-brown plumage, and its wings and tail are black barred with white. On its head is a long crest of chestnut-brown feathers with black tips. Its bill, black and very long, seeks out insects and other animals. It lives a solitary existence in open country and is very timid. The nest is made in a hole in a tree, and this is identifiable by its filthy condition and repellent smell, in striking contrast to the beauty of the bird itself. The excrement of both parents and chicks accumulates, putrefies, and attracts flies.

Wood hoopoes (Family Phoeniculidae)
The six wood hoopoes of Africa have more markedly curved beaks than the Hoopoe and live in large societies in forests. They have a strong, musky smell. They lack a crest and have long graduated tails of metallic colours. They differ from the Hoopoe in certain anatomical details, but some ornithologists place them in the same family.

Hornbills (Family Bucerotidae)
The dark-plumaged hornbills of the tropical forests of Africa and tropical Asia are ungainly looking birds whose bills vie with the toucans' in size. In most species the bill has a 'helmet' or a rough protuberance above it, and in many species this is an air-filled hollow and in some rather solid and ivory-like. The sounds uttered by the birds are loud and raucous. With the exception of the Ground Hornbill, all hornbills, which mate for life, have a common pattern in their behaviour: once the nest is made in a tree hollow, the cock immures the hen in it, blocking the opening with clay until only the tip of her bill emerges. Thereafter he feeds her and, later, the chicks, as long as they are inside. The young birds grow slowly and take several months to mature. When they are about half grown one of the parent birds enlarges the hole in the nest so that the female can emerge to help the male search for the fruit, berries, and insects which habitually form their diet.

The Great Hornbill (*Buceros bicornis*), found in South-east Asia, is 150 centimetres long.

Woodpeckers and allies
(Order Piciformes)

Plainly birds of the woodlands with second and third toes directed forwards, while the first and fourth point backwards. (Such pairing of the digits is termed zygodactylous.) Some families are primarily vegetarian, but most are insectivorous, all nest in holes. One family is parasitic.

Jacamars (Family Galbulidae)

These are graceful birds up to thirty centimetres long that range in humid forest regions from Mexico to Brazil. They have long, tapering bills and iridescent plumage, and in these respects they are not unlike humming-birds. They are noisy and full of activity. Frequent sallies from a tree perch to take brilliantly coloured insects are typical. They nest in burrows in a bank or hillside, where they lay three to four white eggs. The young are covered in a heavy white down, quite unlike the majority of naked piciform hatchlings.

Puffbirds (Family Bucconidae)

Thirty species constitute this family found in the tropical forests of Central and South America. The puffbird's head is disproportionately large, the plumage of most species is drab grey or brown, and its tail short. The overall effect is of a squat 'puffy' bird. A habit of raising the feathers until the bird looks rather like a huge powder-puff strengthens this impression. When alarmed, the birds immediately flatten the feathers against their bodies. They are quiet birds, rarely found in flocks. Nesting is of two types: in holes dug in termite nests, and ground burrows. Two or three glossy white eggs are incubated by both birds. One of the commonest species is the White-necked Puffbird (*Notharchus macrorhynchus*) of Central and South America, which is about twenty-five centimetres long.

Barbets (Family Capitonidae)

The sturdy, non-migratory barbets get their common name from the bristly nostril feathers round their bill. They are noisy and markedly arboreal, rarely descending from their perches at treetop level. All are weak in flight. Some species live on a vegetarian diet, others take insects. Distribution is pan-tropical, with high development in Africa. Asia, Africa, America, each has species peculiar to it. No genus or species occurs in more than one of the continents. Most are brilliantly coloured and active, but others, cryptically coloured merge inconspicuously into a background of dead leaves, are much slower in their movements. All are cavity-nesters, pecking out hollows in dead tree-trunks.

Honey-guides (Family Indicatoridae)

Like cuckoos, the honey-guides are social parasites and lay their eggs in the nests of other birds, where the young are raised by foster-parents. They are small birds found in the tropical forests of Asia and Africa. One species, the Greater Honey-guide (*Indicator indicator*) is particularly well known for its remarkable skill in finding the nests of wild bees. Its fluttering and calling in the bushes attracts the attention of any interested party, man, honey-badger or other mammal, and reveals the position

of the nest. The birds wait for the comb to be left behind in the opened nest. Unique secretions in the stomach enable them to digest the wax. The honey-guides are insectivorous too.

Toucans (Family Ramphastidae)

A large, ludicrous, brightly coloured bill, serrated at the edges and in some species as long as the body, makes the arboreal Toucan one of the most striking of the piciforms. But the bill size is deceptive: its apparent solidity and weight are broken by a honeycomb of fibres within the bulky outer case. There is some doubt about the adaptive origin of the large bill. Certainly the bird's frugivorous habits do not explain its massive structure. The long tongue is bristled at the tip.

The largest species, with the largest bills, are those of the genus *Ramphastos*, inhabitants of lowland forests. The black of their bodies is relieved with gaudy throat patches, bright bills and tail coverts. Species of the genus *Pteroglossus*,

The Hoopoe (*Upupa epops*) is widely distributed in Europe, Africa and Asia. Although it flies strongly it has a wavering, irregular flight. On the ground it runs and walks about with its head bobbing up and down. The name 'Hoopoe' comes from its cry of *hoop-hoop-hoop-hoop*.

The Yellow-horned Hornbill (*Tockus flavirostris*) eating a snake. This is one of a number of small hornbills that live in savannah and thornbrush regions of Africa. They are usually seen in small groups feeding on the ground. Apart from small reptiles they eat fruit and insects and may take eggs and young birds.

their strong wedge-shaped bill to extract insect larvae. The prey is then probed from the crevices with the long, sensitive, pointed tongue, which is cylindrical in cross-section. Its entire surface is sticky and bears small hooks at the tip. It is used as an organ of touch and taste. The tongue of the Green Woodpecker can be protruded for a length of twenty centimetres, five times as long as the bill itself, to explore cavities for insects. The anatomical structure of a woodpecker's tongue is curious in that it is prolonged to the back of the head by two ligaments which then curve upwards and forwards over the top of the skull to terminate, according to species, near the base of the bill, in the upper mandible or, more rarely, behind or below the eye.

The hunt for food is usually over a restricted territory, which is scoured daily. The entire surface of each tree is examined from top to bottom. The flight from tree to tree is both jerky and noisy. On the ground the bird has an ungainly way of hopping after insects and worms. The holes it drills in search of food are wrongly supposed to damage trees. In fact it attacks only wood that is already riddled with the borings of wood-eating insects. Its stomach is always crammed with the pests of cultivated lands and forests.

Woodpeckers' cries are short and resounding. In the Green Woodpecker the call resembles a crazy laugh, which has earned the bird the nickname 'yaffle'. During the mating season characteristic drumming sounds are made with the bill on a tree branch or a resonant, dead stump.

Woodpeckers lead markedly solitary lives, but come together in pairs for the breeding season. Male and female remain together throughout the entire period of nesting, incubation and the rearing of the young. The nest is hollowed out in the heart of an old tree and is lined with chips of wood. Some six eggs are produced, brown spotted or white.

North America has numerous species of typical woodpeckers: the Yellow-bellied Sapsucker (*Sphyrapicus varius*), the Red-headed Woodpecker (*Melanerpes erythrocephalus*), the Golden Fronted Woodpecker (*M. aurifrons*) and—one of the best known—the Yellow-shafted Flicker (*Colaptes auratus*) which is an ant-eating species common in the eastern United States. Further west this last species is replaced by the Red-shafted Flicker (*C. cafer*). A singular habit is found in one species, the Acorn Woodpecker (*Melanerpes formicivorus*): it gathers acorns and stores them for the winter in individual holes dug into the boles of trees, telephone poles, agave, and yucca stems. The method of storing is very systematic. The first hole is made near the base of the plant and then filled with an acorn. The second hole is made a little higher up, again packed with an acorn, and so on to the top of the stem. One wooden, electric power pole contained over 2,000 acorns stored in this manner.

European coasts have three spotted species, the Great Spotted Woodpecker (*Dendrocopos major*), the Lesser Spotted Woodpecker (*D. minor*), the Middle Spotted Woodpecker (*D. medius*); and also the Green Woodpecker (*Picus viridis*), the Grey Woodpecker (*P. canus*), the Black Woodpecker (*Dryocopus martius*) and the Three-toed Woodpecker

The Keel-billed or Sulphur-breasted Toucan (*Ramphastos sulfuratus*), one of the most conspicuous of the toucans that inhabit the dense low-lying forests of Central and South America. They live in noisy flocks feeding on fruit and berries. In spite of its size the bill is very light and useless in defence against hawks, the toucans' main enemies.

The Great Spotted Woodpecker (*Dendrocopos major*) of Europe and Asia showing its striking black and white plumage. Typically a woodland species, it is also seen in parks and orchards, and is becoming a frequent visitor to bird tables where it will feed on household scraps. Its main food, however, is insects and the fruits of trees.

usually called aracaris, are smaller and the most gregarious. Other species inhabit the higher altitudes of the mountain forests.

Woodpeckers (Family Picidae)
This is a widely distributed family over two hundred species subdivided into three main groups: the Picinae or true woodpeckers, the Picumninae or piculets, and the Jynginae or wrynecks. General characteristics are large head, short legs, long, sticky tongue, insectivorous feeding habits, and harsh cries. The true wookpeckers are essentially tree-climbing birds. The wrynecks, on the other hand, are perching rather than climbing birds. The piculets perch and climb.

The Green Woodpecker (*Picus viridis*) of Europe and the Great Spotted Woodpecker (*Dendrocopos major*) of Europe and Asia are typical examples of the Picinae, clinging to a tree trunk with their claws, using the stiff, spiky tail feathers as additional support. In this position, using the large robust head, they hammer away at the bark with

(*Picoides tridactylus*). The last-named species also occurs in North America where it is called the Northern Three-toed Woodpecker as there is a closely related species there, the Blackback Three-toed Woodpecker (*P. arcticus*). Black, white and red are the dominant colours in the plumage of *Dendrocopos*.

There are marked geographical variations in colour and size within this widespread group. Yellows and reds predominate in the warmer regions, while in humid conditions the darker colours are commoner because warmth and high humidity lead to excessive development of pigment and a reduction in size of the birds. Cold and dry conditions seem to have the opposite effect, producing bigger birds and brighter colours. This is an interesting example of the direct influence of the environment on living creatures.

Two species of wrynecks complete the family: the Eurasian Wryneck (*Jynx torquilla*) and the African Wryneck (*J. ruficollis*). Unlike the true woodpeckers these less specialised birds neither climb nor drill holes in trees though they do nest in cavities or holes in trees. They are, rather, perching birds, finding their food on the ground not in the trees. Ants form the staple of their diet. They take their common name from their habit of twisting their neck when disturbed. Plumage is a cryptic mottle of greys and browns. It is supposed that the wrynecks are primitive woodpeckers.

Perching birds (Order Passeriformes)

About 5,100 of the 8,700 known species of living birds are classified as perching birds or passerines. This group is currently highly successful. Other groups have been dominant in the past, each in turn replaced by a more successful form. Passerines owe their success to adaptation to a wide variety of habitats and to exploiting different ways of feeding. Their evolution has been so rapid and so diversified that the order contains about sixty-five families.

The true inter-relationships of many of these families are largely unrecognisable, particularly as parallelism and convergence are common; that is, unrelated birds with similar habits have come to resemble each other. For example, the American orioles and blackbirds (Icteridae) share their habitat preferences with the Old World starlings (Sturnidae) and have much the same build. More striking, they have the same kind of bill, a factor once regarded as a reliable basis for classification, but now known to be extremely plastic from an evolutionary point of view. Among the flower-peckers (Dicaeidae) many different bill-shapes are found, some almost conical like a seed-eater's, others slim like a warbler's. Apart from a few reasonably well defined groups such as larks (Alaudidae), it seems that behaviour, especially nest building, provides a better clue to relationship than the structure of the birds themselves.

The passerines are all land birds, and the principal features common to the whole order are the four toes, all at the same level and never webbed. The hind toe is highly developed but not reversible. Song, too, shows remarkable development, particularly in the suborder Oscines, the true song birds.

All passerine birds are altricial and are hatched

with only a trace of down on the feather tracts of the dorsal surface. At its fullest development this natal down presents a soft, fluffy appearance over the helpless nestlings. It is gradually pushed outwards by the tips of the feathers of the juvenile plumage, and portions of the down may frequently be seen adhering to the young birds when they leave the nest. Although the flight feathers are hardly discernible when the chick hatches some passerines are ready to fly in less than ten days.

Primitive perching birds (Suborders: Eurylaimi, Tyranni, and Menurae)

Broadbills (Family Eurylaimidae)
The broadbills are brightly coloured insectivorous birds inhabiting the tropical forests of Africa and Asia. The greatest number of species is found in the islands of the Malayan archipelago. One of the commonest in this area is the Green Broadbill (*Calyptomena viridis*), which is largely frugivorous. It is a dark grass-green colour with black bars on

The Yellow-shafted Flicker (*Colaptes auratus*) one of the best known woodpeckers in North America, widespread in the eastern United States, where it is also known as the Yellowhammer or Goldenwing. It has distinctive yellow markings on the wings and tail feathers, in contrast to the Red-shafted Flicker (*C. cafer*) in the western states which has red markings. Most authorities, however, now regard all flickers as one species.

439

The Black-headed or Hooded Pitta (*Pitta sordida*) of tropical southeast Asia, like all pittas has brilliantly-coloured plumage. Pittas feed on the forest floor and, in spite of their showy appearance, are more often heard than seen. They build large, untidy nests of sticks and roots on or near the ground.

the wings. The feathers are soft but look slightly waxy, so that the bird harmonises with the wet shiny leaves of its habitat. It sits silenty for hours in the shadows of a tree and only occasionally makes short foraging flights for insects, after which it returns to its perch. In contrast, the Black-and-yellow Broadbill (*Eurylaimus ochromalus*), of the same area, is whitish, with black wings with yellowish-white barring, and rather vinous-coloured underparts. The males perch for long periods singing a loud melodious song. Broadbills build a long, hanging nest of woven grasses and fibres, suspended from a branch by a slender rope of the same materials.

Kingbirds and allies (Suborder Tyranni)

Woodcreepers (Family Dendrocolaptidae)

Woodcreepers, or woodhewers as they are often called, are about fifty species of small neotropical birds, twenty to thirty-eight centimetres long, and predominantly brown in colour. They range throughout the forests and brushlands of Mexico, Central America and all but the southern tip of South America. They resemble woodpeckers in having a long bill and stiff-shafted tail feathers, and they lay white or whitish unspeckled eggs in tree cavities, although they do not excavate the nest-hole themselves. The Ivory-billed Wood-creeper (*Xiphorhynchus flavigaster*) is a typical species. It is a solitary bird, cryptically coloured in brownish tones, and never seen away from the woods. It invariably utters a loud, melancholy cry as it passes from tree to tree. It always alights on the trunk close to the ground, clinging to the bark in a vertical position, supported by its tail and with its head thrown back to give the extremely long beak free play. Thus positioned, it progresses

upwards by short hops, exploring the crevices in the wood for small insects and spiders. When it reaches branch height, it flies off to the next tree. Its manner of seeking food is very similar to that of the Old World tree creepers. It is especially fond of the very large carpenter ants which live in the decaying parts of trees.

Ovenbirds (Family Furnariidae)

Chiefly renowned for the unusual clay, oven-shaped nests they build, ovenbirds, of which there are some 200 species, are found in most habitats in southern Mexico and Central and South America from forests to semi-desert, and from rocky mountain slopes to the sea shore. The so-styled North American Ovenbird is actually a wood warbler.

The Red Ovenbird or Hornero (*Furnarius rufus*), which is extremely widespread, is a stout little bird with a slender, slightly curved beak nearly two centimetres in length, and strong legs suited to its terrestrial habits. The upperparts are a uniform rufous brown, the tail slightly redder, and the underparts pale brown. Its food consists of insect larvae and worms, for it is an exclusively terrestrial feeder.

In favourable seasons a pair begin nest building in the southern autumn and continue sporadically in mild spells during the winter. Otherwise nest building starts in early spring. The site selected may be a stout horizontal branch, the top of a post, the roof of a house or even the ground. The nest is made of mud, to which root fibres are added to make it more durable. When finished it has the shape of a kiln or old-fashioned baker's oven, but with a deeper and narrower entrance. There is an inner nesting chamber so walled off that, while a man may get his hand into the entrance, he cannot twist it to reach the eggs in the inner cavity.

The inner compartment is lined with dry soft grass, and five white eggs are laid. The 'oven' is thirty centimetres or more in diameter, and sometimes weighs as much as four kilograms. Both birds share the incubation. The young are extremely noisy and, when half-fledged, can be heard although they are still within the nest. After emerging from the nest the young remain with the parents for up to three months. Only one brood is raised each year, and a new oven is built for each, although old deserted ovens will survive for two or three years.

Ant-thrushes (Family Formicariidae)

This family contains over two hundred species confined to the area between southern Mexico and central South America. The birds range in size from that of a Wren to as large as a Jay, but most are about the size of chats and thrushes, which they resemble. They tend to skulk in the undergrowth of the forests and brushland and in some respects have the same ecological preferences as the pittas of eastern tropical forests. Their name reflects the common habit of accompanying ant-armies in order to feed on the insects the well-organised ants flush from the litter on the forest floor. The nest, unlike that of the ovenbirds, is usually a simple cup, semi-pendent on a low branch or in a bush near the ground. A few species build a covered nest on the ground and some line a tree-cavity. Ant-thrushes are usually solitary, sometimes occurring in pairs, and are somewhat sombre in appearance, with black, greys and browns predominating. They are strongly terrestrial birds and consequently have very weak flight.

Ant-pipits (Family Conopophagidae)
Also known as gnat-eaters, the ten or eleven species of this family belong to the Amazonian rainforests. Small, stocky and wren-like, they keep to thick impenetrable cover, and little is known of their habits.

Tapaculos (Family Rhinocryptidae)
The ground-dwelling tapaculos related to the antbirds, may be found throughout South America and in Central America, in grassland, scrub or forest, from sea-level up to 3,000 metres. Most species are inconspicuous browns and greys, stoutbodied and up to twenty-five centimetres long. They feed on insects and seeds, scuttling for cover as soon as disturbed, and seldom flying. At most they flutter a few metres. Their breast muscles are poorly developed and their legs strong. For example, the Barrancolino (*Teledromas fuscus*), of Argentina, is only seven centimetres long but is capable of taking fifteen centimetre strides. A special feature of the family is that each nostril has a movable flap, the function of which is unknown. Nesting habits are varied: some species are cavity-nesters, others are tunnel-burrowers, yet others build with grasses.

Pittas (Family Pittidae)
Known also as jewel-thrushes, the pittas inhabit the tropical forests of the Old World, particularly in the islands of the Malayan archipelago, including New Guinea, and the rainforests of Queensland in Australia. They are brightly coloured birds of the forest floor, where they live on insects, grubs and land molluscs. They resemble thrushes in their skulking habits, their size and even the brown-speckled young, but differ in having bright plumage, stubby tails, fairly long, strong legs, and only a piercing whistle instead of a melodious song. One of the most widespread species is the Red-breasted Pitta (*Pitta erythrogaster*), which ranges from the Philippines throughout the Moluccas to New Guinea and its associated islands. Most species of pitta are sedentary and seldom fly. The African Pitta (*P. angolensis*), however, breeds as far south as the Transvaal and outside the breeding season is found as far north as Uganda.

Asities and false sunbirds (Family Philepittidae)
There are four species of these birds on the island of Madagascar. Two are plump long-legged fruit-eaters, the Velvet Asity (*Philepitta castanea*) and Schlegel's Asity (*P. schlegeli*), which look like pittas. They inhabit the humid forests on the eastern and western sides of the island. The other two species, the Wattled False Sunbird (*Neodrepanis coruscans*) and the Small-billed False Sunbird (*N. hypoxantha*), are so like sunbirds they were originally classified with them. They have a habitat similar to that of sunbirds but they are of more slender build, with shorter legs and a long down-curving bill with which they sip nectar and take small insects. The Small-billed False Sunbird is known only from seven skins in museums and appears to be in danger of extinction, as its forest habitat is disappearing rapidly.

New Zealand wrens (Family Acanthisittidae=Xenicidae)
Only three of the four known species of these wren-like birds are left. Two are now rare, the Bush Wren (*Xenicus logipes*) and Rock Wren (*X. gilviventris*) having been preyed upon by introduced rats, cats and stoats. The third is the Rifleman (*Acanthisitta chloris*), which is yellowish green, and feeds on insects and spiders in much the same manner as tree-creepers. There was a fourth species, the Stephens Island Rock Wren (*X. lyalli*), but the lighthouse keeper's cat exterminated them. All three extant species are insectivorous.

Tyrant flycatchers or kingbirds (Family Tyrannidae)
The tyrant flycatchers are common throughout the New World, about 365 species being currently recognised. They destroy many insects in gardens and orchards. In America these are commonly referred to as 'flycatchers', but since the flycatchers of the Old World, quite a different family, have prior claim to the name the Tyrannidae are better known as tyrant flycatchers to avoid confusion.

The Vermilion Flycatcher (*Pyrocephalus rubinus*), a tyrant flycatcher of Central and South America, is easily identified by its bright red and black plumage. The male is seen to best advantage during his beautiful courtship flight. For a small bird he is often surprisingly bold in defending his territory.

The Superb Lyrebird (*Menura novaehollandiae*) lives in the rain forests of eastern Australia. The male builds circular mounds on which he sings and dances, displaying his lyre-shaped tail feathers, during the breeding season. The female builds the nest, incubates the single egg and rears the chick which stays in the nest for at least six weeks.

Nesting habits are varied, with a general emphasis on cup-shaped nests set in trees or bushes, but hole-nesting and ground-nesting is the pattern in some species.

Plumage is olive-green, grey or brown, black and white; a few species are brightly coloured. There is little sexual dimorphism. Wings are pointed and tails slightly forked. Bristles at the base of the beak are prominent. Some species, like the Scissor-tailed Flycatcher (*Muscivora forficata*), have a deeply-forked tail. This species owes its name to the habit of opening and closing its long outer tail feathers while in flight. These feathers are ten centimetres longer than the neighbouring two. The total length of the adult male is thirty-five centimetres, of which the tail contributes twenty-five. The head and back are pearly grey and the crown and wing-linings salmon pink. The underparts and all the tail feathers are white, with the exception of the black-tipped central pair. The Scissor-tail is found usually in open, sparsely wooded country, where it watches for insects and catches them in flight like an Old World flycatcher. It also feeds on small fruits.

The Eastern Kingbird (*Tyrannus tyrannus*) is a large black and white tyrant flycatcher, and is the best known of this family. It is very much in evidence during the summer in American orchards and farmyards. These noisy birds, always ready for a quarrel and usually coming off best, seem to delight in driving off crows, even when they have no eggs in the nests on which the crows might prey.

Many species are crested, particularly those of the genus *Myiarchus*. The best known is the Great Crested Flycatcher (*M. crinitus*), mainly of eastern North America but also found in Texas, and in the winter in South America. In has a prominent crest, grey throat and breast, yellow underparts and a rufous tail, and it nests in cavities in trees, laying four to six buff-coloured eggs scratched and spotted with a variety of rich shades of brown and lavender.

Other common species of Canada and the United States are the Eastern Phoebe (*Sayornis phoebe*), Say's Phoebe (*S. saya*) which breeds as far north as central Alaska, the Least Flycatcher (*Empidonax minimus*), the Eastern Wood Pewee (*Contopus virens*), the Western Wood Pewee (*C. sordidulus*), and the bright red species with a black back, wings, and tail, the Vermillion Flycatcher (*Pyrocephalus rubinus*).

Sharpbills (Family Oxyruncidae)
A few skins, gathered from tropical America and deposited in various museums, represent nearly all that is known of the single species of Sharpbill (*Oxyruncus cristatus*). About the size of a starling, olive-green above, yellowish with dark spots below, and with a yellow and scarlet crest, the Sharpbill has a straight, sharp-pointed bill and feeds on fruit.

Manakins (Family Pipridae)
In some of the fifty-nine known species there is a curious and unexplained modification of the wing primaries. In shape and appearance this group of small, brightly coloured birds of South America resembles the tits, although the two families are unrelated. The wing feathers of many species are so modified as to produce a rattling noise in flight, so that the first intimation of the presence of one of these birds is a sharp whirring sound, followed by two or three sharp snaps. There is marked sexual dimorphism and an elaborate lek courtship pattern that varies according to genus. In one species, *Chiroxiphia linearis*, sometimes called the Fandango Bird, the central pair of tail feathers is very long. At the time of courtship a number of males assemble at a given point, where each prepares a display ground for itself. Then the birds placidly await the arrival of a female, when each male indulges in astonishing acrobatics in its own area. The competition continues until the hen selects one for a mate. The female builds the woven nest, slung in a low fork, and cares for the young completely by herself.

Cotingas (Family Cotingidae)
Also known as chatterers, the cotingas are distributed from northern Argentina to the southern border of the United States. Bellbirds, fruit-crows, tityras, becards, cocks-of-the-rocks and the strange Umbrella-bird are all embraced in this group as diverse in colour as it is in size and form.

The sexual dimorphism marked throughout the family is well demonstrated by the male Umbrella-bird (*Cephalopterus ornatus*), a jet black bird the size of a crow with a long feathered lappet and a huge umbrella-like crest on its head that projects beyond the lip of the bill. Another ornamented species is the White Bellbird (*Procnias alba*) of the Guianas. This snow-white bird has a black fleshy caruncle about seven centimetres long rising from its forehead. When excited, it erects the spike-like caruncle and utters a sound like a bell.

In the genus *Rupicola* or cocks-of-the-rock, living in the Amazon basin, both sexes have an erectile crest that covers the whole of the top of the head and extends right to the tip of the bill. The cocks are a bright orange, and the females are brownish. The cock birds perform in turn a dance on a prominent clearing, around which the hens gather to select mates.

Plant-cutters (Family Phytotomidae)

The three species of plant-cutter are pests to agriculture, for a reason unusual in birds: they damage far more than they eat. Sparrow-like in appearance, they live in the open woodlands of South America, from Peru to Argentina. They not only feed on vegetation, but with their finely toothed saw-like bills they cut off leaves, buds and shoots, and even sever small plants at the base.

Lyrebirds and scrub-birds (Suborder Menurae)

Lyrebirds (Family Menuridae)

There are two species, the Superb Lyrebird (*Menura novaehollandiae*) and the smaller Prince Albert's Lyrebird (*M. alberti*). The first is the largest of the passerines and looks very like a pheasant. It lives solitarily in the eucalyptus forests of eastern Australia, where it is rigorously protected. The species is terrestrial and rarely takes wing. The male is plainly clad in grey and rufous, but possesses a long tail made up of sixteen plumes, each of the outer pairs curved in the shape of an 'S'. When the bird displays it spreads the tail feathers fan-wise forward over its body. The inner tail feathers lack barbules and resemble the strings of a lyre stretched between the S-shaped outer pair. The male builds a mound of twigs on which he sings and displays. The female builds the nest unaided and she broods the single egg while the male remains nearby and sings to her. The single youngster stays with the parents for up to three years, and as one egg is laid each year it means that a family party may consist of both parents, a young chick, another one year old, and a third two years old. It is believed that the birds mate for life. The males are renowned for their powers of mimicry, and can imitate the songs of other birds, the screeching of parrots, and the sounds made by dogs and man. They have even been known to reproduce the sound of a train-whistle.

Scrub-birds (Family Atrichornithidae)

Although related to the lyrebirds, the scrub-birds resemble large wrens. There are two known species, both unique to Australia. The Noisy Scrub-bird (*Atrichornis clamosus*) of western Australia is the larger, measuring twenty-two centimetres long. The Rufous Scrub-bird (*A. rufescens*) of eastern Australia is eighteen centimetres long. This is a rare species, decimated by the destruction of its habitat, and survives mainly in the Lamington National Park. In 1961 the Noisy Scrub-bird, thought to be extinct, was rediscovered. Scrub-birds are near-flightless and rarely show themselves, although the ringing whistle of the male can be plainly heard. Their mimicry is almost as skilled as the lyrebird's.

Higher perching birds or song birds (Suborder Passeres = Oscines)

Larks (Family Alaudidae)

Larks differ from all other song-birds in that the posterior surface of the tarsometatarsus (the longest part of the exposed 'leg') is reticulate. They have conical beaks and are mainly insectivorous. One obvious and well-defined character

The Woodlark (*Lullula arborea*) feeding its chicks. It is a summer visitor to the south and west of Britain. Less territorial than most larks, it inhabits open spaces with trees where it can perch. Both sexes are alike, having a flattened crest and a pale eye-stripe. Its thin beak is adapted to an insectivorous diet and contrasts with the short finch-like beaks of the seed-eating African larks.

is a hind toe with an immense straight claw. This makes perching difficult but walking easy. Other predominant features are the superb song and colour adaptation to environment. In a ground-dwelling family the second feature has particular importance in evading predators. The best examples are found in Africa where species living in red sand areas have reddish plumage, those living in pale desert are appropriately paler, while those in dark lava areas are very much darker plumaged. The species rarely enter the 'wrong' colour zone.

The well-known Skylark (*Alauda arvensis*) of the Old World has been introduced several times unsuccessfully into the eastern United States and successfully on Vancouver Island, British Columbia, as well as New Zealand and Hawaii. It soars vertically to a great height and hovers there singing for a long time, a mere speck in the sky, but still audible. It is while the bird is in flight that the song reaches its best. Suddenly it drops like a stone, and the next moment begins another soaring ascent towards the sun. On the ground it walks and runs quickly. It feeds on insects and seeds.

Normally sociable, the Skylark becomes pugnacious in the breeding season, the male birds fighting each other and behaving almost like gamecocks. After mating, the birds build simple nests in depressions in the ground. They may have two or three broods each year, with normally three or four eggs in a clutch. Both cock and hen share the duty of sitting on the eggs and feed the nestlings with worms, and insect larvae.

Four other species of lark are very closely related to the Skylark, but belong to different genera. The Woodlark (*Lullula arborea*) is smaller and, with the Short-toed Lark (*Calandrella brachydactyla*), inhabits waste ground, lightly tree-clad slopes and woods. The other two are larger; these are the Crested Lark (*Galerida cristata*), with an erectile crest, and the Calandra Lark (*Melanocorypha calandra*), recognisable by the dark patch on either side of its neck. The former likes the verges of roads, while the latter prefers bare, dry ground.

In North Africa there is the Desert Lark (*Ammomanes deserti*), which has a long, frail bill and sandy-grey plumage harmonising with the ground,

The Swallow (*Hirundo rustica*) or the Barn Swallow, as it is known in America, at its nest. The nest is made of mud lined with grass and is usually built on a roof beam or against a wall. Usually two clutches, of four to six eggs, are laid, very occasionally three. Swallows migrate to Africa in the autumn, returning the following April, quite often to the same nest-site.

in which it scratches like the gallinaceous birds, and there are bush larks (genus *Mirafra*), and finchlarks (genus *Eremopterix*).

Although there are many species of lark in the Old World, there is only one in America: the Horned Lark or the Shorelark (*Eremophila alpestris*). This also occurs in Eurasia and northern Africa. It has two small black 'horns' formed from crown feathers, and a black collar below a light throat. In flight it looks light-bellied with a black tail. There are slight differences in colour in the various regional subspecies found throughout North America. Being birds of prairies and open spaces that were once separated by continuous forests, their movements have tended to change as the forests have been cleared. Thus during the winter when the birds migrate from the interior to the warmer coasts more than one subspecies may be seen together. In the more southern states and in Britain and Europe they are sometimes known as shorelarks because when they visit these areas they are frequently found on the shore.

Swallows and martins (Family Hirundinidae)

This is a really cosmopolitan family of small, insectivorous birds, about ten to twenty-two centimetres long and highly gregarious. Only the polar regions and New Zealand are excluded from this distribution. Long, pointed wings, darkish

plumage and forked tails are the general outward characteristics. They are well adapted to an aerial life. Flight is strong, swift and graceful, and food is taken on the wing through the very wide gape. This makes migration inevitable for most of those species living in temperate climates, for in winter their wholly insect diet is not available; one American species in northern areas during the winter subsists on the waxy fruit of the bayberry.

Three genera are cosmopolitan, the barn swallows (genus *Hirundo*), the cliff swallows (*Petrochelidon*) and the sand martins or bank swallows (*Riparia*). Some are confined to the Old World: the palaearctic House Martin (*Delichon urbica*), the Red-rumped Swallow (*Hirundo daurica*) of southern Europe and Africa; others, mostly hole-nesters, belong to the New World: the Tree Swallow (*Iridoprocne bicolor*), the Purple Martin (*Progne subis*) of temperate areas, the Golden Swallow (*Kalochelidon euchrysea*) found in Jamaica; the Grey-breasted Martin (*Progne chalybea*) ranging from Texas south to Argentina.

In Britain, during March or April, the first swallows and martins return, and by May all are preparing to breed. Most nests are made of mud, sometimes mixed with saliva, and lined inside with soft materials. In them are laid four to six white eggs (speckled in some species). Incubation lasts about twelve days, during which the cock feeds the sitting hen. When the chicks hatch they are first fed with insects.

In autumn the swallows assemble in flocks on roofs and telephone wires. They leave during the night, the European birds to Africa, and some American populations to Mexico and central South America. They fly by night and rest by day to escape predators. They appear to have a delicate sense for atmospheric changes. Often flocks fly off at the onset of a cyclone and escape storms that might be fatal. Swallows ringed in Great Britain have been recovered in Senegal, Guinea, Egypt, and even at the Cape of Good Hope. Few swallows or martins cross the Mediterranean on a wide front, but follow one of three routes: via Spain and Morocco, Italy and Tunisia, or the Balkans and Asia Minor. They cross the Sahara using the oases as staging posts. They reach their destination in October, winter in their second homeland and return to the first the following spring. Throughout southern Europe swallows are becoming unaccountably rare. In Paris 100 years ago, 2,000 nests were counted on roof-tops in a single street, but today not one is to be found there.

The Swallow (*Hirundo rustica*) which breeds in Eurasia and North America and winters in Africa, southern Asia, and South America, is known in America as the Barn Swallow: the Tree Swallow (*Iridoprocne bicolor*) is very common through most of North America. It is a hole-nester and winters as far north as it can find ample bayberries.

AFRICAN RIVER MARTIN (*PSEUDOCHELIDON EURYSTOMINA*): This is a single aberrant species of martin. It differs from typical swallows and martins in having complete bronchial rings, and there are other peculiarities. A large black swallow with red beak and red eyes, it is highly localised. It was believed to be rare, but in 1921 its breeding ground was discovered on sandy shoals in the middle reaches of the Congo River, where the water level is low in the dry season. There the colonies nest, each nest being a chamber lined with dead leaves and twigs, at the end of a downward-slanting tunnel, where three white eggs are laid. Later, as the waters rise again, the birds migrate 800 kilometres to the Nyana River. Their food is mainly winged ants. The species is presently recognised as a subfamily, Pseudo-chelidoninae, of the true swallows.

Pipits and wagtails (Family Motacillidae)

The pipits have the same brown plumage speckled with black as the larks, but they are distinguished by more slender bodies, longer, thinner legs, finer bills, and by being more strictly insect eating. The commonest British species are the Meadow Pipit (*Anthus pratensis*) and the Tree Pipit (*A. trivialis*). The former is more common in fields and marshy land, the latter on heaths, trees and bushes. The Meadow Pipit spends most of its time on the ground, whereas the Tree Pipit is most often seen in the branches of trees. Both, however, nest on the ground. There is also the Rock Pipit (*A. spinoletta*), which is not so common, for it normally breeds on the coast, less frequently inland in the mountains, and comes down to the wet lands of the valleys only in winter. In the western hemisphere this same species is known as the American Water Pipit. It breeds in the Canadian arctic, winters in open spaces as far south as the Gulf of Mexico, and is the most common member of the family.

Another American species is Sprague's Pipit (*A. spragueii*), which is mainly a bird of the plains and prairies, although it winters throughout most of the southern United States. It is distinguished from the Rock or Water Pipit by its straw-coloured legs, its striped back and less active tail.

Several pipit characteristics are exaggerated in the wagtails of the Old World, so called because of the movement of their tails when they walk. There are three very widespread species: the Pied or White Wagtail (*Motacilla alba*) with black and white plumage, slender legs, and a long tail; the Yellow Wagtail (*M. flava*), which has yellow underparts; and the Grey Wagtail (*M. cinerea*), which has a very long black tail. There are few birds so pleasant to watch. A wagtail runs very quickly along the water's edge, and even in the water, provided that the water does not rise above the tarsus. It walks with its body horizontal, the tail often held aloft for fear of wetting it. When perching, it straightens its body and lets the tail hang. When walking it wags its tail up and down. Its flight is easy and swift, undulating, jerky; often it will cover a considerable distance at one unbroken stretch. Its song is simple and pleasant; its food insects and aquatic molluscs. It makes its nest at the water's edge.

Cuckoo-shrikes and minivets (Family Campephagidae)

Many of the seventy-two species of this family have superficial resemblances to both shrikes and cuckoos. All have a shrike-like bill with bristles at the base, and all have the rump feathers matted, partly erectile, and with rigid and pointed shafts. Ranging from sparrow- to pigeon-sized, they are distributed from Africa, across southern Asia, to the Solomons. They live mainly in forests, where they feed mainly on insects and berries.

The Barred Cuckoo-shrike (*Coracina lineata*), of Australia to the Solomons, is twenty-four centimetres long, and mainly grey with underparts barred in black and white, recalling the Common Cuckoo. The Red-shouldered Cuckoo-shrike of Africa (*Campephaga phoenicea*) is slightly smaller, and mainly black with a red shoulder patch.

The Flamed Minivet (*Pericrocotus flammeus*), of India to the Philippines, is similar in size. It is black but has scarlet underparts, rump, outer tail feathers, and scarlet patches on the wings.

Bulbuls (Family Pycnonotidae)

The bulbuls are moderate-sized birds that live in the forests, open country or gardens of tropical Africa and Asia. There are about one hundred and twenty species, predominantly brown to olive in colour, few species having bright plumage. For their size they have remarkably small feet and legs, a feature that has no disadvantages, however, since bulbuls seldom come to the ground. Bulbul nests are cup-shaped. The chief item of diet is

The Red-eyed Bulbul (*Pycnonotus nigricans*) of southern Africa. The African bulbuls are mostly green or yellow with slender bills and rounded tails. They live in thick forest and undergrowth and feed much more on insects than do other bulbuls. They are sometimes called Greenbuls or Brownbuls.

The Grey Wagtail (*Motacilla cinerea*) seen at its nest with young. It has slate-grey plumage with contrasting yellow underparts. In summer the male has a black throat and a white eye-stripe and white moustachial stripes. This wagtail is widespread in Europe, parts of Asia and Morocco. In Europe it is mainly a resident or only a short-distance migrant but over part of its range the population winters in Africa and Arabia.

445

The Red-backed Shrike (*Lanius collurio*) is the only shrike to breed in the British Isles. The male is seen here feeding the young. The female lacks the male's black face. Like many members of the family it impales its catch on thorns earning it the name of 'butcherbird'.

Leafbird (*Chloropsis aurifrons*) is green above, greenish yellow below, with a golden-red forehead, blue throat and black patches on head and breast.

Shrikes or butcherbirds, and allies (Family Laniidae)

There are about seventy species of these predominantly Old World birds, which are aggressive and carnivorous. The bill is strong, conical and hooked, with a notch on either side of the tip of the mandible. Together with their strong, sharp-pointed claws this gives them a predatory look. Like pipits and wagtails, they have three toes in front and a hind one which is separate. The shrikes or butcherbirds are well equipped for hunting, though much of their diet is insectivorous. The largest of them are about the size of a European Blackbird or American Robin but sturdier. They resemble birds of prey when attacking other small birds or mammals, but unlike the birds of prey they carry their prey in their beaks not in their claws. They have short wings, long tails and their colouring varies. A shrike's nest is an intricately made bulky, cup-shape built in a tree or bush. The parent birds tend their chicks over a relatively long time, a feature suggestive of birds of prey.

Among the European species the Great Grey Shrike (*Lanius excubitor*) has an ash-grey hood, the Woodchat Shrike (*L. senator*) is black with a rufous nape, and the Red-backed Shrike (*L. collurio*) is entirely rufous. All three have a pinkish-white belly and black wing feathers edged with white or chestnut. They inhabit olive groves, woods, hedges and isolated trees. They are generally solitary outside the breeding season and jealously guard their territory. They perch motionless in a tree, waiting to hurl themselves at their victims, killing them with blows of their beaks and carrying them off into a bush. The Red-backed Shrike, like many members of the family impales its catch on thorns, and in these 'larders' may be found dead beetles, grasshoppers, mice, lizards and frogs, which the birds eat at their convenience.

The Great Grey Shrike (*L. excubitor*) is one of the two species found in America, where it is known as the Northern Shrike. It breeds in southern Canada and migrates to the United States each winter. It is essentially a northern bird and is replaced in the south by the Loggerhead or Migrant Shrike (*L. ludovicianus*). Generally, the commoner of the two in the United States in winter is the Northern Shrike, and in summer the Loggerhead. The Northern Shrike is slightly larger than the Loggerhead and its breast is faintly barred instead of plain grey. The feathers at the base of the bill are grey rather than black.

The Bornean Bristle-head (*Pityriasis gymnocephala*), is twenty-five centimetres long, greyish black with red on the head and throat. This strange species is now considered a subfamily of the true shrikes Laniidae. Its head is partially naked and warty, the rest of it clothed with bristle-like feathers.

Helmet-shrikes (Family Prionopidae)

An exclusively African group is formed by two genera and several species of helmet-shrikes or wood shrikes. They are shrike-like birds found mainly in Africa, south of the Sahara, living in

fruit, although insects are frequently eaten. Some species resemble flycatching birds and these have well-developed bristles around the gape, but in the main these bristles are poorly developed, as would be expected among frugivorous birds. They are noisy birds, and according to species, the voice may be harsh or pleasant, but the most famed songsters of the orient belong to this family.

One of the best songsters is the Yellow-crowned Bulbul (*Pycnonotus zeylanicus*), which approaches the size of a Eurasian Jay. It has a straw-coloured head with a black line through the eye, a white throat, brown upper parts and mottled underparts, and it makes an attractive pet. It lives in scrub country, sometimes gardens, and along watercourses in Malaya, Sumatra, Java and Borneo. Another bulbul very common in the same area is the Yellow-vented Bulbul (*P. goiavier*). This is a thrush-sized bird, brown above, whitish below, with white eyebrows, face and throat, and a black stripe through each eye. As its name implies it is characterised by a sulphur yellow vent and under tail coverts. It also has a crest which is variously developed among the family.

Fairy bluebirds, ioras, leafbirds (Family Irenidae)

These very colourful birds from the size of a thrush to that of a pigeon, are fruit-eaters living in the tree-tops in forests from southern Asia to the Philippines. The male Blue-backed Fairy Bluebird (*Irena puella*) is iridescent black and ultramarine. The Common Iora (*Aegithina tiphia*) is nearly fifteen centimetres long, black above, yellow below, with yellow on the head, a greenish-yellow rump and white wing-bars. The Golden-fronted

forests and feeding mainly on insects. Most are black above, white or buff below, and their distinctive features are the stiff feathers on the forehead projecting forward over the nostrils and the wattle surrounding each eye. The White Helmet-shrike (*Prionops poliocephalus*) is twenty-two centimetres long. It builds in the forks of trees a nest of grass, rootlets, bark fibres and spiders' webs, and sometimes the nests are in groups. Birds in the flock nesting communally will incubate each other's eggs and feed the chicks at random. It is even said that up to three adults will drive a sitting hen off her nestlings, and each then feed them in turn, the last settling on them to brood them. A group of six Spectacled Shrike (*P. plumata*) has been observed engaged in communal nest building, four bringing nest materials and two making the nest.

Vanga-shrikes (Family Vangidae)
Confined to Madagascar, the vanga-shrikes are closely related to the helmet-shrikes. The eleven species differ more than usual within a family, especially in the shape of the bill. All keep to the trees, feeding on insects, frogs and lizards found among foliage or on bark. The Helmet Bird (*Euryceros prevostii*) has a huge compressed bill, and the Sicklebill (*Falculea palliata*) a long, down-curved bill in marked contrast to this.

Waxwings (Family Bombycillidae)
The Bohemian Waxwing (*Bombycilla garrulus*) differs from the shrike in its soft, thick plumage, its crest, long wings and short tail. It is a fairly uniform rufous colour, lighter on the belly than on the back, and the feathers of wing and tail end in a patch of white or yellow. The secondary feathers have reddish, waxy-looking tips, giving rise to the name 'waxwing'.

The Waxwing nests in the northern forests of the Old and New Worlds, and makes only brief, irregular appearances in more southerly temperate latitudes. In the winter season it subsists almost exclusively on berries and other fruit, but during the breeding season it consumes mostly insects.

During some winters the Bohemian Waxwing is locally common in Great Britain, but these invasions occur sporadically and the number of birds varies. They arrive from Scandinavia in parties of a dozen or so and move around the country stripping bushes of their berries.

In America, in addition to the Bohemian Waxwing, there is a smaller species, the Cedar Waxwing (*B. cedrorum*). It is plainer coloured and has no white in the wing or chestnut red on the under tail coverts. Whereas in North America the larger species is found principally in western Canada, the Cedar Waxwing is common farther south and is seen commonly if somewhat irregularly throughout the eastern United States.

The silky flycatchers are here included in the family Bombycillidae. They are slender birds with crests, and are found from the south-west borders of the United States to Panama. The four species are often placed in a separate family Ptilogonatidae.

The Hypocolius (*Hypocolius ampelinus*) is distributed around the northern end of the Persian Gulf, and feeds largely on figs, mulberries and dates.

This rather peculiar bird has been considered the sole member of a separate family Hypocoliidae.

Palm-chat (Family Dulidae)
The single species (*Dulus dominicus*) in this family of starling-sized birds is localised on the West Indian islands of Hispaniola and La Conave. These birds live in flocks in trees, feeding on flowers and berries. Members of a flock crowd close together when perching and this social behaviour is evident also in nesting, a communal nest being built by about four pairs. Some authorities consider this species as a member of the Bombycillidae.

Dippers or water-ouzels (Family Cinclidae)
The five species in this family are all somewhat wren-like in stance, but their habits are unique. They are to be found mainly by mountain streams from Great Britain, Europe, through central Asia to Japan, and in western America from the Yukon to the Argentine. They are the most exclusively aquatic of all the perching birds and swim underwater, even walking on the bottom of streams in search of small crustacea, molluscs, small fishes and particularly insect larvae. A remarkable adaptation is that the 'third eyelid' (the nictitating membrane) is transparent, so that a dipper can close its eyes underwater and still see. It is something of a mystery how these lightweight birds can stay underwater, especially as air is inevitably trapped in their plumage when they dive under the surface. Yet they manage to do so and without the plumage becoming waterlogged, which would prevent the birds emerging and flying off. Their nests are always built close to

The Waxwing (*Bombycilla garrulus*) known in North America as the Bohemian Waxwing. In winter the Waxwings move south through Europe from their breeding areas in the northern forests, sometimes in enormous flocks of several thousands. They move from one area to another stripping the trees of fruits and berries. At one time these irruptions were looked on with superstitious fear as the forerunners of disaster.

447

A Common Wren (*Troglodytes troglodytes*) coming to its nest with food for its young ones. The cock builds a number of nests, one of which is chosen by the hen, who lines it before laying her eggs. In severe weather as many as forty-six wrens or more have been seen roosting together in a hole or nestbox. Even so in hard winters the wren populations become seriously reduced.

water, usually behind a waterfall, in hollows, under walls or banks, even on a rock or fallen tree in the middle of a stream. They have even been seen to fly through a waterfall to get at the nest. The European Dipper (*Cinclus cinclus*) has an undeservedly bad reputation among salmon fishers, for it is thought by many to rake over redds (troughs in which the female salmon lays her eggs) to eat some of the eggs or fry.

Wrens (Family Troglodytidae)

About sixty-three wren species are currently recognised. They are essentially American and are all dull-coloured birds in shades of olive, brown and black, a few having a little white in the plumage. The bills are slender, often somewhat longish and curved. In most species the tail is short and frequently cocked over the back. The most widespread species is the Common or Winter Wren (*Troglodytes troglodytes*), occurring in the Old World. Long ago, it or its ancestors succeeded in crossing the Bering Straits and it gradually spread westwards to Britain and southwards to North Africa. Nowadays it is found wherever there is low cover and is frequently seen darting from shrubbery or a hedgerow. The song of most species is highly developed. In many the female joins the male in song, and antiphonal singing has been recorded. Some build nests in hollows, but others build bulky, ball-shaped nests out of sticks, moss and grass, lined with feathers.

The best known American species, the House Wren (*T. aedon*), ranges from southern Canada to the southern United States and in winter extends into south central Mexico. It has taken to constructing a neat cup-shaped nest atop a mass of twigs in bird houses and in any natural hollow. It sets up its summer home in almost every garden where the owners supply the house, and in return supplies continuous, rollicking song and vigorous action against any insect pests that there might be.

Mockingbirds, catbirds, thrashers (Family Mimidae)

Ranging from southern Canada southwards to all but the extreme south of South America, these are mainly solitary birds, or occur in pairs. Although most are arboreal they usually feed on the ground, and some are largely terrestrial. The Common Mockingbird (*Mimus polyglottos*) is as large as a thrush but more slender and longer-tailed. These birds not only have a well-developed song of their own but, as the name implies, they can mimic or mock nearly any other bird song or call. They will sing all day and even at night, without seeming to take time to hunt for worms or insects. The Catbird (*Dumetella carolinensis*) does not repeat its song. Its chief call is a distinctive, cat-like mewing note, usually heard issuing from thickets. The Brown Thrasher (*Toxostoma rufum*) is a slim bird. It is larger than a thrush and its underparts are not spotted. It also has a longer tail and yellow eyes. Like the Catbird it is found mainly in thickets, and even its song resembles that of the Catbird, although it is more musical and is repeated once.

Accentors or hedge-sparrows (Family Prunellidae)

The accentors are a family of North African, European and mainly central Asian birds. Because of the similarity between the plumage of the House Sparrow and that of *Prunella modularis*, this species, common in most of Great Britain, is generally known as the Hedge Sparrow, and less frequently by the more distinctive name, Dunnock. It is in no way related to the sparrows, but has a close affinity with the Old World flycatchers and thrushes. The bill is more slender than that of the House Sparrow and the head, throat and neck are greyish, the underparts greyish-white.

Babblers, Old World warblers, thrushes, bald-crows, Old World flycatchers, gnatcatchers, etc. (Family Muscicapidae)

All the subfamilies listed below have been, and still are, considered by many ornithologists as full families. There are, however, so many species so intermediate between these groups that the divisions have merely served as convenient size aggregations enabling the experts to discuss and study them more easily. They are listed here as subfamilies and one has but to substitute '*idae*' for the -*inae* in order to raise them to full families should the need or desire arise at any time.

Babblers (Subfamily Timaliinae)

The babblers, or babbling thrushes, have a distribution rather similar to the bulbuls, but also extend to Australasia. However, like the bulbuls some species in this subfamily closely resemble birds of other families, particularly the Old World flycatchers (Muscicapinae) and the Old World warblers (Sylviinae). Consequently some are dificult to identify as one cannot always be certain to which family the bird one sees really belongs. A good example is provided by the Malay Nun-babbler (*Alcippe poiocephala*), which apart from its slightly rounder, more slender bill, cannot be distinguished in life from the Olive-backed Jungle Flycatcher (*Rhinomyias olivacea*) unless the observer is familiar with the behaviour of these two species. Babblers further resemble the more unrelated bulbuls by being poor flyers, with short, rounded wings. There the similarities end, for as a rule the legs and bill are very stout and the birds are entirely insectivorous. Moreover, many live on or near the ground, particularly in thickets and dense jungle undergrowth. They have one characteristic which clearly separates them from the flycatchers and the thrushes, which many resemble, and that is the unspotted plumage of the young.

The ground-babblers are almost entirely terrestrial and are somewhat like small rails. the Malay Rail-babbler (*Eupetes macrocerus*) lives in the dense Malayan jungle and behaves very much like pittas, it moves fast on the ground and is difficult to spot. The jungle babblers are mainly dull-covered birds of Africa and Asia and some look very much like warblers. A widespread Asiatic species, Abbotts' Jungle Babbler (*Trichastoma abbotti*), which is olive brown above and pale below, is a common lowland bird, particularly along the sea coast, even entering wooded gardens. The ball-like nest is built close to the ground.

Then there are the scimitar- and wren-babblers. The former, which have scimitar-shaped bills, occur in Asia, Australia and New Guinea. The latter are small birds with long, strong legs and feet. Another group is the tit-babblers, small, almost tit-like birds, found almost entirely in trees, bamboos and long grass. These often have hair-like feathers on the back that give them a soft, fluffy look. The last group is the song-babblers, some of which are known as laughing or jay-thrushes. They are noisy birds and, unlike other

The Common or Northern Mockingbird (*Mimus polyglottos*) is probably the best-loved songbird in North America. It usually sings from a high perch and its song is said to rival the Nightingale's. Mockingbirds will attack any intruder that enters their territory, even humans. Outside the breeding season they live in noisy flocks.

The Hedge Sparrow or Dunnock (*Prunella modularis*) feeding its young. It is common throughout Europe and the Near East but is often overlooked because of its unobtrusive appearance and habits. It is typically a bird of open woods and forests and of scrubland but in the British Isles it is found in parks, gardens and hedgerows.

babblers, their plumage is often brightened with scarlet, green, yellow and other colours. Many of them have a pleasant song. The Silver-eared Mesia (*Leiothrix argentauris*) is one of the most attractive. It has an orange forehead, black crown, eye stripe and moustache, silvery-grey ear coverts, orange-red shoulders, olive back, scarlet throat, rump and upper breast, brownish abdomen, and dark grey wings and tail marked with yellow and some red. This species ranges from the Himalayas to Indo-China and Malaysia, where it moves around the mountain undergrowth in parties.

Bald crows (Subfamily Picathartinae)

The two species of *Picarthartes* have not been seen by Europeans. Their native haunts in West Africa

Male Asiatic Paradise Flycatcher (*Terpsiphone paradisi*) seen on its nest. It breeds from Russian Turkestan eastwards through India to China and south and east to Malaysia and Borneo. Plumage varies in colour considerably in the various sub-species. The vernacular name comes from the long tail-feathers recalling the plumes of the birds of paradise.

are difficult to find and the birds are of uncertain relationships. Originally classified with the crows they resemble starlings anatomically, while in their build, nesting habits and method of progressing by long hops they recall the babblers. They are the largest birds to build a mud nest which they construct on the face of a rock. The Grey-necked Rockfowl or Bald Crow (*Picarthartes gymnocephalus*) and the White-necked Rockfowl or Bald Crow (*P. oreas*), up to thirty-five centimetres long, differ largely in the bare yellow skin of the head in the former and the pink skin of the latter.

Parrotbills (Subfamily Paradoxornithinae)

There are fourteen species of parrotbills, also known as suthoras, living in central and south-east Asia. They have no clear relationship with other families. Smallish with inconspicuous plumage, they inhabit scrub or grassland, feeding on insects, seeds and berries. Their feature is their parrot-like bill, yet they are probably near relatives of titmice.

Wren-tit (Subfamily Chamaeinae)

A single species of Wren-tit (*Chamaea fasciata*) is placed in this separate subfamily largely because its relationships are not clear. Many authorities feel it is definitely a babbler of subfamily Timaliinae. Small, brown, with a long barred tail, and living in low scrub on insects and fruit, it recalls both wrens and titmice. Wren-tits remain in pairs throughout the year, and probably for life. They are found only in western North America.

Old World flycatchers (Subfamily Muscicapinae)

This subfamily comprises 300 or 400 species, distributed over the forests, woods and orchards of the Old World. Most flycatchers are about the size of a sparrow, but have a bill somewhat similar to a swallow, that is, short, flattened, wide-split, and equipped with bristles, which act as a funnel for scooping insects through the open gape. Flycatchers keep watch for insects, especially flies, which they seize in flight, but towards the end of

summer, when insects are less plentiful, some take to eating a little soft fruit. Then they leave for the south, and from September to March none is to be seen north of the Mediterranean. Convergent evolution in food habits leading to very similar methods of capturing insect food led the early Europeans in America to consider the tyrant flycatchers as belonging to the same group.

Two flycatchers are common in Great Britain. The Spotted Flycatcher (*Muscicapa striata*) is a dull grey-brown, somewhat paler below with brown-black streaking on the throat. It is usually seen from May to August in trees and bushes in reasonably open country, particularly parklands. It sits upright on the outer branches of a tree, occasionally flitting outwards after an insect and returning to the same perch. The way the bird flutters up to a swarm of gnats, takes an insect, then returns, only to repeat the performance, could give the impression that it is incapacitated in some way. The nest is usually built in the hollow of a tree and may consist of little more than a lining of moss, wool and feathers. Generally six blue-green eggs are laid and both parents share the incubation.

The other common British species is the Pied Flycatcher (*Ficedula hypoleuca*), which is found mainly in wooded valleys in Wales, northern England and southern Scotland. This species is black above and white below and has white also on the forehead and wings. Although one of the commoner flycatchers, it is not very numerous in comparison with some other summer visitors.

Many more species of flycatcher are found in the tropical forests of Africa and Asia, some brightly coloured. In Asia there is a large number of species with predominantly blue upperparts. The male Verditer Flycatcher (*M. thalassina*), apart from a black forehead and throat, is entirely verditer blue. This species lives in fairly open forests from northern India and Burma to Indonesia.

Another group is the monarch flycatchers, which also belong to the Muscicapinae. They differ from other true flycatchers in taking their insect prey from the branches of trees instead of sallying forth on wing. Although strongly territorial in behaviour in the breeding season, they often roam in small flocks in the winter. There are many species throughout the tropical forests. One of the most striking is the Black Paradise Flycatcher (*Terpsiphone atrocaudata*). Although only about fifteen centimetres long, the males of this species have tails thirty-eight to forty-three centimetres in length. Mainly black with purplish maroon-coloured shoulders and a white abdomen, this bird breeds in Japan and in winter flies south along the south China coast to Malaya and Sumatra.

Two groups of flycatchers are centred mainly in the Australasian region. First, the fantails (genus *Rhipidura*), which are easily distinguished by their small bills and feet, short but wide wings and their long broad tails which they cock up and partly open, flitting from branch to branch. Secondly, the whistlers (genus *Pachycephala*), which have a round, stout head and a short, thick, shrike-like bill and a robust body. They are brightly coloured with yellow, white and grey predominating. They are usually to be found singly or in pairs searching the lower levels of the forests for insects.

Old World warblers or true warblers (Subfamily Sylviinae)

The warblers are a large subfamily of perchers that includes the birds known in America as gnat-catchers. They are small birds with straight, conical bills that have a few feathers at the base and are slightly notched towards the tip. They are mainly insectivorous though they eat some fruits, especially in winter. Big trees do not tempt them, and they tend to be clumsy on the ground. As they have short wings, their flight is not strong and they are seen mostly in bushes or reeds, creeping about in search of their favourite food. There too they nest and sing. Their nests vary in shape, but they are always built with skill and grace.

The Sylviinae are divided into many genera, some containing numerous species. It is easiest to divide them into two biological groups: the bush or leaf-warblers, and those that prefer the reeds or marshy ground, the reed-warblers.

The warblers are mainly brown and grey, and male and female often have differently coloured crowns. The species are so numerous that only a few can be mentioned: the commonest in Europe are the Garden Warbler (*Sylvia borin*) and the Blackcap (*S. atricapilla*). The former is a reddish brown with lighter underparts; the latter has a brown back, grey-blue belly and head, and the cock has a fine crown of deep black. Both have a sweet song. Their nests are cup-shaped, made of dried grasses and hung from the lower branches of a hedge or bush. The warblers are sedentary in the south of Europe, only migrating north to nest from April to September.

Warblers of the genus *Phylloscopus*, a name which means 'inspector of leaves', have shorter bills that are also 'pinched' towards the tip. The plumage is a uniform green for the upper parts and yellowish underneath. In habits they differ little from birds of the genus *Sylvia*, except that they are more often seen in tree-tops and that their nests are spherical with an opening in the side. Their song is not as musical. Another species is the Willow Warbler (*P. trochilus*), which is a migrant in northern Europe, though sedentary further in the south.

Bush-warblers (genus *Hippolais*) are experts at imitating other birds' songs, and sometimes produce a regular potpourri of them.

Reed-warblers (genus *Acrocephalus*) generally have a reddish-brown plumage. The several species, including the Reed-warbler (*A. scirpaceus*) and the Marsh-warbler (*A. palustris*), haunt ponds, marshes and the banks of rivers, where they climb up and down the stems of reeds and water-plants. Their call is not pleasant, being rather like a croak. Their nest, which is in the shape of a purse, is of woven reeds. Both cock and hen sit on the eggs. The related Sedge-warbler (*A. schoenobaenus*) has black markings on its back, and the Fan-tailed Warbler (*Cisticola juncides*) also has black markings on a reddish back. Finally, the grasshopper warblers (genus *Locustella*) live on the ground rather than amongst vegetation and build crude nests.

Another group of species include the kinglets or goldcrests, from both Old and New Worlds. The Goldcrest (*Regulus regulus*), the smallest European bird, is a dull green above and pale greenish yellow below. It receives its name from the bright golden-orange streak edged with black along the centre of the crown. It is an inconspicuous bird with a rather plaintive, high-pitched call and is commoner in pine woods than elsewhere. A similar bird is the Golden-crowned Kinglet (*Regulus sapatra*) of the spruce belt of southern Canada and the northern United States. It differs from the Goldcrest mainly in having a white streak above each eye extending to the black edging of the orange along the crown.

The tailor-birds (genus *Orthotomus*), of which there are several Asiatic species, are also warblers. They owe their popular name to the way they sew together several leaves of the tree in which they nest, edge to edge, to make the walls of the nest. An Australian genus, *Malurus*, includes several small birds, some with brilliant, metallic colouring, mostly black, blue, green and violet. They are known by a variety of names: Australian wrens, emu-wrens, grass-wrens and bristle-birds.

The Spotted Flycatcher (*Muscicapa striata*) is a common summer visitor to Eurasia. Their reliance on flying insects for food prevents these flycatchers from remaining in Europe for the winter so they start leaving for Africa at the end of July, returning the following spring.

The Sedge Warbler (*Acrocephalus schoenobaenus*) seen at its nest in the reeds. It breeds over much of Europe and Asia and winters in Africa, south of the Sahara. It prefers to nest in reed-beds or in marshy areas on the edges of lakes or rivers but will sometimes use forestry plantations or cornfields if near water.

Others of this subfamily are the American gnat-catchers, the Blue-grey Gnatcatcher (*Polioptila caerulea*) being common in the woodlands of the United States. It is smaller than a Blackcapped Chickadee, blue-grey above and whitish blue, and has a long, black tail with white outer feathers.

Wren-thrush (Subfamily Zeledoniinae)

The Wren-thrush (*Zeledonia coronata*) lives in deep forests in Costa Rica and western Panama, 1,800 to 3,000 metres above sea-level. Although the size of a Wren, and having much the same habits, it also recalls the babblers of south-east Asia and Australia in its habit of skulking on the ground in inaccessible forests. Many authorities consider it a thrush of subfamily Turdinae.

Thrushes, nightingales, robins, Old World blackbirds (Subfamily Turdinae)

Representatives of this large subfamily are found in all parts of the world, especially in the temperate areas, where it occurs in fields and open country as well as in woods, arid regions and along the water's edge. In Europe and North America most are migrants that come north to breed and spend the winter in warmer countries. They eat mainly worms and insects and their larvae, but many species also feed on berries and fruits. The song is usually highly developed. It is difficult to find distinct common characteristics. Their toes are not joined; they tend to have slender rather than conical bills; and they are more insectivorous than frugivorous. Their affinities are with the Old World flycatchers and warblers. The Turdinae comprise the European Blackbird, thrushes, Nightingale, robins, bluebirds, Blue-throated Warbler, redstarts, wheatears and chats.

The European Blackbird (*Turdus merula*) is one of the most common European birds. It is seen everywhere and heard whistling from morning to evening during spring and early summer. Distinctive by reason of its all-black plumage and yellow bill, the cock cannot be confused with any other European bird. The hen is brown with mottled underparts. Partial albinos are not infrequent. Another species, more common in mountainous districts, the Ring Ouzel (*T. torquatus*), is distinguished by a broad, white crescent on its breast. These two build their nests low down and with great care, using moss, blades of grass and dry leaves, which they weave together. They then line the inside wall with damp earth, making a smooth waterproof covering. They lay four to five greenish eggs on which the cock and the hen sit in turn, whereas the hen Blackbird normally does all the incubating. Both species generally have two broods, one in March, the other in May, and it is not unusual for a Blackbird to have three, or even four, broods in a season, for they are prolific birds.

The thrushes differ from the European Blackbird in that both cock and hen are conspicuously marked on the underside with dark spots on a light ground. The Mistle-thrush (*T. viscivorus*) is the largest and perhaps the most common in Europe, where it gets its name from its predilection for the white viscous berries of the mistletoe, and on the Continent it sometimes roosts in mistletoe. By evacuating the seeds with its droppings, the Mistle-thrush helps to spread this parasite.

The Song-thrush (*T. philomelos*) is somewhat smaller than the Mistle-thrush. It sings short musical phrases, often a series of variations on or around the distinctive song of the species. It is sometimes called the nightingale of the north.

The smallest of the European thrushes is the Redwing (*T. musicus*). It is the only one with a buffish-white eye stripe, but gets its vernacular name from its chestnut-red flanks. Unlike the other thrushes, the Mistle-thrush and Song-thrush, the Fieldfare (*T. pilaris*) and Redwing belong to the higher latitudes, migrating south in autumn, and are most numerous in Britain in autumn and winter. The cock takes little part in building the nest except to help choose the site and to transport some of the materials, but even that is not the rule.

The Rock-thrush (*Monticola saxatilis*) and Blue Rock-thrush (*M. solitarius*) live in open rocky areas and on bare mountainsides of Europe and southwestern and central Asia, though they have been known to nest in niches in towers and tall buildings. They are wary, solitary birds. The plumage of the Blue Rock-thrush is deep blue-grey, except for the wings and tail, which are deep black. It has a lovely song, though not the equal of the Nightingale or its close relatives.

Another member of this group is the very common American Robin (*T. migratorius*), very like the Song-thrush except for its grey back and its brick-red breast, which is its sole similarity to the European Robin. In the male the head and tail are blackish; in the female, paler. It breeds from the tree-limit in Canada southwards to southern Mexico. It is partially migratory and many winter in the southern United States.

Other American thrushes that resemble birds of this group, but are a little smaller, belong to the genus *Catharus*. The Veery (*C. fuscescens*) is the most uniform in colour, rusty above, pale below with indistinct spots on the breast. Its song is a distinctive breezy whistle. Common in damp woods from Canada to the central United States, it migrates to South America during the winter.

A similar bird is the Hermit Thrush (*C. guttatus*), which has more distinctive spotting on the breast and a conspicuous reddish tail. It breeds in the evergreen-hardwood forests of southern Canada and the central United States and winters in the more southern States. The song is clear and flute-like, consisting of a key note followed by four or five phrases at different pitches. Another similar bird is the Wood Thrush (*H. mustelina*), but this has conspicuous spotting on the breast and sides and a reddish head instead of a reddish tail as in the Hermit Thrush. It also has a wider range in North America, where it is found in deciduous woodlands. It usually winters in places like Florida.

Another group of European Turdinae comprises four main species, all small in size, sombre in colouring, and easy to distinguish by their markings. The Nightingale (*Luscinia megarhynchos*) is of a uniform reddish brown, deeper on the back than on the underparts. The European Robin (*Erithacus rubecula*) differs from the latter in having a bright red throat and breast. These same parts are of a lovely azure blue in the Bluethroat (*Luscinia svecica*), which also has a central white patch and tri-coloured collar. Finally there is the Redstart (*Phoenicurus phoenicurus*) with its distinctive red tail and black throat. The top of its head and its back are of an ashen blue.

All four live in woodlands, parks and heaths. They are solitary and not sociable, quarrelling and fighting among themselves in the breeding season. Each cock then selects a territory which it will defend most energetically. They make rather crude cup-shaped nests on or near the ground.

In addition there are a number of small, brightly coloured members of the thrush family. One of several similar species, the Eastern Bluebird (*Sialia sialis*) is common in semi-open country and is found throughout most of temperate eastern North America. It is a little larger than a Sparrow and the male is blue above with a red breast. In Asia there are other similar birds, usually known as robins or shortwings. The Siberian Blue Robin (*Luscinia cyane*), which is slaty blue above and white below, breeds in Siberia and Japan and winters principally in the islands of the Indo-Australasian archipelago.

In these same islands live a group known as shamas. One of the commonest is the White-rumped Shama (*Copsychus malabaricus*), which is black with a chestnut abdomen and a white rump. Its tail is longer than its body and is black, apart from the outermost feathers which are white. It lives in thickets in the forests and is regarded as one of the best song-birds in the world.

Another group in the subfamily Turdinae is the forktails found throughout the Orient. They can be distinguished by their deeply forked tail, which is opened and closed repeatedly like a pair of scissors. Their size is about that of wagtails, particularly the Pied or White Wagtail (*Motacilla alba*), which they resemble not only in continuously flicking the tail as they walk but in being mainly black and white in colour. One of the most widespread species is the White-crowned Forktail (*Enicurus leschenaulti*), which extends from the Himalayas to the China Sea. This bird is black but has a white crown, rump and abdomen, and a white bar on the wings and white tips to the long, black tail feathers. It is usually to be found along fast-flowing streams flying from boulder to boulder, searching the water for insect larvae.

The last group of the Turdinae comprises the wheatears and the chats, most of which live in stony, rocky or sandy parts and make their nests in a hole in the ground. Like the Nightingale, they are fairly strictly insectivorous and thus of help to farmers. There is nothing remarkable about their song. An example is the Wheatear (*Oenanthe oenanthe*), which has a white rump and white sides to its tail. Then there is the Stonechat (*Saxicola torquata*) with a black head, white half-collar and an orange breast contrasting with the deep brown of its upperparts.

Titmice and chickadees (Family Paridae)

The members of this family are small birds with stocky bodies and short, conical bills. Their nostrils are covered by feathers, and they have strong claws, especially on the hind toe.

In the woods and copses they are never still, constantly flying from tree to tree, examining the branches, and swinging and hanging like acrobats

to do so. No corner, however remote, escapes them as they seek out insects as well as their larvae and eggs. A fly passing by is caught as it goes. Enormous quantities of insects must be eaten to feed their broods, which are always large.

The Paridae build strong, intricate nests, which are usually spherical with a round opening near the top. Moss, lichen, feathers, hair, and spiders' webs are some of the materials with which they weave. Each of their two clutches comprises six to fourteen finely speckled yellowish-white eggs.

The plumage patterns in the Paridae are variable, but with grey, black and white predominating in many species. Among the European birds there are first the two tits with greenish upperparts and yellow belly: the Great Tit (*Parus major*), which has a black head and white cheeks; and the Blue Tit (*P. caeruleus*), which has a white head with

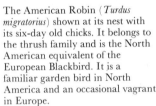

The American Robin (*Turdus migratorius*) shown at its nest with its six-day old chicks. It belongs to the thrush family and is the North American equivalent of the European Blackbird. It is a familiar garden bird in North America and an occasional vagrant in Europe.

The European Robin (*Erithacus rubecula*) is a familiar and popular bird of gardens and parks in Britain but on the Continent it is a shy bird frequenting woods and forests. It is a resident bird in Britain but Robins breeding in many parts of northern Europe migrate to the Mediterranean region in winter.

The Blue Tit (*Parus caeruleus*) is largely confined to central and western Europe. It is a familiar and popular bird at the bird table showing great enterprise and ability in reaching hanging coconuts and fats and taking peanuts from meshbags. The Blue Tit's normal diet is insects of all kinds, as well as the larvae and eggs.

The Long-tailed Tit (*Aegithalos caudatus*) shown here feeding its young. The nest, often built in a gorse bush, is a beautiful and compact domed structure made of mosses and bound together with hair and spider's webs. The species is widely distributed across Europe and Asia.

The Whinchat (*Saxicola rubetra*) is a migratory species breeding throughout most of Europe and western Asia, as far north as the Arctic Circle, and wintering in tropical Africa. It nests on the ground in open grassland, marshes and heaths. It can be distinguished from the similar Stonechat by its pale eye-stripe and white sides to the base of the tail.

blue crown and a black collar. Then come those that are less common, the Coal Tit (*P. ater*), the Marsh Tit (*P. palustris*), and the rare Willow Tit (*P. atricapillus*), all of which are more sombre with brownish upperparts and black crowns. The last two are almost indistinguishable, but the head of the Willow Tit is duller. There is also the Crested Tit (*P. cristatus*), which has a crest of black feathers edged with white, and in Great Britain is confined to Scotland. Finally, one that looks almost like a little ball of feathers, the Long-tailed Tit (*Aegithalos caudatus*), has a coat of black and pink, a white apron, white head, and black eyebrows. There is, too, the Penduline Tit (*A. pondulinus*) of southern Europe, which has red upperparts and white belly and which makes a purse-shaped nest hung from reeds.

The Willow Tit of Europe also occurs in North America, where it is known as the Black-capped Chickadee. In America it is one of the most common and beloved birds at home feeding stations. A similar species, but somewhat smaller, is the Carolina Chickadee (*Parus carolinensis*). These two species replace each other geographically. The former range across Canada and parts of the northern United States, while the latter extends southwards throughout the more southern United States to the Gulf of Mexico. The Brown-capped or Boreal Chickadee (*P. hudsonicus*) is similar but its plumage is brown or brownish where it is black or grey in other species. Finally in North America is the Tufted Titmouse (*P. bicolor*) with a grey, crested crown and grey back. The name chickadee is derived from the songs of the Black-capped Chickadee, or Willow Tit of Europe (*P. altricapillus*), and the other 'chickadees'.

Another branch of the Paridae consists of a number of Asiatic forms, as well as one European species, the Bearded Tit (*Panurus biarmicus*). It is an attractive bird with ashen grey head, vivid red underparts, and the sides of its head are graced with a pair of black 'moustaches'. It lives in secluded reed beds. The pairing bond between the sexes appears to be very great.

Tree creepers and nuthatches
(Families Certhiidae and Sittidae)

These two families belong to the same ecological group as the true climbers like the woodpeckers. However, while the woodpeckers have two toes in front and two behind, tree creepers, wall creepers and nuthatches have three in front and one behind. Their form of adaptation for climbing consists of an extraordinary development of the claw of the thumb, which is strong and hooked. It is a veritable climbing iron which supports them when climbing vertically and enables the nuthatch to climb head downwards. The creepers particularly have long slender bills for searching out insects and spiders. All are mainly insectivorous and spend their lives climbing about the trunks of trees or rock faces inspecting all the cracks and crannies in search of food. They have long tongues which end either in a tuft of hair-like filaments or in little hooked papillae which help them to catch larvae and insects.

The Certhiidae and Sittidae are not sociable, living alone except during the breeding season. They further resemble the woodpeckers by building their nests in a lined tree or rock cavity, which they pad with moss, lichen and feathers; but they do not excavate the hole themselves.

There are three European species of Certhiidae. The first is the Tree Creeper which is also the Brown Creeper of North America (*Certhia familiaris*). The Short-toed Tree Creeper (*C. brachydactyla*) is more common on the Continent. The Tree Creeper or Brown Creeper is a small bird with a long down-curved beak, reddish-brown plumage with black and white streaks on its upper parts and a light grey belly. Its hunting technique is most interesting: beginning at the foot of a tree it climbs in straight lines and spirals, but in such a way as to leave no part unexplored. Each branch is similarly inspected. When the bird reaches the top of the tree, it takes to the air and glides down to the foot of the next tree, where it starts again on another climb. Ivy-clad walls are also good hunting grounds for it. The whole business is performed in silence. The Tree Creeper has a very brief and unremarkable call, which sounds like a weak, high-pitched *seeee*. The mating and nesting season is from March to June. There are two successive broods, the first containing from six to nine eggs and the second from three to six. The eggs are white and brown.

The third species is the Wall Creeper (*Tichodroma muraria*), a bird common only in the mountains from the Alps and Pyrenees to the Himalayas. It has a grey-black plumage with crimson patches on its wings, and is said to prefer bare rocks and harsh, arid Alpine regions. It visits the long trails of plants growing down the rocks, but only to look for insects, and always seems to be in a hurry to get back to the bare places. The Wall Creeper never climbs in trees and does not like the ground, living only in the air or on the rocks. If it sees an insect on the ground, and cannot reach it from its rock, it will take off, fly down, and alight for an instant just to seize its prey, and the next moment it will be back on its wall of rock looking for a suitable place in which to eat its prey. It eats the small beetles that feign death and let themselves roll down the rock and into some inaccessible place, and the spiders that try to escape by letting themselves down on their thread. These it catches as they fall through the air.

Included in the family Sittidae are two groups formerly considered separate families: the Australian nuthatches (subfamily Neosittinae) of about five species restricted to New Guinea and Australia and the Coral-billed Nuthatch (*Hypositta corallirostris*) of Madagascar, the only member of the subfamily Hyposittinae.

The European Nuthatch (*Sitta europaea*) is common in the woods and copses of much of Europe. Unlike the creepers it has a straight beak. Its plumage is grey on the upper parts, the underparts are rufous, and it has a long, black eye stripe. Like the Tree Creeper, the Nuthatch darts about the trunks and branches of trees, climbing up and down incessantly, being the only bird to descend head first, which the woodpeckers never do, and ceaselessly uttering its little cry of *tait tait*. Children, being more forthright, generally call nuthatches 'upside-down birds'. The Nuthatch is not as completely insectivorous as the Tree creeper. In addition to insects and larvae it will eat

The Short-toed Tree Creeper (*Certhia brachydactyla*) seen feeding its young in the nest usually built behind loose bark on a tree trunk. The species is much less widely distributed than the Common Tree Creeper, being restricted mainly to south western and central Europe and a narrow coastal strip in North Africa. It inhabits open deciduous woodlands, parks, gardens and hedges.

The White-breasted Nuthatch (*Sitta carolinensis*) lives in deciduous woodlands in North America from southern Canada to northern Mexico. It nests in hollows in trees or stumps, even in nestboxes. Like the European Nuthatch and Tree Creeper it searches the bark of trees for insects.

seeds, even those of conifers, which it knows how to extract. In fact the name is derived from an old English word meaning 'nut hacker' because they hack hard-shelled seeds open with their bills. Having selected a hole in a tree and enlarged it, if need be, the hen Nuthatch lines the opening with mud worked with her beak, and so makes it narrower.

There are four species of nuthatches in North America. The White-breasted Nuthatch (*Sitta carolinensis*) has a black cap, and its black eye is set in a white cheek. It has a wide range and is found in most woodlands and orchards. In contrast the Red-breasted Nuthatch (*S. canadensis*) has a broad, black stripe through the eye and prefers the evergreen forests. It breeds from the limits of spruce trees in Canada to north Minnesota, Michigan and in the Appalachian Mountains to North Carolina. The Brown-headed Nuthatch (*S. pusilla*), with a brown cap coming down to the eyes and a white spot on the nape, has a more restricted range. It is a resident only of the open pine woods from Florida and the Gulf of Mexico, as far north as coastal Delaware and southern Missouri. Finally there is the Pygmy Nuthatch (*S. pygmaea*), small as the name implies, similar to the Brown-headed Nuthatch, which is found in the mountains of western North America.

Australian tree creepers (Family Climacteridae)

This is a group of six species, all in the genus *Climacteris*, found in Australia and New Guinea. They were formerly placed in the true tree creeper family Certhiidae, but some basic differences have led to their being considered a separate family. The bill is longer and more decurved, the legs and toes are long with strong claws, the tail feathers are not stiffened, and there is noticeable sexual dimorphism not present in Certhiid species. Species included are the Red-browed Tree Creeper (*Climacteris erythrops*) and the White-throated Tree Creeper (*C. leucophaea*) both of eastern Australia.

Flowerpeckers (Family Dicaeidae)

About fifty species of flowerpeckers are found only

in the oriental and Australasian regions. Those of the genus *Anaimos* look rather like kinglets (or goldcrests). Others, such as the Scarlet-backed Flowerpecker (*Dicaeum cruentatum*), which is mainly black with buffish-white underparts and a brilliant scarlet head and back, look somewhat like a sunbird, but with a short bill. Unlike the sunbirds the flowerpeckers feed on seeds as well as insects. The Scarlet-backed Flowerpecker has a wide Asiatic distribution and can be found wherever the tropical parasitic mistletoe *Loranthus* grows, the berries of which form its favourite food.

Sunbirds (Family Nectariniidae)

Most sunbirds are very small and are usually seen fluttering around flowers. There are over one hundred species. They look very like humming-birds, having an iridescent plumage and long, curved bills. They are found throughout the tropical parts of the Old World and are the counterpart of the humming-birds in the New World. Like them they feed on nectar, but will also eat small insects found inside blossom. Indeed, insects trapped in the nectar are an essential part of their diet. The nests are usually purse-like structures hanging from a branch. In many species the males lose their brilliant plumage in the non-breeding season, and have an eclipse plumage resembling that of the immature males or even that of the female.

One widespread Asiatic species is the Yellow-backed Sunbird (*Aethopyga siparaja*), which is a brilliant, metallic scarlet above and on the breast, with a bright yellow rump, the abdomen being greyish. In some areas these birds have a metallic blue tail and forehead.

White-eyes (Family Zosteropidae)

Superficially resembling the unrelated American vireos, these small warbler-like birds are predominantly olive-green above, with a yellow throat and white abdomen, although some species have varying amounts of grey, brown or black. With the exception of a few aberrant species they are all characterised by a ring of white feathers around each eye. The white-eyes extend from Africa south of the Sahara eastwards to Asia and southwards to Australia, where they live particularly on the edges of the forests, in secondary growth, plantations and mangroves. They feed on insects, and small fruits, and will probe flowers for nectar with their brush-like tongues.

Honey-eaters (Family Meliphagidae)

There are 160 species of honey-eaters, distributed over the south-west Pacific from Australia to Hawaii. Small, with slightly down-curved bill, honey-eaters have a highly specialised tongue. It is extensile and brush-like just behind the horny, pointed tip, and can be used as a probe, brush and sucking-tube for taking nectar and the insects assembled to drink it. The birds also carry pollen as they brush past the flowers and are believed to play a major part in pollinating the Australian eucalyptus forests. The Parson-bird or Tui of New Zealand (*Prosthemadera novaeseelandiae*) has two white feathers on either side of its throat. The New Zealand Bell-bird (*Anthornis melanura*) is insignificant except for its bell-like call. Other honey-eaters,

Sunbirds are tiny, brilliantly-coloured birds with a tubular tongue adapted for nectar feeding. They are found in the tropics of the Old World. This male Firetailed Sunbird comes from Nepal but most sunbirds are concentrated in Africa.

The Yellow-tinted or Pale-yellow Honeyeater (*Meliphaga flavescens*) lives in open country with scattered trees and scrub in tropical northern Australia and New Guinea. It is never found far from water as it likes to drink and bathe frequently in the heat of the day. It feeds on honey from flowering eucalyptus and also takes insects.

however, are more richly coloured, and one, the Moho (*Moho nobilis*) of Hawaii, was wiped out through being trapped for its feathers.

Buntings and allies (Family Emberizidae)

This family includes many species which were formerly placed in the family Fringillidae. Recent behavioural and anatomical studies have shown that the grouping followed here is most natural. It includes many species especially in America, referred to as sparrows as well as the buntings, some grosbeaks, towhees, juncos and longspurs, etc. The birds in this family are generally sparrow-like but it also includes many brightly coloured species. There is still much disagreement as to whether or not some species belong in this family or in the Fringillidae; possibly one hundred species or more make up the Emberizidae. To agree with the old arrangements the subfamilies listed below, except for Emberizinae and Pyrrhuloxiinae which would maintain their subfamily rank but in the Fringillidae, should be raised to family status and the tanagers placed closer in order to the Fringillidae. It is one of the most numerous (over 500 species) and widespread of the families.

Buntings and Cardinal grosbeaks
(Subfamilies Emberizinae and Pyrrhuloxiinae)

The Yellowhammer or Yellow Bunting (*Emberiza citrinella*) of Europe and the Ortolan Bunting (*E. hortulana*) are likewise not distinguished for their song. None-the-less the Yellowhammer is a beautiful bird with its head and neck a fine lemon yellow. The habitat of both Yellowhammer and Ortolan Bunting is farmlands, roadsides and open country.

In addition to the large number of North American members of the Emberizidae called 'sparrows' there is another group known as juncos. The relationships between some of the species are so close, owing to interbreeding, that it is not always possible to know to which species an individual actually belongs. For this reason the birds are sometimes merely known by field observers as juncos. One common bird of the coniferous and mixed forests of North America which may be more readily identified is the Slate-coloured Junco (*Junco hyemalis*). It is greyish above with a white underside and outer tail feathers. In winter it migrates to the warmer parts of the United States.

One of the best known of the American finches is the Cardinal (*Cardinalis cardinalis*), which is smaller than a thrush, but has the typical conical bill of a finch. The males are red all over except for some black around the base of the bill. The Cardinal can be readily distinguished from some of the tanagers which it superficially resembles, by its characteristic crest and heavy red bill. It is nonmigratory and is found chiefly in the states south of the Great Lakes. Another American species is the Painted Bunting (*Passerina ciris*) which is probably the gaudiest of all the birds of the United States. It is about the size of the House Sparrow and the males have a bluish-violet head, green back and red rump and underparts. It breeds mainly in central United States and winters further south.

Many American members of the Emberizidae are known as sparrows. They look very much like House and European Tree Sparrows, although these belong to the unrelated weaver-bird family Ploceidae. One of the best known is the Vesper Sparrow (*Pooecetes gramineus*). It differs from a House Sparrow by having white outer tail feathers, a whitish eye-ring and a chestnut-coloured patch at the bend of the wing. A bird of meadows, fields and prairies, it breeds in southern Canada and the more northern United States, wintering further south to the Gulf of Mexico.

Tanagers (Subfamily Thraupinae)

This subfamily comprises over 200 species of New World birds extending throughout the North and South American continents except for the extreme north and south. The Scarlet Tanager (*Piranga olivacea*) is a common representative of this family in eastern North America as well as being a popular cage-bird in Europe. The male in his breeding plumage is handsome, bright scarlet, with black wings and tail; in autumn and winter he moults into one resembling the females. Like all tanagers the bill is short and conical, rather like that of a sparrow. The female is a dull green above, yellowish below with brownish-black

The Little Bunting (*Emberiza pusilla*), little more than twelve centimetres long, breeds in the tundra regions of Siberia and part of northern Finland and Sweden. In the autumn it migrates south-east to winter in northern India and China. It is an inconspicuous little bird feeding mainly on the ground on seeds and insects. It builds its nest in a depression in the ground.

The male Common Cardinal (*Cardinalis cardinalis*) of North America is unmistakable with its bright red plumage and black throat. The Cardinal is a favourite at the bird table eating a wide variety of food put out. The male sings throughout the year and in the breeding season mated birds may be heard singing antiphonally.

457

wings. Birds of this family vary in size from being smaller than a sparrow to as large as a jay, but the North American species are all about the same dimensions, that is, a little larger than a House Sparrow. Most feed mainly on small fruits but will also take flowers and insects. Although the males of the different species are brightly coloured in a variety of hues, those of the northern species are predominantly red, the Summer Tanager (*P. rubra*) being a uniform rose-red all over. One exception is the Western Tanager (*P. ludoviciana*), which breeds in the mountains from British Columbia to southern California. In this species the male is yellow with black shoulders, wings and tail, and a red face in the breeding season. The nest is usually a shallow cup built upon horizontal branches of trees at varying heights from the ground. Three or four bluish-grey eggs spotted with brown are laid in the nest. All these northern species are migratory, most of them wintering in central South America. The tanagers include some of the most vividly coloured species known: the Blue-crowned Chlorophonia (*Chlorophonia occipitalis*) and the Paradise Tanager (*Tangara chilensis*) are among the more notable examples.

Plush-capped finch
(Subfamily Catamblyrhynchinae)

The sole member of this subfamily, *Catamblyrhynchus diadema*, ranges over much of tropical South America. Finch-like fifteen centimetres long, it is remarkable for its erect, golden-brown crown feathers which are like a stiff velvet pile. Almost nothing is known of its habits. Present-day systematists consider this is an aberrant tanager of the Thraupinae subfamily.

Swallow-tanager (Subfamily Tersininae)

The Swallow-tanager (*Tersina viridis*) is the sole member of this subfamily. It is a colourful, starling-sized and tanager-like bird that ranges over much of tropical America, feeding on insects and fruit. It is remarkable for its bill and its swallowing capacity. The bill is broad, hooked at the tip and has sharp edges. When eating fruit the Swallow-tanager cuts it up with its bill and swallows large lumps, its elastic throat pouch taking on strange shapes in consequence.

Wood-warblers (Family Parulidae)

Some species look very much like vireos, other resemble kinglets, and some species of wood-warblers differ so little from each other that it takes years of experience to be able to identify them in the field. The problem is complicated as many species wear a more sombre dress in the fall than in the spring and therefore resemblances are accented in autumn when even the songs, usually reliable identification guides, are stilled.

Before the birds reappear from their wintering grounds, mainly in tropical America, they have moulted into bright, distinctive plumages and are singing. One of the most distinctive in spring is the Black-and-white Warbler (*Mniotilta varia*) named for its stripes of black and white. It may be seen creeping along trunks and branches in the leafy woodlands of most of Canada and the United States. In winter it migrates to Florida or to the tropics. It is sometimes confused with the Black-

poll Warbler (*Dendroica striata*), although the latter has no white stripe on the head and has white instead of black cheeks. It breeds in spruces chiefly in Canada and winters in South America. One of the brightest of this family is the Myrtle Warbler (*D. coronata*), which is grey, striped with black above, white below, and has a bright yellow crown, wing-patch and rump. Normally it breeds in the conifer belt of Canada and in the northern United States, wintering in the southern United States. This species has achieved fame in recent years because one spent the summer in England. Stragglers of American species do occur from time to time in Europe but this bird was unusual because of its small size and good condition. It may have been swept across the Atlantic by a gale, or it may have rested in the rigging of an eastbound ship and so crossed the Atlantic with comparative ease. Nevertheless, this tiny bird somehow managed to reach Europe, and spent the whole summer in the garden of a house at Exeter in Devon. Generally when birds from America reach Europe they are so physically exhausted that they die shortly after arrival.

There are about one hundred and twenty species of these generally small, often bright-coloured birds of the Americas. Most North American species are migratory, breeding in the more temperate regions and returning to the tropical areas for winter. Spring migration in the United States is often spectacular with myriads of these birds passing through in relatively few days. Common names are very confusing as not all species are called warblers. There is the Yellow-throat (*Geothlypis trichas*) and the Yellow-throated Warbler (*Dendroica dominica*); the American Redstart (*Setophaga ruticilla*), not at all related to the Eurasian Redstart; the water-thrushes of the genus *Seiurus* which are vaguely thrush-like; and the related Ovenbird (*Seiurus aurocapillus*) which looks thrush-like but builds an oven-shaped nest of grasses. Well-known, widely distributed species in the United States include the Tennessee Warbler (*Vermivora peregrina*), Nashville Warbler (*V. ruficapilla*), Yellow Warbler (*Dendroica petechia*), Magnolia Warbler (*D. magnolia*), Black-throated Green Warbler (*D. virens*). and the Yellow-breasted Chat (*Icteria virens*).

Hawaiian honeycreepers (Family Drepanididae)

There are twenty-two species of honey creepers peculiar to the Hawaiian islands. All are small with inconspicuous plumage and with tongues specialised for taking nectar. They differ in details of wing, tail and leg, but above all in the shape of the beak. In some it is finch-like, in others slender and curved, or parrot-like, even crossed at the tip. The assumption is that ancestral birds crossed the 3,200 kilometres from America, and that their descendants have become adapted and altered to the many contrasting habitats on the islands, a parallel with Darwin's finches on the Galapagos Islands.

Vireos (Family Vireonidae)

The vireos are confined to the New World, ranging throughout North America and into central South America. They are very similar to the Old World white-eyes and, like them, many have an eye-ring,

The Chestnut-backed Tanager (*Tangara laviniga cara*) is confined to Central and South America. Most of the small tanagers of the *Tangara* genus live in the tops of tall trees in the tropical forests. They move around in small troops, quite often in the company of honeycreepers, feeding on berries and fruits. Little is known of their breeding habits.

usually white in colour, but normally a white spot links this ring with the base of the bill. They are usually solitary, hunting for food among foliage where they move around rather deliberately. Six species are fairly widespread in the United States. Although difficult to distinguish, they can be identified by a process of elimination. Three of these species have two distinct wing bars, while the other three have none. Of the species with wing bars, the Blue-headed or Solitary Vireo (*Vireo solitarius*) with it blue-grey head is probably the easiest to recognise. It is usually the first vireo to be seen in the spring when it returns from the coast of the Gulf of Mexico to breed in the evergreen-deciduous forest belt of the northern United States and southern Canada and higher altitudes in the Appalachians.

Another species with two wing bars is the readily identified Yellow-throated Vireo (*V. flavifrons*), which is the only American species with a bright yellow throat and breast. It breeds in most deciduous forests in the United States. In winter it migrates south to southern Mexico or into South America. The last species with two wing bars is the White-eyed Vireo (*V. griseus*) which differs from the Yellow-throated Vireo mainly in having a whitish throat and breast and a white iris. It breeds in a broad belt across the centre of the United States and winters further south.

Of the three species without wing bars, the Red-eyed Vireo (*V. olivaceus*) is most readily identified because it has a grey cap and a black-edged white stripe above each eye, the red iris being difficult to see except at close quarters. Its range and habitat are much the same as those of the yellow-thoated Vireo. The Warbling Vireo (*V. gilvus*) is very similar but lacks the grey cap, and the stripe above the eye is less distinct. It breeds in tall shady trees from southern Canada southwards to all but the southernmost parts of the United States, and spends the winter in the tropics. The next species without wing bars is the Philadelphia Vireo (*V. philadelphicus*), which differs from the Warbling

Vireo chiefly in having a yellow breast and, to a lesser extent, abdomen. The eye-ring is almost absent. The identification of this species is dificult save by observers who know it or its song well and can differentiate between the vireos and the wood-warblers which this species resembles. It breeds in deciduous forests and edges of clearings in a zone across the temperate parts of North America, wintering in South America. There are six other species in the United States, including the two species of pepper-shrike and four species of shrike-vireo, formerly placed in their own families. In all there are forty-five known species.

American blackbirds and orioles
(Family Icteridae)

The vastly different kinds of plumage pattern in this family make it difficult to make any general

The Red-eyed Vireo (*Vireo olivaceus*) lives high up in the trees of the deciduous woodlands of central and eastern North America and winters in northern South America. Although a common little bird it is not often seen because of its inconspicuous rather drab plumage and its secretive ways. Its distinctive song is monotonous and made up of short, whistled phrases.

The Ovenbird (*Seiurus aurocapillus*) of North America belongs to the American wood-warbler family, not to the Furnariidae, a family noted for building oven-like nests of mud. It is seen here bringing food to its young in the domed oven-shaped nest of leaves and grasses which is built in an open place on the forest floor. Ovenbirds live in the undergrowth of woods and thickets feeding on insects, worms, spiders, centipedes and other small ground-living creatures.

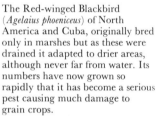

The Red-winged Blackbird (*Agelaius phoeniceus*) of North America and Cuba, originally bred only in marshes but as these were drained it adapted to drier areas, although never far from water. Its numbers have now grown so rapidly that it has become a serious pest causing much damage to grain crops.

statements. They usually have long, sharp-tipped bills and many resemble starlings. They are found throughout the New World, except in the extreme north, and are as varied in habits as in appearance. Some are gregarious, others solitary; some have harsh calls, others have a well-developed song. There is hardly a source of food that is not exploited by some member of the family: nectar, fruit, seeds, fishes, amphibians, crustaceans, insects, small birds and mammals. There are over ninety species recognised.

One of the commonest American blackbirds is the Common Grackle (*Quiscalus quiscula*), which is about thirty centimetres from bill to tail. Its

plumage is an iridescent blackish-purple colour, which gives it an oily appearance like that of a starling in summer plumage. Its tail appears to have a crease along the centre, giving it a keel-like structure. Brewer's Blackbird (*Euphagus cyanocephalus*), the male of which is black with a purple sheen on the head and greenish over the rest of the body, somewhat resembles the grackles but has a shorter, more normal-shaped tail, and the male has white eyes. This species is essentially a bird of the prairies and meadows, particularly of the western United States. It nests either in bushes or the lower branches of trees, and even on the ground. The nest is made of sticks, roots and grasses and in it are laid three to five dull white eggs with brown speckling. By far the most abundant land bird in America, possibly in the world, is the Red-winged Blackbird (*Agelaius phoeniceus*) which breeds in reedy marshes from northern Canada to Cuba and Costa Rica.

Many species resemble the Old World orioles. For example, the Baltimore Oriole (*Icterus galbula*) is very similar in size and markings. It is about the size of a starling, and the male has a black head and shoulders, wing and inner tail feathers; otherwise it is orange in colour. This species breeds in groves of trees such as elms in the eastern parts of southern Canada and the eastern United States, and winters in Central America. A common grassland species is the Eastern Meadowlark (*Sturnella magna*), which is brown with speckles on the back, conspicuous black and white streaks on the crown, and bright yellow below with a black 'V' across the breast; the three outer pairs of tail feathers are white. It is a long-legged bird, which walks on the ground looking very much like a Lark or Pipit. It lives and nests in the open fields and in grassy areas, usually in small flocks. The almost indistinguishable species, the Western Meadowlark (*S. neglecta*) replaces it in western North America.

One species found over most of North America is the Bobolink (*Dolichonyx oryzivorus*). The male is black below with white patches on wings and back and a yellowish nape. During the breeding season it is hard to find any other bird that sings so continually. It is sociable and several pairs may be found nesting in the same piece of meadowland, filling the air with their sweet, wild music. They build their nest in a shallow depression in the ground; it is lined with grass and frequently so covered as to be almost arched over to conceal the eggs. Four to five greyish-white eggs speckled with lilac are laid. The bill of this species is rather short and conical.

Some members of this family, the oropendolas, troupials, and some of the orioles, build more complex nests than the Bobolink. These are called 'hangnests' and build large, complex nests that hang from the branches of trees. In contrast a number of species build no nest at all, but are parasitic like the Eurasian Cuckoos. The most common species is the Brown-headed Cowbird (*Molothrus ater*) of southern Canada and most of the United States. The males are black with a brownish head, while the females are a uniform grey; the bill is short and conical, like that of a sparrow. Like the female Cuckoo the hen Cowbird lays one or occasionally two eggs in the nest of a smaller bird. The foster-parents brood and rear the young, which never know their true parents.

Finches, Darwin's finches
(Family Fringillidae)

With about 125 species, this family is one of the more widespread and common of the Passeriformes, being absent only from Madagascar and the Australasian region. These are small birds with stocky bodies, free toes and short, conical bills. They eat chiefly seeds, and their nests are generally basket-shaped. Some are migrants, and some, such as the Canary (*Serinus canaria*), have a beautiful song.

The type genus of this family is *Fringilla* of which two species, the Chaffinch (*F. coelebs*) and the Brambling (*F. montifringilla*), are fairly common in Britain and Europe. Both may be frequently seen in woods, orchards and farmlands. The former is undoubtedly the more lovely, with its pinkish-brown front, blue-grey hood, brown wings with double white bars, brown tail, and greenish rump. As well as being handsome it is lively and has a fine song.

The Hawfinch (*Coccothraustes coccothraustes*) is found in the cooler parts of the northern Old World from Ireland to Japan. It is quite a large bird with a huge bill that occupies most of its face. Its main colour is a rich brown with metallic tints, and it has bold white shoulder patches. During the summer it will crack open cherry-stones with its bill and eat the kernels. This is a remarkable feat for it usually requires a force of about thirty kilograms.

As its name suggests, the Greenfinch (*Chloris chloris*) is green except for its wings, which are a mixture of grey, black and yellow. It is a partial migrant and its habitat is gardens, shrubberies and farmlands. The characteristic note of the cock is like someone whistling with indrawn breath.

Very close to these is the Bullfinch (*Pyrrhula pyrrhula*), which is always easy to recognise by its grey back, the fine red of its underparts, and by its lustrous black head. It is rather a shy bird that spends most of its time in woods and its song is noted for its melancholy.

Another of the Fringillidae, which although resident in Britain is more typical of northern Europe, is the Red or Common Crossbill (*Loxia curvirostra*), which irrupts when larger numbers than usual come south every few years. It has red plumage and the tips of its mandibles cross. It is found in coniferous woods, where it picks open cones and eats the seeds. Its habitat is the vast extent of the spruce, pine and larch forests of Europe and North America. There is a second species that occurs in America, the Two-barred Crossbill (*L. leucoptera*) with similar habits and habitat to those of the Red Crossbill.

The European Goldfinch (*Carduelis carduelis*), which has been introduced into parts of eastern North America and Bermuda, gets its name from the Latin word for thistle (*Carduus*), for seeds of which it shows a preference. The main characteristic of its colouring is its scarlet face. The Siskin (*C. spinus*), on the other hand, which is as common in North America as in Europe, is yellowish and quite close to the Serin (*Serinus serinus*) with which it would easily be confused but for the top of the

head being far darker. The Serin has recently begun to breed in Britain, while the European Goldfinch is a partial migrant. The Canary is closely related to the Serin, and comes from the islands of that name. The American Goldfinch (*C. tristis*) is common in eastern North America where it is often called the 'wild canary'.

The Linnet (*Carduelis cannabina*) has a pinkish breast and a red crown. Its habitat is open country with hedges. It is a partial migrant, as is another species, the Mountain Linnet or Twite (*C. flavirostris*), which is similar but distinguishable in winter by its yellow bill. Their habits are little different from the rest, and their basic diet is seeds.

The Greenfinch (*Carduelis chloris*) breeds over much of the western half of Eurasia. In Britain it is a familiar finch of parks and gardens and breeds regularly in inner London. It feeds on seeds of wild plants and grasses but also on cultivated grain. During the winter large flocks of Greenfinches gather, some are resident but some migrate up to several hundred kilometres.

The Woodpecker-Finch (*Camarhynchus pallidus*) of the Galapagos Islands has a long stout bill which it uses to probe into bark for insects. It is unusual among birds in being a tool-user. If it cannot reach a particular insect it will use a cactus spine or a thin twig to poke out or impale the insect.

The House Sparrow (*Passer domesticus*) must be one of the most familiar birds in the world as it has become more or less completely dependent on man and his buildings. Although a native of Europe and Asia it has been taken by man to North and South America, southern Africa, Australia and New Zealand. In many places it has become a pest.

The Black-headed Weaver (*Ploceus cucullatus*) is one of the most familiar and widespread weavers in subsaharan Africa. It nests in colonies in trees usually near water and often in association with other species of weaver. All weavers build oval or spherical nests expertly woven from grasses and vegetable fibres.

Darwin's finches of the Galapagos, usually placed in a subfamily, the Geospizinae, are adapted for a variety of ways of life. They presumably evolved from an ancestor from the American mainland.

Waxbills, grassfinches, mannikins and Java sparrows (Family Estrildidae)

This family contains 107 species of small seed-eaters which were formerly assigned to the families Fringillidae and Ploceidae. They are all found in the Old World, and are distinguished by their complicated nests with a spout-like entrance to one side in which white eggs are laid, the young from them maturing in a year. In the Ploceidae, which have equally complicated nests, the eggs are bluish and the young take two years to mature.

Some of the Estrildidae are favourite cage-birds, like the Zebra Finch (*Poephila guttata*) of Australia, barred black and white with a chestnut ear-patch.

The parrot-finches also belong here. Another cage-bird is the Java Sparrow (*Padda oryzivora*) which, with the mannikins, such as the Moluccan Mannikin (*Lonchura molucca*), both of Indonesia, live either near human habitation or on the edge of the forest. They are commonly seen in gardens eating seeds, but have achieved notoriety because they persistently plague the paddy fields. When the rice is ripening large numbers of these birds are to be seen in the fields, often eating half the yield.

One group of birds formerly included in the family Ploceidae and now placed in the Estrildidae is the waxbills. These are small, Old World birds, best known in northern countries as attractive cage-birds, particularly those of the genus *Estrilda*. The males are predominantly a buffish grey with white spots, often with scarlet back, head or bill.

Sparrows and weaver-birds (Family Ploceidae)

The 136 or more members of this family, the sparrows, weaver-birds and widow-birds, closely resemble the finches (Fringillidae) in three respects: free toes, conical beak, and a diet mostly of seeds.

The House Sparrow and Eurasian Tree Sparrow are the only European representatives of the family. The way they spread wherever there are human habitations is well known and they have done this even in countries where they have been introduced, as in North America and Australia. The most familiar species is the House Sparrow (*Passer domesticus*) with its ash-blue crown. A black patch from throat to chest distinguishes the male from the female. This patch is not so large in the Eurasian Tree Sparrow (*P. montanus*), the head of which is browner and shinier. Only the House Sparrow is found in towns. In the countryside the House Sparrow is found in villages and the Eurasian Tree Sparrow in fields and copses. The Eurasian Tree Sparrow was introduced into America near the city of St Louis and, thriving there, has spread to southern Illinois.

Buffon described the House Sparrow as being 'uncomfortably familiar and vulgarly lively'. It is justly accused of doing damage to fields and orchards and also—though this is not certain—of hindering the propagation of the insect-eaters by taking possession of their nests. As the Sparrow is both a seed-eater and an insect-eater, the advantages must be weighted against disadvantages.

Sparrows have at least three broods a year. Cock and hen together make the nest, weaving it of all sorts of materials and choosing the most unexpected sites, such as gutters, ventilation holes, old-fashioned street lamps, farm outbuildings, and even roofs of houses. When they build in trees, the nests are spherical and of sound construction. The nest of the House Sparrow is almost invariably a mess of grasses and a wide variety of debris.

An example of seasonal sexual dimorphism is found in the whydahs (*Euplectes*), plentiful over much of Africa, which are all-black outside the breeding season. But during this season (from May to September) the cocks acquire a fiery red breast and a huge tail that makes them clumsy.

Weaver-birds (*Ploceus* spp.) are spread throughout Africa. They are expert weavers and make their nests with vegetable fibres, shaping them into long pendant pouches. The opening is at the top

462

and a long sleeve open at the bottom gives access to the nest. There may be dozens of these nests jammed one against the other in a single tree.

Finally, there are the sociable weaver-birds, whose collective nests are the work of hundreds of individuals. From a distance these nests look like a thatched roof hung from a tree. At close quarters the holes of the individual nests can be seen along the edge of the 'roof', in and out of which there is a continual traffic of birds. One of the most widespread species is the Quelea (*Quelea quelea*), which is sparrow-like and thirteen centimetres long. It is particularly common in East Africa, where hundreds of thousands of birds will suddenly descend on a field and within a short time completely strip the ripening crops. One nest may fill a whole tree and contain hundreds of females rearing their young. The males are polygamous and a large colony may contain only a few males, each with an immense harem. The weight of the nest is sometimes so great that the tree soon collapses.

Starlings and oxpeckers (Family Sturnidae)

Starlings (*Sturnus vulgaris*) go about in great flocks, often with crows, thrushes and even pigeons. Particularly in non-breeding seasons they fly continuously about the fields, and at the end of the day huge flocks of them return to the cities to roost. In recent years starlings have irrupted noticeably. They have spread from Europe southwards to Africa, eastwards to Asia, and some have been found on Pacific Islands. The few originally introduced into the United States have multiplied to such numbers that they are as great a problem in many American cities as they are in Europe. Another member of the Sturnidae to visit southeast Europe, sometimes straying as far west as Britain, is the Rose-coloured Starling (*S. roseus*). It is predominantly pink with a black and violet head.

Members of this family generally live in warmer climates. The mynahs, which live in Asia, tend to live in flocks, like most starlings, and breed in cavities in trees. The celebrated Talking Mynah is the Hill Mynah or Indian Grackle (*Gracula religiosa*), a widely distributed oriental species frequently imported into western countries as a cage-bird. About the size of a Jackdaw, it is black with a white patch on the wings. It has a thick orange bill and short yellow legs. There is bare yellow skin on the face and behind the eye, extending to the nape. It feeds entirely on fruit, and makes an attractive cage-bird, with a long, melodious whistle. Other mynah species may also be taught to talk.

In Africa two species of the genus *Buphagus* are always found in association with large game mammals, especially cattle. They are known as oxpeckers and perch on the back of game, feeding on the ectoparasites in the mammal's coat, and even on the larvae embedded in the skin. As soon as any predator approaches, the birds swirl upwards calling, so giving warning of danger to their host.

Old World orioles (Family Oriolidae)

These birds should not be confused with the American orioles of the family Icteridae. They are sturdy jay-sized birds, arboreal and insectivorous. Their bills are longer and more pointed than those of the finches and sparrows, though less slender than those of the Old World blackbirds or warblers. Distribution is typically tropical in Eurasia, Africa, Indonesia, the Philippines, and Australia.

The family is represented in Europe by the Golden Oriole (*Oriolus oriolus*), a lovely black and yellow migrant, which arrives in May and leaves again in August for Africa. The general colour and pattern are so similar to that of the Baltimore Oriole of the eastern United States that it led to this member and others of the family Icteridae being called 'orioles'. It is wild, noisy and bold, with a sonorous, rather lovely song heard in the morning and evening. The nest is a skilfully woven bowl lined with moss and lichen hung in the fork of two branches for stability and protection.

Drongos (Family Dicruridae)

The twenty species of drongos are noted for their aggressiveness. All but one are black with iridescent green or purple plumage. The tail is long and varies in shape. Most are the size of a jay, with a hook-tipped beak ornamented with rictal bristles. They feed on insects, hunting them in the manner of flycatchers but with a seeming ferocity. Long pointed wings give strong flight. In defence they will take on even hawks and eagles, and such is their success in driving off intruders that a tree containing a drongo's nest is likely to contain those of less stout-hearted birds as well because of the protection afforded. Curiously, these are not attacked by the drongos. Some are also clever mimics of other bird-songs, and will attack snakes, uttering the calls of other birds.

One species, the Papuan Mountain Drongo (*Chaetorhynchus papuensis*), has twelve tail feathers. The remaining species, distributed from Africa, across southern Asia, to the Solomons and southwards to Australia, have only ten. The King Crow (*Dicrurus macrocercus*), which ranges from India to Java and Formosa, is black with red eyes and a forked tail. The forked tail is most marked in the Racket-tailed Drongo (*D. paradiseus*) of India and Malaya, which has a shaggy crest and 'rackets' at the tip of the tail.

Wattled crow, huia, and saddleback (Family Callaeidae)

These three New Zealand species have long tails and legs, a somewhat velvety plumage and brightly coloured wattles.

The Wattled Crow (*Callaeas cinerea*), or Kokako, said to be New Zealand's best songster, lives in the forests and feeds on leaves, buds and berries, holding them under one foot and tearing them with the other. The beak is sharp-pointed and slightly down-curved.

The extinct Huia (*Heteralocha acutirostris*) is noted for the difference between the male with its straight, sharp beak, and the female with her long down-curved bill. It is said that a pair of huias would combine in food-getting, the male chiselling away rotten wood and the female inserting her long bill into the tunnel to extract the grub, but there is no foundation for this in the published literature.

The Saddleback (*Philesturnus carunculatus*) is glossy black with bright chestnut tail and wings.

463

The Magpie-lark (*Grallina cyanoleuca*) common throughout Australia, has shiny, sleek black and white plumage. It is found wherever there is water and in the autumn large flocks can be seen feeding around the edges of dams and other wet places. It is mainly insectivorous but will eat large numbers of snails when available.

The Satin Bowerbird (*Ptilonorhynchus violaceus*), best known of the bowerbirds, is confined to eastern Australia. The male has glossy black plumage with an iridescent blue sheen. The female is much drabber, a dull grey-green. The male's bower is a platform of sticks and twigs about thirty centimetres long enclosed within two walls fifty centimetres high, decorated with flowers and other, usually blue, objects.

The Saddleback feeds on insects and fruit, and has a straight, sharp-pointed bill.

Magpie-larks (Family Grallinidae)

There are four species of these birds: three in Australia and one in New Guinea. Both the Mudlark of Australia (*Grallina cyanoleuca*) and that of New Guinea (*G. bruijni*) are black and white, and live along the edges of muddy lakes. Their nest is a mud bowl, strengthened with hair or fur, and lined with feathers and grass. The Apostle-bird (*Struthidea cinerea*) is mainly black, but with some white. It is jay-sized and goes about in parties of twelve. The nest is also bowl-shaped and of mud. The White-winged Chough (*Corcorax melanorhamphus*) also makes a mud bowl, several individuals combining to build it, and several females laying their eggs in it when it has been completed.

Wood-swallows (Family Artamidae)

Another group of birds having apparent affinities with the shrikes are the wood-swallows. The ten are found throughout south-east Asia to Australia and even as far as the Fiji Islands. They also have stout bill, legs and feet. Their pointed wings and their habit of taking insects while on the wing make them appear rather swallow-like.

The colour pattern in some species also increases the resemblance to the swallow family. The Greater Wood-swallow (*Artamus maximus*), of the forests of New Guinea, is a dark slate-grey colour with a white rump and underparts, very much like the House Martin. This species is gregarious and several shallow, cup-shaped nests are often built in the same tree. When a young bird clamours for food it may be fed by any of the adults present.

Bell-magpies, Australian butcherbirds, piping crows (Family Cracticidae)

This is a family of about ten species distributed over Australia, Tasmania and New Guinea. All are jay or crow-sized and some have the beaks and habits of shrikes.

The melodious note of the bell-magpies is one of the commonest bird songs in Australia. Three species represent the group: the White-backed Bell-magpie (*Gymnorhina hypoleuca*), the Black-backed Bell-magpie (*G. tibicen*), and the Western Bell-magpie (*G. dorsalis*). Distribution of the three rarely overlaps.

The Western Bell-magpie (*G. dorsalis*), with black and white plumage, has remarkable territorial behaviour. Groups of six to twenty males and females occupy a territory of up to fifty hectares all the year round, defending its boundaries from rival groups of bell-magpies and mobbing intruders, even human beings. Mating is promiscuous. The hens build the nests and care for the young unaided. The male helps to feed them only when they leave the nest. They have a ringing, bell-like call and at the breeding-time groups call in chorus. This dies down as soon as the egg-laying begins.

The piping crows (genus *Strepera*), also called currawongs, are large birds found in wooded habitats, in pairs during the breeding season and at other times in flocks. Plumage is predominately black, white and grey.

The third genus, the Australian butcherbirds (*Cracticus*), share with the true butcherbirds (*Laniidae*) the habit of impaling insects, lizards and small birds on thorns to anchor the carcasses during feeding. In contrast to this practical but robust behaviour is their very pleasing song, particularly that of the rather distinctive Pied Butcherbird (*C. nigrogularis*), an inland species.

Bowerbirds (Family Ptilonorhynchidae)

Closely related to the birds of paradise, bowerbirds are so called because they build canopies and galleries for courtship. This family of about eighteen species is restricted to the New Guinea/Australia area. These are built on the ground with interwoven twigs and are ornamented with shells, flowers, pebbles, bleached bones and feathers, particularly blue ones. After courtship and mating take place, the female leaves to build her nest, while the male remains near the bower displaying to other females.

Birds of paradise (Family Paradisaeidae)

Birds of paradise, which are found only in New Guinea and adjacent islands, live mainly on insects, although they also eat fruits. They are characterised by a sexual dimorphism, which attains its fullest expression in the breeding season. They are polygamous, as is often the case where there is a marked sexual dimorphism. The Greater Bird of Paradise (*Paradisaea apoda*), found only in New Guinea and the Aru Islands of Indonesia, is a typical example. In full nuptial plumage the male has a velvety black breast with emerald tints; the crown of his head and nape are lemon yellow; the upper part of his throat is emerald green with golden lights; and his tail, wing feathers and belly are chestnut. Long filiform feathers, with separated barbs, grow from the flanks. They are a beautiful orange-yellow, shading into wine red at the extremities, and the bird can curve them in graceful scrolls or press them close to its body. The hen by comparison is dull.

The cock King of Saxony Bird of Paradise (*Pteridophora alberti*) has two feathers springing from its crown. These are twice as long as the body, beyond which they extend in graceful curves. The male Twelve-wired Bird of Paradise (*Seleucidis melanoleuca*) has six feathers growing from each flank that are reduced to mere filaments.

The courtship of the birds of paradise is a colourful sight. The cocks display in such a manner as to exhibit their plumage to its fullest advantage before the hens, fluffing out their feathers and at the same time prancing and bowing, and in some species performing acrobatic manoeuvres on their perches. Only their raucous, guttural cries seem out of place.

Crows, magpies, jays (Family Corvidae)

These large perching birds have free toes and powerful bills. Many Corvidae live in large flocks, and have a loud and sometimes lugubrious cry. The dominant colour of the species in the crow group is black. The jays, as a group, sport brighter colours. The crow is chiefly insectivorous, picking up grubs when the fields are being worked. During harvest-time it is granivorous and in winter it

The Grey Butcherbird (*Cracticus torquatus*) has a wide distribution in much of the Australian bush and also in Tasmania. It is considered to be one of the best Australian songsters. It is a friendly bird and can be enticed into gardens but it has been known to kill pet caged birds and drag them out through the wires of the cage to be added to its 'larder'.

The Raggiana Bird of Paradise (*Paradisaea raggiana*) lives in the wet lowland forests of New Guinea. Like all members of the genus it has long lacy plumes extending beyond the tail. In the breeding season the male calls to the females and starts his courtship dance opening his wings to show the beautiful red feathers. He then arches his body forward so that his tail plumes cascade into an alluring show.

becomes omnivorous, eating seeds, earthworms, grubs of all kinds, birds and even carrion.

Some of the crow family have entirely black plumage and legs. The most impressive of these is the Common Raven (*Corvus corax*), which can be sixty-three centimetres or more from beak to tail. It has become rare in Europe and in America, and is only found on cliffs or in mountains except in the more arctic regions. The Carrion Crow (*C. corone*) lives in woods and fields, and the Rook (*C. frugilegus*) has a pointed and not hooked bill. It is the most widespread of them all, and lives in colonies or rookeries.

In North America the bird known as the Common or American Crow (*C. brachyrhynchos*) is yet another all-black species which is remarkably like the Carrion Crow in appearance, voice and also in its behaviour.

Another North American species, the Fish Crow (*C. ossifragus*), is seldom found far inland, and may be distinguished by its voice. Instead of the loud, clear open 'caw' of the adults of the European and American crows, it utters a hoarser, shorter 'car' as if it were accustomed to talking through its nose.

Other Old World members of this family have black plumage but red feet; these comprise the genus *Pyrrhocorax*. The Cornish Chough (*Pyrrhocorax pyrrhocorax*) has a long red beak, and the

Alpine Chough (*P. graculus*) has a short, yellow bill. Both live in mountains, but the Cornish Chough is also found in cliffs and rocks. The Alpine Chough can live at great heights, and one was seen by the Mount Everest expedition in 1953 at 8,100 metres.

The Hooded Crow (*Corvus cornix*) has a grey back and underparts. It is a close relative of the Carrion Crow with which it interbreeds. Nowadays the tendency is to regard both as belonging to the same species (*C. corone*), but forming separate sub-species. The Jackdaw or Belfry Crow (*C. monedula*) has grey only on the nape. It is one of the most common crows and is frequently seen in towns.

Crows and rooks are among the earliest breeders of the year. They mate from January on, build their nests of twigs in February, and lay their eggs at the beginning of March. They seem to be monogamous. While the hen sits on her four or six greenish eggs, the cock stays near her and supplies her with food. Later, when the chicks are hatched, the two birds look after them together.

The House Crow (*Corvus splendens*), common in India and Ceylon, owes its scientific name to the metallic tints of its plumage, and is an expert thief that will steal anything.

The Black-billed Magpie (*Pica pica*), also a member of the Corvidae, is actually pied. It has a black back and pure white shoulders and belly, and its tail is very long. In Europe where there is only the one species, it is the Magpie; in North America there is also the Yellow-billed Magpie (*P. nuttalli*). Unlike crows and rooks, magpies seldom gather in more than small parties, and then only in winter, living in pairs during the rest of the year. Both magpies' flight is heavy and laboured owing to their short wings, and their cries are an incessant chattering. They are even greater thieves than the rooks, with a marked predilection for bright objects. In other habits magpies differ little from other crows.

The Old World Nutcracker (*Nucifraga caryocatactes*) differs from other Corvidae in that its bill is conical and no longer than its head. It is brown speckled with white, and inhabits the colder parts of Europe, including the conifer forests of the Alps, Jura and Pyrenees, where it feeds mainly on nuts and the seeds of pines and spruce. It will also eat insects, worms and small birds. Like the squirrel, it prepares for the winter by burying acorns in the ground, after first literally stuffing its crop with them. In America this genus is represented by Clark's Nutcracker (*N. columbianus*) which has similar habits.

The European Jay (*Garrulus glandarius*), another member of the crow family, has a bill of medium length, and gay plumage. The wing coverts are barred with light blue, dark blue and black and the body is pinkish brown. It lives in woods and eats acorns, beechnuts, berries and fruit, as well as vast numbers of grubs, caterpillars and other pests. It is a great robber of nests.

The numerous jays, in addition to being more colourful, are commonly crested to varying degrees and have proportionately longer tails than do the sombre crows. In America there is the noisy, rather well-named Blue Jay (*Cyanocitta cristata*) common east of the Rocky Mountains

The Jackdaw (*Corvus monedula*) ranges across Europe and much of western Asia. A smallish member of the crow family, it is an inveterate chatterer and a pet Jackdaw will manage to include a number of words in its vocabulary. Strangely, although its song consists of a medley of many natural calls it seldom if ever copies the call of another bird.

from southern Canada to the Gulf Coast; the great-crested Steller's Jay (*C. stelleri*) which is largely blue, but looking as if the fore third of the bird were dipped in black ink; and the crestless Green Jay (*Cyanocorax yncas*) which has a blue head, black cheeks and bib, and yellow outer tail feathers composing its otherwise green plumage. The Green Magpie (*Cissa chinensis*) of southeastern Asia with its red bill and legs is another beautiful representative of the crow family.

USEFULNESS OF BIRDS: We cannot leave the passerines without mentioning their usefulness. Agriculture and forestry have many enemies, the worst being insects and their larvae. The harm done by locusts, Colorado beetles, weevils, different kinds of caterpillars, especially the processionary ones, wood-boring insects, moths and other pests hardly needs stressing and, as Michelet once said, 'Without birds the world would be at the mercy of insects.'

When one considers the quantities of insects and larvae destroyed every year by some of our small birds, the truth of this statement is evident. A Goldcrest, for example, eats more than three million insects every year. A Blue Tit, which is much the same size, destroys more than six and a half million for its own needs and at least twenty-four million to rear its brood of twelve to sixteen young. To obtain them it makes at least 450 sorties a day in the neighbourhood of its nest. Under the same conditions a swallow flies more than 640 kilometres a day and destroys millions of flies in the course of a season. A nestful of wrens consumes 9,000 insects before leaving the nest. A wren has been observed to bring thirty grasshoppers to its chicks in the space of an hour. Young jays con-

sume half a million caterpillars in a season.

It is more difficult to defend the grain-eating and fruit-eating birds which are accused with some justification of being harmful to agriculture. But even most of these birds feed insects to their nestlings and by consuming weed seeds as well as grain are mainly beneficial to man. They all have their part in the critical balance of nature with which man is inextricably bound. On the whole the few fruits and seeds a bird eats are a small price to pay in view of the general usefulness of birds in protecting crops from the much greater ravages of insects.

Most members of the crow family take readily to human companionship, even to the point of frequenting houses. The House Crow (*Corvus splendens*) of southern Asia is particularly tame and bold when not persecuted and is always found near human habitations, feeding largely on scraps of food thrown out.

The Common or Eurasian Jay (*Garrulus glandarius*). Jays habitually hide food, usually in the ground, and this is especially true of the autumn acorn crop.

Mammals (Class Mammalia)

Although man is far removed from mammals such as whales, dolphins and porpoises, he has much in common with them, for the two distinguishing attributes of mammals are the presence of hair and milk-secreting glands. Hair is never entirely absent, even in whales, which are aquatic, while milk is found even in the monotremes, which lay eggs.

A typical mammal is a warm-blooded, air-breathing, four-footed vertebrate with a hairy skin rich in glands. Its teeth are usually rooted in sockets in the bone. It has fleshy lips (initially for suckling), a uvula and epiglottis, a larynx, a complete diaphragm and lungs with alveoli or air-cells. The heart has four cavities, and the aorta curves upwards to the left instead of the right as in birds. The brain is well developed. The middle ear has three bones and a tympanic cavity. Mammals are viviparous (except for monotremes) and the foetus is enclosed in both an amnion and an allantois. The young are nourished after their birth by a milk secretion from their mother's mammary glands.

Structure, adaptation and behaviour

Skin and cutaneous structures

In contrast to that of birds, the skin of mammals is comparatively thick, particularly in such types as the elephant, hippopotamus and rhinoceros. The epidermis is a stratified epithelium whose outer horny layers are continually renewed from the soft and protoplasmic layer beneath, and it is largely from this layer that hair, nails, claws, hooves, horns, whalebones and scales are derived.

The underlying dermis is thicker than the epidermis and contains blood vessels. The dermis ensures the growth of the skin appendages mentioned above. It also contains sweat glands and sebaceous glands that lubricate the hair. There are various kinds of scent glands and, in the female, the mammary glands. The fibres of the dermis are usually short and irregularly matted as in felt, though there are exceptions, like the long fibres in the laminated dermis of sharks.

Beneath the dermis is a layer of connective tissue richly supplied with fat. This layer provides a protection against cold and is therefore particularly thick in mammals such as seals and whales living in cold waters. It also serves as a reserve of energy.

Hair may be stubbly, woolly, silky or velvety, but basically it is of two types: a short, soft underfur and longer, coarser guard hairs. In domestic sheep the underfur has been developed as wool but in most mammals the visible coat of fur is the guard hairs which form a waterproof cover over the heat-retaining underfur. Where horny fibrous material predominates we have horsehair, hog's bristles and, as an extreme, the quills of porcupines, and the spines of hedgehogs.

The colour of the pelage is extremely variable too. It may be uniform or patterned and it may differ according to sex, age, season or habitat.

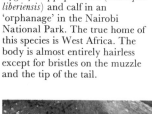

Pygmy Hippopotamus (*Choeropsis liberiensis*) and calf in an 'orphanage' in the Nairobi National Park. The true home of this species is West Africa. The body is almost entirely hairless except for bristles on the muzzle and the tip of the tail.

Some wild pigs, for example, are born striped but later acquire an adult coat of uniform colour. The ermine is reddish brown in summer and snow white in winter in the colder parts of its range. Desert animals are fawn or beige while polar species are white. Such adaptations to environment are described as protective coloration.

Skeleton

If one bears in mind the human skeleton, it is not difficult to grasp the essential details of the skeletons of other mammals. The vertebrae are usually biplanar and separated by intervertebral discs (epiphyses) which make possible the bending movements of the vertebral column. This nearly always consists of seven cervical vertebrae (the same number in the giraffe's long neck as in the whale's extremely short one), after which comes a variable number of thoracic, lumbar, sacral and caudal vertebrae. The sacral vertebrae are fused together to form the sacrum, to which the pelvic girdle is attached. The caudal vertebrae are reduced in man and the anthropoid apes to a coccyx consisting of a few rudimentary vertebrae. Ribs are attached to the thoracic vertebrae.

The skull includes the cranium, which may or may not bear a sagittal crest or frontal horns, and the face, which is generally muzzle-shaped, the most important part being the lower jaw or mandible whose condyles, very variable in form, fit precisely the cavities in which they articulate.

The bones of the limbs vary considerably according to the method of locomotion. Except for cetaceans and the Sirenia, which have completely lost their posterior limbs, all mammals are

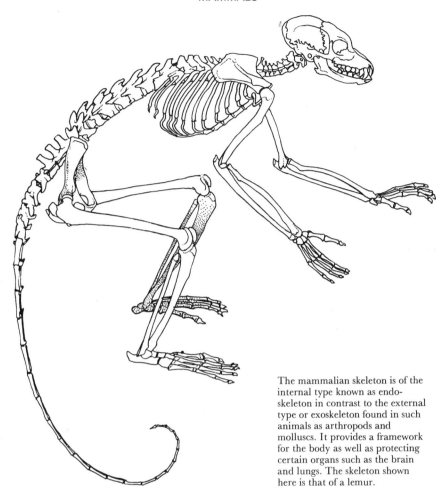

The mammalian skeleton is of the internal type known as endoskeleton in contrast to the external type or exoskeleton found in such animals as arthropods and molluscs. It provides a framework for the body as well as protecting certain organs such as the brain and lungs. The skeleton shown here is that of a lemur.

Leopards (*Panthera pardus*) were once distributed throughout southern Asia and Africa but are today much reduced in numbers and range. Powerful for their size they are good tree-climbers, often dragging a heavy kill up into a tree out of reach of a marauding Lion.

469

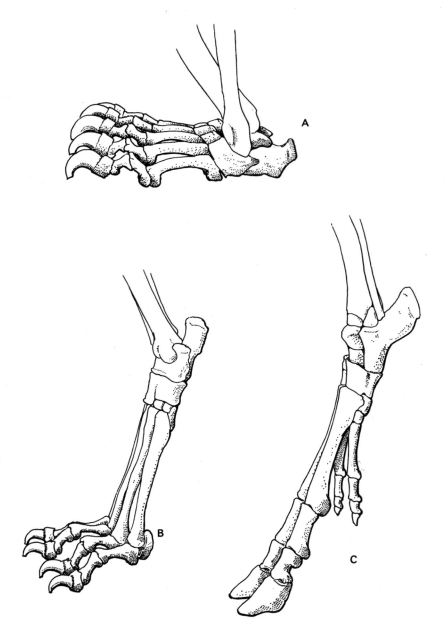

The basic foot posture is the plantigrade type (A) found in monkeys and bears. Predatory animals have evolved a more advanced digitigrade mode (B) which enables them to move stealthily, and a further development in ungulates, the unguligrade mode (C), is an adaptation to running.

much further specialised for running, the digits have become reduced, first to four, then to three, two and even one in the case of the horse.

A limb bearing five digits is known as a pentadactyl limb, as in the elephant. It is the basic form from which all others have evolved. In a pentadactyl foot the middle toe is the strongest and is provided with a stronger nail. Most of the Perissodactyla (e.g. tapirs and rhinoceroses) have tridactyl feet, in which the middle digit of each foot has become accentuated and carries an increasing share of the weight of the body, while the first and fifth digits have been reduced until they no longer touch the ground.

In the monodactyl foot the second and fourth digits have in turn become reduced and are raised from the ground. The successive stages in the evolution of the monodactyl limb from the primitive pentadactyl limb are illustrated by the five-toed foot of the elephant, the tridactyl foot of the rhinoceros and the monodactyl foot of a horse.

As well as the odd-toed ungulates there are orders with an even number of toes. A pig's foot has four toes, the third and fourth (middle) ones being better developed than the second and fifth (lateral) ones. The weight is carried by central toes, relatively stronger than the others. From the tetradactyl foot of the pig there is a further reduction to the didactyl foot of a camel. These two lines of development have given rise to two series of ungulates: in the odd-toed ungulates (Perissodactyla) the predominance of a central digit has led to an uneven number of toes; in even-toed ungulates (Artiodactyla) third and fourth digits are equally predominant. This specialisation is an adaptation paralleled in other mammals. Bats have taken to flight, cetaceans and Sirenia to swimming, kangaroos and jerboas to jumping, moles to burrowing and monkeys to climbing.

Feet play a very important part in the recognition of animals in the field. An experienced tracker distinguishes with absolute certainty between the prints left by dog and fox, closely related as they are, or between those of the Pine Marten and the Stone Marten. From the tracks of all four feet, and the trails made by a succession of tracks, sometimes not only the sex, but the age, gait and state of health can be deduced with accuracy, and the speed at which the animal was travelling may also be deduced.

Teeth

Almost all mammals, even some of the misleadingly named edentates, have teeth. Each tooth consists of a crown and a root, the latter being in an alveolus or pit in the jawbone. Teeth are always arranged in a single line along the jaws, sometimes closely set, sometimes spaced. Only in rare cases (some edentates and dolphins) are all the teeth alike. Generally they vary in shape with their position in the jaw and their consequent function. Typically, the mammalian dentition includes incisors, canines, premolars and molars.

Most mammals have two successive sets of teeth, milk teeth and permanent teeth, but in some one set is eliminated. Milk teeth occur in the insectivores only in the embryo, are absent in most marsupials. Cetaceans have only one set, which may be described as milk or permanent teeth.

tetrapodal. Their limbs follow the pattern seen in the batrachians, reptiles and birds. The coracoid bones are generally lacking, however, or rather are reduced to the coracoid processes of the scapula. In the running mammals the clavicles also have disappeared.

In the most primitive condition, running mammals stand on the whole length of the foot. This is the plantigrade method of locomotion still used by man, apes, monkeys and bears. The first action in running is to raise the heel and instep, so that only the lower surfaces of the digits touch the ground. This is the digitigrade position adopted by dogs and cats. Much is gained in both silence and suppleness. In some mammals this process has been advanced still further until they stand right on the tips of their toes, which are then provided with immensely enlarged nails or hooves. This is the unguligrade condition found in the ungulates, such as elephants, pigs, horses and cows.

Plantigrade and digitigrade animals generally have four or five digits, while in the ungulates, they

Dentition is usually correlated with diet, so there are omnivores, carnivores, insectivores, herbivores and rodents or gnawing animals. In the first three the dentition is complete, consisting of incisors, canines and molars. Owing to the absence of canines dentition is generally incomplete and discontinuous in herbivores and always so in rodents.

The form of the teeth also varies with the diet. In omnivores, carnivores and insectivores teeth are short and limited in growth. In these the dentine has a permanent covering of enamel and the molars have rounded or pointed cusps. This type is called bunodont. The adaptation to a herbivorous diet is usually marked first by the continuous growth of the teeth and the fusion of the cusps into longitudinal or transverse ridges. This gives the lophodont type found in tapirs and rhinoceroses. Finally, in the third type the crests become very worn away, revealing the dentine below. Between the crests dentine is deposited. Thus the crowns become smoothly worn surfaces on which bands of roughly crescent-shaped enamel surround patches of dentine and are themselves surrounded by cement. This is the selenodont type of dentition found in oxen and horses.

The number of teeth is expressed in a dental formula in which the incisors, canines, premolars and molars are given in turn, the upper figure being for one half of the upper jaw, the lower for half the mandible. For instance:

$$\text{Pig I.} \frac{3}{3} \quad \text{C.} \frac{1}{1} \quad \text{Pm.} \frac{4}{4} \quad \text{M.} \frac{3}{3}$$

$$\text{Ox I.} \frac{0}{3} \quad \text{C.} \frac{0}{1} \quad \text{Pm.} \frac{3}{3} \quad \text{M.} \frac{3}{3}$$

By adding all the numbers in the formula and multiplying by two, the total number of teeth is found: forty-four in the pig, thirty-two in the ox.

Alimentary tract

Beginning with the mouth, there are the fleshy lips and a highly muscular tongue, the palate extending into a soft palate and the epiglottis which closes the nasal passages when swallowing. The muscular cheeks and the salivary glands surrounding the buccal cavity also belong to this system. The stomach is more or less differentiated. The gut is divided into a small intestine (ileum) and a large intestine (colon). A caecum is present, larger in some species than in others, and there is a large liver and pancreas.

All these organs are subject to variation from one mammalian order to another. The salivary glands are highly developed in herbivores, much less so in carnivores, and not present at all in wholly aquatic mammals. The stomach is divided by a constriction in rodents, while in ruminants it consists of several compartments: rumen (paunch), reticulum (honeycomb), omasum (manyplies) and abomasum. The intestine is very long in herbivores and omnivores. Whereas a sheep has twenty-seven metres of gut, a Lion has less than six. Carnivores and insectivores have no caecum, while rodents have a voluminous one.

African Elephant (*Loxodonta africana*) and calf. They clearly show the primitive pentadactyl limbs.

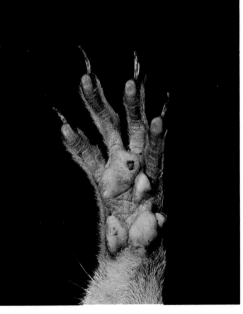

Underside of the forefoot of a Grey Squirrel (*Sciurus carolinensis*) showing the long sharp claws and the pads that contribute so much to this rodent's climbing abilities and sure-footedness in trees.

471

Lioness yawning and in doing so permitting a glimpse of a typical carnivore dentition including the well-developed canine teeth.

Bunodont

Lophodont

Cement (shown black)

Dentine

Enamel

Selenodont

The form of the teeth varies according to diet. In omnivores, carnivores and insectivores the molars have rounded or pointed cusps (A: bunodont type). Herbivorous animals have cusps fused into ridges (B: lophodont type). In ruminants the crests wear away, exposing the underlying dentine which is surrounded by crescent-shaped bands of enamel (C: selenodont type).

The gall bladder is lacking in many rodents and ungulates.

The contents of the stomach are an excellent guide to diet. Analysis tells us that a badger, for instance, may occasionally take game, but that it lives mostly on earthworms, molluscs and insects. It feeds on the underground nests of wasps and, still more commonly, the larvae of the cockchafer, of which 200 have been found in a badger's stomach killed shortly after its first meal of the night. On the vegetable side, it eats mainly acorns and beech nuts.

Respiration and circulation

The throat consists of a larynx with several cartilages (Adam's apple), vocal cords, glottis and epiglottis. The windpipe (trachea) carries air to the bronchi, through which it passes to the bronchioles and then to the pulmonary alveoli which, like the diaphragm, are fully developed only in mammals.

The heart has four chambers. The single aorta, rising from the left ventricle, arches to the left and not to the right as in birds. The red corpuscles are circular, biconcave and without a nucleus, in contrast to the elliptical, biconvex and nucleated corpuscles of the other vertebrates. Only the Camelidae have elliptical corpuscles, but these are

also without a nucleus. The complete circulation of the corpuscles, combined with active breathing, enables mammals to keep an even temperature of 37·2–40°C. The exceptions here are the monotremes, whose temperature is maintained as low as 27·2–28·3°C, and hibernating animals, whose temperature is lowered during their long period of winter sleep.

Ductless glands

Mammals are richly supplied with ductless or endocrine organs, such as the thyroid, parathyroid, thymus, suprarenals and hypophysis or pituitary body. They secrete hormones into the blood and these act on the growth or function of other organs. The ovaries and testes also operate as ductless glands. The thyroid and parathyroid are in the neck at the level of the thyroid cartilage (Adam's apple) and represent the remains of gill clefts. They secrete an iodised hormone called thyroxine which controls body growth. The thymus lies at the base of the neck and represents the remains of the last gill cleft. It also affects growth, but only in the young, for it shrivels in the adult. The suprarenals or adrenals are situated on the kidneys and secrete adrenalin, a stimulant of the heart and nervous system. The pituitary is a complex gland under the brain and appears to control other endocrine organs, including the sexual glands.

Nervous system and sense-organs

The nervous system of mammals is the most highly developed in the animal kingdom. It is dominated by the brain, especially the cerebrum or cerebral hemispheres and the cerebellum. In rodents and insectivores the cerebral hemispheres are smooth (lissencephalous). Others, with more or less highly convoluted brains are gyrencephalate. The two cerebral hemispheres are connected by two bridges of white matter, the fornix and the corpus callosum. The cerebellum has a median vermis or lobe between two lateral or floccular lobes. The pyramidal cells of the cerebrum and the cells of Purkinje of the cerebellum progressively acquire a high degree of complexity. The senses have attained varying degrees of perfection in the various groups. In some, smell is the most highly developed; in others, hearing or sight.

The sense of touch is generally highly developed through the host of tactile corpuscles scattered in the skin. Snouts and muzzles are particularly rich in them and are often equipped with sensitive hairs such as the whiskers of a cat. Taste is located in the taste-buds of the tongue. As many as 8,000 have been counted in a dog and 35,000 in an ox. Smell depends above all on the complexity of the turbinal bones, which serve to increase the surface of the nasal passages. Mammals alone have an external ear and tympanic ossicles, of which two are derived from the mandibular arch of an ancestral vertebrate, and the third ossicle, the stapes, from the hyoid arch. The cochlea has two to four spiral turns and contains the very complex organs of Corti.

The eyes of other mammals are much like those of man, except that in most they are set in the sides of the head, which makes vision largely monocular and affects the ability to estimate distance. In the retina the proportion of rods (sensitive to dim light) to cones (sensitive to colour and detail) varies according to whether the species is diurnal or nocturnal. Eyelashes are always highly developed. The third eyelid or nictitating membrane of birds is represented by a fold at the inner angle of the eye and may be well developed. Certain burrowing mammals have their eyes covered with skin.

Reproduction

UROGENITAL SYSTEM: The excretory and reproductive organs of mammals are similar to those of birds and reptiles. The kidney is a metanephros, the urine flowing through their independent ureters. The sperm-ducts coming from the testes are the former ureters of the mesonephros. Similarly the oviducts for the ovaries may be regarded as former ureters of the pronephros. It is interesting to note the way in which 'old stock' is made use of in the course of evolution. An organ no longer required for its original function may instead of disappearing become adapted to a new one.

Kidneys are nearly always compact and of typical kidney shape, though they may sometimes be lobed as in the elephant and ox, or even broken up into clusters. Except in monotremes, the ureters open into the posterior part of the urinary

bladder, which is the base of the embryonic allantois dilated into a reservoir. From the bladder the urine is evacuated through a urethra. The urine itself is liquid and much richer in urea than in uric acid, and to this extent is in sharp contrast with that of reptiles and birds.

The testes arise first in the lumbar region, but in the course of development their position changes.

The Water Vole (*Arvicola amphibius*), of Europe, exposing to view the pair of incisors, in both upper and lower jaws, characteristic of rodents as a whole.

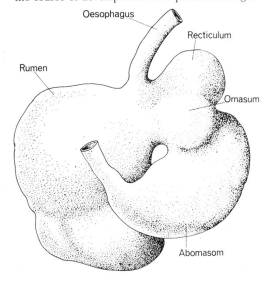

Oesophagus

Recticulum

Rumen

Omasum

Abomasom

The ruminant stomach is a compound organ specially adapted for the digestion of plant material. This is accomplished by a long process in which the food is subjected to bacterial action and is regurgitated before it passes finally to the rennet stomach to be acted on by gastric juices.

Red Fox (*Vulpes vulpes*) among
bluebells, showing the alert eyes
and ears of a predatory mammal.
The long whiskers of the Fox are
sensitive tactile organs which
enable it to prowl about in
complete darkness.

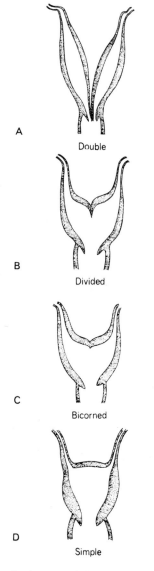

A
Double

B
Divided

C
Bicorned

D
Simple

In the most primitive type of
uterus the oviducts are completely
separate and form two distinct
uteri (A). Both the divided and
bicorned types (B and C) are
more advanced and represent
intermediate stages towards the
development of the single uterus
(D) in which the oviducts are
completely joined.

In some mammals they are lodged in the pelvis
and the fact that in these orders the testes are
internal and therefore invisible gave rise to the
name Cryptorchidia, which grouping includes
elephants, edentates and cetaceans. The testes of
this group may descend into the scrotum only
during the rut and afterwards return to their
position within the pelvis. This is a natural
protection against sterility that would be caused
by the high body temperature. The testicle contains a multitude of seminiferous tubules embedded in connective tissue. Semen descends these
and then passes eventually through the epididymis
and a duct known as the vas deferens, to be
discharged into the urethra.

The urethra is thus a passage for both urine and
semen. Surrounded by carvernous tissue, erectile
when suffused with blood, it constitutes the penis,
the organ of coition. In many mammals, particularly carnivores, there is a rod-like os penis or penial bone. And in many orders the penis is provided
with spines so placed as to cause the male
difficulty in withdrawing after coitus. Between
ejaculations spermatozoa, stimulated by the secretion of the prostate gland surrounding the base of
the uretha, accumulate in the seminal vesicles.

Unlike the testes, the ovaries always remain
within the pelvis and have no direct connection
with the oviducts or Fallopian tubes, which end
near the ovaries in a fringed and ciliated funnel.
Ova are discharged from the ovary into the
abdominal cavity. They find their way into the
funnel and pass through the oviducts to the uterus.
In most mammals, fertilised ova attach themselves
to the uterus and develop. If the ovum does not
reach the funnel extra-uterine gestation may take
place. This is fairly common, but in humans it
generally leads to abortion. The uterus ends in a
vagina, which the male organ enters in coitus.

Several stages of evolution may be observed in
the reproductive organs. In monotremes and marsupials the two genital tracts remain distinct
throughout their length, so that there are two
vaginas and two uteri. In placental mammals the
two vaginas merge into a single organ, but the two
uteri may remain distinct as in rodents, or be
incompletely fused as in insectivores, carnivores
and ungulates. Complete fusion into a single sac is
achieved only in primates. According to the stage
reached, uteri are said to be double, divided,
bicorned or simple. The aperture of the uterus is
surrounded by a circular muscle, or sphincter. The
vagina is provided with glands, protective lips and
an excitatory clitoris, an organ homologous to the
glans penis and sometimes provided with a clitori-
dean bone.

In early embryonic stages the urogenital tracts open into a sort of cloaca, which is simply a dilation of the end of the intestine. Monotremes never advance beyond this stage and thus show an affinity with birds and reptiles. In other mammals a partition (perineum) is soon formed and this divides the cloaca into two, the urogenital tract on the ventral side and the intestine terminating in an anus on the dorsal side.

MATURATION OF THE OVA: Monotremes are oviparous, marsupials ovoviviparous and placentals viviparous. In ovoviviparous mammals the egg is relatively large and contains sufficient yolk to nourish the embryo in the first stages of development, but there is no attachment to the uterine wall. The gestation period is very short and the young is born in an early stage of development and makes its way into the female's pouch or marsupium. In placental mammals the process is quite different. The ovum, which is very small and without food reserves, becomes attached to the uterine wall, and later the developing embryo is nourished by the maternal blood through a special organ, the placenta. The gestation period is long and birth does not take place until the foetus has reached an advanced stage of development.

In the female placental mammal the production of ova follows a regular oestrous cycle of varying length. For example, it is thirty-one days in a cow, fourteen in a guinea-pig and four or five in a mouse. Dogs, cats and goats have two oestrous cycles a year, while the hibernating marmot and hedgehog have only one. The oestrous cycle covers maturation and extrusion of the ovum, followed by the formation and rejection of the corpus luteum.

The active part of the ovary, unlike that of the testes, is the outer part. The centre is more or less degenerate, the ova differentiating and maturing just under the surface. Each ovum develops in a protective follicle. As many as 300,000 of these follicles have been counted in a woman, but normally most of these degenerate and only 400 reach maturity, liberating their ova in successive menstrual cycles. In the mature follicle a hollow is formed which fills with liquid. In this an ovum appears and grows to about 0.25 millimetres in diameter. This is very much smaller than that of birds, reptiles or even monotremes, because the ovum of a placental mammal is devoid of yolk.

Although the ovum is small, its follicle may reach a diameter of between one and two centimetres, so that finally it protrudes from the surface of the ovary. In a woman usually one develops in each menstrual cycle, but in certain animals there may be several. When sufficiently swollen the follicle bursts and the ovum is extruded near the funnel of the Fallopian tube, which it then descends. This process is termed ovulation.

After sexual intercourse the spermatozoa swim up into the funnel of the Fallopian tube, and meet the descending ovum. If the egg is fertilised it attaches itself to the wall of the uterus which has been prepared by the action of the hormone progesterone liberated by the corpus luteum and the follicle liquid. In this case the corpus luteum persists and continues to supply progesterone which controls the relations beween the foetus and its mother.

If the ovum is not fertilised it passes on through the uterus and is discharged. The corpus luteum degenerates quickly, the wall of the uterus discharges its accumulation of mucus and blood, and then heals, and the cycle begins again.

GESTATION: This really begins at the moment of fertilisation and includes the few days which elapse before fixation of the fertilised ovum. Since it has no yolk the whole of the egg divides, first into a morula, then into a blastocyst. In the cavity of the blastocyst the part which gives rise to the embryo is called the inner cell mass. The swollen egg membrane forms the primary chorion.

There may be simple fixation to the wall of the uterus or, as in humans, implantation. In both cases a double foetal membrane is formed; first an amnion, a protective sac round the embryo containing an amniotic fluid, then an allantois or respiratory membrane. Both are attached to the embryo through the umbilical cord. In placental mammals the primary chorion and allantois are soon fused to form a secondary chorion from which fine processes or villi protrude into the uterine wall, which becomes thickened and congested at that point. Its blood vessels dilate or even disrupt into sinus-like spaces into which grow the villi from the embryo. The organ produced by this double reaction is the placenta. Part of this organ is foetal and part maternal.

There are several sorts of placenta. In mares and sows the villi are spread over the whole surface of the chorion, forming what is called a diffuse placenta. In ruminants the villi are scattered all over the chorion in tufts (cotyledonary placenta). Each tuft or cotyledon is like a press fastener attaching the foetus to its mother. In rodents, proboscidians and carnivores the cotyledons are concentrated in a zone (zonary placenta). In primates the villi are grouped in a disc (discoidal placenta).

Pouch of a marsupial, here a female Virginian Opossum (*Didelphis virginiana*), exposing the young inside still at a very immature stage of development.

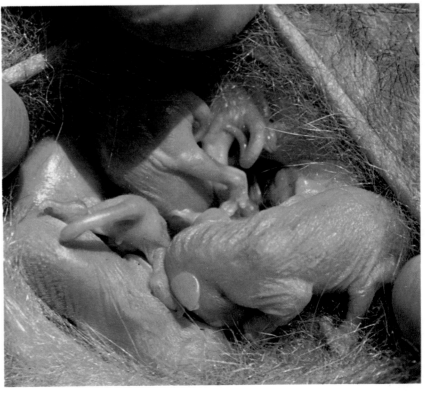

Zebra in the Etosha National Park, South-West Africa. In contrast to the development of some mammals a newly born zebra has to be prepared to run with the herd within a very short time of being born.

It is through the placenta that all alimentary, respiratory and excretory exchanges between the foetus and its mother are effected. Since there is no actual blood connection they depend on diffusion. It is not a matter of simple filtering. The exchanges are continually checked and regulated by the placenta. The blood on the maternal side is generally richer in glucose, sodium chloride, phosphates and calcium. Some toxins and even certain microbes can pass from mother to foetus, but others fail to do so. Vaccination of the mother, for example, leaves the foetus unaffected. Hormones pass only towards the end of gestation. In addition to these functions the placenta produces hormones necessary to the regulation of pregnancy.

In all placental mammals the development pattern of the embryo is constant. The heart is one of the first organs to be formed. At an early stage it begins beating automatically and regularly. (The pulse is about twice the adult rate, 140 instead of 70 in human beings). Red blood corpuscles are more numerous in the adult than the embryo, and in the embryo they originate in the liver not, as later, in red bone marrow. Since the foetus does not breathe, all gaseous exchanges take place by way of the placenta, the lungs playing no part. It is of interest that at some point in the development there must be a sudden change from one respiratory system to another, and there are changes also in the circulation. The alimentary tract, though receiving no food, secretes digestive juices and bile and contains at birth excremental matter called meconium. The kidneys function in the embryo,

secreting a small quantity of urine which accumulates in the bladder. This accounts for the immediate micturation of the young at birth. The foetal ductless glands, particularly the pituitary and thyroid, are active. All these operations are regulated by medullary and bulbar reflexes, the brain hardly functioning and remaining inert for several days after birth. The length of the gestation period varies: twenty-one months in the elephant, five in the goat and two in the dog. After gestation follow labour and parturition.

PARTURITION AND LACTATION: When the foetus has reached the end of its uterine development, the pituitary, ovarian and placental hormones, which have played such a big part in gestation, intervene once again to cause expulsion. Pain is caused by the progressive stretching of the cervix and the simultaneous contractions of the uterine muscles. With the rupture of the chorion and the amnion the fluid escapes, after which the foetus makes its appearance, still attached to the placenta by the umbilical cord, which breaks in some and needs to be severed in others. The scar left forms the navel. A few hours later the placenta itself is extruded.

The stage of development at which animals are born is subject to much variation. Guinea-pigs are no sooner born than they start running around looking for food and are capable of regulating their temperature. But many mammals are more or less incapable of fending for themselves at birth. The mother has to look after them and, if necessary, keep them warm. These differences depend chiefly on the degree of nervous development.

One of the most important mammal features is the possession of mammary glands by the female, conditioned by hormonal secretions from the ovary and pituitary. These should not be confused with mammillae or teats, the number of which is variable. In the foetus there is a mammary crest running up each side of the body from the groin to the shoulder, on which mammary buds may form. For each bud there is an elementary mammary gland and a mammilla, but several buds may fuse into a single gland which will, however, (as with the cow) have several teats. On the other hand a large number of buds may abort, which explains the wide diversity in the number of mammillae in various species.

The largest number of teats is found in the Tenrec of Madagascar, the female having eleven pairs. In cats there are four, in cows two or three, in sheep and goats one or two pairs. In horses, donkeys and whales there is only one pair situated far back (inguinal), while the single pair in primates, bats, elephants and sirenians is pectoral. The secretion of milk is induced by placental, ovarian and pituitary hormones. Immediately after birth the secretion (colostrum) is rich in proteins, but after the first few sucklings milk production becomes fully established. Milk is a complete food for mammals. It contains, dissolved in water, various mineral salts, a sugar (lactose), various proteins (casein, lactalbumin, globulin) and fats. The table below shows the extent to which the quantity (in grams) of these substances can vary per litre. A woman's milk is three times richer in fat than an ass's, so that the latter is much more easily digested by delicate stomachs. The milk of ewes and sows is much less sweet than a woman's but much richer in both proteins and fat. The creamiest milk is that of cetaceans and it enables the young to develop at an extraordinary rate. Cow's milk is one of the best balanced, since it contains about forty grams of the principal ingredients per litre.

Composition of milk of various species
(Given in grams per litre)

Species	Sugar	Proteins	Fats	Salts
Ass	66	17	11	4
Buffalo	38	62	125	8
Camel	33	30	55	7
Cat	50	92	35	11
Cow	45	35	40	9
Dog	40	70	85	11
Elephant	72	32	190	6
Ewe	50	67	70	8
Goat	47	33	40	6
Horse	60	20	12	4
Porpoise	13	110	460	6
Reindeer	29	100	175	14
Sow	32	75	45	10
Whale	4	95	200	10
Woman	75	11	35	3

The duration of lactation varies enormously: a few weeks in a guinea-pig, a little over one month in a dog, over four months in cows and mares, and six to twelve months in whales.

Sexual dimorphism

In mammals the males commonly differ from the females in obvious external characters such as their greater size, stronger voice, production of hair, manes and beards, growth of horns and often bigger canine teeth. The mammary glands are well developed in the females, but only rudimentary in the males. In the Duckbilled Platypus (*Ornithorhynchus*) the males have poisonous spurs on their hind feet, and in marsupials the females have a marsupium in which to shelter their young. These differences are termed secondary sexual features.

Secondary sexual features are influenced by hormones from the testes and ovaries. Castration before puberty stops the development of sexual characteristics. After puberty it causes their

Sexual dimorphism is present in most animals, the males developing secondary sexual characters which distinguish them from females. Only the males of true deer such as the Fallow Deer (*Dama dama*) have antlers and there are usually differences in size and pelage between the sexes. Males also have a stronger voice and more aggressive temperament.

477

The Hazel Dormouse (*Muscardinus avellanarius*) spends half the year in hibernation, in a sleep so profound that if the animal is removed from its spherical nest of dry grass and rolled across a table it still shows no sign of waking.

Many animals burrow in the ground to produce living quarters. Few do so as extensively as the European Badger (*Meles meles*). The deep and extensive burrow, known as a sett, sometimes can be used by successive generations for centuries. A single sett may have up to fifty entrances leading to tunnels and chambers at different levels and may measure a tenth of a hectare in extent.

involution. In humans eunuchs retain certain juvenile characters, such as long legs, narrow shoulders and pelvis, absence of beard or pubic hair, childish voice and subnormal intelligence. Often they tend to grow fat, that being a feminine character. In an old woman whose ovaries have degenerated, or a younger woman whose ovaries have been removed, the breasts are reduced in size and there is a tendency to grow facial hair.

The same applies to domestic animals, in which castration is widely practised to make them easier to handle (horse, ox, pig) or to make them fatten quickly (ox, sheep, rabbit). In species in which only the male has horns, castration stops their growth. For example, castrated billy goats look like females, and their scent glands regress. Conversely, grafting testicular or ovarian tissues on to castrated animals restores their sexual characters. Testicular or ovarian extracts or synthetic hormones can be injected to give the same result.

The control of the reproductive functions in vertebrates, and particularly in mammals, depends on an abundant flow of many hormones from the pituitary body and the thyroid and genital glands. The pituitary, lying under the brain, acts on the thyroid by thyrotropic hormones, and on the gonads by gonadotropic hormones. Thus stimulated, the testes are able to produce spermatozoa and, at the same time, the testicular hormones that are known to determine the secondary sexual characters, sexual instinct and rut.

With the ovaries it is more complex. First of all, there are the follicle-stimulating hormones from the pituitary and the corpus luteum whose secretion, progesterone, acts on the uterus, preparing it for gestation. The mammary glands are in turn conditioned by oestrogen and progesterone as well as by prolactine coming directly from the pituitary. Lastly, the thyroid acts on the growth of the foetus, and later on that of the child.

Mating and nest building

Although mammals are superior to birds in the development of their psychological faculties, they are not so specialised in their reproductive habits. The courting and nuptial displays so frequent in birds, particularly in the galliforms, are absent in mammals. The males generally confine themselves to fighting other males for territories. There is then some semblance of caressing, promptly followed by intercourse. In mammals there is every degree of attachment from monogamy to open polygamy, and lifelong associations are rare. In most cases monogamy does not last a season, the male passing from one female to another in the same rutting period. Roe deer and foxes are far from deserving their widespread reputation for perfect conjugal fidelity.

Nest building is common among creatures of medium or small size. The earth of the fox or the sett of a badger includes a chamber for whelping, and the female rabbit also prepares a separate isolated brood chamber. The squirrel makes a nest in the trees. Young Beavers are brought up in a lodge. The most perfected nest is that which a Harvest Mouse constructs with woven leaves and suspends from cornstalks. Even so, this is far from the immense variety of bird nests.

Egg-laying mammals (Order Monotremata)

Egg-laying mammals, which belong to the order Monotremata in the subclass Prototheria, are the most primitive mammals and those most closely related to reptiles. They are oviparous, but nourish their young after hatching with milk. They have a cloaca, two uteri, a beak, no teeth and a pectoral girdle with coracoid bones.

The form of the girdle supporting their forelimbs relates them to lizards and to the early Mesozoic reptiles of South Africa, for they have an interclavicle and two coracoids in addition to the shoulder-blades and collarbones of other mammals. The interclavicle is a single T-shaped bone joining the clavicles in front of the chest. In the monotremes the coracoids reinforce the clavicles, whereas in viviparous mammals they are represented only by the coracoid processes of the scapulae. Oviparous mammals thus display a reptilian feature that has survived in the evolutionary process.

Like marsupials the monotremes possess a pair of bones which rise from the anterior edge of the pelvis into the abdominal muscles. These are rudimentary or vestigial marsupial bones, analogous to those which support the marsupium in opossums and kangaroos. They may indicate the former existence of a pouch as ample and permanent as that in present-day marsupials. In echidnas the pouch develops only during the breeding period and in this the single egg is placed.

The monotreme beak may be long and round or short and flat. In the young it may have milk teeth (molars) which are not replaced when shed. These molars have numerous cusps reminiscent of Mesozoic fossils.

Unlike other mammals in which the anus and urogenital aperture are separate, oviparous mammals have a cloaca like birds and reptiles. The genital organs are also primitive. The oviducts are separate right down to the urogenital sinus, which leads to the cloaca. Their temperature is constant, but does not exceed 28·3°C.

Eggs are spherical and have a horny shell containing a thin layer of white round a large yellow yolk. As each egg passes down the oviduct it is bathed in an abundant mucous secretion, which it absorbs by osmosis through the shell. This secretion enables it to increase in size from that of a pea to that of a cherry. When laid the eggs

Detailed data on the mammalian types

Type	Max. length (cm)	Max. height (cm)	max. weight (kg)	Gestation (days)	Litters (per year)	Number in litter	Max. life-span (yrs)
Antelope	260	174	1,000	215–275	1	1–2	20
Ass	268	158	410	375	1	1	45
Badger	76	—	15	180	1	3–5	15
Barbary Ape	75	70	13	210	1	1	27
Bat (Flying Fox)	46	168(wing-span)	0·9	60	1	1	15
Bear (European Brown)	200	250(erect)	400	210–250	1 every other year	1–2	30
Bear (Polar)	260	268(erect)	600	250	1	1–2	34
Beaver	100	—	30	128	1	2–6	20
Bison	300	180	1,500	275	1	1	30
Boar (Wild)	170	100	300	112	1	3–15	30
Buffalo	290	190	1,000	340	1	1	16
Camel	338	180	700	350–400	1	1	40
Cat (Domestic)	54	30	4	60	2	3–6	20
Cat (Wild)	70	—	7	60	1	3–6	10
Chamois	146	80	40	165	1	1–2	20
Chimpanzee	—	140(erect)	75	270	1	1	50
Coypu	61	—	7	100	2–3	5–8	5
Dog	140	100	100	65	2	2–16	20
Elephant (African)	774	366	7,000	640	1 every other year	1	70
Elephant Seal	695	—	3,000	330	1	1	20
Elk (European)	280	210	1,000	250	1	1–2	25
Fallow Deer	150	88	70	240	1	1	25
Ferret	40	—	1	60	2	5–10	13
Fox	80	37	10	54	1	3–8	14
Gibbon	—	100(erect)	12	210	1	1	23
Giraffe	472	347	1,000	440	1 every other year	1	28
Goat	165	80	80	150	1–3	2–3	10
Guinea-pig	35	—	0·8	60	2–3	2–6	5
Hare	70	—	5	42	2–4	2–5	10
Hedgehog	30	—	0·8	60	1–2	3–7	5
Hippopotamus	347	158	3,000	240	1–2	1	41
Horse	330	25	1,300	335	1	1–2	60
Hyaena	150	140	75	93	1	2–4	25
Ibex	150	90	109	150	1	1–2	30
Kangaroo	150	182	100	40	1	1	13
Lion	200	100	250	106	1	2–4	40
Llama	240	120	134	330	1	1	20
Lynx	120	—	15	70	1	2–4	10
Lemur	50	—	—	60	1	1–2	20
Manatee	300	—	500	270	1	1–2	8
Marmoset	20	—	0·2	140	1	1–3	20
Marmot	60	—	5	40	1	2–6	18
Mole (European Common)	15	—	0·1	40	1–2	3–7	3
Moufflon (European)	130	70	50	150	1	1–2	—
Mouse	10	—	0.025	21	4–6	4–8	4
Opossum	55	—	5·5	13	2	9–12	8
Orang-utan	—	130(erect)	80	260	1	1	50
Otter	90	—	22	63	1–2	2–5	15
Ox	300	150	1,500	280	1	1–2	25
Panther	120	70	65	93	1	2–5	21
Pig	250	120	600	115	2–3	6–20	15
Porcupine	55	—	15	112	—	2–3	20
Porpoise	200	—	50	360	1	1	15
Rabbit (Tame)	100	—	12	30	6–7	10–15	10
Rabbit (Wild)	46	—	1·5	30	3–4	4–10	13(5–6 average)
Red Deer	220	130	350	235	1	1–2	30
Roe Deer	140	80	45	280	1	1–2	15
Rat (Grey)	24	—	0·5	22	2–7	5–14	5
Reindeer	230	140	200	246	1	1	15
Rhinoceros	488	180	2,000	560	1 every other year	1	40
Seal (Common)	200	—	255	276	1	1–2	30
Sheep	150	80	150	150	1	1–2	14
Shrew	7	—	0·008	20	1	5–10	2
Squirrel	22	—	0·4	32–40	2	3–6	15
Tapir	200	100	300	390	1 every other year	1	30
Tiger	200	100	218	106	1 every other year	1	25
Weasel	24	—	0·13	60	1–2	3–8	8
Whale (Blue)	3,290	—	120,000	330	1 every other year	1	30
Whale (Sperm)	2,680	—	80,000	480	1	1	25
Wolf	110	80	60	63	1	3–9	16
Zebra	190	150	318	375	1	1	30

The Duckbill or Platypus (*Ornitho-rhynchus anatinus*) is an egg-laying mammal found in eastern and southern Australia and Tasmania. It is equally at home in the freezing waters of the Australian Alps and the warm tropical rivers of Queensland. However, it spends only a few hours each day in the water; most of the time it stays in its burrow in the river bank.

are placed in the marsupial pouch. The Platypus, however, lays its eggs in a nest and broods them. After hatching, the young are reared on milk from teatless mammary glands, which correspond not to the sebaceous glands of other mammals, but to the sweat glands. The milk is discharged into the marsupium or into a fold of skin in which the young is held by its head.

On each hind foot in the male there is a horny and mobile spur which is pierced by a narrow canal leading from a poisonous gland. As it is present only in the male it is difficult to regard it as a defensive weapon. The idea of its serving to hold the female during coitus is not borne out by the practice. Another theory suggests that through the spurs the male injects the female with a toxin which reduces her resistance to coupling.

The monotremes, then, are a survival of an ancient animal type. There are only two living types, the Duckbilled Platypus and the Spiny Anteater, both of which are confined to Australia, Tasmania and New Guinea.

Duckbilled Platypus

The Duckbill or Duckmole (*Ornithorhynchus*) is a native of the rivers of Tasmania and southeastern Australia, where it is also known as the Water Mole. Its various names refer only to superficial resemblances. It might equally well have been called the Australian Beaver, as it looks much like a smaller form of beaver, particularly with its flattened tail and its habit of lying in burrows whose entrance is underwater. Its short, velvety fur is reddish brown above and greyish below.

The Duckbill is one of the marsupial animals well adapted to aquatic life. It has very short fur and lacks an external ear. Its clawed paws have five digits and are broadly webbed like a duck's

feet. Its broad, flat beak, covered with a highly sensitive skin, is a wonderful instrument for grubbing in the sand or muddy river bottoms. The broad, flattened tail serves as a horizontal rudder in diving or surfacing.

The Duckbill is also a burrowing animal. Its burrow in the river bank consists of a long gallery opening both above and below water and leads to a spacious chamber lined with dry grasses. Here the female lays and hatches two eggs, rarely more. They are white, soft and compressible, with a leathery shell. The newborn young are weak and naked and are taken head first into a fold of their mother's skin, where the milk is discharged.

Two features of this animal are the presence of temporary molar milk teeth, which disappear in the adult state, and the absence of cerebral convolutions. The male is distinguished by its greater size and by the spurs on its hind legs.

The first specimen was discovered in New South Wales in 1797. It was thought to be an aquatic mole and seemed the most extraordinary mammal in existence, with a duck's beak affixed to the head of a quadruped. Dissection of another specimen revealed many of its strange features, but it was not until some years later that its very primitive mammary glands were discovered and its oviparous habit definitely established.

Echidna

The second monotreme to be discovered was an Echidna (*Tachyglossus aculeatus*), also called the Porcupine Anteater or Spiny Anteater on account of the spines on its back. Unlike the Duckbill it is a land animal, its habitat being the sandy and rocky parts of Australia, Tasmania and New Guinea. The feet are not webbed but have plantar pads (i.e. on the sole of the foot). Being a burrower, it has strong claws. It has a rudimentary tail and a convoluted brain. Its snout is long and cylindrical with a sticky vermiform tongue with which it captures ants. The sexes are externally alike. The one or two eggs laid by the female are placed in a rudimentary marsupial pouch, which develops to coincide with laying. The mammary secretion is discharged into this pouch. The young have neither milk teeth nor teeth germs. The Echidna's gait is ungainly because of its claws, but it can move with great rapidity. In a few moments, particularly if frightened, it can burrow well out of reach. Alternatively, it can roll up like a hedgehog. There is a second species, the Long-beaked Echidna (*Zaglossus bruijni*), in New Guinea.

Primitive mammals
Pouch-bearing mammals
(Order Marsupialia)

The infraclass Metatheria or pouch-bearing mammals is decidedly more advanced than the monotremes and therefore further removed from the common stem of mammals, birds and reptiles. In this group the clavicles are not reinforced by coracoid bones. There is no beak and dentition is permanent. A muscular wall (perineum) separates the anus from the urogenital apertures. Mammary glands are grouped in true mammae ending in mammillae or teats. In addition to these anatomical advances, the eggs hatch in the oviducts instead of being laid. Marsupials or pouch-bearing mammals thus deserve a higher zoological position than the monotremes.

These animals are, however, still far from the level of the placental mammals. Their teeth, although not replaced by a beak, are not replaced by a second dentition either. The only change is the addition at a certain age of large molar teeth to the initial incisors, canines and premolars. Only the four last premolars are replaced, but it is now agreed that this is not really the substitution of one set for another, since the new tooth is a milk premolar that has been held in reserve, Marsupials are therefore fully entitled to be described as monophyodont, having only one set of teeth.

Another primitive character in marsupials is that in the female the oviducts are only joined towards the end, where they form a vagina, divided into two by a median partition. Otherwise they are quite separate, each having a swelling or uterus quite unconnected with the other.

Whereas the monotremes lay eggs, the marsupials retain theirs in the uterus until after hatching. But there is no placenta connecting the embryo to the mother and the foetus is born at such an early stage that the period of uterine gestation must be followed by a further period of development in the pouch. In the largest of the kangaroos the newborn is, at most, the size of a haricot bean, and in the opossum it is even smaller (a dozen do not fill a teaspoon). The only senses functioning—and these only in an elementary way—are touch and smell.

In most marsupials the female has an abdominal pouch, or marsupium in which the mammae are lodged. Into this the newborn offspring makes its way, climbing through the mother's fur after emerging from the vagina. On arrival there it grasps a mammilla in its mouth, which is ringed by a powerful muscle, and it does not leave it during the whole period of lactation. It has no power to suck and would die of inanition but for the muscular action of the mammae, which from time to time squirt milk into its mouth. To enable it to breathe freely during this suckling, its larynx is extended by a tube to the nasal fossae.

In the jumping and arboreal marsupials the pouch opens forwards; that is, upwards when the animal jumps or climbs, and in running and walking types the opening is often to the rear. Sometimes the pouch is no more than folds in the skin, and sometimes even these are so slight that there is virtually no pouch at all. The marsupial bones are often said to support the marsupium, but their more probable function is to support the weight of the intestines, and they are most likely a survival of certain bones in reptiles.

Distribution

Marsupials were the dominant mammals in the Mesozoic era, when they appear to have been spread over the whole of the existing continents. Their small size and arboreal habit must have enabled them to keep out of reach of the great reptiles that were then the lords of creation. In the Cretaceous period they began to disappear in Europe, probably in competition with the more advanced placental mammals. In the Cainozoic era the only marsupials found in Europe are some

forms allied to the present-day American opossums, but these also disappeared under growing pressure from placental mammals.

Present-day marsupials are restricted in distribution, being confined to Australasia and South America, with one species overflowing into North America. It is certain that the survival of marsupials in the first of these areas is due to the geographical isolation of Australia and New Guinea from the mainland of Asia, from the Cretaceous period onwards. In Europe it appears that the marsupials gave way to better adapted placental mammals; but they maintained themselves in Australasia, which was already out of those mammals' reach. A surprising contrast is presented between the faunas of Celebes and Borneo (two islands between which lies a deep marine depression, corresponding to what has been called Wallace's Line), for while there are no marsupials in the Celebes, in all the islands west of Wallace's Line, in Borneo, Java and Sumatra, the mammals are placental. This line therefore marks the boundary between two long-separated worlds, Australasia and Asia.

The preservation of the American marsupials is more difficult to explain, for in that area they exist side by side with placental mammals which should theoretically have destroyed them. One possibility is that the placental mammals reached South America in comparatively recent times—in the middle of the Cainozoic, for instance—having come from Asia to North America over land connections which have since subsided. Another factor which suggests the late arrival of placental mammals in South America is that until relatively recent geological times North and South America were separated and there was a more or less continuous sea where Central America now lies. If

The Long-beaked Echidna (*Zaglossus bruijni*), living in the high, humid forests of New Guinea, is a very large echidna growing up to a hundred centimetres long. An outstanding feature is its very long snout and its very long tongue, which is over twenty centimetres in length. It is thought to live on worms, ants and termites.

The Common or Virginian Opossum (*Didelphis marsupialis*) is the only marsupial in the United States, from where it is spreading northwards into Canada. At birth the young are only a centimetre long. After being suckled in the pouch for about three months they come out and ride on their mother's back. The arboreal habits of this opossum are strikingly illustrated in this picture.

A Murine Opossum (*Marmosa*), of South America, with its babies on its back, climbing a tree. Its long prehensile tail is wrapped loosely round a branch when climbing and it sometimes hangs by the tail alone. There are about forty species in the genus *Marmosa*. They eat mainly insects and fruit.

these views are correct then the presence of one marsupial, the Virginian Opossum in North America, would be because this species had extended its range northwards after North and South America had once more become connected.

Being the most numerous mammals in Australia, the marsupials have been able to occupy every part of it, adapting themselves to the many different habitats. Accordingly we find paralleled in them all the means of locomotion and every kind of feeding habit found elsewhere in the world among the placental mammals. Thus there are running, jumping, burrowing, arboreal and even aquatic marsupials. Some are carnivorous or insectivorous, others herbivorous; and among the latter there are those that feed on roots, on leaves, on fruit and on nectar. Some resemblances to placentals are so perfect that experts have often

been mistaken. The Thylacine is very like a wolf, while others resemble civet cats or weasels. Among herbivorous types are counterparts of marmots, squirrels, rats, mice, dormice and jerboas. A charming Australian form, the Koala, resembles a small bear, and marsupial moles are remarkably like the placental moles.

It might be thought possible to classify marsupials according to these various adaptations, grouping them, for instance, as insectivores, carnivores, rodents, herbivores, as has been done with the placental mammals. Such a clasification is not possible for marsupials, for it would bring together distantly related types and separate close relatives. Zoologists have therefore generally divided marsupials according to their dentition into two suborders, the Polyprotodontia and the Diprotodontia.

The Polyprotodontia have numerous teeth at the front of the mouth; in other words, they have many incisors. They also have canines developed into fangs and molars with cutting crowns. In short, they have a dentition similar to that of such widely diverse placentals as cats and hedgehogs, which they also resemble in their carnivorous or insectivorous diet. They are found in both Australia and America and include opossums, dasyures, theylacines and bandicoots, only the first named being found in North and South America.

The Diprotodontia, on the other hand, have in the lower jaw only two incisors. Canines are either absent altogether or are only rudimentary, and the flattened molars have many fine tubercles, suitable for crushing vegetable matter. These are the herbivorous and frugivorous types, paralleling the squirel, dormouse or antelope. Only a few are insectivorous. All Diprotodontia live in Australasia, the most important being the kangaroos, phalangers, wombats and koalas. Examples of dental formulae are:

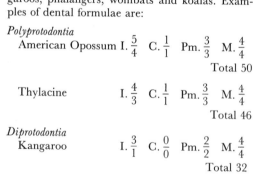

Polyprotodontia
American Opossum I. $\frac{5}{4}$ C. $\frac{1}{1}$ Pm. $\frac{3}{3}$ M. $\frac{4}{4}$
Total 50

Thylacine I. $\frac{4}{3}$ C. $\frac{1}{1}$ Pm. $\frac{3}{3}$ M. $\frac{4}{4}$
Total 46

Diprotodontia
Kangaroo I. $\frac{3}{1}$ C. $\frac{0}{0}$ Pm. $\frac{2}{2}$ M. $\frac{4}{4}$
Total 32

American opossums (Family Didelphidae)

The American marsupials are arboreal and altogether different from the Australian opossums or phalangers, being polyprotodont and not diprotodont. They have numerous incisors in both upper and lower jaws, their canines are well developed and their molars sharp. They are mainly insectivorous and carnivorous rather than herbivorous, though they also eat grain, carrion and fruits and cause considerable damage to crops.

The Common or Virginian Opossum *(Didelphis marsupialis)* ranges from south and east of the United States—where it is the only marsupial— to the Argentine. It grows bigger than a cat and is rat-like. It has a pointed snout. Its long, almost bare tail is prehensile. It frequents fields, orchards and farmyards. Carrion, insects, small vertebrates, mushrooms, fruit, berries, grain and—rarely—poultry compose its diet. Its wiliness recalls the fox. When struck it feigns death, lying inert with tongue lolling out and eyes closed.

In the cooler climate of their habitat, the opossums found in the United States have thick fur, varying through every shade from black to white, while in the same species in tropical America the coat is frequently found to be dark or black.

Opossums are sedentary. It has been found, by using marked animals, that they rarely wander from their locality, that males are rather more numerous than females, and that adults live in isolated pairs.

In wooded districts the opossum is arboreal, sleeping in tree hollows, but in the open plains in burrows, enlarging burrows dug by other animals to about 1.5 metres deep. Sometimes it lives with other animals such as the armadillo. Its fur is much sought after, particularly in December and January, when it is at its thickest. It is estimated that a million are caught yearly in Texas alone.

Even after such extensive hunting for close on a century, opossums are not threatened with extinction, because, like the phalangers and koalas of Australia, their superiority lies in their fecundity. The female generally bears two litters of nine each year, usually in February and June. After a thirteen-day uterine gestation, the newly born young climb through their mother's fur and enter the pouch, where they stay for about three months.

The family includes numerous South American species, some of which are no bigger than rats or mice. Some are arboreal, some terrestrial, one is even aquatic.

Among the small arboreal opossums are the murine opossums (genus *Marmosa*) ranging from Mexico to Brazil, which have no pouch at all. The young make their way on to the mother's back as soon as they let go of the teats. The mother climbs along the branches with a whole litter on her back. There is, hoewever, no truth in the well-established idea that they maintain their position by winding their tails round the mother's tail.

The terrestrial short-tailed opossums (genus *Peramys*) of Guiana, Brazil and the Argentine, have short tails which are not prehensile. This family also includes the only marsupial adapted to an aquatic life, the Water Opossum (*Chironectes minimus*) of Argentina to Mexico, whose habits are so like those of the otter that earlier naturalists classified the two in the same group. Its hind feet are webbed, and its bare tail is scaly and non-prehensile. It burrows in river banks and feeds entirely on other aquatic animals. The female has a pouch which it is able to close while diving.

Dasyures (Family Dasyuridae)

These are terrestrial, often carnivorous animals, which in habits and instincts are the counterpart of weasels, martens, wild cats and wolves among the placental mammals, and hold on the Australian continent the same ecological position as those animals do elsewhere. The teeth number forty-two (as in dogs) or forty-six, including fang-like canines and sharply cusped molars. Among the smaller kinds are the Australian Eastern Native Cat (*Dasyurus quoll*), which is the size of a Domestic Cat, and the marsupial rats (genus *Phascogale*).

The native cat is readily recognised by its grey or brown coat marked with almost pure white spots. It is a handsome animal with a reputation for savagery and destructiveness on the farm. Although not truly arboreal, it may spend the daytime in trees and bring forth its young there. There is also the arboreal Tiger Cat, or Spotted-tailed Native Cat (*Dasyurops maculatus*), nearly 120 centimetres long, fifty centimetres of which is tail.

Marsupial rats can be distinguished by their uniform coats and their general resemblance to rats or mice. The females lack a pouch. Marsupial rats and marsupial mice live in all sorts of rocky and craggy sites, feeding on smaller rodents.

The Tasmanian Devil (*Sarcophilus harrisii*) whose reputation for savagery has been much exaggerated, was once widespread in Australia but is now confined to Tasmania. It is stockily built and powerful, with a large head and strong jaws and teeth, but it rarely exceeds a metre in length. Although a land animal it forages along river banks and beaches.

The Northern Short-nosed Bandicoot (*Isodon macrourus*) of northern and north-east Australia. All bandicoots have long noses, but those of the short-nosed bandicoots are shorter than most. With these long noses they dig small conical-shaped holes in the ground searching for food such as insect larvae, worms and spiders.

Included in the Dasyuridae are two big and ferocious animals, the Tasmanian Devil (*Sarcophilus harrisi*) and the Thylacine or Tasmanian Wolf or Tiger (*Thylacinus cynocephalus*), in both of which the pouch opens backwards. Although the Tasmanian Devil is now confined to Tasmania it used to live in Australia. It is badger-like with a large bear-like face, powerful jaws, short strong limbs and strong claws. Its colour, dark brown or black is relieved by only a few white patches. Tractable in captivity, it has the reputation of being savage in the extreme in the wild state, its chief victim being sheep, though it attacks anything, and one has been known to kill fifty-four chickens, six geese, an albatross and a cat in two nights.

The Thylacine (*Thylacinus cynocephalus*) is also now confined to Tasmania. It is sometimes known as the Tasmanian Wolf. Its coat is red-brown with dark transverse stripes on the rear part of the back. Nocturnal in habit and with a highly developed scent, it formerly lived by hunting kangaroos and wallabies; then came the flocks of sheep and it readily switched to an easier prey. The thylacines have now been exterminated in Australia and driven back into the most inaccessible territory in Tasmania. They may now be extinct since nothing has been seen of them for so many years.

The Banded Anteater or Numbat (*Myrmecobius fasciatus*) has a pointed snout and long, extensile, worm-like tongue with which it catches ants and termites. It has fifty teeth, a number exceeded only in porpoises and dolphins. Its red-brown coat is marked on the back with white transverse stripes. The tail is long and velvety. As the female lacks a pouch, the young simply hang from the teats, protected by the long hair of the mother's abdominal fur. A second species used to be recognised, the south Australian Banded Anteater or Rusty Numbat (*M. rufus*) but this is now generally accepted as conspecific with *M. fasciatus*.

Marsupial mole (Family Notoryctidae)

The Marsupial Mole (*Notoryctes typhlops*) was not discovered until 1889. It is mole-like, with a pointed snout, short close fur and powerfully clawed front feet. Its eyes are buried beneath closed eyelids, and it feeds on insects. Its method of progression is as follows: after a short distance on the surface it dives into the soil, opening a passage with its muzzle and fore paws and closing this behind itself with the hind paws. Thus no permanent tunnel is left. After proceeding several metres at a depth of less than a metre, it comes up to the surface again and repeats the manoeuvre. A second species used to be recognised, the north-western Marsupial Mole (*N. caurinus*) but is now generally accepted as conspecific with *N. typhlops*.

Bandicoots (Family Peramelidae)

In this family are grouped the true bandicoots (genus *Perameles*), the bilbies or rabbit bandicoots (genus *Thylacomys*), the short-nosed bandicoots (genus *Isodon*), and the pig-footed bandicoots (genus *Choeropus*). One of the most common species in Tasmania is the Tasmanian Barred Bandicoot (*Perameles gunni*), whose hind quarters are marked with a few black stripes arranged symmetrically on either side of a longitudinal black band. Like other bandicoots it is extremely swift and lively in its movements. Sometimes it is kept as a pet and soon becomes one of the family. Sleeping all day, it becomes intensely busy at night, running and jumping in all directions. It is a charming animal, despite the harm it does to gardens.

Bandicoots have numerous incisors, as well as canines and sharp molars. The snout is pointed and the diet omnivorous, most of their food being animal (insects and worms). Their liking for roots and tubers earns them the farmer's dislike. They remain underground until dark and return there by daybreak, having meanwhile covered a considerable distance in their jumping gait which, though less developed, recalls that of a kangaroo. As in the latter their hind legs (particularly the feet) are elongated.

Phalangers, Australian possums, cuscus (Family Phalangeridae)

The members of this family are adapted to an arboreal life. Many of them resemble dormice or squirrels, and almost all have a prehensile tail. Their fore paws are the same size as the hind paws, and some have lateral membranes which serve as parachutes. Their teeth tend to be of the insectivorous type, with canines and sharply cusped molars. In fact their food varies from leaves and insects to bird eggs and the birds themselves. As species called the Honey Possum (*Tarsipes spenserae*) drinks nectar.

The most typical are the cuscuses and phalangers that range from Australia to Celebes. Their tails are barred along half their length and highly prehensile. Their fur is short, woolly and sometimes pleasantly spotted. One of the most widespread species is the Brush-tail or Vulpine Possum (*Trichosurus vulpecula*), which is about the size of a fox and haunts wooded hollows in Australia and Tasmania. It is nocturnal in habit and rarely seen, but is hunted by moonlight for its valuable fur. Hunted for the same reason are the ring-tailed opossums (genus *Pseudochirus*), which are distinguished from all others by building a nest much like the squirrels.

The Great Glider Possum (*Schoinobates volans*) inhabits the forests and tall woodland areas of eastern Australia. All gliders have a flap-like extension of their body skin which can be stretched between fore and hind limbs. The Greater Glider differs slightly from the others in that the membrane stretches from albow to ankle and it glides with its arms bent inwards from the elbow.

Another group, known as the flying phalangers, living in eastern Australia and Tasmania, have fur of a thickness and beauty which make it extremely valuable. The gliding possums or flying phalangers resemble flying squirrels, but are readily revealed as marsupials by their ventral pouches. Their likeness to flying squirrels is not through relationship but similarity of environment. The resemblance is heightened by the long bushy tail, which contrasts sharply with that of most other phalangers that have prehensile tails.

The typical genus is *Petaurus*, which includes the Sugar Glider (*P. breviceps*) or Short-headed Flying Phalanger. This is a charming animal the size of a squirrel, with a grey back and white front, living in southeastern and eastern Austalia, as well as in New Guinea. Another is the Feather-tailed Glider or Pigmy Flying Phalanger (*Acrobates pygmaeus*) barely fifteen centimetres long overall, half of which is tail. This marsupial dwarf is rather like a mouse with a busy tail and a membrane stretched out between the extended limbs. *Burramys parvus* was known only from fossils until discovered alive in 1966.

Koalas (Family Phascolarctidae)

The Australian Koala (*Phascolarctos cinereus*) is like a toy come to life. It is small, weighing five to eight kilograms in the adult state. It is extremely clean, very affectionate and the young play together delightfully.

The young Koala is very small when born and spends six months in its mother's pouch, after which it is carried on her back until half grown. This heavy load does not deter the mother from climbing to the tops of the gum trees (eucalyptus), where mother and child gather their favourite leaves and flowers, the scent of which impregnates their bodies. Its voice is very like the wail of a child.

Its smell makes the Koala inedible, but the fur was once as much in demand as that of the phalanger. The fur of both is known in the trade as possum. Intensive hunting of Koalas and phalangers began towards the end of the last century, and between 1919 and 1922 eight millions were killed. In order to save these animals from extermination a national park has been created in Queensland and another in Victoria. Considering the unique fauna of Australasia, the importance of this cannot be overstated.

Wombats (Family Phascolomidae)

There are two species of wombat, the Common Wombat (*Vombatus hirsutus*) and the Island Wombat (*V. ursinus*) differing only in size and colouring. In addition there is a somewhat similar hairy-nosed wombat (*Lasiorhinus latifrons*). Wombats are somewhat badger-like, but their dentition is similar to that found in rodents. The two incisors in each jaw, which are enamelled on the outer side only, are ground by wear into sharp cutting edges. The canines are completely lacking. The molars are provided with transverse crests which emphasise the dental resemblance to rats or rabbits. Wombats are omnivorous, though vegetable food predominates, as their teeth would suggest. They are again like the rodents in living socially and in riddling the earth with their

The Koala (*Phascolarctos cinereus*) is a slow-moving, heavily built marsupial, superficially bear-like in appearance. Although once considered an endangered species, today it is one of the few marsupials whose numbers are definitely increasing. This is largely due to increased public interest and an active management programme.

The Hairy-nosed Wombat (*Lasiorhinus latifrons*) inhabits the woodland savannah and grassy plains of more arid, inland Australia. It digs complex burrow systems or warrens in which, very often, the entrances of a number of burrows meet together at a crater about a metre deep, large enough for a vehicle to fall into. Above ground, the entrances to a warren are connected to a network of trails leading to feeding areas and to other warrens.

The Red Kangaroo (*Macropus rufus*) is the best-known and most widely distributed of all kangaroo species. When on the move it can cover anything from five to eleven metres at a jump and it can sometimes reach a speed of forty kilometres an hour.

Kangaroos almost typify the unusual fauna of Australia but as sheep grazing extended into their natural habitat they became unpopular, as competition arose between these indigenous animals and the introduced sheep. The result has been that the graziers, as the sheep farmers prefer to be called, have been forced into a running battle to prevent the kangaroo from out-grazing the sheep.

burrows. The Tasmanian species, *V. ursinus*, is so bristly that its fur is used as a doormat.

Kangaroos (Family Macropodidae)

Their peculiar gait and the size of their marsupial pouches have made the kangaroos the best-known of the marsupials. Their jumping movements might almost be taken as symbolic of the rapid advance of Australia during the last century, and indeed they figure prominently on stamps and coats of arms. Outside Australia they are found only in Tasmania and New Guinea and they inhabit a few of the neighbouring islands as well.

The two largest species are the Red Kangaroo (*Macropus rufus*) and the Great Grey Kangaroo (*M. giganteus*), the males of which weigh 100 kilograms and are nearly 150 centimetres long from the muzzle to the root of the tail. The Red Kangaroo lives chiefly in the highlands of southern and eastern Australia, while the Great Grey Kangaroo frequents the lower-lying prairies.

The kangaroos have two lower incisors which project forward and have bevel-edges, and upon these play the six smaller incisors. In place of the canines is a bare ridge or diastema, like the bar in the horse's mouth. Behind, hidden by the cheeks, are six grinding teeth in each half jaw. They are flat and tuberculate, suitable for prolonged chewing of the vegetable materials cropped by the incisors, for kangaroos are herbivorous in the literal sense.

The peculiar structure of the limbs and tail determines their attitude when browsing, resting or running. The fore legs are short and, in the smaller species, serve to pick up food and carry it to the mouth. Kangaroos have been observed to use the fore limbs when fighting or playing among themselves. The normal method of defence is, however, to kick out with the powerful hind legs.

The hind legs are unusually long. Still more important, they are made up of three more or less equal parts, thigh, shin and foot. The great length of the foot has an elongated metatarsus, and a powerful central toe, which is much more developed than the others. With this strongly clawed toe it can disembowel a dog attempting to attack. The hind legs are Z-shaped like those of the frog, grasshopper and other jumping animals.

When the kangaroos are in motion they cover five to eleven metres at a jump, the body being carried horizontally and remaining at about the same height from the ground throughout the jump. All the work is done by the hind legs, while the tail curves upwards and serves as a counterpoise. the jump is entirely in a forward direction and not upwards, a method far less fatiguing than lifting the body at each movement.

At rest, the weight is carried by a tripod consisting of the hind legs and the tail. The latter is long and very strong and is used in ordinary locomotion, when, with the animal starting on all fours and its tail, the hind legs are lifted slightly and thrust forward until level with or even beyond the fore legs. Then the fore legs follow, bringing the animal back to the position it started from. It is not easy to realise the contribution made by the tail when the hind legs are moving forward. It carries the greater part of the weight of the body, hardly less than when the animal leans back on it

The name 'wallaby' is reserved for the smaller species of kangaroo in which the feet of the adult are less than twenty-five centimetres long. One of the larger species is the Swamp Wallaby (*Wallabia bicolor*), *bicolor* referring to the contrast between its dark brown back and the rich rusty yellow underparts. Although often found in thick swamps and mangrove shallows, it is truly a bush wallaby haunting hillsides and mountain tops.

The Black Tree Kangaroo (*Dendrolagus ursinus*) of the dense, tropical rain-forests of New Guinea. Closely related to the other kangaroos, it has become adapted to an arboreal life with cushion-like soles to the feet covered with roughened skin which prevents slipping on smooth surfaces. The hands are large and powerfully nailed for grasping and the tail acts as a balancer.

Rufous Rat-Kangaroo (*Aepyprymnus rufescens*), of Queensland and northern New South Wales, lives on the open plains and among dense forest grasses. It is nocturnal and builds a grass nest in which to shelter during the day, emerging at night to forage for roots and plants.

in an attitude of self-defence, freeing the hind feet for use as weapons.

When lying down a kangaroo generally takes one of two positions. It may either lie on its stomach, the hind legs on each side and the fore legs together, which is the best position for sudden movement, or when absolutely assured that all is well, it will lie in complete comfort right on its side with all its legs together. Even so, it will often keep its head raised for observation. These animals are indeed very mistrustful and easily frightened, and they rely on hearing and smell for their safety.

Reproduction is slow, as a rule, since most have only one offspring each year, but a new baby is born almost as soon as the previous one leaves the pouch. When it is born, after some forty days of uterine gestation, it crawls up through the fur until it reaches the pouch and attaches itself to a teat. There it remains uninterruptedly for two months. During the third month it begins to go out and look for food, returning to the pouch between its expeditions.

Kangaroos sometimes invade the pastures of sheep and cattle. Hunting them is done on horseback with the aid of specially trained rough-haired greyhounds. A twenty-seven kilometre chase has been recorded, the last three kilometres being in the sea, for kangaroos are excellent swimmers.

Besides the two species mentioned, there are some fifty others ranging in size from the Red and Great Grey Kangaroos down to the smallest, commonly called wallabies, some of which also belong to the same genus (*Macropus*) as the larger kangaroos, others to the related genera *Petrogale*, *Onychogalea* and *Lagorchestes*. The petrogales or rock-wallabies live in the rocky regions of southern Australia. The Yellow-footed or Ring-tailed Rock-wallaby (*P. xanthopus*) is handsomely coloured with yellowish feet and ears, and banded tail. The nail-tailed wallabies (genus *Onychogales*) have a nail at the end of the tail, which has given to one of their species the name of *O. unguifera* (the specific name means 'nail-bearer'). The hare-wallabies (genus *Lagorchestes*) derive their name from their resemblance to the hare. In addition to these wallabies there are kangaroos which are no bigger than rats, the rat-kangaroos, commonly living in

gardens and potato-fields where they find abundant food. There are also the tree-kangaroos (genus *Dendrolagus*) whose manner of life recalls that of the oppossums of South America. They are plentiful in New Guinea, living in the densest parts of the forest, but in Australia are found only in Queensland. They are very agile, using the tail as a balancer. They sometimes make extraordinary leaps from branch to branch or to the ground.

Placental or true mammals

True mammals or Eutheria are characterised by the possession of a placenta ensuring nutritive and respiratory exchange between mother and foetus through villi growing out from the allantois which penetrate special blood vessels of the uterine wall, the oxygen and other products passing through the thin partition separating the two blood systems.

As a result of the placenta the young can be born in a more advanced condition. Moreover, if uterine gestation is long, the suckling period can be shortened, and, while it lasts, the young need no longer be attached to the mother's mammae. Suckling takes place at regular intervals.

Another feature of the placentals is that they have one womb, which may be divided, bicorned or simple but never double as in the marsupials.

The placentals are also called Eutheria to indicate their place at the summit of the animal kingdom, but not all have reached the same degree of evolution. Insectivores and edentates, for example, are decidedly primitive.

Insect-eating mammals
(Order Insectivora)

In keeping with the small size of the creatures on which they live, the Insectivora are themselves small. The Hedgehog is one of the largest; the smallest is Savi's Pigmy Shrew (*Suncus etruscus*), which is only 3·8 centimetres long without the tail and is the smallest known mammal.

Insectivores are often confused with rodents, but the resemblance is only superficial. Insectivores have long snouts richly supplied with vibrissae, which are probably tactile in function. Their dentition is generally complete, and the incisors are not bevel-edged, but all teeth are pointed or tuberculate, suitable for seizing and crushing insects. The total number may be forty or forty-four, but in shrews it is only twenty-eight or thirty-two, as some incisors and premolars have disappeared. Here are some dental formulae:

Mole   I.$\frac{3}{3}$ C.$\frac{1}{1}$ Pm.$\frac{4}{4}$ M.$\frac{3}{3}$ Total 44

Hedgehog   I.$\frac{3}{2}$ C.$\frac{1}{1}$ Pm.$\frac{3}{2}$ M.$\frac{3}{3}$ Total 36

Shrew
(European   I.$\frac{3}{1}$ C.$\frac{1}{1}$ Pm.$\frac{3}{1}$ M.$\frac{3}{3}$ Total 32
Common)

'The hedgehog, the shrew and the mole', according to Vogt, the German zoologist, 'are the three types representing the Insectivora in our regions . . . The two jaws bristle with points and cusps, and there are dagger-like teeth, sometimes in the place of canines, sometimes right behind, on the crowns of molars. Sharp cones with points resembling the teeth of a saw alternate with teeth like the blade of a pocket-knife. This conformation indicates teeth designed to seize and transfix hard-shelled insects, like the Coleoptera... The Insectivora neither masticate nor crush. Their teeth bite and perforate. The crowns are not blunted by the grind of mastication; what rubbing there is only sharpens them'.

Apart from this highly specialised dentition, the Insectivora have retained a number of primitive characters: their feet have five-clawed toes and are plantigrade, they have shoulder girdles that have well-developed clavicles, small unconvoluted brains, internal testes, bicorned uteri, and numerous teats. The young are born very weak, and remain several weeks in the nest.

Contrasting with these characters is one which relates the Insectivora to the primates and thus to man: discoidal placenta.

The Insectivora vary greatly in their pelage, the length of their tail and in their habits. They may

A family of hedgehogs, including mother and young. Although so rotund and short-legged, the European Hedgehog (*Erinaceus europaeus*) is surprisingly agile. It can run fast when put to it, climb well and swim expertly. In the colder parts of its range it hibernates for four to five months in winter. Its nest is usually sited under a pile of dead vegetation, logs or thick undergrowth.

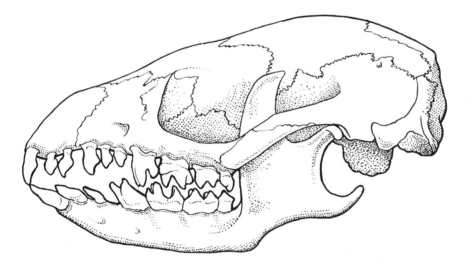

The skull of typical insectivores (moles, hedgehogs and shrews) is primitive in shape, with a small brain-case and elongated jaws bearing between forty-four and forty-eight teeth. The incisors and canines are sometimes not clearly distinguished from each other. In contrast, the molars and premolars are specialised for an insectivorous diet, the triangular or rectangular crowns bearing sharp cusps.

be terrestrial, arboreal or aquatic; they may be jumping or burrowing, nocturnal or diurnal. Several hibernate.

There are a great many species distributed over the world, with the exception of Australia, where their place is taken by the insectivorous marsupials.

Hedgehogs (Family Erinaceidae)

These are characterised by an armature of spines all over the back and sides, which can be erected by powerful skin muscles. They can roll up into a ball, so that the unprotected parts—the belly, legs and head, which may be either naked or hairy—are enclosed. They have thirty-six teeth, pointed or cusped, in either case sharp enough to deal with their food—insects, molluscs, reptiles, worms and small rodents. This diet makes them animals of great utility, and it is a pity they are not more common in fields and gardens. They have a taste for eggs and chicks, raiding nests on the ground, such as those of pheasants, partridges and gulls, and for this reason they are persecuted by game-keepers in some areas.

Hedgehogs are nocturnal. During the day they lie hidden under bushes, in hollows at the base of trees, or in crevices in rocks.

A feature of a hedgehog is its relative immunity against snake bites. A dose of poison that would be fatal to another animal of its size leaves it completely unaffected, and this resistance enables the European Hedgehog to kill vipers.

The gestation period is thirty to forty-nine days and litters consist of from two to seven. At birth the young are blind and have soft spines. At the end of a month they are like their parents, but without the capacity to roll themselves up. This, their ultimate means of defence, comes much later.

These remarks apply primarily to the species *Erinaceus europaeus*, which is widespread over western Europe, but with minor variations it is equally true of *E. roumanicus* of central Europe, and of the several other species in Asia and Africa.

Other species of Erinaceidae include the gymnures, long-tailed, somewhat rat-like and lacking spines, found in India and south-east Asia. The Moonrat or Raffle's Gymnure (*Echinosorex gymnurus*) is over thirty centimetres long without the

489

The Water Shrew (*Neomys fodiens*) is well adapted for swimming. Its feet are broad with toes bordered with stiff hairs, making them efficient paddles. The long tapering tail is flattened from side to side and has a keel of bristles along its underside, making it an efficient rudder. The Water Shrew feeds on small aquatic animals which it brings to the bank to eat.

The Pigmy Shrew (*Sorex minutus*) is the smallest of the northern European shrews and extends also into Asia. It measures six centimetres long. The Pigmy Shrew lives in the same terrain as the Common Shrew, an instance of two related species sharing the same habitat successfully.

tail, which is twenty centimetres. The Lesser or Short-tailed Gymnure (*Hylomys suillus*) is less than half the size.

Shrews (Family Soricidae)

This family comprises at least 170 species, spread over Europe, Africa, Asia and North America. They are mainly small and easily overlooked, for which reason their study was neglected until fairly recently. Instead of being nocturnal, as was formerly supposed, they have a three-hourly rhythm of activity, with alternate feeding and rest every three hours that continues throughout the day and night.

For their size shrews are remarkably savage and always ready to bite. Though less numerous their teeth resemble the hedgehog's and are extremely sharp. They have moderately long tails and musk glands on their flanks, which give off an odour believed to save them from being eaten by many animals. They are, however, the prey of owls, storks and vipers.

The family is divided into red-toothed shrews and white-toothed shrews. Amongst the former is the Common Shrew (*Sorex araneus*) of Europe and North Asia, which is about six centimetres long and has a tail of 3·8 centimetres. It is a brownish black above, turning to nut brown on the sides and then to greyish white below. This species, like most shrews, is solitary in habit and readily attacks any member of its species poaching on its territories. Couples only come together for mating. The female builds a nest of leaves and moss in a hole in the ground, in which one gives birth, after gestation of thirteen to twenty days, to a litter of from five to ten. They may be born at any time from May to July. The mother has six teats.

In winter shrews do not hibernate but remain active, seeking their food wherever insects are found.

A still smaller species is the Pigmy Shrew (*S. minutus*), found all over Europe including Great Britain, and in central Asia. It is five centimetres long with the tail another 3·8 centimetres. The Alpine Shrew (*S. alpinus*) lives in the Alps, the Jura mountains and the Pyrenees. It may be found at heights up to 2,400 metres. The Eurasian Water Shrew (*Neomys fodiens*) is about eight centimetres long with a 7·6 centimetre tail. It is found in Britain, over the greater part of Europe, and in Asia Minor and Siberia. It lives by water and is a good swimmer. It has a 'keel' of bristles along the ventral side of the tail.

The North American shrews are also red-toothed shrews, though the colour is really more of a chestnut brown. There are a great many varieties, the Northern Water Shrew (*Sorex palustris*), little shrews (*Sorex* spp.), the Pigmy Shrew (*Microsorex hoyi*), the Short-tailed Shrew (*Cryptotis parva*), the Big Short-tailed Shrew (*Blarina brevicauda*) and many others, all with habits similar to those described above.

Of the white-toothed shrews, *Crocidura russula* is 7·6 centimetres with a 3·8 centimetre tail, and is found in central Europe and the Mediterranean region as well as in central Asia and northeastern Siberia. It does not occur in Britain, but a related species, *C. cassiteridum*, is found in the Scilly Isles, possibly introduced from the Continent. Some

African and Asiatic members of the *Crocidura* are as big as rats. The habits in this genus are a little different from those of the other shrews. They frequent fields and gardens and often seek refuge in farm-buildings during winter. Because of their smell they are often called musk rats, but they should not be confused with the rodents that have the same name.

Contrasting with the larger *Crocidura* is Savi's Pigmy Shrew (*Suncus etruscus*), the smallest mammal in the world. The head and body measure 3·8 centimetres with a 2·5 centimetre tail and weigh less than three grams.

Tenrecs (Family Tenrecidae)

This family belongs to the island of Madagascar and is related to both the hedgehogs and the shrews. The best-known species, the Common Tenrec (*Centetes ecaudatus*), is the largest of the Insectivora, the body being thirty to forty centimetres in length. It is covered with a mixture of hair, bristles, and a few spines. The tail is rudimentary; the teeth number thirty-eight. The tenrec feeds on earthworms. They are nocturnal and become dormant during the hottest and driest season of the year. The female has the reputation of being the most prolific of all mothers, giving birth to litters of from fifteen to twenty, to feed which she has twenty-two teats.

In Madagascar tenrecs are hunted for their flesh. They have also been introduced into Mauritius and Reunion, where they are semi-domesticated. There are two other genera, *Remicentetes* and *Ericulus*, the former including the Banded Tenrec (*H. semispinosus*) and the Black-headed Tenrec (*H. nigriceps*). In *Ericulus*, the hedgehog tenrec, the whole of the back and the short tail are covered with spines.

The rice tenrecs (*Oryzoryctes* and *Nesoryctes*) are mole-like animals related to the tenrecs, and also live in Madagascar. They do a certain amount of damage to crops as they burrow for insects.

Solenodon (Family Solenodontidae)

There are only two species in this family and they are restricted to the West Indies: the Agouta (*Solenodon paradoxus*) and the Almique (*S. cubanus*). Despite their long tails (as long as the body) and the absence of spines, they are very like tenrecs. They are nearly sixty centimetres long overall. Sleeping by day, they spend the night grubbing for insects and other small animals with their long, almost trunk-like snouts. More omnivorous than other insectivores, they have been shown, by the contents of their stomachs, to live on insects, worms, small reptiles, roots and fruit. Both the Agouta and the Almique were plentiful before the Mongoose was introduced to combat snakes, but they are now very rare.

Moles and golden moles
(Families Talpidae and Chrysochloridae)

The habit of burrowing has been acquired independently by several insectivores, but these two families have reached the highest degree of specialisation in this direction.

The European Common Mole (*Talpa europaea*) has a short, thick, cylindrical body ending directly, with no neck, in a conical head. The eyes are

The European Common Mole (*Talpa europaea*) is a burrowing member of the Insectivora which feeds mainly on earthworms. It will often store worms which it has immobilized by biting off the front end. Sometimes hundreds of worms have been found in one store. Its life is almost wholly subterranean but it will come to the surface when food is scarce, as, for example, during a drought.

The Common Tenrec (*Tenrec ecaudatus*), the largest living insectivore, is the most widely distributed and most common of the tenrecs. It has a fairly long snout, short stout limbs and large flattened claws on all digits, used in digging its burrow. The spines on the nape form a crest which is erected when the animal is alarmed.

buried in the fur and are barely the size of a pin's head. Microscopical examination has shown them to be in an embryonic condition, and just capable of distinguishing day from night. The external ears are vestigial and too small to hamper movements through the ground. The ear channels open abruptly on the surface, but can be closed. The tail is much reduced. The black fur is thick, short, velvety, and without set, as is most suitable for a subterranean animal.

The instruments for burrowing are the fore limbs, which are specially adapted for the purpose. Their articulation is carried forward by the lengthening of the scapula and the sternum. The bones of the arm are short, strong and have many processes to allow for the insertion of the very powerful muscles. The hand possesses a sort of additional digit (the falciform bone of the wrist), making it still more spade-like.

The hind limbs, not used for burrowing, are gathered in under the body. The forty-four teeth (the maximum number found in heterodont mammals) are sharply pointed, as in other insectivores, fitting the mole well for its carnivorous diet. Its food is mainly earthworms with some insect grubs, and it would on that account be regarded as a most beneficial animal were it not for the damage done to plants by its burrowing.

The mole is rarely seen, not because it is nocturnal but because it rarely comes above ground. It is one of the ablest of all burrowers. In ordinary soil it can drill its way through fifteen

The Short-nosed Elephant Shrew (*Nasilio brachyrhynchus*) is found only in Africa from Zaire and Kenya southward to Namibia, Botswana and Mozambique. Its habitat varies from dry, thorn-bush country and grassland to thin forests with thick undergrowth. There are usually two young in a litter, furred and with their eyes open at birth.

metres and more in an hour, and in the rutting season it can do fifty. The mole pushes itself into the earth, pushing the earth away with its spade-like hands. If the passage dug is only for temporary use the earth is thrown up into molehills above the ground, marking the passage at more or less regular intervals. Permanent runs, however, are made by compression of the earth. No molehills are formed to reveal their presence. The walls are made smooth entirely by the friction of the body of the aminal.

Each mole lives in a separate fortress, generally placed under a wall or between the roots of a tree. Opening it up carefully one finds a central chamber about ten centimetres in diameter with several tunnels leading from it, including an emergency outlet leading to one of the main exits. The latter run about twenty centimetres below the surface and twist and twine in innumerable ramifications, as the mole continues to elaborate in the course of its wanderings. Digestion is very rapid and the mole has a voracious appetite. If deprived of food it very soon dies.

Fiercely unsociable, the mole will not suffer the proximity of any of its kind except in the mating season. In this respect it has no equal apart from the shrew. Mating is in the spring and gestation lasts thirty to forty-two days, after which a litter of three to seven is born in a specially constructed chamber. Despite their unsociability, moles have been bred in captivity in France, owing to an ingenious system whereby the animals are kept in dark cubicles.

The European Mole is found over most of Europe and in northern and central Asia. The somewhat smaller Blind Mole (*Talpa caeca*), whose eyes are covered with skin, is found in southern Europe and the Caucasus, There are the North American species: the Eastern American Common Mole (*Scalapus aquaticus*), which has webbed feet though it is not aquatic; the western moles (*Scopanus townsendi* and *S. orarius*); and the Star-nosed Mole (*Condylura cristata*) with an extraordinary fleshy star-shaped sensitive outgrowth on the end of the nose; and the Shrew Mole (*Neurotrichus gibbsii*), which is the smallest. The habits and diet closely resemble those of the European Common Mole.

In South and Central Africa the Talpidae are replaced by the Chrysochloridae, the golden moles, whose fur has a coppery sheen. The Cape Golden Mole (*Chrysochloris asiatica*) differs little in structure from the European Common Mole, except that the fore limbs are articulated normally, whereas the Common Mole's are articulated well forward, the hands have not got the 'extra' digit and, instead of the nails being equal, one is greatly developed, making the hand pick-like instead of spade-like. The Golden Mole does not make an elaborate fortress.

Other well-known species are the Red Golden Mole (*Amblysomus hottentottus*) from eastern South Africa, Peter's Golden Mole (*A. obtusirostris*) from Portuguese East Africa, and the Giant Golden Mole (*Chrysospalax trevelyani*) of South Africa, which is nearly twenty-three centimetres long.

As an example of convergence the moles and golden moles should be compared with the utterly unrelated Marsupial Mole (*Notoryctes typhlops*).

Desmans (Family Talpidae)

The Pyrenean Desman (*Galemys pyrenaica*) is rather like an elongated, long-tailed mole and belongs to a subfamily, Desmaninae, with a long and extremely mobile snout. The desmans are aquatic, and with their webbed feet are better adapted to their environment than the water shrews. The ears are buried in the fur and the animals smell strongly of musk. They burrow in the banks of water-courses. In the Pyrenean Desman the tail is laterally compressed at the end, but in the other species, the Russian Desman (*Desmana moschata*), it is compressed for most of its length. This is a much bigger animal, twenty-five centimetres long without the tail, and twice the size of the Pyrenean Desman. It is found in the basins of the Volga and the Don and in some Siberian rivers.

Otter shrew (Family Potamogalidae)

The only species in this family, the Otter Shrew (*Potamogale velox*), lives in Central and West Africa. Its feet are not webbed and it swims largely with its long, laterally compressed tail, which is thirty centimetres long, like the body. It resembles an otter in appearance and habits. It hides between stones, waiting for passing fishes, on which it pounces with astonishing rapidity. It takes its prey ashore to eat.

Jumping or elephant shrews (Family Macroscelididae)

The hind legs of elephant shrews, which are adapted to jumping, are much longer than the fore legs, and consist of three more or less equal parts: thigh, shin and foot. Elephant shrews are rat-sized animals, and their resemblance to the jerboas would be striking were it not for their mobile trunk-like snouts. They have long, scaly tails and large eyes and ears. They are diurnal and may be seen in bright sunshine hopping after insects. At night they take refuge from the cold in holes in the ground or in the burrows of other aminals. The five genera are all from Africa: *Macroscelides*, *Elephantulus*, *Nasilio*, *Petrodomus* and *Rhynchocyon*.

Tree-shrews (Order Tupaioidea)

First classed as insectivores, then as prosimian primates, tree shrews are now given their own order because of their primitive characters.

Raffle's Tree Shrew (*Tupaia ferruginea*), one of several species in south-east Asia, resembles a squirrel in shape and size, in its fur, its bushy tail, the vivacity of its movements, and its grip on branches and food, but it is distinguished by its long, pointed snout and its teeth, which remain typical of the insectivores. What is most interesting, however, are those characters which foreshadow the primates, and in particular the lemurs, family Lemuridae.

The first digit can be opposed to the others, which heralds the hand, the prehensile organ which reaches perfection in the monkey, ape and man. The face is reduced in size relative to the cranium, which is rounded and higher, and the brain undergoes a corresponding development, the visual part outstripping the olfactory part. This is an adaptation to arboreal life, in which the quarry is seen at a distance rather than scented. With the development of the visual senses the orbits are set

further away from the nasal fossae.

The caecum appears in the Tupaiidae, and is retained in the primates. The placenta remains discoidal. Lastly, whereas most of the insectivores have large litters, the tree-shrews give birth to no more than two, and the number of teats is reduced to four, which is another step towards the primates.

Flying lemurs (Order Dermoptera)

The Colugo, Cobego or Flying Lemurs (*Cynocephalus variegatus* and *C. volans*) were once classed as insectivores, but are now placed in a separate order, Dermoptera, between the insectivores and bats. They are closest to the insectivores. The two species range over Malaya, southern China, Indonesia and the Philippines. The gliding membranes show affinities with lemurs and bats, and they have even been classed as a carnivore on account of their dentition. They resemble bats also in having only one young, which clings to its mother's breast or belly.

The Common Tree Shrew (*Tupaia glis*) of southern Asia, Sumatra, Java and Borneo is about thirty-five centimetres long and like the other tree shrews bears a superficial resemblance to a squirrel. Although its teeth are typical of the Insectivora, the Common Tree Shrew is omnivorous, eating a wide variety of both animal and plant foods. The individual pictured here is grooming its tail after resting.

493

The Colugo or Flying Lemur (*Cynocephalus variegatus*) clinging upside down from a branch. As well as sleeping by day in this manner, it will also hang upside down in a tree to feed, pulling the leaves and fruit towards its mouth with its forelimbs. When the Colugo is moving around, the gliding membrane is drawn down under the forelegs so it will not catch on branches.

By day the Flying Lemur sleeps like a bat, hanging by its feet from a branch. Waking at dusk, it starts foraging for fruit and other vegetable foods. The large caecum and divided stomach alone suffice to indicate its herbivorous habit. Its molars have rounded cusps and its incisors slope outwards and are comb-like in structure, presumably for shredding vegetable matter.

The Flying Lemur's most outstanding feature is a highly developed gliding membrane not only between the fore limb and the hind limb, as in the phalangers and the flying squirrels, but also including the whole of the tail and the toes. Had the fingers lengthened to sustain the membrane, something in the nature of a bat's wing might have resulted. As it is, the Flying Lemur can do no more than glide from tree to tree, though it can cover distances of some eighty metres on occasion.

Bats (Order Chiroptera)

The Chiroptera have sometimes been regarded as birds or 'unclean fowl' and sometimes as rodents, as the French *chauve-souris* and German *Fledermaus* indicate. In 1748 Linnaeus went to the other extreme, classing them with the primates. They are now classed as a separate order, possibly derived from an insectivore-like ancestor, and this placing is confirmed by their teeth. It is, however, noteworthy that the oldest fossil bats, found in the

Eocene, were as fully evolved and structurally adapted for flight as any recent forms, so the living order is of great antiquity.

Their characteristic feature is, of course, the wings, or, technically, the alar membranes attached to the limbs and tail. The bones which support the wing are those of the typical fore limbs: the humerus from shoulder to elbow, then the radius and ulna, carpals, metacarpals and digits. All except the carpals and the thumb are greatly elongated. The second, third, fourth and fifth digits, with their corresponding metacarpals, have become long, thin, flexible supports.

The alar membrane is divided into three parts: a thin strip in front of the arm, running from the shoulder to the base of the thumb; the main part, the patagium, between the arm and the forefinger on the anterior side and the hind limb on the posterior side (this is really the wing, and something similar existed in the pterodactyls or flying reptiles, but in that case the wing was supported by the little finger, the remaining digits being free for grasping); and a posterior part, the interfemoral membrane, stretching between the two spurs, one on each hind limb, and including the whole or part of the tail, according to the species.

This is very different from a bird's wing, which consists of feathers inserted into the skin of various part of the limb. And where the bird's hand is much reduced the bat's has been developed to support the greater part of the wing.

The bats fly almost as well as birds, and some perhaps just as well. Their ability varies greatly with the different genera, just as it does in birds. The serotines and horseshoe bats have a low and rather sluggish flight, but the noctules, with their long, pointed wings, are the equal of swifts in speed and agility, and occasionally may be seen hunting with them in the evening.

Camera studies of the flight of bats show it to be divided into two movements. First the wings, half folded, are raised above the back. Then they are spread out full and brought sharply downwards. This cycle may be repeated as many as fifteen or twenty times a second during a regular flight.

Unlike bird's which are generally diurnal, most bats are nocturnal, coming out to hunt in the twilight. Numerous studies have been made of the way in which they are able to avoid obstacles in the dark, particularly in confined spaces. Two American scientists, Galambos and Griffin, have shown that the flight of bats is directed by a system not unlike sonar or radar, using ultrasonic waves outside the range of the human ear. Ultrasonic sounds are emitted at a rate of about ten to the second when the animal is at rest, and thirty to sixty when it is flying. The wave-frequency is normally between 30,000 and 130,000 per second.

Bats are by this means able to asses the position and distance of every object in their path by noting the delay between the emission of the sound and the return of its echo. The large larynx with powerful muscles inserted on bones and not cartilages is associated with this vocal ability. It is a structure that has no parallel among other mammals. Most insectivorous bats emit their ultrasonic squeaks through the open mouth; the horseshoe bats (and possibly others not yet investigated), which use the nose, are exceptions. In the horseshoe bats the larynx is extended into the nostrils.

In most species, in front of the ear (already very large) there is a fleshy lobe called the tragus, or earlet, which corresponds to the tragus of the human ear. It may either be spear-shaped or club-shaped. In the long-eared bats, for example, a membranous fold runs over the forehead from one ear to the other. The Rhinolophidae or horseshoe bats, with simple ears, also have nose leaves, which are more or less complicated folds of skin standing up over the nose and filling much of the space between the eyes. Some species, such as the vampires and the false vampires, have both tragi and nose leaves. The nose leaves act as a sort of megaphone for the transmission of ultrasonics. The tragi and pinnae are sensitive 'ear-trumpets'. They help to collect the returning echoes and assist in determining the position from which they are coming.

Little is known concerning the rest of the bat's sensory system. As in most nocturnal animals, the retina has only rods and no vascular system. It is believed that bats can see only a short distance, and only moving objects. Little is known of their sense of taste and smell. Their tactile sense seems to be keen, to judge by the sensitive vibrissae on their muzzles, ears and wings.

Bats are divided into three groups, according to diet: fruit-eating, insectivorous, and blood-sucking. Although there are intermediate forms between the first two, the teeth are generally modified in accordance with the diet. All bats have incisors and canines followed by premolars and molars. The only important difference is that in the fruit bats the crowns of the molars are flattened, while in the insectivorous group they have sharp crests arranged in a 'W'. In the blood-sucking bats the teeth are fewer, but are highly modified. The number of teeth varies from twenty to thirty-eight. For example, the dental formula of a horseshoe bat is:

$$\text{I.} \frac{1}{2} \quad \text{C.} \frac{1}{1} \quad \text{Pm.} \frac{2}{3} \quad \text{M.} \frac{3}{3} \qquad \text{Total 32}$$

Bats are insatiable, and their exceptional need for food is due to the extent and nature of their skins. With the great expanse of wing, the large ears and the nose leaves, the skin area is out of all proportion to the volume of the body. The wings, moreover, are richly supplied with blood vessels. As a result, a great quantity of heat is lost, which has to be replaced by intense feeding. It is to reduce the loss of heat that bats sleep in clusters in buildings, hollow trees and caves in which they shelter by day. This explains the curious contrast between the individualism of mouse-eared bats during hours of activity and their communal association in sleep.

Many bats hibernate in winter, when there is no longer enough insect food to keep them active. Their temperature falls until it is only slightly above that of their surroundings; breathing becomes very slow and circulation sluggish. Alternatively, a few species such as the Red Bat (*Lasiurus borealis*) of North America migrate to a warmer climate on the approach of winter.

Through the great expanse of skin bats also lose a lot of moisture and are obliged to drink fre-

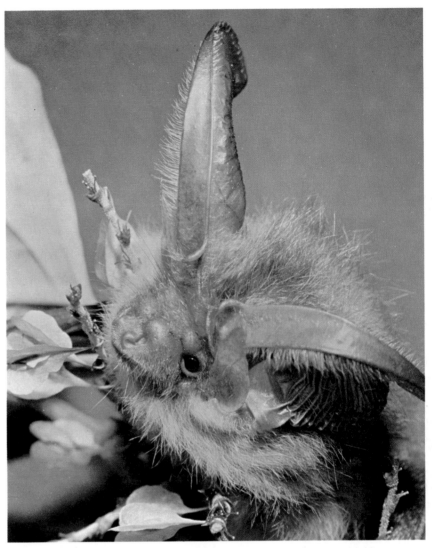

quently. To prevent the skin becoming dry and chapped, it is lubricated by an oily secretion from glands situated between the eyes and nostrils. The caves in which many bats hibernate must remain at a constant temperature and a constant level of humidity. In a dry place and deprived of water a bat will soon die and become mummified in a short space of time.

It is well known that bats at rest hang head downwards. Awake, they hang by both hind feet, or by one, with the other tucked under the wings, which are folded over the body. In both cases the head is visible. (It is in the same position, hanging by the leg, that the Collared Fruit Bat has its meals in captivity). They also clean themselves in this position, using their free hind foot to clean their teeth. One foot is enough to hang by when they are asleep, the other limbs and the head disappearing beneath the wings. A bat is found head upwards on two occasions: climbing up or down a wall, and during its evacuations, when it hangs by both alar claws with the hind limbs separated.

Most bats are very awkward on the ground, unable to do more than crawl, although they do so with a fair speed when disturbed. The vampires and the long-eared bats are more capable of walking on all fours. A vampire placed on the ground stands on its hind feet and front knuckles

The Long-eared Bat (*Plecotus auritus*) flies among the branches of trees, hovering to catch insects. It ranges from Britain to Japan and southwards to north India, Israel and Egypt. Unlike most bats it can walk and climb easily.

A group of European Mouse-eared Bats (*Myotis myotis*) roosting in a barn. Like all insectivorous bats, the mouse-eared bats have cusped molars suitable for holding and crushing insects. They have been observed hopping over the ground feeding on dung beetles, having apparently located these by smell.

The Borneo Horseshoe Bat (*Rhinolophus borneensis*) seen hanging upside-down in its roost in the Niah Great Cave, Sarawak. Horseshoe Bats use echo-location in flight to find prey and avoid obstacles, but they emit squeaks through the nose instead of the mouth as in most other species of bats. The horseshoe-shaped nose-leaves are used to receive echoes.

with the thumbs turned outwards, no doubt for additional stability.

In cave habitats different species adopt different positions. The horseshoe bats and the mouse-eared bats generally hang from the ceiling. The long-eared bats, barbastelles and pipistrelles, hang on the walls, low down, or tuck themselves in crevices.

Male bats differ from females only in their genital organs, which are plainly visible. The penis is long and pendent and in many species there is a penial bone, analogous to that found in many carnivores. The testes are lodged in a depression of the skin. In the females the vulva is hidden beneath the fur. The uterus is bicorned or simple, and there is a single pair of pectoral teats. In the horseshoe bats there are false teats in the groin for the young to hold on to.

Mating takes place once a year, amongst most north temperate zone bats in autumn, shortly before hibernation. Fertilisation is delayed for several months, from October to March, and occurs only when the female awakens. It has been shown that during this period spermatozoa remain in the uterus, where they are nourished by a substance secreted from it walls. The vagina, on the other hand, is completely blocked by the swelling of its internal epithelium.

Gestation lasts about two months, varying according to the species. Larger forms have longer gestation periods. Generally only one young is born at a time. Parturition is rapid, the young emerging hind feet first, and falling into an apron, as it were, formed by the interfemoral membrane. The mother licks it, attaches it to her ventral fur, and bites through the umbilical cord.

The most striking fact is that every one of a host of female bats hanging in a cluster from the roof of a cave gives birth at almost exactly the same time. Casteret noticed this collective parturition and he offers a very simple explanation: when the bats awake from hibernation, they wake each other up; and, since fecundation has been delayed till this moment, gestation starts simultaneously.

The newborn bats are naked and blind, but have milk teeth, which are replaced after six weeks by the permanent dentition. As regards the period of lactation, we have a description by Pouchet, a physiologist contemporary with Pasteur, who writes of the horseshoe bats: 'Each female carried a single young, which clung tightly to its mother. . . Only by careful examination could it be seen that the young was grasping its mother with the claws of its feet, which were dug into her sides just below the armpits. It lay on her abdomen, looking backwards, its head stretching out beyond the membrane joining her hind limbs and her tail. . . On my first visit I found a large number of young on the ground, while during the second day they were all firmly attached to their mothers. The first time, they had been too young, and being weaker, were easily shaken off by their mothers' rapid swerves in flight; during my second visit they hung on firmly and could not be dislodged without considerable force. The bats of this species do not seem to have much affection for their young for, when they are captured and the young annoy them by their movements, they bite them angrily. When the bats are resting, hanging from the vaults of

Fruit Bats are tree-dwelling species of the tropical and sub-tropical Old World. During the day they hang in trees and depart on feeding expeditions only at night. Then they visit fruiting trees in swarms, to feed voraciously.

their caves, the young are probably in a different position, no doubt the other way up, so that their heads are within reach of the teats; they only take the position we have described during their mother's flight, when they move about on her body with ease, gripping her fur with their wing claws and feet.'

It should be mentioned that the bats described here were disturbed. The females normally leave their babies behind when they go hunting.

At four months the young bat is fully grown but has not acquired its adult fur. Only when two years old is it in all respects an adult. It will probably live between five and ten years, at maximum twenty.

From many long-term observations it has been established that certain species of bat capable of prolonged flight undertake seasonal migrations. In the more temperate latitudes of Europe caves are not inhabited by bats in winter, and even those in the south of France are scantily inhabited between September and March. But, like migratory birds, bats appear suddenly in places at more or less regular dates, leaving again after a brief sojourn. Three species of North American bats, for instance, have been found in the Bermudas for a few weeks of the autumn. Individuals of these species have been seen for a few days in late August or early September under the lantern of a lighthouse in Massachusetts. And flights of bats have been seen in daylight, often in the company of swallows,

moving always in a more or less southerly direction. Noctules, which had left the neighbourhood of Moscow in the middle of August, were seen two weeks later flying 720 kilometres to the south, having covered over fifty kilometres per day.

More accurate results have been obtained by ringing or banding, which is done in much the same way as with birds, and migrations of up to 800 kilometres have been noted. According to Casteret, the mouse-eared bats found from April to August in the Tignahustes cave in the Pyrenees are females and their young, which spend the winter in Morocco where they rejoin the sedentary males. They return again in spring after mating and hibernating.

Migration has been observed in many other long-eared bats, besides the mouse-eared bats. It has been observed in the noctules, the barbastelles, the long-eared bats, and in Schreiber's long-winged bats. Examples have also been found in the horseshoe bats, poor flyers though they appear to be. In contrast, the pipistrelles are sedentary types, rarely moving their habitat by more than twenty kilometres.

Ringing also allows the results of experiments to be observed. Bats have been taken as much as 500 kilometres from their habitat and then released to see if they would find their way home. Some individuals have been successful, proving that bats have the same unexplained sense of direction found in birds.

The False Vampire Bat (*Megaderma cor*) is found in Africa from Ethiopia to Tanzania. These bats are called false vampires to distinguish them from the true vampires of the New World, for although they are large and carnivorous they do not suck blood in the traditional style of the vampires of fiction.

The Serotine Bat (*Eptesicus serotinus*), of Europe, temperate Asia and west Africa, is one of the larger European bats. Roosting colonies of these bats are small, rarely exceeding twenty, although occasionally numbering up to a hundred.

The Pipistrelle Bat (*Pipistrellus pipistrellus*) ranges across Europe and much of Asia. Although only eight centimetres long, it is of robust build and has a wing-span of twenty centimetres. It is a very active bat flying on a regular beat and frequently uttering a shrill squeak as it snaps at small flies.

The order Chiroptera contains some 750 species and is divided into two suborders, the Megachiroptera and Microchiroptera. The Megachiroptera are large fruit-eating bats with flattened molars. The second digit has three phalanges and usually ends in a claw. There are no tragi or nose leaves. Examples are the flying foxes, Long-tongued Fruit Bat and Collared Fruit Bat. The Microchiroptera are small or medium-sized (mainly insectivorous) bats. The molars have cutting crests. The second digit has one or two phalanges but no claw. Tragi are present. There are seventeen families, among them horse-shoe, mastiff, vespertilionid and blood-sucking bats.

Fruit bats
(Suborder Megachiroptera)

Fruit bats are distributed over the tropical and sub-tropical areas of the Old World. Essentially arboreal, they hang in trees during the day, emerging at night to forage among fruit trees for mangoes, guavas and bananas. They are said to fly as much as fifty kilometers to the scene of their devastations, returning the same night to their tree shelters, where they fill the air, sometimes for hours, with their quarrelling until they have found a comfortable spot. Some of these bats are occasionally active during daylight.

The principal fruit bats are the flying foxes, particularly the Indian Flying Fox (*Pteropus giganteus*) from India, Burma and Ceylon, which is thirty centimetres in length with a wingspan of 130 centimetres and the Kalong (*P. vampyrus*) from the East Indies, the largest of all bats, forty centimetres long with a wingspan of over 150 centimetres. Other species are found in Madagascar, Oceania and Australia.

Other fruit bats are the epauletted bats (*Epomorphorus*), so called from the tufts of white hair on the shoulders of the males, which are found in Central and South Africa; the related Hammerhead Bat (*Hypsignathus monstrosus*) from Central and West Africa, with a greatly enlarged snout; and the long-tongued fruit bats (*Macroglossus* and *Megaloglossus* found in India, New Guinea, Australia and Africa.

Insectivorous bats
(Suborder Microchiroptera)

These are the most numerous, the most varied and the only bats to be found in Europe. Nearly all hunt on the wing, catching their prey either directly with their mouths or with their hind legs, using their interfemoral membranes as scoops. However, there are a few which pick insects off foliage and hover round bushes and hedges in search of them. Others feed on spiders, which they catch on their webs. The larger ones are not content with insects and are ready to prey on birds and other bats smaller than themselves. Some feed on frogs and fishes. The insectivorous and carnivorous forms can be distinguished from one another by their nose leaves, tragi and tails.

False vampires (Family Megadermatidae)

Bats of the genus *Megaderma* have both nose leaves and tragi but no tail. After the flying foxes they are the largest bats, some having a wingspan of fifty centimetres. They are extremely bold and fierce and they have a vicious bite. One of the largest species, *M. gigas*, is found in Australia; others inhabit various parts of Africa and Asia.

Horseshoe bats (Family Rhinolophidae)

Horseshoe bats have nose leaves and a tail but no tragi. The Greater Horseshoe Bat (*Rhinolophus ferrum-equinum*) inhabits southern and central Europe (spreading westwards as far as England) as well as North Africa and Asia. Its head and body are six centimetres long and its wingspan thirty-eight centimetres. The English form, with a smaller wingspan of thirty-four centimetres, is generally regarded as a distinct subspecies. The Lesser Horseshoe Bat (*R. hipposideros*) is little more than half the size. Horseshoe bats owe their name to the shape of their nose leaves. They frequent church towers, where they live in colonies, and come out to hunt in the twilight. At the approach of winter they migrate to a warmer climate or take refuge in caves.

Long-eared bats and allies (Family Vespertilionidae)

Most of the bats found in Western Europe, the United States and Canada belong to the family Vespertilionidae, which is numerous in both the temperate and the tropical regions of both hemispheres. They include the long-eared bats, mouse-eared bats, noctules, serotine and pipistrelles.

The Long-eared Bat (*Plecotus auritus*) is a small bat, easily recognised by its ears, which are almost as long as its body and joined together at their base by a membranous fold running over the forehead. It flies about at night in gardens or among trees and picks insects from the leaves while hovering in flight. In summer it lives alone or with a mate in tree hollows. In winter it seeks a more secluded shelter. It is one of the few bats that walk and climb.

Two common species are the European Common Mouse-eared Bat (*Myotis myotis*) and the Noctule or Great Bat (*Nyctalus noctula*). The latter is the largest bat commonly found in Great Britain, having a wingspan of thirty-eight centimetres. The Mouse-eared Bat has an equal wingspan but although abundant in Europe is seldom found in England. The chief difference between the two species is in the tragi, which are long and pointed in the Mouse-eared Bat and short and swollen in the Noctule. Both are fast and high flyers, sweeping over fields, gardens, woods and rivers as they hunt for insects. During the day they are hidden away in caves or tree hollows. In autumn and spring they undertake distant migrations. In North America the most common and widespread of the mouse-eared bats is the Little Brown Bat (*Myotis lucifugus*) which hibernates in caves and in summer roosts in attics and farm buildings in which it becomes a considerable pest.

The Serotine (*Eptesicus serotinus*) is somewhat shorter than the preceding species and has shorter, broader wings. It is a much less able flyer. Solitary in habit, it is little noticed. The Big Brown Bat (*E. fuscus*) is found through most of North America. It resembles the Little Brown Bat except in size. It is fairly common in the United States. The Pipistrelle (*Pipistrellus pipistrellus*), in spite of its small

size (four centimetres long), never fails to attract attention by its rapid flight close to houses, into which it sometimes ventures in its search for flies. The Eastern Pipistrelle (*P. subflavus*) of North America is the smallest American bat, being about six centimetres long. There are over twenty-five species of this family in the United States.

American leaf-nosed bats (Family Phyllostomatidae)

This is a large South and Central American family with one or two North American forms, such as the Californian Leaf-nosed Bat (*Macrotus californicus*). These are insectivorous and occasionally fruit-eating bats, but were at one time thought to be blood-suckers. Hence the family's alternative name 'vampire-bats'. It includes the Great False Vampire (*Vampyrus spectrum*) from Guiana and Brazil, which is fifteen centimetres long and has a wingspan of some seventy centimetres, the related Javelin Vampire (*Phyllostomus hastatum*), and two subfamilies, the Glossophaginae or long-tongued vampires and the Stenoderminae or short-nosed vampires. This last-named subfamily corresponds to some extent to the flying foxes of the Old World.

Hare-lipped bats (Family Noctilionidae)

Also known as bulldog or fishing bats, these have very long legs used for seizing fishes. They are the only bats to feed predominately on fishes.

Mastiff bats (Family Molossidae)

Mastiff bats are thick-set and snub-nosed. When the wings are folded the fore arm can be used for walking. There are five species in North America, including the Californian Mastiff Bat (*Eumops californicus*), the largest bat in the United States,

The Tent-building Bat (*Uroderma bilobatum*) is a leaf-nosed bat ranging from southern Mexico through Central America to Brazil and the island of Trinidad. The nose-leaf consists of a horseshoe-shaped basal part, with rounded lobes on either side, and an erect lancet-shaped portion. These bats roost in palm fronds or banana leaves, often forming their own shelters by biting partly through the ribs of a frond so that part of it hangs down like a tent to give the bats protection.

499

and one species in Europe, Rafinesque's Wrinkle-lipped Bat (*Tadarida teniotis*) with swallow-like wings, found in the Mediterranean region.

Blood-sucking bats (Family Desmodontidae)

These too are sometimes called vampire bats, but unlike those just mentioned, the Desmodontidae actually feed on blood. In most texts it is agreed that these bear officially the common name of 'true vampire bats' because of their diet. No sucking is involved. The bat punctures the skin of its victim with its extremely sharp upper incisors, and when the blood runs the bat has merely to lap it up. The bat's saliva prevents the blood coagulating and it can flow indefinitely.

The Great Blood-sucking or Great Vampire Bat (*Desmodus rotundus*) is distributed from Mexico to Paraguay. It is a small bat, the head and body being about seven centimetres. The Lesser Blood-sucking or Lesser Vampire Bat (*Diphylla ecaudata*) is found in the same regions.

It is surprising that these bats can puncture the skin of an animal unobserved, and it has been suggested that some anaesthetic process is involved. Scientific investigation, however, has shown that the secret lies simply in the neatness of the operation. Younger bats are less skilful and

sometimes cause pain. Blood-sucking bats are unable to digest any food other than blood, as the stomach is reduced to a long slender tube. The caecum in which the blood is digested is very big and the excreta are always blackish and liquid. The teeth are almost reduced to a pair of razor-sharp upper incisors and canines, while the cheek teeth are greatly reduced in number and size and are functionless. The Desmodontidae are good walkers and runners.

The Primates (Order Primates)

Primates, the order to which man belongs, remain primitive in many respects. They are pentadactyl, plantigrade animals with clavicles, a complete dentition and unspecialised molars. In all the features the horse is more highly evolved. But primates have two organs of exceptional importance: a voluminous and complicated brain and a supple hand with opposable thumb. It was formerly the custom to place the primates on the top rung of the zoological ladder, but present usage is to place them much lower in the mammalian scale because of their generalised and therefore primitive (in terms of evolutionary history) physical structure.

Although their advance to the evolutionary stage of the anthropoid apes and the hominids dates from comparatively recent times, the primates go back to the beginning of the Cainozoic era, beyond which their origins should be sought, in all probability, from the ranks of the then most highly developed insectivores. No one can deny the close resemblance of the tree shrews of southern Asia to the tarsiers of the same region, animals equally insectivorous and equally arboreal, but which have earned a place among the primates by virtue of their remarkable cerebral development.

It is perhaps arboreal life which has conditioned the development of the primates, and thus of man. To climb better the hand needed to be perfect for grasping. Sight outstripped scent; from which followed the enlargement of certain parts of the brain to the detriment of others. Increasing agility involved the cerebral cortex in further development. The incompatability of arboreal life and large litters ended by these being reduced to one or two and with that the teats were reduced to two.

If the primates are descended from arboreal insectivores, it could be that the forests which covered the continents through the Mesozoic and Cainozoic eras may well have been the true cradles of humanity. So far as we can tell, man belonged to the trees until he had acquired the brain and the dexterity to conquer the rest of the earth.

The first requirement for life in the trees is the modification of the fore limbs for climbing, including more especially the opposable thumb, which makes the hand what it is. Another adaptation to arboreal life, though not found in all primates, is the prehensile tail.

The primates, like their insectivorous ancestors, have a complete dentition. They have cutting incisors and fang-like canines. The molars, however, vary according to diet. In the insectivorous forms they have cutting crests for crushing the chitinous integuments of insects. In the fruit-eating primates, they have flat crowns with rounded tubercules. The most common dental

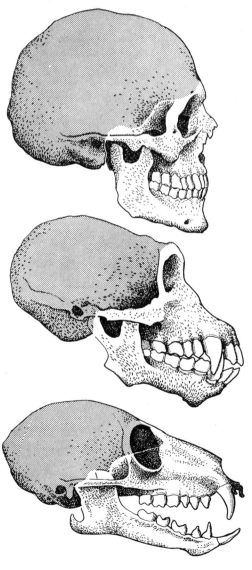

Development of the primates is characterised by an increase in brain size and a shortening of the jaw. A large proportion of the human skull (*top*) is taken up by the brain-case (shaded portion) and the jaws are short. Chimpanzees (*centre*) have a smaller brain-case with a sloping forehead and heavy, projecting jaws. In lemurs (*bottom*), the most primitive of the primates, the face is long with a fox-like muzzle and the brain-case is small and flattened.

formulae are:

Lemurs and New World monkeys

$$\text{I.}\frac{2}{2} \quad \text{C.}\frac{1}{1} \quad \text{Pm.}\frac{3}{3} \quad \text{M.}\frac{3}{3} \qquad \text{Total 36}$$

Old World monkeys, anthropoid apes, and hominids

$$\text{I.}\frac{2}{2} \quad \text{C.}\frac{1}{1} \quad \text{Pm.}\frac{2}{2} \quad \text{M.}\frac{3}{3} \qquad \text{Total 32}$$

In most mammals the face is bigger than the cranium, the brain being small and the jaws elongated into a muzzle. In one group, the primates, there is shortening of the jaws in varying degrees and progressive enlargement of the cranium as the brain develops. In the smaller primates the brain has few convolutions, but in the larger forms it is almost as complex as the human brain. Certain lobes of the cerebrum develop more than others, particularly the occipital lobes, seat of the visual centres, and the frontal lobes, seat of the higher reflective powers. Even so, the forehead in the majority of monkeys remains sharply sloping, if it can be said to exist at all. It is only in the Orang-utan, the Gibbon and man that it is really developed.

The face is so shaped as to bring the eyes forward and closer together, so that they both look in the same direction. This binocular vision enables primates to judge distance, to see things in relief. Organically the eyes of all the primates are constructed on the same plan as in man.

Within the primates, there is a wide variety of social organisation, from the solitary Orang-utan to the huge troops of baboons. In most species, 'society' is organised into 'multi-male' groups of several adult males and females and their young. Others have one-male 'harems' or 'family' groups of one adult of each sex. In man, there is no mating season, sexual activity is practically uninterrupted and a constant bond is formed.

There are two suborders which, in order of evolutionary progression, are the Prosimii and the Anthropoidea, the first including the lemurs, aye-aye, lorises, potto, bush-baby and tarsier, the second including the monkeys and apes.

Lemurs and allies (Suborder Prosimii)

Lemurs (Family Lemuridae)

To some extent intermediate between insectivores and monkeys, the lemurs are sometimes grouped with prosimians. The German name of half-apes (*Halb-Affen*) indicates very clearly their position. They are easily distinguished from true monkeys by their fox-like muzzles, which are covered with hair like the rest of the body, and their very large but inexpressive eyes. Their arms are much longer than their legs, and their fur is soft and woolly. They are generally nocturnal in habit. Their brains are not well developed and show no sign of convolutions. Linked with this fact, their faces lack the mobility, expressiveness, and intelligence associated with monkeys. Physically, however, they are excellently adapted to their arboreal existence. The thumb and great toes are opposable to the other digits, and are of unusual size.

The dentition of the lemurs closely follows that of the insectivores, except that it is more markedly

The Ring-tailed Lemur (*Lemur catta*), of Madagascar, measures 120 centimetres long including the tail. It lives in thinly wooded, dry and rocky country, whereas most lemurs live in thick forests.

adapted to a fruit diet. The number of teeth is generally thirty-six. The lower canines lie alongside the lower incisors, which are slightly separated and slope forwards, suited to peeling fruit.

The lemurs also differ from the monkeys and apes in having a bicorned uterus, a diffuse placenta, and in many species, additional teats, placed abdominally.

At the beginning of the Tertiary era lemurs were spread all over the world, and were represented by large forms. After the Oligocene period they began to disappear from Europe and America as the true monkeys made their appearance, and are now found only in Madagascar, where traces of many extinct forms are found.

The Ruffled Lemur (*Lemur variegatus*) has thick, woolly fur, piebald black and white, with a white ruff. It is more than a metre long, of which more than half is tail. The Mongoose Lemur (*L. mongos*) is about the same size, its general colour being fawn with a black ring on the forehead. The Crowned Lemur (*L. coronatus*) is yellow, grey and white, with a red-gold line across the forehead. The Ring-tailed Lemur (*L. catta*) is greyish, with dark rings round the eyes and a long, ringed tail. It is slightly bigger than the Mongoose Lemur. It is kept as a domestic animal in Madagascar and Mauritius, where it is given the run of the house

The Slow Loris (*Nycticebus coucang*), of India, Sri Lanka and southeast Asia, has short, thick limbs and is a slow and deliberate climber. It hunts insects and small animals at night. It seldom leaves the trees, being awkward on the ground.

Loris (*Loris tardigradus*), with extremely thin legs, and the Slow Loris (*Nycticebus coucang*), which has rather short, thick limbs.

The term 'slow lemurs' is sometimes used to include the lorises and their African equivalents, the Potto (*Perodicticus potto*) and the Angwantibo (*Arctocebus calabarensis*). They, too, are slow in movement and have only rudimentary index fingers, but they do have a tail of sorts, a mere stump in the Angwantibo, and five centimetres in the Potto. They live in forests, their only protection from predatory animals being their strictly arboreal and nocturnal habits.

Bush-babies, also known as night-apes or galagos, are African, with several species distributed between Senegal and the east coast. They are attractive creatures, with their soft, thick, silky fur, which has been justly compared to that of the Chinchilla. All have tails which are longer than the body and generally bushy. The muzzle is short, the eyes large and the hind legs much longer than the fore limbs, giving them prodigious leaping powers. A characteristic feature is their ability to fold their large, naked ears, pricking them again at the least hint of danger. They have the strange habit of constantly licking the palms of their hands and the soles of their feet as they climb amongst the trees.

Nocturnal, they sleep by day, prowling at night in search of insects, fruit and eggs. They are particularly fond of crickets, grasshoppers and the Praying Mantis. When alarmed, they either jump from tree to tree or remain absolutely still, in which case they look like lumps of moss. Though rarely giving birth to a litter or more than one, the females have four teats, two being inguinal.

The most important species are the Bush-tailed or Great Galago (*Galago crassicaudatus*) of East Africa, which is over thirty centimetres long with a tail slightly longer, and the Senegal Galago (*G. senegalensis*), which ranges across the continent to Ethiopia and Mozambique.

Sifakas, indris, avahis (Family Indriidae)

These animals are characterised by the possession of thirty teeth, the lower canines and one premolar in each half jaw having been lost. The sifakas have short arms, long legs and tail, and ears almost completely hidden beneath thick silky fur. They are diurnal animals and like basking in the sun. Their diet is largely frugivorous and they seem to prefer unripe fruit, which they always peel with their sharp, sloping incisors. By way of contrast they chew leaves and flowers with their molars.

Besides their strong limbs, sifakas have branchial membranes which up to a point function as parachutes. They are fringed with long hairs. Thus aided, they can jump over ten metres with such ease that they seem to have the power of flight. They are not confined to forests, and on occasion move about in bush and open country. Their arms, though ending in long, slender hands, are too short for them to go on all fours like monkeys or the other lemuroids, and they are therefore obliged to progress by jumps. With each jump the arms go up in the air, reminding one of children at play. Oddly enough, their hands, well adapted to grasping branches, are practically useless for holding objects. If a banana is put down

and makes no attempt to escape. All it needs are warmth and fruit. In the wild state it lives on rocky plains, not in the forests. It loves basking in the sun and will do so for hours without moving.

The gestation period of lemurs is two months, and usually a litter of one is born, rarely two. For three months the baby lemur remains attached to its mother's breast with its legs round her waist and its hand firmly grasping the hair on her shoulders. It maintains that position no matter what acrobatic feats its mother performs. Later it climbs on her back like a jockey. Only at the age of seven months can it get about on its own.

Other lemurs have been compared to squirrels, rats, mice and weasels. The Mouse Lemur (*Cheirogaleus pusillus*) is rat-sized. The more truly mouse-like species, the Lesser Mouse Lemur (*Microcebus murinus*), is classed among the dwarf lemurs. The first of these is forest-dwelling, living at the tops of the highest trees in a nest like that of a Crow. The second is a plains-dweller, lodging in holes in the ground and in rock crevices. Both are nocturnal, living on both insects and vegetable food. At the approach of the dry season when food is scarce, they eat enormously, fattening themselves up, food reserves being stored in their tails which become club-shaped. They then retire to their nests and live on their own reserves until the rains start again. This is a form of aestivation strictly comparable to the hibernation of marmots and dormice in temperate latitudes.

Lorises (Family Lorisidae)

The lorises are inhabitants of India and Ceylon and south-east Asia. They have no tails, and the index fingers are vestigial. In these features they differ from the lemurs. But they differ most of all in their slow movements, creeping about the trees at night, approaching their insect prey with the utmost caution. During the day they sleep, rolled up in a hollow. The best known are the Slender

beside them, they do not pick it up but bend down to seize it with their mouths, helped by the fingers and palms of their hands, but not by the thumbs. Sifakas are quiet and very gentle creatures, yet the males fight bitterly at mating time, as their ears often show.

One of the most handsome species is the Crowned Sifaka (*Propithecus diadema*), which has particularly beautiful fur, a sumptuous black on the back and orange-yellow below. The diadem is white, and the tail gradually changes from orange to grey at the tip. There is only one extant species of Indris, *Indri brevicaudata*. It is a metre long, almost tail-less, with occasional bipedal gait. The Indris has a thick, silky fur, black back, fawn hind quarters and a black stripe down the legs. These contrasting colours break up their outline, making it difficult to see them as long as they remain still.

The Indris has much the same habits as the Sifaka, living a diurnal life in small communities on a vegetarian diet in the forests of eastern Madagascar. It is the largest lemur, reaching a length of nearly a metre. Its tail is a mere two centimetre stump.

From the same habitat comes the Avahi (*Avahi laniger*) with a thick woolly grey-brown coat and a forty-centimetre tail, which is ten centimetres longer than the body. It contrasts with the other members of the family in being nocturnal and slow in movement. Living alone or in couples it has received very little attention from naturalists.

Aye-aye (Family Daubentoniidae)

The Aye-aye (*Daubentonia madagascariensis*) is the only member of this family. It has lost all cannines and most of its premolars, being left with twenty-two teeth. Another singular feature of its dentition is that, like the rodents, it has close-set sloping incisors which have no enamel on the inner surfaces, and it gnaws. Buffon and Cuvier therefore classed it among the rodents, and it was only much later that its rank as a primate was established.

Outwardly the Aye-aye is much like some of the lemurs. About the size of a cat, it has a thick silvery fur and a long bushy tail. Its arms are much shorter than its legs, its eyes are fairly large and its ears large, thin and rounded. A striking feature is the slenderness of its bony fingers. The third finger, in particular, is no thicker than a wire, and is used for hooking insect larvae out of holes, and for extracting the contents of bamboos and sugar cane.

As is so often the case with nocturnal tree-climbers, not much is known of its habits. By day it is in its nest in the tree-tops. By night males and females prowl together among the trees, tapping the banches to drive out insects, scratching off bits of bark, gobbling up any eggs that may be found, and devastating wild hives to obtain the honey. The Aye-aye can easily be kept in captivity on a diet consisting mainly of eggs, milk and fruit.

Tarsiers (Family Tarsiidae)

The Tarsier (*Tarsius* spp.) has a curious mixture of characters—some of them very primitive and some highly advanced. Its diet is mostly of insects and more than others it has preserved the habits of its insectivorous ancestors. But it shows evolution-

The Tarsier (*Tarsius* sp.) lives in the forests of the Philippines, Borneo and Sumatra. By night they hunt insects, lizards and small birds, taking acrobatic leaps of up to five metres through the trees. They also eat fruit. The single young is born well-furred, with its eyes open and capable of climbing.

ary development in the flattened face, the round skull, and orbits of the eyes completely separated from the temporal fossae. The placenta is discoidal. These characters relate it closely to the true monkeys, and more especially place it in the line of man's descent. It is often regarded as his ancestor.

The Tarsier is about fifteen centimetres long, with a twenty-five centimetre tail, which is almost hairless except for the terminal tuft. The legs are elongated, particularly the tarsal bones, and specialised for jumping. The tips of the fingers and toes are expanded to form adhesive pads. The face is dominated by the enormous close-set eyes. The pupils are closed during the day, dilating at night, when the Tarsier leaps about like a frog, holding on to smooth branches by means of the tactile pads on the finger-tips. Having caught its prey, it shuts its eyes and skins it with sharp teeth. The Tarsier is found in the Philippines, Sumatra and Borneo.

Monkeys and apes
(Suborder Anthropoidea=Simiae)

Anthropoids are frugivorous primates with flattened, bare faces, small eyes with orbits completely closed laterally. The digits always end in nails and the teats are exclusively pectoral. They are diurnal in habit, and are divided into four families: Cebidae (New World monkeys,) Callithricidae (marmosets), Cercopithecidae (Old World monkeys) and Pongidae (anthropoid apes).

New World monkeys (Family Cebidae)

In the immense forests which stretch from the southern edge of Mexico to the northern edge of the Argentine, and from the western mountain ranges to the Atlantic, live a profusion of monkeys, very different from the prosimious and Old World monkeys. They have bare, flattened faces, a good cranial capacity, small eyes, simple uterus, discoidal placenta, and two pectoral teats. Their fur is

The characteristic chorus of the Howler Monkeys is heard at dawn and again at dusk, just as birds, in the breeding season, indulge in a dawn chorus and a less vociferous version just after sundown. In both it is assumed that the calling serves basically to advertise possession of a territory.

Opposite top
The Common or Black Spider Monkey (*Ateles paniscus*) is found in Mexico through Central America to the upper Amazon. It is very slenderly built and its long arms and extremely long tail enable it to climb and swing through the trees with great agility.

Opposite bottom
The Squirrel Monkey (*Saimiri sciureus*) of Central and South America is probably the most common primate in the whole of the Americas. It lives in large bands of up to a hundred individuals, travelling across the scrub woodlands which it prefers to the deep forest. A single young is born which is carried by either parent.

thick and woolly. Several species are nocturnal, and some have claws on one or more of their fingers. Known as the Platyrrhini ('broad-nosed'), together with the marmosets, they have nostrils widely separated by a thick septum. They always have three premolars in each half of both jaws, and twenty-four milk teeth. Normally there are thirty-six teeth in the permanent set but the latter may be reduced to thirty-two by atrophy of the wisdom teeth.

Other less constant features distinguish the New and Old World monkeys. Their thumbs, for example, are usually atrophied, and their tails are long and usually prehensile. In a general way, too, they have a less lively intelligence than Old World monkeys. They are duller, less turbulent and less quarrelsome, lacking gaiety, and even morose. Their only psychological superiority is the great affection they have for their masters. They are gentle and easily tamed.

TITIS, SAKIS, UAKARIS: These members of - the Cebidae have thirty-six teeth and all the digits end in nails, there being no longer any trace of the lemuriod claws inherited from insectivores. They are no bigger than a large squirrel. The tail is long in the titis and sakis, short in the uakaris, and is never prehensile. The fur is thick and of various colours. The White-collared Titi (*Callicebus torquatus*) is a glossy black with a white face, collar and hands. It ranges from northern Brazil to Ecuador and Peru. The Masked Titi (*C. personatus*) inhabits the upper Amazon.

The sakis have long, curly hair and a bushy tail. They are found in the South American forests, chiefly in Brazil. There are two genera: *Pithecia* which includes the White-headed Saki and Humboldt's Saki, and *Chiropotes*, which has the Black Saki and the White-nosed Saki.

The brightly coloured uakaris are characterised by their short, bushy-ended tails. The three species, the Black-headed Uakari (*Cacajao melanocephalus*), the Red Uakari (*C. rubicundus*) and the Bald Uakari (*C. calvus*), are remarkable in being confined to a comparatively small tract of forest in the Amazon basin, without distribution of the three overlapping. Few cases of such clear-cut distribution are known among mammals.

All these forms are gregarious. They live high in the trees of the Amazonian forests, feeding on fruit and insects, and rarely come down to the ground.

HOWLER MONKEYS: The striking character of howling monkeys is their voice, which can be heard miles away. The howling is produced by saccular diverticula of the larynx more developed than in any other monkeys, even the spider monkeys. The bone is enormously enlarged and cavernous, forming a sort of bony trumpet. It can easily be seen to move up and down as the animals howl.

Howler monkeys are the largest of the New World monkeys, the male being the size of a fairly large dog. They are bearded and have prehensile tails, longer than the body. In the Black Howler Monkey (*Alouatta caraya*) only the old males are black, the females and young being pale yellow.

They range from Ecuador to Paraguay. The Red Howler Monkey (*A. seniculus*), from the north and north-west of the subcontinent, varies from red-brown to purple-black. The jet black Guatemalan Howler Monkey (*A. villosa*) lives in the cold, damp forests of the mountains at heights up to 3,000 metres.

The coats of Red Howler Monkeys kept in captivity change colour in contact with water, red turning to orange, and that again to yellow. It may happen also in the wild state under the influence of rain, and this would explain the different reports of the colour of these animals. In captivity they are found to be liable to chest diseases and dysentery.

CAPUCHIN MONKEYS AND SQUIRREL MONKEYS: Close to the howler monkeys in the classification system are the capuchin monkeys, so-called for the 'cowl' of thick hair on the crown of the head. There are many species spread over Central and South America, where they are also called sapajous. The long tail is only slightly prehensile. The coat is variable in texture, being woolly, silky or bristly according to species.

The most important species is the White-throated Capuchin (*Cebus capucinus*), which is white on the head, shoulders and chest, with a dark brown cowl, and a pale, flesh-coloured face. It lives well in captivity, is cunning, and very quickly learns to imitate man's actions.

In the wild state capuchin monkeys are predatory and vicious and are accordingly detested by the local inhabitants. They are worse poultry raiders than the fox. They are far from exclusively carnivorous, however, and their ravages in fields and orchards are considerable.

The Squirrel Monkey (*Saimiri sciureus*) is one of the most widely distributed monkeys of South America, and it is considered one of the most charming and beautiful. Like the capuchin monkeys, it has a long but only slightly prehensile tail, but it is above all remarkable for its large skull. Relative to its body, its brain is bigger than man's. Hardly bigger than a squirrel, this monkey is a yellowish green, somewhat darker on the head, and with red lower part limbs. In captivity it eats meat. In the wild, it lives a gregarious life hunting for lizards, eggs and, above all, for insects. There are three others species, including the Red-backed Squirrel Monkey (*S. oerstedii*), from Panama, whose back and sides are glossy red and limbs olive-brown.

SPIDER MONKEYS AND WOOLLY MONKEYS: The spider monkeys are slim monkeys with long limbs (the arms are longer than the legs), and a very long, strongly prehensile tail. Their generic name *Ateles* means 'imperfect' and refers to the absence of thumbs. Yet, with only four fingers, all working in the same direction, they are wonderful climbers, comparable in this respect only to the gibbons. And like the gibbons they jump from branch to branch, swinging from hands and feet, whose digits are more or less permanently bent. The tail is almost a fifth hand, serving to hold on to the branches and to explore crevices for anything edible they may contain. It is when they are hanging by their tails with all their limbs free that they resemble spiders.

There are several species of spider monkey living in Brazil, Guyana, Ecuador and Peru. Their

The Emperor Tamarin (*Saguinus imperator*), of the forests of South America, is distinguished from other marmosets by its very long drooping white moustache under which the whole nose and mouth areas are unpigmented. Tamarins live in territorial family groups in which the female is more aggressive than the male in maintaining the territory against intruders.

coats vary from black all over in the Black-faced Spider Monkey (*A. paniscus*), to reddish-brown in the Long-haired Spider Monkey (*A. belzebuth*), in which the hair falls cloakwise over the flanks. This is the most northerly of the New World monkeys, being found in Mexico. The spider monkeys live in groups of about forty to fifty, which sometimes break up temporarily into smaller groups in the course of the day. The smaller group may be composed of a female and her young, several females and their young brought up together, a single male with his mates and offspring, or several males in temporary association. In the forest these small groups remain within call of each other, and on the threat of danger the whole group can be reassembled by particular calls. Whatever their subsequent colour the young are always completely black for the first six months, at the end of which they are weaned.

The woolly monkeys (genus *Lagothrix*) are fairly widespread in the northern half of South America. The long tail is almost as prehensile as in the spider monkeys. Thumbs are present, and here again the arms are longer than the legs. A grey woolly coat covers the whole body except the palms of the hands, soles of the feet, and ears. On the face it is reduced to a sort of plush. Humboldt's Woolly Monkey (*L. lagothrica*) is one of the largest of the New World monkeys.

DOUROUCOULIS: The variety of the New World monkeys is further enriched by some curious species, recalling the lemurs with their large eyes and nocturnal habits. Alternatively called night-apes or owl-faced monkeys, the soft, curly-haired douroucoulis constitute the genus *Aotes*. They are the only nocturnal monkeys and seem to be blinded by daylight. They remain hidden in hollow trees during the day, coming out at sunset to prowl for insects, eggs, birds and fruit. They make charming pets and keep the house free of mice and insects. The tail, which is longer than the body, is not prehensile. There are several species in Central and South America. The Night Ape (*Aotus trivirgatus*) is grey-brown, somewhat redder below, with three black stripes along the head. It ranges from Guyana to Brazil and Peru.

Marmosets and tamarins (Family Callithricidae)

The marmosets are characterised by the atrophy of the wisdom teeth, bringing the total down to thirty-two. This family has preserved more primitive features than the Cebidae, such as the presence of claws on most of the fingers, a non-prehensile tail and litters of more than two.

The Common Marmoset (*Callithrix jacchus*) is about twenty centimetres long, and has a bushy tail over thirty centimetres long. The fur is soft. Each hair is black at the base, yellow in the middle and white at the tip, and the general impression is a greenish yellow, set off by white ear tufts. It inhabits the mouth of Amazon, where the trees echo with their cries as they run after fruit and insects. A peculiarity of this species is the males' care of their offspring, which are carried hanging to the ventral fur, then on the hip, and finally, when they are older, on the shoulders. The mother's part is merely to suckle the young.

Other species of true marmoset are the Black-tailed Marmoset (*C. argentata*) and the Pigmy Marmoset (*Cebuella pygmaea*).

The Lion Marmoset (*Leontocebus leonicus*) from the Amazon basin is about forty centimetres long overall, half of which is the tail. It has a yellowish mane. Of the same genus is the Silky Marmoset (*L. rosalia*), which is about twice the length of the Lion Marmoset and distributed from Brazil to Panama. It is orange-coloured with a brown mane.

The related tamarins (genus *Saguinus*) are expert climbers and can drop long distances without harm. One was observed to fall at least fifteen metres, and alight on its feet. The tamarins, which have no ear tufts or tail rings, live on fruit, eggs and insects.

Members of the Callithricidae may be kept in captivity, but are prone to develop rickets and tuberculosis without cod-liver oil and sunray treatment. The marmoset is a somnolent creature, spending much of its day sleeping. Another activity is grooming. Each hair is separated—its own or that of another marmoset—with the fingers, nails and lips to remove the least speck of dirt or dandruff. The work is done with intense concentration. Marmosets rarely quarrel, the chief squabbles among males being on sexual grounds. Sometimes discord enters families, but such instances are exceptional, and no fights between marmosets of opposite sex have been observed. Marmosets are easily frightened by a sudden sound or movement, and panic quickly spreads among them. In captivity these animals show no affection for their keepers.

Old World monkeys (Family Cercopithecidae)

The domain of the Old World monkeys is vast and comprises all the warmer zones of the eastern hemisphere, with the exception of Madagascar and Australasia (the homes of the lemurs and the marsupials respectively). They are distinguished from New World monkeys by two characters. Known as the Catarrhini, they have nostrils which are close together and point downwards as in man, the septum between them being thin. Secondly, they have only two premolars in each half of both upper and lower jaws. The milk teeth number twenty and the permanent set thirty-two, including wisdom teeth, which are rarely lacking. The dental formula is:

$$I. \frac{2}{2} \quad C. \frac{1}{1} \quad Pm. \frac{2}{2} \quad M. \frac{3}{3} \qquad \text{Total } 32$$

As complimentary characters the Old World monkeys generally have a well-developed thumb, and ischial callosities (bare buttock patches) that are very often highly coloured. The tail is seldom short and never prehensile. Many have cheek pouches in which food can be stored. More vegetarian in diet than the New World monkeys, they have often a divided stomach like that of the ruminants. Never more than two are born to a litter.

In some species the mother takes her young off, away from the father. For weeks she tastes every scrap her offspring puts into its mouth, teaching it what food is suitable and what to be avoided. It is not sufficient to attribute this behaviour to instinct. The higher the level of intelligence, the smaller the part played by instinct and the greater the need for education. The young monkeys, it has been observed, though provided with the physical means, is not a born climber and undergoes a long apprenticeship on lower and less dangerous branches, watched attentively by its mother. Her affection does not preclude discipline, however, and, if necessary, the young one is seized by the neck or ear and soundly slapped.

LANGURS: In the forests of Borneo, Java, Sumatra, Ceylon and India, and in Tibet, where they may be found at altitudes up to 4,000 metres, live large troops of langurs or languars, very slim monkeys, somewhat resembling the spider monkeys, but without a prehensile tail.

In the genus *Presbytis* the thumb is rudimentary, there are no cheek pouches, and the stomach is divided into several compartments for the digestion of the vegetable food.

The best-known species is the Entellus Monkey or Hanuman (*P. entellus*) a large monkey with a silver-haired body, black face, ears, hands and soles of the feet, and a face fringed by grey-white whiskers. The Entellus Monkey is sacred to the Hindus.

The Himalayan Langur (*P. entellus schistaceus*) is a race of the Hanuman which lives at altitudes of over 1,800 metres. Also closely related is the Capped Langur (*P. pileatus*) from south-east Asia. The Black-crested Langur or Banded Leaf Monkey (*P. melalophos*) has a dark crest on the head.

Of the same family is the Snub-nosed Monkey (*Rhinopithecus roxellanae*), which has a small turned-up nose. It lives in Tibet and is one of the most northerly of all monkeys, a large part of its habitat being under perpetual snow. The male Proboscis Monkey (*Nasalis larvatus*) has a swollen, pendent nose, generally over eight centimetres long, hanging down over the mouth. Sometimes it curves inward so as almost to touch the chin. The females and young have snub noses. It lives in the humid forests of Borneo, for preference near rivers, and is fond of swimming. It is called locally by the name meaning 'white man'.

COLOBUS MONKEYS: These are African. The anatomical character which distinguishes the colobus

monkeys from the langurs is the extreme reduction of their thumbs. But they are generally recognised by their long, silky fur hanging down their sides like a sumptuous garment. The tail ends in a beautiful, long tuft. They have been much hunted for their fur, and this has almost caused the extermination of one species, the Guereza (*Colobus abyssinicus*), which were killed by the thousand until protective measures were introduced. This beautiful monkey is black, with white round the face, and long white hairs on flanks and tail. The young are white all over. There are several other types, variously coloured, and many species are red or reddish-brown. The Black Colobus (*C. satanas*), from West Africa, is entirely black. This is a large monkey about 100 centimetres long with a tail half as long again. The Ursine Guereza (*C. polykomos*) is from the same region, while the Mantled Colobus (*C. palliatus*) is from East Africa.

Throughout their range, which covers the whole of Central Africa from coast to coast, the colobus monkeys live entirely in forests seldom leaving the high tree-tops, where they find ample supplies of

The Pygmy Marmoset (*Cebuella pygmaea*) is one of the smallest and most primitive of primates. It is only about twelve centimetres long with a twenty centimetre tail. It lives in the equatorial rain forest of the upper Amazon and feeds on insects, fruit, birds and birds' eggs. Nothing is known of its social behaviour in the wild.

The Hanuman or Entellus Langur (*Presbytis entellus*), of India, Sri Lanka and Nepal, is the largest of the langurs. Although langurs are typically 'leaf-monkeys' the Hanuman will also eat fruit, berries and domestic crops. It lives in a wide variety of habitats from dry scrubland and tropical forest to high mountains up to 3,000 metres.

The Long-tailed Macaque or Crab-eating Monkey (*Macaca fascicularis*) lives near the coast in the tidal creeks and mangrove swamps of south-east Asia and has now been introduced into Mauritius. A good swimmer and diver, it often crosses fair stretches of water, and has established itself on isolated islands. It feeds on shellfish.

The Japanese Macaque (*Macaca fuscata*) has been the subject of considerable field studies in recent years, especially of its social behaviour. In the course of these studies it was seen that one monkey hit upon the idea of washing the sweet potatoes supplied to them. Observers were able to watch the habit spread to other members of the troop.

fruit and leaves, the two staple elements of their diet.

MACAQUES, GUENONS, PATAS MONKEYS, MANGABEYS: A very large number of species belong to this group, which includes many of the most widespread monkeys and the most frequently seen in zoos, where they are always a very popular spectacle. They nearly all have long, non-prehensile tails, which are always covered to the tip with short hairs. They have well-developed thumbs, fore limbs and hind limbs of equal length, simple stomachs and cheek pouches.

Their habits in the wild state are well known. They are gregarious, and in bands of several dozens, each led by an experienced male, they scour their chosen hunting ground, which they defend fiercely against other bands intent on poaching. The leader is a well-tried, cunning chief, which always goes on ahead, sometimes climbing to survey the horizon. His cries report the result of his inspection, and if all is well, the band continues, perhaps to a cornfield, where they scatter, though remaining under the control of the leader. First the cheek pouches are filled with corn, then the monkeys wander about, inspecting, testing, eating. The damage done by these animals is enormous, and they are among the most detested of their kind.

When all seems peaceful the mothers allow their young, hitherto clinging to their chests, to go off and play with one another, while they sit and watch. A trembling, wailing cry from the chief is the danger signal, at which the mothers call in their young. The troop bands together again and, snatching a last handful of food, makes for the nearest tree.

A favourite occupation, as with so many other monkeys, is grooming one another's coats. At night all take refuge in the tree-tops, out of reach of leopards, snakes, and eagles, the monkey's great enemies. The numerous species in this group belong to about six genera, nearly all African.

The Asiatic genus *Macaca* is found in China and Japan, India, Burma and Malaya, but one species is found in North Africa and Gibraltar. The macaques are thick-set monkeys and stand the cold well as they are accustomed to high altitudes, some of them living well above the snowline.

The Rhesus Monkey (*Macaca mulatta*) is widespread in northern India and south-east Asia. It is gregarious and very agile and the adults are powerful. The long-haired coat is greyish in colour. There are red ischial callosities.

There are three races of the Pig-tailed Macaque (*N. nemestrina*), spread over Assam, Burma, Thailand, Malaya and the East Indies. This is a strongly built species, with the head and body sixty centimetres long, and the tail over fifteen centimentres. It is more terrestrial in habit than other species, but is still a good climber, and in Sumatra it has been trained to pick coconuts. In Malaya botanists have used it to collect specimens from tall trees. The most northerly species are the Japanese Macaque (*M. fuscata*) and the Assamese Macaque (*M. assamensis*), both of which are acustomed to −8 to −10°C.

Of special interest is the Barbary Ape (*M. inua*), sometimes called the Pygmy Ape or Magot, which is almost tail-less and has a long snout. It belongs to the mountains of Morocco and Algeria, but is better known as a resident of Gibraltar, where it appears to have been introduced from Barbary. It is the only monkey found in Europe. A hundred years ago, when the number of apes in Gibraltar had fallen to three, several young specimens were imported from Morocco. By the beginning of this century there were over a hundred, but they became a nuisance, and protection was suspended. Those left today are all tame and in private keeping.

Elsewhere in Africa the Cercopithecidae are represented by guenons (genus *Cercopithecus*), of which there is a larger number of species, differing in little but their coloration and markings. Included among the guenons are the Talapoin (*C. talapoin*) of the Congo and Angola, a small yellow-green monkey, only eighty centimetres long, including thirty-five centimetres of tail; the Moustached Monkey (*C. cephus cephus*) from eastern Nigeria to the Congo, with an olive-green to blue-grey body, a bright blue face and a white mark like a moustache across the upper lip; and the Diana Monkey (*C. diana*) from Liberia, which has a black head, legs and tail, grey body, red-brown rump, white neck and breast and a white band on the forehead. The Mona Monkey (*C. mona*), a handsome guenon from West Africa, has been introduced into St Kitt's and Grenada in the West Indies.

The Patas Monkey (*Erythrocebus patas*) is closely related to the guenons, but it is not arboreal. It is orange above, white below, and has a black face. Its many races are distributed from Senegal to Ethiopia and East Africa, in dry savannas where trees are within reach for emergencies.

The mangabeys are like long-snouted guenons, mostly with dark coats of uniform colour. The Crested or Grey-cheeked Mangabey (*Cerocebus albigena*) has a brush of long hair on the head, black in the middle merging into grey. It is fairly widespread from Cameroun to Uganda. Most of the other species, such as the Collared Mangabey, Crested Mangabey and Agile Mangabey, are restricted in their distribution.

BABOONS AND MANDRILLS: These Old World monkeys are confined to Africa, except for one species of baboon. All its members are big and have a general likeness, fostered by their adaptation to terrestrial life. They always move on all fours. With their long muzzles, terminal nostrils and strong teeth they have something in common with the dog. Their canines are as fang-like as those of the Leopard, which they sometimes attack. They are caricatures of a dog, however, in the same way as the Gorilla is a caricature of man. Many have mantle-like manes. Their ischial callosities are enormous and highly coloured. Sometimes, as in the drills, the genital regions are naked and brightly coloured, and the snout is similarly coloured. The heavy-browed eyes are small. The tail is of moderate length in baboons and thinly haired, but in the drills it is a stump.

The Sacred Baboon (*Papio hamadryas*) is one of the best known. It is found in Somalia and on both sides of the Red Sea and lives gregariously in mountainous regions. The males are pale silver with a flowing mantle-like mane, the females are smaller and browner. The ischial callosities are

The Pig-tailed Macaque (*Macaca nemestrina*) of Burma and Sumatra is the largest of the macaque monkeys, with a heavy body and short tail which is held up in a loop. In the wild macaques move in troops and are as much at home on the ground as in the trees.

The Rhesus Monkey (*Macaca mulatta*) is one of the most familiar of the macaque monkeys. The organ-grinder's monkey, for example, was usually a Rhesus Monkey. Rhesus Macaques are intelligent and have a strong sense of curiosity. They soon learn to manipulate simple tools and distinguish colours and shapes. Pictured here are two engaged in their favourite occupation of social grooming.

Female Olive or Anubis Baboon (*Papio anubis*), with her offspring. The typical species is the Hamadryas or Sacred Baboon of the north-east of Africa and Arabia. The Anubis Baboon, closely related to it, ranges across Central Africa from West to East Africa. It can be recognised especially by its long muzzle.

The Mandrill (*Papio sphinx*) is the most arresting of the baboons, with its vivid colouring both front and rear. It is a forest creature, moving in troops on the forest floor and occasionally climbing trees to investigate whatever arouses its curiosity.

Opposite
A Grey or Silvery Gibbon (*Hylobates moloch*) of Java and Borneo. The gibbons are the smallest of the apes, rarely growing taller than a metre but with arms which reach the ground. When walking bipedally the arms are held above the head, in an attitude of surrender. Gibbons travel at great speed through the trees and can usually outdistance any of their enemies but are fairly helpless if caught on the ground.

bright red. Other species are the Anubis Baboon (*P. anubis*), living in rocky districts of West and Central Africa; the Yellow Baboon (*P. cynocephalus*); and the Chacma Baboon (*P. ursinus*) from South Africa, which is grey-black with a black face and no mantle. This last feeds on reptiles, scorpions and insects, but will eat roots at a pinch, and kills newborn lambs to drink the milk in their stomachs.

The Mandrill (*Papio sphinx*) has been described as the ugliest and most brutal of monkeys. The muzzle is purple, and the enormous cheek swellings are pale blue. A ring of bristles frames the face. The coloration, particularly of the genital regions and buttock patches, must be regarded as a secondary sexual character, apparently attractive to the more dully coloured females. The Drill (*M. leucophaeus*) is like the Mandrill except for its black face. They come from Cameroun and Gabon.

The Gelada (*Theropithecus gelada*) is related to the baboons but has nostrils on the side of the snout instead of at the end. It lives in the mountains of northern Ethiopia. The Dusky Gelada Baboon (*T. obscurus*) also lives in mountains but in southern Ethiopia.

The baboons and mandrills live in rough and rocky regions of Africa and Arabia at heights of 3,000 to 4,000 metres. They are rarely found in forests, where they would hardly be able to climb trees. Their troops muster sometimes as many as 200 or 300 individuals under the leadership of the old males. They are highly gregarious and their devotion to family and community is highly developed. Whether monogamous or polygamous the males guard their mates jealously and punish any infidelity with death. Rarely, on the other hand, does a male pay court to a female not his own. The young are strictly brought up by their mother, and sometimes taken to task by their father. When very young they cling constantly with hands and feet to their mother's breast, with one teat in the mouth, at which they suckle from time to time. Later they ride with great assurance on her back. Grooming, a sign of sociability common to all monkeys, is practised still more assiduously by the young.

They are highly organised, and it has been claimed that they have their chiefs, lieutenants, sentinels, vanguards and rearguards. Their expeditions have always a foraging intent. They are omnivorous, and if they render service in keeping down insects and gorging themselves on invading crickets, they also do heavy damage to fruit, grain, buds and roots. They are also great egg-stealers.

They defend themselves ferociously if attacked and can stand up to leopards and the best trained hounds. They do not often attack man, but are regarded as dangerous, particularly the mandrills, whose strength, agility and teeth make them the tyrant of the forest, fearing no enemy.

Anthropoid apes (Family Pongidae)
Anthropoid apes are the primates closest to man, anatomically, physiologically and psychologically. They are represented today by two Asiatic groups, the gibbons and Orang-utans, and two African groups, the Gorillas and Chimpanzees. In the Cainozoic era the group contained other forms, e.g. *Dryopithecus* and *Palaeopithecus*. It was from this

group that the stem which eventually led to *Homo sapiens* branched off, probably in the Miocene.

The chief anatomical characters which link anthropoids with man, and at the same time distinguish them from the other primates, are the absence of tail, the more or less upright posture and the high degree of development of the brain.

We have already seen monkeys in which a tail was lacking—the Barbary Ape, for instance—but these are exceptional. In the anthropoids, on the other hand, it is the invariable rule and one of the distinguishing characters. The number of caudal vertebrae is reduced, as in man, to three or four, and they are more or less fused together to form the vestigial tail called a coccyx.

Though they often walk on all fours, the anthropoids have reached the stage at which they can no longer be called quadrupeds. Incidentally, except in the gibbons, even on all fours, their weight is not supported by the palms of the hands and soles of the feet, as in other monkeys. Only the outer edge of the soles and the knuckles of the second digits rest on the ground. The limbs of the anthropoids are much nearer in structure to man's than to the monkey's, the chief difference being in their relative lengths: arms shorter than legs in man, about equal in the chimpanzees, and longer in the gorillas, orang-utans and, particularly, in the gibbons, Another indication of the upright posture of anthropoids, however imperfect it may be, is given by the spinal processes. Whereas in quadrupeds those on the anterior part of the spine slope backwards and those in the rear slope forwards, in the anthropoids and in man they all slope backwards.

The cranial capacity of anthropoids also approaches that of man, even though still inferior. But brain size is not the only relevant factor; there are also the convolutions, whose basic disposition is the same in the anthropoids as in man. The Orang-utan's brain is indeed very near to man's and the Chimpanzee's brain even shows a suggestion of the gyrus of Broca, the centre of articulate speech. It can also be seen from the behaviour of these apes, particularly the Chimpanzee, that they possess a developing intelligence comparable to man's. It might even be justified to group the gibbons, Orang-utans, Gorillas and Chimpanzees in a separate suborder intermediate between the monkeys and the hominids. The more generally accepted classification is followed here.

GIBBONS: Gibbons are the least anthropoid of the group. Though possessing a large brain in proportion to their weight, they are definitely less intelligent. They differ from other anthropoids in having much longer arms, and they are the only ones to have ischial callosities. They are placed by some naturalists in a distinct family, the Hylobatidae, which some would even exclude from the Anthropoidea.

The gibbons are not very widely distributed, being found only in Burma, Thailand, Indo-China, Malaya, Sumatra, Java and Borneo. In this limited area there is one genus, with some half dozen species. The genus *Hylobates* includes the Hoolock Gibbon (*Hylobates hoolock*), the Lar Gibbon (*H. lar*), and the Black Gibbon (*H. concolor*). The first two species are both about a metre in height and their weight is not often above

MAMMALS

Opposite
The Orang-utan (*Pongo pygmaeus*), is found only on the islands of Sumatra and Borneo. It is a forest-dweller usually found in lowland forest swamps. Its movements are unhurried. It either walks on the branches or swings leisurely from branch to branch with its hands.

Gorillas (*Gorilla gorilla*) are the largest and most powerful of the primates, but in spite of its great strength and fearsome appearance, a Gorilla is not dangerous unless provoked. It never kills to eat, its natural diet being fruit and vegetables. The mountain Gorilla is black and is found in the Gabon and Zaire. The lowland or coast Gorilla, of the same region, has an iron-grey colouring.

six kilograms. The Siamang (*H. syndactylus*) is slightly taller and definitely heavier, sometimes reaching eleven kilograms. It can be recognised by its deep black colour and red-brown chin.

The gibbons are slender, swift-moving animals, living almost entirely in the trees. They are the only apes which normally stand and walk upright when they are on the ground. They have a throughly plantigrade stance, moreover, not merely using the outer edges of the foot, and they keep balance with the aid of the arms, which they hold outwards shoulder high. The arms are so long that the hands almost touch the ground. The hands themselves are much longer than the feet, and the fingers are hooked inwards towards the palms. Sometimes a few of the toes are fused together. These characters correspond to the arboreal life. They haunt mountainous forests, the Siamang being found at heights of up to 3,000 metres in Sumatra. They move easily among the branches, swinging by their arms, and launching themselves confidently to a branch a good ten metres away. It is claimed that they can change their direction in mid-air. They are, in contrast, among the few species incapable of swimming.

They are very noisy creatures, chanting in chorus from morning till night. Some species, like the Hoolock, are called after the sounds they make. The Siamang is the loudest, its cry being a sort of barking, amplified in a laryngeal cavity at the front of the throat.

Like that of other anthropoids, their diet is largely frugivorous and herbivorous, but on occasion they eat insects, spiders, birds' eggs and small vertebrates. They have been seen to catch birds on the wing. In captivity they easily get used to eating meat, both cooked and raw. The gibbons drink in an extremely primitive manner, dipping their fore arms in the water and then licking the fur dry. It is possible, however, that some species drink with their lips in water, or they may even lift water to their mouths in cupped hands.

Sexual maturity is attained in from five to eight years. Gestation lasts seven months and there is generally a litter of one. Lactation lasts about seven months, during which the infant is carried about continually by its mother, and only after weaning does it begin to venture away from her. The young cannot fend for themselves until the age of three or four, so that, with a new infant arriving yearly, a permanent family is formed consisting of the parents and three or four off-spring. In Indo-China it is not rare to find polygamous families of two or three females with a single mate, the offspring all being brought up together.

At night gibbons sleep hidden among leaves; they do not construct any kind of nest or shelter. In captivity they are very friendly, and their emotions are revealed immediately by cries, gestures and facial expressions. One observer has noted five different cries of pleasure, and at least four of discontent or fear. Gibbons are nevertheless the least educable of the anthropoids. Except for a few tricks that come easily to them, it is usually impossible to teach them anything at all, though there are exceptional cases that have been recorded.

ORANG-UTANS: There is only one species, *Pongo pygmaeus*, strictly confined to the low-lying forests of Sumatra and Borneo. Orang-utan is Malay for 'man of the woods', and the facial resemblance to man is marked. The Orang-utan is the only anthropoid whose head has developed upwards, producing a high, arched forehead. It is also the only one to have, like man, twelve thoracic vertebrae and twelve pairs of ribs. There, however, the likeness ceases. Its arms are longer than those of the Gorillas and Chimpanzees, the legs shorter, and the canines more fang-like. In cranial capacity it is mid-way between Gorillas and Chimpanzees.

Except in a few places, such as the face and palms of the hands, the Orang-utan is covered with long, mahogany-coloured hair, which is longer and thicker in the male than the female. The male is also larger, has a huge laryngeal cavity forming a sort of goitre, which hangs down over the chest, and two fatty cheek swellings. It stands 140 centimetres high and weighs about seventy kilograms.

Much less agile than the gibbons, the Orang-utan never indulges in acrobatics. Even when

512

pursued, it moves with a somewhat leisurely haste, feeling its way more with man-like prudence than monkey-like dash. On the ground it moves clumsily, generally on all fours, but sometimes it walks upright, moving its arms to keep balance.

The Orang-utan lives chiefly on buds and fruit. Like most mammals it drinks directly with the mouth. To sleep, it constructs what is generally called its nest, a platform of small branches collected in the fork of a tree and trampled down. It sleeps on its back or side, with its legs curled up and its arms folded under its head. In cold or wet weather it covers itself with leaves. The nest is a temporary shelter, though used by one animal, or a mother with her young, for several nights.

Adult males live apart, except in the mating season, and have no sense of family responsibility. Sexual maturity is reached in both sexes at the age of ten. Gestation is a fortnight shorter than in man, and only one offspring is born at a time, the weight at birth being about a kilogram. Lactation lasts a year-and-a-half.

Orang-utans are friendly animals in captivity, except for old males, which become bad tempered and even dangerous. They are active, playful and affectionate, sociable even to the extent of sharing their quarters with animals of quite different species. They are almost as responsive to education as Chimpanzees. After six months' training, one Orang-utan learnt to use the word 'papa' correctly, and a little later the word 'cup', which it used whenever it wanted water. That is more than has been obtained from any other anthropoids.

GORILLAS: It is generally recognised that there is only one species (*Gorilla gorilla*), the Mountain Gorilla being regarded merely as a subspecies. The Gorilla is found in the depths of the forests of Cameroun, Gabon and the Congo, and the Mountain Gorilla high up in the mountains north of Lake Kivu and on the Uganda border in the same area.

The Gorilla is the biggest and strongest of all the primates. A male may easily be 180 centimetres tall and weigh 200 kilograms. A specimen kept for many years in the Berlin Zoo attained the record weight of 288 kilograms. It is not surprising that animals of such dimensions should have inspired tales of sacked villages and abducted women and children although, in reality, Gorillas are gentle creatures.

Allied with its size is a strikingly ferocious appearance. The ears are small and rather human in shape, but the eyes are deeply sunk under beetling brows, and in the males the head has a high sagittal crest to which powerful jaw muscles are attached. This ridge gives additional height to the skull, but that must not be taken to indicate cranial capacity, which is indeed less than that of either Orang-utans or Chimpanzees. The lower jaw is as massive as that of Orang-utans and the teeth are equally strong, with particularly large and fang-like canines. The limbs are more human in their proportions than those of Orang-utans, though the arms are still considerably longer than the legs. Upright stance and, still more, an upright carriage are almost impossible. The Gorilla stands on the outer edge of its feet and the knuckles of the hand. It has nevertheless become an almost terrestrial animal. Although the females and the

young climb trees, they do so cautiously, but the fully grown male has become too heavy for arboreal life.

The Gorilla's family life shows a marked advance on that of Orang-utans, for the male lives with his females and offspring, and sometimes several families combine to form a small tribe of some forty head. Forced to be nomadic in order to find the great quantity of fruit they need, gorillas come to a halt only at night, sleeping in the trees or on the ground with a hastily improvised mattress of branches and leaves for a nest. The male animal may sit on a heap of leaves with his back against a tree and his arms crossed over his chest.

Accompanied by the female, he is a dangerous creature and will not hesitate to attack an intruder. He may be content to frighten it off with an aggressive display of power, beating his breast and barking hoarsely, and finishing with a resounding roar.

Gorillas reach sexual maturity at the age of about twelve. Little is known of the sexual life, for they seldom breed in captivity. Young gorillas grow very rapidly, to judge from observations made at the Berlin Zoo. A young male, weighing fifteen kilograms on its arrival at the zoo, weighed over 270 kilograms when it died seven years later.

For long the Gorilla was taken to be the least intelligent of the anthropoids. Despite its relatively small brain, however, it seems that the Gorilla is on about the same mental level as the Orang-utan. It does not have the active curiosity of the Chimpanzee nor its perseverance in experiment, but it is attentive. Although slow to learn, it remembers what it has learnt. These animals evidently show greater individual variation in both character and intelligence than other anthropoids. Some individuals show excellent response. Others, however, have proved sullen and irritable.

CHIMPANZEES: There is only one species of Chimpanzee (*Pan troglodytes*), though divided into several races in the area it occupies, which stretches from Sierra Leone and along the west coast of Africa across to the Great Lakes east of the Congo. One race known as the Dwarf Chimpan-

An old male or silverback of the Mountain Gorilla (*Gorilla gorilla*). The Mountain Gorilla is the largest and most powerful of all the primates but, in spite of its great strength and fearsome appearance, it is not dangerous unless provoked. Its natural diet is vegetarian and its disposition is pacific.

Opposite
The Chimpanzee (*Pan troglodytes*) has a very highly developed brain and anatomically is very close to man. It can be found in most of equatorial Africa, where the usual unit is a family group with a single male at the head and a harem of several females, which he protects and jealously guards.

The Giant Anteater (*Myrmecophaga tridactyla*) is a native of the tropical grasslands of Central and South America. Anteaters feed almost exclusively on termites, ants and soft-bodied grubs. With the strong sharp claws of the front feet they can tear holes in the tough resilient walls of termite nests, as effectively as a man wielding a pick-axe.

zee, to the south of the Congo River; used to be regarded by some as a distinct species (*Pan paniscus*). It is the most widespread of the anthropoids and the best studied, particularly since tropical laboratories have enabled it to be kept under observation under the best possible conditions.

Anatomically, the Chimpanzee tends towards man in its brain, dentition and the relative length of its limbs. Whereas the arms of other anthropoids are longer than their legs, those of the Chimpanzee are about the same length. This is a step towards man, whose legs are longer. It has the most highly developed brain of the anthropoids, with convolutions hardly different from man's. This advance in cerebral structure is reflected in the Chimpanzee's behaviour, which shows an intelligence undoubtedly superior to that of any other primate. Physiological factors, such as similar blood reactions and an acceptance of grafted tissues, are further indications of proximity to man.

The various races differ considerably in outward appearances. As one writer has observed: 'Like us, these apes differ markedly among themselves in skin colour, which ranges with age and exposure to sunlight, from Caucasian white to Negro black; in coat colour from jet black to faded brown or dirty grey; in size from pygmy to giant; in skull shape from round to long; in ear shape and size from small to large and erect to lop. . . Nevertheless, the typical Chimpanzee is recognisable enough, with its large, turned-out ears, and characteristic eyes. The coat is generally dark, or a mahogany brown. A typical size is 150 centimetres for a male, the female being thirty centimetres shorter.'

The Chimpanzee is less arboreal than gibbons or Orang-utans, but more arboreal than the Gorilla. It moves quite fast in the trees; on the ground it slouches along on all fours, rarely holding itself upright. When it does walk on two feet, it is apt to hold its hands behind its back, probably to counter the natural forward tilt of the body. In the forests which are their natural habitat chimpanzees live in groups or bands of variable composition which belong to a large society, of sixty to eighty animals. The bands move about a home range and there is little sign of social ranking in the band.

During the day these chattering groups forage around for fruit and other vegetable food. At night nests are built in the fork of a tree—really a platform on which the Chimpanzee can huddle. They wake up after sunrise. Drinking is direct, with the lips immersed in water, as by Gorillas and Orang-utans. Like the gibbons, Chimpanzees dislike water and are incapable of swimming.

The sexual life of Chimpanzees is well known, since they have often bred in captivity. The adult state is reached in seven or eight years in both sexes. The menstrual cycle is twenty-six or twenty-seven days, and gestation lasts between eight and nine months. Only one young is born at a time, weighing about 1·8 kilograms. It clings first to the mother's belly, then to her back. Later, it leaves her to play with other babies. It will continue to associate with its mother after her next baby is born. Growth is more rapid than in man, but life is shorter. From observations made Chimpanzees are old at thirty and they die at about fifty.

Chimpanzees thrive better than any other anthropoid in captivity; and, provided they are captured young and brought up with others of the same kind, they show the most remarkable mental and affective qualities.

Chimpanzees have learnt to imitate closely a number of operations performed by humans; to put on clothes, to eat and drink at table, to sweep, wash up, use keys, hammers and other tools, to ride bicycles, and smoke. Although these operations may be simply the result of acute observation and imitation, there are others in which Chimpanzees have used genuine initiative and powers of reflection, in other words they have shown genuine intelligence. If tempting food is put out of reach in a Chimpanzee's cage, the animal will promptly place two or three boxes on top of each other to provide a platform from which it can grasp the food, even if it has never seen such a thing done before. Similarly, set in a cage with a set of extending rods inside and a desirable object outside, the Chimpanzee will immediately estimate how many sections of rod to put together to reach the object. Using the rod could be the result of collective, hereditary experience; fitting the sections together indicates individual intelligence.

The following experiment was carried out in the United States in 1936. An automatic machine delivered a raisin every time a counter was put in the slot. Another machine delivered a counter each time a lever was pulled. Very quickly the Chimpanzee picked up the idea, getting counters from one machine and using them in the other. To make the experiment more difficult the machines were than adjusted to work at different times. When the one with the raisins operated, the other was out of action and vice versa. Once again the Chimpanzee was quick to grasp the situation, providing itself with a hoard of counters and then waiting patiently, for hours if necessary, until the machine with the raisins was working again. The animal thus showed a real understanding of the nature of money—a symbolic object of no value in itself, but capable of ultimately satisfying a desire.

The Chimpanzee's intelligence is based on perpetual curiosity, the perception of the significance of a fact, and the capacity to initiate speculative reactions. Its memory is good, recalling after an interval of years a person, a place or how to operate a machine. The range of its emotional life is considerable, and it is able to express surprise, interest, disgust, fear, anger, joy, sadness and even despair, the latter being evinced by fits of sobbing. Only tears are lacking. Their affection is manifested by hugs and kisses.

It is interesting to compare the psychology of a child with that of a young anthropoid. An American scientist, Kellog, has done this in the United States. He brought up his own son from the age of ten months with a female Chimpanzee, which at the start was seven-and-a-half months old. Both were treated alike, given the same things to play with, taken on the same walks, put to bed at the same time. Very soon the Chimpanzee had shown herself much more precocious. She responded much sooner to orders like 'Come here', 'Sit down', 'Stand up', and to simple questions such as 'Where's Donald?' In manual skill and strength she was well ahead of the boy and was quicker to realise where a sound came from. Before long, however, Donald began to catch up and then to outdistance her. He was the first to abandon mere scribbling for an attempt at drawing and he was the one who began to pronounce words.

Allen and Beatrice Gardner brought up Chimpanzee, Washoe, as one of the family. They communicated with her using ASL, the American Sign Language, used by the deaf and dumb. Unlike the finger-spelling of British Deaf-and-Dumb language, this is a system of gestures, each of which stands for a whole word or concept. For example, 'flower' is described by holding the fingertips of one hand together and smelling them. Washoe now has a vocabulary of some 150 signs, and invents her own signs and meanings. She learned to give the sign for 'open' when she wanted to go through any door and then, amazingly, used it when she wanted a water tap turned on. She also coined the phrase 'open-food-drink' for a refrigerator, and when she heard a dog bark she 'said': 'hear-dog'.

Ant-eaters, sloths, armadillos (Order Edentata)

Edentata ('toothless') is not a literally correct appellation for this order, particularly when we taken into account the sloth and the armadillo, whose jaws carry as many molars as, if not more than, man's. Admittedly some, such as anteaters, have no teeth, but the name really indicates that in the whole group there are no outwardly visible teeth, no member having either incisors or canines. Even the molars are very simple teeth, lacking enamel, and open at the bottom of the root. The families in this group have no other character in common.

Formerly the order Edentata included the pangolins, but these are now regarded as of separate stock and have been reclassified to the order Pholidota. The Pholidota have a normal joint between the last dorsal and first lumbar vertebrae. The females have a bicorned uterus, and a diffuse placenta not unlike that of a mare. The males have external testes and a well-developed penis ending in a glans. Pholidota are found only in the Old World, in Asia and Africa, and the only living forms are the pangolins.

The Edentata differ from the Pholidota in that the joint between the last dorsal and the first lumbar vertebrae is quite abnormal. There are the usual articular processes and, in addition, the joint is reinforced by additional processes, the function of which is not understood. The female has a divided uterus, which is only one step removed from the double uterus of the marsupials. The placenta, on the other hand, is discoidal, and thus more advanced than that of the Pholidota. The males have internal testes, a small penis and no glans. The Edentata are exclusively New World creatures. They include the anteaters, sloths and armadillos.

Anteaters (Family Myrmecophagidae)

These edentates are readily distinguished by their long fur and extremely elongated snouts. Some have a long, prehensile tail, used for climbing, and one has a bushy tail. They resemble the pangolins in two features only: the long digging claws on the fore feet and their viscous, vermiform tongue.

The largest of all the edentates, the Great Anteater (*Myrmecophaga tridactyla*) attains an overall length of more than 240 centimetres. From the middle of the chest to the rump dark brown predominates, with alternating bands of black and white on the head and fore feet giving an optical grey. A black triangle running back from the throat separates the two areas so effectively that it is difficult at first sight to see that they belong to the same animal. A mane of long hairs rises in the middle of the back, flowing over and mingling with the long hairs of the enormously bushy tail. The Anteater is one of the strangest-looking creatures, and its feeding habits do nothing to deny this impression. From the end of its already very long snout proceeds the worm-like tongue, which can stretch for a good twenty centimetres further. It darts into the breaches it has made in nests and is withdrawn repeatedly, each time with hundreds of insects sticking to it, and each time it emerges from the mouth it is bathed in fresh viscous saliva.

The claws are used only to demolish the termite hills and not, as in the pangolin, for burrowing. In fact the Anteater has no very constant abode. Sleeping in the grass during the day, sheltered from the sun by its tail, it spends the night foraging, or, in the pairing season, seeking a mate.

The Tamandua or Collared Anteater (*Tamandua tetradactyla*) is the second largest of the New World anteaters. It ranges over a wider area than the Giant Anteater, being found from Mexico to Paraguay. It is arboreal and has a prehensile tail. A great many insects are caught at one time with its long extensile tongue, which is kept moist with saliva.

The Three-toed Sloth or Ai (*Bradypus tridactylus*) ranges over South and Central America, from the Amazon northwards to Honduras. It is more lively than the Two-toed Sloth (*Choloepus didactylus*) although both are characteristically extremely lethargic. In trees they hang suspended, but rarely for long periods preferring to prop themselves in branches with their backs well supported.

Opposite top
Armadillos are habitual diggers and scratchers, foraging for insects and a variety of small animals living at the surface of the soil. They also eat fruit, leaves and shoots, and although they destroy many noxious animals they tend, in some areas, to become agricultural pests. This is especially true of the Nine-banded Armadillo.

Opposite bottom
The Fairy Armadillo or Pichiciego (*Chlamyphorus truncatus*) lives in Patagonia and the Argentine pampas. It is the smallest of the armadillos, measuring only fifteen centimetres in length. Mole-like, it has powerful front legs and small eyes, with less armour than the other species. It lives underground. Armadillos live on a variety of food: insects, plants, carrion, snakes and lizards.

The female bears only one at a time, carrying it on her back throughout lactation.

The Tamandua (*Tamandua tetradactyla*) is arboreal and has a prehensile tail. With its white, yellowish and ochrous colouring, it is easily hidden among the leaves when hunting. In moments of danger it will try to escape. If that is impossible it sits down and tries to hug its adversary with its arms. This attitude is said to be the origin of its nickname, *Dominus vobiscum*, because of its supposed likeness to a priest at the altar.

The Two-toed Anteater (*Cyclopes didactylus*) is about the size of a squirrel, and is essentially arboreal. It inhabits the hottest parts of Brazil, Guiana and Venezuela, but because of its nocturnal habits is rarely seen.

Sloths (Family Bradypodidae)

Much is now known about the Tree-toed Sloth observed over a long period by a New York scientist, W. Beebe, in the station of Kartabo, Guyana.

In repose or slow movement in a tree it may be likened to a tuft of hay or lichen, or a hanging ant's nest. Its long hair is a mixture of many tints of black, brown, yellow, orange or white. The hairs are grooved and inhabited by algae which turn yellow in periods of drought and green under damp conditions, thus contributing - to the camouflage of the Sloth among the foliage at different seasons.

The likeness to a hanging nest is increased by the fact that the animal spends most of its active life hanging down, face upwards, from the branches by the three long claws on each of its feet. Neither shaking the branch nor hauling on the animal can dislodge it, even if it is asleep, when it is usually rolled up in a ball. When shot it remains hanging until it rots. Jaguars and eagles, its chief enemies, are often defeated by its remarkable

camouflage and immobility. Its vital resistance is considerable, serious wounds healing quickly and only rarely becoming infected.

It has a short, stumpy tail, and a head as round as a monkey's, with a face devoid of expression. The eyes, in particular, are round, lacking in mobility, very short-sighted, and surrounded by a ring of dark lashes giving the appearance of spectacles. The small mouth has thick, horny lips, which hold the leaves during mastication. Above the mouth is a sort of snout pierced by two nostrils. There is no outward sign of ears, the pinnae being so small they are lost in the hairs.

It has eighteen teeth, five molars above on each side and four below. They are rounded, separate from each other and hollowed out, simple teeth that slowly grind the leaves held by the rugged lips and then pushed back by the tongue—also rough.

A sloth's most striking feature is its sluggish movement or complete inactivity. Everything is done as though in slow motion. Not only do the limbs follow one another very slowly but the head, though quite mobile, turns with the utmost deliberation. Undoubtedly there are physiological causes for this congenital lethargy. Circulatory weakness and slow reflexes have both been suggested. The slowness of their movements has been perpetuated in their common name, but has sometimes been exaggerated. It has even been claimed that they pass their whole lives in a single branch. One sloth, kept under observation for 168 hours, fed for eleven hours, climbed for about eighteen, remained motionless during ten and slept for 129. In other words, the creature's day consisted of nineteen hours of rest and five hours of activity. Its speed of movement in a tree has been estimated as two kilometres an hour.

Sometimes sloths make for water and cross big rivers. They swim with their fore feet at a speed of some 550 metres an hour. It is on land that they are the slowest, crawling clumsily at about half their swimming speed. Sloths are also slow in masticating and digesting their food, and therefore eat very little. They absorb only one-seventh of the food of a young fawn of the same weight.

Sloths seem to have no feelings, whether of anger, hatred, love, friendship, dislike, fear or courage. Even in coupling there is no sign of eagerness. Generally they are silent and only when attacked, or when the young are separated from their mothers, do they emit a plaintive wail, which is the origin of the name *ai*, by which the Three-toed Sloth is also known.

There are only four occasions on which sloths really react positively: when attacked they defend themselves with teeth and claws; when two find themselves on the same branch they attack each other fiercely until one is killed or driven away; separated from its mother the young one cries until the mother looks for it and finds it or until some other preoccupation makes her forget it; and at least once a year sloths undertake a journey, the reason for which remains unknown. At such times they will be seen crossing a river, though the trees on the far side are the same, and no advantages can be found to provide a motive. One specimen marked by Beebe was found to have covered a distance of 6·5 kilometres in two months. Sloths are therefore far from being completely indolent, and this is particularly applicable to the Three-toed Sloth (*Bradypus tridactylus*).

The Two-toed Sloth or Unau (*Choloepus didactylus*) inhabits the same tropical parts of America and is a smaller form. It moves less slowly, is more responsive, more sociable and more easily kept in captivity than the three-toed species.

The skeletons of these two animals, the Ai and the Unau, are very different, which justifies their being placed in different genera. The Ai has a short tail and its fore limbs are longer than the hind limbs. Unlike every other mammal, it has nine cervical vertebrae; it also has thirty ribs. The Unau has six or seven cervical vertebrae, forty-eight ribs and no tail. As Buffon says: 'In living things the interior establishes the pattern of nature and is its true form. The exterior is a mere surface or garment.'

Armadillos (Family Dasypodidae)

In this group the hair coat is replaced by strong, bony plates covered with horn. A scapular shield protects the shoulders, and a pelvic shield the rump. Between these two, the plates are arranged in transverse bands joined to one another, but are sufficently mobile to allow the animals to roll themselves into balls. The top of the head and the exposed parts of the limbs are also covered with scales, and the tails also are armoured.

The feet are plantigrade and have four to five strong burrowing claws, by means of which the armadillos can very quickly disappear into the ground out of sight of their enemies. They also burrow to provide homes for themselves, and the claws are useful in digging up worms and insects.

The teeth consist of very simple molars without enamel or roots, but they may be very numerous; a hundred in the giant armadillos. Since there are no incisors, food is caught by the viscous cylindrical tongue, as in the pangolins and anteaters.

Just as the Opossum is the only representative of the marsupials in North America, the Nine-banded Armadillo (*Dasypus novemcinctus*) is the only edentate whose habitat extends to the United States. It is also the best known variety, owing to the researches of the local authorities in Texas. It attains a length of over seventy-five centimetres and a weight of 5·8 to 6·75 kilograms. It has nine mobile bands between the scapular and pelvic shields, and thirty teeth.

The Nine-banded Armadillo has a peculiar reproductive feature. The female always bears a litter of four, which are always of the same sex and exactly alike. Research has shown that these are really identical quads; that is, derived from the division of a single egg. Moreover, they are attached umbilically to a single placenta. In scientific terms this is a case of polyembryony happening normally and regularly. In other mammals it is accidental.

The Nine-banded Armadillo lives on insects and their larvae, worms and millipedes, which make up ninety-three per cent of its stomach contents.

Although always terrestrial the armadillo does not fight shy of water. It is a heavy animal and does not swim easily, but in a short time it blows out its stomach and intestine with air, which gives it additional buoyancy. This air-swallowing has not yet been explained. It often falls a prey to dogs,

peccaries or coyotes, against which its armour plating is not an adequate defence. Unable to run away, the armadillo seeks to dig itself in, failing which it feigns death like the Opossum.

The Nine-banded Armadillo has spread rapidly into the United States during this century. Formerly it came no farther north than Mexico, but in 1880 it crossed the Rio Grande and entered Texas and by 1939 specimens were being reported in all the southeastern states. Its tentative progress towards New Mexico and Oklahoma was without great success as it was unable to stand up to cold and died if subjected to even a short period of frost.

Many other varieties of armadillo are found in various parts of Central and South America. The Giant Armadillo (*Priodontes gigas*) is the largest, being almost 152 centimetres long overall. It has twelve movable bands between the scapular and pelvic shields. The Tatouay (*Cabassous unicinctus*) is distinguished by having a tail covered only by delicate scales. The Six-banded Armadillo (*Euphractus sexcinctus*) inhabits the same part of South America. Farther south in Argentina down to Patagonia, is the Hairy Armadillo (*Euphractus villosus*), whose scales are covered by abundant hair, growing interstitially.

The Three-banded Armadillo (*Tolypeutes tricinctus*) thrives in the hottest parts of the American continent. It is also called Apara, Mataco and Bola, the last because of the speed with which it rolls up into a ball to avoid attackers.

The Fairy Armadillo or Pichiciego (*Chlamyphorus truncatus*) is thirteen centimetres long without the tail. It is a curious species. The shell is attached to the body only along the mid-dorsal line, and beneath it the whole body is covered by a perfectly round, flattened horny shield, from which the tail, equipped with a spoon-shaped tip, projects. It lives underground and as a burrower has often been compared to a mole. Its fore feet have digging claws. Its distribution is relatively small and limited to the sandy plains in parts of western Argentina.

Pangolins (Order Pholidota)

Scaly anteaters are distinguished from all other mammals by their covering of scales. The back, sides, top of the head, upper part of the limbs and both surfaces of the tail are completely protected by numerous scales arranged in longitudinal and transversal rows. The scales are formed of modified hair and overlap like tiles from front to back. With their sharp point and edges, these scales form an unsurpassed protective shield. They are placed so that the animal can still roll itself up into a ball as a protective measure.

The gait is plantigrade. Each foot has five digits terminating in powerful claws. The central claw of each front foot is greatly enlarged for burrowing, and also used for demolishing termite hills when searching for food. But the claws hamper walking. Though standing on the soles of their hind feet the pangolins can only stand on the outer edges of their fore feet because of the claws rolled up underneath.

Pangolins' heads are narrow and triangular. The mouth is small and the long, extensile vermiform tongue is viscous and used for catching ants and termites. Pangolins are completely toothless as no teeth are needed to deal with their diet.

The Temminck's or Cape Pangolin (*Manis temmincki*) lives in the East African savannahs from Ethiopia to the Cape, and is one of the terrestrial pangolins. When in danger the animal defends itself by rolling into a ball and exposing the sharp edges of its scales to a would-be aggressor. Pangolins have no teeth and feed mainly on termites and ants with their extraordinary tongues.

Solitary except in the breeding season, when they form small groups, the Brown Hare (*Lepus capensis*), of Europe, Asia and Africa, is an extremely timid animal which relies on its acute hearing and great speed to escape danger. A full-grown hare can reach a speed of seventy kilometres an hour.

As a protection against ants and termites the pangolins have no external ears and their nostrils can be closed. Their eyes have thick lids to shield them from bites. By flicking up their scales the pangolins can scatter any insects that have slipped into the crevices. The salivary glands stretch down into the chest and discharge a heavy mucous secretion. The tail is long and very mobile despite its scale covering. In several varieties it is prehensile and can be coiled round a branch.

The Giant Pangolin (*Manis gigantea*) is a native of tropical Africa and grows to an overall length of 152 centimetres. It is the largest of the family and its size makes tree-climbing impossible.

The small-scaled Tree Pangolin (*M. tricuspis*) and the Black-bellied Pangolin (*M. longicaudata*) are also African species and arboreal. Their tails are strongly prehensile, gripping branches by scaleless callous parts towards the end, and their claws are sharpened for gripping. They look for columns of ants among the leaves or attack their hanging nests. The Indian Pangolin (*M. crassicaudata*) is mainly terrestrial. The Chinese Pangolin (*M. pentadactyla*) and the Malayan Pangolin (*M. javanica*) are both arboreal.

Little is known of reproduction among pangolins. Probably the females have only one young at a time. It hangs on to the mother's tail using the claws in terrestrial species and the tail in arboreal ones. The scales of the newborn pangolins are soft and take a few weeks to harden.

Hares, rabbits, pikas (Order Lagomorpha)

These animals possess an additional pair of incisors situated inside the normal pair. The total number of teeth is thus higher than that of the rodents. The typical formula is:

$$\text{I.}\frac{2}{1} \quad \text{C.}\frac{0}{0} \quad \text{Pm.}\frac{3}{2} \quad \text{M.}\frac{3}{3} \quad \text{Total 28}$$

Hares and rabbits (Family Leporidae)

This is the principal family of the Lagomorpha, comprising some seventy species spread all over the world, for where they are not native, as in Australia, they have been introduced by man. Three pairs were let loose in New South Wales and a few years later there were hundreds of millions. It has been calculated that one couple alone can have over thirteen million descendants in three years. They eat all types of vegetable matter.

The Brown Hare (*Lepus capensis*) has a great capacity for running and jumping. Its powerful hind quarters and unusually long hind legs enable it to run at an estimated speed of sixty-five kilometres an hour. A racing greyhound only gains on it when the hare begins to tire. The hare has very long ears with a black patch at each tip. The fur is ruddy brown above and white beneath, but there are many varieties. The young hare always has a white star on its forehead and the underside of the tail is also white. The eyes are yellow. They are usually between fifty-eight and sixty-eight centimetres long without the tail, and weigh between three and five kilograms. In central Europe some are much bigger. The Brown Hare is common all over Europe except in Scandinavia and northern Russia.

There is little difference between the sexes, and they can only be distinguished at a distance by a slight difference in movement when they bolt from cover. The male or jack comes out more noisily and boldly, his ears pointing different ways. The female comes out in a crouching attitude with flattened ears, and she keeps close to the ground unless she can find some rut to give her cover. Even on close examination the sex cannot be determined easily. The testes and the penis are concealed beneath the skin and amongst the hair. The vulva is very close to the anus and has a clitoris which often resembles the male organ.

The principal rutting season is from December to March and the males engage in strange combats in which tufts of hair are pulled out. Although not as fertile as rabbits, hares generally have four litters a year of one to four young. Gestation lasts about forty-two days. The young are born with

their eyes open and their bodies covered with hair. No nest is prepared. They are simply dropped on the ground and, except for suckling morning and evening for a fortnight, left to manage for themselves. Growth is rapid, the adult state being reached in a year.

Hares, unlike rabbits, are in no way social. Nor do they burrow, contenting themselves with a depression in the grass, their 'form' as it is called, and in this they rest during the day. They are always on the alert. Hearing and smell warn them of danger, and they remain motionless in hiding or bolt at full speed. Otherwise they venture forth mainly at night, to feed in fields of clover, lucerne or cabbage, still on the alert, however, and sometimes sitting up on their hind quarters to have a good look round. Their enemies are foxes, wild cats, polecats, weasels and birds of prey. Dogs pursue them; poachers snare them.

Close to the Brown Hare is the Mountain Hare, also called the Varying Hare or Alpine Hare (*L. timidus*), found in Alpine regions at heights of 1,500 to 3,000 metres, and also in northern Europe, Scandinavia, Scotland and Ireland. Its rusty-brown coat turns white in winter to give protective colouring, except in the case of the Irish Hare which is a subspecies (*L. timidus hibernicus*). The ends of the ears remain black in all seasons. In habits it is more like a rabbit than a hare, especially in taking to holes when scared.

The Arctic Hare (*L. arcticus*) of Canada, Alaska and Greenland burrows into the snow for shelter. Other North American leporids are the Jack Rabbits (*Lepus californicus* and others) of the western plains, which, from their very long ears and powerful hind legs, as well as by their habits, are obviously hares and not rabbits at all. They are often very numerous and do heavy damage to crops and grazing ground. They are preyed upon by coyotes and eagles, but the reduction of these predators by control schemes has enabled them to keep up their numbers. They are often gregarious. Another common woodland species is the Snowshoe Rabbit or Hare (*L. americanus*). It is also known as the American Varying Hare and is in fact a hare allied to the European Varying Hare. It has a white wintercoat and develops very hairy soles which help to spread its weight on the snow. The Canada Lynx feeds mainly on the Snowshoe Rabbit and its numbers fluctuate in close relation to the great population changes of the Snowshoe Rabbit, often over a ten-year cycle.

The cottontails (*Sylvilagus*) are a numerous group of rabbit-like animals found all over North America and parts of South America. They are very much like the European Rabbit in appearance and habits, having comparatively short ears and legs and preferring to seek safety under the cover of thickets and brushwood or swamps rather than in fast, open flight like hares. Their young are born blind, naked and helpless in fur-lined nests, often in a hole dug by some other animal. Unlike the European Rabbit, cottontails do not excavate burrows for themselves. There are eight species known, the most widespread being the Eastern Cottontail (*S. floridanus*).

WILD RABBIT: The ears of the Wild Rabbit (*Oryctolagus cuniculus*) are always shorter than the head and have no black patches at the tips, this character distinguishing it from the various hares. Its fur is a rusty grey mixed with longer black guard hairs, buff-coloured flanks and brown tail with white underneath. The coat varies with climate and the nature of the country. There are also individual exceptions, as in the occasional black, biscuit-coloured or albino rabbits.

The Wild Rabbit is always smaller and lighter than the hare, with a body rarely over forty-five centimetres long and 1·3 kilograms in weight. The chief difference, however, is in its habits, for rabbits are particularly gregarious animals and burrowers. They are found only in large numbers, living in complex, ramifying burrows, with galleries running from one to another and with many entrances. The scientific name indicates the burrowing habit. *Oryctolagus* comes from two Greek words meaning 'burrowing hare'.

Timid and apprehensive, the Wild Rabbit spends the greater part of the day underground, usually coming out to feed from dusk to dawn. In a cornfield its advance may be traced from the outside inwards (the opposite of the hare's) and the straws left in its wake are chamfered through obliquely to ten centimetres from the ground. It goes for many things besides corn, ravaging fields of lucerne, cabbage or beet. In the winter it gnaws the bark off trees and attacks their roots. Its burrows also undermine the soil. All told, then, the Wild Rabbit is one of the most serious pests.

It has many enemies: the fox, badger, buzzard, wild cat, marten, weasel, polecat, wild boar, dog, and man with his guns, snares and ferrets. That it has been able to stand up to such an onslaught is the measure of its extraordinary fertility, surpassed only by that of the rat.

A female generally has three or four litters a year (after a gestation of one month), bearing from four to ten at a time. The newborn rabbit is fertile in four to six months. At some distance from the burrows the female digs a shallow hole for a brood-chamber, so shallow that a man thrusting in his hand can touch the bottom, which is a soft nesting place lined with dried grasses and covered with down from her own stomach. After the birth she carefully conceals the opening and returns to the common burrow. Every night for three weeks she comes to the brood chamber to feed her offspring. By that time they are to fend for themselves, and another litter is already forming in her body.

DOMESTIC RABBITS: The Domestic Rabbit is derived from the Wild Rabbit and is not very ancient. There are many varieties. Some are uniform in colour and others have mixed colours or even distinctive patterns. The Polish, for example, is completely white, but is not simply an albino. There are also various silver-grey breeds which all have a dense fur of uniform colour and projecting guard hairs with black or white tips.

Rabbits of distinctively contrasting colours belong to the Russian or Dutch breeds, the former being white with black extremities. In the Dutch breed the head and hind quarters are of uniform colour (which may vary), while the muzzle, forehead, neck, shoulders, chest, fore legs and hind feet are pure white. There are also patchy races like the English, which is white with patches of another colour on the body, muzzle, ears and round the eyes.

Breeders are also concerned with structure, weight, fertility, and aptitude for crossing. While the Dutch, Polish and Russian breeds are of smaller build, the silver-grey breeds often reach 4·5 or 5 kilograms and the Flemish Giant reaches 7·6 or 9 kilograms with a length of a metre.

Some varieties have curious features. The Lop-ear, for instance, has very long pendent ears, sometimes reaching a length of sixty-three centimetres. Another curious breed is the Angora, characterised by a long, silky fur. Angora is a term applied to other animals, like guinea-pigs, cats, goats, when they have the same silky coats. An Angora rabbit is a beautiful creature, looking like a little heap of snow. But they exist in other colours too, even deep black. Some have remarkably thick silky tufts at the tips of the ears.

Some rabbits have been successfully bred without guard hairs in the fur, which can thus be used without 'plucking'. These are the Rex breeds, and include such well-known breeds as Castor Rex, Chinchilla Rex, Blue Rex and Ermine Rex.

Pikas (Family Ochotonidae)

This family consists of only one genus, *Ochotona*. Known variously as pikas, mouse-hares, calling hares or rock rabbits, they resemble rabbits but have short ears and are no larger than guinea-pigs. Most of them are found in the mountains of central Asia and in the Himalayas, where they have been found on Everest at heights of up to 5,250 metres. Outside Asia they are found only in the Rocky Mountains of North America. They all inhabit rocky slopes and screes, where they shelter deep under the stones from their constant enemies, hawks and foxes. They are active by day, cutting and carrying quantities of green herbage which they stack in the sun to dry before storing it for the winter among the stones. They do not hibernate. The name 'calling hare' comes from their habit of sitting up watchfully, constantly uttering a bleating note, either to give warning of some impending danger or to keep in touch with each other.

Rodents (Order Rodentia)

Although rodents may resemble certain marsupials or insectivores they are easily identified by their dentition, which makes up a multi-purpose tool as well as a means of obtaining and masticating food. 'Rodent' means 'gnawing animal' and rodents will gnaw all manner of hard substances as well as food. They have a pair of long incisors in each jaw and these project at the front of the mouth, giving them an unmistakable family likeness. Their incisors bear enamel only on the front surface.

Although a few rodents, like the porcupines, beavers and, the largest of all, the Capybara, may measure up to a metre without the tail, the majority are modest in size or even small. Some of the dwarf mice of Africa have bodies only eight centimetres long, only slightly bigger than shrews, the smallest living mammals.

The dentition in this order is incomplete, canines being absent. Between the incisors and the molars there is a wide gap, or diastema, very much like the bars of a horse's jaw on which the bit rests.

Squirrels and rats have big curved incisors, generally yellow or orange. There is one pair in

Opposite top
The Black-tailed or Californian Jackrabbit (*Lepus californicus*) is a common American hare, occurring in great numbers in the west from the state of Washington down into Mexico. Jackrabbits are very prolific and produce several litters a year, each consisting of about six young which are born with their eyes open and a full covering of fur.

Opposite middle
The Snowshoe Rabbit (*Lepus americanus*) lives in well-timbered country. It grows extra hair on its feet in the winter which enables it to travel easily over the snow. It is also called the Varying Hare because its colour ranges from the agouti coat of spring and summer to white in winter.

Opposite bottom
The Desert Cottontail (*Sylvilagus audubonii*) one of seven to eight species of cottontails, so called because of the fluffy appearance of their tails. They are very much like the European Rabbit in appearance and habits except that the babies are born above ground in a shallow excavation lined with the mother's fur and concealed from above by dry grass.

each jaw. These may be regarded as typical of constantly growing teeth. Their extraordinarily long roots reach right back into the jaw bones until they are above the upper molars or below the lower ones, and they have throughout life an opening at the root for the entry of important nutritive vessels. As these teeth grow they are ground down by use; and, since they are enamelled only on the outer side, they wear unevenly and become bevelled or chisel-shaped. It is essential that wear should keep pace with growth. Indeed, some rodents gnaw not only their food, but almost anything they can get hold of, even metals. Teeth that are constantly growing must be constantly worn down, or they become a serious danger. If wear stops for any reason (age, paralysis, the absence of an opposing tooth) a tooth may perforate the palate or grow right out of the mouth and into the eye, causing death.

Behind the diastema on each side is a row of molars, the number of which varies according to the species. Generally, premolars tend to disappear. In more advanced types they are completely absent. The large molars, too, are reduced in number in some Australian water rats. There are thus in rodents wide differences in the total number of teeth, varying from twenty-two in the squirrel to ten in the New Guinea Mouse (genus *Mayermys*). Here are some representative dentitions:

Squirrel $\quad$ I. $\frac{1}{1}$ $\quad$ C. $\frac{0}{0}$ $\quad$ Pm. $\frac{2}{1}$ $\quad$ M. $\frac{3}{3}$ $\quad$ Total 22

Guinea-pig $\quad$ I. $\frac{1}{1}$ $\quad$ C. $\frac{0}{0}$ $\quad$ Pm. $\frac{1}{1}$ $\quad$ M. $\frac{3}{3}$ $\quad$ Total 20

Rat $\quad$ I. $\frac{1}{1}$ $\quad$ C. $\frac{0}{0}$ $\quad$ Pm. $\frac{0}{0}$ $\quad$ M. $\frac{3}{3}$ $\quad$ Total 16

Beaver rat
(*Hydromys*) $\quad$ I. $\frac{1}{1}$ $\quad$ C. $\frac{0}{0}$ $\quad$ Pm. $\frac{0}{0}$ $\quad$ M. $\frac{2}{2}$ $\quad$ Total 12

New Guinea Mouse
(*Mayermys*) $\quad$ I. $\frac{1}{1}$ $\quad$ C. $\frac{0}{0}$ $\quad$ Pm. $\frac{0}{0}$ $\quad$ M. $\frac{1}{2}$ $\quad$ Total 10

The molars are less uniform in structure than the incisors. In the lower types (squirrels, rats) they are limited in growth and covered with tuberculae, which wear only slightly in the course of life. It is in the more highly evolved types (beavers, voles, Capybaras, porcupines) that teeth go on growing and are ground down until they show a pattern of enamel folds with dentine inside and cement outside.

The form of the teeth affects the condyle of the jaw, to the extent that the form of the one can be deduced from the form of the other. Since rodents' teeth have to rub against one another in a fore and aft direction the condyles of the mandible have to be cylindrical in shape, sliding in gutter-shaped cavities in the squamosal bones.

The forward and backward movement of the lower jaw is different from the up and down movement in man, and different muscles are accordingly developed for mastication: in rodents it is the cheek muscles or masseters, in man the temporal muscles. With different use, there is a different structure.

The consistency of the rodent's manner of biting contrasts with the great variety of limb structures, which are adapted sometimes to running, sometimes to jumping, swimming or grasping. As a rule the fore limbs are the less modified and possess three to five digits, which the animal uses with great dexterity for holding food. The hind feet have three to five digits, which may be webbed or otherwise modified. Clavicles exist only in the climbing forms (squirrels). In jumping forms, such as jerboas, the metatarsals in the foot are fused and greatly elongated. Some squirrels have lateral skin folds which are used in gliding, like parachutes, but this does not alter the limbs in any way, unless it is by the provision of a cartilaginous spur stretching from the wrist to the edge of the skin folds.

Rodents have a very long intestine and a highly developed caecum, in which an important part of the digestion must take place. The stomach is sometimes simple, sometimes formed of several

The Naked Mole-rat (*Heterocephalus glaber*), which measures about ten centimetres, is the smallest of the mole-rats and is almost entirely hairless. It is a burrowing rodent and, unlike moles which are carnivorous, feeds mainly on roots and bulbs. It inhabits the hot, sandy regions of Somalia and northern Kenya.

The Tuco-tuco (*Ctenomys mendocinus*) is a large rodent about twenty-three centimetres long. Adapted to a burrowing habit, it has a cylindrical body, short limbs bearing large digging claws and small eyes and ears. It makes extensive burrows in open country and is widespread in Argentina, Chile and some parts of Brazil.

compartments, like that of a ruminant. The brain is small and the cerebral hemispheres smooth. The uterus is always divided, except in a few species, in which it is double. Numerous teats extend from the chest to the groin. The placenta is discoidal. The young are generally born blind and hairless and have to remain several days in the nest before being able to get about. Two exceptions here are young guinea-pigs and the coypus, which are active from birth and are soon able to forage for themselves.

Rodents have a peculiar and sometimes very strong odour, particularly the males. This comes from scent glands near the anus which should not be confused with the genital glands.

Great activity coupled with small size makes them insatiable feeders, for small animals have a relatively large surface area compared to their bulk resulting in a large heat loss which must be replaced by energy from food.

Rodents have a strongly developed building instinct. Some, like beavers, are real engineers. What they can accomplish in dam constructing, canal cutting and lodge building is truly astonishing. Most of them burrow either to make food stores or habitations. The underground dwellings of some rodents are sometimes as complex as that of a mole.

They have an instinct for hoarding provisions of all sorts, which doubtless helps during a lean season. At the onset of winter their stores are packed with grain, fruit and roots, and much of it is often untouched when springtime arrives.

The fecundity of some rodents is unrivalled among mammals. Physiologically the males are extremely well equipped and the females are capable of an uninterrupted series of gestations and of bearing a large number of young at each litter. Rats, for instance, are adult and capable of reproduction at the age of three months. The number of litters a year varies from two to seven, 'with three to fourteen in each. Thus the yearly offspring of a pair number not less than six and may amount to ninety-eight, all capable of the same rate of reproduction as soon as they mature.

Wherever food is plentiful rats breed and multiply rapidly. Some also carry disease, by harbouring vectors such as fleas in bubonic plague. As a scourge to humanity, rats stand next to insects, which accounts for the continual efforts made to keep them under control. In his fight against rodents, man has valuable allies. Hunting by night, owls consume large numbers of rodents, and by day the hawks and snakes do also.

Although many rodents are a nuisance, some are protected or even bred for their food value or their fur. Among the edible rodents are squirrels and others less appreciated, such as guinea-pigs and cane-rats. Furs come from Coypus, squirrels, beavers, muskrats, chinchillas and others.

There are some 3,000 different species of rodent, spread all over the world and adapted to the most varied habitats. They can be found in deserts and marshlands, in plains and mountains, in open country and in dense equatorial forests. Their mode of life and method of locomotion vary accordingly. In spite of these differences and their morphological effects, rodents are among the most difficult mammals to classify by precise characters,

yet their heterogeneity is more apparent than real.

The classification of the Rodentia used here is based upon that proposed by Sir John Ellerman in his two-volume work *The Families and Genera of Living Rodents*, published by the British Museum (Natural History) in 1940. The order is divided into four suborders which are diagnosed on anatomical detail but more especially on two features: whether the tibia and fibula are fused or separate and whether the zygomatic arches are stout or delicate. The first suborder, the Bathyergomorpha (African mole rats), contains few representatives. Only the lower part of the tibia and fibula is fused, and the zygomatic arch is delicate. The next is the suborder Hystricomorpha, the porcupines and their relatives, with separate tibia and fibula and stout zygomatic arches. The third is the Sciuromorpha, the squirrels and beavers, again with tibia and fibula separate but with delicate zygomatic arches. The fourth is the Myomorpha, the rats, mice and allies, with fused tibia and fibula and delicate zygomatic arches.

The Coypu (*Myocastor coypus*), is an aquatic rodent which is a native of South America. It is farmed for its fur, which is known as nutria. Now Coypus are found in feral colonies all over Europe, having either escaped from the farms or as in Russia been released deliberately, where they are artificially fed in winter then trapped for their fur.

The Agouti (*Dasyprocta aguti*) inhabits forests and thick cover from Mexico to Peru. It is also found in the West Indies. Agoutis are stout-bodied rodents, well-adapted for speed, having long slender legs. They move with a swift, bounding gait. They also swim well.

The American porcupines comprise about a dozen species, but the best known is the North American Porcupine (*Erithizon dorsatum*). It is covered with an armour of finely barbed spines, which when relaxed are almost concealed in a coat of long brown hair. It can climb well and spends much of its time in trees.

The Prehensile-tailed Porcupine or Coendou (*Coendou prehensilis*), of Central and South America, is more arboreal than the North American species. Its spines are shorter and are not concealed by hair. The long, prehensile tail is capable of supporting the animal when it hangs from a branch.

African mole rats
(Order Bathyergomorpha)

The Bathyergidae (six genera) is the only family in this suborder. All species are mole-like in shape and habits, but the size of the body and the claws, as well as the colour and nature of the fur, vary considerably. The family is widespread over Africa. It includes the species *Bathyergus suillus*, which is up to twenty-five centimetres long and has immense fore claws. It lives among the coastal sand dunes of South Africa and is known as the Mole Rat. The fur is slate-coloured to fawn. The eyes are small, the tail short and the claws of the fore feet and the projecting incisors are powerful and used in digging. Its diet consists mostly of bulbs and roots.

The most extraordinary is the Naked Mole Rat (*Heterocephalus glaber*) of northern Kenya and Somaliland. It is ten centimetres long, with a tail 2·5 centimetres long, and is entirely naked except for a few scattered hairs. Blind and without external ears, it shuns the light and burrows in the sandy soil, where its presence can usually be detected by the numerous small craters it makes in the ground.

Porcupines and allies
(Suborder Hystricomorpha)

Coypu (Family Echimyidae)

Besides the Coypu this family also includes other very primitive rodents of the New World. The tucotucos (*Ctenomys*) are small and particularly numerous in Chile and Argentina, making extensive burrows in open country. The hutias (genus *Geocapromys*) are restricted to the West Indies, with one species in Jamaica, one in the Bahamas and a third on Little Swan Island. The Hutia-conga (*Capromys pilorides*), of Cuba, forty-six centimetres long, is nocturnal and arboreal. A dwarf species, *C. nana*, first known from fossil skulls, still survives. Another relic from the past still surviving on San Domingo, is *Plagiodontia*, with two species, the second discovered as recently as 1926. In Africa the family is represented by the Grass-cutter or Cane Rat and the Rock Rat. The first, *Thryonomis swinderianus* of West Africa, has a harsh bristly fur, always lives near water and swims well. The Rock Rat (*Petromus typicus*) of south-west Africa has a flattened skull and remarkably flexible ribs, that enable it to squeeze through narrow crevices in the rocks.

The Coypu (*Myocastor coypus*), sometimes called the Swamp Beaver on account of a superficial resemblance to the beaver, is native to the temperate regions of South America but is well known in Europe, where it is bred for its fur, known as nutria. Looking like an enormous rat it has a body averaging some forty-six centimetres in length and six kilograms in weight. In habits the Coypu resembles the Water Vole and like it is found in its natural state by rivers and lakes. It is easily kept in captivity, so long as some marshy ground is available, with a stretch of open water in which it can bathe. It has advantages over the Musk Rat, which is also farmed for its fur, since it does not burrow much or try seriously to escape, and is extremely fertile. The female can have up to three litters of five per year. The four or five pairs of teats are placed high up on the flanks, almost on the back, enabling the young to suckle from the mother's back when she is swimming. The young are active from birth, like guinea-pigs, and they grow very rapidly. The Coypu is strictly herbivorous.

Its fur is one of the best that can be obtained from animals bred in a temperate climate and has only a few guard hairs to be removed. The undercoat is short, thick and downy, chestnut brown in colour, varying from light to very dark. With so many advantages, it is not surprising that the animal has been introduced in many European countries and in the United States. Some Coypus have escaped and since their domestication they have also been introduced as wild animals, and must now be regarded as part of the European and American faunas. Although not troublesome in small numbers, in recent years the Coypu has become a nuisance causing considerable damage through feeding on root crops and burrowing into dykes.

Agouti (Family Dasyproctidae)

A South American rodent resembling the hare in size and shape, the Agouti (*Dasyprocta aguti*) is brown with a tawny or yellow rump. Its fur is good enough to be valued locally, i.e. chiefly in Brazil and Guyana. The numerous species of the one genus *Dasyprocta* are alike in habits, and many may be only subspecies of *D. aguti*. Agoutis live in small parties and are essentially nocturnal, frequenting forest clearings. The female is very prolific and is capable of breeding in all seasons.

Porcupines (Families Erethizontidae and Hystricidae)

All the members of the Erethizontidae (New World porcupines) and the Hystricidae (Old World porcupines) have spines or quills in addition to ordinary hair. These spines are sharply pointed hairs, of enormous size and with the fibrous material greatly exceeding the soft medulla. Erectile, they serve as organs of defence, controlled by powerful muscles in the skin. Such muscles are also present in rudimentary form in man, and in animals such as cats, which bristle when angry.

The New World porcupines include the Canadian Porcupine and the South American tree porcupines. Their quills are never very long and are concealed among the fur. All are arboreal and in some the tail is prehensile. They move about cautiously in trees, sleeping during the day and feeding at night on a wide variety of vegetable matter including leaves, buds and bark.

The Canadian Porcupine (*Erethizon dorsatum*) ranges from Alaska across Canada and, in the United States, to central California, New Mexico and eastwards to Virginia. It is 105 centimetres long, including fifteen centimetres of tail, with long brownish black fur sprinkled with long white hairs concealing short barbed spines. The hind foot has a well-developed big toe. The species *Echinoprocta rufescens* of Colombia is very like the Canadian Porcupine, but the typical South American porcupines are represented by the Prehensile-tailed Porcupine (*Coendou prehensilis*), which has a long prehensile tail with stiff bristles at its root that assist by gripping the tree trunk when the animal is climbing. Its hind foot has a broad fleshy pad opposable to the four toes.

The Common or Crested Porcupine (*Hystrix cristata*) is to be found in southern Europe, North Africa and Asia Minor. It is of fair size, up to seventy centimetres in length and twenty-seven kilograms in weight. The tail is short. The dominant feature is the crest of white-tipped grey quills and a similar covering of quills which are hollow and open at the end. Loosely implanted, they easily become detached. This gave rise to an early belief that the Porcupine could cast its quills at its enemies like darts. Solitary in habit, it remains in the deep burrow it has dug for itself during the day, coming out at night to look for roots, fruits and other vegetable matter. When attacked it erects its quills, prances and grunts, but does not use its teeth. A bold person can easily catch it by seizing the crest.

Mating takes place at night and has rarely been observed. In Uganda the explorer Gromier watched the male's nuptial display by the light of a

The Pacarana (*Dinomys branickii*), of the mountain forests of the Andes, is one of the largest rodents. It lives mainly in burrows and among rocks. Little more is known about this animal and it appears to be becoming very rare.

The Chinchilla (*Chinchilla laniger*) was much hunted, almost to extinction, for its valuable fur. In the 1900's the South American government banned their hunting and later, successful farms were set up. As a result, the price of Chinchilla fur dropped sufficiently to protect the remaining population.

The Capybara (*Hydrochoerus hydrochaeris*) is common and widespread in South America and is found in woodland close to lakes and swamps. The largest of all living rodents, it is semi-aquatic with partially webbed feet, a sparse coat and thick deposits of fat in the skin.

525

The Patagonian Cavy or Mara (*Dolichotis patagonum*) is a rodent about the size of a Brown Hare. Mainly herbivorous, it inhabits the pampas of Patagonia and Argentina, sheltering in burrows dug with its large hoof-like claws. The three or four young are born in a burrow.

Red Squirrels (*Sciurus vulgaris*) are abundant over Europe and Asia but in parts of the British Isles, especially in deciduous woodland, they have been replaced by the Grey Squirrel (*S. carolinensis*). Red Squirrels preferring coniferous areas. They do not hibernate, but they do store food and are less active in the winter.

torch. The crest was erect and the back and tail quills were flicked up and down with a peculiar clicking sound. This was accompanied by a grunting not unlike that of a pig. After two month's gestation the female gives birth to two or three young, which are born without quills. These appear gradually, replacing the initial soft fur.

Other Old World porcupines are found in Asia and Africa. In the brush-tailed porcupines (genus *Atherurus*) of south-east Asia and Africa the tail ends in a tuft of horny hairs simulating spines.

Paca (Family Cuniculidae)

The Sooty Paca or Spotted Cavy (*Cuniculus paca*) of Mexico and Brazil and the Mountain Paca (*C. taczanowskii*), of the Andean forests, make up this family. The Sooty Paca is easily distinguished by its brown coat, ornamented on each side by three to five lines of pale spots. Its habits are like those of the Agouti, but the female has only one young in the middle of each summer—a very exceptional circumstance among the highly fertile rodents.

Pacarana (Family Dinomyidae)

This family includes only the one species of Pacarana (*Dinomys branickii*) of the mountain forests of the Andes. It is similar to the Paca, but more heavily built. It is black with whitish spots and has a well-developed tail.

Chinchillas and viscachas (Family Chinchillidae)

These animals are highly prized for the beauty and the texture of their fur.

The Chinchilla (*Chinchilla laniger*) is the most valued. Its pearl-grey fur is one of the most beautiful, and has more hairs per square centimetre than any other animal. It is about the size of a squirrel, which it also resembles in shape. Long the prey of hunters, the Chinchilla has taken refuge in the most arid mountainous regions, where occasionally it may be seen among the rocks and stones. It is difficult to capture one and a couple of experienced trappers will not catch more than six or so in two years. The Chinchilla is protected in Chile, but is widely bred for its fur on farms in North America and Europe.

The Mountain Chinchilla or Mountain Viscacha (*Lagidium viscaccia*), which frequents the foothills of the Andes, is much larger, nearer a hare in size, and has poor quality fur. It lives gregariously near arable land in ramifying burrows, which undermine the ground. Viscachas live much like rabbits. At sunset they play in the open, while male sentries keep an alert watch and give warning of the slightest danger. The Plains Viscacha (*Lagostomus maximus*) is larger than the Mountain Viscacha and has coarse fur. It lives on the pampas of Argentina.

Cavies (Family Caviidae)

The Guinea-pig, the Patagonian cavies and the Capybara make up this family. The Guinea-pig came originally from Peru, where it still exists in the wild state in the form of the Brazilian or Peruvian Cavy (*Cavia aperea*). From Peru the animal was introduced by man into every country of the world. The first specimens were brought to Europe in the middle of the sixteenth century. It has been show that all the varieties of the Domes-

MAMMALS

tic Guinea-pig (*Cavia porcellus*) have been produced by selection. They differ from one another chiefly in the colour and texture of their fur, which may be short and soft, short and bristly, or long and curly (Angoras). In one curious race their hair is distributed in little tufts.

Whatever their race Guinea-pigs are always recognisable by their stocky, rounded bodies without noticeable necks or tails. Their overall length varies from twenty to thirty centimetres and they live from three to five years. Gestation takes sixty days and there are two to three litters a year with two to six young in each. The young can see at birth and run about, and they do not suckle long. The mother has two teats.

The Capybara or Carpincho (*Hydrochoerus hydrochaeris*) is the largest of all the rodents, growing to the size of a small pig (122 centimetres long and fifty-four kilograms in weight). A sort of gigantic guinea-pig, it is essentially aquatic in habit, and lives in bands by rivers and lakes in tropical America. It is easily tamed and bred and is less sensitive to cold than the Guinea-pig. In captivity all it needs is some grassland with enough water to bathe in and a hut to shelter in at night or in bad weather. It eats hay, oats and all sorts of greenstuff. In the wild state the female bears one litter a year from three to eight. Domestication increases fertility. Birth is easy and, as with Guinea-pigs, the young are self-sufficient.

Another close relative of the Guinea-pig is the Patagonian Cavy or Mara (*Dolichotis patagonum*), which in its general appearance and with its long ears resembles a hare, and is sometimes called the Patagonian Hare. But it has longer legs and the fore legs are about the same length as the hind legs, which does not facilitate jumping. In this respect it is more like a small antelope. The Patagonian Cavy is one of the familiar animals of the Argentinian pampas. It lives in herds, excavates and eats grass.

Squirrels and allies
(Suborder Sciuromorpha)

Squirrels, prairie dogs, marmots
(Family Sciuridae)
There are no less than seventy species of true squirrels distributed in all parts of the world except Madagascar and Australia. Like all climbers, these small arboreal rodents, with their bushy, plume-like tails and ears often tufted, have well-developed clavicles.

The European Red Squirrel (*Sciurus vulgaris*) is well-known in woods, parks or gardens, more especially where there are conifers. Few animals equal it in agility and gracefulness. It seems to glide along branches, jumping from one to another with astonishing skill. Long, sharp claws enable it to climb tree trunks, and on the ground strong hind limbs make jumps of several metres commonplace.

Its food includes acorns, beechnuts, pine seeds, leaf buds and toadstools. It is often destructive and like most rodents, buries surplus food at random, finding it again by smell.

For shelter and breeding, the female makes a covered nest of cleverly interlaced twigs lined with moss. It is not unlike a Magpie's nest, and in fact a deserted Magpie nest may be used as a foundation. The period of gestation is thirty-two to forty days and there are two litters a year, each consisting of three to six. The young are born blind, and the eyes do not open for over a week. The females has four pairs of teats.

In spite of its small size—it weighs less than half a kilogram—the Red Squirrel is treated as game in some countries, though more for the sake of its fur than its flesh. In southern and central Europe it is pure white below and brownish red above, turning to grey in winter, but in northern Europe it is silvery grey all over, and this is the squirrel fur most sought after by the furriers.

Squirrels thrive in captivity and in many countries they are common in parks where they often become tame through being fed.

The European Red Squirrel's capacity for migration is remarkable. The conditions which prompt this are not clear; probably the need for some particular kind of food. Usually sedentary and unsocial in habit, squirrels collect at times in large bands and travel hundreds of kilometres, overcoming the most varied obstacles. Though generally avoiding water, they do not hesitate at such times to cross big rivers. They have even been seen swimming in the Gulf of Finland. Many die of exhaustion and hunger, and many are killed as

The Eastern Grey Squirrel (*Sciurus carolinensis*) is a native of North America. Both Red and Grey Squirrels are essentially arboreal and, in contrast to the terrestrial ground squirrels, they have a long, bushy tail which is used as a balancer when climbing and also acts as a rudder when the squirrel is jumping from tree to tree.

The Southern Flying Squirrel (*Glaucomys volans*) from North America is not capable of true flight. Its furry membranes are used only to glide from tree to tree. Unlike other squirrels, the flying squirrel is nocturnal, sheltering during the day in hollow trees and in buildings. It does not hibernate.

The Golden Mantled Ground Squirrel (*Citellus lateralis*) is found in open country throughout much of North America and Asia. They excavate extensive burrows often housing colonies, like rabbit warrens. Ground squirrels have internal cheek pouches in which they carry seeds for storage in their burrows. After fattening up in autumn they go into deep hibernation.

they pass through densely populated regions. In Russia and Siberia these migrations sometimes take the form of a veritable exodus. In North America the Grey Squirrel migrates in the same way.

Wherever there are forests, particularly in the tropics of both Old and New Worlds, tree squirrels have evolved in a great variety of forms. The tiny pygmy squirrels (genus *Myosciurus*), of Cameroun in West Africa, and the tufted-ear forms from Borneo (genus *Nannosciurus*) are no larger than mice. The giant squirrels of India and Malaya (genus *Ratufa*) are as big as cats and are brightly coloured in shiny black, red, cream and fawn. In southeastern Asia some squirrels are terrestrial rather than arboreal, probing among the dead leaves for insects. These have long, slender snouts and their cheek-teeth have degenerated, as if they were evolving as rodent anteaters. Among the North American species is the well-known Grey Squirrel (*Sciurus carolinensis*) which, as an introduced species, has thrived exceptionally well in the British Isles, supplanting the smaller and less enterprising native Red Squirrel (*S. vulgaris*). The American Red Squirrel or Chickaree (*Tamiasciurus hudsonicus*) is not as closely related to the European Red Squirrel as one might imagine from the name.

Classed near true squirrels are a number of flying squirrels. They do not actually fly but have a membrane along each flank which serves as a parachute when they glide from tree to tree. The membrane starts at one wrist, from which it stretches to the hind foot and on to the root of the tail, where it joins the membrane from the other wrist. The anterior edge may be strengthened by a cartilage. Jumping from the top of a tree, a flying squirrel may glide some metres before alighting.

There are many genera, the largest being the Flying Squirrel (*Petaurista*) of Asia, not to be confused with the Lesser Flying Phalanger (*Petaurus*) of Australia. *Petaurista* is generally over forty-five centimetres long, but some Malayan forms are very small. The European and North American flying squirrels live in northern pine forests and are active throughout the winter. A notable feature of all flying squirrels is that they are nocturnal, while all true squirrels are diurnal. There are two North American flying squirrels, both slightly smaller than the Red Squirrel: the Northern Flying Squirrel (*Glaucomys sabrinus*) and the Southern Flying Squirrel (*G. volans*). Contrasting with *Petaurista* are the terrestrial forms. Although sometimes seen in trees, they live in holes dug among the roots of trees, or even in treeless plains. They are intermediate between the typical squirrels and the marmots, and have lost the typical squirrel characters of a very bushy tail, tufted ears, and soft silky fur. The best known are the chipmunks, or striped gophers. The North American Eastern Chipmunk (*Tamias striatus*) inhabits the birch and pine forests of the United States. Its back is marked with longitudinal black and yellow stripes. It has cheek pouches in which food, such as grain and fruit, can be carried to a storing-place near or in which it spends the winter. Stocks amounting to many kilograms have been found. The dozen or so chipmunks of western North America, though similar in appearance to the Eastern Chipmunks, are placed in a separate genus of their own known as the *Eutamias*.

Amongst the terrestrial squirrels are the ground squirrels (genus *Citellus*). They too have cheek pouches and hoard grain and other vegetable foods underground. They are regarded as more serious pests than the chipmunks, for they infest the great corn lands of the Old and New Worlds. The largest species is the Souslik (*Citellus citellus*), of central Europe, frequenting Poland and Hungary and extending into Russia and Siberia, where it riddles the ground with deep burrows.

Many species of ground squirrel inhabit the more barren parts of North America from the Alaskan and Canadian arctic tundras to the southwestern deserts and Mexico. They live in colonies, and in cold regions go into deep hibernation after fattening up in the autumn. Most of them are sandy or plain coloured, but the Thirteen-lined Ground Squirrel (*C. tridecemlineatus*) is a notable exception, having rows of spots and stripes.

PRAIRIE DOGS: Further removed from the squirrels and completely terrestrial is the famous Prairie Dog (*Cynomys ludovicianus*), which was given its common name by the early Canadian and American trappers because of its yelping and barking.

In some parts of the western United States these animals live in large communities. Each hole, some six metres from the nest, is surmounted by a cone-shaped mound of thrown-up earth. This is the exit from a main shaft with horizontal branches off it, one for each inhabitant. Some burrows house up to fifteen individuals. One member of the community seems always posted on the mound, while the others pursue their occupations, but recent observations suggest that there is no deliberate posting of sentries. Any individual happening to be on a mound may give the alarm, whereupon all the others dive below, staying there until the danger is over.

Unlike the ground squirrels, Prairie Dogs have small cheek pouches and do not hoard. When cold weather comes they go below and sleep continuously in almost complete hiberation until it is over.

MARMOTS: The best known of the marmots has from ancient times been the Alpine Marmot (*Marmota marmota*), a somewhat heavy, short-legged animal, but one which is nevertheless able to run, jump and climb among rocks with surprising speed and agility. Its tail is short, furry and ends in a black tuft. Its head is broad and rounded, its eyes prominent and its ears medium-sized. A heavy moustache runs along its upper lip. It has the same dental formula as a squirrel and the same tuberculate molars. The fur is thick but coarse and dull coloured, varying from red-brown on the back to pale grey and rust-coloured on the ventral side. It is rather less than sixty centimetres long, without the tail, and weighs about five kilograms.

In summer Alpine Marmots live in the most inaccessible parts of the Alps, the central Asian and Himalayan ranges, from an altitude of 1,800 metres up to the snow-line. They live in small social groups of ten to fifteen, and their earths may be found anywhere, even near glaciers. From early morning they can be seen gambolling in the sun, watched over by a sentry who, at the least hint of danger, gives a sharp whistle, repeated regularly,

The Prairie Dog (*Cynomys ludovicianus*), of North America lives in huge colonial burrows called 'towns', but each member has its own den and intruders are driven away. Prairie Dogs were formerly very numerous, their 'towns' sometimes extending for over a 150 kilometres but they are now found only in remote places.

The Alpine Marmot (*Marmota marmota*) of Europe is a ground-living, burrowing rodent of the squirrel family. It feeds on a variety of green vegetation but lacks the cheek pouches found in most other ground squirrels. A nest of dry grass is made in a burrow and the whole family will hibernate together for up to six months.

529

One of the most primitive rodents, the Sewellel or Mountain Beaver (*Aplodontia rufa*) is restricted to the Pacific coast of the United States. It is a good swimmer and lives near streams in damp, wooded country, feeding chiefly on vegetable matter. It is not related to the true beavers and the pelt is useless commercially.

On land, beavers have a slow awkward gait. They walk on the sole of the foot with the heel touching the ground. The dishevelled appearance of this beaver is due to the long guard hairs which mask and protect the short soft underfur that has made beavers the object of trapping and hunting for centuries.

and so loud that it often disturbs neighbouring game. They feed on plants, which they gnaw like rabbits. Besides romping, they spend a lot of time grooming themselves. The breeding season is in the spring. Gestation lasts from thirty-five to forty-two days, and a litter consists of from two to six. The female has ten teats.

By the autumn Marmots have become very fat, and as winter approaches they go down into the fields that are being abandoned by the shepherds and begin digging burrows to hold a dozen or fifteen individuals. A gallery, which may be ten metres long, leads to a large chamber stocked with hay. Here, in a general huddle they spend the winter fast asleep.

Other marmots are found in the Rocky Mountains of North America but not all marmots live on remote and wild mountain-sides. The familiar Woodchuck or Ground-hog (*Marmota monax*), of North America, lives in woodlands and on farms, where its depredations on crops make it a pest at times. It is not as gregarious as the mountain or rock marmots, and its keen sense and readiness to dive into its deep burrow at the approach of

danger enable it to survive in spite of persecution. Like other marmots it sleeps the winter through, deep underground, and emerges at the first sign of spring.

HIBERNATION: Since marmots are typical of hibernating mammals, this is a suitable point at which to study hibernation, the means by which many mammals avoid the rigours of winter. To understand this phenomenon it must be remembered that there are two sorts of animals: poikilotherms—those whose temperature varies with their surroundings (fishes, frogs and, to some extent, reptiles); and homoiotherms—those whose temperature remains constant (birds and mammals). Truly hibernating animals stand physiologically between the two groups. Bears and badgers though sleeping deeply and frequently in winter, do not appreciably lower their temperatures. True hibernators on the other hand have a constant temperature in summer and a variable one in winter and all belong to one of the three orders: the rodents (Prairie Dogs, marmots and dormice), the insectivores or Chiroptera (bats).

The marmots generally hibernate as soon as the temperature falls below 15·5°C., and sleep so deeply that they seem dead, but in fact they wake up occasionally to urinate and defecate. And in some cases if the temperature falls below a certain point, the animals wake, shake themselves and warm themselves up, otherwise they would die. Their torpor is never as complete as that of insectivores.

In deepest sleep the marmots breathe very slowly and the circulation of the blood is reduced. Normally they take sixteen breaths a minute, with a pulse rate of eighty-eight. At a temperature of 10°C. these figures are reduced to two and fifteen respectively. During experimentation a ground squirrel reached a temperature of 0·5°C. without suffering injury.

During hibernation, a marmot lives off its own reserves of fat. This change in the source of energy affects the urine, which is normally alkaline, but becomes acid during hibernation. The proof that its fat is being consumed is given by the respiratory quotient (the relation between the carbon dioxide being given off and the oxygen being taken in). During a marmot's hibernation it is in the region of 0·5. As soon as the animal wakes up it rises towards unity, showing a large consumption of carbohydrate. The liver in particular at once draws on its reserves of glycogen, and as a result its temperature rises. This increase spreads throughout the body and in a few hours the marmot's temperature rises from 10°C to 37·3°C.

It is obvious that any animal must lose weight during hibernation, and it has been shown that in 160 days a marmot loses a quarter of its original weight. The reduction is naturally less in hibernators like the ground squirrels and hamsters, which wake up from time to time to eat their hoard.

Mountain beaver (Family Aplodontidae)

This curious North American mammal, commonly known as the Mountain Beaver, has no close relationship with the true beavers. It is a primitive rodent, perhaps in the ancestral line to the squirrels, called the Sewellel as well as Mountain Beaver (*Aplodontia rufa*), and is the sole species of its family. It lives in the coastal areas of the western United States up to altitudes of 2,700 metres, making extensive burrows, usually near water. In mountain regions it is found in the wider soft-soiled valleys. It is a brown animal, about the size of a rabbit, almost tail-less. One of its characteristics is the habit of storing green food in its tunnel for the winter.

Beavers (Family Castoridae)

The body of the beaver is thick-set and supported by short, strong legs. Its short, thick head is carried by a sturdy and very flexible neck. The nostrils and auditory canals are provided with valvules which close the apertures when the animal is immersed. The mouth shuts behind the incisors, so that the latter can be used while water is excluded. The hind feet are webbed for swimming. The fore feet are not webbed, and they are flexible enough to function almost as hands. The tail too is adapted for an aquatic life, being broad and flat like a paddle and covered with epidermal scales. Though not used as a trowel in building operations (as has sometimes been claimed), it is of great use in swimming and diving and is also used to beat the ground or the surface of the water, possibly as a signal to others.

The pelage consists of long, strong guard hairs, amongst which is a thick silky underfur much valued in the fur trade. Its natural colour is a slightly rusty brown, somewhat lighter on the head and underparts.

Dentition is less complete than that of squirrels and marmots, the beaver having only twenty teeth instead of twenty-two. On the other hand its molars are selenodont and are constantly growing at the roots. The life-span of an American Beaver is fifteen to twenty years. Adults attain a length of a metre, excluding the tail, and a weight of over twenty-seven kilograms. Males are polygamous, and the females have a single litter of two in the spring after a gestation of four months. They have two pairs of pectoral teats, and lactation lasts a month. But the young do not leave their parents for two years, when they are ready to breed.

The life of the beavers is entirely bound up with trees, rivers and lakes. Their food consists of the bark and shoots of willow, poplar, alder, elm and oak, mixed as the season allows with all sorts of riparian vegetable produce. To obtain bark they sometimes fell trees of considerable size. It used to be believed that they made the tree fall in the most advantageous position by cutting the appropriate side but this has been disproved many times. When the bark is eaten the tree yields the sticks, beams, struts and stakes required for their engineering operations. It is well known that the beavers are engineers and builders unparalleled in the animal kindgom. With only their teeth and hands they are capable of constructing lodges, dams and canals.

Dams are built to impede the flow of rivers and thus make artificial lakes in which the animals build their dwellings. The dams are of all shapes and sizes. One was discovered 500 metres long and four metres high; others are only a few metres in length. When the river is placid the dam is built to run straight across, but if the current is strong, the dam is bowed to turn into it to resist the pressure.

Beavers would thus appear to have an innate understanding of stress and strain forces. The banks of the dam are constructed to slope at an angle of forty-five degrees on the downstream side, though they may be vertical on the other. The dam is built of pieces of wood, sometimes of considerable weight, which are floated as nearly as possible into place and then manipulated. Beavers have no means of driving in stakes. Instead they weigh down timber with heavy stones. As the wood is interlaced it is made impermeable and hardwearing with a mortar of clay and dead leaves. The building of a dam begins in summer when the flood is at its lowest and continues until the first cold weather. Repair work is constant, except when everything is frozen. Outlet sluices are built for the disposal of overflow water, and canals along which building timber can be floated.

Beaver lodges are completely artificial constructions, either on the side of a lake or on a small island. From a distance they look like round heaps of tree branches and mud, but examined closely they can be seen to be built, like the dams, of interlaced branches and a mortar of clay and dead

A beaver dam, sited in the Highwood Valley of Alberta, Canada, constructed by the American Beaver (*Castor canadensis*). The beaver is highly skilled in the damming of streams and the construction of its home, known as a 'lodge'. The technical skill used in this work is only rivalled by that of man, yet the beaver's actions are instinctive and owe little to intelligence.

Merriam's Kangaroo Rat (*Dipodomys merriami*) inhabits the deserts from south-west California to central Mexico. It can survive long periods without drinking, relying for moisture on tubers which grow below the ground. It has long hindlegs and progresses by a series of long leaps, using its tail as a balancer.

leaves. Their outer dimensions may be about 487 centimetres in diameter and about 152 centimetres in height. There is no visible opening. The large and comfortable chamber inside is reached by two sloping galleries which come up from entrances below water-level. One, the narrower and steeper, is used by the animals for entry and exit. The other, wider and less steep, is the 'beaver entrance' up which the wood for winter food is taken.

It is in the lodge that the beaver family spends the winter. There, when all is frozen, they can remain in warmth and comfort, out of reach of the prowling Wolverine, lynx, wolf or other hungry animal. They do not need to expose themselves even for food, as they have previously stored a stock of wood at the bottom of the pond. Some beavers, called locally 'bank beavers' have constructed simple lodges or dug burrows in the banks of larger streams and rivers as is the habit of the European Beaver.

The following figures compiled in a Canadian National Park give an idea of the work beavers can accomplish: in fifteen months two adults cut down 266 trees, mostly poplars and willows, the trunks of which varied in diameter from two to thirty centimetres; they built three seventeen-metre dams across a river; they constructed a lodge of 330 cubic metres, and stored up a wood pile ten metres long, 2·6 metres broad and a metre high.

Formerly all the northern half of North America was inhabited by thousands of millions of American Beavers (*Castor canadensis*). They were much hunted for their fur, but protective laws passed in the nineteenth century allowed them to invade afresh areas from which they had been exterminated. Now, in some places in the eastern United States, beavers have become numerous enough to be referred to as pests by highway construction crews who find beaver dams causing flooded roads from time to time.

In the Old World the Beaver (*C. fiber*) has not fared so well, although at one time it ranged from Scandinavia to Spain and from Britain to Siberia. There are many proofs of its former distribution. Its bones are found in old river and peat deposits which date from Neolithic times.

Today Beavers have been exterminated in western Europe except in a few places: on the lower Rhône, the middle Elbe, and in the southern part of Norway. Until recently they tended to live in small colonies and seemed to have lost all their building instinct. Their lodges were supplanted by simple earths cut into river banks, with an underwater entrance and another gallery above ground to provide ventilation. Piles of timber stocked near the earths were taken for lodges.

However, the animals are now protected by law, and reserve breeding grounds have been established. There are already indications that the building instinct of the European Beaver can be revived. Beavers have been seen amassing wood above one of their earths in the Ile de la Piboulette (Bas-Rhône) and in Poland they have built rudimentary lodges. In Norway they are already displaying their full architectural powers and they are increasing in that country, which shows that they are living under favourable conditions.

Pocket gophers (Family Geomyidae)
The name of these North American rodents is derived from the French *gaufre*, which originally indicated a honeycomb pattern and referred to the way they riddled the soil with innumerable holes. The 'pocket' mentioned in their name is the cheek pouch in which they carry food for storing underground. The principal species is the Northern Pocket or Grey Gopher (*Thomomys talpoides*), which was once widespread in western Canada and the western United States and which is considered destructive and wide-scale measures have been taken for its repression. There are seven species of this genus in the United States and Canada. In most classifications the pocket gophers of the eastern United States are usually referred to the genus *Geomys*.

Kangaroo rat (Family Heteromyidae)
There are five genera and about twenty species in western and southern North America. Closely resembling the Old World Jerboa in form and habits, the Desert Kangaroo Rat (*Dipodomys*

The Springhare or Cape Jumping Hare (*Pedetes cafer*) is found in the short-grass plains of eastern and southern Africa. As in all bipedal mammals the hindlegs, and especially the hindfeet, are very long and the front feet disproportionally short. Springhares are slow breeders. The litter consists of one, occasionally two, young.

deserti), of the southwestern deserts and semi-deserts of the United States avoids the intense heat of the desert sun by spending the day in deep tunnels, emerging at night to search for seeds and other vegetable matter among the sparse, dry vegetation. If alarmed, its long hind legs carry it back to its burrow very rapidly. It even has the Jerboa's black and white tuft of long hair at the tip of its long tail, which, again like the Jerboa's, is used as a third leg when the animal stands on its hind feet. Capacious cheek pouches enable it to carry quantities of seeds to its burrow.

The related Spiny Pocket Mouse (*Perognathus spinatus*) is much smaller with a spiny coat. These mice are not adapted for leaping, but have ample cheek pouches from which their name derives.

Rats, mice, voles (Suborder Myomorpha)

Scaly-tails (Family Anomaluridae)
These highly specialised rodents, the scaly-tailed flying squirrels of tropical Africa, were once thought to be aberrant squirrels, but are now regarded as a distinct family. They are confined to the high forests, where they sleep in hollow trees during the day and emerge at dusk to make long gliding flights from tree to tree in search of food, mainly fruit and nuts. Like the true flying squirrels they have a wide gliding membrane on either side of the body, stretching from wrist to ankle, but the stiffening cartilaginous spur rises from the elbow, not the wrist. In addition there is a series of hard, pointed scales under the base of the tail, which give additional support to the animal clinging to the smooth-boled forest trees.

Most scaly-tails are of moderate size, the largest (*Anomalurus peli* from West Africa) being the size of a Domestic Cat, and conspicuously black and white. The pygmy scaly-tails (genus *Idiurus*) are no larger than mice, and have a delicately feathered tail which apparently allows them to alter course in flight. The base of the tail has a file-like surface instead of scales, but it must serve the same purpose. They are found from Ghana to eastern Zaire. The very rare Flightless Scaly-tail (genus *Zenkerella*), is known only from a few specimens found in southern Cameroun. It is the size of a large Dormouse, pure grey in colour and has no gliding membrane.

Cape-jumping hare (Family Pedetidae)
The single species in this family *Pedetes cafer* is another large, specialised rodent. It is not a hare, but it is about the size of that animal. It has long hind legs and is rather like a giant jerboa or miniature Kangaroo in its leaping powers. It lives in colonies in extensive burrows in open grassland in East and South Africa, feeding at night on vegetable matter of all kinds.

Gundis (Family Ctenodactylidae)
There are four genera of these little-known rodents of north and north-east Africa. Their exact position in the order Rodentia is difficult to define. They are like guinea-pigs in size and form, and have claws covered with stiff bristles, which may assist them in digging in loose sand. The two inner toes of the hind feet have horny combs and stiff bristles that are used in combing the fur.

Jerboas (Family Dipodidae)
In these the adaptation is for jumping, the hind legs being unusually long. The foot, which is as long as the shin or thigh, shows particular elongation. The metatarsal bones are fused. The tail, too, is long and helps to support the animal when squatting. The fore limbs are short and used for grasping. The animal moves by a series of rapid bounds with which it covers great distances in its search for food in the sandy and semi-desert regions. Its coat is always fawn-coloured, and harmonises with the terrain.

In the steppes and deserts of the Old World is a profusion of jerboas of many kinds but the best known are the jerboas of the dry regions of North Africa, Egypt, Arabia and Syria. The most common is the Egyptian Jerboa (*Jaculus jaculus*), one of the most gentle and charming animals.

Jumping mice (Family Zapodidae)
Most of these are found in North America, chiefly in Canada and the northern United States,

The food of the Common Dormouse (*Muscardinus avellanarius*) is much the same as that of a squirrel. It particularly enjoys hazel nuts which it eats by gnawing a hole in the shell and extracting the kernels. Hibernation is from late October until April, each individual hibernating on its own. During this winter sleep the pulse is very slow and feeble and the muscles are held rigid giving the dormouse the appearance of being dead.

The Crested Rat (*Lophiomys imhausi*) which inhabits Ethiopia and Kenya has grizzled, black and white hair which can be erected to form a crest along the middle of the back, flanked on either side by a naked line. It is an arboreal rodent with considerable climbing aptitude, as indicated by its flexible fingers.

Bamboo Rats (*Rhyzomys* sp.) lead a subterranean existence, excavating and exploring under the roots of the bamboo, which is its principal food. At night the rodent climbs up the stalks, stripping off slivers of bamboo and carrying them back to its burrow.

The Brown Rat (*Rattus norvegicus*) is the Common Rat found in most cities of the temperate zone. The female is very fecund, able to start breeding when three months old. Gestation takes three weeks, each litter comprising four to ten blind, deaf and naked young. As many as twelve litters may be born in a year.

although they are also found further south. There are two American genera: *Zapus* and *Napaeozapus*, the latter a forest species. Of the same family is the Birch Mouse (*Sicista subtilis*), of eastern Europe and Asia and the Szechwan jumping mice (genus *Eozapus*) of China.

Dormice (Family Muscardinidae)

Members of this family have twenty teeth, like some of the squirrels. The dormice are confined to the Old World. The species found in the dormice family in western Europe are the Fat Dormouse, the Garden Dormouse and the Common Dormouse.

Dormice are intermediate between squirrels and rats. Like the first, they are essentially arboreal and vegetarian and sometimes, as with the Fat Dormouse, have a thick, bushy tail. On the other hand their general appearance and pointed snouts resemble rats. They hibernate for about half the

year and even during the summer months spend much of their time sleeping.

The Fat Dormouse (*Glis glis*) is thirteen centimetres long, excluding its bushy tail, and is bright silver-grey on the back and yellowish white underneath. It hides during the day and goes foraging at night for fruit of various kinds, nibbling at far more than it can eat and doing much harm to orchards. When winter comes it rolls itself up in a hole lined with moss and dry grasses.

Found in central and southern Europe, where it is still eaten in some places, the Garden Dormouse (*Eliomys quercinus*) is a little smaller than the Fat Dormouse, with a black and white tuft of hairs on the end of the tail. Its fur is tawny grey above and whitish grey below, and there is a black patch on each side of the head, stretching from the eye to the ear. Its habits are much the same as those of the Fat Dormouse, but it can stand a colder climate.

The Common Dormouse (*Muscardinus avellanarius*) is the only dormouse native to Britain. It is no bigger than a House Mouse, and is tawny yellow with white below. It is widely distributed from Britain to Turkey and from Scandanavia to Tuscany.

Several species of dormice (genus *Graphiurus*) live in Africa from the Cape to Somaliland and Senegal. Most of them are quite small and grey all over but one species, the Cape Dormouse (*G. ocularis*), has a bold pattern of black and white on the face. The Spiny Dormouse (*Platacanthomys lasiurus*) is found in southern India. Its back is covered with spiny bristles. The Blind Dormouse (*Typhlomys cinereus*) of Indo-China apparently spends all its life inside rotten logs searching for insects, and has almost lost the use of its eyes.

Crested rat (Family Lophiomyidae)

The Crested Rat (*Lophiomys imhausi*), formerly regarded as a cricetine, is the only species in this family. It is characterised by a highly specialised skull in which the temporal fossae are roofed by plates of bone rising from the frontals, parietals and jugals. The Crested Rat of Ethiopia and northern Kenya is stout-bodied, thirty centimetres long with a tail slightly less than this, covered in long black and white hair. The hair along the midline of the back can be raised to form a crest, flanked on either side by naked skin. It is nocturnal, vegetarian, slow-moving, and lives in rocky ravines, but little else is known of its habits.

European mole rat (Family Spalacidae)

Species including *Spalax microphthalmus* forming this family live in the great plains of central and southern Europe as well as in south-west Asia and North Africa. They burrow with incredible rapidity, using the head as a drill, a habit which could not have developed had not both eyes and ears becomed atrophied. Their burrows are palatial, including galleries, store-rooms and chambers for living in, for mating, for birth (nest) and even latrines which are cleared out when full. Solitary by nature *Spalax* is intolerant of its own kind, except an individual of the opposite sex, and then only temporarily. The male lives with the female just long enough for mating, after which he must leave her, or be driven savagely away.

Bamboo rats (Family Rhizomyidae)

These burrowing rodents of northern India, China and Malaya (genus *Rhizomys*) have thick-set bodies thirty-six centimetres long, a strongly built head and prominent orange incisors.

Common rats and mice (Family Muridae)

This family of rats, mice and Eurasian voles is now divided into eight subfamilies.

Old World rats and mice (Subfamily Murinae)

In murines the number of teeth is reduced to sixteen, the premolars being absent. The tail is extremely thin and covered by only very fine hairs or scales. The animals are omnivorous and therefore well suited to become commensal with man, for they are able to live exclusively on what he can provide unknowingly from his house, farm and warehouse or factory.

Rats and mice need man's help for the simple reason that they are neither habitual hoarders nor hibernators, those being the normal alternatives for rodents in temperate or cold climates. They must either sleep through the unproductive months of winter, or put by stores for them.

Rats and mice are among the most fertile of mammals. Gestation varies between three and four weeks according to the species. Litters consist of from three to fourteen and come between two and seven times a year. According to a reliable estimate a pair of rats could, under ideal conditions, have twenty million descendants in three years.

The subfamily Murinae runs into some 250 species and is distributed throughout the world. No murines are native to the New World; those found there have been introduced by man. In Britain there are six species; the Black Rat, the Brown Rat, Wood Mouse, Yellow-necked Mouse, House Mouse, and Harvest Mouse.

The Black Rat differs from the Brown Rat not so much in colour as in shape of body. In the Black Rat (*Rattus rattus*) the tail is longer than the body and the ears are more than half as long as the head. In the Brown Rat (*R. norvegicus*) the tail is shorter than the body and the ears one-third the length of the head. The Brown Rat is bigger than the Black Rat, reaching a length of up to twenty-five centimetres without the tail, and a weight of over half a kilogram.

The Black Rat made its appearance in Europe in the thirteenth century, following the return of the Crusaders who brought it from Asia Minor. In the south of Europe it remained an open-air animal, but in the north it lost no time in taking up its quarters with man. Down to the seventeenth century they were responsible for plagues, which from time to time decimated the population. The Brown Rat, also from Asia, appeared in Europe during the eighteenth century, reaching England by 1729 and North America by 1775.

Although the two tended to avoid each other, the Black Rats preferring the dry upper parts of a house (such as lofts) and the Brown Rats the lower and damper parts (such as basements and cellars), nevertheless the Brown Rat has driven the Black Rat out of many places in Europe and America.

The Long-tailed Field-mouse or Wood Mouse (*Apodemus sylvaticus*) lives in fields, woods, or

The Long-tailed Field Mouse or Woodmouse (*Apodemus sylvaticus*) is as much an inhabitant of the field, garden and cultivated land as it is the woodland. A feature of the maternal behaviour, shared with many small mice, is that when alarmed, the female will run with half-grown babies hanging to her teats, and keeping in step.

The European Harvest Mouse (*Micromys minutus*), is one of the smallest rodents. A typical attitude of the Harvest Mouse is to grip adjacent cornstalks with the hind-feet and wrap its prehensile tail around one or both of the stems, leaving the front paws free for holding food.

The Striped Grass Mouse (*Lemniscomys striatus*) is abundant throughout most of Africa. It is found in a variety of habitats up to about 2,000 metres, especially grassland where its stripes act as camouflage. It is slightly larger than the House Mouse and is diurnal.

The Common European Hamster (*Cricetus cricetus*) is larger than the familiar Golden Hamster. It is a pugnacious animal found in eastern Europe and western Asia, where it nests in underground burrows. It spends the winter in semi-hibernation, having stored large quantities of grain and roots.

gardens. It is considerably smaller than either of the rats and its hind legs are much longer than the fore legs. Unlike the other members of the family it burrows and hoards, and like its relatives does a great deal of damage. It is a rather rusty colour. A close relative is the Yellow-necked Mouse (*A. flavicollis*), which is similar in appearance and habits, but more robust and vigorous, and more given to entering houses in winter.

The House Mouse (*Mus musculus*), is one of the oldest known species of domestic rodents, its association with man may well go back to prehistoric times. Though charming enough, it is a formidable pest. Normally these mice are grey, but albinos are bred in captivity.

The Eurasian Harvest Mouse (*Micromys minutus*) is six centimetres long, excluding the tail. This

pretty little animal, bright red-brown above and white below, lives in wheatfields or among coarse herbage. Its lightness enables it to climb up the stalks to nibble the seeds or grains. At the beginning of summer it builds a round, hanging nest woven of bits of grass and shredded corn leaves that could easily be taken for a bird's nest. The opening is at the side. The interior is lined with petals and vegetation which keep the nest warm. In winter the Harvest Mouse retires into a hayrick.

Africa can boast the smallest mouse and the biggest rat. The Gambian Pouched Rat (*Cricetomys gambianus*) is over thirty centimetres in length with a tail of equal length, and thus much larger than a Guinea-pig. It is very destructive because of its voracious hoarding in deep burrows. In southern Asia its place is taken by the Bandicoot Rat (*Bandicota bengalensis*), which measures up to forty centimetres long with the tail.

Hamsters and New World rats and mice (Subfamily Cricetinae)

Hamsters and the New World rats and mice have molars like those of rats, limited in growth and with tuberculate crowns. They are considered a distinct family by many mammalogists. The Common Hamster (*Cricetus cricetus*) ranges from western Europe to Siberia and southwards to Iraq. Its fur is brown, flecked with yellow and white, except for the underside, which is quite black.

A most interesting feature is the Common Hamster's burrowing and hoarding. Dug under fields or in any dry or sandy ground, its underground works are not very deep (some thirty-five to seventy-five centimetres) and consist of a large central chamber with radiating galleries leading to smaller chambers either for habitation or for excretion. The Hamster is an extremely clean creature which scrupulously avoids soiling its living quarters. A summer burrow serves for breeding. Another one, constructed for the winter, is a marvel of organisation, with separate chambers for corn, potatoes, carrots, beetroot, chestnuts and nuts. The total weight of stored food may amount to 100 kilograms. The burrows are indicated by the corn-scattered mounds over them, in the middle of which is the principal entrance. Other entrances encircle the burrow.

The Common Hamster uses its incisors to carry the larger provisions, like potatoes, while corn is stowed in its cheek pouches, which are afterwards emptied with the aid of its fore paws. The foraging is always nocturnal. The Hamster also hunts insects, lizards, snakes, mice and young birds. It is pugnacious on occasions, even to man.

In the autumn the Common Hamster descends into its burrow and blocks up all the means of access. Then rolled up in a ball on a bed of straw it goes to sleep. It does not hibernate very deeply, however, and from time to time it wakes up to eat. The Hamster ranks high as a nuisance, and is the constant object of repressive measures, including the use of special dogs trained to hunt it, as well as the flooding or fumigating of the burrows.

The Golden Hamster (*Mesocricetus auratus*) stands in marked contrast to the Common Hamster. It was first known from one specimen in 1839 and was not seen again until 1930 when an adult

female and twelve young were found in Syria. Some of the progeny were sent to England in 1931 and soon this animal became popular as a pet and as a laboratory subject, partly because of its high rate of breeding. Whereas the Common Hamster has eight mammae, the Golden Hamster has from fourteen to twenty-two. The gestation period is only fifteen days and the young are fully adult at eleven weeks.

NEW WORLD RATS AND MICE: All the native 'rats' and 'mice' existing in the New World before the introduction of Old World rats and mice are members of the same subfamily as the Hamster, and although superficially many show close resemblances to their murine counterparts in the Old World, their dental patterns are quite different. They afford many good examples of convergent evolution. South America particularly has a great variety of these cricetines, inhabiting every type of country from tropical forests and swamps to open treeless plains and up to the snow-line in the Andes. In North America the most abundant members of the group are the deer mice or white-footed mice (genus *Peromyscus*), which bear a striking resemblance in form, colour and general habits to the common European Long-tailed Field-mouse (genus *Apodemus*). Many varieties of these species are found from coast to coast and from the northern tree-line south to Mexico. The most interesting American cricetines are the wood rats or pack rats (genus *Neotoma*), large soft-furred, rat-like animals, (one species has a bushy tail) various species of which are found mainly in the western United States. They have a habit of collecing any bright objects which catch their eye, and carrying them away to decorate their nests, which are large structures of sticks built on the ground or among bushes and trees, or sometimes among rocks. They have even been known to carry off every small portable article from deserted log cabins, replacing them with pebbles. Hence the alternaive name, trade rats. In desert regions the lodges of pack rats may be so adorned with pieces of cactus as to be an almost impenetrable refuge. There are seven species in the genus, all with rather similar habits.

Voles, lemmings, muskrats
(Subfamily Microtinae)

Voles never live in association with man. They might loosely be called country rats, some even living in desert conditions. They are heavy and short-limbed, and are distinguished from true rats by their blunt muzzles, small ears and eyes, and tails (never more than half the length of the body), as well as by their constantly growing molars whose crowns show a series of alternating right and left handed folds of enamel. Many consider them part of the Cricetinae; they seem to be closer to the Cricetinae than to the Murinae.

Like the lemmings, voles are prone to cyclic fluctuations in numbers. The reasons for this are not fully understood, but voles have been known to increase rapidly in a locality and, when their populations are at a maximum, to do enormous damage to the vegetation. These 'vole years' lead to high concentrations of birds of prey, particularly short-eared owls, which feed almost exclusively on the voles. Other predators are drawn to

the affected area also, and the phenomenal rise in the populations of voles is followed by a 'crash'. The original cause is almost certainly connected with a good food supply, which leads to more and bigger litters and a rapid maturing of the successive generations. A single pair can have 200 descendants in a year, and as the numbers build up, the food supply runs short. The overcrowded or saturation conditions under which the voles are living then lead to more fighting and less breeding. The 'crash' may therefore be due to a combination of circumstances: dwindling food supply, higher mortality among adults, abnormally low breeding rate, and the onslaught of predators.

At times they undertake mass migrations and the damage they do is enormous. They crop the grass bare and attack the bark of young trees, severely damaging young plantations. If a single vole eats only thirty grams of grain per week and if, at a modest estimate, there are 1,600 animals to the hectare, that makes a weekly loss of about fifty kilograms to the hectare—about 10,000 kilograms a month over a fifty-hectare field.

The Field Vole of Europe (*Microtus arvalis*) is related to the Short-tailed Vole or Meadow Vole (*M. agrestis*), which is also found in Britain. The other well-known species in western Europe is the

The Deer Mouse or White-footed Mouse (*Peromyscus maniculatus*) is found throughout America and resembles the Long-tailed Field Mouse in appearance, habits and habitat. It lives in communities and makes runs in leaf litter or just below the surface, feeding on vegetable matter, especially nuts, fruit and berries.

The Grasshopper Mouse or Scorpion Mouse (*Onychomys torridus*) occurs in the more arid parts of North America. It has a much shorter tail than most other mice. Its diet consists almost entirely of insects, especially grasshoppers and scorpions; it often catches its prey by leaping on it.

The Bank Vole (*Clethrionomys glareolus*) is common over most of Europe. It inhabits warm dry banks, hedgerows and wooded country where it constructs shallow runs in the earth, often with many entrances and exits. Active day and night, it can swim, dive and climb bushes.

The Steppe Lemming (*Lagurus lagurus*), of European Russia, central Asia and the western United States is mainly nocturnal but individuals may move about in the daytime. It is a burrowing rodent and is active the year round. Up to five litters are born during the summer, with usually four to seven young.

Water Vole (*Arvicola amphibius*). The Short-tailed Field Mouse or Vole is just over ten centimetres long without its tail, which is about four centimetres long, brown-grey above, grey-white below. The deep brown Water Vole has a body twenty centimetres long, the tail being about half that length. The Meadow Vole or Mouse (*M. pennsylvanicus*) of the northern United States and Canada is the most abundant vole in North America.

Their burrows comprise multiple galleries, living-rooms, nests and store-rooms. The Water Vole, incorrectly called the 'Water Rat', lives by the water, feeding on the aquatic plants and bark, occasionally eating frogs and fishes. Over much of the continent of Europe it is replaced by a related species, *A. terrestris*, which is entirely terrestrial and mole-like in its habit of burrowing, but is otherwise similar to *A. amphibius*.

The Bank Vole (*Clethrionomys glareolus*) is common over most of Europe. Members of the genus *Clethrionomys* differ from true voles in having

rooted molars. The Northern Red-backed Vole or Mouse (*C. grapperi*) and other species of the genus are common in the Arctic and cool-temperate forests of North America where they often forage in the tree branches.

Besides these types which live in the plains, there are mountain voles of which the best known is the Snowy Vole (*Microtus nivalis*), found sometimes in the Alps, Pyrenees, and Massif Central at heights of over 3,000 metres. In winter it remains in a burrow, where it has stored provisions.

The Northern Vole (*M. oeconomus*) inhabits eastern Siberia and Kamchatka. Its specific name refers to its hoarding habits, which are carried to such a point that local inhabitants can live in winter by raiding its stores. It is often numerous enough to be a major pest.

LEMMINGS: A close relative of the voles and a member of the same subfamily, the Norway Lemming (*Lemmus lemmus*) inhabits the mountainous wastes of northern Norway and Lapland and is given to extraordinary mass migration at times.

'Every third or fourth year', according to one observer, 'this rodent, generally timid and nocturnal and hardly ever seen on the vast barren plateaus of Scandinavia, appears openly in broad daylight, busily searching for food which becomes scarcer as the animals' numbers increase. It overflows from its natural habitat, pouring down into the valleys, driving straight forward, the foremost pushed on by those in the rear, the whole number seemingly obsessed by the desire to forge ahead. The valleys broaden, rich in crops, also in villages, men, and dangers of every sort, but the lemmings ignore them all, swarming onward, more concerned, once the migration has started to advance than to enjoy what it finds. The psychosis of exodus is thus realised earlier and more intensely than in the squirrel, but otherwise there is little difference.'

There is still a great deal we do not know about these animals. But we do know that in Scandanavia the migrations always start from one of five different centres and always proceed in the same directions. The northern ones, for instance, always go to the Lofoten Islands or to the Gulf of Bothnia. The initial cause of the movement seems to be overpopulation, just as it is the cause of the swarming of bees.

Migration appear to occur more or less regularly. There are 'lemming years', just as there are years when the cockchafers flourish. The important factor seems to be a cyclic variation in fertility. Normally there are two litters of five each year, but every so often there are four litters of six to eight, and such a fecund summer is invariably followed by an autumn migration. The problem becomes more complex when we note that lemming migrations are linked with movements of other animals not closely connected with them. Thus 'lemming years' are also years of shrews, capercaillies, and even certain butterflies, whose caterpillars strip whole birch forests of their leaves. This periodic acceleration of fertility in animals which have nothing in common but habitat cannot be a coincidence. The Brown Lemming (*L. trimucronatus*), the Bog Lemming (genus *Synaptomys*) and the Collared Lemming (genus *Dicrostonyx*) of northern America have similar emigrations.

MUSKRATS: The Muskrats (*Ondatra zibethica*) is a
sort of vole living in Canada and United States. It
is the size of a small rabbit and weighs about 1·3
kilograms when adult. Its fur resembles a beaver's,
thick, soft and shiny, brown above, grey below. In
its habits also, such as its riparian burrowing and
its lodges, it is similar to a beaver.

Essentially a water rat, the Muskrat spends its
life in ponds and rivers, feeding on aquatic vegetation. With its strong incisors and claws it digs deep
burrows in river banks, dykes and weirs, with two
openings, one under the water, the other above.
Sometimes it builds a lodge of grasses and reeds
cemented with mud.

The popular name 'Muskrat' is due to an
odorous substance, comparable to a beaver's cas-
toreum, secreted by its iguinal glands.

Because of the value of its fur it was introduced
into Europe in 1905, but the Muskrat does much
damage to man-made earthen dams, dykes and
canals with its burrowing habits. From Prague,
where it was first introduced, it has spread over a
large part of central Europe. The related Florida
Water Rat (*Neofiber alleni*) is sometimes called the
Round-tailed Muskrat.

Mole-rat (Subfamily Tachyoryctinae)
Once placed with the bamboo rats, the mole-rats
(genus *Tachyoryctes*) are now assigned to this separate subfamily. Twenty-three centimetres long,
these burrowing rodents of East Africa live as far
up Mount Kenya as the bamboo zone. They have
long, silky fur, which is bright tawny or a rich
chestnut.

Sand rats (Subfamily Gerbillinae)
Gerbils or sand rats inhabit the drier parts of
Africa and Asia. They are nocturnal, remaining in
their burrows during the day and coming out at
night to feed on seeds and grain. The various
species resemble rats or mice. They are sandy or
pale buff above, with white underparts and feet.
Gerbils leap on their hind legs, kangaroo fashion,
using the long tail, characteristically tufted, as a
counterpoise. The name gerbil is usually applied
to species of the genera *Gerbillus*, *Tatera* and others,
which all hoard food. The Fat-tailed Gerbil (*Pachy-
uromys duprasi*) does not hoard. Living in North
Africa, it is of heavier build and its club-shaped
tail contains a reserve of fat against times of
scarcity. The name 'jird' is given to related species
of the genus *Meriones* which are inhabitants of
North Africa and south-west Asia.

Australasian water rats
(Subfamily Hydromyinae)
One of the most specialised of the Myomorpha,
the New Guinea Water Rat (*Crossomys moncktoni*)
has large webbed hind feet, small fore feet, vestigial ears and a tail fringed with hairs for use in
swimming. There are about thirteen genera and
many species in the subfamily which is found from
the Philippines to New Guinea and Australia.

Shrew-rat (Subfamily Rhynchomyinae)
The Shrew Rat (*Rhynchomys soricoides*) is the only
species in this subfamily. It is found only in the
Philippines and has a long, narrow head, minute
teeth, and probably feeds on soft bodied insects.

The Muskrat (*Ondatra zibethica*)
ranges over North America
wherever the habitat is suitable. It
is an aquatic animal, living among
the water plants by streams and
rivers, in fresh and salt water. Its
food consists mainly of water
plants but frogs, fish and freshwater mussels are also taken.

The East African Mole Rat
(*Tachoryctes splendens*) ranges from
the sandy plains to the bamboo
forests. A burrowing rodent it
makes long tunnels, biting away
obstructions with its protruding
incisor teeth and throwing the
loose earth backwards into mounds.
The coloration is quite variable.

The Gerbil (*Tatera valida*) inhabits
the drier parts of Africa and Asia.
It lives underground in communal
burrows and is mainly nocturnal,
though not entirely so. Living far
from water they rely for moisture
on that contained in seeds, grain
and roots.

Blue whale

Greenland right whale

Pigmy right whale

Humpback whale

Bottlenose whale

Sperm whale

Cetaceans vary considerably in shape and size. The largest is the Blue Whale (*Balaenoptera musculus*), with an elongated body thirty metres long and a deeply furrowed throat. The huge head of the Greenland Right Whale or Bowhead Whale (*Baleana mysticetus*) accounts for a third of the total length of sixteen to twenty metres. The largest of the toothed whales, the Sperm Whale (*Physeter catodon*) is twenty-three metres long and has a square head and snout. The Humpback Whale (*Megaptera novaeangliae*), thirteen to sixteen metres long, has a squat body and elongated, irregular-shaped flippers. The Pygmy Right Whale (*Caperea marginata*), which grows to about six metres long, is the only right whale with a dorsal fin. The Bottlenose Whale (*Hyperoodon ampullatus*), about ten metres long, has a distinctive 'forehead' formed by bony crests on the skull.

Banana mice (Subfamily Dendromyinae)

Species of the genus *Dendromus*, the banana or tree mice, are delicately built and have a long prehensile tail. They have three toes on each fore foot, and are light fawn-buff with a dark stripe down the back. They live in Africa, and hide in the folds of banana leaves or among the fruit. Related to them are the South African fat mice (genus *Steatomys*), which live in sandy burrows. They have very fat bodies and short tails, and are extremely lethargic, features which are linked with their hibernating habit without parallel among African mammals.

Whales (Order Cetacea)

Cetaceans are the mammals most completely adapted to an aquatic life. Their morphological resemblance to fishes is so close that for a long time naturalists classed them together, but comparative anatomy shows that they are mammals undoubtedly descended from terrestrial animals, through which they may be related to the ungulates. Another suggestion is that they may have come from an early group of carnivorous mammals known as the Creodonta.

Cetaceans swim well and are well streamlined. Like the best swimmers among fishes—the Mackerel or the Tunny—they progress broad end forward.

A uniform layer of fat concentrated in a part of the dermis covers the whole body. This is the blubber which serves to conserve heat and to provide an auxiliary source of energy.

Cetaceans have no external ears or projecting nostrils to hamper movement through the water. The very small opening leading to the ear-drum is filled with a wax plug. The body is completely hairless, except for a very few hairs on the muzzle and those which in some whales have been modified into whalebone. This acts as a filter for the food of the right whales and rorquals. The hairless skin has neither sebaceous glands nor sweat glands.

Streamlining has involved the shortening of the neck, so that the head is continuous with the body. The seven cervical vertebrae, which in giraffes occupy a length of two metres, are very much compressed in the whales and often fused into a single disc, which is only a few centimetres thick, even in very large individuals. The head therefore cannot be moved in relation to the body.

The fore limbs or flippers are well developed, and there may be a dorsal fin but this is little more than a fold of skin and is not supported by a skeleton. There is nothing corresponding to the anal and-pelvic fins of fishes.

Dissection of a whale's flipper reveals the same skeleton as that found in the fore limb of a terrestrial mammal, with the following modifications: the scapula is consolidated and simplified; the humerus, radius and ulna are reduced in relative size, while the hand is elongated by the multiplication of phalanges; the digits are no longer separate but enclosed in fibrous tissue; the muscles, except those of the shoulder, are atrophied. The flippers can only move up and down. They are not propellent. Their function is to act as stablisers.

The real locomotory organ is the tail, which has two horizontal flukes projecting on each side, and is thus entirely different from the vertical tail of a fish. Operated by powerful muscles, the flukes serve as a propellor and as a horizontal rudder regulating horizontal movement in the water. Most cetaceans have a small dorsal fin which apparently keeps steady on a course. The right whales are slower than others and have no dorsal fin.

Unlike seals and other pinnipeds, cetaceans have no hind limbs at all. But vestiges of a pelvis, and sometimes of a femur and tibia remain inside the body, and these alone are enough to prove that this order is originally descended from four-footed terrestrial mammals.

As with other aquatic mammals, their teeth tend to be simplified. The dolphins and porpoises have between 100 and 200 conical teeth, all alike and not solidly rooted in the jaws. Their function is merely to grasp the fishes on which they feed. In the sperm whales, or cachalots, there are functional teeth only in the lower jaw (about twenty-five on each side), which fit into sockets in the upper jaw. It is thought that this is a convenient arrangement for dealing with the slimy cephalopods on which they chiefly feed. The beaked whales have only a few teeth, sometimes only one, in each half jaw. The narwhal is peculiar in having only two teeth in all, in the middle of the upper jaw; one of them grows to some two metres in the male and forms a tusk.

The mouth is large in the Odontoceti, or toothed whales. In the Mysticeti, or whalebone whales, it is enormous to accommodate the plates of whalebone, or baleen, which take the place of teeth. Each baleen plate is triangular in shape and secured by its base in the gum of the upper jaw, its convex side turned outwards and its concave side inwards. It is composed of agglutinated hairs which diminish in length from the convex to the concave side, where they form a freely projecting fringe that increases in length as the animal ages. There may be hundreds of these plates one to two metres long according to the species, latticed one behind the other.

When not in use the baleen is covered by the underlip which projects above the lower jaw. To feed, the whale opens its mouth and swims into the shoals of fish or shrimp-like animals, known as 'krill', on which it lives. When sufficient has been taken in, the mouth is closed and the water expelled through the baleen plates. The food is retained on the inside, then removed by the tongue and swallowed. This operation is performed repeatedly to make one meal, at the end of which a large whale may have ten tonnes of small creatures in its stomach, sometimes of the same species.

Odontoceti, or toothed whales, are more varied and more numerous. The progressive atrophy of the teeth begun in the Odontoceti concludes with their complete absence in the Mysticeti. In both, teeth or whalebone are preceded by milk teeth which never erupt, and disappear before birth.

The cetaceans may be divided into three groups according to diet; whalebone whales, feeding on small animals such as crustaceans and pteropods in the plankton floating in the sea, and accordingly called planktonophagous; fish hunters or ichthyophagous whales; and those that feed largely on cephalopods, described as teuthophagous. Members of this last group often bear on their heads the scars made by the suckers of cephalopods, and contents of their stomachs reveal a large number of 'beaks' and cuttle-bones from those they have eaten. Taxonomically, however, there are only two groups, or suborders: the Mysticeti and Odontoceti.

Cetaceans have a divided stomach, the first compartments playing the part of a masticatory gizzard, while the others secrete gastric juices.

The most striking adaptation the Cetacea have undergone is undoubtedly in their respiratory and vascular systems. These animals dive to depths of 100 to as much as 1,200 metres and some, like the sperm whales, can stay below for an hour. Before diving the whale takes in a large provision of air. Its lungs are comparatively small and carry only a small proportion of oxygen needed for a dive. More is stored in the blood and muscles and it is conserved by the whale closing down non-essential activities, such as digestion, and employing anaerobic respiration in the muscles while submerged. The blowhole can be closed, as also the glottis, and each bronchial passage has a sphincter.

On diving the heart beat slows and the blood circulation shuts down except to the most essential organs: the brain, nervous system and heart. A whole network of arteries and veins contributes to this end. In man signs of asphyxia are quickly produced because the medulla is highly sensitive to carbonic acid gas in the blood. In the Cetacea, on the contrary, the medulla is particularly insensitive to this stimulation.

When a whale surfaces, the top of the head where the blowhole is placed emerges first. From this shoots the 'spout' which rises high in the air. It was once thought that the spout was simply water. It is now commonly accepted that the spout is caused by condensation of moist warm breath meeting the cold air. A more recent discovery is that it is made up of droplets of mucus and it has been suggested that it is probably a mechanism by which the body expels nitrogen from inhaled air.

The blowholes are the only respiratory outlets. The larynx does not open into the back of the mouth, as in other animals, but directly into the nasal fossae. This permits the cetacean to open its mouth while swimming and to swallow food, without the risk of either the food or water entering the windpipe.

The brain is relatively small, but has many complex convolutions. The nasal fossae function solely as air passages and have lost all sense of smell. The ears have no pinnae. The auditory passages are very narrow and finish flush with the skin, just behind the eyes. Hearing is extremely sensitive and many whales also produce a variety of sounds. Dolphins have a very sensitive system of echolocation and this may be true of the larger toothed whales.

The eyes are small relative to the size of the animal. In a whale twenty-seven metres long they are barely the size of a saucer. Placed far back, at the angle of the mouth, they do not give binocular vision. The crystalline lens is spherical, as in fishes, and accordingly adapted to the refractive index of water. Eyelids are rudimentary and have only limited power of movement. Lachrymal glands secrete a fatty substance which protects the cornea and conjunctiva against the action of sea water.

In the males the testes are internal, and the penis lies in a ventral groove. In the female the uterus is bicorned and the placenta diffuse, as in the horse. Teats are inguinal, situated on either side of the vulva. One, rarely two, young are born at a time.

Whereas cow's milk contains forty grams of cream to the litre and approximately the same amount of proteins, whale's milk contains 200 grams of cream and only twenty of proteins. It is thus very rich and full of calories, enabling the young to grow with great rapidity, and to resist the cold until they have developed the thick protective layer of blubber.

Behind each teat is a reservoir in which a supply of milk can be held. This is controlled by a muscle which ejects the milk promptly as soon as suckling begins. The whole operation is therefore very rapid. A fold of skin around the teat forms a valve which prevents water entering the youngster's mouth.

The suborder Mysticeti ('moustached') includes the right whales and rorquals. The first have neither dorsal fin nor ventral grooves; the second have a dorsal fin and a varying number of grooves on the throat and chest. Both are generally big and feed on small animals.

The Odontoceti ('toothed') include those like the sperm whales and the beaked whales, which have teeth in the lower jaw only; those like the dolphins, porpoises, belugas, killer and pilot whales, which have teeth in both jaws; and the narwhals, which have only a single tooth developed as a tusk in the upper jaw. This suborder varies in size. Some feed on fishes, some on seals or porpoises, and some on squid.

Whalebone whales (Suborder Mysticeti)

Right whales (Family Balaenidae)

The absence of a dorsal fin and grooves on throat and chest distinguishes right whales from all other cetaceans. The colour varies from slate-grey to black according to the species. There are three genera: *Balaena, Eubalaena* and *Caperea*. The Greenland Right Whale or Bowhead (*Balaena mysticetus*) is now rare, but is still found in the Arctic. Its total length varies from fiften to eighteen metres, and that of its whalebone from three to four metres. The Biscayan, or Atlantic, Right Whale (*E. glacialis*) is the same size, but the whalebone is shorter. It too is rare.

In the Greenland Right Whale the head accounts for one-third of the length, but only for a quarter in the Atlantic Right Whale. The Southern Right Whale (*E. australis*) is a little more abundant but nothing much is known about the Pygmy Right Whale (*Caperea marginata*) of southern seas.

The jaw and lips are curiously formed. The two halves of the upper jaw form a 'V' and at the same time are strongly arched. They hold the baleen plates, which number roughly 300 on each side. The lower jaw is also V-shaped but more or less horizontal. It is the lower lip which rises to meet the upper lip to cover the whalebone. When the whale is feeding, however, the lower lip is extended into a sort of scoop to gather up innumerable animalcules that go to make up its diet. The throat of the Right Whale is no bigger than a stovepipe.

Rorquals (Family Balaenopteridae)

The presence of a dorsal fin and ventral grooves distinguishes rorquals from right whales. The head is smaller and the jaws, which are not arched, are less wide apart, since the baleen plates are shorter. The lower lip does not come up so

The Southern Right Whale, of the South Atlantic, is usually called *Eubalaena australis* but there is probably only one species of black right whales, *E. glacialis*. The black right whales are similar to the Greenland Right Whale but the head, mouth and baleen plates are smaller. They are now rare everywhere.

high and the flippers are more pointed. In general, rorquals are more slender and streamlined. Because of their greater speeds, they are more difficult to reach and capture. Unmolested until the invention of the harpoon-gun, the rorquals became the chief objective of the whaling industry, in Arctic or Antarctic waters during the summer, or in the warmer waters to which they are driven by the formation of pack ice in winter.

There are several species: the Blue Whale, the Fin Whale, the Sei Whale, the Minke Whale, Bryde's Whale and the Humpback Whale.

The Blue Whale, Sulphur-bottom, or Sibbald's Rorqual (*Balaenoptera musculus*), is the biggest of the cetaceans, and the largest animal in the world. It is a dark slate-blue all over except for the colourless tips and undersides of the flippers. The number of ventral grooves varies from eighty to 100. They enable the throat to expand when the animal swims, mouth open, through the krill on which it feeds. The tongue contracts on the floor of the mouth then squirts the water out through the whalebone.

The Blue Whale used commonly to reach a length of twenty-four to thirty metres and weigh as much as 1,500 men or twenty-four elephants. As a result of intensive whaling, the thirty-metre whale is no longer seen and a twenty-four-metre individual is a rarity. The weight of a large Blue Whale was made up as follows: fifty tonne of muscle, eight tonne of blood, one tonne of lungs, and sixty tons of skin, bones and viscera. The heart weighed 585 kilograms and measured about a metre each way. It is impossible to imagine a creature with so much weight to support living out of water. If stranded it would soon die as the weight of the body would compress the lungs and prevent it from breathing.

The Fin Whale (*B. physalus*), or Common Rorqual, is more abundant than the Blue Whale, but smaller. Its maximum recorded length is twenty-four metres. Gracefully streamlined and very fast, it has been called the 'Ocean Greyhound'. The dorsal fin is more developed than in the Blue Whale. It is dark above, white below, and has a curiously unsymmetrical head. Besides feeding on plankton it often goes for herring or cod.

Smaller still is the Sei Whale (*B. borealis*), whose maximum length falls short of eighteen metres. Its common name has been given it because it appears off the north coast of Norway at the same time as the Sei, a sort of Whiting. It has from thirty to sixty ventral grooves. The body is grey above, with a white belly.

The Humpback Whale (*Megaptera novaeangliae*) is not a true rorqual (those in the genus *Balaenoptera*) although it is placed in the same family. It differs from the others in the low hump on the back, the bosses on the snout, and the very long flippers which may be one-third the length of the animal, or roughly five metres. It is ugly compared to the true rorquals. It has a maximum of twenty ventral grooves. It is black above and white below, sometimes with black spots.

A great deal of careful research has been done in southern waters by scientists. Specimens have been marked so as to follow the migrations of certain species from year to year. The movements of schools of rorquals have been followed through

the months, and much statistical work has been done to establish the poportions of the sexes and age of puberty.

The rorquals are almost world-wide in distribution, but they do not occupy all their area at every season. The widest in their movements are the Blue Whale and the Fin Whale. Sei Whale and the Humpback Whale are more confined to warm or temperate waters, and not so often found in polar regions, so that they play a less important part in Antarctic whaling operations. They are inclined to venture close to European coasts, where occasionally one becomes stranded.

In summer, that is from May to October in the northern hemisphere and from November to April in the southern hemisphere, the rorquals frequent the polar seas, which with the melting of the pack ice positively swarm with planktonic crustaceans. These are the relatively large *Euphausia* and *Calanus*, of which the rorquals consume enomous quantities. It is during this period of the year that the whaling season is at its height.

When winter comes, and with it the spread of pack ice, most of the rorquals move to warmer waters. There is nothing absolute about the dates given above. Each species acts differently, and different sexes and age groups in the same species may also act differently.

Mating takes place towards the end of wintering, but it has rarely been witnessed. According to

The Fin Whale, Common Rorqual or Finner (*Balaenoptera physalus*) is worldwide in distribution. Unlike their relative the Blue Whale, Fin Whales swim in schools and are rarely found singly. The gestation period is about ten months and it is interesting that the ovum of these whales is no bigger than that of the smallest mammals but in nine months it grows to a whale one-third the length of its mother.

The Humpback Whale (*Megaptera novaeangliae*) has many similarities to the rorquals but is placed in a separate genus. The picture shows the whale's characteristic long pectoral fin. In spite of its large size, up to fifteen metres in length, the Humpback Whale may often be seen leaping and rolling back into the water. It is widely distributed in the oceans and follows the rorqual migratory pattern.

one observer writing about the Humpback Whale, the males and females frequently slap each other with their huge flippers. They are doubtless friendly pats but can be heard kilometres away in calm weather. They also turn over on their sides and rub each other with their flippers.

There is no direct evidence to confirm that rorquals are monogamous or polygamous, but the relative numbers of males and females may give some indication. If at birth the number of males is slightly in excess, as is generally the case with mammals, that excess soon disappears with a higher mortality rate in adolescence. By the time the adult state is reached males are definitely less numerous than females, and would thus be expected to tend towards polygamy. But the fact that the females bear young only every second or third year would seem to indicate that less than half were available for mating, thus suggesting monogamy. Monogamy appears to be more likely in the Blue Whales, which are generally seen in couples, than in the Fin Whales, which go about in schools.

A female gives birth once every two or three years, and never to more than one calf at a time. Gestation varies from ten to eleven months according to the species. At birth the young are from four to five metres in length, although the calf of the Blue Whale is somewhat larger. For six months they are fed exclusively by their mothers. Fed on such rich milk, the calf grows at an incredible pace. A young Blue Whale, for example, seven metres in length at birth, will grow to fifteen metres by the time it is weaned seven months later. At puberty, in the third year, males reach twenty-two metres and females twenty-four metres. The prime of life is reached in ten to fifteen years. The length of life is estimated to be about fifty years.

The parasites that afflict cetaceans are connected with their migrations. Various crustaeans (Cirripedes, copepods and amphipods) attach themselves to the skin during the wintering in warmer waters and disappear on return to Arctic or Antarctic seas. Conversely, the skin may become covered in cold water with a coating of algae and diatoms which disappear in temperate water.

Californian grey whales (Family Eschrichtiidae)
The Californian Grey Whale (*Eschrichtius robustus*) has no dorsal fin but has two ventral grooves. Its maximum length is 13·5 metres. It lives in the North Pacific, migrating regularly from the Arctic to warmer waters, where it breeds in shallow bays. It used to live in the North Atlantic and the western North Pacific.

Toothed whales (Suborder Odontoceti)

Sperm whales (Family Physeteridae)
Because of their size sperm whales or cachalots are often confused with right whales. The one living species is, however, quite different. First, it has no whalebone with which to catch its food, but is a toothed whale, with teeth in the lower jaw only— forty teeth in all, each about twenty centimetres long, approximately three kilograms in weight, and fitting into sockets in the upper jaw. This dentition is suitable for dealing with the slimy squid on which they feed.

Another characteristic distinguishes the cachalots from the right whales and rorquals: they have a massive blunt snout, thrust forward beyond the mouth. In it is a cavity, developed from one of the nasal fossae, which contains a thin, colourless, transparent oil. On contact with air this oil solidifies to form a white wax called spermaceti, which was at one time thought to be the animal's brain, but was later shown to be a wax.

Another product of sperm whales is ambergris, found as an intestinal concretion. This solid grey substance has a disagreeable odour yet with time acquires properties which make it highly prized as a base for the most precious perfumes. It is now agreed that it is somehow connected with the cephalopods on which the whale feeds. Lumps of it, weighing anything from a few grams to many kilograms, are often evacuated and found floating on the sea or cast up on the shore. The largest, taken from a whale off the Azores in recent years weighed about 270 kilograms.

Sperm whales have no real dorsal fin but a series of low humps on the rear third of the body. Like all the Odontoceti they have single blowhole. Males may be up to eighteen metres long, but females are very much shorter. They are black above, grey on the sides, and white below.

Unlike the other species so far described, they are aggressive, Not only do they attack squids and on occasion hunt fishes, but will even assault a whole boat manned by whalers, crushing it like matchwood in their powerful jaws. When tormented by a harpoon wound, the whale may even charge a ship, smashing the hull.

Battles between sperm whales and giant squids occasionally take place on the surface and have been witnessed from ships. On one occasion a squid of huge dimensions was grasping the whale's head with its long muscular tentacles. Under this painful clutch the whale flung about wildly, beating up mountains of spray with its formidable flukes. Some time later the head of the squid was seen floating on the surface.

In their reproductive habits sperm whales seem to behave rather differently from rorquals. Gestation lasts for sixteen months. Birth is always of a single calf which is suckled for one year. They are definitely polygamous, and a male is always accompanied by several members of the more numerous female sex.

Only one species of Sperm Whale is known (*Physeter catodon*), which is common in temperate and tropical waters from about 40°N. to 40°S. Males range much further, however, and may be caught in the Antarctic.

In the eighteenth century sperm oil was used principally for lighting, and the substitution of paraffin in lamps probably saved the cachalots from extermination. Hunting declined in the second half of the last century, but as rorquals were hunted out, the sperm whales are being caught in increasing numbers and are again killed in greater numbers than any other species.

Pygmy sperm whales (Family Kogiidae)
The only species in the family are the Pygmy Sperm Whale (*Kogia breviceps*) of the Atlantic, Pacific and Indian oceans, and the Dwarf Sperm Whale (*K. simus*) of the tropics. They are similar in habits and life-history to the Cachalot.

Porpoises (Family Phocaenidae)
The Common Porpoise (*Phocaena phocaena*) is the smallest cetacean of European waters, measuring

A Grey Whale (*Eschrichtius robustus*) breaching. This whale shows characters of both the right whales and the rorquals. It is a shallow water, inshore species and in the past has suffered from persecution by inshore fishermen. It is now found only in the North Pacific where it is protected and its numbers are increasing.

Sperm Whales (*Physeter catodon*), disorientated in shallow water and washed ashore at Cape Schanck, Victoria, Australia. The Sperm Whale, the largest of the toothed whales, is a deep water species, rarely found in depths less than 100 metres. It can dive deeply to at least 450 metres, where it hunts the giant squid.

just under two metres and never weighing more than fifty kilograms. Black above, shading to white below, it has a low dorsal fin. The flippers are not large, but it is nonetheless an excellent swimmer. It has 100 teeth and pursues shoals of herring, sardines and mackerel.

The Common Porpoise is widely distributed over the North Atlantic, English Channel, North Sea and Baltic. It is often found near the coast and in estuaries, and sometimes swims up rivers for 150 kilometres or more. Both in European waters and along the Atlantic coast of the United States it is the commonest of all cetaceans. It is regarded as edible in some northern countries.

Mating takes place in the summer, gestation lasting a year. The young are born in June and July and are about half the length of the female. According to one observer the mother swims on her side when suckling so that when she comes to

streamlined with the body and the animal looks the swift and predacious creature it is. The Killer Whale attacks seals, porpoises, dolphins, all manner of fishes and birds such as penguins. The stomach of one contained the remains of thirteen porpoises and fourteen seals. In schools killer whales will not hestiate to attack other large whales, biting great chunks out of them and relishing the tongues.

This pirate is world-wide. It can be encountered off Greenland, in Bering Strait, in the Antarctic, and off the coasts of Europe, where it is sometimes stranded. Not much is known of its reproductive habits, which probably differ little from those of other Delphinidae.

The False Killer Whale (*Pseudorca crassidens*) is a related type. It appears at rare intervals, but then in considerable numbers, off coasts throughout the world. It is about five metres long on average, and entirely black. It seems to feed on cephalopods.

Another group of species are the pilot whales, also called the caa'ing whales, blackfishes and grindhvals. As indicated by the generic name *Globicephala*, the heads are globular. Beneath the protuberant forehead the muzzle forms a very small beak. The pilot whales are entirely black and have about forty teeth, long dorsal fins and flippers. They vary from six to eight metres long.

Pilot whales are inoffensive animals, feeding mostly on cuttlefishes. They live in schools of several hundred, which appear to obey a leader. When attacked they press tightly together and can easily be driven ashore by lines of small boats. They are hunted for their oil, their gregarious habits making them an easy prey. *Globicephala melaena* lives in northern and southern seas but is replaced by the Short-finned Pilot Whale G. *macrorhyncus* in tropical seas.

Risso's Dolphin (*Grampus griseus*), which must not be confused with the Grampus because of its scientific name, is another form found off the coasts of Europe. It too has a rudimentary beak under a rounded forehead and has long, pointed flippers. It measures up to four metres in length and lives in large schools, which sometimes come inshore and do much damage to fishing nets. A haul of sardines is particularly attractive to them. Some from colder regions may migrate to African waters during winter, but those in the Gulf Stream seem to be sedentary.

The Common Dolphin (*Delphinus delphis*) has a pronounced beak separated from the snout by a groove. It is easily mistaken for a fish, particularly a Tunny, which it resembles in coloration: dark blue above, white below, with wavy lines down each side, and a dark line from the eye to the corner of the long and pointed beak. Its length does not exceed 2·5 metres and it has 100 teeth.

Common Dolphins are among the swiftest of the cetaceans. They pursue shoals of herring and sardines, devouring immense quantities. Sometimes several thousand otoliths from the ears of their prey may be found in their stomachs. Dolphins are abundant in the North Sea and in the Mediterranean, frequenting all warm and temperate waters.

The dolphins and porpoises are the highly intelligent mammals of the seas, now familiar performers in marine shows.

The Killer Whale or Grampus (*Orcinus orca*) has a very bad reputation for ferocity which is probably unjustified. It has, however, a voracious appetite and will take anything that swims in the sea. Killer Whales can be playful and are easily trained as shown here in an oceanarium in Miami, U.S.A.

The ancestors of dolphins, and of the related porpoises and whales, were entirely land-living, but they have become so completely adapted to an aquatic life that, apart from being compelled to rise to the surface and open the blow-hole to take in air, they are as completely at home in water as any fish. It is of interest therefore that in their playful moments they should leap out of the water. It is comparable with the truly terrestrial animals, including the human species, that seem to enjoy immersing themselves in water for relaxation.

the surface to breath the young can breathe too. However, recent observations in the United States show that this happens only when the calf is very young, and is not invariable even then. Usually the calf surfaces independently, takes a breath and then goes down to the mother for its feed.

There are various species. One in the Indian Ocean and the Far East, the finless Black Porpoise (*Neophocaena phocaenoides*), is black all over and has no dorsal fin. In habits it is much the same as the Common Porpoise. It often ascends rivers and has been known to swim for 1,600 kilometres up the Yellow River, or Hwang Ho.

Dolphins (Family Delphinidae)

The Killer Whale or Grampus (*Orcinus orca*) is the largest of the Delphinidae, the male reaching a length of ten metres, and the female only half as long. The Killer Whale differs from the Common Porpoise in having a very high dorsal fin and broad, rounded flippers. It has close on fifty teeth, and is black all over except for a white patch over the eye and a white ventral band. The head is

There are many species of dolphin and some are freshwater species inhabiting a few of the larger rivers of the world.

The genus *Lagenorhynchus* includes the Whitesided Dolphin (*L. acutus*) and the White-beaked Dolphin (*L. albirostris*) found in all seas. The Bottle-nosed Dolphin (*Tursiops truncatus*), which grows to 3·5 metres and occasionally enters the Thames, is restricted to the North Atlantic and the Mediterranean. Known in the United States as a porpoise, it is now famous for the tricks it performs before visitors to seaquariums. The Rough-toothed Dolphin (*Steno bredanensis*), found in the Atlantic and the Indian Ocean, is somewhat longer than the Common Dolphin and has a longer beak. The long-beaked river dolphins (genus *Sotalia*) frequent estuaries in South America, Africa and Asia. The spotted dolphins form two species of the genus *Stenella*, frequenting the Atlantic coast of North America. Another American dolphin is the Right Whale Dolphin (*Lissodelphis borealis*), found off California.

Beaked and bottle-nosed whales (Family Ziphiidae)

The beaked whales have all their teeth in the lower jaw, and the snout is elongated into a beak. They vary between four and twelve metres according to species. Their teeth are vestigial except for one or two pairs but in the young of both sexes, and in females of all ages, these remain embedded in the gums, so that they appear toothless.

The two best-known members of the family are the Bottle-nosed Whales (*Hyperoodon ampullatus* of the North Atlantic and *H. planifrons* of the South) and Cuvier's Beaked Whale (*Ziphius cavirostris*), which is cosmopolitan. Specimens are occasionally found stranded on the coasts of western Europe. Their length varies from six to nine metres. The two others are Sowerby's Whale (*Mesoplodon bidens*), which is under five metres in length and found in the North Atlantic, and Baird's Whale (*Berardius bairdi*), twelve metres long and ranging from the Bering Strait to California.

White Whale and Narwhal (Family Monodontidae)

The White Whale or Beluga (*Delphinapterus leucas*) lives in Arctic waters and is more like a porpoise than a dolphin, since it has no beak. In the adult state it is completely white, has eighteen teeth in each jaw and measures from three to five metres long. It lives on fishes, crustaceans and cephalopods. The White Whale is hunted on the northern coasts of Europe, Asia and America. Its flesh, fat and leather(sold as 'porpoise hide') are of commercial value. It is rarely seen in temperate waters.

A somewhat close relative of the White Whale is the Narwhal (*Monodon monoceros*), which also inhabits Arctic waters and is very rarely seen elsewhere. It is distinguished by the black spots on its white skin and by its singular dentition. All the tooth buds are present in the foetus but they have disappeared by birth, with the exception of the two upper centrals (incisors). In the females these teeth remain undeveloped within the skull. In the males one of them, generally the one on the left, grows enormously, directed forwards into a

straight twisted tusk which may reach a length of 2·5 metres. Sometimes it is the right hand tooth which develops, and in rare cases both tusks grow equally. When that happens they are both twisted in the same direction. A few cases have been reported of females growing tusks, but this is quite abnormal. The tusks are to be classed as secondary sexual characters. No practical use has been established for them though various suggestions have been made. The Narwhal tusk contributed to the legend of the unicorn, and the animal itself has consequently been dubbed the 'Sea-unicorn Fish'.

The Narwhal reaches a length of from 3·5 to 4·5 metres, excluding the tusk. It was formerly hunted for the ivory of its tusk, which among the superstitious brought fantastically high prices, but nowadays when it is slaughtered in the ice floes it is chiefly for the excellent oil obtained from it.

River dolphins (Family Platanistidae)

Some very old forms of cetaceans have survived owing to their adaptation to a freshwater existence. They have lost all contact with the sea and must not be confused with those marine types of Delphinidae which enter estuaries or even swim far up a river for a season or the Irrawadi Dolphin (*Orcaella brevirostris*) which is classed with the true dolphins. The river dolphins vary in length from 1·5 to three metres. The shortest is the La Plata Dolphin (*Pontoporia blainvillei*). All have a long, almost bird-like beak, but furnished with teeth. The Gangetic Dolphin (*Platanista gangetica*) frequents the Brahmaputra, Indus and Ganges. It is quite blind, the eyes being mere vestiges.

The Amazonian Dolphin (*Inia geoffrensis*) lives in the upper reaches and tributaries of the Amazon; and the Chinese River dolphin (*Lipotes vexillifer*) was discovered this century in Tung Ting Lake on the Yangtze Kiang.

Flesh-eating animals (Order Carnivora)

Although some other animals are carnivorous this order is reserved for certain groups whose anatomy and other physical characters, as well as their instincts, make them stand out as flesh-eaters. There is one suborder: Fissipeda (carnivores with separate toes) which includes dogs, cats, otters, badgers and weasels, which in their perfect adaptation to hunting and devouring their prey have a marked family likeness.

Hunting demands both strength and agility. The Domestic Cat, to say nothing of its more powerful cousins, the Leopard and the Tiger, has a strong yet supple body, whose muscles can be seen to move beneath the skin.

The paws are of moderate size, and have neither the rigidity of the ungulates nor the mobility of the hands and feet of the primates. They are used for many purposes, such as walking, running, jumping, and sometimes even tree-climbing, which they do with the aid of claws, but have neither opposable thumbs nor prehensile fingers like primates.

In the Cat and its closest relations running is facilitated by the raising of the palms and soles off the ground. The Cat is thus digitigrade: it walks on tiptoe. Hence the silence and delicacy of its tread. Some carnivores are less well adapted in this respect. The Pine Marten, for instance, lifts only its heels and wrists off the ground and is thus

semi-plantigrade. The Bear is too heavy even for that and is plantigrade like the primates.

There are similar differences in claws. Cats and a few other carnivores have retractile claws, which can be withdrawn by special muscles when not in use and thus kept sharp for gripping prey. A Lion's paw can be the gentlest or the cruellest. The claws of bears, dogs or hyaenas are not retractile and generally play only a secondary role in capturing prey.

It is their dentition, however, which distinguishes carnivores from other mammals. Typically they have six upper and six lower incisors, flanked by long canines that form fangs. Behind the canines is a more or less complete set of molars. The last upper premolar and the first lower molar are much enlarged and have a cutting edge. These are the carnassials, or flesh teeth.

In the Cat the other teeth, both those in front of and those behind the carnassials, play a much smaller part and are reduced in number to thirty. Other carnivores have an increased number, particularly in the postcarnassial molars. Polecats and hyaenas have thirty-four teeth, otters thirty-six, weasels and badgers thirty-eight, the Civet Cat forty, bears and dogs forty-two, and the Bat-eared Fox (*Otocyon megalotis*) of South Africa forty-eight. As the teeth become more numerous the postcarnassials increase in size. In bears they are bigger even than the carnassials, and are the only crushing teeth this animal possesses to deal with the vegetable food which forms the greater part of its diet. Here are some typical dental formulae:

Cat   I. $\frac{3}{3}$ C. $\frac{1}{1}$ Pm. $\frac{3}{2}$ M. $\frac{1}{1}$ Total 30

Hyaena   I. $\frac{3}{3}$ C. $\frac{1}{1}$ Pm. $\frac{4}{3}$ M. $\frac{1}{1}$ Total 34

Civet   I. $\frac{3}{3}$ C. $\frac{1}{1}$ Pm. $\frac{4}{4}$ M. $\frac{2}{2}$ Total 40

Dog, Bear I. $\frac{3}{3}$ C. $\frac{1}{1}$ Pm. $\frac{4}{4}$ M. $\frac{2}{3}$ Total 42

The shape of the jaws and head varies with the dentition: cats with thirty teeth have round heads, dogs with forty-two, long heads. There are also modifications to the skull imposed by the greater development of the jaw muscles. The zygomatic arch, which extends from the cheekbone to the occiput, must also be very strong to permit the insertion of the masseter and be arched to allow for the passage of the temporal muscle. The condyles of the jaw allow only vertical movement of the mandibles. No lateral or backwards and forwards is possible. Carnivores have thus a very powerful bite, but cannot use their teeth to grind or chew their food.

The nature of the diet is correlated with the structure of the alimentary tract. The stomach is simple, the intestines short and the caecum generally absent. The carnivore's urine contains uric acid and urea, which gives off ammonia when fermenting. It also taints the flesh, usually making it inedible.

Males have external testes and a penis which may have a bone (os penis) and often turgid ridges or spines to prevent quick retraction after coitus.

Females have a bicorned uterus, a variable number of abdominal teats and a zonal placenta.

In cerebral development, sense-organs and habits there is a high degree of correlation with the mode of feeding. The brain is well developed and its convolutions indicate the mental capacity of the carnivores; they have courage, patience and cunning.

Even the smaller carnivores are ferocious beasts of prey, which live by killing a large number of other animals. They are regarded as a nuisance because they attack farmyard animals, but the predator plays an important part in the natural economy, keeping in check the numbers of herbivores and omnivores, especially mice, rats and voles. Those domesticated often show a remarkable capacity for affection, although they can be cruel and bloodthirsty.

Carnivores have the keen sense of smell, sharp sight and sensitive hearing which are necessary in tracking down and attacking quarry. The eyes are large and typically have round pupils, although they may sometimes be reduced to slits. They are mobile and capable of instantaneous adaptation to the slightest changes in light. Behind the retina, on the choroid, is a reflecting layer which makes the eyes apear luminescent and may possibly facilitate night vision. The whiskers or vibrissae probably serve as sensitive organs of touch.

Dogs (Family Canidae)

Although at one time taken as the typical example of the family Canidae, the Domestic Dog (*Canis familiaris*) does not from a strictly zoological point of view qualify for this. There seems to be no wild form in existence from which it can with certainty be claimed that the Domestic Dog has been derived. It was at one time thought that the dingoes of Australia were truly wild but it is fairly certain now that they are feral domestic dogs. As a rule such dogs burrow and live gregariously, hunting rodents and scavenging generally. They have lost the habit of barking, and this may well be a return to an earlier habit before domestication.

So great are the differences between the various breeds of dogs today that it is impossible to make a clear and simple list of what might have been the original characters of the species. The Domestic Dog seems to be closely related to the wolf and jackal, from which it is almost indistinguishable. Crosses have been obtained with both these animals. In the first case most crosses are the issue of male wolf and female dog, the reverse being much rarer. Both with wolf and with jackal the hybrids are fertile. With the fox it is quite otherwise, and it is very difficult to get the two animals to mate.

A dog is thus less closely related to a fox, as is also shown morphologically. In a fox the forehead and nose are in a straight line, the pupil of the eye is oval or slit-shaped, and the tail is bushy. In a dog, wolf and jackal, the forehead is appreciably distinct from the head, the pupil is circular and the tail much less bushy.

A dog has elongated jaws with forty-two or forty-four teeth. There are flattened molars in front of the carnassials, indicating a diet which is less than purely carnivorous. Domestic dogs eat plenty of biscuit and vegetable food and feral dogs have a mixed diet of all sorts of refuse.

A dog is digitigrade and has five toes on the front foot and four on the hind one. It often has a dew-claw above the hind paws which is the rudiment of a fifth toe. These are commonly removed. Claws are not retractile, and are consequently blunt. On this account the tread is noisy compared to that of a cat.

Dogs are nubile towards the end of their first year, and from then on bitches come on heat twice yearly, normally in August and December to January, the period lasting about a fortnight. The long duration of coupling results from the presence of erectic folds on the penis which when turgid prevent retraction. Forced retraction will probably cause a lesion or even the fracture of the os penis.

Gestation lasts about two months, with a few days' difference for the various breeds. The size of the litter is from two to sixteen. Pups are blind and only just strong enough to crawl to their mother's teats, which number eight to ten. A bitch's milk is rich in cream and proteins and more nourishing than a cow's. The growth of a litter is rapid. Pups open their eyes at ten days and walk easily at twenty, when they already have incisors and upper canines. At a month, all the milk teeth have been cut. Weaning is done at six weeks. Permanent teeth appear at five months.

Dog breeds

Breeds are classified according to employment of the dog. They are: hounds, gun dogs, spaniels, terriers, non-sporting dogs, sheepdogs, watchdogs, draught animals and toy dogs.

HOUNDS: Formerly enormous dogs were used, capable of attacking boars and wild bears. Their descendants are mastiffs and Great Danes, which are used as watchdogs and sometimes for draught, their place in the field being taken by animals of smaller size.

The greyhound is one of the oldest breeds. Formerly bred for coursing hares, it is now far

The Dingo is restricted to Australia where it is the only remaining wild carnivore. Dingoes are believed to be descendants of domestic dogs brought to Australia in prehistoric times which have reverted to the wild state. They prey on sheep and are usually shot on sight.

The Foxhound breed has been evolved over the centuries to produce a hound almost perfect for hunting the Fox in Britain. It now has a worldwide reputation. A Foxhound has to have the stamina and condition to endure long tiring days hunting in the pack, sometimes covering up to 110 kilometres in a day in pursuit of a fox.

The use of dogs for sledge-pulling is very important in the Arctic. Most of these dogs are known as 'Huskies' but there are many different types. Here Huskies are shown pulling a komatic, linked by a fan hitch typically used by Eskimos of western Baffin Island in northwest Canada.

more popular on the race-track. As it is built for speed, all unnecessary weight has been eliminated. The lungs are very large, and it is the only dog to have the left ventricle larger than the right.

The bloodhound is another very ancient breed, considered by some to be the oldest hound in existence. It used to be employed in tracking deer through forests, speed not being necessary. It was also used to track down the offender when deer were killed and stolen. The hound is a very gentle dog and makes an excellent pet.

Three centuries of foxhound breeding have produced a hound that is the best adapted for its purpose. The foxhound has great powers of scent and was formerly used in the southern United States for tracking escaped convicts. The beagle is a smaller variety that can be followed on foot.

The main hound breeds are: the basset, a short-legged hound, believed to be of French extraction; the whippet, produced by crossing a terrier with

an Italian greyhound and then breeding back to the English greyhound; the dachshund, imported from Germany, though it may have originated in France or Ethiopia; and the borzoi or Russian wolfhound, brought to England in the last decade of the nineteenth century.

GUN DOGS: The characteristic of these dogs is that they do not rush at their game. The pointer, for instance, stands absolutely still on scenting game and does not move until the game is flushed. It is probably of Spanish origin and is somewhat like the foxhound but slimmer.

The setter is probably of both pointer and spaniel ancestry. The chief varieties are English, Gordon and Irish.

SPANIELS: There are many varieties of spaniel. The cocker spaniel is the smallest of them and one of the most popular of all dogs. Next in popularity is the springer spaniel. The Irish water spaniel is a very useful gun dog in marshy country.

There are four varieties of retrievers: curly retriever, flat-coated retriever, golden retriever, and Labrador, the latter being the origin of the other three (with the possible exception of the golden) by crossbreeding with spaniels or setters. Originally bred solely for retrieving game, it was subsequently found that they could learn to do the work of other gun dogs as well. This is particularly true of the Labrador.

TERRIERS: These dogs were originally intended for hunting burrowing animals and pursuing them into their earths or dens. They have been used for hunting fox, badger and rabbit, but on the whole terriers are regarded much more as household pets than as working dogs. The fox terrier is typical of this group. Its origin is obscure, but the foxhound is probably one of its ancestors. Originally bred for fox-hunting it is now an excellent ratter.

The Airedale is the largest of the terriers, probably descended from the English working terrier. It is very much at home in and about water, perhaps because of the admixture of otterhound blood.

The bull terrier was originally a cross between a bulldog and a terrier and was a heavier, stronger animal than its modern descendant, which has an admixture of other breeds.

The cairn terrier is the ancestor of most Scottish terriers, the best known being the Scottish terrier (formerly the Aberdeen) and the Skye terrier with its long flowing coat.

The Australian terrier was bred in that country towards the end of last century, probably by crossing other terrier breeds. It has been known in England for some time.

The Boston terrier is the only breed to have originated in the United States. It was produced in the last century, reputedly from bulldog and bull terrier with some admixture of French bulldog. It was recognised as a breed in 1893 and now enjoys great popularity in the United States.

NON-SPORTING DOGS: Many dogs have been developed for various duties: to act as sheepdogs, watchdogs, police dogs or for life-saving; others are used as draught animals.

The Alsatian became known in England after the first world war. It is very intelligent and responds well to training, making an excellent police dog. It has a certain amount of wolf blood

and can be dangerous if not well disciplined.

The collie is equally good as sheepdog or watchdog, but the Old English sheepdog is claimed by some to be the best of all sheepdogs, though it is less agile than the collie.

The bulldog is now kept as a house dog and is noted for its gentleness and reliability, but if it is set on to an intruder it bites and does not let go. The poodle is reputed to be the most intelligent of all dogs. It can be trained as an excellent gun dog, which it originally was, being used for duck-shooting.

The mastiff is a very ancient breed. It was used as a cattle dog and then a draught animal and it is still used as such in the north of France and Belgium. Usually it is kept as a watchdog. The Great Dane is one of the fleetest and most powerful of dogs. It too is sometimes put in harness on the Continent.

The Dalmatian or plum pudding dog seems more at home in stables than in the house. It used to be a familiar sight running under carriages behind the horses' heels.

The Welsh corgi is used for herding cattle and sheep, but is actually a 'heeler', running behind cattle and snapping at stragglers. Its short legs are of advantage, as it stands too low for the cattle to reach with their horns.

The two famous life-saving breeds are the Newfoundland and the St Bernard, the first saving men from drowning in the sea, the second rescuing those lost in mountains and snow. The St Bernard, too big to become a common pet, stands apart with immense prestige, owing to the great work done for the hospice of St Bernard in Switzerland, where the great Barry, who died in 1815, was credited with having saved fifty lives. The breed may have originated in the mountains of central Asia, but it was brought to Europe at a very early date. The most majestic of all dogs, it weighs up to 100 kilograms. When the Norwegians discovered Newfoundland in the eighteenth century, there were no dogs on the island, and the Newfoundland breed no doubt descends from dogs from Scandinavia and Labrador. Physically it has much in common with the St Bernard.

The use of dogs in harness is of great importance in the extreme north. Excellent sledge dogs have been bred in the Arctic, the best-known breeds being the Alaskan Malemute, the Eskimo and the Samoyed.

The chow or chowchow comes from China, where it was bred for its fur and meat. The name is pidgin English for 'food'.

TOY BREEDS: Some of these breeds are ancient. The pug, for instance, is supposed to have come from China, but has been bred in Europe for hundreds of years.

The Pomeranian is another very old breed, dogs of similar type being depicted at least as long ago as the second century B.C. When it was first brought to England, it was as large as an ordinary terrier, but selective breeding has produced a smaller dog. Towards the end of the last century weights of seven kilograms or more were common, while many are now just over a kilogram.

The King Charles spaniel has a more obscure origin, little being known of it until it was made fashionable by Charles II.

The Pekinese was unknown outside China for some 2,000 years. Some specimens brought to England in 1860 founded the European stock.

The Brussels griffon is a lively dog, more terrier in type and less of a 'toy' than other breeds. It is an excellent ratter.

Wild dogs, wolves, jackals (Family Canidae)

Unlike the Dingo of Australia there are some wild dogs that have never undergone domestication.

The Indian Wild Dog or Dhole (*Cuon alpinus*) looks like a shaggy Alsatian but differs from domestic dogs in having forty teeth and more

The Great Dane, standing seventy-five centimetres at the shoulder, was first used in Germany for hunting boars. It is not trained for sport in Great Britain but is occasionally used as a guard dog. In spite of its size it is a remarkably fast runner.

A pack of Cape Hunting Dogs (*Lycaon pictus*), of the African savannahs, feeding off their kill. They hunt as a team, usually consisting of twelve to twenty dogs, but sometimes much larger. They run down their prey such as wildebeest, zebra or gazelle and then tear the carcase to pieces.

The Maned Wolf (*Chrysocyon brachyurus*), of Paraguay, Argentina and Brazil, resembles a giant fox and has extraordinarily long legs for the size of its body. Although it has a shaggy, reddish coat and fox-like head, it behaves more like a specialised wild dog. Large enough to kill sheep, it hunts alone, not in packs.

The Wolf (*Canis lupus*), one of the supposed ancestors of the domestic dog, ranges throughout the tundra and temperate and coniferous forests of the northern hemisphere. A powerful and intelligent animal, it has always been greatly feared and ruthlessly slaughtered to protect domestic stock.

numerous teats. It is reddish above and whitish below, and measures about a metre long without the tail. Dholes hunt in small packs and, like wolves, are undaunted by the largest game. They neither howl nor bark, but utter little yaps.

Cape hunting dogs (*Lycaon pictus*) are African wild dogs. The head is like that of a hyaena and the body is marked with irregular patches of colour, no two individuals being coloured alike. They also hunt in packs and attack the largest antelopes. Formerly they did much damage to domestic herds, but they are now greatly reduced in number. They live in the savannas from the Transvaal to as far north as Lake Chad and Somalia.

The Bush Dog (*Speothos venaticus*) is a nocturnal South American species, living in the forests of

Brazil and Guyana. It is about sixty centimetres long and has short legs and tail.

The Maned Wolf (*Chrysocyon brachyurus*) is the largest of the South American wild dogs. It is 130 centimetres long with a forty centimetre tail, and has a mane on the nape of the neck and down the back. It is found on the pampas of southern Brazil, Paraguay and the Argentine.

The Cordillera Fox (*Cerdocyon magellanicus*) is nearly a metre long without the tail and ranges from the extreme southern areas of South America as far north as Ecuador. The Crab-eating Fox (*C. thous*) is a jackal-like wild dog living in open country between Venezuela, Guyana and the south of Brazil. It has sometimes been domesticated by the Indians, but more often crossed with dogs to improve the latter as hunters. Azara's Fox (*Dusicyon azarae*) is another wild dog, whose pelt is known to the fur trade as Patagonian fox, Rio fox, or Provincia fox.

WOLVES: The Common European Wolf (*Canis lupus*) looks like a lean-flanked Alsatian with a more powerfully built skeleton, a longer nose, stronger jaws, eyes more oblique, ears always pricked, and a bushy tail always hanging down between the legs. Its coat varies in thickness according to the climatic conditions in which it lives, and is generally a brownish grey, with a touch of black. A black line runs along the back and down the front legs; the belly is greyish white. An adult male stands a little over seventy-five centimetres high at the shoulders and weighs between forty-five and sixty kilograms. It differs from the dog in howling instead of barking.

Wolves have one litter a year. Mating takes place at the end of January and beginning of February. Gestation lasts about two months. When the time for her litter approaches, the she-wolf chooses a thicket near a stream or pool and there lines her den with dead leaves, moss and hairs from her belly. In April or May from three to nine cubs are born; they are blind and are suckled by the mother for six weeks. She takes the utmost care of them, carrying them about in her mouth when necessary. Before they are weaned the cubs eat a certain amount of half-digested food disgorged by the mother. The father remains with his family until the cubs are well grown up, and if anything happens to the mother he looks after them and provides them with food. The cubs reach adult state at the end of a year, but are not fully grown until the age of two.

Wolves once ranged over the whole of Europe. The last English wolf was killed during the reign of Henry VII. In Scotland they remained much longer, the last being killed in 1743, and the last in Ireland a little later. In France wolves have now been virtually exterminated, but only in recent times, and they still exist in Italy, Spain, Hungary, the Balkans and the Carpathians. From Scandinavia they are spread in considerable numbers all the way to China and formerly to Japan. The American Wolf is now generally regarded as a variety of *Canis lupus*.

Wolves inhabit both hill and plain. They may appear suddenly where they have not been seen for many years, their speed of movement being considerable—fifty to sixty kilometres in one night. In populated areas they hunt at night, elsewhere by day. They feed on other animals. They will follow migrating herds of caribou, and they are ready to eat carrion. In packs they attack animals much more powerful than themselves.

They are extremely cunning, and observation has proved that they are capable of true team work: one of a pair may create a diversion while the other snatches a kid. Whole packs have been said to divide, one half in direct pursuit of the quarry, the other seeking to cut off its line of retreat. Wolves generally avoid humans, but will attack them when pressed by hunger.

Two subspecies of the Common Wolf are known as the Indian Wolf. They are the Woolly Wolf (*Canis lupus chanco*) found in the Himalayas and central Asia, and the small Indian Wolf (*C. l. pallipes*) of the plains. They are the same size, both smaller than the Common Wolf. These wolves are never in large packs, and they seldom howl. Their usual cry is something like a feeble bark.

The North American Timber Wolf or Grey Wolf was originally widespread over the whole country, and is still reasonably common in the subarctic regions of Canada and Alaska. When the game animals on which it lived, particularly deer and bison, were replaced by man's flocks and herds constant war was waged on it by gun, trap and poison. Animal ecologists now tend to the view that the wolf should be allowed to survive in remaining wilderness areas as a natural means of eliminating the diseased and weakly among the caribou herds. In the far north many wolves are adaptively coloured white or cream and a litter may contain mixed colour types. Packs such as have been described from Russia and eastern Eruope have rarely been reported in the New World, where wolves usually hunt in family parties. They have distinct hunting ranges, sometimes extending for a hundred kilometres or more.

JACKALS: The Oriental Jackal (*Canis aureus*), which is the most widespread, has sometimes been called the Common Jackal and may be taken as typical. A slender, long-legged animal, it is surprisingly sturdy, with a rather short, bushy tail, a pointed muzzle and relatively small carnassials. It is black-brown above, merging into whitish below. From North Africa and south-east Europe it has spread through southern Asia as far as Burma and Thailand. It prefers high ground and may be found up to 1,500 metres. Its howling and yapping is most disagreeable. It will enter villages in search of anything edible.

Both in habit and anatomy jackals stand between wolves and foxes, often hunting in packs like the first and being nocturnal like the second. They are a menace to poultry yards and sheep. Sometimes they will follow on the heels of larger carnivores to feast on their leavings. They are useful scavengers and, with the hyaenas and the vultures, do much for sanitation.

The Black-backed Jackal (*C. mesomelas*), a reddish-flanked and fox-like species, is much hunted for its fur. It is found from Ethiopia and the Sudan to the Cape. In habits it is much the same as *C. aureus* and, like the latter, is easily tamed.

Resembling the Oriental Jackal, but with a rather more pointed fox-like face, is the Side-striped Jackal (*C. adustus*), which is found from Ethiopia and Morocco to the Transvaal.

The Coyote, Bush Wolf or Prairie Wolf (*Canis latrans*) still haunts the western plains of North America. Smaller than the Timber Wolf and more adaptable to changing conditions, it is able to survive in spite of settlement of much of its former wilderness range. Its keen senses and fast speed enable it to live almost anywhere; it feeds on mice, hares, rabbits, deer, occasionally sheep and even fruit. In some areas it has crossed with domestic dogs and the resulting progeny are not always easy to distinguish from the original wild animal.

Foxes and fennecs

Foxes are not sufficiently different from dogs, wolves and jackals to form a separate subfamily. They are recognisable by their relatively long bodies and short legs. They have pointed snouts,

The Grey or Timber Wolf (*Canis lupus*), of North America, belongs to the same species as the European Wolf. It exists in numerous local races, differing in size and in colour from black to white. In the picture Timber Wolves are trying to take a Mule Deer carcase away from a Grizzly Bear:

The Black-backed Jackal (*Canis mesomelas*), of the plains of central and South Africa, has a distinctive black saddle along its back and a black stripe along the length of its tail. Jackals hunt mainly at night, feeding on carrion and small animals. They are generally solitary but occasionally band together in a small pack.

The Coyote or Prairie Wolf (*Canis latrans*) is a North American wild dog closely related to the wolf, but smaller. Mainly due to its cunning and opportunism the Coyote has expanded its range from its original home on the Western Plains of the United States to as far east as New England.

The American Red Fox has long been considered to be a separate species *Vulpes fulva* but usually today it is regarded as being the same species as the Old World Red Fox (*V. vulpes*). It is found throughout North America except the extreme north of Alaska. There are many colour phases and mutations, including the well-known Silver Fox.

big erect ears and oval pupils. The long bushy tails (brushes) are carried horizontally or raised when running. Coats vary considerably.

The Old World Red Fox (*Vulpes vulpes*) is red-brown above and white below, the backs of the ears and the feet being dark. The coat does not change greatly with environment and the winter coat provides a valuable fur. The height to the shoulder is forty centimetres and the weight of large specimens varies from seven to ten kilograms. They have forty-two teeth. Anal glands are well developed, accounting for the well-known scent, and there is also a gland near the root of the tail, which may be responsible for the characteristic 'foxy' smell.

Foxes generally live in burrows, or earths, either digging them themselves, or utilising those made by badgers or other hole-digging animals, which are driven off or, occasionally, allowed to share the accommodation. When no underground quarters are available, foxes may live in 'kennels' above ground, that is, in hollows under stones or trees. Often foxes have a principal earth or den, with several chambers and several exits and various alternative refuges to which they can resort.

During the day the fox generally lies low, venturing forth to hunt at night and even then with extreme caution. It is ready to prey on birds and rabbits, as well as on moles, field mice and voles, which are its more normal food. Attacks on poultry tend to be localised. Near a lake it will stalk aquatic birds; in a river it will catch fishes and crayfishes, and recent research has shown that a fox eats a surprising amount of grass and wild fruits.

Its methods of hunting are varied. Sometimes it will chase its quarry, or it may stalk its victim, or lie in wait for it. Its sight, smell and hearing are extremely keen. Its voice is varied—howling, barking, growling, yelping, and a sort of raucous scream made at mating time by both sexes. The bark is a thin sound; it may be heard when two foxes are hunting together, or from the cubs.

The mating season is in the middle of winter, when the males emit a strong odour from their anal glands. Some fighting takes place between the males, but it is not serious. In the spring it is not rare to find several foxes in a vixen's earth. Opinions on the sexual relations of foxes are diametrically opposed. According to some the fox is monogamous, according to others polygamous, and both are authenticated.

Coupling takes place in the same way as with dogs. Gestation lasts about fifty-six days. A few days before the end the vixen prepares a place on which to litter by spreading a layer of dead leaves and hair. The litter consists of three to eight cubs, which are blind but well-coated. Their eyes open at the end of a week. Before the end of lactation, which lasts two months, the mother supplements the cubs' diet with half-digested flesh which she regurgitates for them. Lactation over, she continues to feed them, first on dead game, then live game, and finally she takes them hunting to teach them the way. The vixen is an exemplary mother, running any risk and facing any danger in defence of her offspring. The cubs remain with her until October, becoming adults the following year.

The Old World Red Fox is spread over the greater part of Europe and much of northern Asia. Taking its place across the Atlantic is the North American Red Fox (*V. fulva*), which is similar but larger and with longer hair. One variety is the Silver Fox, a black fox with silver-tipped hairs. The Cross Fox is a variety of the two red foxes, with a black cross on the shoulders.

The Grey Fox (*Urocyon cinereoargenteus*), which is not unlike the Red Fox but flecked with grey, is found in several varieties from the Great Lakes, on the border dividing the United States and Canada to northern South America. Usually a forest animal, it is sometimes found sheltering among the cacti on desert plains and semi-desert areas. In woodland areas it resorts frequently to climbing trees, an exercise at which it is adept.

The Arctic Fox (*Alopex lagopus*) is smaller with a white winter coat, and a brown or slate-coloured summer coat. In one phase, however, the coat is a smoky grey all the year round. This is known as blue fox in the fur trade. Closely related is the Corsac (*Vulpes corsac*), of the steppes round the Caspian, and as far east as Mongolia.

The African Silver Fox (*V. chama*), which lives in open sandy plains, is another small fox less than sixty centimetres long, excluding the tail. The Pale Sand Fox (*V. pallida*) is found in the Sudan.

The Fennec (*Fennecus zerda*) is a small fox about forty centimetres long without the tail, character-ised by its enormous ears. It lives in North Africa and Arabia and feeds on jerboas, rodents, birds, lizards, locusts and fruit. Very sociable animals, Fennecs are easily domesticated and become affec-tionate pets. They are hardly suitable for more northerly climates, however, as they are very sensitive to cold.

Most foxes provide good fur. The most valuable comes from northern latitudes, with silver fox the most valuable of all. With demand increasing and wild life rapidly being exterminated, fox farms were started towards the end of last century in Canada, and were followed by others in the most northerly parts of the United States, Norway, Sweden and elsewhere. Foxes thrive in captivity, and breed as freely as in the wild state.

Bears (Family Ursidae)

Bears are the largest animals in the order Carniv-ora and, curiously, the least carnivorous. They have heavy bodies and short, strong legs, and are able to stand upright and grasp things with the front paws. They have a short thick neck, a rounded head, pointed muzzle, short ears, small eyes, and an extremely short tail. They are com-pletely plantigrade. The soles of the feet are always naked except in the Polar Bear, in which hairy soles assist walking over icy surfaces. The paws each have five toes and non-retractile claws. Sight is poor but the senses of smell and hearing are acute. The cheek-teeth are weak and have flattened crowns.

The dental formula is the same as in dogs, with a total of forty-two teeth, but the postcarnassial teeth have developed into large-crowned, flat,

crushing teeth, completely different from the cut-ting carnassials and precarnassials of other carni-vores. Only in one species, the Polar Bear, does animal flesh form any considerable part of the diet and even this species will occasionally eat large quantities of vegetable matter if flesh is scarce.

The Polar Bear (*Thalarctos maritimus*) is essen-tially an aquatic animal, rarely found south of 70°N. It is becoming rare on the southern coasts of Spitsbergen and Novaya Zemlya, where the ice disappears completely during the summer. It is therefore the most completely polar of all animals and the most completely adapted to withstand the cold. It is quite at home on floating ice, which may carry it far from its original locality. It can swim strongly, sometimes covering many kilometres, and hunts between the ice floes for seals, walruses, whale calves and fishes, which form the bulk of its food. It also takes carrion, and even vegetable food when there is nothing better to be had. Agile on land, it is able to capture the Blue or Arctic Fox, lemmings and even birds. It rarely attacks human beings unless itself attacked, when it becomes a re-doubtable foe, up to three metres long and weigh-ing up to 640 kilograms. It is much less prone than other bears to stand erect on its hind feet.

The Polar Bear does not hibernate; it goes into what is now called winter dormancy. Certainly the Eskimos hunt it all the year round. At the end of the year the female gives birth in a snow den to one or two cubs no bigger than rabbits and very weak, like all bear cubs. By the end of the summer they can fend for themselves. Many stories have been told by whalers and explorers of the she-bear's love for her offspring; and when she is looking after them she is greatly to be feared.

The Bat-eared Fox (*Otocyon megalotis*) lives on the dry plains and savannahs of Africa. It is an unusual canid with very large ears and with forty-six to forty-eight teeth instead of the normal forty-two of most dogs and foxes. Bat-eared foxes are usually seen in pairs or small groups. They feed on small mammals, birds, lizards and insects such as termites.

The Polar Bear (*Thalarctos maritimus*) is a powerful animal, three metres long. More slender in build than most bears and with a longer head and neck, it is also the most carnivorous, feeding on seals and young walruses. Its feet have hairy pads that assist movement over the icy wastes of its Arctic habitat. It has good vision and a keen sense of smell.

Opposite top
The Grizzly Bear which used to be classed in a separate species (*Ursus horribilis*) is now considered only a subspecies of the Brown Bear (*U. arctos*). It has the reputation for being, at least at times, particularly ferocious but it is now extinct over most of its former range.

Opposite bottom
The North American Black Bear used to be included in *Ursus* but is now classed as *Euarctos americanus*. It is smaller than the Brown Bear, and is particularly agile with even full-grown adults still able to climb trees.

The Brown Bear (*Ursus arctos*) is still the most common of the bears, despite its elimination from the greater part of Europe. It may still be found in the wilder parts of the Pyrenees and Alps, Scandinavia, Lapland, Transylvania and Russia, while other races of the same species are spread eastwards, such as the Syrian Bear, the Isabelline or Kashmir Brown Bear, the Blue or Snow Bear, and the Japanese Bear. These races vary in colour from almost black to red, brown and yellowish, while the Syrian Bear is grey with a white collar. Formerly regarded as different species, now they are all accepted as varieties of *U. arctos*.

The height to the shoulder when they are on all fours varies from eighty to 120 centimetres, the total height erect from 150 to 245 centimetres, and the weight from 200 to 400 kilograms. Females are somewhat smaller and more slender in build. The present-day Brown Bear is smaller than the long-extinct Cave Bear (*U. spelaeus*), which was a contemporary of early man.

The Brown Bear keeps to the most inaccessible parts of the great forests, where it is solitary except in the mating season, dividing its time between sleeping, hunting, eating and bathing. It can climb trees, grasping the trunk with its limbs, and it can walk out easily on horizontal branches. On the ground it ambles like an elephant, moving the two right limbs together, then the two left. Like most large plantigrade animals it cannot jump, but is so strong that it can take a cow or deer in its mouth and carry it uphill.

The Brown Bear eats roots, grasses, leaves, buds, mushrooms and fruit. It occasionally does much harm to crops by eating budding wheat, oats and maize. It digs out anthills to eat, and will walk into a river to scoop out fishes with a flipping action of the paw, but it is particularly fond of honey. It will slash open a wild hive and, regardless of the bees, pounce on the honeycomb. The

only notice it takes of the bee stings is to roll itself on the ground or rub itself against the trees to get rid of the insects.

Brown and Black Bears will eat other animals when the occasion occurs, and on rare occasions a rogue individual has attacked domestic stock, leaping at them from behind after frightening them with its roaring or tiring them with a long pursuit. But they will not attack man unless first attacked by him. Surrounded by hunters and hounds a bear becomes a fearsome adversary.

In October or November, having acquired a layer of fat beneath the skin in the course of the summer, a bear looks round for a lair in which to hibernate. If it has spent the summer at high altitudes it will come down to lower ground and trudge for many kilometres in search of a suitable place, such as a cave, hollow or thicket; possibly the one it occupied the previous year. It will normally be in its lair before the first fall of snow. It sleeps either coiled up or sitting, but its sleep is not as profound as that of the Marmot or Dormouse and is interrupted by periods of wakefulness. The only thing it has in common with the complete hibernants is that the Brown Bear neither eats nor drinks until March or April, when it comes out of its lair thin and scraggy.

It was formerly a common belief among some bear hunters that before 'hibernation' the Brown Bear cleaned out its intestine by thorough purging and then blocked up the rectum with a wad of grass, which could not be expelled until the spring. However, it is now realised that this 'faecal plug' is simply the accumulated residue of vegetable matter, and not a deliberate provision.

In the spring male and female come together for a while for breeding, after which both resume their solitary existence. A male bear never stays with its mate long enough to see the birth of the cubs or to take any part in raising them. Gestation lasts for

180-250 days; and in December or January one or two cubs are born, blind, helpless, twenty centimetres long and weighing 0·6 kilograms. This takes place during hibernation. The mother neither eats nor drinks, yet for the remaining three months of winter she suckles and cares for them. Of her six teats only the two pectoral teats give milk, the others being mere vestiges, relics of ancestors with larger litters. Soon the short hair of the cubs grows into a proper coat, which has a white 'V' over the chest and shoulders. This usually disappears later, though a trace of it may be left in the adult state.

At the end of hibernation the mother emerges with her cub or cubs. Where there are two they are always of opposite sex. Another bear, two years old, is usually with them, a cub from the previous year that has not yet left its mother and has hibernated with her. It helps to bring up the new cubs. At the end of the summer it goes off on its own but does not reach sexual maturity until the age of four.

Taken young enough, Brown Bears can be domesticated and trained to perform. They are intelligent and, in spite of their normally solitary lives, can become very attached to their owners. Their tempers are uncertain, however, and they tend to become irascible in old age.

AMERICAN BEARS: North America has several species of bear so similar to the Brown Bear that some zoologists have regarded them all as races of one species. Certainly they are linked by a relationship which goes back no further than the time when land animals could pass from one continent to another over what is now the Bering Sea. Here all brown bears are treated as one species.

One of the largest is the Grizzly Bear, the 'Old Ephraim' which plays so big a part in the stories of Fenimore Cooper, Mayne Reid and others, who depicted it as a terrifying animal, following the herds of bison, stealing horses from camps, and even attacking man without provocation. The name refers, however, not to the bear's temper but to its grizzled coat, but in spite of its name it is really more brown than grey. Today the Grizzly seems to have been almost exterminated in the United States, except in Alaska and in national parks such as the Yellowstone, but is still found in British Columbia and the Yukon. It is larger than the European Brown Bear.

In the far north, in Alaska and the islands off the coast there are the Big Brown Bears which are the biggest and strongest of all American bears. The Kodiak Bear, a subspecies found on the islands of Kodiak, and another subspecies, the Kenai Bear from the Kenai peninsula, may be three metres or more long and weigh up to 740 kilograms. The Big Brown Bear is restricted in its range to southern Alaska and northwestern British Columbia.

The American Black Bear (*Euarctos americanus*) is much smaller, about 150 centimetres in length, ninety to 225 kilograms in weight, and has commonly a glossy black coat but in some geographical areas it is brown rather than black. Living in forests it is a more agile climber than the Big Brown Bear. It hibernates in northern latitudes and breeds only every other year. It may do considerable damage to some crops, and is becoming a menacing pest about garbage dumps in some

The Crab-eating Raccoon (*Procyon cancrivorus*), of South America, is larger and shorter haired than the North American species, and not so common. Raccoons are omnivorous, but they prefer aquatic life such as frogs and fish and as its name implies the Crab-eating Raccoon is said to eat crabs.

The Coati or Coatimundi (*Nasua narica*), of Mexico and northern South America, has a long mobile snout and a striped, bushy tail like the raccoon to which it is related. The Coati travels in groups searching for food. It is omnivorous feeding on rodents, insects, fruits and seeds.

parts of America. It is much hunted and becoming rarer in some areas, but it is well represented in the national parks.

Kermode's Bear (*E. a. kermodei*), a subspecies of the Black Bear, is small and pure white except for some buff on the head and in the middle of the back. It is found on only Gribble Island and its immediate neighbourhood in British Columbia.

The Spectacled Bear (*Tremarctos ornatus*) of South America ranges from Venezuela to Chile. A black bear, it owes its name to the tawny rings round its eyes.

There are three further species of Asiatic bears: the Himalayan Black Bear, the Malayan Bear and the Sloth Bear.

The Himalayan Black Bear (*Selenarctos thibetanus*) is found from Persia to the Himalayas, and in Burma, Indo-China, Manchuria, Korea and Japan. It has a pointed snout and a black coat with a V-shaped mark of pure white on the chest.

The chin is white too. The height hardly exceeds two metres and its weight 120 kilograms. In summer it may be found at heights up to 3,600 metres. It is a forest-dweller and a partial hibernant.

The Malayan Bear or Sun Bear (*Helarctos malayanus*) is not very different in appearance, except for a yellowish chest patch. An extremely active bear, just over 120 centimetres in height, it is so agile in climbing trees that it has been compared to an ape. It is not in the least dangerous to man, and is found in Burma, Thailand, Indo-China and parts of Indonesia.

The Sloth Bear (*Melursus ursinus*) is an aberrant type with a narrow snout and long, mobile lips. Its teeth are reduced to forty by the loss of two upper incisors. It has a rough, coarse coat, naked face and long tongue which enables it to feed on ants and termites. The mobile lips form a tube through which it sucks up insect food with a loud snuffling sound. It is an ugly brute, yet comic in its movements and Hindu jugglers teach it tricks and take it round villages. It reaches a height of nearly two metres and over 135 kilograms in weight and frequents forested hills in India and Sri Lanka. When they are small the cubs are often carried on their mother's backs.

Raccoons (Family Procyonidae)

The Raccoon (*Procyon lotor*) is about the size of a badger. It has a grey-brown coat, a tail ringed with black, and a dark band across the face and eyes, giving it the appearance of being masked. It is intelligent and, besides being terrestrial, it is both aquatic and arboreal, being almost as much at home in the trees as a squirrel. Though standing in a plantigrade manner it actually walks with its heels off the ground. It has the curious habit of apparently washing its food before eating, but this has only been seen in captivity. Recent research has shown, however, that on entering water it 'paddles' with its fore paws whether these hold food or not. When they do hold food the action looks like washing. Moreover, if away from water or if the water is more than a few centimetres deep, this action is inhibited and there is no sign of this so-called washing. In the wild state the Raccoon preys upon anything in farms, turning as readily to the orchard as to the chicken run, but although much hunted it is still plentiful in many areas. Throughout its range it feeds extensively on crayfishes. Raccoons are among the most completely nocturnal animals. They hibernate only in the most northerly part of their range, which covers North America up into Canada. The fur (and the animal colloquially), known as Coon, was once widely used by American frontiersmen and sporadically returns to favour.

The Crab-eating Raccoon (*P. cancrivorus*) is found in South America, chiefly on the east coast. It is said to eat crabs.

Coatis or coatimundis are South and Central American procyonids with very long snouts. The Ring-tailed Coati (*Nasua rufa*) is red-brown and is confined to South America, while the Coatimundi (*N. narica*) is somewhat more northerly, ranging from Mexico to Peru. They walk with their long tails upright, and climb easily to hunt for birds and lizards. They grub for insects and larvae with their noses and are easily bred in captivity but generally remain unfriendly and refractory.

The Kinkajou (*Potos caudivolvulus*) is another procyonid ranging from Mexico over Central and South America. The long tail, which is longer than the body, is prehensile, making the animal look something like the Spider Monkey which is often its neighbour in the trees. It is interesting to see this case of convergence of animals that are nevertheless so widely separated in zoological classification.

The Cacomistle ('cunning-cat squirrel') or Ring-tailed Cat (*Bassariscus astutus*) somewhat resembles a marten, with a beautifully banded black and white tail. Rather over thirty centimetres long with a tail as long again, it lives in Central America and the southern United States. It is nocturnal and arboreal. The fur is known as ring-tail cat.

Pandas (Subfamily Ailurinae)

Sometimes classed in a separate family of its own, but here treated as representing a subfamily, the Lesser Panda (*Ailurus fulgens*) is a completely plantigrade animal up to sixty centimetres in length without its long bushy tail. It looks rather like a large cat, and has thirty-eight teeth. Spread from Nepal to Yunnan, in Asia, it lives an arboreal life, often at high altitudes, feeding on fruit, buds and leaves, though it will also eat eggs, insects and their larvae. The specific name *fulgens* is due to the glossy red fur on its back, the lower parts being black. The face is white, with a dark stripe from each eye to the corner of the mouth, and the tail is ringed.

The Giant Panda (*Ailuropoda melanoleuca*) is also included in this subfamily. It was discovered in Szechwan, western China, towards the end of the last century by the French missionary Père David on the farthest reaches of the eastern Himalayas. Although it has a marked resemblance to a bear, with its large heavy body and very short tail, it is rather smaller than the Brown Bear. Its fine coat is divided into large patches of black and white and its diet is vegetarian, consisting largely of bamboo shoots, but it is now known to eat small mammals, birds and fishes in the wild. Very little is known of its habits in the wild state, but in captivity it is a friendly and playful animal.

Opinion is swinging towards regarding the Giant Panda as a bear but it seems no firm conclusion has been reached.

Weasels, otters, badgers, skunks (Family Mustelidae)

This is a large family composed mostly of small, long-bodied, short-legged animals, with thick, silky fur, and possessing anal glands giving off a fetid odour. However, their feet and dentition show considerable variety. Some are digitigrade, others plantigrade. The number of toes may be four or five, and claws may or may not be retractile. The number of teeth varies from twenty-eight to thirty-eight. Most of the Mustelidae are completely carnivorous. They destroy vermin, especially rodents, but some occasionally take poultry. They are fur-bearers, some providing the most beautiful of all furs, such as the Ermine, Pekan or Fisher, Sable, Skunk or Mink.

The Pine Marten (*Martes martes*) has a supple, graceful body covered by dark brown fur turning paler below, with a creamy-white to orange patch on the throat. It measures up to seventy centimetres total length, including twenty-three centimetres of tail, and has thirty-eight teeth.

The Pine Marten is found in woody regions in the northern half of Europe (Britain, France, Germany, Scandinavia, Poland and Russia) and extends into parts of Siberia. Further south it is scarcer, barely reaching the north of Italy, Greece, the Crimea and the Caucasus. It is a very agile climber, and its depredations are considerable. It goes for squirrels, rabbits, hares, dormice, mice, pheasants, partridges and many other birds, which it surprises in their nests. Its taste for squirrels explains why it is commonly found in pine woods. It will also eat fruit. When food is scarce, it might venture into the farmyard, but it is too rare in Britain to be a menace.

Three or four young are born in April, after nine weeks of gestation. As is usual with carnivores they

The Giant Panda (*Ailuropoda melanoleuca*) in the wild inhabits the bamboo forests in mountain regions of a small area in southwestern China. It does not feed exclusively on bamboo shoots as was first believed, but also eats rodents, small birds and fishes. The few Giant Pandas that have reached Western zoos have been very popular.

The Pine Marten (*Martes martes*), inhabits the thick pine forests of the northern hemisphere. It is one of the most agile and graceful of the Mustelidae leaping skilfully from branch to branch in the trees hunting squirrels and birds. It also eats rodents, insects, fruit and eggs.

are helpless and blind. The nest is a hollow in a tree or an old bird nest lined with moss. The young grow rapidly and leave the mother after two months.

The Sable (*M. zibellina*) is a northern species found in northern Asia from the Urals to Japan. The most valuable of them have blue-black fur with silver tips.

The Beech Marten (*M. foina*) is a close relative and is distinguished by its grey-brown fur with white throat mark. Its range is more southerly than that of the Pine Marten. It is absent from Britain and Scandinavia, but occurs in various parts of Asia. Less of a forest animal and less shy of man, it is commonly found in barns, stables and haylofts, from which it emerges at night to raid its surroundings, often killing much but taking only one of its victims back to its lair. It also consumes fruit and honey.

The American Marten (*M. americana*) is very similar to the Pine Marten, though somewhat

differently coloured. Its fur is known as American sable. It is known as the Pacific Marten (*M. a. caurina*) on the west coast of North America. The Fisher (*M. pennanti*) is a large variety, dark in colour and about the size of a fox. The body is a metre long, including a tail of forty-five to fifty centimetres. It is a nocturnal forest animal, hunting on the ground as well as in the trees, and is found in Canada, the extreme northeastern United States and down the west coast to California, but is becoming rare. One of its favourite prey is the Porcupine, and it also hunts squirrels.

Another large marten, though smaller than the Fisher, is the Himalayan Marten (*M. flavigula*) of southern China, India, Burma and Malaya. It is seventy-five centimetres long, and has a tail of forty-five centimetres. Dark on the back, it has a yellow throat.

The Black-footed Ferret (*Mustela nigripes*) of North America is yellowish above, mixed with brown on the head and back, and slightly paler below. The legs are blackish. It was formerly found over most of the western and central Great Plains but is now very rare, having suffered from poisoning campaigns directed against larger predators and prairie dogs, in whose colonies it lives.

The Polecat (*Putorius putorius*) might well be taken as the model of the Mustelidae. Almost everything about it is typical: the long body on short legs, the flattened triangular head, the snout moderately long and rounded at the end, the small sharp eyes, and the short furry tail. One exceptional feature is that the brown fur is darker on the belly than on the flanks and back. It is up to sixty centimetres or more long, including a tail of twenty centimetres, and has thirty-four teeth.

It exists in Wales, France and central Europe, and up to Sweden and Finland. It lives under log piles, in hollow trees, or in abandoned burrows. In winter it hides during the day in farm buildings, emerging only at night to hunt. It destroys large numbers of rodents and reptiles, even attacking vipers, and may do great damage in the farmyard, killing tame rabbits, hens and pigeons. When attacked by dogs it defends itself by emitting the contents of its anal glands. Its fur, called polecat or fitch, was used in England for civic robes.

The Polecat can be trained to catch rabbits, but the domesticated form is usually employed. This is the Ferret—often erroneously given a distinct scientific name, *P. furo*—an albino, which is a yellowish white, and is said to be descended from a subspecies of North African polecat. The Ferret has two litters a year, with five to ten in each litter. The Polecat has only one litter annually, but hybrids follow the Ferret in having two.

To ferret for rabbits the animal is muzzled and put down one of the holes, all the others having been blocked. The rabbits are terrified and can be caught as they come out.

The Russian Polecat (*P. peversmanni*), smaller than the common form, lives in southern Russia and western Siberia. The Marbled Polecat (*Vormela peregusna*) is distributed from the Balkans across Asia to Mongolia.

A close relation of the Polecat is the Mink (genus *Mustela*), an aquatic mustelid of which there are several species. It is somewhat smaller than the Polecat, more slender and graceful, and

The Polecat (*Putorius putorius*) has a long, slender body like the weasel but is larger and its cream-coloured underfur is overlain by long black-tipped hairs. It is still common over much of Europe but has been largely exterminated in Britain. Its lithe agility and speed enable it to surprise its prey which it kills by pouncing and biting the neck.

with a darker fur. In its habits it recalls the Otter, digging burrows by the banks of wooded lakes or forming a lair under forked roots or piles of rushes. It dives and swims admirably and is capable of pursuing fishes. Otherwise it lives on frogs, snakes and rats, and an occasional waterbird or even poultry from a farmyard. A litter of three or four is born in April or May after a gestation of nine weeks.

The Old World Mink (*M. lutreola*) is not found in England and is rare in France, but from there it ranges eastwards to central Europe and northern Asia. Its fur is not so much used as that of the related Siberian Weasel or Kolinsky (*M. sibirica*), from Siberia, China and Japan. The North American Mink (*M. vison*) is similar to the Old World Mink, but it is bigger and the coat is thicker and softer. This is the most important mink in the fur trade, the best coming from Labrador and Hudson Bay. The great majority of the skins usually come from mink farms, both in North America and in Europe.

The offensive odour common to all this family is still worse in the Striped Skunk (*Mephitis mephitis*), which has two musk glands situated at the base of the tail, from which it can squirt an irritating and nauseous liquid a distance of three metres. Contrasting with its repulsive odour is the beautiful coat of glossy black fur with a white stripe on each side running into the tail. A skunk is about the size of a small cat and is rather slow-moving, spending most of the day underground. There are two species of *Mephitis* in various parts of Canada, the United States and Mexico, the Striped Skunk coming from southern Canada as well as most of the United States and the Hooded Skunk (*M. macroura*) from the southwestern United States and Mexico. The Spotted Skunk or Civet (*Spilogale putorius*) is smaller.

A similarly striped fur and the same obnoxious smell are found in the Zorille or Cape Polecat (*Ictonyx striatus*), a mustelid living in rocky country throughout Africa. The similarity of these two species is remarkable considering their wide geographical separation. They have the same nocturnal life and burrowing habit, and they hunt the same type of small mammals and birds, with occasional recourse to the farmyard.

Amongst the Mustelidae with thirty-four teeth, two forms stand apart on account of their small size and their elongated, almost serpentine bodies. They are the Common or European Weasel (*Mustela nivalis*) and the Stoat (*M. erminea*). The European Weasel is about sixteen centimetres long and has a tail of about five centimetres. The Stoat is about ten centimetres longer in body length and its tail is about thirteen centimetres long and has a black tip. Tawny brown above and white below, in northern countries stoats turn white in winter, but they generally do not do so in Great Britain except in Scotland. The European Weasel, too, occasionally turns white in cold climates. In Ireland there is a related subspecies of Stoat (*M. erminea hibernicus*), but known in Ireland as a weasel, which never turns white.

Weasels and stoats have much the same habits. Almost as active by day as by night, they run swiftly, climb with great agility, survey the surroundings with their sharp little eyes, and pounce

The Striped Skunk (*Mephitis mephitis*) is common and widespread over much of North America. If disturbed it stamps with its forefeet and raises its black-and-white plumed tail high in the air. If this intimidation display fails it shoots out from its anal glands the obnoxious fluid for which skunks are so well known.

The Weasel (*Mustela nivalis*) extends from Britain to Japan and southwards into North Africa. It used to be thought that the American weasel was a separate species, *M. rixosa*, but it is now regarded as conspecific with *M. nivalis*. Its fur occasionally turns white in winter over the northern parts of its range.

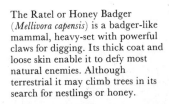

The Ratel or Honey Badger (*Mellivora capensis*) is a badger-like mammal, heavy-set with powerful claws for digging. Its thick coat and loose skin enable it to defy most natural enemies. Although terrestrial it may climb trees in its search for nestlings or honey.

Opposite
The American or Canadian Otter
(*Lutra canadensis*) photographed on
a river bank with a largemouth
bass. It is larger than the European
Otter. Both American and
European Otters are playful
animals often sliding down mud
banks or playing in the snow.

furiously on any living creature within their reach. Their voracity is unbounded and, like so many of their congeners, they are extremely courageous, commonly preying on animals much larger than themselves. Rabbits are the favourite food of stoats. When suddenly alarmed, or if cornered, they eject an obnoxious fluid from their anal glands.

The breeding habits of the two species are also much alike. Litters of from three to eight are born in April or May after two months gestation. The young do not leave their mother for seven or eight months, going off only when they are nearly adult and fully able to fend for themselves.

Partly on account of its small size the European Weasel is not valued for fur, and is allowed to go fairly unmolested, being useful for keeping down vermin. That is not the case with the Stoat, at any rate not in latitudes in which its coat turns into ermine, as in Russia and Scandinavia. In North America, the Stoat, called there the Short-tailed Weasel or Ermine, is found through the northern half of the continent. Also widespread in America are the Least Weasel (*M. rixosa*), and the Long-tailed Weasel (*M. frenata*).

The wolverines and badgers are among the largest of the Mustelidae. The Ratel or Honey Badger (*Mellivora capensis*) ranges from India to Arabia and over all Africa south of the Sahara. The underside of the body is black, sharply contrasting with the grey back. It is both a burrower and arboreal, nocturnal in habit, feeding on small mammals, birds, reptiles and insects. With its powerful claws it tears open the termitaries to get at termites. Its second name indicates its passion for honey. As soon as it discovers a nest of wild bees it opens it up and plunders it. It has no fear of bee stings, being protected by its hairs and by a thicker layer of subcutaneous fat. The association between the Ratel and the honeyguides (small birds which locate wild bee nests and lead the Honey Badger and also man to the site) is not well authenticated.

The Ratel is seventy-five centimetres long without the tail, which is about twenty-five centimetres.

The Wolverine or Glutton (*Gulo gulo*) is found in both the Old World, from Scandinavia to Kamchatka, and in the New World, from the Arctic to the northwestern parts of the United States. It was common in France and England during the Ice Age, but retreated northwards as the climate grew warmer. It is 120 centimetres long, including the long bushy tail, and is thickly built and somewhat like a bear cub. The fur is dark brown but paler at the flanks. It well deserves the name of glutton. When it gets the chance it attacks almost anything it meets, even prey as large as moose, when deep snow hinders their movements; otherwise it contents itself with lemmings, hares, birds, frogs, fishes and berries. Though slow and clumsy it wins its prey by patience and cunning. In winter it inspects the snares set for it and neatly removes the thongs to eat them, or eats the trapped animals. It is a good climber and swimmer. It is remorselessly hunted, partly for the sake of its fur, which is valued especially in the Far North for its protective qualities.

Otters are mustelids more completely adapted to an aquatic life. The long body, short legs, teeth and anal glands are a reminder of their close relationship to the Polecat and Pine Marten, but otters have other characters correlated with moving under water. The head is flattened, and vibrissae or whiskers are stout as in seals; the ears are small and provided with a membrane to close them when diving. The feet have five toes, webbed for three-quarters of their length, with non-retractile claws. The broad, flattened tail is usually said to be used for steering in water, but in fact it takes part with the body in the sinuous swimming movements. The short, dense fur is impermeable to water; dark brown and glossy on the back and only slightly paler on the throat.

The Common or Old World Otter (*Lutra lutra*) is widespread, being found in Europe (including the British Isles), North Africa, northern Asia and in parts of India, where it cohabits with the somewhat smaller Indian Small-clawed Otter (*Aonyx cinerea*), which is also found from the East Indies to the Himalayas and China. Another otter of India and Malaya is the Smooth-coated Otter (*Lutrogale perspicillata*). In Africa there is another 'clawless' form, the Cape Otter (*Aonyx capensis*), in which the claws are merely rudimentary. The North American Otter (*Lutra canadensis*) is widely distributed, but the fur, more valuable than that of the Common Otter and known as Virginian Otter, comes from the northeast of Canada, from Newfoundland to Hudson Bay.

The Common Otter's hole, known as a holt, is burrowed out of the bank of a lake or water course, the chamber being above water-level while the entrance is below. The only openings above ground are imperceptible air-holes, and its presence is only given away by the mewings of the cubs and the smell of the fishes which the mother brings them to eat. The only other indication of the Otter's whereabouts are the remains of fishes, of which the fleshy parts have been eaten, and the grey dung full of fishbones and scales which are always left in the same spot, a white stone or some other barren place.

The Wolverine or Glutton (*Gulo gulo*) is the largest and fiercest member of the weasel family. The short muscular legs end in clawed feet, which, as in the Polar Bear, have hairy soles that assists its movement over snow and icy surfaces.

The Otter's movements on land are clumsy, but it makes up for this in the water, where it swims with a serpentine movement of the body and tail, the limbs being pressed to its sides. The hind feet are used mainly in manoeuvring in water. It is a marvellous diver and can stay several minutes under water, owing to its great lung capacity. It generally hunts from the bank, spotting its prey and diving upon it with great accuracy. At other times it swims along the bottom, foraging for fishes and crustaceans among the plants and stones. It is alleged to do much damage to fishing and is consequently trapped for its fur, but careful investigation in recent years suggests that its principal food is eels and crayfishes. A Common Otter may journey long distances at night, either in water or over land, seeking new rivers or lakes. In Czechoslovakia they have been seen crossing mountain chains, staying for a while in each lake and then moving on.

The Common Otter's cry is a sort of half-scream, half-grunt which it utters only rarely. In the mating season males and females call each other by a prolonged, shrill whistle. In May the female gives birth to a litter of from two to five young after nine weeks of gestation. She feeds and cares for them tenderly. If taken young and fed on bread and milk, an Otter becomes very tame and learns to fish for its master, bringing him its catch. Even an adult otter can sometimes be tamed in a few months. Even to the point of being taught to answer to its name.

The Common Otter reaches a length of seventy-five centimetres with a tail forty-six centimetres long, and may weigh up to eleven kilograms, but the largest recorded was 168 centimetres long and weighed 16·5 kilograms.

The Sea Otter (*Enhydra lutris*), found in the North Pacific, is a much bigger animal growing to nearly 120 centimetres with a thirty centimetre tail, and weighing up to eighty or ninety pounds. Both morphologically and in its habits it forms a transition between the land carnivores and the seals. The skin of the Sea Otter is loose and the fur is fine, dense, rich and rather long, of a dark brown colour with a few long guard hairs. It is one of the most valued furs. As a result of extensive hunting the animal was almost exterminated, but protective measures have led to its numbers increasing. Sea Otters are seldom found more than a kilometre from the shore, and they favour particularly the neighbourhood of coastal reefs and extensive kelp beds, where the sheltered waters enable them to spend much of their time floating lazily on their backs. They do not often come ashore, but in stormy weather will haul out on to the rocks. The single young is born on the rocks but accompanies its mother into the sea very soon. The food is almost entirely sea urchins, molluscs, crabs and a few fishes, found on the sea bed and eaten at the surface as the animal floats on its back, using its chest as a dining table. Sea Otters have been known to bring a large stone to the surface together with the shellfishes, and use it to smash open hard shells by clasping the stone in their paws and bringing it down smartly on the shellfishes resting on their chest. The cheek teeth are extraordinarily powerful in order to cope with such food. Sea Otters are gregarious and diurnal,

and can often be seen playing. They are increasing noticeably under strict protection along the Californian coast, as well as in the Aleutian Islands in the extreme North Pacific.

Once classed with bears, true badgers are now included as a subfamily Melinae in the Mustelidae. They resemble bears in their massive build, plantigrade walk, omnivorous diet and placid behaviour. They belong clearly to the Mustelidae in the number of their teeth (thirty-eight), in the possession of anal glands, and in other anatomical details. A particular characteristic is their burrowing habit, for in that they are highly skilled, their 'sets' not only being very deep

The Sea Otter (*Enhydra lutris*), of the North Pacific, is exclusively marine, seldom coming ashore. Unlike other otters it has seal-like flippers, small compact forepaws and a short tail. It is one of the few tool-using mammals, bringing up a stone from the ocean bed to serve as an 'anvil' on which to break an urchin or mussel shell.

563

but covering a large area. They have powerful, non-retractile claws well suited for digging, and their coats are thick and coarse. Their sense of smell is much keener than that of sight or hearing.

The Common Badger (*Meles meles*) may grow to just over a metre, including twelve centimetres of tail, and to a weight of over thirteen kilograms, the boars being somewhat heavier than the sows. A squat animal with a flattened head, and small ears and eyes, it has a grizzled coat somewhat indeterminate in colouring, owing to each hair being yellow at the base, then black and then greyish, as may be seen in any genuine badger-hair shaving-brush. The head is white, the snout black, and two black lines, starting in front of the eyes, run backwards over the ears to fade away on the back. The throat is black too. The hairs are erectile, and when alarmed the Badger makes the whole or various parts of its coat stand on end, so that it seems nearly twice its normal size. The Common

Badger is cunning and not easily trapped, and hunting it is a laborious business, involving digging, unless gas is used to drive it out.

The burrow differs from a fox's earth in its absolute cleanliness. Badgers use specially dug holes for latrines above ground and tolerate no refuse of any kind whatever in the burrow, the living quarters of which are lined with dried grasses or straw. The cubs are born there in the spring. The eyes open at the end of a week and they are weaned at one month, when they are about the size of a wild rabbit. At that age their coats are less coarse and can be used as fur. Badgers are easily tamed and are friendly and clean about the house. Their only vice is to occasionally let loose odour at dogs which may worry them.

Common Badgers are essentially nocturnal, though they may sometimes be seen in the morning trotting home from foraging. They feed on voles, moles and any small vertebrates. They dig out nests of young rabbits and eat quantities of earthworms. They are said to raid partridges' nests and to steal young leverets, but they are still more attracted by vegetable food. They are as fond of honey as any bear, and will gobble it up regardless of bee stings.

In most parts of their range Common Badgers are active through the winter and only stay below ground in very bad weather. They are believed to hibernate, if only partially, in some of the more northerly parts of their ranges.

On the whole the Badger is more beneficial than a nuisance to the farmer. It will, for instance, dig up the larvae of cockchafers and helps to control the numbers of rabbits and other pests.

The Common Badger is found over almost the whole of Europe. The American Badger or Taxel (*Taxidea taxus*) is silver-grey and black above, yellowish below, and the dark head has a median white stripe. Heavily built, but slightly shorter than the European Badger, it is more markedly carnivorous and lives largely on ground squirrels and prairie dogs which it digs out. It is distributed over most of North America. The fur is of negligible commercial value although, before synthetics, it was highly prized for shaving-brushes.

The Japanese Badger (*Meles anakuma*) is somewhat smaller and shorter-haired, and provides a fur known as Nami. The Ferret Badger (*Melogale moschata*) from Assam, Burma and southern China is partly arboreal. In China its fur is called Pahmi. The Hog Badger (*Arctonyx collaris*) ranges from the Himalayas to Yunnan and has a pig-like snout.

Civets, genets, mongooses (Family Viverridae)

The members of this family have some features in common with cats, but differ in their shorter legs and the length of the muzzles. They do not have the cat's round head because their teeth, thirty-six to forty in number, require longer jaws. Two groups included in the family are the civets and genets, which are digitigrade and, unlike cats, do not have retractile claws. The civets are further characterised by the perfume of that name secreted by their anal glands.

The two principal species of civet are the African Civet (*Civettictis civetta*) and the Large Indian Civet (*Viverra zibetha*), which resemble each

Badgers lack the ferocity of the related weasel, leaving their underground den or sett only at night. The Common Badger (*Meles meles*), below, is found over most of Europe and western Asia. The broad black stripe on each side of the head distinguishes it from the American Badger (*Taxidea taxus*), bottom, which has a narrow central stripe. The Common Badger lives in wooded regions, while the American species is found in open country. Both badgers feed chiefly on insects, earthworms and small vertebrates, as well as vegetable food.

other in their grey coats with black markings, their erectile manes, and the shortness of their tails. They live in bushy regions, hidden during the day and by night hunting or raiding farmyards. Civets have often been kept in captivity to obtain their scent, which is expressed from the glands about twice a week with a small spatula. To expel it naturally the Civet must rub against a stone or tree-trunk. Both species are about 120 centimetres long overall. Civet, a musk-like perfume, is also obtainable from the Tangalung (*V. tangalunga*), a smaller Asiatic civet, and from the Rasse, or Small Indian Civet (*Viverricula indica*), which has been introduced into Madagascar. In America the unrelated Spotted Skunk (*Spilogale putorius*) is also called the Civet.

The Palm Civet (*Paradoxurus hermaphroditus*) is an oriental viverrid about the size of a cat, with a tail as long as the body. There are many races in India and Ceylon and further east. The closely related Masked Palm Civet (*Paguma larvata*) has an overlapping but somewhat more northerly range, to the east and southeast of the Himalayas. A second species, *P. lanigera* has a woolly winter coat and is found in Tibet. There is one species in West Africa, the African Palm Civet (*Nandinia binotata*), which is nocturnal and arboreal and lives in forests.

Related to the Palm Civet is the Binturong (*Arctictis binturong*) of Asia, one of the very few mammals outside Australia and South America to have a prehensile tail.

The Otter Civet (*Cynogale bennetti*), is an aquatic form, found in Malaya, Sumatra, and Borneo, which has soft, thick fur and a long moustache. The feet are webbed and it feeds largely upon fishes and frogs. It has a limited capacity for tree-climbing.

The genets, and in particular the Feline or Small Spotted Genet (*Genetta genetta*), are easily distinguished from civets by their tails, which are considerably longer, though with similar black and white rings. Their coats are somewhat alike; their scent glands, though present, are little developed. They are found in Spain, southern France and throughout Africa, where they live in forests, but more often in open country, preying upon any small mammals and birds they can catch. They are all good climbers and, like the civets, are active at night, resting by day in trees and hollows.

Another type of viverrid are the mongooses, which are plantigrade, have non-retracile claws, and a different form of scent glands. There are many species, the largest being rather bigger than a cat, but most are quite small.

The Ichneumon or Egyptian Mongoose (*Herpestes ichneumon*) was a sacred animal in ancient Egypt and was often mummified. Before the introduction of cats it kept the house free of rodents. It feeds on all sorts of animals, including reptiles, and lives in thick vegetation by rivers, from north-east to South Africa. A subspecies in Spain and Portugal is called the Spanish Mongoose.

The Banded Mongoose (*Mungos mungo*) is dun-coloured, with dark bands across the back. Its range is from tropical Africa southwards. Two other African species are the White-tailed Mongoose (*Ichneumia albicauda*), of southern Arabia and Africa south of the Sahara, and the Marsh or Water Mongoose (*Atilax paludinosus*), found in Africa south of the Sahara.

The Crab-eating Mongoose (*Herpestes urva*) is nearly sixty centimetres long without the tail. It is found in marshy valleys in the Himalayas, Assam, Burma and Malaya, where it lives on crabs, frogs and fishes. Two other Asian species are the Common Indian Mongoose (*H. edwardsi*), related to the Ichneumon but smaller, and an allied form, the Small Indian Mongoose (*H. javanicus*). Both are fairly widely distributed in southern Asia.

The battle between mongoose and snake has been too well described by Kipling to be repeated here. One species, the Small Indian Mongoose, was introduced into Jamaica and Martinique, which were infested with vipers. The mongooses thrived on them, but eventually became a nuisance through stealing poultry, and became sub-

The Blotched or Tigrine Genet (*Genetta tigrina*), common throughout Africa, differs from *G. genetta* by having larger spots on a more yellowish ground colour. A notable feature of genets is their white face markings which stand out clearly on a dark night presumably allowing one genet to recognise another. The same feature occurs in other nocturnal animals such as badgers and foxes.

Most mongooses have speckled grey or brown fur but the Banded Mongoose (*Mungos mungo*) has dark bands across the back. All mongooses are alert and agile with lightning fast reflexes, necessary assets for those species that kill snakes. Very little is known of their breeding habits in the wild.

ject to vigorous control measures themselves. They are easily domesticated, making charming and intelligent pets.

The Meerkat (*Suricata suricatta*) is a peculiar species of mongoose. A small and slender animal with a narrow snout extending well beyond the lips, it is a terrestrial South African animal and lives on small rodents and snakes.

The fauna of Madagascar includes Viverridae not found elsewhere. The most interesting is the Fossa (*Cryptoprocta ferox*), not to be confused with the genus *Fossa*, which is a Madagascan civet. The Fossa is the largest carnivore in Madagascar, being 150 centimetres long overall, including a little over sixty centimetres of tail. The legs are

short, as in all the Viverridae. It has thirty-two teeth and a pointed nose, and its coat is a rich, warm brown. A last representative of a disappearing fauna, the Fossa lives in inaccessible regions, and little is known about it. Though largely a terrestrial animal, it climbs trees to hunt lemurs, and although it has the reputation of being one of the most ferocious killers, recent observations suggest that this is somewhat undeserved.

Hyaenas (Family Hyaenidae)

Present-day hyaenas are the degenerate representatives of a formerly much more important family which included European forms. Fore-shadowed in the Eocene by indecisive forms such as *Pterodon*, it took shape in the Miocene in *Ictitherium* and *Hyaenictis* before finishing in the Pliocene in forms that can be regarded as the direct ancestors of the striped and spotted hyaenas of today.

Hyaenas are Carnivora adapted for carrion-feeding. The fore parts are well developed, but the hind quarters, so powerful in the springing Felidae, are considerably reduced in the hyaenas, being both lower and less muscular than the shoulders. The head is generally rounder than in the Viverridae, owing to a shortening of the jaws and broadening of the zygomatic arches, under which the temporal muscles pass. There are only thirty-four teeth, but they are extremely strong and with powerful jaw muscles capable of crushing bones.

The claws, which are not used for hunting, are blunt and non-retractile, though they are strong and serve for digging. Hyaenas are four-toed, digitigrade animals, which have coarse, rough coats, composed chiefly of guard hairs. Many have an erectile mane along the top of the back.

With their low hind quarters, somewhat crooked legs and brutal faces, hyaenas are among the most unattractive animals, the impression being heightened by their ugly coats and offensive odour.

The largest is the Spotted Hyaena (*Crocuta crocuta*), a direct descendant of the Cave Hyaena (*Hyaena spelaea*), whose fossil bones and dung are found in profusion in Paleolithic beds. The present habitat comprises the whole of Africa except the north and the Congo basin. It does not frequent deserts nor equatorial forests, preferring bush with some rocky ground accessible in which it can find a lair. The coat is reddish grey with brown spots. There is no mane.

The other two species of true hyaena have dark erectile manes, contrasting with the lighter colour of the rest of the body. One is the Striped Hyaena (*H. hyaena*), the other the Brown Hyaena (*H. brunnea*), which is, apart from the mane, more or less uniform in colour. The first, with dark stripes on a dull grey ground, ranges from Central Africa to India; the second is confined to southern Africa.

Spotted hyaenas keep to their lairs by day and prowl by night, when their raucous barkings or hysterical laughter can be heard. They follow the great hunters to batten on their leavings, but they also hunt for themselves. Travelling in packs they attack herds of antelopes and sometimes a horse, donkey or cow, biting at the mammary glands or abdomen in the attempt to tear out the viscera. In villages they consume refuse and even dung. They

The Pygmy or Dwarf Mongoose (*Helogale parvula*), of subsaharan Africa, is the smallest of the mongooses never reaching more than forty-five centimetres in length. It feeds by day in groups of up to a dozen, sheltering at night in burrows or termite mounds. A characteristic of this mongoose is that it drinks by dipping a forepaw into the water and licking it.

The Meerkat or Suricate (*Suricata suricata*) lives in colonies in burrows on the dry sandy veld of South Africa. As seen in this photograph it has the charming habit of sitting back on its haunches and basking in the sun.

disinter bodies which are not deeply buried, and at times even attack children. If they do not cause death directly they leave infected wounds which may soon become fatal. They prefer open country whereas the Striped and Brown Hyaenas live in drier country with thick bush, are more solitary and take smaller prey.

Once a year the female gives birth to three or four cubs, which are brown with no markings.

Aardwolf (Family Protelidae)

The Hyaenidae are divided into two groups, the true hyaenas already dealt with, and the subfamily Protelinae which contains only one species, the Aardwolf (*Proteles cristatus*). This animal resembles the Striped Hyaena in general shape, striped coat and dorsal mane, but it is of slighter build, has five toes on the hind feet and much less powerful teeth. The jaws are weak and the molars reduced to simple rounded points. They do not crush bone.

About as big as a fox, the Aardwolf lives in an earth with two or three exits which it digs for itself. It sometimes feeds on carrion and small creatures, but almost entirely on termites. It ranges from South Africa to Angola and Somalia.

Cats (Family Felidae)

The word cat may be used loosely to denote any member of the family Felidae and thus to include lions, tigers, leopards and jaguars as well as lynxes, servals, bobcats and pumas, in addition to the domestic animal. On the other hand it may be reserved, as in this book, for the Domestic Cat and those wild cats that closely resemble it in size, shape and habits. The larger members of the family are referred to as the Big Cats.

All the Felidae are distinguished by a round head, thirty teeth and digitigrade feet with retractile claws. The only exception is the Cheetah, with non-retractile claws.

WILD CATS: The European Wild Cat (*Felis sylvestris*) is exclusively a forest-dweller. It is the wild cat of the north and east of Europe, and it is also found on open ground in the Scottish Highlands, several regions of France and Corsica. It resembles the domesticated tabby cat, but is more heavily built. Its fur is yellow-grey with dark transverse stripes over most of the body and a black stripe down the back. The tail is marked with black rings and a black tip which is blunted. There is a good growth of whiskers. It is entirely nocturnal and has a general appearance of ferocity and strength.

During the day it may tuck itself away in the fork of a tree or lie out on a branch, the colour of its fur blending with that of the bark. At night it hunts in the usual cat manner, but with stealth, depending on the rapidity of its final pounce. It is dangerous both to man and his dogs, since it attacks without provocation. When wounded it defends itself with obstinate fury.

The Wild Cat becomes sociable during the mating season. Pairs come together in the early spring, and after two months' gestation three or four young are born in April or May. They are as wild as their parents, ready at all times to scratch and bite. All attempts to tame them have been in vain.

There are many other species of wild cat in the Old World. Some have uniform coats like the Golden Cat or Temminck's Cat (*Felis temmincki*) of south-east Asia. Others are spotted: the Fishing Cat (*F. viverrina*) of India and south-east Asia; the Jungle Cat (*F. chaus*), widely distributed from north-east Africa through southern Asia to Indo-China; and the Caffer Cat (*F. lybica*) of which there are several races in Syria and between Egypt and the Cape. It is yellowish buff with dark markings. The Indian Desert Cat (*F. l. ornata*) is a race of the Caffer Cat, and the Leopard Cat (*F. bengalensis*) of the eastern half of Asia is the commonest of the small cats of India. Some of these have been suggested as ancestral forms of the Domestic Cat (*F. catus*), but the origin and evolution of this animal cannot be traced with certainty.

The Spotted or Laughing Hyaena (*Crocuta crocuta*), of subsaharan Africa, is the largest and most aggressive of the hyaenas. It has been seen to drag a ninety kilogram carcase for a 100 metres. Although Spotted Hyaenas usually feed on carrion they also attack domestic stock and hunt wildebeest and other antelopes.

The Brown Hyaena (*Hyaena brunnea*), of southern Africa, is halfway in size between the Spotted and Striped Hyaenas. It has a long-haired erectile mane. It lives near the shore feeding on marine carrion and any refuse left by the tide.

The Scottish Wild Cat (*Felis silvestris grampia*) is a subspecies of the European Wild Cat. It has been exterminated except in the Scottish Highlands where in recent years its numbers have increased. It is extraordinarily ferocious and virtually untameable, even when taken as a kitten.

The Siamese is one of the most popular breeds of short-haired domestic cats. The colour of the fur changes from pure white in the kitten to a pale fawn in the adult with dark brown points. The eyes are very bright blue. The Siamese was the sacred, royal or temple cat of Thailand and was first introduced into England in 1884.

DOMESTIC CATS: Although little is known for certain about the origin of Domestic Cats, there is no evidence to show that they are descended from the European Wild Cat, although the two interbreed. They show a number of similarities, including the strong resemblance that a striped tabby cat has to the wild cat in coat pattern. The Caffer Cat (*F. lybica*) is also a possible ancestor, but its kittens, like those of *F. sylvestris*, are virtually untameable.

Domestic Cats in Europe tend to fall into the category which Americans call the 'alley cat', characterised by its long, thin tail, straight ears and short hair, the colour varying in individuals completely concealing their ancestry. They may be black, white, brown, grey, ginger, tabby and tortoiseshell. The Domestic Cat is the best mouser and ratter, a great point in its favour.

There seems to be no foundation for the claim that some cats have an Asiatic origin and may be descended from Pallas's Cat (*Felis manul*) or from close relatives of that species. The skulls of such Domestic Cats show no similarity to those of the Asiatic species named. Some of those for which such a claim is made are the long-haired Angora race, characterised by its fine thick fur, particularly round the neck, chest and and tail, generally of a light and uniform colour; and the Chinese Cat with pendent ears and long, silky fur. It is rarely imported into Europe. Another of the same ancestry is the Siamese Cat. It has a kinked tail and its colour varies from pale fawn to chocolate with dark markings. Its eyes are a deep blue. The origin of this race is unknown. Its habits are in many ways more dog-like than other cats, and it has great individuality and independence.

There are at least two tail-less breeds: one from the Isle of Man, the Manx Cat and an excellent mouser, and another from Japan.

Another race which contrasts with the Common Cat is the Abyssinian Cat, which is longer in the face and ears. It is a ruddy brown, the hairs being 'ticked' with dark brown or black. Like the Siamese it is a short-haired breed.

Cats do not lend themelves well to scientific breeding. No animal is more vagabond by nature, and it is difficult to keep races pure. If there are two races in any region, they will blend in time.

Female cats have two periods of heat in a year, when a number of males gather round at night calling. Scratching seems to be associated with this. At the moment of coupling the male seems to be attacking the female, but as soon as coition is complete it is the she-cat that turns on her mate.

Gestation lasts fifty-five or fifty-six days, and five or six kittens are born in April and August. The mother has eight teats. Kittens are blind at birth and utterly dependent on their mother. She feeds them, keeps them clean, and above all protects them from the male, which would be only too ready to devour them.

The Serval (*Felis serval*), of Africa south of the Sahara, generally frequents grassy scrub country, where it easily blends with the landscape because of its fawn coat with longitudinal rows of black spots. Its tail is ringed with the same colours. It is one of the fastest runners of all the Felidae and can catch birds on the wing, even when they are almost two metres from the ground. Its favourite food is guinea-fowl, but it takes other birds, as well as hares and rodents. It also attacks young antelopes, and, like other carnivores, it will quickly take advantage of an easy access to the farmyard.

LYNXES: The summer coat of the European Lynx (*Lynx lynx*) is rufous above, whitish below, and is more or less spotted; the winter coat is paler. The Pardel Lynx (*L. pardinus*), one of the smallest and most handsome members of the group, is a more thickly spotted type. It is also found on the French slopes of the Pyrenees, and it may possibly be found in Greece and Turkey.

The Caracal (*Lynx caracal*) is long-legged and better built for running than other cats. Its coat is a uniform fawn, shading to white below and to black at the tips of the ears. It lives in the deserts or savannas of North Africa and western Asia, hunting all sorts of animals, including gazelles, which it can outstrip for a time. Its agility is so great that it was used in pigeon-catching contests by Eastern princes. Although it is lynx-like, with ear-tufts, it is nearer to the Serval.

The Serval (*Felis serval*), of subsaharan Africa, is a slender, beautifully marked cat with very long legs and ears that are very large compared with most of the Felidae. It has a second colour phase in which its stripes are replaced by a fine powdering of specks. This phase is known as the Servaline.

The Caracal or Desert Lynx (*Caracal caracal*) is one of the most beautiful of all the cats but today is much less common than formerly. In former times it was trained for hunting in India in much the same way as was the Cheetah.

The Bobcat (*Lynx rufus*), the widespread wild cat of America, is up to a metre long and stands up to sixty centimetres at the shoulder. Because of their adaptability and wide variety of diet, bobcats have largely survived the spread of agriculture. They are good tree climbers as this young Bobcat illustrates.

Tigers (*Panthera tigris*) are northern Asiatic animals that have spread to the south. Intolerant of heat, they seek shade at midday or lie in water to keep cool. The most powerful of the big cats, the Tiger will sometimes take to attacking man for food when age reduces its speed and strength.

Lynxes have short tails and can be recognised by their tufted ears. While Servals, like other cats and most other felids, have thirty teeth, lynxes have only twenty-eight.

The European Lynx (*Lynx lynx*) ranges throughout central and northern Europe and is also found in Siberia and Mongolia, wherever large forests give sufficient cover from hunters and trappers. Formerly it existed in Gaul and Germany, but is now extremely rare in these regions. Only some sixty lynxes have been killed in the French Alps and Pyrenees in the last three-quarters of a century, and they appear to be no commoner in Switzerland and Germany.

An agile climber, the European Lynx takes heavy toll of animals, from small mammals and birds to rabbits, hares and deer of all varieties. When food is scarce in the forest a lynx will leave it and attack sheep and goats. It stalks like a household cat, creeping up cautiously and noiselessly. Then suddenly it leaps on the back of its victim, usually killing by biting into the neck. Among a flock of sheep it will sometimes kill a large number for no obvious reason.

Lynxes are not very prolific. Two to four cubs are born between April and May in some den or thicket in the densest part of the forest. They are blind at birth and their mother, having suckled them, continues to feed them after they are weaned on mice, voles and small birds, until they have grown strong enough to hunt for themselves.

The Canadian Lynx (*L. canadensis*) is the largest North American lynx. It resembles the European Lynx, but generally has somewhat longer hair and broader feet. Its pelt is valuable as a fur. It is found in the pine forests of Canada and the northern United States, where its chief food is the Snowshoe Rabbit, but it has tended to disappear as human settlement has spread.

Further south in the United States is the Bobcat or Bay Lynx (*L. rufus*), also known as the Wildcat, which is considerably smaller but equally fierce. It is a uniform rufous colour as a rule, but is sometimes striped or spotted. A subspecies, the Barred Bobcat (*L. r. fasciatus*), has black markings and rings on the legs. It is found in the west of the United States down to northern California. Bobcats kill many young deer by leaping on their backs.

LEOPARDS: The Leopard (*Panthera pardus*) of Africa and Asia has a strong resemblance to a domestic cat. It has the same beauty, strength and agility, and like the cat, has a round head, short nose and long, thin tail. Its claws are extremely sharp and long, and its teeth are stronger, relative to its size, than a lion's. Its coat has a yellowish background covered with dark spots, the shape and disposition of these varying according to the region even in individuals. No two skins are ever alike. On the flanks, head and legs the spots are scattered without order, but on the back they tend to be set in little groups or rosettes. The spots are smaller in the African than the Asian Leopard, and further apart in the Mountain Leopard of India than in that living in the plains, but all are merely subspecies. So great is the variety that attempts have been made to distinguish different species by patterns on the coat.

This variability in marking may perhaps be explained by the fact that the Leopard is the most widely distributed of all the Felidae. It is found in Africa from the Mediterranean to the Cape.

In Asia the Leopard has a greater range than the Tiger, stretching from Asia Minor to China and from southern Siberia to the East Indies. Black Panthers occur in the East Indies and India, and are melanistic forms of the same species.

The only other species called leopard but not really a true leopard is the Snow Leopard or Ounce (*Uncia uncia*), which has black spots on a whitish ground. It lives in the mountains of central Asia and the Himalayas, usually above 2,400 metres feeding on wild sheep and ibex, as well as domestic sheep and goats on occasion. Its soft, thick fur and very long, thick tail make it possibly the most handsome of all Big Cats.

The Leopard is perhaps the most athletic of the Felidae, being equally good at running, jumping, tree-climbing and swimming across rivers. It hunts ceaselessly and will prey on birds and monkeys as readily as antelopes or cattle. It is rarely seen, even by its victims. Leopards that take to man-eating can be more dangerous than Lions or Tigers. In the Central Provinces of India, a Leopard killed over 200 people in the course of two years, even coming into homes to find its prey.

Pairs are formed only in the mating season. In February or March, after three months' gestation, two to five cubs are born, generally in a dense thicket or rocky hollow.

In captivity Leopards are tameable only when young. As they grow older their wild nature is always ready to reassert itself, and it is never possible for the tamer to trust them as he may trust Lions and Tigers. Few are consequently tamed.

TIGER: There is only one species of Tiger (*Panthera tigris*), and for a very long time it was known only from South and East Asia. It ranges north-east from Persia through Turkestan, Mongolia and southern Siberia to Korea. On the other side of the Asiatic highlands it stretches through India, Tibet, China, Thailand and Indo-China. At some very distant date the Tiger reached the Malay Peninsula, then Sumatra and Java, possibly by swiming. Borneo and the other islands of Indonesia have no Tigers. Nor has Sri Lanka, and the assumption is that the Tiger has spread through India since the time when Sri Lanka became separated from the mainland.

It is easy to understand that, covering such a wide range in both territory and climate, the species should have been modified and should be present in so many varieties. There is a great deal of difference between a Bengal Tiger and a Siberian one. The first is short-haired and dark with many strongly-marked stripes. The second is long-haired and has a paler coat, whose stripes are fewer and less striking. Each variety has undergone a long adaptation to local conditions. Within a given region there is considerable difference

between specimens and even within a family, though the general pattern of the stripes is constant. Very rarely white or black tigers are born.

Male Tigers measure over a metre in height at the shoulder, the females a little less. The length may be up to three metres and weight varies from 100 to 225 kilograms. The Siberian subspecies is the largest variety.

The life of the Tiger is best observed in Bengal, Burma, Thailand or Indo-China, and especially in such regions as Baria in Indo-China or Nha-Trang in Annam, where the forest is interspersed with clearings. The Tiger is less of a forest animal than the Leopard, though more so than the Lion. During the day it remains hidden in the forest, emerging in the evening and early part of the night to stalk its prey, lying in wait by paths through forest or to water, or along the banks of rivers. It takes whatever is available, whether ox or wild boar, deer or peacock, and it will fish with its paws if nothing is found on land. It may even turn to tortoises or other reptiles. Prey that is too large to be eaten at a single meal is dragged away into a thicket to which the Tiger returns on successive days. If the meat begins to putrefy, the Tiger does not seem to notice, being less particular in this respect than the Leopard or the Lion. Near villages a Tiger will raid herds, and once it takes to cattle it generally becomes man-eating as well.

The reproductive habits of the Tiger follow the same pattern as the Leopard's. After three months' gestation two or three cubs are born. They are blind and completely dependent on the mother. When she has weaned them she still provides their food. Sometimes she hunts with her mate, the male thus playing an indirect part in the care of the offspring. By the end of six months the two or three cubs have been reduced to one or two. The missing cubs may have fallen to the ferocity of their father, but it is equally possible that the mother regulates the number of her progeny. Even if she raised only one family in two years and only one of the litter survives, she can leave twenty desendants. Tigers will breed in captivity, and in a

Lions (*Panthera leo*) are still numerous in Africa south of the Sahara but in Asia only a few survive in the Gir Forest Reserve in India. They live in groups called 'prides' which can vary in size from three to thirty individuals, usually comprised of a male, several lionesses and their young.

The Puma or Mountain Lion (*Felis concolor*) is still widespread over many parts of North and South America, where its adaptation to a wide range of habitat and diet has probably saved it from extinction. Like most of the large predatory animals it is solitary and mainly active at night, relying on stealth and surprise to secure its prey.

The Jaguar (*Panthera onca*) is the counterpart in South America of the leopard and the largest of the New World cats. A good swimmer and fond of water, it will follow its prey into the river, and will not hesitate to attack an alligator.

few instances crosses between a Lion and a Tigress, called Ligers, have been obtained, having stripes like the mother but otherwise about half way between the two.

LION: The Lion (*Panthera leo*) has been intimately connected with human history, even in Europe. In prehistoric times there was a Cave-dwelling Lion (*Felis spelaea*) and in historical times Lions still inhabited the Balkan peninsular.

Since then the Lion has steadily retreated before the advance of man. It has disappeared from the Near East, while in Algeria, Tunisia and Morocco the last Barbary Lions were killed in the last century. Further south it still exists in the savannas between Senegal and East Africa, and southwards to the Transvaal, wherever there is still an abundant herbivorous fauna. It is not found in deserts or in thick forest. The Cape Lion, like the Barbary Lion, has long been extinct in that part of the world.

A Lion is usually about a metre tall at the shoulders and a Lioness is some fifteen centimetres shorter. It may be up to three metres long and weigh 180–225 kilograms. It is at present the largest African carnivore.

Colour and body size differ little in the various races or subspecies, of which many have been recognised. The Barbary Lion was large and yellowish and had a long, thick mane. The Senegal Lion is smaller and more tawny with much less mane. The Cape Lion was the largest of all, grey-yellow with a dark mane. The Masai Lion of Kenya is buff-coloured with a yellow mane. The Somali Lion is small, with a reduced mane and a pale grey-yellow coat. The Indian Lion, as also the extinct Persian and Mesopotamian Lions, is smaller than the African. All are so closely related that they are regarded as one species.

Even where it is abundant the Lion is rarely seen during the day, largely because its colour blends well with the landscape. In rocky country it conceals itself in a hollow.

The Margay (*Felis wiedi*), one of the smaller South American cats, is closely related to the ocelot with a similar attractive appearance. Its fur is bright cream-yellow, spotted with jet black. It is often captured when young and reared as a pet, especially in the United States.

The Lion hunts at night, creeping silently in order to surprise a stray animal or a sleeping herd. Often it waits by a waterhole, as it has more patience than desire for running. Its favourite prey are antelopes and zebras, which offer little resistance. It may try for a young giraffe but adult ones can put up a stout defence, as do buffaloes. If a Lion misses its prey it rarely gives pursuit.

Lions are the only sociable members of the cat family. They live in 'prides' composed of a few females with their cubs and one or two males.

Although the Lion hunts in silence its roar may be heard in the early hours of the morning and sometimes continues all day. Others may join in and as many as ten raucous voices have been heard in concert. The roar is used to keep touch.

Gestation lasts three months and two or three cubs are born at a time. They are as big as cats and have their eyes open. The cubs are weaned at six months, and by the end of a year they are about the size of big dogs. In the males the mane usually starts growing at about the age of three years.

PUMA: The Americas have species of the cat family that are not found elsewhere: the Puma which looks much like a small Lioness, and the Jaguar and Ocelot which resemble the Leopard. There are also several small wild cats.

The Puma, Cougar or Mountain Lion (*Felis concolor*) is distinguished from other American felids by its uniform, Lion-like colour and could be described as a short-legged, maneless Lion. It formerly roamed from Alaska to Cape Horn, being equally at home on the pampas, prairie, in coniferous forests of the north or in jungles. But hunting and the spread of agriculture have eliminated it from many parts of North America and it survives mainly in reserves and national parks. Recently a recovery in numbers has been noted in a few parts of the eastern United States, where deer have increased greatly.

It is a good climber and when hunted it takes refuge in a tree, making no attempt to defend itself.

Its diet is varied and it has been suggested that it may have exterminated the horse in America before the discovery of that continent. The Puma's depredations may be severe, for on occasion it kills far beyond its needs. One is reported to have killed fifty sheep in a single night.

The animal hunts mainly at night, showing a daring skill which equals that of the Tiger. The Puma rarely attacks man and, like the Jaguarundi, can easily be tamed and domesticated.

JAGUAR: If the Puma is the Lion of the New World, the Jaguar (*Panthera onca*) is the Leopard. Its coat is yellow, becoming whitish on the underparts, and it is marked with black spots mainly arranged in rosettes of four to five around a central spot. It is, however, bigger than its African and Asiatic counterparts, being only a little smaller than the Tiger, and is often called a Tiger (*El Tigre*) in South and Central America, where it lives on the wooded banks of rivers, and in marshes covered with tall grasses. Hidden by day, it hunts by night, preying on all sorts of animals, aquatic as well as terrestrial: water-birds, aquatic tortoises, fishes, caimans and monkeys; but its favourite food is horses and ruminants.

The largest and fiercest South American carnivore, the Jaguar shows no fear of man, unlike the Puma, and may even become a man-eater. It does much harm and is hunted relentlessly.

OTHER AMERICAN CATS: The next largest felid of America is the Ocelot (*Panthera pardalis*), far smaller than the Jaguar and with a more ornamental coat. Also known as the Painted Leopard, it is golden on the head and down the middle of the back, and silvery on the flanks, with rows of somewhat metallic spots on the body and dark longitudinal stripes on the head and neck. The Ocelot lives in South American forests, often near a village where it can prey on farmyard animals. Although nearly a metre long, excluding the tail, it is harmless to man and will even run away from a dog. It does not provide interesting hunting

because it presents no challenge. In captivity it is as playful as a kitten.

The American Tiger Cat or Margay (*P. tigrina*) is a related species with the same habits. It is no bigger than the domestic cat and is found in northern Brazil and from Cayenne to eastern Venezuela.

The Jaguarundi (*Felis yagouaroundi*) is a metre to 1.2 metres long, including the tail. Slenderly built and somewhat otter-like in shape, it has two colour phases: one dark grey (Jaguarundi) and one red-brown (Eyra), which occupy the same locality, ranging from Argentina to southern Texas.

The American Felidae are solitary and the sexes associate only during the mating season. Two or three cubs are born at a time. They are blind and are nursed with great care by the mother.

CHEETAH: Although included in the Felidae, the Cheetah (*Acinonyx jubatus*) shows certain dog-like characters. It has long legs, does not climb, and its claws are blunt and non-retractile. Also known as the Hunting Leopard, it has been trained for hunting from very early times.

The single species is spread over all the hot, dry regions of the Old World, from Algeria to Morocco to Mauretania and the Transvaal, and in the east to Ethiopia, Egypt, Arabia, Syria, Persia and India. Being spotted, it has often been confused with the Leopard. Like the latter, it was once believed to be a hybrid, a cross between a Panther and a Lioness.

The fact that there are no fossil remains of the Cheetah in Africa points strongly to its Asiatic origin and indicates that it must have later spread westwards, either independently or through its association with man. It is now commoner in Africa than Asia.

In the wild state Cheetahs hunt in small groups for gazelles and antelopes, first stalking them stealthily and then rushing at them with great speed and pouncing on them. They prefer the blood and the entrails and do not often touch the rest of the carcass. They rarely return to a previous day's kill.

Seals, sea-lions, walruses (Order Pinnipedia)

With a few exceptions such as the Beaver, Otter and Hippopotamus, adaptation to an aquatic existence has been achieved by only three groups of mammals: the Cetacea, Sirenia and the Pinnipedia. The relationships of the first two are uncertain, but the Pinnipedia can be regarded as aquatic carnivores. Some authorities claim that there is a very close relationship between earless seals and otters, and between eared seals and bears. It can be said that the Pinnipedia and the Carnivora represent divergent branches from a common ancestral stock, the Creodonta, the smooth-brained Precarnivora that lived in the Eocene and Oligocene and did not possess carnassial teeth.

Of these three groups the pinnipeds are the least modified. Admittedly, their bodies are fish-like, but they have retained hairy coats and four limbs and are able to move about on land. Indeed some essential parts of their life, including mating and birth, are carried out on land.

The pinnipeds are divided into three families: true or earless seals (Phocidae), eared seals (Otariidae) and walruses (Odobenidae). They are fairly plentiful in the oceans and in more or less enclosed seas such as the Baltic, Mediterranean, and Black Seas, and there are seals even in inland waters like the Caspian and Lake Baikal.

The spindle-shaped body is often masked in the larger seals by rolls of subcutaneous fat. The head is round and carried on a distinct neck, so that it can be moved relative to the body. The fur covering the skin is generally short-haired and slopes backwards, making for easy movement through water.

The Cheetah (*Acinonyx jubatus*) has long been credited with being the fastest land animal over short distances. Less nocturnal than most of the big cats, it is active during the day but will also hunt at night if the moon is full.

The paddles of the pinnipeds represent the first stage in the evolution of the flippers of cetaceans. They are still limbs capable of being used for movement on solid ground. With the shortening of the humerus and the bones of the fore arm, however, we see in the true seals the progressive loss of suppleness in the elbow and wrist, only the shoulder retaining mobility. The digits remain visible and are provided with nails. In the eared seals adaptation has gone further in this respect. The digits have become indistinct and the nails reduced until they have disappeared, and the whole limb has lengthened and become sickle-shaped, but the number of digits and phalanges has not increased.

Unlike the cetaceans and the sirenians which have broad flukes at the end of the tail, the tails of pinnipeds are vestigial. The hind limbs, situated well back and overlapping the stumpy tail perform the same functions as a whale's flukes. In the Phocidae the hind limbs serve only for swimming. but in the eared seals they can be held out at right angles to the body and act as legs on land.

The dentition of the pinnipeds is different from that of the carnivores. Incisors are generally present in both jaws, but they are always more numerous in the upper than in the lower jaw. The upper canines are fang-like or may even become tusks, as in the Walrus. The molars are all alike, and have either a single root or a median lobe and an anterior and a posterior root. The crowns have cutting edges, suitable for dealing with fishes, crustaceans and molluscs on which the animals mostly feed. Some typical dental formulae are:

Eared Seal   I. $\frac{3}{2}$ C. $\frac{1}{1}$ Pm. $\frac{4}{4}$ M. $\frac{1}{1}$ Total 34

Sea Elephant I. $\frac{2}{1}$ C. $\frac{1}{1}$ Pm. $\frac{4}{4}$ M. $\frac{1}{1}$ Total 30

Walrus   I. $\frac{1}{0}$ C. $\frac{1}{1}$ Pm. $\frac{3}{3}$ M. $\frac{0}{0}$ Total 18

Like all carnivorous animals the pinnipeds have a simple stomach, relatively short intestine and a little-developed caecum. The brain is large and much convoluted, indicating intelligence, and all sense-organs are well developed. The sense of smell has not been lost, as it has been in the cetaceans.

The testes are external in the eared seals but internal in the Phocidae. The males resemble the land carnivores in having an os penis, and the female in having a bicorned uterus and a zonal placenta. Gestation varies between nine and twelve months, according to the species. One or two calves are born at a time, and one or two pairs of teats are situated abdominally.

The pinnipeds are much hunted, particularly in Arctic regions, for their flesh, skins and edible fat. Their enemy is the Grampus or Killer Whale.

Pinnipeds live well in captivity, reaching ages of ten to forty years. They can be trained to perform in various ways, including balancing.

Earless seals (Family Phocidae)

Earless seals have no obvious external ears. Only a small vestige remains lodged in the canal leading to the inner ear. They have very short necks, nailed digits, palms and soles covered with hair and hind limbs, which are swept back beside the tail and of no use in locomotion on land. Even the fore limbs are little used on land, the animals wriggling and moving forward in a series of jerks. Even so they can cover more than a kilometre an hour on the ice. One in Norway is reported to have travelled fifty-six kilometres in a week on snow.

The Common or Harbor Seal (*Phoca vitulina*) is dun-coloured above, lighter below and flecked all over with browner spots or marblings. Varying in length from 150 to 200 centimetres, it lives in the northern parts of the Atlantic, in the North Sea, Baltic, the Arctic Ocean and the North Pacific. It is sometimes seen in the English Channel and even

The Common Seal (*Phoca vitulina*), known as the Harbor Seal in North America, lives in estuaries and on sandbanks. It is widely distributed and many subspecies have been named for the various geographic groups. The adults feed on fish, squid, whelks and mussels but, after weaning, the cubs feed on shrimps.

Crabeater Seals (*Lobodon carcinophagus*) are the most abundant seal of the Antarctic, living in colonies and moving north in winter on the drifting ice pack and south in summer when the heavier ice breaks up. Its name is misleading as it feeds on krill.

in the Bay of Biscay. One colony has settled down in the estuary of the Somme in northern France. On rare occasions it has been found in the Mediterranean, and the Pacific subspecies has been seen as far south as California.

Harbor Seals are very slow breathers and, though normally they stay below far more than a minute or so, they can remain submerged for very much longer. When they sleep, which they generally do in shallow water, they come up to breathe periodically, their movements being no doubt unconscious. When underwater, their nostrils and ears are closed.

In different circumstances the Common Seal barks or grunts. It is monogamous but is often found in large schools, particularly when resting

on sandbanks. Pups are born on lonely beaches and rocks in May or June away from predators and enemies. They are born with the adult coat instead of the usual fluffy pupcoat or lanugo.

The Ringed Seal (*Pusa hispida*) is dark grey, paler below, with whitish rings. It is more or less confined to Arctic waters, rarely coming into North Sea. Those commonly found in the Gulf of Bothnia should be regarded as a relict fauna of a time when the species had a wider range. Still more so should those inland species and subspecies, the Saimaa Seal (*P. h. saimensis*) of Lake Saimaa in Finland, Caspian Seal (*P. caspica*), Baikal Seal (*P. sibirica*) and Ladoga Seal (*P. h. ladogensis*) whose ancestors lived in those lakes when they were connected with the open sea.

The Greenland or Harp Seal (*P. groenlandica*) is a handsome animal with a black and white coat, living on drift ice in the Arctic and coming down to Norway and Newfoundland in the winter. It is rarely seen off British coasts. Greenland seals move about in large numbers and undertake regular migrations to the same spots. Sometimes several thousand congregate together, as in the mating and pupping seasons. These are polygamous.

The Grey or Atlantic Seal (*Halichoerus grypus*) reaches up to three metres in length. It is grey and spotted, the underside being paler. Grey seals are most frequently seen around the Scilly Isles, on the Pembrokeshire coast, and off the coast of Scotland from the Clyde to the Orkneys and Shetlands. There is also a colony on the Faroe Islands. The northern British Isles contain two-thirds of the known population. They are said to do much harm to fisheries, but this is doubtful.

The Monk Seal (*Monachus monachus*) is a plain grey above and white below. It has thirty-two teeth instead of thirty-four, and the nails are reduced to rudiments. Males may be over 245 centimetres long. The Monk Seal is found in the Black Sea, the Mediterranean, particularly in the Adriatic and round the Greek islands, and in the Atlantic near Madeira and the Canaries. The West Indian Monk Seal (*M. tropicalis*), formerly abundant but now rare, and the Pacific Monk Seal (*M. schauinslandi*), living in tropical parts of the Pacific, are closely related, but are sometimes regarded as separate species and possibly extinct. Little is known of the habits of the Monk Seals.

Closely related to the Monk Seals are: the Crabeater Seal (*Lobodon carcinophagus*), a small Antarctic seal up to 260 centimetres in length; a smaller one, the Ross Seal (*Ommatophoca rossi*), and the Weddell Seal (*Leptonychotes weddelli*), up to 300 centimetres long, and the Leopard Seal (*Hydrurga leptonyx*), which is the largest Antarctic seal except for the Elephant Seal. The female is longer and may reach 365 centimetres.

The Hooded Seal (*Cystophora cristata*) males can inflate their nostrils to form a hood or crest. This is a secondary sexual character, apparently serving no useful purpose, since the hood, being soft, cannot be used as a weapon in the violent combats between rivals. The males are over 245 centimetres long and the females almost sixty centimetres shorter. They inhabit the Arctic waters and drift ice from Spitsbergen to Canada, but are also seen occasionally off the coasts of Britain and

France on the eastern side of the Atlantic and New England on the other.

In the elephant seals (*Mirounga leonina* and *M. angustirostra*), adult bulls have a pendulous nose which can be inflated to form a proboscis fifty centimetres long. This also is a secondary sexual character. Old bulls also have a bony crest rising between the muscles on the top of the skull, making the latter extraordinarily strong.

Elephant seals are at least twice the size of other seals, and they are the largest of all pinnipeds. Bulls may reach 610 centimetres and more, cows 365 centimetres, and weights vary from two to three tonnes. A single large specimen can furnish a tonne of oil from the thick layer of blubber which envelops it, and which shows in the rolls of fat round the neck. The skin is a blackish grey and the teeth are reduced to thirty, with only two incisors in the lower jaw.

In September the cows arrive on the coast at the end of their eleven-month period of gestation. They form in tight groups on the beaches and wait. Soon each gives birth to a single calf, which is nearly 120 centimetres in length though very thin. The calf barks and digs its nose into its mother's flank, looking for one of the four abdominal teats. The adult males arrive at the beaches.

In October the bulls fight for the possession of the cows. The contestants meet head on, seeking to bite each other's heads and necks with their upper canines; wounds are rarely fatal. The most vigorous bulls acquire the largest 'harems', for polygamy is the rule. Then the 'rookeries' of virgin cows arrive and join existing 'harems'. The calves, which are still with their mothers, have grown to nearly 150 centimetres and increased in weight. They shed their original black woolly coats and acquire sleek ones of pale grey.

Coupling goes on continually throughout November. With his teeth the bull seizes the cow by the neck and clasps her with his flippers. Coitus lasts a quarter of an hour and may be repeated several times. After two months of lactation, the calves leave their mothers and make off, gathering in a quiet spot where they play and learn to swim.

After living on their reserves of fat for a month the adults put to sea for refreshment. The calves, too, begin to hunt for squid, but return daily to sleep on shore. From January to February the cows return to the beaches to shed their coats, followed by the bulls. The calves show no change, except that they grow bigger. The shedding of coats, which lasts about six weeks, is painful, strips of skin coming away with the hairs. The animals isolate themselves as much as they can and rub against the ground to get relief by scratching. Between May and July the elephant seals put to sea, joining the great migration in search of cephalopods, which are their principal source of food. Sexual maturity is reached at the age of two, but no bull under the age of five has a chance of forming a harem.

In the eighteenth century Southern Elephant Seals (*M. leonina*) were swarming in the Antarctic, around Cape Horn, the South Shetlands and South Georgia, and round to the Kerguelen Islands and the Macquarie Islands on the other side of the Pole. The uncontrolled hunting of the nineteenth century so nearly exterminated the species that few were left in recent times. Only the complete cessation of sealing has enabled the elephant seals to become numerous again in many areas, and exploitation is now under strict control.

A closely allied species, the Elephant Seal (*Mirounga angustirostris*), is found along the Pacific coasts of California and Mexico.

Eared seals (Family Otariidae)

As the name indicates, eared seals differ from the true seals in the possession of obvious external ears, but there are other differences: their necks are longer and more clearly marked; their palms and soles are naked: their fore limbs are long and supple and, with hind limbs which can move away from the tail, they are capable of what may be

A male Northern Elephant Seal (*Mirounga angustirostris*) seen in threat display with his grotesque inflated proboscis. This is an enlargement of the nose and when fully developed overhangs the mouth. It may also act as a resonating chamber.

The Californian Sea-lion (*Zalophus californianus*) lives along the Californian coasts and offshore islands, on the Galapagos Islands and off the coast of Japan. Both males and females are a dark chocolate brown and the older bulls have very high foreheads caused by the development of a very high sagittal crest on the skull.

The Northern, Pribilof or Alaskan Fur Seal (*Callorhinus ursinus*) is the best known of the fur seals. Although its breeding is restricted to the far north it migrates southward in winter, the Pribilof seals going down the Canadian and American coasts and returning in April. The adult males establish their harems on the same breeding beaches year after year.

The Walrus (*Odobenus rosmarus*) lives in family herds of cows, calves and young bulls of up to a hundred individuals. Except in the breeding season the adult bulls form separate male herds. Walruses have now changed from frequenting coastal beaches to hauling out on ice-floes owing to persecution by man.

called quadrupedal locomotion. They always have thirty-four teeth.

Eared seals are divided into two groups; sea-lions and fur seals, sometimes called sea bears. The first have a coarse coat of nothing but hairs, the second have a thick dense underfur beneath the guard hairs.

The Southern Sea-lion (*Otaria byronia*) frequents the Galapagos Islands, ranging down the coast of Peru and Chile and up that of Patagonia as far as the River Plate. The males are over two metres long and have a mane. The females are smaller.

The Californian Sea-lion (*Zalophus californianus*) is slightly larger and the males have no mane. A distinctive character is the way the forehead rises sharply from the nose, like the profile of the Flying Lemur or the 'stop' of certain breeds of dog. This is the most abundant species today and the one most commonly seen in zoos. Its coat is dark brown and it has a shrill bark.

Steller's Sea-lion (*Eumetopias jubatus*) is considerably larger, the males being up to four metres in

length and 585 kilograms in weight. They are much darker than the females and have no manes. Unlike other eared seals they move on land with difficulty, due to their great weight. The animal is found all along the Pacific coast from San Francisco to Hokkaido, but was much reduced in numbers by the hunting of the nineteenth century. It was discovered in the eighteenth century on the Pribilof Islands by Bering, and described by Steller.

Two species of minor importance are the Australian Sea-lion (*Neophoca cinerea*) of Australia, and the New Zealand Sea-lion (*N. hookeri*) of the Auckland, Campbell and Snares Islands.

The fur seals, which are not true seals, are of modest size. The bulls are up to two metres long, with a weight of up to 276 kilograms, and the cows are under 1.5 metres and weigh sixty-two kilograms. Males and females have a darkish grey coat, which consists of coarse guard hairs and a thick underfur.

There are several species of fur seal, one in the north and the others in the south. The Alaska Fur Seal (*Callorhinus ursinus*) has, with those on the Japanese seal islands, a similar range to that of Steller's Sea-lion, being most numerous betwen Alaska and Kamchatka, and having its rookeries on the fog-bound Pribilof Islands, where the present seal population is estimated at between two and three millions. Under a carefully controlled system of exploitation about 80 per cent of the three-and four-year-old non-breeding males may be killed each year after being driven to the appointed killing beaches. The removal of this proportion annually has no effect on the total population, as there are always enough adult breeding bulls to mate with the available cows.

The Southern Fur Seal (*Arctocephalus australis*), greatly reduced in numbers and strictly protected, is found only in the Falkland Islands and round the neighbouring coast of South America. Allied species are the Cape Fur Seal (*A. pusillus*), the New Zealand Fur Seal (*A. forsteri*), and the Fur Seal (*A. philippii*), the Australian Fur Seal (*A. doriferus*), the Kerguelen Fur Seal (*A. gazella*) and the Gough Fur Seal (*A. tropicalis*).

The northern and southern species have much the same habits, allowing for a shift in the timetable owing to the difference in the seasons. Their stay on land is shorter and less complete than that of the sea elephants, lasting only a few months and being frequently interrupted by a return to the sea for hunting. Even the nursing mothers put to sea in their search for food.

Each year in May the waters of the Bering Sea surrounding the island of St Paul, one of the Pribilof Islands, suddenly seethe with life, as the fur seals shoot through the waters to the east coast of this island. Here the first seals always land, finding their way there from all parts of the North Pacific as if guided by a compass. They waddle up the shore, snort, shake themselves, and settle down to rest. They have been at sea for nine months and the first to arrive are the males, their sleek heads rising 1.5 metres above the sand. Fierce fights flare up between these bulky bulls, as each tries to stake a claim to a convenient piece of the beach. They heave against each other like wrestlers, panting and biting, and chase each other over the slippery

rocks. As more seals arrive the fights get worse and their roaring is sometimes so loud that it can be heard above the thunder of the waves.

By the end of May the whole island is divided as if by a fine network of invisible boundaries. The old bulls with their scarred bodies are spaced at regular intervals, each guarding his territory. They look harmless enough, lying with their heads thrown back and noses in the air, but each has half an eye on his neighbours. They lie like this for days, waiting for the females.

In June the females arrive, later than the bulls because they go farther south during the winter, often as far as Santa Barbara on the coast of California. Each of the old bulls gathers round him as big a herd of females as he can. Battles break out repeatedly as the bulls defend their territories from intruding neighbours, and especially when one of the young unmated bulls ventures near the boundary of one of the harems.

Whereas young sea elephants leave their mothes at the age of two months, young fur seals, like all the eared seals, need maternal care for a longer period. They are suckled for three months and their mothers leave them at intervals to feed at sea. The mothers leave them at about four months to begin their southward migration, and many of the young do not survive their first year.

Walruses (Family Odobenidae)

Walruses resemble true seals in having no external ears. Like eared seals they have a distinct neck, naked palms and soles, and hind limbs which can be used for walking on land. They differ from both in having only eighteen teeth. In both sexes these include upper canines developed into downward-pointing tusks sometimes as long as sixty-eight centimetres.

Walruses average 320 centimetres with a maximum of 490 centimetres, and weigh up to 1,350 kilograms. The cows reach 245 centimetres in length and weigh up to one tonne. In the young the fur is yellowish-brown, but this gets paler and later disappears. Bulls are invariably scarred from their fights in the mating season. Gestation lasts eleven months, at the end of which one calf is born.

The cry of the Walrus may be described as barking, lowing or neighing, according to the circumstances. Its diet is mainly molluscs, with some fishes.

The Atlantic Walrus (*Odobenus rosmarus*) is found in Arctic waters from the Kara Sea westwards as far as Labrador and Hudson Bay. The Pacific Walrus (*O. divergens*) has longer and slightly divergent tusks and inhabits the Bering Sea and neighbouring waters. Many consider these to be one species.

Aardvark (Order Tubulidentata)

Formerly classed with the edentates, the Aardvark is now placed in a separate order with only one family (*Orycteropidae*), which consists of the species *Orycteropus afer*. They have many characteristics that place them above the edentates: they are digitigrade instead of plantigrade, they have permanent teeth preceded by milk teeth and, like the Carnivora, a zonary placenta. The name of the order, Tubulidentata, refers to their molars, the only teeth they possess, which are made up of tiny

tubes radiating from a common centre. The teeth themselves are rootless and without enamel, and are presumed to be primitive.

The name Aardvark is Afrikaans for 'earth-pig'. The Aardvark resmbles a pig, being about the same size and having pig-like bristles, but its ears are donkey-like, its elongated muzzle ends in wide nostrils and its tail is long and heavy. It lives on termites and the long claws, which are used in opening up termite hills, indicate a burrowing habit; the generic name *Orycteropus* means 'burrowing foot'. Like the pangolins and anteaters with which it was formerly classified the Aardvark

The Aardvark (*Orycteropus afer*) is a large African burrowing animal, ranging from Ethiopia to South Africa. With its powerful limbs and sharp claws it excavates long burrows into which it retreats when danger threatens.

The Asiatic or Indian Elephant (*Elephas maximus*) is smaller than the African with relatively small ears and a domed forehead. Little is known of this elephant in the wild but it has been semi-domesticated in Asia for centuries.

The African Elephant (*Loxodonta africana*) is larger than the Indian species. Elephants were formerly abundant throughout Africa, even in the area now covered by the Sahara desert and elephants from North Africa were used by Hannibal to cross the Alps. They are now absent from North Africa and from most of South Africa. In the rest of the continent they have a discontinuous distribution and their numbers are dwindling with expanding human populations.

has a narrow, elongated mouth with a viscous vermiform tongue. It affords a good example of convergence in structure of animals of similar diet or method of locomotion.

Elephants (Order Proboscidea)

Elephants have five digits on each foot, which means they have retained the pentadactyl limbs of the ancestral mammals. They are themselves ancestral types in many ways, in spite of the adaptation of their nostrils and upper lips to form a proboscis and the peculiar characters of their teeth.

Size and weight are the most striking characteristics of elephants. The largest of them from tropical Africa reaches an average height of 320 centimetres to the shoulders in the male, and 280 centimetres in the female. These heights may be exceeded, although it is seldom more than 335 centimetres and reports of 365 centimetres must be treated with reserve. One adult bull in the United States National Museum is the only known specimen 365 centimetres at the shoulders. The Indian Elephant is smaller, with an average of 275 centimetres for the bulls and 215 centimetres for the cows, and occasionally a bull reaching 305 centimetres. An African male elephant estimated to be thirty years of age weighed nearly 4·5 tonnes, and one about sixty years of age was discovered to weigh nearly six tonnes.

The Indian Elephant rarely lives for more than seventy years and the African Elephant for fifty years. The age can be judged approximately from the rims of the ears and the wear of the teeth.

In spite of its thickness and hardness an elephant's skin is very sensitive to insect bites and readily chaps under exposure to the sun. Wild elephants therefore bathe frequently, afterwards rolling in the mud. In captivity their skins have to be greased. Hair grows very scantily, except in the tuft at the end of the tail.

The trunk, which is an elongated nose, is prehensile and highly sensitive. The network of muscles composing it gives it great flexibility and strength. With its trunk an elephant can carry a tree or take a lump of sugar. The elephant uses it to touch and smell, carry food and water to its mouth, give itself a shower-bath and powder itself with sand. It is a multi-purpose organ and an elephant can be trained to use it to bolt and unbolt doors or untie ropes. For the more delicate actions the extremity is used. The African Elephant has at the tip of its trunk an upper and lower triangular projection which can be used for gripping, whereas the Indian Elephant has only one.

The upper incisors or tusks extend on either side of the trunk. They grow to a great length, particularly in the males. They may be straight or curved upwards and enamel is only present at the tip and is soon worn away. The right-hand tusk is generally more worn than the left as it is used more, the elephant being predominantly 'right-handed'.

The heaviest tusk known is one in the British Museum, which is 312 centimetres in length, measured along the outer curve, and weighs 102 kilograms. At the beginning of this century it was not unusual to find tusks weighing sixty-five kilograms. Since then the average has dropped, owing to the activities of ivory hunters, and tusks taken today in Equatorial Africa rarely exceed sixteen kilograms. The tusks of the Indian Elephant are smaller and now average four to ten kilograms. Elephants with only one tusk are sometimes found, this being the result of an accident. More rarely animals may be found with three or even four tusks, the result of damage to the growing tooth germ when young.

Elephants have neither lower incisors nor canines. The molars are enormous and are subject to a curious system of replacement. There are six molars in each half of both upper and lower jaws, but only one functions at a time. Pushing out the stump of its predecessor, each in turn will be pushed out by the one to follow. Each molar seems to be formed of many tall plates stuck together, but it is a single large tooth deeply ridged. Being covered with cement, the tooth appears smooth and uniform when it breaks through the gum. As it wears, however, the crest of each ridge appears, divided by cement (lophodont tooth). Then this splits to become an enamel frame, and finally we see a series of lines of dentine surrounded by enamel, each separated from the next by a layer of enamel, so that the lophodont tooth has become selenodont, showing a 'table' as in the horse. The enamel folds are parallel in the Indian Elephant and lozenge-shaped in the African. The number varies with the species and the particular tooth in question.

The weight of the tusks and molars is so considerable that the skull is lightened in compensation. Each bone is hollow, having a huge sinus which communicates with the neighbouring one and thus eventually with the nasal fossae. In spite of a large head, the elephant has a relatively small brain. However, it is highly convoluted, and this may account for the remarkable memory and intelligence with which the animal has been credited.

The size of the external ear, particularly in the African Elephant, is not connected with hearing only. When the animal charges it fans out its ears, augmenting its terrible aspect; and it also uses them for chasing away flies. They also present a large surface area for losing body-heat, and elephants wave their ears to keep cool. The eyes are tiny for an animal of that size, but they are quick and alert. As they are placed so far on the side of the head it is unlikely that they are capable of binocular vision.

The enormous weight of the animals is carried by massive columnar legs. The feet may be forty-five centimetres across in the largest specimens. The sole of the foot is formed of soft and elastic horny layers, which account for the animal's soft and silent tread. The nails are on the front of the foot, there being four or five on the fore feet and three or four on the hind feet.

The elephant walks with an ambling gait. The two right feet move forward together, then the two left. In this it is like the camel, the bear and the giraffe. With dogs and horses, on the other hand, the right fore foot goes forward with the left hind foot, and vice versa.

Elephants can make good speed over a short distance with a fast amble, and they are very much at their ease in the water. Amongst other anatomical characteristics which may be mentioned are the simple stomach, internal testes, penis retracted in a sheath, bicorned uterus and zonary placenta.

The African Elephant (*Loxodonta africana*), the biggest and noblest of land animals, can reach a height of 335 centimetres and a weight of nearly six tonnes. It can be recognised by its arched forehead, large ears and two triangular appendices or 'lips' on the end of the trunk. The molars have lozenge-shaped enamel folds. African elephants are now confined well within the tropics and are rarely seen beyond seventeen degrees of latitude in either hemisphere. Elephants inhabit both forest and savanna. In times past, the elephant was found throughout Africa. The species is now restricted in range, but efforts are being made to prevent its extinction by reserving suitable habitats in national parks.

The Indian or Asian Elephant (*Elephas maximus*) is markedly smaller than the African, its height never much exceeding 305 centimetres. It can be recognised by its concave forehead and knobbly head, small ears, single appendix or 'lip' at the end of the trunk, and the parallel enamel folds of the molars. In the wild state it inhabits India, Sri Lanka, Assam, Burma, Thailand, Kampuchea, Laos, Vietnam, the Malay peninsular, Sumatra and Borneo.

Elephants live in family units of an old female, her eldest daughter and their youngsters. Bulls live apart either in separate herds, or solitarily. Large herds of over 100 sometimes gather temporarily. A female giving birth is accompanied by other females and they stay with her until the newborn young is capable of following its mother. In effect, these females act as midwives. If an elephant falls into a trap, its companions have been known to do all in their power to release it. If one is wounded one or more of its companions, or even the whole herd, may attempt rescue.

Elephants eat a great deal and have constantly to be moving off in search of new pastures. The forest does not always offer them sufficient food. They take refuge among trees during the heat of the day, then come out into the tall grasses for a richer harvest of elephant grass. They like the marshes. Migration usually takes place in the rainy season when they are relatively safe and they travel long distances in search of new feeding grounds.

Elephants travel at a walk in single file. An experienced female leads; the males come in the rear, following far behind. Trunks hang listlessly, or gather a few leaves in passing; ears flap, driving away flies. Only when alarmed do elephants move more quickly. In the forest the track they make is often the only track available to man. It is, of course, strewn with broken branches, barkless tree trunks, and endless droppings in which can be seen undigested food remains.

In their relations with man, elephants are dominated by fear. A herd may be spontaneously aggressive, and a rogue will attack without the least pretext. As a rule, however, elephants flee as soon as they scent man, and they do so at a quickened stride which soon takes them out of reach. When wounded or cornered the elephant really becomes dangerous.

Sexual maturity is reached by the age of fifteen

The Rock Hyrax or Dassie (*Procavia capensis*) is a small, herbivorous mammal found throughout most of Africa as well as in Syria and southern Arabia. Dassies live in colonies on rocky cliffs or among boulders on hilltops. They spend much of the day basking in the sun but are ready at the slightest alarm to bolt for cover.

years in bulls, but cows are capable of breeding at seven years. Coupling is probably nocturnal in the wild state and is accomplished without any signs of excitment. Heat is only betrayed by a certain note of trumpeting and by the fact that the sexes seek each other. After a few caresses with the trunk, the male mounts the female. Elephants breed readily in captivity.

The length of the gestation period is twenty to twenty-six months, and there is only one calf at birth, rarely twins. A female can give birth at intervals of four or more years for the rest of her life, which means that a female Indian Elephant living the full life span can bring nearly fifteen elephants into the world.

Birth is generally quick and with very little pain, in spite of the size of the foetus. A newborn elephant can be a metre tall and weigh ninety kilograms. Dropped on to soft damp ground or a bed of leaves, it lies for a few hours before standing up. The skin is pinkish, hairy and in folds. After two days it can walk. Lactation lasts for four to six years and continues for months after the young has begun to eat grass. Elephant milk is very sweet and rich in cream. Growth appears to be rapid. One elephant weighed 290 kilograms at the age of fifteen months and was 110 centimetres tall. Two years later it weighed 725 kilograms and measured 160 centimetres. Elephants grow after reaching the adult state.

Hyraxes (Order Hyracoidea)

Hyraxes are about the size of a marmot and like the latter have incisors which slope forward. Their hooves differ only in size from those of a rhinoceros. They have five toes on the fore feet and three on the hind feet. They were formerly classified as ungulates, their fossil ancestors showing relationship with tapirs, rhinoceroses and even elephants. There is only one family, Procaviidae.

Hyraxes are found in Africa, Arabia and Syria, living in large colonies, much like rabbits. Members of the genius *Procavia* (rock hyraxes) are adapted to rocky habitats, those of *Dendrohyrax* (tree hyraxes) to life in the trees. Tree hyraxes can climb easily owing to the furrowed cushions under their feet. They have incisors like rodents and live on grass, buds, seeds and fruit. They are very

prolific, with several young in each litter. The females have two to six teats according to species.

Sea-cows (Order Sirenia)

At one time cosmopolitan in distribution, sea-cows are now confined to tropical coastal waters and estuaries. There are two families, represented by the manatees (Trichechidae) of the Atlantic and Caribbean, and the dugongs (Dugongidae) of the Indian Ocean. Steller's Sea-cows (*Hydrodamalis stelleri*), a dugong, was at one time plentiful in the extreme north of the Pacific, but was exterminated by the end of the eighteenth century.

The Sirenia are almost as completely aquatic as the Cetaea and these two orders have many characters in common. Both are fishlike in shape and both have a practically hairless body. The fore limbs are converted into flippers and hind limbs are represented only by a vestigial pelvis. Tail flukes are horizontal, unlike a fish's tail. Sea-cows have small eyes covered by a nictitating membrane. There are no external ears and the nostrils can be completely closed by sphincters. The head is grotesque and the snout has huge mobile lips fringed with bristles. Dentition is incomplete, there being no canines, and it shows varying degrees of degeneration. Testicles are internal and females have a bicorned uterus and diffuse placenta. Gestation lasts a year and one calf is born at a time.

Being herbivorous, sea-cows keep to the coast or to estuaries, in which they swim a considerable way upstream, grazing on aquatic vegetation. They have long intestines and very developed caecum. They are reputed to be both harmless and stupid. At the present time schools are becoming smaller, less frequent and increasingly restricted in range.

Manatees are less completely adapted to an aquatic life. They still have scattered hairs on their bodies and nails at the tips of their flippers, and the latter have retained enough suppleness to play a part in the gathering of food. Their tails are rounded and not notched as in dugongs. Both canines and incisors are lacking. The latter remain rudimentary, buried below the horny covering of the gums and molars appear successively, replacing each other as in elephants.

Manatees vary in length from two to four metres and in weight from 270 to 900 kilograms; the Florida Manatee (*Trichechus manatus*) reaches four metres and weighs 900 kilograms. It is slate-grey in colour. This species, also known as the Lamantin, was formerly widespread along the coasts of the Gulf of Mexico and the West Indies. The Amazonian Manatee (*T. inunguis*) is found from Venezuela to northern Brazil and has entered the Amazon and the Orinoco. Although it has not yet disappeared, it has become much rarer and schools are more thinly scattered. The West African Manatee (*T. senegalensis*) has also become greatly reduced and is nearly extinct. It is only found along the west coast between 16°N. and 10°S. and in the estuaries of the Senegal, Niger and Congo.

Dugongs differ from the manatees in being more like cetaceans. Their bodies are completely naked and their flippers lack nails. They are used only in swimming. The tails are notched at the centre. Dugongs have two upper incisors, developing in the male into tusks about 25 centimetres long. The molars are few and show various signs of degeneration, such as the absence of enamel and no demarcation between root and crown.

The Dugong (*Dugong dugon*) frequents the shores of the Indian Ocean. It reaches a length of 365 centimetres and a weight of 675 kilograms. Mating has been observed in February and March in fairly shallow water, the female lying on her back. Gestation takes one year. The Red Sea and Australian dugongs are now regarded as the same species as the Indian Ocean Dugong. Like the manatees, dugongs are greatly reduced in numbers. They have completely disappeared from Mauritius and the coasts of Madagascar.

Steller's Sea-cow (*Hydrodamalis stelleri*) was abundant in the Bering Sea and off Kamchatka and the Aleutian Islands when it was discovered in 1741. All that is known of it comes from Steller's description and from various museum skeletons for it is now probably extinct. It was very like a dugong, but had a horny plating over the gums and palate instead of teeth and was also considerably larger, reaching a length of six metres. Its skin was peculiarly rough and crinkled.

Odd-toed ungulates
(Order Perissodactyla)

The Perissodactyla or odd-toed ungulates include all the ungulates with three toes (if only on the hind feet as in tapirs) or a single one. They are the tapirs and rhinoceroses, horses, asses and zebras, in which the pentadactyl foot has become either tetradactyl, tridactyl or monodactyl.

The teeth of Perissodactyla have either projecting ridges or crushing surfaces; that is, they are either lophodont or selenodont. In tapirs and horses dentition is complete, but in adult rhinoceroses canines and often incisors are lacking. Here are the dental formulae:

Tapir, Horse I. $\frac{3}{3}$ C. $\frac{1}{1}$ Pm. $\frac{3}{3}$ M. $\frac{3}{3}$ Total 40

Rhinoceros (Asiatic) I. $\frac{2}{2}$ C. $\frac{0}{0}$ Pm. $\frac{4}{4}$ M. $\frac{3}{3}$ Total 36

Rhinoceros (African) I. $\frac{0}{0}$ C. $\frac{0}{0}$ Pm. $\frac{4}{4}$ M. $\frac{3}{3}$ Total 28

Horses, asses, zebras (Family Equidae)

All of these are monodactyl, the functional digit being the middle one. The second and fourth digits still exist, though only in vestigial form as thin, tapering splint bones, situated close to the upper end of the metacarpus or metatarsus of the third digit. These vestiges are of great anatomical importance, since they afford proof of descent from an earlier type with three digits. These splint bones sometimes bear phalanges, and even tiny hooves. Bucephalus, charger of Alexander the Great, was tridactyl or three-toed, recalling the

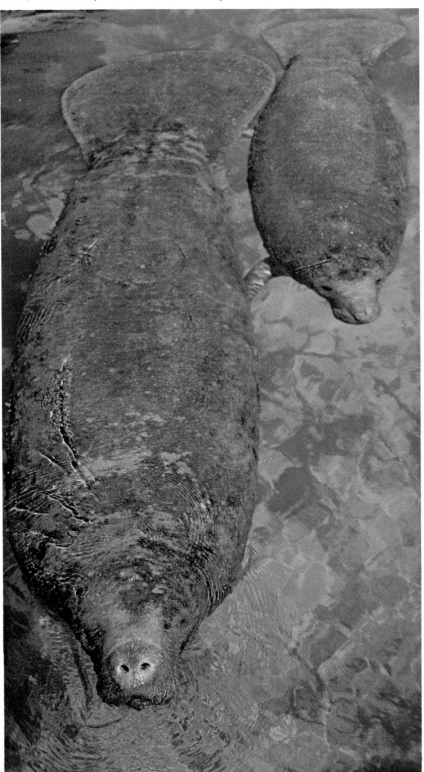

A female Manatee (*Trichechus manatus*) pictured with her calf. This species of manatee lives in the coastal, estuarine and river waters of the Caribbean. Like all sea-cows it is completely aquatic, even breeding in the water. It feeds not only on aquatic vegetation but will also reach up for soft plants growing along the banks.

Przewalski's Horse (*Equus przewalski przewalski*) used to inhabit the steppes and semideserts of southern Siberia, Mongolia and western China. It is probably now extinct in the wild although occasional sightings are reported in the Gobi desert.

A female African Wild Ass (*Equus asinus*) shown here with her foal. All wild asses live in steppe country, semi-desert or desert, but they need to drink every few days so depend on surface water. They are thought to live in family herds led by a stallion.

immediate ancestor of the horse, the late Cainozoic and early Quaternary *Pliohippus*.

The different parts of a horse's limbs must be clearly understood. The upper parts of a horse's limbs, down to the elbow or the knee, are enclosed within the outline of the body, their joints being revealed only to the touch. The visible parts of the legs begin with what correspond to our forearms and shins. Thus, what is commonly called the knee in a horse is really the wrist and the equivalent posterior joint, the hock, is really an ankle. The next bone, the cannon bone, corresponds to the metacarpus or metatarsus. The pastern joint is between the foot and the toe, and the pastern is composed of the first two phalanges. The last of the phalanges is incorporated into the hoof, which consists of a wall and a sole, the latter being divided on the posterior side to make room for the frog.

The horse's teeth are of the greatest interest. Along the front of both jaws is a row of six cutting incisors called the middles, intermediates and corners. Between these and the premolars is a space (diastema) where the bit is placed. Stallions have rudimentary canines or tushes next to the incisors. The side of the jaw contains a row of three premolars and three molars, bringing the total number of teeth up to forty in stallions and thirty-six in mares. Both the incisors and molars are long permanently growing teeth ending in a table with a characteristic pattern of enamel folds. The following is the state of the incisors at different ages:

Eruption of milk teeth	middles	8 days
	intermediates	5 weeks
	corners	6 months
Disappearance of cusps	middles	1 year
	intermediates	15 months
	corners	2 years
Eruption of permanent teeth	middles	2½ years
	intermediates	3½ years
	corners	4½ years
Disappearance of cusps	middles	6 years
	intermediates	7 years
	corners	8 years

These two principal characters mark horses, asses and zebras as an independent family, but there are others which help to identitify them. All parts of their bodies are harmoniously proportioned: they have neat feet, powerful hind quarters, a long but not exaggerated neck, somewhat triangular head and soft, tender muzzle. The eyes are high in the head and the ears, whether long or short, are always pricked and alert. When the ears are erect this indicates calm, ears straining forward denote fear and ears flattened back anger.

The coat may be uniform or striped. Wild horses and asses generally have a uniform colour which blends with the natural steppes and desert.

Asses are sometimes slightly striped on the leg and have a transverse stripe across the shoulders.

The mode of life does not differ greatly from one species of Equidae to another. The animals live in herds led by an old stallion, which warns them of danger. Their days are passed in grazing or migrating to new pastures. In the rutting season the stallions fight, using the teeth as well as hooves. Mares do not breed every year and never give birth to more than one foal at a time. Gestation lasts from eleven to thirteen months. Mares have two inguinal teats, and their milk is as rich in lactose as human milk. All species of the Equidae are capable of cross-breeding, the resultant hybrids being loosely called mules, although a mule is strictly the offspring of a mare and male ass. Authorities now place all species in the genus *Equus*.

The Wild Horse (*Equus caballus*) is now represented by only one race, the Mongolian Wild Horse or Przewalski's Horse (*E. c. przewalskii*). It is unquestionably a horse, as is proved by its short ears, round hooves, horny warts or 'chestnuts' on the inside of each leg and tail hairs growing the whole of its length. It is not a tall horse, being only 137 centimetres at the withers. It is isabelline in colour with a more or less black mane and tail.

Formerly found in Mongolia and Sinkiang, with a small herd along the Tahkin Shara–Nurce range, the Mongolian Wild Horse should not be confused with the Tarpan which formerly inhabited southern Russia and eastern Europe, and became extinct about two hundred years ago.

The African Wild Ass (*E. asinus*) differs from the Wild Horse by its long ears, shorter upright mane and narrow hooves. The tail has only a tuft of hair and there are no 'chestnuts' on the hind legs. The Ass brays instead of neighing and is less graceful than a horse. Divided into two races, the Nubian and the Somali, wild asses are found only between the Sudan and Somalia. The wild asses of the Sahara appear to be feral stragglers that have taken to the bush.

There are also some semi-asinine types usually classed as asses. The Syrian Wild Ass (*E. hemionus hemippus*) is now very scarce, if not actually extinct. The Onager (*E. h. onager*) of Persia and India is not uncommon in certain areas. In addition there are the Kulan or Chigetai (*E. h. hemionus*) of Transcaspia and Mongolia, and the Kiang (*E. h. kiang*) of Tibet and Sikkim. All these are more or less dun-coloured and vary in height from 120 to 130 centimetres at the withers. After the zebras they are the most abundant of wild Equidae. Several are mountain types. The Kiang wanders at heights of of 3,900 to 5,400 metres and its dung is gathered for fuel.

Zebras were used by the Romans in circuses and were called horse-tigers (*Hippotigris*) because of their stripes. The name is still used as an alternative to the generic name of *Equus*. In many ways they are closer to asses than horses, having long ears, short stiff manes, tufted tails and 'chestnuts'

Grevy's Zebra (*Equus grevyi*) is the largest of all wild equids standing up to 150 centimetres at the shoulder. The social organization of this species is completely different from that of other zebras as the stallions are territorial. All zebras rely on their keen eyesight and sense of smell to avoid danger, but if attacked they defend themselves vigorously with their hooves and teeth. Their chief enemy is the Lion.

The Damara Zebra (*Equus burchelli antiquorum*), a subspecies of the Plains or Common Zebra lives in southwest Africa, Botswana and Zululand. The leg stripes in this subspecies are much reduced and are often completely absent. The stripe pattern of the body is often irregular.

In the Camargue, subtropical delta land in southern France, live many semi-wild horses grazing not only on the grasslands but also feeding on aquatic plants in the half-flooded meadows. They roam freely in great herds.

confined to the front legs. Like *Equus asinus* they are native to Africa.

The Mountain Zebra (*E. zebra*) formerly inhabited the mountainous areas of South Africa. It has been greatly reduced by hunting and now exists only in small numbers in reserves. It is striped all over except under the body and inside the legs, and is easily recognised by the stripes on the crupper which have a very distinctive grid-iron pattern.

Grévy's Zebra (*E. grevyi*) has narrow black stripes close together, and a white crupper. It is the largest of the zebras, up to 153 centimetres at the withers. Its habitat is Ethiopia, Somalia and northern Kenya.

The Common Zebra or Burchell's Zebra (*E. burchelli*) is distributed between Ethiopia and the Orange River. The pattern of stripes varies considerably even among individuals of the same herd, and numerous subspecies have been based on it. Today only three subspecies are recognised. Selous's Zebra, of the Zambezi Basin, from Victoria Falls, Zimbabwe, Mozambique, northwards to southern Malawi, has close-set stripes over the whole body and legs. Grant's Zebra, also known as Boehm's Zebra, found from Zambia to the Sudan and Ethiopia, has body and legs still completely and evenly striped, but with the stripes more widely spaced, and between the Zambezi and the Orange River in Chapman's Zebra the lower leg tends to be without markings. On the body some of the stripes have become shadow stripes between the others.

The reduction in the striping was taken to its extreme in the Quagga (*E. quagga quagga*) of the Cape, which had no stripes except on the head and neck. This race became extinct nearly a hundred years ago, although formerly numerous.

DOMESTIC HORSE: Attempts at domestication have at one time or another been made on all species of the Equidae, but it is above all the horses and the African Wild Ass, the ancestor of the domesticated donkey, that have proved the most successful. Some asses, particularly the Onager, have done excellent service both as pack animals and for riding.

The domestication of the horse does not seem to go back beyond the Bronze Age. The Aryan peoples introduced the Arab horses into Europe, and the English perfected the racing horse. Horses were brought to America in the fifteenth century.

SADDLE- AND RACEHORSES: The Arab is thought to be a native of the central Asiatic plateau from which it has spread out in all directions, but it is actually in Arabia that it is found in its purest state. In Turkey, Persia and the Caucasus pure-blood Arabs may also be found, but also half-breed horses of less value. The Barb, which is a similar horse, probably an offshoot of the same stock, was developed in North Africa and has played an important part in the ancestry of the English thoroughbred.

Breeding to obtain the fastest possible horse has produced an animal with elongated limbs, slender figure, a very well-developed chest and greatly reduced belly. Not only have the limbs been made longer, but the body has also been raised by the straightening of the humerus and the femur. From fourteen-and-a-quarter hands (145 centimetres) the horse had by the eighteenth century grown to fifteen-and-a-quarter hands and is now fifteen-and-three-quarter hands. Through this high degree of specialisation the thoroughbred has lost the elegance of line of its Arab ancestors, but the speed has been raised to 15.6 metres per second, though this cannot be maintained for long.

English thoroughbreds have been crossed with Anglo-Arabs to produce a horse much in demand for improving stock. Where endurance is required horses are nearly always half-bred, and the English hunter is one of the best saddle-horses in the world. In the American West the quarter-horses, being one quarter thoroughbred, are widely used on ranges.

The breeding of racehorses has been carried on for over two centuries in North America. Bull Rock, a son of the Darley Arabian, was imported in 1730 and since then a large number of thoroughbred stallions and mares have been introduced.

HARNESS BREEDS: The hackney is an old local breed from the eastern counties of England, much improved in the last century by the introduction of thoroughbred blood. It is a strong and heavy breed and was much used as a coach-horse. Other breeds of the same type are the Yorkshire coach, Hanoverian and Oldenburg. The light roadster type represented by the American Standard Breed has been bred primarily for speed. This American breed, improved by an admixture of thoroughbred blood, has been much stimulated by racing.

DRAUGHT HORSES: The most important heavy draught horses are the Shire, Clydesdale, Suffolk, Belgian and Percheron.

The Shire is a large horse of seventeen hands and is the commonest farm horse in England. It is descended from the knight-carrying horse, the English Great or Black Horse, which in turn was descended from stock improved by Flemish blood.

The Clydesdale is the same height as the Shire, but is less massive in build and not as strong. On the other hand, it has speed and agility. In the early eighteenth century it was known in Lanarkshire as a mixture of local stock and horses from England, some of Flemish breed.

The Suffolk is common in East Anglia but is less widely distributed than the Shire and Clydesdale. It is a good, hardy farm horse, standing sixteen-and-a-half hands, and is unsurpassed for the amount of work it can do on the minimum of food.

The Belgian is the direct descendant of the old Flemish heavy horse. Two races have contributed chiefly to the modern breed, the Ardennes and the Frisonne. It is an excellent breed for dray work.

The Percheron also contains Flemish blood, but with much improvement from Arab stock to make a medium-weight draught horse about the same size as the Suffolk. It is most commonly used in the United States and Argentina.

PONIES: The small size of ponies is due to the poor conditions of their habitat: the Mongolian and Manchurian deserts and Norwegian, Welsh or Scottish mountains. The breeding of ponies has declined in England since the mechanisation of coal mining. Generally found in mountains or heathlands, the chief breeds are: the Shetland, which is less than nine hands in height; the Highland, a sturdy breed; the Dales and Fell breeds, very sturdy and make excellent riding-ponies when crossed with small Arab and thoroughbred sires; the Welsh, a very old stock improved in the eighteenth century by the introduction of Arab and thoroughbred blood; the Welsh cob used for riding in Wales; the Dartmoor, Exmoor and New Forest, and so on. The hackney pony is closely related to the hackney, and the polo pony is related to the thoroughbred.

DONKEYS AND MULES: Donkeys originally came from Africa and they are particularly suited to a hot, dry climate. Their only relatives in the wild state are in Ethiopia and Somalia. From Egypt the domesticated animal spread through Asia Minor and Turkey into the Balkans before reaching the rest of Europe in the ninth century. The donkey reached the United States in 1868.

Donkeys are placid and hardy, which makes them more suitable than horses for some purposes. They are better as pack animals than for draught purposes. Although hardy, they are sensitive to cold.

Most donkeys are the result of so much crossing that it is impossible to define their race with any precision. Donkeys often show signs of stripes at the feet, a dark line down the back, and a cross line over the shoulders. These ancestral markings are much commoner in Egyptian donkeys, which are much nearer to the Wild Ass.

Strictly speaking, a mule is a cross between a he-ass and a mare. A cross between a she-ass and a stallion is called a hinny. As these animals do not cross naturally, recourse has to be made to artifices of ancient origin.

France and the United States are at the present day the greatest producers of mules. The mule is generally bigger than the hinny, as size is derived more easily from the larger female.

Tapirs (Family Tapiridae)

Tapirs have four toes on each fore foot and three on each hind foot, a short movable trunk and extremely simple lophodont molars.

The Brazilian Tapir (*Tapirus terrestris*) stands a metre at the shoulder and is two metres in length. It looks at first glance like an enormous pig. Its

The Brazilian Tapir (*Tapirus terrestris*) is the smallest tapir, weighing up to 180 kilograms. It lives in the tropical and subtropical forests of South America, from Colombia to Paraguay and northern Argentina. The young are striped and spotted and weigh only four kilograms at birth.

skin is without folds and its coat is short and thick—a woollen velvet as it has been rightly described. It is dark brown with a white fringe to its ear.

Strictly nocturnal, tapirs spend the day in the densest thickets, only coming out in the evening to bathe and forage in rivers and marshes. The crust of mud with which they are commonly coated is a protection against insect bites. They feed on a variety of leaves and fruits, doing damage to sugar plantations and destroying young cocoa trees.

Gentle, timid, peaceful and mistrustful of man, those are the dominant traits in their character. Normally solitary and silent, they grunt when disturbed and emit a piercing whistle in the rutting season. Then the males and females seek each other out and stay together for a few weeks, after which they separate again. The mother alone cares for and brings up her offspring, never more than one, which is born after thirteen months of gestation. At birth the coat is ornamented with rows of white spots which later disappear.

There are three other American species, similar in appearance and habits: the Mountain Tapir (*T. roulini*), of the Andes of Colombia, Ecuador and Peru, at 4,200 metres and Baird's Tapir (*T. bairdii*), of Mexico to Ecuador up to 1,800 metres.

The Malayan Tapir (*T. indicus*) is particularly common in Thailand and Sumatra. It differs from the American species in its parti-coloured coat, which is black with a sort of white blanket over the loins and rump. The young are marked like the young of South American tapirs.

Rhinoceroses (Family Rhinocerotidae)

The principal characters of rhinoceroses are the massive body and limbs, the very thick skin, which often suggests armour-plating, and, most striking of all, the horns (one or two) situated on the median line of the head. These horns are really an agglomerated mass of hairs solidly attached to a roughened patch of bone. The feet are tridactyl and have three hooves, the middle one being the most developed. The canines are lacking and, in the two African species, so are the incisors after a certain age. The molars are lophodont.

587

The Black or Hook-lipped Rhinoceros (*Diceros bicornis*) used to range all through East and South Africa but now exists mainly in national parks and reserves of East Africa with small numbers in bush country in the north and south. It is dark grey and can be recognised by its prehensile, hooked upper lip with which it draws leaves, twigs and herbage into its mouth.

Hearing and smell are the most developed senses of this animal, which for acuteness of smell comes second only to the elephant. Its sight is very poor. When it attacks a man—and it does so without provocation, being very aggressive—it is always directed by smell. The rhinoceros always walks with its nose turned into the wind and when alarmed its first charge is upwind.

The rhinoceroses have very small brains in proportion to their size and are far from being intelligent, but they are all the more dangerous on that account, being quite unpredictable.

The other African species is the White or Square-lipped Rhinoceros (*Diceros simus*), but this is a misnomer except when it is covered with dry mud, for its grey colour is no paler than that of the Black Rhinoceros. Its most marked features are its square upper lip and its flattened nose. The lower lip is horny, no doubt for gathering the siliceous grasses on which it feeds. It grazes in the same way as the Bovidae and, in contrast with the Black Rhinoceros, it is diurnal, peaceful and sociable, being generally found in small parties in thin woodland or grassy open spaces.

The White Rhinoceros is the largest terrestrial mammal after the elephant and giraffe, being five metres long, two metres tall, and weighing three to four tonnes. The anterior horn is the longest, usually ninety to 140 centimetres, the record being 157·5 centimetres.

Formerly common in South Africa, the White Rhinoceros has been so hunted that it is now reduced there to reserves in Zululand. Elsewhere it is only found in a part of Uganda and the Sudan west of the Nile, as far as the point where the territories of Sudan, the Central African Republic and Zaire meet. Even there it survives only because it is protected.

The Sumatran Rhinoceros (*Dicerorhinus sumatrensis*) is another two-horned rhinoceros and is found in eastern Asia. Smaller than the other species, it is only about 137 centimetres tall at the shoulder. It is also found in Burma, Sumatra, Borneo and the Malay peninsula. Its habitat is much the same as that of the Malayan Tapir.

The Indian Rhinoceros (*Rhinoceros unicornis*) is a single-horned species, which usually grows to about 426 centimetres in length and a height of nearly 180 centimetres. The length of the horn measures up to sixty centimetres. The nose has transverse grooves. The most remarkable feature of this, the largest rhinoceros of Asia, is the thickness of its skin, which has deep folds and is covered with granulations imitating scales. The colour of the skin, when it can be seen through the mud, is a uniform grey-brown. In behaviour it is much like the White Rhinoceros. Its habitat, constantly decreasing, is now confined to the plains of Assam, Nepal and Bhutan.

The commoner of the African species is the Black or Hook-lipped Rhinoceros (*Diceros bicornis*), which is found mainly in Angola, Rhodesia, north-western Transvaal, Kenya, Tanzania and Uganda. Its favourite habitat is round the great East African lakes. A few may also be found in Ethiopia and Somalia. In its natural state it is one of the most impressive of animals. It may be over 335 centimetres (excluding the tail), 170 centimetres at the shoulder and weigh over two tonnes. On its nose is an enormous horn with another, generally smaller, behind it. The larger averages about sixty centimetres long. Fifty years ago much longer horns were found, the record being 136 centimetres. The thick skin is more grey than black. It is not folded and is almost devoid of hair. The mobile upper lip is rather like a parrot's beak in shape. The ears are rounded and the tail is short.

Partially nocturnal, it lives a solitary life and does not move about much, frequenting the savanna, but never penetrating the forest, although seeking shade on its edge. It can feed on the most thorny or leathery plants. Like the Tapir, and for the same reason, it bathes in muddy water, coming out with a thick protective coating of mire over its body.

The only other one-horned rhinoceros is also an Asiatic species, the very rare Javan Rhinoceros (*R. sondaicus*). It has quite a short horn and a curiously granular skin. It was once distributed from Burma through Malaya to Java, but it is no longer found on the mainland, and so far as is known the only survivors are a small number in a reserve in western Java.

The gradual disappearance of the rhinoceroses is the result of centuries of hunting. Until the present century few official efforts were made to stop the export trade. They have been hunted for their flesh, their skin and most of all for their horns, which among superstitious and primitive peoples are credited with aphrodisiac properties and taken as a medicine.

Even-toed ungulates (Order Artiodactyla)

Formerly grouped together as ungulates, the order comprising the cloven-hooved or even-toed herbivores such as pigs, hippopotamuses, camels, giraffes, deer, cattle, sheep and antelopes is one of the most numerous group of mammals. Those belonging to the suborder Suiformes (pigs and hippopotamuses) are known as non-ruminants. Although they have either cloven hooves or an even number of toes, they do not have complex stomachs, nor do they ruminate (chew the cud).

Pigs and hippopotamuses (Suborder Suiformes)

Suiformes are bunodont; in other words, the crowns of the molars have rounded tubercles. Tusk-like canines are also present. In wild boars and hippopotamuses dentition is complete. In adult wart hogs incisors and anterior premolars are commonly lacking.

Wild Boar	I. $\frac{3}{3}$ C. $\frac{1}{1}$ Pm. $\frac{4}{4}$ M. $\frac{3}{3}$	Total 44
Hippo- potamus	I. $\frac{2}{2}$ C. $\frac{1}{1}$ Pm. $\frac{4}{4}$ M. $\frac{3}{3}$	Total 40
Wart Hog (young)	I. $\frac{1}{3}$ C. $\frac{1}{1}$ Pm. $\frac{2}{1}$ M. $\frac{3}{3}$	Total 30

Wild pigs (Family Suidae)

Wild Boars, bush pigs, Wart Hogs, the Babirusa and peccaries are distinguished from hippopotamuses by several characters. They are of moderate size, the body is covered with bristles and the elongated head ends in a snout. They have bunodont molars and an omnivorous diet. They are terrestrial. The females are extremely prolific, with many teats and large litters. Their voice is the well-known grunt.

The principal and best-known species is the Wild Boar (*Sus scrofa*), which still ranges over a wide area, from Europe to central Asia and from the Baltic to North Africa. The Indian Wild Boar (*S. s. cristatus*), a subspecies, is found in India and Sri Lanka. All the breeds and varieties of domestic swine are descended from this species.

The Wild Boar is by no means a ponderous, clumsy creature like the domestic pig, but a well-proportioned animal, built for fighting and running. The rather narrow body is carried on relatively thin legs. The elongated shaggy head ends in a movable, cartilaginous disc, the snout, in which the nostrils are set. It can penentrate thickets which no other animal of its size would attempt since it is protected by a very thick skin, on which scattered bristles grow in summer. In the winter coat there are more bristles, as well as a thick under-hair. The tail is straight and pendent, and never coiled up as in the domestic pig. The eyes are small and bright, and the ears are large, mobile and always pricked. Smell and hearing are the best developed senses.

The teeth deserve special attention. The outer incisors, like the front premolars, play an unimportant part and eventually fall out. The molars are much the same as in the common pig, but the canines are striking. The lower canines rise straight up outside the mouth, then curve backwards until they point towards the eyes. They are real tusks and the Wild Boar has only to lift its head sharply to rip open an adversary. Fitting them closely inside are the upper canines, which, besides sharpening the tusks, also serve as weapons.

Boars are generally sociable, living in herds which consist of the females and young under guidance of an old sow. The older males live solitarily.

The Indian Rhinoceros (*Rhinoceros unicornis*) used to range over large areas of India but the main population today survives in the Kaziranga Sanctuary in Assam. The two shown here are wallowing in mud in a national park in Nepal. Without sufficient protection rhinos will soon die out, especially the Asian species.

The European Wild Boar (*Sus scrofa*), from which the domestic pig is derived, lives in open woodlands, spending much of its time rooting in the earth and eating anything plant or animal it finds. It turns with ferocity on anyone disturbing it.

The Wart Hog (*Phacochoerus aethiopicus*) lives in open country over most of Africa but mostly subsaharan. It shelters in old antbear burrows and goes about in family groups, feeding on roots and grasses and other plants. It will sometimes go down on its knees and shuffle along when feeding, but when alarmed can run fast, tail held high.

The Babirusa (*Babyrousa babyrussa*) is found only in the Celebes and Molucca Islands. It lives in dense marshy forests and bamboo thickets travelling in small groups. It feeds mostly on green vegetation, roots, tubers and fruits.

In Europe Wild Boars make their lairs in quiet spots in woods. In the evening they all come out, making for the places where they know they can find food. They grub the ground with their snouts and are particularly fond of beetroot, potatoes and Jerusalem artichokes. Above ground they gather acorns, beechnuts, chestnuts and any kind of fallen fruit, but they also feed on insects and their larvae, earthworms, reptiles, birds and their eggs, and small mammals. They appear to be immune to snake-bites. Occasionally they do considerable damage in fields adjacent to forests and, like many other animals, spoil far more than they consume.

Either before or after feeding, Wild Boars generally make for some muddy lake or swamp in which to wallow, this mud-bath being necessary to rid them of parasites.

Occasionally migrations are observed, the reason for which is unknown. Besides their long nocturnal wanderings in search of good feeding grounds, Wild Boars sometimes appear in regions where they have been unknown for years.

The rutting season is in December and January. The males then join the herds and many fights take place for the attention of the females. Boars are sometimes deeply wounded in these duels and tusk fragments are left in the wounds. Once they have mated, the males retire again. The females remain in the herd during their pregnancy and, after three or four months, they too move off, looking for a quiet spot in which to give birth. The first litter is usually of three or four young; succeeding litters may number a dozen and occasionally even more. The young are striped, born with their eyes open and able to stand. Their growth is rapid. At the end of a fortnight they can begin to forage for themselves, though they go on suckling. At six months they lose their longitudinal white stripes and become a uniform dun colour, and at one year old they acquire the colour of adults, a blackish brown. They still remain in the herd, however, until the age of two, and it is only then that their canines develop and show outside the mouth. The largest Boars are a metre high at the shoulder, and weigh anything up to 150 kilograms.

There are many species of *Sus*, including the Celebes Wild Pig, Javan Wild Pig, Bornean Wild Boar, White-whiskered Swine and the Pygmy Hog, and in Africa there are several wild pigs sufficiently different to be classed as separate genera.

Close to the Wild Boars are the bush pigs (genus *Potamochoerus*) of which the Red River Hog (*P. porcus*) is typical. Very like the Wild Boar in general outline, shape of snout, bristles and mane, and with the same longitudinal stripes in the young, it is brighter and more variegated in colour, being dun-coloured above and black below with a contrasting white mane and a grey face. The ears are pointed and end in tufts of hair. Spread over Africa, with a related form in Madagascar, this bush pig lives in herds in reed beds and thickets and, like the Wild Boar, does great damage to crops.

Another wild pig, very different from the above and living in much the same area, is the Wart Hog (*Phacochoerus aethiopicus*), which derives its name from the large wart-like excrescences on the cheeks. Everything about the animal is ugly, from its grey, more or less naked skin to its misshapen head with enormous sickle-shaped upper canines and grotesque warts.

The Forest Hog (*Hylochoerus meinertzhageni*) is another African pig and was first discovered in 1904 in the depths of the Kenya forests. It is now known to range across equatorial Africa to Liberia. It is like the Wart Hog, but little is known about it.

Suidae of quite different types are found both in south-east Asia and in America. In Celebes and the Molucca Islands is the Babirusa (*Babyrousa babyrussa*), a native name meaning pig deer and suggested by the enormous curved canines, particularly the upper one, which is the longest and grows upwards, sometimes curling round almost in a circle. It is not to be confused with the Hog Deer, which really is a deer. No explanation has yet been found for these exaggerated canines. Orthogenesis is the name suggested for an evolutionary impetus, which sometimes carries a succession of changes far beyond what is useful and the canines of the Babirusa may be an expression of this.

The Babirusa has habits much like other Suidae, though it is one of the most aquatic, frequenting marshy forest. Fertility is rather low, only one or two offspring being born at a time.

Peccaries (Family Tayassuidae)

In Central and South America the Suiformes are represented by the Peccaries, which are small animals with very thin legs. Though looking like tiny Wild Boars, the peccaries show some curious transitional characters towards the ruminants. Their stomachs, for instance, are made up of several divisions, and the two median bones of the foot are fused into a cannon bone. There is a scent gland on the rump. The coat is a blackish brown, with a white collar in the case of the Collared Peccary (*Pecari tajuco*), found in South America from as far south as Paraguay, northwards to the extreme south of the United States. Another species is the White-lipped Peccary (*Tayassu pecari*), found in varying races from Paraguay to Mexico, the colouring differing according to race.

Large herds roam the forests, their habits differing little from those of other wild pigs. They have the same omnivorous diet and gregarious tendency as the Wild Boar. Like the Babirusa, the peccaries are not prolific, having never more than two young in a year. They band together in the face of danger and will tree a man or a jaguar if attacked. They are hunted for sport and meat, and are called javelins or, in Spanish, *javelinas*.

DOMESTIC PIGS: The old European farm pig was derived from the Wild Boar and in spite of probable crossing there are still very close physiological connections between these two, including absolute interfertility.

At least two races have been formed, a European and an East Asian one, perhaps by divergence from stocks, the Asian race from some oriental wild pig or pigs, but probably chiefly from the White-whiskered Swine.

Serious breeding began in England in the eighteenth century. Some Siamese hogs were crossed with native Yorkshire stock in 1760 and selection eventually produced the White Yorkshire. This pig has a long body but short legs and head and a flattened face. Only the upright ears are reminiscent of the Wild Boar. The White Yorkshire has considerable powers of digestion and of building up fat and growth is incredibly rapid. From one kilogram at birth a sucking pig reaches a weight of nearly four kilograms at the end of a fortnight, 15·75 kilograms after two months, 67·5 kilograms after six months, 120 kilograms after a year and finally some 305 kilograms.

The White Yorkshire has a small chest capacity for its size and is delicate. It is not always easy to breed these hogs to serve. The sows are not very fertile and are bad milkers. The breed is divided into three sub-breeds, Large, Middle and Small, but the last of these has now been abondoned on account of these defects.

Other British breeds are the Black Berkshire, the Suffolk (black or white), and the Red Tamworth. The pigs of the United States are descended chiefly from the Berkshire and other British breeds. In Europe some races have been crossed with the White Yorkshire, but such crosses are not necessarily advantageous. What is gained in rapidity of growth may be lost in reduced fertility. Sows of pure Norman or Limousine breed remain among the best breeders known.

Gestation lasts 115 days, allowing the sow to have two or even three litters a year, each of six to twenty young. Lactation lasts for six weeks to two months, after which fattening may be started at once. A sow breeding continuously for ten years could, if all her daughters did likewise, have seven million descendants in that time.

The chief pig-farming countries are the United States, England, Yugoslavia, Hungary, Germany and Denmark and other European countries.

Hippopotamuses (Family Hippopotamidae)

The hippopotamuses have become more at home in water than on land. On shore they labour along with their bellies almost scraping the ground, apparently overpowered by their own weight, which can amount to some four tonnes. The Great African Hippopotamus (*Hippopotamus amphibius*) is nearly 150 centimetres high at the shoulder, but the legs are less than sixty centimetres long. The skin alone, which is thickly lined with fat, weighs almost 500 kilograms and is deeply folded at the neck and chest.

The hippopotamuses swim easily, often with little showing but the top of the muzzle. Nostrils, ears and eyes are placed high on the head, so that the animals can breathe and keep watch while the rest of the body is submerged. The nostrils have muscular valves which close them and the large upper lip completely seals the mouth. Hippopotamuses can remain submerged for several minutes, swimming underwater or walking along the bottom. The blue-grey skin helps to camouflage them in the water, and they come out on land mainly at night. Their feet, like those of all the Suiformes, end in four digits enclosed in round hooves, but the lateral toes touch the ground and are almost as well developed as the median toes.

When a hippopotamus yawns one gets the first glimpse of its teeth, a few incisors and canines, which are placed far apart and are long only in the

Opposite
The Domestic pig is a supreme example of a domestic animal used entirely for man's own ends, for at least 5,000 years. Although primarily a prolific source of meat and cooking fat, pigs have been used in the past as draught animals, for rounding up cattle and retrieving game. When rooting for food they are admirable for clearing rough ground.

The One-humped or Arabian Camel (*Camelus dromedarius*) has long, slender legs adapted for speed. Inhabiting the hot, arid deserts of North Africa and the Near East, it has one hump containing fatty tissue which can be used as an energy store. Because of its fleshy lips the camel can eat hard thorny food and will exist on almost any kind of dry vegetation. The picture shows a day-old camel with its mother.

Opposite
A yawning Hippopotamus (*Hippopotamus amphibius*) showing his lower canines, which may be as long as sixty centimetres, are curved and stick up like tusks. The 'Hippo' is typically aquatic, coming on land only at night to pasture. Females and juveniles occupy separate areas of the river from the males, each of which has his own area adjacent to the central territory occupied by the females and young. The 'yawning' is an aggressive gesture, a prelude to attack.

lower jaw. The incisors are straight and lean forwards. The canines are curved and stick up like tusks. Each may be nearly sixty centimetres long and may weigh 2·5 kilograms. The remaining teeth are generally invisible, hidden by the inner edge of the lips, but there are numerous powerful molars. A clover-leaf pattern in enamel on their tables is the result of the partial wearing down of four tubercles. In this respect the hippopotamus stands midway between the bunodont pigs and the selenodont ruminants.

There is very little hair on the hippopotamuses. A few hairs are thinly scattered about all over the skin, and the tails have a terminal tuft of bristles, stiff as wire.

The Great African Hippopotamus is almost confined to the big African rivers and lakes, living in small herds and spending most of the day dozing. Intensive hunting has made it cautious, so that it tends now to frequent places where reeds offer concealment. It comes on land, especially at night, to pasture. Cultivated fields attract it particularly. The Great African Hippopotamus seems to be a much less dangerous animal than the rhinoceros and rarely attacks without provocation. Its cry is a lowing or rather a belling, a deep bass *ba-ho-ho-ho*, which carries a great distance.

It migrates regularly, working upstream during the rainy season and coming downstream during the dry season to look for fresh pastures. The males each occupy separate territories and fight fiercely to maintain them. The females and juveniles live in harmony in an area which is surrounded on most sides by the territories of the males. One young is born at a time after a gestation of eight months, and it is carefully tended by its mother.

Hippopotamuses at one time inhabited the whole of Africa, below the Sahara in the west and up to the Nile delta in the east.

The Pygmy Hippopotamus (*Choeropsis liberiensis*), the only species in the family, lives by the rivers of West Africa. It is only a tenth the size of the Common Hippopotamus, the weight being no more than 250 kilograms. Its habit is more terrestrial, and it lives singly or in pairs.

Animals similar to *Hippopotamus amphibius* were at one time distributed throughout Europe and Asia. There is evidence that they were hunted with stone weapons in the Seine and Rhine regions. One species, whose fossil remains have been found in Europe, was much bigger than the living species.

Camels and llamas (Suborder Tylopoda)

Camels and llamas have only two functional toes on each foot. The body is carried on long, slender legs ending in two toes, beneath which is a broad, callous and elastic pad. The under-developed hooves are more suggestive of nails. The feet are adapted to walking on desert sands or for the ascent of slippery and dangerous paths. The neck and head are both elongated, the latter ending in a deeply cleft upper lip. Horns are lacking. Incisors and canines (tushes) are present in the upper jaw. The stomach has three divisions. There is no gall bladder. The red corpuscles of the blood are elliptical like those of the oviparous vertebrates. The placenta is diffuse. The dental formula is:

$$I. \frac{1}{3} \qquad C. \frac{1}{1} \qquad Pm. \frac{3}{3} \qquad M. \frac{3}{3} \qquad Total\ 36$$

Camels (Family Camelidae)

The Bactrian Camel (*Camelus bactrianus*) is distinguished from other members of the family by the possession of two humps of fatty tissue, one over the shoulders and the other over the hind quarters. The coat is thick, woolly and of a ruddy-brown colour. There is a deep fringe of hair under the neck and the upper parts of the fore legs are shaggy. The height to the shoulder is nearly 180 centimetres.

A few wild herds exist in the Gobi desert that were for long believed to be feral, but are now thought to be an original wild stock. Otherwise the the Bactrian Camel is known in the domesticated state only. It is the steed of the whole of central Asia, and it also provides milk, meat and leather.

The Arabian or One-humped Camel often called the Dromedary (*C. dromedarius*) exists only as a domestic animal. There is reason to believe that it was Asiatic in origin and not African, as is often supposed. It is fifteen centimetres taller than the Bactrian Camel and has a shorter, though equally woolly coat. Its colour is fawn or beige, matching the colour of its environment. Everything in the Dromedary is adapted for life in the desert: the broadened feet, eyelashes that protect the eyes from wind-blown sand, nostrils that can be closed, lips thickened to withstand the coarsest plants, the hump with its reserve of fat and the ability to survive for long periods without water.

The camels are said to be stupid, obstinate and malicious, and have an ugly voice as well as an offensive odour. However, the service they do is undeniable.

As pack and saddle animals the camels have no equal and have been used from early times. The Arabian Baggage Camel, heavier in build than the Racing Camel for which the name Dromedary should be reserved, can carry a load of 140 to 200 kilograms sixty kilometres a day. The Dromedary or Racing Camel can do two or three times that distance, but carrying only a rider.

Camels and dromedaries have become accustomed to kneeling down for loading or unloading, and they have acquired callosities over the sternum and at the knees and other joints which touch the ground. These are not hereditary, but are acquired by each generation.

In both the Bactrian and the Arabian Camel the period of gestation is about a year and only one colt is born.

The One-humped Camel has been successfully used in the desert regions of Australia where it is now feral in considerable numbers. Attempts have also been made without success to introduce it into southern Europe and North America.

LLAMAS: There are two species of wild llama, the Huanaco or Guanaco (*Llama huanacos*) and the Vicuña (*L. vicugna*). They are found in the Cordillera of the Andes and extend southwards to Patagonia and Tierra del Fuego. They differ from camels in being much smaller and having no dorsal humps.

The most widespread of the wild llamas is the Guanaco, which in the rainy season frequents the uplands, coming down to the plains and into the valleys when it is dry. It has also spread farthest south. The Guanaco stands about 120 centimetres at the shoulder and 160 centimetres to the top of the head. Its general bearing is more that of a long-necked, long-legged sheep. The head, too, is elongated and ends in an overhanging, deeply cleft upper lip. The ears are long and very mobile. The wool is short on the head and legs, long and fine on the body and is not easily usable owing to the impossibility of separating the guard hairs. The colour is chiefly red-brown, whitish below, with black forehead and head patches.

The Guanacos live in small herds composed of a male, several females and young of various ages. As climbers they recall the ability of the Chamois and the Ibex. They have great curiosity which impels them to examine anything unusual. When danger threatens the male emits a bleat similar to, but harsher than, a sheep's. At this signal all the females move off, driving the young with their heads, while the male acts as a rearguard.

The rutting season is marked by violent battles between the males. Gestation lasts eleven months. The young is born fully developed, covered with hair and with eyes open. The mother suckles it for six to twelve weeks and cares for it for another eight. Then, if it is a male, it is driven off by the head male and joins the other males, the young and those beaten in combat.

The Vicuña is a smaller, better proportioned animal, which is becoming rarer on account of hunting and is now found only in the highest and most lonely heights of Peru. In habits the Vicuñas are very like Guanacos, but they are more timid, a cord stretched across a mountain path being enough to stop them. Their wool is of very high quality and consequently much sought after.

The domesticated Llama, of the High Andes of Peru, provides wool and meat as well as being a beast of burden. Llamas breed readily with the two wild species, the Guanaco and Vicuña to give fertile young.

The Vicuña (*Lama vicugna*), one of the two wild species of llama, lives in the western High Andes of South America. It is the smallest, most graceful and most agile of the South American camelids, living in family groups of a stallion and up to twenty mares. Within this century Vicuñas became near to extinction but now with protection their numbers are increasing.

Opposite
The Giraffe (*Giraffa camelopardalis*) inhabits Africa south of the Sahara. A browser and cud-chewer, it feeds almost entirely on leaves from acacia, mimosa and wild apricots. It is able to go for many weeks without water.

593

A Red Deer stag (*Cervus elaphus*) belling in the rutting season. The stags cast their antlers each year and from the bony stalk or pedicel a new pair grows. The new antlers are covered with a velvety skin in spring and summer, when the stags are said to be 'in velvet'. When the velvet is shed the antlers harden and the stags grow restless and begin to 'bell', heralding a new rutting or breeding season.

The commonest domestic species is the Llama, the characteristic animal of the high Altiplano of Bolivia and of the highlands of Peru, Ecuador, Chile and Argentina. It is believed to be a descendant of the Guanaco, domesticated for many centuries. They have no means of self-defence except to spit in an adversary's face. The colour is variable and they have a callosity on the chest.

As a pack animal the Llama played an important part in South America before the introduction of the horse and the mule. Even now it is the beast of burden on the mountain tracks of the Cordillera. Its pace is slow but steady, and can be maintained for a considerable time. A Llama can carry forty-five kilograms fifty kilometres a day for five days, and after a day's rest can do the same again. It can subsist on an absolute minimum when travelling.

Castrated males are used for transport. The females and a few males are kept in the pastures for breeding. The females are poor milkers. The wool, though long and strong, is coarse and is too inextricably mixed with guard hairs to be made use of except for carpets and the coarsest stuffs.

On the Altiplano by Lake Titicaca, on the borders of Bolivia and Peru, is another domestic species, the Alpaca, more restricted than the Llama and specialised in wool production. It is smaller than the Llama, more sheep-like, and the breast has no callosities. The wool is very long and fine, and was the material from which the Incas originally made most of their textiles.

Ruminants (Suborder Ruminantia)

This suborder includes the greater part of the hooved animals formerly included in the ungulates. They have two and sometimes four toes and they differ from members of the Artiodactyla already considered not only in having divided stomachs but in ruminating their food (chewing the cud). Generally they have frontal horns and

lack upper canines. Their molars have grinding surfaces and are of the selenodont type. The Ruminantia include deer, Giraffe, Okapi, cattle, sheep, goats and finally antelopes.

The Artiodactyla differ from the Perissodactyla not merely in the number of their toes, but above all in having the third and fourth digits equally developed, and more developed than the second and fifth. These last two are still quite large in the Suiformes, though no longer touching the ground, except in the hippopotamuses. In the chevrotains and deer these digits are still present, though greatly reduced. In the remainder they have either disappeared completely or are represented by mere vestiges, like the splint bones of a horse. This is the truly didactyl foot, ending in two nails that have become hooves. These latter groups, and more loosely the whole of the suborder are thus known as bisulcate or cloven-footed.

Another important character of the foot is that the third and fourth metacarpals in the front foot and metatarsals in the hind foot have united totally or partially to form a single strong bone, the cannon bone. This unification takes place in the foetus. As in the number of their toes, the chevrotains are behind the other ruminants in this also, their metacarpals and metatarsals being sometimes fused and sometimes separate. In some the bones of the hind foot (metatarsals) are fused while those of the fore foot (metacarpals) are separate.

The ruminant's cannon bones must not be confused with that of the horse, in which it is a single bone, a strongly developed third metacarpal or metatarsal. The cannon bone of a ruminant—of an ox, for example—is the result of fusion, a double bone whose dual origin is generally betrayed by a longitudinal groove or alternatively a terminal bifurcation.

Many ruminants have a pedal gland between their phalanges secreting an oily odoriferous liquid. Some have another gland (preorbital) below the eye. Its blackish secretion acquires a special smell in the rutting season and must be regarded as a secondary sexual character.

All the ruminants, with the exception of the chevrotains, musk deer, and the Chinese River or Water Deer, have horns, which are valuable weapons in defence and attack, except in the case of the Giraffe, which has bony outgrowths covered by ordinary skin and hair.

Nearly all deer have antlers, single or branched bony appendages covered at first by a soft, hairy, deciduous skin called velvet, which is responsible for laying down the bone. Later, this skin dries and falls away, the horn remaining hard and clean until it is shed in the following spring, when the whole process begins again, generally with more elaborate branches or tines. This shedding is due to an organic growth at the base of each antler causing a constriction of all blood vessels carrying blood to the antlers. Except in reindeer and caribou, only males have antlers.

Other ruminants. such as buffaloes, cattle, sheep, goats and antelopes, are called the hollow-horned ruminants. In these there is a bony core over which the horn is laid down. The horns are nourished from the interior and continue to grow throughout life. Often they are present in both sexes, but sometimes, as in some antelopes, only in the male. Their length, position on the head, ornamentation and manner of coiling and twisting vary greatly.

The dentition of ruminants is always incomplete. The upper incisors are absent and in many cases the canines also. Upper canines only are found in the few hornless ruminants. In the lower jaw the canines are shaped like the incisors, with which they join to form a cutting edge of eight teeth. That is one of the initial differences from the horse, which has a cutting edge of only six incisors. Another and more important difference is that the horse also has upper incisors and grazes with a scissor action, while the ruminants have to tear away the grass, holding it between their incisors and the hardened toothless gum above.

The front teeth are named similarly to those of horses: middles, first intermediates, second intermediates and corners. The order of their eruption and displacement and the degree of wear are likewise used to estimate the age of a ruminant, though with these animals there is often added evidence from the horns.

There are three premolars and three molars in each half of both upper and lower jaws. Generally they are tall teeth, prismatic in cross section, ending in a grinding surface or table, on which appear the crescent-shaped and more or less continuous enamel folds of the typical selenodont tooth. These are former crests worn down by mastication. They are D-shaped on the premolars and B-shaped on the molars. Between the enamel folds is the dentine, and on the outside, the cement. The appearance is similar to horses'.

The enamel folds are generally longitudinal, and thus they act like a file when the lower jaw is worked from side to side in the manner so well known in ruminants. Here are the dental formulae of typical ruminants:

Chevrotain $\quad$ I. $\frac{0}{3}$ $\quad$ C. $\frac{1}{1}$ $\quad$ Pm. $\frac{3}{3}$ $\quad$ M. $\frac{3}{3}$ $\quad$ Total 34

Ox, Giraffe $\quad$ I. $\frac{0}{3}$ $\quad$ C. $\frac{0}{1}$ $\quad$ Pm. $\frac{3}{3}$ $\quad$ M. $\frac{3}{3}$ $\quad$ Total 32

The dominant feature of the ruminants is the possession of a compound stomach, the food passing through several compartments before reaching the intestine. These are the rumen or paunch, the reticulum or honeycomb stomach, the psalterium or manyplies, and finally the abomasum or rennet stomach (see page 473).

The paunch is the largest, a huge compartment for storing hastily swallowed food. Its epithelium is covered with papillae, whose function is to raise the temperature and thus promote the bacterial fermentation that takes place there. This fermentation breaks down cellulose upon which digestive juices are ineffective.

An offshoot of the paunch constitutes the honeycomb stomach, so called from the intersecting folds of the epithelium which form a reticulum, the function of which is to assemble food in pellets ready for regurgitation, for the food has to go back into the mouth for rumination, in which process it is ground to pulp. This is done while the animal is at rest and may take several hours.

After rumination the food is swallowed again and this time it passes from the bottom of the gullet along a temporary fold of the stomach into the manyplies, which derives its name from the lamellated epithelium. Its function is certainly masticatory, affecting a further trituration of the food before its passage into the fourth and last compartment, the rennet stomach. This is a genuine stomach comparable to our own, in which the food is acted upon by gastric juices. When a calf sucks, milk passes straight through to the rennet stomach, to be curdled and digested.

Ruminants have unusually long intestines, thirty-three metres in sheep and fifty metres in oxen, when compared with carnivores.

They have well-developed and highly convoluted brains but show no special mental faculties.

Most ruminants have external testes and a retractile penis. Females have a bicorned uterus. The placenta is cotyledonous except in the horned ruminants. The young are generally born with their eyes open and are able to stand. One or two are born at a time. There are two or four inguinal teats sometimes joined to a single udder.

The suborder is divided into three groups according to whether they are hornless, have solid horns (antlers), or have hollow horns. Hornless ruminants are the chevrotains (Tragulidae). These have a number of archaic characters: upper canines and/or incisors; lateral toes and separate metacarpals; and the absence of a manyplies. Except for giraffes, solid-horned or antler-bearing ruminants are confined to the family Cervidae (deer), the Chinese Water Deer and Musk Deer being hornless exceptions. The giraffe's horns, though homologous to antlers, are greatly reduced. The hollow-horned group consists of the family Bovidae, using the word in its widest sense to include buffaloes, wild cattle, bison, sheep, goats, antelopes and a few minor forms.

Chevrotains (Family Tragulidae)

These are hornless, but their upper canines have been elongated, in the males, into small tusks protruding from the mouth. The feet have two well-developed toes and two smaller lateral toes.

Chevrotains or mouse-deer (genus *Tragulus*) are among the smallest ruminants, being no more than twenty to thirty centimetres at the shoulder. They are timid, solitary except in the breeding season, and live in the forests and bushy regions of India, Java and Sumatra. The Malayan Chevrotain (*T. javanicus*) has a coat of a uniform colour, differing in this respect from the Indian Chevrotain (*T. meminna*) which is spotted, and still more from the African Water Chevrotain (*Hyemoschus aquaticus*), of Sierra Leone through Cameroun to the eastern Congo, which is dark brown with white longitudinal stripes and spots. The latter lives on river banks and feeds on aquatic plants. In some respects it is intermediate in type between pigs and deer; the metacarpals of the fore legs are unfused.

True deer (Family Cervidae)

Although connected with the hollow-horned ruminants by a certain number of transitional types, such as the Giraffe and the American Pronghorn with its branched deciduous horns, the deer form a distinct and homogeneous family. Its principal members are the deer, Elks, Reindeer, wapitis or Red Deer, muntjacs and Sikas.

The Malayan Chevrotain (*Tragulus javanicus*), of the tropical forests of southeast Asia, showing how the upper canines in the male are elongated to form small tusks protruding from the mouth. Chevrotains are the smallest of all the artiodactyls and are often called mouse deer.

A Fallow Deer buck (*Dama dama*) which shows clearly its broad, flattened antlers with several small tines. In October the bucks gather the does into harems and there is a certain amount of fighting, but this is mostly show. During the winter Fallow Deer gather in mixed herds of both sexes.

The appendages on the head, generally confined to males, are antlers and contain no horn in their structure. They are bony outgrowths formed originally from connective tissue, and are distinguished by two major characters: they are generally branched and they are shed each year, a new set then grows. Antlers are at first covered with a skin or velvet which plays the part of a periosteum in the promotion of their growth. Once they are formed and completely ossified, the skin dries and is rubbed off. The growth of antlers is due to a secretion from the inside of the skin, while in hollow horns it is due to the action of the outside of the skin on the surface of the core.

They are secondary sexual characters and their growth depends ultimately on the hormones secreted by the genital glands. A castrated fawn never grows any antlers at all. An old stag in decline has less-developed antlers each year, that is, they become shorter and have fewer snags or tines. If it lives long enough they will finish up as simple beams like those of its first year. Conversely a hind, having become sterile, may grow rudimentary antlers as well as acquiring a dewlap and canines like a male. Such processes may be pathological.

The feet of the Cervidae are less developed than those of other ruminants, since they still have four toes. The third and fourth digits are well developed, while the second and fifth are small and do not touch the ground.

The dentition of the Cervidae is similar to that of cattle, except that the upper canines are generally well developed in males, giving them thirty-four teeth instead of thirty-two. The first premolars are round and very small.

The Cervidae are well-proportioned animals with strong yet graceful legs. The muzzle is naked. The ears are usually large and beneath the eyes are scent glands, which in the male secrete an odoriferous liquid. These tear glands, or face glands, have nothing to do with lachrymal glands. The pelage consists of coarse guard hairs and a fine undercoat, varying in colour with the seasons. The males have long hair, something like a mane, beneath their necks. Fawns are usually spotted with white. Tails are generally short and are held erect in moments of excitement. Heights to the shoulder vary greatly, from thirty-three centimetres in the pudu to over 180 centimetres in the European Elk and the North American Moose.

MUSK DEER: The Musk Deer (*Moschus moschiferus*), of eastern Asia, is larger than the Chevrotain, being nearly fifty centimetres in height. Its thick, spring coat fits it for a life in exposed situations in the mountains. The male has a musk gland in front of the navel, which is highly odoriferous and still sought after for making perfume. Living in high and rocky ground the animal is not easily shot and is more often trapped.

EUROPEAN DEER: The Red Deer (*Cervus elaphus*) is still fairly common in most European countries. It is well known in the Highlands of Scotland and on Exmoor, and it is also to be found in north-west Africa and south-west Asia. It has been introduced into New Zealand.

When a calf is born, in May in western Europe, it is no taller than a kid. Its general colour is a golden red-brown, with longitudinal lines of white

The Musk Deer (*Moschus moschiferus*), of northern India and part of eastern Asia, in which the males are devoid of antlers but are armed with long upper canine tusks. It is a solitary deer, living in forest and scrubland up to 3,300 metres, which has been much hunted for its musk, used in the manufacture of soap and perfume.

spots. Weak at birth, it gains strength rapidly and from July can romp with its kind. At the age of six months the sexes begin to differ visibly.

The hinds continue to grow, but otherwise undergo little change. The young stags can be distinguished by their wider foreheads, which make the muzzle look narrower, and by a straggling growth of long hairs under the neck. Only in the course of the winter do two humps appear on the forehead, the first sign of the formidable headgear to come later.

These humps are the pedicles, which are never shed, never lose their skin, and continue to grow year by year. The young grow simple unbranched antlers the first year. In each succeeding year, a new tine is added up to a maximum of ten or eleven tines, some of which may be arranged in a cup or a crown at the top. Sometimes antlers are flattened as in Fallow Deer, and are then known as palmate.

The antlers of the Red Deer often measure a metre in length and weigh nine kilograms, and in central Europe still larger antlers are found. The present record comes from a stag killed in Hungary, one of whose antlers measured over 120 centimetres and weighed 14·5 kilograms. The animal itself varies in height from 120 to 140 centimetres at the shoulder, and in weight from 135 to 340 kilograms. Deer are excellent jumpers, being capable of jumps of 180 to nearly 300 centimetres in height and ten to twelve metres in length. They are also excellent swimmers.

The calf's white spots disappear at the age of five or six months, when the permanent colouring is assumed: in summer reddish-brown with white below, in winter darker brown above and almost black below. The coat is longer in winter and the males then have the long hair under the neck.

Red Deer feed chiefly in the evening or at night, in spring on all the budding greenstuff, later on young wheat and oats, and still later on carrots, beet, and even cider apples, which they seem to find particularly attractive. In autumn when hunting begins they become more cautious, leaving the wooded country less readily. When they do, they return in a roundabout way, confusing their tracks. Once in their resting place they are difficult to see because of their colouring.

From the social point of view, their life is divided into three periods. From November to February there are two sorts of herds of twenty to thirty head, the stags consorting in one and the hinds and calves in the other. In February the stags begin to drop out of their herd to cast their horns, first the old ones, then the younger, age by age, down to the youngest in June. In May, after a nine-month gestation, the hinds isolate themselves to bear their one or two calves, which they tend and suckle until the autumn.

In August they come on heat and the stags come in search of them, sometimes travelling long distances. As soon as a stag joins a herd of hinds its first action is to chase away any of its own sex. Its bellowing, which may be heard a kilometre away, is a means of warning off any pretenders which may be nearby and which might try to usurp his territory.

The fights between the males at rutting time usually take place from the middle of September to the middle of October. Often they are fierce, and may even end in death to one or both the contestants. The victor settles down with his harem in the neighbourhood of water, for though he eats nothing he needs to drink constantly. He spends his time serving the hinds and does not leave them before each has been covered several times. Then he trots off, either in search of further adventures or just goes away. When his bellowing period is over he becomes silent again until the following year.

The Fallow Deer (*Dama dama*) is native to Mediterranean countries, but even there is rare in a truly wild state. The herds existing in Spain, Sardinia, Greece and Asia Minor are semi-domesticated. In the British Isles and other northern countries the Fallow Deer exists as a park animal. Taken all in all, it may be said to be in the process of extinction. Recently the Mesopotamian Fallow Deer has been rediscovered.

Barely ninety centimetres in height at the shoulder, the Fallow Deer weighs only sixty-five kilograms. The antlers are composed of a rather short beam with a brow tine and a bez tine, and end in a palm edged with a number of points which increase in number as age advances. Another difference between it and the Red Deer is that, except in winter, it has a similar coat to that which it had at birth, spotted with white. On the buttocks on either side of the tail is a white patch bordered with black.

Amongst the Fallow Deer rutting comes a little later than in the Red Deer, not until October and November. The fights between stags are milder, and the challenging note is unlike that of Red Deer.

Beautiful as they are in parks it is not always practicable to keep them, because of all the damage they do, particularly in eating the shoots of young trees.

Unlike the Fallow Deer, the Roe Deer (*Capreolus capreolus*) has a wide distribution, from Scandinavia and Britain to southern and central Europe, Siberia and China. There are three races, the European Roe Deer (*C. c. capreolus*), the

Siberian Roe Deer (*C. c. pygargus*) and the Manchurian Roe Deer (*C. c. bedfordi*). These races get larger as they go eastward. In central Europe the animals are considerably bigger than they are in France and Britain, where they are eighty centimetres at the shoulder with a weight of forty-five kilograms.

The Roe Deer is a step further removed from the Red Deer. The short antlers are pointed and grow almost vertically from the forehead. There are no brow tines and only three tines altogether, situated high up. The antlers are furrowed and pearled. Sometimes the heads are misshapen, possibly owing to a derangement of the ductless glands.

The adult coat is red-gold in summer, browner in winter, sometimes approaching black, with the legs and belly always lighter, and white buttock patches. The males also have a white patch under the throat, in the winter coat.

The Roe Deer has no face gland, nor does the male bellow. The cry is a sort of barking, while the female makes bleats. Roe Deer do not form herds. The most that are found together are a buck and two or three does with their kids. Even those families are often split up. In the middle of winter the roebuck goes off to shed his horns and grow new ones. Then comes a sort of pre-rutting period from March to July when the males, greatly excited, engage in fights. The rutting season is in July and August. During it the roebuck is not bound to any one doe but will serve any female that attracts him by her bleating. It is only after the rutting season is over that the 'family' is constituted, though the kids are not necessarily the offspring of the buck at the head of it. After up to nine months gestation (usually 140 to 160 days) the females retire into solitude to give birth to their young, generally two kids of opposite sex. Contrary to what has often been claimed, there is no monogamy, even temporarily, among Roe deer.

The extinct Irish Elk (*Megaloceros giganteus*) was a gigantic Fallow Deer which lived in Europe, and especially Ireland, in Neolithic times. The antlers were enormous, measuring nearly 335 centimetres from tip to tip. With such a spread of horns the animal would have been forced to live on the plains. Its fossils are found chiefly in Irish peat, in which it probably sank when attempting to grass. What brought about its demise is still unknown.

NORTH AMERICAN DEER: The Red Deer has its counterpart in America, with much the same habits. This is the Wapiti, or American Elk, sometimes considered as belonging to the same species as the Red Deer (*Cervus elaphus*), but more often regarded as a separate species (*C. canadensis*). Several races exist, chiefly in Canada but also in the United States. The Californian Wapiti, sometimes called the Dwarf Elk, is regarded in America as a distinct species. The Arizona Wapiti belonged to the mountains of Arizona and New Mexico, but it is doubtful whether any now remain. However, wapitis have been reintroduced into this region, and are protected by certain landowners.

The White-tailed Deer (*Odocoileus virginianus*), sometimes called the Virginian Deer, is the commonest species in North America, Guiana, Bolivia and Peru. It is even found very near to New York City. It is a graceful, somewhat slightly built animal, about ninety centimetres high at the

The Roebuck (*Capreolus capreolus*) has short three-tined antlers which grow almost vertically from the forehead. Roe deer are dainty and agile, living in open woodlands. Their ability to move stealthily through dense cover makes the chance of seeing them unlikely especially as they feed mainly at dusk and dawn.

withers. Its wide distribution is reflected in the number of races, each adapted to its particular environment. In the north the coats are markedly reddish in summer, turning to grey in autumn. With this coat it would be hard to see but for the white tail, or 'flag' as it is called, which is generally raised when running. The antlers are variable, five to six points being common, and there is always a brow tine.

Herds of these animals naturally tend to come into contact with cultivated croplands and there has been some conflict of interest between the game authorities and the farmers. To help solve the problem a census is taken each year, which shows the great abundance of the White-tailed Deer and enables game managers to decide how long the season should be to bring the herds under control. In some parts of Texas, for instance, from 100 to 520 are found to the square kilometre. The females, incidentally, would normally be about as numerous as the males, but after repeated hunting seasons have reduced the number of bucks the situation is commonly reversed. The Mule Deer (*O. hemionus*) ranges over western North America from Alaska to New Mexico. It is sometimes regarded as constituting two species, although the tendency now is to speak of two subspecies. They are distinguished from the Virginia Deer partly by the long mule-like ears and black-tipped tail, partly by the different bounding gait and by the greater tendency to associate in herds; and they seem to be less woodland-dwellers. The height is about 110 centimetres, and the antlers are larger and more branched. When protected from hunting, as also happens with the White-tailed Deer, the numbers have sometimes become excessive, resulting in winter starvation, with consequent disease decimating the herds.

SOUTH AMERICAN DEER: In South America there are several types of Cervidae whose antlers tend to be rudimentary. The Pampas Deer (*Ozotoceros bezoarticus*) is about the size of a Roe Deer and like it has antlers with only three points. The Marsh Deer (*Blastocerus dichotomus*), which is the largest South American form, has antlers with five points. The brockets (genus *Mazama*) are small deer, sixty centimetres at the shoulder, with short, unbranched antlers. There are several species spread over the sub-continent. In the pudu, also, the antlers are short, simple spikes. The Chilean Pudu (*Pudu pudu*), the smallest American deer, is thirty-three centimetres at the shoulder. The Ecuadorian Pudu (*P. mephistophiles*) is larger.

ASIATIC DEER: Asia has many species of deer and is probably the cradle of the family. Some are closely related to European and American types. The Maral (*Cervus elaphus maral*), which some would put in a separate species, is a large Red Deer, 140 centimetres in height, and spread over south-west Asia. The wapiti are represented by the Turkestan Deer, the Altai Deer in central Asia, and the Isubra, or Manchurian Wapiti, in northern Manchuria. These subspecies are intermediate between the Red Deer and *C. canadensis*, which is why the American Elk and Red Deer are considered one much-varied species. All have complex antlers.

The Axis Deer or Chital (*Axis axis*) with three-tined antlers, is found in India and Sri Lanka, and a deer with similar antlers is the Sambar (*Rusa unicolor*), which ranges from India to the Philippines. The Hog Deer (*Axis porcinus*), so called on account of its low build, is a common deer in India. Its height varies from sixty-centimetres to seventy-four centimetres. The Chinese River or Water Deer (*Hydropotes inermis*) of eastern China has no antlers, but it has tusk-like upper canines. It lives in river valleys in the long grass. The muntjac or barking deer (genus *Muntiacus*) has short, two-tined antlers at the ends of long, bony, skin-covered pedicles, or burrs. It also has tusk-like upper canines. There are several species of muntjac in India and further east, living alone or in pairs in deep jungle, where they probably provide good hunting for tigers and other carnivorous animals.

In marshy regions of India and south-east Asia are the Swamp Deer, or Barasingh (*Cervus duvauceli*) and the related species, Schomburgk's Deer, Eld's Deer, or Thamin. The last two are

A doe and fawn of the White-tailed Deer (*Odocoileus virginianus*) which is the most widespread deer in the Americas. It is so called because of its long white tail which is raised erect when fleeing from danger and serves as a warning signal to other deer.

There are two species of Pudu in South America. One is the smallest of all deer, the Chilean Pudu (*Pudu pudu*), the fawns of which have three rows of spots running from the shoulder to the base of the tail, plus spots on the shoulders and flanks. Both species possess short spike-like antlers.

The Axis, Chital or Indian Spotted Deer (*Axis axis*) is a common deer of India and Sri Lanka. It has also been introduced into the Hawaiian Islands. Associating in large herds, mating takes place in April or May. After a gestation period of seven to eight months, usually two young are born in dense cover. The mother feeds nearby and nurses the infant until it has sufficient strength to roam with the herd.

A female Reeves' Muntjac or Barking Deer (*Muntiacus reevesi*). This deer has the widest distribution of the three species from China. It also has a wide distribution in central England, where it has become feral. It is also known as the rib-faced deer because of the slit-openings of the facial scent glands.

collectively referred to as the brow-antlered deer. In these the curved brow tine forms a semicircle with the beam.

Père David's Deer (*Elaphurus davidianus*) is named after the French missionary who observed them in the gardens of the Emperor's palace near Peking. These were destroyed during the Boxer rebellion, but specimens had already been taken to Europe, and the species still exists at Woburn Park in England and in various other zoos, and some of those from Woburn were sent to Chinese zoos.

Of the Asiatic Cervidae the best known in Europe is probably the Sika or Japanese Deer (*Cervus nippon*), since it was introduced into Europe by the gift of a stag and three hinds by the

Emperor of Japan to President Sadi Carnot of France, from which a stock has been raised that has finally spread to other countries. It is a small deer, barely ninety centimetres in height and weighing at the most fifty kilograms. Its coat is like the Fallow Deer's, spotted with white in summer, plain in winter, but with the lower parts always lighter than the upper. The striking feature of the Japanese Deer, however, is its very white buttock patch. The antlers are smaller and simpler than those of the Red Deer. The Formosan and Manchurian Deer are closely related, while the Pekin Deer (*C. nippon hortulorum*), from China and Manchuria, is considerably larger standing 110 centimetres high at the shoulder.

Only one species of deer is found in Africa. This is called the Barbary Stag (*C. elaphus barbarus*), but is a race of Red Deer found in Algeria and Tunisia, and its survival is unlikely.

ELK (MOOSE) AND REINDEER (CARIBOU): These two northern Cervidae were spread over the greater part of Europe at the end of the glacial period, and were only driven gradually to their present habitat.

The European Elk (*Alces alces*), which some zoologists believe differs only in race from the American Moose (*A. americana*), is the largest of all deer. Its height to the withers, usually over 180 centimetres occasionally reaches 235 centimetres, and its weight may be up to 800 kilograms. The males have a long Roman-nosed head with overhanging upper lips. A beard hangs beneath the throat. The cows are smaller, not so heavy, and are without antlers. In both sexes the coats are coarse and dark brown except for the legs, which are white. The hooves are broad, which spreads the weight when the animal is standing on snow. The antlers are palmate.

In its habits the Elk does not differ greatly from the Red Deer, apart from its predeliction for deciduous woodland, marshes and peat-bogs. The food is almost entirely young shoots and twigs of deciduous saplings, especially willow and aspen, which the animal's great stature enables it to reach easily. It is not gregarious as a rule. Its bellowing is deep and brassy and has two notes. Gestation lasts eight to nine months and one or two young are born.

The European Elk has only disappeared from western Europe in historical times. It was still in France in the third century. Today it is confined to Scandinavia, East Prussia, Finland, northern Russia and Siberia. In America the Moose narrowly escaped extinction in the last century. Now, as a result of protection, it is not uncommon in Canada and the northernmost parts of the United States. It is larger than the European Elk and it has finer antlers, which may reach a span of 200 centimetres.

Reindeer (*Rangifer tarandus*) are the only deer to have been really domesticated. Within the Arctic Circle they play the same part as cattle do in more southerly latitudes. There are several domesticated races, including the Scandinavian and the Finnish reindeer. The introduction of domestic reindeer into North America is of fairly recent date. It has been found impossible to keep the New World Caribou (*R. arcticus*) in captivity, although the two species are so alike in most other ways.

Reindeer and Caribou are instantly recognisable by their very long antlers, the beams and brow tines sweeping out in almost a semi-circle. The brow tines and surantlers are slightly palmate. This is the only deer in which both sexes bear antlers, those of the males being larger. The hooves are splayed like the European Elk's or Moose's for walking on snow. The coat is brown, with white or grey on the lower parts and on a buttock patch. The height of the Newfoundland Caribou is about 130 centimetres to the shoulder and it weighs up to 225 kilograms.

Caribou are divided into two types: the barren-ground group such as the Greenland Caribou, and the woodland and forest group such as the Newfoundland Caribou.

The Reindeer never lives alone. Formerly wild herds of several thousands could be seen, but hunting has reduced their numbers and herds of this size are rarely found now.

Giraffe and okapi (Family Giraffidae)

The horns of these two animals are bony outgrowths covered by skin, and comparable with either the bony centres of hollow horns or the pedicles of antlers. In other characters the Giraffidae stand between the hollow-horned and the solid-horned ruminants. The dentition is similar to that of oxen.

The head is elongated and ends in long, thin lips. The black and prehensile tongue can extend some fifty centimetres and is used with the lips to pluck leaves neatly from trees, thus avoiding the thorns. The nostrils have muscles to close them. The large brown eyes are velvety and protected by long lashes. The ears are very mobile. On the forehead are two or three horns (the 'third' horn is much smaller and located centrally on the forehead below the prominent pair), covered with ordinary skin, except at the tips where they are black and callous.

There is a short mane along the back of the neck, the slope of which, continued down the animal's back, is the dominant feature of the Giraffe's profile. The front legs are only slightly longer than the back ones, the height of the fore part of the body being largely due to the heavy muscular development of the base of the neck. The very long neck results from an increase in the length of the vertebrae, and not from additional ones.

The legs and hooves have nothing really distinctive to separate the Giraffe from the bovines. The tail hangs down to the hocks, which are really the heels, and ends in a thick tuft of bristles.

Earlier forms of the Giraffe may have been bigger, but in the existing types the males do not exceed 550 centimetres and females are some ninety centimetres shorter. Only when the animal throws its head right back are these heights somewhat exceeded. The height to the withers is 250 to 335 centimetres according to sex. The tail is over ninety centimetres long. The hooves are fifteen centimetres in height in males, but only ten centimetres in the females. Weights vary from a half to one tonne.

The pattern of the coats of Giraffes is so diversified that many varieties have been named. The coloration often varies considerably between

different animals of the same herds. Formerly it was believed that there were two: the Giraffe (*Giraffa camelopardalis*) and the Reticulated Giraffe (*G. reticulata*), which is confined to East Africa and has a fine nut-brown coat with a network pattern of fine white lines. Today it is generally agreed these represent only one species (*G. camelopardalis*).

Giraffes are still fairly plentiful on savannas where there are acacias and climbing leguminous plants. These may be found from 10°N. to 20°S. and from Lake Chad to eastern Africa. Herds of twenty to thirty are not uncommon, each containing several males but many more females. Only old males are excluded and live in isolation.

The Moose (*Alces alces*) is a very large long-legged deer of cold northern climates. Known as elk in northern Europe and Asia, and moose in North America, it is the largest living deer. It feeds in summer in lakes and rivers.

The Reindeer (*Rangifer tarandus*) of Europe and Asia is known as the Caribou (*R. arcticus*) in America. Bulls fight savagely for a harem of from five to forty cows. Rutting takes place in September or October, one to two calves being born in the summer. These can walk after two hours and are weaned after two months.

The Okapi (*Okapia johnstoni*) inhabits the dense rainforests of eastern Zaire and first became known to Europeans in 1900. A primitive member of the giraffe family, it stands 150 centimetres at the shoulder and has shorter limbs and neck than the Giraffe. Only males have horns.

A Giraffe is very awkward when stooping to drink, which it can only do by flexing its front legs, or straddling them. Its gait is interesting. It does not exactly amble, which means moving the two right legs and then the two left. With the Giraffe the front foot leaves the ground before the hind one and comes down before it. It is this lack of simultaneity which makes the Giraffe's gait so peculiar.

Giraffes do not often use their low fluttering voice, but they have a keen sense of hearing. Sight and smell are also well developed, as is the intelligence. Danger is scented at a considerable distance and evasive action taken. They can travel faster than a horse and can maintain their speed longer. If cornered they can give a good account of themselves with their hooves. A single Lion can rarely get the better of a Giraffe.

Otherwise they are gentle creatures. When their two enemies, man and lion, are out of sight they are very sociable in habit. They are often to be seen in company with zebras, gnus or Ostriches. They also have the company of ox-peckers (*Buphaga*), the perching birds that ride on their backs feeding on ticks and other parasites. Gestation lasts fourteen or fifteen months and never more than one is born at a time.

The Giraffe was the only known member of its family until 1900, when the famous naturalist Sir Harry Johnston found specimens of the striped leg skin of the Okapi in the Congo. Later a whole skin and two skulls were found. A British zoologist described them under the name of *Okapia johnstoni*.

The Okapi is unquestionably a cousin of the Giraffe and, although not a common animal, it is represented in most of the big zoos. Its head is the same shape and it has the same lips and tongue. It also has, though in less degree, the same slope of the back. But it differs in several points which make it seem like a half-formed Giraffe or a precursor to it. Its neck is no longer than that of some antelopes and its horns, present only in the male, are pointed and naked at the tips.

An interesting thing is that the Okapi presents today an almost exact picture of the ruminant which actually preceded the Giraffe, *Palaeotragus*, which lived in Greece in Miocene times. The Okapi thus looks like a lingering survivor of that distant genus. The stripes on the hind quarters, contrasting with the rest of its hazel coat, must not be allowed to suggest any relationship to the zebra.

Pronghorn (Family Antilocapridae)

A peculiar antelope-like animal of uncertain affinities, the Pronghorn (*Antilocapra americana*) is the sole representative of its family. Although persecuted by hunters, it still exists in herds in the Far West of North America, where they are protected. Under proper management they have increased to a point where a limited open hunting season is possible in some states. The Pronghorn is the only hollow-horned ruminant to have branching horns, the outer sheath of which is shed and renewed each year. It looks like a young stag with a beam and one tine. The Pronghorn also has the reputation of being the fastest ungulate in North America. Its top speed is eighty kilometres per hour over short distances.

Wild cattle (Family Bovidae)

The ox is typical of the Bovidae and still more of the subfamily Bovinae. It has a massive, heavy body and short neck, beneath which hangs the dewlap. The muzzle is broad, bare and wet. The tear glands, or interdigital glands, are lacking, and the hollow horns are generally smooth, or grooved only at the base. The tail is long and tufted at the end. There are four teats on a single udder.

The wild species living today all belong to the single genus *Bos*, including the Gayal, Gaur, and Banteng, which are all Asiatic and differ from the European Domestic Ox (*Bos taurus*) mainly by the lumps on their backs. Their habits are always the same. They generally live in small herds of between five and twenty, each led by a bull, and consisting of its females and their young. Banished from the herd on reaching the adult state, the latter live alone until they in turn establish a herd. A certain number of old males also live in isolation, waiting for any occasion to satisfy their sexual impulses. Wild cattle generally rest early in the morning and in the middle of the afternoon, when they chew the cud. They normally sleep at night, but adopt a nocturnal mode of life in areas where they are not left in peace.

The Gaur (*B. gaurus*) inhabits the wooded and mountainous regions of India, Burma, Thailand, Indo-China and Malaya, generally in inaccessible spots. It measures 195 centimetres at the shoulder and has long horns arched over the head. It has no dewlap. It is very dark in colour except on the ventral side, and has white stockings on the lower leg. The horns are flattened, broad at the base, strongly curved inwards at the tips and up to 110 centimetres from tip to tip. It is not easily domesticated though attempts have been made.

The Gayal (*B. frontalis*) is a domesticated form of the Gaur. It is similar in colour to the Gaur, but is a few centimetres shorter and has a dewlap. The horns are also shorter and more divergent. The meat is of good quality, as is the leather.

The Banteng (*B. sondaicus*) distributed from Thailand to Indonesia is most like the Gayal both in appearance and habits though somewhat slighter in build and with thinner horns. Both sexes have white stockings stretching some way up the legs. There are wild herds as well as domesticated ones, which are considered the best cattle of the East Indies.

The Aurochs (*B. primigenius*) was a form of wild cattle living in Europe, Asia and North Africa in the late Cainozoic era, only becoming extinct in the seventeenth century. Primitive cave-drawings of the Aurochs are more rare than those of the bison. It is still possibly represented by three races of modern domestic cattle: the Spanish, Camargue and Corsican.

DOMESTIC CATTLE: Among the creatures most useful to man, domestic cattle (*B. taurus*) rank as the most powerful of draught animals. A yoke of oxen each of 700 kilograms, can draw a load of five tonnes a distance of twenty-five kilometres in a day, admittedly at a speed of about three kilometres per hour. Horses could go faster, but they could not pull the load. For heavy ploughing oxen are unrivalled.

Cow's milk has the best balanced content, the sugar, protein and cream content being about equal (about forty grammes of each to the litre). It is thus less creamy than goat's milk and less sweet than ass's milk. Cream is the most valuable constituent, and in animals bred for milk production every effort is made to increase the cream content. Other races are bred for beef, which may come from oxen, bullocks or even cows. As regards veal, the flesh from calves which have been grazing either during or after lactation will be redder and less tender than that from sucking calves. There is rarely more than one calf, born after nine months gestation. Lactation lasts six months, after which the calf is weaned.

Domestic cattle are classed according to whether the profile is straight, hollow or rounded, the body long, short or medium, by the length of the head, the length and shape of the horns, the nature of the coat, and so on.

Only a few races can be mentioned. Of the dual-purpose cattle, valuable alike for beef and dairy products, none is better than the Normandy. It is of great size, and in milk production it is generally accepted that a Normandy cow can yield just over

3,350 litres a year and well over 135 kilograms of butter. In Belgium and Holland races have been bred in which the quantity of milk was the first consideration and yearly figures of 4,000 and 4,500 litres and more have been reached, but the fat content is not high and the meat is of poor quality. The Holstein-Friesian breed is common in England as well as in the United States, Canada, Australia, South America and South Africa.

The Jersey is another dairy breed whose beef is poor. Although it is a breed of Norman and Breton descent, in this case the aim is a milk as rich as possible in cream. The Guernsey is a somewhat larger breed than the Jersey, and both are known in the United States. Another common dairy breed is the Ayrshire, which is strongly represented in Canada, and may also be found in the United States, South Africa, Australia, New Zealand, Central America and Europe. The Brown Swiss, one of the oldest breeds, is sometimes used in the United States but more so in Italy, Austria and Hungary.

The commonest British beef breed is the Short-horn from Durham. It is one of the most wide-

The Pronghorn (*Antilocapra americana*) is restricted to North America, being found chiefly on the open western plains, where it lives in large herds. It is the only horned animal that sheds its horn sheath. It does this each October. The long white hairs on its rump patch can be erected to form a disc that can be seen at a distance flashing in the bright sunlight like a heliograph.

The Gaur (*Bos gaurus*) is the largest species of wild ox. In bulls the horn-tips turn upwards, but in cows they point inwards and occasionally cross. Gaur range in herds of from five to twenty. During the heat of the day they rest in the grassy areas in thick forest, emerging to feed in the early morning and evening.

A Hereford bull with Hereford x Friesian heifers. Domestic cattle (*Bos taurus*) have become increasingly important over the centuries with the increase in human populations. The first cattle were probably domesticated over 6,000 years ago in Asia and today selective breeding enables many types of cattle to be produced for a particular habitat or purpose.

spread breeds in the world. It is numerous in the United States and Argentina.

The Hereford is the result of centuries of breeding and selection from the original stock of the county. It is very hardy, perhaps owing to its thick coat. Polled Herefords have been produced in England and in the United States and have been exported to Canada, Mexico, South America, Australia and the Philippines, where they have adapted well.

The Aberdeen Angus is another polled breed, smaller than most beef breeds but of the best quality. Less often imported than the Shorthorn and the Hereford for the improvement of stock, it is nevertheless popular in the United States, Canada, New Zealand and Argentina.

The Devon and Red Poll have also been imported in many countries. More local in distribution are the wide-horned, shaggy Highland cattle, the hardiest of all the British breeds.

Another species of domestic cattle is the Zebu (*B. indicus*), called the Brahman in the United States. Cattle of this breed have pendent ears and a fatty hump. They are sometimes called humped cattle. They flourish in humid or arid districts and are resistant to infectious diseases. Male zebus are also crossed with ordinary cows to improve the stock. The Afrikander, a local South African humped breed, is probably descended from the Zebu. It is bred primarily for the production of good trek cattle. The Santa Gertrudis is another humped breed, produced by crossing Brahman bulls with Shorthorn cows.

The ancestry of domestic cattle, now assigned the scientific name *Bos taurus*, is obscured in the mists of antiquity. There seems to be little doubt that three species, all extinct in the wild, were implicated: the Aurochs (*B. primigenius*), the Zebu (*B. indicus*) and the Indian Ox (*B. namadicus*). At

some period or other cattle of the genus *Bibos* may have been crossed with man's primitive stock. At the present time there is no living member of the genus *Bos* except under rather rigid domestication.

BUFFALOES: The word 'buffalo' is used in the United States for the North American Bison. The species described here is the Buffalo of the Old World.

Buffaloes have much the same general appearance as oxen. Like oxen, Buffaloes have thirteen pairs of ribs, but they lack a dewlap and the forehead is rounded. The shape of the horns is also different. The horns drop slightly and sweep widely outwards before curving upwards. They have ridges near the base and the ends are rounded. The testes are not pendent. The hair is very short, leaving the skin almost naked. The colour is black sometimes a little reddish or greyish, and paler on the ventral side.

All Buffaloes have a liking for marshes, in which they wallow and cake themselves with mud as a protection against insects. When rubbed away the mud will normally take the ticks with it, in much the same way as surgical plaster is used to remove hairs in a beauty parlour.

The Domestic Buffalo of Europe (*Bubalus bubalis*) has the shortest and most splayed horns of any variety. It is common in the Balkans, Greece, Italy, Asia Minor, Egypt, and in the southern Soviet Republics. Properly known as the Indian or Water Buffalo, also as the Arna or Carabao, a few are still found wild in a few places in India, Assam, Indo-China and Borneo. In addition, they are found feral in Sri Lanka and northern Australia.

The Domestic Buffalo has the advantage over the ox of being able to stand the most humid climate and the most marshy soil, and to resist the infections normal to such country, being less prone to insect-borne diseases. Their wide flattened hooves give them a good grip of soft land. They are very hardy and can live entirely on reeds, rushes, sedges, and all sorts of aquatic plants. They stand cold so well that they can be kept permanently in the open, without any kind of shelter.

Like the horses and oxen of the Camargue, Domestic Buffaloes are kept in herds of 200–300, and one can provide some 1,600 litres of milk a year, which is as much as a cow of ordinary quality gives. The milk is twice as rich in cream as a cow's, and thus gives twice the quantity of butter, but the latter suffers from the grave disadvantage of not solidifying, except at low temperatures, and thus being usable only in winter. Buffalo cheese is appreciated all round the Mediterranean. It is from this milk that the genuine oriental yoghurt is made. The bullock is a gentle and obedient animal, useful for draught purposes.

Related to the Indian Buffalo or Arna are two other Asiatic species: the smaller Tamarau (*Anoa mindorensis*) from the Philippines and the still smaller Anoa (*A. depressicornis*), the Wild Dwarf Buffalo of Celebes which is only 100 centimetres high. Its horns are straight and sweep back like those of an antelope.

The African Buffaloes are generally classed in the separate genus *Syncerus*, and there has been some controversy as to the number and distribution of the species. It has, however, been recently shown that the size, colour, shape and disposition of horns vary according to the habitat frequented, which may be anywhere between Lake Chad and the Cape, and between Senegal and Ethiopia. Moreover, in this vast expanse they are found in dense tropical forests, half-open country, and in the savanna. With such difference of environment and consequently of diet, it is only to be expected that they should vary in muscular strength, hardiness, and in the shape of their horns, and what were formerly supposed to be separate species are now known to be varieties or subspecies of the same species (*Syncerus caffer*), widespread throughout Africa south of the Sahara. In fact, the horns may vary considerably in a given herd and even in a given individual at different ages.

The Dwarf or Forest Buffalo (*S. caffer nanus*) is the smallest race, being only 110 centimetres to the shoulder and weighing only 200 kilograms. It lives in the marshy forests of West Africa, where it is known as the Bush Cow. Authorities differ as to whether it is a distinct species or a race of *S. caffer*. The Cape or Black Buffalo, living in the open country of Central, South and East Africa, attains a height of 150 centimetres at the shoulder and a weight of 790 kilograms. Between these two there seems to be insufficient difference to prevent hybridisation in the regions where they overlap, which is one reason for supposing them to be conspecific. The Forest Buffalo, a very wild type that has never been domesticated, lives in herds of up to a thousand.

The African Buffalo is still abundant, although it is widely persecuted. Hunting Buffalo can be a dangerous sport. If irritated, let alone attacked, the beast will charge, and it can disembowel an enemy with its horns or trample it to death. The Africans hunt it with spears and poisoned arrows, or trap it, for the sake of its meat and leather. Apart from man, its only enemy is the Lion.

BISON: The North American Bison, though locally called buffalo, should not be confused with the African Buffalo. The Bison form a particular group of bovines characterised by the enormous development of their shaggy fore quarters, topped

The Zebu, Brahman or Oriental Domestic Cattle (*Bos indicus*) are derived from the Indian wild cattle. They have long horns, a hump and a pronounced dewlap under the throat. Zebu do well in hot climates and seem to have a resistance to insect pests, often attributed to their repellant sweat.

The African Buffalo (*Syncerus caffer*) is widespread throughout Africa south of the Sahara and is found near water, grass, and sufficient cover. It goes to drink usually in the morning and evening and feeds during the early part of the night. Later it will rest and chew the cud. During the heat of the day it retires to the forest shade.

The heavy fore-quarters and massive head are the outstanding features of the North American Bison or Buffalo (*Bison bison*). Large bulls stand two metres at the shoulder and may weigh nearly one-and-a-half tonnes, but they are not aggressive and rarely make an unprovoked attack.

The Yak (*Bos mutus*) lives in the Tibetan highlands among cold, desolate surroundings. These animals do not thrive in the lower warmer parts of Asia. Bulls travel alone or in groups of two or three, cows and calves form big herds from twenty to two hundred. In late autumn the rut takes place, when the bulls fight fiercely, although fatalities rarely result.

by a hump just behind the neck. The long, shaggy hair covers the head, neck, shoulders and breast, and runs down the fore limbs. It may even be prolonged down the back as far as the root of the tail. This unusual growth of hair is more pronounced in the male than in the female. The horns are rather small, circular in cross section, and set very far apart on the rounded forehead. Unlike the oxen and the African Buffaloes they have fourteen pairs of ribs. The voice is also different, more like a groaning than a lowing.

The species most frequently shown in zoos is the North American Bison (*Bison bison*), in which the typical characters are carried to extreme. Its shaggy winter coat falls off in patches in the spring, and gradually the summer coat appears. It is very short and thin. The colour is dark brown in winter and lighter in summer. The largest males reach a height of nearly 180 centimetres at the withers and a weight of a tonne-and-a-half.

A grass feeder, the Bison formerly existed in enormous herds on the prairies of western Canada and the United States. It passed its time in grazing, chewing the cud, sleeping, or going down to the water-holes. In the autumn those in the north moved south in vast herds. Whole plains were then covered with them as far as the eye could see. They pressed on, disregarding rivers or railways, the latter having at times to suspend their services; and these legions were followed by wolves, coyotes, and eagles and vultures.

In the spring, movement was in the reverse direction and was the prelude to calving and then pairing. After a gestation of nine to nine-and-a-half months, the cows give birth to a single calf between July and October, when the bulls fight for possession. First there is a preliminary stamping, then they charge at each other head on, coming together with a resounding crack which may involve three tonnes weight.

Although outwardly placid, the Bison is readily aroused and can be violently aggressive. In captivity it has to be approached with caution. Although its vision is poor, its sense of smell and hearing are very sharp, and in the wild they enable the American Bison to detect an enemy at a fair distance. Against wolves, the bulls gather round the cows, which themselves encircle the young. When roused, the Bison's normal reaction is to flee and whatever gets in the way of a stampeding herd rarely escapes.

When America was discovered Bison were distributed over about a third of the continent, from well into Canada in the north to the border of Mexico, their principal habitat being the basins of the Mississippi, the Missouri and the Ohio. From the central region they extended eastward to the Appalachians and beyond, and westward at one point over the Rocky Mountains. It has been estimated that there must have been some sixty million in the country.

The extermination of Bison began towards the end of the eighteenth century. By 1820 there were relatively few Bison left east of the Mississippi, and the construction of railways in the last quarter of the century hastened the process. Not until 1905 was the American Bison Society formed with the object of preserving the animal from total extermination and reserves were established in the United States and Canada. By 1935 there were about 20,000 Bison in North America, more than half being in Canada. Their numbers are now large enough to guarantee their survival and to permit a controlled harvesting of the surplus.

The European Bison or Wisent (*B. bonasus*) is closely related to the American Bison and was abundant in Europe in the late Cainozoic era. It is more graceful than the North American species. It has a smaller head, more slender horns, a less pronounced hump, longer legs, and the whole body is markedly less shaggy.

In the first centuries of the Christian era Bison still inhabited the forested regions of western Europe, but various factors led to their gradual elimination and by the eighteenth century the species had been reduced to two herds of a few hundred head. An international society for the preservation of Wisent was founded in 1932 and the herds are now increasing.

YAK: Related to the Bison, the Yak (*Bos mutus*), which lives in the Tibetan highlands, has a rounded forehead, horns wide apart, and a hump over the shoulders, covered with long hairs and a fringe of long black hair on the flanks. It resembles the Bison in having fourteen pairs of ribs and in groaning rather than lowing.

Living at heights of 3,900 to 6,000 metres the Yak has a special protection against cold in the long hairs which fall from its sides almost to the ground, looking like a strange garment in which the tail and legs are concealed. It is a slightly reddish black with white muzzle, forehead and tail and measures up to 180 centimetres at the shoulder.

The Yak is unsurpassed among bovines for its capacity to survive under the bleakest mountain conditions. It can walk and climb great distances, as is essential in a habitat where food is scarce. Often it grazes only just below the snow-line. It can sleep on the snow, and even the newborn young can withstand these harsh conditions.

The Yak is hunted for its flesh and hair, and it makes a good pack or saddle animal when domesticated. Its creamy, aromatic milk is excellent. Even its dung is dried and used as fuel. Civilisation in Tibet seems to depend largely on two animals, the Yak and the wild ass known as the Kiang.

MUSK-OX: In the far north of the American continent, and round the north and east coasts of Greenland, lives a ruminant which in the Ice Age was spread much further south and was also distributed in Europe and Asia. This is the Musk-ox (*Ovibos moschatus*), called *Ovibos* because it is more or less intermediate between oxen and sheep, and *moschatus* because it has a musky odour.

With the compact neck, equiline profile, hairy muzzle, thin lips and small pointed ears, it is by no means unlike a big, long-haired ram. The flattened horns, however, implanted low on the skull are more like those of the African Buffalo, though they fall much lower and rise again merely to the level of the eye. The brown coat remains long all the year round, the hairs hanging down and half-concealing the legs, which thus look shorter than they are. In this respect they remind one of the Bison and still more of the Yak. There is also a fine undercoat.

Anyone visiting the barren Arctic wastes of the New World might well be astonished that they could nourish herds of Musk-ox, which are up to 150 centimetres at the shoulder and weigh up to 310 kilograms. There is nothing but the products of a very short summer and, in winter, the mosses and lichens hidden beneath the snow. They have no shelter of any sort, not even trees, to protect them from the furious blizzards of those latitudes, nor have they much defence against the famished wolves which are always on the lookout for a straggler. For hardiness they have no rival, and in any case their strength is in unity. They huddle together against the cold, sharing their warmth. Against wolves the herd forms a phalanx, presenting a unified series of extremely daunting horns to the enemy.

Their most deadly enemy is the Eskimo, who hunts them for their flesh, despite the taste of musk, as well as their hair and leather. In order to prevent the Musk-ox becoming extinct, the Canadian and the Danish Governments have taken steps to protect the last remaining herds. A reserve has been established between Hudson Bay and Great Slave Lake, and there is another in Greenland. The Musk-ox is worth preserving, not merely as a zoological curiosity, but also because it can be used for hybridisation with domestic animals so as to increase their resistance to the cold.

Sheep, goats, goat-antelopes (Subfamily Caprinae)

Sheep are smaller than the Musk-ox and have transversely ribbed horns which tend to curl in spirals with the points turning outwards as they rise. The mouth is narrow and the lips thin. There are only two teats. Inter-digital glands are present in some varieties, as are face glands. The sheep has a very characteristic profile and like goats has a bleating voice.

The Moufflon and related wild sheep are found exclusively in the mountainous districts of Europe, Asia, Africa and North America. The Barbary Sheep, Arni or Aoudad (*Ammotragus lervia*) is

furthest removed from the domestic species. It has long hair on its neck and fore limbs. The horns are almost equally developed in both sexes and sweep in a wide semicircle away from the head. In appearance and habits the Barbary Sheep resembles a goat. It is very hardy and can withstand great differences in climate. Its habitat extends from the highest peaks of the Atlas to the Red Sea. Its ability to go without water is extraordinary.

The remaining wild sheep belong to the same genus (*Ovis*) as the domestic variety. The true Moufflon (*O. musimon*) is the European wild sheep, living in Corsica and Sardinia, where it owes its survival to the roughness of the scrub, though only a few scanty herds are still to be found. It has short wool and long, curved horns. Its rusty colour becomes darker in winter. Pairing is in the autumn, ewes giving birth to two lambs which are capable of running about almost immediately after birth.

The Bighorn (*O. canadensis*) lives in North America from Alaska to Mexico and in north-eastern Siberia. It grows to a height of nearly 120 centimetres at the shoulder and a weight of over 135 kilograms. It lives in herds of about fifty on the wildest and most inaccessible mountains, having an unsurpassed ability for climbing and jumping.

The Argali (*O. ammon*) is closely related to the Bighorn and is the largest of the sheep family, attaining a height of over 120 centimetres. Its horns sweep round in a complete circle. It is found in central Asia and Bokhara and Altai to Tibet and Mongolia. Marco Polo's Argali of the Pamirs has the longest horns. They grow outwards in an open spiral, the record length being 190 centimetres.

Other eastern forms are the Red Sheep or Urial (*O. orientalis*), also known as the Cyprian Sheep. It is regarded as one of the ancestors of the domestic species and lives in western Asia.

DOMESTIC SHEEP: The use of Domestic Sheep (*O. aries*) goes far back into antiquity. In many areas there are native stocks which are hardy and capable of a fair production of milk, mutton, wool

The Musk-ox (*Ovibos moschatus*) is found in north-east Canada and Greenland. It was threatened with extinction largely because of its habit of forming phalanxes for mutual defence, this was effective against wolves but not modern firearms. The shooting of an entire herd was an easy matter since the animals did not attempt to escape.

The Bighorn or Rocky Mountain Sheep (*Ovis canadensis*) is the only wild sheep in the mountains of western North America. It is gregarious, but males and females form separate herds. A mountain-dweller, it moves with swift bounds, having soft foot pads which absorb impact and also provide a grip.

and leather, but in the great sheep-rearing countries such unspecialised stocks have given way to breeds developed and improved for a particular purpose.

The Merino is the most important fine-wool breed. It has a short head with wool down the forehead and sometimes even descending the nose. The skin of the neck has lateral folds. Only the rams have horns, which are twisted into a spiral at the sides of the head. Originating in Spain, but now distributed throughout the world, the Merino is a hardy animal in a dry climate. It has served as a foundation stock for the formation of many breeds (e.g. Rambouillet, Negretti, Saxony) and has played a great part in the development of Australia as the greatest wool-producing country in the world.

The British breeds are divided into longwools and shortwools. The longwools are white-faced, with the exception of the Wensleydale, and hornless. The English Leicester was one of the first sheep to be bred scientifically in England. It crosses well with merinos to give an excellent wool. The Border Leicester is a cross between the English Leicester and the Cheviot. The Lincoln Longwool has been much exported and the sheep in Argentina are largely Lincoln. Other longwool breeds are the Wensleydale, Cotswold, Devon Longwool, Romney Marsh and Roscommon, the latter being an Irish breed.

The shortwools produce better mutton and short, fine quality fleeces. The Southdown is the oldest of British breeds and of great importance. It is a black-faced sheep, and is popular in Commonwealth countries and the United States. Other black-faced breeds are the Hampshire Down and the Suffolk breed, produced originally from Norfolk ewes and Southdown rams, and the Oxford Devon, produced by crossing Hampshire Down and Suffolk. The Shropshire, which is also black-faced, has become a popular farm sheep in the Middle West. Other shortwool breeds are the Dorset Down, Dorset Horn, Ryeland and Kerry Hill.

The mountain breeds are smaller than the longwools and most of the shortwools. They are hardy animals and give very good mutton. The Cheviot is one of the oldest British breeds and its wool is used for the best Scotch tweeds. The Welsh Mountain also has good wool but the Scotch Blackface has coarse, hairy wool used for carpets.

Several white-faced shortwools have originated in other countries. The Corriedale is a New Zealand breed obtained by crossing Lincoln rams with Merino ewes. Two French breeds of international standing are Le Contentin and Ile de France. The Columbia and Panama are both United States breeds, as is the Romeldale from California. The Texel is a Dutch breed common in Europe and the Oldenburg White Head is a German breed.

The fur type of sheep comes from the wild and rugged western slopes of the Pamirs. At the beginning of this century a few rams and ewes were exported from Bokhara, and have founded the various herds now scattered over the world, the principal ones being in the United States, Canada, Poland, Austria and South Africa. The tight curls of wool soon begin to straighten and

Dall's Sheep (*Ovis dalli*) is one of the thinhorn sheep and is pure white. It occurs in north-west Canada and Alaska where large numbers are found living in sight of huge glaciers.

therefore the lamb has to be killed during the first few days of life.

GOATS: Closely related to sheep, goats are lively, swift, climbing animals with a strong odour, particularly in the male. They are distinguished from sheep by the following characters: narrower head; bearded chin in the male; horns close at the base, sweeping upwards and backwards, and transversely ridged or twisted like a corkscrew; no face gland; short, upturned tail.

The principal species are the Wild Goat or Pasang (*Capra hircus*) and the various ibexes. The Alpine Ibex (*C. ibex*) is a short-legged, squat and sturdy animal with powerful horns, which are triangular in section and strongly ridged. The winter coat is thicker and darker than the summer one. A big male may be almost ninety centimetres tall and weight up to 110 kilograms. It has no beard. This splendid animal, the Steinbok of the Alps, became extinct except for a colony in the Gran Paradiso National Park in Italy and perhaps one near Salzburg. It has since been reintroduced into Switzerland, Bavaria, Austria and Yugoslavia and lives in small herds high among the glaciers. Males, particularly old ones, may be seen perched on a pinnacle, while the females and young keep below among the rocks and bushes. At night all come down into the forest. Their skill in climbing and jumping is the marvel of all mountaineers. An Ibex can stand comfortably on a peak only just big enough for its four feet and can jump over chasms with incredible accuracy.

Pairing takes place in winter after furious fights between the males. After five months' gestation the female gives birth to a single kid in May or June, and a few hours after birth it is already an able climber with an unerring foothold.

The Nubian Ibex or Beden (*C. i. nubiana*) and Asiatic Ibex or Sakin (*C. i. sibirica*) are subspecies of the Alpine Ibex. The Asiatic Ibex is a large animal with very long horns.

The Spanish Ibex (*C. pyrenaica*) has compressed horns which lack knots and sweep outwards as well as backwards in a rather impressive display.

The Wild Goat (*C. hircus*), which is also called the Passang or Persian Wild Goat, is believed to be the ancestor of the Domestic Goat. It is more angular than the Ibex and has compressed horns with sharp edges. It lives in the mountains of Asia Minor up to heights of 3,900 metres.

DOMESTIC GOATS: The Domestic Goat belongs to the same species as the Wild Goat (*C. hircus*). Its hardiness, resistance to disease and the ease with which it can be kept have made it the 'poor man's cow'. A big Alpine Goat of seventy-five kilograms gives an average of 550 to 780 litres of milk a year. Relative to the animal's size, this is twice or three times the yield of a good cow. Excellent butter and many cheeses can be made from the milk. Moreover, it is easier to digest than cow's milk and never harbours tubercular infection. The Domestic Goat is more prolific than the Wild Goat, giving birth to two or three kids at a time.

The most important milk-producing breed is the Swiss or Alpine Goat, and there is a good deal of its blood in most European goats. The Swiss race is divided into two breeds: Saanen and Toggenburg. The native English Goat, small short-legged and long-haired, has been improved to give a higher milk yield by the use of pedigree males, mostly of Swiss extraction. This breeding has been so successful that England has now the best and heaviest milk stock in the world. The chief breeds in England today are the Saanen, Toggenburg, British Saanen, British Toggenburg and Anglo-Nubian, based on stock from India and Egypt. The Scotch, Welsh and Irish types have also been improved, although they show more of their local ancestry than the English. The Eastern or Nubian breed, with long, drooping ears, is an oriental one which has been imported into England and other countries. In South Africa the 'Boer' Goat is a Swiss-Nubian cross. The United States breeds largely Toggenburgs, Saanens, Nubians, and French Alpines. There is also an American breed, the Rock Alpine.

The Kashmir and Angora are 'wool' goats. The Kashmir goat comes from Tibet. Its thick, white coat consists of long guard hairs and a highly

The Mountain Goat (*Oreamnos americanus*) lives in the Rockies and coastal ranges of North America. It is not a true goat but a goat-antelope. An animal specialised to live on steep, wet, and often snow-covered mountains. It has massive, muscular legs with large broad hooves, which have a hard sharp rim, enclosing a soft inner pad, well suited for climbing over rocks and ice.

The Alpine Ibex (*Capra ibex*) has close-set horns, triangular in section and measuring 150 centimetres long. The prominent ribbing on the flattened anterior edge distinguishes it from the Spanish Ibex. Although it has been reintroduced into its former ranges in the Alps, it is now only found in a truly wild state in the Italian Tyrol.

The Chamois (*Rupicapra rupicapra*) inhabits the mountain ranges in Europe and Asia Minor. The females and their young gather in herds of between ten and fifty. Old males live solitary lives for the greater part of the year, only joining the herd in autumn for the rutting season, when they drive the young males from the herd, occasionally killing them.

Elands (*Taurotragus oryx*) drinking at a waterhole in the Wankie National Park in Zimbabwe. During the dry season herds of a hundred or more come together and wander in search of food. Recently elands have been domesticated for milk production and in the future they may become economically beneficial animals in Africa.

valued silky underwool. The Angora breed from Turkey is similar, but in this case it is the long, silky guard hairs that are valued. The breed has been successfully introduced into Algeria, Mexico, South Africa, Australia and the United States. In the latter country three-quarters of the mohair produced comes from Texas.

GOAT-ANTELOPES: Intermediate between the goats and antelopes, some goat-antelopes look like goats, smell like them and share their climbing powers, but they have muzzles like oxen and antelopes and are never bearded. Sometimes their necks are maned. The horns in some recall those of cattle, while in others the horns foreshadow those of antelopes.

Several species of gorals (genus *Naemorhaedus*) are goat-like, but both sexes bear horns. They live in the Himalayas, western China and Korea. The remarkable Takin (genus *Budorcas*), which combines features of the ox, goat and antelope, comes from the highlands of central Asia. Its Roman nose, eyes high in the head, and horns placed at the top of the forehead give it an extremely unusual appearance. The serows (genus *Capricornis*), distributed from the Himalayas to China, Formosa and Japan, and south to Malaya and Sumatra are all mountain animals and are closely related to the gorals.

The Rocky Mountain Goat (*Oreamnos americanus*) of North America is the only ruminant to keep a white coat all the year round. It has a shaggy coat and both sexes have short, black horns, about twenty-three centimetres long. Rocky Mountain goats live on the craggiest and most remote mountain slopes, usually well above the tree-line. They associate in small groups, and the males are often solitary. They are only found in the mountains of the West from the northwestern United States along the Pacific coast to Alaska.

The Chamois (*Rupicapra rupicapra*) is the only European species in this heterogeneous group. Smaller than its rival in jumping, the Ibex, it is even more graceful. Its horns are not only smaller, but are differently shaped. They are not ridged and are set close together on the forehead, from which they project almost at right angles and are quite straight until they curve sharply backwards near the top. Both sexes bear horns. The colour of the Chamois varies with the season. In summer it is beige-grey, in winter black with white patches on the head, neck and flanks. It stands eighty centimetres high and weighs up to forty kilograms, the female being somewhat smaller.

The Chamois is found in the Alps, Pyrenees (this variety being called the Izard), Apennines (Abruzzi), Balkans, Carpathians and Caucasus, at heights of from 750 to 2,250 metres. Herds, of both sexes, vary in numbers from ten to fifty, and sometimes more. Only old males live alone. Summer is spent in the heights. Rutting takes place in the autumn and lasts until December, and during it there are many fights among males. When the snow falls all come down to shelter in the forests. Gestation lasts five to six months, a single young being born at the end of the spring.

The tahrs (genus *Hemitragus*) may also be classed with the goat-antelopes. They have very short horns and quite a different odour in the male, but are otherwise much like the goat. There are a Himalayan species and two others, from southern India and southeastern Arabia.

Antelopes (Subfamily Antilopinae)

This group of animals might be said to include all the hollow-horned ruminants that cannot easily be classified elsewhere. The size of antelopes varies from that of a hare to larger than an ox. Some have face glands, a dewlap and a mane, but others are without any of these.

Horns may be present in both sexes or only in the males. They are always simple and persistent, but otherwise differ greatly. They may be long or short, straight with simple ribs, spiralled, or straight with a spiral keel. They may curve forwards or backwards, be U-shaped, or V-shaped or start divergent and then become convergent, like the horns of a lyre. The base can be adjacent or widely separated. One curious antelope is the Chousingha, or Four-horned Antelope, of southern India, the males of which have four small horns.

There is as much variety in their habitats. They may be found in the heart of tropical forests, in semi-open country, in savannas and even in deserts. Those living on the plains are usually found in herds, while those living in thick cover are generally solitary or in pairs. Antelopes live on grass, leaves and shoots, but the diet varies with the habitat, which also influences the distances they must go for both food and water. Some are capable of going without water for several days, and the Arabian Oryx is believed to be able to go indefinitely without drinking, obtaining water from the desert succulents it eats. As soon as they hear or smell an enemy of any sort, they invariably make off at a trot or gallop. Many of them are faster than either horse or greyhound, but they cannot maintain their speed for long. Antelopes are often hunted for their flesh, and some species of duikers are valued for their leather.

Rutting takes place once a year and always involves fights between the males. This has always been supposed to be for the possession of the females, but recent observations of the Uganda Kob leave no doubt that in that one species the fights are purely territorial. The females have two teats or four, but they bear a single young which they tend carefully.

The Eland (*Taurotragus oryx*) is a large antelope with straight spirally twisted horns and a dewlap. It lives in open country in East Africa and at one time ranged as far south as the Cape. Adult males are 165 centimetres at the shoulder. The Giant Eland, or Lord Derby's Eland (*T. derbianus*), is still bigger and is the largest of the antelopes, being nearly 180 centimetres at the shoulder and weighing over a tonne. The straight, twisted horns may be seventy-five to a hundred centimetres long, the female's being no shorter though somewhat more slender. Elands are easily tamed and have been bred for their milk and meat.

The Nylghai or Blue Bull (*Boselaphus tragocamelus*), which lives on the open plains in India, has points of resemblance to the ox, deer, goat and camel, these resemblances being indicated in its specific name. It is the biggest Asiatic antelope, the height to the withers being 140 centimetres. The low hind-quarters give the back a considerable incline. The horns, found in males only, are small and slightly curved forwards.

The Kudu (*Tragelaphus strepsiceros*) and the Lesser Kudu (*T. imberbis*), both live in more or less open country in eastern and southern Africa. Though smaller than the Eland, the Kudu is more imposing with its very long, spiral horns and the white stripes on its grey or pale tawny body. It is perhaps the most beautiful and striking of the great antelopes of Africa.

The Hartebeest (*Alcelaphus buselaphus*), on the other hand, is a large, awkward animal with V-shaped or lyre-shaped horns coming from a lumpy forehead, which makes the face look unduly long. There are several species living on the African savannas. The wildebeestes or gnus of Africa have their eyes set high, the face tufted, and the horns (in both sexes) sweep downwards like those of a buffalo.

The most horse-like antelopes are in the genus *Hippotragus*, which stand about 150 centimetres at the shoulder, and have long horns curving backwards. The Roan Antelope (*H. equinus*) is greyish-roan and is found chiefly in West and southeastern Africa. The Sable Antelope (*H. niger*) is somewhat smaller, but with still longer horns, which reach 150 centimetres in length. It is found in Kenya and the Transvaal. An even longer-horned form, the Giant Sable Antelope (*H. niger variani*), with horns up to 165 centimetres long, is found in Angola.

Among the medium-sized antelopes—that is, those not much more than a metre in height—are the Bushbucks, Bongos, oryxes, gazelles, all of Africa; and the Asiatic Saigas, Chousinghas and the true antelopes.

The Bushbuck (*Tragelaphus scriptus*) is a graceful animal living in savanna or forest. It is dark red with white spots and stripes, which have earned it the name of harnessed antelope. Only the males

The Greater Kudu (*Strepsiceros strepsiceros*) of East and South Africa stands 150 centimetres at the shoulder and has magnificent spiralling horns. It keeps to the bush, camouflaged by its striped grey coat. When hunted it seeks refuge in water, being a powerful swimmer.

The White-bearded Brindled Gnu or Blue Wildebeest (*Connochaetes taurinus albojubatus*) ranges from Kenya to South Africa. It prefers a habitat of open grassy plains with water nearby. Gnus usually gather in herds of five to fifteen animals but occasionally much larger herds are found. They have keen sight and sense of smell, which they use to avoid their greatest enemy, the Lion.

The Gemsbok (*Oryx gazella*) of southwest Africa ranges in bands of two to a dozen, but occasionally as many as sixty are noted together. Both sexes have long straight horns. All four species of the genus *Oryx* are hunted for these rapier-like horns.

The Gerenuk or Waller's Gazelle (*Litocranius walleri*), of East Africa, has an elongated neck and has the habit of standing erect on its hind legs to browse tall bushes.

have lyrate horns, about 40 centimetres long. Another specialised bushbuck is the Nyala (*T. angasi*) of Zululand, one of the most handsome of all the antelopes.

The Bongo (*Boocercus eurycerus*) is only found in the deep recesses of equatorial forests, from West Africa to the Aberdare Mountains of Kenya. Few white men have ever seen it.

The Sitatunga (*Limnotragus spekei*), also known as Marsh-buck or Water-koedoe, is more adapted to marshy ground, with its long, spreading hooves which prevent it from sinking. It is only found in

the dense papyrus swamps of tropical Africa and so presents a sharp contrast to the Saharan types, the oryxes, Addaxes and gazelles.

The White Oryx (*Oryx algazel*), which is a somewhat larger antelope, has very long horns in both sexes, curving gracefully; hence its alternative name, Scimitar Oryx. It is found in the deserts of western Sudan. Other species are the Gemsbok (*O. gazella*), of south-west Africa, the Beisa of East Africa (*O. beisa*), and the Arabian Oryx (*O. leucoryx*), which now appears to be almost extinct.

The Addax (*Addax nasomaculatus*), which lives in North African deserts, has, in both sexes, long, ribbed horns in an open spiral.

Gazelles (*Gazella* spp.), proverbial for their beauty, are among the most widely distributed of the Antilopinae. The horns, generally lacking in the female in Asiatic forms but usually common to both sexes in the African forms, are V-shaped or lyrate, with the points generally turned forward. All are sandy-coloured and most have white rump patches. Their speed is remarkable. A gazelle can keep up a speed of over sixty-five kilometres an hour for fifteen minutes and more. Hunting it is accordingly very difficult, but nonetheless the size of the herds has suffered considerable reduction. There are many species spread over North Africa, western Asia, India and Central Asia. The Dorcas Gazelle (*G. dorcas*), spread over North Africa, is one of the smallest gazelles, being barely sixty centimetres up to the shoulder.

The Mhor or Dama Gazelle (*G. dama*), also native to Africa, is considerably larger. The Chinkara or Indian Gazelle (*G. bennetti*) is slightly over sixty centimetres in height and is one of the Asiatic forms with horns in both sexes. The Zeren, or Mongolian Gazelle (*Procapra gutturosa*) is seventy-five centimetres in height. The Goa or Tibetan Gazelle (*Procapra picticaudata*) inhabits the plains of the Tibetan plateau at heights of 3,900 to 5,400 metres. There are numerous other species.

Closely related to the gazelle is the Gerenuk (*Litocranius walleri*) with long thin neck and legs. Also known as the Giraffe-necked Gazelle, it stands erect on its hind legs in order to reach the foliage. There are sub-lyrate horns in the males only, and it spreads from southern Ethiopia to Tanzania. Another close relative is the Dibatag or Clarke's Gazelle (*Ammodorcas clarkei*) with similarly elongated limbs and neck.

Two other true antelopes from Africa are the Impala and the Springbok. The Impala (*Aepyceros melampus*) is a good-sized antelope, ninety-eight centimetres high living today mainly in East Africa, but elsewhere in national parks. The male has long, lyrate horns. The leaping powers of the Impala are extraordinary; possibly the purpose is to confuse an attacking Lion. The Springbok (*Antidorcas marsupialis*) is a South African species also famous for its jumping. It is found mainly in the Kalahari and Angola.

The duikers are short-legged African antelopes of small or medium size, recognisable from the tuft of hair between their very short horns (often in the female too). All have a uniform red-brown or grey coat and live south of the Sahara in forests and thickets. They are hunted for antelope skins.

The Saiga (*Saiga tatarica*) is now confined to the steppes of the Volga and the Caspian Sea but was formerly present in Europe. There are Pleistocene remains in south-east England. It is a heavy, somewhat sheep-like animal, with a very rounded nose sticking out in front of the mouth like a rudimentary trunk. The nose is over-developed and very mobile, particulary in males, and can be regarded as a secondary sexual character with no useful purpose. The males have horns, lyrate in form. The young are said to bleat like lambs.

The Chousingha (*Tetracerus quadricornis*) is a medium-sized antelope, which has four horns. Another is the Blackbuck (*Antilope cervicapra*), in which sexual dimorphism is carried very far. The males are nearly black with long, spiral horns, the females light beige and hornless. It inhabits the plains of India, especially where the grass is tall.

There are also very small types of antelopes. The Klipspringer (*Oreotragus oreotragus*) is fifty centimetres at the shoulder and is found from the Cape to the Sahara. A group called the neotragines includes the Pygmy or Royal Antelope (*Neotragus pygmaeus*), the smallest of all ruminants, which is only thirty centimetres at the shoulder and lives in West Africa. The Suni (*N. moschatus*) from East Africa is thirty-four centimetres. Other small antelopes include the five tiny dik–diks (genus *Madoqua*) and the Rhebok (*Pelea capreolus*). The Grysbok (*Raphicerus melanotis*) from South Africa is fifty-five centimetres high and is very similar to the Steinbok (*R. campestris*) from the same area.

Antelope herds are now much smaller and less numerous than they used to be and some species have already become extinct owing to excessive

hunting by man. Many other forms of wild life, ranging from the Duckbilled Platypus to the African Elephant, owe their continued existence to protection in national parks and nature reserves, which play an important part in preserving for us the great diversity of species comprising the animal kingdom.

The Springbok or Sprinkbuck (*Antidorcas marsupialis*), of South Africa, can leap three metres into the air in stiff-legged jumps when alarmed. As it does so it opens a fold of skin on its back lined with white hairs and this serves as a warning signal to the rest of the herd. At the same time the white hairs on the rump are erected, reinforcing the signal.

The Impala (*Aepyceros melampus*) ranges from Kenya to South Africa. It remains close to dense trees and bushes with easy access to water, and when alarmed it can take long leaps of up to ten metres to disappear into the nearest cover. Large herds of up to fifty form in winter, but in summer Impala travel in smaller family groups.

Classification List

Phylum Protozoa
Class Mastigophora
  Subclass Phytomastigophora
    Order Phytomonadida
    Order Euglenoidida
    Order Cryptomonadida
    Order Chrysomonadida
    Order Dinoflagellata
  Subclass Zoomastigophora
    Order Protomonadida
    Order Polymastigida
    Order Trichomonadida
    Order Opalinida
Class Sarcodina
  Subclass Rhizopoda
    Order Rhizomastigida
    Order Amoebina
    Order Testacida
    Order Foraminifera
    Order Heliozoida
    Order Radiolarida
Class Sporozoa
  Subclass Gregarinomorpha
    Order Archigregarinida
    Order Eugregarinida
     Suborder Cephalina
     Suborder Acephalina
  Subclass Coccidiomorpha
    Order Eucocciida
     Suborder Adeleidea
     Suborder Eimeriidea
     Suborder Haemosporidia
Class Cnidosporidea
Class Ciliata
  Subclass Holotricha
    Order Gymnostomatida
     Suborder Rhabdophorina
     Suborder Cyrtophorina
    Order Suctorida
    Order Trichostomatida
    Order Hymenostomatida
    Order Peritrichida
    Order Astomatida
  Subclass Spirotricha
    Order Heterotrichida
    Order Hypotrichida
    Order Entodiniomorphida
Phylum Mesozoa
  Order Dicyemida
  Order Orthonectida
Phylum Porifera
Class Calcarea
Class Hexactinellida
Class Demospongiae
Class Sclerospongiae
Phylum Cnidaria
Class Hydrozoa
  Order Athecata
    Family Tubulariidae
    Family Clavidae
    Family Corynidae
    Family Bougainvilliidae
    Family Hydridae
  Order Thecata
    Family Campanulariidae
    Family Lafoeidae
    Family Sertulariidae
  Order Limnomedusae
  Order Trachymedusae
  Order Narcomedusae

  Order Siphonophora
  Order Hydrocorallinae
    Suborder Milleporina
    Suborder Stylasterina
Class Scyphozoa
  Order Semaeostomeae
  Order Rhizostomeae
  Order Coronatae
  Order Cubomedusae
  Order Stauromedusae
Class Anthozoa
  Subclass Octocorallia
    Order Alcyonacea
    Order Gorgonacea
    Order Pennatulacea
  Subclass Zoantharia
    Order Actiniaria
    Order Corallimorpharia
    Order Scleractinia
    Order Zoanthiniaria
  Subclass Ceriantipatharia
    Order Antipatharia
    Order Cerianthidea
Phylum Ctenophora
Class Tentaculata
  Order Cydippida
  Order Lobata
  Order Cestida
  Order Platyctenea
Class Nuda
  Order Beroida
Phylum Platyhelminthes
Class Turbellaria
  Order Polycladida
    Suborder Cotylea
    Suborder Acotylea
  Order Tricladida
    Suborder Maricola
    Suborder Paludicola
    Suborder Terricola
  Order Protricladida
    Suborder Crossocoela
    Suborder Cyclocoela
  Order Eulecithophora
  Order Perilecithophora
  Order Archoophora
  Order Temnocephala
Class Monogenea
Class Digenea
Class Cestoda
  Subclass Cestodaria (=Cestoda
    Monozoa)
  Subclass Eucestoda (=Cestoda Merozoa)
Phylum Nemertina (=**Rhynchocoela**)
Class Anopla
  Order Palaeonemertini
  Order Heteronemertini
Class Enopla
  Order Hoplonemertini
  Order Bdellonemertini
Phylum Aschelminthes
Class Nematoda
  Subclass Aphasmida
    Order Chromadorida
    Order Enoplida
  Subclass Phasmida
    Order Rhabditida
    Order Strongylida
    Order Ascaridida
    Order Tylenchida

  Order Spirurida
Class Rotifera
  Order Seisonidea
  Order Bdelloidea
  Order Monogononta
    Suborder Ploima
    Suborder Flosculariacea
    Suborder Collothecacea
Class Gastrotricha
  Order Chaetonotoidea
  Order Macrodasyoidea
Class Kinorhyncha
Class Priapuloidea
Class Nematomorpha
  Order Nectonematoidea
  Order Gordioidea
Phylum Acanthocephala
Phylum Entoprocta
Phylum Bryozoa
Class Phylactolaemata
Class Gymnolaemata
  Order Cyclostomata
  Order Cheilostomata
  Order Ctenostomata
Phylum Phoronida
Phylum Brachiopoda
Class Inarticulata
Class Articulata
Phylum Mollusca
Class Monoplacophora
Class Amphineura
  Subclass Polyplacophorea (=Loricata)
  Subclass Aplacophorea
Class Gastropoda
  Subclass Prosobranchea
    Order Archaeogastropoda
    Order Neritoidea
    Order Mesogastropoda
    Order Neogastropoda
  Subclass Opisthobranchia
    Order Cephalaspidea (=Bullomorpha)
    Order Aplysiacea (=Anaspidea)
    Order Thecosomata
    Order Gymnosomata
    Order Notaspidea
     (=Pleurobranchomorpha)
    Order Acochlidiacea
    Order Sacoglossa
    Order Acoela (=Nudibranchia)
  Subclass Pulmonata
    Order Basommatophora
    Order Geophila (=Stylommatophora)
Class Scaphopoda
Class Bivalvia (=Lamellibrancha=
  Pelecypoda)
  Subclass Protobranchia
  Subclass Lamellibranchia
Class Cephalopoda
  Subclass Nautiloidea
  Subclass Coleoidea
    Order Sepioidea
    Order Teuthoidea
    Order Octopoda
    Order Vampyromorpha
Phylum Sipuncula
Phylum Echiuroidea
Phylum Annelida
Class Polychaeta
    Family Phyllodocidae
    Family Tomopteridae

    Family Nephtyidae
    Family Glyceridae
    Family Aphroditidae
    Family Polynoidae
    Family Nereidae
    Family Syllidae
    Family Eunicidae
    Family Amphinomidae
    Family Ariciidae
    Family Cirratulidae
    Family Magelonidae
    Family Arenicolidae
    Family Capitellidae
    Family Maldanidae
    Family Spionidae
    Family Chaetopteridae
    Family Sabellariidae
    Family Oweniidae
    Family Pectinariidae
     (=Amphictenidae)
    Family Ampharetidae
    Family Terebellidae
    Family Sabellidae
    Family Serpulidae
Class Oligochaeta
Class Hirudinea
Phylum Arthropoda
Class Onychophora
Class Pauropoda
Class Diplopoda
Class Chilopoda
Class Symphyla
Class Insecta
  Subclass Apterygota
    Order Thysanura
     Family Lepismatidae
     Family Machilidae
    Order Diplura
     Family Campodeidae
     Family Japygidae
     Family Projapygidae
    Order Protura
    Order Collembola
     Suborder Arthropleona
      Superfamily Poduroidea
      Superfamily Entomobryoidea
     Suborder Symphypleona
      Family Sminthuridae
  Subclass Exopterygota
    Order Ephemeroptera
     Family Baetidae
     Family Siphlonuridae
     Family Caenidae
     Family Ecdyonuridae
    Order Odonata
     Suborder Zygoptera
      Family Agriidae
      Family Coenagriidae
     Suborder Anisozygoptera
     Suborder Anisoptera
      Family Aeshnidae
      Family Libellulidae
      Family Gomphidae
      Family Petaluridae
    Order Plecoptera
     Family Eustheniidae
     Family Pteronarcidae
     Family Leuctridae
     Family Capniidae
     Family Nemouridae

Phylum Arthropoda continued
  Family Perlidae
Order Grylloblattodea
Order Orthoptera
  Family Tettigoniidae
  Family Stenopelmatidae
  Family Gryllidae
  Family Gryllotalpidae
  Family Acrididae
  Family Pneumoridae
  Family Tetrigidae
  Family Tridactylidae
  Family Cylindrachetidae
Order Phasmida
  Family Phylliidae
Order Dermaptera
  Suborder Forficulina
  Family Forficulidae
  Family Labiidae
  Family Labiduridae
  Suborder Hemimerina
  Suborder Arixeniina
Order Embioptera
  Family Clothodidae
  Family Embiidae
Order Dictyoptera
  Suborder Blattodea
  Suborder Mantodea
Order Isoptera
  Family Mastotermitidae
  Family Kalotermitidae
  Family Hodotermitidae
  Family Rhinotermitidae
  Family Termitidae
Order Zoraptera
Order Psocoptera
  Suborder Eupsocida
  Family Psocidae
  Family Mesopsocidae
  Family Pseudocaeciliidae
  Suborder Trogiomorpha
  Suborder Troctomorpha
Order Mallophaga
  Suborder Amblycera
  Family Menoponidae
  Suborder Ischnocera
  Family Philopteridae
  Family Trichodectidae
  Suborder Rhynchophthirina
Order Siphunculata
  Family Echinophthiriidae
  Family Hoplopleuridae
  Family Linognathidae
Order Hemiptera
  Suborder Heteroptera
    Section Geocorisae
  Family Pentatomidae
  Family Coreidae
  Family Pyrrhocoridae
  Family Lygaeidae
  Family Tingidae
  Family Reduviidae
  Family Nabidae
  Family Anthocoridae
  Family Cimicidae
  Family Miridae
  Family Saldidae
    Section Amphibicorisae
  Family Gerridae
  Family Veliidae
  Family Hydrometridae
    Section Hydrocorisae
  Family Naucoridae
  Family Belostomatidae
  Family Nepidae
  Family Notonectidae
  Family Corixidae
  Suborder Homoptera
    Section Auchenorrhyncha
  Family Cicadidae
  Family Cicadellidae
  Family Membracidae
  Family Cercopidae
    Group Fulgoroidea
  Family Delphacidae
    Section Sternorrhyncha
    Group Aphidoidea
  Family Psyllidae
  Family Coccoidae
  Family Pseudococcidae

  Family Aleyrodidae
Order Thysanoptera
  Suborder Terebrantia
  Suborder Tubulifera
Subclass Endopterygota
Order Neuroptera
  Suborder Megaloptera
  Family Sialidae
  Family Corydalidae
  Family Raphidiidae
  Suborder Plannipennia
  Family Sisyridae
  Family Hemerobiidae
  Family Chrysopidae
  Family Mantispidae
  Family Myrmeleontidae
  Family Ascalaphidae
Order Mecoptera
  Family Panorpidae
  Family Bittacidae
Order Lepidoptera
  Suborder Zeugloptera
  Family Micropterygidae
  Suborder Monotrysia
  Family Eriocraniidae
  Family Hepialidae
  Family Incurvariidae
  Suborder Ditrysia
  Family Sesiidae
  Family Tinaeidae
  Family Gracillariidae
  Family Plutellidae
  Family Orneodidae
  Family Cossidae
  Family Psychidae
  Family Zygaenidae
  Family Tortricidae
  Family Eucosmidae
  Family Olethreutidae
  Superfamily Pyralidoidea
  Family Galleriinae
  Family Crambinae
  Family Phycitinae
  Family Pyralidae
  Family Pyraustinae
  Family Lasiocampidae
  Family Saturniidae
  Family Bombycidae
  Family Nymphalidae
  Family Lycaenidae
  Family Pieridae
  Family Papilionidae
  Family Hesperiidae
  Family Geometridae
  Family Sphingidae
  Family Noctuidae
  Family Notodontidae
  Family Lymantriidae
  Family Arctiidae
Order Trichoptera
  Family Rhyacophilidae
  Family Hydroptilidae
  Family Hydropsychidae
  Family Phryganeidae
  Family Limnephilidae
  Family Leptoceridae
Order Diptera
  Suborder Nematocera
  Family Tipulidae
  Family Psychodidae
  Family Culicidae
  Family Cecidomyiidae
  Family Bibionidae
  Family Mycetophilidae
  Family Simuliidae
  Family Chironomidae
  Suborder Brachycera
  Family Stratiomyidae
  Family Rhagionidae
  Family Tabanidae
  Family Asilidae
  Family Bombyliidae
  Family Empididae
  Family Dolichopodidae
  Suborder Cyclorrhapha
  Family Syrphidae
  Family Phoridae
    Section Acalyptratae
  Family Agromyzidae
  Family Psilidae

  Family Tephritidae
  Family Chloropidae
    Section Calyptratae
  Family Oestridae
  Family Calliphoridae
  Family Tachinidae
  Family Muscidae
  Family Hippoboscidae
Order Siphonaptera
Order Hymenoptera
  Suborder Symphyta
  Family Xyelidae
  Family Siricidae
  Family Diprionidae
  Family Pergidae
  Family Orussidae
  Family Tenthredinidae
  Suborder Apocrita
    Section Parasitica
  Family Ichneumonidae
  Family Braconidae
  Family Cynipidae
  Superfamily Chalcidoidea
  Family Trichogrammatidae
  Family Mymaridae
  Family Agaontidae
  Superfamily Proctotrupoidea
  Family Scelionidae
  Family Platygasteridae
    Section Aculeata
  Family Dryinidae
  Family Chrysididae
  Family Scoliidae
  Family Tiphiidae
  Family Formicidae
  Family Pompilidae
  Family Vespidae
  Family Sphecidae
  Family Prosopidae
  Family Andrenidae
  Family Megachilidae
  Family Apidae
Order Coleoptera
  Suborder Adephaga
  Family Carabidae
  Family Cicindelidae
  Family Paussinae
  Family Haliplidae
  Family Dytiscidae
  Family Gyrinidae
  Suborder Archostemata
  Suborder Myxophaga
  Family Cupedidae
  Suborder Polyphaga
  Family Hydrophilidae
  Family Histeridae
  Family Silphidae
  Family Staphylinidae
  Family Passalidae
  Family Lucanidae
  Family Geotrupidae
  Family Scarabaeidae
  Family Elateridae
  Family Buprestidae
  Family Cantharidae
  Family Lampyridae
  Family Dermestidae
  Family Anobiidae
  Family Cleridae
  Family Nitidulidae
  Family Coccinellidae
  Family Tenebrionidae
  Family Meloidae
  Family Cerambycidae
  Family Chrysomelidae
  Family Curculionidae
  Family Scolytidae
Order Strepsiptera
Class Crustacea
Subclass Cephalocarida
  Family Hutchinsoniellidae
Subclass Branchiopoda
Order Anostraca
Order Notostraca
Order Conchostraca
Order Cladocera
  Family Daphniidae
Subclass Mystacocarida
Subclass Copepoda
  Order Calanoida

  Family Diaptomidae
  Family Centropagidae
Order Cyclopoida
  Family Cyclopidae
  Family Notodelphyidae
Order Harpacticoida
Order Caligoida
Order Monstrilloida
Order Lernaeoida
Subclass Branchiura
Subclass Ostracoda
Order Myodocopa
Order Cladocopa
Order Platycopa
Order Podocopa
Subclass Cirripedia
Order Thoracica
Order Rhizocephala
Order Ascothoracica
Subclass Malacostraca
Superorder Phyllocarida
Order Leptostraca
Superorder Hoplocarida
Order Stomatopoda
Superorder Syncarida
Order Anaspidacea
Order Stygocaridacea
Order Bathynellacea
Superorder Peracarida
Order Spelaeogriphacea
Order Thermosbaenacea
Order Mysidacea
  Suborder Lophogastrida
  Suborder Mysida
Order Tanaidacea
Order Isopoda
  Suborder Asellota
  Family Asellidae
  Suborder Flabellifera
  Family Limnoriidae
  Family Sphaeromidae
  Family Anthuridae
  Suborder Gnathiidea
  Suborder Valvifera
  Suborder Phreatoicidea
  Suborder Oniscoidea
  Family Ligiidae
  Family Armadillidiidae
  Suborder Epicaridea
  Family Entoniscidae
  Family Bopyridae
Order Amphipoda
  Suborder Hyperiidea
  Suborder Gammaridea
  Family Gammaridae
  Family Talitridae
  Suborder Caprellidea
  Family Caprellidae
  Family Cyamidae
  Suborder Ingolfiellida
Order Cumacea
  Family Pseudocumidae
Order Euphausiacea
Order Decapoda
  Suborder Natantia
    Section Penaeidea
  Family Penaeidae
  Family Sergestidae
  Family Leuciferidae
    Section Caridea
  Family Atyidae
  Family Alpheidae
    Section Stenopodidea
  Family Stenopodidae
  Suborder Reptantia
    Section Palinura
    Section Astacura
  Family Homaridae
  Family Astacidae
  Family Parastacidae
  Family Austroastacidae
    Section Anomura
  Family Paguridae
  Family Coenobitidae
  Family Lithodidae
  Family Galatheidae
  Family Porcellanidae
    Section Brachyura
  Family Dromiidae
  Family Calappidae

CLASSIFICATION LIST

Phylum Arthropoda continued
Family Portunidae
Family Potamonidae
Family Xanthidae
Family Pinnotheridae
Family Grapsidae
Family Oxypodidae
Family Majidae
Class Arachnida
Order Scorpiones
Order Pseudoscorpiones
Order Opiliones
Order Acari
Family Eriophyidae
Order Palpigradi
Order Uropygi
Order Schizomida
Order Amblypygi
Order Araneae
Suborder Orthognatha
(=Mygalomorpha)
Suborder Labidognatha
(=Araneomorpha)
Family Araneidae (=Argiopidae)
Family Theridiidae
Family Agelenidae
Family Thomisidae
Family Lycosidae
Family Salticidae
Order Solifugae (=Solpugida)
Order Ricinulei
Class Merostomata
Class Pycnogonida
Phylum Pentastomida
Phylum Tardigrada
Phylum Chaetognatha
Phylum Pogonophora
Phylum Echinodermata
Class Asteroidea
Class Ophiuroidea
Class Echinoidea
Class Holothuroidea
Class Crinoidea
Phylum Chordata
Subphylum Hemichordata
Class Enteropneusta
Class Pterobranchia
Subphylum Urochordata
Class Ascidiacea
Class Thaliacea
Class Larvacea
Subphylum Cephalochordata
Subphylum Vertebrata
Superclass Agnatha
Class Cephalaspidomorphi
Order Petromyzoniformes
Class Pteraspidomorphia
Order Myxiniformes
Superclass Gnathostomata
Class Chondrichthyes
Superorder Selachimorpha
Order Heterodontiformes
Order Hexanchiformes
Order Lamniformes
Family Rhincodontidae
Family Orectolobidae
Family Odontaspidae
Family Lamnidae
Family Scyliorhinidae
Family Carcharinidae
Family Sphyrnidae
Order Squaliformes
Family Squalidae
Family Pristiophoridae
Family Squatinidae
Superorder Batoidimorpha
Family Pristidae
Family Rhinobatidae
Family Torpedinidae
Family Rajidae
Family Dasyatidae
Family Potamotrygonidae
Family Myliobatidae
Family Mobulidae
Subclass Holocephali
Order Chimaeriformes
Family Chimaeridae
Family Rhinochimaeridae
Family Callorhynchidae
Class Osteichthyes

Subclass Dipneusti
Order Ceratodiformes
Order Lepidosireniformes
Family Lepidosirenidae
Family Protopteridae
Subclass Crossopterygii
Order Coelacanthiformes
Family Latimeriidae
Subclass Brachiopterygii
Family Polypteridae
Subclass Actinopterygii
Order Acipenseriformes
Family Acipenseridae
Family Polyodontidae
Order Semionotiformes
Family Lepisosteidae
Order Amiiformes
Family Amiidae
Order Osteoglossiformes
Order Mormyriformes
Order Clupeiformes
Family Clupeidae
Family Engraulidae
Order Elopiformes
Order Anguilliformes
Order Notacanthiformes
Order Salmoniformes
Suborder Esocoidei
Suborder Salmonoidei
Suborder Argentinoidei
Suborder Stomiatoidei
Order Gonorynchiformes
Order Cypriniformes
Suborder Characoidei
Suborder Cyprinoidei
Order Siluriformes
Order Myctophiformes
Order Polymixiiformes
Order Percopsiformes
Order Gadiformes
Order Batrachoidiformes
Order Lophiiformes
Order Indostomiformes
Order Atheriniformes
Suborder Exocoetidei
Suborder Cyprinodontoidei
Suborder Atherinoidei
Order Lampridiformes
Order Beryciformes
Order Zeiformes
Order Syngnathiformes
Order Gasterosteiformes
Order Synbranchiformes
Order Scorpaeniformes
Suborder Scorpaenoidei
Order Dactylopteriformes
Order Perciformes
Suborder Percoidei
Suborder Mugiloidei
Suborder Sphyraenoidei
Suborder Polynemoidei
Suborder Labroidei
Suborder Blennioidei
Suborder Icosteoidei
Suborder Ammodytoidei
Suborder Gobioidei
Suborder Acanthuroidei
Suborder Scombroidei
Suborder Stromateoidei
Suborder Anabantoidei
Suborder Channoidei
Suborder Mastacembeloidei
Order Gobiesociformes
Order Pleuronectiformes
Family Psettodidae
Family Citharidae
Family Bothidae
Family Pleuronectidae
Family Soleidae
Family Cynoglossidae
Order Tetraodontiformes
Family Balistidae
Family Ostraciontidae
Family Tetraodontidae
Family Diodontidae
Family Molidae
Class Amphibia
Order Apoda [Order Gymnophiona
of some authors]
Family Caeciliidae

Order Caudata (=Urodela)
Suborder Cryptobranchoidea
Family Hynobiidae
Family Cryptobranchidae
Suborder Ambystomatoidea
Family Ambystomatidae
Suborder Salamandroidea
Family Salamandridae
Family Amphiumidae
Family Plethodontidae
Family Proteidae
Suborder Sirenoidea
Family Sirenidae
Order Anura (=Salientia)
Suborder Amphicoela
Family Ascaphidae
Suborder Opisthocoela
Family Pipidae
Family Discoglossidae
Family Rhinophrynidae
Suborder Anomocoela
Family Pelobatidae
Family Pelodytidae
Suborder Diplasiocoela
Family Ranidae
Family Rhacophoridae
Family Microhylidae
Family Phrynomeridae
Suborder Procoela
Family Pseudidae
Family Bufonidae
Family Atelopidae
Family Hylidae
Family Leptodactylidae
Family Centrolenidae
Class Reptilia
Order Rhynchocephalia
Order Testudines (=Chelonia)
Family Testudinidae
Family Emydidae
Family Kinosternidae
Family Platysternidae
Family Chelydridae
Family Chelidae
Family Trionychidae
Family Chelonidae
Family Dermochelidae
Family Pelomedusidae
Family Carrettochelyidae
Order Crocodylia (=Loricata)
Family Gavialidae
Family Crocodylidae
Family Alligatoridae
Order Squamata
Suborder Sauria (=Lacertilia)
Family Gekkonidae
Family Agamidae
Family Iguanidae
Family Lacertidae
Family Teiidae
Family Helodermatidae
Family Varanidae
Family Chamaeleonidae
Family Scincidae
Family Cordylidae
Family Anguidae
Family Amphisbaenidae
Suborder Serpentes (=Ophidia)
Family Boidae
Family Typhlopidae
Family Colubridae
Family Elapidae
Family Viperidae
Family Crotalidae
Family Hydrophidae
Class Aves
Order Struthioniformes
Order Rheiformes
Order Casuariiformes
Family Dromaiidae
Family Casuariidae
Order Apterygiformes
Order Tinamiformes
Order Sphenisciformes
Order Gaviiformes
Order Podicipediformes
Order Procellariiformes
Family Diomedeidae
Family Procellariidae
Family Hydrobatidae

Family Pelecanoididae
Order Pelecaniformes
Family Phaethontidae
Family Pelecanidae
Family Sulidae
Family Phalacrocoracidae
Family Anhingidae
Family Fregatidae
Order Ciconiiformes
Family Ardeidae
Family Cochleariidae
Family Balaenicipitidae
Family Scopidae
Family Ciconiidae
Family Threskiornithidae
Family Phoenicopteridae
Order Anseriformes
Family Anhimidae
Family Anatidae
Order Falconiformes
Family Cathartidae
Family Accipitridae
Family Pandionidae
Family Falconidae
Family Sagittariidae
Order Galliformes
Family Megapodiidae
Family Cracidae
Family Tetraonidae
Family Phasianidae
Family Numididae
Family Meleagrididae
Family Opisthocomidae
Order Gruiformes
Family Mesitornithidae
Family Turnicidae
Family Pedionomidae
Family Gruidae
Family Aramidae
Family Psophiidae
Family Rallidae
Family Heliornithidae
Family Rhynochetidae
Family Eurypygidae
Family Cariamidae
Family Otididae
Order Charadriiformes
Family Jacanidae
Family Rostratulidae
Family Haematopodidae
Family Charadriidae
Family Scolopacidae
Family Recurvirostridae
Family Phalaropodidae
Family Dromadidae
Family Burhinidae
Family Glareolidae
Family Thinocoridae
Family Chionididae
Family Stercorariidae
Family Laridae
Family Rynchopidae
Family Alcidae
Order Columbiformes
Family Pteroclidae
Family Columbidae
Order Psittaciformes
Family Psittacidae
Order Cuculiformes
Family Musophagidae
Family Cucilidae
Order Strigiformes
Family Tytonidae
Family Strigidae
Order Caprimulgiformes
Family Steatornithidae
Family Podargidae
Family Nyctibiidae
Family Aegothelidae
Family Caprimulgidae
Order Apodiformes
Family Apodidae
Family Hemiprocnidae
Family Trochilidae
Order Coliiformes
Order Trogoniformes
Order Coraciiformes
Family Alcedinidae
Family Todidae
Family Momotidae

CLASSIFICATION LIST

Phylum Chordata continued
Family Meropidae
Family Leptosomatidae
Family Coraciidae
Family Upupidae
Family Phoeniculidae
Family Bucerotidae
Order Piciformes
Family Galbulidae
Family Bucconidae
Family Capitonidae
Family Indicatoridae
Family Ramphastidae
Family Picidae
Order Passeriformes
Suborder Eurylaimi
Family Eurylaimidae
Suborder Tyranni
Family Dendrocolaptidae
Family Furnariidae
Family Formicariidae
Family Conopophagidae
Family Rhinocryptidae
Family Pittidae
Family Philepittidae
Family Acanthisittidae
(=Xenicidae)
Family Tyrannidae
Family Oxyruncidae
Family Pipridae
Family Cotingidae
Family Phytotomidae
Suborder Menurae
Family Menuridae
Family Atrichornithidae
Suborder Passeres (=Oscines)
Family Alaudidae
Family Hirundinidae
Family Motacillidae
Family Campephagidae
Family Pycnonotidae
Family Irenidae
Family Laniidae
Family Vangidae
Family Bombycillidae
Family Dulidae
Family Cinclidae
Family Troglodytidae
Family Mimidae
Family Prunellidae
Family Muscicapidae
Family Paridae

Family Certhiidae
Family Sittidae
Family Climacteridae
Family Dicaeidae
Family Nectariniidae
Family Zosteropidae
Family Meliphagidae
Family Emberizidae
Family Parulidae
Family Drepanididae
Family Vireonidae
Family Icteridae
Family Fringillidae
Family Estrildidae
Family Ploceidae
Family Sturnidae
Family Oriolidae
Family Dicruridae
Family Callaeidae
Family Grallinidae
Family Artamidae
Family Cracticidae
Family Ptilonorhynchidae
Family Paradisaeidae
Family Corvidae
Class Mammalia
Subclass Prototheria
Order Monotremata
Infraclass Metatheria
Order Marsupialia
Family Didelphidae
Family Dasyuridae
Family Notoryctidae
Family Peramelidae
Family Phalangeridae
Family Phascolarctidae
Family Phascolomidae
Family Macropodidae
Infraclass Theria
Order Insectivora
Family Erinaceidae
Family Soricidae
Family Tenrecidae
Family Solenodontidae
Family Talpidae
Family Chrysochloridae
Family Potamogalidae
Family Macroscelididae
Family Tupaiidae
Order Dermoptera
Order Chiroptera
Suborder Megachiroptera

Suborder Microchiroptera
Family Megadermatidae
Family Rhinolophidae
Family Vespertilionidae
Family Phyllostomatidae
Family Noctilionidae
Family Molossidae
Family Desmodontidae
Order Primates
Suborder Prosimii
Family Lemuridae
Family Cheirogaleidae
Family Lorisidae
Family Indriidae
Family Daubentoniidae
Family Tarsiidae
Suborder Anthropoidea (=Simiae)
Family Cebidae
Family Callithricidae
Family Cercopithecidae
Family Pongidae
Order Edentata
Family Myrmecophagidae
Family Bradypodidae
Family Dasypodidae
Order Pholidota
Order Lagomorpha
Family Leporidae
Family Ochotonidae
Order Rodentia
Suborder Bathyergomorpha
Suborder Hystricomorpha
Family Echimyidae
Family Dasyproctidae
Family Erethizontidae
Family Hystricidae
Family Cuniculidae
Family Dinomyidae
Family Chinchillidae
Family Caviidae
Suborder Sciuromorpha
Family Sciuridae
Family Aplodontidae
Family Castoridae
Family Geomyidae
Family Heteromyidae
Suborder Myomorpha
Family Anomaluridae
Family Pedetidae
Family Ctenodactylidae
Family Dipodidae
Family Zapodidae

Family Muscardinidae
Family Lophiomyidae
Family Spalacidae
Family Rhizomyidae
Family Muridae
Order Cetacea
Suborder Mysticeti
Family Balaenidae
Family Balaenopteridae
Family Eschrichtiidae
Suborder Odontoceti
Family Physeteridae
Family Kogiidae
Family Phocaenidae
Family Delphinidae
Family Zephiidae
Family Monodontidae
Family Platanistidae
Order Carnivora
Family Canidae
Family Ursidae
Family Procyonidae
Family Mustelidae
Family Viverridae
Family Hyaenidae
Family Protelidae
Family Felidae
Order Pinnipedia
Family Phocidae
Family Otariidae
Family Odobenidae
Order Tubulidentata
Order Proboscidea
Order Hyracoidea
Order Sirenia
Order Perissodactyla
Family Equidae
Family Tapiridae
Family Rhinocerotidae
Order Artiodactyla
Suborder Suiformes
Family Suidae
Family Tayassuidae
Family Hippopotamidae
Suborder Tylopoda
Family Camelidae
Suborder Ruminantia
Family Tragulidae
Family Cervidae
Family Giraffidae
Family Antilocapridae
Family Bovidae

Glossary

aboral: situated on the side of an animal furthest from the mouth.

abyssal: living in the depths of the sea.

actinula: hydrozoan larva consisting of a short-bodied polyp.

adipose fin: fin on dorsal surface of a fish, posterior to the dorsal fin, and containing fatty tissue.

adoral: near the mouth.

aglyphous dentition: without venomous fangs.

albino: abnormal animal lacking dark pigment from its skin, hair or feathers, and eyes.

alimentary canal: the tube in which digestion of food takes place in the body of an animal.

allantois: sac-like outgrowth from the posterior part of the alimentary canal of embryo reptiles, birds and mammals. Its surface is concerned with the exchange of the gases involved in respiration and, in mammals, with nutrition and nitrogenous excretion. In some cases nitrogenous waste accumulates in the allantois.

altricial birds: having young which are very immature and helpless when hatched.

alveolus (pl. alveoli): a small pit or cavity, e.g. the sacs in mammals' lungs at the surfaces of which gaseous exchange takes place.

amino-acids: group of fatty acids, some of which form the fundamental constituents of proteins.

amnion: sac which surrounds embryo reptiles, birds and mammals. Contains fluid which provides an aqueous environment for the developing animal.

amplexus: embrace during mating as shown by anuran amphibians.

anabiotic: able to return to life after apparent death.

anadromous fishes: those which spend most of their adult life in the sea but which enter rivers in order to spawn.

anal fin: the unpaired fin on the middle line of the ventral surface of a fish.

antennules: the first small pair of antennae on the head of a crustacean.

anterior: situated towards the head end of an animal.

aorta: the main artery carrying blood from the heart to the body.

aortic arches: paired arteries which in fishes carry blood to and from the gills. In higher vertebrates some of these vessels are adapted to other functions and the remainder are lost.

apterous: wingless.

apterygote: belonging to the group of insects which are primitively wingless.

arboreal: tree-dwelling.

auditory meatus: ear opening.

auricle: chamber in the heart which receives blood from the veins, and from which blood passes to the ventricle.

axial skeleton: the skull and vertebral column.

barbs: the filaments which make up the vane of a feather.

barbels: slender sensory processes which grow from the jaws of some fishes.

barbules: very small filaments attached to the barbs of feathers. Barbules from adjacent barbs hook together.

benthic: living on the sea bed.

bicorned: having two horn-shaped parts.

bilateral symmetry: the condition in which an animal's body, when divided along one plane only, can be divided into two parts, each of which is a mirror image of the other.

binocular vision: two-eyed vision which permits judgement of distance.

bipectinate: bearing comb-like projections on each side.

bipedal: walking on two legs.

biplanar vertebrae: those with a flat surface at both the anterior and the posterior ends.

blastocyst: early stage in the development of the mammalian embryo. Hollow ball of cells which is thickened towards one side.

branchiostegal rays: skeletal supports within the gills of a fish.

bronchus (pl. bronchi): large tube leading from the trachea to the lung of a vertebrate.

buccal: of the mouth.

caecum (pl. caeca): a blind branch of a hollow structure, such as the alimentary canal.

Cainozoic era: the fourth and most recent of the great geological eras.

carapace: exoskeleton covering the dorsal surface of an animal.

carinate: keel-shaped or, in the case of birds, having a keel-shaped process on the breast-bone.

carnassial teeth: the shearing last upper premolar and first lower molar teeth of members of the Carnivora.

carnivorous: flesh-eating.

carpal bones: wristbones of tetrapod vertebrates.

casque: an enlargement of the dorsal surface of the upper bill of a bird.

caudal: of or near the tail of an animal.

cement: bone-like material covering the roots of vertebrate teeth. In the case of some mammals also found on the crowns of teeth.

centriole: small granule to be found just outside the nucleus of many living cells.

centrum (pl. centra): the principal solid bony part of a vertebra.

cercus (pl. cerci): jointed process arising on the abdomen of some invertebrates.

cere: fleshy protuberance over the upper part of the bill of some birds.

cerebellum: part of the vertebrate brain. A thickening of the dorsal wall of the hind brain.

cerebral hemispheres: cerebrum.

cerebrum: paired outgrowths of the vertebrate fore brain. Primitively concerned with olfaction, but in higher vertebrates with coordination and control of many activities.

cervical vertebrae: neck vertebrae.

chaetae: bristles made of chitin.

cheek teeth: premolar and molar teeth.

chela (pl. chelae): pincer, e.g. that of a crab.

chelate: bearing pincers.

chelicera (pl. chelicere): chelate appendage on the head of a spider.

chitin: horny material, typically found in the arthropod exoskeleton and often present in other invertebrates.

chitinous: made of chitin.

chloroplast: dense, chlorophyll-containing inclusion within a cell.

chorion: membrane enclosing the embryonic structures of reptiles, birds and mammals.

choroid: vascular layer of the vertebrate eye between the outer covering and the retina.

chromosome: thread-like body bearing genes within the cell nucleus.

cilium (pl. cilia): cytoplasmic thread projecting from the surface of a cell.

ciliated: bearing cilia.

clavicle: collar-bone.

cleavage: the series of cell-divisions by means of which a zygote becomes an embryo.

cloaca: posterior part of the alimentary canal into which genital and excretory ducts or, in the case of some echinoderms, some gill-like structures, lead.

cochlea: the part of the vertebrate inner ear which turns sounds into nerve impulses.

coelenteron: the body cavity of a polyp or medusa.

coelom: the body cavity typical of the higher invertebrates and all vertebrates.

coelomate: having a coelom.

commensal: living in close association with another living organism without either marked beneficial or harmful effects to either party.

condyle: protuberance on a bone which fits into a socket on an adjacent bone.

conjunctiva: transparent epidermis covering the eye and lining the eyelids of vertebrates.

contour feathers: feathers which cover the surface of a bird's body and to a large extent determine its apparent shape.

convergence or convergent evolution: the appearance of similar structures or adaptations in organisms which are unrelated, but are adapted to the same mode of life.

coracoid: bone which links the shoulder-blade and breast-bone in some vertebrates.

cornea: the transparent anterior covering of the vertebrate eye.

corpus luteum: ductless gland which develops in that part of a mammalian ovary which has just liberated an ovum.

cotyledonous placenta: placenta in which the villi are arranged in patches.

covert feathers: contour feathers adjacent to the primary and secondary flight feathers and over the ear opening of a bird.

cranium: the part of the skull which surrounds and protects the brain.

crepuscular: active at dusk and just before dawn.

Cretaceous: the geological epoch comprising the most recent part of the Mesozoic era.

cryptic colouring: camouflage.

ctenidium (pl. ctenidia): structure having a comb-like appearance, e.g. the gills of some invertebrates.

ctenoid scales: scales with rough edges.

cycloid scales: scales with evenly curved edges.

cytoplasm: all the protoplasm of a cell except that contained in the nucleus.

degenerate: having become secondarily simplified in the course of evolution.

dentine: the hard, bony substance of which teeth are principally composed.

dermal: relating to the skin of an animal.

dermis: the inner layers of the skin.

diaphragm: the muscular partition which, in mammals, separates the abdominal and thoracic cavities.

diffuse placenta: placenta with scattered villi.

digitigrade: walking on tip-toe, e.g. dogs and cats.

diphycercal: tail fin which is equally developed on both the dorsal and ventral sides of the vertebral column.

discoidal placenta: placenta with villi clustered within a disc-shaped area.

diurnal: active by day, as opposed to nocturnal—by night.

diverticulum (pl. diverticula): blind outgrowth branching off from a cavity.

dorsal: towards the back of an animal, i.e. the surface which in the majority of animals is directed away from the earth's centre.

ear ossicles: small bones which convey sound vibrations through the vertebrate middle ear.

ecdysis: moulting the outer layers of the body-covering.

ecology: the study of the relationship between an organism, its neighbours, and its surroundings.

ectoderm: the outer layer of cells of multicellular animals.

ectoparasite: parasite which lives outside the body of its host.

ectoplasm: the clear, outer cytoplasm of a cell.

embryo: an immature organism developing within the egg, or within the womb of its mother.

enamel: the hard material which typically covers the crown of a tooth.

endocrine glands: ductless glands which secrete hormones.

endoderm: the inner layer of cells of a multicellular animal.

endoplasm: the granular, innermost part of the cytoplasm of a cell.

endopod: the inner arm of a two-branched arthropod appendage.

endopterygote: insect in which the wings develop internally, and in which the specialised larva differs greatly from the adult in appearance.

endoskeleton: internal skeleton.

endosome: mass of nuclear material within a cell.

enteron: coelenteron, or the alimentary canal of higher animals.

enzyme: a catalyst which promotes chemical change within a living organism.

Eocene: epoch of the Cainozoic era. Preceded by the Palaeocene and followed by the Oligocene.

epidermis: outermost layer or layers of cells of an organism.

epiglottis: flap of tissue which in mammals covers the anterior end of the glottis during the act of swallowing.
epithelial: pertaining to epithelium.
epithelium: cellular tissue covering a surface.
epizootic disease: epidemic disease amongst animals.
Eustachian tube: tube which in land vertebrates connects the middle ear to the throat.
exopod: the outer arm of a two-branched arthropod appendage.
exopterygote: insect in which the wings develop externally and the juvenile form is not unlike the adult in appearance.
exoskeleton: external skeleton.
Fallopian tube: oviduct of a mammal, leading from the body cavity to the uterus.
femur: thigh-bone of a limbed vertebrate, or the third joint of the leg in some arthropods.
feral: having escaped from domestication and become wild.
fibula: the outer and more slender of the two bones of the shin in limbed vertebrates.
flagellum (pl. flagella): whip-like cytoplasmic process projecting from a cell.
flame cell: flask-shaped cell with a bunch of cilia at the centre. It has an excretory function.
fovea: thin part of the retina of the eye at which vision is most acute.
frugivorous: fruit-eating.
gall bladder: bladder in or near the liver of vertebrates. Stores bile which is important in the digestion of fats.
gamete: germ cell which, on fusing with another, gives rise to a new organism. An ovum is a female gamete and a spermatozoon is a male gamete.
ganglion (pl. ganglia): a group of nerve cells outside the brain and the spinal cord.
genes: the units which are responsible for the inherited characteristics of an organism. Genes are situated in linear order along the chromosomes within the cell nucleus.
gill rakers: small projections on the gill arches of some fishes. They serve to strain food particles from the water.
glottis: the opening from the windpipe to the throat.
glycogen: carbohydrate stored in the liver of animals.
Golgi apparatus: material contained in a network of vacuoles present in the cytoplasm of many animal cells.
gonad: reproductive gland which produces gametes and sex hormones.
gonadotropic substances: hormones which affect the activity of the gonads.
graminivorous: feeding upon grain or other seeds and grass.
granivorous: grain-eating.
habitat: the environment inhabited by an organism or group of organisms.
haemocoel: body cavity containing blood. Commonly found in arthropods and molluscs.
haploid: having half the number of chromosomes typical of most body cells. Gametes are haploid.
haptor: disc or sucker of a trematode.
hemimetabolous: having incomplete metamorphosis, as in the exopterygote insects.
hemipenes: paired male copulatory organs.
herbivorous: plant-eating.
hermaphrodite: having both male and female reproductive organs.
heterocercal tail: tail of a fish in which the vertebral column runs into the larger, dorsal lobe.
heterodont: having teeth of varying shapes and functions in different parts of the mouth.
holarctic: having a distribution which includes Europe, northern Asia and North America.
holometabolous: having complete metamorphosis with a resulting great difference in form between larval and adult forms, as in the endopterygote insects.
homocercal tail: tail of a fish in which the dorsal and ventral lobes are equal in size.
homothermic: maintaining a steady body temperature. Warm blooded.
hormone: substance secreted by an endocrine gland and, when transported by body fluids, producing an effect on another part of the body.
humerus: the upper bone of the fore limb of a limbed vertebrate.
hyoid: skeletal structure in the floor of the mouth of higher vertebrates. Derived from part of one of the gill arches of fishes.
inguinal: in the groin region.
insectivorous: insect-eating. Many insectivorous organisms also consume other invertebrates in addition to insects.
instar: stage between two moults during the larval development of an insect.
intracellular: inside a cell.
isabelline: having light brown coloration. Desert-dwelling animals are often isabelline.
ischial callosities: leathery patches to be found on the buttocks of many of the higher primates of the Old World.
karyosome: an aggregation of nuclear material within a cell.
kinety: row of granules each situated at the base of a cilium.
lachrymal gland: tear gland, the secretion of which moistens the eye in the higher vertebrates.
lappets: lobe-like structures, e.g. the wattles of domestic fowls.
larva (pl. larvae): any animal in an immature but self-supporting form which differs significantly from that of an adult.
larynx: the vocal organ in the windpipe of a mammal.
laryngeal: pertaining to the larynx.
littoral: pertaining to the shore.
lophodont: having cheek teeth with ridged surfaces.
lumbar: pertaining to the lower spine.
lyrate: lyre-shaped.
lysosome: a particle situated in the cytoplasm of a cell and consisting of a membrane containing several enzymes.
mammilla (pl. mammillae): nipple.
mandible: in invertebrates, a jaw-like appendage. In vertebrates, the lower jaw.
mandibular: pertaining to the mandibles.
mantle: fold of skin covering part of the body of molluscs and some other invertebrates. Usually secretes the shell, and may also protect the organs which are situated in the cavity beneath.
manubrium: handle-like structure, e.g. the region which projects round the mouth of a medusa.
marsupium: pouch situated on the abdomen of some female mammals.
masseter: jaw muscle found in the higher vertebrates.
maxilla (pl. maxillae): one of the paired mouth-parts of arthropods, or one of the upper jaw-bones of vertebrates.
maxillules: the first pair of maxillae in an arthropod where more than one pair exists.
medulla oblongata: the vertebrate hind brain excluding the cerebellum. Merges with the spinal cord.
medusa: disc-shaped free-swimming form of cnidarian.
meiosis: cell division during which the number of chromosomes is halved resulting in haploid cells. Occurs during gamete production.
meiotic: of meiosis.
membranella (pl. membranellae): membrane formed of a fused row of cilia.
mesogloea: layer of jelly-like material between the endoderm and the ectoderm of a coelenterate.
mesonephros: type of kidney which is functional in fishes and amphibians, and the embryos of higher vertebrates.
Mesozoic: the third of the great geological eras, coming between the Palaeozoic and the Cainozoic.
metabolic rate: the speed at which the chemical changes within an organism proceed. These include both the building up and the breaking down of protoplasm. Metabolic rate can be assessed by measuring the production or disappearance of substances involved in one of the chemical reactions concerned, e.g. by measuring the rate at which carbon dioxide is produced during respiration.
metacarpal bones: the bones of the metacarpus.
metacarpus: the region between the wrist and the digits in the fore limb of limbed vertebrates.
metamerism: repetition of segments along the long axis of an animal's body. Exhibited by many invertebrates, e.g. annelids and arthropods, and also by vertebrates.
metamerically: by means of metamerism.
metamorphosis: change of shape, e.g. the transformation of an organism from larval to adult form.
metanephros: type of kidney which is functional in the higher vertebrates.
metatarsus: the region between the ankle and the digits in the hind limbs of limbed vertebrates. Sometimes also applied to comparable parts of the insect limb.
metathorax: the third and last segment of the thorax of an insect.
metazoan: animal consisting of two or more layers of cells.
mimetic: imitating another species.
Miocene: epoch of the Cainozoic era. Preceded by the Oligocene and followed by the Pliocene.
mitochondria: rod-like protoplasmic structures contained in living cells.
mitosis: cell division during which the chromosomes divide so that the cells which are produced have the same number of chromosomes as the original.
molar teeth: teeth at the back of the mouth of a mammal. The more posterior cheek teeth. Molar teeth are not present in very young mammals. The molars of omnivores (like man) and herbivores are adapted for grinding, whilst those of meat-eating types are adapted for crushing and shearing.
monotypic genus: genus containing only one species.
morula: early stage of embryonic development when cleavage has resulted in a solid ball of cells.
mucosa: epithelium containing glands which produce mucus.
myomere: muscle which is under the control of the will and which is contained within a segment of an animal which exhibits metamerism.
myotome: muscle block contained within a segment of a developing animal which exhibits metamerism.
nanoplankton: microscopic plankton.
nares: the nostrils of vertebrates.
nauplius (pl. nauplii): oval planktonic crustacean larva bearing three pairs of appendages.
nematocyst: chitinous capsule containing a coiled thread capable of being ejected and stinging.
neoteny: the retention of larval characteristics.
neotropical: having a distribution which includes parts of Central and South America.
nephridium (pl. nephridia): tube-like excretory organ of many invertebrates.
nephrocyte: cell which stores up excretory products.
nephrostome: the ciliated internal opening of some excretory organs, such as certain types of nephridia.
neurotoxin: poison which attacks the nerves.
niche: the place within the plant and animal community that an organism is adapted to occupy.
nictitating membrane: the inner, third eyelid present in many land vertebrates.
nidicolous birds: those which remain in the nest for some time after they are hatched.
nidifugous birds: those which leave the nest soon after they are hatched.
notochord: skeletal rod present at some stage of the development of all chordates. In most vertebrates it is replaced by the vertebral column.
nymph: immature hemimetabolous insect, not unlike the adult in appearance but lacking wings.
nymphal: pertaining to a nymph.
ocellus (pl. ocelli): simple eye found in many invertebrates.
oesophagus: the anterior part of the alimentary canal immediately preceding the stomach.
olfaction: the detection of chemical particles by means of the nostrils or nose. In land animals the sense of smell.
Oligocene: epoch of the Cainozoic era. Preceded by the Eocene and Palaeocene epochs and followed by the Miocene and Pliocene in the Tertiary period.
omnivorous: eating both plant and animal matter.
opisthaptor: a posterior disc or sucker on a trematode.
opisthoglyphous dentition: with venomous fangs at the back of the mouth.
opisthosoma: the posterior, legless part of the body of spiders and mites.
opposable digit: digit capable of being held against other digits on the same limb, giving a grasping action.
organelle: specialised part of a protozoan cell, e.g. a flagellum.
organ of Corti: the specialised epithelium of the cochlea of a mammal.
osmoregulation: control of the amount of water within an organism.
osmotic pressure: the apparent pressure which causes fluids to pass from weaker to stronger solutions when these are separated by membranes of a type common in living organisms.
os penis: the bone within the penis of certain mammals.
osphradium (pl. osphradia): molluscan sense-organ consisting of specialised ciliated epithelium.
ossicle: a small bone.
ossified: converted to bone.
ovary: a female gonad.
ovum (pl. ova): a female gamete. Ova, unlike male gametes, are unable to move of their own accord.
oviduct: the tube through which ova are carried from the ovary or coelom to the exterior.
oviparous: egg-laying.
ovipositor: tube protruding from the body of a female. Used in egg-laying.
ovoviviparous: producing eggs which hatch within the mother's body before they are laid.
paedogenesis: breeding whilst some organs of the body are still larval in character. An extreme form of neoteny.
palaeognathous birds: birds such as the large flightless birds and tinamous which have a primitive palate. Once thought to be related, but the resemblance is now believed to be due to convergence.
Palaeolithic: occuring in the Old Stone Age.
palatine: bone forming part of the roof of the mouth of a vertebrate.
palmiped: a webbed-footed bird.
palp: a sensory appendage.
pancreas: digestive gland of vertebrates which also has endocrine functions.

parapodium (pl. parapodia): muscular projection from the side of the body of a polychaete worm. Parapodia are paired and segmentally arranged.

parenchyma: living tissue made up of irregular-shaped cells.

parthenogenesis: the development of an unfertilised egg or eggs.

parthenogenetic: exhibiting parthenogenesis.

pectoral: in the region of the chest.

pectoral fins: the anterior lateral paired fins of fishes, usually situated just behind the head.

pectoral girdle: the skeletal structure within the body which supports the pectoral fins of fishes, and the fore limbs of limbed vertebrates.

pedicellaria (pl. pedicellariae): small, often stalked, chalky pincer-like structure found on the surface of echinoderms.

pedipalp: paired appendage on the head of spiders. May be locomotory, sensory, used for seizing prey, or (in males) modified for reproductive purposes.

pelagic: living in the middle or near the surface of the sea or lakes.

pellicle: a thin, non-living outer covering.

pelvic fins: the posterior paired fins of fishes.

pelvic girdle or pelvis: the skeletal structure within the body which supports the pelvic fins of fishes or the hind limbs of limbed vertebrates.

pentadactyl: having five digits.

pentadactyl limb: the typical limb of amphibians and higher vertebrates.

pericardium: the space surrounding the heart, or sometimes the membrane enclosing it.

pericardial: pertaining to the pericardium.

periosteum: layer of tissue covering the bones of vertebrates.

perisarc: the chitinous or horny layer which often covers the soft parts of hydrozoans.

peristalsis: waves of contraction passing along muscular tubular structures, e.g. the alimentary canal, moving the contents.

peristaltic: of peristalsis.

peritoneal space: the part of the vertebrate coelomic cavity which contains the viscera.

phagocytosis: the flowing process by means of which the cytoplasm of some cells engulfs particles.

phagocytic: capable of phagocytosis.

phalanges: bones inside the digits of vertebrates.

phytophagous: plant-eating.

pinna (pl. pinnae): the outer ear of a mammal.

piscivorous: fish-eating.

pituitary gland: endocrine gland situated between the base of the brain and the roof of the mouth in vertebrates.

placenta: the structure by means of which, in most mammals, substances involved in respiration and nutrition pass between the mother and the developing embryo.

plankton: small organisms that drift passively in water.

plantigrade: walking with the metacarpal or the metatarsal region making contact with the ground.

planula: aquatic invertebrate larva in which a ciliated ectoderm surrounds the endoderm.

plastron: skeletal structure protecting the ventral surface of an animal.

pleopod: flattened appendage on the abdomen of an arthropod used in swimming.

Pliocene: epoch of the Cainozoic era preceded by the Miocene and followed by the Pleistocene.

pneumatic bones: bones which contain cavities filled with air.

polyandrous: having, as a female animal, more than one mate.

polygamous: having more than one mate. Polygyny, in which a male consorts with several females, is more common than polyandry.

polymorphism: the existence of visibly distinct types within the same species, possibly, but not necessarily, representing different stages of the life-cycle.

polyp: sedentary form of hydrozoan, e.g. sea anemone, or sometimes a similar individual forming part of a colonial organism.

polypoid: taking the form of a polyp.

posterior: situated away from the head end of an animal. The opposite of anterior.

precocial birds: young ones which are well developed and active as soon as they are hatched.

prehensile: able to grasp.

premolar teeth: teeth immediately anterior to the molars in the mouth of a mammal. Premolars usually have a simpler structure than molars, but have the same function. Unlike molars, premolars are represented in the first set of teeth of a young mammal.

primary feathers: flight feathers borne on the parts of a bird's wing which correspond to the human wrist, palm and fingers.

primitive: at an early stage of evolutionary development, or having changed little since that stage.

progenesis: the maturation of the gametes within an organism before it has reached physical maturity in other respects.

prolegs: short, unjointed appendages borne on the abdomen of caterpillars.

pronephros: type of kidney functional only in embryonic vertebrates.

pronotum: the chitinous covering of the dorsal surface of the first segment of an insect's thorax.

pronucleus (pl. pronuclei): the nucleus of either a male or a female gamete before fertilisation.

prosoma: the anterior part of the body of spiders and mites.

prostomium: the part of an annelid which is anterior to the mouth.

protandry: in hermaphrodite animals the condition of producing first male, and then female gametes.

protein: any of a group of complex compounds of carbon, hydrogen, oxygen and nitrogen, and sometimes other elements. Proteins are essential constituents of all living cells.

prothorax: the first segment of the insect thorax.

protonephridium (pl. protonephridia): organ consisting of one or more flame-cells present in many invertebrates.

protoplasm: the living substance of a cell, consisting of both the cytoplasm and nucleus.

pterygote: belonging to the group of insects which are either winged, or have winged ancestors.

pulmonary: pertaining to the lungs.

Quaternary: the most recent geological period. The last subdivision of the Cainozoic era.

radius: one of the two bones in the forearm of limbed vertebrates.

radula: horny, toothed strip in the mouth of a mollusc used for rasping food.

raptoral: predatory, or adapted for seizing prey.

reflex: simple, involuntary form of behaviour in which a stimulus evokes a simple response.

regeneration: the restitution by an organism of tissues or organs which have been lost.

remiges: the large flight feathers of a bird's wing, both primaries and secondaries.

retina: the light-sensitive layer of nerve-cells which receives the image formed by the lens of an eye.

retrices: the large flight feathers of a bird's tail.

ribosomes: particles situated within the endoplasm of a cell and concerned with protein synthesis.

rictal: pertaining to the mouth of a bird.

rods: light-sensitive cells present in the retina of the vertebrate eye. Rods are sensitive to dim light but do not permit great acuity of vision.

sagittal crest: elongated ridge of bone along the middle line of the dorsal surface of the vertebrate skull.

saprophagous: feeding on dead or decaying organic matter.

scapula (pl. scapulae): the shoulder-blade.

schizogony: reproduction by fission.

scolex: the organ of attachment on the end of a tapeworm.

sebaceous glands: mammalian dermal glands which produce an oily secretion.

secondary feathers: flight feathers borne on the part of a bird's wing which corresponds to the human forearm.

sensilla: a small sense-organ.

sessile: fixed and immobile.

seta (pl. setae): a chitinous bristle also known as a chaeta.

sexual dimorphism: a difference in appearance between the males and females of the same species.

siphonoglyph: ciliated groove in the mouth of an anthozoan.

somatic: pertaining to the body of an animal rather than the gonads and gametes.

somite: one of the segments of an animal which exhibits metamerism.

specialised: having changed greatly during the course of evolutionary development, and become highly adapted to a special function or mode of life.

sphincter: a circular muscle which encircles an orifice or tubular structure.

spiracle: a respiratory aperture, or in elasmobranch fishes an opening on the head through which water enters before passing over the gills.

squamous: scale-like.

statocyst: an organ of balance consisting of a sac lined by sensory cells and containing a solid chalky particle.

statolith: the solid particle contained by a statocyst.

sternum: the ventral part of the exoskeleton of an arthropod, or the breast-bone of a vertebrate.

stolon: a stalk-like structure.

stridulation: the production of noise by rubbing parts of the body together.

subpellicular: occurring under the pellicle.

symbionts: organisms which exhibit symbiosis.

symbiosis: an association between two dissimilar organisms which is beneficial to both.

systematic position: the position of an organism within the system of classification used for living things.

systematist: a biologist specialising in the classification of organisms.

tarsal bones: ankle bones of tetrapods.

tarsus (pl. tarsi): the tetrapod ankle, or in some arthropods the end of the limb.

taxonomy: the science of classifying living organisms.

telson: the last segment of the abdomen of an arthropod. Absent in adult insects.

territorial behaviour: defense of an area by an individual or group against other members of the same species.

Tertiary: that part of the Cainozoic era between and including the Palaeocene and the Pliocene, but excluding the more recent Quaternary.

testis (pl. testes): a male gonad.

tetrapod: a four-limbed vertebrate.

theca: a case enclosing an organ.

thorax: the part of an animal posterior to the head, often bearing appendages used in locomotion. The thorax of an insect, for example, bears the legs and, where these are present, the wings. In vertebrates the thorax contains the heart and lungs or gills, and bears the anterior pair of limbs or paired fins.

thyroid gland: endocrine gland situated central to the throat in vertebrates.

tibia: the inner of the two bones of the shin in limbed vertebrates, or the fourth joint of the leg in some arthropods.

trachea (pl. tracheae): an air-tube in some invertebrates, or in air-breathing vertebrates the tube leading from the glottis to the bronchi.

tragus (pl. tragi): a fleshy protrusion in front of the ear-opening of a mammal.

tuberculate: covered with small, rounded bumps.

tympanum: a drum-like structure, e.g. an ear-drum.

ulna: one of the two bones in the forearm of a limbed vertebrate.

ungulate: a mammal bearing hoofs or, if lacking them, closely related to hoofed forms. Members of the orders Artiodactyla and Perissodactyla are ungulates.

ureter: the duct which conveys urine from the kidney to the cloaca or bladder.

urethra: the duct which conveys urine from the bladder to the exterior.

uropod: appendage found on the segment immediately in front of the telson in some crustaceans.

uropygial gland: the preen gland of a bird.

uterus (pl. uteri): the womb of a female mammal.

uterine: relating to the uterus.

uvula: the fleshy protrusion at the back of the roof of a mammal's mouth.

vacuole: a fluid-filled space within a cell.

vane of a feather: the flattened part of a feather consisting of the barbs held together by their interlocking barbules.

vascular: pertaining to vessels which convey fluids—e.g. blood—within the body.

vector: an animal which transmits parasites or disease to members of another species.

vegetative reproduction: asexual reproduction. Parthenogenesis does not come into this category being a degenerate form of sexual reproduction.

ventral: the opposite of dorsal. Towards the belly of an animal.

ventricle: chamber in the heart with thick muscular walls. Receives blood from the auricle and pumps it to other parts of the body.

vermiform: worm-shaped.

villus (pl. villi): a small pointed protrusion such as the vascular processes of the mammalian placenta.

viscera: the soft organs in the body cavity.

visceropallium: the visceral mass covered by the mantle on the dorsal surface of a mollusc.

vitellarium: a gland which forms yolk.

viviparous: giving birth to live young.

vomer: a bone forming part of the floor of the cranium on the vertebrate skull.

wattles: fleshy appendages on the chin or throat of a bird.

yellow spot: pigmented area of the retina surrounding and including the fovea.

zonal placenta: placenta with villi forming a girdle round the embryo.

zygodactylous: having two toes directed backwards and two directed forwards as in birds such as parrots.

zygomatic arch: bony arch below the eye socket in the mammalian skull.

zygote: the cell produced when two gametes fuse.

Further Reading List

General

Alexander, R. McNeill. *The Chordates*. Cambridge University Press, London, New York, 1975.

Allee, W.C. and others. *Principles of Animal Ecology*. W.B. Saunders, 1949.

Baker, R.R. *The Evolutionary Ecology of Animal Migration*. Hodder & Stoughton, London, 1978.

Buchsbaum, R. *Animals Without Backbones*. University of Chicago Press, 2nd ed., 1976.

Cloudsley-Thompson, J.L. *Terrestrial Environments*. Croom Helm, London, 1975.

Grove, A.J. and Newell, G.E. *Animal Biology*. University Tutorial Press, 9th ed., 1966.

Hegner, R.W. and Engelmann, J.G. *Invertebrate Zoology*. Macmillan, New York, 2nd ed., 1968.

Hinde, R.A. *Animal Behaviour*. McGraw-Hill, New York, 2nd ed., 1970.

Hyman, L.H. *The Invertebrates* (5 vols). McGraw-Hill, New York and London, 1940.

Krebs, J.R. and Davies, N.B. *Behavioural Ecology*. Blackwell Scientific Publications, Oxford, 1978.

Macan, T.T. *Freshwater Ecology*. Longmans, London, 1963.

Manning, A. *An Introduction to Animal Behaviour*. Edward Arnold, 3rd ed., 1979.

Marshall, N.B. *Developments in Deep Sea Biology*. Blandford, Poole, 1979.

Ricklefs, R.E. *Ecology*. Nelson, 1973.

Romer, A.S. *The Vertebrate Story*. University of Chicago Press, Chicago and London, 4th ed., 1959.

Romer, A.S. and Parsons, T.S. *The Vertebrate Body*. W.B. Saunders, Philadelphia, London and Toronto, 5th ed., 1977.

Sebeok, T.A. *How Animals Communicate*. Indiana University Press, 1977.

Smith, J.E. and others. *The Invertebrate Panorama*. Weidenfeld & Nicolson, London, 1971.

Thorson, G. *Life in the Sea*. Weidenfeld & Nicolson, London, 1971.

Weisz, P.B. *The Science of Zoology*. McGraw-Hill, New York, 2nd ed., 1973.

Wells, M. *Lower Animals*. World University Library, London, 1968.

Wilson, E.O. *Sociobiology*. Harvard University Press, 1975.

Young, J.Z. *The Life of the Vertebrates*. Oxford University Press, 2nd ed., 1962.

Protozoans

Jones, A.R. *The Ciliates*. Hutchinson, London, 1974.

Sleigh, M. *The Biology of Protozoa*. Edward Arnold, London, 1973.

Flatworms, Flukes and Tapeworms

Croll, N.A. *The Behaviour of Nematodes*. Edward Arnold, London, 1970.

Riser, N.W. and Morse, M.P. *Biology of the Turbellaria*. McGraw-Hill, New York, 1974.

Rotifers

Donner, J. *Rotifers*. Warne, London and New York, 1966.

Cnidarians

Mackie, G.O. *Coelenterate Ecology and Behaviour*. Plenum, New York and London, 1976.

Muscatine, L. and Lenhoff, H.M. *Coelenterate Biology*. Academic Press, 1974.

Molluscs

Morton, J.E. *Molluscs*. Hutchinson, London, 5th ed., 1979.

Tebble, N. *British Bivalve Molluscs*. H.M.S.O., London, 1976.

Yonge, C.M. *Oysters*. Collins, London, 1960.

Yonge, C.M. and Thompson, T.E. *Living Marine Molluscs*. Collins, Glasgow, 1976.

Wells, M.J. *Brain and Behaviour in Cephalopods*. Heinemann, London and Stanford University Press, 1962.

Segmented Worms

Dales, R.P. *Annelids*. Hutchinson, London, 1963.

Edwards, C.A. and Lofty, J.R. *Biology of Earthworms*. Chapman and Hall, London and John Wiley and Sons, New York, 2nd ed., 1977.

Laverack, M.S. *The Physiology of Earthworms*. Pergamon, London and New York, 1963.

Mann, K.H. *The Leeches*. Pergamon, London and New York, 1962.

Arthropods

Manton, S.M. *The Arthropoda*. Clarendon Press, Oxford, 1977.

Insects

Askew, R.R. *Parasitic Insects*. Heinemann, London, 1971.

Blaney, W.M. *How Insects Live*. Elsevier Phaidon, Oxford, 1976.

Borror, D.J. Delong, D.M. and Triplehorn, C.A. *Introduction to the Study of Insects*. Holt, Rinehart & Winston, New York, 4th ed., 1976.

Borror, D.J. and White, R.E. *A Field Guide to the Insects of America North of Mexico*. Houghton Mifflin, Boston, 1970.

Chapman, R.F. *The Insects: Structure and Function*. English Universities Press, London, 1969.

Chinery, M. *A Field Guide to the Insects of Britain and Northern Europe*. Collins, London, 1973.

Daly, H.V. Doyen, J.T. and Ehrlich, P. *Introduction to Insect Biology and Diversity*. McGraw-Hill, New York, 1978.

Essig, E.O. *Insects and Mites of Western North America*. MacMillan, New York, 2nd ed., 1958.

Frost, S.W. *Insect Life and Natural History*. Dover, New York, 1959.

Hill, D.S. *Agricultural Insect Pests of the Tropics and their Control*. Cambridge University Press, 1975.

Imms, A.D. *Insect Natural History*. Collins, London, 3rd ed., 1971.

Mackerras, I.M. (ed.). *The Insects of Australia*. C.S.I.R.O., Melbourne, 1970 (Supplement, 1974).

Richards, O.W. and Davies, R.G. *Imms' General Textbook of Entomology*. Chapman & Hall, London, 10th ed., 2 vols., 1977.

Selman, B. *et al.*, *Insects: An illustrated survey of the most successful animals on earth*. Hamlyn, London, 1979.

Smith, K.G.V. (ed.). *Insects and other Arthropods of Medical Importance*. British Museum (Natural History), London, 1973.

Wigglesworth, V.B. *The Life of Insects*. Weidenfeld & Nicholson, London, 1964.

Wigglesworth, V.B. *The Principles of Insect Physiology*. Chapman & Hall, London, 7th ed., 1972.

Wilson, E.O. *The Insect Societies*. Harvard University Press, Cambridge, Massachussetts, 1971.

Crustaceans

Green, J.A. *A Biology of Crustacea*. H.F. & G. Witherby, London, 1963.

Schmitt, W.L. *Crustaceans*. David & Charles, Newton Abbot, 1973.

Sutton, S. *Woodlice*. Ginn & Co., 1972.

Warner, G.F. *The Biology of Crabs*. Elek Science, London, 1977.

Waterman, T.H. (ed.). *The Physiology of Crustacea* (2 vols). Academic Press, New York and London, 1960–61.

Whittington, H.B. and Rolfe, W.D.I. (eds). *Phylogeny and Evolution of Crustacea*. Museum of Comparative Zoology, Cambridge, Mass., 1963.

Spiders

Bristowe, W.S. *The World of Spiders*. Collins, London, 1958.

Comstock, J.H. *The Spider Book*. Cornell University Press, 1965 (reissue).

Evans, G.O. Sheals, J.G. and Macfarlane, D. *The Terrestrial Acari of the British Isles* (vol. 1). British Museum (Natural History), London, 1961.

Gertsch, W.J. *American Spiders*. Van Nostrand (D.), Princeton, New Jersey and London, 1949.

Echinoderms

Clark, A.M. *Starfishes and their Relations*. British Museum (Natural History), London, 1962.

Nichols, D. *Echinoderms*. Hutchinson, London, rev. ed. 1966.

Fishes

Berg, L.S. *Freshwater Fishes of the U.S.S.R. and Adjacent Countries* (3 vols). Israel Program for Scientific Translations, Jerusalem, 1962, 1964, and 1965.

Böhlke, J.E. & Chaplin, C.C.G. *Fishes of the Bahamas and Adjacent Tropical Waters*. Livingston Publishing Company, Wynnewood, Pa., 1970.

Budker, P. *The Life of Sharks* (trans. P.J.P. Whitehead). Weidenfeld & Nicolson, London, 1971.

Frank, S. *The Pictorial Encyclopedia of Fishes*. Hamlyn, London, 1971.

Gilbert, P.W. Mathewson, R.F. and Rall, D.P. (eds). *Sharks, Skates, and Rays*. Johns Hopkins Press, Baltimore, 1967.

Hart, J.L. *Pacific Fishes of Canada*. Fisheries Research Board of Canada, Ottawa, 1973.

Hoar, W.S. & Randall, D.J. (eds). *Fish Physiology*. Academic Press, New York & London, vols 1–7, 1969–1978.

Hoese, H.D. & Moore, R.H. *Fishes of the Gulf of Mexico*. Texas A & M University Press, College Station, Texas, 1977.

Lagler, K.F. Bardach, J.E. Miller, R.R. & Passino, D.R.M. *Ichthyology* (2nd ed.) John Wiley & Sons, New York, 1977.

Lindberg, G.U. *Fishes of the World. A Key to Families and a Checklist*. John Wiley & Sons, New York; Israel Program for Scientific Translations, Jerusalem & London, 1974.

McDowall, R.M. *New Zealand Freshwater Fishes a guide and natural history*. Heinemann Educational Books (NZ) Ltd, Auckland, N.Z., 1978.

Marshall, N.B. *The Life of Fishes*. Weidenfeld & Nicolson, London, 1965.

Marshall, N.B. *Explorations in the Life of Fishes*. Harvard University Press, Cambridge, Mass., 1971.

Marshall, T.C. *Fishes of the Great Barrier Reef and coastal waters of Queensland*. Angus & Robertson Ltd, Sydney, 1966.

Nelson, J.S. *Fishes of the World*. J. Wiley & Sons, New York & London, 1976.

Nikolskii, G.V. *Special Ichthyology* (2nd ed.) Israel Program for Scientific Translations, Jerusalem, 1961.

Nikolsky, G.V. *The Ecology of Fishes*. Tropical Fish Hobbyist Publications Inc. Neptune City, N.J., 1978.

Norman, J.R. & Greenwood, P.H. *A History of Fishes* (3rd ed.). Ernest Benn Ltd, London, 1975.

Scott, W.B. & Crossman, E.J. *Freshwater Fishes of Canada*. Fisheries Research Board of Canada, Ottawa, 1973.

Smith, J.L.B. *The Sea Fishes of Southern Africa*. Central News Agency Ltd., South Africa (6th ed.), 1970.

Sterba, G. *Freshwater Fishes of the World*. (trans. D.W. Tucker). Studio Vista, London, 1966.

Thomson, D.A., Findley, L.T. & Kerstitch, A.N. *Reef Fishes of the Sea of Cortez*. J. Wiley & Sons, New York, & Chichester, 1979.

Tinker, S.W. *Fishes of Hawaii*. Hawaiian Service Inc, Honolulu, 1978.

Wheeler, A. *Fishes of the World an Illustrated Dictionary*. Macmillan Publishing Co. Inc., New York, 1975; and Ferndale Editions, London, 1979.

Wheeler, A. *Key to the Fishes of Northern Europe*. F. Warne & Co. Ltd, London, 1978.

Amphibians and Reptiles

Bellairs, A. *The Life of Reptiles* (2 vols). Weidenfeld & Nicolson, London, 1969.

Bustard, R. *Sea Turtles*. Collins, London, 1972.

Carr, A. and the Editors of *Life*. *The Reptiles*. Time-Life, 1963.

Goin, C.J. and O.B. *Introduction to Herpetology*. W.H. Freeman, San Francisco and London, 1962.

Harless, M. and Morlock, H (eds). *Turtles: perspectives and research*. John Wiley, New York, 1979.

Heatwole, H. *Reptile Ecology*. University of Queensland Press, 1976.

Klauber, L.M. *Rattlesnakes, their habits, life histories and influence on mankind*. University of California Press, 1956.

Mertens, R. *The World of Amphibians and Reptiles*. McGraw-Hill, 1960.

Minton, S.A. and M.R. *Venomous Reptiles*. George Allen and Unwin, London, 1971.

Noble, G.K. *The Biology of the Amphibia*. Dover, New York and London, 1954.

Parker, H.W. and Grandison, A.G.C. *Snakes–a natural history*. British Museum (Natural History) London and Cornell University Press, Ithaca and London, 2nd ed., 1977.

Porter, K.R. *Herpetology*. W.B. Saunders, 1972.

Birds

Brown, L. and Amadon D. *Eagles, Hawks and Falcons of the World* (2 vols). Country Life Books and Hamlyn, London, 1968.

Burton, J.A. (ed.). *Owls of the World*. Peter Lowe, 1978.

Cameron, A. and Harrison, C.J.O. *Bird Families of the World*. Elsevier Phaidon, Oxford, 1978.

Delacour, J. *The Pheasants of the World*. Country Life Books, London and Charles Scribner's Sons, New York, 1951.

Delacour, J. and Amadon, D. *Curassows and Related Birds*. American Museum of Natural History and Chanticleer Press, 1973.

Dorst, J. *The Life of Birds* (2 vols). Weidenfeld & Nicolson, 1971.

Forshaw, J.M. *Parrots of the World*. Lansdowne, Melbourne, 1973.

Gilliard, E.T. *Birds of Paradise and Bowerbirds*. Weidenfeld & Nicolson, London, 1969.

Goodwin, D. *Pigeons and Doves of the World*. British Museum (Natural History), 2nd ed., 1970.

Goodwin, D. *Crows of the World*. Cornell University Press, New York, 1976.

Gruson, E.S. *A Checklist of Birds of the World*. Collins, London, 1976.

Hancock, J. and Elliott, H. *The Herons of the World*. London Editions, 1973.

Marshall, A.J. (ed.). *Biology and Comparative Physiology of Birds* (2 vols). Academic Press, New York and London, 1960.

Mayr, E. and Greenway, J.C. jr (eds). *Check-list of the Birds of the World*. A continuation of the work of J.L. Peters, below.

Nelson, J.B. *The Sulidae: Gannets and Boobies*. Oxford University Press, 1978.

Peters, J.L. *Check-list of the Birds of the World*. Harvard University Press, 1931–1951.

Ripley, S.D. *Rails of the World*. M.F. Feheley Publishers, Toronto, 1977.

Ristall, R.L. *Finches and other Seed-eating Birds*. Faber, London, 1975.

Stonehouse, B. (ed.). *The Biology of Penguins*. Macmillan, London, 1975.

Thomson, A.L. (ed.). *A New Dictionary of Birds*. Nelson, London and McGraw-Hill, New York, 1964.

Todd, F.S. *Waterfowl*. Seaworld Press and Harcourt Brace Jovanovich, New York and London, 1979.

Welty, J.C. *The Life of Birds*. W.B. Saunders, 1962, Constable, 1964.

Mammals

Anderson, H.T. *The Biology of Marine Mammals*. Academic Press, London and New York, 1969.

DeBlase, A.F. and Martin, R.E. *A Manual of Mammalogy*. W.C. Brown, Dubuque, 1974.

Ewer, R.F. *The Carnivores*. Weidenfeld & Nicolson, 1973.

Fox, M.W. (ed.). *The Wild Canids*. Van Rostrand Reinhold, New York, 1975.

Frith, H.J. and Calaby, J.H. *Kangaroos*. C. Hurst, London, Humanities Press, New York, F.W. Cheshire, Victoria, 1969.

Groves, C.P. *Horses, Asses and Zebras*. David & Charles, Newton Abbot, 1974.

Harris, C.J. *Otters*. Weidenfeld & Nicolson, London, 1968.

Hinton, H.E. and Dunn, A.M.S. *Mongooses*. Oliver and Boyd, Edinburgh, 1967.

Kummer, H. *Primate Societies*. Aldine, Chicago, 1971.

Leuthold, W. *African Ungulates*. Springer-Verlag, Berlin, Heidelberg and New York, 1977.

Mochi, U. and Carter, T.D. *Hoofed Mammals of the World*. Charles Scribner's Sons, 1971 and Lutterworth, 1974.

Napier, J.R. and P.H. *Handbook of Living Primates*. Academic Press, London and New York, 1967.

Osman Hill, W.C. *Evolutionary Biology of the Primates*. Academic Press, London and New York, 1972.

Reynolds, V. *The Apes*. Cassell, London, 1968.

Rowell, T. *Social Behaviour of Monkeys*. Penguin, Harmondsworth, 1972.

Schaller, G.B. *The Serengeti Lion*. University of Chicago, 1972.

Scheffer, V.B. *Seals, Sealions and Walruses*. Stanford University Press and Oxford University Press, 1958.

Schultz, A. *The Life of Primates*. Weidenfeld & Nicolson, London, 1969.

Stoddart, D.M. (ed.). *Ecology of Small Mammals*. Chapman and Hall, London and John Wiley, New York, 1979.

Tyndale-Biscoe, H. *Life of Marsupials*. Edward Arnold, London, 1973.

Walker, E.P. *Mammals of the World* (2 vols). The Johns Hopkins Press, Baltimore and London, 3rd ed., 1975.

Whitehead, G.K. *Deer of the World*. Constable, London, 1972.

Yalden, B.W. and Morris, P.A. *The Lives of Bats*. David & Charles, Newton Abbot, 1975.

Young, J.Z. *The Life of Mammals*, Clarendon Press, Oxford, 2nd ed., 1975.

Acknowledgements

All the photographs in this book
were provided by Bruce Coleman Ltd.

Photographers

Helmut Albrecht facing page 513; Ken Balcomb 543, 545 top; Des Bartlett 190, 361 top right, 425 top; Jen and Des Bartlett 231, 290 centre, 345, 360 top, 361 top left, 361 bottom, 363, 380 bottom, 393, 414 top, 427 bottom, 429 top, 492, 497, 517 bottom, 522 bottom, 532, 533 bottom, 577 top, 610 bottom; Wolfgang Bayer 319 bottom; S.C. Bisserôt 102, 113 bottom, 121 top, 125, 128, 130 top, 152 centre, 213, 291 bottom, 293 top, 344 top, 471 bottom, 491 bottom, 496 bottom, 498 bottom, 499, 502, 601 bottom; Chris Bonington 131 bottom, 550 bottom; Rod and Moira Borland 56, 89 bottom, 518; Mark Boulton 90 bottom, facing page 383, 567 top, 579 bottom, 584 bottom, 589 top, 606; Bill Brooks 605 bottom; Nicholas Brown 127 top, 132 bottom, 134 top, 151 top, 161; John R. Brownlie 122 bottom, 285 bottom, 313 bottom, 442, 549; J. & S. Brownlie 545 bottom; Jane Burton 34, 38 top, 38 bottom, 44 centre, 46 bottom, 50 bottom, 82, 88, 89 top, 93, 98, 104 top, 109 bottom, 116 top, 116 centre, 117 bottom, 119 top left, 119 centre left, 119 bottom left, 119 top right, 119 bottom right, 121 bottom, 123 bottom, 124, 126, 127 bottom, 133 bottom, 135, 142 top, 143 top, facing page 147, 152 top, 155 top, 157, 164 top, 165, 168, 170 top, 170 bottom, 172, 191 top, 191 bottom, 194 bottom, 200 top, 201, 207, 220 top, 221, 242, 246, facing page 252, 253, 257, 259 bottom, 262, 265 top, 268, 272, 274 left, 274 right, 275 top, 276 top, 284 bottom, 288 top, 288 bottom, 289 right, 299 top, 305, 312 bottom, 317 top, 317 centre, 317 bottom, 334 centre, 348 top, 473, 474, 490 top, 491 top, 498 top, 498 centre, 522 top, 525 centre, 539 centre, 550 top, 568 top, 568 bottom, 600 bottom, 604; Bos and Clara Calhoun 338, 396, 402, 433, 455 bottom, 561 top; R.I.M. Campbell 290 bottom, 373, 472, 569 bottom, 605 centre; Robert C. Carr 143 bottom right, 150 bottom, 599 top; Ron Cartmell 571; B.J. Coates 129 bottom, 142 bottom, 422, 440, 456 bottom, 465 bottom, 481; Bruce Coleman Ltd. 234, 297 top, 303, 304, 311 top, 313 top, 330, 334 bottom, 375 top, 378, 431 top, 464 bottom, 465 top, 483 bottom, 484, 503, 511, 523 top, 572 bottom, 584 top, 602, 612 bottom; Neville Coleman 49 bottom, 185 bottom, 196 bottom, 200 bottom, 209, 256 bottom; Alain Compost 174 bottom, 423, 487 bottom, facing page 512; J.A.L. Cooke 109 top, 118, 134 bottom, 154 top, 158, 160 top, 184; Gene Cox 40, 61, 64 top, 64 centre, 64 bottom; Eric Crichton 599 bottom; Gerald Cubitt 605 top, 613 top; Stephen Dalton 114 top, 114 centre, 138 top, 331, 346 bottom, 347, 438 bottom, 444, 448; Peter Davey 585 top; Adrian Davies 83, 90 top, 92 top, 117 top, 478 bottom; B. Davies 129 top, 141 centre; Neville Fox-Davies 50 top, 87, 103, 111, 115, 146, 179; A.J. Deane 144 top, 312 top, 370 bottom, 371 top, 385 top, 386, 401, 407, 408, 412, 419, 432, 434 bottom, 478 top; Jack Dermid 176 bottom, 178 bottom, 269, facing page 283, 294 top, 326 centre, 460 top; Nicholas Devore 609 top; Ernest Duscher 369 bottom, 418, 461 top, 462 top; Jessica Ehlers 552 top; Francisco Erize 359 top, 366 top, 376 top, 425 bottom, 483

top, 485 top, 485 bottom, 486 top, 486 bottom, 488, 514, 515, 516, 524 top, 524 bottom, 525 top, 525 bottom, 542, 544, 556, 576 bottom, 578 top, 587, 590 centre, 603 bottom, 607, 612 top; Inigo Everson 162, 169 top, 171; John Fennell 223, 278 top, 346 top; M.P.L. Fogden 138 bottom, 180 top, 180 bottom, 182 bottom, 183 bottom, 188, 281, 284 centre, 300 top, 301 centre, 306 bottom, 310 top, 319 top, 324, 325, 328, 428, 430 bottom, 531 bottom, 534 top; Jeff Foott facing page 146, 204, 220 bottom, facing page 392, 417 bottom, 563 bottom, 573, 576 top, 577 bottom, 583; Michael Freeman 298 bottom, 507 top; C.B. Frith 132 top, 150 top, 167, 175 bottom, 176 top, 279, 319 centre, 320, 322 bottom, 327 top, 392, 508 top, 509 top, 509 bottom; C.B. & D.W. Frith 175 top; Robert Gillmor 417 top; Sven Gillsater 342; Eduardo Gonzales 294 bottom; Mary Grant 507 bottom, 570 bottom, 597; Dennis Green 352 bottom, 426 top, 454 bottom; Giorgio Gualco 217; Keith Gunnar 531 top; James Hancock 280; M.P. Harris 360 bottom; Anthony Healy 113 centre, 133 top, 148, 154 bottom; Pekka Helo 430 top, 457 top; Peter Hinchcliffe 122 top; Udo Hirsch 273 bottom, 275 bottom, 285 top, 290 top, 292, 367 bottom, 370 top, 372, 374, 391 top, 467 bottom, 490 bottom, 547, 552 bottom, 593 top; D. Houston 348 bottom, 364; Carol Hughes 155 centre, 329 top; David Hughes 116 bottom, 130 bottom, 194 top, 296 top, 296 centre, 300 bottom, 314 bottom; E. Breeze-Jones 388; M. Philip Kahl 375 bottom, 403 bottom, 436 bottom, 476, 510 top, 553 bottom, 558 bottom, 574–575, 588; Jon Kenfield 49 top, 70, 196 top, 197, 240, 250, 260 bottom; Stephen J. Krasemann 293 centre, 457 bottom, 517 top, 520 top, 557 top; H.A. Lambrechts 427 top, 437 top; Gordon Langsbury 377 bottom, 415 bottom, 451 top, 453 bottom, 466; Wayne Lankinen 387, 426 bottom, 528 bottom, 564 bottom, 603 top; Cyril Laubscher 445 top; Antti Leinonen 447; Norman R. Lightfoot 468; Rocco Longo 289 left, 349 bottom; Lee Lyon 513, 561 bottom, 592; John Markham 131 top, 151 bottom, 183 top, 271 bottom, 301 bottom, 316, 443, 449 bottom, 454 top, 535 top; Derek Middleton 362 top, 411; C.C.S. Miller 495; A.J. Mobbs 299 bottom, 308 top: Colin Molyneux 376 bottom; R.K. Murton 424 bottom, 431 bottom, 446, 451 bottom; Norman Myers 302, 326 top, 326 bottom, facing page 382, 501, 559 top, 580; Owen Newman 533 top, 535 bottom, 538 top, 564 top; M. Timothy O'Keefe 33, 51 top, 52, facing page 62, 100 bottom, 224, 296 bottom; Charlie Ott 276 bottom, 333 bottom, 343 bottom, 353, 380 top, 520 centre, 601 top; David Overcash 141 bottom; Oxford Scientific Films 58; Alan Parker 413; J.M. Pearson 551 bottom, 569 top; Roger T. Peterson 436 top; G. Pizzey 337, 464 top, 480; Dieter and Mary Plage 385 bottom, 469, 600 top; G.D. Plage 235, 344 bottom, 365, 393, 456 top, 565 bottom, 585 bottom; S.C. Porter 349 top, 371 bottom, 414 centre, 420, 454 centre, 534 bottom; Allan Power 47 bottom, 81, 195 top, 212, 229, 230, 232, 239 bottom, 248, facing page 253, 254,

260 top, 263, 265 bottom, 266, 267; S. Prato 123 top, 350; M.P. Price 297 bottom, 579 top; Mike Prior 450; Masood Qureshi 368 bottom, 471 top, facing page 593; Hans Reinhard 174 top, 211, 216, 219, 236, 237, 241, 243, 244, 245, 249, 256 top, 270, 277 top, 283, 284 top, 295 bottom, 298 centre, 307, 308 bottom, 309 top, 318 bottom, 323 top, 323 bottom, 327 bottom, 329 bottom, 356, 399 bottom, 429 bottom, 445 bottom, 489, 496 top, 519, 526 bottom, 536 bottom, 551 top, 559 bottom, 560, 561 centre, 586, 589 bottom, 590 bottom, 594, 598, 611 bottom; Hector Rivarola 114 bottom, 120, 134 centre, 143 centre, 145, 339, 341; Alan Root 403 top, 461 bottom; W.E. Ruth 608 bottom; Leonard Lee Rue III 185 top, 295 top, 295 centre, 318 top, 333 bottom, 352 bottom, 368 top, 379 bottom, 391 bottom, 395, 437 bottom, 439, 453 top, 475, 477, 482 top, 505 top, 527, 529 bottom, 530 top, 539 top, 554 bottom, 557 bottom, 563 top, 566 top, 570 top, 572 top, 578 bottom, 590 top, 596 bottom, 608 top, 609 bottom, 610 top, 611 top, 613 bottom; Frieder Sauer 12 top, 12 bottom, 13, 14, 15 top, 15 bottom, 16, 20 top, 20 bottom, 22, 23, 24, 25 top, 25 bottom, 26, 30, 31, 37, 41, 42 left, 42 right, 43, 44 top, 44 bottom, 45, 46 top, 47 top, 53, 55, 67, 69, 71, 72 top, 72 bottom, 76, 77, 99 top, 100 top, 143 bottom left, 193, 202, 310 bottom, 315, 321 top; Robert Schroeder 94, 187; Harold Schultz 482 bottom; John Shaw 136 bottom, 152 bottom, 164 top, 271 top, 273 top, 459 bottom, 523 bottom; Reinhard Siegel 455 top; James Simon 529 top; M.F. Soper 291 top, 322, 359 bottom, 362 bottom, 410, 424 top; Sinclair Stammers 160 bottom, 178 top; Lynn M. Stone 322 top, 409; Marty Stouffer 528 top; Stouffer Productions 537 top, 553 top; Diana and Rick Sullivan 367 top, 582; Sullivan and Rogers 555, 567 bottom; Kunio Takano/Orion Press 508 bottom; Jan Taylor 314 top; Kim Taylor 10, 19, 59, facing page 63, 99 bottom, 104 bottom, 112, 144 bottom, 163, 311 bottom; Norman Tomalin 169 bottom, 228 bottom, 306 top, 381, 434 bottom, 530 bottom, 596 top; Simon Trevor 383, 462 bottom, facing page 592; D. & K. Urry 335, 343 top, 415 top; Joseph van Wormer 377 top, 390, 399 top, 404, 405, 416, 449 top, 459 top, 460 bottom, 520 bottom, 554 top, 562; Peter Ward 113 top, 136 top, 137, 139, 141 top, 155 bottom, 277 bottom, 278 bottom, facing page 282, 321 bottom, 379 top, 389, 467 top, 494, 504, 536 top, 539 bottom, 558 top, 566 bottom; John Wallis 487 top; Rod Williams 293 bottom, 301 top, 309 bottom, 358, 438 top, 493, 510 bottom, 537 bottom, 538 bottom; W.H.D. Wince 400; Bill Wood 51 bottom, 92 bottom, 96, 97, 192, 195 bottom, 199, 228 top, 239 top, 255, 258, 259 top, 261; Gunther Ziesler 182 top, 238, 282, 334 top, 369 top, 382, 414 bottom, 421, 441, 505 bottom, 506, 526 top, 593 bottom; Christian Zuber title page, 512, 546, 565 top.

Drawings by Peter Morter

Index

Figures in italics refer to illustrations

627